GOVERNING A CHANGING AMERICA

TO THE STUDENT:

A Study Guide for the textbook is available through your college bookstore under the title Study Guide to accompany GOVERNING A CHANGING AMERICA by Susan MacManus, Charles Bullock and Donald Freeman. The Study Guide can help you with course material by acting as a tutorial, review and study aid. If the Study Guide is not in stock, ask the bookstore manager to order a copy for you.

GOVERNING A CHANGING AMERICA

Susan A. MacManus
UNIVERSITY OF HOUSTON

Charles S. Bullock, III
UNIVERSITY OF GEORGIA

Donald M. Freeman
UNIVERSITY OF EVANSVILLE

IN COLLABORATION WITH
Loch Johnson
UNIVERSITY OF GEORGIA

John Wiley & Sons
NEW YORK   CHICHESTER   BRISBANE   TORONTO   SINGAPORE

Cover Photos

Top, front and back: Fred J. Maroon/Photo Researchers.

Front, bottom from left: Mike Mitchell/Photo Researchers;
Thomas S. England/Photo Researchers; Robert Perron/Photo
Researchers; Will McIntyre/Photo Researchers.

Back, bottom from left: Richard Weymouth Brooks/Photo
Researchers; Nancy Brown/The Image Bank; Georg Gerster/
Rapho-Photo Researchers; Richard Hutchings/Photo Researchers.

Library of Congress Cataloging in Publication Data:

ISBN 0-471-05594-8

Printed in the United States of America

10 9 8 7 6 5 4 3 2

PREFACE

Over the years, new people, values, issues, and technologies have continually changed the face of America. What is striking is the ability of our system of government, devised over two centuries ago, to adapt to these changes. For some the changes have been too slow; for others, too fast. Yet while our nation, its people, and its governments are constantly in flux, our democracy remains intact.

This book focuses on the ability of the American political system to react to changes in the makeup, attitudes, needs, and demands of the nation's population. Specifically, it shows how changes in our society create new issues and problems that policymakers must attempt to solve. It also demonstrates the system's responsiveness and provides a positive, upbeat view of our democratic system.

Governing a Changing America is unique in several respects. First, the book does not start with the traditional, frequently boring, historical discussion of the nation's founding. We have discovered from our years of teaching that such approaches tend to alienate students rather than excite and encourage them to read the rest of the book. Instead, we begin with an introductory chapter designed to show how much our country has changed before describing the constitutional framework that has accommodated these transformations. We rely heavily on U.S. Bureau of the Census materials to document shifts in the demographic, socioeconomic, political, and institutional makeup of America. Longitudinal attitudinal surveys are used to trace changes in Americans' attitudes toward each other (e.g., increasing tolerance), toward government and its officials, and toward other nations.

Our second chapter, ''America's Changing Needs and the Process of Making Public Policy,'' links changes in the population discussed in the introductory chapter to the emergence of new problems and issues that confront the nation (and world) today: the economy, energy and environment, and lifestyle. Instead of simply identifying these problems as important, we provide extensive substantive background material on each. This background material is vitally important for the student to understand the issues involved in making decisions regarding these problems.

Our changing economy has presented the makers of public policy with three critical issues: (1) how to deal with a stagflation economy, (2) how much government regulation to impose to strengthen the economy, and (3) how to ease tensions among the classes (poor, middle class, wealthy). Changes in the world's supply of natural resources have presented policymakers with dilemmas about how to decrease our nation's dependency on foreign products, develop alternative energy sources, and achieve greater energy efficiency, while at the same time protecting the environment. The lifestyles and values of many Americans have also changed. As a consequence, policymakers must address such issues as: (1) how to change the public's expectations about its standard of living, including such factors as home ownership, temperature control, and food consumption, (2) how to create a satisfactory balance between work and leisure from the perspectives of both the individual and the economy, (3) how to balance affirmative action with equal opportunity in the workplace, (4) how to meet the health and income needs of America's aging population, and (5) what role the government should play in the individual's exercise of lifestyle choices. These issues are woven into every chapter to demonstrate the role each governmental institution (Congress, the Presidency, the Bureaucracy, the Judiciary) plays in the policymaking process and how individuals can influence the process. The close interrelationship of these various policy questions is also demonstrated through numerous examples and case studies.

Throughout the book we rely on research findings from other disciplines as well as from our own. For example, the introductory chapters and the media, budgeting, domestic policy, foreign policy, nominations and campaigns, and elections chapters incorporate data from the business, economics, communications, and science and technology fields. We also rely on our extensive practical experiences as policy analysts for various public agencies such as the U.S. Departments of Commerce, Health and Human Services, Housing and Urban Development, Labor, several congressional subcommittees in both the House and the Senate, and numerous state and local governments. We have also served as policy analysts for private agencies and groups, including The Brookings Institution, National Academy of Public Administration, Princeton Urban and Regional Research Center, the American Public Welfare Association, the Joint Center for Political Studies, and one of the major news networks. Each of these experiences has broadened our understanding and appreciation of the dynamics of the policymaking process, as well as the outcomes.

Another unique feature of the book is its coverage of America's minorities, which focuses on their increasing political influence. From chapter content, to case studies, to the Appendix (which includes The Seneca Falls Declaration of Sentiments and Resolutions, and the Emancipation Proclamation), we attempt to show how our nation has reacted to established minorities as well as to newly emerging groups such as the handicapped.

There is also a strong economic tone to the book. Recognizing the increasingly close tie between government and the economy, we have attempted to inform the student how the two relate, both nationally and internationally. Issues such as protectionism, the flat-rate tax, government spending on defense versus social programs, jobs programs, government loans to declining industries, PAC spending in election campaigns, and Reaganomics are just a few that we discuss in the book.

In summary, our approach is a policy approach. The difference in this perspective, compared with that of other texts, is that we focus on the *dynamics* of the policymaking process, rather than merely on the outcomes. Changes in the population are linked to changes in the political arena that are linked to changes in issues and, ultimately, to decisions regarding those issues. Particular care has been taken to make political processes and governmental institutions relevant to the personal lives and everyday experiences of the reader.

This book was greatly enhanced by the comments and critiques of a number of our professional colleagues throughout the country as well as at our respective universities. We are especially indebted to John Alford, Lenore Alpert, James Anderson, David Brady, Lee Epstein, Robert Erikson, Darwin Gamble, Joan Grafstein, Dennis Johnson, John Kay, Sam Kirkpatrick, Joan Lomax, David Neubauer, Karen O'Connor, Bruce Oppenheimer, Glenn Parker, Virginia Perrenod, C.K. Rowland, Sarah Slavin, Robert Stein, and Kent Tedin.

We are also greatly appreciative of the efforts of a number of individuals who helped in the preparation and typing of the manuscript: Patricia Cobb, Pearl Durkee, Peggy Elliott, Ina Freeman, Jeannine Hall, Earlene Huck, Sharon Fitzgerald Lukish, Ann Martin, Kay Trine, and Yolanda Villareal. Very special thanks go to Barbara Langham and Andrea Zaricznyj for their outstanding editorial efforts.

Finally, this book could never have been completed without help and encouragement from publishing professionals. We sincerely thank the following individuals at John Wiley & Sons, Inc.: Wayne Anderson, formerly political science editor, now publisher; Mark Mochary, political science editor; Maryellen Costa, administrative assistant; Stella Kupferberg, photo editor; Kathy Bendo, picture editor; Jan Lavin, production supervisor; Carolyn Moore, marketing manager, Rafael Hernandez, assistant design director, and Daniel Otis, manuscript editor. We would also like to thank Joanne Daniels (now with Congressional Quarterly Press) for her initial encouragement to undertake the project.

CONTENTS

GOVERNING A CHANGING AMERICA

CHAPTER 1

THE CHANGING FACE OF AMERICA: A CHALLENGE TO DEMOCRACY

Government's Role in a Changing Society: Making Public Policy ■ Changes in the Population ■ Changes in Values ■ Changes in Political Participation ■ Two Theories of Policymaking: Elitism and Pluralism ■ Why Study Government? Learning How to Influence Policymaking

America has changed drastically since its founding in 1776. Who among the country's founders would have—could have—predicted that its population would grow from 2.7 million in 1780 to 227 million in 1980? What would George Washington, for example, have thought if told that many of America's farms and much of its wilderness would become concrete and glass cities crisscrossed by highways? Or that blacks, descendants of the slaves he had at Mount Vernon, would be members of Congress, state legislators, and mayors of large cities? Or that some women, no less genteel than his wife, Martha, would be carpenters, doctors, Supreme Court justices? Imagine his surprise at hearing that America would face the possibility of running out of energy sources and that government, rather than families, would assume primary care of the poor and the elderly! More startling to him might be our nation's capability to blow up the world.

Yet America continues to change. Even 20 years ago, who could have predicted the tremendous increase in women working outside the home? the climb in divorce rates? the rise of families with only one parent? Who could have foreseen even the *question* of drafting women into the armed forces? widespread citizen tax revolts? the massive movement of people into the Sun Belt? the declining birth rate? the huge influx of immigrants—Cubans, Vietnamese boat people, Mexicans?

Despite these big changes, America has remained a democracy. The American system of government, devised 200 years ago, has been able to adapt. When change has occurred, government leaders have reacted to—and in some measure accommodated—the new needs and demands of various individuals and groups. In fact, *politics is really the struggle to make policies that meet the needs and demands of people*. The primary role of government, then, is to make public policy. The difficulty, of course, is the frequent conflict over *whose* needs are most important.

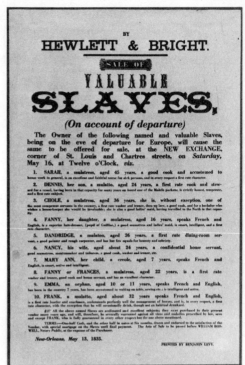

Once regarded merely as property to be sold rather than as citizens with voting rights (left), blacks in America are now very active and influential in politics. In several large U.S. cities, blacks such as Harold Washington of Chicago (right) have been elected mayor.

GOVERNMENT'S ROLE IN A CHANGING SOCIETY: MAKING PUBLIC POLICY

The *policymaking process consists of three stages: policy formation, policy implementation, and policy evaluation*[1] (see Figure 1.1). Not only must a policy be drawn up and adopted, but it must also be carried out and then evaluated.

Suppose that the Houston City Council is faced with the needs of two groups of citizens: one group wants to build a park for teenagers; the other wants to buy vans for transporting the city's wheelchair-bound citizens around town. If the Council members favor building a park, they must also decide:

1. What type of park to build (a neighborhood playground or softball–tennis complex);
2. Where the park will be (inner city, suburb);
3. When it will be built (next year or five years from now);
4. How it will be financed (higher taxes, bond sale, grant from the federal government).

Policy Formation

Such decisions as those facing the Council are part of the first stage of the policymaking process. *Policy formation involves both the identification of a particular need and the adoption of a policy to meet that need.* The formation of policy is influenced throughout by individual citizens or groups of citizens trying to convince the policymakers (in this case, the Houston City Council) that their needs are most urgent and their ideas the best.

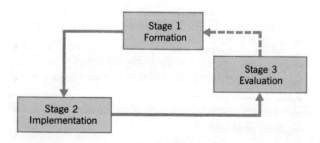

FIGURE 1.1
The Public Policymaking Process

The final decision about building the park or buying the vans lies with the City Council. While policy *formation* depends on individual citizens or groups of citizens telling government officials what they want or don't want, the power to *adopt* the policy lies with government officials alone. They have the final responsibility for deciding which need is greater—a decision that may be based on the relative political strength of the two groups of citizens. If the Council members make a decision that a majority of the city's population strongly disagrees with, they can be voted out of office. In a democracy, government officials are held accountable for their policymaking activities by citizens using the power of the ballot box.

Policy Implementation

Once the Council makes a decision, the policy must be carried out, or implemented. Suppose the Council decides to buy the vans. Implementation of this city policy will involve such activities as:

1. Putting out bids to van dealers;
2. Determining the lowest bidder;
3. Having the city's financial officer certify that money is available;
4. Having the city attorney draw up a purchase contract;
5. Having the city planner determine the routes of the vans based on the needs of the city's handicapped residents;
6. Hiring van drivers and supervisors;
7. Informing the handicapped of the new service.

Policy implementation, then, is the actual carrying out of a policy decision by government officials. Employees of all government departments and agencies (whether it be the U.S. Department of Defense, the Texas Department of Human Resources, or the Kansas City Garbage Department) spend most of their working hours implementing government policies that directly or indirectly affect the public.

Policy Evaluation

When policies are implemented, they must accomplish the original intent of the government policymakers. Suppose that the Houston City Council decides to build a neighborhood playground. According to the Council members, the primary reason for their decision is to prevent an increase in juvenile delinquency in the neighborhood. Thus, the park will accomplish its purpose if the rate of juvenile delinquency in the neighborhood declines. To find out, the Council may direct that an evaluation of the park's impact on neighborhood youth be made. This is *policy evaluation: the measuring of the impact or consequences of policy implementation.* Policy evaluation lets citizens hold public officials accountable for their policy decisions. Just as importantly, it informs officials whether the old policy should be revised or replaced with a completely different one.

Suppose that after the park is built, a group of neighborhood residents complains that the park has been taken over by older, unemployed teenagers who vandalize surrounding homes and cars. And let's say that when the city recreation department completes a study of park activity, it finds that instead of reducing juvenile delinquency, the park actually increases it by serving as a recruitment ground for youth gangs. What will the Houston officials do? In the short term, they can make new policies for the parks—or for the city's unemployed youths. For example, they can:

1. Expand planned activities in the park (baseball tournaments, soccer matches, swimming lessons);
2. Increase police patrols in the neighborhood;
3. Have the city take part in a federally funded program to hire unemployed teenagers.

In the long term, the evaluation helps the Council make better, more informed policy decisions regarding any further park construction in neighborhoods with high concentrations of unemployed youths.

Policymaking and the Survival of Democracy

Making public policy is the primary responsibility of any government. The same is true of a president, governor, mayor, school board member, or other public official. A *public policy* is any decision, backed by the authority of a government, that determines who in the population gets what, where, when and how.[2]

Equally important from the citizen's perspective is *why* a particular policy is made. Understanding *why* often helps determine later whether the policy was good or bad in terms of accomplishing what was originally intended.

The policymaking process is dynamic and on-going, which is why American democracy has survived. At any given time, numerous policies are being formulated, implemented, and evaluated by governments at all levels—national, state, and local. In its chief role of policymaker, government has changed policies in response to changing needs and demands of citizens. This brings up some important questions. How has America's population makeup changed? What effect have these changes had on new policies? Have these changes affected the participation of Americans in the policymaking process? How has government responded?

CHANGES IN THE POPULATION

Growth and Migration Patterns

America has grown rapidly from a population of 2.7 million in 1780 to 227 million in 1980. However, the population growth rate now shows signs of a decline. Between 1960 and 1970 it was 13.4 percent, whereas between 1970 and 1980 it was only 11.4 percent. This growth rate was the lowest in American history, except for the decade of the Great Depression.

Shifts have also occurred in where Americans live. Over the years, more and more people have moved away from farms to urban areas. By 1980, 74.8 percent of all Americans lived in densely populated urban areas. But recent migration patterns have shown that there is a "back-to-the-country" mood among many Americans. For one thing, there has been a mass migration of Americans out of the older, crowded, declining industrial states of the Frost Belt to the newer, more spread out, economically prosperous states of the Sun Belt. As a result of these population shifts shown in the 1980 census, Sun Belt states gained 17 representatives in Congress at the expense of Frost Belt states, which lost the same number. This shift substantially weakened the power in the House of the older, industrial cities of the Northeast and strengthened that of the newer, sprawling Sun Belt areas (see Table 1.1).

During the 1960s and 1970s a large number of Americans moved out of cities into suburbs—or even farther. Most of this outward movement can be explained by the movement of business and industry into suburban areas, where taxes are typically lower than in the central cities. Between 1962 and 1978, nonmetropolitan areas gained 56 per-

TABLE 1.1

Shifts of Power from Frost Belt to Sun Belt Cities, 1923–1983*

	1923		1943		1963		1973		1983**	
	City Reps.	Area Reps.	City Reps.	Area Reps.	City Reps.	Area Reps.	City Reps.	Area Reps.	City Reps.	Area Reps.
Frost Belt Cities										
Boston	5	6	4	5	3	6	3	6	2	6
New York	24	1	24	1	19	6	17	5	14	4
Philadelphia	7	2	7	3	5	3	5	3	4	3
Baltimore	4	0	4	0	4	1	3	1	2	2
Detroit	2	3	6	2	5	3	5	6	4	6
Chicago	10	1	10	1	11	4	8	8	7	7
Sun Belt Cities										
Miami	1	1	1	0	2	1	3	3	3	4
Houston	1	2	1	3	2	3	3	4	4	2
Dallas	1	3	1	4	1	4	3	3	4	3
Los Angeles	2	3	10	3	15	6	17	7	17	7
San Francisco	2	3	2	5	2	8	2	8	2	8

SOURCE: *National Journal,* November 14, 1981, p. 2037.

*The table lists the number of members representing 11 major cities at four points in the past six decades as well as those representing districts that included counties adjoining the center city; 1983 estimates are based on the 1980 census and early redistricting action. Except for Chicago, the city total also includes all parts of the county that contains the major city; the San Francisco area includes all counties in the immediate bay area. Districts that include both the city and outlying area are counted only in the "city" category.

**With the exception of Houston and Dallas, 1983 figures are estimated.

Newly arrived immigrants, like these Vietnamese refugees awaiting customs procedures at the Oakland Airport, tend to locate in large cities. According to some experts, this massive influx of new immigrant groups into our large cities is helping to offset the outmigration of long-time city residents to the suburbs.

cent of all new manufacturing jobs, of which 30 percent were in the South alone. Naturally people move to where the jobs are—if they can afford to move.

In the 1960s a proportionately greater number of whites than blacks moved to the suburbs. But during the 1970s greater proportions of blacks made the move. Between 1970 and 1980, the black suburban population increased by 1.8 million—a 44 percent gain. At the same time, the white suburban population increased by only 10.6 million, or 13 percent. The movement of blacks into suburbia has been attributed to the passage of laws (the making of public policy) preventing discrimination in housing, employment, and education. Most blacks who moved to the suburbs were wealthier and more educated than those who remain in central cities, but on average they were still poorer than their white suburban counterparts.

In addition to the 14.6 million who moved to the suburbs during the 1970s, another 7.3 million moved into rural areas. Most said they moved to get away from the noise, crime, and pollution associated with congested big cities. By "getting closer to nature," many thought they could live a healthier life.

There is some question among population experts about whether these trends—population decline and migration to the suburbs and rural areas—will continue in the 1980s. The President's Commission for a National Agenda for the Eight-

ies predicts that "the scattering of Americans into sprawling suburbs and rural areas will continue in the next few years despite scarce and expensive energy needed for transportation."[3]

Arthur P. Solomon, Director of the Joint Center of Urban Studies at Harvard, has a different view. He predicts that migration to the suburbs will slow down because of changing lifestyles brought about by the economic squeeze, the energy crunch, and the growing number of working adults who choose not to have children.[4] These changes, plus the rapid influx of Cubans, Mexicans, and Vietnamese refugees, may reverse the trend (see Figure 1.2).

No one knows which prediction will come true, but one thing is certain: changes in population affect the policymaking activities of governments. The size of the population often determines how much federal aid a state or local government will receive to fund a child-care program, for example. Similarly, population migration often affects the type of policies that government officials implement. An example is the mass migration of more affluent citizens out of the nation's Frost Belt cities into the Sun Belt. Cities that lose population have to concern themselves with funding their activities in the light of a shrinking tax base. Cities gaining population must try to expand utilities and other services to new residents as soon as possible.

Besides the shifts in where people live, important changes have occurred in the age, education,

Average annual legal immigration to U.S.

Period	Immigration
1900-10	820,239
1910-19	634,738
1920-29	429,551
1930-39	69,938
1940-49	85,661
1950-59	249,927
1960-69	321,375
1970-79	446,518
1980	808,000 (est.)

Immigrants to U.S. by region

1959	Region	1979 (latest)
60.9%	Europe	13.4%
8.9%	Asia	41.4%
1.1%	Africa	2.6%
0.5%	Oceania	1.0%
19.8%	Latin America	38.6%
8.9%	Canada	3.0%

An additional 500,000 to 1 million persons are believed to enter the U.S. illegally each year.
Note: Totals may not add because of rounding.

FIGURE 1.2
New Wave of Immigrants and New Origins
SOURCE: "New Wave of Immigrants." Reprinted from *U.S. News and World Report.* Copyright © 1982 by U.S. News and World Report, Inc. Used by permission.

income, occupation, employment, and racial and ethnic characteristics of America's population. These changes have also necessitated changes in policymaking.

Age

One of the most marked changes is the aging of America—or, as some say, the graying of America. During the past decade more than two full years were added to the average individual's life expectancy. At the same time, the birthrate declined. The "baby boom" (a rapid increase in the birthrate) has been replaced by a "baby bust," because young people today are getting married later and having fewer children. The result of the declining birthrate and higher life expectancy is an aging population. The percentage of the population over age 65 grew from 9.8 percent in 1970 to 11.3 percent in 1980.

Pressing policy issues will emerge because of this aging trend. One of these issues is the increasing strain on the Social Security system. More of the elderly are becoming eligible to draw benefits from the system, but fewer young people are growing up to contribute to it.

Another issue is the provision of health care for the elderly. This is a difficult, delicate matter because many Americans feel that health care is the responsibility of the family rather than of the government. But can the government ignore the growing number of senior citizens whose families cannot or will not help at the time of their lives when they may most desperately need support?

A third pressing policy issue is the decreased demand for schools brought about by the declining birthrate. Government policymakers may be forced to choose which schools to close and what types of educational programs to cut first. Both are very difficult choices.

Education

Today's average American has far more formal education than his or her ancestors had. In 1850 only 47.2 percent of all school-age persons were enrolled in school. By 1980 this figure had risen to almost 90 percent. In 1870 only 2 percent of the population had graduated from high school, but by 1980 this figure was more than 65 percent. Likewise, the number of college graduates has increased dramatically. In addition, major changes have occurred in *who* goes to college.

In the 1970s, many blue-collar (skilled labor) jobs began to pay more than many white-collar jobs. As a result, greater numbers of high-school-age persons opted to go to technical school or to enter the work force right after graduation rather than go to college. College enrollment levels did not drop much, however, largely because of the influx of a new group of students—women. Between 1970 and 1980 the number of women 14 to 34 years old enrolled in college increased by 71 percent, compared with only a 14 percent increase for men. This trend of women going to college co-incided with the trend toward fewer children, later marriages, higher divorce rates, and increasing numbers of displaced homemakers (nonworking, middle-aged women suddenly left alone because of widowhood or divorce).

Changes in the public's educational aspirations, the economic pinch, and the declining birthrate will continue to create critical issues for policymakers in the 1980s. They will have to decide, for example, whether the national, state, or local level of government will bear primary responsibility for public education costs, how to fund public schools (with either the unpopular, locally raised property tax or state sales and income taxes), and, as we have already noted, which schools to close and what types of educational programs to cut.

Income

Median family income rose from $3,319 in 1950 to $22,390 in 1981. This may seem like a big jump, but much of the increase is due to inflation (a decline in the buying power of the dollar). Even so, a *Washington Post* survey of 2,505 Americans taken at the end of the 1970s found that 81 percent felt they were better off than their parents had been at the same age.[5] The same survey revealed that the economy is nevertheless the biggest worry of most Americans. An overwhelming majority confessed that they are worried about whether they will have enough income to live on when they retire.

Not everyone has benefited equally from the prospering of America. There are still greater proportions of blacks, Hispanics, and women below the poverty line than there are white males. In fact, even though levels of income have risen dramatically since World War II, the degree of inequality has remained about the same. Roughly three of every ten blacks (32.5 percent) and two of every ten Hispanics (25.7 percent) live in poverty compared to only one of every ten whites (10.2 percent).

More women, particularly female heads of household (single or divorced women with children), live in poverty than men. In addition, even though more women have entered the work force in recent years, women still earn less than men. However, some progress is being made. For example, among younger workers earning gaps tend to be smaller. But women still have a long way to go.

TABLE 1.2

Male–Female Earnings by Occupation, 1981 Weekly Medians

Occupation	Women's Pay	Men's Pay
Clerical workers	220	328
Computer specialists	355	488
Editors, reporters	324	382
Engineers	371	547
Lawyers	407	574
Nurses	326	344
Physicians	401	495
Sales workers	190	366
Teachers (elementary)	311	379
Waiters	144	200

SOURCE: "How Long Till Equality?" Copyright 1982 Time Inc. All rights reserved. Reprinted by permission from Time.

In 1979 the median earnings for women were $10,550, or about 60 percent of the men's median income of $17,514. The earnings gap was even greater in certain occupations, such as sales (see Table 1.2). Some of this continuing gap can be explained by the fewer years of work experience and lower educational levels of women, which limit the types of jobs they can hold and the wages they can make. However, some of the gap is the result of sex discrimination in hiring and promoting and the lack of child-care facilities.

The wide variations in the incomes of Americans create important policy issues for governments. They must make policies that help lift persons out of poverty but that at the same time do not destroy their incentive to work. In making policy decisions involving economic well-being, governments often cannot avoid class and racial issues, which make decisions doubly difficult. These class and racial issues will be discussed later in the chapter.

Occupation

Major shifts have occurred in the occupational structure of the United States largely because of marked changes in the incomes associated with certain types of jobs. A decline in the size of the blue-collar work force during the 1960s reversed in the 1970s. Shortages of skilled laborers such as plumbers, painters, carpenters, electricians, and mechanics drove their wages way above those of white-collar workers such as teachers, clerical and office workers, and middle managers. By 1980, the average weekly earnings of these skilled laborers were well above those of most white-collar

Left, Doctor Sally Ride was America's first woman astronaut sent into space. She might never have been given the opportunity to train for this position without passage of Title VII of the 1964 Civil Rights Act prohibiting job bias on the basis of sex. Right, Elizabeth Dole was appointed U.S. Secretary of Transportation by President Ronald Reagan. As a woman Cabinet member, heading a very technical department, she is an example of how much the occupational opportunities for American women have improved in recent years.

workers, the exceptions being professionals (doctors, lawyers) and persons in the upper levels of management. Some have labeled this new group of affluent Americans the "new rich blue-collar."

The shift in incomes associated with certain occupations stimulated enrollment in technical schools and community college skill programs. Suddenly, going to college was no longer so necessary to earn a decent wage. In 1979, 17,268,000 persons were enrolled in vocational programs across the country, while only 11,570,000 were enrolled in colleges and universities. This trend is expected to continue into the 1980s. It is estimated that fewer than 20 percent of all new jobs in the 1980s will require college degrees.

Another change has been the entry of women into occupations that previously had been "for men only." Passage of the Equal Pay in Employment Act of 1963 (requiring equal pay for equal work) and Title VII of the 1964 Civil Rights Act (prohibiting job bias on the basis of sex) and the

higher pay associated with "men's jobs" attracted many young women into nontraditional blue-collar, craft-type jobs. However, most women workers are still clustered in the poorest-paying occupations. According to one report, in 1979 over 80 percent of all women workers were concentrated in low-paying, dead-end clerical, sales, service, and factory jobs.[6] Eleanor Holmes Norton, head of the Equal Employment Opportunity Commission (EEOC) during the Carter administration, predicts that such job segregation will be one of the most important women's issues in the 1980s. According to her, women's work has traditionally been undervalued and continues to be so.

An example of undervalued women's work is the case of Linda Cooper, a production editor for a small New England publishing firm.[7] Cooper considers her job of turning manuscripts into books just as valuable as that of the firm's manufacturing coordinator, who purchases the paper for the books and selects the printers. But her job,

Cooper says, is usually filled by a woman and paid less than the other, which is generally filled by a man and leads to promotions and more responsibility. What Cooper is raising is the issue of pay *parity*—fair pay for work of equal value.

Another occupational issue is the value of housework. Many women's movement leaders are pushing for recognition of the social and economic value of the work done by the American homemaker. Because of the high dollar value of housework—hiring workers to do all that a homemaker does around the house is expensive—women's movement leaders maintain that all social security and pension benefits earned by the husband should accrue (be credited) equally to the wife and the husband.

Settling these occupational policy issues will not be easy. Determining the value of certain jobs will be both complex and costly. The ultimate decisions will probably rest with the Supreme Court.*

Employment

Overall, more Americans are working today than ever before. The percentage of employed working-age Americans rose from 56.8 percent in 1950 to

---

*In *County of Washington* v. *Gunther* (1981), the Supreme Court did address the comparable worth issue but did not make a final determination as to the value of specific jobs. The Court merely held that the Civil Rights Act of 1964 would allow women to sue employers for pay discrimination when their jobs were comparable to those performed by men.

59.9 percent in 1981. However, such overall employment figures at times misrepresent the employment picture. This is true when there are increases in the unemployment rate due to changes in the condition of the economy. For example, during the height of the recession of 1981 to 1983, the unemployment rate rose and some 12 million Americans were temporarily out of work. Overall employment figures also hide two important long-term trends: the entry of women into the work force and the rising level of unemployment among the country's minority youth, especially young blacks in America's big cities.

The year 1978 marked the first time in American history that more than half of all women over 16 years of age were working.[8] The percentage of women in the labor force doubled in just 20 years (from 1960 to 1980) as fewer women married, more couples divorced, and more families needed two incomes to meet the rising cost of living. Yet as we've already seen, women's wages remained lower than men's, and fewer women were able to hold full-time jobs. Women are still more likely than men to work part-time (21 percent versus 5 percent), usually because of home and family responsibilities. Those responsibilities of course greatly narrow the types of jobs women can hold and the wages they can earn.

The rapid entry of women into the work force has created new issues for policymakers. Pregnancy disability rights, equal pay for equal work, and provision of child-care services are issues that

Government-sponsored training programs are designed to make unemployed, unskilled minority youths employable. However, these programs are very expensive and if taxes must be raised, policymakers run the risk of alienating taxpayers by approving such programs.

have emerged because of changes in employment patterns.

The rising rate of unemployment among the country's minorities, particularly youth, has also created new demands on the makers of public policy. These youths, most of whom are high-school or junior-high-school dropouts, do not have the technical skills needed to get a job. Yet the longer they remain out of school and unemployed, the more difficulty they have finding a job, the more depressed they frequently become, and the more likely it is that they will turn to lawbreaking and violence. Areas with high youth unemployment rates are the country's breeding grounds for crime and riots.

Public programs designed to reduce unemployment rates among minority youth are expensive. They're also often unpopular with the average middle-class American worker, who probably feels overtaxed. Policymakers must attempt to pay for training and employment programs for needy youth yet avoid raising taxes and fueling the hostility of America's increasingly vocal middle class.

Racial and Ethnic Composition

Population experts predict that by 1990 blacks and Hispanics will represent one-fifth of all Americans. By 2080 it is expected that Hispanics will make up 23.4 percent of the population, blacks will make up 14.7 percent, and Asians 12 percent

if current fertility and immigration rates continue.[9]

Other experts predict that Americans will continue to be as divided along class, racial, and ethnic lines as they have been during the past 40 years.[10] The nation's minorities and ethnics are typically poorer and more dependent on society than are its white citizens—people of northern European origin. Proportionately, they are the most often in need of costly social services and, at the same time, the least able to help pay for them. Any further increase in their numbers, without some advances in helping today's poor become more self-sufficient, will hurt the overall economy, particularly if the cost of living continues to rise as rapidly as it has in the past. In addition, a failure to make policy that will reduce the unemployment of minority populations may stimulate the return of race riots, which characterized urban areas in the 1960s. (The majority of America's minorities live in urban areas.) Such riots could cost taxpayers even more than employment and training programs.

The changing racial and ethnic makeup of the population has also changed the political makeup of governments across the nation. Because of passage of the Voting Rights Act of 1965 and increased political participation by minorities (especially blacks), members of minority groups have been elected to city councils, school boards, state

The ethnic composition of America is consistantly changing. Hispanics are one of the fastest growing ethnic groups. By 2080 it is expected that Hispanics will make up 23.4 percent of the U.S. population if their current fertility and immigration rates continue.

legislatures, judgeships, and Congress. Minorities have also been appointed to high government posts such as the president's cabinet and the Supreme Court. As a result, new issues have been placed on the policymaking agenda of America's national, state, and local governments. Here again is evidence that the democratic system can respond positively to changes in people's needs and expectations. Of course, these changes do not always come as fast as some would like.

CHANGES IN VALUES

The changes in population and the problems created as a result have historically resulted in the emergence of new values—ideas, principles, or qualities—that may at first conflict with older, more traditional values. But over time, new values may become acceptable as people get used to them (see Table 1.3). Many things considered de-

sirable and taken for granted today were once viewed as highly undesirable; examples would include electricity, the right of women and blacks to vote, Social Security, and Medicare.

Some of the fiercest conflicts in the policymaking arena involve issues that split the population along moral, religious, or ethical lines—all parts of an individual's value system. The policy issues most often characterized by such splits are those dealing with individual rights and the power and scope of government. Many of these issues will be discussed in more detail in the chapters on civil liberties and civil rights, but this discussion will introduce value conflicts that have characterized America in recent years.

Values Concerning Individual Rights

New values have most often conflicted with older, more traditional ones in such areas as lifestyle rights, rights to control one's own body, the right to privacy, and the right of free expression.

TABLE 1.3
Changing Social Norms

Questions: Today there are many different kinds of lifestyles which people find acceptable, such as a husband staying home and caring for the children while the wife goes to work. How do you feel about this? Do you find it acceptable for other people but *not* for yourself, acceptable for other people *and* yourself, or not acceptable at all? (Respondents were then asked a series of questions about other behavior, as shown below.)

	Not Acceptable at All (a)	Acceptable for Others but not for Self (b)	Acceptable for Others and Self (c)	(b + c)
A single woman having and raising a child	26%	40%	34%	74%
The husband staying home and caring for the children while the wife goes to work	26	36	38	74
Premarital relationships	36	23	41	64
A mother of young children going to work for career purposes and self-fulfillment when the money is not needed	39	27	34	61
Enrolling very young children in day care centers or nursery schools to give the mother more leisure time	49	24	27	51
Young people with children living together in what they call the "extended family"	54	34	12	46
Homosexual relationships	59	35	6	41
Divorced women asking their parents to raise the children while they build a new life	71	19	10	29

Source: Survey by *Time*/Yankelovich, March 1978. Reported in Ruth Clark and Greg Matire, "Americans, Still in a Family Way," *Public Opinion* 2 (Oct/Nov 1979), Table 3, p. 19.

 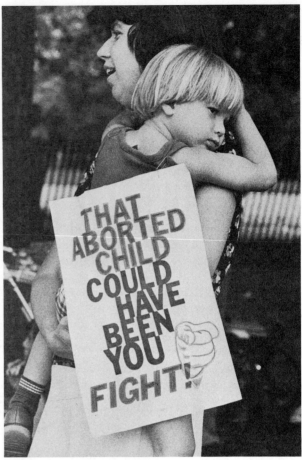

One of the most controversial lifestyle issues has been abortion. Pro-choice advocates (left) argue that a woman should have the right to choose whether she wants an abortion; such a choice is an individual right, not to be determined by government. Anti-abortionists (right) argue that abortion is morally and ethically wrong. They equate abortion with murder and argue that since it is a crime, government should outlaw it.

Among the most widely publicized conflicts in the 1970s were lifestyle issues—premarital sex, cohabitation of unmarried couples, and homosexuality. Although most Americans still do not choose these lifestyles for themselves, recent surveys show that they have become more tolerant of the right of others to adopt them (see Table 1.3).

A poll by the *Washington Post* in 1979 found that 63 percent of all Americans had become more tolerant than they were a mere ten years earlier on such social issues as liberalized divorce laws, unmarried couples living together, and homosexuality.[11] The traditional values of marriage and the family still prevailed, however. A *Time* survey found that most Americans still value the health

and well-being of their families above everything else (see Table 1.4).

TABLE 1.4

The Continued Strength of Traditional American Values

Question: What role does each of the following values play in your life? Is . . . very important, fairly important, or not very important? The figures represent the percentage of the people surveyed who considered the value very important.

Family	92%	Patriotism	70%
Friendship	81	Religion	66
Work	78		

SOURCE: Survey by *Time*/Yankelovich, March 1978. Reported in Ruth Clark and Greg Matire, "Americans, Still in a Family Way," *Public Opinion* 2 (Oct/Nov 1979), Table 1, p. 16.

Gay rights is a lifestyle issue that first became widely publicized in the 1970s. While most Americans do not favor such a lifestyle for themselves, recent surveys indicate that society has become increasingly more tolerant of those who do choose such lifestyles.

Yet the American family is also changing as more and more women are working. Of the citizens surveyed by the *Post*, 43 percent said that the men in their families were taking more responsibility for household work than they did in the past. While a majority of women favored greater equality between the sexes, they still expressed some doubt about what this new equality would do to family life. Two-thirds of them thought that the decline of traditional male and female roles would be harmful to children.[12]

Numerous issues concern the individual's right to control his or her own body. These include the right of a female to have an abortion, the right of an individual to receive treatment by a drug not condoned by the government (e.g., laetrile), the right to use a controlled substance (e.g., marijuana), the right to eat certain foodstuffs (e.g., saccharin), and the right to die (to order hospital life support systems to be removed). Of these issues, perhaps the most controversial has been abortion. Many see abortion as more a moral or religious issue than the others.

Americans have always valued their right to privacy. In recent years a number of new privacy issues have come up because of the emergence and development of highly computerized information systems of both government (see Table 1.5) and industry. For example, an individual's right to privacy can be interrupted by mail (the unwanted ''junk'' variety) or by telephone (through exchanges of computerized mailing and donor lists). Also at issue is the way businesses can exchange information of a highly personal, confidential nature without the individual's consent. In a more traditional vein are issues involving the wiretapping of private conversations and the right of two consenting adults to engage in whatever form of sexual expression they desire in the privacy of their own homes.

New freedom-of-expression issues have also emerged because of changes in the population. Examples include an individual's right to view pornography, to travel to foreign countries despite a presidential ban, and to ask for contributions for a religious group or charity in a public airport.

How are issues concerning individual rights resolved? In a democracy, elected officials have the responsibility of weighing public opinion—that is, comparing the strength of public support for new values with support for older, more traditional ones. Elected officials are also responsible for making policy that they think will be supported by a majority of the population they represent (unless, of course, such policy conflicts with certain individual rights set down in the Constitution).

Assessing public opinion, as we shall see in chapter 5, is complicated when one group expresses its values and opinions more vigorously than others. Such lopsided expression may give the policymaker an inaccurate picture of public opinion. Even so, public officials are held accountable for their policymaking activities. If they make unpopular decisions, they can be removed from office and replaced by others more in tune with the public's needs and demands.

TABLE 1.5

How Private Are Our Lives?

Files on People

Departments of Education and Health and Human Services	1,033,999,891
Department of Treasury	780,196,929
Department of Commerce	431,427,589
Department of Defense	333,951,949
Department of Justice	201,474,342
Department of State	110,809,198
Department of Agriculture	33,727,730
Copyright Office	28,408,366
Department of Transportation	24,023,142
Federal Communications Commission	20,870,078
Department of Housing and Urban Development	20,340,642
Department of Labor	16,785,015
Department of Interior	16,708,016
Office of Personnel Management	16,016,779
Department of Energy	8,929,999
Executive Office of the President	30,655
All other federal agencies	452,043,345
Grand total	3,529,743,665

Or 15 files on average for each American

SOURCE: "Files on People." Reprinted from *U.S. News and World Report.* Copyright © 1982 by U.S. News and World Report, Inc. Used by permission.

Values Concerning the Power and Scope of Government

Government has become involved in a wider range of activities over the years. The effect of this expansion has been to "create more pressure on [government], raise greater expectations of its performance, complicate its essential job of representing and reconciling conflicting interests, encounter more contradictions, and generate more disappointment."[13]

Americans have always differed in their opinion of how big and how strong government, particularly the national government, should be. In the 1970s concern grew that the national government was gaining too much power at the expense of state and local governments. Many people questioned whether someone in Washington could understand their problems as well as a policymaker who lived closer to them. As the national government expanded its role in policymaking, people feared they were losing their power over what happened to them.

In the 1970s Americans also became disenchanted "with government and the political system's attempt to respond to that loss of faith."[14] Between 1966 and 1979 the public's confidence in such government institutions as Congress and the executive branch (the presidency and the bureaucracy) fell by 50 percent and reached an all-time low. These feelings, according to some, were direct reactions to the "major growth of the federal government in the 1960s when Washington took over many of the functions previously under local or private control."[15]

The disturbing thing about this tremendous drop in the public's confidence in the national government was that it continued to increase even as the government was attempting to make the system more open. For example, new laws were passed that called for open meetings of government agencies, financial disclosure by top government officials and private lobbying groups, appointment of special prosecutors in certain types of cases, zero-based budgeting, civil service reform, and regular review of federal regulations.

In fact, decreasing confidence in national government institutions was a key issue in the 1980 presidential election. One study of the election concluded that the preelection climate was characterized by:

the conviction that government in general, and the federal government in particular, was not doing anything to make people's lives better, despite the higher taxes most were paying. . . . What made Reagan so attractive to the voters of 1980 [as opposed to incumbent Jimmy Carter] was his ability to express their own frustrations at the failures of government to function with more efficacy.[16]

The public's dissatisfaction with the size and scope of the national government in relation to state and local governments also carried over into the congressional races. In 1980 Republicans seized control of the Senate by defeating such established liberal Democratic senators as George McGovern, Gaylord Nelson, Birch Bayh, and John Culver.

An immediate result of the 1980 elections was congressional approval of Reagan's proposed cuts in the federal budget and support for creation of federal block grants that returned control of some federal aid dollars to the states. The fact that congressional support for Reagan's proposals came from members of both political parties led one expert to conclude that "political leaders, for all their seemingly sharp differences on domestic and foreign policy, seem to agree on the importance of responding to the public's discontent."[17] But the public has remained discontented. Even in the light of these changes, a number of Americans appear to be uninterested in participating in the political process—whether at the national, state, or local levels.

CHANGES IN POLITICAL PARTICIPATION

Several changes in the political activity of Americans have occurred in recent years. Fewer persons are voting, more people are calling themselves independents rather than Democrats or Republicans, and more people are becoming active in special interest groups.

Drop in Voting

In each of the past six presidential elections, the percentage of eligible voters who actually cast ballots has dropped. In 1960, 63.8 percent of the eligible voters voted. By 1980 this figure had dropped to 53.2 percent—seventy-six million eligible Americans failed to vote. Moreover, this drop in participation has characterized elections at all levels—national, state, and local.

The drop in voting has been greatest among young persons (under age 34) and among ethnic and racial minorities.[18] Even though persons under the age of 34 made up over 40 percent of the voting-age population, they were only 27.6 percent of the turnout in the 1978 congressional elections. Similarly, even though the percentage of

blacks who register to vote is the same as that of whites, fewer blacks actually vote on election day. In 1980, 60.9 percent of all whites of voting age reported that they voted compared to only 50.5 percent of all voting-age blacks. Hispanics are even less likely to register or vote. Only 36.3 percent of all eligible Hispanics reported they registered to vote (compared to 68.4 percent of whites and 60 percent of blacks), and only 29.9 percent said they actually voted on election day. In chapter 9, which examines elections and voting behavior, we will see some of the reasons for these findings.

The ironic thing about this downward trend in voting, according to political columnist James Reston, is that "it occurred during a time of unprecedented expansion in the nation's communications (television, radio, news magazines) and also during a period of widespread liberalization in the procedures and statutes governing registration and voting."[19]

A study made by the American Bar Association's Committee on Election Reform blamed the downward trend in voting on:

political mistrust [a carryover from Watergate, Koreagate, Brilab, Abscam], the decline of allegiance to political parties, a widespread feeling of 'helplessness' among the people to change anything by voting, particularly among the poor and poorly educated, and the complexities of the absentee ballot voting system at a time when the people [are] moving from one place to another as never before.[20]

Decline in Political Party Voting

Another change has been the declining significance of political parties. Fewer people consider themselves Democrats or Republicans and more prefer to call themselves independents. Many also prefer to vote a split ticket (a Democratic candidate here and a Republican candidate there) instead of voting a straight ticket (all Republican or all Democratic). This trend toward independence is particularly evident among young voters. More than half of all new voters classify themselves as independents.

Here is one description of the movement away from political parties:

There was a time when many people felt that 'anybody in your party was terrific and everybody in the other party was a skunk.' No more. . . . More likely, every-

The owner of this car is obviously a strong Democrat, as evidenced by the bumper stickers. Today there are fewer such individuals who identify exclusively with one political party and more who call themselves independents and vote a split ticket.

one is a skunk. Public esteem of politicians of both parties is low. . . . Party labels still count, but less. Issues matter more than before, and stereotypes of regional and ethnic voting patterns are no longer very relevant.[21]

Some scholars believe that another reason parties are declining is the ''professionalization'' of politics. ''The election process is increasingly overrun by professional pollsters, advertising consultants and even bureaucrats at the Federal Election Commission (FEC). New campaign styles and strategies, based heavily on these technologies, have substituted for party organization.''[22]

Other scholars believe that political parties are being taken over by activists who are ideologically extreme—either much more conservative or much more liberal than the majority of the party followers.[23] Extremists appall the average party member. Examples of extremism in candidate selection are the nominations of Barry Goldwater by the Republicans in 1964 and George McGovern by the Democrats in 1972. Neither of these candidates represented the views of a majority of his party.

What Do These Changes Mean?

The significance of these changes in voting behavior has been heavily debated by political scientists and election specialists. Some feel that high voter turnout is essential to the maintenance of a democracy. They warn that a low turnout means that ''politics will be dominated by professional media manipulators beholden to no one.''[24] These professionals, they warn, could make a winning candidate out of an unknown; furthermore, the candidate could turn out to be ''unstable, demagogic, and even an authoritarian.'' Others do not think a high turnout is necessary to ensure the continuance of a democracy. They believe that the voters ''are not stupid. . . . They will vote when they think it matters.''[25]

At the very least, a drop in the level of voting means that fewer people, for one reason or another, are actually exercising their right to participate in the process of choosing their official policymakers. But indications are that even though people are not voting as much, they are participating more in another type of activity: the special interest group.

Rise in Interest Group Participation

An ***interest group*** *is an organized group of citizens who hold the same views about what type of policy the government should adopt on a specific issue.* Just about every issue has interest groups with completely opposite views about what government should do. Examples include the ''pronuke'' and ''antinuke'' groups, ''right-to-life'' groups (against abortion) and ''prochoice'' groups (for it), and pro-gun control and anti-gun control groups. Most important policy issues today are characterized by debate between opposing groups.

Some say that interest groups are healthy for a democracy, that in fact they *are* democracy in its purest form: people exercising their freedom of expression. As such, interest groups are advanced as proof that American government is ''of, by, and for'' the people. But others say that the rise of interest groups may actually be killing democracy. For example, some congressional leaders feel that the rising number of single-issue groups makes it difficult, if not impossible, to work out compromises on policy issues and keeps *any* decision from being made.[26] This is because each lawmaker is pressured by different single-interest groups who can affect his or her reelection.

Participation in interest group activities is on the upswing. Most important policy issues today are characterized by debate between opposing groups. Both advocates (left) and opponents (right) of nuclear power use protest tactics to get their messages across to the public and its policymakers.

The Link Between Participation and Policymaking

People who participate in the political process—whether by voting, belonging to a political party or interest group, attending city council meetings, or serving on citizens' advisory committees—are more likely to influence the policymaking process than those who do not participate. Because not everyone participates, some people are more influential than others. Whether this limited participation is harmful for democracy is a subject of debate. However, unequal rates of citizen participation have always existed in American politics.

More disagreement arises over whether each person has an equal *chance* to influence the policy-making process. In other words, political scientists differ about the power of the individual to influence policy.

TWO THEORIES OF POLICYMAKING: ELITISM AND PLURALISM

Power is the ability to determine who gets what, when, where, and how. *Political power* is the ability to influence the public policymaking process. Some political scientists maintain that only a handful of citizens really have the power to influence public policymaking and that "elites, not masses, govern America."[27] The theory of *elitism* holds that powerful individuals from the better educated and higher socioeconomic levels of society usually hold important positions in industrial, financial, military, or governmental institutions and thus wield a disproportionate share of power. Political scientists who believe in the elitist theory of political power do not think that such a power structure necessarily harms the powerless. Instead they argue that elites must be aware of, and respond to, the needs of the masses to maintain the system of government that keeps them powerful.

Letter-writing and petition-signing are two of the most common tactics used by interest groups to demonstrate strong grass-roots support for their positions.

Other political scientists believe in a pluralist theory of power.[28] According to the view of *pluralism, any citizen, particularly if he or she is a member of an interest group, has the power to influence policy. However, it is not always the same citizens who are interested in and who influence policy debate.* In other words, no one group holds all the power. Certainly the pluralist theory of policymaking is more consistent with traditional ideas about democracy—popular participation of all citizens, government by majority rule, and the right of dissent through freedom of speech, press, assembly, and petition.

Regardless of which theory you believe best describes power in America, few disagree that some people participate in politics more than others. Often people participate simply because they are interested in politics. On the other hand, when people do not participate, it is sometimes because they are frustrated about what the government is or is not doing. They begin to feel that involving themselves in politics is useless, that their vote doesn't really matter, that all candidates are alike, or that no matter what they do, life doesn't get any better. We have already seen that more and more people are becoming frustrated with politics and policymaking.

WHY STUDY GOVERNMENT? LEARNING HOW TO INFLUENCE POLICYMAKING

People may fail to participate in the policymaking process because they feel that they don't know how to. They don't understand the structure of government, the nature of the policymaking process itself, or how they can make their voices heard in the policy arena. The purpose of this book is to help you understand all of these important elements. We will examine the structure of American government, see how the different political institutions—presidency, bureaucracy, legislature, and courts—figure in the policymaking process, and demonstrate how these institutions can be made to respond to the changing needs and demands of Americans. By learning how the American system of government works, you will be better equipped to exercise your right to participate.

Throughout the chapters to come we will focus on policies that respond to three of America's most critical areas of concern: 1) changing lifestyles, 2) energy shortages, and 3) a fluctuating economy. In chapter 2 we will take a closer look at these needs so that in later chapters we can better understand how policies relating to them are being formed, implemented, and evaluated.

SUMMARY

Government's role in a changing society is to make public policy. A public policy is any government decision that determines who gets what, where, when, and how. The American system of government has survived because it has adapted its public policies to the changing needs of its people. The dynamic nature of the policymaking process (policy formation, policy implementation, and policy evaluation) permits this adaptation.

America has undergone some major changes since 1776. Its population has grown from 2.7 million in 1780 to over 227 million in 1980. What was once largely a rural society has become a highly urban society. However, more recent migration patterns reflect a "back-to-the-country" mood as Americans increasingly move to the suburbs and beyond. They are also moving out of the Frost Belt to the Sun Belt. In addition to these migrational changes, the American population has become older, better educated, wealthier, more racially and ethnically mixed, and more concerned with pay parity and affirmative action as more women have entered the work force. Americans have become more tolerant of the rights and life-styles of others but less tolerant of big government. In terms of their political participation, fewer Americans are voting in presidential elections, more consider themselves independents as opposed to Democrats or Republicans, and more are participating in the activities of special interest groups.

There are two theories about the power of the individual to influence policy. Elitism theory holds that powerful individuals from the better-educated and higher socioeconomic levels of society hold more important positions and have more influence over policymaking than the average citizen. The pluralist view holds that citizens have the power to influence policymaking, particularly as members of interest groups, but recognizes the fact that it is not always the same citizens who are interested in each policy issue. Inherent in each theory is the notion that some citizens are more influential than others, usually those who best understand the policymaking process.

KEY TERMS

elitism
interest group
pluralism
policy evaluation
policy formation
policy implementation
policymaking process
political power
politics
power
public policy

SUGGESTED READINGS

Advisory Commission on Intergovernmental Relations. *Citizen Participation in the American Federal System.* Washington, D.C.: Government Printing Office, 1980.

Anderson, James E.; Brady, David W.; and Bullock, Charles L., III. *Public Policy and Politics in America.* North Scituate, Mass.: Duxbury Press, 1978.

Crotty, William J., and Jacobsen, Gary C. *American Parties in Decline.* Boston: Little, Brown, 1980.

Hadley, Charles D. *Split Ticket Voting in America: Realignment, Dealignment, or Status Quo?* New York: Pergamon Press, 1981.

Ippolito, Dennis S., and Walker, Thomas G. *Political Parties, Interest Groups, and Public Policy: Group Influence in American Politics.* Englewood Cliffs, N.J.: Prentice-Hall, 1980.

Ladd, Everett Carll, Jr. *Where Have All the Voters Gone? The Fracturing of America's Political Parties.* New York: W. W. Norton, 1978.

Moe, Terry M. *The Organization of Interests: Incentive and the Internal Dynamics of Political Interest Groups.* Chicago: University of Chicago Press, 1980.

Nie, Norman H.; Verba, Sidney; and Petrocik, John R. *The Changing American Voter,* 2d ed. Cambridge, Mass.: Harvard University Press, 1979.

Sale, Kirkpatrick. *Power Shift: The Rise of the Southern Rim and Its Challenge to the Eastern Establishment.* New York: Vintage Books, 1975.

Snyder, David Pearce, ed. *The Family in Post-Industrial America: Some Fundamental Perceptions for Public Policy Development.* Boulder, Colo.: Westview Press, 1979.

AMERICA'S CHANGING NEEDS AND THE PROCESS OF MAKING PUBLIC POLICY

A Pressured Economy ■ The Energy "Shortage" ■ Changes in Lifestyles ■ The Citizen's Role: Policy Influencer ■ Evaluating Public Policies: Improving Democracy

In the 1980s America's most pressing needs arise from an uncertain economy, high demands for energy from limited resources, and the changing lifestyles of the population. These needs will require responses from government in the form of policy. What are the most difficult issues that policymakers must resolve? What is the role of the citizen in the decision-making process? What determines whether a public policy is successful or not? These questions will be addressed in this chapter.

A PRESSURED ECONOMY

The American public is worried about the economy. As Table 2.1 reveals, in recent years the commonmost replies to the question "What do you think is the most important problem facing the country today?" have been "the high cost of living" and "unemployment." The picture of the economy at the beginning of the 1980s was none too bright:

America entered the 80's with a shrinking dollar, a productive population whose real incomes . . . were beginning to recede, and whose taxes were growing heavier

through inflation creep that edged them into higher tax brackets. [1]

In spite of their belief in a free enterprise system, Americans expect the government to play a key role in regulating the economy. When unemployment levels are high, protestors push for government programs to create new jobs.

TABLE 2.1

Most Important Problem Trend: Public's Top Concerns, 1935–1981

Question: "What do you think is the most important problem facing this country today?"

1981:	High cost of living, unemployment	1958:	Unemployment, keeping peace
1980:	High cost of living, unemployment	1957:	Race relations, keeping peace
1979:	High cost of living, energy problems	1956:	Keeping peace
		1955:	Keeping peace
1978:	High cost of living, energy problems	1954:	Keeping peace
		1953:	Keeping peace
1977:	High cost of living, unemployment	1952:	Korean War
1976:	High cost of living, unemployment	1951:	Korean War
1975:	High cost of living, unemployment	1950:	Labor unrest
1974:	High cost of living, Watergate, energy crisis	1949:	Labor unrest
		1948:	Keeping peace
1973:	High cost of living, Watergate	1947:	High cost of living, labor unrest
1972:	Vietnam	1946:	High cost of living
1971:	Vietnam, high cost of living	1945:	Winning war
1970:	Vietnam	1944:	Winning war
1969:	Vietnam	1943:	Winning war
1968:	Vietnam	1942:	Winning war
1967:	Vietnam, high cost of living	1941:	Keeping out of war, winning war
1966:	Vietnam		
1965:	Vietnam, race relations	1940:	Keeping out of war
1964:	Vietnam, race relations	1939:	Keeping out of war
1963:	Keeping peace, race relations	1938:	Keeping out of war
1962:	Keeping peace	1937:	Unemployment
1961:	Keeping peace	1936:	Unemployment
1960:	Keeping peace	1935:	Unemployment
1959:	Keeping peace		

Source: *The Gallup Report,* no. 198 (March 1982), p. 13.

The same problems characterized the economies of other countries because of their growing dependence on one another. Robert S. McNamara, former director of the World Bank and U.S. secretary of defense, has said:

> *The fortunes of the developed and developing countries alike must face up to such immense and complicated problems as population growth, food production, creating more jobs, energy, urbanization, reducing absolute poverty, and expanding international trade and financial flows.*[2]

The very character of America's economy has changed in recent years. Instead of economic abundance and growth, we seem to be facing a period of economic scarcity and decline. The consequences of scarcity and decline may be political, diplomatic, or possibly even military. One example of this has been America's experience in buying oil from the *Organization of Petroleum Exporting Countries (OPEC), an organization of oil-rich nations that meets regularly to decide how much oil to produce and what price to charge.*

Our changing economy has presented the makers of public policy with three critical issues: 1) how to deal with a stagflation economy, 2) how much government regulation to impose to strengthen the economy, and 3) how to ease tensions among the classes (poor, middle-class, wealthy).

A Stagflation Economy

According to government, TV, and newspaper reports, the United States always seems to be battling either inflation or recession. During a period of *inflation, prices and wages rise sharply and employment levels are high.* This produces a constant increase in the cost of living. It also reduces the purchasing power of the dollar because a dollar buys less. The reduction in the purchasing power of the dollar reduces the value of an individual's savings, which encourages more short-term buying, which in turn fuels inflation. During a *recession, the economy slows down, wages and prices do not rise as rapidly, but the unemployment rate increases sharply.* Fluctuations in the economy may be caused by a number of factors: international crises, crop failures, natural disasters, strikes in major industries—even changes of season (e.g., Christmas is a big buying time and employment levels are high).

Most theories about how government can help combat economic instability are based on the assumption that at a particular point there is either a recession or inflation—but not both. Even public opinion polls, in soliciting people's feelings about the economy, ask the question in an "either-or" format: "Do you favor trying to curb inflation *or* trying to reduce unemployment?" The problem is that since the early 1970s the American economy has been characterized by rising prices *and* rising unemployment rates—a phenomenon known as stagflation. A period of **stagflation** *is characterized by sluggish growth, extraordinary rates of inflation, a shrinking dollar, rising food and fuel bills, and substantial levels of unemployment.*

Since World War II, makers of public policy have assumed that the basic way to remedy inflation is to decrease the money supply—that is, to tighten credit by raising interest rates (thereby cutting purchasing) and to reduce government spending. This slows down the economy, reducing the rate of increase in wages and prices. Similarly, public policymakers have assumed that the way to end a recession is to increase the money supply—that is, to make credit easier to get by lowering interest rates (thereby expanding purchasing) and to increase government spending. These assumptions are based on economic principles set down by the English economist John Maynard Keynes in his famous book, *General Theory of Employment, Interest, and Money* (1936).[3] **Keynesian economic theory,** sometimes referred to as demand-side economics, *focuses on influencing individual and governmental buying patterns to stabilize the economy, based on the belief that demand creates supply.*

The problem with the Keynesian approach is that it does not cure stagflation, which is characterized by both inflationary and recessionary tendencies. Many now believe that Keynesian theory is outdated. Historian Arthur M. Schlesinger, Jr., among others, has attacked the policy of using recession to combat inflation and then using inflation to combat recession as "foolish and futile."[4]

Schlesinger's criticism of Keynesian economics appears to be justified, based on evidence from the late 1970s. During that decade, the inflation rate inched upward so that by 1979, 87 percent of the population felt that inflation had "become one of the facts of life and was here to stay."[5] Inflation was eroding the purchasing power of hard-earned dollars. Between 1970 and 1978, median family income after inflation rose by only 6.5 percent, as compared to a 34 percent increase in the 1960s. In response, the government imposed wage and price controls, but these did little to reduce inflation. The failure of Keynesian economics to deal with stagflation had a lot to do with the popularization of another approach to managing the economy—supply-side economics.

Supply-side economists reject the Keynesian notion that demand creates supply. Instead, they believe that supply creates demand—a principle often attributed to Jean Baptiste Say (Say's Law) but made famous by Ronald Reagan ("Reaganomics" is supply-side economics). **Supply-side economics** *suggests that the way to move the economy out of stagflation is to stimulate production (supply) by cutting taxes and government spending, reducing government regulations and red tape, increasing individual incentives to produce, and stimulating investments and savings.* If people are taxed less, they will save more and spend more, which will result in expansion, greater production, more jobs, and more tax revenue for the government. This theory was so appealing to a large number of people and their representatives that Reagan was able to get Congress to enact the Economic Tax Recovery Act of 1981, which reduced taxes, cut the federal budget by billions of dollars, and cut back on government regulations, especially in the area of energy and the environment. (We will examine this in more detail in chapter 17 on the budget.)

These actions, along with those of the Federal Reserve Board—the independent regulatory agency charged with controlling the nation's money supply through regulation of its banks—reduced inflation considerably in the early 1980s. However, these supply-side policies could not prevent a sharp rise in unemployment to near-record levels. Supporters of supply-side economics blamed much of this on the activities of the Federal Reserve Board, whose guiding economic philosophy is yet another type of economic theory—monetarism.

Monetarism *is a free-market theory based on the principle that the way to control the economy is through controlling the money and credit supply.* This is done through regulating the interest rates charged to the nation's banks when they borrow from the Federal

Reserve System, our system of national banks. Monetarists such as Milton Friedman believe that fluctuating the money supply is far preferable to fluctuating government taxing and spending policies (characteristic of both Keynesian and supply-side theories). Monetarists also believe that inflation is a much more serious, long-term economic problem than unemployment.

But monetarism, like Keynesian and supply-side economics, revealed its shortcomings in dealing with a stagflation economy in the recession of 1981 to 1983. The Federal Reserve Board's determination to keep interest rates high (tight money supply) reduced inflation but stimulated unemployment. Supply-side economists blamed monetarism for negating supply-side policies (tax reductions) intended to stimulate production.

The truth, then, is that none of these theories—demand-side, supply-side, or monetarist—has been effective in dealing with a stagflation economy. The result is a growing skepticism on the part of the public and its policymakers that *anything* will work. Much of this cynicism, according to economist Robert J. Samuelson, stems from the fact that economic theories are simplified for presentation to the public and "assume magical qualities; they imply that all good things (low inflation, high employment, rising living standards) are possible *simultaneously* (emphasis added)."[6]

Also, public expectations are that results will be quick in coming. When they aren't, public policymakers are blamed, and for their own political lives they must often abandon strategies that may make sense economically but not politically. As Samuelson notes, the result has been a "demolition derby for economic theories in the past 20 years. One after another, they've been bashed and consigned to the scrap heap."[7]

Significantly, in terms of a changing America and a changing world, few of these theories have squarely faced the fact that all nations' economies are intertwined. No nation is self-sufficient—each is somewhat dependent on others as buyers or sellers of goods and services. Today, no nation's policymakers have total control over their country's economy. We learned this lesson well when political problems in the Middle East over which we had no control interrupted our oil supply and greatly affected our economy.

Even more problematic is the fact that international economic interdependencies are hampering the development of traditional foreign policy. As Samuelson notes:

> *Economic and political alliances no longer neatly correspond. . . . The traditional ideological and strategic orientation of foreign policy has given way before economic interests. . . . International banks, multinational companies and global traders now effectively create their own foreign policies.*[8]

Despite the difficulties stemming from an interdependent world economy, American policymakers are held responsible for the state of our economy. Because of this, they are constantly searching for solutions to our economic problems—solutions that typically involve some form of government intervention despite the popular notion that our nation's economic system is a pure free-enterprise system.

Government Involvement in the Economy

A *free-enterprise system* is one that "assumes that the best of all possible solutions to economic problems can be sought if we leave, to the fullest extent, economic decisions to private firms and private individuals, and make sure that a high degree of competition prevails everywhere."[9] Such a system is also referred to as capitalistic, laissez faire, or private-enterprise. Under this system private individuals and firms—not government—decide what to produce, how to produce it, and who will get the product.

Obviously, our economy is not a pure free-enterprise system. The government is involved in many economic decisions concerning what will be produced, how it will be produced, and who will get the product. There are five major areas of government involvement:

1. Protection of individual economic, political, and religious rights and freedoms through the courts and the administration of laws;

2. Provision of goods and services in the interest of all, such as highways, national defense, and education;

3. Regulation, to ensure fair economic competition and to protect public health and safety;

4. Promotion of economic growth and stability through various economic policies and programs;

5. Direct support to individuals such as programs to reduce hardship for people who

cannot meet their minimum needs because of special circumstances or lack of employment.[10]

The United States actually has a mixed economic system. Under a *mixed economic system, the private sector (consumers and producers) and the public sector (government) coexist, but the government is expected to take a role in the nation's economic affairs to ensure full employment and continued economic growth.* The key question confronting policymakers is how extensive this role can be and still remain consistent with the basic principles of free enterprise.

Determining the proper balance between public and private involvement in the economy is very difficult. People's approaches vary according to their ideological predispositions. Liberals believe that government should play a major role in regulating the economy and in ensuring that everyone attains at least a certain minimal standard of living. Traditionally, liberals have favored increased federal spending—that is, growth in the public sector. Conservatives, on the other hand, favor expansion of the private sector and reduced public-sector involvement. They believe that a market free from government intervention is the best guarantee of a healthy economy. Historically, our nation's economic policies have fluctuated between these two positions as the national mood has changed.

The election of Ronald Reagan in 1980 seemed to suggest that the nation's mood had changed. Reagan came to office with what he viewed as a mandate to reduce the role of the public sector and increase that of the private sector. Reagan's guiding philosophy was that government's role in the economy should be directed toward stimulating expansion of the private sector rather than toward expanding itself by increased government spending. His initial approach was supply-side: he recommended cutting taxes so that the private sector could increase savings and investments, thereby improving the economic health of the nation. He also recommended that the private sector take back responsibility for certain social services that the federal government had gradually taken on since the New Deal. To stimulate this, Reagan recommended and Congress approved large budget cuts. Not surprisingly, some disagreed with this approach.

With any policy change involving the distribution of scarce resources (e.g., money), some see their interests being hurt and others see their interests being helped. The initial Reagan economic program was no exception. The expanded economic role of the national government in the past two decades greatly increased the number of individuals and groups with a stake in policy decisions. As each new aid program was created, a new constituency with an interest in protecting and expanding the program arose. Thus each new program increased the number of people who felt that government should take an active interest (especially monetary) in their problem area. Washington has become a hotbed of interest group activity. Business, state and local government, farm, women's rights, and other groups are there pushing for new programs, regulations, or tax changes. The result is that government policymakers are finding it increasingly difficult to be fair to all. Tensions among groups are created when economic and political conditions call for budgets to be cut.

Diffusing Tensions Between the Classes

In looking ahead to the 1980s, Vernon Jordan, former president of the National Urban League (one of America's leading black interest groups), remarked that our nation's biggest challenge was how to deal with values in an era, not of plenty, but of scarce resources and inflation.[11] Likewise, Arthur Schlesinger forecast:

As increasing energy costs and declining populations threaten to slow the rate of economic growth, we will not have the economic surplus to lubricate social change. Our economy will tend toward a zero-sum game, where one person's gain is another person's loss; *and the result can only be an alarming increase in tension between classes* (emphases added).[12]

Tension between the economic classes is dangerous because it can lead to alienation and loss of faith in our government and economic system. The tax revolt of the 1970s gave a preliminary indication of how this can happen. California's citizen-initiated Proposition 13 evidenced a public loss of faith in government's ability to give relief to taxpayers and to reduce its own taxing and spending levels. This feeling spread rapidly around the nation and helped propel Ronald Reagan to the White House on the basis of his promise to cut federal taxes and spending.

The problem with cutbacks is that a majority of

the population tends to favor cutting back programs for society's "have-nots." When programs must be cut, people most commonly feel that welfare and other social services should be cut first. This greatly upsets the poor, who feel that they are being abandoned. Yet this response accurately reflects the frustrations of many middle-class taxpayers, who feel that they're carrying an unfair share of the tax burden. Predictably, tensions between society's "haves" and "have-nots" have escalated in recent years as cuts in federal moneys for social programs have been made.

The Reagan administration's economic program brought the issue of class tension to the forefront. Sixty percent of the 1982 cuts in direct payment to individuals (entitlements) were in programs that largely benefit the poor (food stamps, Medicaid, Aid to Families with Dependent Children). Despite attempts to convince the poor (and their representatives) that the "truly needy" would not suffer because a "safety net" would be retained, Reagan was heavily criticized for being insensitive to the needs of the poor. At the same time, Reagan's cuts were praised by many middle class taxpayers, at least until some of them were victims of rising unemployment. To say the least, this was a very difficult situation for a policymaker to be in.

Tensions between the classes intensified following the publication of an extensive interview with Reagan's budget director, David Stockman. Conceding that the supply-side economic policies adopted by the Reagan administration would probably widen the income gap between rich and poor, Stockman went so far as to condemn supply-side economics for being nothing more than a "Trojan horse" for tax relief to the rich.[13]

But Stockman also argued that previous attempts to narrow the gap between the rich and the poor (redistributive federal spending policies, or Keynesian approaches) were ruining the economy, making future entitlement programs unlikely. This message, however, did not reach most Americans, who instead heard only the criticism of "Reaganomics." (The role of the media in setting the economic policy agenda will be discussed in chapter 10.) Consequently, the image of Reagan's policies as helping the rich through tax cuts and investment credits and hurting the poor by cutting back welfare and social services became even more fixed.

Tensions between the poor and the rest of society were also heightened when Reagan announced his plan to make welfare, specifically Aid to Families with Dependent Children, a state responsibility, as it was originally. This was part of his New Federalism proposal (which will be examined in more detail in chapter 4). However, there are wide variations in state public-assistance programs. Some states have historically spent more on poverty programs than others—often because they have been able to afford to spend more. Many advocates for the poor fear that the tax bases of some states are inadequate to support welfare programs. Others fear that political pressures from the middle and upper classes—the majority of the nation's voters—will keep state officials from increasing taxes to cover the cost of such programs.

Supporters of Reagan's plan to return welfare to the states argued that much of the slack would be picked up by the private sector. Their conviction—and Reagan's—was that government involvement in social services and public-assistance programs had reduced the incentive for private individual effort. They also felt that government-run programs were not very effective at getting services to those who really needed them and that voluntary organizations could do better—a position many Americans tended to agree with.

Indeed, a survey conducted by the Roper Organization in November, 1981, revealed that most Americans believed that human services could be better provided by private agencies than by government. This same survey showed that more Americans felt that the best way to tackle problems facing the nation, such as unemployment and health care, was through the efforts of large corporations rather than through taxes raised by the government. The underlying assumption was that if the private sector were willing and could afford to pick up where government left off (big "ifs"), the poor might actually be served better because the programs designed to help them would be operated more effectively than they had been by the federal government. But the nagging question remained: could the private sector afford this? And was it *willing* to do so? At the same time that it was being pressured to rescue the nation's economy, the private sector was also being asked to help government solve the nation's energy and environmental problems.

THE ENERGY "SHORTAGE"

Long gas lines, spiraling prices, and fuel shortages following the Arab oil embargo in 1973 and 1974 and strikes by Iranian oil field workers in 1978 and 1979 made Americans aware for the first time of the limited nature of our most important energy source—oil. During the 1970s, the term "energy crisis" became a household word, and Americans made some painful adjustments once they were convinced that the crisis was real.

Nevertheless, a Roper survey found that in late 1979 only 28 percent of the population felt that gasoline and oil shortages *were* in fact real. Fifty-one percent felt that the oil crisis had been contrived for economic and political reasons. Table 2.2 shows that most laid the blame on the oil companies. However, by 1982 many Americans had generally come to accept that energy shortages were a real problem and would continue to be a problem so long as the political conditions in the Middle East remained unstable.

Meanwhile, our policymakers must formulate and implement policies that will:

1. Decrease our nation's dependency on OPEC for oil;
2. Develop alternative energy sources;

Oil and gas shortages in the 1970s led to restrictions on operating hours, long gas lines, and higher prices at service stations across the U.S. Americans quickly learned how dependent we are on petroleum. The term "energy crisis" became a household word.

TABLE 2.2

Was the Oil Crisis Real?

Here is a list of statements about the gasoline and oil shortage [respondent given card]. Which *one* of those statements comes closest to expressing your opinion?

    A. There is a very real shortage and the problem will get worse during the next 5 to 10 years.
    B. There is a real oil shortage but it will be solved in the next year or two.
    C. There was a short-term problem, but it has been largely solved and there is no real problem any longer.
    D. There never was any real oil shortage—it was contrived for economic and political reasons.

| | | Statements | | | Don't |
		A	B	C	D	Know
1974:	May	21%	12%	8%	53%	6%
1976:	May 8–15	25	9	9	48	9
	Nov 6–11	26	11	8	46	9
1977:	Apr 30–May 7	40	15	6	33	6
	Oct 29–Nov 5	33	14	9	39	5
1978:	Apr 22–May 3	32	8	9	45	6
	Oct 28–Nov 4	31	10	9	43	7
1979:	Jan 6–20	29	8	8	48	7
	Apr 28–May 5	25	12	6	51	6
	Sep 22–29	28	9	7	51	5

SOURCE: Al Richman, "The Polls: Public Attitudes Toward the Energy Crisis," *Public Opinion Quarterly*, Winter 1979, p. 578.

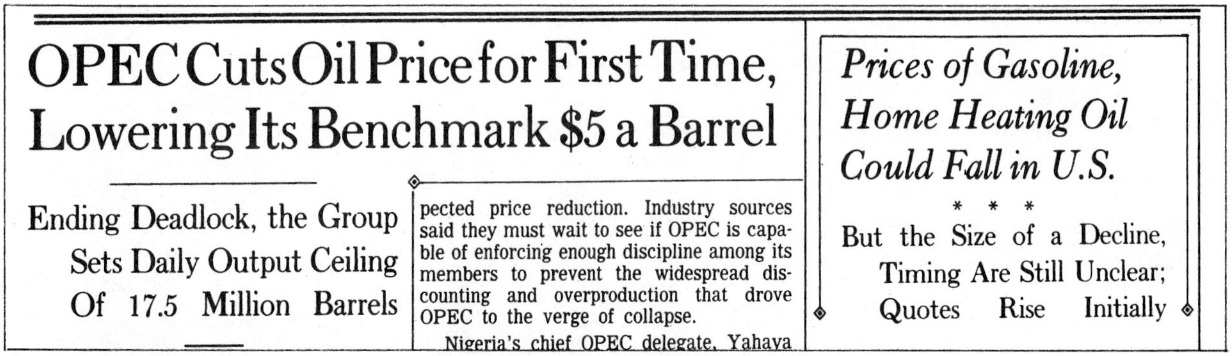

OPEC Cuts Oil Price for First Time, Lowering Its Benchmark $5 a Barrel

Ending Deadlock, the Group Sets Daily Output Ceiling Of 17.5 Million Barrels

pected price reduction. Industry sources said they must wait to see if OPEC is capable of enforcing enough discipline among its members to prevent the widespread discounting and overproduction that drove OPEC to the verge of collapse.

Nigeria's chief OPEC delegate, Yahaya

Prices of Gasoline, Home Heating Oil Could Fall in U.S.

* * *

But the Size of a Decline, Timing Are Still Unclear; Quotes   Rise   Initially ◈

American dependence on OPEC (the Organization of Petroleum Exporting Countries) for imported oil is reflected in these headlines. Even after the oil crises of the 1970s, Arab oil remains an important source of imported oil.   (Wall Street Journal, March 15, 1983)

3. Achieve greater energy efficiency and conserve more of our energy.

This is easier said than done, especially when we are not in the midst of a crisis.

Decreasing Our Dependency on OPEC

Historically, the United States has imported one-third of its oil. Prior to the 1970s, most of our imported oil came from the Western Hemisphere (Canada, Mexico). But by the 1970s, most was coming from OPEC countries, especially Saudi Arabia, Nigeria, Libya, Algeria, Indonesia, and Iran. Even after the oil crises, Arab nations remain our primary source of imported oil. The primary reason for our nation's continued reliance on foreign oil is simple: oil production at home cannot satisfy demand.

America is heavily dependent on petroleum and petroleum-based products for gasoline and home heating fuel. Petroleum is also used to make kerosene, chemical fertilizers, pesticides, plastics, synthetic rubber, and synthetic fibers. Americans still use more oil than just about everyone else in the world, despite the fact that we have cut back consumption considerably since the oil crisis of 1978 and 1979. More than half of the difference between United States and foreign consumption can be attributed to variations in transportation. The average American travels greater distances than the average European, and American cars have generally tended to get fewer miles to the gallon. Houses in the United States are much larger than those of other countries, and Americans prefer higher house temperatures in winter and cooler temperatures in summer. This heavy demand for oil has unfortunately exceeded the supply.

Production of oil in the United States has not increased significantly in recent years (see Figure 2.1). According to figures released by the National Supply Company, we have the lowest average well production of the world's fifteen major producing nations. We also have the lowest estimated reserve life—9.5 years for oil, 10.1 years for gas. Oil industry representatives blame this on the high costs of drilling ($2.8 million for a shallow well, $180 million for a large, semisubmerged offshore well) caused by government restrictions

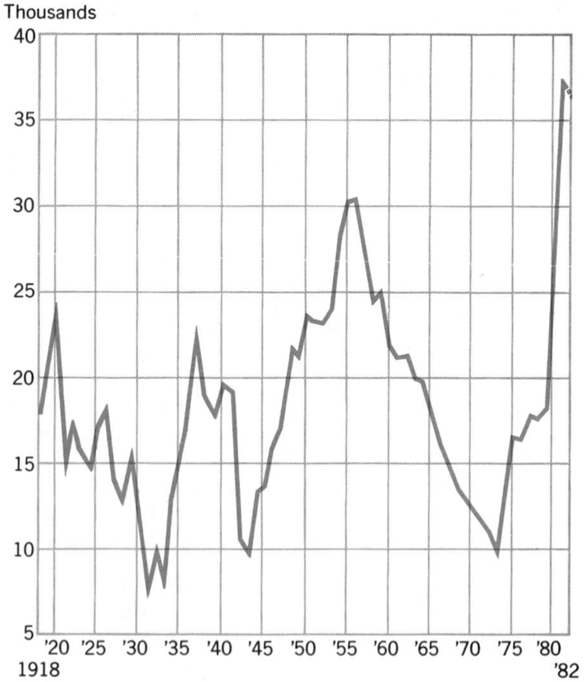

FIGURE 2.1

U.S. Oil Wells Drilled

SOURCE: *Houston Chronicle,* June 20, 1982; based on data from Economic Advisory Services. © Houston Chronicle.

Dependence on oil is heaviest among Americans. More than half the difference between U.S. and foreign consumption of petroleum is due to transportation variations. The average American travels a greater distance to work in a car that gets fewer miles to the gallon.

on areas open to exploration. (Government officials are equally pressured by environmental groups to keep certain areas, such as federally owned wilderness lands, off limits to exploration.)

Aside from the high costs of drilling an oil well, there are disagreements within the oil industry itself about the real potential for greater production of oil and gas. Some have warned that America's reserves of oil and gas will be 90 percent depleted by the year 2000. But others believe that a 1000-year supply of gas lies in the Gulf of Mexico, that there are 50 to 100 billion barrels of oil in Alaska, and that another 105 billion barrels can be recovered in existing oil fields once technologies are developed to tap the supply. For now, though, United States production continues to lag behind

demand, and it appears that our nation will remain fairly dependent on foreign oil throughout the 1980s.

The task facing policymakers, then, is to develop contingency plans in the event of another major cutoff of oil from the Middle East like that of 1973. Such a cutoff would cost the United States economy hundreds of billions of dollars in lost production and higher inflation. Fuel prices would soar and long lines at gas stations would reappear.

One means of insuring America against any major economic upheaval from a cutoff of Middle Eastern oil has already been set up. In 1981 President Reagan accelerated the filling of the Strategic Petroleum Reserve (in salt dome caverns in Texas and Louisiana). When the federal government created the reserve in 1975 after the first oil crisis, plans were to stockpile 1 billion barrels of oil as a cushion against a possible loss of Middle East oil. President Reagan speeded up the daily rate so that by the beginning of 1983 over 300 million barrels (equal to 150 days of imports from the Middle East) had been stored.

A stockpiling strategy apparently has political advantages as well as economic ones. The fact that the United States has a strategic stockpile of oil deters OPEC from imposing another embargo. But the Strategic Petroleum Reserve is merely a short-term solution to the problem of United States dependence on foreign oil. Even the Reserve has not been enough to keep some from predicting another major oil crisis in this decade. As Daniel Yergin put it,

> *A third oil crisis is highly likely before the end of the 1980s, one far more serious than the two already expe-*

rienced. By the year 2000, oil prices may be more than twice what they are today. The result could be a test of the American system on a scale matched only in this century by that of the Great Depression. [14]

The concern of many experts is that Americans do not really think that such a crisis is imminent. A 1982 Associated Press–NBC News poll showed that while over 75 percent believe we are too dependent on foreign oil, only half believe that we face an energy shortage.[15] The president of the Shell Oil Company expressed the fears of many others in the energy industry: ''It makes me nervous that many people think the United States is immune to another oil-price shock.''[16] What has energy industry representatives concerned is the public's apparent loss of interest in the development of alternative energy sources. Without public pressure on the president and Congress to offer incentives to business to develop alternative en-

Coal is one of the most promising alternative energy sources. The U.S. has 31 percent of the world's recoverable coal reserves. Strip mining is the most common method of recovery; it is heavily criticized by environmentalists.

ergy sources, it may be almost impossible to reduce our dependency on foreign oil.

Development of Alternative Energy Sources

Alternative energy sources appear to be the key to United States energy self-sufficiency. While everyone seems to recognize that alternative energy sources are the best solution in the long run, in the short run it is hard to develop them. Three factors slow development: 1) environmental concerns, 2) high costs that are unrecoverable in the short term, and 3) lack of a sense of urgency.

Development of two of the nation's most promising alternative energy sources—coal and nuclear energy—has been hampered by environmental concerns. Still the potential remains. The United States now has 31 percent of the world's recoverable coal reserves. These reserves represent 81 percent of all our energy resources, yet coal provides less than one-fifth of the energy used in the United States. Much of the coal that is used is consumed by utility companies, but many more industries would use coal if it were more readily available and the costs of converting were not so astronomical.

Coal industry representatives claim that government policies, particularly clean air and environmental regulations, make it difficult to increase coal production. Environmentalists and the Environmental Protection Agency (EPA) have demanded that industries converting from oil to coal not be allowed to exceed their current levels of emissions. They are concerned that these plants would add enough sulfur dioxide (a poisonous gas) to the atmosphere to increase the acidity of rainfall, creating a health hazard to humans, fish, and forests. A pollution control device called a "scrubber" can absorb most of these poisonous fumes, but it is expensive and often undependable.

Transportation problems also threaten to limit coal's usefulness as an alternative to petroleum. The primary means of transporting coal is by rail. Presently, transportation accounts for 25 to 30 percent of the cost of coal to the user, and deregulation of the railroads could send that percentage much higher. An alternative to rail transportation is the pumping of a liquid "slurry" mixture of water and crushed coal through pipelines to utility companies. While this would reduce costs substantially, environmentalists (and the railroad in-

dustry) oppose it. Environmentalists fear the misuse of Western lands and the possibility that coal pipelines would interfere with water reserves needed for irrigation.

Nuclear energy is also plagued with environmental problems. Once thought to be the major alternative to petroleum, nuclear energy has a doubtful future, largely because of the Three Mile Island nuclear reactor accident in Pennsylvania in March 1979 (see Figure 2.2). The United States currently has 75 nuclear reactors, which provide about 11 percent of the nation's electricity, the equivalent of 1.3 million barrels of oil a day. However, in 1981 only 4 new nuclear plants reached commercial operation, while 44 projects were delayed and 6 reactors were canceled.

Once thought to be a major alternative to petroleum, nuclear energy has a doubtful future, largely because of the Three Mile Island nuclear reactor accident in Pennsylvania in March 1979.

Question: I'm going to read you several statements relating to ways that have been suggested to improve our energy situation. As I read each statement, please tell me whether you strongly favor it, mildly favor it, mildly oppose it, or strongly oppose it. ...more nuclear power plants to generate electricity.

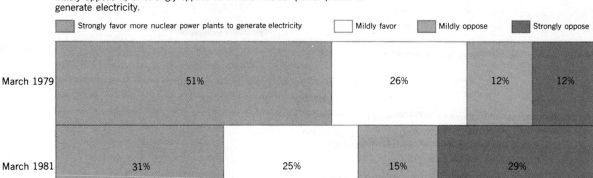

FIGURE 2.2

Changing Attitudes Toward Nuclear Power Plants

SOURCE: *Public Opinion,* February/March 1982; based on a survey by Opinion Research Corporation for the LTV Industries and Companies, latest is that of March, 1981, p. 38.

While environmentalists are most concerned about plant safety and nuclear waste disposal, they also question whether nuclear power production increases the likelihood of nonpeaceful uses of nuclear technology. Due to the expanded lobbying efforts of such antinuclear groups as Ground Zero, the role of nuclear power in providing a bridge from the era of cheap and plentiful fossil fuels (oil, coal) to the use of renewable sources such as the sun and wind may be less important than was originally planned. A 1981 Associated Press–NBC News poll found that 53 percent of the population wants no new nuclear plants built in the United States.[17]

Few Americans believe there is any relationship between adequate energy supplies and protection of the environment. One study of public opinion polls found that "Americans want the environment protected *and* they want . . . an adequate energy supply. There is not one iota of evidence suggesting that the public thinks it must choose between the two."[18] However, if plans for alternative energy sources such as solar and synthetic fuels do not pan out, the public may very well find that it must choose, or at least make do with a little less of each—energy and a healthy environment.

Synthetic fuels (synfuels) are fuels most often made from coal, tar sands, and oil shale. Coal can be converted into natural gas, gasoline, and other liquid fuels. Oil shale is a finely textured rock that when crushed and heated becomes a type of oil that can be refined. Shale oil is one of the most promising synthetic fuels, and United States shale deposits are enormous. One oil shale formation, the Green River formation in Colorado, Wyoming, and Utah, is said to hold more than 20 times as much synthetic oil as there is in conventional crude oil reserves in the entire country.

Synfuels are favored by many energy experts, who see them as the least painful way to transform an oil-based economy to one fueled by renewable energy resources such as solar power and nuclear fusion. But synfuels development is stymied by the "cost-price paradox"—the cost of producing synfuels is so high that their market price makes them noncompetitive. For example, experts estimate that a barrel of oil can be squeezed from oil shale for about $40. But with the price of oil at about $29 a barrel, shale oil remains an unprofitable commodity.

Recognizing the high cost of developing synfuels, the government in 1980 created the U.S. Synthetic Fuels Corporation, a quasi-governmental agency, to help finance the new industry. It was originally expected to spend up to $88 billion so that by 1992, 1 to 2 million barrels of synfuels would be produced daily. However, the Corporation's budget was greatly slashed by President Reagan in his move to reduce the size and scope of

Solar energy and wind power are two of the most promising "new" sources of energy, particularly in the Sunbelt. This home in New Mexico features a solar water heater and a windmill that pumps the heated water supply throughout the house.

the federal government. His energy secretary spread the word that the administration's philosophy was that private companies, not the federal government, should determine the feasibility of energy projects. This approach has not helped the private sector solve the cost-price problem inherent in the development of synfuels. The nation needs alternative *liquid* synfuels for its airplanes, boats, trains, trucks, and cars, because it will be years before solar energy will be developed to supply liquid fuel.

The most promising new source of energy may well be the sun. Solar development is less hampered by environmental or cost concerns. Already, solar hot-water heaters and solar heating and cooling systems are economically feasible in certain parts of the country. Even though they are initially expensive, operating costs are so much lower that in time the systems pay for themselves. According to one report, a $1500 solar hot-water system will pay for itself in just ten years.

Development of these major alternative energy sources—and of others, such as wind power, natural steam (geothermal) power, and ocean tide power—has been slowed because of a lack of urgency, a worldwide decline in oil prices, and a glut in the world oil supply in the early 1980s. We have been lulled into a false sense of security, say many energy analysts. They warn against drifting along without doing anything to solve the problem until

another crisis hits, because then it will be too late to do anything. Nor will conservation efforts by themselves be enough.

Conservation of Energy: Becoming More Energy-Efficient

In recent years, the United States and other industrialized nations have cut back their demand for petroleum. Part of the cutback is attributable to individual conservation efforts prompted by high energy costs. The rising costs of heating and cooling a home and driving a car have led many Americans to become more energy conscious. Many have added insulation to their homes, turned down their thermostats, and bought more efficient cars and home appliances. As a result of these moves, United States oil consumption dropped 15.3 percent between 1978 and 1981.

Most experts see this trend as continuing. Few predict that consumers will go back to their old ways. (How many people will go back to driving "gas hogs" again?) One recent national survey of consumers found that 93 percent say they are trying to conserve energy.[19]

Conservation efforts have reduced energy consumption, but they have not done much to alleviate our dependence on foreign oil. Even if such a dependence were eliminated, our policymakers would still face another big energy-related problem at home—how to deal with the differentials in energy supply that exist within our own national boundaries. This problem has intensified in recent years and is described by some as an "energy Civil War."

Preventing Another "War Between the States"

The tension between energy-rich and energy-poor states has steadily mounted. Energy-poor states are worried that if the price of energy suddenly escalates, the energy-rich states will benefit greatly from increases in revenue from severance taxes, royalty payments, corporate and personal income taxes, sales taxes, and property taxes.

Today 12 states produce all the energy they need (see Figure 2.3); the other 38 must import energy. Among the 38 "have-nots," particularly those in the Northeast and Midwest, there is fear that the "haves" could conduct what would amount to economic warfare against the rest of the country. One United States senator from Mis-

souri has even compared the energy-rich American states to OPEC, saying, "They will begin doing exactly what the OPEC countries are doing, building up their economic base at the expense of the rest of the country."[20]

The division between the "have" and "have-not" states basically follows the line between the Sun Belt and the Frost Belt (with the exceptions of Alaska and Florida). Frost Belt states in recent years have seen many of their industries move south and west. They are afraid that even more industries will leave and head for energy-rich states. Such fears have already put both camps in something of a fighting mood. Representatives of energy-poor states have pushed for revision of federal aid formulas, which they say disproportionately benefit the energy-rich states because of the formula link between most federal aid programs and state tax receipts. Energy-rich states counter this attack with arguments that they are merely catching up on revenues lost in the past because of

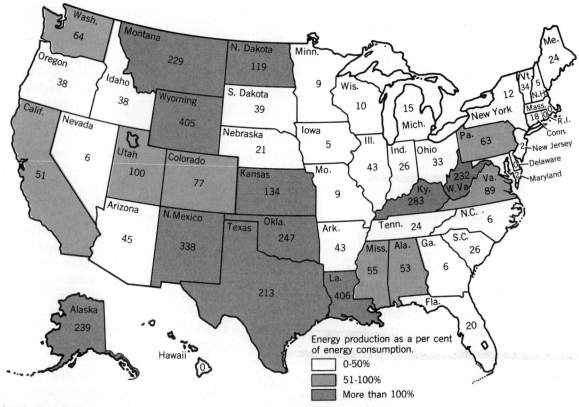

FIGURE 2.3

The Energy Haves and Have nots

SOURCE: *National Journal*, March 22, 1980, p. 469.

federal controls on oil and natural gas. The energy issue could well provoke another "war between the states."

To avoid this regional showdown, some energy specialists are recommending development of new technologies on a regional basis. "Iowa could make alcohol from its corn, Illinois could make gasoline from its coal, New York could make fuel out of its garbage, and Wisconsin could produce fuel from its dairy whey," suggested one.[21] But, again, there remains the question of who should plan, coordinate, and fund such developments. Should it be government or private industry? During the past two presidential administrations, two vastly different approaches have been tried.

Who Should Make Our Energy Policy—Government or Industry?

In 1977, during the Carter administration, the U.S. Department of Energy was created. It was hailed as the solution to the problem of the scattered, uncoordinated federal energy effort that existed prior to Carter's taking office. The Senate report recommending the formation of the Energy Department justified it by stating that:

[Energy] policy can neither be effectively developed nor implemented without a single entity with an overview of all of the nation's energy-related programs and needs [that] can mold these efforts together into the plan and concerted effort to resolve the nation's energy problems.[22]

During his administration, Carter developed a national energy plan designed to move the nation toward energy self-sufficiency through conservation efforts and the development of alternative energy sources, especially synfuels.

Ronald Reagan, Carter's successor, ran on a platform that called for the abolition of the Energy Department and the reassignment of many of its functions to other departments, as shown in Figure 2.4. In Reagan's eyes, the Energy Department had hindered energy production rather than increased it because it imposed numerous costly regulations on the energy industry. He proposed getting government out of the energy business and letting the private sector take over. One of his first acts as president was to deregulate all price and allocation controls on gasoline and domestic crude oil. In each budget proposal that he submitted to Congress, he recommended greatly reduced funding for energy-related activities. Pre-

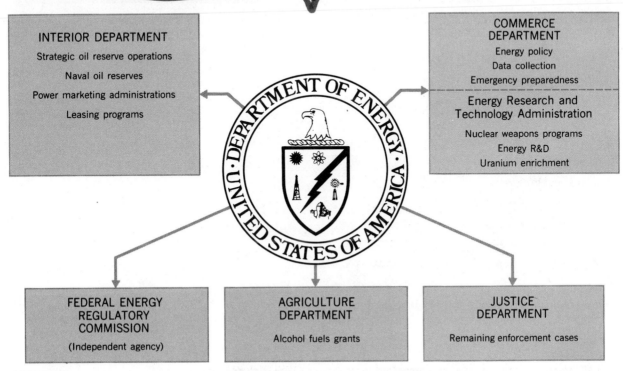

INTERIOR DEPARTMENT
Strategic oil reserve operations
Naval oil reserves
Power marketing administrations
Leasing programs

COMMERCE DEPARTMENT
Energy policy
Data collection
Emergency preparedness

Energy Research and Technology Administration
Nuclear weapons programs
Energy R&D
Uranium enrichment

FEDERAL ENERGY REGULATORY COMMISSION
(Independent agency)

AGRICULTURE DEPARTMENT
Alcohol fuels grants

JUSTICE DEPARTMENT
Remaining enforcement cases

FIGURE 2.4

The Reagan Proposal to Abolish the Department of Energy

SOURCE: *National Journal,* January 2, 1982, p. 39.

dictably, his free-market approach was attacked by those favoring an active role for government in the making of energy policy.

One critic of Reagan's energy policy commented:

The Reagan administration has a blind faith that the market system will work perfectly in an international crisis and doesn't see the economic cost of the two [previous] oil shocks in terms of inflation and unemployment. [23]

Another criticism of the plan to abolish the Energy Department is that it will slow down conservation efforts, contingency planning for energy emergencies, and the search for alternative fuels. Critics argued the nation would be left with no central agency for the formulation and execution of a national energy policy.

We have seen that in the area of energy, our policymakers must still decide how to make policies that substitute abundant energy resources such as coal and the sun for those in relatively short supply. They must also decide how to develop synfuels while maintaining environmental standards. They must meet these challenges before another interruption in the world's petroleum supply occurs. The difficulty is that, for now, energy appears to be a less immediate threat to the lifestyles and values of Americans than the economy is. But of course the two issues are highly related.

CHANGES IN LIFESTYLES

As the economy has changed, the lifestyles and values of Americans have changed as well (see Figure 2.5). In an article entitled ''National Growth: The Question of the 80s,'' two public-opinion specialists have observed:

Starting in the late 1960s and gathering momentum in the 1970s, Americans began to change their philosophy of life—their sense of what is important and what isn't. . . . In the past, people were motivated mainly by earning more money, adding to possessions, gaining

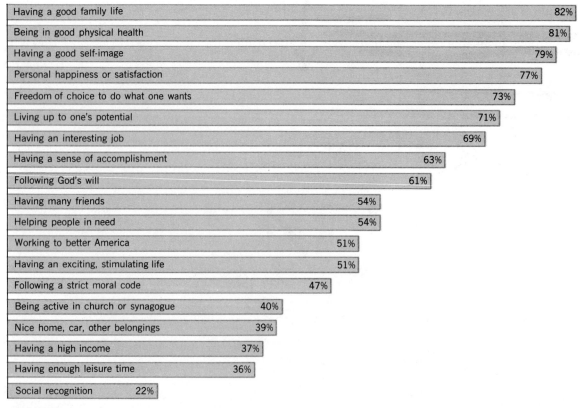

Having a good family life	82%
Being in good physical health	81%
Having a good self-image	79%
Personal happiness or satisfaction	77%
Freedom of choice to do what one wants	73%
Living up to one's potential	71%
Having an interesting job	69%
Having a sense of accomplishment	63%
Following God's will	61%
Having many friends	54%
Helping people in need	54%
Working to better America	51%
Having an exciting, stimulating life	51%
Following a strict moral code	47%
Being active in church or synagogue	40%
Nice home, car, other belongings	39%
Having a high income	37%
Having enough leisure time	36%
Social recognition	22%

FIGURE 2.5

What's Important to Americans? (Percent Rating Importance Very High or High)

SOURCE: *The Gallup Report,* No. 198 (March, 1982), p. 5.

economic security, and providing material comforts for the family. But, increasingly in recent years, new motives of self-fulfillment have gained in importance.

People want more but are willing to give less for it. They desire more personal freedom, more time off, more self-expression, more flexibility, more of a say in how things are done, more variety, more opportunity—more of everything. . . . Money and status still count, but they are not as powerful or universal as they used to be. Increasingly, Americans want something different out of life.[24]

This desire for something different has generally come about because changes in the economy have caused many Americans to believe that the United States has reached its economic peak. In a survey by Yankelovich, Skelly, and White, 62 percent of the respondents agreed with the statement that "Americans should get used to the fact that our wealth is limited and most of us are not likely to be better off than we are now."[25]

These changes in the economy, lifestyles, and values of Americans have created important and difficult issues for policymakers, including the following: 1) How can the public's expectations about its standard of living be changed in light of money and energy shortages? These include traditional expectations related to home ownership, transportation, temperature control, buying on credit, and food consumption. 2) How can a satisfactory balance be created between work and leisure from the perspectives of both the individual and the economy? 3) How can affirmative action be balanced with equal opportunity in the workplace? 4) How can the health and income needs of America's aging population be met? 5) What role should the government play in the individual's exercise of lifestyle choices?

As we shall see, the public is often divided on these value-laden issues, and this makes decisions difficult for policymakers. In addition, individuals are often inconsistent and contradictory in their opinions on certain lifestyle issues, which has the effect of sending mixed signals to policymakers.

Changing Standards of Living

The declining value of the dollar, coupled with rising unemployment and energy costs, makes it difficult for an individual to achieve what has long been considered an average standard of living. Historically, Americans have expected to own their own home and car (or cars), to live in comfort (heat in the winter, air conditioning in the summer), to buy food at only slightly higher prices than they paid the year before, and to use credit cards to buy whatever items they wanted without having to wait until they had saved enough cash. Yet the likelihood that a young person will be able to afford a home is much less today than it was even a few years ago. First-time home buyers made up 48.1 percent of all home buyers in 1977 but only 32.9 percent by 1979. Similarly, the likelihood of buying a new car every few years is lessening. In 1983 the average car in use was 7 years old compared to 5.6 years in 1970.

Americans have generally begun to revise downward their ideas of an acceptable standard of living. One survey shows that by a 79 to 17 percent margin, they think more emphasis should be placed on "teaching people to live with basic essentials" than on "reaching a higher standard of living."[26] But they still are reluctant to give up the things they traditionally have regarded as essential to a "good life." People do not want to give up their family cars, their vacation vehicles, their central heating, their own single-family home, or their credit cards. While they are prepared to use fans instead of air conditioners, to keep their cars a little longer, to eat out less, and to charge less, they still expect to acquire the same basic goods and services. Policymakers are expected to provide government-financed loans to homebuyers, keep utility rates low, subsidize the American automobile industry, and stimulate farm production—all while keeping taxes low!

" 'Mr. and Mrs. Sheldon Carter Sloane request the pleasure of your company at the reception of their daughter, Harriet, and Mr. Edward Arlo Sander in announcement of their living together . . .' "

Balancing Work and Leisure

In the 1970s, many Americans began to revise their thoughts about what success really is. According to one study, a number of Americans thought that they had devoted too much time and attention to the task of making a living and not enough to the question of how to live.[27] Leisure has become a more important part of our lives and values. In fact, we increased our free time from 296 minutes per day (4.9 hours) to 330 minutes per day (5.5 hours) between 1965 and 1975 (see Table 2.3), and the figure was even higher by the 1980s. A more recent study of 4000 persons across the country, conducted by the Opinion Research Corporation on behalf of the U.S. Department of the Interior, found that more Americans are participating in outdoor recreational activities. More than half had gone fishing, and about seven in ten had walked or jogged for exercise, driven for pleasure, had a picnic, or visited zoos and amusement parks.[28] Much of this free time was spent in publicly financed and operated parks or recreational facilities.

While a majority of Americans want more leisure time, there is no indication that they question the value of work or are any less satisfied with their work than in the past. Sixty-one percent believe that people should place more emphasis on working hard than on what gives them pleasure. More than 90 percent still believe that hard work is important if one wants to succeed, even though fewer persons believe that hard work alone will guarantee success. Work satisfaction has remained fairly stable as well. In 1963, 89 percent of the population said that they were satisfied with their work. In 1978 the figure was a comparable 87 percent.[29]

TABLE 2.3

Changes in the Use of Free Time Among Americans (in minutes per day)

Activity	Total 1965	Total 1975
Organizations:		
Education	8	10
Religion	9	11
Voluntary	6	6
Social Life:		
Entertainment out	27	28
Visiting, conversation	55	49
Recreation:		
Outdoor	8	9
Hobbies, games	14	17
Mass Media:		
Television	89	130
Radio	4	2
Records, tapes, etc.	1	2
Books, magazines, and so on	14	15
Newspapers	22	14
Other:		
Rest, relax, and so on	4	9
Correspondence	6	2
Other	11	5
All associated travel	18	21
Total	296	330

SOURCE: *Public Opinion,* August/September 1979, p. 43. Survey by John Robinson, 1965, 1975.

Jogging is a popular form of exercise and relaxation for Americans of all ages. Leisure time activities have become a more important part of people's lives in recent years.

TABLE 2.4

The Decline in America's Productivity: Growth Rates of Real Output, 1960–1981* (percent)

	Total		Per Capita		Per Unit of Labor Input	
	1960–1973 (1)	1973–1981 (2)	1960–1973 (3)	1973–1981 (4)	1960–1973 (5)	1973–1981 (6)
United States	4.2	2.3	3.0	1.2	3.1	0.9
Japan	10.5	3.8	9.3	2.9	9.9	3.6
Germany	4.8	1.9	3.9	2.0	5.8	3.3
France	5.7	2.5	4.6	2.2	5.9	3.4
United Kingdom	3.2	0.5	2.7	0.5	3.8	1.8
Italy	5.2	2.4	4.4	2.0	7.8	1.4
Canada	5.4	2.4	3.7	1.7	4.2	0.4

SOURCE: Herbert Stein, "The Industrial Economies: We Are Not Alone," *The AEI Economist,* May 1982, p.1; based on the following data: Cols. 1, 2, 3, 4: International Monetary Fund, *International Financial Statistics,* various issues. 1981 partly estimated by the American Enterprise Institute.
Col. 5 and col. 6, 1973–1979: John W. Kendrick, "International Comparisons of Recent Productivity Trends" in *Essays in Contemporary Economic Problems,* William Fellner, ed., 1981–1982 edition (Washington, D.C.: American Enterprise Institute, 1981), p. 128.
Col. 6, 1979–1981: Organization for Economic Cooperation and Development, *Economic Outlook,* December 1981, p. 46.

*Note: Data for France, Italy, and the United Kingdom are based on gross domestic product. Data for the other countries are based on gross national product.

What have changed are the public's attitudes about what constitutes a satisfying job. No longer is salary the most important factor. In a survey for *Time Magazine,* when asked whether a person should choose the highest paying job even if it was not the most satisfying job, 58 percent of the population said no.[30] Sixty-nine percent of the respondents in a 1982 Gallup survey rated having an interesting job as very important; only 37 percent rated having a high income as very important.[31] Opinions about people's pride in their work and their pace of working have also changed. Most Americans (64 percent) feel other Americans are taking less pride in their work. This declining pride is said to be associated with a similar decline in the productivity levels of American workers. (A *productivity decline exists when fewer and fewer things are produced for the same amount of labor and money*.) America's productivity rate has been declining over the past two decades (see Table 2.4).

A report of the Joint Economic Committee of the U.S. Congress concluded that "the average American is likely to see his/her standard of living drastically decline in the 1980s unless the United States accelerates its rate of productivity growth."[32] Poor productivity causes higher prices and higher unemployment and makes American businesses less able to compete with foreign businesses. A decline in productivity hurts individual Americans as well, including retired and low-income Americans, as costs rise for food, health care, transportation, and taxes; teenagers, as college costs skyrocket; high-school dropouts, especially minority youth, as American industry is unable to absorb them into the work force; young couples, as home prices and interest rates accelerate; unskilled and semiskilled workers, as layoffs occur and new jobs become scarce; and other wage earners, as pay increases are canceled by price increases.[33]

The productivity issue is both economic and political. Declining productivity has resulted in a huge loss of income and shaken our confidence in ourselves and our institutions.

In the 1980s policymakers are being forced to deal with the public's conflicting demands for more leisure and a better, more productive economy. On the one hand, policymakers are being pressured to improve working conditions and allow more job sharing, flexible working hours, and four-day work weeks. On the other hand, they are being pressured to design policies to improve the productivity levels of American workers, such as offering greater salary incentives and revising civil service systems.

Equal Opportunity in the Workplace: Affirmative Action versus Reverse Discrimination

The changing makeup of the workforce—specifically, the rapid entry of women and increases in minority populations—has resulted in pressures to open up the workplace to allow the new groups to take nontraditional jobs and move up the organizational ladder by promotion to the executive level. These pressures will grow stronger in the 1980s, as will the reactions of white males.

As with other lifestyle issues, the public sends mixed signals to policymakers on the important issue of equal opportunity in the workplace. While a clear majority of the population—72 percent—approves of married women working, 47 percent agree with the statement that "women's place is in the home."[34] Similarly, a *New York Times*–CBS News poll showed that while a majority of whites (nearly two-thirds) favored programs that would require large companies to set up special training programs for minority workers, 60 percent disapproved of programs that imposed quotas by requiring businesses to hire a certain number of minority workers.[35] The key issue here is not so much sex and race discrimination as employing and promoting on the basis of individual merit and qualifications. In line with traditional values regarding the work ethic and individual self-determination, white males expect hiring and promoting decisions to be made on the basis of considerations other than color and gender.

Affirmative action programs are programs designed to increase employment opportunities for minority groups that were disadvantaged in the past because of discrimination and poor educational opportunities. Reverse discrimination is the practice of discriminating against whites, particularly males, in order to increase opportunities for minorities that were previously disadvantaged. This issue first came up in the Allan Bakke suit which challenged a special admissions program for disadvantaged applicants to attend the University of California Medical School at Davis. Bakke, in *Regents of the University of California v. Bakke,* challenged the school's practice of reserving 16 of 100 student openings for blacks, Hispanics, and Orientals, which resulted in admission of applicants with lower qualifications than his own. He argued that he had twice been denied admission on account of his race and that this violated the Fourteenth Amendment's equal protection clause. He further contended that this denial was in direct violation of Title VI of the 1964 Civil Rights Act, which forbids racial discrimination in any federally assisted activity (the university was a recipient of federal funds). This, said Bakke, was reverse discrimination. Ultimately, the U.S. Supreme Court, on June 28, 1978, sided with Bakke—but only partially. The Court ruled that Bakke must

be admitted because it was unconstitutional to use race as the *sole* criterion for admission. However, the Court also held that race could be one of many criteria used, which effectively upheld the constitutionality of affirmative action programs.

Since the Bakke case, a number of suits have been filed by white males challenging federal regulations loosening hiring and promotion systems, particularly those related to seniority (e.g., *United Steelworkers v. Weber*, 1979). Others have been filed challenging federal requirements that a certain percentage of federal grants be set aside for minority businesses (e.g., *Fullilove v. Klutznick*, 1980). Daniel Leach, former vice-chairman of the Equal Employment Opportunity Commission (EEOC), charged that these are attempts to throttle all efforts to bring women and racial minorities into the economic mainstream.[36] (These cases will be discussed in more detail in chapter 15 on civil rights.)

The U.S. Supreme Court has generally upheld the *principle* of affirmative action; however, the Court has found it difficult—as have most employers—to determine at exactly what point affirmative action turns into racial discrimination. After the Court ruled that Bakke had been discriminated against but that it is constitutional for admissions officers to give some consideration to an applicant's race, one black columnist concluded, "The outcome of the celebrated case is . . . an awkward compromise that pleases no one."[37]

The Court still has not settled the difficult issue: to what extent is it legal and proper for individual white Americans to be discriminated against so that minorities can have a better chance of having a good life?

As the economy gets tighter and minority groups grow in strength, greater conflicts may arise between white males and women and minorities. Government policymakers, like the Supreme Court, will have difficult decisions to make concerning individual rights to employment and advancement opportunities and the proper degree of government involvement in the private sector.

An Aging Population: Retirement Income and Health Care Problems

The future of America will be influenced by how well the nation deals with the problems associated with an aging population. One economist has said: "America is getting older, and much of our well-being and sense of self-respect depend on how well we mature. A nation unable to care for its elderly invites upon itself a wounding sense of frustration and failure.''[38]

The percentage of the population above age 65 is growing. Between 1970 and 1980 it rose from 9.8 percent to 11.3 percent. At the same time, the birthrate dropped. The effect of these trends will be greater pressure on younger persons to support the growing number of aged persons. In 1980 there were 3.3 workers for each Social Security recipient, but by the year 2025 this ratio will shrink to two to one (see Figure 2.6). These figures concern younger Americans. A report by the President's Commission on Pension Policy indicated that nearly two-thirds are worried that their retirement incomes will not be adequate. They fear that the Social Security system will collapse by the time they reach retirement. Many are also worried, in light of today's rapidly rising health and hospital costs, about what will happen to them if they get sick.

Most elderly persons depend on Social Security for their retirement income. Over 35 million Americans receive a monthly Social Security check, which for most of them is their sole source of income. *Social Security is an insurance program administered by the federal government. It is financed by a payroll tax, half of which is paid by a person's employer and half by the employee. The money goes into three separate trust funds: the Old Age and Survivor's Insurance Trust Fund (out of which retirement benefits are paid), the Disability Trust fund (for benefits to the disabled who can no longer work), and the Hospital Insurance Trust Fund (for Medicare payments).* There is no single issue that directly affects more Americans than Social Security payroll taxes and the benefits they provide. As more

money is needed to support the elderly and their survivors, the payroll tax must be increased, taking more money out of the pockets of younger workers. The Social Security system has shown signs of strain for some time. The reserves in the Old Age and Survivor's Insurance Trust Fund have been declining steadily, necessitating emergency legislation by Congress.

Among the more important issues that policymakers began to tackle in 1983 with regard to retirement income for the elderly were the following:

1. Should the Social Security system be financed with other types of taxes in addition to the payroll tax?

2. Should the Social Security system be adjusted to account for changing job and demographic patterns, such as the increasing number of divorced and working women? (Higher divorce rates and large gaps between the life spans of men and women leave millions of elderly women with little or no retirement money under the current system.)

3. Should Social Security benefits be treated as taxable income for federal income tax purposes? (They are currently not taxed.)

4. Should the benefit formula be changed so that workers who receive low wages will receive enough benefits to keep them above the official poverty level?

5. Should the minimum retirement age be raised?

6. Should the federal government require employers to set up private pension funds on behalf of their workers?[39]

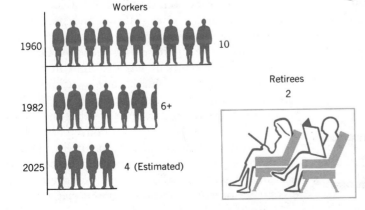

FIGURE 2.6
Workers Available to Support Two Retirees
SOURCE: Copyright 1982, *The Houston Post*. Reprinted by permission. Post graphic by Bud Bentley.

Another critical issue will be how to care for the health needs of the aged. Health and medical costs are the biggest expense item in the average retiree's budget. They are also big costs to the government.

Many health specialists argue that current government health programs for the elderly (Medicare, Medicaid) are biased in favor of those who have physical disabilities or require institutional medical care in nursing homes or hospitals. Yet physical disabilities prevent only about 15 percent of the elderly from going about the normal tasks of daily life. Most of their health problems involve the psychological and social problems related to frailty, which is not considered a disease.

Some health specialists have proposed a system of in-home health and social services at the community level. Because most elderly people who are unwell have chronic ailments that do not necessarily incapacitate them, they might be happier and healthier if they could remain at home in their own community, closer to family and friends. Unfortunately, the price tag of such a program is estimated at over $10 billion. With an aging population and a declining economy, it will be very difficult to fund such a program even if a majority of policymakers support the idea.

The cost of health care for the elderly is only one problem that confronts policymakers. Another is maintaining the family's role in caring for its elderly. One assistant secretary for planning and evaluation in the U.S. Department of Health and Human Services (HHS) told a House subcommittee on health and the environment that "the most significant contribution of long-term care services is in fact made by an individual's own family and friends. . . . A clear policy and fiscal concern is that public programs build on, not substitute for, the assistance provided by these informal care givers."[40] Yet the government cannot ignore those elderly whose families cannot or will not help them when they are ill.

In light of our aging population, young Americans must expect to provide progressively greater support for the elderly in the coming years.

Changing Personal Lifestyle Choices

Individualism has always been one of America's strengths. Alexis de Tocqueville in *Democracy in America* observed nearly 150 years ago that the United States virtually invented the concept of individualism.[41]

The American idea of liberty is that an individual should be free to develop and act in the ways that he or she finds most rewarding. Yet, as we saw in chapter 1, new values and new lifestyles are not immediately accepted by a majority of the population—and some are never accepted. And although each individual is entitled to equal protection of the law under the Fourteenth Amendment to the Constitution, sometimes many years pass before new values are reflected in new laws and the individual holding new values is protected.

Many new values regarding such lifestyle issues as abortion, marijuana, pornography, cohabitation of unmarried couples, and homosexuality were first adopted by college students in the 1960s. Abortion, premarital sex, and cohabitation have been more readily accepted by the general population than some other behaviors, at least insofar as upholding individual choice. In contrast, homosexuality and pornography are still opposed by an overwhelming majority of the population. Although the public's attitudes toward some of these issues may be softening, policymakers still have not written them into law. For example, marijuana has not been legalized, abortion is restricted for welfare mothers, and an individual's right to view pornography remains fairly limited.

Because the acceptance of many of these values and lifestyles is a fairly recent phenomenon, their impacts on individuals and society as a whole are not yet known. For example, the long-term effects of breakdowns in the traditional family on young children and future generations are an unknown, as are the effects of unlimited access to pornography on sexual criminality and the effects of marijuana on sterility. The importance of policy evaluation is clear in the area of personal lifestyle choices.

Issues concerning individual lifestyle choices will be among the more difficult and perplexing decisions facing policymakers throughout the 1980s. Not only is there the sensitive issue of whether the government has the right to control an individual's use of his or her own body, but also the country as a whole seems to be turning more conservative. Indications are that the youth of the 1970s and 1980s are more conservative than their counterparts of the 1960s. In a poll of 23,200 high-school juniors and seniors, 86 percent did not favor having a child without being married, 85 percent preferred a traditional marriage (as op-

College graduates of the 1960s (left) were much more radical than their counterparts of the 1970s and 1980s (right).

posed to living together), 51 percent opposed abortion, and 66 percent favored censorship of certain movies and written materials.[42]

Much of what is adopted as public policy in the area of lifestyle choices will depend on the political clout of the groups pushing for policies. Interestingly, it is often through *group* politics that the *individual* rights of Americans are protected. A clear understanding of the policy process can help an individual see how to push for adoption of untraditional values or the preservation of more traditional ones.

THE CITIZEN'S ROLE: POLICY INFLUENCER

In his book *Designing Public Policy*, Laurence E. Lynn says, "Policy reflects our character as a people, our methods of self-government, and basic changes in society and the economy."[43] To maintain a democracy—a government "of the people, by the people, and for the people"—citizens must participate in the policymaking process. If citizens do not convey to policymakers what they want and expect, the policymakers cannot make policies that respond to the public's demands, nor can they be held accountable for their failure to do so.

As you will recall from chapter 1, a public policy is any decision backed by the authority of a government that determines *who* in the population gets *what*, *where*, *when*, and *how*. You will also recall that the three stages in the policymaking process are *formation*, *implementation*, and *evaluation*. Citizen participation in each of these stages is important, but opportunities for participation are perhaps greatest at the formation stage.

The formation of a public policy (see Table 2.5) involves identifying a general problem or need, setting specific goals to address the need, determining the means by which the goals can be met, and, finally, formally adopting the policy (which must be done by government officials).

Policy needs often emerge as a consequence of changes in the environment. These changes can be the result of changes in geography (natural disasters, variations in supply of natural resources, climatic shifts), changes in the characteristics of

TABLE 2.5

Elements of Policy Formation

I. Identification of Policy Need

II. Establishment of Goals of the Policy
  A. Problems (needs) to be addressed by the policy
  B. Priority of the policy need in relation to other problems
  C. Specific population(s) to be benefited

III. Establishment of the General Means to Achieve the Policy Goals
  A. Alternative approaches to achieving goals (how policy might be implemented)
  B. Identifying the key actors who will carry out the policy (how policy will be implemented)
  C. Resources that must be expended to carry out policy (how much it will cost in terms of time, money, energy)
  D. How policy success will be measured (how it will be evaluated)

IV. Adoption of the Policy by Formal Government Policymakers

SOURCE: Adapted from Robert T. Nakamura and Frank Smallwood, *The Politics of Policy Implementation.* Copyright © 1980 by St. Martin's Press, Inc.

the population (size, location, age distribution, wealth distribution, health), cultural changes (values and lifestyles), or changes in the economic system.[44] These changes create new demands for public policymakers. For example, we have seen that geographical, demographic, economic, and cultural changes have created demands for new programs for the aged, new energy sources, government protection of new lifestyles, and new theories to deal with a stagflation economy.

Obtaining citizen consensus of broad policy needs, such as those stated above, is fairly easy. However, when specific goals and specific means of achieving them must be established, much more disagreement among the citizenry is likely to occur. A real policy issue emerges on the public policy agenda "when a [constituency] with a problem seeks or demands governmental action, and there is public disagreement over the best solution to the problem."[45] At this point individual citizen participation is most important and can have the greatest impact on policy formation and implementation. Decisions by public policymakers on how to structure a program, how much to spend, who will benefit, who will pay for it, who will implement it, and what criteria will eventually be used to measure its success often depend greatly on the pressure put on them by certain individuals or groups.

An individual citizen can try to influence or exert pressure on public policymakers in numerous ways, including:

1. Voting and campaigning for candidates who share similar policy viewpoints;

2. Lobbying for certain issues and programs;

3. Voting for specific legislative (policy) proposals (bond issues, constitutional amendments, taxing and spending proposals);

4. Serving as a member of an official citizen's committee;

5. Attending and speaking out at conferences and public hearings;

6. Responding to questionnaires and surveys from public officials and agencies;

7. Writing or phoning public officials to express one's views;

8. Participating in public protests and demonstrations;

9. Filing a lawsuit or making an administrative appeal;

10. Joining groups of people who share similar policy preferences.[46]

Certainly the person who participates in any one of these activities has a much greater chance of influencing policy decisions than the person who does not.

The chances of getting one's policy preferences adopted and implemented (even if one's preference is to let things continue the way they are or to do nothing at all) are even greater when others in the population share the same viewpoint and col-

Citizen participation in the policymaking process is essential for the maintenance of democracy. One of the most exciting forms of participation is working in the campaign headquarters of a candidate whose positions on important issues coincide with your own.

lectively try to influence decision makers. The old saying "there's strength in numbers" is true. Because policymakers are simultaneously bombarded with numerous policy issues, because they don't have the time, resources, or information to weigh the costs and benefits of all policy proposals, and because they must try to represent the majority of their constituents, they are more likely to be influenced by groups than by individuals.

Belonging to a political party (Democratic, Republican, Socialist Worker, Libertarian, or other) or to a special-interest group (National Organization for Women, Common Cause, Sierra Club, Right-to-Life, National Urban League, American Legion) is often an effective way of influencing policy formation and implementation. However, some groups are generally more effective than others. According to James Anderson in *Public Policy-Making*, the influence of groups depends on "the size of the group's membership, its monetary and other resources, its cohesiveness, the skill of its leadership, its social status, the presence or absence of competing organizations, [and] the attitudes of public officials."[47]

In the chapters that follow, we will show how various individuals and groups have influenced presidential, congressional, bureaucratic, and judicial policy decisions related to energy, the economy, and changing lifestyles. We also hope to persuade you that you can have an influence on the policymaking process and that such participation is important to the democratic system of government.

Evaluation of government policies (such as safety regulations on automobiles) by individuals like Ralph Nader and his Nader's Raiders help determine whether a policy is satisfactory, should be revised, or should be replaced with a new one.

EVALUATING PUBLIC POLICIES: IMPROVING DEMOCRACY

Policy evaluation is the measuring of the consequences of policy implementation. It is another very important part of the policymaking process. Without evaluation, policymakers might continue to make inefficient, unresponsive, and inappropriate policy decisions. Policy evaluation helps determine whether an old policy should just be revised or be replaced with a completely different one. Evaluation can also help citizens hold public officials accountable for their policy decisions.

Who Evaluates Policy Impacts?

Evaluations can be of two types, internal and external. In an *internal evaluation, the government itself conducts case studies, committee hearings and investigations, audits, and so on. External evaluations are conducted by public and private research institutions* (universities, The Brookings Institution, RAND Corporation, American Enterprise Institute, and others) *under contracts from the government. External evaluations can also be conducted by individuals or citizen groups* (e.g., "Nader's Raiders," the Citizens Conference on State Legislatures) *and by public and private research institutions that undertake such evaluations on their own without a government contract* (e.g., League of Women Voters).

What Questions Must Be Asked and Answered?

In evaluating a policy, the overriding question is, "Did the policy achieve the goals set down at the time of its adoption?" In other words, did the policy do what policymakers intended or did it have unanticipated, undesirable impacts? Was it effective or ineffective? Below are some specific questions that must be answered before a final determination can be made of whether a policy met its goals:

1. Did the policy benefit all or only some of those it was originally intended to benefit?
2. Did the policy reach some that it was *not* intended to benefit? (If so, the policy had ''spill-over effects.'')
3. Was the policy administered honestly by those responsible for its implementation?
4. Was the policy implemented on time?
5. Did implementation cost what it was supposed to in terms of money and energy?
6. Did the quality of the good, service, or program produced by the policy meet the expectations of the beneficiaries, the public, and the policymakers?

Evaluation Difficulties

The difficulty of answering the above questions varies with the type of policy and its evaluators. Generally, it is easier to evaluate policies with goals which can be quantified—that is, measured numerically. For example, an energy-related policy with a goal of having 50,000 more home owners install solar heating and cooling systems between 1985 and 1990 would be easier to evaluate than a lifestyle policy with a goal of improving the quality of life for America's elderly by 1990. Policies with predominantly quality-oriented goals are generally much more difficult to evaluate.

In addition, the less quantifiable the goal, the less objective the evaluation can be. When policy evaluators have to use somewhat impressionistic data such as interviews with program administrators and program clients, they are more susceptible to bias in their evaluation. And, of course, there are always evaluators who conduct evaluations for subjective reasons—they may want to show either that a pet policy works or that a policy they scorn does not.

The possibility of such subjective evaluations is why external evaluations by different research institutions, citizen groups, and private individuals are necessary on a regular basis. Interestingly, the

public today is letting policymakers know that they expect such evaluations and that they hold policymakers accountable for failing to alter policies that are shown to be nonproductive, inefficient, and generally poor.

In the following chapters, we will see how evaluations over the years have caused policymakers to modify old policies and make new ones more consistent with a changing America. We will also demonstrate the role of evaluation in making economic, energy, and lifestyle policies.

SUMMARY

In the 1980s America's most pressing needs arise from an uncertain economy, high demands for energy from limited resources, and the changing lifestyles of the population. These needs present the nation's policymakers with some difficult choices in their quest to develop policies that are responsive to people's needs and demands.

In the area of economic policy the key issues are 1) how to deal with a stagflation economy, 2) how much government regulation to impose to strengthen the economy while still protecting the basic principles of free enterprise, and 3) how to diffuse tensions between the classes. These issues are more complex than ever before because of the greater scarcity of resources and the increasingly interdependent world economy.

In the energy arena, the challenges confronting policymakers are how to 1) decrease our nation's dependence on foreign oil, especially from OPEC countries, 2) develop alternative energy sources, and 3) achieve greater energy efficiency through conservation while at the same time protecting the environment. Making energy policy that will protect our nation in the long run is often very difficult because the short-term costs seem extraordinarily high, especially since there is no imminent crisis. Also, there are fundamental differences among policymakers and members of the public as to who is more effective at making energy policy—the government or the private sector.

Lifestyle issues may be even more difficult to resolve because they touch on individuals' own values and moral preferences. Policymakers are confronted with important issues such as 1) how to change the public's expectations about their standard of living in light of money and energy shortages, including traditional expectations related to home ownership, transportation, temperature control, and credit buying; 2) how to create a balance between work and leisure that is healthy from the perspective of both the individual and the economy; 3) how to balance affirmative action with equal opportunity in the workplace; 4) how to provide for America's aging population; and 5) deciding what role the government should play in the individual's lifestyle choices (such as childbearing and living arrangements).

For policymakers to be responsive to the population, individuals must take an active role in letting them know their policy preferences. The individual can influence the policymaking process in several ways, including voting, campaigning, lobbying, and speaking out at public hearings. By calling for evaluations of existing policies, the individual can also hold public officials accountable for the policies they do make.

KEY TERMS

affirmative action programs
external evaluation
free-enterprise system
inflation
internal evaluation
Keynesian economic theory (demand-side economics)
mixed economic system
monetarism
Organization of Petroleum Exporting Countries (OPEC)
productivity decline
recession
reverse discrimination
Social Security system

stagflation
supply-side economics
synthetic fuels (synfuels)

SUGGESTED READINGS

Berk, Richard A., and Berk, Sara F. *Labor and Leisure at Home: Content and Organization of the Household Day.* Beverly Hills: Sage Publications, 1979.

Burns, Arthur F. *The Condition of the American Economy.* Washington, D.C.: American Enterprise Institute, 1979.

Caplovitz, David. *Making Ends Meet: How Families Cope with Inflation and Recession.* Beverly Hills: Sage Publications, 1979.

Doran, Charles F. *Myth, Oil and Politics: Introduction to the Political Economy of Petroleum.* New York: The Free Press, 1977.

Lawrence, Robert, ed. *New Dimensions to Energy Policy.* Lexington, Mass.: Lexington Books, 1979.

Lyle, Jerolyn R. *International Influences on U.S. Inflation: Too Few Goods or Too Much Money?* Lexington, Mass.: Lexington Books, 1981.

Palley, Marian Lief, ed. *Race, Sex, and Policy Problems.* Lexington, Mass.: Lexington Books, 1979.

Pampel, Fred C. *Social Change and the Aged: Recent Trends in the United States.* Lexington, Mass.: Lexington Books, 1980.

Steinman, Michael, ed. *Energy and Environmental Issues: The Making and Implementation of Public Policy Issues.* Lexington, Mass.: Lexington Books, 1979.

Yankelovich, Daniel. *New Rules: Searching for Fulfillment in a World Turned Upside Down.* New York: Random House, 1981.

CHAPTER 3

THE DEVELOPMENT OF THE AMERICAN CONSTITUTION

Roots of the American Constitution ■ The Articles of Confederation ■ The Philadelphia Convention of 1787 ■ The Constitution of 1787 ■ The Constitution Today and How It Changes

Not all policies are equally long lasting. Really important policy issues tend to dominate political conflict—at all levels of government—for decades. For example, slavery directly influenced policymaking for three-quarters of a century. In the second half of the nineteenth century, policymakers seemed to fight endlessly over the protective tariff and the ratio of gold to silver in establishing the basis of the currency. Major policies such as these have impacts that can reach far into the future. Slavery gave us sectionalism, racism, and all the social and economic costs of both. The tariff and currency policies of the nineteenth century had much to do with the wars and economic problems of the twentieth century.

Many of these important policy debates have stemmed from different interpretations of the rules of policymaking laid down in the Constitution. A *constitution defines how policy will be made and who will make it; it contains fundamental laws, allocates power and responsibility, and provides ways for conflicts within the political system to be resolved*. Additionally, a constitution removes certain types of policy questions from consideration under any circumstances. For example, Congress is forbidden to enact laws abridging the freedoms of speech, press, and assembly.

This chapter is about the American Constitution. In the pages that follow we will consider a small portion of the heritage that made the Constitution possible. We will also examine the Declaration of Independence and the Articles of Confederation. Finally, we make note of the ways the Constitution has been changed to fit the needs of a changing people. The Constitution is our national agreement on the process of policy formulation, implementation, and evaluation. With all its rich overlays of meaning, it is also the best evidence of our adjustments to changing population, circumstances, and technology.

ROOTS OF THE AMERICAN CONSTITUTION

At some point in the 1760s the colonists in North America began to think of themselves as Americans; however, before that they were English, with

TWO
TREATISES
OF
Government:

In the former,
The *false Principles*, and *Foundation*
OF
Sir *ROBERT FILMER*,
And his FOLLOWERS,
ARE
Detected and Overthrown.
The latter is an
ESSAY
CONCERNING THE
True Original, Extent, and End
OF
Civil Government.

LONDON,
Printed for *Awnsham Churchill*, at the *Black
Swan* in *Ave-Mary-Lane*, by *Amen-
Corner*, 1690.

John Locke, the English philosopher, wrote *Two Treatises of
Government* in 1660. His book stressed the idea of a social con-
tract between the ruler and the ruled, an underlying theme of the
American Declaration of Independence.

all the constitutional rights of English citizens.
The roots of American constitutionalism reach to
England and Western Europe, with a rich heritage of political theorizing and practical training
in self-government. Four examples illustrate our
indebtedness to the past.

First of all, much of American thought about
limited government and a written constitution
comes from *Two Treatises of Government,* a book
written in 1690 by the English philosopher John
Locke. Locke was trying to soothe the national
conscience in the second *Treatise,* for the English

had deposed James II and put William and Mary
on the throne, and this drastic move had left the
English sense of orderliness and propriety somewhat shaken. Locke resurrected and developed
the old idea of a *social contract, an agreement between
the ruler and the ruled, with both having mutual obligations.* Almost all of Locke's theory reappears in the
American Declaration of Independence.

The second is the *separation of powers, which is
the principle that the three great functions of government—
legislative, executive, and judicial—be assigned to separate and independent agencies to avoid a dangerous concentration of power.* The clearest statement of this
doctrine appears in a book written in 1748 by a
French Baron and political philosopher, Charles-
Louis de Secondat de Montesquieu. In his *Spirit of
the Laws,* Montesquieu praises the English Constitution for separating the functions of government
and argues that merging the three in one person
or group is the very definition of tyranny. Out of
this notion, we created the American presidency,
the Congress, and an independent national judiciary.

Third, although there were other theorists who
contributed to American thought, there was also a
pragmatic side to our heritage. In challenging the
power of the state to dictate a person's religion,
ordinary people in England and Western Europe
contributed greatly to the idea of limited government. Training in politics and government was
given to many nonclerical members of Protestant
sects. This prepared a new stratum of leaders beyond the ordained, titled, and propertied classes.

Finally, the colonists lived in North America
under English law from 1607 to 1776. During this
period, the English Constitution and common-
law tradition were followed; when revolution
came, that tradition was continued. Of course,
adjustments were made to fit English institutions
to the American setting. Practical experience in
living so remote from the English homeland encouraged experimentation. The pattern of conflict
that then emerged between Colonial legislatures
and royal governors inspired the development of
American institutions. When reviewing the acts
of the legislature, governors sat with their advisory councils, and this practice produced an "upper house" to review actions of the "lower
house." This became *bicameralism, in which the
legislature is divided into two houses.* Also out of the
Colonial practice came the *checks and balances*

system, *the notion that the doctrine of separation of powers should be amended to provide each branch of government with enough power to control and limit the powers held by the other branches.*

The Politics of Separation and the Continental Congresses

The American colonies and England entered a prolonged period of political conflict following the French and Indian War. That conflict became both irreconcilable and increasingly bitter between 1763 and 1776. England felt that the colonists had shirked their fair share of responsibility during the French and Indian War. When the war was over, England's debts and worldwide responsibilities had grown so large that she demanded the colonists share, through taxes, the responsibility for their defense. This demand was resisted in the colonies.

Conflict between the colonies and England changed the structure of political institutions in the colonies. At first, resistance to English authority was unorganized, but it was serious enough to force changes in acts of Parliament. Then, in the 1770s, colonial *Committees of Correspondence produced a network of communications between persons and communities resisting English authority.* This network alerted the colonists when the British closed Boston Harbor in 1774 (in retaliation for the Boston

Tea Party) and also proposed an economic boycott. Out of the resistance movement came *Continental Congress meetings of delegates from all the colonies to consider British actions:* the first met in September 1774 in Philadelphia, and every colony was represented except Georgia.

The words *independence* and *revolution* were forbidden in all but the most private conversations of the delegates to the First Continental Congress in 1774. However, by the spring of 1775 when the Second Continental Congress was convened, discussions of fighting had begun. Gradually, as delegates to the Congress left and were replaced, moderate and conservative delegates were replaced by men less patient with England. Still, although the Second Congress prepared for war and named a commander-in-chief for its army, it adopted a petition on July 5, 1775 aimed at reconciliation, begging the king to prevent further hostilities against the colonies. Yet one day later the Second Congress assumed some governmental functions, including the operation of a post office department.

The Continental Congresses were important for the leadership they provided the colonies and for the government they created for the United States between 1774 and 1781. The Second Congress, having witnessed the deteriorating relationship with England, called on the colonies to form their own governments, and finally declared American

Taxation policy has always been controversial. England's taxation of the colonies was one of the basic causes of the Revolutionary War. Here, John Malcolm, a tory (pro-English) tax collector, is shown being tarred and feathered by colonists in Boston in 1774.

independence of England. The men who served as delegates to the Continental Congresses were among the leading citizens of the colonies; they were men of property who held positions of influence under English rule. They were hardly a cross-section of the male population of the colonies, and they were not selected in a uniform process—but they were the new nation's first policymakers. Without trying to assess the quality of the Congresses, we can give them credit for providing an interim government, declaring our independence, and ushering in an important era of constitution writing.

The Declaration of Independence

On June 7, 1776, Richard Henry Lee introduced a resolution to the Second Continental Congress declaring the independence of the United States. While the resolution was being debated, a committee of five was chosen to write a *Declaration of Independence, a document formally declaring the independence of the colonies from England and justifying the separation.* Thomas Jefferson became its principal author. Lee's resolution was adopted on July 2; the Congress debated the language of the Declaration on July 3; and the document was adopted as modified on July 4.

The Declaration has four parts: 1) preamble, 2) political philosophy, 3) enumeration of specific grievances against George III, and 4) conclusion. The influence of John Locke's contract theory on the Declaration is unquestionable. However, some years later Jefferson wrote that he did no research before writing, and that no written work influenced the document. This can only be explained by the fact that Locke's work had become so well known in American intellectual circles and his theories so widely accepted that Jefferson had only to synthesize, in good literary style, what everyone had been discussing for a decade or more. Consequently, without turning to Locke, Jefferson managed to quote the English theorist directly in the Declaration. The political philosophy section of the Declaration was most influenced by Locke and of all parts it is the most often quoted:

> *We hold these truths to be self-evident, that all men are created equal, that they are endowed by their Creator with certain unalienable Rights, that among these are Life, Liberty, and the pursuit of Happiness. — That, to secure these rights, Governments are instituted among Men, deriving their just powers from the consent of the governed, — That whenever any Form of Government becomes destructive of these ends, it is the Right of the People to alter or to abolish it, and to institute new Government, laying its foundation on such principles and organizing its powers in such form, as to them shall seem most likely to effect their Safety and Happiness.*

Without precisely stating the case, Jefferson had argued that men made government through a contract; that governments were created to ensure the basic rights of man; and that when government violated the terms of the contract, the people

On July 4, 1776, delegates to the Second Continental Congress signed the Declaration of Independence, a document formally declaring the independence of the colonies from England and justifying the separation. Thomas Jefferson was the principal author of this important document.

might justly initiate a revolution and replace the old government with a new one.

The contract theory could be used to justify a revolution, but it implied far more. It implied that the powers of government are limited and must be defined so that all would know the terms on which a government had been established. This is the essence of constitutionalism and of written constitutions. Revolutionary theory was thus joined with the Colonial heritage of compacts and charters, the written agreements by which the colonists had governed themselves for almost two centuries.

Our Declaration of Independence was also a propaganda document and an appeal for help to England's historic enemies. The men who signed it knew they had to have allies if they were to defeat the English. Accordingly, the Declaration lays the whole business of misgovernment on King George III and brands him a tyrant. Not one direct mention of Parliament appears in the document. To make good theory and good politics, the Declaration does not demand the rights of Englishmen; it demands the natural rights of man. In the preamble, Jefferson says that "a decent respect to the opinions of mankind requires that [a revolutionary movement] declare the causes which impel them to the separation." Obviously the Declaration was a communication with Americans and with American friends in Parliament; but the first intent was to sell the movement to an audience in Europe.

In Jefferson's first draft of the Declaration he indicted the King for waging "cruel war on human nature itself" by carrying people into slavery. Unfortunately, the objections of colonists from the South and of shipping interests from the North caused the passage to be deleted. Jefferson recognized the inconsistency of slavery with the principles of the Declaration. An early attack on the slave trade might have spared the United States much suffering later on. Still, the movement to abolish slavery often relied on the language of the Declaration for inspiration, and another century later the same document was an inspiration to the black movement for equality in America.

THE ARTICLES OF CONFEDERATION

Richard Henry Lee's resolution of June 7, 1776, contained two parts; in addition to the motion for a declaration of independence, he moved that "a plan of confederation be prepared and transmitted to the respective Colonies for their consideration and approbation." It was appropriate that the motion for independence be offered together with a call for constitution-making; the resulting document was certainly well suited to the liberal goals of those who made the Revolution. Liberals cherished individual liberty and feared strong central governments—they believed that citizens would be safer and better protected by the smaller state governments than by a distant, large, national government comprised of representatives from the several states. Government under the Articles of Confederation represented a reaction to the British Constitution, to the central government it embodied, to the power wielded by the British government, and especially to executive authority under the English Constitution. The Articles of Confederation government was expected to be "a perpetual union," as its full title suggested, but it had a life of only eight years, 1781 to 1789. In 1789, the conservatives won a victory in the writing of a new constitution that would protect most of their interests. They had always favored a stronger national government but had lost control of the Second Continental Congress and had been beaten by the movement for independence.

Acting on Lee's resolution, the Congress appointed a committee to draft a constitution. The draft of the Articles of Confederation delivered to the Congress on July 22 was principally the work of John Dickinson, a Pennsylvania conservative. Congress debated the Dickinson draft, changed it to weaken the powers assigned to the national government, and on November 17, 1777 sent it to the states for ratification. The deadline for ratification was March 10 of the following year. However, more than three years of debate and negotiation followed in the state legislatures. On March 1, 1781, the last states instructed their delegates in Congress to ratify. The next day the Second Continental Congress changed its journal to read "The United States in Congress Assembled."

The Articles of Confederation provided a government much like that under the Continental Congresses. It was to be a confederation—a league or alliance among sovereign states united for common purposes. Articles 2 and 3 of the constitution contain the essence of the alliance:

ARTICLE 2 *Each state retains its sovereignty, freedom and independence, and every power, jurisdiction,*

and right, which is not by this confederation expressly delegated to the United States, in Congress assembled.
ARTICLE 3 *The said states hereby severally enter into a firm league of friendship with each other for their common defence, the security of their liberties and their mutual and general welfare; binding themselves to assist each other against all force offered to, or attacks made upon them, or any of them, on account of religion, sovereignty, trade, or any other pretense whatever.*

The policymaking power of Congress was limited to 1) determining peace and war, 2) conducting foreign relations, 3) maintaining a post office, 4) regulating the standards for coins, and 5) establishing uniform standards in weights and measures. Maintaining the army and navy involved a complex partnership between the Congress and the states, in which the national government 1) determined military needs, 2) appointed top-ranking officers, and 3) requisitioned equipped soldiers from the state militia. Congress could regulate trade with Indians if they were not residents of states. It could also regulate international commerce, but only through its treaty-making power and only if treaties did not interfere with the state power to regulate commerce and tax imports and exports.

There were few restrictions placed on the states under the Articles. The states were forbidden a series of military and diplomatic powers except as approved by Congress. Likewise, some aspects of state sovereignty were abridged by the Articles: each state was required to recognize the public records and judicial proceedings (wills, marriages, divorces, property titles, and the like) of all other states; to grant citizens of other states the privileges and immunities of citizenship (travel, commerce, and access to the government, for example); and to return fugitives from justice. These three clauses were carried over to the Constitution of 1789 almost intact. Furthermore, the states could not make alliances or agreements with one another without the prior approval of Congress. Appeals from disputes between states were to be settled by a complex arbitration process using congressmen as the court of arbitration.

Other aspects, especially how government was to be organized under the Articles of Confederation, are described in Table 3.1, which compares the Articles with the Constitution of 1789.

Viewed from the perspective of 200 years' hindsight, government under the Articles might seem woefully inadequate. Most analysts dwell on the limited powers assigned to the national government and on the alleged structural defects. But the Articles of Confederation were exactly the government its framers wanted. They believed that republican government was possible only in a small geographical area and that large governments, remote from the people, endangered republican principles. They also believed that the states were of an appropriate size to sustain a republican form of government and that a national government was needed solely to carry out those functions the states could not easily provide separately.

The Articles of Confederation kept the power of the national government at about the same level it had been during the Revolution. This represented a victory for liberal, republican principles and for those who had come to dominate the Second Continental Congress. Once the war was won and the Articles of Confederation government was in place, the revolutionaries expected to continue their movement at the state level. Their confidence was based on the social revolution that had taken place simultaneously with the political and military revolution. Loyalist property had been confiscated and redistributed; many of the "first families" who had made up the privileged class of Colonial times had boarded English ships and returned to England. The privileged position of the Church of England in the colonies was gone, along with the last vestiges of feudalism. Although the decisions for independence and a constitution had been made by an elite sitting in both the Congress and in the state legislatures, the Revolution had been democratized substantially during the war. Nevertheless, the full realization of all egalitarian principles was in some cases decades or centuries away.[1]

The Rise and Fall of the Articles of Confederation (1781–1789)

The 1780s were dominated by a constitutional struggle between two groups. On the one side were the *Federalists, who secured the Articles of Confederation government, favored a reliance on legislatures, and preferred state power to power concentrated in a central government.* On the other side were the *Nationalists, who favored a strong central government, preferred*

TABLE 3.1

Comparative Analysis of the Articles of Confederation and the Constitution of 1789

	Articles of Confederation	Constitution of 1789
Proposing agency	Second Continental Congress	Constitutional Convention called to amend the Articles of Confederation
Ratifying agency	State legislatures instructed their delegates in the Second Continental Congress to ratify	Special ratifying conventions in the states, called by state legislatures
Proportion required for ratification	Unanimous vote of the states	9 of 13 states required for ratification
Amending process (A) Proposal	Unanimous vote of the state delegations in Congress	Either by two-thirds vote of both houses of Congress or by a convention called by Congress on request of two-thirds of the states
(B) Ratification	Unanimous vote of the states through instructing their delegations in Congress	Either by a majority vote in three-fourths of the state legislatures or by conventions in three-fourths of the states
Type of federalism adopted	A confederation of sovereign states	A federation in which the people are sovereign
Allocation of powers in the federal system	(1) Limited enumerated powers assigned to the national government	Broad enumerated powers assigned to the national government
	(2) Undefined or unenumerated powers are assigned to the states; the United States can exercise only powers expressly delegated to it	Implied powers are assigned to the national government through the "necessary and proper" clause and the omission of "expressly" from the Tenth Amendment
	(3) Few powers are denied either level of government—states are denied the power to make foreign and national security policy and are barred from treating other states as if they were a foreign power	Both the national and state governments are denied significant powers and policy options; limitations on states' sovereignty are carried over from the Articles; the slave trade is protected for 20 years; states are barred from interfering with commerce or impairing the obligation of contract
	(4) Limited shared powers are developed: both levels of government cooperate in raising and equipping the army; both can borrow money, emit bills of credit, and appropriate funds	There is a wide sharing of powers and functions in areas not exclusively assigned to one level of government or denied to one of the levels
Legislative authority (A) Composition	A unicameral Congress of states, in which each state has one vote; each state is required to send a minimum of two delegates, and is permitted to send a maximum of seven, to Congress	A bicameral Congress, representative of the states and the people; an unamendable section guarantees each state equal representation in the Senate; seats in the House of Representatives are allocated on the basis of population (with slaves counted as three-fifths of a person)
(B) Selection	Delegates are selected by state legislatures	Senators are selected by state legislatures.* Representatives are selected by the vote of those in each state eligible to vote for the most numerous branch of the state legislature

TABLE 3.1

Comparative Analysis of the Articles of Confederation and the Constitution of 1789 *(continued)*

	Articles of Confederation	Constitution of 1789
(C) Status of members	Paid by the states; subject to recall by the states; one year term of office; limited to no more than three years in any six consecutive years	Paid by the United States; fixed term of office; subject to discipline and expulsion by the full membership of their respective houses
Executive authority	There is no established or independent executive; Congress is authorized to appoint a committee of the states composed of one Congressman from each state; Congress authorized to set up other committees and civil officers as necessary to manage the general affairs of the United States; when Congress is not in session, the committee of the states (or any nine members) is authorized to act for the Congress in its place; Congress is authorized to appoint one of its members to preside as president, limited to a term of no more than one year in any three consecutive years	A presidential office is created, with a strong executive system; there is a separation of powers, with the executive established as independent of the Congress. The president is elected for a fixed term of four years, and reelective without limit;** the presidential election process is established as semi-independent of the Congress, though the Constitution makers expected the final selection of the president would frequently be made in the House of Representatives; one of the many powers assigned to the independent president is that he/she can require reports in writing from heads of executive departments; a full-blown bureaucracy under his/her leadership is implied
Judicial authority	There is no established or independent judiciary; Congress serves as the court of appeals for conflicts between the states through a process best described as arbitration; Congress is empowered to establish courts to handle maritime and admiralty cases and to determine the rules for deciding such cases	A national Supreme Court is established and Congress is empowered to create inferior courts in the national court system; separation of powers provides substantial independence of executive and legislative authority; judges are protected by lifetime appointment and guarantees against reduction of salary
Essential nature of governmental organization	A weak national government, with major obstacles in place to prevent strengthening the government at the expense of the states	A strong national government, with potential for further strengthening of the government at the expense of the states' powers, especially through judicial interpretation of the Constitution
Policy advantage or victory	The federalists or radicals who made the Revolution and dominated the writing of the early state constitution	The nationalists and the conservatives who feared democratic trends
Guarantees of rights and liberties	Left entirely to the state constitutions or to traditions upheld by the courts	Before the addition of the Bill of Rights through the amending process, only a few basic rights were protected in the Constitution, with reliance on the state constitutions and on traditions upheld through the courts
Essential nature of the movement for the document	Revolutionary	Counterrevolutionary

*Direct election of Senators required of all states by the Seventeenth Amendment, ratified April 8, 1913.

**President limited to no more than two terms or a total of ten years by the Twenty-second Amendment, ratified February 27, 1951.

republican to democratic government, and placed a greater reliance on the executive and judicial functions of government as compared to the legislative. The Congress of the Articles of Confederation was dominated at first by the Nationalists and later by the Federalists. Because delegates to the Congress served a one-year term and could serve no more than three out of any six consecutive years, a turnover of leadership every three years was ensured. Furthermore, both the Federalists and the Nationalists were periodically and cyclically dominant in the state legislatures, whose members were also typically limited to a one-year term. The state legislatures selected congressmen, could recall them, and regularly instructed their delegations in Congress on important matters.

As the strength of either the Federalists or the Nationalists grew or declined in Congress, policy changed. Both groups agreed that the Congress needed more power; they disagreed on *how* that power should be acquired. Initially, the Nationalists preferred either to liberally interpret new implied powers for the central government or to amend the Articles of Confederation. Later this group became convinced that a radically new constitution was required. The Federalists, on the other hand, sought grants of power from the states for limited time periods, without amending the Articles.

The Political Impact of the Postwar Economy
Economic conditions after the Revolutionary War were mixed, but the Nationalists controlled the newspapers and dominated the political dialogue to such an extent that early historians inaccurately portrayed the United States economy as unusually poor. The truth is that the United States had a quite normal postwar boom followed by a period of overexpansion of credit. This produced a negative short-term balance of trade, and, understandably, a depression which began in 1784. After the war, American harbors were filled with ships—not only those of our wartime allies, but also England's. The United States had excellent exports in tobacco, wheat, and corn, but the demand at home for European manufactured items was so great and European credit so easy to secure that Americans went on a buying spree and quickly overextended themselves. The English government tried to impose punishing restrictions on the purchase of American commodities, but the restrictions were not observed. The postwar boom continued, but not for long.

Inflation in a new nation without a standard currency produced a severe shortage of silver and gold coins, which in turn produced a demand for paper money (in use in 7 of the 13 states by 1786). But paper money suffered from depreciation and from a variety of discounting procedures used by banks. The depression of 1784 was also blamed on the English import restrictions and the English practice of dumping goods on the American market, so the states adopted protective tariffs (although in an uneven pattern). Deflation and an economic slowdown followed the depression, but these trends were mostly felt by New England and the shipping trade. It was the nation's first experience of the so-called postwar boom-bust-recovery cycle. Today this inflation-recession cycle still challenges the nation's economists.

The Group Struggle for Policy Advantage The interest groups that in the 1780s made demands on government—both at the state and national levels—were not as well organized as their counterparts of the 1980s. However, then as now, producer interests came to dominate consumer interests. The three major clusters of early American producer interests were 1) farmers; 2) merchants, creditors, bankers; and 3) manufacturers.

In the 1780s, the nation was 80 to 90 percent agricultural. Much of rural America suffered little from the war and in fact experienced a boom after it. Initially, farmers wanted to sell crops abroad at good prices without government interference. However, when the commercial depression came they then sought relief from the banks and from government. On the other hand, the merchants, creditors, and money lenders opposed all relief for farmers and instead asked for navigation laws favoring American shipping. As for the manufacturers, they wanted a protective tariff, not caring who transported goods as long as American products enjoyed an advantage over European competition. These interests produced rivalries among the states and resulted in interstate trade restrictions. Much of the basic constitutional policy struggle of the 1780s was a struggle between the New England, Middle Atlantic, and southern states for an economic advantage in the parallel (although not perfectly matching) areas of shipping, manufacturing, and agriculture.

Myths About the Failure of the Articles of Confederation Government The notion that the government under the Articles of Confederation was debt-ridden is mostly a myth. According to historian Merrill Jensen, author of *The New Nation* (one of the best studies of the Articles of Confederation), as much as $400 million of debt had been wiped out by the middle of 1783. The remaining domestic and foreign debt at the end of the Confederation was about one-tenth that amount—about $12 per capita. The Congress was not penniless; although its income fluctuated yearly, it received money, mostly from the states. The Congress had no power to tax, but it could sell public land and requisition money from the states.

With the income it received, the Congress had three major budgetary obligations. These were 1) to pay the costs of ongoing government operations, 2) to pay the interest on the entire debt, and 3) to liquidate as much of the principal indebtedness as possible with the remaining revenues. The debt was of enormous political significance, and the most serious question raised about it was how it would be liquidated. The Nationalists wanted to consider the debt a national obligation, but the Federalists were committed to keeping that kind of power out of the hands of the national govern-

ment, since English constitutional history suggested that the power to tax drew to it other, wider-ranging powers. Many of the states had actually assumed much of the national debt due their own citizens, and some of the states bought up the depreciated Continental certificates. Since American citizens were not used to paying taxes, the states were unwilling to impose heavy duties to fund the debt; still, by 1784 some of the states were attempting to resolve the problem of the national debt.

Toward a New Constitution

Despite the fact that the Articles prohibited the states from negotiating with one another and from entering into agreements without the permission of Congress, Virginia and Maryland sent delegates to Alexandria in March, 1785, to consider problems relating to navigation of the Chesapeake Bay and the Potomac River. At month's end the delegates moved to Mount Vernon, where George Washington hosted (but didn't join) their deliberations. They reached solutions on a wide range of policy questions and referred them back to their state legislatures. Soon, other states were invited to join in far-reaching policy discussions.

The Annapolis Convention After the *Mount Vernon Conference*, a second meeting was proposed by several states, and Virginia invited all of the 13 states to a meeting to be held at Annapolis in September of 1786. Nine states named dele-

TERMS of SALE of LOTS in the CITY of WASH-INGTON, the Eighth Day of *October*, 1792.

ALL Lands purchased at this Sale, are to be subject to the Terms and Conditions declared by the President, pursuant to the Deeds in Trust.

The purchaser is immediately to pay one fourth part of the purchase money; the residue is to be paid in three equal annual payments, with yearly interest of six per cent. on the whole principal unpaid: If any payment is not made at the day, the payments made are to be forfeited, or the whole principal and interest unpaid may be recovered on one suit and execution, in the option of the Commissioners.

The purchaser is to be entitled to a conveyance, on the whole purchase money and interest being paid, and not before. No bid under Three Dollars to be received.

In the early days of the Republic, Congress did not have the power to tax, but it did have the power to sell public lands to raise money. Public lands in Washington, D.C., were commonly offered for sale under the terms cited above.

gates to the **Annapolis Convention**, but delegations from only five reached the site. The meeting was chaired by John Dickinson, writer of the first draft of the Articles, and was so poorly attended that no major substantive issues were discussed. However, the 12 delegates adopted a resolution, drafted by Alexander Hamilton, calling on all of the states to send delegates to a convention to meet in Philadelphia on the second Monday in May of the next year. This meeting was to consider not only commercial problems but ''all matters'' necessary to strengthen the constitution of the national government.

Thus Mount Vernon, Annapolis, and Philadelphia represented three orderly and progressive steps toward the goal of a new constitution to which so many Nationalists were dedicated. Opponents suspected that the true agenda at Annapolis was the calling of the **Philadelphia Convention**, not some list of commercial or trade problems.

The movement for a new constitution was reinforced by two other events: 1) the complete failure of all efforts to grant the Articles of Confederation Congress more power, and 2) Shays's Rebellion.

The Failure to Grant Congress More Power The quest for more congressional power had begun a month before the ratification of the Articles. The Second Continental Congress had proposed an amendment to the Articles granting Congress the power to impose a 5 percent import tax on all goods coming into the United States. Rhode Island was the only state to decline ratification of the amendment, but under the Articles the objection of a single state was enough. There were other incidences of states blocking amendments designed to expand congressional power. New York blocked an amendment which would have granted financial powers to Congress for twenty-five years without necessitating frequent amendments to the Articles. And sectional trade differences kept various states from ratifying amendments that would have given Congress the power to regulate trade.

From 1781 to 1787 congressional leaders offered a variety of strategies to correct the perceived ills of the Articles. In May of 1786, for example, Charles Pinckney introduced a resolution in Congress for a Grand Committee to consider the affairs of the nation and either call a convention or themselves propose amendments to the

Articles. The debate lasted for weeks. Finally, a committee was appointed, and its report included a list of amendments that would have greatly strengthened the national government without changing its basic organization. Congress did not act on this report, perhaps because those committed to change had shifted their attention to the Annapolis Convention.

Shays's Rebellion If there was one event that could be called the catalyst for the meeting in Philadelphia which drafted the Constitution, it would be **Shays's Rebellion**—a local uprising in Massachusetts that began in August of 1786 and was crushed in February of 1787. Shays's Rebellion was a debtors' revolt against high taxes, high court fees, a hard-money policy (gold and silver coins), and a legislature that was insensitive to debt-ridden farmers' problems. It was also against sheriffs, lawyers, and judges who conducted the legal system's foreclosure processes (farmers had lost their farms and homes). The protest began in town meetings, expanded to bands of Shaysites who blocked foreclosures, and grew to include the mobilization of armies by the insurgents and the Massachusetts state government.

The seriousness of Shays's Rebellion can be measured by two notable facts: 1) Congress authorized calling up an army of 1340 men, although they were never used; however, some 4000 Massachusetts state militiamen were. 2) The major military maneuvers that brought the rebellion to an end involved efforts of the Shaysites to capture the federal arsenal at Springfield. Of course, the movement for a convention was well under way before the revolt; but Shays's Rebellion frightened the ''good people'' of the United States, produced evidence to support the Nationalists' propaganda about the weaknesses of the Articles of Confederation, and reinforced the elites' fears of mob rule. Five states selected delegates to the Convention at Philadelphia during the course of Shays's Rebellion, and others completed the selection process shortly thereafter. Thus, the rebellion stimulated interest in the Philadelphia Convention, as did the Annapolis Convention activities.

The report of the Annapolis Convention was sent to the states and to the Congress meeting in New York. At first the Congress ignored the matter, but then, on February 21, 1787, it passed the resolution calling on the states to send delegates to Philadelphia

> *for the sole and express purpose of revising the Articles of Confederation and reporting to Congress and the several state legislatures such alterations and provisions therein as shall when agreed to in Congress and confirmed by the states render the federal constitution adequate to the exigencies of government and the preservation of the Union.*

The Convention that was to meet in Philadelphia had a much broader mandate from Annapolis than it had from the Congress.

THE PHILADELPHIA CONVENTION OF 1787

The Convention in Philadelphia represents a strange blending of continuity and change. Most analysts dwell on change, and certainly there was much of that. However, our analysis will first focus on the continuity that the Convention represents. The constitutional struggle over the power, policy responsibility, and functions to be assigned to the national government began *before* the American Revolutionary War. It continued right on through the war, during the entire Confederation period and into the Philadelphia Convention. This unceasing debate extended to the struggle for ratification and beyond to the Civil War, to the rise of the social service state after the Depression of the 1930s, and on into the 1980s.

Thus the debate over the creation of a national Department of Education in 1979 resurrected elements of a debate that is at least four centuries old, if we date the American experience back to our Colonial heritage. Opponents of a Department of Education asked whether the creation of a cabinet-level department wouldn't ultimately take from the states the last remnants of their role in licensing and setting the standards and general direction of education. Wouldn't the federal government first fund, then advise, and finally regulate one of the last exclusive policy domains of the states?

The basic struggle over a national identity had continued after 1775, but the debate was limited by a number of constraints. First, the communications and transportation systems of the 1770s and 1780s were far from ideal for a national debate; for example, delegates to conventions and Congresses were frequently late or did not show up at all. Second, this was a pre-party era, and

few national organizations existed—especially organizations sufficiently developed to support a serious debate. Third, the Revolutionary War substantially dislocated public life and distracted leaders from addressing many basic policy questions. Fourth, as we've already seen, the distinctive restraints put on holders of public office at the state and national levels prohibited any sustained leadership. There was no executive at the national level, and there were only weak executives at the state level. Typically, legislators served a one-year term and were barred from extended periods of service; at the national level they were permitted to serve no more than three out of six years. Finally, the question of a national identity was itself a difficult one over which men of good will substantially differed. Given these constraints, the outcome of the Convention of 1787 was remarkable. Both in their deliberations and in their later politicking for ratification, the delegates achieved well beyond reasonable expectations.

The Convention was marked by controversy and conflict. The record of the debates is a record of hard bargaining; of victories won and then withdrawn to hold the delegates together; of differences so serious that they almost caused adjournment in defeat; of compromise; of a final product three members would not sign even as witnesses of the unanimous vote of the states; and of a final draft that pleased no one completely. Ultimately, though, the delegates found that there were more issues on which they agreed than on which they disagreed, and their commitment to maintain the union in the form of a national government was the overriding goal that kept them at Philadelphia. But the final product that they sent to the states and to the Congress was controversial. The Philadelphia Convention became the Grand Convention only years later when the Constitution and its makers were overlayed by myth and mystique, fabricated on both truth and fiction.

Many of the delegates to the Philadelphia Convention were the same men who had made the Revolution, served in the Continental Congress, and who would serve the government to be established under the new Constitution. Benjamin Franklin and George Washington, the two most famous men in the United States, were delegates. Robert Morris, the financial genius of the American Revolution, John Dickinson, the author of the first draft of the Articles of Confederation, and the

"*Remember, gentlemen, we aren't here just to draft a constitution. We're here to draft the best damned constitution in the world.*"

Drawing by P. Steiner, © 1983 by The New Yorker, Inc.

incumbent governors of three states attended the Convention. The following statistics are revealing: of the 55 men who went to Philadelphia, 7 served in the First Continental Congress; 8 signed the Declaration of Independence; 30 had seen some type of military service; 42 had served at one time or another in the Articles of Confederation Congress (9 of them in the current Congress meeting in New York); all but 2 or 3 had held public office in the colonies or states; and about 20 had helped to write their state constitutions. When the first government under the Constitution of 1787 convened in 1789, the continuity was equally impressive: the president, 8 members of the House, 11 members of the Senate, and 2 members of the cabinet had been delegates to the Convention in Philadelphia.

All in all, the continuity of the Philadelphia Convention with America's past and future was impressive. Where the Convention broke with the past, the delegates embraced only those changes that they felt would be acceptable to the segments of the population that cared most about government, politics, and policy on a day-to-day basis. Quite a few radical changes proposed for the constitutional structure were abandoned, including a national government veto of acts of state legislatures. We can examine the dynamics of change at the Convention from four different perspectives: 1) the characteristics of the delegates, 2) the setting, 3) the organization and rules, and 4) the major decisions.

The Delegates to the Convention

The delegates attending the Philadelphia Convention were an elite, no more or less representative of the population than other elites who had served in past Congresses or state legislatures. Their selection had been left entirely up to the state legislatures, who generally followed the two-to-seven-member delegation rules for selecting the Congress under the Articles of Confederation. To go to the Convention was an honor, and appointments were much sought after. That it was a mark of distinction to be selected was widely recognized, and the delegates were quite aware of their dignified status. This "collective reputation" of the men at Philadelphia later proved to be a crucial factor in the ratification struggle: many people reasoned that so reputable a body of leaders surely deserved a decent hearing. Also, as a result of their collective experience, the delegates knew and trusted one another. Without mutual trust and respect, it is very doubtful that the Convention could have continued its deliberations from May 25 until September 17.

Other social characteristics of the delegates can be summarized as follows:

1. *Geography*   One important study of the Convention identified 55 major geographical areas in 1787. Of these, two-thirds were represented at Philadelphia. The backcountry was the one region notably underrepresented, and much of the opposition to the "national view" came from there.

2. *Politics*   In this pre-party era there were approximately 30 stable political factions in the new nation. Of these, probably 80 percent were represented, but many of the delegates were independent of any established faction.

3. *Family*   As few as 10 percent of the delegates began life at the bottom stratum of society. For the most part, they came from important if not highly influential families.

4. *Wealth*   Eighty percent of the delegates were at least comfortably well-off, and over 20 percent were rich. Their most substantial investments were in real estate and slaves (16 delegates owned slaves). Of course, their investments were far more diverse and included bank securities, bank loans, shipping, and manufacturing.

5. *Occupation*   It is not easy to classify the 55 delegates precisely by occupation, but our best information shows: planters or large-scale farmers, 13; lawyers, 13; merchants, 8; state officeholders, 12; doctors, 3; small farmers, 2; retired, 2; and unclassifiable, 2.

6. *Education*   For a time in which few men, even the very well-to-do, attended college, the delegates were distinguished by their education. Over half had earned their bachelor's degree; others had studied the law formally and informally; some had honorary degrees; and a few had done graduate work at home or abroad. Although only 13 were practicing lawyers, more than two-thirds of the delegates had studied in the office of an attorney.

7. *Religion*   According to historian Clinton Rossiter, "Most were nominally members of one of the traditional churches in their part of the country . . . —and most were men who could take their religion or leave it alone."[2] The rationalist and secular spirit of the age had clearly influenced them.

8. *Age*   The average age was slightly over 43.

To sum up, the delegates at Philadelphia comprised an elite. In general, they were educated, well-to-do, from the best families, and were either professionals, affluent farmers, merchants, or public officeholders. They attended the "right" churches. They were young, and yet they represented a wealth of political experience. And except for the backcountry regions and the anti-Nationalists, they were representative of the major geographical areas and political factions of the day. However, the young nation had an abundance of leaders of the first rank who were not at Philadelphia. Thomas Jefferson and John Adams were out of the country, and many of the men who were important to the Revolution—including John Hancock, Sam Adams, Richard Henry Lee, and Patrick Henry—were not delegates.

In all, 74 delegates were chosen; 55 attended at one time or another; and 29 could be considered full-time participants. New Hampshire selected a delegation of four, but only two attended, and they did not arrive in Philadelphia until July 2 (they were due May 14). Rhode Island refused to name delegates and never participated.

The Convention's Setting

Philadelphia was the nation's largest and most exciting city. It was a center of commerce and manufacturing, of education, of communications, and of the arts. It was at the center of the country; occasionally, when the Convention recessed for one of its committees to work, some delegates could make a quick trip home. Four other conventions were meeting in Philadelphia, and yet the city, with some effort, could find accommodations for delegates and provide a meeting hall.

Organization and Rules

Called to meet on May 14, the Convention was embarrassed by a problem that had plagued the Congress repeatedly, and for which it had been much criticized by the Nationalist faction: there was no quorum. Only two states' delegations had arrived at the statehouse. Not until May 25 did five more delegations arrive to constitute a quorum of seven states. During the 11 intervening days, James Madison led the Virginia delegation in the preparation of a proposal which was largely his own writing. This session, named the Virginia Caucus, proved to be one of the most important meetings of the Convention; the proposal that it drafted was the *Virginia Plan*, which dominated early Convention deliberations. The proposal was introduced as a series of resolutions about which Max Farrand, the leading scholar of the Convention, wrote: "Amended and expanded they became the Constitution of the United States."[3]

When a quorum did appear on May 25, the first order of business was the selection of a chairman and the adoption of rules for the Convention. Only two men commanded a level of respect that would ensure their consideration for the chairmanship—Benjamin Franklin and George Washington. Robert Morris, acting for Franklin's state of Pennsylvania, nominated Washington, who was elected by a unanimous written ballot. In addition to a chairman, the Convention selected a secretary, a doorkeeper, messengers, and a three-man committee to prepare standing rules and orders. The secretary, William Jackson, kept a rather sketchy journal, and James Madison took his own notes, which along with the notes of other participants have been published as *The Records of the Federal Convention of 1787.*[4]

The rules as recommended by the committee and amended by the Convention were mainly the rules used by the Articles of Confederation Congress, but in four respects these rules were critically important to the success of the Convention:

1. Initially, some leaders of the large states opposed voting by states, which would have put the states on an equal footing with one another, but delegates from Virginia persuaded them to abandon this opposition because of the friction it might produce between the large and the small states. In agreeing to vote by states, the leaders hoped to build a foundation for later concessions from the small states.

2. Some rather strict rules of decorum were established that had the effect of compelling gentlemanly conduct even during brutal exchanges in debate.

3. The rules were designed to encourage deliberation and to delay closure of debate until every aspect of an issue had been explored.

4. The rules provided the delegates with privacy and freedom from external pressure. To quote from the journal, the rules provided "That no copy be taken of any entry on the journal during the sitting of the House without leave of the House. That members only be permitted to inspect the journal. That nothing spoken in the House be printed, or otherwise published, or communicated without leave."[5]

The secrecy rule was not perfectly observed by all the delegates, but no important violation occurred. This rule was perhaps the most important one adopted by the Convention; the delegates were free to debate, negotiate, and compromise without fear of immediate reaction from their constituents. If decisions had been made public during the heat of their most bitter debates, the leaders might have been less willing to compromise. The secrecy rule was maintained even by the printer who printed the draft copy and the final versions of the Constitution. When the Convention ended, the journal and all of the records were entrusted to George Washington until the Congress should make some decision concerning their final disposition.

Convention Decisions

On May 29, Governor Edmund Randolph opened the substantive business of the Convention by reviewing the Nationalist position on the weaknesses of the Articles of Confederation. Then he introduced the work of the Virginia Caucus—the Virginia Plan, sometimes known as the Large-State Plan or the Randolph Plan. By implication, the Virginia Plan abandoned any idea of amending the Articles of Confederation. The essence of the Large-State, Nationalist Plan can be outlined as follows:

1. *A bicameral national legislature.*

   Both houses allocated on the basis of taxes or population.

   The first house directly elected by the people.

   The second house elected by the first house from a list of nominees prepared by the state legislatures.

   Both houses elected to a fixed term of office.

   Both houses paid from the national treasury.

2. *Powers assigned to the legislature.*

   All those exercised by the Articles of Confederation Congress and all others better exercised at the national than at the state level.

The power to veto acts of state legislatures conflicting with the national Constitution.

The power to use force against states not fulfilling their duty under the Constitution.

3. *A national executive (unclear whether singular or plural).*

Selected by the legislature.

Term of office fixed.

Ineligible for reelection.

4. *A national council of revision.*

Composed of the executive and members of the national judiciary.

Charged to review acts of the national and state legislatures before they became operative.

Empowered to veto all acts of the national and state legislatures (veto is final unless the act is passed again by the legislature).

5. *A national court system.*

One or more supreme tribunals and inferior courts to be established by the national legislature.

Members to serve during good behavior (life) and to receive an irreducible salary.

Jurisdiction over admiralty and maritime cases, cases involving foreign nationals, diversity of citizenship cases, cases involving the national tax system, impeachments of national officers, and breaches of the national peace and harmony.

6. *Provisions for the states.*

Admission of new states into the union provided for.

Each state guaranteed a republican form of government.

Territorial integrity of each state guaranteed.

7. *An amendment process.*

Provision for changing the Constitution when needed (implies a more flexible process than under the Articles).

8. *A binding oath.*

National and state officers bound by an oath to uphold the Constitution.

9. *A ratification process.*

The new Constitution to be ratified by state conventions elected by the people.[6]

From May 29 until mid-June the Convention deliberations centered solely on the Virginia Plan. Then, on June 14, the small states revolted. On the 13th the Committee of the Whole had reported back to the Convention the revised Virginia Plan. The small states were unhappy with both the speed of the revision process and the contents of the revisions. William Paterson's request for a delay is the only entry in the journal on June 14. He announced that it was the wish of several delegations, especially his own state of New Jersey, that another—purely federal—plan, quite different from the Virginia Plan, be prepared and introduced.

On the next day, as promised by Paterson, new resolutions were proposed. Collectively, they became known as the *New Jersey Plan*, or the Small-State Plan, or Paterson Plan. This Small-State, Nationalist Plan called for many of the reforms previously proposed as amendments by the Articles of Confederation Congress. Its essential components can be listed as follows:

1. *A unicameral national legislature.*

Voting by state.

2. *Powers assigned to the legislature.*

All those exercised by the Articles of Confederation Congress, plus new powers including: imposing import duties, stamp taxes, and postal fees; regulating interstate and foreign commerce; and requisitioning taxes from the states in proportion to the population (slaves to be counted as three-fifths of a person).

Power to devise ways of collecting from states in arrears on their taxes.

Power to pass major legislation without a unanimous vote (requisite vote not specified).

3. *A plural national executive (exact number not specified).*

Selected by the legislature.

Term of office fixed.

Ineligible for reelection.

Removable by Congress on the request of a majority of state governors.

Empowered to appoint other national officers and to direct all military operations.

Empowered to compel states' compliance with national laws and treaties.

4. *A national supreme tribunal (with no inferior courts).*

Appointed by the executive.

Members to serve during good behavior (life), and to receive an irreducible salary.

Original jurisdiction over impeachment of national officers, and appellate jurisdiction over admiralty and maritime cases; cases involving treaties, ambassadors, and foreign nationals; and cases involving the regulation of trade or the collection of national taxes.

5. *Preeminence of national enactments.*

Laws and treaties of the United States declared the supreme law of the land, with state judiciaries bound to uphold them.

6. *Provisions for the states.*

Admission of new states into the union to be provided for.

States to be furnished with uniform rules for naturalization.

States to impose the same standards of justice on out-of-state citizens as they would on their own residents.[7]

Other plans were introduced at the Convention, but the Virginia and New Jersey Plans received the most attention, the Virginia Plan being the principal basis for Convention deliberations.[8] On June 19 the key provisions of the Virginia Plan were adopted by the Convention in a vote of seven to three, with one state divided.

In the weeks that followed, the Convention came perilously close to dissolving. On many key matters the Convention was united, but it became obvious to all delegates that differences over representation in the Congress had to be compromised. The small states were adamant that they retain equal votes with the large states, as was proposed in the New Jersey Plan and had prevailed under the Articles of Confederation. The Virginia Plan, which had in the main been accepted by the Convention, proposed a bicameral Congress based on population only. On July 16, the Convention broke this impasse by voting (five to four, with one state divided) for the so-called *Great Compromise* or *Connecticut Compromise: seats in the lower house (the House of Representatives) were to be allocated on the basis of population; in the upper house (the Senate) the states were to be equally represented.* After

the vote was taken, the disappointment of the large states threatened to adjourn the Convention. However, sober leadership secured an adjournment only for the balance of the day, and private negotiations and small caucuses kept the Convention together.

There were many other compromises made. However, the compromise on representation was crucially related to the major division in the country at the time—between the interests of the small states and those of the populous and prosperous large states. Another example of Convention politics is the *three-fifths compromise. The slave states wished to have slaves counted for the allocation of seats in the House of Representatives, but not for the apportionment of taxes. The Convention ultimately decided to count each slave as three-fifths of a person for both apportionment and taxation.* We cannot try to discuss the many other compromises reached at Philadelphia. However, scholars who have devoted much time to an analysis of the Convention report that the Constitution ultimately adopted represents a 50-50 compromise between the Virginia and New Jersey Plans.

In formal sessions between the 17 and 26 of July the Convention approved those resolutions that had been adopted in the Committee of the Whole. Then it appointed a five-man Committee of Detail, referred all proposals and adopted resolutions to it, and adjourned for the committee to work. The instructions of the committee, which we quote here, provided clear standards for American constitution making.

> *In the draught of a fundamental constitution, two things deserve attention:*
>
> 1. *To insert essential principles only, lest the operations of government should be clogged by rendering those provisions permanent and unalterable, which ought to be accomodated [sic] to times and events.*
> 2. *To use simple and precise language, and general propositions, according to the example of the several constitutions of the several states.*[9]

The Committee of Detail did a splendid job of merging all the decisions into one document. It then ordered from the printer enough copies for the delegates. When the Convention reconvened on August 6, it considered the draft, section by section. On August 31, a Committee of Postponed Matters, composed of one member from each state, was appointed and charged to propose solutions for the many, sometimes nasty, details that had plagued the Convention. It was this Committee that designed the electoral college method of selecting the president of the United States.

On September 8, the last of the committees—the five-member Committee of Style—was appointed and charged to revise the complete document and put the several parts under their proper headings. Gouverneur Morris of Pennsylvania, a member of the Committee of Style, became the "penman of the Constitution," because he was primarily responsible for the final draft. The Committee of Style was also responsible for the language of the preamble to the Constitution. Because the Committee could not be sure which states would ratify, they replaced the cumbersome listing of states with the well-known phrase "We the people of the United States." From September 12 to 15 the Convention gave the document its last review, and on the 15th approved it by a unanimous vote of the states and ordered a hand-written parchment copy prepared for signatures on September 17.

THE CONSTITUTION OF 1787

Decisions and Nondecisions

The Constitution of 1787 became the first policy decision of a reborn nation. Within it there are many decisions and nondecisions that have influenced policy and structured conflict in the United States over the past two centuries. The most sweeping and important decision implicit in the Constitution was the reassignment of power between the states and the nation. The United States was changed from a confederation of sovereign states—each state with a veto power over any serious policy change—to a federation of states resting on popular sovereignty. The longstanding notion of *sovereignty was that a nation or state was defined by its absolute power to make and enforce policy within its boundaries*. As sovereign states the former English colonies in North America had joined together to create the Articles of Confederation. The Constitution of 1787 adopts the notion found in the Declaration of Independence and much eighteenth-century political theory of *popular sovereignty*—that is, *ultimate political authority rests with the people, who retain the power to create, alter, or abolish government*.

The new national government had both a full set of powers, enumerated in the Constitution, and the potential for the development of *implied powers* through the "elastic clause"—which empowered Congress to "make all laws which shall be necessary and proper for carrying into execution" its list of enumerated powers. Under the Articles, United States government policies affected people indirectly, coming as they did through the state governments. Under the Constitution of 1787, both the national and the state governments were empowered to govern individuals. In those policy areas that had caused much of the conflict among the states during the Confederation period, only the national government would be empowered to act. The states were to pass no laws impairing the obligation of contracts, were barred from making monetary policy, and were prohibited from making policy regarding interstate and foreign commerce. To put it simply, the capacity of the states to wage commercial and financial war on each other were significantly reduced, though not completely eliminated.

Among the nondecisions found in the new Constitution, two of the most important relate to voting and to slavery. Rather than specifying qualifications for voting in national elections, the Constitution makers delegated that decision to the states. Those persons qualified by state law to vote for delegates to the "most numerous branch of the State Legislature" could vote in national elections. In each state this was at the time the most generous standard being used to grant the vote; however, rules governing who could vote varied from state to state. In future years each expansion of the eligible electorate began at the state level. Ultimately constitutional amendments, Supreme Court decisions, and national executive intervention were required to eliminate a wide range of state discrimination.

In the long run, the nondecision on slavery proved far more costly to the nation. The slave states were protected in at least three respects: 1) by implication, slavery was recognized and given constitutional standing, 2) Congress was forbidden to stop the importation of slaves for 20 years, and 3) a fugitive-slave law was included in Article IV as one of a series of required interstate relationships. Future generations of Americans might condemn the Constitution makers for failing to end slavery in 1787, but the votes of both the slave states and the shipping states might have been lost on this one policy question. Perhaps the lesson to be learned from this is that nondecisions are in reality important choices, sometimes having grave consequences.

Concerning the Constitution of 1787 we can say that in its symmetry and balance it is a product of the eighteenth century. Like the architecture and music of that time, there is order, balance, and consistency of theme in the document. Power was divided between the nation and the states; and at the national level, three coequal branches of government were balanced with one another. A cooperative relationship (or harmony) among all levels and branches of government was an essential requirement for the making and implementation of all major policies.

Motives of the Constitution Makers

As for the motives of the men who wrote the Constitution, we should reemphasize four points made earlier: 1) the framers were experienced, first-rate politicians who compromised on the most serious differences between the states and the sections; 2) they produced a highly controversial document; 3) however, in the generations following 1787, a kind of reverence for the Constitution and its framers developed and grew; and 4) after the Civil War, in a period of triumphant nationalism, reverence for the Constitution developed into a sort of civic piety or civil religion.

Early in the twentieth century, a new generation of historians questioned the tenets of the civil religion. In 1913 historian Charles A. Beard wrote the first major dissenting critique of the Constitution makers. He found that:

The movement for the Constitution of the United States was originated by four groups of personalty [that is, personal property] interests which had been adversely affected under the Articles of Confederation: money, public securities, manufactures, and trade and shipping.[10]

He further argued that a small, active group of men initiated and carried out the whole effort; that no popular vote was taken on the matter at any stage; that most of the delegates at Philadelphia derived economic advantages from the new system; that the Constitution removed private property rights from the reach of popular majorities; that as a result of the voting laws of the day, perhaps as few as one-sixth of the adult males participated in the selection of delegates to ratifying

conventions; that the same economic beneficiaries who wrote the Constitution manipulated the ratification process; and that in the ratification struggle, the line of cleavage for and against the Constitution was between those with substantial property interests on one side and the small farmers and debtors on the other.

At first Beard's book shocked the nation; however, it drew greater acceptance from relativist historians and economic determinists in the decades that followed. Relativists believe that every age must reinterpret history in the light of new evidence and new theories and that historical events develop new meanings in each succeeding generation. Economic determinists believe that economic forces determine not only the form of government but also the social organization and intellectual and moral conditions of its citizens. Beard's critics later pointed out that his documentation on such matters as ownership of public securities was marred by error and that the line of cleavage over ratification was geographical or sectional rather than purely economic.[11] Errors notwithstanding, however, the book suggests that the motives of the Constitution makers should be given a careful examination.

Other critics have devoted more attention to what they might call the unauthorized behavior of the Constitution makers. The argument goes as follows: the delegates were authorized to propose amendments to the Articles of Confederation; they ignored this mandate and became framers rather than amenders; they locked the doors, met in secret, and protected their journal from public scrutiny; they deliberately violated the Articles of Confederation in providing that only nine states need ratify the new Constitution; and, finally, they did not submit their work to Congress for its approval but instead submitted the Constitution to the states via Congress.

Still another line of attack suggests that the Constitution was an elitist document, deliberately antidemocratic in design. It is undeniable that the delegates were an American elite. Further, under the new national government, only the House of Representatives was directly elective—by an electorate limited by varying state voting restrictions. The Senate could be reached by the people only through their election of state legislators, and the chain of influence on the president was much longer. Direct influence of the federal judiciary was too remote to even contemplate. Those who argue an elitist, antidemocratic motivation can quote the delegates to bolster their case. A good example is found in a speech by Elbridge Gerry of Massachusetts delivered on the floor of the Convention on May 31, 1787:

> *The evils we experience flow from the excess of democracy. The people do not want virtue; but are the dupes of pretended patriots. In Massachusetts it has been fully confirmed by experience that they are daily misled into the most baneful measures and opinions by the false reports circulated by designing men, and which no one on the spot can refute.*[12]

There were, undoubtedly, different motivations for different delegates. However, their debates afford surprisingly little evidence to support an antidemocratic, an economic, or any one of the other conspiracy theories of motivation. After the Convention, the delegates returned to their states, made presentations to their state legislatures, and wrote an extensive and detailed set of explanations of their work at Philadelphia. The Convention was a political event, and the delegates were politicians. They knew that the records were to be privileged and that they could therefore be quite candid in the debates; yet there is little support for a conspiracy theory in the journal entries, in Madison's notes, or in other accounts of the Convention. Their collective and individual reputations were at stake in the reports they gave when they returned to their states—what they said publically and privately was deemed noteworthy by their peers and recorded to a considerable degree. In light of the extent of this publicity, it seems likely that questionable motives would have been exposed. Under the circumstances, we can safely interpret the Convention primarily as a political event and, on the whole, accept the delegates' own record of motivation. Political scientist David G. Smith has summarized this view very well.

> *In the context of their society and their experience with the colonial and revolutionary governments, the delegates' activities in behalf of the new government seem to have been directed primarily at a simple, coherent set of political objectives. They seem to have been aiming at (1) withdrawing particular objects of contention from local majorities; (2) attempting to secure a common interest; (3) securing the support for the "representative republic" of a stratum of "wise and virtuous" leaders who would put republican principles above personal and factional interest; and (4) devising a scheme of representation and checks and balances that would complete that government and prevent it in turn from developing cumulative tendencies toward an extreme.*[13]

Rightly or wrongly, it seems that the delegates at Philadelphia truly believed that the government under the Articles could not succeed and was in the process of dying. When it seemed that the Convention might break up, just after the proposal of the Great Compromise, they talked about "saving the union." This was the commitment that kept them together.

Ratification and the Bill of Rights

The ratification process provided in Article VII of the Constitution did not require approval of the Congress, shifted ratification from the state legislatures to ratifying conventions, and required ratification by only nine states to go into effect. Thus the Convention set the rules of the political struggle to follow. Letters of transmittal, signed by George Washington as president of the Convention, spelled out the ratification process in detail and outlined the transition process by which leaders under the Articles of Confederation would ultimately turn the government over to officers elected under the Constitution of 1787.

After adjournment of the Convention on September 17, those delegates who were also members of Congress rushed from Philadelphia to New York to help ensure a good reception for the Constitution by the Congress. The delegates had hoped that the Congress would transmit the Constitution to the states with a recommendation for ratification, but they had to settle for a simple, noncommittal transmission. Under the circumstances, it is remarkable that the Congress paid the salaries of the secretary, doorkeeper and messenger employed by the Convention and also paid the printing costs. Equally remarkable was the fact that before the Convention met, Congress had extended the free-postage privilege to delegates quite as though they were equal in standing to members of Congress.

Given the limited transportation and communications systems of the day, it is also remarkable that ratification was accomplished in only ten months. Before a convention could be called in each state, the legislature had to pass enabling legislation specifying the number of delegates as well as the process of electing them.

The battle for ratification was managed by a small group of men. They used timing, other forms of manipulation, and propaganda as part of the strategy. They knew that 1) some states were ready to ratify, would ratify easily by a wide margin, and would give the movement a momentum; 2) other states would require a full-blown propaganda effort; and 3) only nine states were necessary to ratify the Constitution, but Virginia and New York were essential to the union since they were large and their absence would cut the republic into two noncontiguous land masses; and 4) the overall ratification campaign had to be successful at a level that would ensure the legitimacy of the new government, and had to be carried out without totally alienating the opposition. At first they argued that reservations and amendments to the document were unacceptable. However, later in the campaign they accepted proposed changes and agreed the proposals would be laid before the new Congress and considered through the amendment process.

The debate over the Constitution took many forms. It was the custom of the day to offer theoretical analyses of major public questions in the form of articles signed with Latin names. As a part of the propaganda effort in New York, Hamilton, Madison, and Jay wrote a series of articles signed "Publius." Collected and supplemented, they were published later as *The Federalist papers, which summarize the deficiencies of the Articles of Confederation and defend the most important aspects of the Constitution*. Over the years, scholars, government leaders, and judges have frequently consulted *The Federalist* papers to improve their understanding of the intent of the Constitution makers. *The Federalist* papers are considered to be one of this country's few original contributions to political theory.

There are many reasons for the success of the effort for ratification, including the following:

1. The collective reputation of the men who wrote and signed the Constitution—especially George Washington and Benjamin Franklin—carried great weight. It could easily have been reasoned that no other body of men could have drafted a better Constitution.

2. The pro-Constitution group rather quickly preempted the name *Federalist* and placed opponents on the defensive as *Anti-Federalists*.

3. The Federalists had written the rules for ratification; they were better organized and had a unified strategy.

4. The Federalists included in their ranks a substantial number of influential people: the clergy, teachers, writers, editors, and lawyers.

5. The Federalists had shown flexibility from the beginning. At the Convention they had carefully judged what was possible and rejected the unacceptable. When they realized that ratification was not possible without reservations, especially a Bill of Rights, they yielded and promised that the first Congress would consider such amendments as were necessary.

6. They had correctly judged elite and public support for a move to a second, higher level of nationhood.

7. In state after state, the Federalists were able to convince the ratifying convention delegates that *they*, the Federalists, were the true friends of the Revolution.

The Anti-Federalists contributed substantially to the Federalist victory. Though many important public figures opposed the Constitution, they could not agree on a unified strategy. They discussed at least three strategies: 1) to propose amendments to the Articles of Confederation and follow the legally established amending process, 2) to let the Articles of Confederation go, reject the Constitution of 1787, and create three viable confederacies, or 3) to call a second Convention to make changes in the Articles more acceptable to those opposing the Constitution.

It would appear that the ratification fight was a close contest, even with only nine states required for ratification (see Figure 3.1). At first, Rhode Island refused to call a ratifying convention, and North Carolina's convention voted 184 to 84 to reject. If the Federalists were a minority, as some critics have charged, the ratification struggle is an outstanding example of what a well-organized minority can accomplish. But accomplish it they did

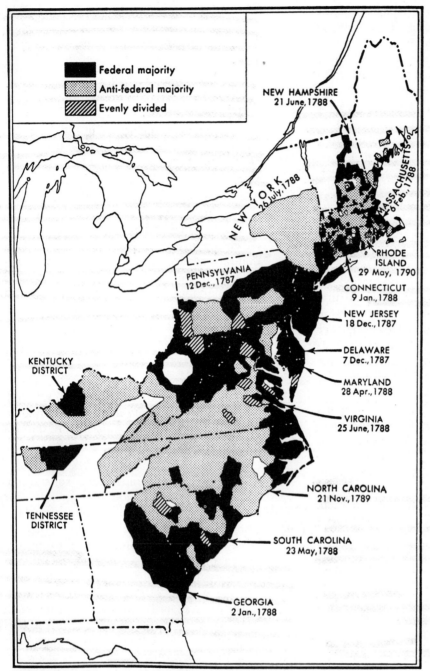

FIGURE 3.1

Ratifying the Federal Constitution

SOURCE: Richard B. Morns, Ed. *Encyclopedia of American History*. New York: Harper & Row Publishers, 1965, p. 118.

and the nation had a new Constitution and a new form of government.

In the first session of the new Congress the Federalists delivered on their campaign commitments. Led by Madison, friends of the Constitution drafted a ***Bill of Rights*** *consisting of the first ten*

amendments to the Constitution. Twelve articles of amendment were proposed to the states in September of 1789 and ten were ratified; they became operative on December 15, 1791. The first two articles were rejected. They pertained to the size of the House of Representatives and the compensation of members of Congress—certainly atypical of the weighty matters addressed in the articles approved.[14]

The Nature of the Document: 3 × 3 Government

Federalism and separation of powers are crucial concepts to describe how the framers assigned power in the new Constitution. *Federalism allocates power geographically to the nation and to the states*. Separation of powers allocates national power according to the three functions of government: legislative, executive, and judicial. Figure 3.2 illustrates the resulting 3 × 3 matrix of the government of the United States. Each citizen lives under a national, state, and local government, and at each level of government legislative, executive, and judicial functions are assigned to distinct units of government. The way that power or authority is structured in the 3 × 3 matrix has important consequences for politics and policymaking. At the national level, changing a policy by legislation requires the approval of both houses of Congress and the signature of the president—and the agreement of the courts, if the law is challenged. Interest groups, political parties, and citizens know that they must cope with all three branches of government. Also, they must frequently persuade both the national and the state governments if they wish to make an important change in policy.

Federalism was the product of the most significant compromise reached at the Constitutional Convention. In 1787 federal government was a novelty on the world scene; but in a way, it was not so novel to the Constitution makers at Philadelphia. Federalism had in fact evolved in relationships between England and the North American colonies; furthermore, the experience of intergovernmental relations during the Confederation prepared the new nation for federation under the Constitution of 1787. Federalism seems to be particularly appropriate as a compromise between an extreme concentration of power and a loose confederation of independent states. It has proved to be popular in building constitutional governments for the former colonies of the nations of Western Europe. The initial compromise need not be ironclad: the precise nature of the union, or federation, is spelled out through politics and intergovernmental relations over the years.

Because federalism is a crucial political arrangement in the United States, we devote all of chapter 4 to it. The principle of separation of powers as practiced in the United States will be fully described in chapters 11, 12, and 14 which discuss Congress, the presidency, and the judiciary.

THE CONSTITUTION TODAY AND HOW IT CHANGES

At the end of this text is printed the Constitution of 1787 (as amended). However, these words are constantly being reinterpreted as our nation's political, social, and economic conditions change. As a basic policy framework, the Constitution was written for a small, agricultural nation located mainly in the territory we now call the eastern seaboard. Yet, only a few changes by amendment have been made to the Constitution. The broad, general language of the original Constitution has made the document very flexible and reduced the need to formally amend it. For example, the

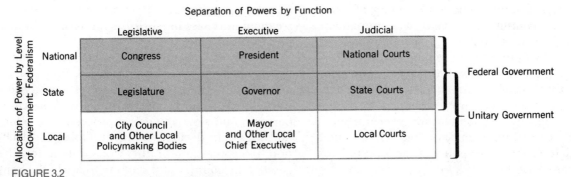

FIGURE 3.2

The 3 x 3 Matrix of Formal Power Dispersal

United States Congress has gone on to authorize such unforeseen agencies and programs as the National Aeronautics and Space Administration, which sent an astronaut to the moon, the Communications Satellite Corporation, a collaboration of public and private interests that built Telstar, which permits 50 nations to send and receive television signals around the world; and the Department of Energy, which has invested billions of dollars in the development of synthetic fuels to relieve American dependence on fossil fuels from abroad. Each of these actions was possible because of liberal interpretations of the various clauses in the Constitution. While the words of the Constitution have changed very little, their meaning and their applications have changed in countless ways.

On the reference shelves of any good library you can find still another version of the Constitution. Printed by the Congressional Research Service of the Library of Congress, *The Constitution of the United States of America: Analysis and Interpretation* is annotated with decisions of the Supreme Court interpreting its meaning. For each word, phrase, clause, or sentence of the Constitution cited in the annotated version, an analysis of current meaning along with the relevant Supreme Court decisions is given. The *interpreted* or *unwritten Constitution is the meaning of the Constitution that goes beyond its literal words*.

We've already seen that the men who wrote the Constitution intended to insert essential principles only, and to use simple and precise language. The Constitution, according to its makers, was to be the basic policy statement for a more perfect union, but they fully expected it to change in use. In fact, many of the men at Philadelphia became leaders in the new government and began immediately to interpret and thereby change the document. There is no mention in the Constitution of a "meeting of heads of departments"—which we now call the Cabinet. The full meaning of "citizenship," "commerce," "veto," "commander-in-chief," "general welfare," "spending power," and dozens of other terms remained to be interpreted as the Constitution was used. The inferior courts, the executive bureaucracy, and congressional operating procedures remained to be designed by political action in future governments.

So the Constitution makers laid a foundation on which succeeding political generations of Americans have built a skyscraper. From the be-

ginning, Chief Justice John Marshall viewed the written Constitution properly as the first stage of a process that would continue and either progress or decay. Studying Marshall's greatest judicial decisions, we can almost hear him say, "We must remember that it is a Constitution we are expounding."

Constitutional change is a day-to-day process, and important changes are the result of decades of small, seemingly insignificant, and subtle events. The agents of change may never be identified by even the most patient observer. However, for the purposes of our investigation we shall use a simplified, threefold classification of change procedures.

1. Executive, legislative, and judicial interpretation.
2. Custom and usage.
3. The amendment process.

Executive, Legislative, and Judicial Interpretation

Executive Interpretation An early illustration of constitutional interpretation proceeding from the executive branch is an ironical one involving President Thomas Jefferson and the Louisiana Purchase. Jefferson, as a critic of the Washington and Adams administrations, had taken a strict constructionist political stance. (A *strict constructionist interpretation opposes any policy for which a specific and explicit constitutional authorization cannot be found.*)

At the time, western Americans were very anxious to secure both freedom to navigate the Mississippi River and control over New Orleans—and westerners could be very aggressive people. Jefferson sympathized with the westerners; therefore, when Spain turned the territory over to France, the Jefferson administration negotiated a treaty of purchase in April 1803, offering $15 million for Louisiana.

Finding no constitutional authorization of the purchase, Jefferson at first ordered drafts for an amendment authorizing it. However, his advisers warned that time did not permit use of the cumbersome and slow amending process. The reluctant president decided to accept a loose construction interpretation of the Constitution for the good of the country and sent the treaty to the Senate for ratification. In the Senate the only serious opposition was political, based on Federalist party fears that new states in the South and West would support the Jeffersonian Republican party. The Senate ratified the purchase by 26 to 5 and the Supreme Court approved the procedure in *American Insurance Company* v. *Canter* (1828).[15] Later administrations were happy with this precedent, which permitted other purchases of vast territories, expanding the United States.

Another more recent illustration of executive interpretation of the Constitution is the Ford and Carter administrations' efforts to fight inflation in the 1970s. These efforts consisted of plans based mostly on voluntary compliance with guidelines established in presidential speeches. Both presidents publicly denounced mandatory wage and price controls, even though inflation worsened at a double-digit rate throughout most of that decade. Mandatory wage and price controls are economically unsound for at least two major reasons: 1) imposing controls requires a considerable bureaucracy, which takes time to put in place, and which can never provide fully equitable treatment for all citizens; and 2) during times of mandatory controls, there is a tendency for the maximum prices and wage increases to become the new minimum, thus actually driving up, uniformly, prices and wages. Moreover, if the government does elect to freeze prices and wages, plans to do so must be kept secret until the order is given or all persons affected will try to rush in adjustments before the freeze takes effect. Finally, a freeze of prices and wages does not attack the cause of inflation, and once the freeze is lifted, pent-up pressures for increases simply produce another, more dramatic round of inflation. This applies to the entire Western world, and executives in other nations have been faced with precisely the same problems with inflation that have challenged American presidents in recent decades.

Thus President Carter reinforced his calls for voluntary compliance by establishing a modest anti-inflation agency headed by economist Alfred Kahn. Furthermore, the White House inserted itself in labor-management contract negotiations and canceled government contracts with firms not in compliance with anti-inflation guidelines. Carter was not the first president to use government contracts as a weapon against uncooperative elements of the industrial and business communi-

ties. In the early 1960s John F. Kennedy had forced the steel industry to roll back steel price increases by withholding contracts from companies that increased prices and granting contracts to those companies that canceled earlier increases. According to the Constitution, the Congress of the United States is authorized to make policy, while the president is authorized to administer policy; but over time and by degrees strong presidents have developed an independent authority for the presidency that would probably impress Alexander Hamilton.

Congressional Interpretation The Constitution gives the president the power to appoint judges and the principal officers of the country with the advice and consent of the United States Senate. Traditionally, presidents have followed the norm of *senatorial courtesy, consulting senators in their own party before making an appointment in the senators' state*. The practice of senatorial courtesy has radically changed the effect of the Constitution on the appointment power. The first use of senatorial courtesy occurred in the Washington administration of 1789. Benjamin Fishoun, the president's nominee for the post of Officer of the Port of Savannah was rejected by the Senate because the nomination did not meet with the approval of the senators from Georgia.

Senatorial courtesy does not cover all appointments. Those most affected are appointments to districts or programs that fall within a particular state. For example, federal district court judges are selected under the rules of senatorial courtesy, but not court of appeals judges or Supreme Court justices. Senators from the president's party control appointments to federal offices within their states. For many posts, the president and the senator or senators consult and reach an agreement on appointments; for others, the senator literally makes the choice, and the president sends it to the Senate for confirmation.

In 1979, 152 newly created federal district court judgeships were to be filled, and Senator Edward M. Kennedy, then chairperson of the Senate Judiciary Committee, suggested to Senate colleagues that judicial merit commissions be used to help improve the quality of nominees. Some senators resented interference in their domain; one very prominent senator said, ''I will send up one name on a slip of paper, and that will be it.''[16]

Since the advent of the *social service or welfare state which stresses an enlarged role for government through economic and social programs to protect individual security and general welfare*, Congress has been delegating more and more of its policymaking power to the executive branch. This trend is characteristic of all nations of the Western world. Congress defines a given policy goal, outlines the program necessary to achieve the goal, creates an agency to handle the program (or assigns the program to an established agency), and authorizes the program to be carried out. Of course, agencies or units of the administration must follow the procedures that Congress has spelled out and administrators must treat all citizens equally under the law.

When Congress first began to delegate its powers to the executive in the 1930s, the resulting legislation was very controversial, as reflected in the often contradictory opinions of individual members of the Supreme Court. Today, however, Americans have become accustomed to rule-making by a vast national bureaucracy, and most Americans can find more policy intimately affecting their daily lives in the *Federal Register* (the place where proposed and final administrative rules and regulations must be published) than in the *Statutes at Large* (the place where all acts of Congress are published at the end of each session). However, the Reagan administration pledged to reduce bureaucratic policymaking, especially federal regulation of private businesses and state and local programs. With some pride, the Reagan bureaucrats canceled regulations in force and reduced the size of the *Federal Register*.

Judicial Interpretation   Interpretation of the Constitution seems today to be the special province of the courts, but this was not always the case. Early in our nation's history, all three branches of the government fully expected to share this burden. In fact, 50 years after the Supreme Court assumed the power of judicial review, both the Congress and the president believed themselves equal with the courts in judging the constitutionality of official acts of government. Judicial review is the power of the courts to declare acts of the legislative and executive branches unconstitutional, and it was first claimed by the courts in *Marbury v. Madison* (1803). Although judicial review is discussed in great detail in chapter 14, we'll examine here two decisions of the Supreme Court handed down in this century that illustrate the influence of the courts on the interpreted Constitution.

At the deepest point of the Great Depression of the 1930s, the gold clause cases reached the Supreme Court. Before the Depression, nations of the Western world had used gold as the basis for international monetary exchange. As the Depression deepened, all nations, including the United States, abandoned the gold standard. However, as a standard procedure, private contracts included a requirement that loans (both principal and interest) be repaid in gold, using the standard of weight and quality in use at the time the money was borrowed. Though by an act of Congress the dollar was no longer redeemable in gold, thousands of private contracts demanded payment in that metal.

The gold reserves of the country were seriously reduced by this demand—in 37 days in 1933, about one-eighth of the nation's gold was drawn from the Federal Reserve Banks or the Treasury for export or for hoarding. In June of that same year, Congress passed a joint resolution declaring all gold-payment contracts contrary to public policy and void. Private parties then went to court to obtain orders that these contracts be honored. One petitioner asked that his railroad bonds be redeemed, not at the $22.50 face value, but at $38.10 each under the gold contract. One particular government bond would be worth not the face value of $10,000 but, under the gold contract, $16,931.25.

The cases were argued before the Supreme Court from January 8 to 10, 1935. The Court repeatedly delayed its decision, finally dividing five to four but upholding the congressional resolution as it applied to private contracts and gold certificates. In a twisted piece of logic, the Court first said that it was beyond the power of Congress to change the value of United States bonds, but then it invoked technical rules of damage (compensation), saying federal bondholders had not demonstrated actual damage and therefore could only collect the face value of bonds. Conservative Justice James C. McReynolds was so angered by the decision that, in reading his own dissenting opinion, he exploded, ''This is Nero at his worst. The Constitution is gone!'' The Court thus upheld the powers of Congress to set monetary policy, even when the policy destroyed contracts made in good faith by business-persons around the country. It is also very likely, of course, that the Court thereby

The Burger Court's *Roe* v. *Wade* (1973) decision is regarded as one of the most significant and far reaching examples of Constitutional interpretation. In this case, seven of the nine justices created a national abortion policy based on their interpretation of the Fourteenth Amendment to the Constitution.

saved the nation and its business community from complete financial ruin.[17]

Constitutional lawyers, both conservative and liberal, are agreed that the most significant and far-reaching decision to come from the Supreme Court in recent years is *Roe* v. *Wade* (1973). This decision is also the Burger Court's most controversial. (The Burger Court is the name given to the Supreme Court headed by Chief Justice Warren Burger.) Pro-choice and anti-abortion groups have been fighting over the abortion decision since it was handed down. In *Roe* v. *Wade,* seven of the nine justices created a national abortion policy through their interpretation of the Fourteenth Amendment. According to them abortion is a private matter and under this amendment an individual's right to privacy cannot be eliminated by state action. (Most laws outlawing abortion were made at the state, not at the national, level.) However, the Court did qualify this decision.

Justice Harry A. Blackmun, speaking for the majority, found that the right to an abortion was not absolute and that the state had an increasing, legitimate interest in elective abortions the longer the pregnancy continued. The Court declared that control over abortions depended on the particular trimester (three-month period) of the pregnancy: 1) during the first trimester, the decision rested entirely with the mother and her physician, without state interference; 2) because of the increased risk to the health of the mother posed by abortion after the first trimester, the state could regulate the abortion procedure; and 3) in the last stage, the state was acknowledged to have an important and legitimate interest when a viable fetus, with potential for life outside of the womb, existed within the mother. In the last stage, the state could even outlaw abortions, except as required to ensure the life and health of the mother. Interestingly, the Supreme Court in *Roe* v. *Wade* was returning the United States to policy in use when the Constitution was adopted. In English common law, abortions performed in the early stages of pregnancy were certainly not a criminal offense.[18]

Interpreting the Constitution Through Custom and Usage

By custom and usage we mean those settled practices and interpretations that go beyond changes in the Constitution made by the executive, legislative, and judicial branches.

Political parties and organized political interest groups are not mentioned in the Constitution. However, the existence of political parties has entirely changed the operation of the electoral college in selecting presidents. Also, the two-party competition that has existed since about 1795 has become so much a part of the American government that many voters believe that a two-party system is required by the Constitution. The Constitution provides only for geographical represen-

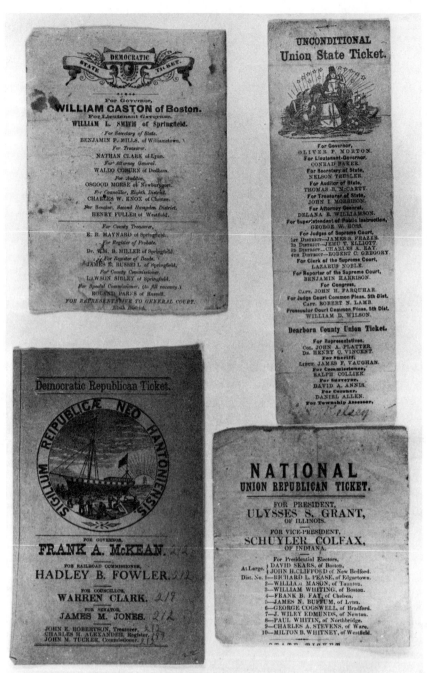

Our two-party system has existed at both the national and state levels since about 1795. Political parties have become so much a part of American government that many voters believe they are actually required by the Constitution; they are not. Parties are an example of how custom informally changes the implementation of the Constitution.

tation, but organized groups supplement *geographical* representation with *functional* representation—that is, organized groups establish lines of communication between government and such interests as agriculture, labor, and business. The Constitution provides for *republican* government, but parties and organized groups have virtually transformed the United States into a *democracy*.

The acceptance of the Constitution by the American people is perhaps one of the best illustrations of custom and usage. Certainly it was controversial in 1788 and 1789, but affection for the document grew in the nineteenth and twentieth centuries, and those who question it in our time are thought strange indeed. Political candidates may attack a particular administration, the president, or the president's programs, but an attack on the Constitution would be an act of political suicide.

The presidential system of government differs notably from the parliamentary system in the executive's term of office—our president has a fixed term, but when a prime minister loses a vote of confidence in Parliament, the government is forced to call an election. However, custom and usage may be developing an American version of a "no-confidence" vote. Since World War II, four presidents have suffered a severe loss of power and influence as the result of public criticism and poor evaluation in public-opinion polls. The media translate the public view into a concrete assessment of the administration.

In 1952 Harry Truman and in 1968 Lyndon Johnson withdrew from races the media proclaimed they could not win. Richard Nixon resigned his presidency one step ahead of an impeachment trial. The adversities of Jimmy Carter in 1979 and 1980 were reminiscent of the crisis of confidence that befell Truman, Johnson, and—to a lesser extent—Nixon. Carter's standing in the polls fell lower than Nixon's at its lowest; when Carter made cabinet changes that, ironically, had been demanded by the media only a short time before, the result was compared to Nixon's "Saturday night massacre" (the night Nixon fired three levels of leadership in the Justice Department before he got to an officer who would fire Watergate Special Prosecutor Archibald Cox); and an opposition senator suggested that Carter was showing signs of mental strain and that he should take a rest before he collapsed. In each of these four cases, the president's authority and leadership were seriously impaired long before he left office.

Changing the Constitution by Amendment

The framers designed the amending process (Article V) to make the Constitution difficult but not impossible to change. In achieving this goal, they were extremely successful. Of the thousands of amendments introduced in either the House or the Senate, only 34 have been proposed to the states by Congress and only 26 have been ratified. The pace of changing the Constitution by amendment has been uneven—61 years lapsed between the ratification of the Twelfth and Thirteenth Amendments and 43 years between the Fifteenth

and Sixteenth Amendments. However, when the demand for change is great, a cluster of amendments may emerge within a short time period; for example, the four amendments inspired by the Progressive Movement were ratified between 1913 and 1920. Amendments have been a response to one of two needs: 1) the need to correct an error in the Constitution, either in policy or governmental organization, and 2) the need to respond to demands for a new policy which requires constitutional revision. The commentary provided with the following list of amendments is far too brief, but it suggests the trends in motives for constitutional revision by amendment.

Amendment(s)	Occasion and Content (and Dates)
1–10	Pledge required to secure ratification of the Constitution; Bill of Rights (1791).
11	Constitutional error discovered in *Chisholm* v. *Georgia* (1793); forbids suits against a state by a citizen of another state or another country (1793).
12	Constitutional error discovered in election of 1800; provides for separate ballots for president and vice-president in the electoral college (1804).
13–15	Civil War amendments; abolished slavery and ensured civil and voting rights for ex-slaves (1865–1870).
16–19	Progressive Movement amendments; income tax, direct election of senators, prohibition, and women's right to vote (1913–1920).
20	Corrects error in Constitution on nonmatching terms for president and Congress; abolishes lame-duck sessions of Congress (1933).
21	Admission that neither the Constitution nor act of Congress can change a nation's drinking habits; repeal of the Eighteenth Amendment, prohibition (1933).
22	Resentment over Franklin D. Roosevelt's breaking of the George Washington tradition of no more

Women were granted the right to vote by the Nineteenth Amendment to the Constitution, ratified on August 18, 1920. Advocates of women's suffrage successfully argued that the exclusion of women from the electoral process was a fundamental error in the original Constitution.

Two of the most controversial constitutional amendments were the 18th (instituting prohibition) and the 21st (abolishing prohibition). These amendments were examples of constitutional changes made in response to public demands for new policies more consistent with the moral "tastes" of Americans.

than two terms for a president; constitutionalizes the two-term tradition (1951).

23   Corrects error in conception of the District of Columbia; provides electoral vote in presidential elections for residents of the District of Columbia (1961).

24   Civil-rights revolution; outlaws the poll tax as a requirement in national elections (1964).

25   Corrects error in presidential succession rule; provides for filling a vice-presidential vacancy and furnishes guidelines for presidential disability (1967).

26   Movement to remove voting requirements; lowers the voting age in national and state elections to 18 (1971).

The Twenty-third, Twenty-fourth, and Twenty-sixth Amendments were the products of the ferment of the 1960s which produced the civil-rights revolution and a demand for the removal of most barriers to voting. The ferment of the 1960s also resulted in two other proposed amendments: 1) the Equal Rights Amendment, which forbade discrimination based on sex; and 2) a second District of Columbia Amendment, which, for representation purposes only, would treat the District of Columbia like a state—that is, assign the District seats in the Senate and House of Representatives.

Amendments to the Constitution, though few in number, have made substantial changes in the document. Through the amending process, far-reaching guarantees of civil rights and civil liberties were included in the Constitution. Standing alone, the Sixteenth Amendment, providing Congress with the power to tax incomes, had an impact on political and economic affairs bordering on revolutionary. The income tax permits Congress to tax, approximately, on the ability to pay. Of course, today's tax structure is not totally based on an individual's, but the income tax remains central to an equitable taxing policy. One of the leading authorities on public policy, Robert L. Lineberry, described its importance:

> There is, in the mighty arsenal of government policy in America, only one policy that explicitly incorporates a thoroughgoing redistributive assumption. That is the federal (only the federal) income tax. . . . The federal income tax lives up to its name as a progressive tax, taking proportionately more from the rich than from the poor. Despite all the well-founded hoopla about tax loopholes for the rich, the progressivity of the federal tax structure is undeniable. Because leveling is a matter of degree, the American tax structure could be much more redistributive, of course, than it actually is. [19]

Redistributive policies are those government actions which distribute again the benefits allocated by the economic system. Imagine the sort of government and society we would have if the United States had moved from a simple, agrarian economy to modern corporate capitalism without the income tax as a redistributive mechanism. The degree of income inequality among Americans would be staggering. The substantial accumulations of personal wealth produced by the industrial expansion of the nineteenth century were moderated, and the emergence of high levels of income inequality was limited by progressive taxation. Imagine the popular response to the government during the Depression of the 1930s if the taxing of incomes had not been on a progressive (redistributive) basis.

The Amendment Process Amendments may be *proposed* in two ways: 1) by a two-thirds vote in both houses of Congress, or 2) by a constitutional convention called by Congress at the request of the legislatures of two-thirds of the states.

Amendments may also be *ratified* (adopted) in two ways: 1) by a majority vote in both houses of the legislatures in three-fourths of the states, or 2) by a majority vote in conventions held in three-fourths of the states. The courts have determined that ratification is a political question, and it is the right of Congress to determine further details in the process. Congress may stipulate a time limit for ratification, which it has increasingly chosen to do, typically using seven years as the limit. The president may not veto an amendment, and the governor of a state has no role in the amending process. Ratification may be done only by the legislature or by a convention; a state may not use a referendum to make the decision. After a legislature has declined to ratify, it may change its mind and ratify. However, once having ratified an amendment, a state may not withdraw its ratification.

Every amendment adopted thus far has been proposed by Congress and ratified by state legislatures, except the Twenty-first, which repealed prohibition. Because of the extraordinary political pressures exerted on state legislators by the "dry" forces, state legislatures were spared the risk of handling this ratification assignment. Popularly elected conventions were used in this one instance.

The amending process is usually a pretty dull matter, hardly exciting to the average student of American government. However, the politics of the amending process has recently turned up at least two interesting controversies: 1) the legality of the action of Congress in extending the time deadline for ratifying the Equal Rights Amendment, and 2) a national effort to call a constitutional convention to propose an amendment calling for a balanced federal budget. The call for a constitutional convention has frightened a good many constitutional authorities because there are so many unanswered questions about its authority.

The Equal Rights Amendment (ERA) was first introduced in Congress in 1923 as a follow-up to the successful women's suffrage movement. Although the ERA was introduced in most sessions of Congress and even received a positive vote occasionally in one of the two houses, it had no serious chance of adoption through the 1960s. In the

The Constitution and Second-Class Citizenship for Women

Even with the ratification period extended by Congress, the Equal Rights Amendment died on June 30, 1982, three states short of becoming a part of the Constitution. Phyllis Schlafley and the Stop-ERA supporters held an elegant celebration to proclaim the amendment "not only dead now but forever in this century." The Pro-ERA organizations had been especially outspoken during the last months of the ratification struggle, and on July 14, 1982, their supporters in Congress reintroduced the Equal Rights Amendment.

The *Time* magazine piece on the failure of ratification for ERA was entitled "How Long till Equality?" In part it read:

> Neither . . . increasing numbers of women politicians, nor their male colleagues could manage to get women something that once looked elementary, something that should have been so simple: a constitutional guarantee of equal rights under the law.
>
> There are also the numbers, statistics like measured mile markers, flashing along a dawn drive toward a still distant reckoning. There were 301 women state legislators in 1969, 908 in 1981; 5,765 female elected officials in 1975, 14,225 just four years later. And yet, those 908 legislators are only 12% of the members of state legislative bodies. Only 19 of the 435 members of the U.S. House of Representatives are women, and two of the 100 Senators.
>
> The numbers mark distance traveled and distance yet to go. Eighty percent of all women who work hold down "pink-collar jobs" and get paid about 66¢ of a man's dollar. Seventy percent of all classroom teachers are women, yet for the same job, they make an average of $3,000 a year less than their male colleagues. More than a third of all candidates for M. B. A. degrees are women: the numbers encourage. Only

5% of the executives in the top 50 American companies are women: the numbers numb.[1]

Cartoon caricatures on the plight of women abound. One favorite shows boy and girl infants peeking down into their diapers and saying "So that explains the difference in our salaries." Or consider the Bennett editorial cartoon for the St. Petersburg *Times* in which the doctor greets the father in the waiting room with "Congratulations, Mr. Smithers . . . you're now the proud father of a six-pound, four-ounce, second-class citizen."

Opponents of the ERA argued that the Constitution's equal protection and due process clauses were all the insurance of fair treatment required for anyone. If the Supreme Court were suddenly to embrace the notion that sex is a constitutionally suspect classification, then the ERA would not be needed. Race, ethnic background, and perhaps religion are classifications that are clearly suspect. That is, if the government classifies citizens on the basis of race, ethnic background, or religion, it will have the burden of demonstrating the appropriateness of the classification. The states are mostly barred from classifying persons as either citizens or aliens. However, the United States Supreme Court has waffled on what they call gender-based classifications. Not until 1971 did the United States Supreme Court declare a law unconstitutional because of a classification based on sex, and the Court has since tiptoed carefully through the legal thicket of gender-based discrimination.[2] Through the Supreme Court's power to interpret the Constitution (that is, judicial review), it could give women their long-sought victory almost overnight.

[1]"How Long till Equality," *Time*, 120 (July 12, 1982), p. 20.
[2]Jack W. Peltason, *Corwin & Peltason's Understanding the Constitution*, 9th ed. (New York: Holt, Rinehart and Winston, 1982), pp. 189–206.

1970s it seemed that ERA's time had come—it passed in the House in 1971 by a vote of 354 to 24 and in the Senate in 1972 by a vote of 84 to 8. Only two hours after it was proposed by Congress, Hawaii ratified the amendment, and by the end of 1972, 22 states had ratified. Then the process slowed down: 8 states ratified in 1973, 3 in 1974, and only 1 in 1975, for a total of 34.

The movement was stopped in its tracks, not by men, but by women. The early success, directed by the League of Women Voters and the National

Organization of Women, was countered by the Stop-ERA movement directed by Phyllis Schlafly; and women with more traditional values turned up in state capitols to oppose ratification of the ERA. By the end of 1977, 35 states had ratified, but 3 states had passed resolutions rescinding their ratification, and the seven-year deadline for ratification was becoming an insurmountable hurdle. Pro-ERA forces mounted an effort to extend the ratification deadline—a tactic never used before. The extension of the ERA ratification deadline passed both houses of Congress by margins much reduced from the required two-thirds, but supporters of the extension argued successfully that the deadline was in the enabling legislation, not in the amendment itself. The distinction was not clear to many opponents of ERA, but the wording of the amendment clearly does not mention the deadline.

Section 1—Equality of rights under the law shall not be denied or abridged by the United States or by any state on account of sex.

Section 2—The Congress shall have power to enforce, by appropriate legislation, the provisions of this article.

Section 3—This amendment shall take effect two years after the date of ratification.

Since the deadline was not in the language of the amendment, a simple majority vote in Congress was sufficient. The extension adopted was for three years (to June 30, 1982), and though opponents of the ERA pleaded for the right of states to rescind during the extension, the practice was not authorized.

In December, 1981, the anti-ERA forces won a brief victory when a district court judge ruled the deadline extension unconstitutional and backed the right of states that had previously ratified to rescind their decision. A month later, the Supreme Court stayed the district court's ruling and agreed to hear the case, but the high court's 1981–1982 calendar was so crowded that review was postponed until the fall of 1982, well after ERA had failed to secure the required three-fourths of the states approval.

Although the nation has not had a constitutional convention since 1787, in 1979 the National Taxpayers Union claimed that 27 of the required 34 states had formally requested that Congress call one to consider an amendment calling for a mandatory balanced federal budget. Thus far, the necessary 34 states have not made this request, but it remains a popular proposal, particularly as the size of the federal budget deficit grows. But what worries a lot of constitutional scholars is what will happen if a convention is called since we have not had one since 1787.

The mere suggestion of a constitutional convention brings up the spectre of a repeat of the Philadelphia Convention of 1787, which ignored its congressional mandate, threw out the Articles of Confederation, and wrote a brand new Constitution. Beyond this central fear, there are many unanswered legal questions concerning this option in the amending process.

1. What constitutes a valid call for a convention? Must state petitions be transmitted to Congress? Must all state petitions be identical in wording? Who makes the decision on the validity of each state's petition?

2. Within what time period must the requisite number of state petitions be received to constitute a valid call?

3. Must Congress respond to a valid call with a convention? Can Congress ignore the call? Can Congress propose an amendment rather than calling a convention?

4. Would the courts enforce a valid call?

5. How would delegates to a convention be apportioned? What would be the size of the convention? Would votes be cast by individual delegates or by state delegations? How would delegates be selected? May members of Congress serve as delegates?

6. Could Congress limit the scope and authority of the convention? If a convention did exceed its authority, could Congress block proposed amendments from state action? Worded differently, must a convention submit proposed revisions through the Congress to the states, or can a convention send its recommendations directly to the states?

We have no precedent other than the Philadelphia Convention to follow, and Congress has never provided a set of rules to guide a constitutional convention. Former Senator Sam J. Ervin authored a Federal Constitutional Convention Procedures Bill in 1967 to provide answers to all the above questions. The bill was considered without success in 1967 and 1969; it passed the Senate unanimously in 1971 and 1973, but the House took no action. Distinguished constitutional lawyers disagree over almost every aspect of the convention question. Yale scholar Charles L. Black, Jr. has said that consideration of a constitutional convention procedures bill is unwise—that on such matters one Congress cannot bind a future Congress.[20]

SUMMARY

In this chapter we have seen that the Constitution was one of the first major policy decisions of the United States. The Constitution is a policy about *how* policy will be made and *who* will make policy. Therefore, the provisions spelled out in the Constitution have had enormous and continuing policy consequences. The Constitution makers influenced future conflict and political evolution through the structure of the government that they provided. They gave the new national government the authority necessary to deal with the issues that the 13 member states confronted collectively. They removed from state action the policy areas that had produced the greatest intergovernmental conflicts under the Articles of Confederation, and they removed selected policy areas from the jurisdiction of any government, national or state.

The Constitution has a rich ancestry in England and Europe, in Colonial America, and in the first state and national governments of the United States. We were Englishmen before we were Americans. Both the movement for independence and the movement for the Constitution of 1787 rested substantially on interpretations of the English Constitution, the writings of English theorists, and English institutions that had been transplanted to the colonies. When the Constitution makers began their labors in Philadelphia, they relied not only on their English heritage but also on a long list of their own experiences, including Colonial self-government, the Committees of Correspondence, the two Continental Congresses, the early state constitutions, and the Articles of Confederation.

The United States was governed under the Articles of Confederation from 1781 until 1789. The national government provided by the Articles was weak—it had no executive, no judiciary, a Congress whose members were paid by the states and voted as members of state delegations, and extremely limited authority to raise taxes. All efforts to enlarge the powers of the Congress failed, mainly because of the requirement that amendments be ratified by a unanimous vote of the states. Post-Revolutionary War economic cycles created a political climate which permitted the Nationalists to launch a concerted movement for a new constitution, although the record of the Articles government was pretty good.

Many analysts have been quite critical of the government of the United States under the Articles of Confederation, but federation under the Constitution of 1787 would probably not have been possible without trying confederation first. It is very likely that the United States adopted as much national government as the people would tolerate in 1781 and 1787.

The story of the Constitutional Convention which met in Philadelphia in 1787 is one of conflict, hard bargaining, and compromise. The delegates were reputable men of great experience. Of the many compromises they reached, the most important was the Connecticut Compromise, which settled differences between the large and small states over representation in Congress. Not one of the delegates to the Convention was totally pleased with the Constitution; nevertheless, they agreed to campaign for it and designed a strategy that included a mixture of manipulation and propaganda. The propaganda campaign centered on publicizing a series of articles explaining the document known as the *Federalist* papers. Another element of the winning strategy was to agree to the amendments to the Constitution that we call the Bill of Rights.

Though analysts tend to concentrate on the change in government between the Articles of Confederation and the Constitution of 1789, there was also continuity. The constitutionally mandated relationships between the states were almost identical to those listed in the Articles. The Constitution maintains a republican form of government—that is, one in which the people do not make policy directly but instead influence policy through their elected representatives. In assigning power and providing an organization to manage conflict, the Constitution makers relied heavily on separation of powers and federalism (the "3 × 3 matrix" of government). That was an important change. Another important change can be found in the "locus of sovereignty"—the states were no longer sovereign members of a confederation; the new Constitution was based on popular sovereignty, with final authority resting in the people themselves.

There is an interpreted, or unwritten, Constitution in addition to the literal text. The Constitution has gathered meaning over almost 200 years

by 1) executive, legislative and judicial elaboration, 2) custom and usage by the American people, and 3) amendment, as provided in Article V.
A viable constitution is never static; viewed properly, the written document is only the first stage of
a process of constitution building that never really
ends.

KEY TERMS

Annapolis Convention
Anti-Federalists
bicameralism
Bill of Rights
checks and balances
Committees of Correspondence
Constitution
Continental Congresses
Declaration of Independence
federalism
The Federalist *Papers*
Federalists
Great Compromise or Connecticut Compromise
implied powers
interpreted Constitution or unwritten Constitution
Mount Vernon Conference
Nationalists
New Jersey Plan
*Philadelphia Convention or Constitutional
   Convention of 1787*
popular sovereignty
senatorial courtesy
separation of powers
Shays's Rebellion
social contract
social service state or welfare state

sovereignty
strict constructionist
three-fifths compromise
Virginia Plan

SUGGESTED READINGS

Beard, Charles A. *An Economic Interpretation of the Constitution of the United States.* New York: The Macmillan
Company, 1919.

Becker, Carl. *The Declaration of Independence: A Study in
the History of Political Ideas.* New York: Alfred A.
Knopf, 1942.

Cortner, Richard C. *The Supreme Court and Civil Liberties
Policy.* Palo Alto, Calif.: Mayfield Publishing Company, 1975.

Hofstadter, Richard. *The American Political Tradition.*
New York: Alfred A. Knopf, 1948.

Jensen, Merrill. *The Articles of Confederation: An Interpretation of the Social-Constitutional History of the American
Revolution, 1774–1781.* Madison, Wis.: The University of Wisconsin Press, 1940.

McDonald, Forrest. *We the People: The Economic Origins
of the Constitution.* Chicago: University of Chicago
Press, 1958.

Peltason, Jack W. *Corwin & Peltason's Understanding the
Constitution,* 9th ed. New York: Holt, Rinehart and
Winston, 1982.

Rossiter, Clinton. *1787: The Grand Convention.* New
York: The Macmillan Company, 1966.

Smith, David G. *The Convention and the Constitution.*
New York: St. Martin's Press, 1965.

Wills, Garry. *Inventing America: Jefferson's Declaration of
Independence.* Garden City, N.Y.: Doubleday, 1978.

CHAPTER 4

FEDERALISM

The Constitutional Design of the Federal System ■ A Changing Federal System ■ How Grants Aided the Rebalancing of the Federal System ■ The Reagan Proposals: A Return to an Equal Partnership?

L*eave to private initiative all the functions that citizens can perform privately; use the level of government closest to the community for all the public functions it can handle; reserve national action for [areas] where state and local governments are not fully adequate.*[1]

Such were the instructions, not from President Ronald Reagan to Congress in 1980 as one might have guessed, but from the Kestnbaum Commission on Intergovernmental Relations to President Dwight Eisenhower and Congress in 1955. Similar words might also have been uttered by two of America's founders, Thomas Jefferson and John Calhoun.

While these instructions appear simple and straightforward, they are difficult to achieve. Decision makers at each level of government often have quite different ideas about which of them should do what. Throughout American history, they have disputed which has the power to make certain policy decisions. The dispute arises because of the ***federal system of government***, *in which*

power is divided between a central government and regional governments.

Officials from each level of government frequently interact with each other on various policy issues. During President Carter's administration, he (left) met with Hugh Carey (center), New York's Governor, and Ed Koch (right), Mayor of New York City, to determine how state and local officials would react to his positions on key issues.

America's founders disagreed about whether the national government or the states should be more powerful in making public policy. In the spirit of compromise, they created a system of shared and separate powers. The system established national and state levels of authority but did not totally separate the functions of the two. Over the years, the distinctions between the responsibilities of the two levels have become less clear. Today, the federal system is described as a "mishmash of governmental responsibilities and regulations" and "a bewildered and bewildering maze of complex, overlapping, and, often, conflicting relationships among the [different] levels of government."[2]

In spite of the blurred responsibilities, citizens and elected officials in 1980 shared a widespread concern that the national government had become too dominant and too powerful. The Advisory Commission on Intergovernmental Relations, which is composed of representatives from all levels of government, concluded that the national government's influence had become too intrusive, too unmanageable, too ineffective, too costly, and above all, too unaccountable.[3] Governors and state legislators alike began calling for the courts to bolster their interpretations of the Tenth Amendment to the U.S. Constitution, which reserves all powers not granted to the national government to the states. President Reagan, himself a former governor, entered the White House in 1981 with a promise to restore balance to what was perceived as a top-heavy federal system.

In the 1980s, we can expect debates in Congress, state capitals, city halls, county courthouses, and school board headquarters across the country on which level of government has the power to make certain policy decisions. These decisions will fall in three major policy areas: the economy, energy and the environment, and lifestyle.

Determining which level of government should hold the primary monetary and programmatic responsibility for various functions is often very difficult. This difficulty stems from the way our nation's founders wrote the Constitution. This chapter will examine 1) how the Constitution has divided power between national and state governments, and 2) how these constitutionally established powers have responded to changing conditions in America—what some refer to as "pragmatic federalism."

THE CONSTITUTIONAL DESIGN OF THE FEDERAL SYSTEM

At the Constitutional Convention, the delegates voted to adopt a federal system of government. The federal system constitutionally distributes power between a national government and the various state governments "in a way that protects the existence and authority of each."[4] America's founders chose this system instead of a *unitary system, in which all policymaking powers are assigned to the central (or national) government* (as in Great Britain and Sweden), or a *confederation, in which the constituent governments (the states) create and assign policymaking powers to a national government* (as in the United States under the Articles of Confederation).

Once the federal system was in place, however, each state government adopted a unitary system for giving policymaking powers to governments within its own boundaries. Even today, cities, counties, towns, school districts, and other local governments derive their authority from their respective state governments. In fact, the federal Constitution contains no mention of local governments.

The Distribution of Power

National Government Powers The national government has both delegated and implied powers. The *delegated powers are those specifically granted to the national government in the Constitution.* In Article I, Section 8, Congress is given the power to:

1. uniformly tax persons, goods, and imports.
2. spend.
3. borrow.
4. regulate interstate and foreign commerce and trade with the Indian tribes.
5. enact uniform naturalization and bankruptcy legislation.
6. establish a national currency and regulate the value of foreign and domestic currencies.
7. fix standards of weights and measures.
8. enact laws for the punishment of counterfeiters of currency and securities.
9. establish post offices and post roads.
10. enact patent and copyright laws.

Robert White, former U.S. ambassador to El Salvador, urges a Senate Committee to approve economic, instead of military, aid to that nation. Opponents of military aid have warned Congress that this exercise of its delegated power to appropriate (spend) money may ultimately lead to U.S. troop involvement similar to that in Vietnam in the 1960s and early 1970s.

1. establish a federal court system below the Supreme Court.

2. enact laws covering maritime cases and violations of international law.

3. declare war, grant letters of marque and reprisal (government permission to private parties to attack enemy ships; not used since the eighteenth century), and provide rules governing capture on land and water.

4. raise, fund, and establish rules for the army and navy.

5. provide rules for calling up and using states' militia to enforce the law, suppress insurrections and repel invasions.

6. govern the District of Columbia and all other property purchased for use by the national government.

Had Article I, Section 8 included only such ex-

plicit powers, the courts and legislative bodies would probably never have had many battles about whether the national government had exceeded its authority. But the Constitution's writers ended the section with the "necessary and proper" clause, which gave the national government the power "to make all Laws which shall be necessary and proper for carrying into Execution the foregoing Powers, and all other Powers vested by this Constitution in the Government of the United States, or in any Department or Officer thereof." This clause states an implied power—that the national government can do whatever is necessary to carry out its delegated powers. *Implied powers are national government powers that are not specifically spelled out in the Constitution but are inferred from powers that are spelled out.* This clause is sometimes referred to as the "elastic clause" because it allows the national government to expand its authority to meet the changing needs of the nation. Because it was intentionally written in general and vague terms (in contrast with the preceding parts of Article I, Section 8), application of this power has always been open to interpretation—and controversy.

The first important constitutional test of the clause came before the U.S. Supreme Court in 1819 in *McCulloch v. Maryland*. The case involved the constitutionality of the Second Bank of the United States and the power of the state of Maryland to tax the Bank. The First Bank had been incorporated by an Act of Congress as one portion of Treasury Secretary Alexander Hamilton's plans to stabilize the country's fiscal affairs. When the Bank was incorporated, Congress had a prolonged and bitter debate over its constitutionality. The Second Bank, chartered in 1816, had adopted policies that resulted first in a period of speculation and inflation and then a period of deflation, retrenchment, and tight control. Many charges were leveled at the Bank, and the states decided to enact policies restricting its activities. Maryland passed legislation requiring the Bank to either print its notes on stamped paper, which was heavily taxed, or pay an annual lump sum tax of $15,000; each violation of the law drew a penalty of $500. McCulloch, the cashier in the Bank's Baltimore branch, issued notes without paying the tax. Maryland sued, and the suit was appealed to the Supreme Court.

The debate before the Court pitted Federalists against strict constructionists. The former argued

The Supreme Court, under the leadership of Chief Justice John Marshall (above), was responsible for broadening the scope of power of the national government through its liberal interpretation of the "necessary and proper" clause of Article I, section 8 of the Constitution. In the famous *McCulloch* v. *Maryland* (1819) case, the Court ruled that Congress' power to charter a national bank could be "implied" from the "necessary and proper" clause.

for a broad interpretation of congressional (national government) powers and the latter insisted upon a literal interpretation of powers listed in Article I, Section 8 (a position favoring the states). Chief Justice John Marshall wrote the Court's opinion upholding congressional power to charter the Bank, stating that 1) he found no mention of a bank in the list of delegated powers, but 2) a bank could be created to implement some of the delegated powers, and 3) the power to create the Bank could be implied from the ''necessary and proper'' clause. He noted that the clause was placed among the powers of Congress and that its language appeared to enlarge, not diminish, those powers. In this one decision, Chief Justice Marshall firmly established both the doctrine of implied powers and the doctrine of national supremacy. Under the doctrine of national supremacy,

states were prevented from interfering with national programs and policies.

Powers Denied the National Government   In Article I, Section 9, after the section delegating powers to Congress, the Constitution lists powers denied Congress. These denied powers protect the rights of both individuals and states. The national government is forbidden to:

1. suspend the writ of *habeas corpus* during times of peace. (The writ of *habeas corpus* ensures that any person taken into custody must be brought to court and formally charged with an offense, thereby prohibiting arbitrary arrest and imprisonment.)

2. enact bills of attainder. (A bill of attainder is a legislative act that defines the actions of a specific individual as criminal, effectively preventing him or her from having a judicial trial.)

3. pass *ex post facto* laws. (An *ex post facto* law retroactively makes something a crime that was not a crime at the time it was committed, increases the punishment for a crime, or changes the rules of evidence to the detriment of the individual accused of the crime.)

4. apportion poll taxes, property taxes, or other taxes on persons except in proportion to the census mandated every ten years.

5. tax exports.

6. give any advantage at all to one port over another.

7. spend public funds without congressional authorization and proper accounting procedures.

8. grant titles of nobility.

The Constitution also forbids any public official to accept a title, office, or payment of any kind from a foreign government without the consent of Congress. As originally written, the section espoused a national pro-slavery policy. Among the denied powers was one prohibiting the national government from ending the slave trade before 1808. In tying taxes to the census, the framers added one more dimension to a pro-slavery policy; this limitation barred Congress from taxing slavery out of existence. (The eradication of slavery required a constitutional amendment.)

State Government Powers The founders did not draw up a list of government powers for states as they did for the national government. Because the founders represented states, which were still the most powerful units of government under the Confederation, they were more concerned about spelling out exactly what the national government could and could not do.

They already had a fairly clear picture of the policymaking role of the states. At that time, states typically had the responsibility for caring for the health, safety, and welfare of their citizens; providing for public education; establishing and maintaining roads; and establishing rules of eligibility for voting and for the conduct of elections. They also legislated on charters of incorporation for banks, businesses, and cities; provided for all local governments; and made policy on all public matters inside state boundaries.

Historical accounts of discussions by Constitution framers in 1787 reveal that they assumed any powers not specifically assigned to the national government were reserved to the states or to the people (except for powers expressly denied to the states in Article I, Section 10, of the U.S. Constitution). Not until the Bill of Rights was drawn up in 1791 was this inferred jurisdiction actually written into the Constitution. The Tenth Amendment states that ''the powers not delegated to the United States by the Constitution, nor prohibited by it to the States, are reserved to the States respectively, or to the people.'' As we have already seen, among those powers delegated to the United States (the national government) by the Constitution are those which are ''necessary and proper'' to carry out its functions. Over the years, as the powers of the national government have been expanded and justified as ''necessary and proper,'' the powers reserved to the states have shrunk. The result has been a push among state and local officials to restore some of these lost powers.

National Protections and Assistance to the States The agreement of the founders to establish a federal system meant the states had to give up some policymaking power they had previously exercised under the Confederation. But they did guarantee states a place in the national government. One guarantee the Constitution provides the states is *territorial integrity*. New states can be admitted by Congress but they cannot be created out of territory under the jurisdiction of an exist-

Officials from different states meet regularly to address important issues of mutual concern. At the 1981 meeting of the National Governors' Conference, Governors George Busbee of Georgia (left) and John Dalton of Virginia (right) confer on an issue of vital importance to both states.

ing state without its consent. For example, two states could not be created out of the State of Texas without its approval.

A *republican form of government* is also guaranteed. Although the Constitution does not define ''republican'' government, the concept almost certainly means a government operated through elected representatives—a representative democracy. Thus, when Congress seats the elected representatives of a state, it thereby certifies that a republican form of government exists.

States are *protected against foreign invasion and domestic violence* by the national government. Protection against foreign invasion is clear enough, but protection against domestic violence may not be. The Constitution requires the state legislature or governor to call on the national government to intervene in situations of domestic violence such as riots or looting. In several situations, however, the president has sent in troops to maintain order without a request from the state involved—for example, in the 1957 school integration controversy in Little Rock. A president can justify such intervention on the basis that it upholds a national law or protects national property.

Finally, each state is guaranteed *equal representa-*

tion in the U.S. Senate. A state's equality in the Senate is protected by a unique constitutional statement. Article V, which provides for amending the Constitution, limits the amending power this way: "no state, without its consent, shall be deprived of its equal suffrage in the Senate." Authorities generally doubt that this one provision is unamendable; nevertheless, the Constitution framers clearly so intended. The Senate is a constant reminder of federalism and the important place of the states in the union.

Powers Denied the States Most powers denied the states in Article I, Section 10, are those expressly delegated to the national government in Article I, Section 8. First, American states are not to behave like nation-states in diplomatic and military affairs. They are denied the power to enter into any treaty, alliance, or agreement with a foreign power; maintain an army in times of peace; engage in war unless invaded or threatened with invasion; or grant letters of marque and reprisal.

Neither are the states permitted to interfere with national commerce and finance. The states are forbidden to coin money or print paper money; authorize payment of debts in a medium other than gold and silver; pass a law impairing the obligation of contracts; levy import or export duties except with the consent of Congress, and then only to the extent necessary to maintain ports and port facilities; and tax ships and shipping without the consent of Congress.

Three constitutional limitations on the national government also apply to the states: they are barred from passing *ex post facto* laws, enacting bills of attainder, or granting titles of nobility. Finally, the Constitution limits the states by prescribing their relations with each other (Article IV, Sections 1 and 2). States must not regard each other as hostile, and one state may not treat the citizens of another state as if they were aliens. Specifically, each state must give "full faith and credit . . . to the public acts, records, and judicial proceedings of every other state." In other words, the *"full faith and credit" clause ensures that wills, property titles, marriages, divorces, court awards (such as child custody), and other authoritative records listed in one state must be honored in other states.* Some conflict over these principles has occurred over the years. Varying marriage, divorce, and child support laws in the states have been a common source of conflict. However, the principles are honored.

The Constitution also states that "the citizens of each state shall be entitled to all privileges and immunities of citizens in the several states." The *"privileges and immunities" clause establishes that citizens of all states shall be treated equally.* The conditions affected have not been listed authoritatively, but they include such things as travel into and within a state, access to the courts and to public authorities, and legal protection. A state may, however, charge nonresidents higher tuition to attend its colleges and universities and higher fees for fishing and hunting licenses. States may also insist on a minimum residency for voting in state and local elections.

*Extradition—returning fugitives from justice in one state to the state where the crime was committed—*is another type of interstate interaction which is nearly automatic. But some states have refused to cooperate when, for example, the law was questioned or the fugitive has become a model citizen.

Finally, "No state shall, without the consent of Congress . . . enter into any agreement or compact with another state. . . ." This protection of the union from alliances between the states seems to be of little concern to Congress today. Congress has approved a number of *interstate compacts, cooperative agreements between states.* One of the oldest compacts is that between the states of New York and New Jersey to run the New York Port Authority. In practice, the U.S. Supreme Court has ruled that congressional consent is required only if the compact will affect a power of the national government.

Powers Shared by the National Government and the States Nowhere in the Constitution does the term "shared powers" (or "concurrent powers") appear. However, as constitutional scholars point out, the fact that the Constitution created both national and state governments, neither of which can abolish the other but both of which must govern their constituencies, means they share the powers essential to the conduct of any government. These essential powers are taxing, spending, borrowing, and enforcement of the law. And, as we have already seen, a state may perform the same functions as the national government under certain conditions: if it does so constitutionally, if the national government has elected not to exercise its power to perform the function, if state laws do not conflict with national

Law enforcement is a power exercised, or shared, by all levels of government. Here, a representative of the FBI (left) and the chief of detectives of the New York Police Department appear at a press conference to solicit citizen assistance in the apprehension of the couple suspected of extortion in the famous Tylenol poisoning case.

1. State government domination: 1789–1862
2. Equal partnership: 1862–1913
3. National government domination: 1913–1978
4. Equal partnership: 1978–?
5. State government domination: ?

State-Dominated Federalism (1789–1862)
Before the Civil War the national government performed only the broadest of functions, all truly national in scope (e.g., the postal service, defense, foreign affairs, coining money). The states did most of the government policymaking much as they did under the old confederation.

Probably the key event that started the erosion of state domination was the 1819 *McCulloch* v. *Maryland* decision mentioned earlier, which asserted the principle of national supremacy. Decline of states' power continued through the mid-1800s (the period of the Civil War). In 1869, the

laws, if state action does not interfere with national programs or policies, or if the national government has approved the state action. However, if and when the national government decides to occupy the field delegated to it by the Constitution, the principle of national supremacy prevails.

As we have seen, the Constitution has established many specific policy domains for the national and state governments. But the "necessary and proper" clause and the Tenth Amendment have created a "gray area" that makes it unclear which government level has policymaking power. Changing interpretations of these *implied* powers have allowed the federal system to respond to changing conditions in America.

A CHANGING FEDERAL SYSTEM

The federal system was state-centered during the nation's early years, but it has evolved into a national-centered system. However, there is some evidence that the nation may be headed back toward a state-centered system. If so, the nation will have come full circle. The flexibility of the Constitution has made this cycle possible.

The Phases of Federalism
Attaching exact dates to phases of national and state government relations is difficult, but the time frame may be generalized as follows:

The Civil War ended the period of state-dominated federalism and began the equal partnership (dual federalism) period. During the equal partnership period (1862–1913), the national and state governments were viewed as separate but equal. Each was responsible for different, but equally important, policy areas.

U.S. Supreme Court ruled in *Texas* v. *White* that "the Constitution, in all of its provisions, looks to an indestructible union, composed of indestructible states."[5] A new period had begun: the national government and the state governments were partners in the federal system.

Equal Partnership (1862–1913) Around the turn of the century, policymaking areas were viewed as separate and equal. *Dual federalism rulings* (which actually began as early as 1836 but continued to the mid-1930s) *sought to create a clear line of authority between the two layers of government*. An example is the U.S. Supreme Court's *Tarbel* ruling in 1871:

> There are within the territorial limits of each state two governments [state and national], restricted in their spheres of action, but independent of each other, and supreme within their respective spheres. Each has its separate departments, each has its distinct laws, and each has its own tribunes for their enforcement. Neither government can intrude within the jurisdiction of the other or authorize any interference therein by its judicial officers with the action of the other.[6]

Some scholars have called an expansion of dual federalism, *layer-cake federalism*. *The "cake" has three layers (national, state, and local) of which each is assigned distinctive policy areas*. Enough competition exists between different levels to ensure the separation of the three layers.

National-Dominated Federalism (1913–1978)—The beginning of this period is linked with ratification of the Sixteenth Amendment, which gave Congress the power to impose an income tax (1913). As we shall see later, this financial windfall enabled the national government to begin "sharing" revenue with state and local governments. The national government greatly expanded its policymaking sphere through the strings and guidelines attached to these moneys.

As the responsibilities of the three levels of government began to overlap, relations between governments became increasingly tangled. Professor Morton Grodzins described the American system of government not as a layer cake, but as a "*marble cake, characterized by an inseparable mingling of differently colored ingredients, the colors appearing in vertical and diagonal strands and unexpected whirls.*"[7]

The federal aid trend peaked in 1978, perhaps signaling the end to national-dominated federalism. But a closer look at the growth of grants and their effect on governments offers a lesson in how the federal system adapts to changing conditions and periodically rebalances itself.

HOW GRANTS AIDED THE REBALANCING OF THE FEDERAL SYSTEM

"Q. What has 500 parts, costs $83 billion and is condemned by almost everybody?
A. The chaotic system of 500 federal grant programs."[8]

A federal *grant-in-aid* is a "*payment of funds by one level of government [national] to be expended by another level [state and local] for a specified purpose, usually on a matching basis and in accordance with prescribed standards or requirements.*"[9] For example, the national government may give a city $500,000 to restore a historic building provided the city can come up with another $500,000 of its own funds or money given by private citizens. The national government may attach strings to the grant, perhaps requiring that bids be solicited from minority construction companies or specifying certain building codes. No state or local government has to accept these funds; participation in any grant-in-aid program is voluntary.

Why Federal Grants?

George Hale and Marian Palley, in *The Politics of Federal Grants*, list the following benefits of grants:

1. They help equalize the level of public services among the states and localities. Transferring federal funds from wealthier states to poorer states helps equalize service to citizens across the United States.

2. They take pressure off state and local revenues. The federal income tax provides a great deal of revenue, and grants return some of these revenues to state and local governments. Grants allow state and local governments to provide services to their citizens that would not be possible with state or local funds alone.

3. They establish national standards or minimum levels of service in such areas as pollution control and minimum income. Thus, they help the national government meet its

charge to provide for the common welfare of all people.

4. They improve the overall level of government performance since federal administrators generally have more training, education, and skills than state and local administrators and it is these federal administrators who design grant programs.[10]

These statements explain why national government officials offer grant programs but not why state and local government officials apply for and accept federal aid. The main reasons are economic. Poorer governments with declining populations and tax bases do so out of necessity. The funds are desperately needed just to provide basic services such as police and fire protection, sanitation, and health care. Better-off states and localities seek federal funds because: 1) their taxpayers deserve back a fair share of the taxes they pay to the national government, and 2) by using federal funds, they can avoid raising state and local tax rates and continue to attract new residents and industries.

Types of Grants and Methods of Distribution

Federal grants are of three types: categorical, block, and general revenue-sharing (see Table 4.1). The oldest and still most common is the *categorical grant, which can be used only for a specific, narrowly designed program,* such as a reading program for blind preschoolers or for construction of a particular type of highway. The design of categorical aid programs is almost exclusively in the hands of federal administrators and members of Congress. They leave state and local officials little discretion

in deciding how the moneys will be spent. In 1980, nearly 80 percent of all federal aid dollars were in the form of categorical grants.

A *block grant is a payment to a state or local government for a general function such as health, education, or law enforcement.* The money must be spent on activities related to the appropriate broad function, but state and local officials determine what these activities will be. For example, the national government might give a state government $20 million for social programs. State officials could decide to spend it for child care for poor families, training for child-care workers, and family planning information for poor families.

A *general revenue-sharing grant is a lump sum of money returned to state and local governments to do with what they want.* It gives state and local officials complete discretion in spending the funds. For example, a city may decide to use the money to build a new jail, to buy park land, or to simply add it to a depleted city treasury to keep from raising property taxes. This type of grant is relatively new; it was first authorized in the State and Local Fiscal Assistance Act of 1972.

The distribution of grants may be either project-based or formula-based. When federal aid is distributed on a *project basis, state or local governments compete with all other interested state or local governments for funds.* The actual decision on who gets how much is made by administrators in the agency responsible for handling the grant, such as the Department of Housing and Urban Development, the Department of Labor, or the Department of Commerce. State and local governments applying for project-funded grants have to play the "grants game." They usually lobby federal

TABLE 4.1

Selected Characteristics of Major Types of Federal Grants

Type of Grant	Recipient Discretion	Program Scope	Funding Criteria
Categorical			
a. Project	Lowest	Narrow—program	Federal Administrative Review
b. Formula	Low	Narrow—program	Legislative formula
Block	Medium	Broad—functional area	Legislative formula
General Revenue Sharing	High	Broadest—government operations	Legislative formula

SOURCE: George E. Hale and Marian Lief Palley. *The Politics of Federal Grants.* Washington, D.C.: Congressional Quarterly Press, 1981, p. 12.

bureaucrats and hire personnel who can prepare polished, detailed grant applications. Since many small jurisdictions cannot afford to play this game, they get left out of a number of project-funded grant programs.

Formula-funded grants distribute moneys to all eligible jurisdictions on the basis of a formula set by Congress. With this method, decisions are made by members of Congress, not federal agency officials, even though these officials may make recommendations to Congress.

Formula-based grants are more popular than project-based grants with most state and local officials. As Table 4.1 (p. 93) shows, block grants and revenue-sharing grants are given exclusively on a formula basis. Categorical grants can be distributed on either a project or a formula basis. By 1980, two-thirds of the categorical grants were distributed by formulas. As we shall see later in the chapter, a great deal of competition has emerged in Congress over who will devise the formulas.

The Beginning of Cash Grants

Cash grants by Congress to state governments began around the end of the nineteenth century. Before that time, grants had been in the form of land, not money. (The Morrill Act of 1862, for example, granted portions of public lands to each state. States could sell the lands to raise money for land-grant colleges such as Michigan State University.)

In 1887 Congress passed the Hatch Act, which provided the first annual cash grants to states to build agricultural experiment stations. By 1902, however, cash grants still amounted to less than 1 percent of all federal expenditures.[11]

The Impact of the Sixteenth Amendment The real stimulus to federal grants-in-aid was the Sixteenth Amendment, which gave the national government the power to tax income. This tax put a huge amount of money into the U.S. Treasury quickly because of its elasticity—the income tax could grow at the same rate as the economy. By 1922, just nine years after its passage, the income tax accounted for 60 percent of all national government revenues.[12] With this new money, Congress created the first major grant-in-aid programs—the Federal Aid Highway Act of 1916, the Smith-Hughes Act of 1917 (vocational education), the Vocational Rehabilitation Act of 1920, and the Shephard-Towner Act of 1921 (maternal

and infant care). In general, these federal funds were merely supporting services traditionally provided by state governments; they were not creating new services or functions.

Establishing the Constitutionality of Grants-in-Aid Even though states did not have to participate in these early grant programs, some state officials openly complained that such programs were improper intrusions into areas traditionally reserved for the states. It wasn't long before states began challenging federal grants-in-aid—and the strings attached to them—in the courts. In 1923, two cases brought before the U.S. Supreme Court (*Massachusetts* v. *Mellon* and *Frothingham* v. *Mellon*) sought to keep Treasury Secretary Andrew Mellon from spending funds authorized by Congress under the Shephard-Towner Act. In these rulings, the Court upheld the constitutionality of federal grants-in-aid.

The Impact of the Great Depression (1933–1944)

Soon state and local officials' concern about the legitimacy of federal grants and intrusion into state policy arenas gave way to economic necessity. Shrinking revenue bases and the urgent need to help poverty-stricken constituents made federal aid desirable rather than despicable. State officials complained very little about the national government's entry into the welfare policy arena, which was traditionally dominated by the states. Between 1933 and 1938, Roosevelt's New Deal created a number of new programs related to public assistance, unemployment compensation, child welfare, employment, and public housing. By 1935, the national government was spending $2.2 billion to counter the effects of the Depression.[13]

A new type of federal aid emerged during this period—aid going directly from the national government to the cities, bypassing the states. Cities were often hit even harder than states by the Depression. Mayors were frustrated with state legislatures that met only every other year and were heavily dominated by rural legislators. (Not until 1964, in *Reynolds* v. *Sims*, did the U.S. Supreme Court rule that state legislatures must be apportioned on a "one person, one vote" basis.) Because of this frustration with their respective state governments, a number of mayors formed the U.S. Conference of Mayors in 1933. They believed their cries for help were more likely to be

Federal aid to state and local governments was an important component of Franklin D. Roosevelt's New Deal program, designed to aid the nation's recovery from the Great Depression. Federal funds were used to hire those out of work to build public facilities, like this new park pavilion, in communities throughout the U.S.

heard in Washington than in their own state capitals. Their first lobbying success came with passage of the Housing Act of 1937. Under this act, the national government funded municipal public housing programs if the cities agreed to go along with the guidelines *and* if their state governments passed legislation authorizing them to enter into a direct agreement with the national government. State officials did not like being bypassed, but they often had no choice. Although they worried about the long-range consequences to their own policymaking powers, the need for money prevailed.

The Impact of Foreign Threats to U.S. Security (1945–1960)

The number of federal grants-in-aid continued to increase even after the Great Depression ended and a number of New Deal emergency aid programs were eliminated.

Many grant programs created during and after World War II were designed to protect the country against external threats. As one author notes,

During World War II and the Cold War that followed, federal grant-in-aid programs continued to expand while taking on labels that made them appear to be part of the defense effort. Aid to public schools came in a program to assist school districts experiencing rapid population growth because of military bases, defense industries, or federal installations. In 1956, the Interstate and De-

fense Highway Act greatly expanded aid for the construction of the interstate highway system. In the National Defense Education Act of 1957, federal grants and loans were authorized for higher education [in response to Russia's launching of its satellite Sputnik].[14]

The Impact of Domestic Threats to U. S. Security (1960–1968)

The most dramatic increase in the number of grants and in total grant dollars occurred during President Johnson's administration. This period is sometimes called the "period of grant explosion."[15] In 1965 and 1966 alone, Congress enacted 130 new grant-in-aid programs, the heart of Johnson's Great Society program. The grant-in-aid system also changed in function. Federal funds shifted from commerce and transportation programs (36 percent of total grants in 1963 to 23 percent by 1968) to health and human services programs (13 percent of total grants in 1963 to 40 percent in 1968).

The shifts in federal aid's functional emphasis were triggered by several major domestic events: 1) the emergence of black political power in many cities; 2) the banding together of diverse urban, consumer, civil rights, environmental, and other groups in the wake of Vietnam and the assassinations of the Reverend Martin Luther King and Senator Robert Kennedy; and 3) social unrest and violence in many cities and on college campuses.[16]

President Johnson referred to his program to combat domestic unrest as *creative federalism*. This program called for *"the development of new and expanded [national government] partnerships with state and local governments and private enterprise to tackle many of the pressing problems of urban society—poverty, crime, unemployment, illiteracy, substandard housing, disease, and physical decay."*[17]

To distressed observers at the state level, it appeared that under creative federalism, the national government's approach to state and local problems was to declare a national objective, design an aid program to meet it, and establish a new office or agency in Washington to administer it. State officials were also upset at the growing number of grants designed to bypass them. In particular, state representatives were concerned that states were becoming merely "administrative adjuncts" of federal agencies.[18]

To many national and local officials, bypassing the states seemed justified and necessary. According to one intergovernmental relations specialist, "State elected and appointed officials were corrupt, incompetent, and racist; state constitutions were long, complex, and antiquated; governors were weak, underpaid, and overworked; and legislatures were unrepresentative, backward, and cumbersome."[19]

The Impact of Changes in Presidential Leadership (1968–1978)

The election of President Richard Nixon in 1968 marked a beginning attempt to change the tide of burgeoning federal aid. Whereas Johnson's creative federalism had tried to impose nationally designed solutions, Nixon's *new federalism* sought to return decision-making powers to the governments closest to the people.

Nixon proposed to 1) consolidate a number of categorical grants into block grants, and 2) create a new type of grant—general revenue sharing. In 1969, he called for $11 billion worth of categorical grant moneys to be lumped into block grants for six purposes: education, urban development, rural development, transportation, job training, and law enforcement. However, he was successful in getting Congress to pass only a few of these proposals. Nixon was more successful in pressing Congress to pass the State and Local Fiscal Assistance Act of 1972, which gave general revenue back to state and local governments with no

strings attached. The argument for general revenue sharing grants is that they allow state and local governments to determine where the funds can best be spent to aid their constituents. Studies have shown that state and local governments spend revenue-sharing money for the same kinds of things they spend their own money for. The promise to return decision-making powers to state and local officials made this a popular grant program. However, beginning in 1981, states were no longer eligible for general revenue sharing grants. In its 1980 renewal of the State and Local Fiscal Assistance Act of 1972, Congress decided to leave the states out since many state governments had large surpluses in their treasuries at that time.

Nixon's successor, Gerald Ford, also pushed for consolidation of grants. In 1976, he proposed four major block grants: in health, education, child nutrition, and social services. All were rejected or ignored by a Democrat-controlled Congress, which accused Ford, as they had Nixon, of trying to end the Democrats' social programs.

Even when a Democrat was elected president in 1976, he entered the White House promising to simplify the grants system. President Carter wanted to eliminate many guidelines and much of the administrative red tape that accompanied grants. But he was no more successful than his Republican predecessors.

The Impact of the Bureaucracy (1968–1980)

Some attribute the inability of Presidents Nixon, Ford, and Carter to revamp the federal grants system to the existence of *iron triangles, informal networks of middle-level bureaucrats, congressional staff members, and lobbyists who rely upon each other for information.* These groups made it difficult to really change the grants system, particularly to reduce the number of categorical grants. Each group lobbied the others to protect against drastic changes in grant program structure or funding levels.

As controllers of the paper flow, bureaucrats exercised a great deal of power over the grants system structure. A 1979 report by the Office of Management and Budget indicated that federal agencies were making use of 4,916 forms, reports, and record-keeping requirements.[20] The *Code of Federal Regulations* increased from 23,000 pages in 1950 to nearly 84,000 pages in 1978. The number of pages published annually in the *Federal Register*, another indicator of federal regulatory activities, jumped from about 20,000 in 1960 to 60,000 by the late 1970s.[21]

The real burden has fallen on the state or local government applying for aid. The cost and time involved in just meeting the *cross-cutting requirements (requirements attached to each federal grant)* is staggering—not to mention the cost and time of designing a program. For each grant application

TABLE 4.2

Cross-Cutting Requirements on Federal Grants

Nondiscrimination

Age Discrimination in Employment Act of 1967
Architectural Barriers Act of 1968
Civil Rights Act of 1964, Title VI, VII
Education Amendments of 1972, Title IX
Education for All Handicapped Children Act of 1975
Equal Pay Act of 1963
Executive Orders 11141 (1963) and 1246 (1965), Nondiscrimination in Employment by
   Government Contractors and Subcontractors
Executive Order 11764, Nondiscrimination in Federal Programs, 1968
Executive Order 11914, Nondiscrimination Against the Handicapped, 1976
Rehabilitation Services Act of 1973, Section 504
State and Local Fiscal Assistance Act of 1972
Urban Mass Transportation Act of 1964, as amended 1970, Section 16

Environmental Protection

Clean Air Act of 1970 and Federal Water Pollution Control Act, 1970
Endangered Species Act of 1973
Flood Disaster Protection Act of 1973
National Environmental Policy Act (NEPA), 1969
National Historic Preservation Act of 1966

Planning and Project Coordination

Demonstration Cities and Metropolitan Development Act of 1966
Intergovernmental Cooperation Act of 1968, Title IV

Relocation and Real Property Acquisition

Uniform Relocation Assistance and Real Property Acquisition Policies Act, 1970

Labor and Procurement Standards

Davis-Bacon Act (1931, as incorporated into individual grants)
Office of Federal Procurement Policy Act, 1974
Urban Mass Transportation Act of 1964, as amended, Section 13c
Work Hours Act of 1962

Public Employee Standards

Anti-Kickback (Copeland) Act (1934, 1946, 1960)
Hatch Act (1939, 1940, 1942, 1944, 1946, 1962)
Intergovernmental Personnel Act of 1970

Access to Government Information and Decision Processes

Citizen Participation (numerous grant programs in past three decades)
Family Educational Rights and Privacy Act of 1974 (Buckley Amendment)
Freedom of Information Act, 1974
Privacy Act of 1974

SOURCE: George E. Hale and Marian Lief Palley. *The Politics of Federal Grants.* Washington, D.C.: Congressional Quarterly Press, 1981, p. 103; based on information from the following sources: *The Federal Grants Reporter,* National Reporter Systems, 1976; Evelyn Idelson, "1976 Perspective of Title VII," *County News,* April 19, 1976, p. 9; and U.S. Advisory Commission on Intergovernmental Relations, *Categorical Grants: Their Role and Design* (Washington, D.C.: GPO, 1977), p. 235.

(and a state or locality may submit hundreds), the applying government must document its compliance with all 59 requirements, which relate to nondiscrimination, environmental protection, planning, labor and hiring, public employee standards, and citizen access to government information (see Table 4.2).

While these requirements may not seem so bad from a program standpoint, they are costly from a financial standpoint. A study for Congress's Joint Economic Committee by Murray L. Weidenbaum estimated that the public and private sectors spent at least $100 billion complying with federal regulations during 1979. The Department of Commerce placed the figure even higher, at between $150 billion and $200 billion.[22]

Meeting requirements often means a receiving government will not be able to use funds as it originally intended. A classic example came from John D. Rockefeller IV when he was governor of West Virginia:

> We wanted to build housing for the poor with federal money. First, we couldn't build the housing where we wanted because it was in a flood plain. So we chose a site atop the Appalachian mountains. Then, we still couldn't qualify for federal aid unless we put in access roads. Then Washington applied the cruncher: "The roads must have sidewalks," they told us. So now we have roads running up the mountains of West Virginia with sidewalks on both sides.[23]

Sometimes a government eligible for aid under a formula grant program will decide it's not worth it. In New York City, the Metropolitan Transportation Authority voted to pass up $400 million a year in federal transit aid rather than comply with laws requiring special access for the handicapped. According to MTA officials, they did not object to the requirement's intent, but rather the cost of meeting it, which was estimated at $1.5 billion.[24]

These regulations have also increased the number of state and local lawsuits testing the constitutionality of various grant-related strings and guidelines. By 1980, courts across the country had made some 500 decisions related to the receipt and use of federal assistance. Most cases have been decided in favor of the national government on the basis of the spending power assigned in Article I, Section 8, of the Constitution.

Ironically, at the same time state and local officials were bitterly lambasting growth of federal aid

and mountains of red tape, they themselves were either directly or indirectly lobbying to keep the funds flowing.

One type of lobbying was by *public interest groups (PIGs), national associations of state and local officials.* Groups such as the National Governors Conference, National Conference of State Legislatures, Council of State Governments, U.S. Conference of Mayors, National League of Cities, International City Management Association, and the National Association of County Officials pressured Congress to renew or redesign grant programs, particularly block grant programs like Community Development and the Comprehensive Employment and Training Act (CETA).

Another type of lobbying in the 1970s resulted in conflict between various state and local governments (see Figure 4.1). The most widely publicized fights were those between Frost Belt and Sun Belt states and between distressed, declining cities and healthy, growing cities. Most fights centered on federal aid formulas. Great arguments took place on the House and Senate floors about precisely which census statistics (e.g., population size, population growth, income, or race) should be plugged into a particular grant formula. This led to the era of *printout politics in which federal aid distribution is determined mainly by formulas set in Congress rather than by federal agencies.* Now, each time a new formula is proposed, each member of Congress gets a computer printout showing how much money will go to his or her district compared to other members' districts. The result has been less redistributing of funds to needy persons and areas and more spreading of benefits across all congressional districts.

Thus we see that while collectively states favored reducing strings and guidelines, eliminating bypass, and reducing the amount of aid available, individually they fought to get as much money as possible. This helps explain the difficulty Presidents Nixon, Ford, and Carter had in prying apart the iron triangle. It wasn't until taxpayers began their attack that state and local government officials began to refrain from talking out of both sides of their mouths.

The Impact of the Taxpayers' Revolt (1978–1980)

The revolt of California taxpayers in 1978 resulted in the passage in June, 1978, of Proposition 13 (also known as the Jarvis-Gann amendment after

1982
Taxes paid per $1.00 federal aid *

	$1.00
Alabama	$ .80
Alaska	.57
Arizona	1.18
Arkansas	.72
California	1.11
Colorado	1.26
Connecticut	1.41
Delaware	.86
Florida	1.33
Georgia	.82
Hawaii	.94
Idaho	.85
Illinois	1.18
Indiana	1.22
Iowa	1.18
Kansas	1.28
Kentucky	.79
Louisiana	.89
Maine	.66
Maryland	1.03
Massachusetts	.86
Michigan	.96
Minnesota	.94
Mississippi	.60
Missouri	1.12
Montana	.67
Nebraska	1.16
Nevada	1.17
New Hampshire	1.21
New Jersey	1.27
New Mexico	.69
New York	.56
North Carolina	.98
North Dakota	.73
Ohio	1.19
Oklahoma	1.09
Oregon	1.08
Pennsylvania	.98
Rhode Island	.81
South Carolina	.92
South Dakota	.60
Tennessee	.82
Texas	1.46
Utah	.81
Vermont	.56
Virginia	1.13
Washington	1.11
West Virginia	.67
Wisconsin	.79
Wyoming	1.16
Dist. of Columbia	.24

*Calculations do not count all federal aid received

FIGURE 4.1

Winners and Losers in the Fight for Federal Funds

SOURCE: Tax Foundation study cited in *Houston Chronicle*, May 27, 1981; 1982 data from *Texas Town & City*, Vol. LXIX, No. 9, September 1982. © Houston Chronicle.

its cosponsors). This amendment to the California Constitution 1) reduced the maximum property tax rate to 1 percent of the 1975–1976 assessed

value of the property; 2) restricted future assessment increases to 2 percent per year (unless the property was sold, in which case the property could be put on the tax roll at its current market value); and 3) prohibited the state legislature from raising any state tax above its previous level (to replace revenues lost by the property tax cut) unless a two-thirds popular vote approved the increase.

Tax revolts spread across the country like wildfire. Government officials soon learned that middle-class Americans were fed up with the growth of government in general. Taxpayers were tired of paying more taxes to support government activities at all levels but getting less for their money. They lashed out first at local and state governments only because those levels have the necessary mechanisms, the initiative and the referendum. Voters could petition to place an issue directly on a ballot under the initiative procedure and to call an election under the referendum procedure. As citizens in state after state imposed taxing and spending limits on their state and local governments, officials in these governments blamed the national government for putting them into a fiscal bind by not controlling inflation and national government spending. By 1981, 31 state legislatures had voted to ask Congress to call a constitutional convention to require the national government to balance its budget. (The balance-the-budget movement will be discussed further in chapter 17 on the Budget.)

THE REAGAN PROPOSALS: A RETURN TO AN EQUAL PARTNERSHIP?

The trends in intergovernmental relations between 1960 and 1980 (see Table 4.3) helped bring about a crisis of confidence in our federal system. In a damaging critique of the status of federalism in 1980, the Advisory Commission on Intergovernmental Relations concluded that the system had "become dangerously overloaded, to the point that [its] most trumpeted traditional traits— flexibility and workability"—were critically endangered.[25] But instead of short-circuiting or blowing a fuse, the system started cooling off. Elected officials quickly reacted to citizen calls for less government spending and lower taxes. President Reagan proposed to restore balance to the federal system by means of budget cuts, block grants, functional and fiscal reassignments, heavier reliance on the private sector, and the re-

President Reagan, like others before him, attempted to restore some order to the highly fragmented federal grants-in-aid system. He proposed to cut funding for grant-in-aid programs, consolidate numerous categorical grants into a few block ones, and eliminate burdensome, costly paperwork requirements.

vision and reduction of costly federal rules and regulations (see Table 4.4). His program designed to strengthen the power of state and local governments also became known as "new federalism." Not all of these proposals were implemented at once. Budget cuts and block grants came first.

TABLE 4.3

ACIR's Key Intergovernmental Trends of the Past 20 Years (1960–1980)

1. Growth in government and expansion of governmental roles into many areas formerly in the purview of the private sector.
2. Massive growth in the size, scope, and intrusiveness of federal aid.
3. Troubled cities and urban areas.
4. Increasingly significant role of the courts in intergovernmental areas accompanying a concern for equity in the system.
5. Growing local government (particularly cities) dependence on state and federal aid.
6. Strengthened states in general and more powerful state revenue systems in particular.
7. Disaffection with government and growing concern for government accountability, manifested in the late 1970s by Proposition 13 and other "tax revolt" activities and responses.
8. Increased intergovernmental lobbying—governments lobbying government.
9. Increasing numbers of regional bodies.
10. Emergence of the Frost Belt-Sun Belt regional competition, also the growing tensions between the "haves" (the oil rich states) and the "have nots" (the consumer states).

SOURCE: Carl W. Stenberg. "Federalism in Transition: 1959–79." *Intergovernmental Perspective*, 6 (Winter 1980), p. 8.

New Federalism, Stage 1: Budget Cuts and Block Grants

Reagan proposed dramatic changes in both the form and level of funding for federal aid. He began by proposing to cut grant outlays to state and local governments to $86.4 billion, down 13.5 percent from the $99.8 billion called for in Carter's 1982 budget proposal. By 1983, grants-in-aid to state and local governments were to be cut to $81.4 billion, only 11 percent of the total federal budget.

Most of the proposed budget cuts were in housing, employment, nutrition, education, transportation, and capital improvement (such as sewage treatment plant construction) programs (see Table 4.5). Reagan regarded most of these programs as the responsibility of state and local governments, not the federal government. In other words, he felt the federal government should ultimately get out of the business of funding such programs and turn them back to the states.

Reagan also proposed replacing numerous categorical grants with block grants. Initially, he proposed consolidating 84 categorical grants into 7 block grants: 2 for education, 2 for health, 2 for social services, and 1 for community development. According to officials in his administration, these 84 categoricals by themselves accounted for 616 pages of laws, 1,400 pages of regulations, more than 10,000 separate grants, 88,000 grant sites, 7 million hours of paperwork, and several thousand federal employees.[26] By consolidating

TABLE 4.4

Reagan's Original New Federalism Proposal*

Stage	Strategy	Time Frame
Stage 1	Budget cuts Block grants	1981–83
Stage 2	Turnback of programs to states Swap of programs with states Creation of federalism trust fund	1984–91
Stage 3	Phase out of federalism trust fund	1988–91
Stage 4	Turnover of certain federal tax sources to states	1991
Stages 1–4	Private sector initiatives Revision and reduction of federal rules and regulations	1981–?

*As proposed in 1981 Budget Reconciliation Act and 1982 State of the Union address (January 26, 1982). Many of these proposals have been altered as they have gone through the policymaking process.

Student Aid: For the Truly Needy or for Everybody?

Under his new federalism, President Reagan proposed to "restrict eligibility for higher education aid to students to those most in need and concentrate campus-based student aid funds on work-study rather than on additional grants and loans."[1] Reagan's proposal clearly demonstrates targeting aid rather than spreading benefits. Under his program, the federal government's role in higher education would be to target aid to the truly needy students. The underlying assumption is that it is the role of state and local governments to make aid available to middle-class students.

The Reagan administration's view is that student aid has gotten out of hand in recent years. Grants, direct loans, loan guarantees, and work-study stipends expanded from $250 million in budget authority in 1965 to $6.3 billion in 1981. According to a Reagan administration spokesperson, "What started as help for poor students to afford a college education has become support for middle-class students who don't need it and who abuse it."[2] A position paper prepared by the Department of Education reported that 40 percent of the 12 million students in degree-granting institutions of higher education receive federal aid. While family income increased 30 percent between 1978 and 1981, family contributions to their children's college costs decreased 6 percent. On top of that, fewer students were trying to support themselves by working part-time or in the summer.

Despite the administration's emphasis on the "truly needy," higher education lobbying groups, including the United States Student Association, questioned both the administration's figures and motives. They debated the figure that showed a decline in family contributions, and they questioned the administration's motives in light of its proposed elimination of the supplemental grants, direct loans, and state incentive grant programs—small programs specifically designed to help the poor.

However, higher education groups and the administration agreed on the numbers regarding the Guaranteed Student Loan program (GSL). This program grew from $357 million in 1977 to $2.5 billion in 1981 and was expected to cost over $3.9 billion in 1983. The number of loans rose from 1.1 million in 1978 to nearly 4 million in 1982. This program is the fastest growing entitlement program in the nation, growing even faster than Social Security. An *entitlement program is one that makes grants available automatically to eligible recipients who meet the requirements and conditions established by congressional statute.* Federal spending on the GSL program, most of which is paid in the form of interest subsidies to banks, grew at an average rate of 82 percent a

[1]Executive Office of the President, Office of Management and Budget, *Budget of the United States Government Fiscal Year 1983* (Washington, D.C.: Government Printing Office, 1982) pp. 5–106.

[2]Rochelle L. Stanfield, "Student Aid Lobby Learns New Trick to Fight Reagan's Spending Cutbacks," *National Journal*, 14 (July 17, 1982), pp. 1262–63.

year between 1976 and 1981, according to the Senate Budget Committee.[3]

The GSL program, created in 1965 primarily to help poor students, became a middle-class program following passage of the Middle Income Student Assistance Act of 1978. This act made all students eligible for GSLs, regardless of family income. This explains the tremendous increase in program costs between 1978 and 1981. In an attempt to move the program back to the targeted one and to cut back on costs, the 1981 budget reconciliation law mandated that a "need" test be conducted on students from families with incomes over $30,000. As a consequence, some 1 million students either lost their aid completely or had it reduced.

Reagan's proposals have aimed at cutting even deeper into middle-income student aid subsidies. Widely publicized incidents of program abuse by doctors, lawyers, and other professionals who haven't paid back their student loans certainly hasn't helped middle-class students. Many members of Congress now see abuses as the rule rather than the exception. Moreover, some Congress members fear that if the growth of the GSL program is not curbed, the program will eventually absorb all available federal resources for higher education, leaving nothing for the truly needy.

In spite of these facts, higher education groups fought successfully to keep Congress from cutting $762 million in 1983 spending for GSLs. How? The year 1982 was a congressional election year and students and their parents represent a huge number of votes: "The belief in the value of a college education, and the frustration at the increasing difficulty of paying for it, run very deep in the middle class, and the politician who ignores that by voting for more aid cuts risks alienating a lot of voters."[4]

Still, further cuts in student aid programs are a real possibility. If they occur, state and local governments will probably have to begin playing their role as the "spreaders" of student aid to middle-class students and leave the targeting of aid to the federal government. What one level of government does in educational policy affects what other levels do—and that affects the lifestyles of millions of American college students.

As this case has demonstrated, the question constantly facing policymakers is this: What responsibilities should be assigned to which level of government and who should pay for them?

[3]Harrison Donnelly, ''Massive Lobbying Campaign Derails Reagan's Proposals for College Student Aid Cuts,'' *Congressional Quarterly*, 40 (May 22, 1982), p. 1167.

[4]Donnelly, *op. cit.*, p. 1169.

TABLE 4.5

The Cuts in Federal Aid

The table shows potential cuts in major federal aid programs in fiscal 1982. The first column shows the reductions ordered by the budget that Congress adopted on May 21. The second shows budget authority required in fiscal 1982 to maintain the programs at current levels. Figures are in billions of dollars.

	Reduction	Authorization
Subsidized housing	− $10.9	$29.9
Public service jobs	− 3.8	3.8
Sewage treatment grants	− 3.6	3.6
Youth employment	− 1.8	5.7
Child nutrition	− 1.5	4.2
Education block grant	− 1.4	6.4
Mass transit	− 1.3	5.1
Social services block grant	− 0.9	6.7
Economic development	− 0.5	0.7
Community development	− 0.5	4.6
Education impact aid	− 0.5	0.9
Health services block grant	− 0.4	1.6
Highway safety	− 0.2	0.2
Arts and humanities	− 0.2	0.3
Highway construction	− 0.2	8.6
Vocational education	− 0.1	0.9
Health planning	− 0.1	0.2
Housing rehabilitation loans	− 0.1	0.1
Juvenile justice	− 0.1	0.2

SOURCE: Rochelle L. Stanfield and Linda E. Demkovitch. "What Budget Cuts Mean for Cities—Lean Years with Less for the Poor. *National Journal*, May 30, 1981, p. 961; based on data provided by the Senate Budget Committee and the U.S. Conference of Mayors.

them into block grants, Reagan administration officials, like their previous counterparts, hoped to eliminate waste.

Reagan also saw block grants as a way to return more responsibility to the states: "The ultimate objective . . . is to use block grants as a bridge leading to the day when you will have not only the responsibility for programs that properly belong at the state level, but you'll have the tax sources, now usurped by Washington, returned to you—ending that round trip of the people's money to Washington and back minus a carrying charge," he told the National Conference of State Legislatures.[27]

As it turned out, Congress in 1982 adopted most of Reagan's initial budget cut and block grant proposals. In fact, Congress created nine block grants instead of the seven requested by Reagan (see Table 4.6). Congress cut $1.2 billion from the categorical programs consolidated into these blocks. Seven more blocks were proposed in the 1983 budget—vocational and adult education, education for the handicapped, employment and training, rehabilitation services, child welfare, rental rehabilitation, and welfare administration. These blocks consolidated more than 34 categoricals and represented a budget cut of $1 billion.

Reactions to Stage 1 Generally, more state than local officials supported the block grant proposals, primarily because the plan was to send the funds directly to the states and let them decide how to divide the money among their localities. As Congress implemented the blocks, however, it left many strings attached—as adopted, they were referred to as "blocks of categoricals" rather than as true block grants. Consequently the primary impact of the blocks was monetary rather than programmatic.

TABLE 4.6
Transition from Categorical to Block Grants

Old Categorical Grants Consolidated 1981	New Block Grants 1982	Nationwide Funding by Federal Fiscal Year (in Millions)		
		1981	1982	Percent Decrease
1. Home Health, Rodent Control, Emergency Medical Services, Flouridation, Rape Crisis, Hypertension Control, Health Incentive, Health Education	Preventive Health and Health Services	$ 130.0	$ 93.2	28.3%
2. Community Health Centers Act, Mental Health Systems Act, two from each: Comprehensive Alcohol Abuse and Alcoholism Prevention, Drug Abuse Prevention	Alcohol, Drug Abuse and Mental Health Services	638.0	485.0	24.0
3. Title XX of the Social Security Act	Social Services	2,991.1	2,400.0	19.8
4. Maternal and Child Health Grants, Supplemental Security Income for Children, Lead Poisoning Prevention, Genetic Disease, Sudden Infant Death, Hemophilia Screening, Adolescent Health Services	Maternal and Child Health	638.0	485.0	24.0
5. Low-Income Energy Assistance	Home Energy Assistance	1,825.0	1,400.0	23.3
6. Various programs of Economic Opportunity Act of 1984 including: Senior Opportunities and Services, Community Food and Nutrition, Energy Conservation and Training	Community Services	374.8	225.0	40.0
7. Small Cities Community Development program (cities under 50,000 population); 701 Planning Grant; Neighborhood Self-Help Development; Territories Program	Community Development	1,080.0	950.4	12.0
8. Community Health Centers; Primary Care Research and Demonstration Grants	Primary Health Care	284.0	214.7	24.4
9. 37 Elementary and Secondary School Categorical Programs (such as desegregation aid, National Teachers Corp., Metric Education, Consumer Education, Education of the Handicapped, Migrant Education, Education of Deprived, Neglected, or Delinquent Children, Education of Gifted Children)	Education	589.4	518.0	12.1

SOURCE: "Block Grant Shares Released." *State Government News*, January 1982; *Fiscal Notes*, Issue 82–4, March 1982, Office of the Comptroller—Texas; *National Journal*, October 10, 1981, p. 1803.

"NOT QUITE THE BUILDING MATERIALS I WAS HOPING FOR"

Copyright 1981 by Herblock in The Washington Post

Local officials, particularly those representing large central cities with significant poor and minority populations, were less receptive to the notion of block grants. They feared that state governments would not spend enough money on minority groups. Local officials, along with urban and social interest group lobbyists, pointed to the history of state neglect that led to national government assumption of responsibility for many categorical programs in the first place. Typical of this view was the comment of one local official from a coal-mining state:

> There was a three year fight before the [national] government provided a black-lung program. Now they're talking of giving it back to the states in the health block grant. But for 30 years, the states systematically avoided doing anything about black lung.[28]

State officials' response to such criticisms is that they have modernized. They point to reform in state constitutions, legislatures, courts, personnel systems, and fiscal systems since 1960. They also cite research showing that states are more responsive to the needs of their cities than is the national government.

What local officials, especially those from small cities, really feared was loss of immediate access to the grant distribution process. The associate director of the National Association of Counties admitted it was "no secret that our organization was opposed to the [Reagan] administration proposal to transfer the Small Cities Community Development [Program] to the states. It took at least three years for the small communities to build up the existing relationship with HUD; we thought that to interpose another level of government in the decision making would be counterproductive."[29] Local officials' fear of loss of influence became even greater when Reagan announced his plans for functional and fiscal reassignments.

New Federalism, Stage 2: Swaps, Turnbacks, and Trust Fund Formation

In his first State of the Union address, President Reagan proposed to rearrange the relationship between the federal government and the states with "a single bold stroke." He called for a "financially equal swap" whereby the national government would trade its responsibility for food stamps and Aid to Families with Dependent Children (AFDC) for the states' responsibility for Medicaid. In addition, he proposed to turn back complete control of some 40 grant programs to the states. Both the "swap" and "turnback" proposals were functional reassignment proposals. To help states pay for these new responsibilities, the president proposed a federalism trust fund, to be financed by federal excise taxes (on alcohol, gas, tobacco, telephones) and the windfall profits tax on oil. This trust fund would be phased out by 1991, at which time the states would be given the exclusive right to impose these excise taxes.

The initial reaction of many state officials to the swap proposal was positive, primarily because of the rapid growth in the costs of the Medicaid program compared with food stamps and AFDC. Ideally, however, governors and state legislators would have preferred that the national government take responsibility for all three programs. They felt that income maintenance programs (such as AFDC, food stamps, and Medicaid) should be a national responsibility because national economic policy largely determines both the number of people on welfare and the level of assistance. On the other hand, many conservatives, including some in the Reagan administration, feared that national government assumption of these three welfare functions would eventually result in a national health care plan.

As is true with any policy proposal, disagreements arose about implementation. One problem with the swap proposal was the financing of the programs. The taxing capacities of the states vary widely, and in the bargaining stage, state and local officials insisted that no state be overburdened by takeover, especially those with high unemployment and large concentrations of poor people. Another issue was how to develop minimum national standards. Some states have more generous AFDC, food stamp, and Medicaid programs than others. Many governors opposed the federal proposal to include "grandfather clauses" requiring states to fund all welfare recipients on their rolls at the time of state takeover at the same level as before the takeover.

The turnback proposal, although less controversial in the eyes of the state officials than the swap proposal, was strongly opposed by local officials. They opposed turnback for the same reason they resisted block grants—fear they would be left out in the cold.

State and local government officials remained unconvinced that the federalism trust funds would be sufficient to fund the swap and turnback proposals. The initial promise was that there would be "no winners and no losers" as a result of these new federalism proposals (see Table 4.7). Individual states that lost money in the swap would gain money as a result of turnback, and vice versa. The net result would be no gains and no losses. The federalism trust fund would be used to offset total losses and equalize individual state gains and losses. This fund, financed by revenues from existing federal excise taxes (oil windfall profits—$16.7 billion, tobacco—$2.7 billion, alcohol—$6.1 billion, telephone—$.3 billion, and gas—$2.2 billion), was to be available to states from 1984 to 1987. It would start being phased out in 1988 (25 percent reduction each year) and be gone by 1991. This phaseout would be Stage 3 of Reagan's new federalism. In 1991, in Stage 4 of the new federalism, states would have the option of imposing the excise taxes on their own and of determining which of the turnback programs to continue to fund.

From the perspective of state and local officials, the problems with the trust fund were numerous. A basic fear was that the initial estimates of program costs and revenue gains were inaccurate and that as a consequence, trust fund payments to the states would be too low to cover losses. There was also concern over the heavy reliance upon the oil windfall profits tax—60 percent of the trust fund revenues would come from it, yet only six or seven states would be able to impose it once the fund dried up. But the most serious concern was whether a formula for distribution of the trust fund moneys could be designed "to avoid great regional disparities that would hurt some states severely and give bonuses to others."[30]

As is characteristic of our system of government, numerous compromises were made. An initial compromise by the Reagan administration was to keep the food stamps program at the federal level. This meant that the swap proposal was narrowed to a trade of AFDC for Medicaid. Ultimately, the swap idea was rejected altogether. Second, the number of programs to be turned back was reduced considerably. Third, part of the trust fund would be supported by general federal revenues rather than by the windfall profits tax on oil. Finally, the administration promised local governments that they would continue to receive the same share of federal funds they get under current programs. Even with these compromises, implementation of Reagan's swap and turn back proposals came slowly.

One reason for the difficulties in reassigning functional responsibilities was the proposal's timing. It was submitted when state and local governments were struggling with the recession *and* trying to cope with the federal aid cutbacks that had occurred as a result of Stage 1.

Another problem was resistance in Congress. Some members of Congress regarded Reagan's new federalism proposals as merely a way of diverting attention from the economic ills facing the nation at that time. Others feared that the shift of responsibility to the states would reduce congressional power.

A third reason for delays was the idea that the programs would be unfair to the nation's poor, in spite of Reagan's vow that "this administration has not and will not turn its back on America's elderly or America's poor, but will preserve the social safety net." (According to the administration,

TABLE 4.7

No Winners, No Losers: State-by-State Figures for Impact of Federalism Plan*

The White House released the following chart showing how states would be affected by its federalism package in fiscal 1984.

The key columns in this chart are under the large heading "Swap Program." The first column—"Medicaid savings"—shows the state share of Medicaid costs that would be assumed by the federal government. The second shows the additional costs imposed on states for Aid to Families with Dependent Children and food stamps.

The difference between the two columns appears as "Net difference." States with negative amounts would lose because of the swap alone; those with positive figures would gain.

The column headed "Turnback programs" shows the amount that states would have received under 40 existing programs being transferred.

The figures under "Trust fund allocation" show what states would get from the new trust fund. They have been set to compensate for state gains or losses under the welfare swap. States that would lose from the swap alone would be given additional trust fund money; trust fund payments would be reduced for those that would gain from the swap alone. For each state, the sum of the "Net difference" columns for the turnback program and swap program is zero. Thus, under the White House reasoning, no state would have a net gain or loss.

The column "Overall total" shows the combined total for each state of the programs and funds involved in the whole package.

	Swap Program			Turnback Program			Overall Total of Both Programs
	Medicaid Savings	Public Assistance Cost	Net Difference	Trust Fund Allocation	Turnback Programs	Net Difference	
Ala.	$ 140	$ 350	$ − 210	$ 713	$ 503	$ 210	$ 853
Alaska	32	53	− 22	188	166	22	220
Ariz.	0	157	− 157	463	306	157	463
Ark.	137	174	− 37	345	308	37	482
Calif.	2,524	2,030	494	2,144	2,638	− 494	4,668
Colo.	161	134	27	331	358	− 27	492
Conn.	277	169	108	283	390	− 108	560
Del.	38	40	− 2	107	106	2	146
D.C.	141	84	57	333	390	− 57	474
Fla.	348	628	− 281	1,433	1,152	281	1,781
Ga.	285	431	− 146	819	674	146	1,104
Hawaii	94	106	− 12	145	133	12	239
Idaho	31	51	− 20	151	131	20	182
Ill.	857	838	18	1,547	1,565	− 18	2,403
Ind.	336	275	61	552	612	− 61	887
Iowa	166	140	26	330	3,356	− 26	496
Kan.	141	94	47	225	272	− 47	366
Ky.	186	367	− 181	690	509	181	875
La.	309	379	− 70	634	564	70	943
Maine	81	102	− 21	240	219	21	321
Md.	342	283	59	507	566	− 59	849
Mass.	669	418	251	732	983	− 251	1,401
Mich.	914	874	39	1,147	1,186	− 39	2,061
Minn.	501	202	299	236	535	− 299	737
Miss.	109	293	− 184	563	379	184	671
Mo.	247	296	− 48	700	652	48	947
Mont.	43	39	4	128	132	− 4	171
Neb.	77	60	17	185	202	− 17	262
Nev.	70	30	39	58	97	− 39	127
N.H.	57	40	16	110	126	− 16	166
N.J.	557	426	132	907	1,038	− 132	1,464
N.M.	57	120	− 64	251	188	64	308
N.Y.	4,002	1,673	2,329	789	3,118	− 2,329	4,791
N.C.	277	375	− 97	820	722	97	1,097
N.D.	45	20	24	83	107	− 24	127
Ohio	744	815	− 71	1,406	1,335	71	2,105
Okla.	228	146	82	249	332	− 82	478
Ore.	128	165	− 38	393	356	38	521

(continued)

TABLE 4.7

No Winners, No Losers: State-by-State Figures for Impact of Federalism Plan* *(continued)*

Pa.	967	875	92	1,658	1,750	− 92	2,625
R.I.	95	78	17	124	141	− 17	219
S.C.	128	282	− 154	553	399	154	682
S.D.	32	33	− 1	124	123	1	155
Tenn.	267	401	− 135	702	567	135	969
Tex.	833	726	106	1,352	1,458	− 106	2,184
Utah	61	60	0	182	183	0	243
Vt.	32	53	− 21	118	97	21	150
Va.	250	288	− 39	617	579	39	867
Wash.	248	240	8	493	502	− 8	742
W. Va.	65	156	− 91	429	338	91	494
Wis.	633	296	337	235	572	− 337	868
Wyo.	17	14	2	75	77	− 2	91
TOTAL	$18,976	$16,382	$2,594	$27,600	$30,194	$ − 2,594	$46,576

SOURCE: *Congressional Quarterly,* January 30, 1982, p. 182; based on figures provided by the White House.

*Figures are in millions of dollars.

the social safety net consists of "those programs, mostly begun in the 1930s, that now constitute an agreed upon core of protections for the elderly, the unemployed, the poor, and those programs that fulfill our basic commitment to the people who serve the country in time of war."[31]) It did not help the image of new federalism when early studies of the Reagan budget cuts and block grants found that the poor, especially the working poor, were most negatively affected by the budget cuts in Stage 1.

In spite of these difficulties in implementing his swap, turnback, and trust fund proposals, Reagan succeeded in moving the system in the direction of an equal partnership between the national government and the states. His successes came not only from his budget cut and block grant proposals but also from regulatory changes and greater reliance upon the private sector.

Other Components of Reagan's New Federalism: Regulatory Changes and Private Sector Initiatives

A first step toward reducing regulations was the creation of a Presidential Task Force on Regulatory Relief, chaired by Vice-President George Bush. By early fall of 1981, the Task Force had announced 52 steps to relax more than 1,200 regulations affecting states and cities.

In early 1981, Reagan also ordered a study of the costs versus the benefits of federal regulations. Under this order, federal agencies must compare costs to the benefits of all new and existing major rules and then pick the least expensive way of im-

plementing rules. (Major rules are those that have an economic impact of $100 million or more, that cause a major increase in costs or price, or that have significant adverse effects on competition, employment, investment, or innovation.) Such cost-benefit analysis quickly resulted in the elimi-

Question: Here is a list of institutions in our society. (Hand respondent card) For each, please tell me if you think the phrase "efficient and well-run" describes it or not. First, the federal government. Does the phrase "efficient and well-run" describe it, or not? (Ask about each)

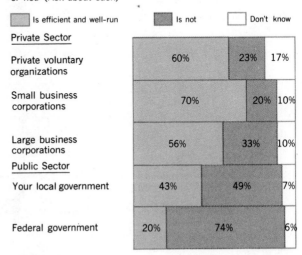

FIGURE 4.2

The Efficiency of Public and Private Sector Institutions

SOURCE: *Public Opinion,* February/March, 1982, p. 29; based on a survey by the Roper Organization/Roper Center for Public Opinion Research for the American Enterprise Institute, November 14–21, 1981.

nation of several expensive cross-cutting requirements, including handicapped access and bilingual education regulations.

Greater involvement by the private sector, including volunteerism, was another important component of Reagan's new federalism. In the president's view, government policies of the past, including many grants-in-aid policies, had stifled private sector self-help efforts. As we saw in chapter 2, many Americans share the president's view that the private sector can solve many problems better than the federal government (see Figure 4.2).

What is the best way to stimulate the involvement of the private sector? The Reagan answer has been to increase productivity. This gives busi-

nesses more resources to help the unfortunate or disadvantaged. To help determine how to increase the productivity of the private sector and volunteerism as well, President Reagan created a Task Force on Private Sector Initiatives.

The initial fear about the private sector initiatives part of Reagan's new federalism was that it was "an unrealistic vision of the private sector rushing in with checkbooks to fill the gap between continuing human needs and diminished federal resources."[32] But public opinion polls (see Figure 4.3) showed that few Americans expected all the cuts to be made up by the private sector.

As for voluntarism, Reagan believed that America needed to rebuild its sense of social obligation, of public-spiritedness, of belonging to and being part of a community. In his opinion, Ameri-

Question: (Hand respondent card) The government has been spending money for each of these areas, but there is now talk of cutbacks. For each one, please tell me if you think support from the private sector-such as corporations, private charities, churches, and individual citizens-will make up for the loss of government support, or not? First, support for the arts. (Ask about each)

	Loss of money will be made up by private sector	Will not be made up	No support loss (vol.)	Don't know
Support for the arts	37%	40%	6%	17%
Basic scientific research	36%	48%	4%	13%
Education in general	33%	54%	3%	10%
Job training	31%	54%	3%	12%
College scholarships	30%	54%	4%	12%
Day care	26%	56%	4%	14%
School lunches	25%	60%	4%	11%
Social services for the elderly	23%	65%	2%	10%

FIGURE 4.3

Perceptions Of Private Sector Ability to Restore Federal Budget Cuts

SOURCE: *Public Opinion,* February/March, 1982, p. 28; based on a survey by the Roper Organization/Roper Center for Public Opinion Research for the American Enterprise Institute, November 14–21, 1981.

As part of his New Federalism plan, President Reagan urged Americans to get more involved in their communities. In his opinion, America needs to rebuilt its sense of social obligation, or public spiritedness, by relying more on volunteers and less on government.

Question: Do you regularly do any type of volunteer work?

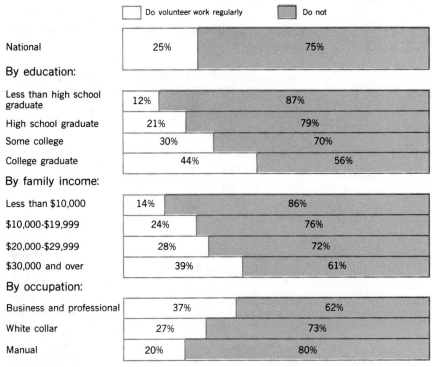

FIGURE 4.4

Who Are America's Volunteers?

SOURCE: *Public Opinion,* February/March, 1982, p. 22; based on a survey by the Roper Organization/
Roper Center for Public Opinion Research for the American Enterprise Institute, November 14–21,
1981.

cans had gotten too used to letting the federal government do everything "in the national interest." Most Americans agree, in principle, that volunteerism is an important value. But only 25 percent report they do volunteer work regularly (see Figure 4.4). Those who do volunteer tend to be the more educated and affluent persons in business and professional occupations.

The initial effectiveness of the private sector initiatives program varied across communities and was very much contingent upon economic conditions. For example, the private sector in Detroit, home of the nation's ailing auto industry, was not as able to get involved in public-private partnership activities as the private sector in Houston, petroleum capital of the United States. Again, critics of the new federalism pointed to this variation as an example of why approaches addressing the national good (centralization strategies) are preferable to those aimed at the community level

(decentralization strategies). It boils down to a philosophical debate: conservatives favor decentralization strategies and liberals favor centralization strategies.

The difficulties in implementing many parts of Reagan's new federalism program make its future unclear. Yet the majority of Americans still feel that state and local governments are able to deal with most problems more effectively than the national government (see Figure 4.5). Since the late 1970s, the American system of government has shifted toward a more balanced federalism. As we approach a more equal partnership, some are asking whether the system will swing back to a state-dominated system as it was in the early days of the Republic. As we have seen, the federal system of government changes as economic, social, and political conditions change at home and abroad. The founders designed the system to do just that.

The States v. Washington

State government	Federal government
Which do you think is more understanding of the real needs of the people of this community?	
67%	15%
Which do you think is more likely to administer social programs efficiently?	
67%	18%
Which theory of government do you favor- concentration of power in the federal government or concentration of power in the state governments?	
56%	28%
Which do you think is more likely to make decisions free of political corruption?	
42%	26%

Of every tax dollar that goes to the federal government in Washington how many cents of each dollar do you think are wasted?

And how many cents of each tax dollar that goes to the government of this state do you think are wasted?

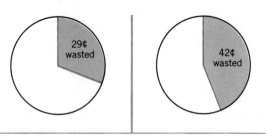

29¢ wasted

42¢ wasted

FIGURE 4.5

The Roots of the New Federalism

SOURCE: *National Journal,* February 27, 1982, p. 375; based on a Gallup Poll conducted September 18–21, 1981; reprinted from *Opinion Outlook,* February 12, 1982.

SUMMARY

America's founders created a federal system of government composed of two levels of authority, national and state. They did not totally separate the functions of the two, however; the system they created involves both shared and separate powers. In the Constitution, some powers are expressly granted to the national government and denied to the states (e.g., declaring war, coining money).

Other powers are denied to the national government and left to the states (election of representatives to the U.S. Congress). Still other powers, such as taxation and law enforcement, are granted to both.

Since the nation's beginning, Americans have often changed their minds about whether the national government or the states should be dominant in the making of public policy. The balance of power has shifted from a state-centered system (1789–1862), to an equal partnership (1862–1913), to a national-centered system (1913–1978). In recent years, there has been evidence that the balance is shifting back to either an equal partnership or a state-centered system as efforts are made to reduce the size and scope of national government activities. These shifts have paralleled changes in the political, social, and economic conditions of the nation. Such shifts are possible within the framework of the Constitution because of the foresight of the founders, who inserted two clauses granting general, "implied" powers to national and state governments. The "necessary and proper" clause for the national government and the Tenth Amendment for state governments have historically been used to justify expansion. Naturally, these clauses have been a source of tension between the two levels of government as each has claimed the other is interpreting its power too broadly.

Interrelationships between different levels of government became more complex with the advent of federal grants-in-aid to state and local governments. This sharing of revenue became possible after the adoption of the Sixteenth Amendment, which gave the federal government the right to levy an income tax. The grants system expanded rapidly, thereby strengthening the position of the national government in the policymaking arena. Over time, this system resulted in a growing resentment toward the national government on the part of many state and local officials and of taxpayers who felt they were losing control over decision-making. In an effort to restore balance to the federal system (i.e., to increase the power of state and local governments while reducing the power of the national government), presidents since Richard Nixon have endorsed some type of new federalism program. The goal of new federalism plans is to decentralize decision-making, primarily by creating large block grants designed to let state and local governments determine their own spending priorities rather than setting such priorities in Washington.

KEY TERMS

block grant
categorical grant
confederation
creative federalism
cross-cutting requirements
delegated powers
dual federalism rulings
entitlement grant
extradition
federal system of government
formula-based grant
"full faith and credit" clause
general revenue sharing (GRS)
grant-in-aid
implied powers
interstate compact
iron triangles
layer cake federalism
marble cake federalism
new federalism
printout politics
"privileges and immunities" clause
project-based grant
public interest group (PIG)
unitary system of government

SUGGESTED READINGS

Barfield, Claude E. *Rethinking Federalism: Block Grants and Federal, State, and Local Responsibilities*. Washington, D.C.: American Enterprise Institute, 1981.

Barton, Weldon V. *Interstate Compacts in the Political Process*. Chapel Hill, N.C.: University of North Carolina Press, 1967.

Break, George F. *Financing Government in a Federal System*. Washington, D.C.: The Brookings Institution, 1980.

Ellwood, John W., ed. *Reductions in U.S. Domestic Spending: How They Affect State and Local Governments*. Rutgers, N.J.: Transaction Books, 1982.

Glendening, Parris N., and Reeves, Mavis Mann. *Pragmatic Federalism*. Pacific Palisades, Calif.: Palisades Publishers, 1977.

Hawkins, Robert B., Jr., ed. *American Federalism: A New Partnership for the Republic*. San Francisco: Institute for Contemporary Studies Press, 1982.

Kettl, Donald F. *Managing Community Development in the New Federalism*. New York: Praeger, 1980.

Martin, Roscoe. *The Cities and the Federal System*. New York: Atherton, 1965.

Patterson, James T. *The New Deal and the States: Federalism in Transition*. Princeton, N.J.: Princeton University Press, 1969.

Pressman, Jeffrey. *Federal Programs and City Politics: The Dynamics and the Aid Process in Oakland*. Berkeley, Calif.: University of California Press, 1978.

Savas, E. S. *Privatizing the Public Sector*. Chatham, N.J.: Chatham House Publishers, Inc., 1982.

CHAPTER 5

POLITICAL SOCIALIZATION, OPINION FORMATION, AND PARTICIPATION

Political Socialization ■ Agents of Political Socialization in the United States ■ The Stages of Socialization ■ Concluding Thoughts about Political Socialization ■ American Political Culture ■ Public Opinion: Expressing One's Views About Politics ■ Political Participation: How One Is Involved (or Uninvolved) in Politics

The Constitution and the federal system are formal, institutional agreements about how the American people will live together as a group of individual citizens. Chapters 3 and 4 were devoted mostly to an analysis of this whole system at what we call the "macro" level. We now want to shift our focus to the "micro," or individual, level and discuss *socialization—how individual citizens acquire societal values*. Of course, the quality of socialization has enormous significance for both society and our government. Widespread agreement on basic values is important: the society and the nation in which we live enjoy a measure of stability because there is substantial agreement in the United States on most basic values.

Americans have agreed as a nation to structure or restrict certain aspects of our individual and collective life. In addition to these formally imposed constraints, we are each affected by informal constraints that are products of our value and belief systems. If you are intrigued by the content of your civic values and curious about how you acquired them, then you will enjoy this chapter. Figure 5.1 summarizes the content of the chapter and

illustrates how the content of public policy is influenced by the socialization process.

POLITICAL SOCIALIZATION

The following verse from *Iolanthe II* was written by Great Britain's William S. Gilbert. He is best known, of course, for the Gilbert and Sullivan comic operas. The verse is clever, quotable, appealing, and wrong.

> I often think it's comical
> How nature always does contrive
> That every boy and every gal,
> That's born into the world alive,
> Is either a little Liberal,
> Or else a little Conservative.[1]

The error is found in the last three lines, for we are born physically and politically naked. We are not innately liberals or conservatives. Political socialization would be much easier to discuss if the process were as simple as Gilbert's lyric is appealing.

Richard Rodgers and Oscar Hammerstein were not only America's greatest Broadway musical

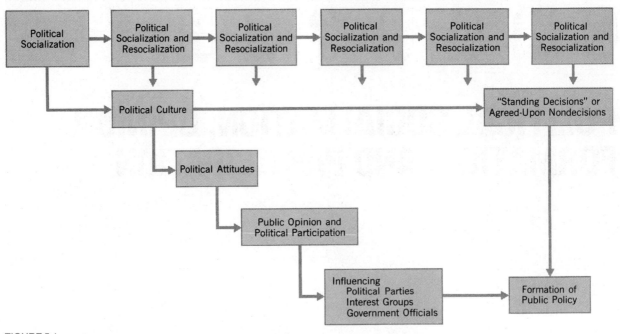

FIGURE 5.1

Political Socialization as a Lifelong Process: Implications for Public Policy

composer–lyricist team, but they were also far better students of socialization theory than Gilbert, as the lyrics of a song from *South Pacific* demonstrate. Recall that there were two love stories intertwined in the musical, both complicated by societal taboos against interracial marriage. The young American soldier fell in love with a Polynesian beauty; the young American Wave fell in love with a handsome widower whose first wife had been Polynesian. In a touching scene late in the musical, these victims of racism try to understand how they acquired their attitudes, and Lieutenant Cable sings "Carefully Taught."

> *You've got to be taught to hate and fear,*
> *You've got to be taught from year to year,*
> *It's got to be drummed in your dear little ear,*
> *You've got to be carefully taught.*
>
> *You've got to be taught to be afraid*
> *of people whose eyes are oddly made,*
> *and people whose skin is a different shade.*
> *You've got to be carefully taught.*
>
> *You've got to be taught before it's too late,*
> *before you are six or seven or eight,*
> *to hate all the people your relatives hate.*
> *You've got to be carefully taught!*
> *You've got to be carefully taught!*[2]

Of course, Rodgers and Hammerstein oversimplify a complicated process, but in many ways they portray socialization very accurately. Attitudes toward other races are largely a product of socialization, and the family is an important agent of socialization.

What is **political socialization**? It is *the process through which the individual acquires his or her particular political orientations—knowledge, feelings, and evaluations regarding his or her political world.* The verb "acquires" is used in the definition to avoid overemphasizing the role of either the individual or the agents in the process of socialization. The individual and the agents interact: people socialize themselves and are socialized by others. Political socialization is a special form of the more general process of socialization; the evolving social self acquires a political self, but the individual is largely unaware of either dimension of his or her development. Only in the classroom and in texts are the two distinguished and examined abstractly.

We are sure that socialization is important. With James C. Davies we believe that "An adult is the lengthened shadow of a child."[3] There are discontinuities in political socialization, however, and the process operates imperfectly in both totalitarian and free societies. In a totalitarian society

Long before entering school, a child knows that he or she is "an American." Patriotic exercises such as parades where the American flag is prominently displayed and saluted help ingrain strong feelings of nationalism at a very early age.

(whether socialist or fascist), the government must control the process, which is a formidable task. In a democratic society, the government leaves socialization mainly in the hands of family, church, schools, media, and individuals. This system requires far less government money and effort, but the content of socialization is much more variable and the balance between stability and change more precarious. That socialization is an imperfect process is demonstrated by "the generation gap." If each generation of Americans reproduced itself perfectly in the next, there would be no generation gap. To put it another way, a core of basic values is transmitted from one generation to another, but beyond the core there is variability within and between generations. The core of basic values transmitted through political socialization we call "political culture," a subject we will take up later in this chapter.

AGENTS OF POLITICAL SOCIALIZATION IN THE UNITED STATES

Socialization is a life-long process; it affects both the "apprentice" and the "mature" citizen. During a lifetime, the citizen not only acquires a political self, but he or she also adjusts the political self through resocialization. **Resocialization** is simply

a process of revising, replacing, or supplementing the individual's personal set of acquired political orientations.

How do the processes of socialization and resocialization work? Mainly they work through interaction between the individual citizen and agents of socialization. The most prominent agents of socialization are the family, schools, peers, and the communications media. At different stages of development, one agent of socialization may be more important than another. For example, the family enjoys a near monopoly of contacts with the preschool child. Figure 5.2 presents a simplified diagram of the relative importance of the agents of socialization throughout the life cycle.

The Family

"Just as the twig is bent, the tree's inclined," goes the old adage from Alexander Pope's *Moral Essays*. The importance of the family in political socialization rests on its near monopoly of influence over the preschool child. Moreover, the family has a central role in the overall socialization of the child. In teaching societal roles, values, and taboos, the family indirectly influences the quality of citizen the child will become. Ties to the family are emotional, highly personal, and have a special, enduring quality. Though Figure 5.2 shows the importance of the family in the socialization

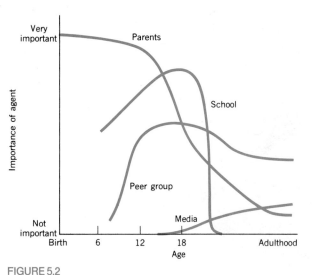

FIGURE 5.2

The Importance of Different Agents of Socialization through the Life Cycle

SOURCE: Bruce A. Campbell, *The American Electorate: Attitudes and Action* (New York: Holt, Rinehart and Winston, 1979), p. 128.

process declining rapidly in late adolescence and early adulthood, for some families interaction continues and there is a mutual influence between parent and child.

The family is most important in conveying consensus values to the child. In this chapter, by consensus values we mean generally accepted political values. While these values are first learned at home, they are reinforced by all of the principal socializing agencies. Long before entering school, the child will know "I am an American," "The United States is the greatest nation on earth," and "The American flag is prettier than the Liberian flag." The child will recognize the nation's heroes, will know about its greatest athletic and military feats, and will probably have visited some of the national patriotic shrines. Simple patriotism and chauvinism will often extend to identifying national enemies (the Russians, in recent years), accepting the American way as the only way, and rejecting virtually all other options for governance and economic practices (world government, socialism, and communism, for example).

The child's first authority relationships come in the family, and it appears that the quality of the relationship between parent and child has a continuing influence: adult males who had poor rela-

tionships with their fathers exhibit unhealthy attitudes toward authority. In the family, the child learns about authority, then transfers what is learned to other authority figures (teacher, principal, police officer, and government official). Many studies have shown that children develop a relatively positive view toward authority early in life, but as they grow older it gradually declines. Logic suggests that long-term citizen obedience to authority may be damaged if 1) the child is treated arbitrarily or capriciously and has no voice at all in family decision-making, or 2) if the family disintegrates as a coherent socializing agency, which some evidence suggests is occurring.

The preschool child also acquires from the family certain important identities: religion, race, social class, ethnicity, and region or subculture. Later, he or she will learn that the nation's Constitution is "colorblind" and will be taught the myth of a "classless society" in the United States, but the identities children share with their family (and others) will shape much of their political life. The reality is that social class and race structure opportunities in our society and have a profound influence on political participation.

We have argued thus far that the family is a very important agent of political socialization, which suggests that politics receives quite a lot of attention in the average home. This is not so. The average family devotes little time to political matters, and except for options that are out of the main stream (such as becoming a communist), parents

Children acquire a political identity just as they acquire a religious identity—through activities in the home.

do not typically care very much what political orientations their children adopt. The family is more likely to devote its guidance efforts to personality development, training, occupational choice, sex roles, and other basic social matters. What direct political content does the family transmit to the child? What influences the political content the family transmits?

All authorities agree that the family transmits basic political and social outlooks, including party identification, better than it transmits more specific and detailed opinions about policy questions. Beyond the rather clear parental influence over the child's party identification, the other measurable, direct, political influence of parents on children can be summarized in the following four statements:

1. The level of political knowledge in the family influences the level of political knowledge acquired by the child.

2. There is a low but positive association between the sense of political efficacy held by parent and child. Efficacy is a feeling that one can have an effect on the political process.

3. There is substantial indirect evidence that the family influences the child's future political participation. This is clearly demonstrated in the backgrounds of the nation's political leaders. Many leaders had politically active families.

4. Parents and children only moderately agree on specific policy questions of the day.

There has been quite a debate over the family's ability to transmit specific policy orientations to children, but there is some evidence to suggest it can. First, in transmitting consensus values to children, parents close many possible options. For example, during the decade-long struggle for a national energy policy, no one of note (and perhaps no one at all) suggested the nationalization of oil and gas deposits in the United States. Belief in a free enterprise system is such a strong consensus value that government ownership was never considered as a viable option to the free market system. Second, though the agreement between parents and children on specific policy questions is only moderate, the relationship is almost always positive. For example, in one study of the similarity of attitudes between parents and college-age

youths, 33 separate issue items were analyzed, 231 separate correlation statistics were calculated, and only 11 were negative. In other words, 95 percent of the time there was some agreement between parents and college-age youths. Persistence of attitudes and opinions from one generation to another is generally understated in empirical studies because 1) there are changes in the way the variables are measured, and 2) there are changes in the meaning of various issues over time. Life is simply not like a constant rerun of the same movie; parents face different political realities from children.

In spite of evidence showing the influence of the family on the child's political values, its real potential has never been realized. Why is this so? First, as already noted, politics is not a central concern of the family and little of its overall social guidance is devoted to political matters. Second, many explicitly political roles and relationships are reserved for adult life. Finally, though the family does dominate the life of the preschool child, the child is not insulated from other, outside influences. By the the time the child is five or six, the school, peers, and the media begin to intrude in the parent-child relationship.

The School

Few children in the world escape some sort of schooling prescribed by society and the state. In the United States, compulsory attendance laws and the development of kindergarten-to-twelfth-grade schools insure that most children receive formal schooling from the ages of five to eighteen. Over half of all high school graduates extend their education to the college level, and so for about half of the new adult population, formal education has been stretched out to seventeen or more years.

The school does a good deal more than transmit information to the child. School-related activities help build character and transmit good citizenship values.

Reinforcing Consensual Values The influence of formal schooling on political socialization is greatest (and least measurable) when it reinforces the consensual values held by the family and society in general. Long before civics courses appear in the curriculum (beginning in about the sixth or seventh grades), the school begins to indoctrinate the student in America's political culture. References are made to "our history," "our

The school is very important agent of socialization. Much of its influence is through ritualistic activities, such as the daily pledge of allegiance. These activities reinforce nationalistic values learned in the pre-school years.

revolution,'' or ''our country.'' Symbols such as our flag, our Constitution, and our Declaration of Independence are introduced, and the birthdays of national heroes often serve as national holidays. From grade school on, students are introduced to consensual political material in nonpolitical contexts. For example, political writings and presidential addresses may be presented as literature in an English course, and just about every student in the land will memorize Lincoln's *Gettysburg Address.*

Beyond the conveyance of consensus values, schools teach what one authority calls the ''ritualistic awe'' of certain practices. The singing of patriotic songs, the saluting of the American flag, and shared reverence for heroes and heroic events are examples of patriotic rituals that often evoke strong emotions. These activities will be performed thousands of times in homeroom, assembly, and athletic contests by the time graduation day arrives.

There are a number of other indirect political learning experiences in school. Early learning about authority and respect for authority learned at home are reinforced by the addition of new authority figures: the teacher and the principal. Students also learn to cope in some fashion with competition for grades, deference, and opportunities, and to cooperate with others in dealing with the system, in interpersonal relations with peers, and

in athletics. Finally, although many scholars have called them shams, students take part in their first elections and learn basic participatory skills in clubs and school organizations.

The Formal Curriculum   The formal civics curriculum taught by social studies teachers complements the informal indoctrination of students to consensus values. However, neither the curriculum nor the teachers influences students very much. Why are preadults not influenced by the civics curriculum and those who teach it? One common explanation is that these courses are redundant for most students; the course content is not new to them. According to advocates of this theory, these courses have an influence only on students coming from relatively deprived family and educational backgrounds.

One other explanation for the ineffectiveness of the civics curriculum may be that teachers are expected to teach an apolitical, noncontroversial course that is unlikely to challenge, inspire, or influence students.

The ''Hidden Curriculum''   In teaching students to be good citizens, the schools may wish to transmit the values of democracy, but one group of scholars argues that this is not possible because the school is not a democratic place. This line of reasoning stresses a ''hidden curriculum'' born of the school's need to maintain order or discipline so it can convey knowledge.[4] The hidden curriculum is summarized as follows:

1. It teaches hierarchical rather than democratic rule. Hierarchy is the notion of a line of authority.
2. The powerless student confronts a teacher who controls the curriculum and a principal who controls the building.
3. Instead of liberty, there is constant surveillance.
4. Instead of supporting the building of social bonds and relationships, the system encourages egoistic competition for grades and status.
5. Instead of a citizen's freedom to make choices and to react spontaneously, there is delay, standing in line, and a fixed curriculum.

Professor Richard Merelman and other scholars have questioned the hidden curriculum theory. He and other critics doubt that the schools are uniformly repressive, that the hidden curriculum is effective, that students accept a dependent status, and that any values learned through the hidden curriculum persist into adult life.

Social Diversity The social composition of the student body also influences the school's role as a socializing agency. Historically, the American public school system has been mass- rather than class-based. With few exceptions, schools served students from a specific geographical area, rather than a particular class, skill level, or religious group. (The major exception, of course, was segregation by race.) Even so, students today attend more heterogeneous schools than their parents and grandparents did. After World War II, consolidation of school districts began to change the size and location of schools, and in the 1960s and 1970s, desegregation orders redressed historical patterns of segregation.

In the mass-based, heterogeneous public school systems, students encounter a cross-section of the community's classes, races, and religions. As a consequence, they confront the stereotypes and prejudices transmitted from the family. The students in the classroom, in the hallways, and on the athletic fields are representative of the people students will meet as adults.

The Christian Right The Christian right has launched a concerted effort to correct what they regard as the decadent lifestyle being encouraged by the nation's public schools. This collection of fiercely independent religious groups is also known as the Moral Majority. The agenda of the Moral Majority includes restoring "morality" to the family and schools. Specifically, they advocate:

1. An amendment to the Constitution restoring the right to pray in school.
2. Local and state laws prohibiting homosexuals from holding jobs in which they might

Dissatisfaction with values taught in the public schools often leads groups of parents to form private schools that teach values more consistent with those taught at home. For example, religious private schools include prayer and Bible-reading in daily activities.

serve as role models for children, such as public school teaching jobs.

3. State laws requiring that biology courses teach ''scientific creationism'' on an equal footing with scientific theories of evolution.

4. That if and when sex education is offered in public schools, parents must consent to their children taking the course, and moral guidance must be given along with instruction on reproduction and contraception.

Not content with ''reforming'' the public school system, the Christian right has created a private school system of its own.

Parents who are dissatisfied with the public school system have an alternative: strict, basic education, taught by Christians in a Christian atmosphere, with large doses of patriotism. The movement has spawned its own publishing houses and firms that sell ''start your own school'' packages showing laypeople and ministers how to go about it. The early catalyst for the Christian schools was the *Brown* v. *Board of Education* (1954) Supreme Court decision declaring separate schools for blacks and whites unconstitutional. A second catalyst was *Engel* v. *Vitale* (1962), which declared the New York State Board of Regents' mandatory prayer for public school children unconstitutional. Forced busing rulings by the courts were another stimulant to the creation of Christian right private schools. Their enrollments had risen to 450,000 by the late 1970s (1 percent of the nation's school-age children).

It is important to note that the Christian schools are only one type of private school. Private and parochial schools have always been available and have provided different forms of education.

Whether public or private, schools still act as important socializing agents. To summarize:

1. A list of cognitive developments takes place in the thirteen years of formal schooling (ages five to eighteen). Thus it is difficult to isolate the influence of schooling over such a long period.

2. The school does not enjoy a monopoly of influence over the student, and the school may be in conflict with other agents of socialization. Other agents of socialization, such as the family and peers, may teach conflicting values.[6]

3. There is little overt political content in the entire schooling process; schools' direct impact on political orientation appears to be minimal.

4. The civics curriculum and social studies teachers have surprisingly little influence, but they do have some impact on the uninformed (primarily students who come from families with little formal education).

5. Schools teach students how to deal with authority, with peers, and with the system, skills that can be transferred to adult political life.

6. The school's greatest impact is in reinforcing the consensual values of the family and the community.

7. If control of the content of socialization is a high priority, perhaps private schools do a superior job because of their homogeneity, their clarity of mission, and their ability to deal with values more openly.

Peers

Peer relationships are typical *primary relationships, close, personal relationships that involve a high level of interaction. Secondary relationships are more formal interactions that occur between members of clubs, professional groups, unions, and business or trade associations.* Peer groups include the family, school chums, college friends, cliques, and also those neighbors and coworkers you get to know quite well. Peer relationships have potential not only for additional socialization but also for resocialization away from early family and school experiences. As shown in Figure 5.2, the importance of peer socialization surges in early adolescence, reaching a peak as the student enters junior high school and diminishing modestly as schooling ends and the responsibilities of adulthood begin. Though there are a number of peer relationships, most research attention has focused on those between students and between married couples.

Student Peer Relationships   Student peer interactions occur through social contacts, shared interests, and communications, most of which are not politically relevant. It is not surprising then that peer relationships have little influence on political orientations. However, on the whole, peers are more important to a teenager's political orientations than are teachers. Peers are a source of information and attitudes. They help one to define

During the high school years, peers are more important determinants of one's political orientations than teachers. Not wanting to be "different," many teenagers express the same opinions as their class leaders (the "in-crowd") on important political issues of the day.

the social world, conceptualize the social self, and define the range of acceptable views on issues. Jennings and Niemi found that high school seniors had an over-all higher level of agreement with peers than parents on two out of the five political matters examined and that they gravitated to the opinions of friends more than to the opinions of their social studies teachers.[5] Peer relationships do not structure political orientations as surely as they do social relationships, but they can be influential if an issue is highly relevant for students. If a particular peer group is interested in politics, its members are more likely to be influenced.[6]

Conjugal Socialization   The term *conjugal socialization refers to the influence of husband and wife on each other.* It will be no surprise to you that there is a relatively high degree of agreement between husband and wife on political matters; this is especially the case with party identification. But how do spouses achieve such high levels of political homogeneity? There are several possible explanations:

1. Selective mating based on political orientations.
2. Similarity in the social backgrounds of marriage partners, which increases the probability that political orientations will be similar.
3. Conversion or change after marriage, with one spouse influencing the other or both

spouses making adjustments in their political orientations.

There may be a bit of selective mating going on these days, but similarity in social backgrounds is a much more likely explanation of agreement between husband and wife at the beginning of marriage. However, even if the new husband and wife have similar backgrounds (even political ones), they are not carbon copies of each other, and so some change must take place.

There is pretty convincing evidence that change occurs in political attitudes after marriage. Some adjustment is made by both mates, but the husband appears to have the advantage. That men "should" take the lead over women in politics is a rather traditional way of viewing things, and men still seem to be having their way. But lifestyles are changing and with them values about political roles. Although wives have not yet achieved parity with husbands in conjugal socialization, the trend is in that direction.

There are, of course, other examples of peer socialization. Adults in the United States are quite mobile, and new neighbors, church parishioners, and coworkers become agents of change. After the school years, peer socialization diminishes only slightly in importance; it remains an important agent of socialization in one's adult years. Peer contacts persist as sources of political information and ideas and continue to influence political orientations.

The Communications Media: Growing in Influence?

This generation of Americans certainly lives in a media age. The major media are television, radio, newspapers, magazines, books, motion pictures, and billboards. There is little doubt that the media's role in the socialization process is becoming more important. However, we may always have underestimated the impact of the media, for several reasons: 1) we have not considered the indirect transmission of attitudes and values from the media by way of parents, teachers, and peers; 2) there are so many media sources that it is hard to distinguish the simple, direct effect of any particular medium; and 3) too often we have not asked people for the source of their ideas and values in a way that elicits the correct answer.[7]

As agents of socialization, the media differ from the family, teachers, and peers because of their passive nature. However, what the media lose through their passivity, they make up through their sheer pervasiveness. The average adult ''spends nearly three hours a day watching television, two hours listening to [the] radio, twenty minutes reading a newspaper, and ten minutes reading a magazine. . . . On an average day, 80 percent of all Americans are reached by television and newspapers.''[8]

Young People and Television   Recent widespread interest in the socializing potential of the media has focused mainly on young people and television. Given the time the average child or adolescent spends in front of a television set, the potential for influence has to be great. Consider the total weekly viewing time estimates for four preadult groups based on Nielsen's survey of February, 1979.

Children aged 2 to 5—32 hours 47 minutes

Children aged 6 to 11—29 hours 3 minutes

Female teens—24 hours 11 minutes

Male teens—24 hours 3 minutes

Those concerned about the influence of television on children have suggested family guidance in program selection, but such guidance is unlikely since TV viewing is not generally a collective family event. Parents report sharing less than 15 percent of their viewing time with their children.

Concern about the impact of television on children is not based on its political content, but rather on the pervasiveness of violence and sex. The concern is based on rather simple reasoning: 1) American television is saturated with sex and violence; 2) children and adolescents spend more time watching television than in contact with teacher, parent, or peer; 3) children and adolescents are highly impressionable; and 4) they are likely to imitate the antisocial behavior they view on television. This concern is not directly political, of course, but deviant behavior has political consequences.

On May 5, 1982, the National Institute of Mental Health released a report on 2,500 studies conducted since 1970 on the link between television and violence. A 1972 report had said that violence on television was conducive to increased aggressive behavior on the part of some children; the 1982 report concluded that there was overwhelming scientific evidence that violence on television could lead to belligerent conduct by children and teenagers.

This report, like those before it, drew an immediate critique from the networks and their National Association of Broadcasters.[9] Television is clearly very sensitive to its critics, and the industry has adopted a policy of self-regulation. Commercial time on children's shows has been cut drastically. Acknowledging a special responsibility for the content of children's programs, the industry has brought in consultants to help design ''prosocial'' programming. Since 1975, the networks have had a ''family viewing time'' policy, by which programs from 7:00 to 9:00 P.M. must be suitable for all groups.

Limitations on Media Influence   Given the power of the media to influence the behavior of children, one would expect this influence to extend to adult political behavior as well. But it does not, for several reasons. The media's inability to have a substantial positive influence on political socialization is a reflection of the nature of the media and the audience they serve. The audience seeks information and entertainment, not sophisticated analysis. The audience is not very political. About 23 million persons in the audience are functional illiterates. Even the information conveyed by the media is not retained very long. The media generally accept the values of their audience and tend to reinforce consensual values. Finally, much of the directly political content of the media is shaped for the medium's particular audience. Newspaper stories are short on background and analysis and long on simple facts. The television evening news is presented by media personalities in a string of "show and tell" episodes, the total content of which is only a fraction of one page of a standard newspaper. Radio must condense current national or local items into five minutes or less every hour. All of the media try to report news that they believe to be "newsworthy," which too often means the sensational and the unusual. A more extensive discussion of the influence of each type of medium on political behavior is presented in Chapter 10.

In summary, then, the media traditionally have been viewed as having a limited role in political socialization and resocialization. Although they vary, most media have a very limited political content. Even so, a wide variety of groups has expressed concern about the influence of the media, especially television. Furthermore, the importance of the media is likely to grow in direct proportion to the decline in social institutions like the extended family and the local community. If schools are distracted from their traditional role in the socialization process and the bond between parents and schools is further eroded, young people may acquire a greater part of their political orientation from the media.

Other Agents of Socialization and Resocialization

Events such as wars, depressions, and scandals may have such a profound impact on society and government policy that they change lives and political orientations. Children socialized under the presidencies of Eisenhower and Kennedy have a far more positive view of government than those who were socialized during the Johnson and Nixon administrations, which were much criticized and often involved in scandal.

The groups we belong to, whether we join or are born into them, may also shape our political outlooks. One's category in society may be so important and so distinctive that one becomes part of a *subculture*—that is, *a group within society that shares status, background, interests, and goals.* In our country, for example, there are Amish, Jewish, black, Chicano, and other subcultures. An individual may join the Boy or Girl Scouts, Junior Achievement, the 4-H Club, Little League, a labor union, or the American Bar Association; each can influence a person's attitudes and behavior in fundamental ways.

Contacts with government, especially during late adolescence and early adulthood, can affirm or contradict one's expectations about the political world. Unprofessional and arbitrary conduct by a police officer or judge could reinforce attitudes held by a minority or disadvantaged youth that government only serves the interests of the affluent. On the other hand, a sensitive and caring public official can have just the opposite effect.

Finally, a change in life situation or social role may affect resocialization. Not only one's marriage partner, but marriage itself has an impact, as do parental, home, and job responsibilities. Aging, all of life's different roles, the acquisition of property (especially a lot of it), changes in health, and varying opportunities can all produce a change in political orientation. Luther H. Hodges, a lifelong Democrat, former governor of North Carolina, and Secretary of Commerce under John F. Kennedy, told of an old friend who was a Methodist and a Democrat when he was young. Later, the friend got a little money, joined the Episcopal Church, and became a Republican. He had certainly been resocialized!

THE STAGES OF SOCIALIZATION

Thus far, we have focused our discussion on the different agents of political socialization, such as the family, school, peer groups, and the media. In this section, we focus more sharply on what we learn at different ages.

Every adult citizen has a cognitive and affective map of his or her political world; that is, each citizen knows about and has feelings about politics and government. True, some citizens have very limited and poorly drawn maps, but even they can survive and often live quite comfortably in the United States. There has been a good deal of research about the stages citizens go through in constructing their personal maps. There are five stages in the socialization process.

Stage one is "politicization"—developing an awareness of external authority. The child's initial experience with authority occurs in the family. To the child, authority figures are very important persons who do good. The father is thought to be the important symbol of authority in the family.

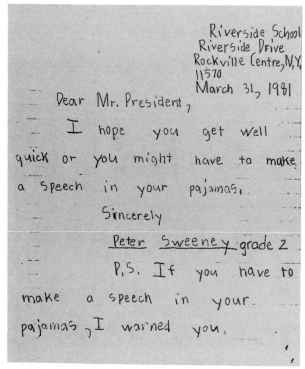

Children view the President as a "benevolent leader" who is hard-working, powerful, honest, intelligent, caring, and good. To maintain these positive feelings, school kids are often encouraged to write a letter to the President.

Gradually, the very young child becomes aware of other authority figures beyond the family, but at first he or she cannot distinguish their different types of authority. Other authority figures in the young child's life include the president and the police officer, among others. Some of the child's positive feelings about authority in the family are transferred to these other authority figures.

Stage two is "personalization." It is when all government is symbolized by persons. At this stage, the child sees the national government in the person of the president. The current president, after all, is highly visible, and past presidents are folk heroes.

The third stage is called "idealization," and the child develops a positive feeling for authority figures. The president is idealized. Children ascribe to the president almost God-like attributes. He is seen as hard-working, powerful, honest, intelligent, caring, liking everyone, and just a good person. When the first studies of children's attitudes were done, Professor Fred I. Greenstein used the term "benevolent leader" to describe how fourth to eight graders regarded President

Dwight D. Eisenhower. This early, positive view of the president and government declines as children move toward adolescence. Studies done all around the world show this decline in positive feeling.

The fourth stage is "differentiation and specification"—the developing ability of the child to separate persons from institutions and assign roles and functions to each. As children mature, they learn to differentiate the president from the presidency and the institutional apparatus of government. The child soon separates policeman from father and father from president by defining the role of each in society.

The fifth and final stage can be called "understanding"—the capacity to use acquired information and experience. By the middle teenage years, the child has acquired a good deal of information and experience. Abstract thought becomes possible. The average person can perform comparative analyses and assess political performances. He or she can also transfer what has been learned in one setting to another. By middle to late adolescence, this five-stage cycle is complete, the political self has been formed, and a newly minted citizen is turned out.

The idealized view of the president and government held by young children is much diminished by the time they reach high school. High school students can separate the president from the presidency; a student can be quite critical of Jimmy Carter or Ronald Reagan and still have great affection for the office of president. In its pure form, the idealized view is gone by adulthood, but a residual form remains. Some scholars have called the residual form "diffuse support" to distinguish it from the more specific support an individual might give to a leader, institution, or policy. *Diffuse support is the sort of bedrock support the government requires to persist through time,* the sort of support the United States has needed to weather a Civil War, many economic crises, and crises of confidence in leadership. Governments around the world covet the level of loyalty or diffuse support enjoyed by the United States.

CONCLUDING THOUGHTS ABOUT POLITICAL SOCIALIZATION

The entire process of political socialization is carried out by relatively free agents, none of which has political socialization as its most important function. There is little coherence in the process, but somehow, out of this "chaos," order emerges.

As one generation's political culture is transmitted to another generation, continuity predominates. There is a conservative bias to the process. Though generation gaps appear, and sometimes generational differences are newsworthy, it is fairly clear that today's young people are their parents' sons and daughters. The change that does occur is uneven, slow, and unsure. The process of socialization seems to work against rapid and uniform change and to promote stability and order. Although such values are widely held in high regard, those who are disadvantaged by current arrangements don't always think the cost of stability is warranted.

Socialization and the Women's Rights Movement

The constraints imposed by the socialization process are perhaps best illustrated by efforts to redefine the role of women in the United States. A cigarette commercial may crudely proclaim, "You've come a long way baby," but it is still clearly a man's world in most respects. In spite of affirmative action policies and the appointment of a woman to the Supreme Court, at the highest levels of government tokenism for women is the rule. There is an unspoken agreement among all of the agents of socialization that women have a well-defined role in society; as long as family, school, peers, and media reinforce each other,

true equality for women will come gradually and with difficulty. Because these agents of socialization are powerful reinforcements of traditional roles, change is difficult. To demonstrate how powerful they are, answer the following questions:

1. *Home*—How do the household duties assigned boys and girls differ? Which sex will be encouraged or permitted to take a part-time job first? Which sex will have more opportunities for independent learning experiences?

2. *School*—When you think about the following opportunities, which sex comes to mind: football quarterback? cheerleader? president of the class? signing up for a physics class? signing up for a home economics class? When a bus caravan is organized to follow a team to a big "away" game, is that game more likely to be played by the boys' football team or the girls' basketball team? Why?

3. *Peers*—Are peers more likely to direct sanctions against independent notions held by a boy or by a girl? What differences in peer expectations of boys and girls might one expect to find in the high school yearbook? Members of which sex are more apt to be tagged "most likely to succeed?"

4. *Media*—Considering television only, what role expectations (and therefore, apprenticeship suggestions) for women do the young

Television plays a very important part in the socialization process, particularly in redefining the roles of certain groups within society. Women newscasters, like Diane Sawyer, co-anchor of the popular CBS Morning News, have helped create a more positive image of women as politically informed citizens.

find in the top 15 television programs? On the basis of these programs, what skills should a young girl acquire?

The role expectations of young girls fostered by each of the agents of socialization are clear. Collectively, the pressures they exert on girls to conform to traditional roles are difficult to overcome. To make significant changes, girls *and* boys need to be exposed to adults playing nontraditional roles at home, school, and work.

The Role of Government

Government has very little direct influence on the socialization process in the United States, in spite of its nominal control of public education and its power to license and regulate the electronic media. Even if the national government wished to guide or control the socialization process to bring about some change in the nation's political culture, it would find this task costly and extremely difficult. The violence and repression required to create Nazi control over the cultural, economic, and political activities of the German people or to produce the cultural revolution of Maoist China are well known examples of the high cost of such experiments.

In the United States of the 1980s, the schools and the media are the agents of socialization most vulnerable to manipulation, which may explain why a variety of groups, liberal and conservative, partisan and nonpartisan, are so sensitive to trends in education and communications. However, the government has not resorted to censorship of school texts or the content of the media even though some of these groups have urged it to do so. Government has no incentive to do so, since it has little to fear from what routinely appears in these sources.

In the main, the socialization process in the United States is in the hands of family, schools, peers, and media, virtually without guidance from the government. This arrangement is part of our political culture.

AMERICAN POLITICAL CULTURE

Political culture is *the core of basic values acquired through political socialization.* The content of American political culture is shown in Table 5.1. Have we accounted for the essential values you associate with America? Does our political culture differ considerably from that of other nations?

TABLE 5.1

Basic Elements of the Political Culture of the United States

National Identity

Identity with other Americans as conationals

Prefer to live in the United States

Identity with national community: trust for leaders and government

Identity with local community; diffuse trust for other people and groups

Symbols

The Fourth of July

The Capitol; the White House; the Washington, Jefferson, and Lincoln Monuments

The Flag

The national anthem

The Constitution

The Declaration of Independence

Abraham Lincoln

Frontier heroes: Daniel Boone, Davy Crockett, etc.

Rules or Constitutional Principles

The rule of law; respect for law, justice, law enforcement

The Constitution as a basic set of rules

Popular rule
    Representative government
    The people ultimately control decisions and policy
    Political participation, feeling of competence, and feeling of efficacy

Rule institutions
    Congress and legislatures
    Legislative predominance over other branches of government
    Respect for and suspicion of the executive
    Federalism
    Competitive, decentralized party system

Beliefs

Liberty; free press, free speech, education; freedom preferred over economic security and duty to the state

Equality; equality before the law; reject aristocracy

Religion; belief in God; religious tolerance; altruism

Property; private ownership; free enterprise system; respect for individual achievement

SOURCE: Based on Donald J. Devine, *The Political Culture of the United States* (Boston: Little, Brown, 1972).

Integrated Political Culture

The United States has an **integrated political culture** rather than a fragmented political culture.

That is, *most people within the nation have similar or compatible orientations, and these are in basic harmony with existing political institutions.* The American national identity emerged before the separation from Great Britain, and though it went through a traumatic period (as noted in Chapter 3), during the Civil War, it survived. Much of the content of American political culture can be traced back almost two centuries. Much of the American belief system can be found in the Declaration of Independence, which had its roots in 18th century liberal thought.

We do have subcultures in the United States. However, their fragmenting effect has been muted throughout most of our political history. We have always had subcultures based on geographic region, race, ethnic background, and religion. None of these, however, seems opposed to the political values presented in Table 5.1; indeed, disadvantaged and minority citizens within the various subcultures frequently cite the values of American political culture when protesting injustice and seeking a change in policy.

Most Americans are able to articulate our nation's political values: freedom, equality, religious tolerance, and the private enterprise system. But they are less capable of applying these values in real life situations. Minority groups have suffered great discrimination at the hands of majorities who ignored the principles of equality and freedom because of overriding personal prejudices.

Nazis and Jews in Skokie, Illinois
In 1978, the city of Skokie, Illinois, became the site of a long struggle between two groups of citizens, Jews and Nazis, over freedom of expression. Skokie is a heavily Jewish suburb of Chicago; many of its residents are survivors of the Holocaust. The Nazi party of America applied to the Skokie city government for a parade permit for a march to celebrate the birthday of Adolf Hitler. The permit was denied, and the Nazi party went to court. Both the state and federal courts were called upon several times to rule on various facets of the march; finally, the right of the Nazis to march was upheld at every level, and all roadblocks were removed. The march never took place, though the whole effort to hold it had taken over a year of court action. Instead of a march, negotiations with the Nazis persuaded them to hold a rally in Marquette Park in Chicago. A small band of 20 to 25 Nazi party members held

their rally on July 9, 1978, surrounded by 2,000 to 3,000 counterdemonstrators shouting their disapproval. The American Civil Liberties Union of Illinois had supported the Nazi case in court, but ACLU support of the cause split the group's ranks and lost them many members.

The point this story illustrates is that many Americans say they favor freedom of expression until confronted with some message they do not agree with or want to hear. On the other hand, the Nazi party had to be aware of the reaction their request for a parade permit would get in Skokie. Wasn't this just a deliberate move to create a fight? In the past, the Nazis have made it clear that they would, if they could, suppress the very freedoms they were exercising in Skokie. Should those who would take away freedom have the right to gain the power to do just that? How far would you go in permitting others to express points of view for which you have no respect at all?

The freedom of Nazis to express themselves by holding marches and rallies has been upheld by the courts. Even though their ideas and values are very unpopular among most Americans, they, too, are protected by the basic constitutional principle of freedom of expression.

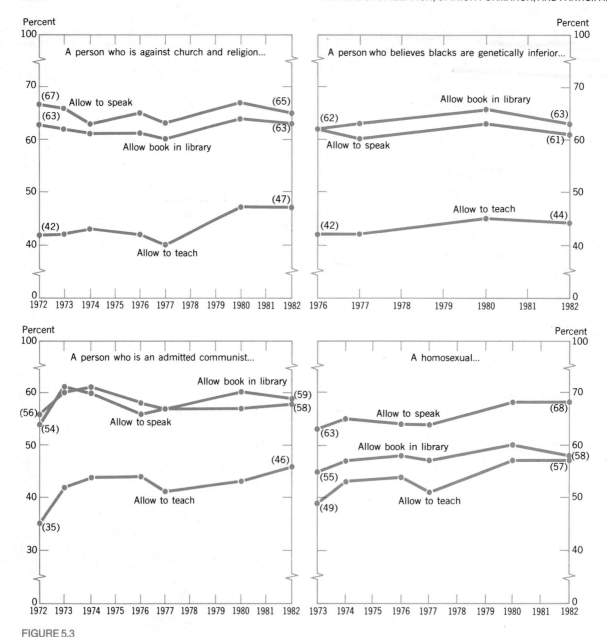

FIGURE 5.3

Tolerance Doesn't Extend to Teaching: A Comparison of Approval for Three Types of Expression by Persons Considered "Bad" or "Dangerous"

SOURCE: "Opinion Roundup, Civil Liberties," *Public Opinion*, 5 (October/November 1982), p. 35.

The inability of Americans to apply basic democratic values, such as freedom of expression, to concrete situations is evident in the data shown in Figure 5.3.

However, there is some evidence that indicates Americans are becoming more tolerant: 1) young persons are far more tolerant than older persons, and 2) college graduates are over twice as tolerant as persons with less than a high school education. The tendency of the young and well-educated to better apply principles to real-life situations has been noted by social scientists for a long time. Another point is also very important: political leaders have always shown a better grasp of the values in the American belief system than have the American people. That is, those who lead the people seem better prepared to preserve basic values than the people themselves.

PUBLIC OPINION: EXPRESSING ONE'S VIEWS ABOUT POLITICS

Through political socialization and resocialization experiences, a citizen acquires the broad political attitudes, orientations, values, and predispositions that characterize the dominant American political culture. These experiences dictate whether an individual will play an active part in the political process. An individual's **attitudes**, *the long-term, fairly stable product of political socialization,* generally determine whether he or she will express an opinion on a political issue. An **opinion** is a *short-term, relatively current evaluation of the political world.* Although not everyone expresses an opinion or participates in politics, those who do have a great deal more influence over public policymakers.

What Is Public Opinion?

V. O. Key, one of this nation's greatest political scientists, wrote, "To speak with precision of public opinion is a task not unlike coming to grips with the Holy Ghost." Key declined to give a formal, highly structured definition, but he described the concept as follows:

> *"Public opinion" in this discussion may simply be taken to mean those opinions held by private persons which governments find it prudent to heed. Governments may be compelled toward action or inaction by such opinion; in other instances they may ignore it, perhaps at their peril; they may attempt to alter it; or they may divert or pacify it. So defined, opinion may be shared by many or by few people. It may be the veriest whim, or it may be settled conviction. The opinion may represent a general agreement formed after the widest discussion; it may be far less firmly founded. It may even be contingent opinion—that is, estimates by decision makers of probable responses to actions they consider taking. Whatever the character or distribution of opinion, governments may need to estimate its nature as an incident to many of their actions. Probably any regime needs to heed at least some opinions outside the government; yet the range of opinions that enter into the calculations of governors obviously varies among societies with their political norms and customs.*[10]

Key stresses the links between the people's political opinions and the behavior of public officials. In democratic countries like the United States, the political culture requires officials to attend closely to the popular view, but even in repressive and totalitarian countries the leaders must be mindful of what the people think.

Of the many formal definitions of public opinion that abound in the texts, the most widely quoted is that by Bernard Hennessy: "***Public opinion*** *is the complex of preferences expressed by a significant number of persons on an issue of general importance.*"[11] This definition includes five elements. By "complex of preferences," Hennessy means the entire range of responses to an issue, including "for," "against," "don't know," and "don't care." Without "expression," an opinion is not public; we eliminate internal, private, or latent opinions. The definition hedges on the size of the "public" in public opinion by saying "a significant number of persons." The size may be of less importance than the effectiveness of those who hold it, and effectiveness may turn on a variety of things, including how strongly the opinion is held and whether those who hold a particular view on an issue are organized. An "issue" is a contemporary conflict or controversy. Rather than one public, there are many publics; a particular public is defined by the issue to which it is related. For example, the controversy over a woman's right to an abortion has been so widely discussed that we can say that we have a national public opinion on the issue. Much more limited publics would be concerned with creating a network of one-way streets in Tucson, Arizona, or raising the standards on the bar examination in the state of Texas.

What Public Opinion Is Not

Public opinion is not uniform, always accurate, or constant. Not all opinions held by persons are equally salient (important to the needs of the person), and behavior does not always follow opinion. Learned commentators sometimes talk about "the public" or "the American people" as if there were a monolithic public view of things, but there are many publics, and a public responding to a particular issue fragments into many groups. For example, there has been a general trend in favor of permitting euthanasia (removal of life-support systems) for terminally ill patients in the

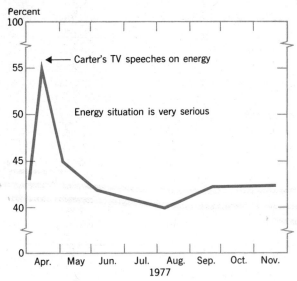

The decline in public approval of the Carter administration paralleled public unhappiness with the president's handling of energy. Only briefly after the major television addresses on energy did a majority of the public believe the energy situation was serious.

FIGURE 5.4

The Carter Administration's Failure to Educate the American Public on the Energy Crisis

SOURCE: Kevin P. Phillips, "The Energy Battle: Why the White House Misfired," *Public Opinion*, 1 (May/June 1978), pp. 11, 12; "Carter overall approval" based on surveys by NBC News/ Associated Press. "Energy situation is very serious" based on data from *Newsweek*/American Institute of Public Opinion (Gallup).

United States: 60 percent of a national sample favored the policy in 1978. However, among persons with a grade school education, only 41 percent favored the policy, while among the college educated, 69 percent supported it. In this case, grade-school and college educated individuals represent two different publics.

Public opinion is also not always accurate. Adolf Hitler's immense popularity in Germany during the late 1930s and early 1940s is testimony to the fallibility of public opinion. A recent American example can be found in energy policymaking. During the 1977 and 1978 energy crisis, a majority of Americans were of the opinion that the energy crisis was not real, even though President Carter and the oil companies tried very hard to convince them that it was (see Figure 5.4).

The myth that public opinion is static should also be discarded. As anyone can see, national public opinion fluctuates in presidential campaign politics as events, personalities, and issues change in importance. To consider another example, American attitudes toward the development of nuclear power as an alternative energy source changed sharply after the Three Mile Island nuclear power plant accident near Harrisburg, Pennsylvania, in 1979. Given such examples, how could one misread public opinion as static? One possible explanation is the failure to separate attitudes from opinions. The American people have a long-standing tradition of support for Congress as the authoritative voice in policymaking (an attitude that is part of our political culture), but they can be quite critical of how Congress is doing its job (a public opinion that varies over time).

Public officials who plan to keep their jobs must be sensitive to their constituents' beliefs about which issues matter most. All opinions are not equally salient. The American voter in 1980 was concerned about inflation, unemployment, foreign policy (especially the taking of hostages by Iran), national defense, and other issues. Reagan and Carter had to bet their political lives on the relative importance of these issues to the electorate. In the long run, inflation outweighed unemployment in the public evaluation of the two candidates, and double-digit inflation under Carter cost him dearly at the polls (see Figure 5.5).

In our earlier discussion of the public's inability to apply basic democratic principles to concrete situations, we illustrated that attitudes and opinions might be inconsistent. Another inconsistency is that behavior may not follow opinion. A classic experiment proving this point was conducted by Richard Lapiere in the 1930s. Lapiere took a Chinese couple all across the United States; they dined at 184 restaurants and stayed at 66 places offering overnight accommodations. Ironically, prior to their visits over 90 percent of these establishments had responded *negatively* to a questionnaire asking them if they would serve Chinese patrons![12]

Describing Public Opinion

If you wished, you could describe each member of your American government class on the basis of age, height, weight, hair color, religion, high school attended as well as other characteristics. After creating a profile of each class member, you could then tally all of the data and know, for example, how many members of the class had black, brown, blond, or red hair. Opinions are like that too, except that we have a different vocabulary for describing them. The following discussion is based on a vocabulary developed by Robert E. Lane and David O. Sears in their brief book entitled *Public Opinion.*[13]

The Attributes of Opinion *Direction.* One can be for or against an option, can approve or disapprove the performance of an official, or agree or disagree with a policy. People can also be neutral, undecided, or say that they don't know or don't care about an issue. Having no opinion counts, too, as we shall demonstrate below.

Intensity. The strength of a person's opinion is also important. A determined minority may influence policy and become the effective public when others don't feel as strongly about it. On the issue of gun control, for example, fewer people are opposed to it than are for it, but those opposed are

much better organized and keep such legislation from being passed.

The Context. How does an individual opinion fit with other people's opinions about the question? Describing the context of an individual opinion requires some analysis: What is the shape or distribution of other opinions? What is the modal position—the opinion held by most people? Are there two or more modes (distinctive options supported by large clusters of people)? What are the outlying or extreme positions on the matter? In 1965, for example, opposition to American involvement in the Vietnam War was an extreme position held by only a small percentage of the population. By 1974, it was the modal opinion.

Stability. For an individual, do the direction and intensity of the opinion remain about the same over time?

Informational Content. How well informed is the

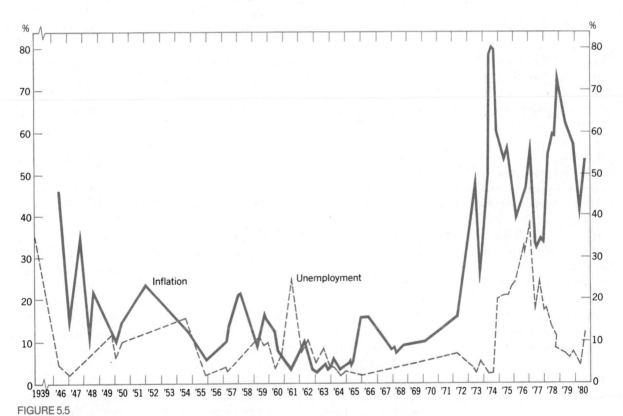

FIGURE 5.5

Inflation and Unemployment as the Nation's Most Important Problem, 1939–1980

SOURCE: Adapted from the *Gallup Opinion Index*, Report Numbers 150–161 (1978), pp. 15–16; Report Number 167 (June 1979), pp. 6–8; Report Number 172 (November 1979), pp. 16–17; Report Number 175 (February 1980), p. 11; Report Number 185 (February 1981). In 1981 the *Gallup Opinion Index* became the *Gallup Report*.

opinion? How many related details has the person mastered? Can the person assess the implications of a policy, action, or event?

Organization and Consistency. Is the opinion integrated with or isolated from the other important opinions the person holds? How broad is the reach of the opinion? For example, if you believe in a free trade policy, does it extend to Japanese automobiles, Italian shoes, and German steel, even when these American industries are having trouble competing with their foreign counterparts? And are the person's opinions consistent within issue areas such as health policy, economic policy, or energy policy?

The Policy Component. What in the opinion is doable? Can the idea be implemented? What policy stand can be inferred from the opinion?

Salience. Is this opinion or opinion cluster one that truly concerns the person? Is it a more important cue for voting, letter writing, or speaking out about politics than other opinions the individual holds?

With this new vocabulary in mind, how would you describe your own opinion about some current issue? By way of illustration, let us consider a hypothetical person, Jane Doe, and Social Security policy. Jane is 60 years old and a widow who was forced back into the labor market when her husband died. She owns a small house and regularly receives a small sum of money from her husband's life insurance policy. Suggested changes in Social Security policy are highly important to Jane (salience), because she has looked forward to retiring, perhaps even taking early retirement, and she is relying on Social Security to be the primary source of her retirement income. She wants the law (policy component) to stay as it is (direction), and she feels strongly about it (intensity). She knows that younger Americans don't want to see the Social Security payroll tax increased, and polls indicate that they would choose to reduce benefits rather than pay higher taxes. She also knows, however, that there are many other people her age and older who feel as strongly as she does (context). She and others like her have held their opinion for some time, and it has grown stronger as they have neared retirement (stability). Jane may not think in terms and phrases such as "actuarially unsound," "trust funds," and "indexed to the cost of living," but she knows what she wants the government to do and feels that the government will betray her and others like her if it

tampers with Social Security (informational content). Almost every other opinion Jane has is linked in some way to her fears about the Social Security system (organization and consistency). We could of course have written this hypothetical case from the point of view of a young, single, relatively affluent Jane Doe who feels she is being taxed to death. How would that description be different?

Patterns of Public Opinion

Politicians and governments also do the sort of opinion analysis that we have outlined above. In a democratic nation, they know that they must respond to the distribution of public opinion to survive. Consequently, it is important that policymakers know how to read and interpret different patterns of public opinion, such as the four shown in Figure 5.6. The first model illustrates supportive consensus. Eighty percent of the individuals surveyed agree or strongly agree on some issue. Presidential administrations typically enjoy a supportive consensus when a foreign policy crisis occurs, but such public approval may not be sustained. President Truman received wide public support for an American "police action" when North Korea invaded South Korea in 1950, but two years later the war was very unpopular and had become "Truman's war." The pattern was repeated with Lyndon Johnson and the war in Vietnam and Jimmy Carter and the hostages in Iran.

A great deal of policymaking at the national, state, and local levels occurs in the context of a permissive consensus. Note that 40 percent are neutral and those with strong opinions on both sides of the controversy total only 17 percent. Such a distribution of opinion gives a great deal of latitude to those who formulate and implement policy. The efforts to deregulate the nation's airline, trucking, and railroad industries took place largely in the permissive consensus mode of national opinion. For example, most Americans cared little about the new policy permitting the airlines to drop many of their unprofitable routes, although some small communities were left with limited or no service. However, if in the long run, airline service costs more and proves less efficient, public opinion on the issue may change.

The last two models illustrate bimodal and multimodal distributions of opinion. In these, diverse opinions are more evident. The bimodal model

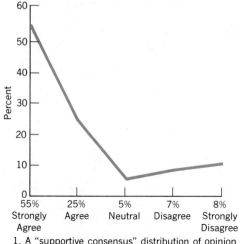

1. A "supportive consensus" distribution of opinion

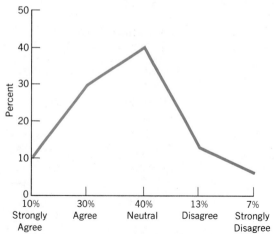

2. A "permissive consensus" distribution of opinion

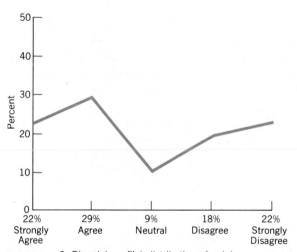

3. Bimodal conflict distribution of opinion

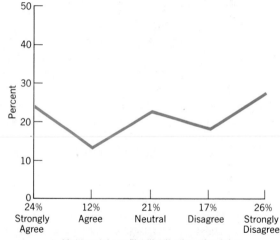

4. Multimodal conflict distribution of opinion

FIGURE 5.6

Patterns of Public Opinion: Four Models

SOURCE: Bernard Hennessy, *Public Opinion*, 4th ed. (Monterey, Calif.: Brooks/Cole Publishing Company, 1981), pp. 83–85.

approximates the distribution of opinion toward President Reagan's "economic recovery" policy in mid-1981. A slim majority of the people (51 percent) either strongly favored cuts in federal spending tied to a 30 percent, across-the-board tax cut over three years, or they were willing to try that policy and give the president a chance. A few people (9 percent) had no view on the issue or were unable to calculate their own response to the policy debate. Finally, a significant minority (40 percent) of the public was opposed somewhat or

very much to the Reagan policy. Note that neither the president nor his opposition could afford to alienate the moderates. In Congress, both sides worked hard to woo the center of opinion.

Perhaps the national struggle between the "freedom of choice" and "right-to-life" views on abortion fits the multimodal model reasonably well. The pro-choice side won its policy victory in the Supreme Court decision *Roe* v. *Wade* (1973), but since that time a strong opposition has emerged. The absolute right to an abortion does

Selling Reaganomics Via Symbolic Politics: Changing Political Attitudes

Former President Jimmy Carter was sold on the importance of political symbolism. At his inauguration, he and the first lady got out of their limousine and *walked* part of the way to the reviewing stand. On other occasions, Carter carried his own suitcase and clothes bag; he wore a sweater and dressed informally for a televised "fireside chat" with the people; and he frequently visited small towns, attended town meetings, and stayed overnight in the homes of "common folks." These were to be symbols of the personalization of the presidency. With the defeat of Carter, such professed modesty disappeared, and Washington society seemed absolutely delighted when what they regarded as a "proper dignity" was restored to the White House.

After all, it seemed, the country had paid long enough for the sins of Lyndon Johnson and Richard Nixon under Gerald Ford and Jimmy Carter; it seemed the time had come for the United States to take pride in itself again, act like the world leader it is, and restore pomp, ceremony, and elegance to events at the White House. The Reagans appreciated the good life and knew how to entertain. The White House was redecorated; expensive new china was ordered; and first lady Nancy Reagan appeared only in the most expensive designer gowns and jewelry (sometimes donated or loaned for the occasion). But what Washington society fully appreciated, the American public did not, and pretty soon the media began to carry a chorus of criticism of the "Louis XIV manner" of the Reagan White House. The press secretary regularly answered the critics, and occasionally the president made a comment in defense of himself or his wife.

Criticism of the president, his family, and the way the White House is run is an old American habit, but the Reagan Administration was particularly vulnerable to this criticism because of cuts being made in social services for the poor and threatened cuts in programs for the elderly and disabled. Of all the groups hurt by program cutbacks in the early Reagan years, blacks suffered the most, and of all social groups this group had been the least supportive of Reagan in the 1980 election.

The image of President Reagan as insensitive to the poor and minorities had to be corrected before the midterm elections of 1982. White House political advisers planned a series of media events in early May. On May 3, the Reagans went to visit Barbara and Phillip Butler, two printers employed by the national government. On January 30, 1977, after the Butlers moved into an attractive subdivision of College Park, Maryland, a young Klansman had burned a cross in their yard. The matter had just returned to public attention because the Butlers had won a civil suit against the offender, but he was nowhere to be found to pay the award. The Reagans spent about 20 minutes alone with the Butlers. The president afterwards said to reporters waiting outside that he had told them "how much I regretted any unpleasantness that they may have had because there shouldn't be any place in our country for that sort of thing."[1]

One week later, on May 10, the president was in Chicago to speak to the students of Providence St. Mel High School. The predominantly black Roman Catholic school had been featured on the CBS news program "Sixty Minutes" because of its remarkable record of success in spite of cuts in support by both the church and government. Fundraising efforts by teachers, students, and administrators plus corporate donations had kept the school open. In a 45-minute question-and-answer session with the students, the president spoke of his personal commitment to racial equality and assured his audience that most people in America shared this view. In response to one question, the president said he had made an error when earlier in the year he had agreed to extend tax-exempt status to private segregated schools. He said he was just trying to reform the Internal Revenue Service and that he didn't know that there were any segregated schools left.[2]

The visits to the Butlers and to St. Mels were only two events in a crowded spring schedule of getting the president out among the people to demonstrate his concern for the poor and minorities. At stake in the whole enterprise was the president's program for economic recovery. No one at the White House believed that Reagan could win over blacks or the very poor, but they did believe that he could somewhat reduce their opposition to Republican and conservative Democratic congressional candidates running and in November of 1982. These media events were also staged for the benefit of middle and upper class whites. Reagan had little hope of their continued support if this image of his lack of concern for the genuinely needy and for victims of discrimination persisted.

As this story demonstrates, elected officials are well aware that they must respond to public opinion, particularly if the opinion is strongly expressed by those who are most likely to be active participants in the political process.

[1]New York *Times*, May 4, 1982, B8.
[2]New York *Times*, May 11, 1982, B13.

not appear to have majority support in the 1980s, although majorities do appear for abortions under some circumstances (if a woman's health is endangered, if she is a rape victim, or if she is likely to bear a deformed child). In this case, the multimodal model makes sense. On the abortion issue there is a large group of people who feel very strongly one way or the other and a smaller group of people who do not feel quite so strongly but still lean for or against abortion. Another large group falls in the middle; its position on the issue depends entirely on the way the question is asked and on the specific circumstances under which abortion would be allowed. For example, this group is in favor of allowing abortions for rape victims but opposes abortion as a method of birth control. The delicate balance between the two sides of this issue can probably be disturbed by any major event that shocks the center group.

The Role of Public Opinion in a Democracy

All public officials, especially in a democracy, need accurate information about what the public wants from its government. Policymakers receive many expressions of personal opinion from individuals, many resolutions from organized groups, and much advice from editorial writers in the media. Presidents and legislators order summaries of their mail, tabulations of telephone calls, and clippings of newspapers, and they have advisers to maintain liaisons with interest groups, constituents, and the various parts of the bureaucracy. Members of Congress take every opportunity to go home and listen to everybody who will tell them what public officials should be doing. Nevertheless, one of the most frequent public criticisms of government officials is that they have lost touch with the people or that they just don't listen.

To tap public opinion, policymakers rely upon a wide variety of *formal and informal measures*. *Formal measures are expressions of opinion to which the government must legally respond.* Examples are primaries, elections, and referenda, because these pick candidates, choose many of our leaders, and change policy. Slightly less important but no less formal and legal are measurements of public opinion from public hearings, citizen's advisory boards, and petitions. *Informal measures* are expressions of public opinion *that have no official status.* Polls are an example. Although the government purchases many polls and leaders certainly pay attention to them, they are not legally binding.

Public Opinion Measurement: Polls, Pollsters, and Predictions

Modern public opinion polling is a direct descendant of *straw polls, informal assessments of public opinion taken by newspapers beginning early in the nineteenth century.* Scientifically speaking, however, there is little relationship between straw polls and those taken by reputable firms such as the American Institute of Public Opinion (the Gallup poll). Modern pollsters draw random samples that permit them to make accurate estimates of public opinion. They are skilled at measuring the public's real attitudes and opinions, and the best pollsters can interpret the data they collect. Unfortunately, unscientific straw polls are still used, largely by the media, for a variety of purposes. They are accurate only if those who take them are truly lucky. The American Broadcasting Company took a straw poll (primarily as a promotional device) on October 28, 1980, asking their viewers to call one of two numbers depending on whether they thought Carter or Reagan had won the presidential debate. Reagan emerged the overwhelming victor, but the poll was much criticized by professional pollsters and Democratic partisans because of its unscientific and misleading nature.

The first public opinion polls were taken in 1935. Now polls are key ingredients in any election campaign. Just about every campaign conducted in this country today relies on at least one poll, and major candidates purchase several at successive intervals. Most nationwide public opinion polls are based on approximately 1500 interviews conducted in person or over the telephone.

Pollsters erroneously predicted Thomas E. Dewey as the victor over Harry S. Truman in the 1948 presidential election.

The size of the sample is not as important as is the way the respondents are chosen, however. As stated earlier, random samples are preferable.

Pollsters have had a few embarrassing moments since 1935. Almost all of the pollsters were wrong in 1948, predicting incorrectly that Republican presidential candidate Thomas E. Dewey would defeat the incumbent president, Harry S. Truman. The 1948 error occurred on the sampling technique being used at that time and the pollsters' failure to measure late shifts of the voters toward Truman. Since 1948 the Gallup poll has had an average error of only 1.6 percent in both presidential and congressional elections. The last-minute collapse of support for President Jimmy Carter led many columnists to charge that the polls had been wrong in 1980—a Reagan win was predicted but in a close election. The pollsters, however, had recorded massive losses for Carter on the weekend before the election, especially among the "undecided voters." Both Carter and Reagan were told what the election outcome would be by their personal campaign pollsters a day or two before the election.

The Dynamics of Public Opinion Formation and Change

When a major policy change is initially suggested, it usually gets one of two receptions: 1) no one takes it seriously, or 2) it is viewed as heretical, so at odds with past practices that it is highly controversial. For example, when the idea of Social Security was first discussed in the United States, its advocates were called socialists. In the depths of the Depression, Social Security was put on the legislative agenda, groups chose sides, and a national debate began. What had been politically controversial suddenly became a serious matter of debate. During the debate, information on the issue was widely shared, and a more informed public emerged. Ultimately, in 1935, a bitter, partisan debate in Congress concluded with the passage of the Social Security Act of 1935. With passage by Congress, Social Security gained a sort of special legitimacy; the debate had officially ended. The new system was gradually accepted by the American people and is now taken for granted. That which had been heresy became the new orthodoxy, a policy so widely and positively accepted that those who would change it today would be called political heretics. As this example illustrates, the cycle of idea (heresy), proposal, debate,

resolution (policy), and acceptance (tradition) seems to characterize all major policy changes.

The rise and fall of Truman, Johnson, Nixon, and Carter illustrate how quickly public opinion can change. In each case, the public's opinion of presidential performance changed from highly positive to highly negative over the course of their administration (see Figure 5.7). Often such major shifts in the direction and intensity of public opinion occur in reaction to major changes in policy.

POLITICAL PARTICIPATION: HOW ONE IS INVOLVED (OR UNINVOLVED) IN POLITICS

Political participation and public opinion are related. Citizens with strong opinions are more likely to participate in the political process than those with only weak opinions or no opinions at all.

What Is Political Participation?

By political participation, we mean actions taken by individual citizens to influence the selection of governmental decisionmakers or to influence the decisions made by the decisionmakers. Therefore, we define **_political participation_** as *actions taken indirectly or directly to influence policy.*

What sorts of actions are included in political participation? On this question there is some disagreement among the authorities. An early work

Polls often influence whether a president will seek reelection. After a careful analysis of public opinion surveys, President Lyndon Johnson decided against seeking a second term.

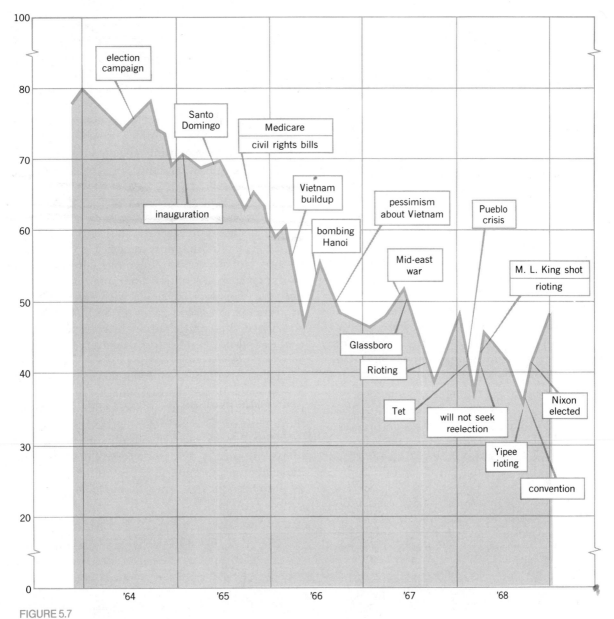

FIGURE 5.7

President Johnson's Approval Ratings

SOURCE: *Gallup Opinion Index*, Report Number 182 (October/November 1980), p. 25.

on political participation in America by Lester W. Milbrath emphasized electoral activities and classified people into types using the metaphor of a Roman gladiatorial contest. Milbrath applied the term "apathetics" to persons not even in the political arena, about one-third of the adult population. "Spectators" were persons only minimally involved in politics, about 60 percent of the American adult population. "Gladiators," the active

combatants, comprised about 5 to 7 percent of the adult population.[14]

In *Participation in America,* Sidney Verba and Norman H. Nie propose quite a different view of "activity." They go beyond electoral activities to include participation in organizations and other efforts designed to directly influence decisionmakers. They identify six different types of participators:

1. The *inactives* (22 percent) take almost no part in political life. Only a few vote, and those who do vote only occasionally.

2. *Voting specialists* (21 percent) vote in presidential and local elections but do almost nothing else.

3. *Parochial participants* (4 percent) take the initiative needed to contact government officials, but only when their own personal needs require that they take action. They vote at approximately the national average, but no better.

4. *Communalists* (20 percent) work with others in their community, form groups, or contact government officials to solve problems, but they abstain from all forms of partisan and campaign activity except voting.

5. *Campaigners* (15 percent) are the exact opposite of the communalists. They are very active in political campaigns but abstain from joining community organizations and community problem-solving efforts.

6. *Complete activists* (11 percent) engage in all types of activities with great frequency. They combine characteristics of the communalists and the campaigners, but they are more active than either of these groups in their special forms of participation.[15]

Verba and Nie were unable to classify about 7 percent of their sample into their types of participants.

Regardless of which classification scheme one uses (Millbrath's or Verba and Nie's), two major points can be made about Americans' political participation. First, few Americans are full participants ("gladiators" or "complete activists"). Second, many Americans are either nonparticipants or, at best, part-time participants.

Neither of these classifications recognizes *unconventional participation, types of political participation that have not gained wide acceptance in the United States, such as violence, civil disobedience, and protest behavior.* In spite of the fact that our nation emerged out of a revolution, most Americans vehemently oppose violence (riots, burnings, physical confrontations, assassination attempts) as a form of political expression. Usually such extreme forms of participation are engaged in by those who are convinced that participation in conventional activities will not be effective in getting their views across to policymakers or the public.

Civil disobedience (willful breaking of a law and acceptance of the consequences) is somewhat more acceptable than violence. The civil rights movement of the 1960s popularized this form of participation as blacks willfully disobeyed laws that were racially discriminatory. The civil rights movement also popularized protest activities such as marches, pickets, sit-ins, and economic boycotts.

Few Americans are as politically active as these poll workers in Boston. Many Americans are either inactive or at best part-time participants in the political process.

Only a very small percentage ever engages in any of these unconventional political activities. However, throughout our nation's history, these activities have been used by individuals and groups excluded from conventional forms of participation.

Constraints on Participation

The Constitution of 1787 delegated to the state governments the authority to grant the right to vote to their citizens. It has been estimated that nationwide only 1 out of every 30 adults was qualified to vote under the first state laws. Although suffrage (voting) laws varied a bit from state to state, the general effect was to limit voting to white, "good" or religious, property-owning men. Gradually, over the course of our nation's history, we have extended the right to vote to groups initially excluded from the electoral process:

1. The religious or "good reputation" requirements disappeared quickly.

2. The property ownership requirement was gradually changed in many states to include all taxpayers, and both requirements had generally disappeared by 1850. By that date, all adult white males could vote.

3. Ratification of the Fifteenth Amendment in 1870 constitutionalized suffrage for black males. With the end of Reconstruction, however, the South systematically disenfranchised blacks.

4. After a long campaign, women were enfranchised with the ratification of the Nineteenth Amendment in 1920.

5. First in a series of court decisions and then through legislation, the barriers to black voting were removed. The decisive legislation (and one of the most effective acts ever passed by Congress) was the Voting Rights Act of 1965.

6. In 1971 the Twenty-Sixth Amendment extended voting rights to people 18 years of age and older.

The remnants of the once extensive list of voting constraints are that a person be: 1) 18 years of age or older, 2) an American citizen, 3) registered, and 4) a resident for a minimum of 30 days. The only other requirements are that a person not be a convicted felon or be institutionalized (confined in a mental institution). Already, a number of recommendations as to how several of these remaining constraints can be loosened have been made.

Never have so many Americans been legally eligible to vote. To minimize the difficulty of registration, many states have provided for deputy registrars and mobile registration units that go from door to door or set up in shopping centers. Some states have registration by mail, and a few states have adopted election-day registration. Since we are a seminomadic people, the residency requirement poses a burden to some otherwise eligible voters, but the residency requirement of 30 days is nothing more than a decent length of time to permit the registrars to update their computer tapes of eligible voters.

Some leaders have argued that in order to increase turnout, the national government should assume the responsibility of registering all citizens and residency requirements should be dropped. However, based on previous experiments at the state level, it is unlikely that these reforms would greatly increase voting levels. In 1976, turnout declined in states that handled voter registration by mail, and the two states that allowed election-day registration experienced only modest increases.[16] In fact, as constraints on voting have been removed, turnout has declined steadily (see Table 5.2). It appears that legal or procedural barriers are sometimes less important determinants of political participation than factors such as income, race, ethnicity, gender, age, or geographic location.

Factors Influencing Political Participation

Class and socioeconomic status (SES) are by far the most important factors influencing political participation in the United States. No matter how we measure SES, those with higher status (usually college graduates) are more likely to participate than those with lower status. Furthermore, higher status persons are most likely to control or dominate the portions of the election system that narrow the final choice for their fellow citizens: voting in primaries, participating in party caucuses, and running the affairs of political parties.

Members of racial and ethnic groups participate at lower rates than their fellow citizens if they are relative newcomers to the country or constitute a deprived subculture. For example, relative

TABLE 5.2

The Cyclical Change in the Nation's Most Important Problem: Trend of Public's Top Concerns, 1935–1980

The question wording is: "What do you think is the most important problem facing this country today?"

Year	Most Important Problem
1980:	High cost of living, unemployment
1979:	High cost of living, energy problems
1978:	High cost of living, energy problems
1977:	High cost of living, unemployment
1976:	High cost of living, unemployment
1975:	High cost of living, unemployment
1974:	High cost of living, Watergate, energy crisis
1973:	High cost of living, Watergate
1972:	Vietnam
1971:	Vietnam, high cost of living
1970:	Vietnam
1969:	Vietnam
1968:	Vietnam
1967:	Vietnam, high cost of living
1966:	Vietnam
1965:	Vietnam, race relations
1964:	Vietnam, race relations
1963:	Keeping peace, race relations
1962:	Keeping peace
1961:	Keeping peace
1960:	Keeping peace
1959:	Keeping peace
1958:	Unemployment, keeping peace
1957:	Race relations, keeping peace
1956:	Keeping peace
1955:	Keeping peace
1954:	Keeping peace
1953:	Keeping peace
1952:	Korean War
1951:	Korean War
1950:	Labor unrest
1949:	Labor unrest
1948:	Keeping peace
1947:	High cost of living, labor unrest
1946:	High cost of living
1945:	Winning war
1944:	Winning war
1943:	Winning war
1942:	Winning war
1941:	Keeping out of war, winning war
1940:	Keeping out of war
1939:	Keeping out of war
1938:	Keeping out of war
1937:	Unemployment
1936:	Unemployment
1935:	Unemployment

SOURCE: *The Gallup Report,* Report Number 185 (February, 1981), p. 13.

to other groups, a smaller percentage of Hispanics register to vote. One reason is that newly arrived immigrants have not been fully socialized into our political culture. A second reason is often the language barrier.

Gender long has been a variable influencing political participation. For most of American history, women were excluded from voting and other forms of activity. Since gaining the vote in 1920, women have gradually increased their level of political participation. The gap between male and female participation rates (at least in terms of voting) has narrowed considerably in recent years; now they are virtually equal. This trend parallels another—the rising educational levels among women.

Age also has an impact on participation. Young adults (18 to 26) have the lowest participation rates of all age groups. Many in this age group are still in school or just getting established in their jobs and households. To them, voting is not as high a priority as these other activities. Participation increases steadily until about 50, after which it declines gradually. After 65, there is a steep drop, generally because of mobility and transportation difficulties.

There is also a social psychology to participation. Those who strongly identify with one of the political parties participate at higher levels than those whose attachments are not so strong and those who think of themselves as independents. Strong identifiers are psychologically involved in politics (that is, tell us that they are "interested" and "care a good deal about the outcome of an election"). They participate at higher levels than those who are less involved. On the other hand, some citizens choose not to participate at all, either because they feel left out of the system (alienation), do not believe their participation will make any difference (cynicism), or just do not care at all about politics (apathy).

Group membership and identification have some influence on participation, especially when the group's concerns are politically relevant *and* the citizen is very active in the group's activities. The simple act of joining a labor union does not indicate higher levels of participation, but being active in the union does. The more organizations a person is active in, the higher his or her level of political participation is likely to be.

Geography or place of residence may also influence political participation. For a long time, political participation in the South was much lower than in the rest of the nation. Lower educational levels, lack of a strong, competitive two-party system, and the exclusion of blacks from the political process are all reasons for this regional variation. All of these factors have changed dramatically,

TABLE 5.3

The Decline in Voting, Presidential Elections, 1964–1980

Group	Percentage of Persons Reporting That They Voted				
	1964	1968	1972	1976	1980
Nation	69.3	67.8	63.0	59.2	59.2
Men	71.9	69.8	64.1	59.6	59.1
Women	67.0	66.0	62.0	58.8	59.4
White	70.7	69.1	64.5	60.9	60.9
Black	58.5	57.6	52.1	48.7	50.5
Spanish origin	*	*	37.4	31.8	29.9
18–20 years of age	39.2	33.3	48.3	38.0	35.7
21–24	51.3	51.1	50.7	45.6	43.1
25–34	64.7	62.5	59.7	55.4	54.6
35–44	72.8	70.8	66.3	63.3	64.4
45–64	75.9	74.9	70.8	68.7	69.1
65 and over	66.3	65.8	63.5	62.2	65.1
Metropolitan	70.8	68.0	64.3	59.2	58.8
Nonmetropolitan	66.5	67.3	59.4	59.1	60.2
North and West	74.6	71.0	66.4	61.2	61.0
South	56.7	60.1	55.4	54.9	55.6
8 years of school or less	59.0	54.5	47.4	44.1	42.6
9–11 years	65.4	61.3	52.0	47.2	45.6
12 years	76.1	72.5	65.4	59.4	58.9
More than 12	84.8	81.2	78.8	73.5	73.2
Employed	73.0	71.1	66.0	62.0	61.8
Unemployed	58.0	52.1	49.9	43.7	41.2
Not in labor force	64.6	63.2	59.3	56.5	57.0

SOURCE: William J. Keefe, *Parties, Politics, and Public Policy in America,* 3rd ed. (New York: Holt, Rinehart & Winston, 1980), p. 108. Modified from the *Statistical Abstract, 1981.*

* Not available.

however, and southern participation rates are rising. For the country as a whole, there is also a difference in the participation rates of those living in large metropolitan areas (big cities and suburbs) and those living in more remote, rural areas. Participation rates are higher in metropolitan areas where the population's educational level is generally higher, elections are more competitive, and distances to the polls are much shorter.

Finally, the type of election being held affects participation rates. For example, presidential elections draw a larger turnout than state or local ones. General elections draw a larger turnout than primaries. Partisan contests (in which candidates run with a party label attached to their name) are more interesting than nonpartisan ones, and people are more likely to participate when they perceive the contest to be important and close.

To Participate or Not to Participate: A Personal Policy Choice

Ultimately, the decision to participate is an individual one. But, as we have already noted, if a citizen chooses not to be active, his or her share of influence goes to others who do decide to participate. As Verba and Nie note: "above all, leaders are responsive to activists. If a particular citizen is not active, particularly in those modes of activity that communicate a lot of information about citizens' preferences, political leaders will pay attention to the preferences of those others who are active."[17] (See Figure 5.8.) Even though our belief system provides for political equality, if "the haves" participate more than the "have-nots," the probable result is greater advantages for those who already have advantages. The question remains: Do you want to be one of the influentials?

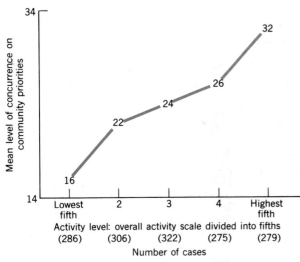

FIGURE 5.8

Individual Participation Scores as Related to Concurrence Between Citizens and Leaders on Community Priorities

SOURCE: Sidney Verba and Norman H. Nie, *Participation in America* (New York: Harper & Row, 1972), p. 305.

SUMMARY

Political socialization and resocialization are lifelong processes of transmitting political culture from one generation to the next. As the individual citizen acquires a social self, he or she also acquires a political self. Socialization is an unstructured process of interaction between the apprentice citizen and agents of socialization, the most important of which are the family, the school, peers, and the communications media. None of the agents of socialization has political socialization as its primary societal role. Each is virtually free of government guidance or control.

Political culture is the core of basic values the citizen acquires through socialization. The United States has an integrated political culture: most of its citizens share its core values and accept its institutional arrangement.

American political culture is a civic culture: popular participation and popular rule are important principles to which we adhere. It is the duty of public officials to follow the citizenry's preferences, and it is the citizen's responsibility to make these preferences known to public officials. The public formally expresses its preferences through elections and informally through personal communications and public opinion polls.

Another important component of American political culture is the "equality" principle: all individuals are equal under the law. It is clear, however, that some people's opinions are more "equal" than others. Those who are full political participants have more influence on policy than those who only vote or those who do nothing at all.

In later chapters of this book, you will see how political parties, interest groups, and public officials respond to public opinion and the patterned political participation of American citizens.

KEY TERMS

attitudes
conjugal socialization
culture
diffuse support
formal measures of public opinion
informal measures of public opinion
integrated political culture
opinions
political culture
political participation
political socialization
primary relationships
public opinion
resocialization
secondary relationships
socialization
straw polls
subcultures
unconventional participation

SUGGESTED READINGS

Campbell, Bruce A. *The American Electorate: Attitudes and Action.* New York: Holt, Rinehart & Winston, 1979.

Crotty, William J. *Political Reform and the American Experiment.* New York: Thomas Y. Crowell, 1977.

Dawson, Richard E., Prewitt, Kenneth, and Dawson, Karen S. *Political Socialization,* 2d ed. Boston: Little, Brown, 1977.

Gallup, George. *The Sophisticated Poll Watcher's Guide,* rev. ed. Princeton, N. J.: Princeton Opinion Press, 1976.

Lamb, Robert B. *Political Alienation in Contemporary America.* New York: St. Martin's, 1975.

Milbrath, Lester W., and Goel, M. Lal. *Political Partici-pation,* 2d ed. Chicago: Rand McNally, 1977.

Niemi, Richard G., and Associates. *The Politics of Fu-ture Citizens.* San Francisco: Jossey-Bass Publishers, 1974.

Public opinion polls are regularly reported in three journals available in most college libraries: *The Gal-lup Report, Public Opinion,* and the *Public Opinion Quar-terly.*

Rosenbaum, Walter A. *Political Culture.* New York: Praeger, 1975.

Weissberg, Robert. *Political Learning, Political Choice, and Democratic Citizenship.* Englewood Cliffs, N.J.: Pren-tice-Hall, 1974.

CHAPTER 6

POLITICAL PARTIES

What Is a Political Party? ■ Functions of Political Parties ■ Characteristics of the American Party System ■ History of American Political Parties ■ Structure of American Party Organizations ■ Decline of the American Party System ■ Future of the American Party System

We have all heard the expression, "There's not a dime's worth of difference between the Republicans and the Democrats." While a lot of folks agree with this statement, the truth is that to a large number of them, party is still an important cue in voting. A 1982 CBS News/*New York Times* survey asked the following question: "In deciding how to vote for Congress this fall, will the political party a candidate belongs to make a great deal of difference, some difference, or not much difference?" Almost two-thirds of those polled said that party would make at least some difference.[1]

Americans are also quite willing to use a party label to describe themselves. When asked by pollsters whether they consider themselves a Democrat, Republican, or an independent, over two-thirds report they are Democrats or Republicans (see Figure 6.1). But do most Americans *really* know what they are identifying with? According to Frank J. Sorauf, a leading expert on political parties:

It is unlikely that [the American adults who insist that they are Republicans or Democrats] have ever worked within the party organization of their choice, much less made a financial contribution to it. They would be hard-pressed to recall its recent platform commitments, and if they did, they would not necessarily feel any loyalty to them. Furthermore, they probably never meet with other Americans who express the same party preferences, and they would find it difficult to name the local officials of their party. In fact, their loyalty to the party of which they consider themselves "members" may be little more than a disposition to support its candidates at elections if all other considerations are fairly equal.[2]

In spite of their apparent lack of understanding of exactly what their party stands for or does and their low level of participation in party activities, most citizens still feel positive enough about one party to label themselves a member.

Americans' opinions about parties vary according to whether they are talking about elected officials or about themselves. On the one hand, they believe that party labels explain very little about elected officials' support for various issues. On the other, they perceive enough differences in the party labels to want to classify themselves and to

FIGURE 6.1

Partisan Identification in the United States, 1937–1983

SOURCE: George H. Gallup, *The Gallup Poll: Public Opinion, 1935–1971* (New York: Random House, 1972); George H. Gallup, *The Gallup Poll: Public Opinion, 1972–1977* (Wilmington, Del.: Scholarly Resources, Inc., 1978). The last reading on the graph is for January, 1983. We acknowledge, with appreciation, the assistance of the Gallup Organization.

use party label as a cue in deciding which candidate to vote for. These inconsistencies stem from the fact that we generally distinguish between the party in government and the party in the electorate. This distinction makes it very difficult to come up with a precise definition of a political party.

In this chapter, we define a political party; describe the typical functions parties play in a democracy; identify the uniquenesses of American parties; trace the development of our two-party system; describe the structure and organization of parties at the national, state, and local levels; examine various theories of party decline; and discuss the challenges facing parties in the 1980s. By the end of the chapter, you should have a much better idea of whether there really is any difference between Democrats and Republicans and what difference it makes to you individually and to the government.

WHAT IS A POLITICAL PARTY?

There is no universally accepted definition of a political party. In his classic parties text, V.O. Key defined a party as a loose association of persons who, through controlling nominations and elections, seeks to gain control of government and exercise power.[3] A leading political dictionary defines a political party somewhat differently: a *political party* is "*a group of individuals, often having some measure of ideological agreement, who organize to win elections, operate government, and determine public policy.*"[4]

The difficulty of devising a definition that applies to political parties everywhere is that "any one person's definition is likely to be rooted in a particular time and orientation [and political culture]."[5] For example, as we shall see later in the chapter, American political parties have unique characteristics that are rooted in our political culture. Recognizing the futility of searching for a single definition, many political scientists resort to describing the functions parties perform as a way of defining them.

FUNCTIONS OF POLITICAL PARTIES

The distinctive roles or functions of political parties include:

1. recruiting and training leaders and candidates.
2. nominating candidates.
3. conducting campaigns.
4. educating and socializing citizens in politics and public affairs.
5. organizing the government if their candidates win or acting as the loyal opposition if their candidates lose.
6. building coalitions, which help reduce the tensions produced by the many natural divisions in our society.
7. shaping policy alternatives.
8. simplifying policy alternatives for presentation to the electorate.
9. bridging the gaps between the three branches of government and, to a lesser extent, the gaps between local, state, and federal governments.
10. operating as instruments of democratic representation for the people to influence their government.

The role of parties in democratic societies is regarded as particularly important.

Functions of Parties in a Democracy

Parties are important for democratic government, primarily because they serve as a link between the people and their government.

As the principal link with institutions of democratic government, the parties perform three general clusters of tasks. They 1) select policymakers, 2) represent interests, and 3) manage the government by formulating, implementing, and evaluating public policy.

Selection of Policymakers Parties play a major role in recruiting, nominating, and electing candidates for public office. *Recruitment may involve going to a potential candidate and urging him or her to run, or it may involve making the party organization available to politicians who themselves plan to run.* In the 19th century, the parties had an iron grip on *nomination, the authoritative designation of an individual as a candidate for public office,* but direct primaries and modern campaign techniques have seriously weakened the control of party leaders over this process. Now the key role parties play is in *elections—the final stage of the leadership selection process, when public officials are officially chosen.* As we have already seen, voters often use party label as one cue in deciding which candidate to vote for.

Interest Representation Usually people join one political party rather than another because the party of their choice stands for something they believe in or is composed of people with whom they identify. In other words, they have an image of each party.

The *party image is the mental picture a voter has of a party.* Party image may encompass long-term, important policy stands; military involvements; major group loyalties or alliances of the party; economic disasters or successes; or the performance of the party in managing the government when in power. The image of the two parties held by the electorate varies in content and clarity. A small segment of the electorate has images of the parties loaded with detail and meaning, but the average citizen has only vague notions of the differences between the two parties. Image is related to basic partisan loyalty, for a major element of image is the citizen's emotional evaluation of what the parties stand for.

Characteristics most commonly used to predict a person's party loyalty are race, occupation, religion, education, and income (see Table 6.1). Others include age, gender, ideology, and place of residence. Of course broad classifications do not include every individual with a particular characteristic, and for some individuals, one characteristic is a stronger determinant of party loyalty than another (for example, gender over education or race over religion). Still, it is possible to note general patterns of identification with each of the two parties:

TABLE 6.1
Social Characteristics of Party Identifiers

	Strong Democrat	Weak Democrat	Independent	Weak Republican	Strong Republican	Others[a]	Totals
Race							
White	12.6%	23.0%	37.3%	15.9%	10.0%	1.4%	100.2%
Black	34.1	35.7	23.5	2.7	1.7	2.2	99.9
Other	4.5	39.4	36.4	9.1	1.5	9.1	100.0
Occupation							
Professional	10.2	23.1	38.8	16.9	10.6	0.3	99.9
Manager, official	12.0	18.4	43.0	13.7	12.7	0.4	100.2
Clerical, sales	12.7	22.9	39.5	14.2	10.5	0.2	100.0
Skilled, semiskilled	19.3	25.7	37.8	11.8	3.7	1.8	100.1
Unskilled, service	17.9	29.5	31.9	12.1	6.8	1.7	99.9
Farmer	19.3	24.1	21.1	22.3	11.4	1.8	100.0
Other (retired, etc.)	12.7	25.7	31.6	15.6	11.0	3.3	99.9
Religion							
Protestant	14.5	22.5	33.7	17.4	10.7	1.1	99.9
Catholic	17.4	31.9	34.5	9.1	6.1	1.1	100.1
Jewish	24.4	31.1	37.0	4.4	3.0	—	99.9
Education							
None through 8 grades	23.2	29.3	22.4	13.6	6.7	4.8	100.0
Some high school	21.4	26.5	32.6	13.5	4.4	1.6	100.0
High school grad	12.9	25.1	39.3	13.4	8.2	1.2	100.1
Some college	9.3	20.8	43.5	15.7	9.8	0.9	100.0
Baccalaureate degree	7.4	18.1	39.8	16.0	18.4	0.3	100.0
Advanced degree	12.9	28.6	32.6	15.2	10.7	—	100.0
Family Income							
$0–$2999	23.2	26.8	28.0	12.4	7.2	2.4	100.0
$3000–$5999	19.3	30.7	27.6	9.8	10.3	2.3	100.0
$6000–$8999	19.0	26.6	32.3	14.4	6.0	1.6	99.9
$9000–$12,999	14.3	24.6	38.1	14.3	6.6	2.1	100.0
$13,000–$19,999	11.0	24.6	45.2	11.6	6.3	1.3	100.0
$20,000 and over	9.9	18.5	37.4	19.9	14.3	—	100.0

SOURCE: Frank J. Sorauf, *Party Politics in America*, 4th ed. Copyright © 1980 by Frank J. Sorauf. Reprinted by permission of Little, Brown and Company.

SOURCE: Survey Research Center of the University of Michigan; data made available through the Inter-University Consortium for Political Research. Data are for 1976.

[a]Includes respondents who prefer other parties, who are apolitical, or who won't or can't answer.

Democrats: blacks; blue collar workers and farmers; Jews and Catholics; the less affluent and less educated; women; liberals; the young; residents of big cities and remote rural areas

Republicans: whites; professionals and managers; Protestants; the more affluent and better educated; men; conservatives; the elderly; suburbanites

From seeing who identifies with each party, it is easy to understand why the Democratic Party evokes an image of being the working class party whereas the Republican Party evokes the opposite image.

Those who prefer not to identify with either party (the independents) are most distinctive in their level of education (highly educated) and, in their incomes (also high). Younger voters tend to fall into this group as well.

A similar comparison of political *party plat-*

A party's platform, the statement of its positions on key issues, is generally drafted by the national party committee but is revised and finally adopted by the delegates to the party's nominating convention.

forms, statements of party positions on selected policy issues (see Table 6.2), reveals that parties also stand for different things, although at times, the differences may not be significant enough to please advocates of a "responsible" party system. A *"responsible" party system is one in which parties offer a clear choice on policy, and officials follow their party's line once elected.*

The difficulty of parties in two-party systems in presenting clear policy choices stems from their need to build a winning coalition, that is, enough supporters to elect enough of its candidates to implement the party's platform. Parties often must solicit support from the political center (moderates). Thus the Democratic and Republican parties try to appeal to all classes, races, ethnic groups, religions, and interest groups, although, as noted earlier, each party has a disproportionate share of one or more segments of each (see Table 6.1).

Regardless of the number of parties in the system, parties represent different types of individuals with different policy preferences. Party memberships and policy positions are constantly changing, and for this reason, public policy is constantly changing, too.

Government Management Parties, through their elected representatives, have a stake in making sure that government operates smoothly and effectively, lest the public lose faith in a democratic system. In managing government, the role of the majority (in power) party differs from that of minority (out of power) parties. The party in power seeks to implement as much of its party platform as possible. Generally it has the organizational advantage, because legislative leadership positions go to members of the majority party and because key appointments in the executive and judicial branches are made by the party whose candidate is elected chief executive (president or governor). The parties out of power criticize the policies proposed or adopted by the party in power. Their hope is that their criticism will swing public opinion to the extent that they will be voted the majority party in the next election.

There are several problems with these cut and dried descriptions of party roles. First, in multiparty systems (for example, Italy), the party in power may actually be a coalition of numerous minority parties. Second, in two-party systems, often one party controls the executive branch while another controls the legislative branch. Third, if the legislative branch is bicameral (composed of two houses), one party may control one house and another party, the other. Fourth, within the same house, legislators may not always use party label as their basis for voting. For example, a bloc of conservative, majority-party members may frequently vote with conservative, minority-party members, in which case ideology, rather than party identification, explains their vote on some policy issue.

Rarely can party leaders in democratic governments force public officials to vote a straight party line. What they *can* do is try to maintain a positive public image for parties in general by expelling incompetent, unethical, corrupt officials from government positions. Such was the case in the 1970s when Republicans and Democrats alike united to force President Richard Nixon's resignation after the Watergate scandal. As stated earlier, all political parties have a stake in maintaining public support for a democratic government in which parties play a significant role. The United States is one such government.

TABLE 6.2

The Party Platform Gap

The Democratic and Republican platforms for the 1980 campaign were even more sharply divergent than the two parties' nominees. Summaries of the major planks on economy, energy, and lifestyle issues.

Democrats	Republicans

The Economy

"The need to guarantee a job for every American who is able to work . . . is our highest domestic priority." The party pledges to take no action that significantly increases unemployment, and also it rejects high interest rates as a means to fight inflation. It endorses an immediate $12 billion anti-recession program to create at least 800,000 jobs. The Democrats call for tax cuts to aid low- and middle-income Americans and stimulate production as soon as such cuts would not be inflationary, and they seek to rebuild American industry by increasing productivity and minimizing the burden of government regulation.

"Unless taxes are reduced and Federal spending is restrained, our nation's economy faces continued inflation, recession and economic stagnation." The platform calls for a balanced budget, supports the Kemp-Roth three-year, 30 per cent cut in personal income taxes and seeks to limit government spending to a fixed and smaller percentage of the gross national product. It advocates indexing tax rates to protect people from "tax bracket creep" caused by inflation, supports tax incentives to stimulate savings and proposes to control inflation by linking the growth of the money supply to real economic growth. Jobs would be created by stimulating growth in the private sector.

Energy

"Conservation is the cheapest form of energy production." The platform proposes a massive program of residential energy-conservation grants. Federal funds should also be used to develop renewable resources, with a goal of using solar power to meet 20 per cent of U.S. energy needs by the year 2000. The plank would stop major oil companies from acquiring coal and solar-energy firms, would "retire nuclear power plants in an orderly manner" and would allow states to reject unsafe radioactive-waste dumps.

The party emphasizes energy production over conservation, proposes to repeal the windfall-profits tax, dismantle all remaining controls on oil and gas and revise "cumbersome and overly stringent Clean Air Act regulations." It advocates accelerated use of nuclear power and the development of breeder reactors.

Lifestyle Issues

Abortion

The plank rejects any constitutional amendment banning abortion and opposes restrictions that deny poor women government funding for abortions.

The GOP calls for a constitutional amendment to protect "the right to life for unborn children," supports curbs on public funding for abortion and pledges to work for the appointment of judges "who respect . . . the sanctity of innocent human life."

Welfare

The Democrats propose that the Federal government assume the state and local burden of welfare costs, reject reductions in programs for the needy for the purpose of fiscal restraint and support full funding for the food-stamp program. The party seeks to provide an "income floor" for the working and nonworking poor and urges that state governments disburse welfare payments equally to "stable and broken" families.

"The Democratic Congress has produced a jumble of degrading, dehumanizing, wasteful, overlapping and inefficient programs that invite waste and fraud but inadequately assist the needy poor." The GOP opposes federalizing welfare and rejects a guaranteed annual income that would "doom the poor to perpetual dependence." The party would tighten food-stamp eligibility requirements and end aid to illegal aliens and the "voluntarily unemployed."

(continued)

TABLE 6.2
The Party Platform Gap *(continued)*

Democrats	Republicans

Health

The platform pledges a comprehensive national health-insurance plan—building on the private health-care and insurance industries—that would cover everything from preventive and diagnostic services to catastrophic illness for every American.

The plank rejects "socialized medicine, in whatever guise it is presented . . ." Americans "should be able to make their own choices about health-care protection. We propose to assist them . . . through tax and financial incentives."

Women's Rights

The party vows to ensure passage of the Equal Rights Amendment and opposes efforts to rescind earlier ratification. The Democratic National Committee pledges not to hold meetings in states that have not ratified the amendment and will "withhold financial support and technical campaign assistance from candidates who do not support the ERA."

"We acknowledge the legitimate efforts of those who support or oppose ratification of the ERA." Ratification is now in the hands of state legislatures, which have a "constitutional right to accept or reject [it] without Federal interference or pressure."

Miscellaneous

The platform calls for prompt completion of a Federal study on the toxic effects of the defoliant Agent Orange . . . pledges to seek a national child-care program . . . promises to protect homosexuals against discrimination . . . condemns the Ku Klux Klan and the American Nazi Party . . . supports gun-control legislation . . . seeks curbs on tax deductions for business lunches . . . urges that Martin Luther King Jr.'s birthday be made a national holiday.

"The Republican Party declares war on government overregulation" . . . it opposes the federally imposed 55-mph speed limit, which "is counterproductive and contributes to the higher cost of goods" . . . supports efforts to restore voluntary prayer in schools . . . condemns forced busing to achieve racial desegregation . . . backs the death penalty . . . supports efforts to crack down on the sale and distribution of drug paraphernalia.

To restore the public's confidence in its elected officials, Republicans and Democrats alike forced President Nixon to resign following the Watergate scandal.

CHARACTERISTICS OF THE AMERICAN PARTY SYSTEM

Few Americans realize that modern political parties were "invented" in the United States long before they emerged in Europe. To this day, the American political party system has certain distinguishing characteristics. One such characteristic is that it is "extra-constitutional," in that the Constitution of 1787 did not mention political parties. In fact, as we shall see later in the chapter, the nation's Founders were originally opposed to parties (or "factions," as they were then called).

Three-Part Membership Structure

Another special attribute is the three-part membership structure *within* each party (see Figure 6.2). Sorauf describes this as a "tripartite system of interactions [among] a party organization, a party in office, and a party in the electorate."[6] The *party organization* includes *the formally chosen party leaders (everyone from the chairperson of the party's national committee to the members of the local precinct committee) who make and carry out decisions in the name of the party.* The *party in office* (or the party in government) *refers to party members who hold elective or appointive public office at any level; party affiliation is an important factor in their acquisition of the position.* As noted at the beginning of the chapter, it is the last group about which most citizens are cynical. Individuals classified as members of the party organization or the party in office are referred to collectively as the party leadership. They interact frequently and, usually, informally.

Followers of parties are often referred to as the *party in the electorate, which has two essential components—organized group followers and mass public followers.* Interest group support for parties is so important that parties regularly court groups and promise them influence in party affairs. To a great extent, however, groups are captives of parties because it is difficult for them to shift their allegiance from one party to another once they have made a public commitment. For example, it is difficult for labor unions to shift their allegiance to the Republican Party after affiliating with the Democratic Party for many years. Beyond the organized group following, a party must have a certain hard core of party identifiers in the electorate. In times of party adversity, this stable base of support keeps the party alive in American politics.

Two-Partyism

The persistence of two-partyism is also unique to the American party system. This devotion to two-partyism has been described by Clinton Rossiter:

> *The most momentous fact about the pattern of American politics is that we live under a persistent, obdurate, one might almost say "tyrannical," two-party system. We have the Republicans and we have the Democrats, and we have almost no one else, no other strictly political aggregate that amounts to a corporal's guard in the struggle for power.*[7]

People have offered many explanations for how and why this two-partyism has occurred.[8] One theory, often referred to as the dualist theory, asserts that there is a natural tendency of democratic politics to create two groups. Historians accepting this theory argue that our two parties were born out of a split that emerged during George Washington's administration between those who favored a strong national government and those who preferred strong state governments. They maintain that once the split occurred, the two-party system was quickly accepted as custom and reinforced by institutional conservatism.

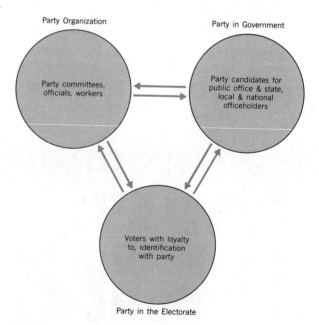

FIGURE 6.2

The Three-Part Political Party
SOURCE: Frank J. Sorauf, *Party Politics in America*, 4th ed. Copyright © 1980 by Frank J. Sorauf. Reprinted by permission of Little, Brown and Company.

Another widely cited theory, which explains why the two party system has continued, is the institutional, or structural-mechanical theory. According to this theory, certain characteristics of our electoral systems, most notably plurality requirements, protect the two parties. ***Plurality requirements** dictate that the candidate who receives the largest number of votes, not necessarily a majority, be declared the winner.* Such requirements give a decided edge to the two parties already in place, each of which has an established party image and a loyal group of supporters. This bias toward the status quo effectively discourages the formation of third (minor) parties. At the national level, the ***winner-take-all*** nature of the electoral college reinforces the two-party system. According to this custom, *the candidate winning by a simple plurality of popular votes in a state receives all of that state's electoral votes.*

Another common explanation for the persistence of the two parties is political socialization or the tendency of parents to pass their party identification on to their children (see Table 6.3). When both parents identify with the same party (the most common situation), their children are very likely to identify with that party. However, when parents differ in their party identification, their children are more likely to be independents or to identify weakly with the party of their father.

Two-partyism has not always prevailed in every region or every state. One-partyism has occasionally been the rule, particularly in the Democratic Deep South. However, in the last two decades, there has been a noticeable trend toward competitive, two-party systems at the state level (see Table 6.4).

Lack of Party Discipline

Another unique characteristic, often offered as a criticism of American parties, is the lack of effective discipline in the party in government. Actually, there is a bit more voting along party lines in legislative bodies than most people realize, especially on national economic, energy, and public assistance (welfare) issues. The data shown in Table 6.5 make this point. Even so, party leaders have no effective way of eliminating party "traitors" from elective positions. That remains a responsibility of the people.

Decentralized Party Organization

Consistent with our federal system of government, American party organizations are highly decentralized. Each level of the party organization (national, state, local) is semiautonomous from the other. A national party chairperson who directs the national headquarters staff and chairs the national committee is not like the head of a corporate board of directors. He or she has no formal power over state or local candidate selection or platform formation. The interactions among party officials at different levels are cooperative, rather than mandatory. For example, the national and state party organizations may work closely together during presidential elections and key congressio-

TABLE 6.3

Intergenerational Similarities in Party Identification

Party identification of children	Party of Mother and Father[a]				
	Both Democrat	Both Republican	Both Independent	Father Democrat, Mother Republican	Mother Democrat, Father Republican
Strong Democrat	24.0%	3.6%	7.1%	9.9%	14.4%
Weak Democrat	38.1	9.1	5.3	22.8	15.8
Independent	26.7	31.3	73.5	42.6	32.9
Weak Republican	7.0	33.6	3.5	11.9	26.3
Strong Republican	3.8	22.0	8.8	12.9	10.5
Other[b]	.5	.4	1.8	—	—
	(N = 1005)	(N = 550)	(N = 113)	(N = 101)	(N = 76)

SOURCE: Survey Research Center of the University of Michigan; 1976 data made available through the Inter-University Consortium for Political Research. Frank J. Sorauf, *Party Politics in America*, 4th ed. Copyright © 1980 by Frank J. Sorauf. Reprinted by permission of Little, Brown and Company.

[a]The table omits a number of possible parental combinations involving small numbers (e.g., one parent allied with a minor party or apolitical).

[b]The category "other" includes loyalists of minor parties, apoliticals, and the usual "don't knows" and "no answers."

TABLE 6.4

States Classified According to Degree of Interparty Competition, 1974–1980

One-party Democratic	Modified One-party Democratic	Two-party	Modified One-party Republican
Alabama (.9438)	South Carolina (.8034)	Montana (.6259)	North Dakota (.3374)
Georgia (.8849)	West Virginia (.8032)	Michigan (.6125)	
Louisiana (.8762)	Texas (.7993)	Ohio (.5916)	
Mississippi (.8673)	Massachusetts (.7916)	Washington (.5806)	
Arkansas (.8630)	Kentucky (.7907)	Alaska (.5771)	
North Carolina (.8555)	Oklahoma (.7841)	Pennsylvania (.5574)	
Maryland (.8509)	Nevada (.7593)	Delaware (.5490)	
Rhode Island (.8506)	Hawaii (.7547)	New York (.5390)	
	Florida (.7524)	Illinois (.5384)	
	Connecticut (.7336)	Nebraska (.5166)	
	New Jersey (.7330)	Maine (.5164)	
	Virginia (.7162)	Kansas (.4671)	
	New Mexico (.7113)	Utah (.4653)	
	California (.7081)	Iowa (.4539)	
	Oregon (.6954)	Arizona (.4482)	
	Missouri (.6932)	Colorado (.4429)	
	Minnesota (.6680)	Indiana (.4145)	
	Tennessee (.6648)	New Hampshire (.3916)	
	Wisconsin (.6634)	Idaho (.3898)	
		Wyoming (.3879)	
		Vermont (.3612)	
		South Dakota (.3512)	

Source: From John F. Bibby, et al. "Parties in State Politics," in Virginia Gray, Herbert Jacob, and Kenneth N. Vines eds., *Politics in the American States*, 4th ed. Copyright © 1983 by John F. Bibby, Cornelius P. Cotter, James L. Gibson, and Robert J. Huckshorn. Reprinted by permission of Little, Brown and Company.

nal and gubernatorial elections held in non-presidential election years, but neither dictates to the other what *must* be done. The high level of decentralization, or fragmentation, of American parties is reflected in the following list of organizational characteristics.

1. There is one national party organization, but the presidential campaign may be run independent of it.

2. The parties in Congress organize their own campaign committees.

3. There are 50 state party organizations.

4. Organizations in some of the major cities are more important (and therefore have more power) than their own state party organizations.

5. There has been a growing tendency over the last three decades for political movements and campaigns to be organized independent from the traditional party organization.

This decentralization has given party organizations a flexibility necessary for adapting to new constituents. Like all our political institutions,

parties are constantly changing to meet the changing needs of the nation. One authority on parties and elections, Gerald Pomper, has gone so far as to say, "To study America is to study American [political] parties."[9] Political parties are, in effect, a reflection of the political history of the United States.

THE HISTORY OF AMERICAN POLITICAL PARTIES

The American Constitution makes no mention of political parties, because the Founders, particularly George Washington, feared that such factions would divide and ultimately destroy the nation. James Madison, however, predicted that they would inevitably develop over economic questions in a country with diverse property interests. In *The Federalist* (paper number 10), Madison explained that different economic groups could be expected to hold different opinions about the role of government and would organize to further policies favorable to themselves. His hope was that the federal system under the Constitution would offset the negative influence of factions.

TABLE 6.5

Democrats or Republicans: What Difference Does It Make? Selected Roll-Call Votes in Congress, 1933–1982*

Legislation	Party	House Vote		Senate Vote	
		For	Against	For	Against
Tennessee Valley Authority	Dem	284	2	48	3
1933	Rep	17	89	14	17
Public Utilities	Dem	203	59	Voice Vote	
1934	Rep	7	83		
Social Security	Dem	287	13	60	1
1935	Rep	77	18	14	5
Soil Conservation	Dem	246	25	49	9
1936	Rep	20	64	5	11
Housing	Dem	239	38	55	8
1937	Rep	24	48	6	8
Agricultural Adjustment Act	Dem	243	54	53	17
1938	Rep	14	74	2	11
Reorganization of Executive Branch	Dem	234	5	59	3
1939	Rep	8	148	1	19
Selective Service	Dem	211	33	50	17
1940	Rep	52	112	8	10
Lend Lease	Dem	236	25	49	13
1941	Rep	24	135	10	17

World War II, 1941–1945

Though party voting did not completely disappear during the war, partisan issues were significantly diminished in number.

Legislation	Party	House Vote		Senate Vote	
School Lunch Program	Dem	164	45	38	4
1946	Rep	110	56	11	17
Taft-Hartley Labor Act	Dem	103	66	17	15
1947	Rep	217	12	37	2
The Marshall Plan	Dem	158	11	38	4
1948	Rep	171	61	31	13
Trade Agreements Extension	Dem	234	6	47	1
1949	Rep	84	63	15	18
Yugoslav Emergency Relief	Dem	182	41	35	7
1950	Rep	43	100	25	14
Public Housing Authorization	Dem	157	44	32	7
1951	Rep	48	125	15	18
Tidelands Oil	Dem	94	70	24	24
1952	Rep	153	18	26	11
Increase Hill-Burton Hospital Funds	Dem	166	29	34	6
1953	Rep	31	173	8	35
Atomic Energy Act Revisions	Dem	36	146	13	25
1954	Rep	195	7	44	2
Exempt Natural Gas Producers from	Dem	86	136	22	24
Regulation, 1955 (Vetoed)	Rep	123	67	31	14
Agriculture: Soil Bank and High Rigid	Dem	189	35	35	4
Supports, 1956	Rep	48	146	15	31
Civil Rights Act	Dem	118	107	29	18
1957	Rep	168	19	43	0
National Defense Education Act (NDEA)	Dem	140	30	37	7
1958	Rep	72	55	29	8
Labor Reform Act	Dem	95	184	15	44
1959	Rep	134	17	32	2

(continued)

TABLE 6.5 *(continued)*

Legislation	Party	House Vote For	House Vote Against	Senate Vote For	Senate Vote Against
Increase Minimum Wage to $1.25	Dem	176	90	47	16
1960 (Not Passed)	Rep	27	121	15	18
Emergency Feed Grain Program	Dem	205	41	47	9
1961	Rep	4	161	11	22
Revenue Act (Revisions)	Dem	218	34	40	14
1962	Rep	1	162	19	10
Revenue Act (Kennedy Tax Cut)	Dem	223	29	Voice Vote	
1963	Rep	48	126		
Economic Opportunity (War on Poverty)	Dem	204	40	51	12
1964	Rep	22	145	20	22
Medicare	Dem	248	42	55	7
1965	Rep	65	73	13	14
Demonstration Cities	Dem	162	60	43	10
1966	Rep	16	81	10	17
Model Cities	Dem	141	82	46	13
1967	Rep	15	159	16	15
Remove Gold Reserve Requirements for	Dem	174	42	30	14
U.S. Currency, 1968	Rep	25	148	9	23
Turn Antipoverty Program Over to the	Dem	60	168	No Vote in	
States, 1969 (Failed)	Rep	103	63	Senate	
Anti-Cambodian Cooper-Church Rider	Dem	120	99	42	11
1970 (Failed)	Rep	33	138	16	26
Discontinuation of Supersonic Transport	Dem	131	114	34	19
(SST), 1971	Rep	84	90	17	27
Minimum Wage Increase	Dem	165	59	43	7
1972	Rep	23	137	22	20
Passage of War Powers Act Over the	Dem	198	32	50	3
Nixon Veto, 1973	Rep	86	103	25	15
Federal Election Campaign Finance	Dem	219	3	37	9
1974	Rep	136	45	16	23
Energy Policy and Conservation	Dem	202	59	50	10
1975	Rep	34	101	8	30
Passage of Labor-HEW Funding for 1977	Dem	247	22	48	4
Over Ford Veto, 1976	Rep	65	71	19	11
Natural Gas Deregulation (For New Gas,	Dem	72	210	16	43
U.S. Only), 1977	Rep	127	17	34	3
National Energy Act (Adoption of	Dem	199	79	43	7
Conference Report), 1978	Rep	8	127	17	10
Creation of Department of Education	Dem	185	77	51	5
1979	Rep	30	124	18	17
Oil Windfall Profits Tax	Dem	217	39	49	8
1980	Rep	85	68	17	23
Economic Recovery Tax Act	Dem	113	94	26	7
1981	Rep	169	1	41	1
Balanced Budget Amendment	Dem	69	167	22	24
1982	Rep	167	20	47	7

SOURCE: Clinton Rossiter developed a similar table in *Parties and Politics in America* (Ithaca, N.Y.: Cornell University Press, 1960), pp. 124–129. We have relied on the Rossiter data and supplemented it with records from the Congressional Quarterly *Almanac*.

*There is a danger in reporting simple roll-call votes because the motives in casting a vote are multiple and do not stem solely from party. In fact, the party differences noted in this table are blurred by the frequent coalitions between Republicans and Southern Democrats. This table illustrates that differences between the Democrats and the Republicans can be noteworthy in Congress and elsewhere. Those "not voting" are omitted, as Congress members who were not identified with the two major parties.

ual

Some of the same leaders who were most wary of political parties (Thomas Jefferson, Alexander Hamilton) were among the nation's first party leaders. According to historian Richard Hofstadter, it was a good thing that parties emerged. In his book, *The Idea of a Party System*, Hofstadter credits parties with transforming the United States into a workable, representative democracy:

In a country which was always to be in need of the cohesive force of institutions, the national parties, for all of their faults, were to become at an early hour primary and necessary parts of the machinery of government, essential vehicles to convey men's loyalties to the state under a central government that often seemed rather distant and abstract. So much so that we may say that it was the parties that rescued this Constitution-against-parties and made it a working instrument in government. [10]

Since the first party emerged, over 900 different party labels have appeared, most lasting only a short time. Of these, only seven can even be classified as significant minor parties, strong enough to carry at least one state in a presidential election. (These parties are listed in Table 6.6.) The number of major parties is even smaller (see Figure 6.3). A major political party is one with sufficient public support to make a serious race for the presidency or to win enough seats to influence Congress. Of these, the modern Democratic and Republican parties are the oldest, although, as we shall see, they too have undergone some major changes at key points in American history.

Major Political Parties

In the development of our major parties, two factors consistently have served as stimuli to change. As Madison accurately forecast, economic issues are one such factor. Another is expansion of the electorate. The ability of a party to survive greatly depends on its ability to absorb immigrants and newly enfranchised voters. Parties with very narrow or élite bases have not survived.

The nation's first two major political parties emerged from an ideological and policy split between two prominent members of George Washington's cabinet--Alexander Hamilton, Secretary of the Treasury, and Thomas Jefferson, Secretary of State. The struggle between the Hamiltonians and Jeffersonians was a classic conflict over policy. They debated both the means and ends of government. They debated the legitimate role of the national government, the intentions of the framers of the Constitution, and the goals of government. In other words, who should be served, how, and to what end?[11] Each engaged in lining up supporters

TABLE 6.6

Significant Minor Parties in American History

1. *Anti-Masonic party*. 1832: 7 electoral votes. A party opposed to the alleged secret political influence of the Masons; later part of an anti-Jackson coalition that formed the Whig party.

2. *American (Know-Nothing) party*. 1856: 8 electoral votes. A nativist party opposed to open immigration and in favor of electing native born Americans to public office.

3. *People's (Populist) party*. 1892: 22 electoral votes. An outgrowth of a movement of agrarian protest opposed to the economic power of bankers, railroads, and fuel industries and in favor of a graduated income tax, government regulation, and currency reform (especially free silver coinage).

4. *Progressive (Bull Moose) party*. 1912: 88 electoral votes. An offshoot of the Republican party, it favored liberal reforms such as an expanded suffrage, social reforms, conservation of resources, and antimonopoly laws.

5. *Progressive party*. 1924: 13 electoral votes. A continuation of the 1912 Progressive tradition with the candidacy of a man (Robert La Follette) who had been one of its founders and leaders.

6. *States Rights Democratic (Dixiecrat) party*. 1948: 39 electoral votes. A southern splinter of the Democratic party, it ran as *the* Democratic party in the South on a conservative, segregationist platform.

7. *American Independent party*. 1968: 46 electoral votes. The party of George Wallace; traditionalist, segregationist, and opposed to the authority of the national government.

SOURCE: From Frank J. Sorauf, *Party Politics in America* 4th ed. Copyright © 1980 by Frank J. Sorauf. Reprinted by permission of Little, Brown and Company.

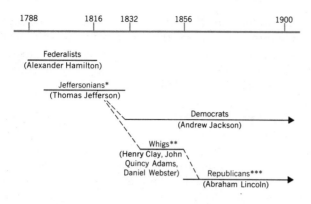

FIGURE 6.3

The American Major Parties and Their Leaders
SOURCE: Adapted from Frank J. Sorauf, *Party Politics in America*, 4th ed. Copyright © 1980 by Frank J. Sorauf. Reprinted by permission of Little, Brown and Company.

in Congress and in the various states. The groups that emerged to support these two men became the nation's first political parties.

Disagreements among key members of George Washington's cabinet, namely Alexander Hamilton (fourth from left) and Thomas Jefferson (second from left), led to the formation of America's first political parties.

The Federalist Party The Federalist Party (1793–1817) was actually the first political party. Its leader was Alexander Hamilton, who personally favored a strong national government (as evidenced by his staunch support for a national bank). Hamilton also opposed any foreign policies that would jeopardize the country's relationship with Britain (in that the national bank depended on tariffs from British imports as its primary source of revenue). Reflecting Hamilton's viewpoints, the Federalist Party was the party of: a stable economy; continuity with English traditions; military preparedness; a strong national government; mercantilism in economic philosophy; and amity toward England and caution toward France in diplomacy.

Hamilton's natural followers were the nation's élite, its natural aristocracy—the most prestigious church leaders; the Society of the Cincinnati (Revolutionary War officers); the leaders of banking, commerce, and manufacturing; planters (farmers with large holdings); the well-to-do in urban centers; and workers dependent on the young nation's limited commercial and manufacturing enterprises. These people had a stake in a strong national government and a stable economy. But the exclusive nature of this first political party was its ultimate downfall. It would not and could not enlarge its membership fast enough to keep it competitive with its rival party, the Jeffersonian Republicans. After losing the presidential election of 1800 to the Jeffersonians, the party's influence swiftly declined and was soon limited to a small sectional base in New England. The party's close identification with the British became a liability when the United States went to war against Britain in 1812. By 1817 the Federalist Party had disappeared altogether.

The Jeffersonian Republican Party The Jeffersonian Republican Party, also known as the Democratic-Republican Party and, eventually, simply the Democratic Party, was founded in 1795. It was composed mainly of agrarians. They accepted the new, liberal economics expounded in Adam Smith's *Wealth of Nations*, which today we call free-enterprise capitalism. The coalition also included people from the Appalachian mountains, Revolutionary War foot soldiers, unskilled laborers, low-status church leaders, and small businesspeople. The party was much stronger in the South, Pennsylvania, and New York than in other parts of the country; it was especially weak in New England.

In contrast to Hamilton and his fellow Federalists, Thomas Jefferson and his followers preferred stronger state governments and a strict interpretation of the Constitution. They were opposed to government policies that favored the economically privileged (such as credit policies of the National Bank). They also were more sympathetic to the French than the British, because they identified with many of the ideals of the French Revolution: universal suffrage and direct popular self-government, among others. Ultimately, their efforts to expand the electorate by convincing states to liberalize their voting requirements (to drop property ownership as a prerequisite for voting) kept their party alive.

Once the Federalists had disappeared, factions soon emerged within the Jeffersonian party. One faction, led by Andrew Jackson, strongly advocated further expansion of the electorate. It welcomed new immigrant groups and actively encouraged the political participation of the common citizen. Following Jackson's election to the presidency in 1828, a number of reforms were implemented to promote greater participation: universal suffrage, popular election of a large number of officials (the long ballot), short terms of office (to encourage turnover of public officials), and an elaborate system of political appointments designed to reward party loyalists. Participatory democracy is a term we often associate with the Jacksonian era.

The party under Jackson became the first really broad-based political party. From this Jacksonian faction the modern Democratic Party emerged. It became known officially as the Democratic Party in 1840.

The Whig Party Many Jeffersonians opposed the democratization of the party. This faction was known as the National Republicans. When Jackson was elected president, many of them left the party and formed the Whig Party. As the Whig Party emerged prior to the 1834 congressional elections, it was a coalition of diverse groups whose only similarity was an intense dislike for the strong executive authority exercised by President Andrew Jackson. In fact, the name of the party was taken from the Whig Party in England, which stood in favor of limiting the power of the king.

This new party was composed of disenchanted Jeffersonians and some fragments of the old Federalist Party. The party drew its strength from merchants and manufacturers of the Northeast, big planters of the South, wealthy farmers of the West, and big business owners in the urban South and West. It also had some support among ordinary people in the West and rural areas in other parts of the country because of the Whig Party's position on transportation improvements. Much of the party's platform was developed by one of its most popular leaders, Henry Clay. Clay developed a program he called his *American System—a plan designed to stimulate a sagging American economy by imposing a protective tariff, maintaining a national bank, and providing transportation between cities and farms at federal expense.* However, President Jackson dismantled the national bank and opposed internal improvements at government expense.

Under the personal leadership of Henry Clay and another strong Whig leader, Daniel Webster, the Whig coalition, loose as it was, managed to capture the White House twice (1840 and 1848), both times by running a popular military hero. But the Whigs always seemed to be the opposition party, perhaps because of their elitist image. By the time the Whigs unsuccessfully ran their last presidential candidate in 1852, the party had already begun to dissolve over the slavery issue. Northern Whigs against slavery (the Conscience Whigs) left the party and joined with a number of other opponents of slavery to form the Republican Party.

The Republican Party The Republican party was born directly out of opposition to the Kansas-Nebraska Act of 1854. Sectional slavery controversies had been dealt with as of 1820 (in the Compromise of 1820) by ensuring artificial equality in the Senate; that is, when new states were admitted to the union, they were admitted in pairs, one slave and one free. The Kansas-Nebraska Act expressly repealed the Compromise of 1820 and adopted popular sovereignty for territories opened for settlement. Under *popular sovereignty, the people settling each territory would decide the question of slavery.* When the Kansas and Nebraska territories were opened for settlement, slave and free forces engaged in an intense struggle to settle and control them, and sectional interests in the United States rapidly polarized. In the Congress, rhetoric centered on the betrayal of the Compromises of 1820 and 1850.

The Republican party has by far the most complex origins of any major American political party. Conscience or Free-Soil Whigs became Republicans, along with many anti-Nebraskan Democrats and remnants of several minor parties. When Abraham Lincoln composed his first cabinet, it included four ex-Democrats, three Whigs, and one man who had belonged successively to the Whig, Liberty-Abolitionist, Free-Soil, Democratic, and Know-Nothing parties. Lincoln himself was a former Whig.

The Republican Party image was sharpened during and after the Civil War. It came to be viewed as the party that preserved the Union, supported Abraham Lincoln, and ended slavery. The party platform advocated free-enterprise capitalism, supported the development of transcontinental railroads, favored a more generous homestead act to settle the West, and encouraged immigration. Although the party wavered occasionally in the 19th century on the issue of tariffs, on the whole it supported protective tariffs, and thus American industrial expansion. It also became the party of conservative monetary policy, which meant: 1) heavy reliance on gold, 2) valuing gold more highly than silver in exchange rates, and 3) limiting as much as possible the use of paper money.

The original Republican coalition included anyone who was unhappy (for any reason) with the government's policy on slavery; it was not exclusively an abolitionist party. The Republicans had general support in the North, no support at all in the South, and developed strength in the Midwest. Farmers and the "better classes" were core supporters. If blacks voted, they voted with the Republicans—the party of Lincoln.

Periods of Majority Party Dominance

Since 1854 the Democratic and Republican parties have contended for power as the nation's two major parties. They have dominated nominations, campaigns, and elections virtually without rivals; in so doing, they have continued an American tradition of two-partyism that dates back to 1795. Historically, however, two-party struggles have rarely been struggles between equals. For long periods, one of the major parties has clearly been the majority party, supported by a more or less stable coalition in the electorate that ensures its position. These periods of majority party dominance are as follows:

1. 1793–1800: Federalist Party.
2. 1800–1860: Jeffersonian Republican (Democratic-Republican or Democratic) Party.
3. 1860–1932: Republican Party.
4. 1932–present: Democratic Party.

The long periods of majority party dominance can be misread as indications of more stability than actually existed. Coalitions on which the majority parties rest undergo change. Sometimes the change is quite marked and the parties are never the same again either in their memberships or their policies.

Elections that signal the transition from one party era to another are critical elections. The term *critical election* was invented by V.O. Key to describe *a rare type of political event that elicits great depth and intensity of electoral involvement and produces a dramatic and durable realignment between the parties*.

Eras of critical realignment, according to Walter Dean Burnham, author of *Critical Elections and the Mainsprings of American Politics*,[12] are characterized by:

1. short, sharp shifts by certain groups of traditional party supporters to the opposite party
2. major third-party revolts, led by those disenchanted with the responsiveness of both major parties
3. serious social and economic problems
4. increases in the ideological, or issue-distances, between the major parties.

Ultimately, party realignments result in major shifts in party loyalties. Thes shifts occur as consequences of major changes in social and economic conditions and the parties' responses to those changes.

Party realignments are rare. There have been only five critical elections. With each, the political landscape was dramatically changed.

1. *1800*—In the first peaceful transfer of power, the Jeffersonian Republicans replaced the Federalists as the normal governing party.
2. *1828*—This election completed the split of the Democratic-Republican party, resulting in the triumph of Jacksonian frontier democracy over the Whig wing of the party.
3. *1860*—The victory of Abraham Lincoln and the Republicans over the hopelessly divided Democrats resulted in the beginning of the

Franklin D. Roosevelt's election in 1832 was a critical election in American history. Significant numbers of Americans shifted their party allegiance to the Democratic Party away from the Republican Party which had been the majority party for over 70 years.

Civil War and the end of slavery as an economic and social system.

4. *1896*—William McKinley and the Republicans defeated the reform-minded Populist-Democrat William Jennings Bryan, ending an agrarian-proletariat challenge to industrial capitalism and the possibility of developing a class-based, mass party system on the European model.

5. *1932*—Franklin D. Roosevelt and the New Deal (to get the country out of the Great Depression) replaced Herbert Hoover, heralding the advent of the social service state and the dramatic expansion of the role of government.

There are those who think America has been in the midst of a realignment period since the citizen tax revolts of the late 1970s. Others have proclaimed that the 1980 election of Republican Ronald Reagan and a Republican majority in the Senate was a critical election. Because it is difficult to make such judgments after one or two elections, we must wait to see whether 1980 will prove to have been a critical election. The mid-term congressional election of 1982 ("won" by the Democrats) suggests otherwise.

The Importance of Minor Parties

So far, we have have given little attention to the hundreds of minor parties that have sprung up in the course of our nation's history. Minor parties often signal to major parties that they are out of touch with a significant number of Americans.

According to Steven J. Rosenstone, Roy L. Behr, and Edward H. Lazarus—authorities on third-party voting in America—there are at least three ways in which minor parties have greatly influenced politics, the outcome of elections, and the behavior of the major parties.[13] First, they attract voters. Of the thirty-six presidential contests between 1840 and 1980, minor parties polled over 5 percent of the vote in one-third and over 10 percent of the vote in one-fifth. In thirteen of the thirty-six elections, third parties controlled enough popular votes in the right states to change the vote of the electoral college. Second, minor parties are policy innovators, raising issues that the major parties would otherwise ignore. Finally, as vote getters and policy innovators, they serve as safety valves for discontent. Discontent registered in a third-party vote protects the established order of things because the government and the major parties can take note and respond.

Third-party voting seems to be high in clusters of elections (see Figure 6.4). It has been noted that third-party voting is high near the end of a party system and signals the coming of a critical election. The graph in Figure 6.4 illustrates that this was true from 1848 to 1860 when the Whig and Democratic coalitions were shattered by minor party voting. The Populist party vote is the

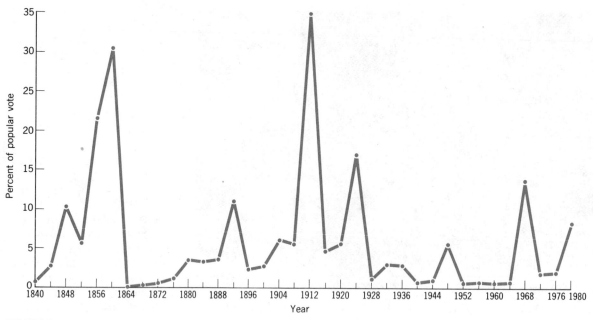

FIGURE 6.4

Third Party Vote for President, 1840–1980
SOURCE: Steven J. Rosenstone, Roy L. Behr, and Edward H. Lazarus, *Third Party Voting in America,* to be
published and copyright ©1984 by Princeton University Press. Fig. 1.1 reprinted by permission of Princeton University Press.

1892 peak before the critical election of 1896.
However, nothing of similar magnitude occurred
just prior to 1932 (the New Deal critical election).
It is also noteworthy that neither the Teddy
Roosevelt Progressive (Bull Moose) surge of 1912
nor the Robert M. LaFollette Progressive vote of

1924 seemed to lead directly to a critical election.

By far the most successful third-party movement since 1932 was George Wallace's American
Independent party. In 1968 the Alabama governor polled 13.53 percent of the vote. The American Independent party represented pent-up

The structure of our electoral system
gives a decided advantage to the two
major political parties. Presidential
candidates, like John Anderson, who
run as independents or third party
candidates rarely win a single electoral
vote because of the winner-take-all
nature of the electoral college.

Southern and working-class anger with many government policies, but its success appears to have been tied to Wallace personally. When Wallace was off the ticket in 1972, his party polled only 1.4 percent of the vote, and this number dropped even more drastically in succeeding years.

In 1980 John B. Anderson ran a media-sustained, highly personal independent candidacy, which seemed to be mainly a protest against the major party nominees. However, he received only 6.6 percent of the popular vote and not a single electoral vote. Undaunted, he decided to run for president again in 1984 from his newly created peace party. He predicted his 1984 candidacy would be easier because his 1980 effort had resulted in the reform of many state laws that had made it very difficult for third party and independent candidates to get on the ballot. Anderson's 1984 candidacy makes us wonder whether we are really at the beginning of another major realignment of our party system and whether the structure of our party system is outmoded.

THE STRUCTURE OF AMERICAN PARTY ORGANIZATIONS

The structure of American party organizations has changed very little in over a century. Party organizations, on paper, appear hierarchical (see Figure 6.5). Each level of the party organization has some influence on the selection of party leaders at the next highest level. Note that power flows *up* rather than down, in contrast to our notions of the power flow in government.

The national party organization has very little control over grass roots party organizations. ''Grass roots'' is a term that refers to government closest to the people, in this case state and local party organizations. In some cases, the only similarity between the national party and the state party is the shared party label and party symbol (the Democrats' donkey, the Republicans' elephant). For example, a Democrat in New York may not necessarily stand for the same policy positions as a Democrat in Georgia, particularly in state and local elections. In fact, some consider

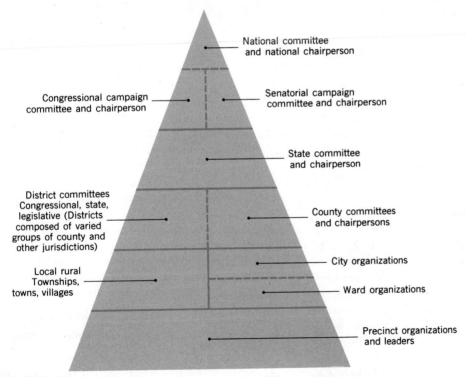

FIGURE 6.5

Structure of a Typical Party Organization
SOURCE: Robert J. Huckshorn, *Political Parties in America* (North Scituate, Mass.: Duxbury Press, 1980), p. 77.

Well aware of the fact that the organizational strength of political parties is at the state and local level, party presidential hopefuls visit state party conventions, fund raisers, and appreciation dinners.

our party system fifty separate party organizations.

The truth is that party organizations are very loose and are often controlled by a few party activitists who, for one reason or another, keep the party going between elections. Elections always breathe new life and new excitement into party organizations; elections are a party's reason for being.

The National Committee

At the top of the party organizational structure is the national party committee. Until 1972, these committees were composed of a national committeeman and committeewoman selected from each state, regardless of the size of a state or its pattern of support for party candidates. These committees were often not very representative of the party membership as a whole. To make them more representative, both parties expanded the size of their committees. The Democrats enlarged their national committee to 342. The new members, in addition to the traditional committeeman and committeewoman from each state, were selected

on the basis of proportional representation. According to the proportional representation rule, if a group (racial, ethnic, gender, or ideological) makes up a certain percentage of the party's membership nationwide, it should make up the same percentage of the party's national committee. (The Democrats adopted similar rules for selecting party delegates to the national convention but ultimately relaxed them because they weakened the influence of a large number of traditionally active party loyalists.)

The national party committee is most active during the presidential election campaign. Between elections, its responsibilities are minimal. A classic study of the national party committees, *Politics Without Power*, describes them as virtually powerless.[14] However, national committees influence party policies between elections in at least three situations.

1. They select the site of the national convention and oversee staff arrangements for it.
2. They monitor public opinion on key issues that emerge between elections and help de-

National political party conventions, held every four years, renew the public's interest in political party activities and reaffirm the strength of the two major parties relative to minor parties.

velop party positions on these issues that will evoke popular support at election time.

3. They fill any vacancies on the presidential ticket that occur after the national convention has adjourned.

A rare opportunity for a national committee to fill a vacancy on the national ticket arose in 1972. George McGovern's running mate, Thomas Eagleton, was forced to resign after it was discovered that he had been hospitalized secretly on several occasions for depression. He was replaced by Sargent Shriver. On that occasion, the national committee had only to approve the choice of candidate McGovern. If the top place on a ticket ever became vacant, however, a new interest in the powers of national committees would certainly emerge.

Another function of the national party committee is to elect the national party chairperson. It usually does so at the end of the national party nominating convention. In reality, the chairperson is hand-picked by the party's presidential nominee. His or her first responsibility is to manage the party's presidential campaign. After the election, the party chairperson's responsibilities change. At that point, the chairperson is expected to lead the party's fund-raising, membership, and public relations campaigns—to keep the party alive between elections. After the election, the individual influence of party chairpersons over the direction of party affairs also changes, depending on whether the party's presidential candidate has won or lost. A national party chairperson actually has more latitude to lead the party if the party's candidate has been defeated, because there is less interference from the White House.

During the Eisenhower and Nixon administrations, the Democrats were fortunate to have three talented national party chairmen—Paul Butler, Larry O'Brien, and Robert Strauss—who helped maintain the loyal opposition. After Jimmy Carter defeated Gerald Ford in 1976, the Republican National Committee chair was sought by five candidates. It was won by former Senator William Brock of Tennessee. Brock took charge of Republican affairs with a vengeance unprecedented in either party. He recruited attractive candidates, intervened in party primaries, and set about building into the national committee organization all the resources necessary to wage a modern campaign. Much of the Republican party's improved political fortunes in 1980 were the result of the "new" Republican National Committee and its catchy slogan, "Vote Republican for a Change." This public relations campaign required close cooperation between national and grass roots party organizations.

State and Local Party Organizations

The structure and duties of state party organizations are generally explicitly spelled out in each state's constitution and statutes. The national party organization, in contrast, is nowhere referred to in the Constitution. Although the details vary, most state party organizations are composed of three basic units: precinct committees, county committees, and a state committee.

Precinct committees are generally regarded as the basic building blocks of the party organization. A precinct is a geographical area, or neighborhood, whose residents vote at a particular polling place. Party members from the same precinct select precinct committee members, a precinct chairperson, and precinct committeemen and women who, in turn, serve as members of the county party committee or whatever level is immediately above the precinct (ward, city, or district) (See Figure 6.5). The same process is used to select state party committee members and state party chairpersons. As Sarah McCally Morehouse, an expert on state political parties, notes:

> The linkage is from the bottom up rather than from the top down. Members of party committees at any level have a power base in an organizational level lower than the level represented by the one in which they sit.[15]

Like the national party organization, state and local party organizations are most active at election time—recruiting and registering new party members, drafting party platform planks, selecting delegates to party conventions, raising funds, and campaigning for the party's candidates. Between elections, state and local party organizations are sustained by a small core of party organization officials (precinct, county, and state committee members and chairpersons).

Who are the party officials? Why do they volunteer their time and money? Especially, why do they get so involved with party work when so few people even know their names? Like other elites, party leaders have a higher socioeconomic status than the general population, come disproportionately from the age group between 35 and 55, and overrepresent the constituencies of their particular parties. Thus, Democratic Party leaders are more likely to be Catholic, Jewish, of Irish, or Polish descent, and members of labor unions; Republican Party leaders are more likely to be Protestant, of German or English descent, and from the upper-income managerial and professional groups.

Party leaders are likely to be self-recruited; they are also self-starters. A classic study by Peter B. Clark and James Q. Wilson identified three major incentives that attract people to leadership roles: 1) purpose (to change party rules or policy goals); 2) gregariousness (to fulfill social needs for congeniality, belonging, and identification); and 3) material benefits (for personal gain, to find a job, to achieve social mobility, or to further a political career).[16] The material benefits of party activity have drastically diminished with the increase in merit appointments, the decline in patronage,

competitive bidding for government contracts, public disclosure, and stricter rules of accountability and public ethics. Indeed, political activity involves considerable personal cost and few material benefits. Filling the ranks, especially at the grassroots or precinct level, becomes more difficult each year.

Another trend that disturbs the party professionals, or old pros, is the rise of **amateur activists**, who are drawn into party work not by material incentives, but by their concern about public policy and their sense of civic duty. **Purist activists** are a special type of the amateur activist; they are so committed to their ideology or principles that they find it difficult to compromise. They would rather be right than win. In the Democratic Party, the amateurs and purists tend to be quite liberal; in the Republican Party, they tend to be quite conservative. In both parties, these newcomers have infused new life into the organizations and helped to reform the parties, but they have also contributed to their fragmentation.[17]

In contrast to the new breed of party activists, **party professionals** value winning and see their role as peacekeepers, coalition builders, and policy compromisers. Building coalitions is increasingly important at the grass roots level where old-time political machines are running out of steam.

Political Machines

A **political machine** is a well-organized, tightly knit, hierarchical party organization whose power stems from its ability to provide personal benefits (food, clothing, jobs, contracts, services, or party leadership positions) in exchange for party loyalty and support. The leader of a political machine is called a **political boss**. Political machines ran many of the nation's big cities—New York, Boston, Philadelphia, Kansas City to name a few—in the 19th and early 20th centuries.

The machine organizations included men and women who could deliver the vote from the block to the precinct to the ward. In exchange, the leaders delivered to their constitutents services and respect, commodities in short supply among the poor, the immigrants, and the unskilled workers who flocked to the cities in search of a better life. The jobs and services the leaders dispensed came from those who wished to do business with the city: utilities, construction engineers, builders, and the like. Because the cities were being built during this period, many contracts, licenses, and franchises were available for exchange. Bosses and

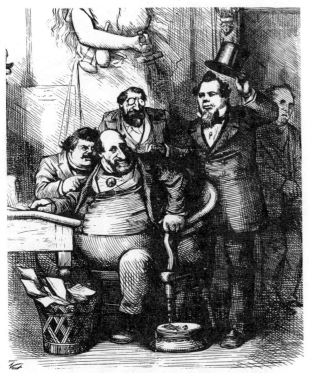

Political machines, such as the Tammany Hall Democratic organization in New York City, run by Boss Tweed (center), were often corrupt. Efforts by reformers to take politics out of government and run it like a business effectively weakened political party organizations.

machines were not altruists; they wanted power and personal gain. However, they did make life in the city more tolerable for many unfortunate and lonely people.

In most cities, political machines declined rapidly after 1930 and disappeared almost everywhere after World War II. The causes of their demise were many and began in the late 19th century. First, civil service reform, with merit appointments, cut down on patronage. Second, laws regulating the granting of contracts and licenses and laws requiring competitive bidding cut down the goods of exchange. Third, the rise of collective bargaining through organized labor improved the quality of life and provided a social contact for city dwellers. Fourth, the decline of immigration after 1920 cut down the group most dependent on the machine. Fifth, and most important, the rise of the social service state after 1932 made government responsible for all of the services formerly provided by the boss and the machine.

The Chicago-Cook County Democratic organization is the last of the big city machines. Techni-

cally, the city's elections are nonpartisan, but the party label of each candidate is well known. The fifty aldermen on the city council do not really run the city; the mayor and a small group of confidants manage the Democratic organization's affairs and the city's as well. In the 1960s and 1970s, the organization, commanded by Mayor Richard J. Daley, impressed all who observed it; and because no one could explain why it had survived the events that destroyed other political machines, it seemed almost indestructible. However, it was damaged by the death of Daley and Jane Byrne's victory in the next election over Daley's successor, Michael Bilandic. In 1983, Representative Harold Washington defeated Byrne's well-financed renomination campaign, and because Washington was black, defections of organization leaders to the Republican candidate were numerous. The unique party organization of Chicago-Cook County is clearly not as strong as it once was.

In spite of the apparent disappearance of political machines, one political scientist, Raymond Wolfinger warns against counting them totally down and out.[18] Rising immigration rates, cuts in government welfare spending, and the weakening of labor unions and civil service systems may hasten the reappearance of political machines. Wolfinger also argues that once party leaders recognize that they have an invaluable service to offer to middle and upper class citizens (namely, assistance in getting through the government's bureaucratic maze), party machines might well be reactivated. As of the early 1980s, however, political party organizations continued to decline.

DECLINE OF THE AMERICAN PARTY SYSTEM

In response to the widespread corruption and the wheeling and dealing associated with political machines and their bosses, a number of good-government groups composed of more affluent, more highly educated individuals led a reform movement. This movement intended to "purge politics from government," to make government run like a business instead of a machine dispensing favors from the corner of a smoke-filled room. In an effort to professionalize, or depoliticize, government, several reforms were implemented that effectively weakened party organizations.

One reform that has weakened party strength

over the years is the *office bloc ballot—a ballot used in a general election that lists the candidates for each office together under the title of each office.* An example of an office-bloc ballot is:

Governor (vote one)

Susan Allison (D)

William Arnold (R)

Michael George (Ind)

Alecia Palaez (Soc)

Cameron Rockwell (Cit)

The format of this ballot is intended to reduce straight party-line (straight ticket) voting and to encourage a voter to consider the credentials of the individual candidate. The office-block ballot was prescribed as an alternative to the more commonly used *party-column ballot.* This ballot *lists the party's candidates for each office in a column under the party's name.* This type of ballot (shown below) obviously encourages straight ticket voting.

Parties were also weakened by the advent of civil service reform, which began at the state level and became a national policy in 1883 with the passage of the Pendleton Act. Originally the number of positions covered by civil service was small, but over the years *patronage appointments—that is, appointments made strictly on the basis of party loyalty and party service—*at all levels of government drastically declined. The big city bosses talked at length about "the curse of civil service reform." Other reforms aimed directly at the big city machines included non-partisan primaries and elections, at-large elections for city councils, and the council-manager form of municipal government.

By far the most drastic reform aimed at political parties was the direct primary. The *direct primary is an intraparty election in which the voters select the candidates who will run under the party's label in the subsequent general election.* In such primaries, candidates not endorsed by the party could defeat party-endorsed candidates, and in one-party states the primary became more important than the election.

The direct primary was divisive, expensive, and gave interest groups an increased influence in the nomination process. It eliminated the leaders' opportunity to put together slates of candidates balancing a wide range of interests and to build and maintain coalitions.

The party decline that had begun with the reform movement at the turn of the century continued into the 20th century. But the most marked decline occurred in the 1960s and 1970s, a twenty-year period when major changes occurred in America. These changes were:

1. a series of domestic and foreign crises, such as the civil rights and Vietnam protests in the 1960s and the Watergate scandal in the 1970s, that effectively alienated many Americans from the party in government;

2. a rise in the number of (independent) voters who either refused to label themselves Democrats or Republicans or frequently split their vote, a trend paralleled by trends toward alienation and higher education (college educations);

3. an increase in the number of single-issue voters concerned about controversial issues neither party was willing to address directly;

4. the growing influence of the media in election campaigns and, consequently, the diminishing influence of party volunteers to contact voters.

To understand how these factors combined to hasten party decline, we will look at each individually.

Crises in the 1960s and 1970s

In these two decades, periods of national frustration were more common than periods of tranquility. The serious national problems during this period included the black social revolution, the urban crisis, the Vietnam War, radical protest movements and increased political violence,

	Dem	*Rep*	*Ind*
Governor	Richard Avriett	Hardie Morgan	Elaine Riegler
Lt. Governor	Julia Barnett	Bruce Galster	Warren Harrison
Sec. of State	Karen Bryan	Ann Martin	Gregory Matthews
County Sheriff	David Herms	Irvin Hightower	Carl Gunther

changing lifestyles, stagflation, and political corruption and abuse of public office. Each of these problems called for a substantial and creative government response. Unfortunately, the problems were interrelated and emerged in clusters, and the government often did not provide very imaginative, daring, or clear resolutions.

Civil Rights Protests and Urban Riots Segregation and discrimination against blacks were centuries old when protests against racism began in the 1950s. The parties had previously paid scant attention to the nation's race relations problem. Not until blacks moved into the streets did government respond. Even then, the response more often came from the courts than from elected officials.

Vietnam Perhaps no other problem in the last two decades damaged public trust in government officials as much as the war in Vietnam. If the parties' chief function is to provide a link between the people and their government, Vietnam is a case study in pathology. In 1964, Lyndon Johnson, the Democratic presidential candidate, denounced the militant policy statements of his opponent, Republican Barry Goldwater; but after the election, Johnson dramatically escalated the American presence in Vietnam. Within two years, Vietnam had become ''Johnson's war.'' In 1968 Republican presidential nominee Richard

Nixon campaigned against the Democrats on the theme that any party that could not end the war in four years did not deserve to be reelected, but the war did not end until well after Nixon had been reelected in 1972.

Radical Protest Movements and Political Violence As opposition to racism and Vietnam mounted and the protest movements moved into the streets, political participation became more violent. The assassination of John F. Kennedy in 1963 at first seemed an isolated piece of madness. But in 1968 Robert F. Kennedy and Martin Luther King were both murdered, and in 1972 George C. Wallace, the American Independent party presidential candidate, was crippled in an attempt on his life. Nor did political violence end

Protests against the Vietnam War during the 1968 Democratic national party convention in Chicago led to violent conflict between anti-war demonstrators and the police. Many people who felt strongly about the war became cynical of the two major political parties because of their waffling on this issue.

The assassination of the Reverend Martin Luther King characterized the turmoil of the 1960s when America was undergoing major social changes. During this period, public cynicism toward elected officials from both political parties increased because of their inability to provide immediate solutions to problems.

there. City officials and members of Congress have been assassinated; two unsuccessful attempts were made on the life of President Ford; and President Reagan was shot in 1981 by a man who also had stalked President Carter. For a time, President Johnson did not announce his travel plans in advance, and during the Johnson and Nixon administrations, the White House was so encircled by protestors that it seemed to be an embattled island, isolated from all support. The nation's college campuses, once almost idyllic places of free inquiry, seemed safely isolated from national controversy. Never so radical as European universities, they changed during a decade of violence in which students at Kent State University were killed by the National Guard.

Changing Lifestyles College students involved in the discontent and protests provided a good deal of the leadership for change. Many adopted a different lifestyle as a form of protest. At first this affected only their hair length and mode of dress, but eventually it challenged family life and basic social conventions. Political candidates like Democrat George McGovern, who appeared on college campuses soliciting votes, were often asked about their views on the legalization of marijuana, abortions, gay liberation, and amnesty for draft resisters and deserters. The fact that a *presidential* candidate would cater to this "radical" group alienated many Americans with more traditional values.

Political Corruption and Abuse of Public Office Political corruption and abuse of public office dealt a severe blow to public confidence in government in the 1970s. A cluster of new words entered the nation's political vocabulary during this period: Watergate, Koreagate, Chappaquiddick, and ABSCAM. How could the electorate trust elected officials when in less than one year both the vice president and the president were forced to resign their offices for two entirely different scandals? *Watergate takes its name from a White House-approved burglary by seven men of the national Democratic Party headquarters located in the Watergate Building, but it stands for a variety of illegal acts committed by officers and agencies of the Nixon administration.* It was Nixon's sponsorship of the cover-up of the burglary that ultimately caused the indictment of top presidential advisers and toppled the administration.

The widespread public cynicism that became the heritage of Watergate led to tougher evaluations of potential presidential candidates. The heir apparent to the Democratic party leadership after 1968 was Massachusetts Senator Edward M. Kennedy, but his usefulness to the Democratic party was seriously damaged in July, 1969, when Mary Jo Kopechne, a young campaign worker for Bobby Kennedy, was drowned in an automobile accident after she and Edward Kennedy left a party together on Chappaquiddick Island, Massachusetts. Though the accident occurred late at night, Kennedy did not report it until the next morning, and his explanations of the event have haunted his career ever since.

Americans were also shocked by scandals involving other members of Congress. In late 1975, the Gulf Oil Company confessed to the Securities and Exchange Commission that over a ten-year period it had doled out over $5 million in illegal campaign contributions to members of Congress. In early 1976, one of the most powerful men in the House of Representatives, Wayne L. Hayes of Ohio, was charged with keeping his mistress on his official government payroll. There were other scandals, too, including the admission by seventeen members of Congress that they had accepted free hunting trips and other favors from large defense contractors. Congress also discovered that beginning in the 1960s, South Korean businessman and lobbyist Tongsun Park had distributed between $500,000 and $1 million a year in cash and gifts to members of Congress and other government officials "to promote a favorable legislative climate for South Korea."

On the eve of the 1980 elections, Congress received another jolt when it was learned that the FBI was involved in a far-reaching investigation of bribery and corruption at all levels of government and that at least seven members of Congress were implicated. *"ABSCAM"* (Arab Scam) *was a nationwide undercover effort to identify corrupt public officials.* Posing as wealthy Arab businessmen, FBI agents invited government officials to meetings at which cash bribes were exchanged for influence. These meetings were recorded on film. Ultimately, one senator and six representatives were indicted and convicted. Subsequently all seven were either defeated by the voters or expelled by a vote of their colleagues in the House and the Senate.

Stagflation   Public confidence in the parties was further eroded by their inability to solve the economic problems of the 1970s. Recession and inflation had been cyclical since World War II, but a new term, *stagflation,* was coined to cover *simultaneous inflation and lack of economic growth.* The long American tradition of economic optimism even in very bad times shifted to pessimism, and for a few years the public seriously doubted that government could do anything to make a difference in the quality of their lives.

In summary, the crises of the 1960s and 1970s eroded public confidence in government, particularly elected officials. Officials from both parties either failed to solve problems or themselves caused some of the problems. Consequently, many citizens began to vote for individuals according to their stance on certain key issues and to rely less on party labels. This trend was particularly strong among young voters.

Independent Voters   In the earliest studies of voting behavior in 1940, scholars discovered that a majority of the American electorate had strong party loyalties. Most Americans thought of themselves as Democrats or Republicans, and few thought of themselves as independents. Those who rejected party labels tended to be less active, less informed, and less likely to vote. Accordingly, party identification was an extremely important variable in explaining the outcome of elections.

After 1960 a pattern of change gradually emerged that scholars have called "party decomposition" (See Figure 6.1). The number of independents increased, and the number of persons who described themselves as "strong" partisans declined sharply. Also, the number of voters who split their ticket between the parties increased. Especially in the 1970s, voters gave increasingly negative evaluations of the parties; issue voting increased as party voting declined.[19]

Rise of Single Issue Voters   Political parties have also suffered at the hands of single issue voters. Many of the issues that emerged during the 1960s and 1970s were precisely the type that typically evoke the strongest personal feelings. They touched on the religious, moral, and ethical values of different groups of people. When such issues emerge, they form the single issue voter's overriding concern, by which he or she judges a political party. However, because political parties must adopt centrist strategies to win elections, they cannot take such strong positions on issues that they will alienate a significant portion of this political center. The Democratic and Republican Parties took the center on such issues as legalization of marijuana, gay rights, civil disobedience, and amnesty for draft evaders. But by refusing to commit themselves on such issues, they alienated from party politics voters who felt very strongly about each of these issues.

This trend toward single-issue voting has continued into the 1980s and parallels an increase in the number and strength of single-issue interest groups. (Interest groups will be the focus of the next chapter.) It also parallels another trend, the growing influence of the media.

The Media and the Modern Campaign   The growing influence of the media and of political consultants has also contributed to the declining role of political parties, especially in campaigns. The old political campaign included parades, rallies, and thousands of party volunteers contacting voters personally. This type of campaign has been replaced by a combination of well-orchestrated media events designed to attract free news coverage and paid commercials on television and radio. The modern campaign is designed and managed by professional political consulting firms that provide a wide range of services, including fund raising to pay for their services. For example, Republican Senator Jesse Helms of North Carolina won reelection in 1978 in a campaign that cost $7.5 million, or $12 per vote, compared to his challenger's $0.26 per vote. Most of the money was raised by mail solicitation in contributions of less than $100. The cost of raising the money was about one-half the amount raised.

The widespread use of the direct primary to nominate candidates contributed to the increased influence of the media and political consultants at the expense of parties. Because party organizations legally are given only a limited role in most primaries, candidates must build their own personal organizations, find funding sources, and secure professional help. Then, when the primary is over, nominees tend to maintain their own organization.

Did the new technology and the pervasiveness of the media reduce the influence of political parties, or did they fill a void left as the parties atrophied? In the late 1970s, the Republican National Committee began to provide modern campaign technology to their candidates, a service that seems to have accounted for some Republican successes of 1980. If the party organizations become useful to candidates again, perhaps their influence will begin to increase.

The modern campaign, based on the use of media and political consultants, poses serious problems for party responsibility. The content and management of campaigns have been separated from the jurisdiction of the parties, but candidates still run on the party label or under the party symbol. A candidate for whom the party wishes no responsibility can win both the nomination and the election. The technology of the new politics is neutral in both values and ethics; it is available to all.

THE FUTURE OF AMERICAN POLITICAL PARTIES

There has always been a tendency among political observers to predict the imminent demise of American political parties. In 1971 for example, David S. Broder, one of the nation's most distinguished journalists, wrote a book entitled *The Party's Over: the Failure of Politics in America*.[20] But as soon the parties are pronounced dead, they revive. For example, the Republican Party was declared headed for extinction when Republican candidate Ronald Reagan won the presidency in 1980 and Republicans won a majority of Senate seats. In the wake of these Republican victories, obituary notices were prepared for the Democratic Party. But in 1982, Democratic candidates won a majority of governorships and of congressional and state legislative seats.

The challenges that parties will have to meet in the 1980s are considerable. One such challenge is restoring confidence in the party system among young and well educated voters. Ultimately the parties will have to take stands on issues of importance to these groups, a task that will become easier when these groups comprise a larger portion of the voting public and their views become the political center.

A second major challenge, very much related to the first, is how to translate many highly technical issues of the day into party-line divisions. In our postindustrial society, more and more private-sec-

tor problems intertwine with public-sector problems, and the problems of various nations also intertwine, making it difficult to determine who should take responsibility and be held accountable for solutions.

A third major challenge involves the ability of parties to adapt in an age of media. Both political parties have begun to use the media to sell themselves and their candidates to the public. They are also using the media to involve citizens in party activities such as fund raising (through telethons) and platform formation (through phone-in talk shows). Party officials are well aware that they must reestablish their usefulness in campaigns if they are to regain their control over the campaign process and make candidates who use the party label more loyal to the party platform once elected.

To meet these challenges, the American party system may have to undergo another major realignment. But it seems highly unlikely that our party system will disintegrate altogether, for parties are as much an American tradition as Mom or apple pie.

It is not our intention to argue that political parties have done a perfect job, for that is hardly the case. However, for almost 200 years they have energized executive, legislative, and other policymakers. Parties have channeled public opinion and served as intermediary between the people and their public officials. The parties have been devoted to building coalitions in a nation with a great diversity of interests. In building coalitions and striking policy bargains, the parties have been masters at gaining public assent to policy. Even the most controversial policy decisions have attained a legitimacy, most of the time, through the bargaining process.

SUMMARY

Most Americans hold somewhat conflicting opinions about political parties. On the one hand, they tend to believe that party makes little difference in the behavior of elected officials. On the other, most willing use a party label to describe themselves and as a cue in deciding how to vote.

Although there is no universally applicable definition of a political party, a party is generally defined as a group of people with similar beliefs who organize to win elections, operate government, and determine public policy. Although there is a debate over the importance of parties, most authorities agree that along with interest groups they are important links between citizens and government. They help transform individual preferences into policy.

American political parties are not provided for in the Constitution, because the Founders feared and distrusted them. But parties soon emerged and were embraced fairly quickly. The American party system has developed unique characteristics. It is extra-constitutional, two-party, centrist, decentralized, and undisciplined. Within each party, there are really three parties—the party in government, the party organization, and the party in the electorate.

The United States has had over 900 political parties, but only four major ones—the Federalists, Jeffersonians (Democrats), Whigs, and Republicans. Each of these major parties emerged over economic issues or issues involving the enfranchisement of new groups of voters. These four, working in pairs, have virtually monopolized politics in this country. Since 1854, the two-party system has been composed of the Democratic and Republican parties.

Periods of party stability are called party systems. Occasionally, changes occur and there are major shifts in party loyalty among certain groups of voters. Such periods are called eras of party realignment. Critical elections signal the end to these eras and the beginning of a new party system, or period of stability. There have been five critical elections in our history: 1800, 1828, 1860, 1896, and 1932. Third parties occasionally increase in importance and act as vote getters, policy innovators, and safety valves for strong dissent.

Party organizations are hierarchical. Each level of the party organization (precinct, county, state, or national) has some influence on the selection of party leaders at the next highest level. Power flows from the bottom up rather than from the top down. The real strength of the parties is at the grass roots (state and local) level. In fact, the national party committee has very little formal power over the fifty state party systems. Party organizations are most active during elections. Between elections, the party is held together by a few party activists (party committee members and chairpersons).

Corruption among big city political machines and their bosses led to a reform movement around the turn of the century. This movement was organized by good-government groups who wanted to professionalize or depoliticize government. Several of their proposed reforms, the office-bloc ballot, civil service, nonpartisan elections, and the direct primary, among others, effectively weakened the strength of political parties. However, the most marked period of party decline was between 1960 and 1980. A series of domestic and foreign crises, a rise in the educational level of the population, the growing influence of the media, and an increase in the number of independent and single-issue voters all combined to weaken parties. Even efforts to reform the party structure (such as democratizing the selection of delegates to party conventions and party committees) weakened the party machinery.

In order to reverse this decline, some of the major challenges parties must meet in the 1980s will be to restore the confidence of young and well-educated voters in the party system, to translate highly technical issues into party lines, and to adapt to the media age. In spite of the difficulty of meeting these challenges and the declining strength of parties in recent years, it is unlikely that American parties will disintegrate altogether. Parties are a long-standing American institution with which a large number of citizens still identify.

POLITICAL PARTIES AND ECONOMIC POLICY: IDEOLOGICAL CONSISTENCY?

Elected officials do not always vote their party's line once elected. Because of this, American parties are described as less ideological and less disciplined than European political parties. Under what conditions do elected officials choose to abandon party lines? A look at three such key votes in Congress can give us some insight.

Three times during the 1970s, Congresspeople were asked to approve major financial assistance packages to corporations (two private and one public) facing imminent bankruptcy: the Lockheed Corporation in 1971, New York City in 1975, and the Chrysler Corporation in

American political parties are often described as undisciplined because elected officials do not always vote their party's position on key issues. These three members of the Senate Finance Committee, Robert Dole, a Republican (left), Harry Byrd, an Independent (center), and Russell Long, a Democrat (right), all voted for a Republican-sponsored tax cut.

1979. Knowing the Republican Party's traditional opposition to government intervention in the free market and to increases in federal grants-in-aid to state and local governments, we would expect to find that Republicans overwhelmingly voted *against* each of these proposals. But did they?

The Republican (and Democratic) party votes on the three issues are shown in the table below. On the Lockheed proposal, a majority of the Republicans in both the House and the Senate voted *for* aid to Lockheed—just the opposite of what we would have expected based on our knowledge of the party's ideological positions. On the Chrysler proposal, however, the vote was in the ex-

pected direction—against. Finally, on the proposal to aid New York City, the vote was in the expected direction only in the House (against); in the Senate, the party was split (half for, half against).

To understand why certain Republicans in Congress abandoned the party line, one has to examine the characteristics of their individual constituencies. For example, Senator John Tower, "Mr. Conservative" among Texas Republicans, voted *for* aid to the Lockheed Corporation (a defense industry) and even led the flood fight for it. His decision to abandon the party line might be explained by the fact that a very large number of federal defense contracts go to businesses in Texas. Likewise, New York Representative Jack Kemp, a fiscal conservative, voted *for* aid to New York City. His vote might be explained by the fact that major financial institutions in New York would have been threatened by New York City's bankruptcy. As a final example, Senator Richard Lugar, a conservative from Indiana, voted *for* aid to the Chrysler Corporation and even wrote key portions of the legislation. His vote may have been influenced by the fact that all of Chrysler's automatic transmissions are built by a plant located in Indiana, a plant that would have closed had Chrylser folded.

This case raises several important questions. First, would the majority of the Republicans in these officials' districts have expected them to vote the party line in spite of the fact that it might hurt the economy of their district? Second, are the Republican party priorities in each of these states in line with the national party platform? Third, did the national Republican Party committee play as important a role in the election of these officials as the state and local party organizations in their respective states? Finally, had we examined the votes of the Democrats who abandoned the party line on each of these proposals, would we have found similar economic explanations?

	Lockheed		New York City		Chrysler	
	For	Against	For	Against	For	Against
House	50.4%	49.6%	51.2%	48.8%	66.6%	33.4%
	(192)	(189)	(213)	(203)	(271)	(136)
Republicans	60.0	40.0	27.5	72.5	41.3	58.7
	(90)	(60)	(38)	(100)	(62)	(88)
Democrats	44.2	55.8	62.9	37.1	81.3	18.7
	(102)	(129)	(175)	(103)	(209)	(48)
Senate	50.5%	49.5%	65.5%	34.5%	54.6%	45.4%
	(49)	(48)	(57)	(30)	(53)	(44)
Republicans	61.4	38.6	50.0	50.0	30.8	69.2
	(27)	(17)	(16)	(16)	(12)	(27)
Democrats	41.5	58.5	74.5	25.5	70.7	29.3
	(22)	(31)	(41)	(14)	(41)	(17)

SOURCE: *Congressional Quarterly Almanac*, XXVII, p. 152 ff., XXXI, p. 441 ff., XXXV, p. 285 ff.

KEY TERMS

ABSCAM
amateur activist
American system
coalition
critical election
direct primary
election
nomination
office-block ballot
party image
party in office
party in the electorate
party organization
party platform
patronage appointment
plurality requirement
political boss
political machine
political party
popular sovereignty
professionals
purist activist
recruitment
"responsible" party system
stagflation
Watergate
winner-take-all principle

SUGGESTED READINGS

Chambers, William Nisbet and Burnham, Walter Dean, eds. *The American Party Systems: Stages of Political Development.* 2d ed. New York: Oxford University Press, 1975.

Crotty, William J., and Jacobson, Gary C. *American Political Parties in Decline.* Boston: Little, Brown, 1980.

Downs, Anthony. *An Economic Theory of Democracy.* New York: Harper and Row, 1957.

Fishel, Jeff, ed. *Parties and Elections in an Anti-Party Age: American Politics and the Crisis of Confidence.* Bloomington, Ind.: Indiana University Press, 1978.

Jewell, Malcolm E., and Olson, David M. *American State Political Parties and Elections.* 2d. ed. Homewood, Ill.: Dorsey Press, 1982.

Ladd, Everett Carll, Jr., with Hadley, Charles D. *Transformations of the American Party Systems: Political Coalitions from the New Deal to the 1970s.* New York: W.W. Norton, 1975.

Mazmanian, Daniel A. *Third Parties in Presidential Elections.* Washington, D.C.: Brookings Institution, 1974.

Ranney, Austin. *Curing the Mischiefs of Faction: Party Reform in America.* Berkeley, Calif.: University of California Press, 1975.

Rosenstone, Steven J., Behr, Roy L. and Lazarus, Edward H. *Third Party Voting in America,* to be published and copyright ©1984 by Princeton University Press.

Sundquist, James L. *Dynamics of the Party System.* Washington, D.C.: Brookings Institution, 1973.

Trilling, Richard J., *Party Image and Electoral Behavior.* New York: John Wiley & Sons, 1976.

CHAPTER 7

INTEREST GROUPS: COMPETITORS IN THE POLICYMAKING PROCESS

Interest Groups in a Democracy ■ Political Interest Groups ■ Government Interest Groups ■ Strategies and Techniques

Japanese-American Citizen League, Gay Rights National Lobby, Christian Voice, United States Automobile Association, Sierra Club, National Coal Association, Environmental Industry Council, Citizen Victims of Chrysler—at first glance, these groups appear to have nothing in common. But all of them sent lobbyists to Washington in the 1980s to influence the policymaking process. In reality, these are but a few of thousands of interest groups that compete to influence policymaking in lifestyle rights, the economy, energy, and the environment.

Because of recent publicity about the activities of lobbyists, interest group activity may seem to be a new political phenomenon. In fact, it is not. Many years ago, V. O. Key noted:

A striking feature of American politics is the extent to which political parties are supplemented by private associations formed to influence public policy. . . . Such groups, while they may call themselves nonpolitical, are engaged in politics; in the main theirs is a politics of policy. They are concerned with what government does either to help or harm their membership.[1]

A ***political interest group*** (also referred to as a ***pressure group***) *is an organization whose members share the same views about the type of policy the government should adopt on a specific issue or several issues.* In contrast to a political party, whose primary goal is to elect people to office, an interest group tries to influence a public policy that directly or indirectly affects its members. In short, parties focus on *selecting* policymakers, and interest groups focus on *influencing* policymakers.

Both political parties and interest groups are important links between the citizen and government policymakers. And just as political parties compete to elect officials, interest groups compete to influence them. Later in this chapter, we will show how interest groups with opposite policy preferences have attempted to influence the policymaking activities of executive, legislative, and judicial officials. Specifically, we will look at interest group activity on one economic issue, whether the American auto industry should be protected at the expense of free trade. This example will expose you to some of the different interest groups active in American politics and the techniques they use to influence policy.

INTEREST GROUPS IN A DEMOCRACY

Are Interest Groups Important in Our Democracy?

Interest groups have always been an important direct link between the citizenry and policymakers. Since America's founding, interest groups have helped "translate social and economic power into political power through the process of articulating specific [policy] demands."[2] As society has changed, interest groups have helped push for changes in legislation. Even so, many disagree about whether interest groups really result in policies that reflect the public interest.

Some people maintain that interest groups represent democracy in its purest form, that is, citizens exercising their First Amendment freedoms of speech, assembly, and petition. They argue that interest groups prove our government is "of, *by*, and for" the people. Groups are beneficial, they contend, because they 1) inform policymakers and citizens about problems and issues, 2) stimulate public debate, 3) help policymakers evaluate the impact of proposed legislation—whom it will help and hurt, 4) monitor the activity of policymakers and thereby act as a check on their power, 5) allow new viewpoints and new groups access to policymakers, and 6) allow minority viewpoints to be expressed. By doing these things, interest groups help "to stabilize political relationships by increasing the public's participation in official policymaking, thereby increasing public satisfaction and identification with the government."[3]

On the other side are those who think the growing number of interest groups may actually damage democracy. Doubts about interest groups were first expressed by James Madison in *The Federalist No. 10*. He pointed out that interest groups, or "factions," were united by a "common impulse of passion, or of interest, adverse to the rights of other citizens, or to the permanent and aggregate interests of the community."[4] Thus, in Madison's view, interest groups demonstrated human selfishness. However, he was also firmly convinced that the federal system of government with its checks and balances would be able to control such groups.

More recent critics are not so sure. According to E. E. Schattschneider, groups have a definite upper-class bias. Joiners are likely to be wealthier, more educated, and higher status individuals than nonjoiners. The result is unrepresentative public policy—policy that does not accurately reflect the public interest.[5]

Growth of Interest Groups   Good or bad, interest groups continue to be an intricate part of America's political system, and their number is growing. Between 1960 and 1980, the population of the United States grew from about 179 million to 227 million, an increase of 26.3 percent. During the same period, as shown in Table 7.1, the number of organizations grew from 8,207 to 13,974, an increase of 70.3 percent—and these figures represent only the growth in national organizations. If we added the groups that exist only in a state or locality, the number would be enormous.

Not all these groups directly involve themselves in the policymaking process by hiring lobbyists, contributing to political campaigns, running television spots and newspaper ads, conducting studies, and staging protests. However, the existence of these groups does demonstrate to policymakers that some segment of the citizenry cares about a particular issue.

Groups exist to represent the interests of just about everyone. There are business groups, labor groups, agricultural groups, racial and ethnic groups, public-interest groups, professional groups, women's groups, and groups representing senior citizens, the handicapped, veterans, and gays. There are even groups representing state and local governments, government employees, and foreign governments.

POLITICAL INTEREST GROUPS

Business Groups

The largest number of political interest groups are business organizations. They have been active in the policymaking process since Colonial days, when they represented the interests of fur traders, merchants, and shippers. In recent years, their number has increased rapidly in response to expansion of federal laws and regulations. Business groups are particularly interested in regulation of industry, labor, international trade, tax policy, banking laws, and government subsidies. Many large corporations try to directly influence the pol-

TABLE 7.1

Changes in Number and Type of National, Nonprofit Organizations (1961–1980)

Type of Organization*	1961		1980		Increase 1961–1980	
	Number	%	Number	%	Number	%
Trade and commercial organizations	2584	31.5	3033	21.7	+ 449	+ 17.4
Commodity exchanges and agricultural	504	6.1	659	4.7	+ 155	+ 30.8
Governmental, public administration, military, legal	279	3.4	494	3.5	+ 215	+ 77.1
Scientific, technical, and engineering	425	5.2	982	7.0	+ 557	+ 131.1
Educational and cultural	812	10.0	2271	16.3	+ 526	+ 64.8
Social welfare	323	3.9	880	6.3	+ 657	+ 203.4
Health and medical	598	7.3	1337	9.6	+ 739	+ 123.6
Public affairs	268	3.3	950	6.8	+ 682	+ 254.5
Fraternal, foreign interest, nationality, and ethnic	487	5.9	438	3.1	− 49	− 10.1
Religious	697	8.5	738	5.3	+ 41	+ 5.9
Veteran, hereditary, and patriotic	140	1.7	205	1.5	+ 110	+ 78.6
Hobby and avocational	228	2.8	867	6.2	+ 639	+ 280.3
Athletic and sports	192	2.3	473	3.4	+ 281	+ 146.4
Labor unions, associations, and federations	239	2.9	227	1.6	− 12	− 5.0
Chambers of Commerce	108	1.3	103	0.7	− 5	− 4.6
Greek-letter societies	323	3.9	317	2.3	− 6	− 1.9
TOTAL	8207	100.0	13,974	100.0	+ 5767	+ 70.3

SOURCES: *Encyclopedia of Associations,* 3d ed., vol. I, *National Organizations of the United States* (Detroit, Mich.: Gale Research Company, 1961); Nancy Yakes and Denise Akey, eds., *Encyclopedia of Associations,* 14th ed., vol. I, *National Organizations of the United States* (Detroit, Mich.: Gale Research Company, 1980).

*Not all of these groups directly try to influence public policy.

icymaking process. The list of corporations that sent at least one lobbyist to Washington in the 1980s reads like a who's who of American companies. In addition, a few corporations set up a Washington office or hire a Washington-based law firm or public relations firm to represent them before congressional committees, executive agencies, and the courts.

Although only a few businesses can afford to open a Washington office, nearly all can afford to belong to at least one trade association. The broadest and best known of these is the United States Chamber of Commerce, which was founded in 1912. By 1980, the Chamber had more than 97,000 members, including 1,321 specialized trade associations and 2,726 state and local chambers; it required a staff of 1,200. From its headquarters across from the White House, the Chamber develops positions on nearly all issues affecting businesses and draws up strategies to get those positions across to policymakers and the public.

Another powerful and well-established trade association is the National Association of Manufacturers (NAM), organized in 1895. By 1980 NAM had 14,000 members, primarily industrial companies, and a staff of 220. Like the Chamber of Commerce, NAM has its headquarters in Washington.

The Chamber of Commerce and the National Association of Manufacturers represent primarily big businesses. Smaller businesses are more likely to join the National Federation of Independent Businesses (NFIB), founded in 1943. NFIB has a membership of 620,000—making it the largest group in terms of membership—and a staff of 120. The National Small Business Association (NSBA) also represents the interest of small business owners; it has 40,000 members.

The Chamber, NAM, NFIB, and NSBA are *umbrella organizations—each is a broad-based group to which a number of other organizations belong.* These groups concentrate on matters of interest to the business community as a whole. Matters specific to an industry are handled by *trade associations,* which are among the more active political interest groups in Washington today. Trade associations *are composed of businesses operating in the same field.* There are trade associations for banking, real estate, and hospitals, for example. The Society of Association Executives reports that the average association in Washington employs 29 people (about half professional employees); their average salary is $21,000. The Society estimates the total payroll of trade associations to be close to $1.2 billion.[6]

Labor Groups

Although business groups outnumber labor groups, labor groups have more members. They have existed since the days of George Washington, but in recent years their membership has declined. Less than one-fourth of the work force now belong to unions. Even so, labor groups continue to wield a great deal of influence in Washington, where many have their headquarters and employ full-time lobbyists. They are interested in a wide range of policy issues such as working conditions, wages, pensions, Social Security, medical insurance, taxation, foreign trade, and immigration.

The best-known labor union is the American Federation of Labor-Congress of Industrial Organizations (AFL-CIO). This umbrella organization joins together 107 separate unions (for example, the Amalgamated Transit Union, the International Association of Machinists and Aerospace Workers, and the Government Employees' Council). It has a membership of more than 14 million and a staff of 600, including its own legislative department and numerous full-time lobbyists. Its headquarters is only two blocks from the White House.

The largest single union not affiliated with the AFL-CIO, is the International Brotherhood of Teamsters, Chauffeurs, Warehousemen, and Helpers of America (the Teamsters Union), with a membership of nearly 2.3 million. Its headquarters is also in Washington—at the foot of Capitol Hill.

Other strong unions not affiliated with the AFL-CIO are the United Mine Workers, with 280,000 members, and the United Automobile, Aerospace, and Agricultural Implement Workers of America (UAW) with 1.5 million members. The UAW's headquarters are in Detroit. Each union, besides having a Washington office, has a legislative department to draft, monitor, and evaluate public policy, and each employs several full-time lobbyists.

Agricultural Groups

Agricultural groups are interested in price supports, production controls, foreign import policy, foreign export policy (wheat sales to Russia), low-cost government loan programs, deregulation of the trucking industry, environmental policy (pesticide control), and energy policy (protection of farmers in any gas-rationing system). There are several broad-based agricultural groups and numerous specialized groups of farmers.

Unions rely heavily on grassroots support (local organizations) for financial and political assistance in getting their messages across to policymakers at all levels.

The three broad-based groups—the American Farm Bureau Federation, the National Grange, and the National Farmers Union—represent the general interests of farmers just as the Chamber of Commerce represents the general interests of business owners and the AFL-CIO represents the general interests of organized labor. Likewise, specialized farm groups such as the National Pork Producers Council and United Egg Producers have functions as business trade associations and specialized unions.

Membership in agricultural groups has been declining for some time. Today, less than 5 percent of the population is engaged in farming. However, farm groups have remained powerful in the policymaking process, for several reasons. For one thing, agriculture is important to everyone. As one farm group's bumper sticker states, "If you eat, you're involved in agriculture." And most Americans admire those who farm for a living. Second, congressional agricultural committees are composed of representatives from Farm Belt areas, who are obviously receptive to the viewpoints of farm groups. Third, farmers have become more vocal in recent years, particularly by staging dramatic protests. In the "tractorcade" of the American Agricultural Movement (founded in 1977), farmers from all parts of the country rode their tractors to Washington to demand pay parity and call attention to sagging farm prices.

Racial and Ethnic Groups

The most powerful and politically active racial and ethnic groups are those making up the largest proportion of the total population—black, Spanish-speaking, and Jewish groups. Most racial and ethnic groups were formed to combat discrimination and poverty. They are interested in civil rights, federal aid, welfare, employment and affirmative action, housing, and voting rights.

There are two well-known broad-based groups representing blacks—the National Association for the Advancement of Colored People (NAACP) and the National Urban League. The NAACP, founded in 1910, is the oldest group. It is also the largest—by 1980, it had 450,673 members and 1,700 local chapters. The National Urban League, founded in 1914, has a membership of 50,000. Both groups maintain Washington offices and hire full-time lobbyists.

Hispanic groups are smaller, much younger,

and less cohesive than black groups. The League of United Latin American Citizens (LULAC), founded in 1929, is the oldest and largest, with a membership of 120,000. Other important Hispanic groups are the Forum of National Hispanic Organizations, La Raza, Mexican American Legal Defense and Education Fund (MALDEF), and the National Association for Puerto Rican Rights. No broad-based Hispanic group is equivalent in power to the NAACP or the Urban League because a number of diverse groups are represented by the term "Hispanic"—Mexican-Americans, Puerto Ricans, Cubans, and Latin Americans. Recently, 57 Hispanic organizations joined together to form the Forum of National Hispanic Organizations, but only three (LULAC, the National Association of Latino Elected and Appointed Officials, and the National Council of La Raza) engage in full-time lobbying in Washington. And, according to some observers, these three lobbying groups compete more than they cooperate with each other.[7]

A number of groups represent American Indians and Eskimos. Some are broad-based, such as the National Congress of American Indians, founded in 1944, and the American Indian Movement, founded in 1968. Others represent specific tribes or nations, such as the Confederated Tribes of Warm Springs, the Navajo Nation, Keweenaw Bay Chippewa Tribe, and the Shoshone-Bannoch

Groups representing American Indians are often concerned with economic issues. For example, Navajo Nation leaders have lobbied very hard to get royalties from oil, natural gas, uranium, and coal found on their lands.

Tribes. The total membership of these groups is far less than the total membership of black and Hispanic groups because Indians make up less than 1 percent of the nation's population.

Jewish groups have different interests from black, Hispanic, or American Indian groups. They are interested more in American foreign policy (aid to Israel) than in domestic policy. The strongest Jewish group is the American Israel Public Affairs Committee (AIPAC), which has about 15,000 members and represents more than 30 different Jewish organizations. By 1979, it had a staff of more than 20, an annual budget of over $750,000, and four registered lobbyists. On any issue involving Israel, AIPAC can tap a network of influential, often wealthy, Jewish citizens across the country who have direct access to policymakers.[8]

Public-Interest Groups

Jeffrey M. Berry defines a *public-interest group* as *"one that seeks a collective good, the achievement of which will not selectively and materially benefit the membership or activists of the organization."*[9] In other words, such groups' programs and policies benefit everyone in society—not just those who formally belong to the group. Berry identified 83 public-interest groups in 1974 and admitted he had probably overlooked many others.

Public-interest groups became highly visible in the 1970s, though they existed long before that. In the past, they were called good government, reform, consumer, legal rights, or taxpayer groups. So many public-interest groups arose in the 1970s, first, because the timing was right. After the Watergate scandal, many citizens were disgusted with government and its failure to control itself, business, and labor. Another reason was the success of two broad-based citizens' groups— Common Cause and Public Citizen—which used new techniques to attract members and influence policymakers.

Common Cause was founded in the summer of 1970 by former Secretary of Health, Education, and Welfare John Gardner. Within six months, the organization had 100,000 members; by early 1974, its membership reached its peak of 300,000. Gardner used a new approach to recruit members. He ran full-page advertisements in major newspapers across the United States and conducted direct mail appeals—in its first year alone,

Common Cause sent out 6.5 million pieces of mail.[10] The goal of Common Cause is to reform government. Over the years, it has pressed for the enactment of "accountability" laws calling for revision and expansion of the lobby registration act, increased financial disclosure by members of Congress, restrictions on incumbents' use of congressional staff and resources in reelection campaigns, and reform of the confirmation process in the Senate.[11]

Public Citizen, Inc., founded by Ralph Nader in 1973, focuses more on issues in the economic, consumer, environmental, legal, and social realms than on government reform. It attacks both business and government, often through the courts. Public Citizen is actually an umbrella organization that raises and distributes money for Nader's other organizations—the Health Research Group, the Litigation Group, Congress Watch, the Tax Reform Research Group, the Critical Mass Energy Project, and the Public Citizen Visitors Center in Washington, to name a few. Unlike Common Cause, which is supported by its members, Public Citizen is supported by contributors, who numbered 200,000 in 1979.

In recent years, supporters of both Common Cause and Public Citizen have gradually been shifting to more specialized public-interest groups such as those dealing with the environment (Sierra Club, National Wildlife Federation, National Clean Air Coalition), tax issues (National Taxpayers Union, Citizens for Tax Justice), and youth (Children's Foundation, Children's Defense Fund). One critic of the public-interest

Environmental groups, like the Sierra Club, are often critical of secretaries of the Interior who are responsible for the management of public lands. James Watt, Secretary of the Interior under President Reagan, was one of the most criticized, in large part for his proposal to auction off public lands.

movement believes the decline of broad-based public-interest groups was inevitable.

> The public-interest movement simply has no resource that can match the power of capital. Unlike both business and labor, the public-interest movement has nothing it can withhold from civil society in order to make credible its political demands. Corporations can refuse to invest, and workers can refuse to work. But what can public-interest organizations refuse to do? Public-interest activists have no activity in society outside of their role as pressure groups; they have no source of power independent of the political process. . . . [In] the long run [public-interest groups] cannot match the power [of business and labor] to halt or curtail economic production.[12]

This means, not that public-interest groups will just fade away, but that public-interest groups have a weaker bargaining position than business or labor. However, as Berry points out, the value of public-interest groups has always been their representation of "constituencies that have been chronically unrepresented or underrepresented in American politics."[13]

Professional Associations

Professional associations, especially those representing legal, health, and education professionals, have a great deal of influence in the policymaking arena—more than their number of members would indicate. They have relatively strong influence because of the prestige and resources of their members. They are unique as interest groups because their membership is limited to persons who have been trained for entry into a specific profession. Among these groups are the American Medical Association (213,940 members), the American Bar Association (250,000 members) and the American Association of University Professors (68,100 members). Some professionals, such as doctors and lawyers, must receive several years of academic and practical training after they receive their bachelor's degree. Teachers, certified public accountants, doctors, and lawyers must also pass licensing examinations.

The first priority of professional associations is to maintain control over who gets into the profession. In recent years, a number of doctors, lawyers, and college professors have expressed dismay over affirmative action requirements, which have been interpreted to mean that professional

schools should admit some minority students even if nonminority students have superior credentials. Members of these professions fear that lowering admission standards will lead to the eventual deterioration of their professions. On the other hand, women, blacks, and members of other minority groups believe that older members are against letting minorities into the professions at all. Our main point is that professionals, regardless of their field, greatly resent policymaking by those they consider less qualified than themselves. They often join coalitions on other social issues, but they exert their full influence only when regulation of their own profession is involved.

Women's Groups

No umbrella organization represents the general interests of all women, because gender is often a less important factor than race, religion, or occupation in determining policy preferences. As noted by V. O. Key, Jr., even before the clash between liberal and conservative women's groups in the 1970s and 1980s, "women's organizations often [had] difficulty in finding issues on which their members [had] a joint concern and in avoiding issues that generate schisms."[14] Particularly problematic are individual rights issues, such as abortion or gay rights, which have strong moral and religious overtones. Less controversial are economic and employment issues, such as equal opportunity and pay parity.

Over the years, women members of larger professional, occupational, racial, ethnic, and religious groups have tended to form subgroups to increase the participation of women in the larger groups. Such groups have an overriding commitment to the larger groups, however. For example, although the American Women's Society of Certified Public Accountants encourages women CPAs to become more active in the accounting profession, the society is primarily committed to furthering the principles and practices of public accounting. When such broader groups come into conflict with each other, as they often do, the women's subgroups also come into conflict.

During the late 1960s, women's liberation and women's rights emerged as issues around which new groups were formed. Groups such as the National Organization for Women (NOW), the Women's Equity Action League (WEAL), and the National Women's Political Caucus were

Women's rights groups became very visible in the 1970s. In 1977, the largest women's conference ever held in America took place in Houston, Texas. Delegates to this conference submitted a list to President Carter of 26 policy recommendations related to women's rights.

formed to push for social, political, and economic equality for *all* women, regardless of race, religion, or political affiliation. These groups easily won the cooperation of many traditional women's groups because they dealt with **role equity** (*providing women political and economic opportunities equal to those of men*) rather than **role change** (*a basic alteration in the distribution of sex roles in society*) or **moral change** (*change in cultural, religious, or ethical values*).[15] However, in the 1970s when NOW, WEAL, and NWPC adopted positions favoring reproductive freedom, acceptance of individual sexual preferences, and other controversial stands, new women's rights groups were formed in opposition. These more conservative groups, led nationally by Phyllis Schlafly, claim that NOW, WEAL, NWPC do not speak for all women, many women still prefer their traditional roles as wives, homemakers, and mothers.

Actually, the splintering of women's groups is typical of all social movements once they progress from the formative, ideological stage to the implementive, political stage. At first, all women's groups strongly agreed on the broad goal of equal opportunity for women, but when they tried to determine how the goal was to be achieved, women with similar religious, social, and political ideas began breaking off into smaller groups. The result is that women have become polarized along liberal and conservative lines. On issues that require role or moral changes, some women's groups push for radical change while other groups defend the status quo. Each side claims to repre-

sent the majority of the women in America.

However, women's groups, both liberal and conservative, still tend to unite on certain issues—strong penalties for those who commit violent crimes against women and children, more comprehensive Social Security coverage for wives and widows, control of pornography that exploits women and children,[16] and better wages and working conditions.

Emerging Activist Groups

In the mid-1970s, a number of new groups representing older Americans, veterans, handicapped persons, and gays were formed. A few groups representing these constituencies had existed earlier, but the new ones were much more inclined toward activism, and they stimulated the older groups to become more active. Together, they began to educate the public about their members' special needs and pressed for legal rights and the elimination of discrimination.

Groups representing older Americans, veterans, handicapped persons, and gays share one feeling—that society treats their members as second-class citizens and regularly discriminates against them in such matters as employment, housing, and access to public facilities and services. To fight this discrimination, these groups have adopted the strategies used by women and blacks in their fight to end sexual and racial discrimination—lobbying, protests, and litigation. These strategies will be discussed more thoroughly below.

GOVERNMENT INTEREST GROUPS   **185**

Groups representing America's elderly became more activist-
oriented in the 1970s. They adopted many of the strategies used
by women and blacks in their fights against discrimination.

GOVERNMENT INTEREST GROUPS

Government Employee Groups

The groups we have examined so far all represent
private individuals. However, a growing number
of groups represent governments and those who
work for them. Government employees, like their
counterparts in the private sector, have traditionally formed organizations to press for higher
wages, better working conditions, better health
and retirement benefits, and more input into the
policymaking process. Originally, these groups
closely resembled social and professional associations, but in 1962 President Kennedy issued an
executive order that officially recognized federal
employee unions and their right to bargain collectively for their members. Since then, most of the
groups have become public-employee unions.

By 1980, there were 88 unions representing federal employees, but most members belonged to
one of four unions—the American Federation of
Government Employees (700,000 members), the
National Treasury Employment Union (115,000
members), the National Federation of Federal
Employees (150,000 members), and the National

Association of Government Employees (130,000
members). There were also two associations of
management-level government employees—Fed
42, founded in 1979, and the Senior Executive
Association, established in 1980.

Many Americans do not like the idea of public
employees being unionized because it creates the
possibility of strikes and service interruptions. It
is the fact that their services are essential that
gives public employees such power at the bargaining table. They can cause schools to close, buses
and subways to stand idle, garbage to pile up, and
the mail to stop. The unions make their demands
at the risk of encouraging public animosity. As a
result, public employee unions often use public
relations campaigns to improve their images.

Groups Representing State and Local Governments

The federal system of government has encouraged
the formation of groups representing state and local governments. The seven big umbrella organizations are the National Governors' Association,
the National Conference of State Legislatures, the
Council of State Governments, the United States
Conference of Mayors, the National League of
Cities, the International City Management Association, and the National Association of Counties.
These groups were formed during the 1960s to
pressure the national government for more grants-
in-aid and more executive control of federally-as-
sisted programs in their jurisdictions. Today they
continue to influence legislation and regulations
that affect how much money they get and how
they spend it.

In addition to belonging to organizations, individual state and local governments often set up
their own Washington offices. The director of the
Missouri governor's office in Washington expressed the states' reasoning this way: "State government is intricately entwined with the federal
government. We live and die with what the federal
government does. We're here to get our fair
share."[17]

Foreign Groups

Foreign governments, like American state and local governments, send representatives to Washington or hire Americans to represent them. As of
August, 1980, about 650 foreign agents had registered as representatives of foreign governments.
Foreign agents fall into two categories. There are

Foreign governments, especially trade states which export large quantities of goods to the U.S., often hire Washington lobbyists to represent their interests.

agents from *client states*—*governments* such as Israel and Korea *that depend heavily on the United States for military, political, and economic aid.* There are also agents from *trade states, which are primarily interested in foreign and commercial activity and exporting more goods to the United States.* The nations with the most agents here are America's chief trading partners—Japan, Canada, France, West Germany, and Mexico.

Foreign agents spend a great deal of time talking to members of Congress and to executive officials who regulate policies in which they have an interest, such as officials in the Defense and Commerce Departments and those on the Federal Trade Commission. Some foreign agents even conduct public relations campaigns to give their countries a good public image and thereby help pass legislation favorable to tourism and exports.

Intragovernmental Groups

True to our system of separation of powers and checks and balances, each government branch has employees whose major responsibility is to inform the other branches of their branch's position on various issues.

Executive Branch The most common intragovernmental activity occurs "when various departments of the executive [branch] 'lobby' the legislative branch. In such instances, the executive departments are behaving in much the same manner as an interest group . . . such as the AFL-CIO

or the National Farmers Union."[18] However, under the Lobbying with Appropriated Monies Act of 1913, executive employees are expressly prohibited from engaging in traditional lobbying activities, such as wining and dining members of Congress or sending them letters or telegrams. Technically, then, these employees are not considered lobbyists, but "liaison personnel."

Whether one calls their activities lobbying or liaison work, executive personnel regularly communicate with those in the other two branches of government. Nearly every executive agency from cabinet departments to offices and bureaus has a congressional relations division. In 1978, the congressional liaison staffs of the 12 cabinet departments alone had 311 employees and cost almost $15 million to operate.[19] These people "track legislation at the subcommittee and committee stage, field questions from members of Congress, and monitor developments within their own departments so they can give prior notice to members [who can influence] their constituents."[20] Most executive liaison personnel cultivate close ties with the members of Congress who hold key positions in the committees they most frequently interact with.

As legislation has grown in volume and complexity, Congress has increasingly turned to executive agencies for help. This help may involve giving committees technical assistance in drafting legislation, conducting evaluation studies of previously enacted legislation, and commenting on proposed legislation. The very fact that Congress often needs the assistance of executive agencies gives these agencies as much or even more power than Congress in the policymaking process.

Legislative Branch   Lobbying on the part of the legislative branch has intensified in recent years as the size of congressional committee staffs has increased. Between 1960 and 1980, the number of professional staff members doubled in the Senate and increased fivefold in the House. These staff members often try to influence employees of the executive and judicial branches. For example, a staff member of the House Appropriations Committee might try to convince a staff member of the Office of Management and Budget that Congressional Budget Office economic projections are more realistic. Likewise, a staff member of the Senate Judiciary Committee might provide a clerk of the Supreme Court with interpretative material aimed at influencing the Court's opinion on an issue under consideration.

Judicial Branch   The courts also have legislative liaison personnel. Judges themselves often contact members of Congress or their staff members to express an opinion about a piece of legislation. Some people view judicial lobbying as totally inappropriate and a direct violation of the constitutional doctrine of separation of powers, but many judges and members of Congress see it as entirely appropriate and beneficial behavior. They think good legislation cannot be drafted unless those who will be affected by it, even if they happen to be judges, have had some input into its preparation.

Intragovernmental interactions like these show how the three branches of the federal government sometimes function as interest groups. All lobbyists try to create a favorable climate for interactions with legislators, are concerned with shaping policy, and use similar strategies and tactics.

STRATEGIES AND TECHNIQUES

With literally thousands of groups vying for attention, what determines which groups will be successful in influencing the policymaking process? Which strategies and techniques catch the attention of government officials? Because different groups have different reputations and varying monetary, personnel, and organizational re-

sources, each group must figure out which combination of strategies and tactics will do the most to further its cause. The four most commonly used tactics are lobbying, campaign politicking, molding public opinion, and litigating (filing lawsuits).

Lobbying

Lobbying is the pressuring of legislative, executive, or judicial policymakers by a person or group acting as the representative of an organized group for the purpose of influencing public policy. Lobbying may occur at any stage of policymaking—formation, implementation, or evaluation.

Ever since the First Continental Congress (1774), when representatives of special interests hung around the lobbies of hotels where delegates were staying, lobbying has been a fact of political life. In the early days, lobbying was confined almost exclusively to influencing those in the legislative branch. Today, members of the executive and judicial branches are also lobbied.

Lobbyists need not be individuals; law firms, advertising agencies, and public relations firms are also hired to lobby. The role of the lobbyist remains the same—to serve as an intermediary between the client interest group and the government. There are a number of ways to gain access to policymakers.

In recent years, as we have seen, many interest groups have moved their headquarters to Washington, set up a regional office there, or hired full-time lobbyists based in Washington. It is in Washington that lobbyists interact frequently with policymakers, track the status of legislation, and mobilize the help of their group's members when it becomes necessary.

Lobbyists know that everyone likes the personal touch. A visit from a friend means more than a form letter from a stranger. Accordingly, lobbyists often personally contact members of Congress. By doing so, they hope to keep lines of communication open and to gain the trust and respect of policymakers. Lobbyists also personally contact congressional and agency staffs—more so today than in years past. Lobbyists have realized that as bills have become more technical, they are more often written by staff members. An important result of personal contacts with policymakers and their staffs may be an invitation for the lobbyist to present his or her opinions about proposed bills or regulatory rules before a congressional committee or federal regulatory agency.

Entertaining, or "social lobbying," is another technique used by lobbyists. This technique, which gave lobbying a bad reputation, was used more often and less discreetly in the past than today. Lobbyists still pay for lunches, but buying a policymaker a lunch does not have the persuasive power it once did. The tremendous increase in the amount of legislation being introduced and the highly technical nature of most of it has made information more important than meals.

Thus, the most effective lobbying technique today is providing policymakers and their staffs with reliable, high-quality information. As one lobbyist put it, this allows him to "continually build up a rapport and credibility. You give [policymakers] bad information once, and you can forget it."[21]

Lobbyists themselves often draft a bill they would like to see passed and then look for members of Congress to introduce it—ideally, as many as possible as cosponsors. At the least, lobbyists want members of the key committees in each house to sponsor their bill. They also distribute copies to sympathetic staffers and urge them to assure Congress members that the bill is a good one.

Another lobbying strategy involves taking the offensive and stealing your opponents' thunder. One public relations firm helped the Glass Packaging Institute (an industrial interest group) portray itself as the defender—not a despoiler—of the environment. This strategy caught environmental groups completely off guard. Before the environmental groups could introduce legislation requiring deposits on bottles and cans (which the Glass Packaging Institute did not want), the public relations firm helped the Institute draft and get sponsors for legislation to tax all firms contributing to litter, with the revenues from the tax to be used for recycling centers. The public relations executive said, "We took the idea of an industry solving its own problems rather than being forced to do so [by environmental groups]."[22] Another successful public relations strategy has been to create "speakers' bureaus" to create positive images of an industry or issue (see Figure 7.1).

Another important part of lobbying is building coalitions. V. O. Key calls this *intergroup lobbying—the process by which lobbyists try to get other groups to join theirs, either permanently or temporarily.*[23] Interest groups often form coalitions to exchange information and coordinate strategies, not just to get fast action on a bill. For example, the AFL-CIO

FIGURE 7.1

Public Relations Strategy of a Major Oil Company

SOURCE: Atlantic Richfield

Speaker's bureaus are lobbying techniques commonly used by industries or groups who are concerned that press coverage of their side of an issue has not been adequate. They are particularly popular among the major oil companies.

invites three powerful independent unions (the United Auto Workers, the Teamsters, and the

United Mine Workers) to its weekly legislative strategy sessions.

Most lobbying activities discussed so far have been *inside strategies, which rely on the internal legislative and political needs of members of Congress, as well as the network of social relationships, to cultivate access and exert influence.*[24] Equally important are *outside strategies, lobbying activities at the grassroots level designed to mobilize interest group members in the home districts of members of Congress.*

There are many grassroots lobbying tactics. One of the oldest and most common is to organize massive telephone, telegram, and letter-writing campaigns. Today, this is often done by computer. Many groups have their membership lists computerized and organized by congressional district, which allows them to fire off legislative alerts quickly. If the problem is less urgent, organizations may use monthly newsletters and publications to urge members to write their representatives and senators. Another common grassroots tactic is to arrange for influential people back home to call a member of Congress or, even better, to personally visit their representative. A final example of a grassroots strategy is for a business or industry located in a Congress member's district to remind the member how many jobs in his or her district a proposed piece of legislation would create, keep, or eliminate. This strategy is a favorite of lobbyists for the defense industry.

Underlying all these tactics are two broad goals: 1) to create the impression that the issue is important to a large number of folks back home, including many powerful people, and 2) to suggest that at election time, the interest group will not forget how their senator or representative voted on this issue and this issue alone. Meeting the second goal is difficult for large groups with diverse interests; meeting the first is difficult for small, single-interest groups.

The strategies and technqiues chosen are often based on the recommendations of the group's lobbyists. "It is the lobbyist's job to select the form of communication most likely to be favorably and accurately received by the intended [policymaker]. This means that the lobbyist must choose the target and content of the message with care and skill."[25] Some lobbyists are more effective than others, often because of their previous experience and their personalities.

Who Are the Lobbyists? Lobbying has become big business. Because of costs and intense competition, lobbyists must be professional. "The bribe-offering, cigar-smoking entrepreneur of the past has been replaced by a smooth-talking, sophisticated business [person] who works the nooks and crannies of power."[26] Lobbying has also become a specialized business. Groups often hire a number of lobbyists, each with a different skill—making contacts, opening doors because of their prestigious name, understanding the timing of the policymaking process, being able to read public opinion, mobilizing members, raising money, or putting people at ease, for example.

Most lobbyists are recruited from fields such as public relations, law, business, or government service. There is no college for lobbyists. As Table 7.2 shows, the recruitment paths for public-interest lobbyists are different from those for private sector (business and labor) lobbyists. Fifty-seven percent of the private sector lobbyists are recruited directly from the administrative or legislative branches of government; only 26 percent of all public-interest lobbyists are recruited from government. Lobbyists are well educated. More than 90 percent have some college education and 65 percent have a graduate degree.

Former members of Congress no longer form an overwhelming majority of lobbyists. Today, only one-third of the Washington lobbying corps consists of former Congress members. Still, many interest groups prefer Congress members, primarily because of their contacts with those still in Congress, their familiarity with the legislative process, and their knowledge of the operations of the committees of which they were members. Recruiting former members is not difficult. Many want to stay in Washington. In the Ninety-fifth Congress, about 25 percent of its 87 departing members remained in Washington to work for corporations, trade groups, consulting companies, or law firms that specialized in legislative matters (see Table 7.3).

Of course, being a former Congress member is no guarantee that a person will be a good lobbyist. An interest group may prefer not to hire former members for several reasons. As interest group leaders explain it,

A lobbyist has to do the grunt work. Members of Congress [are used to having] staff to do the grunt work. . . . A lot of [former members] just like to float around

TABLE 7.2

Prior Career Experience of Public-Interest Group and Business- and Labor-Group Lobbyists

	Public-Interest Lobbyists		Traditional Business- and Labor-Group Lobbyists
	Career Pattern	Most Recent Job	Most Recent Job
Law (private practice)	16%	11%	8%
Business	9	11	17
Government	26	26	57
Journalism	10	2	1
Teaching	6	4	X
Religion	5	4	X
Interest group work	7	14	2
Liberal arts (college background only)	9	14	X
Other	11	12	15
	99%	98%	100%
		(N = 91)	(N = 106)

SOURCE: Jeffrey M. Berry, *Lobbying for the People: The Political Behavior of Public Interest Groups.* Copyright © 1977 by Princeton University Press. Table IV-5 reprinted by permission of Princeton University Press.

TABLE 7.3

They Can't Stay Away from their Old Haunting Grounds
Following is a list of prominent former Members of Congress who continue to live in the Washington area and work as representatives of domestic and foreign clients, dealing mostly in government relations and legislative counseling. Included are the names of their current employers or firms and some of their clients:

Sen. James Abourezk, D-S.D. Now at the law firm of Abourezk, Sobol & Trister. Represents several Middle East clients but is not registered as a foreign agent.

Sen. Edward W. Brooke, R-Mass. Now at the law firm of O'Connor & Hannan. General practice.

Rep. John W. Byrnes of Wisconsin, senior Republican on the Ways and Means Committee. Now at the law firm of Foley, Lardner, Hollabaugh & Jacobs. Government consulting, specializing in congressional relations. Registered lobbyist for the Insurance Association of Connecticut.

Rep. Charles E. Chamberlain, R-Mich. Now at the law firm of Webster, Chamberlain & Bean. Specializes in tax law. Represents about 150 associations. Clients include the American Apparel Manufacturers, the Army Mutual Aid Association, the International Taxicab Association, the National Association of Accountants and the Packaging Machinery Institute. Registers as lobbyist when required.

Sen. Frank Church, D-Idaho, chairman of the Foreign Relations Committee. Now at the law firm of Whitman & Ransom. International law.

Sen. Marlow W. Cook, R-Ky. Now at the law firm of Cook, Purcell, Hansen & Henderson. Represents the Tobacco Institute.

Rep. James C. Corman, D-Calif. Now at Manatt, Phelps, Rothenberg & Tunney. Focuses on legislative law and government relations. Clients include the GATX Corp., manufacturers of railroad tanks, Music Corp. of America, the Tobacco Institute, Northwest Pipeline Co. and the Northrop Corp.

Sen. John C. Culver, D-Iowa. Now at the law firm of Arent, Fox, Kintner, Plotkin & Kahn. Firm represents the Teamsters Union Central States Pension Fund and is a registered foreign agent for "all kinds of foreign clients."

Rep. Robert Duncan, D-Ore. Now at the law firm of Schwabe, Williamson, Wyatt, Moore, Roberts & Duncan. Government consulting. Registered as a lobbyist. Clients include the state of Oregon, the Metropolitan Portland Mass Transit District, the City of Portland, Multnomah County, Ore., the Portland Metropolitan Council of Governments, the General Aviation Manufacturers Association and Mountain States Energy Inc. Also represents the timber industry.

Rep. Bob Eckhardt, D-Texas. Now at the law firm of McCarthy, Sweeney & Harkaway. Registered lobbyist for the Investment Company Institute, Consolidated Natural Gas Co. and the Consumer Federation of America. Also represents Walton & Sons, a Pasadena (Texas) stevedoring company.

Sen. J. W. Fulbright, D-Ark., chairman of the Foreign Relations Committee. Now at the law firm of Hogan & Hartson. General practice and international law.

Rep. Robert N. Giaimo, D-Conn., chairman of the Budget Committee. Now in private law practice, specializing in government relations. Clients include United Technologies Corp. and the Insurance Association of Connecticut. Also co-chairman of the Committee for a Responsible Federal Budget.

(continued)

TABLE 7.3 *(continued)*

Sen. William D. Hathaway, D-Maine. Now at the law firm of Patton, Boggs & Blow. Legislative counseling and anti-trust law. Firm is a registered lobbyist for the Chrysler Corp. Among Hathaway's clients is the Great Atlantic & Pacific Tea Co.

Rep. Clark S. MacGregor, R-Minn. Now vice president for external affairs at United Technologies Corp. Several staff members are registered as lobbyists.

Rep. Jack H. McDonald, R-Mich. Now at McDonald Associates. Government consulting and lobbying services. Registered lobbyist for the American Express Co., the Burroughs Corp., the Dow Chemical Co. and the Dow Corning Corp. Registered as a foreign agent on behalf of the embassies of Japan and Turkey and Nissan, the Japanese manufacturers of the Datsun automobile.

Sen. George McGovern, D-S.D. Now head of Americans for Common Sense. Lectures and teaches courses on U.S. history and foreign policy.

Rep. Wilbur D. Mills, D-Ark., chairman of the Ways and Means Committee. Now at the law firm of Shea & Gould. Tax counseling. Registers when case requires lobbying.

Rep. Paul G. Rogers, D-Fla. Now at the law firm of Hogan & Hartson. Registered lobbyist for savings and loan firms and engineering designers. General practice.

Sen. Richard (Dick) Stone, D-Fla. Now at the law firm of Proskauer, Rose, Goetz & Mendelsohn. International law. Registered as a foreign agent. Clients include Dupont Banana Corp. of Miami, Board of Foreign Trade of Taiwan, Capital Bank of Washington and Capital Bank of Miami.

Rep. Al Ullman, D-Ore., chairman of the Ways and Means Committee. Now at Ullman Consultants. Government relations and legislative counseling.

SOURCE: Dom Bonafede, "Life After Congress—Former Members Stay in Town as Political Insiders," *National Journal,* 14 (September 4, 1982), p. 1509.

seeing their old buddies, hanging out in the Speaker's lobby. . . . The last thing a small [lobbying] firm needs is a former member who thinks he's still running the show.[27]

Given the potential disadvantages of retaining former Congress members as lobbyists, interest groups often look elsewhere for lobbyists. The research abilities of congressional staff members have made them a prime target for lobbying recruitment efforts. Another popular source is former legislative liaison personnel from the executive and judicial branches. The majority of lobbyists, however, are recruited from the interest group they represent. Such lobbyists tend to have a better knowledge of the issues important to the group, the information the group can generate, and the most effective techniques for mobilizing the membership.

Most Americans remain unaware that lobbying has been professionalized. A couple of unethical lobbyists and a few dishonest policymakers can reaffirm most citizens' negative views of lobbyists and intensify demands for tighter regulation of lobbyists.

Regulation of Lobbying Hardly a session of Congress has passed in which some piece of legislation to tighten lobbying regulations has not been introduced. The Federal Regulation of Lobbying Act, passed in 1946, is the major legislation in force today. This act requires disclosure of who is lobbying for whom and how much they are being paid; it does not dictate how lobbying can take place. It requires that any person or group intending to lobby a member of Congress register with the House Clerk or the Senate Secretary and file quarterly expenditure and activity reports.

The act is written in such vague terms that lobbyists have found numerous loopholes to escape from registering. One estimate is that of the 20,000 people in Washington earning at least part of their living lobbying Congress, only 5,500 (28 percent) are actually registered.[28] One reason for this disparity is the narrow definition of lobbying, which excludes lobbying of executive or judicial policymakers. Another reason is the Supreme Court's narrow interpretation of the Lobbying Act in *United States* v. *Harris* (1954). The Court ruled that the Act covers only groups that solicit money for influencing Congress members, not groups or individuals who spend their own money, and that the Act applies only to groups or individuals whose principal purpose is influencing members of Congress through direct contacts with them.

Why has Congress not passed stronger registration laws? One reason is that it is difficult to impose restrictions without infringing on the constitutional rights of free speech, press, assembly, and petition. Another is fear that such restrictions would hurt legitimate lobbies without really curbing the more serious lobby abuses. Finally, the lobbyists themselves have effectively lobbied against it, keeping regulation to a minimum.

Today, there is a move among lobbyists toward self-regulation. The American League of Lobbyists, founded in 1979, has developed a code of ethics in an attempt to improve the public image of lobbyists. Group members see the ethics code as part of the overall professionalization of lobbying, which may eventually involve educational requirements, accreditation of lobbyists, and self-regulation.

Campaign Politicking

Campaign support, monetary or otherwise, has two broad purposes—to make a member of Congress or a president more sympathetic to a group's interests and to elect people who are sympathetic to the group's goals. Political support may also give a group access to a policymaker. The major drawback to getting directly involved in election campaigns is that if the candidate loses, the group's influence may be severely damaged. Some groups try to avoid this by giving to both sides, but this strategy can backfire because the winning candidate may resent a group's contribution to his or her opponent.

Political Action Committees A *political action committee (PAC) is "the political arm of a business, labor, professional, or other interest group, legally entitled to raise funds on a voluntary basis from members, stockholders, or employees in order to contribute funds to favored candidates or political parties."*[29] For years, PACs were used almost exclusively by labor groups. The AFL-CIO's Committee on Political Education (COPE) was one of the first successful PACs, beginning its activity in state and national campaigns in 1956. It not only raises and distributes funds but helps its members learn about candidates and issues, register to vote, and go to the polls. Even though a few business PACs, such as the Business-Industry Political Action Committee (BIPAC), were formed in the 1960s, business did not really begin to use PACs as an influence technique until after 1974.

In that year, Congress passed the Federal Election Campaign Act, which limited individual campaign contributions to $1,000 per election and prohibited unions and businesses from using their own funds for political gifts. The result was that business PACs sprang up everywhere almost overnight. By 1976, there were more corporate PACs than labor PACs, and by 1980, corporate PACs had more dollars to spend than labor PACs.

Under the 1974 law, PACs can contribute up to $5,000 per election on a federal candidate's behalf and spend unlimited amounts of money—independently—on a candidate's behalf. Independent expenditures are those made without any contact between the PAC and the candidate. Because a primary and a general election count as separate elections, PACs can really spend up to $10,000 for a candidate, and of course they can let the candidate know they are doing so. PACs spent more than $186 million on the 1982 congressional elections; they have become indispensable in the lobbying game (see Table 7.4).

Vote Ratings and Hit Lists Publishing vote ratings of Congress members is an increasingly popular, if somewhat indirect, method of affecting the success of a candidate. From the roll call votes taken in Congress, an interest group selects votes on issues it considers important. The group then calculates the percentage of key-issue votes in which a Congress member agreed with the group's position. A score of 100 means the member was in total agreement with the group. A zero score means the member was definitely an enemy.

Vote ratings were first used in 1919 by the National Farmers Union. Before the 1970s, only four major ratings were published annually—the AFL-CIO labor issues index, the Chamber of Commerce business issues index, the Americans for Democratic Action liberal issues index, and the Americans for Constitutional Action's conservative issues index. The rapid growth in single-issue interest groups and the creation of PACs stimulated more groups to use the ratings. By 1980, more than 70 national groups and dozens of state and local interest groups were issuing vote ratings. According to one source, interest groups use rating schemes because they "consider them a valuable guide for their own members, if not for the voters at large; political professionals [PACs] find them useful in allocating campaign money and energy; lobbyists use them to plan and persuade."[30] Lately, though, ratings have found a new use—they are used as the basis for "hit lists."

The first and most famous hit list was the Dirty Dozen. In 1970 a new environmental group, Environmental Action (EA), identified 12 members of Congress who had scored low on the group's list of key environmental votes and appeared to be beatable at the polls. EA went so far as to have

TABLE 7.4

The Leaders of the PACs in Campaign Giving

The table shows campaign activity by many of the most active political action committees (PACs). Shown are total money raised in 1981–82 and contributions to candidates. For two PACs, footnotes show independent expenditures; for all the rest, independent expenditures were less than a sixth of contributions.

	Money Raised	Contributions Democrats	Contributions Republicans
Associations			
American Bankers Association	$ 938,188	$ 418,010	$ 507,200
American Dental Association	733,967	236,150	359,300
American Medical Association	2,443,769	500,911	1,179,159
American Trial Lawyers Association	828,524	278,425	156,755
Associated General Contractors of America	678,593	139,050	538,156
Gun Owners of America	929,055	6,000	67,200
League of Conservation Voters	1,089,354	96,413	10,074
National Automobile Dealers Association	1,274,215	466,629	516,625
National Association of Life Underwriters	1,020,969	154,025	394,598
National Association of Realtors	2,981,906	504,576	1,605,185
Corporations			
American Family Corp.	304,936	105,525	121,750
Bear, Stearns and Co.	435,000	17,300	10,450
Fluor Corp.	301,944	21,300	196,600
General Dynamics Corp.	276,226	68,220	89,720
General Electric Co.	280,566	76,980	81,350
Grumman Corp.	293,150	101,478	85,700
Standard Oil Co. (Indiana)	396,771	26,900	130,477
Tenneco Inc.	474,520	31,250	312,650
Wheelabrator-Frye Inc.	290,908	75,800	76,350
Winn-Dixie Stores Inc.	380,235	153,650	115,725
Labor Unions			
AFL-CIO	1,196,861	780,525	2,500
American Federation of Teachers	1,039,388	311,075	4,100
Communications Workers of America	1,183,803	541,028	4,250
International Association of Machinists and Aerospace Workers	1,578,709	1,277,159	28,250
International Ladies' Garment Workers Union	1,040,448	613,963	8,000
National Education Association	1,380,323	1,118,765	62,650
Seafarers International Union of North America	1,261,125	680,293	130,538
United Auto Workers	1,667,174	1,403,996	13,450
United Food and Commercial Workers International Union	1,129,697	693,102	19,400
United Transportation Union	1,232,599	400,225	40,490
Other Businesses			
Associated Milk Producers Inc.	1,595,801	553,200	289,250
Chicago Mercantile Exchange	898,478	178,400	140,373
Dairymen Inc.	813,160	180,373	54,160
Mid-American Dairymen Inc.	634,997	320,200	149,150
Political Organizations			
Citizens for the Republic	2,386,277	1,000	467,177
Committee for the Future of America Inc. (Walter F. Mondale)	2,088,605	167,433	—
Committee for the Survival of a Free Congress	2,280,031	27,865	127,758
Fund for a Conservative Majority*	2,833,387	1,500	104,319
Fund for a Democratic Majority (Edward M. Kennedy)	2,290,326	177,355	—
National Committee for an Effective Congress**	2,131,563	305,552	250
National Congressional Club (Jesse A. Helms)	9,053,645	4,117	105,238
National Conservative Political Action Committee	9,625,834	21,081	235,849
National Rifle Association	2,013,588	175,895	540,159
Republican Senate Majority Fund (Howard H. Baker, Jr.)	1,828,564	—	354,664

SOURCE: Richard E. Cohen, "Giving Till It Hurts: 1982 Campaign Prompts New Look at Financing Races," *National Journal*, 14 (December 18, 1982), p. 2145; based on data from Federal Election Commission.

*Expenditures of $334,147 for Republicans or against Democrats

**Expenditures of $2,973,072 for Republicans or against Democrats and $196,474 for Democrats or against Republicans

"wanted" posters printed for these 12 members. Since then, a number of other groups, especially New Right groups, have also adopted the hit-list strategy.

Molding Public Opinion

Molding public opinion is an important interest group activity. The long-range objective is to promote a favorable image for an interest group and its cause. The short-range objective is to convince the public to support the interest group's position on a currently controversial issue or an issue subject to government action.[31] Groups spend a lot of time and money to meet these objectives. In 1981 American corporations and trade associations alone spent an estimated $1 billion on issue advertising. Interest groups conduct public relations campaigns the same way companies do when they sell a product. Facts and figures, scientific studies, polls, position papers, press releases, newspaper advertisements, television and radio commercials,

celebrity endorsements, public appearances—all are used to create a positive group image.

The larger, wealthier interest groups often hire public relations and advertising firms to help them sell a positive group image or issue position. These firms have a great deal of technical expertise plus the capacity to use their results most effectively. New groups without a great deal of money cannot afford to conduct elaborate campaigns. Instead, they may distribute brochures and handbills to passers-by or residences or telephone individual citizens to rally support for an issue. These activities require much effort by group members and attract little media attention, however. Many smaller groups use more dramatic, publicity-grabbing techniques such as marches, rallies, boycotts, demonstrations, and sometimes even violence. Such tactics cannot be used repeatedly by the same group because they soon lose their news appeal, and their repeated use may actually lower the public's opinion of the group rather than improve it. In the case of riots and violent protests, the media may choose to give only passing coverage to the group's activity to keep the activity from spreading.

A somewhat newer public relations strategy is *negative advertising, attacking the opposition in an attempt to damage its credibility*. This strategy is particularly popular with ideological groups. For example, after the National Conservative Political Action Committee's success in voting a number of liberals out of office in 1980, the Progressive Political Action Committee (PROPAC) was formed. PROPAC budgeted $1 million for contributions to liberal candidates, public relations services, and the media for attacks on conservative groups and candidates.[32]

Litigation

"Everybody's suing everybody else these days." We usually hear this comment about individuals, but it also describes interest group behavior. Civil rights groups' successful use of the courts in the 1960s popularized this method of influencing policy, particularly among groups without much political clout in Congress or the executive departments. Litigation strategies are also used by groups that have political clout but have lost the policymaking battle in the other branches.

The two major litigation strategies are the outcome-oriented strategy and the amicus curiae

LLOYD WILLIAMS: Hunter Safety Instructor and Outdoor Skills Specialist for the Missouri Department of Conservation; Member of the National Rifle Association.

"The major purpose of my job is to promote the idea of firearms safety. If I can reach kids before they develop bad habits and teach them safe attitudes, I'll have accomplished a lot. But I also stress conservation, respect for wildlife and proper use of the land. All the things that go into making safe hunters and better sportsmen.

"That's why I joined the NRA. They help me to do my job by providing guidebooks, handouts — even films, that encourage responsible hunting. It all boils down to teaching young people to respect nature. After all, when you love the outdoors as much as I do, you want to make sure it'll be around a long, long time." **I'm the NRA.**

NRA works with fish and game agencies throughout North America to train hunter safety instructors. Instruction materials and assistance in organizing and conducting training sessions as well as hunter clinics are provided by NRA. If you would like to join NRA and want more information about our programs and benefits, write Harlon Carter, Executive Vice President, P.O. Box 37484, Dept. LW-27, Washington, D.C. 20013.

Paid for by the members of the National Rifle Association of America.

Larger, wealthier groups, such as the National Rifle Association (NRA), often hire public relations and advertising firms to help them sell a positive group image or position.

Wheelchair protests by handicapped persons called attention to their lack of access to many public facilities because of structural barriers (such as curbs and building entrances with no wheelchair ramps).

strategy. The purpose of **outcome-oriented strategies** is *to modify decisions made by policymakers or to redefine statutes such that they will be more favorable to the group.* For example, when Congress was considering a law limiting draft registration to males, certain individuals and groups lobbied to have women drafted as well. Unsuccessful in their lobbying attempts, the groups went to court to have the law ruled unconstitutional. (The Court ruled against the groups in *Rostker* v. *Goldberg*, 1981.)

The **amicus curiae** (friend-of-the-court) **strategy** is less direct, far less expensive, and currently more popular than outcome-oriented litigation. In this technique, *interest groups, rather than sponsoring litigation, present their viewpoints in court about a case.* An interest group "may wish to inform the

TABLE 7.5

Amicus Curiae Briefs Filed in Rostker v. Goldberg (1981)

Briefs to Affirm	Briefs to Reverse
(Pro-Women Draft)	(Anti-Women Draft)
NOW Legal Defense and Education Fund	National Jewish Commission on Law and Public Affairs—for Orthodox Jewish Coalition on the Draft
Women's Legal Defense Fund on behalf of Women's Equity Action League (WEAL)	Washington Legal Foundation
WEAL Legal Defense and Education Fund	
Federally Employed Women	
National Women's Studies of U.S. Student Association	
Women Lawyers of LA	
Federation of Organizations for Professional Women	
Association of American University Women	
League of Women Voters	
Catholics for ERA	
National Association for Business and Professional Women	
Michigan Education Association	
Women's Caucus	

Court of its stand on the issue, present new material, provide an additional perspective, show widespread support for a particular resolution of the issue, or provide a symbol or indication of organizational activity for its members or the public at large."[33] A group may also file an amicus curiae brief if it is "dissatisfied with the quality or the type of argument filed by the primary parties in the pending action."[34] Permission to file such a brief can be granted by the two parties involved or by the court itself.

Amicus curiae strategies are particularly common in cases involving constitutional rights, especially the "equal protection" clause of the Fourteenth Amendment. In the *Rostker* case, amicus curiae briefs were filed by a number of women's groups, such as the National Federation of Business and Professional Women's Clubs and the League of Women Voters (see Table 7.5). A record of 57 amicus curiae briefs were filed in the *Bakke* case. Bakke was a white male who was not admitted to a medical school because of its minority admissions policy. (See chapters 2 and 15 for a lengthier discussion of this controversial case.)

Protecting American Industry

"Buy American" is the slogan that represents this controversy. A number of American industries, including the steel, clothing and textile, shoe, furniture, and automobile industries, are being threatened by foreign competition. Business and trade associations and labor union groups have united to pressure policymakers to impose restrictions on foreign imports in order to protect American products and keep American jobs. A significant number of citizens agree (see Table 7.6). On the other side are foreign agents (lobbyists), American businesses and trade associations that sell foreign products, and a number of ideological groups that support a free-enterprise economic system. Trade protectionism or free trade? This is one of the most important economic issues confronting policymakers today.

As we shall see, the interest groups involved in this issue generally employ lobbying strategies aimed at directly influencing the policymakers in Washington rather than grassroots letter-writing strategies.

In 1980, Ford Motor Company and the United Auto Workers (UAW) petitioned the United States International Trade Commission (ITC) for restrictions on imported cars and trucks under the escape clause of the Trade Act of 1974. This clause allows an industry to seek protection if it faces serious injury or a threat of such injury from imports. According to the figures presented, imports "accounted for a record 27 percent of U.S. car sales in the first half of 1980, and Japanese cars represented about four-fifths of the figure"[1] (see Table 7.7). Sales of American-made cars dropped, and estimates were that about 239,000 auto workers and 450,000 workers in related industries (such as the steel industry) were on indefinite

[1]Robert J. Samuelson, "Disputes over Car and Steel Imports May Be Heading for Bargaining Table," *National Journal*, August 2, 1980, p. 1266.

TABLE 7.6
The Public's Views on Protectionism

On balance, do you favor or oppose new laws to limit imports from foreign countries into the United States?	Favor	61%
	Oppose	27%
Do you agree or disagree that limiting imports will mean more jobs and production here in this country?	Agree	71%
	Disagree	22%
Do you agree or disagree that limiting imports will mean less competition and higher prices?	Agree	41%
	Disagree	47%
If we pass new laws limiting imports, will other countries retaliate by limiting our exports by a substantial amount, or will this not be a problem?	Problem	34%
	No problem	53%
In your opinion, is there a lot of unfair competition from foreign countries, or is this not a very serious problem at present?	A lot	52%
	Not a lot	26%

SOURCE: *The National Journal*, 15 (January 29, 1983), p. 241; based on data from an October public opinion poll by the Gallup Organization Inc., October-November business executive poll by the Survey Research Center, both for the Chamber of Commerce of the United States.

Business and labor groups have collaborated in an extensive public relations campaign designed to convince Americans to buy American-made products.

layoff by the end of June. Auto industry and labor officials claimed that lower labor costs and fewer government-imposed environmental and safety regulations allowed foreign countries (especially Japan) to produce cheaper cars. According to one report, the Japanese had an average cost advantage over American companies of $1,000 to $1,500 per car. In spite of these arguments, the ITC denied Ford and the UAW's request for import restrictions, ruling that "Detroit's problems were as much a result of economic conditions [the fuel crisis, eco-

nomic downturn], rising interest rates, and failure to meet consumer demands as of imports."[2]

Immediately, the auto industry began lobbying Congress members to get them to impose import restrictions. A bill was introduced to impose a quota allowing only 1.6 million Japanese autos to enter the United States each year. Opponents of this legislation, including the importers and their trade associations, blamed the auto industry itself for its economic predicament. They blamed auto unions for high labor costs, making American cars more expensive. (Between 1970 and 1978, auto industry wages rose about 25 percent faster than all private wages.) They also attacked the quality of American cars and faulted the industry for continuing to produce big, inefficient cars instead of retooling to produce smaller, efficient cars. The senior vice-president and general operations manager of Toyota Motor Sales, U.S.A., Inc. (the nation's largest auto importer) quoted figures that showed that the increase in imports (23,000 units in the first half of 1980) was nowhere near equal to the decrease in domestic sales (down 1.5 million units). He concluded that the overwhelming majority of the lost sales was due to something other than imports.[3]

[2]Judy Sarasohn, "Auto Import Curbs Shelved as Japan Agrees on Limits," *Congressional Quarterly*, May 9, 1981, p. 798.
[3]Norman D. Lean, "Don't Blame the Imports," *National Journal*, October 18, 1980, p. 1770.

TABLE 7.7

New Car Sales: The Rise of the Imports
(in thousands of vehicles sold)

	Cars				Trucks			
	Total	Domestic	Imported	Percent Imported	Total	Domestic	Imported	Percent Imported
1955	7,466	7,408	58	0.8%	1,015	1,012	3	0.3%
1960	6,641	6,142	499	7.5	963	926	37	3.8
1965	9,332	8,763	569	6.1	1,554	1,539	14	0.9
1970	8,405	7,119	1,285	15.3	1,811	1,746	65	3.6
1971	10,250	8,682	1,568	15.3	2,096	2,011	85	4.1
1972	10,950	9,327	1,623	14.8	2,692	2,486	143	5.4
1973	11,439	9,676	1,763	15.4	3,148	2,195	233	7.4
1974	8,867	7,454	1,413	15.9	2,687	2,511	176	6.6
1975	8,640	7,053	1,587	18.4	2,477	2,248	229	9.2
1976	10,110	8,611	1,498	14.8	3,181	2,944	237	7.5
1977	11,185	9,109	2,076	18.6	3,675	3,352	323	8.8
1978	11,312	9,312	2,000	17.7	4,110	3,773	337	8.2
1979	10,550	8,100	2,450	23.2	3,480	3,010	470	13.5
1980*	10,000	7,500	2,500	27.0	3,126	NA	NA	NA

SOURCE: *National Journal*, 12 (March 15, 1980), p. 428; based on data from Motor Vehicle Manufacturers Association (1955 to 1979 figures), Sanford C. Bernstein & Co. Inc. (1980 estimates).

*Estimate.

Proponents of free trade, including a number of public-interest groups, oppose trade protection policies on the grounds that they usually mean higher prices for the consumer. Robert Samuelson, a renowned economist, has concluded that protection means higher prices, consumer subsidy of auto workers and auto companies, and inefficiency. The United States trade representative, testifying in opposition to restrictions on auto imports before the House Ways and Means Trade Subcommittee, argued that "import restrictions [designed to keep out small, fuel-efficient cars] wouldn't help the American industry so much as it would drive prices higher and deprive consumers of opportunities for saving fuel."[4]

[4]Robert J. Samuelson, "Good Work, Doug." *National Journal*, July 19, 1980, p. 1193.

In addition, some foreign policy experts oppose protectionist measures on the grounds that they "risk increasing conflicts among Europe, Japan, and the United States just when our allies need cementing, not further fracturing."[5]

As it turned out, the Japanese government took the offensive when it appeared that Congress would adopt a trade-restriction policy in reaction to the powerful united lobby of auto companies and labor unions. First, the Japanese government voluntarily limited auto sales to the United States over a three-year period. Second, it encouraged Toyota to enter into a joint production effort with an American company—General Motors. However, these were temporary solutions that a number of Congress members, especially those from states dominated by the auto industry, do not see as significantly helpful to American auto manufacturers.

Some basic American values are at stake in the trade issue. Americans overwhelmingly believe in a free-enterprise economic system, but trade protection policies reduce competition and call for government intervention in the economy. It may be that Americans value protection of Americans' jobs more than they value a free-enterprise system. Undoubtedly, this struggle will intensify over the next few years as trade agreements in other industries expire and have to be renegotiated. One thing is certain—interest groups on both sides of the issue (and the oceans) will be involved.

[5]*Ibid.*

SUMMARY

Thousands of interest groups compete with one another to influence policymakers. Proponents of interest groups view them as examples of democracy in its purest form, while critics condemn them as narrow, self-interested groups working against the common good. Nonetheless, the number of interest groups is growing in response to changes in society.

A political interest group pressures policymakers to pass laws and adopt regulations in line with views held by its members. There are groups representing a number of different interests, including business (corporations and trade associations), labor (unions), agricultural interests, racial and ethnic groups, the public interest (also called good government, reform, consumer, legal rights, or taxpayer groups), professional associations, women's groups, older Americans, veterans, the handicapped, and gays.

Another category of interest groups represents governments and the people who work for them. These include government-employee groups, state and local government groups, groups representing foreign governments, and intragovernmental groups (executive, judicial, and legislative liaisons).

Regardless of type, interest groups use four principal influence tactics:

1. *Lobbying* This may involve sending a lobbyist to Washington, setting up a Washington office, contacting policymakers or their staffs personally, drafting legislation, testifying at committee hearings, forming coalitions with other groups, mobilizing the folks back home, or publishing vote ratings.

2. *Campaign politicking* This consists of giving group monetary or other support to election campaigns or forming political action committees so group members can give money as individuals on a voluntary basis.

3. *Molding public opinion* This strategy involves developing public relations campaigns via the media, advertising, leaflets, and telephones to build a positive image of a group.

4. *Litigation* Filing lawsuits to change the interpretation of laws, show support for a point of view, or generate publicity.

Interest groups are particularly active today. As our example of lobbying for protection of the American automobile industry showed, on most important policy issues interest groups with opposing views try to influence the outcome. Since they often use the same strategies and techniques, policymakers are often equally pressured from both sides, and the policy decisions that ultimately emerge may vary only slightly from previous decisions. In the end, however, much of the population is satisfied that our system of government is responsive because alternative viewpoints have been seriously debated by our policymakers. This is the value of interest groups in our society.

KEY TERMS

amicus curiae
client state
inside lobbying strategies
intergroup lobbying
lobbying
moral change
negative advertising
outcome-oriented litigation strategy
outside lobbying strategies

political action committee (PAC)
political interest group
public-interest group
role change
role equity
trade association
trade state
umbrella organization

SUGGESTED READINGS

Caldwell, Lynton K.; Hayes, Lynton R.; and Macwhirter, Isabel M. *Citizens and the Environment: Case Studies in Popular Action*. Bloomington, Ind.: Indiana University Press, 1976.

Greenstone, J. David. *Labor in American Politics*. Chicago: University of Chicago Press, 1977.

Haider, Donald H. *When Governments Come to Washington: Governors, Mayors, and Intergovernmental Lobbying*. New York: The Free Press, 1974.

Howe, Russell Warren, and Trott, Sarah Hays. *The Power Peddlers: How Lobbyists Mold America's Foreign Policy*. Garden City, N.J.: Doubleday, 1977.

McFarland, Andrew. *Public Interest Lobbies: Decision-Making on Energy*. Washington, D.C.: American Enterprise Institute, 1976.

Makielske, S. J., Jr. *Pressure Politics in America*. Washington, D.C.: University Press, 1980.

Malbin, Michael J. *Unelected Representatives*. New York: Basic Books, Inc., 1980.

Melone, Albert P. *Lawyers, Public Policy, and Interest Group Politics*. Washington, D.C.: University Press, 1977.

Milbrath, Lester W. *The Washington Lobbyists*. Chicago: Rand McNally, 1963.

Moe, Terry M. *The Organization of Interests: Incentives and the Internal Dynamics of Political Interest Groups*. Chicago: University of Chicago Press, 1980.

GARY HART PRESIDENT 1984

Mondale for President

with you to correct th
nity to America. To as
ount of:

$25   ☐ $35   ☐

Glenn President 84

ALAN CRANSTON '84

CHAPTER 8

NOMINATIONS AND CAMPAIGNS: PHASE ONE IN THE POLITICS OF SELECTING POLICYMAKERS

The Evolution of Nominating Methods in the United States ■ Nominating the President and Vice President ■ The Old and the New Politics of Campaigning ■ Presidential Campaigns

On the fourth night of the Republican National Convention, July 17, 1980, Ronald Reagan and his entourage left his suite in the Detroit Plaza Hotel and traveled the short distance to the Joe Louis Arena, where the delegates and the party faithful waited to hear his acceptance speech. All of the evening's events were timed to present the party's presidential nominee to the millions who would watch during prime time on national television. The candidate mounted a blue platform trimmed with red and white carnations and emblazoned with the convention's theme, "Together: A New Beginning." Looking out at the demonstrative, adoring crowd, Reagan no doubt thought back to his two previous races for the nomination. In 1968 he made a last-minute bid for the nomination, formally announcing his candidacy on the first day of the Miami convention, but Richard Nixon's support held, and Reagan was defeated. In 1976 Reagan challenged the incumbent, Republican President Gerald Ford, and lost a closely contested race for the nomination. In 1976 Reagan had mounted the podium on the final night of the convention to

endorse the Ford candidacy, but in 1980 the roles of the two men were reversed.

When Reagan finished his 45-minute speech, he stood with his vice presidential running mate, George Bush, to accept the applause of the crowd. Then, one by one, Reagan and Bush were joined by party leaders, including those who had contested them for the party's nomination. The platform mob scene symbolized that consensus had reigned at the convention. The Republicans would leave Detroit unified on their candidates and platform.

Reagan had formally declared his candidacy for the Republican nomination on November 13, 1979, but his campaign for the presidency had long preceded the formal announcement. On the evening of July 16, 1980, he was voted his party's nomination, but a nomination is only an official license to campaign for the job under a party symbol. A month later, the Democratic party renominated President Jimmy Carter and Vice President Walter Mondale. There was never any doubt that either Reagan or Carter would be the next president of the United States, in spite of the candi-

The typical closing scene at a national party convention shows the party nominees and their spouses embracing and waving to the delegates and millions of television viewers in a show of party unity.

dacy of independent John Anderson. However, there was considerable doubt in July and August about which man (Carter or Reagan) would win the election.

In this chapter and the one that follows, we will discuss the politics of selecting those who make policy. This chapter is devoted exclusively to nominations and campaigns. Chapter 9 concentrates on elections and voting behavior. Actually, nominations, campaigns, elections, and voting behavior are interrelated so closely that parties, candidates, and the voting public see them as one process.

The importance of the politics of selecting policymakers cannot be overemphasized. This is a critical step in the ultimate policymaking process. For most individuals, casting ballots for potential policymakers is the most direct form of participation in the policymaking process, for these reasons:

1. The voter is rarely or never able to directly make policy. Occasionally, at the state and local level, an issue will be referred to the people in a referendum, but there is no provision for a national referendum.

2. It is impossible for candidates to spell out precise details on important policy questions. Platforms and pledges given by parties and candidates indicate direction and general tendency far more than specific policy choices.

3. Elections rarely produce clear mandates for particular courses of action.

4. However, American elections do choose those who frame the policies of government.

5. Policymakers, therefore, have considerable latitude in shaping policy.

Rather than deciding what policy the government will adopt, the electorate decides *who* will decide what policy will be adopted.

THE EVOLUTION OF NOMINATING METHODS IN THE UNITED STATES

The entire history of nominations in the United States can be summed up in three words: caucus, convention, and primary. Each method of nominating candidates dominated a period of political history. The displacement of one method by another represented an effort to broaden the number of persons involved in the selection process.

The Caucus

A *caucus is a closed meeting of party leaders to nominate party candidates.* A caucus of influentials, notables, or party leaders was a very popular method of nominating party candidates in the early days of the Republic, particularly at the state level. Because communications and transportation were so difficult, it was advantageous for state legislators of the same party to get together during a legislative session and to select candidates for state offices.

For the first two presidential elections, no nominations were necessary because the electoral college worked as intended by its designers. (The electoral college will be discussed in more detail in chapter 9.) In 1796 a congressional caucus, which operated like the state party caucuses, was used by the Democratic Republicans to nominate their presidential and vice presidential candidates. The caucus system dominated the politics of national nominations until 1824.

Use of the caucus as a mechanism for nominating presidential and vice-presidential candidates rapidly declined. There were several reasons for this decline. First, it was easier for delegates to travel to a convention. Second, members of the party serving in Congress did not represent a full cross section of the party faithful or the party leadership. Finally, the caucus was not in keeping with the trend toward greater participation by all types of citizens. By 1824 the congressional caucus had become so unpopular that almost three-fourths of the members boycotted the meeting.

The Convention

A *convention is a meeting of party delegates to nominate party candidates, make party policy, and prescribe rules for the conduct of party business.* Credit for holding the first national nominating convention, in the modern sense, must be given to the Anti-Masonic party, a minor party whose convention met in 1831. The two major parties followed their example a few months later, in 1831 and 1832.

The convention was quickly institutionalized for national party nominations and was gradually adopted at the state level. Legislative influence over nominations declined while both party leaders' and party members' influence over nominations increased. Unfortunately, the convention was subject to abuse and became as unrepresentative as the caucus. By the second half of the nineteenth century, the convention had come to symbolize boss rule, high-handed manipulation, and oligarchy. As a means of weakening the grip of political machines on the nominating process, re-

formers argued that nominations should be made, not by convention, but by the people.

The Primary

A *direct primary is an intraparty election in which the voters select the candidates who will run under the party's label in the subsequent general election.* The primary is this nation's last and most drastic move toward popular control over nominations. The primary was advocated by two major reform movements at the end of the nineteenth and the beginning of the twentieth century: the Populist Revolt and the Progressive Movement. Populist leaders experimented with the primary in the South, but the first statewide direct primary law was adopted in Wisconsin in 1903 under the leadership of Progressive Governor Robert M. LaFollette. The primary spread rapidly—today, all statewide candidates must be nominated in primaries, except in Delaware and a few southern states in which the Republicans are permitted to use a convention.

Primaries can be classified as partisan or nonpartisan, plurality or run-off, and open or closed. All primaries to select candidates for national office are partisan. However, nonpartisan primaries are used frequently to choose candidates for school boards, state judgeships, and the city councils of small cities. In *nonpartisan primaries, candidates do not run under a party symbol;* in *partisan primaries, candidates must be affiliated with a party.*

In all except ten southern states, a primary is decided on a simple plurality of votes cast. In the southern states that hold a *run-off primary, a majority of all votes is required to secure a nomination, and a second primary between the top candidates is required if no candidate secures a majority in the first primary.* The run-off primary developed in response to the one-partyism in the South.

Finally, *closed primaries are those in which a "party test" is made to gain access to the ballot—a voter may vote only in the primary of the party in which he or she is registered.* In an *open primary* state, *the voter may vote in either party's primary.* Alaska and Washington have primaries in which voters may vote in both parties' primaries so long as they do not vote for the same office in both. Since parties are blamed or praised for their candidates and elected officials, the closed primary naturally follows from the idea of party responsibility. Party leaders generally oppose open primaries because they fear that voters

John F. Kennedy was the first candidate to own his nomination to the presidential preference primaries. They enabled him to prove that a Catholic could be a viable presidential candidate.

from the opposite party will "cross over" and "raid" their primary.

Presidential preferential primaries have spread less rapidly than primaries for state-level candidates. In these primaries, voters express their preference for one of their party's presidential contenders. These results influence how a state's delegation to the party's national convention votes in the presidential nomination balloting. Until 1960 there was no evidence that a presidential candidate owed his nomination to the influence of the primaries. All authorities agree that in that year John F. Kennedy could not have gotten his party's nomination without winning his way through the primaries. By doing so he proved that a Catholic could be a viable presidential candidate.[1] Now winning presidential preference primaries is regarded as critically important for any serious presidential hopeful.

The Current Mix of Caucus, Convention, and Primary

Each of these devices is still in use today. The party caucus is used in Congress to select party leaders and to make important party decisions. A substantial minority of the states continues to have some sort of preprimary party endorsement by a convention. In states that have strong party

organizations, the parties hold "slating meetings," or caucuses to designate preferred candidates in the primaries. Conventions are still widely used by the parties to adopt a platform, promote party candidates, and conduct other party business. Finally, in nominating presidential candidates, a combination of the caucus, convention, and primary is used to select delegates to the national convention, as we will now explain.

NOMINATING THE PRESIDENT AND VICE PRESIDENT

There are about 500,000 elective offices in the United States. Most of these positions are in state and local governments, each of which tends to have its own election timetable. This arrangement means that every year there are nominations to be made and elections to be held. But the election that gets the most attention occurs every four years—the presidential election. Every fourth year we must elect a new president or reelect the incumbent. The event has become so important that its every detail has become newsworthy. In fact, the nomination and election of a president of the United States attract worldwide media attention.

The Invisible Primary

Of the millions of Americans eligible to serve as president in 1980, only four Democrats and eleven Republicans formally declared themselves to be candidates for their respective party nominations. Before the presidential preferential primary season opened in New Hampshire in February, some of the declared candidates were no longer serious contenders; they had lost the invisible primary.[2] The *invisible primary is an informal process of assessing candidacies that takes place long before the first caucus or primary is held.* The first stirrings of a nomination drive can be detected as soon as the smoke clears from the last presidential election. Recent successful campaigns for the major party nominations have begun at least two years before the election (see Figure 8.1), and formal announcements of candidacy have come about one year before the election. By the beginning of 1983, there were already six candidates in the invisible primary for the Democratic nomination in 1984.

Arthur T. Hadley, the political scientist who coined the term "invisible primary," has devel-

Six candidates for the Democratic nomination in 1984 threw their hats into the ring quite early and began making the rounds to state party conventions. Here Senator Edward Kennedy (third from right) stands with the candidates (shown left to right): Senator John Glenn (Ohio), former Florida governor Reubin Askew, former vice president Walter Mondale, Senator Ernest Hollings of South Carolina (whose wife is shown representing him), Senator Alan Cranston (California), and Senator Gary Hart (Colorado).

oped six standards by which a candidate's performance in the race is judged. These standards, or "tracks," as he calls them, include:[3]

1. The psychological track. How does a presidential candidate react to the strain and the temptations of the campaign?

2. The staff track. How good is the candidate's staff, and how well does he relate to them?

3. The strategy track. Precisely how does the candidate intend to get through the invisible primary, the state primaries, the election, and to the White House?

4. The money track. Can the candidate raise enough money to mount a serious campaign? Is his monetary support from a wide range of contributors? Will he qualify for and choose to accept federal campaign funds? This track generally proves to be the most difficult and complex for all candidates.

5. The media track. Does the press believe the candidate has a chance of either winning or influencing the strategy of the victor? This is believed by many candidates to be the key to the invisible primary.

6. The constituency track. Does the candidate have a group of people who believe in the candidate enough to work for him and contribute money?

To be labeled a serious contender, one must turn in a strong performance on each track.

Who Is a Presidential Possibility?

In social background, the contenders for a presidential nomination are hardly a representative cross section of the American people. They are mostly affluent, white, middle-aged, Protestant males. No woman, black, Chicano, or distinctively ethnic candidate has been seriously considered, although the increasingly powerful black vote led Jessse Jackson, a veteran of the civil rights movement, to consider seriously entering the race in 1984. Both parties have mostly nominated members of establishment or mainline Protestant churches, although the taboo against a Catholic nominee has been eliminated. The Democrats have twice nominated a Catholic for president, and the Republicans on one occasion selected a Catholic for vice president. No Jew has been considered for a presidential nomination.

By trade most presidential contenders have been lawyers, although the nominees of both parties in 1980 were not. Of course, genuine contenders for the presidency are really full-time politicians and usually have been so for many years before seeking their party's nomination. Politics and public office-holding become their vocation, their avocation, and the justification for any other job they undertake. Both parties want to nominate good candidates, experienced campaigners, or "winners," whom they hope will also be good presidents if elected. To insure that a person will be a good candidate, they look at his or her past record in office, visibility, popularity in the party, and vote-getting ability.

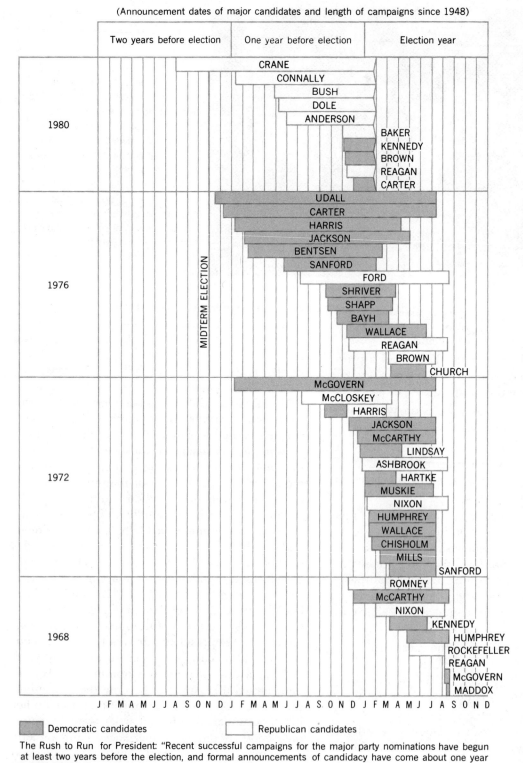

(Announcement dates of major candidates and length of campaigns since 1948)

☐ Democratic candidates   ☐ Republican candidates

The Rush to Run for President: "Recent successful campaigns for the major party nominations have begun at least two years before the election, and formal announcements of candidacy have come about one year before election."

FIGURE 8.1

The Road to the White House: Getting Longer and Longer

SOURCE: Congressional Quarterly, Inc., *Elections '80* (Washington, D.C.: Congressional Quarterly, Inc., 1980), p. 6.

The growing strength of the black vote led civil rights leader Jesse Jackson to call for a black presidential candidate to enter the presidential race in 1984.

Occupants of three public offices seem to have the best chance of gaining the nomination of the two parties: the vice president, a United States senator, or the governor of a large state. Persons holding these offices receive a good deal of media attention and thus establish name identification. Vice presidents have two advantages. First, they have already participated in a national presidential election campaign. Second, they are among the best-known party leaders.

Senators have campaign experience in a complex constituency, especially if they are from a large state. In addition their six-year term permits them to run for president without giving up their post. Furthermore, senators operate in the political and media center of the nation in a legislative body that has preeminence in foreign and national-security policymaking. These areas have been the principal concerns of recent presidents, and a knowledgeable senator may thus seem like a logical nominee.

Until recently, governors have not seemed as well positioned in the race as vice presidents and senators. True, they have about the same campaign experience as senators, and they may get a good deal of media attention, but that attention may be regional in scope and negative in character. Governors also have less freedom to mount a campaign while in office and may create resentment at home if they do. In the last twenty or so years, more than a few strong governors have been so busy trying to cope with their states' problems that they did not have the time or reputation left to mount a national effort. As former governors, Jimmy Carter and Ronald Reagan were exceptions. Both men had completed their terms of office and were free to mount intensive drives for the nomination.

"Winnowing"

During the delegate-selection season, which lasts from early in the year to as late as July or August, a winnowing process takes place, during which all but three or four candidates drop out. The *winnowing process is the process by which the number of candidates is narrowed down so that only a few candidates remain by convention time.* For the candidates it is an endurance test, an obstacle course, and a fight for survival.

The early stage of the delegate selection season is the critical time: candidates must do well or they will be forced out. A large number of candidates confuses an already complicated process, so the "handicappers" of the race assist in the winnowing process by declaring particular candidacies to be 1) long shots, 2) faltering, 3) disorganized, 4) dispirited and running short of money, or 5) hopeless. The media and party leaders establish seemingly arbitrary measures of candidates' success as they proceed from state to state. They may assert that the candidate must do well in states in his own region of the country to have any hope of a success or that a candidate must poll 30 percent of the vote to retain his backers' funding. They may say that since the candidate polled 40 percent of the vote in 1980, he must do as well or better in 1984. Once the front runner has been established, analysts then focus on whether a challenger can defeat him in the next contest.

The winnowing process quickly reduces the number of candidates in the race. Consider how quickly the process worked in the 1980 campaign,

Traditionally the first big test of a presidential candidate's potential as a serious contender has been the New Hampshire primary. Knowing the importance of a good showing, candidates start campaigning in that state several years before the election.

when the Republican Party had a number of early entries. Iowa held the first precinct caucuses on January 21, and New Hampshire held the first presidential primary on February 26. By March 15, there remained only the slightest doubt that Ronald Reagan would be the Republican nominee. Howard Baker had finished third in New Hampshire and fourth in the primaries of Massachusetts and Vermont. John Connally had spent almost $13 million, ending his campaign over $2 million in debt, and had still won only one delegate. Robert Dole, Gerald Ford's vice presidential running mate in 1976, gleaned fewer votes than either Baker or Connally. John Anderson and George Bush also sparred for the title of challenger to Reagan for the nomination, but neither could win out. By early April, Anderson had decided to launch an independent candidacy, and on May 26 Bush withdrew. The biggest single primary day of the year came on June 3, and Reagan had no challenger in the field.

The winnowing process in the party that controls the presidency involves fewer participants and operates somewhat differently. Normally an incumbent president does not experience serious competition for his party's nomination. However, in 1980 Carter was challenged by both Jerry Brown and Ted Kennedy. Brown did so poorly in the early primaries that in two states he ran behind "no preference," and so he withdrew on April 1. Carter forged an insurmountable lead over Kennedy by March 15, but Kennedy still did not quit. On June 3, just like Reagan, Carter won enough delegates to have a clear majority at the convention; but that day Kennedy beat Carter in five out of eight primaries and outpolled Carter by slightly more than 191,000 votes. Still Carter's chief rival refused to quit and carried his ultimately unsuccessful nomination fight to the convention.

As these examples have shown, the winnowing, or weeding out of candidates, is an important stage in the nominating process. It preceeds another critical stage—the nominating convention. Conventions are not always rubber stamps of primaries and, in fact, may be quite controversial.

The "Reformed" Nomination Process

The 1968 Democratic National Convention in Chicago was the end of one era and the beginning of another. Protest groups vehemently criticized the party's delegate-selection process, claiming it effectively reduced the participation of minorities, women, and the poor. To quiet some of the criticism, the 1968 convention "adopted a resolution requiring state parties to give 'all Democrats a full, meaningful, and timely opportunity to participate' in the selection of delegates."[4] The Democratic National Committee implemented this resolution by creating the Commission on Party Structure and Delegate Selection, better known as the McGovern-Fraser Commission. (It was chaired first by Senator George McGovern of South Dakota and later by Congressman Donald Fraser of Minnesota.) The Commission formulated eighteen guidelines for the 1972 delegate-selection process. The three most obvious results of the reforms were 1) a change in the demographic characteristics of the delegates, 2) the proliferation of presidential preference primaries, and 3) the

Rules for selecting delegates to the national Democratic party convention adopted in 1968 have resulted in greater representation of women and blacks at the national party convention.

decline in influence of party professionals, as evidenced by a reduction in the number of elected officials serving as convention delegates.

The McGovern-Fraser Commission's affirmative action guidelines produced more women, more blacks, and more young people at the 1972 convention than had ever been delegates before. The gains realized by these groups have not been perfectly maintained, but today both parties give them better representation than they did before the reform movement. New rules adopted by the Democrats in 1980 required the state delegations to be divided evenly between men and women. The trends in demographic characteristics of delegates from 1968 to 1980 are summarized in Table 8.1.

The Republicans never felt the pressure the Democrats felt to reform their delegate-selection process; nevertheless, a reform-mandated Delegate and Organization Committee reported to the 1972 convention. The Republicans, in general, do not impose rules on their state and local parties, preferring to leave the responsibility for keeping abreast of the times to lower levels of the party organization. However, since primaries are established by state law and the delegate-selection process is regulated in part by state law, changes requested by the Democrats have influenced the Republicans as well. The dramatic increase in the number of delegates chosen by primaries between 1968 and 1980 is presented in Table 8.2.

The reform rules effectively cut in half the number of elected officials serving as delegates to conventions between 1968 and 1972. Further reforms were voted in by the Democrats at their 1980 convention, in part as a response to the complaints of these officeholders that they were being underrepresented.

In the rules for the 1984 convention, the Democrats reinstituted some practices that had been eliminated in 1968. More than 550 of the almost 4,000 delegates will be party officials and activists who will be appointed by the party organization rather than chosen in primaries or caucuses. These appointed ''superdelegates'' will include members of Congress, governors, and leading party officials. In response to the efforts of the Kennedy forces in 1980 to eliminate the binding delegate rule, the 1984 convention will be able to respond to events that unfold during the primary season. The superdelegates will be unpledged, and delegates who run under the banner of a candidate will be allowed to vote for someone other than the individual to whom they are pledged.

Winning Preconvention Strategies

Candidates are well aware of the need to develop successful preconvention strategies. In the past, winning preconvention strategies have been based upon certain fundamental rules of political life, some of which are listed below.

1. The front runner gets the lion's share of media attention, while lagging candidates are either ignored or receive critical attention.

2. Early success can be translated into long-term success. Winning may produce a bandwagon psychology and campaign momentum.

3. Candidates must avoid policy errors in the campaign, especially errors that can easily be summed up in quotable phrases in running reports of the campaign. Three types of policy statements may be deemed newswor-

TABLE 8.1

Changing Characteristics of Delegates to the National Conventions, 1968–1980

	National Convention Delegates								Public	
	1968		1972		1976		1980		1980	
	Dem.	Rep.	Dem.	Rep.	Dem.	Rep.	Dem.	Rep.	Dem.	Rep.
Women	13%	16%	40%	29%	33%	31%	49%	29%	56%	53%
Blacks	5	2	15	4	11	3	15	3	19	4
Under thirty	3	4	22	8	15	7	11	5	27	27
Median age (years)	(49)	(49)	(42)		(43)	(48)	(44)	(49)	(43)	(45)
Lawyers	28	22	12		16	15	13	15		
Teachers	8	2	11		12	4	15	4		
Union official	4	0	5		6	0	5	0		
Union member			16		21	3	27	4	29*	18*
Attended first convention	67	66	83	78	80	78	87	84		
College Graduate	19		21		21	27	20	26	11	18
Postgraduate	44	34	36		43	38	45	39		
Protestant			42		47	73	47	72	63	74
Catholic			26		34	18	37	22	29	21
Jewish			9		9	3	8	3	4	1
Ireland			13		19	14	15	9		
Britain			17		15	28	15	31		
Germany			9		9	14	6	12		
Italy			4		6	5	5	6		
Liberal					40	3	46	2	21	13
Moderate					47	45	42	36	44	40
Conservative					8	48	6	58	26	41
Governors (number)	(23)	(24)	(17)	(16)	(16)	(9)	(23)	(13)		
Senators (number)	(39)	(21)	(15)	(22)	(11)	(22)	(8)	(26)		
U.S. Representatives (number)	(78)	(58)	(31)	(33)	(41)	(52)	(37)	(64)		

SOURCE: Warren J. Mitofsky and Martin Plissner, "The Making of the Delegates, 1968–1980," *Public Opinion,* 3 (October/November, 1980), p. 43; Reprinted by permission of *Public Opinion.* Also ©1980 by the New York Times Company. Reprinted by permission.

*Households with a union member.

thy by the media: 1) a change in policy position, 2) an inconsistency in policy statements, and 3) a policy statement that cannot simply or easily be explained.[5]

4. A nationwide "personal" organization and campaign seem essential to winning the nomination. Solid organization is most important in the first state contests, but candidates must be able to sustain the campaign throughout the preconvention struggle. No longer can a candidate pick and choose the states he will enter. Failure to enter is read as a sign of weakness, and rival candidates will accumulate delegates.

5. Incumbents have a substantial advantage over nonincumbents, although incumbents also have a record on which they can be judged.

6. In a close contest, wise allocation of funds can be decisive. Candidates must determine how much to spend on television, radio, direct mail, and telephone campaigns and when to spend it.

7. A strategy that divides the party or relies on a narrow, unrepresentative coalition may produce nomination by the party but not victory in the general election.

A close look at the winning preconvention strategies of the 1980 major party presidential nominees reveals that both Carter and Reagan paid close attention to these fundamental rules.

TABLE 8.2
Proliferation of Presidential Primaries, 1968–1980

Party and Coverage	1968	1972	1976	1980
Democratic Party				
Number of states using a primary for selecting or binding national convention delegates	17	23	29*	29**
Number of votes cast by delegates chosen or bound by primaries	983	1,862	2,183	2,318
Percentage of all votes cast by delegates chosen or bound by primaries	37.5	60.5	72.6	69.6
Republican Party				
Number of states using a primary for selecting or binding national convention delegates	16	22	28*	33**
Number of votes cast by delegates chosen or bound by primaries	458	710	1,533	1,487
Percentage of all votes cast by delegates chosen or bound by primaries	34.3	52.7	67.9	74.6

SOURCE: Adapted from Austin Ranney, *Participation In American Presidential Nominations, 1976* (Washington: American Enterprise Institute, 1977), p. 6; and "Growth of Presidential Primaries Since 1968," *Congressional Quarterly Weekly Report*, 38 (February 2, 1980), pp. 283–289.

*Does not include Vermont, which held a nonbinding presidential preference poll but chose all delegates of both parties by caucuses and conventions.

**Does not include nonbinding preference votes held by Democrats in Idaho, Michigan, and Vermont and held by Republicans in Montana. Delegates in these states were elected by a separate caucus process. Also excluded to maintain comparability over time are primaries held by both parties in Puerto Rico and the District of Columbia.

The Carter Preconvention Strategy Carter adopted the classic incumbent president strategy. He conducted a *"rose garden" campaign, declining debates and campaign travel while keeping himself before the public in media appearances from the rose garden of the White House.* Trends in international affairs made this an excellent choice. In the year before election day, Iranian "students" captured the American embassy in Teheran and took hostages. The "hostage crisis" permitted Jimmy Carter to look very presidential. Two months later, Russia invaded Afghanistan, allegedly to stabilize that government. Carter initially took a strong stand against these aggressive acts, for which he was briefly popular with the public at large. With this surge of public support, he shot ahead of Kennedy in the polls early in the primary season.

An incumbent president can, to some extent, manipulate events and time his responses to them to match the campaign schedule. Likewise, presidential appointments and the allocation of federal grants may be timed to boost his standing in the

The hostage crisis worked to the advantage of President Carter in his preconvention battle with Senator Edward Kennedy for the Democratic party nomination but against him in his general election campaign battle with Republican opponent, Ronald Reagan.

primary states. Official presidential press conferences may also be called to "explain policy positions" if the president appears to be lagging behind in the polls.

The Carter strategy began to come apart near the end of the primary season. Polls show that voters who made their decision on personal qualities of the candidates voted overwhelmingly for Carter, and voters who made their decision on policy questions voted heavily for Kennedy.[6] As a result of the bitter Carter-Kennedy fight and Kennedy's successes in the late primaries, the coalition that ultimately nominated Carter was not strong enough to make him the winner in the general election. In the fall, a number of Democratic party identifiers either stayed at home or filed a protest vote for a third-party candidate.

The Reagan Preconvention Strategy   On the basis of Reagan's strong challenge against President Ford for the Republican nomination in 1976, he assumed the front-runner position in 1980. Reagan announced his candidacy in December, 1979, in a nationally televised and technically superb statement of his general policy positions. He then adopted a low-key campaign posture. He announced that he would not participate in debates that might divide the party, and he reasserted his long-standing commitment to his eleventh commandment: "Thou shalt not speak ill of a fellow Republican."

Reagan got quite a shock in the Iowa caucuses—Bush out-organized the pack and won a media-pronounced victory. The Bush "boomlet" that followed Iowa forced Reagan to campaign vigorously. In two televised debates in New Hampshire, Reagan recaptured the front-runner's position and never relinquished it.

Reagan's strategy called for a campaign based on personality more than ideology or issues. Although Reagan's positions matched trends in public opinion toward the conservative side, voters often perceived him to be radically conservative. Moreover, the voters knew Reagan, but they did not know him well. Given the voters' perceptions, it was necessary that: 1) Reagan be exposed in some depth to the voters to permit the average person to get some feel for Reagan the man, 2) he not flaunt his longstanding and well-known conservatism, and 3) he demonstrate to voters what sort of a leader he would be as president, namely

"clear, forthright, and decisive." Reagan ended the preconvention season leading Jimmy Carter for the first time in the Gallup poll. The moderate strategy he had followed permitted him to seek the votes of disaffected Democrats and unhappy independents in the fall campaign.

Calling a National Convention: Apportioning Delegates and Selecting Sites

Calling the national convention is an official role of the national committees of the Democratic and Republican parties. In sending out "the call," the states, the territories, and the District of Columbia are told how many delegates they may select and where the convention will be held. The apportionment of delegates is determined by rules laid down by the last party convention, so there is no discretion involved. Both political parties allocate delegates according to two criteria: 1) population, and 2) loyalty to the party as demonstrated by electoral success.

Subcommittees of the two parties' national committees are authorized to select the site of the national conventions. Few cities in the United States have the facilities needed for these huge party affairs—20,000 or more first-class hotel rooms, a large convention hall, and all of the other accommodations needed to entertain the delegates, alternates, their families, and friends of the party. Exceptional transportation and communications facilities are also needed. In the last two decades, the ease of maintaining security and the quality of the local police department have also become important factors in site selection. If the party has an incumbent president, the site committee is ever mindful of his preferences. Everything being equal, the party can also chose a convention site to strengthen its appeal to voters in a particular region of the country.

The National Nominating Convention: A Remnant of a Great American Institution

The national nominating conventions were originally created to nominate candidates for president and vice president of the United States, but they now basically meet to certify decisions reached elsewhere. The last time a national convention took more than one ballot to nominate a presidential candidate was in 1952, when the Democrats needed three ballots to choose Adlai Stevenson. The state primaries and caucuses predetermine the outcome of the conventions' most important decisions, and the candidates' delegates have usually stayed "in line" on any roll-call vote remotely connected with the candidates' nominations.

Despite the fact that primaries have become central to the nominating process, voter participation in the primary states is generally very low. In 1980 voter turnout in the primaries varied from a low of 6.4 percent in Rhode Island to high of 45.6 percent in Wisconsin. The irony is that in spite of their power to control the nomination process, most voters stay home, then grumble and complain about the candidates nominated by the parties.

Organizing the National Conventions

Over time, the two parties have developed conventions that are organized in an almost identical fashion. Both last four days. The standing committees are chosen long before the convention opens because their work begins before the convention. Traditionally four standing committees have been used:

1. *Credentials* prepares the official list of delegates and alternates and settles disputes when delegations are contested.
2. *Permanent Organization* selects the officers of the convention, including the chairperson, secretary, and sergeant at arms.
3. *Rules* makes adjustments in rules and procedures for the convention, deciding the length and number of nominating and seconding speeches, for example.
4. *Resolutions* writes the platform, and in so doing holds hearings to discern the views of various segments of the party, its leaders, and the chief rivals for the nomination.

Floor fights over reports from the credentials, rules, and resolutions committees have been important in the politics of the conventions. In recent years, a trailing candidate (or a stop-the-front-runner coalition) has often relied on a strategy tied to the report from one of these committees. Traditionally, the reports are presented on the second night of the convention.

Two of the most interesting, although unsuccessful, attempts by trailing candidates to use the party's committees (in both cases, the Rules Committee) to derail the front runner, occurred in the last decade.

The Vice Presidential Gamble in 1976 Going into the Republican Convention of 1976, Ronald Reagan trailed President Gerald Ford by a very small margin. Neither candidate had enough votes to win, but Ford was ahead of Reagan, and he was wooing the uncommitted with the awesome goods and trappings of the presidency. John Sears, Reagan's campaign manager, convinced Reagan to gamble on a bold change in convention procedure. Reagan announced his vice presidential choice, Senator Richard Schweiker of Pennsylvania, in mid-July, a month before the convention. The reasons behind this move were 1) the choice of the progressive Eastern running mate would show a willingness to reach out to the moderate wing of the party; 2) if Ford could be forced to choose his vice-presidential candidate, he would be deprived of an important bargaining chip in the search for additional delegates; and 3) doing something, even if it backfired, was better than sitting around and permitting Ford to use the presidency to influence uncommitted delegates. The Reagan forces proposed a new rule at the convention to require all candidates to announce their vice-presidential choice before presidential nominations were made. Reagan lost the rules fight by a vote of 1,180 to 1,068. The gamble was perceived to be a last-ditch effort of a losing campaign, and in fact was an intensely controversial break from tradition.

The Release-the-Delegates Gamble in 1980 After the last primaries were over but before the national convention, Jimmy Carter tried to heal the breach between himself and Kennedy, but his initial phone calls were refused. Kennedy then scheduled a meeting with Carter at the White House and offered to release his delegates if Carter would release his, arguing for a convention of delegates free to vote their conscience about the nomination. The Kennedy logic was: 1) that the early Carter victories had been won while the president basked in public support for his foreign policy ventures; 2) that the consequences of the president's mistakes in policy had only become clear late in the delegate selection process; and 3) that Carter would lose to Reagan in the fall, because the polls and the late delegate balloting had shown Carter to be a repudiated leader of the nation and of his party. When Carter declined to release his delegates, the Kennedy forces proposed the repeal of the "binding rule," which requires delegates to vote for the candidate to whom they are pledged when they are chosen. The Carter forces defeated the rules change by a vote of 1,936 to 1,391, and Kennedy withdrew his candidacy.

Neither the 1976 or the 1980 effort by trailing candidates at the national conventions was successful. However, we will undoubtedly continue to have such tests of strength between candidates when the nomination is at all in doubt.

The Platform: "If Elected, I Promise . . ."

Conventional wisdom holds that platforms are meaningless documents full of high-flown rhetoric, self-praise, and glowing promises that are quickly forgotten. If this is the case, one must wonder why interest groups, the media, and practical politicians take the platform-writing process so seriously.

Fights over party platforms both before and during conventions are evidence that platforms are not trivial documents. However, the nagging question that remains is whether platforms truly represent the parties' policy commitments. Can a voter rationally choose a party and its candidates on the basis of its platform? Does it accurately summarize the party's past record and future intentions? Do the parties fulfill their pledges to a reasonable extent?

In an empirical analysis of party platforms adopted between 1944 and 1976, Gerald M. Pomper concludes that a party's platform:

> *summarizes, crystallizes, and presents to the voters the character of the party coalition. Platform pledges are not simply good ideas, or even original ones. In their programs, Democrats and Republicans are not typically breaking new paths; they are promising to proceed along one or another path that has already become involved in political controversy. The stands taken in the platform clarify the parties' positions on these controversies and reveal the nature of their support and appeals. . . . If victorious, the party coalition will pursue its programs. Endorsement of a proposal in the platform provides evidence of its suitability for governmental action and an argument in its behalf. . . . Fulfillment of platform pledges is common.*[7]

Rather than relying exclusively on someone else's conclusion, we prefer that *you* decide whether party platforms are meaningful to the av-

erage voter by comparing the 1980 Democratic and Republican platform positions on economic, energy, and lifestyle issues.

The 1980 Party Platforms: Economic, Energy, and Lifestyle Issues

In 1980, there was a considerable contrast between the two parties in both platform content and the process of platform formation. Sensing victory in November and enjoying complete control of the Republican convention, Ronald Reagan ordered up a conservative platform that squared with his own convictions and muted issues on which the party was divided. In most respects, it was a traditional Republican document. So effectively did the moderate and conservative wings of the party blur their differences that no minority proposal could secure enough support for a floor fight. In contrast to the Republicans, the Democrats fought in both the platform committee sessions and on the convention floor. Twenty-three minority reports or challenges to particular planks in the platform were filed, most of them by the Kennedy forces. As a result, the platform debate was one of the longest in party history, running for seventeen hours over two days. On Tuesday evening, when the economic plank came up, Senator Kennedy took the floor and electrified the convention with what was perhaps the best speech of his entire career. The Kennedy speech so swayed the delegates that Carter's floor managers were forced to accept all of the Kennedy amendments pertaining to the economy, except a call for wage and price controls. Not until the next day did Carter regain control of the delegates and defeat the remaining challenges. The result was a platform which in many respects did not truly represent its candidate's views; it was, rather, a victory for the liberal wing of the party over its conservative wing. The Republican platform was a victory for pragmatism over ideological purity; the Democratic platform was a public record of the deep ideological divisions that had plagued that party since 1968.

Economic Issues   The centerpiece of the Republican platform's economic plank was an endorsement by name of the ***Kemp-Roth supply-side economics proposal****, a 10 percent, across-the-board cut in individual taxes each year for three consecutive years and a limit on government spending to a fixed share of the*

GNP, with that percentage being reduced by 1 percent each year for three consecutive years. For business, the Republicans endorsed an accelerated depreciation allowance and reduced government regulation. They pledged to control inflation by controlling the money supply (in cooperation with the Federal Reserve Board) and reducing federal spending (according to Kemp-Roth). To produce more jobs, they would rely on economic growth (produced by Kemp-Roth) and the revitalization of basic industry. To the unemployed, they pledged: 1) to preserve the existing system of unemployment benefits, 2) to involve the private sector more in retraining and finding jobs for the jobless, and 3) to give additional assistance to those whose jobs were threatened by foreign competition. Many longstanding Republican pledges were repeated in the economic plank, but as a whole, the focus had shifted: they were committed more to a tax cut than to anything else.

To stimulate production and combat inflation, the Democrats advocated tax cuts and the fiscal prudence needed to live within anticipated revenues. However, they opposed untargeted tax cuts as inflationary, and they opposed a constitutional amendment requiring a balanced budget. For the unemployed, the platform included the following: 1) expanding and strengthening existing counter-cyclical and antirecession programs; 2) a job training program targeted toward welfare recipients; 3) promotion of exports to increase jobs at home; and 4) vigorous opposition to unfair international trade practices. In the floor fight over the platform, the Kennedy forces won assurances that 1) economic policies would not significantly increase unemployment; 2) unemployment and high interest rates would not be used to fight inflation; and 3) a $12 billion antirecession jobs program would be undertaken. The platform was more of a traditional one for the Democrats when Kennedy got through with it.

Energy Issues The Republicans adopted a plank supporting a developmental approach to insure national energy self-sufficiency. To increase the production of oil and gas, they recommended: 1) decontrolling the price of oil and gas at the wellhead, 2) repealing the windfall profits tax for newly discovered and hard-to-get oil, and 3) ending the government's authority to allocate petroleum products, except in emergencies. To insure

self-sufficiency, they recommended: 1) increased use of coal, 2) increased use of nuclear power, and 3) accelerating the build-up of the strategic oil reserve. To permit full use of the nation's energy resources, they recommended easing the "overly stringent" portions of the Clean Air Act.

The policy advocated by the Democrats emphasized conservation and the development of alternative sources of energy. Their goal was an energy supply that was "secure, environmentally safe, and reasonably priced." The range of recommendations included: 1) increased use of coal, 2) accelerated exploration for oil on federal lands, and 3) the development of synthetic and alternative energy sources, such as solar and wind power. They advocated financial incentives to insure residential conservation. Nuclear plants would be permitted to operate only if they met the strict standards of the Kemeny Report (the report on the accident at Three Mile Island). They pledged to "retire nuclear power plants in an orderly manner as alternative fuels became available."

Lifestyle Issues Party differences on lifestyle issues were quite clear. The Republican platform called for a constitutional amendment outlawing abortions, the end of the use of any federal funds to pay for abortions, and the endorsement of right-to-life nominees to the federal courts. In a major reversal, the Republican platform, which had endorsed the Equal Rights Amendment since 1940, in 1980 proposed that the ratification of the ERA be left to the states.

In contrast, the Democratic platform opposed a constitutional amendment to overturn the Supreme Court's 1973 decision permitting abortions. It also called for the use of Medicaid funds to pay for abortions. The party not only endorsed the ratification of the ERA, but went a good deal further. First, it was recommended that the party and other organizations continue to boycott non-ratifying states. Second, the national party organization was ordered to withhold campaign funding from Democratic candidates opposing the ERA.

The Nominations
On the third day of the convention, the secretary calls the roll of the states, in alphabetical order, to hear nominations for "the next president of the United States." Through a strange blending of

custom and strict rules, the nominating and seconding speeches for the candidates are given, and a "spontaneous demonstration" follows. After all of the nominating and seconding speeches have been made, the secretary once again calls the roll of the states, this time for balloting on the nomination. As we have said, in recent years the outcome of the balloting has not been in doubt.

What has remained in doubt at recent conventions is the choice of vice-presidential candidates. By longstanding tradition, the party's presidential nominee picks the party's vice-presidential nominee. The presidential nominee can maintain some suspense and excitement at the convention by withholding his decision until the last minute.

Criteria for selecting the vice-presidential candidate vary, but they certainly include the following: 1) compatibility of the two candidates, 2) "balancing" the ticket, and 3) ability to perform well in the vice presidency, as the job is defined by the presidential nominee. Just what the vice president's role should be became a central issue when a former president considered accepting the vice-presidential nomination in 1980.

Vice-Presidential Selection in 1980: "The Reagan-Ford Ticket"

On the Democratic side in 1980, there was no decision to make on the vice presidency. If anything, Walter Mondale was more popular than Jimmy Carter. He had pleased Carter and his own personal constituency, and there was no reason to rethink the ticket. On the Republican side, Reagan had a "natural" selection to make. George Bush represented the moderate wing of the party; next to Reagan, he had run the best race of any of the Republican contenders; he had strong connections through his father (the late Senator Prescott Bush of Connecticut) with the eastern wing of the party; he had national recognition; and the choice of Bush would broaden the image of the Republican ticket for 1980. On the eve of the convention, six conservative Republican governors endorsed Bush for the vice presidency, but this was just tangible evidence of how badly the Republicans wanted unity and a winning ticket—the conservatives would have preferred a "younger Reagan" in the form of Senator Paul Laxalt of Nevada or Representative Jack Kemp of New York.

Sometime on Tuesday, July 15, the second day of the convention, Reagan proposed to former

A "dream-team" ticket featuring presidential nominee Ronald Reagan and former president Gerald Ford as his vice presidential running mate was proposed in 1980 but never came to pass because the candidates could not agree on what the responsibilities of the vice president would be.

President Gerald Ford that he join the ticket as the vice-presidential candidate. Reagan made the unprecedented move after his strategists considered poll results that showed that of all possibilities, only Ford would add strength to the ticket. Ford gave interviews to CBS and ABC in which he discussed what amounted to a co-presidency; the staffs of the two men negotiated at length over the role and authority Ford would have in the new administration; and, on the floor of the convention, some highly regarded sources pronounced the ticket settled and agreed to. It is hard to tell which side first became disenchanted with the deal. Reagan was shocked by what Ford said in interviews with the media, and no doubt the Reagan people were reluctant to deliver large blocs of power to Ford in exchange for his joining the ticket. Reagan and Ford had planned to go to the convention hall after the presidential balloting on Wednesday night to announce their "dream ticket." At 11:15 Ford declined Reagan's offer; at 11:25 Bush received a call from Reagan. Shortly after midnight, Reagan went to the convention hall to inform the delegates of his choice.

It may be that the most fortunate political event of the campaign for Reagan was Ford's decision not to run. The ticket would have been as confusing as it was unprecedented. Ford would have had to move back to Michigan or the ticket would have had to give up the electoral votes of California (the Constitution forbids the casting of electoral votes for two individuals from the same state).

The National Convention as a Rally

P. T. Barnum never ran a circus as large, colorful, gaudy, and thoroughly outlandish as the American national nominating conventions. The great author and critic H. L. Mencken described the convention in this oft-quoted passage, written in 1924:

> *There is something about a national convention that makes it as fascinating as a revival or a hanging. It is vulgar, it is ugly, it is stupid, it is tedious, it's hard upon both the cerebral centers and the gluteus maximus, and yet it is somehow charming. One sits through long sessions wishing heartily that all the delegates were dead and in hell—and then suddenly there comes a show so gaudy and hilarious, so melodramatic and obscene, so unimaginably exhilarating and preposterous that one lives a gorgeous year in an hour.* [8]

Since Mencken's day the conventions have been shortened, and they have lost some of the character they once had, but the great satirist, if he were alive today, would no doubt recognize the institution.

On some things you can depend: the conventions will open and close with prayer; there will be much patriotic ritual; they will start and end late; truly creative renditions of the "Star Spangled Banner" and "America the Beautiful" will be given each day; and after pounding the gavel, the chairperson of the convention will say at least 9,999 times, "Will the delegates please clear the aisles." The national conventions offer strange mixtures and contrasts: here are gathered several thousand men and women to conduct some pretty serious business, yet they often dress and behave in anything but a businesslike manner. At the Republican convention of 1980, the California delegation wore white stetsons which were slightly larger than the sky blue stetsons worn by the Texans. Delegates from Maine wore yellow fishing hats; from Rhode Island, white sailors' hats; other delegates wore farmers' caps with visors, union hard hats, and so forth.

Conventions are probably best known for their endless hours of speechmaking. Several speeches are institutionalized: the welcoming speech from the mayor of the convention city, the welcoming speech from the governor of the convention state, the keynote speech, the nominating and seconding speeches, and the acceptance speeches of the party's nominees. In addition, there will be speeches by beloved leaders or past nominees. The parties also arrange cameo appearances or short speeches for candidates in the fall elections who might receive a boost in their campaign from the exposure. To break up the speechmaking, both parties bring in movie stars, vocalists, and celebrities. Brief relief from speechmaking also comes from slick film presentations, which may include party history, the convention theme, a bi-

Spontaneous demonstrations interrupt convention proceedings but are good media events which promote positive feelings toward the party among the millions of Americans tuned in.

A presidential nominee's acceptance speech can set the tone for the remainder of the campaign and rally the party faithful for the right to come. This is why parties want these speeches carried on prime time television.

ography of the nominee, or memorials to deceased leaders.

The speeches are unashamedly partisan. The keynote speech and the presidential nominee's acceptance speech have the greatest potential to help the party in the elections; parties want these speeches on prime-time television if everything else is lost to public view. These two speeches set a tone for the campaign, rallying the faithful for the fight to come. The best illustration of the influence these two speeches can have comes from the 1948 Democratic convention. The Democratic party was divided over civil rights and over the liberal agenda of the New Deal purists. The low standing of President Truman in the public opinion polls made prospects for victory seem very poor. Senator Alben W. Barkley of Kentucky was the keynote speaker. A great storyteller and awesome orator with a unique ability to craft quotable phrases, Barkley delivered a masterful address that made the delegates begin to believe again. On the last day of the convention, President Truman finished the job—in simple, down-to-earth rhetoric, he set the theme for the campaign. The Democrats would campaign against "that do-nothing, good-for-nothing, rotten 80th Republican Congress." The Republicans had met in Philadelphia and adopted a platform endorsing many programs Truman had asked Congress to pass, and so in the acceptance speech Truman called Congress back into special session and challenged them to pass the legislation if they believed in what the Republican platform said. Truman selected Barkley as his running mate. They ran on the themes the two men had developed in their speeches and then went on to upset the heavily favored Republican ticket in November.

The Convention as a Media Event

The national conventions are the two parties' most important campaign media events. When the chairperson of the convention tries to clear the aisles, they are as likely to be blocked by media representatives as by delegates. In fact, the delegates are often more fascinated with the media celebrities wandering around the convention hall than they are with the convention proceedings. Representatives of the media delight in their influence and power.

Media coverage has added immeasurably to the democratization of the national nominating process. The candidates and the parties know that what they do at the convention—whether right or wrong—will in many cases be transmitted into the American electorate's living rooms. In this sense, the American people participate in the process of selecting candidates and issues far beyond the primaries and caucuses of the spring.

There are, however, some conflicts between the objectives of the parties and the media. The parties wish to nominate winning candidates and adopt a platform with as much harmony as possible. The media wish to report what they think is newsworthy and important. To them the placid, the orderly, the ceremonial, and the ritualistic have a limited appeal compared to the controversial, the unprecedented, and things-gone-wrong in general.

It is particularly difficult to conduct sensitive negotiations at a convention—the media will not permit them to be private or secret. When news of the Reagan-Ford "dream ticket" got out, the story developed a life of its own, with reporters, analysts, and commentators concentrating on it. Negotiations between the Reagan and Ford staffs became much more difficult.

In the end, though, the media's image of a convention is the bridge between the campaign for nomination and the campaign for election. In 1980, when the two conventions were over, the Republicans left Detroit with the image of a united group ready to make a new beginning; the Democrats left New York with the controversy of the Kennedy challenge not dissipated and its nominee bearing the scars of criticism of his four-year tenure in office. The Republicans would quote Ted Kennedy on Jimmy Carter, and the Democrats would quote George Bush on Ronald Reagan, but the Republicans had the better of the quoting-match.

THE OLD AND THE NEW POLITICS OF CAMPAIGNING

The "new" politics of campaigning is really not all that new—it dates back to at least the 1930s. Essentially, the old politics was a party-centered campaign; the *new politics is based on a candidate-centered campaign*. The distinction between the old and new is based primarily on how the candidate gets campaign messages to the voter. In the following paragraphs we will discuss how the sending of campaign messages has changed, beginning in the early nineteenth century but focusing especially on changes in the last fifty years.

The Impact of Changes in Communications and Transportation

American campaigns have changed most over the last 200 years in response to technological innovation. Consider the changes in the print media:

pamphlets were replaced in the nineteenth century by the large city daily newspapers, which were supplemented by magazines and inexpensive books made possible by high-speed printing presses. The advent of wire services and the instant transmission of stories, data, and photographic images around the world have made every campaign detail instantly available to the communications industry.

Electronic communications have also been revolutionized in this century. Not until the late 1920s did radio begin to influence political campaigning. Herbert Hoover enjoyed a great many advantages over Alfred E. Smith in the 1928 presidential race, one of which was that Hoover had a deep, melodious, confident voice that contrasted dramatically with the voice of Democratic nominee Smith on the radio. The use of radio by Franklin D. Roosevelt is legendary. He also made maximum use of the newsreels that became standard weekly fare in movie picture theatres in the later 1930s and during the war years. Eisenhower, the nation's first television president, dominated the medium in much the same way that Roosevelt dominated radio. Today it is imperative that a presidential candidate project a positive image on television.

The revolution in communications has been matched by changes in transportation. Even after the advent of transcontinental railroads, presidential candidates could not carry on full-blown national campaigns in person. In the nineteenth and early twentieth centuries, much presidential campaigning was done by surrogates, with the candidates frequently conducting *front porch campaigns, staying at home as delegations of influential persons from around the country came to call on them.* Until 1932, presidential candidates did not go to the national convention that nominated them. In that year, Franklin Roosevelt broke with tradition and flew to Chicago to accept his nomination in person. Improved railroad transportation in the 1930s and 1940s made this the principal mode of campaign travel, but gradually air transportation began to revolutionize campaigning. Today, candidates may literally crisscross the continent in a single day, making multiple stops. They take with them a few key staff, and stay in constant touch with a central staff a thousand or more miles away on the ground through sophisticated communication systems.

At the very time communications and transportation so rapidly improved, making it easier for candidates to contact voters directly, the nation's political party organizations began to erode. The party workers who had carried each candidate's message door-to-door to voters were not as plentiful as they had been. To fill the void and to take advantage of the new technology, there emerged a whole new profession, one that encompasses all those specialists, technicians, consultants, and practitioners who help candidates communicate with the electorate: the political consultant.

The New Campaign Technology

Political consultants are the new professionals who sell their skills in modern campaign technology. There are all sorts of political consultants. Moreover, political consulting firms provide a wide range of particular skills and services to their clients. In one of the best early works on the modern campaign and

political consultants, Robert Agranoff listed the various specialists employed in campaigns and classified them by function as they appear in Table 8.3. Beyond this list of skills and expertise normally found in large consulting firms, a good deal more about modern political campaign consultants is known.

First, there has been a steady growth in the political consulting industry since the 1930s.[9] By the mid-1950s, about one-third of the state party committees had employed public relations firms at some time, useing a good share of their campaign funds to pay for their advice. By the 1970s, political consultants had become a campaign necessity. Today, virtually no major candidate would consider a challenged race without the help of consultants.

Second, political consultants have developed a considerable amount of power. The most celebrated and successful ones may even select their

---

Political Management Specialists	**Mount Vernon Associates, Inc.**
Mount Vernon Associates, Inc. is recognized nationally as a leader among successful political management specialists and maintains a proud and successful record of political campaign service.	Mount Vernon Associates, Inc., founded in 1978, is a young, dynamic and proven political management firm headquartered in Houston, Texas and Westport, Connecticut.
The key to Mount Vernon's success is a commitment to personalized service backed by professional performance. The staff at Mount Vernon Associates, Inc. has extensive experience in all levels of campaign politics.	Mount Vernon is visually two groups in one: Political Management Specialists and Public Affairs Professionals.
Mount Vernon Associates, Inc. provides assistance to a limited number of political clients who then benefit from individualized, professional service.	Mount Vernon has the technical capabilities, excellent staff and the proven know-how to give our clients uncompromised quality service.
	Mount Vernon serves political candidates and medium and large size companies. It works with Foundations and Institutes.
	At Mount Vernon there is a serious excitement about offering comprehensive services centering on our concept of total public affairs and management.

Campaign Services

Strategy
The Plan
Budget
The Analysis
Targetting

Candidate
Video Speech Delivery
Training
Appearance/Style
Personal Planning
Scheduling

Research
Opposition
Demographic
Polling Development/
  Analysis Interpretation
Issue

Fundraising
Direct Mail/Events

Organization
Precinct/Block Organization
Staff Training/Hiring
Voter Identification
Voter Registration

Special Projects
Phone Banks
Rallies
Campaign Activity
Advance

Media
Relations
Release Schedule

Advertising
Print/Electronic Ads
Flyers, Brochures, Push
Cards, Stickers, Tabloids

Legal
Federal Election Commission
  Reports
State and Local Reports
I.R.S. Requirements
Bookkeeping

Election Day
Ballot Security
Get out the Vote

Member: American Association
of Political Consultants.

"Their professionalism...is unparalleled."

"I must admit, the first poll we commissioned in my race for United States Congress was frightening. The poll showed me trailing the fourteen year incumbent 57% to 3%. I hired Mount Vernon Associates, Inc. because of their reputation and track record nationwide in campaign management and advertising. Together, we promptly forced our primary challengers to withdraw, and months later I was elected to the United States Congress running head of President Reagan in each precinct.

Mount Vernon put together an organization which produced 3000 blockworkers, succeeded in raising $820,000.00, established a distinctive people-oriented grass root effort and advertising campaign. Their professionalism on behalf of other clients and myself is unparalleled."

U.S. Congressman Jack Fields

U.S. Congressman Jack Fields (Texas)

Political consultants list the various services they can provide for candidates and include testimony from one of their winning clients in their advertising brochures. (courtesy Mount Vernon Associates, Inc.)

TABLE 8.3

List of Selected Specialists Employed In Campaigns

Management	Information	Media
Public Relations Counselor	Marketing Researcher	Journalist
Advertising Agent	Public Opinion Pollster	Media Advance Person
Advance Person	Political Scientist	Radio and TV Writer
Fund-Raiser	Social Psychologist	Radio and TV Producer
Management Scientist	Computer Scientist	Film Documentary
Industrial Engineer	Psychologist	Producer
Telephone Campaign	Computer Programmer	Radio and TV Time Buyer
Organizer	Demographer	Newspaper Space Buyer
	Statistician	Television Coach
		Radio and TV Actors
		Graphic Designer
		Direct Mail Advertiser
		Computer Printing
		Specialist

SOURCE: Robert Agranoff, ed., *The New Style in Election Campaigns* (Boston: Holbrook Press, Inc., 1972), p. 17.

clients, rather than vice versa. A contract with a highly visible political consultant can thus become a test of a candidate's viability for nomination and election. For example, the decision of David Garth, a well-known consultant, to take John Anderson's 1980 independent presidential campaign account gave the race status that it might not have acquired in any other way.

Third, political consultants are expensive. Their fees, the costs of the mass media, and the costs of the technology of the modern campaign account for most of the increase in campaign expenses in the last two decades. The schedule of charges described in the contracts is quite complex, but it typically includes three separate categories: 1) the consulting fee, 2) incurred costs and personal expenses, and 3) commissions. The consulting fee is what is charged just to secure the advice and creative genius of the consultant or firm. The client must then pay for all materials, air time, production, travel, and other expenses of the firm. Finally, a commission (typically 15 percent) is charged on just about everything purchased for the campaign.

Fourth, consultants have on many occasions clearly justified their reputations as miracle workers and equally clearly earned their fees. Overall, the consultant offers not only service but also advice. The distinguished senior senator from Illinois, Charles Percy, was losing his reelection campaign in 1978 until media consultant Doug Bailey devised an "apology strategy" that was aired at the last minute in a startlingly frank, 30-second

commercial that saved the senator's political life. This is the language of the commercial:

The polls say many of you want to send me a message. But after Tuesday I may not be in the Senate to receive it. Believe me, I've gotten the message and you're right. Washington has gone overboard and I'm sure I've made my share of mistakes. But in truth, your priorities are mine too. Stop the waste, cut the spending, cut the taxes. I've worked as hard as I know how for you. I'm not ready to quit now and I don't want to be fired. I want to keep working for you and I'm asking for your vote.[10]

There are thousands of success stories like this one, but there are also stories of failures, and both winning and losing candidates have on occasion been less than grateful for the assistance of their political consultants after election day. Sometimes consultants must sue to collect their fees.

And, finally, having stressed the demand for consultants, their power, their price tags, and their successes, we need to conclude with a statement about the reality of all of this magic and science. The fact is that campaign consultants do not possess foolproof strategies or techniques. What works in one campaign may not work in another. Gimmicks to get the attention of the public quickly become shopworn. The best political consultant may have to rely on intuition and gut feelings when caught in a very close contest or one in which events and trends change too rapidly to permit a careful strategic response. Campaigning is a tough business for both consultants and candidates.

What Does It Take to Win?

From the courthouse to the White House, campaigns for election turn on the candidates' ability to use the resources available to them. What are the principal resources available to candidates? They include: 1) the candidates themselves; 2) the media; 3) trends and events in the real world; 4) mistakes made in the course of the campaign; 5) money; 6) loyalists, party identifiers, and sympathetic organized groups; 7) issues; 8) political consultants and their technology or expertise; and 9) campaign strategy developed by the candidate, the consultants, and his or her staff. Winning is not easy for any candidate, but it is particularly difficult for those running for the big prize—the presidency.

PRESIDENTIAL CAMPAIGNS

To demonstrate how one puts together the winning combination of all the resources available, we now focus on the 1980 presidential campaign.

The Candidates

One of the most interesting aspects of the 1980 campaign was the presence of a strong independent candidate, John Anderson. Anderson's strength in the early campaign came from the fact that he offered people an alternative to Carter and Reagan. Those who wished to lodge a protest against the system had a stylish, intellectually acceptable alternative in Anderson. However, the law of diminishing attractiveness of serious "third alternative" candidates eventually caught up with the Anderson candidacy—that is, voters realized that Anderson could not win, and those who valued their vote had to decide between the remaining two candidates.

Carter's major resource was incumbency. He traveled as president, received media attention as president, and to a limited extent could make things happen. The people knew him, whereas they could only guess what sort of president Reagan might be. Reagan was the challenger and could assume the offensive position. The offensive was a comfortable position, given the Carter record. Carter's staff was more experienced than Reagan's, but Reagan had supplemented his own inner circle of loyalists with men and women who had worked in earlier, successful, national Republican campaigns.

Throughout 1980 Reagan was busy building a moderate image, trying to offset or play down his longstanding image as an extreme conservative. The Carter campaign thus had to devote time and effort to sharpening or clarifying the image that Reagan wished to blur. The Carter strategists believed that Carter himself would have to tell the voters what a "dangerous man" this Republican candidate was. But this was bad advice. In the attacks on Reagan, Carter's own image eroded. The people had always believed the president to be very religious, honest, sincere, and fair—their doubts about him had been about his ability to cope with the difficult issues of the day. Out of the Carter attacks on Reagan came a new image, one of a tough, nasty man. When Carter attacked Reagan, the Republican nominee was ready with a mixed response of anger, indignation, and, "Aw shucks, you couldn't be talking about me."

The Media

Three things are noteworthy about the paid media (political advertisements) in 1980. First, spending on the media campaign soared to new heights. Second, conservative political action committees (PACs) spent large sums of money attacking Carter and liberal incumbent senators. Thus began the strategy of negative advertising (which will be discussed in more detail in chapter 10.) The conservative PACs also spent alot to defend and support Reagan. Third, and most important, the Republican Party conducted an $8 million national advertising campaign to sell a more positive image of Republicans in the United States.

The "free" media (regular news coverage) appeared to be a bit less important in 1980 than in previous elections because there were fewer "medialities" than usual. According to media expert Michael Robinson, *medialities are "events, developments, or situations to which the media have given importance by emphasizing, expanding, or featuring them in such a way that their real significance has been modified, distorted, or obscured."*[11] While there were fewer medialities in 1980, several did have an impact. Robinson identifies five: 1) Reagan's little gaffes, 2) Carter's meanness, 3) the first television debate, 4) the last debate, and 5) the hostages. The hostage crisis was the one he regarded as critical. When the ABC news began to count the days the hostages had been held by their captors and ran a special report on the hostage situation every night, and when all of the media started investing much time and creative reporting to the issue, the story became intertwined with the campaign. On the last weekend of the 1980 campaign, the first anniversary of the taking of the hostages was celebrated from Teheran with media coverage beamed via satellite to television sets in the nation's living rooms. Nothing could have demonstrated better the impotence or feebleness attributed by Republicans to the Carter administration's foreign policy than the events of the hostage-taking anniversary.

The presidential debates also played a key role in the 1980 campaign. The first question about the presidential debates in 1980 was, who should participate? As host of the debates, the League of Women Voters decided to invite all candidates receiving 15 percent of the vote in the public opinion polls, and so on September 9, the League invited Anderson to join a first debate with Carter and Reagan in Baltimore to be held September 21. Carter declined the invitation, giving as his excuse that he would not debate two Republicans. (Anderson was a Republican prior to declaring his candidacy as an independent.) Carter called instead for a head-to-head debate with Reagan. The League of Women Voters refused his request, leaving Anderson and Reagan the only participants in the first debate. Carter was attacked constantly by both men for his absence. After the debate, both Anderson and Carter slipped a bit in the polls, but Reagan did not.

After the September 21 debate, a one-on-one Carter–Reagan debate seemed unlikely. For both the Reagan and Carter strategists, debates did not seem worth the risk they would pose to each candidate. Of course, the closer a debate were to election day, the higher its risk to both camps. The Reagan campaign organization decided that they would have to agree to the debate when Richard Wirthlin's October 14 poll showed Carter 2 percentage points ahead of Reagan, and another trusted GOP pollster, Robert Teeter, found that neither man had the support needed to win. This was a bad position to be in against an incumbent president.

Meanwhile, Anderson's support had dropped to 8 percent in the Gallup poll. Thus on October 14, the League of Women Voters invited Carter and Reagan to debate in Cleveland two weeks later. Carter had been planning to close off the option of a debate, but he was trapped. He had declined to debate his Democratic challengers, ducked the Baltimore debate with Reagan and Anderson, but had repeatedly said he wanted a one-on-one debate with Reagan. Once Carter was offered a chance to debate Reagan, he had to accept.

On standard debating points, Carter won the debate, but these events are not scored like college debates. Carter dwelled on the peace issue, took the offensive through most of the debate, and tried to exploit the great distance between the two men on the issues. Reagan turned aside the Carter attacks with a warm, good-spirited, Irish

Televised presidential debates tend to disadvantage an incumbent president who must defend his record of the past four years. In debates, the underdog generally has the edge.

humor most of the time, but on several occasions denied the charges with the simple expression of an innocent wronged: "There you go again, Mr. President." As much as possible, Reagan dwelled on the economic issues of the campaign, especially on inflation and runaway government spending. Reagan's conclusion was brilliant:

> Next Tuesday is election day. Next Tuesday all of you will go to the polls, will stand there in the polling place and make a decision. I think when you make that decision, it might be well if you would ask yourself, are you better off than you were four years ago? Is it easier for you to go and buy things in the stores than it was four years ago? Is there more or less unemployment in the country than there was four years ago? Is America as respected throughout the world as it was? Do you feel that our security is as safe, that we're as strong as we were four years ago?[12]

When the debate was over, it was clear that neither man had made a major mistake or had been embarrassed by the event. That turned the debate to Reagan's advantage, because he did not need a clear victory.

The Carter strategy had been to paint Reagan as an extremist. Reagan came across to those who watched the debates as neither Dr. Strangelove nor the Mad Bomber. Instead, he seemed like a rather pleasant sort of fellow. On the evening of October 28, it is very likely that Reagan crossed "the threshold of acceptability" that a challenger must cross if he is to replace an incumbent president. Reagan had been in the same forum, on the same platform, with President Carter, and he looked "presidential" enough.

Two years later, it came to light that Reagan had been aided in his seemingly brilliant low-key strategy by his campaign staff's prior possession of Carter's debate notes. Known as the Debategate Scandal, this episode only confirmed what most of the public already suspected—the stakes are so high that campaign staffs will go to almost any length to help their candidate win. But with regard to debates in general, it is important to note that one rule still applies: "If you're ahead, don't debate." Each time a presidential debate has been held (1960, 1976, 1980), the real winner has been the challenger or underdog.

Trends in the Real World

The nation's leading economic indicators did not cooperate with the Carter administration in 1979 and 1980. Since the New Deal, the nation has turned to the Democrats when there has been high unemployment or a recession, but the leading economic problem of 1980 was inflation, and efforts by the incumbent administration to bring down inflation had divided its support in Congress.

In foreign policy, the Carter administration was buffeted unmercifully by trends abroad. The hostage crisis did not end. The president responded to Russian intervention in Afghanistan with limited embargoes on high technology and grain and a boycott of the 1980 Moscow Olympics, but business owners and farmers thought they were being singled out unfairly, and Olympians and their supporters took issue with the president's boycott. The administration's SALT II treaty was in the Senate for ratification when the Soviets moved into Afghanistan; Carter had to withdraw the treaty, which by then had no chance of Senate approval. Even the Carter administration's successes in securing a treaty between Israel and Egypt were overshadowed by votes cast in the United Nations that were perceived as anti-Israel.

Campaign Mistakes and Miscalculations   In addition to the presidential debates discussed above there were three other campaign events of considerable importance.

As we have noted, the Democrats fully expected Reagan to "shoot himself in the foot" with errors and gaffes, and for several weeks during the fall these expectations were realized. Among Reagan's gaffes were the following: 1) he told a group of Protestant fundamentalists in Dallas that he had his own doubts about the theory of evolution; 2) in a speech to the Veterans of Foreign Wars he ad-libbed that the Vietnam War was a "noble cause"; and 3) on several occasions he made references to an official relationship with Taiwan, suggesting a return to some sort of "two Chinas" policy. On October 9, Reagan made one of his biggest mistakes of the campaign, attributing 93 percent of the nation's nitrogen oxides to trees and saying the Mount St. Helens eruption produced more sulphur dioxide than ten years' worth of automobiles. In each of these cases, the candidate had wandered from the script that had been prepared for him by his campaign staff.

One of the most obvious examples of miscalculation in the 1980 campaign involved John Anderson. His strategists decided to spend $2,500,000 to put their candidate on the ballot in every state in the union. Had Anderson spent that money and effort on a national media campaign, it would have bought more exposure and certainly more campaign contributions.

Another miscalculation involved the Republican preparation for an "October Surprise." They feared that Carter would bring the hostages home in mid-October. Elaborate preparations were made for such an event. They sensitized the media to such a possibility, planned their strategy, made radio and television commercials for it, and lined up spokesmen such as Gerald Ford and Henry Kissinger to deliver the official Republican response to a late-breaking hostage event. All this effort was wasted—the hostages did not come home until the day after the election.

Money
Although the candidates had the same amount of money to spend on the campaign (roughly $29.4 million), Reagan enjoyed an advantage from uncoordinated independent spending and from the highly successful Republican unity movement in 1980. On the other hand, Carter had the incumbency, and no one can estimate what that is worth in free media coverage and other resources that are better than money. On the whole, the two campaigns seem to have been pretty even in terms of money and the things money can buy. (Campaign financing will be discussed further in chapter 9.)

Base of Support
As noted in chapter 6, the Democratic party has been the majority party since the early 1930s. This status does not, however, give the Democrats a clear majority. The winning strategy for Carter required that he hold the lion's share of the Democrats and win over some independents.

Reagan, on the other hand, was working to build a new, broader coalition in 1980. Throughout the campaign, Reagan tried to swell the party's natural base by appealing to the discontented, those who had suffered from Carter policies, especially the blue-collar workers in economically hard-hit industrial centers and Catholics unhappy not only with Carter's economic policies but with some of the president's social policies as well. Significant support for the Republicans in 1980 came from new interest groups, including the Moral Majority, the pro-life movement, the anti-ERA forces, and the New Right in general.

Issues in the Campaign
Throughout this text, we have focused on three policy areas: economics, energy, and lifestyle policies. The Reagan campaign focused almost exclusively on economic issues and interpreted many other issues as essentially economic. The Carter administration was unusually vulnerable on economic issues, and so the Reagan focus was strategically appropriate. Reagan committed himself to supply-side economics, but he avoided being trapped into radical supply-side statements and gradually put some distance between himself and supply-side economists. Reagan also argued effectively that government was the problem in the economy. He proposed cutting back government spending and regulations and turning the private sector loose on the problems confronting America.

Carter, in contrast, was busy defending policies he had put in place. He said that he had cut government spending and adopted a tight fiscal and monetary policy to control inflation. He said that he was a victim of trends around the world, especially the high costs of oil. Carter was also put on the defensive because of his own campaign promises four years earlier. In 1976, Carter had run on economic policies against Gerald Ford, claiming that the "misery index" (a measure of the nation's economic ills) had increased under Ford. Carter had also predicted a balanced budget by 1980. These 1976 Carter pledges were revived and used against him in 1980.

Differences between the two candidates on energy issues were largely spelled out in the party platforms discussed earlier in the chapter. Carter relied on the policy of conservation and the creation of new, environmentally safe sources of energy. Under Carter the Department of Energy had been established, decontrol of oil had begun, and a windfall profits tax had been levied. Reagan favored abolishing the Department of Energy, completely decontrolling both oil and natural gas, and repealing the windfall profits tax. The Reagan solution to the energy problem was to get government out of the matter entirely and to turn it over to investors and developers on the assumption that the free market would provide cheaper and more plentiful energy.

Lifestyle issues do not normally occupy a central place in American presidential campaigns, and in this respect 1980 was a fairly normal year. In 1980, other issues mattered more than lifestyle policies, even though the party platforms on issues such as abortion, the ERA, gay rights, and prayer clearly differed. As we have said, the candidates themselves became an issue: which man could be trusted with the presidency?

Political Consultants

There is every indication that both Carter and Reagan were well served by their political consultants. To be sure, there were mild shakeups in the consultant corps of both camps, but Carter and Reagan generally relied on the technology, talent, and advice of people they had known and trusted for some years. The Carter staff that helped him lose the 1980 campaign was about the same group that had helped him win in 1976.

General Campaign Strategy

A *campaign strategy is the way all resources are managed—how candidates, media, trends, events, money, bases of support, issues, and modern campaign technology are blended together*. The real challenge is to find the right mix of all these different types of resources.

With the resources of modern campaign technology, consultants can help the candidates assess their strengths and weaknesses, find out what the public thinks, and devise a media campaign to counter a candidate's liabilities. In the long run, however, they cannot save a candidate from the final judgment of the electorate on election day.

Jimmy Carter's strategists relied on Ronald Reagan to save the president's political life. Carter was to take the high road: he would admit that he had made some mistakes but argue that he had learned from those mistakes and had the experience and training to be president. He would talk about his vision of the future, and the American people would find reason to give him four more years. If Reagan did not make himself the central issue of the campaign, surrogates were to communicate the dangers of a Reagan presidency. There was always hope that some trends would reverse or that the hostages might come home. All else failing, Carter's in-house people believed he might win because he was, in their words, "the luckiest politician in America."

Reagan's strategy was to turn the election of 1980 into a referendum on Carter's record as president. But first he had to tell the voters about himself and let the American people get to know and trust him, in the hope that they would believe him competent to lead the nation.

There is strong evidence that the race was close until the last two or three days, but as election day drew closer, keen observers noticed a difference in the spirit of the two camps. People on the Reagan plane were relaxed, smiling, and confident, but people traveling with Carter were grim, drawn, and quiet. At 4:00 A.M. on the morning of election day, as Jimmy Carter was flying back from the West Coast toward Plains, Georgia, Patrick Caddell, Carter's pollster, told him, "Well, Mr. President, it's gone." By the end of the day, Carter had gone down to defeat.

This close look at the 1980 campaign has shown that the campaign trail is long and the journey rough. Journalist Richard Cohen has aptly described what campaigning has become in an era of high technology:

> *Campaigning is a demanding and often sophisticated business. . . . It is a business that requires skills needed to develop, express, and sell a message—skills that are often far different from the business of legislating or representing constituents.* [13]

SUMMARY

The United States has the world's longest and most complex process of selecting leaders, in part because the voters participate in both the nomination and the election of leaders. Selecting leaders is crucial to the policymaking process, because the electorate rarely has an opportunity to directly influence policy. Instead, we pick the leaders who ultimately shape and finalize policy.

A distinctly American system for nominating candidates has evolved. We began with the caucus, which was supplanted by the nominating convention. In the twentieth century we turned to the direct primary. Most of the thousands of candidates for election in the United States are picked by the primary, but the process of selecting a presidential candidate still involves the caucus, convention, and primary.

We have illustrated the complexity of American politics by describing the presidential selection process in some depth. Long before the first delegate is picked to attend the Democratic and Republican national conventions, an "invisible primary" screens out all of the presidential contenders who are not attracting enough support to be considered serious candidates for the nomination. Those who remain contend in the presidential preference primaries and the caucus and convention delegate selection process that begins in January and ends in June of presidential election years.

The national nominating conventions close out the first phase of selecting our president. Success in the second phase of the selection process, the campaign for election that begins about Labor Day, depends to a great extent on the candidate's success in the first part. Did the candidates have a solid preconvention campaign strategy? Was the convention marked by harmony or disagreement? As the nominee's biggest and most important media event, was the convention a success or a failure? What did the party adopt as its official platform? In recent decades, the conventions have been stripped of many of their functions. The choice of the presidential candidate has been clear before the first ballot since 1952. The presidential nominee by tradition selects the vice presidential nominee.

Political campaigns have been revolutionized by the decline in the importance of political parties and by this century's rapid improvements in transportation and communications. This age of computers, television, jet planes, and sophisti-cated technology has changed the campaign process. With the weakening of parties and the rise of technology, a new profession has evolved—that of campaign consultant. Since their emergence in the 1930s, campaign consultants have grown in number and power, and they have contributed to the high cost of campaigns. Political consultants have worked miracles in some campaigns, but they don't guarantee victory.

The 1980 presidential campaign resembled those of the last twenty or so years and will probably resemble campaigns to come, but it had distinctive elements, too. One major distinction was the strong presence of independent candidate John Anderson early in the contest and his fading a little later than we would have expected. The strategies employed by the candidates varied considerably. Essentially, President Carter tried to make Reagan the central issue of the campaign, and Reagan tried to make the election a referendum on Carter's stewardship in office. Campaign strategy is the wise use of these resources: the candidates, the media, trends and events, money, bases of support, issues, and both in-house and outside consultants. Campaigning is a business.

The Case of the Look-Alike Actors and the Canceled Ad: The Republican Campaign of 1982

The one-minute television spot has become the principal method by which candidates communicate with the electorate in the new style of political campaign. In 1982, as in 1980, the most important issue in the Republican campaign was the state of the economy, but this time the Republicans controlled the White House. The following passage is *Time* magazine's description of the Republicans' 1982 media campaign:

> *The TV commercial opens with a bespectacled attorney reading a last will and testament. Incongruously present are the not so dear departed, hugely enjoying themselves as the lawyer tells the grieving heirs:*
>
> *"To Ronald Reagan we leave a recession, inflation at 12.4% and rising, gas prices sky high." Chortling merrily at the dubious bequest are—could it be?—Democrats Jimmy Carter and Tip O'Neill.*
>
> *Well, not exactly. The 30-second spot, which was shown on 59 stations last week, features Actors Ed Beheler and Edwin Steffe, who bear uncanny resemblances to the former President and House Speaker. The commercial is part of a $10 million advertising campaign, sponsored by the Republican Party, in which the G. O. P. points with pride to its accomplishments and views with alarm the legacy of its Democratic opponents as congressional elections approach. A companion ad shows a couple dusting off their camper and taking a vacation with friends now that inflation has eased. The ad's tag line: "Republicans are beginning to make things better."*[1]

The Democrats protested. They argued that the recession began six months after Reagan entered the White House; furthermore, if things were improving, they wanted to know for whom. While protesting, the Democrats demanded equal time to reply. Actually, they were most angry because they lacked the funds to respond to the Republicans in kind.

This was not the first "look alike" commercial for the

[1] "Viewing with Alarm," *Time*, May 31, 1982, p. 20.

Republicans; the same actor had impersonated Tip O'Neill for the Republican 1980 commercials.

Nor was this the first controversial political commercial ever produced or transmitted to American audiences. The Democrats' infamous "Daisy Girl" spot of the 1964 campaign was followed by their "Strontium-90 Ice Cream Cone" spot; both were denounced by the Republicans. The "Daisy Girl" spot was a one-minute film shown on NBC's "Monday Night at the Movies." It "began with a close-up of a tow-haired moppet plucking petals from a daisy, babbling her count as she went, until the film faded through her eyes to a countdown of an atomic testing site and the entire scene dissolved in a mushroom cloud."[2] The other spot "was a portrait of a deliciously beautiful little girl innocently licking an ice-cream cone, with a gentle, motherly voice in the background explaining about Strontium-90 and pointing out that Barry Goldwater was against the Test Ban Treaty."[3] The Democrats ran some pretty tough commercials in 1964, but these two were more than tough. Each spot ran but a single time.

The 1982 "look-alike" ad was one of a package produced at a cost of $1.7 million for the Republican National Committee and the Republican Congressional Committee. The hard-hitting package was to have been the Republicans' 1982 media campaign, but at first all three networks declined to run them, and Republican leaders both in and out of the White House were ambiva-

lent about using them. However, the package was released with fanfare on May 17. ABC reconsidered its opposition and did run the ad, but it produced a flurry of unfavorable editorials. The first media package was replaced with another set of commercials on June 19.

The ads that replaced the "look-alikes" represented quite a change. Instead of the negative theme of blaming the nation's ills on the Democrats, these ads featured folksy-looking older Americans talking about receiving a 7.4 percent cost-of-living increase in their Social Security checks and a 10 percent cut in income taxes on July 1, 1982. "In one ad, a postman with a bushy white mustache says, 'I'm probably one of the most popular people in town today,' as he delivers Social Security and paychecks. The changes aren't much, he admits, 'but President Reagan has made a beginning. For gosh sakes let's give him a chance.' "[4] On July 15, the Democrats denounced the new Republican commercials as "a big lie" and offered the networks one of their own accusing the Republicans of trying to cut back on Social Security payments.

The limited showing of the "look-alike" commercials accomplished the Republican party's goal. The message the Republicans wanted to transmit got out—the troubled economy of 1982 was inherited from the Democrats. Since the print and electronic journalists made these commercials a news item, the fact that they were released and shown one time became a mediality. The Democrats had done the same thing in 1964, with the same results: the two ads accusing Barry Goldwater of being dangerous on the nuclear war issue were shown, denounced, withdrawn, and featured in news stories for a time. The Republicans studied the Democratic spots of 1964 and learned their lessons well.

[2]Theodore H. White, *The Making of the President 1964* (New York: Atheneum Publishers, 1965), p. 339.
[3]*Ibid.*
[4]"GOP Decides on Different TV Strategy," *Atlanta Constitution*, June 20, 1982.

KEY TERMS

campaign strategy
caucus
closed primary
convention
direct primary
front porch campaign
invisible primary
Kemp-Roth supply-side economics proposal
medialities
new politics
nonpartisan primary

open primary
partisan primary
political consultants
rose garden campaign
run-off primary
winnowing process

SUGGESTED READINGS

Chagall, David. *The New King-Makers*. New York: Harcourt Brace Jovanovich, 1981.

Crotty, William J. *Political Reform and the American Experiment*. New York: Thomas Y. Crowell Co., 1977.

Crouse, Timothy. *The Boys on the Bus: Riding with the Campaign Press Corps*. New York: Random House, 1973.

Drew, Elizabeth. *Portrait of an Election: The 1980 Presidential Campaign*. New York: Simon & Schuster, 1981.

Germond, Jack W., and Witcover, Jules. *Blue Smoke and Mirrors: How Reagan Won and Why Carter Lost the Election of 1980*. New York: Viking Press, 1981.

Keech, William R., and Matthews, Donald R. *The Party's Choice*. Washington, D.C.: Brookings Institution, 1976.

Moore, Jonathan, ed. *The Campaign for President: 1980 in Retrospect*. Cambridge, Mass.: Ballinger Publishing Company, 1981.

Pomper, Gerald; Baker, Ross K.; Frankovic, Kathleen A.; Jacob, Charles E.; McWilliams, Wilson Carey; and Plotkin, Henry A. *The Election of 1980*. Chatham, N.J.: Chatham House Publishers, Inc., 1981.

Ranney, Austin, ed. *The Past and Future of Presidential Debates*. Washington, D.C.: American Enterprise Institute, 1979.

Wayne, Stephen J. *The Road to the White House: The Politics of Presidential Elections*. rev. ed. New York: St. Martin's Press, 1981.

White, Theodore H. *America in Search of Itself: The Making of the President 1956–1980*. New York: Harper and Row, 1982.

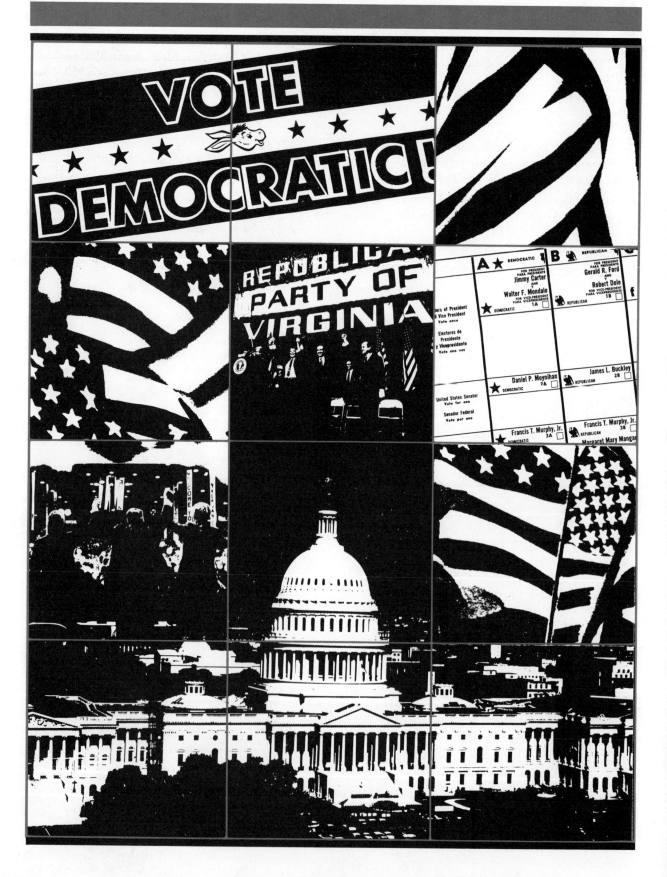

CHAPTER 9

ELECTIONS AND VOTING BEHAVIOR: PHASE TWO IN THE POLITICS OF SELECTING POLICYMAKERS

The Conduct of Elections ■ Three Models of Voting Behavior ■ Voting Decisions in Presidential Elections: 1952 to 1976 ■ The 1980 Presidential Election ■ The Electoral College ■ Campaign Finance ■ Can the Media Win Elections?

On Tuesday, November 4, 1980, the American people picked a president, a vice president, one-third of the United States Senate, and all members of the House of Representatives. In addition, the electorate picked state governors, legislators, mayors, and countless other policymakers. Election day truly symbolizes democracy in action.

The voice of the people registered in the elections of November 4, 1980, was the worst news the Democratic party had received in over 50 years. The presidential vote was Reagan, 43,901,812 (50.8 percent), Carter, 35,483,820 (41.0 percent), Anderson, 5,719,437 (6.6 percent), and others, 1,408,227 (1.6 percent). The electoral college vote was even more striking: Reagan beat Carter 489 to 49, with Carter carrying only six states and the District of Columbia. For the first time since 1952, the Republicans captured control of the Senate with their gain of twelve seats. In the House, the Republicans picked up thirty-three seats, reducing the Democratic majority so sharply there as to leave it clearly in the hands of a conservative coalition for at least two years. The

The longstanding ritual of a presidential election day calls for the candidates to return to their home towns to vote, then pose for photographs and answer the inevitable question, "How did you vote?"

Republican Party and Ronald Reagan had together won a smashing victory. A shadow over that victory, however, was that for the fifth time in a row, the turnout of the electorate had fallen: only 53.9 percent of the voting-age population had bothered to vote.

The key question of interest in this chapter is why individuals choose to exercise their right to vote. Is it because of the procedures for registering, the type of ballot being used, one's interest in politics, party affiliation, the candidates, issues, the media, or some combination of all these?

THE CONDUCT OF ELECTIONS

The national government does not conduct elections. Since the founding of the United States, all arrangements for elections have been made by state and local governments. The national government has, however, defined unconstitutional constraints on suffrage. The states may not deny persons the vote because they are black or female; they may not discriminate against persons because of their religious, ethnic, or language background. States may not impose arbitrary and needlessly long residence requirements (longer than 30 days), impose poll taxes, administer literacy tests, or set the voting age higher than 18. In addition, Congress exercised its constitutional power in 1845 to fix a uniform date for electing the president and members of Congress.

The states have prescribed by law very elaborate sets of rules to guide the conduct of elections and structure the recording and counting of the ballots on election day. To make this process easier, states and localities have been divided into precincts. A **precinct** is a *geographical area, perhaps a neighborhood, whose residents vote at the same polling place.* A voting or polling place is established in the precinct at a public or semipublic place; typically schools, fire stations, and city halls are used, but sometimes voting takes place in barbershops, businesses, or even private homes. Each polling place must be staffed by an adequate number of election officials (called judges, inspectors, or commissioners) whose role is to make sure the election is carried out legally. They check the voters' registration cards, make sure party workers do not pass out literature too near the voting booth, and certify the total number of votes cast in the precinct. Usually state laws require each major political party be

represented among the election officials. In each precinct, there are also poll watchers who are typically employed by the parties and candidates to insure the impartiality of both the conduct of the election during the day and the counting of the ballots when the day is over. At the level above the precinct, there must be a municipal, county, and state board of elections to provide ongoing supervision of the registration and election system. This elaborate and undoubtedly expensive system was established to insure that votes are recorded and counted accurately and without fraud.

The Ballot

The rules for conducting elections are not neutral, and adjusting the rules may benefit certain political parties, interests, or elites. Perhaps the most dramatic change in the balloting system in American electoral history was the adoption of the Australian ballot. An *Australian ballot is a ballot printed at the public expense and cast in secret.* Before the 1880s, ballots were printed by the parties and the candidates in varying colors and sizes; in most cases, the voter could not split the ticket (vote for members of different parties), and voting was usually not secret. With the coming of the Australian ballot, split-ticket voting increased sharply.

The form of the ballot also has consequences for straight and split-ticket voting, as discussed in chapter 6. Most states use a party column ballot, but a reform movement early in this century advanced the cause of an office block ballot, which is used by a substantial minority of the states today. The *party column ballot lists all of the candidates in a column under the party label.* The *office block ballot groups candidates according to the office they seek.* The party column ballot facilitates straight-ticket voting, especially when one mark completes the task of voting. Research suggests that weak partisans, the least aware, and the least sophisticated voters are influenced more than others by the form of the ballot.

Vote Facilitation

Benjamin Ginsberg, a leading student of elections, has suggested that state and local laws governing the process of voting also play an important role in determining whether an individual will vote. Do state and local governments encourage voter participation by making it easy to register? Are polling places well advertised and con-

The ease or difficulty of registering to vote plays an important part in determining whether an individual will participate in the electoral process.

Many states have laws requiring that sample ballots be available to voters. Voters are then allowed to bring these pre-marked sample ballots into the voting booth to speed up the voting process.

veniently placed? Does the government print a voter-education packet and distribute it widely and systematically? Is there an adequate number of voting machines or voting booths so that voters do not have a long wait to vote? Can voters who must be out of town on election day easily secure and cast an absentee ballot? Historic voting studies suggest that these types of considerations facilitate voting among the poor and the least educated, which reduces (but does not eliminate) participation differences between individuals of different socioeconomic status.

THREE MODELS OF VOTING BEHAVIOR

For the average voter, the outcome of the election is what is important: Ronald Reagan beat Jimmy Carter. Election contests symbolize an end to the debate over who will govern and confer legitimacy and acceptance on the winner.

A number of voting studies have been undertaken in an attempt to understand why people vote as they do. At least three models are widely used to analyze voting: the *Monday-morning-quarterback model*,[1] the *American Voter model*,[2] and the *Changing American Voter model*.[3] Although these models generally describe voting in presidential elections, as you will see, they also apply to state and local elections.

The Monday-Morning-Quarterback or Conventional Wisdom Model

Analyses that fall under this model are those that appear on television and in newspapers, magazines, and books in the days and weeks following the election. It is human nature to explain, even when the data to offer an informed analysis are unavailable. Few accurate voting statistics matched to census data for precincts were available until the 1950s, and public opinion polling did not begin until 1935, with national surveys of voting behavior appearing only in 1948. Explanations based on conventional wisdom can be quite erroneous. For example, it was said in 1928 and believed for a long time thereafter that Democratic party nominee Alfred E. Smith was a poor candidate for president against Herbert Hoover. Smith was Catholic, supported the repeal of prohibition, and was "from the wrong side of the tracks." Actually, Smith picked up new support for the Democratic party in the urban, industrial, and Catholic areas of the country and among the foreign-born.[4] More often, the conventional wisdom analyses are at least partially correct. The difference between them and more "scientific" analyses is that conventional wisdom accounts rely upon journalistic accounts of the campaign.

The Monday-morning-quarterback or conventional wisdom approach, then, is not typically based on large stores of data. Journalists such as Theodore White and David Broder describe the campaign and call attention to noteworthy events. Telling the story replaces solid analysis and explanation. Sometimes such accounts miss the mark, but they are generally accurate and portray campaigns and elections in a much more engaging style than dry, analytical, social science reports.

The American Voter Model

This model was first described in *The American Voter* (1960), a book by a group of scholars at the University of Michigan based on extensive survey research. These scholars explain the voting decision as the product of a long-term component, party identification, and a short-term component, election-specific partisan attitudes. In this interpretation, party identification is considered an enduring tendency "to evaluate the elements of politics in a given partisan way." The election-specific attitudes are the new combinations of issues, candidates, and governmental actions presented to the voters at each election.

To put it more simply, no voter comes to an election year without some political preferences, which are a product of the person's political socialization (see chapter 5). During an election year, the voter is presented with candidates, is-

sues, and governmental actions to evaluate; these may either reinforce or challenge the voter's basic political preferences. For example, voters may think of themselves as Democrats but be attracted to the Republican candidate for president.

The Michigan scholars measure the long-term variable by asking respondents whether they think of themselves as Democrats, Republicans, independents, or members of some other political category. They follow up this initial question by asking Democrats and Republicans whether they think of themselves as "strong" or "weak" members of their parties. Those who say they are independents are asked, "Do you think of yourself as closer to the Republican or Democratic party?" Using this sequence of questions, they can classify almost all of their respondents in one of the following categories:

1. strong Democrat
2. weak Democrat
3. independent Democrat
4. independent
5. independent Republican
6. weak Republican
7. strong Republican

As you can see, there is a continuum from strong Democrat to strong Republican; the midpoint is "independent." Those who are "strong" in their party identification are far more likely to vote for their party's candidate than those who are "weak" or "independent." Once the probability of voting for one's party is calculated, a normal vote of the electorate as a whole may be constructed. The *normal vote*, therefore, *is an estimate of the vote based entirely on what social scientists know about the impact of party identification on the electorate's voting behavior.* In other words, if all other considerations are removed and the electorate votes solely on the basis of party identification, we find that one party will be preferred over the other.

The normal vote computation for the national electorate from 1952 to 1960 produced an estimate of about 54 percent Democratic and 46 percent Republican. However, the actual Democratic share of the presidential vote was 44.4 percent in 1952, 42.0 percent in 1956, and 49.8 percent in 1960. The normal vote analysis would have predicted Democratic wins in all three elections, but they lost the first two and barely won the third. This is because short-term variables were running heavily against the Democrats in these three elections. An individual's party identification is not an absolute guarantee that he or she will vote for that party's candidate in a given election.

Clearly, short-term factors have a substantial capacity to deflect the normal vote from its expected direction. What, specifically, are the short-term factors? The Michigan scholars discuss six. Two of the factors are the candidates selected by the two major parties. Another two are the domestic and foreign policy positions of the parties and their candidates. The fifth factor they call ''group-related attitudes''—choices based on whether the party or candidate is good or bad for some group in society (for example, a voter might like the Democratic party because it is good for the poor or dislike it because it always takes the side of blacks). The final short-term factor is the reputation of the two parties as managers of the government when in power.

In summary, putting the long-term party identification factor together with the short-term, election-specific factors, enables the American Voter model better to predict an individual's voting behavior than the Monday-morning-quarterback model.

The Changing American Voter Model

The portrait of the American voter drawn by the Michigan scholars was not very flattering: the ''average'' voter had strong party loyalties, was very unsophisticated when confronted with issues, could rarely use ideological standards in judging political events, and was not very interested in politics or active in political affairs. The *Changing American Voter* model emerged as a revision of the *American Voter* model in 1976. The scholars who developed this model argued that the old American voter model did not take into account changes that were taking place in the electorate. Among these changes were: a dramatic decline in strong party identifiers, a rise in the number of voters who called themselves independent, a decline in the transference of party identification from one generation to the next through socialization, an increase in the proportion of the electorate splitting tickets, and an increase in issue voting. They also noted that the higher levels of issue voting seemed to be associated with the voters' improved

ability to link issues together in ideological or near-ideological frameworks. In contrasting their thesis with the Michigan work, the revisionists wrote,

> *The dynamics of the electoral system depend . . . on the interplay of long-term partisan commitments and the political issues facing the nation. But we assign somewhat more weight to political issues in structuring citizen political behavior than is the case in the ''normal vote'' model of the Michigan researchers.*

They also came to this conclusion:

> *The data do indicate that the new role of issues in the elections since 1964 is, in good part, a reaction to the nature of the candidates offered. If the public is faced with candidates distinguished from each other on the basis of the issues, it will vote on the issues. If the public is offered a more centrist choice, the vote will depend much more heavily on partisan identification.*[5]

These three models of voting by no means exhaust the list, and there is not total agreement in the behavioral sciences about which one best explains the voting decision.

Whether it be the Monday-morning-quarterback, the American Voter, or the changing American Voter model, the key questions are the same. Do voters vote mainly on the issues, the parties, or the candidates? Do voters vote mainly **retrospectively**, on the basis of the previous four years of an incumbent's presidency, or **prospectively**, on the basis of the performance anticipated from a challenger? These are difficult questions to answer, as the following analyses of presidential elections since 1952 show.

VOTING DECISIONS IN PRESIDENTIAL ELECTIONS:

I Like Ike: 1952 and 1956

In both 1952 and 1956, the Republicans nominated Army General Dwight D. Eisenhower for president and Senator Richard M. Nixon for vice president. The Democrats nominated Illinois Governor Adlai Stevenson for president in both years with running mates Senator John Sparkman in 1952 and Senator Estes Kefauver in 1956. Ike was an authentic victorious general who drew crowds wherever he went; Stevenson was less well known and tended to be a bit aloof and talked over the heads of his audiences.

As important as Eisenhower's candidacy was to

the Republicans in 1952 and 1956, voters appeared to vote retrospectively in both years. The Democrats had been in power for twenty years. Their leadership was aging, and petty misbehavior had raised doubts about their integrity. In short, the ability of the Democrats to manage the government was being questioned. Furthermore, the Korean War had become "Truman's War," and there was a general belief that the Truman administration was not handling the "Cold War" with Russia very well, making foreign policy issues a liability to the Democrats. Ike won big in 1952 and bigger in 1956, even though he had a Republican Congress for only two of his eight years as president.

Religion and Image: The 1960 Election

The Republicans in 1960 nominated former Senator and incumbent Vice President Richard M. Nixon for president and ex-Senator Henry Cabot Lodge as his running mate. The Democrats nominated Senator John F. Kennedy and majority leader of the Senate Lyndon B. Johnson for president and vice president. As shown in Figure 9.1, the Republicans enjoyed a net advantage over the Democrats on the basis of the public's assessment of their candidates; indeed, Nixon's advantage over Kennedy in terms of candidate assessment was quite large.

The 1960 election is noteworthy because of the "religious factor" and the first televised debates between major presidential contenders. Because a Catholic had never been elected president, Ken-

nedy's religion was an important factor in the campaign. But one should not overstate its importance: "the fact remains that Protestant Democrats were more likely to behave as Democrats than as Protestants, and Catholic Republicans were more likely to behave as Republicans than as Catholics."[6] In the televised debates, all voters regardless of religious persuasion saw a young, confident, and highly telegenic candidate who just happened to be Catholic challenge the highly visible and experienced vice president of the United States for the presidency. In the first debate, Kennedy convinced many viewers that his youth, lack of experience, and religion posed no serious threat to the nation. In fact, just the opposite image was projected—Kennedy seemed to be a vigorous, competent, and appealing leader who could, to use his slogan, "get the nation moving again." In contrast to the 1952 and 1956 elections, voters in the 1960 election tended to cast their ballots prospectively.

Ideology and the 1964 Election

The Republicans nominated Senator Barry Goldwater and Representative William Miller to be their 1964 presidential and vice presidential candidates. The Democrats nominated the incumbent president, Lyndon B. Johnson, and balanced the "southerner" by choosing Senator Hubert H. Humphrey (Minnesota) as their vice presidential nominee. Johnson's candidacy contributed heavily to the Democratic victory of 1964, but Goldwater's candidacy contributed al-

The 1960 Kennedy-Nixon television debates convinced many viewers that Kennedy's youth, lack of experience, and religion posed no serious threat to the nation. Thus, the debates encouraged voters to cast their ballots prospectively.

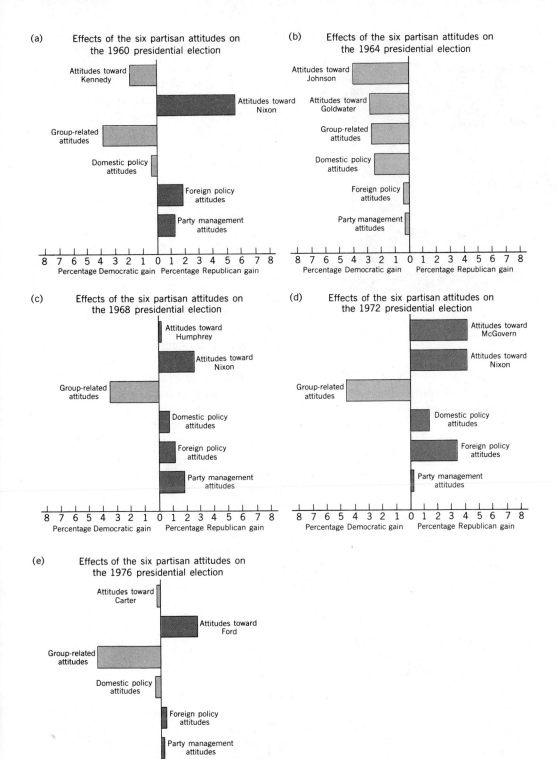

FIGURE 9.1

Short-term Components of the Vote in Five Presidential Elections, 1960–1976

SOURCE: Herbert Asher, *Presidential Elections and American Politics.* 2d ed. (Homewood, Ill.: The Dorsey Press, 1980), pp. 152, 170, 180, 190, and 204. Professor Asher acknowledges the assistance of Michael Kagay and Greg Calderia in preparing these representations.

The unsuccessful Goldwater (R) candidacy against incumbent president Lyndon B. Johnson (D) in 1964 demonstrates how difficult it is for an ideologically-extreme candidate to win a presidential election.

most as much. In Goldwater the Republicans gave the American electorate a choice between a "true conservative" and "politics as usual"; the voters responded by rejecting Goldwater. All six short-term components gave an advantage to Johnson and the Democrats (see Figure 9.1b). Goldwater advocated expanding the Vietnam War so strongly that he lost the Republican party's "peace" advantage, which made even the Democrats seem more reliable as managers of government than Goldwater and his supporters.

One thing is certain: the Goldwater candidacy disrupted some pretty stable voting patterns in American elections for 1964 and the two succeeding elections. How was 1964 different?

1. New issues crowded out the traditional voter concern over domestic policies on standards of living, jobs, and the economy. The most important issues in 1964 were the Vietnam War and race relations.

2. Evaluation of the candidates in ideological terms was four times greater in 1964 than in 1960. A **political ideology** is an abstract view of the world, an elaborate, interrelated, and far-reaching set of attitudes about politics.

3. There was a dramatic increase in attitude consistency among liberals and conservatives; that is, traditional liberals took a liberal position on more issues and traditional

conservatives took conservative positions on more issues. Liberal and conservative positions reached beyond domestic policies to include foreign policies, too.

4. The unique contribution of party identification to the voting decision declined, and issue voting rose.

A Majority Party in Disarray: 1968 and 1972

The Republican Party nominated Richard M. Nixon for president and Spiro Agnew for vice president in 1968 and again in 1972. The Democrats countered with Hubert H. Humphrey and Edmund Muskie in 1968 and George McGovern and Sargent Shriver in 1972. The candidate advantage returned to the Republicans in both these elections: Nixon was a decided asset to the Republican race, while Humphrey (by a small margin) and McGovern (by a large margin) received more negative than positive evaluations by voters (see Figure 19.1c and d). The real stories about the candidates in these two elections were the noncentrist candidacies of George Wallace in 1968 and George McGovern in 1972. Wallace launched a very successful third party challenge that rested on voter discontent over the issues of urban unrest, race relations, crime and violence, and the Vietnam War; the absolute clarity of his stands gave him 13.5 percent of the vote and threatened to send the election to the House of Representatives for a final resolution.

In 1972 McGovern was perceived to be immoderate or extremist in his positions, especially in his stand on the Vietnam War. The division among Democratic voters was most obvious in 1968 in the divergent positions of "hawks" and "doves" on the Vietnam War; by 1972, this division had been further exacerbated by quarrels within the party on social issues.

Voters voted retrospectively in 1968 as they evaluated the Johnson administration and agreed with Richard Nixon that "any administration that could not end the Vietnam War in four years did not deserve to be returned to power." Though the war had not ended by 1972, the Nixon policy of **Vietnamization**—*gradually turning the conduct of the hostilities over to the South Vietnamese*—had brought large numbers of troops home and convinced voters that "peace with honor" was just around the corner. Their retrospective evaluation

Democratic presidential candidate George McGovern was perceived as an extremist, particularly on the Vietnam War, which caused voters to cast their ballots for the incumbent Richard Nixon in 1972.

of his performance was positive enough to return him to office in 1972.

A Return to the American Voter Model: The 1976 Election

In 1976 both the Democrats and the Republicans nominated centrist candidates (see Figure 9.1e). The Republicans nominated incumbent President Gerald Ford for president and Senator Robert Dole for vice president. The Democrats nominated former governor Jimmy Carter and Senator Walter Mondale for president and vice president. Both Carter and Ford made their personal attributes the centerpieces of their respective campaigns: the American people were offered two nice guys they could trust. Honesty, integrity, and decency were values much sought by the people following the Watergate scandal, and both presidential candidates of 1976 were a response to that longing.

Even the authors of the *Changing American Voter* had to admit that the *American Voter* model fit the 1976 election rather well: it looked like a return to the voting patterns that had prevailed before 1964. The unique contribution of party identification rose, but not to pre-1964 levels; issue voting declined, but again not to pre-1964 levels; and ideological evaluation of the candidates plummeted to levels near those of before 1964.

Carter won the 1976 election with 50.1 percent of the popular vote and an electoral vote margin

over Ford of 297 to 240. On the face of it, it seemed that Carter had restored the old New Deal coalition: the South, the big cities, the industrial North, labor union members and their families, Catholics, Jews, and blacks. However, Carter's support from each of these groups was weaker than Roosevelt's had been. For example, Carter's southern support was primarily from black voters whereas Roosevelt's was primarily from southern whites. Likewise, even though Carter enjoyed strong support from Catholics and Jews, traditional Democratic voters, neither of these groups voted as heavily Democratic as they had in the New Deal years. Finally, Carter's support in the industrial North, while strong, was not as strong as Roosevelt's. Clearly, the old New Deal coalition had not been restored because just four years later a significant number of these traditional Democratic voters cast their ballots for Republican Ronald Reagan.

THE 1980 PRESIDENTIAL ELECTION

In 1980, the Democrats once again nominated Jimmy Carter and Walter Mondale. The Republicans nominated Ronald Reagan and George Bush. The public opinion polls predicted a close race between Reagan and Carter, but the Republican nominee won by a margin of about 10 percent. Jimmy Carter became the first elected incumbent president since Herbert Hoover to be defeated for a second term.* Although he was the candidate of the majority party, Carter lost by a wide margin, a margin that helped Republican candidates all over the country. This was unusual. Yet it wasn't an exciting year for the typical American voter. One voter in four waited until the last two weeks before the election to choose among Reagan, Carter, and Anderson. The proportion of the eligible electorate voting declined for the fifth presidential election in a row. The late voting decision and the high proportion of nonvoters indicate how disturbing the 1980 election was for the electorate. A profound public lack of interest in the election and the substantial vote for independent candidate John Anderson are further evidence that many voters were disillusioned with both the issues and the candidates.

---

*Gerald Ford was never elected president. He succeeded to the office when Nixon resigned.

The Monday-Morning-Quarterback Evaluation of 1980

Instant "armchair" analyses of the election produced the following assessments of the Reagan-Carter contest:

1. A massive shift in the ideological alignment of the nation had moved the electorate from the left to the right.

2. The 1980 election was for the Republicans what the 1932 election had been for the Democrats; the New Deal of Roosevelt had been replaced by a New Beginning under Reagan.

3. A realignment of partisan loyalties had occurred, and the Democratic party had been deposed from its long ascendancy as the nation's majority party.

4. The Moral Majority, the Anti-ERA, and the Right to Life movements claimed credit for the Reagan victory and proclaimed the election a mandate for their views on social questions like sex and violence on television, humanistic values in schools, prayer in schools, gay rights, abortion, and the role of women in society.

5. Liberals preferred to interpret the election as a massive repudiation of Jimmy Carter and his presidency; liberals had never cared for the president, and they preferred not to view Reagan's election as a mandate for his policies.

6. Conservatives viewed the election as a long-awaited new era, as a mandate for "getting the government off the backs of the American people," reducing the size of government, cutting taxes, cutting spending in social services, and "closing the window of vulnerability" in national defense by increased military spending.

7. To some, the 1980 election was both a personal and a media contest between Reagan and Carter; for them, the election of an actor who was highly personable and skilled in the use of all communications media was the culmination of the "modern campaign" that makes magicians out of public relations experts and image merchants.

Each of these seven interpretations is off the mark, but separating truth from error in each statement is not a simple task. One's evaluation often hinges on which team one was pulling for.

The American Voter Model and the 1980 Election

The party identification of American voters was virtually unchanged by the 1980 election. The "normal vote" analysis for 1980 produced an estimated vote for the Democratic candidate of 55 percent to the Republican candidate's 45 percent. In other words, the long-term component of the vote has remained stable, and so it is necessary to look to short-term explanations of the election outcome.[7]

Figure 9.2 summarizes the impact of the six short-term components of the voting decision. The direction of the influence of the six components is a real surprise, primarily in the impact of the image of each candidate on the vote. In spite of all of Jimmy Carter's election year troubles, he gained votes for the Democratic cause. More surprising, and contrary to what we would expect, was Reagan's contribution to the Democratic vote. As a candidate, Jimmy Carter was responsible for moving the total vote .93 of 1 percent to the Democratic party's advantage, and Reagan was responsible for moving the total votes cast .70 of 1 percent to the Democratic party's advantage.

The Democrats reaped their traditional advantage from the group-related component. The Republicans were preferred in both domestic and foreign policy. Furthermore, the voters believed that the Republicans could best manage the government. In terms of the *American Voter* model, clearly short-term forces were more influential in determining the election's outcome.

The Changing American Voter Model and the 1980 Election

You will recall that this model assigns greater relative importance to issues in explaining voting patterns and suggests that issues become much more important when a centrist candidate is opposed by an ideologically extreme, or outlying, candidate.

The data from 1980 election studies tend to reinforce Reagan's image as an outlying candidate. Rather consistently, Reagan's position was viewed as being to the right of the Republican party and of the population as a whole. Figure 9.3 illustrates the electorate's evaluation of the candidates' ideological positions. In separate issue areas (includ-

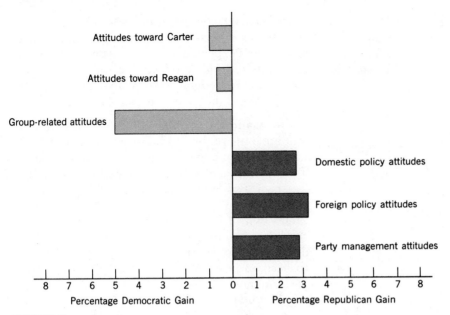

FIGURE 9.2
Effects of the Six Partisan Attitudes on the 1980 Presidential Election
SOURCE: Constructed from figures in Arthur H. Miller and Martin P. Wattenberg, "Policy and Performance Voting in the 1980 Election," Unpublished paper prepared for delivery at the annual meeting of
the American Political Science Association, New York, September 3–6, 1981.

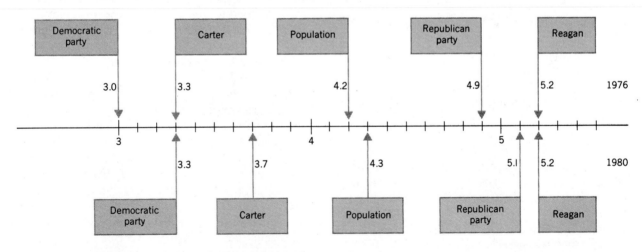

Note: This is an example of how comparisons can be made between elections using a spatial arrangement of the perceptions of voters.
     The scale runs from a low of 1 to a high of 7, with a midpoint of 4; the smaller the number, the more liberal voters perceive parties,
     candidates and themselves to be. "Population"refers to the average "self-placement" of all persons interviewed.

FIGURE 9.3

**Candidate, Party, and Population Placement on the Liberal-Conservative Scale in 1976
and 1980**

SOURCE: John R. Petrocik and Sidney Verba, with Christine Schultz, "Choosing the Choice and Not the
Echo: A Funny Thing Happened to *The Changing American Voter* on the Way to the 1980 Election,"
Unpublished paper prepared for delivery at the annual meeting of the American Political Science As-
sociation, New York, September 3–6, 1981, p. 12A.

ing race, defense and foreign policy, welfare, and women's rights), a similar pattern is sustained—Reagan is to the right of both the Republican party and the population as a whole. If Reagan is an outlier, how did he get elected?

John R. Petrocik and Sidney Verba have suggested that centrist Carter was unable to take advantage of outlier Reagan's distance from the electorate on the issues because of the incumbent president's perceived incompetence. In both 1964 (with outlier Goldwater) and in 1972 (with outlier McGovern), the outlying candidates were evaluated by voters as less competent than their opponents; but in 1980 centrist candidate Carter was perceived to be less competent. Few presidential candidates have run with so heavy a burden of public disapproval of their performance in office, and few have suffered through a campaign with such an unrelenting stream of bad news and negative media coverage.

Petrocik and Verba found no evidence in their data that Reagan was able to moderate his positions sufficiently to become a centrist (although Reagan did not trumpet his strong conservatism during the campaign). They found instead a tendency for the electorate to push Carter's image to the left, even on issues on which the president made no move to the left (national defense spending, for example). It appears that those who disapproved of Carter projected onto the president issue positions that they opposed. Under ordinary circumstances, Carter should have been able to pick up the lion's share of votes on the left and a great many votes in the center. In actuality, Carter did best on the left, but he did very poorly among centrist voters and got precious few votes from the right. It seems, then, that candidate competence may outweigh the "extremist" charge if the two come into conflict.

Beyond the Models: Other Explanations of the 1980 Election

Models generalize rather than tell the full story of why individuals vote the way they do. In the following paragraphs, we will explore party defection, the candidates, social group and sectional voting, issues, and the "mandate" of the 1980 election.

Party Defection Party defection was one of the most significant factors in the 1980 vote. The highest rate of split-ticket voting ever registered in

election surveys occurred in 1980. The rate of defection was especially high among Democrats. A staggering 55 percent of the independent-Democrats defected either to Reagan or to Anderson. Defections in general were related to the voters' feelings about the candidates and the issues.

The Candidates Certainly the most important attribute of the candidate evaluations of 1980 was the electorate's low esteem for Jimmy Carter. The voters believed that they had to choose the lesser of two evils. One enterprising bumper-sticker manufacturer turned out this slogan: "The Evil of Two Lessers." Given that neither candidate inspired confidence, the voters had the difficult task of comparing Carter's actual, or retrospective, performance to Reagan's prospective performance.

In the main, the 1980 election turned out to be a referendum on Jimmy Carter and his stewardship as president. Many of Reagan's votes were votes against Carter and his administration. The voting studies show that overall evaluations of the government and of Carter were quite negative. It is interesting to note, however, that the president's approval ratings in particular problem areas were much lower than his overall approval rating. Near election day, George Gallup found that less than one-third of the electorate approved of Jimmy Carter's handling of his job as president. In October, for example, only 20 percent of those surveyed by Michigan approved of Carter's handling of inflation, but nearly one-third approved of his overall performance as president.

Comparisons of the personal qualities of Carter and Reagan produced an advantage for Carter, who was viewed as more honest, more moral, and less power-hungry than Reagan. Carter inspired more hope, pride, and empathy and less fear than Reagan, but those interviewed also said that Carter caused them to have more feelings of anger, disgust, and uneasiness. Carter was perceived as less able to provide strong leadership. In short, Carter scored higher on qualities related to honesty and integrity; Reagan scored higher on competence and leadership.

On assessments of which candidate could better handle problems facing the nation, opinion was divided, but Reagan did better on the problems troubling the nation most. Carter had a great advantage over Reagan on the issues of war and peace, the conduct of foreign affairs, and support

Comparisons of the personal qualities of the 1980 major party candidates produced an advantage for Carter who was viewed as more honest, more moral, and less power-hungry than Reagan. Unfortunately for Carter, personal qualities of the candidates are but one factor affecting how individuals vote.

Social Group and Sectional Voting As noted in earlier chapters, one of the most enduring attributes of American politics is the variance in participation and voting choice among social and economic groups and the different regions of the country. Table 9.1 reports voting differences based on sex, race, education, occupation, age, religion, party affiliation, union membership, and region from 1952 to 1980. Historically, the Democratic party of the "New Deal coalition" had taken for granted the strong support of the South, Catholics, union members and their families, industrial and manual workers, minorities, and working-class people in general. Republicans were more dependent upon Midwesterners and Easterners, Protestants, highly educated and affluent white collar workers, and corporate executives. Many of these traditional souces of strength were altered in the 1980 election.

In 1980 the Democrats' regional advantage disappeared. Without the black vote, Carter would have done even worse in the South. As it was, he

for minorities, including women. Reagan did much better against Carter on the economic issues, even winning an advantage on the unemployment issue, which had been "owned" by the Democrats for decades. Reagan was also preferred over Carter in military preparedness and in gaining respect for the United States abroad.

Most telling were the reasons voters gave for their choice on election day. The exit polls conducted jointly by CBS News and *The New York Times* in 1980 found that over one-third of the Reagan and Anderson voters voted as they did because they believed, "it is time for a change." The second most frequent reason for a Reagan vote was his "strong leadership," but for Anderson voters it was the candidate's "honesty and integrity." Carter voters said most often that they voted for the president because he was their party's candidate; their second most frequent basis for choosing Carter was his "honesty and integrity."[8] These simple assessments made by the voters in very short interviews confirm what we have already stated—that the public's perceptions of personal attributes of candidates play an important part in determining for whom they cast their vote.

In the 1980 election, Republican candidate Ronald Reagan loosened the Democratic Party's traditional hold on the South in spite of the fact that his opponent, Carter, was a southerner from Georgia.

TABLE 9.1

Vote by Groups in Presidential Elections Since 1952 (Based on Gallup Poll Survey Data)

	1952		1956		1960		1964	
	Stevenson %	Ike %	Stevenson %	Ike %	JFK %	Nixon %	LBJ %	Goldwater %
NATIONAL	44.6	55.4	42.2	57.8	50.1	49.9	61.3	38.7
SEX								
Male	47	53	45	55	52	48	60	40
Female	42	58	39	61	49	51	62	38
RACE								
White	43	57	41	59	49	51	59	41
Nonwhite	79	21	61	39	68	32	94	6
EDUCATION								
College	34	66	31	69	39	61	52	48
High school	45	55	42	58	52	48	62	38
Grade school	52	48	50	50	55	45	66	34
OCCUPATION								
Prof. & business	36	64	32	68	42	58	54	46
White collar	40	60	37	63	48	52	57	43
Manual	55	45	50	50	60	40	71	29
AGE								
Under 30 years	51	49	43	57	54	46	64	36
30–49 years	47	53	45	55	54	46	63	37
50 years & older	39	61	39	61	46	54	59	41
RELIGION								
Protestants	37	63	37	63	38	62	55	45
Catholics	56	44	51	49	78	22	76	24
POLITICS								
Republicans	8	92	4	96	5	95	20	80
Democrats	77	23	85	15	84	16	87	13
Independents	35	65	30	70	43	57	56	44
REGION								
East	45	55	40	60	53	47	68	32
Midwest	42	58	41	59	48	52	61	39
South	51	49	49	51	51	49	52	48
West	42	58	43	57	49	51	60	40
Members of Labor								
Union Families	61	39	57	43	65	35	73	27

SOURCE: The *Gallup Report*, Report Number 183 (December, 1980), back cover of the report.

*1976 and 1980 results do not include vote for minor party candidates.

**Less than one percent.

carried only one southern state, his home state of Georgia. Carter also did well among Hispanic voters, defeating Reagan by a margin of 52 to 43 percent. Only 38 percent of the group voted in 1980, however.

Carter also lost much of the traditionally Demo-

TABLE 9.1

Vote by Groups in Presidential Elections Since 1952 (Based on Gallup Poll Survey Data) *(continued)*

1968			1972		1976*			1980*		
HHH %	Nixon %	Wallace %	McGovern %	Nixon %	Carter %	Ford %	McCarthy %	Carter %	Reagan %	Anderson %
43.0	43.4	13.6	38	62	50	48	1	41	51	7
41	43	16	37	63	53	45	1	38	53	7
45	43	12	38	62	48	51	**	44	49	6
38	47	15	32	68	46	52	1	36	56	7
85	12	3	87	13	85	15	**	86	10	2
37	54	9	37	63	42	55	2	35	53	10
42	43	15	34	66	54	46	**	43	51	5
52	33	15	49	51	58	41	1	54	42	3
34	56	10	31	69	42	56	1	33	55	10
41	47	12	36	64	50	48	2	40	51	9
50	35	15	43	57	58	41	1	48	46	5
47	38	15	48	52	53	45	1	47	41	11
44	41	15	33	67	48	49	2	38	52	8
41	47	12	36	64	52	48	**	41	54	4
35	49	16	30	70	46	53	**	39	54	6
59	33	8	48	52	57	42	1	46	47	6
9	86	5	5	95	9	91	**	8	86	5
74	12	14	67	33	82	18	**	69	26	4
31	44	25	31	69	38	57	4	29	55	14
50	43	7	42	58	51	47	1	43	47	9
44	47	9	40	60	48	50	1	41	51	7
31	36	33	29	71	54	45	**	44	52	3
44	49	7	41	59	46	51	1	35	54	9
56	29	15	46	54	63	36	1	50	43	5

cratic union vote. In 1980 he received only about one-half of the votes of union members.

Carter also carried the manual workers by a bare plurality of 2 percent, but he did very well among voters with only a grade-school education.

Carter lost votes between 1976 and 1980 among all three religions. Notably, his losses were marginally greater among Jews and Catholics, the traditional supporters of Democratic candidates.

Overall, the picture drawn by these voting patterns is: 1) the old group loyalties remained, but they were not nearly as strong as they once were, and 2) they were eroded significantly by the candidates and issues at work in the 1980 election.

The Issues   Reagan and the Republicans owed much of their political advantage in 1980 to their domestic and foreign policy stands, as previously noted in chapter 8. Knowing that the Republicans won, an analyst would predict that voters endorsed the following policy preferences:

1. reductions in the role of government,
2. reductions in government spending on a wide range of programs,
3. reductions of government effort on behalf of minorities,
4. less government involvement in a wide range of social issues,
5. passage of the Reagan-Kemp-Roth tax-cut plan,
6. attainment of energy self-sufficiency even if it increased the cost of energy and decreased concern for environmental protection, and
7. increased national security spending.

However, if the analyst making these predictions had checked public opinion surveys taken just prior to the election, he or she would have found that the predictions were actually more wrong than right.

There was striking support for a reduction in the role of the national government. By a margin of 48 to 15 percent, the people believed that the government in Washington was getting too powerful for the good of the country.[9] By a margin of 41 to 26 percent, the people believed jobs and a good standard of living should be an individual, not a governmental, responsibility. When Ronald Reagan talked about "getting government off the backs of the American people," he was appealing to a set of attitudes that was clearly established in the electorate.

The people's attitudes on government spending were more ambivalent. Those who wished to maintain government services and spending outnumbered those who wished to see a reduction by 38 percent to 27 percent. When offered a list of "government spending programs," the people wished to see cuts in only three out of eleven.

On the question of aid to minorities, the majority of respondents said in 1980 that "they should help themselves" instead of the "government should help," by a margin of 42 to 19 percent. For over a decade, opposition to busing had remained high, and support for aid to minorities had declined.

On social and lifestyle issues, there was not much support for the Reagan position in the electorate. Fifty-eight percent of the people favored an "equal role" for women, compared to 20 percent who said that their "place is in the home." Only 10 percent of those polled said they would "never permit" an abortion, 27 percent would allow an abortion "any time," and 62 percent would permit an abortion for "health" or "personal difficulty" reasons. In other words, Reagan did not hold a mainstream position on these lifestyle issues, but, as stated earlier, lifestyle issues were not as important as economic issues in the 1980 election.

Even so, clear voter support for one of Reagan's economic policies, the Kemp-Roth tax policy was not evident. When asked specifically about the wisdom of cutting taxes by 30 percent over the next three years (the Kemp-Roth proposal), 40 percent of the voters said they had no opinion; only 23 percent favored the reduction. In fact, 54 percent of all respondents had no idea of either candidate's position on tax cuts, and only 22 percent of all people interviewed knew that Reagan favored a 30 percent reduction in taxes.

The voters' positions on energy and the environment did not match Reagan and the Republican platform either. When given a choice between more and cheaper energy or maintaining environmental regulations, 46 percent chose to protect the environment and only 29 percent clearly favored relaxing environmental regulations. When asked whether the government should continue to control the prices of gas and oil or allow the prices to rise to encourage conservation, 67 percent favored continued controls and only 21 percent were ready to see prices increased. The use of nuclear power received the following evaluation: 33 percent approved building more power plants, 42 percent would operate only those already built, and 16 percent would have closed down those already in operation.

There was widespread support among voters in 1980 for the Reagan policy of increased defense spending. Sixty percent favored at least some increase while only 10 percent favored a decrease in military spending. However, the voters were ambivalent on the question of detente with the Russians, and did not support taking a hard line with Russia, in spite of the Russian "invasion" of Afghanistan during the election season.

In summary, the difficulty with such issue analyses is that they do not report which of these issues, if any, was the *most* important in determining which candidate the respondent would vote for. This also poses a problem for the candidate because once elected, it is difficult for the politician to be sure of which issue to pursue most strongly, and quickly.

The "Mandate" of the 1980 Election Given the specific issue stands of the electorate in 1980, why was there not a closer fit between what the voters preferred and what candidate Reagan was advocating? It is especially curious that the electorate seemed unconcerned about taxes, unsure about the candidates' positions on taxes, and really did not favor the 10-10-10 cut pattern. It is even more curious that on a program-by-program basis, the electorate wished to maintain or increase spending in eight out of eleven areas. Could it be that the election of 1980 was not about Ronald Reagan's New Beginning at all? Did the public vote retrospectively, in disapproval of the Carter administration and its policies, or prospectively, endorsing the promise of Reagan's New Beginning?

In considering this question of Reagan's "mandate," it may be useful to look at what was on the electorate's mind during the campaign of 1980. Table 9.2 shows variations in the public's view of the most important problems facing the government in 1980. The electorate was concerned about inflation when the year began, and it grew more concerned by November, but the biggest change in the perceived importance of a problem was the electorate's increasing concern over unemployment. Usually the Democratic candidate is helped by public alarm over unemployment, but we know from our previous discussion that the issue was working for the Republicans in 1980.

Another problem for the Democrats was that the energy shortage, an issue in which Jimmy Carter had invested a great deal of effort and reputation, declined sharply in importance as oil and gas supplies became more plentiful and the threat of shortages seemed to evaporate. Relatedly, Carter's reluctance to talk about getting tough with other nations for fear of endangering the lives of American hostages held by Iran allowed Reagan to take the offensive. As Reagan talked about national defense, however, the importance of that problem grew, doubling by November.

In summary, this analysis of changes in the public's perceptions of serious problems confronting the nation suggests that 1980 may be properly viewed as a referendum on Jimmy Carter. Recall too that the exit interviews with voters emphasized that it was "time for a change." For almost

TABLE 9.2

The Most Important Problem for the Federal Government at Four Time Intervals in 1980*

	January	April	June	November
Unemployment	7%	9%	24%	30%
Inflation	36	48	40	54
Energy shortage	43	35	40	13
Taxes/government spending	7	7	5	11
Other economic problems	17	25	31	21
Social problems	26	21	20	24
Governmental performance	12	12	7	7
National defense	12	8	16	25
Iranian hostages	29	34	25	25
Other foreign policy	48	32	27	31

SOURCE: Warren E. Miller, "Policy Directions and Presidential Leadership: Alternative Interpretations of the 1980 Presidential Election," (with J. Merrill Shanks). *British Journal of Political Science*, vol. 12, July 1982, pp. 299-356.

*The question wording was "As you know, the government faces many serious problems in this country and in other parts of the world. What do you personally feel are the most important problems the government in Washington should try to take care of?" Entries in the table are percentages of voters mentioning a problem area.

half a century, the nation's policy agenda had been largely under the direction of the Democrats. In nominating Reagan, the Republicans chose a candidate who opposed almost everything the Democrats had stood for in the last twenty or thirty years. Voters in 1980 were voting against Jimmy Carter, but they were also saying, ''We have tried it one way for a long time; let's try it another way and see if that works any better.''

Thus we it is not absolutely clear whether the 1980 election was a referendum on Jimmy Carter or a mandate for Ronald Reagan. In this sense, the 1980 election does offer a parallel to the 1932 election. In 1932 the electorate's misery was undoubtedly much greater, since they were dropping into the worst economic depression ever experienced in the industrial era, but in 1980, too, the electorate was beginning to doubt many aspects of the American dream, and that produced a special sort of misery. The electorate of 1932 rejected Herbert Hoover and his policies; it also endorsed Franklin D. Roosevelt's New Deal. The electorate voted chiefly to throw the rascals out, but they also voted to gamble with a change of direction, thinking that anything would be better.

Ronald Reagan's mandate was similar to Franklin Roosevelt's except for the sense of urgency and crisis that sustained Roosevelt's policy ventures. The blueprint for FDR's New Deal was hardly clear in his speeches in the campaign of 1932, but he grasped his ''mandate'' and used it to his advantage. Similarly, it appears that most voters in 1980 had a vague notion at best of Reagan's intentions, but they were willing to give him a chance. He immediately seized upon his overwhelming majority in the electoral college to implement his new policies.

Benjamin Harrison (R) was the last president to be elected in spite of receiving less popular votes than his opponent Grover Cleveland (D) in the 1888 presidential election.

THE ELECTORAL COLLEGE

In 1888 the Democratic ticket of Grover Cleveland and Allen G. Thurman polled 5,534,488 votes, the Republican ticket of Benjamin Harrison and Levi P. Morton polled 5,443,892 votes, yet Harrison was elected president by an electoral college vote of 233 to 168. The Democrats had polled 48.6 percent of the popular vote to the Republican's 47.8 percent, but the electoral college vote percentage was 42 percent for the Democrats and 58 percent for the Republicans. This piece of political history reminds us that popular votes for

president are counted on a state-by-state basis and national vote totals mean nothing at all.

The individuals who wrote the Constitution believed in representative government, but they did not entrust the selection of their ''republican monarch'' directly to the people. Their creation of a college of electors was one of many compromises made toward the end of their deliberations. Many details about how participants in the college were to be selected were left up to the states, and at first many state legislatures picked the electors themselves. Rather quickly, however, the states provided for popular election of electors and imposed the *winner-take-all rule, under which the candidate with a plurality of popular votes gets all of the state's electoral votes.*

Under the original electoral college arrangement, each elector could cast two votes, one of which had to be cast for a candidate outside the elector's own state. Initially, no provision was made for separate ballots for president and vice president. If no candidate received a majority of electoral votes, the selection of the president would move to the House of Representatives where the delegation from each state, acting collectively, could cast one vote. A president would be chosen from the five highest vote-getters; the person coming in second would be vice president. In the election of 1800, however, the Democratic-Republican candidates Thomas Jefferson and Aaron Burr tied in the electoral college, producing a crisis that had to be resolved in the House. The Twelfth Amendment that was subsequently adopted provides for separate ballots for president and vice president, for the House to pick the president in case no person has a majority, and for the Senate to pick the vice president.

The electoral college still does not allow for a direct, popular vote for president. On election day, rather than directly voting for a specific presidential candidate, we are actually voting for a slate of presidential electors who are, in a sense, delegates to the electoral college. These slates are chosen by the state party organization if the candidate is running under a party label or by the candidate if he or she is running as an independent. Technically, then, in November of every fourth year, citizens of each state choose a slate of presidential electors, not the president. A state gets one electoral vote for each of its senators and representatives.

Each of the electors on the winning slate travels to his or her state capital on the first Monday after the second Wednesday in December to officially cast a ballot for president. These ballots are sent to the President of the Senate in Washington. Then, on January 6, a joint session of Congress is held, and the ballots are officially counted. Thus January 6 is really the official presidential election day. If no candidate receives a majority, the election is thrown into the House and Senate.

Very few times in American history has a candidate failed to receive a majority of the electoral votes, but the possibility remains. In such a case, the House of Representatives chooses the president from among the three top vote-getters. Each state delegation has one vote. If a state delegation is tied, it loses its vote altogether. An individual must receive a majority of the votes to be declared president. The process for the selection of the vice president is similar. The Senate chooses the vice president from among the top two vote-getters. Each senator has one vote and, again, a majority vote is required to elect a vice president.

The electoral college has always been a very confusing institution. Predictably, proposals to abolish it or reform it appear every four years. These proposals stem from: 1) biases or distortions inherent in the system, and 2) fears of what the system might produce.

Biases and Distortions in the Electoral College

As the electoral college now operates, there are four distortions of the popular vote. First, there is

Presidential electors chosen by a state's voters in November meet in their state capital the first Monday after the second Wednesday in December to officially cast their ballot for president. Collectively, presidential electors from all the states make up the electoral college.

the small-state bias; regardless of population, each state gets two votes for its senators. Second, there is the large-state bias produced by the winner-take-all principle; the candidate carrying California, by whatever margin, gets all of that state's electoral votes. This gives the ten largest states special clout in presidential races. Third, there is a special advantage for ethnic and minority groups. Because they are concentrated in the largest cities, they often hold the balance of power in the elections held in our largest states. Finally, there is a "lag" bias tied to the decennial census; seats in the House of Representatives are reallocated every ten years, and the further away from a census we get, the more a fast-growing state is underrepresented in the electoral college. Because the Republicans have special strength in plains, mountain-western, and small states, the small-state bias works to their advantage, but the other three biases work to their disadvantage.

Fears about the Electoral College

Public awareness of the electoral college increases in presidential elections in which there is a serious third party candidate who has a chance of carrying one or more states. John Anderson posed no particular threat in 1980 because his 6.6 percent of the vote was scattered all over the country, but George Wallace's 13.5 percent of the vote in 1968 was sufficiently concentrated to permit him to carry five states with 46 electoral votes. The principal fear that arises from a candidacy of this type is that a contingency election will be required—if Wallace's votes had kept one of the two major party candidates from receiving a majority of electoral votes, the election would have been decided in the House of Representatives. Analysts fear the American people would not understand the process and that the legitimacy of the election would be in doubt.

There is also fear that election fraud and mismanagement at the state and local levels could endanger the legitimacy of a very close national election. Finally, there is a fear of the *faithless elector*, *an elector pledged to a candidate who votes for someone else.* For example, in 1976 one of Gerald Ford's electors (from Washington) voted for Ronald Reagan. Faithless electors have been quite rare, however; in all of our history, fewer than a dozen electors have broken faith with the electorate.

Proposals to Reform the Electoral College

The first proposal to reform the electoral college was introduced in the House of Representatives as a constitutional amendment in 1797, and hardly a session of Congress has passed since during which some new proposal has not been introduced. Some changes have been made: separate ballots for president and vice president have been provided (Twelfth Amendment), presidents have been limited to a maximum of two terms or ten years (Twenty-Second Amendment), and the vote has been granted to residents of the District of Columbia (Twenty-Third Amendment). In basic form, however, the electoral college has remained unchanged.

Four major electoral college reform proposals have been considered and rejected by the Congress in the last thirty years. The **Lodge-Gossett** or **proportional plan** *would abolish the office of elector and allocate each state's electoral vote on the basis of the popular vote.* The **Mundt-Coudert** or **district plan** *would also divide up each state's electoral vote—presidential candidates would receive two electoral votes for carrying a state and one electoral vote for each district they carried.* The districts could be the established congressional districts or special districts drawn by the state legislature. The **bonus plan** proposed by a task force in 1978 *would create a national bonus of 102 electoral votes to be awarded to the candidate polling the most votes nationwide, abolish the office of elector, provide for a run-off election in the event that no candidate won the electoral vote, and recommend a set of procedures to insure integrity in the conduct of presidential elections.*[10]

The fourth reform proposes a **direct popular vote** for president. Former Senator Birch Bayh's version of this proposal was the one most widely discussed. It called for *a national run-off between the two top vote-getters in the event that no candidate received 40 percent of all votes cast.* This is by far the simplest and the most democratic of the proposals, but dozens of reasons may be given for not adopting it. Wouldn't a run-off election encourage third party, independent, or "spoiler" candidacies? Assuming that more candidates and parties entered the race, would this not extend an election season that is already too long and complicated? Since the national vote total looms so large in this plan, wouldn't some sort of national administration of presidential elections be required? The electoral college has always produced winners (even if three of the presidents it chose trailed their opponent in popular votes), but a direct popular vote seems to raise further risks for the legitimacy of the choice. What if the result is extremely close? Given the importance of the office, can we afford to have the outcome of a presidential election in doubt?

The principal reason that the electoral college has not been reformed is that it would require an amendment to the Constitution, and no consensus for such an amendment has been achieved. This is because 1) some important groups have a stake in keeping the electoral college the way it is, and 2) institutional conservatism is characteristic in this country ("if it isn't broke, don't fix it"). The contingency procedure has not been needed since the House picked John Quincy Adams in 1824; since 1888, the popular vote winner has become president[11]. Until the electoral college malfunctions again, the country will probably worry about it every four years but make no major change. Changes are more likely to take place in the way candidates finance elections than in the procedure by which they are formally elected.

CAMPAIGN FINANCE

No aspect of presidential campaign policies changed more in the 1970s than campaign finance. The conditions were ripe for drastic reform as political consultants and the media became key ingredients in the process. First, beginning in 1968 the costs of campaigns started rising dramatically (see Figure 9.4). Second, the American public had always been suspicious of the role of money in politics, so support for reform was easy to mobilize. Reforms were first imposed by the Federal Election Campaign Act of 1971 and broadened under the Federal Election Campaign Act of 1974 as a consequence of the Watergate scandal.

According to Herbert E. Alexander, the nation's leading authority on money in politics, recent campaign finance reform legislation has generally called for: 1) public disclosure during the campaign of giving and spending, 2) limits on total spending permitted by a candidate, and 3) restrictions on who may give to a campaign and how much individuals can give.

National Campaign Spending Rules and Public Financing

The Federal Election Campaign Act of 1974 provides for 1) limits on how much individuals and political committees can give to candidates (see Table 9.3); 2) public funding of nomination and election campaigns for the presidency; and 3) disclosure of campaign contributions of more than $10 and expenditures of more than $100. These provisions of the law were upheld by the Supreme Court in *Buckley* v. *Valeo* (1976). Several other provisions of the law were stricken down as a violation of freedom of expression under the First Amendment.

The Rules for Public Funding of Presidential Campaigns

There are strict spending limits for all presidential candiates who decide to accept public funds, and the limits apply to both the nomination and general election campaigns. The source of public funds is the *"check-off" trust fund, the fund created by the Revenue Act of 1971, giving taxpayers the option of contributing one dollar of their income taxes to finance presidential campaigns.* These funds were first used in 1976.

The amount of federal subsidy a candidate is eligible to receive depends on whether he or she is seeking the party nomination or, having won that, is running in the general election. If seeking the party nomination, the federal government will match the amount a candidate raises from individuals who contribute $250 or less, up to a maximum of $5 million. But first the candidate must qualify for the funds by showing that his or her candidacy is a serious one. To qualify, the candidate must raise a minimum of $5,000 in twenty states in individual contributions of no more than $250. The public financing laws were intended to encourage small donations from a large number of people rather than large contributions from a few *"fat cats,"* or *large contributors.*

The public funding provisions also limit the amount candidates may spend in each state to secure their party's nomination. For the important early primary in New Hampshire, for example, they can spend $294,000. These limits challenge each candidate's ingenuity.

Once the candidate has won the party nomina-

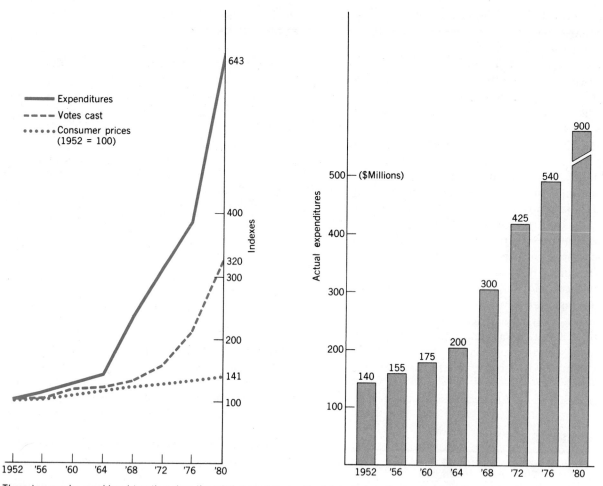

These two graphs considered together show the relationship between the total number of votes cast and the total political spending in presidential election years from 1952 through 1980. Even when the inflationary impact of the rising Consumer Price Index is considered, the increase in political spending far exceeds the increase in the number of voters.

FIGURE 9.4

The Rising Costs of Campaign Spending

SOURCE: Congressional Quarterly, Inc., *Dollar Politics*. 3d ed. (Washington, D.C.: Congressional Quarterly, Inc., 1982), p. 9; based on the following sources: expenditures, Herbert E. Alexander; Consumer Price Index, U.S. Bureau of the Census; votes for president, *America Votes* series.

tion, he or she is entitled to full federal support for the general election campaign, not just matching funds as in the nomination stage. Each major party nominee (defined as a party that received at least 5 percent of the vote in the preceding presidential election) receives the same amount and is limited to spending that amount on the race. Of course, accepting federal funds is the candidate's option. If a candidate turns down federal support, there is no limit on what he or she can spend.

Candidates seeking the nomination of the major political parties in 1980 were limited to spend-

ing $14.7 million ($5 million from private funds, $5 million from federal funds, plus a cost-of-living adjustment, or COLA). Once nominated, Carter and Reagan were limited to spending $29.4 million in their general election campaigns. These limits did not include money spent on legal and accounting services. The law permits candidates to spend any amount of money necessary (besides the funds already mentioned) to comply with campaign finance laws; thus additional money can be raised to cover the costs of attorneys and accountants.

TABLE 9.3

Limits on Campaign Contributions

This table shows the limits on campaign contributions for federal elections. The figures are those in effect following the 1979 amendments to the 1971, 1974, and 1976 financing laws.

Contribution from:	To candidate or his/her authorized committee	*To national party committees[5] (per calendar year)[6]	*To any other committee (per calendar year)[6]	Total contributions (per calendar year)[7]
Individual	$1,000 per election[3]	$20,000	$5,000	$25,000
Multicandidate committee[1]	$5,000 per election	$15,000	$5,000	No limit
Party committee	$1,000 or $5,000[4] per election	No limit	$5,000	No limit
Republican or Democratic senatorial campaign committee,[2] or the national party committee, or a combination of both*	$17,500 to Senate candidate per calendar year[6] in which candidate seeks election	Not applicable	Not applicable	Not applicable
Any other committee	$1,000 per election	$20,000	$5,000	No limit

SOURCE: Congressional Quarterly, Inc., *Dollar Politics*, 3d ed. (Washington, D.C.: Congressional Quarterly, Inc., 1982), p. 26; based on data from the Federal Election Commission.

[1]A multicandidate committee is any committee with more than 50 contributors which has been registered for at least six months and, with the exception of state party committees, has made contributions to five or more federal candidates.

[2]Republican and Democratic senatorial campaign committees are subject to all other limits applicable to a multicandidate committee.

[3]Each of the following elections is considered a separate election: primary election, general election, run-off election, special election and party caucus or convention which, instead of a primary, has authority to select the nominee.

[4]Limit depends on whether or not party committee is a multicandidate committee.

[5]For purposes of this limit, national party committee includes a party's national committee, the Republican and Democratic Senate and House campaign committees and any other committee established by the party's national committee, provided it is not authorized by any candidate.

[6]In 1976 only, and solely in the case of contribution limits established in the 1976 amendments (those indicated by double asterisk), the calendar year extends from May 11 (date of enactment of the act) through Dec. 31, 1976.

[7]Calendar year extends from Jan. 1 through Dec. 31, 1976. Individual contributions made or earmarked before or after 1976 to influence the 1976 election of a specific candidate are counted as if made during 1976.

*See footnote 6.

Candidates work hard to comply with every detail of the law, but in 1980 both the Carter and Reagan campaigns broke some of the rules and had to return money to the public funding account. As their difficulties in complying with the spending limit laws demonstrate, candidates must be very careful in managing the money they do have. They must allocate funds so as not to exceed the limits of the law at the same time as they desperately want to spend as much as they are entitled to spend.

Public Funding of the Political Parties and Minor Party Candidates

To eliminate the past practice of ''selling'' the national convention to the city offering the best deal,

each major political party now receives $3 million plus COLA for its convention. The host city may offer limited support services. Minor party and independent candidates receive no money during the election campaign, but they are entitled to retroactive funding on the basis of a complex formula by which the minor party vote is compared to the average vote of the two major parties. In 1980 John Anderson qualified and received $4,242,304 of retroactive funding. Because he polled more than 5 percent of the vote in 1980, he will get some public funding if he runs again in 1984.

Public Funding of Congressional and State Campaigns

Jimmy Carter backed public funding of congressional campaigns, but before his administration could secure passage other problems distracted the president. With the advent of the Reagan administration and a Republican Senate in 1980, hope for public funding was all but dead. Although Ronald Reagan received public funding for his campaigns for president in 1976 and 1980, his opposition to this policy is longstanding. The president demonstrated his lack of support in 1983 by declining to contribute one dollar for himself and his wife on his income tax forms under the "check-off" provisions of the law. Furthermore, according to one public opinion survey, there is little public support for government funding of congressional campaigns.

Seventeen states provide for public funding of campaigns. Of these, thirteen use an income tax check-off similar to that adopted by the United States in 1971. One major difference between federal and state public funding is that the state funds go to the political parties rather than directly to the candidates, which strengthens party organizations.

The Increasing Costs of Election Campaigns: The Congress

While the costs of running presidential campaigns have been rendered relatively stable by spending limits, no such limitations have been imposed on congressional campaign spending. This spending rose by 44 percent between 1976 and 1978 and by another 25 percent between 1978 and 1980. Table 9.4 reports the top spenders in 1980 for House and Senate seats. Note that one-half of the top spenders lost their races. The congressional campaigns of 1982 were the most expensive in American history.

Spending by all congressional candidates rose more than $100 million, or 42 percent, between 1980 and 1982. As the figures in Table 9.5 reveal,

TABLE 9.4

Top Congressional Spenders in 1980

Senate			
Candidate	State	Won/Lost	Expenditure
1. Alan Cranston (D)*	Calif.	Won (56.5–37.1%)	$2,808,057
2. George McGovern (D)*	S.D.	Lost (58.2–39.4%)	2,757,201
3. Birch Bayh (D)*	Ind.	Lost (53.8–46.2%)	2,751,004
4. Bess Meyerson (D)**	N.Y.	Lost (40.7–31.5%)	2,398,611
5. Alan J. Dixon (D)	Ill.	Won (56.0–42.5%)	2,346,897
6. Dan Quayle (R)	Ind.	Won (53.8–46.2%)	2.289,838
7. Charles E. Grassley (R)	Iowa	Won (53.5–45.5%)	2,183,028
8. Russell B. Long (D)*†	La.	Won (57.6–38.8%)	2,166,838
9. Bill Gunter (D)	Fla.	Lost (51.7–48.3%)	2,164,560
10. Elizabeth Holtzman (D)	N.Y.	Lost (44.9–43.5%)	2,149,390

House				
Candidate	District		Won/Lost	Expenditure
1. Robert K. Dornan (R)*	Calif.	27	Won (51.0–46.5%)	$1,937,209
2. Jim Wright (D)*	Texas	12	Won (59.9–39.3%)	1,193,622
3. James C. Corman (D)*	Calif.	21	Lost (48.7–48.2%)	905,231
4. Jack Fields (R)	Texas	8	Won (51.8–48.2%)	800,343
5. John Brademas (D)*	Ind.	3	Lost (55.0–45.0%)	744,068
6. Richard H. Huff (R)	Ariz.	2	Lost (58.1–40.4%)	696,954
7. Morris K. Udall (D)*	Ariz.	2	Won (58.1–40.4%)	688,173
8. David L. Robinson (D)	Ill.	20	Lost (56.0–44.0%)	674,974
9. Al Ullman (D)*	Ore.	2	Lost (48.8–47.5%)	670,390
10. Bill Patman (D)	Texas	14	Won (56.8–43.2%)	665,984

Source: *Congressional Quarterly Weekly Report*, April 10, 1982, p. 815.

*Denotes incumbent.

**Meyerson finished second in the four-way Democratic primary, behind Elizabeth Holtzman. Voting percentage refers to Holtzman's and Meyerson's shares of the primary balloting.

†The voting percentage refers to the non-partisan primary, which Long won with more than 50 percent of the vote. As a result, no general election was held.

TABLE 9.5

Election '82: Who Spent All the Money?*

Here is a summary of spending by House and Senate candidates in 1981–1982 by party and by incumbents, challengers and contestants for open seats (in millions of dollars).

	Incumbents	Challengers	Open seats	Total
Senate	$53.9	$ 47.7	$37.7	$139.3
Democrats	30.5	19.7	16.9	16.1
Republicans	23.4	27.8	20.7	71.9
Other	0.0	0.2	0.1	0.3
House	$103.7	$ 52.8	$47.9	$204.4
Democrats	54.9	27.2	21.2	103.3
Republicans	48.8	25.5	26.6	100.9
Other	0.0	0.1	0.1	0.2
Total	$157.6	$100.5	$85.6	$343.7

SOURCE: *National Journal*, April 30, 1983, p. 908.

*Figures are in millions of dollars.

incumbents generally spent more than challengers or contestants for open seats.

The Increasing Costs of Election Campaigns: State and Local Offices

Gubernatorial races have also gotten expensive. Consider, for example, the 1980 reelection campaign of West Virginia Democratic Governor John D. (Jay) Rockefeller IV. West Virginia is hardly the largest state in the union, but Jay Rockefeller spent $11.6 million to defeat his opponent, who spent about $1.1 million. Together, the two candidates spent $17.18 for every voter in the election. Political scientist Thad Beyle reports that there were twenty-three winning gubernatorial candidates from 1977 to 1980 who spent over $1 million; the list was about equally divided between Democrats and Republicans. In fact, the average cost for a governor's chair from 1977 to 1980 was $3.5 million.[12] Even state legislative races and big city mayoral contests have become very expensive, often exceeding the cost of winning a congressional seat. Yet, few laws limit spending in these races.

PAC Spending in National Campaigns

A *political action committee* (PAC), as defined in chapter 7, is "*the political arm of a business, labor, professional, or other interest group, legally entitled to raise funds on a voluntary basis from members, stockholders, or employees in order to contribute funds to favored candidates or political parties.*"[14] Under the Federal Election Campaign Act of 1974, PACs can contribute up to $5,000 per election on a federal candidate's behalf and spend unlimited amounts of money—independently—on a candidate's behalf. *Independent spending* is *campaign activity uncoordinated with the campaign organization of the candidate benefiting from the effort.*

On January 19, 1982, Common Cause and the Federal Election Commission lost two decisions before the Supreme Court challenging independent spending. The provision for PAC independent spending had allowed an additional $13.7 million to be spent on the 1980 presidential campaign (in excess of the $29.4 million allowable under public finance laws). Both Carter and Reagan got substantial (and quite legal) boosts from PAC independent spending, although Reagan got the lion's share ($10 million). The court's ruling upholding such spending ensures that it will play an important role in the 1984 presidential contest.

That PAC spending in national campaigns has increased in the last decade is indisputable. Figure 9.5 shows that contributions have grown sevenfold in eight years.

PAC contributions to House and Senate candidates have doubled since 1972; they now supply about one campaign dollar in every four spent to elect members of Congress. In 1980, Democratic candidates enjoyed a 53 to 47 percent advantage over Republicans in PAC contributions, and incumbents enjoyed an advantage over challengers (61 to 39 percent). Labor PACs were distinctively pro-Democratic and well above the average in supporting incumbents. On the other hand, nonconnected (ideological) PACs favored Republicans and nonincumbents by a margin of two to one.

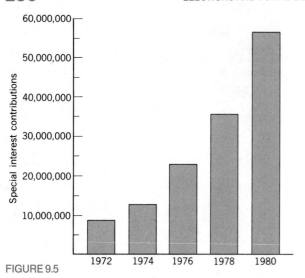

FIGURE 9.5

Growth of Special Interest Contributions to Federal Candidates

Source: Congressional Quarterly, Inc., *Dollar Politics*. 3d ed. (Washington, D.C.: Congressional Quarterly, Inc., 1982), p. 18; based on data from Common Cause.

Independent spending by both PACs and individuals is summarized in Table 9.6. The most active independent spenders were the nonconnected PACs, and their impact is clear in the data. Nonconnected PACs tended to engage in negative spending against Democrats by about a five to one ratio. (Negative spending involves giving money to defeat a candidate but not necessarily giving money to his or her opponent.) For Republicans, positive spending outweighed negative spending by more than a hundred to one. The "targeted" liberal Democratic senators' protests against these independent PAC expenditures would have led one to believe that more than $1.2 million was involved, but this amount (which was only a small fraction of total congressional campaign spending) was important because of its negative nature and because it was focused on a handful of leaders.

The public is far more supportive of campaign spending by ideological PACs than by labor union or corporate PACS (see Table 9.7). In a survey taken by Louis Harris, a greater percentage of respondents said they prefer that campaign contributions come from the candidates themselves and environmental, women's rights, and conservative PACs rather than from labor union and corporate PACs. They are most strongly opposed to contri-

TABLE 9.6

Independent Spending Divided by Candidate Type

The table shows how the $16 million in independent expenditures made during the 1979–80 election cycle was divided among Senate, House and presidential candidates. According to federal election law, an independent expenditure is money spent to support or defeat a clearly identified candidate. Such an expenditure must be made without cooperation or consultation with the candidate or the candidate's campaign. the columns titled "For" show expenditures to support a candidate; those entitled "Against" refer to spending meant to defeat a candidate. The "No." columns indicate the number of candidates to whom the spending was directed.

Because some candidates had expenditures made both for and against them, the figures for the total number of candidates are smaller than the sums of the "No." columns.

Candidate Type	Democrats				Republicans				Others				Total	
	For	No.	Against	No.	For	No.	Against	No.	For	No.	Against	No.	Total	No.
House	$190,615	91	$ 38,023	32	$ 410,478	205	$ 45,132	6	$ 479	1	$ 0	0	$ 684,727	321
Senate	127,381	24	1,282,613	15	231,678	58	12,430	5	0	0	0	0	1,654,102	89
Presidential	123,058	2	736,796	3	12,537,522	3	65,040	2	271,978	7	11,050	2	13,745,444	15
Total	$441,054	117	$2,057,432	50	$13,179,678	266	$122,602	13	$272,457	8	$11,050	2	$16,084,273	425

Source: Congressional Quarterly, Inc., *Dollar Politics*, 3d ed. (Washington, D.C.: Congressional Quarterly, Inc., 1982), p. 81.

butions from "rich people," fearing that money may buy undue influence for these individuals.

In spite of all the horror stories about campaign spending, American campaign costs are not gen-

TABLE 9.7

The Public's Views on Sources of Campaign Contributions*

	Good	Bad	Not sure
Candidates who contribute to their own campaigns	63%	31%	6%
Environmental political action committees	54	35	11
Women's political action committees	53	40	7
Conservative political action committees	40	46	14
Labor unions	34	60	6
Labor union political action committees	27	64	9
Big companies	26	67	7
Firms that do business with the government	23	69	8
Big company political action committees	20	71	9
Rich people who want to protect their interests	16	77	6

SOURCE: "Views on Private Contributors . . ." *National Journal*, February 26, 1983, p. 472.

*In November 1982, Louis Harris and Associates Inc. asked: "Now let me ask you about different groups and types of people who contribute money to political campaigns. Now for each, tell me if you feel it is a good or bad influence on politics and government." The responses to the survey are reported in the table.

erally higher than those in other countries. Moreover, as Herbert Alexander has said, the total cost of all campaigns in 1976 was less than the advertising budgets of either Procter and Gamble or General Motors. The total costs were a fraction of 1 percent of the costs of operating our governments.

Does Money Win Elections?

There is no simple answer to the question of whether money wins elections. In all four of Franklin D. Roosevelt's presidential races, FDR was outspent by the Republicans. Nixon outspent Kennedy in 1960 ($10.1 to $9.8 million), and Goldwater outspent Johnson in 1964 ($16.0 to $8.8 million). Kennedy barely squeaked by Nixon, but Johnson overwhelmed Goldwater. Remember also that exactly half of the top spenders in the House and Senate races of 1980 lost (Table 9.4).

The wisdom of the literature about campaign finance can perhaps be summed up in three statements. First, despite the fact that half of the top spenders lost in the 1980 elections, the candidate who raises and spends the most money usually wins. This does not necessarily mean that the candidate won *because* he or she raised the most money, however. It more often means that strong candidates, especially incumbents, can attract more funds. An incumbent may receive contributions because those who give want access to his or her office after reelection. The money raised and spent, therefore, may be entirely unrelated to the "price" which should be paid for an effective campaign.

Second, money is only one strategic resource in a campaign. We have already mentioned that incumbency is an advantage. Name familiarity is also important (especially if the candidate's image is positive), as are skill in the use of media, a good staff, excellent contacts with community leaders, and other resources. All of these can help to offset limited campaign funding.

Third, when and how a candidate spends the money that she or he does have is often critical. A campaign that is starved for funds early but that receives a surge of funds late in the race may have a chance for victory. Likewise, deciding whether to spend more of one's campaign funds on organization than on fundraising, travel, advertising, or consulting may influence the outcome of the election (see Table 9.8).

The mere fact that a candidate has the most money, then, is not enough to ensure election. One must be wise in spending it. Often the most difficult decisions involve use of different types of media.

CAN THE MEDIA WIN ELECTIONS?

Like campaign finance, the role of the media in elections is a complex subject. And, as with finance, we would have to say that good media coverage alone does not guarantee success. The chapter that follows will treat the media in some depth, so we will not attempt a full analysis of the political impact of the media. However, several points should be made.

First, the media are by no means monolithic or homogeneous in values. The values reflected in the print media, radio, and television vary tremendously. The greatest political differences, however, are those that exist between ownership and management on the one hand and the people who produce the content of the media on the

TABLE 9.8

A Comparison of Candidate Campaign Spending Strategies: Five Congressional Races

	Winner	Loser
U.S. SENATE		
	California	
	Wilson	Brown
Organization	$1,430,556 (21%)	$1,117,400 (21%)
Fund raising	540,346 (8%)	217,409 (4%)
Travel	162,302 (2%)	40,160 (0.7%)
Advertising	4,037,198 (57%)	3,928,721 (74%)
Consultants	805,115 (12%)	15,028 (0.3%)
Total	$6,975,517	$5,318,718
U.S. HOUSE OF REPRESENTATIVES		
	New Jersey—9*	
	Torricelli (D)	Hollenbeck (R)
Organization	$124,475 (53%)	$97,447 (54%)
Fund raising	11,492 (5%)	5,355 (3%)
Travel	5,949 (3%)	1,128 (1%)
Advertising	80,390 (34%)	53,078 (29%)
Consulting	11,465 (5%)	23,880 (13%)
Total	$233,771	$180,889
	Oregon—5*	
	Smith (R)	McFarland (D)
Organization	$257,131 (54%)	$131,506 (70%)
Fund raising	17,563 (4%)	5,148 (3%)
Travel	4,444 (1%)	699 (1%)
Advertising	115,424 (25%)	41,720 (22%)
Consulting	77,254 (16%)	8,397 (4%)
Total	$471,816	$187,470
	Virginia—9*	
	Boucher (D)	Wampler (R)
Organization	$116,199 (55%)	$157,531 (50%)
Fund raising	8,138 (4%)	21,774 (7%)
Travel	8,448 (4%)	16,959 (5%)
Advertising	26,832 (13%)	95,279 (30%)
Consulting	50,265 (24%)	24,779 (8%)
Total	$209,882	$316,322
	Florida—9*	
	Bilirakis (R)	Sheldon (D)
Organization	$158,803 (56%)	$188,272 (50%)
Fund raising	8,608 (3%)	19,154 (5%)
Travel	3,747 (1%)	22,377 (6%)
Advertising	89,357 (32%)	135,131 (36%)
Consulting	22,961 (8%)	10,050 (3%)
Total	$283,476	$374,983

SOURCE: Paul M. Keep; "Wilson v. Brown: The Costliest Senate Race Ever" and "In Four House Races, Organization Gets the Money," *National Journal*, April 16, 1983, pp. 784, 786.

*Congressional district numbers.

other. The conservative values of ownership and management are offset to some degree by the more liberal values of the "working professionals"—those who seek out and report the news.

Second, some experts argue that the **controlled media**—by which we mean *the paid media, the con-* *tent and scheduling of which the purchaser can control*—have less influence than the **uncontrolled media**, *the free media (news stories and broadcasts) that are largely under the control of the working professionals but may be influenced or even manipulated by an effective campaign strategy*. What can kill a candidate is not be-

President Carter received much more unfavorable news coverage throughout the 1980 presidential campaign than his opponent Ronald Reagan which was one factor that led to Carter's defeat.

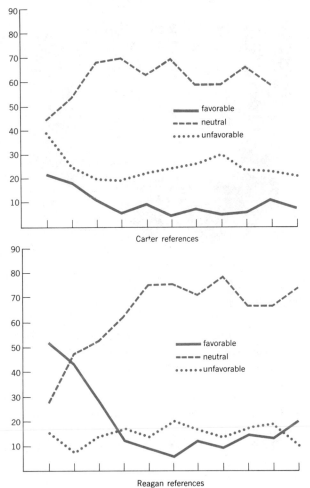

Carter references

Reagan references

FIGURE 9.6

Direction of References on the National Evening News

SOURCE: John R. Petrocik and Sidney Verba, with Christine Schultz, "Choosing the Choice and Not the Echo: A Funny Thing Happened to *The Changing American Voter* on the Way to the 1980 Election," Unpublished paper prepared for delivery at the Annual meeting of the American Political Science Association, New York, September 3–6, 1981.

ing mentioned at all or receiving negative coverage in the uncontrolled media. The 1980 presidential election is an excellent illustration of the power the uncontrolled media can have. In Figure 9.6 are displayed references to Carter and Reagan coded either as neutral, favorable, or unfavorable. Carter received unrelentingly unfavorable news coverage, which was a key variable in explaining his defeat. In contrast, Reagan enjoyed a highly favorable press at the time of his nomination and a modestly favorable press in the last days of the campaign.

Press coverage by the uncontrolled media is not totally objective, for reporters are unavoidably influenced by their own socioeconomic backgrounds and political beliefs. Recognizing this, those who manage political campaigns work particularly hard to influence the reporters assigned to cover their candidates.

Third, regardless of whether the uncontrolled media are really more important, candidates agree that the controlled media (paid advertising) are critical, especially for challengers who must get their names before the public. During the 1982 congressional campaigns, candidates spent $285 million: $25 million on radio; $170 million on television; $27 million on newspapers; $25 million on polling; and $38 million on direct mail.[14]

Paid media are the big-ticket item in most national and state campaigns. Candidates simply don't believe they can afford *not* to rely on the media.

SUMMARY

Nominations, campaigns, and elections are important because they select policymakers. For the average citizen, participation in primary and general elections is the most direct influence on public policy.

"Well, Senator, we've sharpened your image, and your recognition factor is way up. Unfortunately, they're all against you."

Drawing by Stevenson; © 1976 The New Yorker Magazine, Inc.

The conduct of elections historically has been the province of state and local governments. But the federal government has influenced the election process through voting rights legislation, constitutional amendments, and court interpretations. Of most concern now are state procedures that encourage voting.

There are three models for explaining voting behavior: 1) the *Monday-morning-quarterback* model, which relies heavily on journalistic analyses; 2) the *American Voter* model, which includes party identification and short-term campaign variables; and 3) the *Changing American Voter* model, which gives relatively more weight to issues. None of the models works perfectly.

The 1980 presidential election was influenced by a great variety of factors. Party identification and social group and sectional loyalties were important, although less so than in 1976. Personal qualities of the candidates as well as their stances on economic and national security issues were more important determinants of voting behavior in the 1980 election.

American presidential elections are directly decided not by popular votes but by electoral college votes cast by presidential electors from each state. The electoral college is a confusing institution that is biased toward small states and big cities. Proposals to reform it are made every four years, including the recommendation that the president be popularly elected.

While money and the media influence campaigns, their impact is often overstated. Neither money nor the media alone wins elections. More important is how and when each is used in combination with other available resources.

Energy Policy as the Motive for Split-Ticket Giving

The following quotations come from a case study of lobbying written by Bill Keller for *Congressional Quarterly Weekly Report*. This story illustrates very well the dark side of the motives for contributing to political campaigns. In this case, the source of campaign contributions was a firm interested in synthetic fuel production, especially a project for which they needed federally guaranteed loans.

The 1980 presidential election was cause for dejection at the Los Angeles headquarters of Tosco Corp.

The company had worked hard to win President Carter's [endorsement] on a federal loan guarantee for a proposed shale oil venture in western Colorado, but time was running out. Now it seemed likely the idea would have to be sold to a whole new cast of politicians—including a new president who had campaigned as a free-market enthusiast . . .

To make matters worse, the company lacked good Republican connections. Tosco executives had been betting on the Democratic Party. Just six weeks before the election, Tosco chief executive Morton M. Winston had donated $10,000 to the Democratic National Committee and company chairman Isadore M. Scott another $5,000. The company's political action committee and much of the executive hierarchy had pitched in to help Carter.

But any gloom at Tosco was dispelled nine months later, when President Reagan announced the government would stand behind Tosco's borrowing of $1.1 billion. And last November (1981), the government went further and agreed to be not just the guarantor of the loan, but the actual lender.[1]

Keller goes on to tell the Tosco story. Tosco was one of three firms with so-called "fast track" projects that had

[1]*Congressional Quarterly Weekly Report*, March 27, 1982, p. 675.

been favored by the Carter administration. Tosco's partner in the project was Exxon Corporation; they were to ultimately produce 48,000 barrels per day of liquid petroleum from shale on Colorado's western slope. There was some conflict in the Reagan team over this and similar projects: some favored the projects because they would be a move toward energy independence; others felt such projects should be funded by private investment.

Tosco's executive vice president, Camilla S. Auger, put together a lobbying team with a wide range of skills and substantial depth of experience in politics. The lobbying effort had been responsible, at least partially, for the passage of legislation under which the contract for the project had first been negotiated. After the election, the lobbying team was broadened to insure that the project would be continued. The team included persons who knew and were known by both the Carter and Reagan White House staffs. One member was a defeated congressman who had helped write the legislation under which the project had been authorized. In short an exceptional lobbying effort was launched to initiate and then to maintain the project.

Let us return to Bill Keller's own words to conclude this case study of "giving with a purpose."

Since the Republicans took over the White House and the Senate, Tosco—like many other companies—has developed a new outlook toward the Republican Party.

According to Federal Election Commission records, Tosco's PAC last April (1981) donated $10,000 to the Republi-

can Party's Senate-House dinner. (The comparable Democratic committee received $1,000.)

In August, according to California Republican Party records, Tosco Chairman Scott, chief executive Winston, Vice President Auger and other executives—Carter contributors a year earlier—trooped over to the Century Plaza Hotel in Los Angeles to shake Reagan's hand at a $500-a-ticket Republican Party fund-raising reception.

Auger would not discuss the apparent shift in Tosco's leanings, except to say: ''We do not make contributions on the basis of ideological perspective or commitments of the individuals. We make contributions to people on both sides of the aisle on the basis of who is making a significant contribution to public policy in areas that are of interest to the company.''[2]

As a postscript to this study, you may wish to know that the joint venture between Tosco and Exxon collapsed in May of 1982, a victim of escalating costs (even before designs for the plan were complete) and plentiful supplies of oil in the world market. Tosco had to repay the loan to the national government, but it still made a tidy profit on the venture because of the contract it had with Exxon.[3]

There are many similar stories that could have been told. It is easy to see why the public has become somewhat cynical about the world of campaign finance.

[2]*Op. cit.*, p. 679.
[3]*Congressional Quarterly Weekly Report*, May 29, 1982, p. 1250.

KEY TERMS

American Voter *model*
Australian ballot
bonus plan
Changing American Voter *model*
check-off trust fund
controlled media
direct popular vote plan
faithless elector
fat cats
independent spending
Lodge-Gossett or proportional plan
Monday-morning-quarterback model
Mundt-Coudert or district plan
normal vote
office block ballot

party column ballot
political action committee (PAC)
political ideology
precinct
prospective voting
retrospective voting
uncontrolled media
Vietnamization
winner-take-all rule

SUGGESTED READINGS

Abramson, Paul R.; Aldrich, John H.; and Rohde, David W. *Change and Continuity in the 1980 Elections.* Washington, D.C.: Congressional Quarterly Press, 1982.

Alexander, Herbert E. *Financing Politics: Money, Elections and Political Reform.* 2nd ed. Washington, D.C.: Congressional Quarterly Press, 1980.

Ginsberg, Benjamin. *The Consequences of Consent: Elections, Citizen Control, and Popular Acquiescence.* Reading, Mass.: Addison-Wesley, 1982.

Ippolito, Dennis S. *Congressional Spending: A Twentieth Century Fund Report.* Ithaca, N.Y.: Cornell University Press, 1982.

Kessel, John. *Presidential Campaign Politics: Coalition Strategies and Citizen Response.* Homewood, Ill.: Dorsey Press, 1980.

Key, V.O., Jr. *The Responsible Electorate: Rationality in Presidential Voting.* Cambridge, Mass.: Harvard University Press, 1966.

Lipset, Seymour Martin, ed. *Party Coalitions in the 1980s.* San Francisco, Calif.: Institute for Contemporary Studies, 1981.

Malbin, Michael J., ed. *Parties, Interest Groups, and Campaign Finance Laws.* Washington, D.C.: American Enterprise Institute, 1980.

Page, Benjamin I. *Choices and Echoes in Presidential Elections: Rational Man and Electoral Democracy.* Chicago: University of Chicago Press, 1978.

Sandoz, Ellis, and Crabb, Cecil V., Jr. *A Tide of Discontent: The 1980 Elections and Their Meaning.* Washington, D.C.: Congressional Quarterly Press, 1981.

CHAPTER 10

THE MEDIA: REPORTERS OR CREATORS OF THE POLICY AGENDA?

What Do Americans Expect of Their Media? ■ The Media Age ■ Reporters, Gatekeepers, and Media Stars: Deciding What's News and How to Present It ■ The Relationship Between the Media and Government

---

Nation's Press is 'Full of Itself' Former Editor Tells Publishers.'' These words headlined a story quoting the former executive editor of the Detroit *Free Press* and author of the screenplay for *Absence of Malice,* a movie about a newspaper reporter. He had told the American Newspaper Publishers Association that the press has grown too powerful and undisciplined, that the public has become defenseless against the ability of the press to affect their lives. The press "no longer shapes public opinion . . . it has supplanted it,'' he said.[1]

''Former NBC Chief Says Press Serving Better Than Ever.'' In this story, a former NBC News president was quoted as telling the Society of Professional Journalists (Sigma Delta Chi) that ''The American press serves its public better than it ever has, and certainly better than the rest of the world's press.''[2] He praised the press for being more involved, more responsible, and more courageous than ever before.

These two stories, which appeared within three days of each other, reflect an age-old debate: does the press create issues and events, or does it merely report them? In other words, are press reports the cause or the effect of what gets on the public policy agenda? Which role should the press play, and how much power should it have?

The amount of power the press should have has always been more of an issue than how much it actually has. Many years ago, Edmund Burke was quoted as saying, ''There are three estates in Parliament but, in the reporters' gallery yonder, there [sits] a fourth estate more important far than they all.''[3] Even today, the term *fourth estate is used to refer to the media.* Many observers consider our press to be a fourth branch of government—as powerful as any of the other three, making it the most powerful press in the world. As Theodore White put it,

The power of the press in America is a primordial one. It sets the agenda of public discussion; and this sweeping power is unrestrained by any law. It determines what people will talk and think about—an authority that in other nations is reserved for tyrants, priests, parties, and mandarins.[4]

Many believe the power of the media (television, radio, newspapers, magazines, movies, home information systems, and similar means of communications) is increasing. They attribute this to the media's increasingly important role as the transmitter of information to the public and its leaders. Today, Americans are heavily dependent upon the media for information about every aspect of their lives. The media cannot always change attitudes that are a product of family, church, school, and other experiences, but they can make it more likely that we will talk and think about certain issues. In other words, the media may not tell us what to think, but they do tell us what to think about. Changes in public policy issues brought before Congress, state legislatures, or city councils often parallel changes in the topics covered in the media. But here again, it's often difficult to determine which comes first. One thing is clear—without publicity, changes in the direction or content of public policy are unlikely. Thus, the media play an important role in the process of change and often reinforce trends toward change.

If we are to influence the public policy agenda, we must learn how the media operate and how different media influence individuals and public policymakers. In this chapter, we will review the major news media (television, radio, and newspapers), their presentations of the news, and their relationship to government.

WHAT DO AMERICANS EXPECT OF THEIR MEDIA?

Since our country was founded, Americans have staunchly defended the principle of *freedom of the press, a right established in the First Amendment to the Constitution, which reads "Congress shall make no law . . . abridging the freedom . . . of the press."* Yet we often struggle with questions about how the press should gather information and what the press should print or report.

Above all, Americans expect their press to be fair. A survey of public attitudes toward freedom of the press concluded that most Americans "want and expect the communications media to provide equal coverage to opposing political candidates and to present both sides of controversial issues."[5] Eighty percent of those polled believed that Republican and Democratic party candidates should receive the same amount of press coverage. Nearly 70 percent felt that major third-party candidates such as John Anderson in 1980 should get

as much television coverage as the two major party candidates. Seventy-five percent did not believe a newspaper has the right to give opponents of a controversial policy less coverage than proponents get. The public also believes that fringe and minority groups should be able to express their views, no matter how unpopular, in the mass media. For example, 61 percent believed a communist has a right to say what he or she thinks on a television talk show, 57 percent felt that a group of homosexuals has a right to newspaper coverage of their arguments against laws that they feel are discriminatory, and 59 percent felt that members of the Nazi party have a right to publish their own newspaper.

While most respondents initially said they support government-imposed fairness laws, they responded somewhat differently when asked whether "rules requiring fairness and equal time are a threat to freedom of expression because they give the government too much power." Many had not thought about the issue in this way.

The difficulty these respondents had in figuring out how to allow freedom of the press while providing equal treatment of minority positions and individuals is a function of the unique position our country's founders created for the press. The press is the only profit-making institution that is singled out in the Constitution for protection. As one Pulitzer Prize-winning journalist has noted, the founders "gave us an extra-governmental institution, the press, which is at once almost absolutely free and almost absolutely unaccountable."[6] At times this unique position creates some rather awkward dilemmas for the press as well as the public. The press must make a profit to survive, but ethical standards suggest it should cover unpopular persons and events. Reporting unpopular news, however, may cause advertisers to withdraw their financial support. In the same way, a group of citizens not tolerant of this viewpoint can boycott programs and advertisers. One such group, the Coalition for Better Television, organized a boycott of the National Broadcasting Company (NBC) and all products sold by its parent company, the Radio Corporation of America (RCA). The group opposed programs such as *Hill Street Blues* and *Gimme a Break* that dealt extensively with drugs, sex, violence, and alcohol.

The public also has some seemingly contradictory opinions about freedom of the press when it conflicts with individual rights to privacy. While the public strongly supports aggressive press investigations of public and private officials, it disapproves of certain tactics used in *investigative reporting—in-depth gathering of the news to protect the public interest.* One Gallup poll showed that 79 percent approve of investigative reporting and 66 percent would like to see even more of it.[7] At the same time, however, the public has many reservations about the techniques reporters use to gather information: 65 percent disapprove of reporters not identifying themselves as such, 58 percent disapprove of reporters using hidden cameras and microphones, and 52 percent disapprove of running stories that quote unnamed sources.

Americans, then, want the media to be free to investigate and report, but they fear that an unrestricted press may violate individual civil liberties. As we shall see in chapter 16, many civil liberties cases appealed to the courts have dealt with this touchy issue. The number of such cases has increased dramatically in recent years, primarily because of the media industry's growth. This growth has been stimulated by technological innovations such as cable television, satellite discs, videocassette recorders, home computers (see Table 10.1),

and by deregulation of the industry by Congress and the *Federal Communications Commission (FCC), the independent regulatory agency responsible for regulating the media industry, primarily radio and TV.*

THE MEDIA AGE

American adults spend nearly half of their leisure time watching television, listening to the radio, or reading newspapers and magazines. The average citizen is exposed to some form of the mass media for seven hours each day. Exposure to news is far less, since most television news programs last no more than one hour and most radio news broadcasts take a mere five or ten minutes each hour. But entertainment programs also expose us to social and governmental issues. If programs such as *Dynasty, Dallas, Falconcrest,* and *General Hospital* bring up abortion, we think about abortion, even though we may personally disagree with the positions taken in these ''soaps.'' The same process occurs if we read a lead story in *Sports Illustrated* discussing drug use among athletes or go to a movie in which Jane Fonda discovers a dangerous nuclear power plant. Drugs and nuclear power plants are important public policy issues.

The influence of politically relevant information varies because the media use different techniques. We tend to trust and rely on some media more than others. The major sources of news and the ones we trust the most are television and newspapers (see Figure 10.1).

TABLE 10.1

Projected Annual Growth in Profits of the Media Industry, 1980–1985

20% or More

Cable television
Pay cable television services
Subscription television
Satellite services
Super stations
Videodisc

12–20%

Newspapers in high-growth markets
Television stations in high-growth markets
Special interest publications
Entertainment product
Information product and books
Print distribution

8–12%

Newspapers in good growth markets
Television stations in good growth markets
Television networks
General magazines
Radio

SOURCE: John S. Reidy, *Evolution of the Media in the 1980s* (New York: Drexel Burnham Lambert, Inc., 1979), p. 4.

The average adult spends nearly three hours a day watching TV. Regardless of whether they watch the news or an entertainment program, Americans are exposed to many social and governmental issues through television.

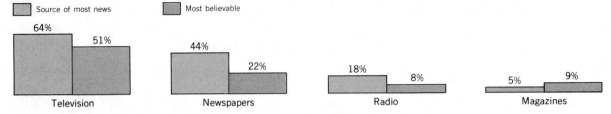

Questions: First, I'd like to ask you where you usually get most of your news about what's going on in the world today–from the newspapers or radio or television or magazines or talking to people or where?

If you got conflicting or different reports of the same news story from radio, television, the magazines and the newspapers, which of the four versions would you be most inclined to believe –the one on radio or television or magazines or newspapers?

☐ Source of most news   ☐ Most believable

Television	Newspapers	Radio	Magazines
64% / 51%	44% / 22%	18% / 8%	5% / 9%

Note: Percentages (for sources of news) add to 131% due to multiple responses. For trend line on these questions, see Public Opinion, August/ September 1979, pp. 30-31. Between 1962 and 1964, television passed newspapers as a source of most news. Between 1958 and 1960, television passed newspapers as the most believable medium.

FIGURE 10.1

News Sources and Their Credibility Rankings

SOURCE: *Public Opinion*, 4 (October/November, 1981), p. 36; based on a survey by the Roper Organization for the Television Information Office, November 15–22, 1980.

Television: The Most Popular Medium

Television replaced newspapers as the most pervasive communications device in the 1960s. The average adult spends 2 hours and 55 minutes a day watching TV; kids watch for four hours a day (see Figure 10.2). *TV Guide* is the nation's best selling magazine. Advertisers spend almost $12 billion a year buying air time to sell their products. Critics of certain television shows attribute undesirable behavior such as crime, violence, sex-role stereo-

Question: On an average day, about how much time, if any, do you personally spend watching TV?

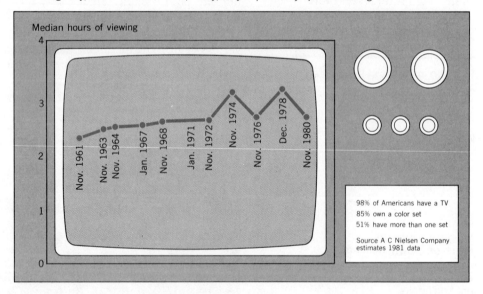

98% of Americans have a TV
85% own a color set
51% have more than one set

Source A C Nielsen Company estimates 1981 data

	Nov. 1961	Nov. 1963	Nov. 1964	Jan. 1967	Nov. 1968	Jan. 1971	Nov. 1972	Nov. 1974	Nov. 1976	Dec. 1978	Nov. 1980
National	2:17	2:34	2:38	2:41	2:47	2:50	2:50	3:02	2:53	3:08	2:55
By selected groups:											
College educated	1:48	—	2:04	2:10	2:17	2:19	2:12	2:23	2:24	2:31	2:14
Upper economic levels	2:02	—	2:14	2:21	2:24	2:30	2:29	2:47	2:40	2:52	2:44

FIGURE 10.2

Time Spent Watching TV on an Average Day: Adults

SOURCE: *Public Opinion*, 4 (October/November, 1981), p. 35; based on a survey by the Roper Organization for the Television Information Office, latest that of November 15–22, 1980.

typing, and racism to exposure to these programs. Others praise TV for presenting programs that make the public more aware of minority issues and emerging social problems.

In light of the evidence on TV's power, who could doubt the ability of TV to "sell" political candidates or influence public thinking on important public policy issues? Surprisingly, some scholars do, but this may be true in part because most research has focused almost exclusively on the role of TV in presidential elections.

The Impact of Television on Campaigns and Elections Research has shown that voters are rarely influenced by nightly network news coverage of the candidates. This is because the evening news focuses on campaign events such as shaking hands, kissing babies, mingling among factory workers, and being booed by protestors rather than the candidate's stance on issues or his or her previous record and experience. If the networks are not looking at candidates' personalities, they are focusing on who's leading whom. In other words, TV networks devote most of their attention to the hoopla and "horse race" aspects of campaigns. In addition, TV viewers retain much less from watching a news broadcast than they do from reading a newspaper. TV news stories are shorter, typically equivalent in length to the first two paragraphs of a newspaper story.

Voters may pay more attention to TV coverage of political party conventions, presidential debates, and political advertisements than they do to the evening news. Even so, this probably doesn't change the way viewers vote. Political advertising, for example, accounts for only 1 or 2 percent of the vote.[8]

Apparently, TV coverage of any type is more likely to influence a person's vote if he or she is not strongly identified with a particular political party or candidate. A staunch party or candidate supporter is likely to tune out coverage of other parties and candidates. It appears, however, that the media may be loosening the party's hold on voters.

The real power of TV in the election process is in candidate selection, which often begins two to three years before the election. TV can make unknowns into front-runners and front-runners into unwanteds by the attention it devotes to each early in the race. In the 1980 campaign, for example,

> *the media, marching almost in lockstep, dissected Edward M. Kennedy's personal history to the point of exploitation, pumped up and set adrift the candidacy of John B. Anderson, pounced on Reagan's verbal gaffes, chastised Carter for the 'meanness' of his campaign strategy and virtually ignored minor party candidates Ed Clark and Barry Commoner.[9]*

Perhaps the only consolation from the candidates' perspectives was that they were all treated equally poorly by the press!

Recognizing the media's candidate-making power, most candidates direct their activities toward creating a public image. "Politicians are tutored on how to project on television. Their images are remodeled, their speeches written and their appearances timed with television in mind," admits one media specialist.[10] Thus, from the start, the emphasis is on style over substance, image over issues, because TV is not geared to in-depth coverage of campaign substance any more than it is geared to in-depth coverage of public policy issues.

The Impact of Television on Public Policy Issues Until recently, little attention has been devoted to TV's influence as a policy agenda-setter. Today, few observers doubt that it has such an

Television evening news focuses more on campaign events such as kissing babies than on a candidate's stance on issues.

Recognizing that on television, the emphasis tends to be on style rather than substance, politicians are tutored by media specialists on how to dress, speak, and gesture.

impact, but they disagree about whether it sets the agenda objectively and fairly. Critics refer to TV as "the boob tube," "the tin kazoo," a "cultural wasteland." They decry television coverage of public affairs because it

1. is too homogeneous in its focus. Almost all stations get their stories from three networks (NBC, CBS, ABC) and two wire services (Associated Press, United Press International). Competition is limited.

2. is too superficial and lacks depth. Sensationalism wins out over public affairs due to the ratings' relationship to a station's (or network's) profits.

3. is too negative toward governmental institutions and public officials. This creates cynicism and distrust of government and threatens our democratic system.

4. teaches a politics of violence and stimulates deviant behavior by glorifying and publicizing the activities of social deviants.

5. reinforces viewers' prejudices rather than eradicating them. People simply screen out what they don't want to see or hear.

6. avoids highly controversial issues and programs that might scare off viewers and advertisers.

7. focuses too much on celebrities and superstars and rarely covers lesser-known individuals and groups with important messages to relate.

On the other hand, supporters identify TV as a vital sociological, political, and cultural force; as the best agent of change in a changing society. They laud television coverage of public affairs on the grounds that it

1. reaches a broad population base, including children, functional illiterates, the poor and the wealthy, the uneducated as well as the educated.

2. can convey emotions as well as information because of its visual nature.

3. can reach around the entire world in a relatively short time.

4. encourages competition and better quality because networks and stations must react to the ratings.

5. has stimulated participation in the political process.

6. informs people about many topics outside their own experiences. On these issues, it can be effective in creating public opinion.

7. is affected by the profit motive, which allows citizens to control the programming.

8. has been broadened considerably by the development of new technologies such as cable TV—again because of the profit motive.

These contradictory claims about television coverage of public affairs suggest that we should take a closer look at several key issues: competition, superficiality, negativism, treatment of minorities, and television's ability to change public opinion.

Does Competition Exist in the Television Industry? TV is the most centralized (and most expensive) of the mass media. Power over the industry as a whole is concentrated at the top. For years, critics of TV have tracked the ownership of individual stations and the general dominance of the industry by centralized national networks, and for years NBC, CBS, and ABC have been regarded as the media power brokers.

The criticism that TV is too "homogenized" stems mostly from the programs distributed by the national networks to their local affiliates. Even though local affiliates have the right to reject network news and programming, they use network programs for about 65 percent of their total broadcast time. During prime-time evening hours, it is even higher—around 83 percent. Local stations have to rely upon network news and programming because of the high, often prohibitive costs of producing their own.

According to some, the problem is that "there's not a dime's worth of difference between ABC, CBS, and NBC." The explanation often given for this look-alike effect is that the networks read the same audience polls and simultaneously adjust their presentations to meet public demands.

While competition may not stimulate diversity in network programming and news coverage, competition from nonnetwork stations, cable channels, public television, videocassettes, and pay TV *does* offer the public some choices. Recent surveys show that the three networks have lost more than 10 percent of their viewers and that since 1976, their share of viewers during prime time has fallen from 91 to 83 percent. And with this fall has come a drop in network profits from $406 million to $325 million. The loss is attributed to the staleness of network programming, which tends to rely on the same stars and formats such as police dramas and domestic comedies.

The new forms of electronic media, especially the video networks, offer the viewer more specialized programs, ranging from news, religious programming, sports, and erotica, to shows for ethnic minorities and children. Some have referred to this as *narrowcasting—directing programming and advertising toward homogeneous audiences.* However, others are already warning of the potential dangers of narrowcasting, the most critical being the fragmentation and polarization of society. Political scientist Benjamin Barber has said,

> *Each group, each class, each race—can have its own programs. . . . The critical communication between groups that is essential to the forging of a national culture and public vision will vanish; in its place will come a new form of communication within groups, where people need talk only to themselves and their clones.* [11]

In conclusion, it appears that no one can say precisely how much competition exists in the TV industry or what effects this competition has. It is equally difficult to draw convincing conclusions on the depth of TV news coverage.

Is TV News Too Superficial, Too Sensational? Walter Cronkite has often referred to network news as a "headline service" providing 30-second reports and 5-minute analyses of highly complex issues such as the economy in a "showbiz" fashion. Obviously, TV news coverage must be entertaining—TV is primarily an entertainment medium. The goal of TV news is to capture the greatest share of the audience as reflected in rating points. One rating point can often mean a million dollars worth of advertising to a station.

TV news gives priority to events that can be filmed. TV news films the dramatic and the exciting because this is what keeps the public tuned in and the advertising dollars coming. Local news programs are most vulnerable to criticisms of sensationalism. In a tongue-in-cheek article, "Eyewitless News," in the *Columbia Journalism Review,* Ron Powers describes the local TV news as focusing on "Unending reports on sex fantasies. And runaway wives. And UFOs. And celebrities. And fires. And murders. And accidents. And, yes, the weather and sports." [12] Does local TV news really cover more sensational stories than public affairs stories? Yes and no. A 1980 study found that during a typical 30-minute local evening news show, only 14 minutes were devoted to news (the rest was spent on weather, sports, and commercials). During this 14 minutes, only 33 percent of the time was spent covering sensational stories. [13] But the study also showed that TV stations used more sensationalistic stories when their ratings started to drop.

This strategy is questionable, primarily because so many people rely on TV as their exclusive source of news. One journalist said, "Television news is entering the beer-and-pizza era. Give them what they want, not what's nutritious. What's good for them and what's attractive and tasty are not always the same." [14] Some think that by responding to public wants, the media is failing in its responsibility to inform the public about important issues:

> *American television does not meet the needs of a political system whose well-being depends upon an informed citizenry. . . . It is bad news for democracy. TV disseminates superficial, frequently irrelevant information that is not an appropriate basis for political action.* [15]

This suggests that if TV news is too superficial, we should turn to other media sources for more in-depth, balanced coverage. We should recognize that television news is dominated by the same concerns that make the rest of television primarily an entertainment medium.

Is TV Too Negative? "Good news is not news." The reason for this is the same as for sensationalism, say defenders of the news. People are more likely to pay attention to bad or bizarre news because it makes them feel better about their own personal lives. But lately, criticism of the press's negativism has intensified, even among journalists who see potential dangers in adversary journalism to American society. Said one:

> If we are always downbeat—if we exaggerate and dramatize only the negatives in our society—we attack the optimism that has always been a well-spring of American progress. We undermine public confidence and, without intending it, become a cause rather than just a reporter of national decline. . . . [For example,] by creating rising expectations that economic reality cannot fulfill, television peddles the impression that the nation is a failure.[16]

Another theory is that too much negativism on TV turns the public against, not the government, but the press itself. This is the *video malaise theory, which maintains that people trust their own senses and eventually come to doubt the credibility of a medium that is consistently negative.* Again, the key issue is if there's too much negativism, who's to blame—the public or the press?

Does TV Treat Minorities Fairly? Since the early 1970s, a great deal of interest has surrounded TV's presentation of gender, racial, and ethnic groups. Minorities are concerned because of evidence that stereotyped portrayals on TV perpetuate sexual and racial prejudices.

TV viewers develop attitudes toward social groups through a process involving two steps: recognition and respect. Recognition is a function of how often a group appears on television—how many times minority characters appear in shows, for example. Respect is a function of the status of the formal roles (leadership, occupation, income, etc.) to which group members are assigned, especially in comparison with other groups. Casting a great many women in TV roles, for example, will not decrease stereotyping if they are portrayed as housewives discussing laundry detergent.

The underrepresentation of women and racial minorities of both sexes is well documented. One study examining characters on prime-time TV shows concluded that "whatever the story line, television maintains societal stereotypes in its portrayal of power."[17] Some say that minorities will be treated fairly only when they own TV stations. Today, less than 2 percent of all TV and radio stations are controlled by minorities, despite the adoption in 1978 of special minority ownership policies by the Federal Communications Commission. Radio and TV stations are very expensive, beyond the reach of most minorities. Even a small radio station costs more than $500,000, and the average TV station costs far more.

Does TV Change Opinions or Merely Reinforce Them? According to the *selective perception theory, TV viewers screen out what they disagree with.* This suggests that TV merely reinforces attitudes already held by the public—a point to which we'll return. A fascinating study of TV's attitude-changing ability involved Archie Bunker, the lead character in *All In The Family.*

> Producer Norman Lear and the leadership of CBS believed that the crude, bumbling, working class conservative, superpatriot, racist Archie Bunker would be an effective weapon against prejudice. Bigotry would be made to appear ridiculous. . . . But evidence soon developed that many viewers applauded Archie's bigotry, believing he was 'telling it like it is.' They missed the satire altogether.[18]

Our key point, however, is that those who tuned in to watch the program were more prejudiced to be-

It is important to minorities that more of them be cast in serious professional roles to help eliminate racial prejudices and stereotypes.

gin with. Those who found it offensive chose not to watch it. Clearly, TV reinforces our opinions on social, economic, and political issues—if we already have well-formed opinions. The "softer" our opinions are on issues, the more likely it is that TV can change them. This is what gives hope to those who see TV as a primary stimulant to social change.

It should be obvious by now that TV has its good and its bad points in the policymaking process. It is important to rely upon other media sources to supplement the news and information obtained from TV.

Radio: A More Localized Medium

Radio today performs two roles: 1) it is an advertising medium, and 2) it transmits entertainment (chiefly music and sports) and information (mostly news) into the home, office, and car. Most radio advertising and news stories are generated locally rather than nationally as with TV. While major networks link radio stations together (CBS, NBC, ABC, and Mutual), only 62 percent of all radio stations are affiliated with the national networks; the figure for TV stations is 88 percent. The national radio networks influence programming less than the television networks anyway. Radio networks today are little more than news and feature services, having reached their peak in the pretelevision days.

Many thought that TV would destroy radio altogether. This has not happened; in fact, the number of radio stations has increased, doubling between 1960 and 1980. The growth of radio can be attributed to its local character, improved technology, better programming, and an increase in the number of FM stations. Other important factors that have kept radio alive are station specialization and ease in changing station format. In most large cities with diverse populations, stations cater to the tastes of different age, ethnic, religious, and educational populations. Stations can change their format when public tastes change.

Format specialization appeals to advertisers, whether they be businesses, political candidates, or interest groups. It allows them to tailor their messages to specific audiences. For example, a candidate running for office can run an advertisement on a religious station stressing his or her position on the issue of prayer in schools. On an "easy listening" station, a candidate might state his or her position on Social Security. Of course, the same criticisms leveled at cable TV for "narrowcasting" can be applied to radio, but few people rely solely on radio for news (see Figure 10.1, p. 268). Another advantage radio offers to political candidates and citizen interest groups is price. Radio spots are much cheaper during prime time (see Table 10.2).

Most people regard radio as the key provider of initial information about crises such as floods, fires, civil disturbances, and wars. This is usually done by interrupting regular programs with bulletins. Citizens' reliance upon radio for fast-breaking news explains why the government depends upon radio to transmit emergency messages during disasters and disorders. But there's a technical reason, too. Radio can operate off emergency power sources more easily than TV and it can reach people via battery-operated transistor radios when electric power supplies are cut off.

Radio plays another role for government—it is

TABLE 10.2

A Comparative Analysis of Media Commercial Costs

Medium	Unit of Sale	Cost per Thousand (Viewers, Listeners, Readers)
Network television:		
All day average	30 seconds	$2.75
Prime time	30 seconds	4.00–5.00
Daytime	30 seconds	1.50–2.00
Spot radio	30 seconds	1.85
National magazine	One page, 4-color	3.50
Newspaper	Composite*	2.15

SOURCE: John S. Reidy, *Evolution of the Media in the 1980s* (New York: Drexel Burnham Lambert, Inc., 1979), p. 151.

*500 lines (about one-quarter page) black and white in each of the top 100 markets in terms of adults.

an instrument of international propaganda. In *Radio Power: Propaganda and International Broadcasting,* Julien Hale explains why:

> *Radio is the only unstoppable medium of mass communication. It is the only medium which reaches across the entire globe instantaneously and can convey a message from any country to any other. Combined, these qualities ensure that it plays an indispensable role in international communications, and keeps its place as the most powerful weapon of international propaganda.* [19]

The purpose of government-supported operations such as Moscow Radio, the Voice of the Arabs, Radio Free Europe, and the Voice of America is to penetrate where they're not wanted. Radio used in this manner is more important as an instrument of diplomacy than as a conveyor of entertainment and news bulletins.

For most Americans, radio's key role in the public policy process is to break the news rather than to interpret or analyze it. For depth, we choose the printed media—newspapers and magazines.

Newspapers: Scrutinizers, Criticizers, Analyzers, Synthesizers

Newspapers have been important in the distribution of news and information to Americans since the days of the Colonial penny presses. Penny presses made newspapers available to large numbers of people because they were sold for a penny (rather than six cents, the going rate for a mail-delivered subscription newspaper) by youngsters on street corners. The newspaper industry has a tradition of being able to adapt to changes in American society. As was the case with radio, many feared that newspapers would be replaced by television. But television has actually worked to the benefit of newspapers by creating an appetite for more information. According to media specialist David Shaw, when TV came along, "newspapers had to do what television news programs did not do: explain and interpret causation, rather than merely show results. . . . Newspapers had to scrutinize and criticize and analyze and synthesize." Newspapers have become more determined to "look beyond the superficial who, what, when,

The Economic Summit Found No New Answers

By Don Oberdorfer
Washington Post Staff Writer

WILLIAMSBURG, May 30—Leaders of world's largest industrial democracies ended three days of intensive discussion of global problems today with statements of renewed unity and common purpose but with no new answers to a staggering array of international problems.

East-West political and military confrontations, the high state of Mideast tension, continuing warfare between Iran and Iraq, internal struggles in Central America, battles over Cambodia, fighting in Afghanistan, other dangerous or bloody situations and the global economic situation were discussed by heads of government or their foreign ministers.

Asked if summit leaders had done anything that could ameliorate world problems, Secretary of State George P. Shultz pointed to Sunday night's joint statement on arms control in the political field and today's declaration in the economic area.

All of this, Shultz said, "presents a picture of a group of countries that are deeply concerned, capable, have resources, will use them, know how to use them [and are] determined.

"I think it is a very strong message, both to ourselves and our own people and the people around the world about the kind of leadership that the world is going to get from the countries represented."

Italian Foreign Minister Emilio Colombo, answering a similar question, said the summit's principal accomplishment in the political field was "verification of certain facts and gravity of these facts" for all of the leaders concerned and a determination flowing from this realization that unified action is essential.

The pronouncements sounded as if the leaders discovered anew in this colonial village what Benjamin Franklin said in 1776: "We must all hang together, else we shall all hang separately."

Of various global problems discussed, the East-West confrontation, especially on nuclear arms, was given by far the greatest time and attention, most of which was consumed in negotiating and drafting the joint statement on arms control.

The difficult problem, several officials said today, was drafting a paper broad enough to win

NEWS ANALYSIS

approval of France, which is not a member of the NATO military command and has a mind of its own on most international questions, and of Japan, which had not been associated with joint statements on western security.

That this could be done at all, despite strains involved, was considered a significant achievement.

Nobody was under the illusion, though, that the statement will have much practical effect on U.S.-Soviet negotiations in Geneva on European-based nuclear missiles or parallel negotiations there on strategic nuclear weapons.

The statement, its authors acknowledged, was aimed as much at international public opinion, especially that in allied countries, as at Moscow.

The leaders also discussed a meeting between President Reagan and Soviet leader Yuri V. Andropov, but there was no indication that Reagan has changed his noncommital and lukewarm view of such a summit.

Late this afternoon, Reagan met West German Chancellor Helmut Kohl in a special meeting to discuss Kohl's visit to Moscow July 4 to 8. It will be the first major visit by a western leader to the new Soviet chief.

Private dinner talk last night among the leaders concentrated on the Mideast situation, but only the sketchiest reports of the discussion were available. Colombo said the six other nations had agreed to support Shultz' recent Mideast peace mission by making new approaches of their own to Syria urging a Syrian withdrawal from Lebanon.

Due to the unusually high state of tension in the Mideast, including continuing Israeli alarm about Syrian troop movement, Shultz kept one eye warily cocked on that region.

He said tonight that on the basis of U.S. intelligence reports, "the level of tension seems to have subsided a little bit." Nonetheless, U.S. officials are anything but relaxed about the continuing trouble in and around Lebanon.

A consensus emerged, a participant said, that overtures from Iran about improved relations should be answered positively. And consensus was reported on reconsidering sanctions against Poland following the visit to Warsaw of Pope John Paul II next month.

For all of the talk, the problems remain—most of them probably until the next annual summit and beyond.

Newspapers provide more in-depth analysis of important events and issues than either radio or television. (© The Washington Post, May 31, 1983)

and where to the causative how and why.''[20] The ''hows'' and ''whys'' are obtained through in-depth investigative reporting. As the investigative role has become more important, the ideological and partisan roles played by newspapers such as editorializing and endorsing candidates have lessened. Today, newspapers are more influential in setting the policy agenda through the process of deciding what stories to run than in swaying citizens' votes.

The Influence of Newspapers on Voter Choice

Newspapers' influence on voter choice varies with the specific newspaper, the type of election (presidential, state, or local), the closeness of the race, the level of information the potential voter already has on a candidate or issue, and the pattern of previous endorsements. Voters can be influenced by editorial endorsements, cartoons, and the op-ed page. The op-ed page is the page opposite the editorial page, which generally includes letters to the editor, columns by nationally syndicated writers such as James Kilpatrick and Marianne Means, and articles by guest contributors.

Newspaper editorial endorsement of candidates is on the decline. In 1932, the *Editor and Publisher* poll of presidential endorsement showed that 93 percent of the nation's daily newspapers endorsed a candidate; by 1976, this figure was down to 74 percent.[21] Prestigious newspapers such as the *Los Angeles Times* and the *Wall Street Journal* have abandoned the practice of endorsing candidates. The editor of the *Washington Post* editorial page stated the problem this way: ''If you endorse early in the campaign, you place a burden on your reporters because the politicians and the readers perceive them as no longer being totally objective, as reflecting your editorial position.''[22]

Another reason for the decline in newspaper endorsements is their ineffectiveness. Fewer than a third of all newspaper readers read the editorial page at all. Of those who do, the vast majority ''are the very people whose intelligence, tenaciously held political views, and access to other sources of information render them the least likely to be converted.''[23] Even so, endorsements can make a difference in certain types of elections, including local races with few issues and little controversy and elections involving ballot propositions (proposed constitutional and charter amendments). In these situations, the voter has

little information about the candidates or issues because they have not received wide publicity. Therefore, they trust the paper on such matters because they figure the paper has better information and more experience than they do.

Newspaper endorsements can carry weight in state and national elections when they are ''against-the-grain'' endorsements. If a newspaper has consistently supported Democratic candidates and it suddenly endorses a Republican candidate, the Republican candidate will benefit. The against-the-grain endorsement will give him or her credibility with a large bloc of voters who might otherwise have been hostile or indifferent.

The influence of the op-ed page is much more difficult to measure. The op-ed page has become much more diverse in terms of content and authorship since the 1960s. During that decade, many newspapers, beginning with the *New York Times,* opened their op-ed pages to outside contributors, ranging from Pulitzer Prize winners to housewives. The purpose was ''to introduce some new voices . . . people other than professional journalists, who might have some interesting things to say about what was happening in our society.''[24] Op-ed pages have become controversial, provocative, intellectual marketplaces.

Op-ed pages serve an important political function. They increase the access of resource-poor groups to the media, enabling them to bring issues of importance to the poor to the attention of the public and its policymakers. According to some, this increases feelings of political effectiveness among minority groups. The popularity of the op-ed concept is evidenced by the fact that the op-ed editor of the *New York Times* receives over 300 unsolicited manuscripts a week. The op-ed pages of major newspapers such as the *Washington Post, New York Times,* and *Wall Street Journal* are particularly important because they are read by a large number of reporters and high level federal officials.

Newspapers also rely on cartoons and photographs to transmit political information to their readers. While there have been no extensive studies of the impact of such visuals on an individual's vote, public officials and candidates have long attributed much power to them. Boss Tweed, a powerful politician of New York Tammany Hall fame, once instructed his assistants to ''Stop them damn pictures. I don't care so much what the papers write about me. My constituents can't read. But, damn it, they can see pictures.''[25] The cartoonist who successfully took on Boss Tweed was Thomas Nast, probably the most famous cartoonist in American history. Nast is credited with creating the Democratic donkey and the Republican elephant, though he actually created only the elephant. Nast's current equivalent in terms of popularity may well be Garry Trudeau, creator of the *Doonesbury* comic strip. The comics have always been a source of political commentary: Harold Gray's *Little Orphan Annie* is one of the longest running.

As important as editorial endorsements, op-ed pages, and cartoons may sometimes be in influencing a voter, they still have less influence than news stories. ''You give me a choice between all those news stories and an editorial endorsement and I'll take the news stories anyday,''[26] says a former chairperson of the California Democratic Party. Political campaign strategists are firmly convinced that day-in and day-out coverage during a campaign influences voters most. Some research lends credibility to this feeling among campaigners. A study of the 1972 presidential election found that people who regularly read newspapers increased their awareness of campaign issues by 35 percent, compared to only 18 percent among less frequent readers.[27] On the other hand, heightened awareness does not always change people's minds about candidates, and other studies have shown that on average, readers read only 10 percent of the stories in the paper.

Political experts generally agree that newspapers rarely influence more than 3 to 5 percent of the vote in a given election. When one considers how many elections are won by close margins, however, the importance of newspapers appears more significant. Their influence may increase in the immediate future as the industry adopts new technologies.

Newspapers and New Technologies   The newspaper industry has become highly computerized in recent years. Reporters now write their stories on CRT units (cathode ray tubes, or television screens) and editors edit the stories electronically, which makes the editorial process much more efficient. The rise in the popularity of home computers and the development of two-way interactive communications (VideoText) systems means that the technology now exists to provide

electronic home delivery of most newspaper contents. Experts predict that the 1980s will begin a new era in which news in print is delivered to the home via the television.

Computers already permit newspapers to make use of **geographic zoning** *to target their news coverage and advertisements to certain communities within large metropolitan areas.* Different stories and ads appear in different sections of the city. This technique is similar to specialization within the TV and radio industries. It allows political candidates, interest groups, and government to tailor their messages to narrow audiences.

The combination of home computers and two-way communications systems will also expand the influence of individuals on the public policy process by increasing opportunities for expressing a policy preference. Instant electronic polls soliciting the public's opinions on topics from nuclear energy to city council budgetary decisions are already being conducted and publicized by cable TV systems such as QUBE. Newspapers will do the same when VideoText systems are in place.

New technologies will not lead to the death of newspapers, in part because newspapers, unlike TV, own the materials they publish. But most significantly, VideoText-type systems will allow newspapers to combine their in-depth coverage with the visual power of TV. This combination may have a significant influence on voters. One unintended consequence of VideoText may be the further reduction of competition among newspapers and the increase of competition among newspapers, TV, and radio as they all move toward specialization and two-way communications.

Newspapers and Competition   The newspaper industry, like TV and radio, has been criticized for becoming too standardized. Standardization has been caused by great dependency upon two national wire services for news stories, a decrease in intracity newspaper competition, and an increase in the concentration of ownership.

Newspapers rely heavily upon the national wire services, AP and UPI, for national and international news. Virtually every American daily newspaper uses one or both of these services. (Radio and TV stations also use the wire services but are less dependent upon them for news.) The services were started in 1848, when the Associated Press was established by six New York newspapers to share the costs of collecting international news.

Between 10 and 80 percent of a newspaper's stories are from the wire services, depending on the size of the paper's own news staff.

The power of the wire services as agenda-setters is clear—studies have shown that on any given day, the same proportion of national and international stories carried on the wires will probably be carried in the local newspaper.[28] If, on a given day, 24.5 percent of the wire service stories involve international news, then 24.5 percent of a local newspaper's coverage that day will be international. Of course, the larger the local paper's news staff, the less likely this is to be true. But smaller papers simply cannot afford to gather their own national and international news.

The concern is that this centralization results in uniformity. The wire services set the trends in news gathering. When a newspaper sends reporters to cover stories broken first by the wire services, they are virtually accepting as newsworthy whatever the wire services have identified as news. Recognizing the need to diversify, prestigious larger newspapers such as the *New York Times, Wall Street Journal, Chicago Tribune,* and the *Los Angeles Times* have created their own wire services to offer more in-depth, interpretive stories to local newspapers. This is an especially valuable service to citizens in cities with only one daily newspaper.

Intracity competition among newspapers is on the decline. In 1923, 502 cities had two or more competing newspapers with different owners. More than 100 of these cities had three or more

papers. By 1978, only 35 cities had competing dailies, and only 2 cities (New York and Philadelphia) had as many as three.[29] In other words, in 55 years, the percentage of cities with competing daily newspapers dropped from 39 to 2.3 percent.

This numerical drop overdramatizes the situation somewhat. The cities that have competing newspapers tend to be the largest urban areas and represent more than 28 percent of the total United States daily newspaper market. Furthermore, as the ***umbrella hypothesis*** suggests, *even in cities with only one daily newspaper there is competition from suburban newspapers, weekly newspapers, "shoppers," and other specialized media.* The originator of this hypothesis, James Rosse, also notes that while we may not have *intracity* newspaper competition, we do have *intercity* competition, which means that the standardization problem may not be as grave as some have assumed.[30] It should be remembered that newspapers compete with radio and TV, too.

The growth of newspaper chains and the concentration of ownership may be a more serious problem. More than 60 percent of America's daily papers, which account for 72 percent of total circulation, are controlled by national and regional chains.[31] The 12 largest chains (see Table 10.3) account for more than one-third of the total daily newspaper circulation in the United States. Four chains—Knight-Ridder, Newhouse, Tribune, and Gannett—account for almost 25 percent. In recent years, these national chains have been buying small city and suburban news-

TABLE 10.3

America's Largest Newspaper Chains

12 Largest Chains in Titles		12 Largest Chains in Circulation	
Gannet	75	Knight-Ridder	3,481,112
Thomson	55	Newhouse	3,244,182
Knight-Ridder	32	Tribune	3,124,020
Newhouse	29	Gannett	2,866,835
Freedom	24	Scripps-Howard	1,875,877
Harte-Hanks	22	Dow Jones	1,854,418
Scripps-Howard	17	Times Mirror	1,767,798
Cox	15	Hearst	1,411,922
Dow Jones	14	Cox	1,119,261
Copley	10	New York Times	1,048,493
Tribune	8	Thomson	983,717
Hearst	8	Capital Cities Communications	970,239

SOURCE: From *Goodbye Gutenberg: The Newspaper Revolution of the 1980s* by Anthony Smith. © 1980 by Oxford University Press, Inc. Reprinted by permission. (New York: Oxford University Press, 1980), p. 52; based on data from *New York Times* (April 2, 1978) and Lane, Colin, Hochstin Co. from ABC (Summer 1977).

papers. If this trend continues, Rosse's umbrella hypothesis will be disproved as the same owners come to control both big city and suburban newspapers.

Media Conglomerates

A *media conglomerate is a large corporation* (such as General Electric, RCA, or Westinghouse) *with diversified nonmedia holdings that buys into the media industry* (see Table 10.4). There is most concern over *cross-ownership,* which occurs *when a conglomerate buys into different sectors of the media industry.* A single corporation could conceivably own TV stations, radio stations, newspapers, book and magazine publishers, and film companies. RCA, CBS, Time, Inc., Newhouse, and Hearst are companies involved in cross-ownership.

Cross-ownership is most controversial when it involves some combination of TV, radio, and newspapers. Since most people depend upon these media for news and information, the fear is that cross-ownership will create a media monopoly. Such a monopoly would be contradictory to the intention of the First Amendment, which protects diversity of opinion. Inherent in this argument is the assumption that local and diverse ownership of the media is the best way to protect Americans' right of access to a wide range of facts and opinions.

In the mid-1970s, the FCC established limits on cross-ownership of radio and TV. No company or individual can own more than seven AM radio stations, seven FM radio stations, and seven TV stations. FCC rules further limit multiple and cross-media ownership within the same markets.

Some feel that the FCC has not gone far enough in regulating media ownership. They advocate action by the U. S. Department of Justice under its antitrust powers to break up the media conglomerates. The issue of government regulation of the media is always difficult, however, because it brings up the debate about the public's right to know versus the press's right to freedom from government control. The debate ultimately involves the individuals who decide what will be news.

REPORTERS, GATEKEEPERS, AND MEDIA STARS: DECIDING WHAT'S NEWS AND HOW TO PRESENT IT

Every day, those who report the news in the different media must decide what news to report. This is a difficult task in today's complex world.

What Is News?

Members of the presss have a tough time providing a definition of "news." Said one, "News is more easily pursued than defined, a characteristic it shares with such other enthralling abstractions as love and truth."[32] The most famous definition is that given by John Bogart, an editor of the *New York Sun,* many years ago: "When a dog bites a

TABLE 10.4

Major Media Holdings of Conglomerate Firms

Revenue Rank	Corporation	Rank in Fortune 1000 Mfg. Companies	Percent Revenues from Advertising	Broadcast Holdings AM	FM	TV	Other Media Holdings Books	Mags	Newsps	Film	Cable
1.	General Electric	9	(not avail.)	6	2	3	—	—	—	—	—
2.	Westinghouse	26	3%	7	2	5	—	—	—	—	—
3.	RCA	30	19	4	4	5	X	—	—	—	—
4.	CBS	91	57	7	7	5	X	X	—	—	—
5.	General Tire/Rubber	122	5	6	5	4	—	—	—	—	—
6	Fuqua Industries	—	7	2	—	3	—	—	—	—	—
7.	ABC	152	83	7	7	5	—	X	—	X	—
8.	Time Inc.	198	43	—	—	1	X	X	—	X	X
9.	Warner Comms.	214	5	—	—	—	X	X	—	X	X
10.	Times Mirror	219	55	—	—	2	X	X	X	—	X
11.	Schering-Plough	—	3	6	6	—	—	—	—	—	—
12.	Knight-Ridder	293	98	—	—	4	—	—	X	—	—
13.	Jefferson-Pilot	—	8	5	4	2	—	—	X	—	—
14.	McGraw-Hill	314	35	—	—	4	X	X	—	—	—
15.	Dun & Bradstreet	—	42	—	—	5	X	X	—	—	—

SOURCE: Benjamin M. Compaine, ed. *Who Owns the Media? Concentration of Ownership in the Mass Communications Industry* (New York: Harmony Books, 1979), p. 97; based on data from *Media Decisions* (October 1978), p. 64.

man, that's not news because it happens so often. But, if a man bites a dog, that is news.''[33] Another oft-cited definition comes from a former managing editor of the *New York Times*. He classified as news ''anything you find out today that you didn't know before.''[34] Probably the most realistic definition of news comes from David Brinkley of ABC News: ''News is what I say it is.''[35]

Although most journalists are unable to come up with a specific definition (not unlike political scientists when asked to define ''politics''), they do have a sense of what is newsworthy. Nearly every journalism textbook offers a checklist of criteria for determining what is newsworthy. Graber, in *Mass Media and American Politics*, provides the following list of criteria for choosing news stories:

1. High impact on readers and listeners (stories with relevance to the most people);

2. Violence, conflict, disaster, or scandal (things that excite audiences);

3. Audience familiarity with the subjects of stories (stories involving famous names, places, and events);

4. Closeness to home (most people are interested in what happens near them);

5. Timeliness and novelty (events that are new and out of the ordinary).[36]

Ultimately, it's up to reporters, editors, and publishers to decide what is news. The media's power as public policy agenda-setters is again obvious. What is less apparent is that journalists' decisions are colored by their experiences and thus are not purely objective. Leo Rosten, journalist and author of a study of the Washington press corps, concluded that ''since objectivity in journalism is an impossibility, the social heritage, the 'professional reflexes,' the individual temperament, and the economic status of reporters assume a fundamental significance.''[37]

Recognizing that pure objectivity is not possible, the key issue, then, is how representative or unrepresentative are these ''judgement calls''? Richard Harwood, former editor of the *Trenton Times*, says, ''the real question we have to ask ourselves . . . is whether the picture of the world we select and produce every day is a truly representative picture. [We might also ask] whether it should be.''[38] To answer, one must take a closer look at those who make news-related decisions and the techniques they use.

The combination of violence, a famous person, and a very unusual event made John Hinckley's attempted assassination of President Reagan a major news story.

The Reporters

Reporters are ''at the cutting edge of the news, where initial decisions are made about what events or aspects of a situation will enter the flow of the news and which will wither away, unknown and unseen, because a reporter left them out of the story, or a camera person turned the lens another direction.''[39]

Reporters don't just randomly chase around the town, the country, or the world in search of a newsworthy story. Instead, the overwhelming majority work on the *beat system,* in which *reporters are assigned to the people, places, and events that are probable sources of news of interest to the public.* On the national level, typical beats are institutions such as the White House, Congress, the State and Defense Departments, the Supreme Court, and issues such as energy, science, and economics (see Table 10.5). At the local level, the most common beats are city hall, the police station, local hospitals, schools, and the courts.

Reporters working beats are rarely told exactly what story to write. They are expected to generate news on their own initiative and are responsible for deciding what to cover and how to cover it. Stories covered by beat reporters are more likely to be carried by newpapers or TV, since beats are

Sam Donaldson is a beat reporter. He is assigned to cover the White House for ABC on a daily basis.

created in response to audience interest. One study found that in the *New York Times* and the *Washington Post*, stories from regular beats outnumber other stories two to one and are more likely to make front-page headlines.[40]

The beat system, while practical in terms of time and money, has been criticized for its heavy bias toward coverage of governmental institutions and the resulting dependency on official sources. Reliance upon official sources (which will be discussed in more detail later) is, as Paletz and Entman note,

> *ingrained from the first professional steps when reporters are instructed to cultivate their sources [and] necessary because reporters soon discover that public officials make what are believed to be (by editors, other public officials, other reporters) the important political decisions and often offer easy access to information about their activities.*[41]

Such a rationale does not necessarily mean that reliance upon official sources for information is always in the best interest of the public, however. The fact that the Watergate story was uncovered by two general news reporters rather than government beat reporters indicates the dangers of excessive reliance on official sources.

A second criticism of the beat system is that it

TABLE 10.5

The Beat System at the National Level

High-prestige Beats

Diplomacy (1)
Class A general assignment (2)
Law (3)
Politics (4)
White House (5)

Medium-prestige Beats

Congress (6)
Science (7)
Energy (8)

Low-prestige Beats

Domestic agencies (9)
Regulatory agencies (10)
Economics (11)
Class B general assignment (12)
Regional (13)

SOURCE: Stephen Hess, *The Washington Reporters* (Washington, D.C.: The Brookings Institution, 1981), p. 49.

The beat system tends to result in pack journalism. Reporters covering the same beat, city hall for example, report the same story, often from almost identical prospectives since they interact with each other on a daily basis.

tends to result in *pack journalism, the tendency of different reporters to write very similar political stories.* Naturally, if all radio and TV stations in town assign reporters to the city hall beat, the stories they report are going to be similar—at least in basic content, if not style. The real problem with pack journalism is not so much that reporters cover the same stories, but that they spend so much time together that they eventually adopt almost identical perspectives.

Unlike beat reporters, *general assignment* reporters are stationed in the newsroom but are free to roam around gathering information. They are *either assigned stories by their editor or they suggest their own stories and have them okayed by their editor. These reporters are more likely to be "investigative," or "interpretive" reporters*—and are most likely to be accused of being biased. Interpretive reporters are often criticized for failing to distinguish between the objective and the subjective, between facts and what they wish were facts. On the other hand, they are more likely to win journalism prizes for their in-depth work, as Bob Woodward and Carl Bernstein of the *Washington Post* did for their stories on Watergate.

Both beat and general assignment reporters often write their stories with their editor's preference in mind. Sixty percent of the subjects of one study admitted slanting their stories, to some extent, to their editor's preferences.[42] Apparently editors have a great deal of power in deciding not only which stories will run but what their content will be.

The Gatekeepers

Gatekeepers are the editors and producers who decide what will be printed or broadcast. On the average, gatekeepers see five times as many stories as they can use everyday. By deciding which stories to run, they let reporters know which stories are likely to be printed or broadcast and which will not be. A gatekeeper's decision can be overturned by those above him or her, but this occurs infrequently.

One common criticism of gatekeepers is that they rely too heavily on other news organizations for their sense of what's news. As one author put it, "Morning papers provide story ideas to editors of afternoon papers and evening broadcasts. Afternoon and evening media provide a sense of the latest developments for the morning media."[43] For national and international news, they rely heavily on the wire services. Editors usually defend themselves against these criticisms by claiming that their decisions closely parallel the relative interest of the general public. But is this so?

A Harris survey of 1,533 adults, 86 top editors and news directors, and 76 reporters and writers found that media personnel did not accurately assess public priorities in news coverage (see Table 10.6). Media personnel greatly· underestimated the public's desire for national and world news but overestimated the desire for state and local news, sports, and entertainment.[44] The primary explanation for this gap lies in the personal characteristics of what some call the "media elite."

Deciding what stories to cover, air, and print each day is the responsibility of editors and producers—the gatekeepers. Since for every story they choose, they must exclude four others, they effectively determine what is news.

TABLE 10.6

Press Assessment of Public Priorities in News Coverage

Kind of News	Percent of the Public that Wants It	Percent of Editors, Journalists, Who Think Public Wants It	Percent by which Editors, Journalists, Misjudge the Public
National	60	34	−26
Sports	35	75	+40
World affairs	41	5	−36
Local	74	88	+14
Entertainment, art, cultural	29	45	+16
State	27	62	+35

SOURCE: "Press Assessment of Public Priorities in News Coverage," from *Electronic Democracy: Television's Impact on the American Political Process* by Ann Rawley Saldich. Copyright © 1979 by Praeger Publishers. Used by permission.

Characteristics of the Media Elite

The *media elite* consists of journalists and broadcasters at the nation's most influential national media outlets. There have been several studies of this group, the first being Rosten's 1937 book, *The Washington Correspondents*. This study was updated in 1981 by two major studies, Hess's *The Washington Reporters* and Lichter and Rothman's "Media and Business Elites."[45] These studies, like Rosten's, found that the media elite differs considerably from middle America.

Lichter and Rothman studied 240 journalists and broadcasters at the nation's most influential media outlets, including the *New York Times*, the *Washington Post*, the *Wall Street Journal*, *Time Magazine*, *Newsweek*, *U.S. News and World Report*, the four TV network news departments (including the Public Broadcasting System, the government-subsidized TV network), and major public radio broadcasting stations. They found that the media elite is composed mainly of white males in their 30s and 40s. They are highly educated, well-paid, primarily from northern industrial states, especially from the Northeast corridor. They do not regularly go to church or synagogue and describe themselves as liberals.

The liberal bias is evident in their voting records for president. Of those who say they voted, the proportion who supported the Democratic presidential candidate has not dropped below 80 percent for the past several elections. They are liberal in their views toward social and international issues (see Table 10.7) and strongly support environmental protection, affirmative action, women's rights, homosexual rights, and sexual free-

dom in general. Over half agree that American exploitation has contributed to Third World poverty.

When asked who exerts the most influence in this country, the media elite listed business first, followed closely by the media and labor unions, with consumer groups, blacks, and feminists lagging far behind. When asked who they would *like* to exert the most influence, the order was as follows: media, consumer groups, intellectuals, blacks, business, feminists, and unions.[46]

Similar results emerged from Hess's study of the Washington press corps—the reporters who cover national government (see Table 10.8). (The latest count shows that roughly 10,000 journalists and news writers work in Washington, including

The media elite is not representative of American society as a whole. These journalists and broadcasters are predominantly white males in their thirties and forties, with more liberal leanings than the public at-large.

TABLE 10.7
Media Elite Attitudes on Social Issues

	Strongly Agree	Agree	Disagree	Strongly Disagree
Economics				
Big corporations should be publicly owned	4%	9%	23%	65%
People with more ability should earn more	48	38	10	4
Private enterprise is fair to workers	17	53	20	10
Less regulation of business is good for USA	16	47	24	13
Government should reduce income gap	23	45	20	13
Government should guarantee jobs	13	35	33	19
Political Alienation				
Structure of society causes alienation	12	37	32	20
Institutions need overhaul	10	18	31	42
All political systems are repressive	4	24	26	46
Social-Cultural				
Environmental problems are not serious	1	18	27	54
Strong affirmative action for blacks	33	47	16	4
Government should not regulate sex	84	13	3	1
Woman has right to decide on abortion	79	11	5	5
Homosexuality is wrong	9	16	31	45
Homosexuals shouldn't teach in public schools	3	12	31	54
Adultery is wrong	15	32	34	20
Foreign Policy				
U.S. exploits Third World, causes poverty	16	40	25	20
U.S. use of resources immoral	19	38	27	16
West has helped Third World	6	19	50	25
Goal of foreign policy is to protect U.S. businesses	12	39	28	22
CIA should sometimes undermine hostile governments	26	19	36	19

	None	Democracies	Friends	Anyone
To what countries should we sell arms?	19	29	48	4

SOURCE: S. Robert Lichter and Stanley Rothman, "Media and Business Elites," *Public Opinion* (October/November 1981), p. 44.

some 450 foreign correspondents.) Hess found, for example, that the Washington press corps has four male reporters for each female reporter. Blacks make up less than 4 percent of the Washington press corps, and other minorities are virtually unrepresented. The Northeast remains overrepresented, despite the population shifts of the 1970s and 1980s.

The new generation of Washington press corps reporters, though still relatively small, is a younger, more socially conscious group that includes blacks and women and represents a wider assortment of journalistic enterprises. Publications such as *Rolling Stone* and *Playboy* now cover Washington stories, for example. Many of these reporters advocate a subjective, adversarial form of journalism. This may lead to further criticisms

of the press's unrepresentativeness, or it may speed changes in the value systems of "middle Americans." At present, 75 percent of all Americans think TV and newspaper reporters are doing an excellent or good job.[47]

The Media Stars
Well-known journalists, especially TV personalities, not only present the news—they make it. Said one reporter, "The competition between Dan Rather and Roger Mudd for Walter Cronkite's anchor chair on *CBS Evening News* was a national event more avidly followed than the appointment of a secretary of state."[48] Numerous books have been written about the rise to stardom of Cronkite, Rather, Barbara Walters, Harry Reasoner, Mike Wallace, Tom Snyder, and others.

TABLE 10.8

Characteristics of Washington Reporters by Place of Employment

Characteristic of Reporter	Employer				
	Wire Service	Network Television	Radio	Magazine	Newspaper
Male	90.0%	81.4%	77.8%	78.8%	84.9%
Female	10.0	18.6	22.2	21.2	15.1
White	97.5	95.3	85.2	96.9	97.6
Black	2.5	4.7	14.8	3.1	2.4
Urban	66.7	76.3	64.0	71.0	74.2
Rural	25.0	15.8	20.0	16.1	22.2
Age					
20–29	15.0	2.3	51.9	12.1	15.1
30–39	40.0	39.5	25.9	36.4	40.1
40–49	17.5	39.5	22.2	15.2	30.2
50 and over	27.5	18.6	0.0	36.4	14.6
Regional Influence					
Northeast	37.9	39.5	33.7	32.4	38.2
North Central	24.6	25.6	9.6	27.0	32.8
South	28.6	26.3	49.3	31.6	17.6
West	8.9	8.6	7.4	9.0	11.4
Education					
High school only	2.5	0.0	3.7	3.0	1.4
Some college	5.0	4.7	11.1	0.0	4.2
College degree	67.5	32.6	66.7	39.4	40.6
Some graduate work	5.0	27.9	3.7	24.2	15.6
Graduate degree	20.0	34.9	14.8	33.3	38.2
Number of responses to each of above	(40)	(43)	(27)	(33)	(212)
College Selectivity					
Highly selective	31.6	36.6	19.2	41.9	37.6
Selective	55.3	48.8	38.5	38.7	40.0
Not selective	13.2	14.6	42.3	19.4	22.4
Number of responses	(38)	(41)	(26)	(31)	(210)
Undergraduate Field of Study					
Humanities/liberal arts	51.4	57.5	34.6	48.4	59.3
Journalism	43.2	27.5	50.0	25.8	29.2
Science/technology	5.4	15.0	15.4	25.8	11.5
Number of undergraduate fields	(37)	(40)	(26)	(31)	(209)
Graduate Field of Study					
Humanities/liberal arts	22.2	37.5	. . .	30.8	23.6
Journalism	66.7	45.8	. . .	46.2	50.0
Science/technology	11.1	16.7	. . .	23.1	26.4
Number of graduate fields	(9)	(24)		(13)	(106)
Specialist	41.2	50.0	16.7	36.4	28.6
Generalist	58.8	50.0	83.3	63.6	71.4
Number of responses	(17)	(20)	(18)	(11)	(77)

SOURCE: Stephen Hess, *The Washington Reporters* (Washington, D.C.: The Brookings Institution, 1981), pp. 153–154.

TV news personalities are highly-paid media stars who not only present the news but make it. Competition for these positions is stiff but the personal rewards are great—instant name recognition, trust, and respect from millions of TV viewers.

Competition for audiences has forced national TV networks and local TV stations to bring entertainment and credibility into the newsroom via the personalities of those reporting the news. A description of this phenomenon as it occurs in the local TV newsroom appears in Ron Power's *The Newscasters*:

> *People in the News. Faces and Places. Personalities. These became the new staples of the local newscast, with the items themselves being delivered by People with beautiful Faces in wondrous Places (the futuristic, color-coordinated new sets), People who were themselves Personalities. People who were members of News Teams, who wore identical tailored blazers (or smart designer blouses and scarves); or, in some cases, people who dressed conspicuously apart from the rest of the Team and were certified as Personalities apart. People who grinned wryly at one another; who traded banter about their personal lives (golf games) at the commercial*

> *break; who, by their very dress and manner and sense of fulsome consumer-well-being, spoke a new national language of comfort and assurance, of a peace that passeth for understanding.*[49]

The personalities of national network newscasters are quite different from those of local newscasters because of differences in audience perceptions of what each should be. Network news is regarded as more objective and more serious than local news, which is more entertaining, regularly covering sports and weather as well as news.

Each network's TV producer carefully selects anchorpersons and reporters to promote the notion that its news is most objective.

> *Correspondents are authoritative and factual, unemotional, uninvolved, dispassionate. . . . Anchorpersons exude qualities of common sense, rationality, and sanity. . . . They, too, are trained to appear reasonable,*

undramatic, low-key. Added to their credibility is the formal way they are announced. ('This is the evening news with. . . . '), their dress, their vocal inflection and resonance, the camera's respectful distance, and the concluding nightly benedictions they bestow ('Thank you and good night. ').[50]

Ironically, TV newscasters rarely write their own stories. Yet millions of Americans view them as among the most knowledgeable, most trusted people in the nation. They rarely express a personal opinion, but when they do, they often have a great influence. Lyndon Johnson is said to have decided to forego a second term after hearing Walter Cronkite disavow the Vietnam War. In any event, it's clear that for many Americans, the deliverer of the news makes a difference in what they think about the news. The public, however, has little insight into where the news comes from. Most would be surprised about how much comes from government officials.

THE RELATIONSHIP BETWEEN THE MEDIA AND GOVERNMENT

The ties between the media and government are both symbiotic and adversarial—their relationship is one of mutual dependency and mutual suspicion. To perform their functions adequately, they need each other, but their goals conflict and they operate under different constraints.

Mutual Dependents

The press, particularly in Washington, relies heavily upon official sources for information. In an analysis of the news sources used by the *Washington Post* and the *New York Times*, Sigal found that 58.2 percent of all information came from routine sources such as press conferences, official proceedings, and press releases.[51] Yet of all the nation's newspapers, these two are considered to be among the most critical of government.

Reliance upon official viewpoints is greatest among beat reporters. It is also greater when government assistance is needed in collecting or verifying data.

The *Washington information establishment*, the primary source of information for the Washington press corps, *is comprised of official directors of public information such as press officers, press secretaries, public affairs directors, assistant secretaries for public information, plus unofficial public relations advisers and government department and subdepartment heads*, who practice

their own unilateral brand of publicity, often without the knowledge of their own public information personnel.[52] The task of official government publicists is to influence opinion, to communicate persuasively, and create consent. They seek a favorable story or no story at all.

The lines of communication between the press and government publicists include the following:

1. The official press release
2. The background explanation or "white paper"
3. The summary of an official speech
4. The summary of proceedings at a hearing or committee meeting
5. The press conference
6. The personal or private interview
7. The interview conducted for a few select reporters
8. The off-the-record "leak" or "backgrounder"
9. The official event
10. The special forum, such as a weekly news program.[53]

A survey by Steinberg of Washington reporters showed that the majority found personal interviews to be the most useful sources, especially when they yielded confidential information (see Table 10.9).[54] Hess's study of the Washington press corps came to the same conclusion, finding that Washington journalists conduct almost five interviews per story and glean more useful information from these personal interviews than from official government documents.[55] However, reporters on more technical beats, such as science, economics, and the Supreme Court must rely more heavily on government documents.

To get a story, a reporter must know who to ask, who will answer the phone, who is likely to offer information. Nearly half report that they consider middle-level bureaucrats the best source. Not one reporter listed public information officers! Middle-level bureaucrats are preferred because "they tend to be more anonymous and more insulated as sources of news and less subject to quotation or attribution."[56]

Reporters gain the most information when they can offer their sources some anonymity. To protect their anonymity, sources can give *off-the-record information*, *which is for the reporter's general un-*

TABLE 10.9

A Survey of the Washington Press's Attitudes toward Government as a Source of Information

Category	Number	Percentage (%)
I. Of the following, which is most productive source of news: press releases; press conferences; personal interviews; confidential information?		
Press releases	0	0
Press conferences	3	10.4
Personal interviews	9	31.0
Confidential information	7	24.1
Personal interview and confidential information	10	34.5
II. Which of the following is usually the best source of information: information officers; top-level officials; middle-level officials?		
Information officers	0	0
Top-level officials	5	17.2
Middle-level officials	14	48.3
All three categories	3	10.3
Congress	1	3.5
Don't know	1	3.5
Top and middle level	5	17.2
III. Do you find the brochures and annual reports put out by the government useful sources of news?		
Yes	4	13.8
No	8	27.7
Occasionally	14	48.2
Rarely	2	6.9
Annual reports only	1	3.4
IV. In your opinion, is there an effort to manipulate news flow by the government agencies?		
Yes	21	72.4
No	3	10.4
Occasionally	5	17.2
V. Are your sources of news in government generally—and truthfully—responsive to your questions?		
Yes	19	65.5
Mostly	7	24.1
Occasionally	2	7.0
Don't know	1	3.4

SOURCE: Charles S. Steinberg, *The Information Establishment: Our Government and the Media.* © 1980 by Hastings House, Publishers, Inc.

derstanding and is not to be reported in any form or *deep background information, which reporters can use only on their own authority*; and *background information*, which reporters can use *in stories without naming the specific source. They can, however, name a general source such as "an administration official."* Twenty-eight percent of the interviews by the Washington press corps are conducted off the record or as background. The percentage increases for stories that are more important or that concern national security.

Critics of nonattribution condemn the practice because it prevents officials from being held accountable. Reporters defend it on the grounds that they would not get the information otherwise and that the gains in the public interest outweigh the losses.

A *leak is information given to a reporter by a public official or private individual that was not intended for publication at that particular time.* Leaking can also be part of the public information strategy used by public officials. Charles Peters, editor-in-chief of the *Washington Monthly*, notes that leaking can be an effective way to push a point of view or to create a favorable or unfavorable atmosphere for certain policies. The most common reason for leaking, however, is to strengthen the survival network, he says. "Officials and reporters build their networks through mutual favors: 'I'll leak this piece of news to you if you'll give my boss front-page coverage on a certain issue. You get a front-page story, and my boss gets publicity.' "[57]

In general, reporters find Congress more accessible than the executive branch, for many reasons. First, legislators and their aides are more willing to talk than executive branch personnel. Says Hess, "The people in [Congress] view publicity as the lifeblood of elective politics; those in [executive] bureaus and agencies most often think of press attention as trouble."[58] Second, reporters find it easier to talk to members of Congress and their staffs. "They're more like us. Bureaucrats don't talk English, they get wrapped up in technical terms."[59] Third, the size, complexity, and geographical dispersion of the executive branch overwhelms general assignment reporters.

The relative coverage of the president and Congress differs by medium. The president is instantly recognizable and so suits the needs of television, a visual medium. With 535 representatives, Congress is more suited to the regional needs of newspapers. The Supreme Court and courts in general get little press coverage, although signs indicate that this is changing because of the growing number of controversial decisions. In general, however, judges rarely grant interviews, hold news conferences, or leak information to the press, fearing that media attention will destroy their image of impartiality. Nevertheless, the courts depend upon the media to communicate their decisions to the population and to maintain their legitimacy as an institution. The relationship between the press and the judiciary is less adversarial than the relationship between the press and the executive and legislative branches, however.

Adversaries

The adversarial relationship between the press and the government has existed since our nation's beginning. It is a result of the First Amendment, which prohibits the government from interfering with the freedom of the press. Over the years, the press has interpreted the Amendment to mean that it must serve as a proxy for the people and be the public's watchdog over government.

People in government wish to retain public support and maintain their power. Naturally, they sometimes do not want to release information they regard as contrary to the national interest or harmful to the country's security. Likewise, they do not want to release information that may threaten their job security, reelection, or reappointment—information likely to be interpreted by the press and the public as evidence of wrongdoing. Public officials generally regard the press as biased against government, profiting financially from the publication of negative rather than positive news.

The suspicions between the press and government officials have stemmed largely from their misuse of each other. The Watergate and Vietnam episodes convinced many reporters that the government sometimes lies and withholds information. During these episodes, the press was intentionally given inaccurate or incomplete information by high-ranking public officials. Public officials, in turn, have become convinced that the press twists facts to make stories reflect ideological biases. *TV Guide* called one documentary broadcast by *CBS Reports* a "smear" of General Westmoreland. In the film, Westmoreland was ac-

"...AND YOU CAN MISQUOTE ME ON THAT!"

TABLE 10.10

A Statement of Principles: American Society of Newspaper Editors

Preamble: The First Amendment, protecting freedom of expression from abridgment by any law, guarantees to the people through their press a constitutional right, and thereby places on newspaper people a particular responsibility.

Thus journalism demands of its practitioners not only industry and knowledge but also the pursuit of a standard of integrity proportionate to the journalist's singular obligation.

To this end the American Society of Newspaper Editors sets forth this Statement of Principles as a standard encouraging the highest ethical and professional performance.

Article I—Responsibility: The primary purpose of gathering and distributing news and opinion is to serve the general welfare by informing the people and enabling them to make judgments on the issues of the time. Newspapermen and women who abuse the power of their professional role for selfish motives or unworthy purposes are faithless to that public trust.

The American press was made free not just to inform or just to serve as a forum for debate but also to bring an independent scrutiny to bear on the forces of power in the society, including the conduct of official power at all levels of government.

Article II—Freedom of the Press: Freedom of the press belongs to the people. It must be defended against encroachment or assault from any quarter, public or private.

Journalists must be constantly alert to see that the public's business is conducted in public. They must be vigilant against all who would exploit the press for selfish purposes.

Article III—Independence: Journalists must avoid impropriety and the appearance of impropriety as well as any conflict of interest or the appearance of conflict. They should neither accept anything nor pursue any activity that might compromise or seem to compromise their integrity.

Article IV—Truth and Accuracy: Good faith with the reader is the foundation of good journalism. Every effort must be made to assure that the news content is accurate, free from bias and in context, and that all sides are presented fairly. Editorials, analytical articles and commentary should be held to the same standards of accuracy with respect to facts as news reports.

Significant errors of fact, as well as errors of omission, should be corrected promptly and prominently.

Article V—Impartiality: To be impartial does not require the press to be unquestioning or to refrain from editorial expression. Sound practice, however, demands a clear distinction for the reader between news reports and opinion. Articles that contain opinion or personal interpretation should be clearly identified.

Article VI—Fair Play: Journalists should respect the rights of people involved in the news, observe the common standards of decency and stand accountable to the public for the fairness and accuracy of their news reports.

Persons publicly accused should be given the earliest opportunity to respond.

Pledges of confidentiality to news sources must be honored at all costs, and therefore should not be given lightly. Unless there is clear and pressing need to maintain confidences, sources of information should be identified.

These principles are intended to preserve, protect and strengthen the bond of trust and respect between American journalists and the American people, a bond that is essential to sustain the grant of freedom entrusted to both by the nation's founders.

SOURCE: From QUESTIONING MEDIA ETHICS by Bernard Rubin. Copyright © 1978 by Praeger Publishers. Used by permission.

cused of suppressing estimates of growing enemy troop strength in South Vietnam before the 1968 Tet offensive. To make their case, CBS "ignored contrary evidence, rehearsed the interview of a friendly source, grilled unfriendly witnesses much more harshly than friendly witnesses, sought out and interviewed more persons who agreed with the broadcast premise, and allowed a friendly source to retape his interview to make it stronger."[60] Obviously, some government publicists and reporters should adhere more strongly to ethical standards (see Table 10.10).

Historically, suspicion of motives has been greatest between presidents and the media. From George Washington to Ronald Reagan, presidents have complained about the press. Even Thomas Jefferson, a leading advocate of press freedom during the founding of the nation, became critical of the press once he was elected president. Jefferson once suggested that editors divide their papers into four chapters, headed "truths," "probabilities," "possibilities," and "lies," and added that "the first chapter would be very short."[61] Likewise, the press has printed derogatory remarks about most presidents. Tyler was described as an "executive ass," Grant as "Kaiser Ulysses," and Nixon as "King Richard," to cite just a few examples.

"Wars" between the press and the president generally stem from the power each attributes to the other. Presidents are well aware of the media's role in elections (see chapter 12 on the presidency), and the press knows how much control the president can command over it. Columnist John Herbers described the president's control as follows:

The President easily commands media attention regardless of whether he is horseback riding with the Queen of England or making a statement on a critical issue of the day.

> *He can command, and generally receive, prime time on national television to say almost anything he wishes. He can control where and when he is photographed. He can hinder or help reporters, columnists, and editors by supplying or withholding information. He can use the press as a whipping boy, blaming it for his troubles by accusing it of incomplete coverage and of misrepresenting his policies. The president can also shape news conferences to his own ends simply by calling on reporters he knows will ask only soft questions or who can be counted on to defuse tense moments by providing comic relief.[62]*

Press coverage of presidents focuses largely on their programs and public policies, but press attention to Congress tends to focus on partisanship (when it creates conflict) and personalities (when they are involved in graft, junkets, and "lovenesting").

Members of Congress criticize the press's failure to publish their votes in subcommittees and committees on procedural matters, which are often more vital than votes on final passage. The press rarely reports a Congress member's key role in getting legislation passed or defeated. Said the press secretary of one member of Congress, "They don't care what we do because they don't think their [audience] is interested. What we do doesn't sell papers [or TV advertising] unless it's sexy or about sex."[63] The House of Representatives addressed this issue by authorizing the televising of House sessions in 1979. The Senate is still debating the issue, fearing that deliberations will be stymied by senators' efforts to become "media stars."

For years, the adversarial relationship between the press and the courts was limited to editorial criticism of court rulings, columnists' attacks on court decisions and procedures, publication of letters to the editor blasting court rulings, and stories citing public opinion polls showing public disfavor of rulings. It was not until the publication of Woodward and Armstrong's *The Brethren*,[64] an insider's look at the personalities of the Supreme Court justices, that reporters recognized that the Supreme Court is not above and beyond politics. The book's popularity has stimulated investigative reporting in the judicial branch.

Recognizing both the press's power to change attitudes and the need for popular and elite acceptance of Court rulings, justices have adopted two strategies: "accentuate the majesty of the Court and minimize access to its inner workings."[65] Fortunately for the Court, most reporters have no legal training and are not equipped to do in-depth investigative reporting.

In one area, however, the press consistently adopts an adversarial approach to the judiciary—cases involving freedom of the press. Press freedom cases often involve conflicts between the rights of the press and individual rights (see chapter 16 on civil liberties). In such cases, media coverage definitely leans toward freedom of the press, and editorial coverage blasts court rulings that the press views as negative.

Finding the right balance between press freedom and individual rights is difficult, but no more so than finding the right balance between the mutual dependency and adversarial relationships that exist between the press and governmental institutions. Over the years, the pendulum has swung first in one direction and then the other. It is fortunate for the public that it is free enough to swing.

SUMMARY

The media play a very important role in establishing the policy agenda. By reporting the news, they help mold public opinion and public policy. Because of its power, it is often called "the fourth estate."

Americans staunchly defend the principle of freedom of the press established in the First Amendment. The public expects the press to be fair and to give minority groups and candidates equal access to the media. At the same time, the public fears government-imposed fairness and equal-time requirements because they are at odds with the ideal of absolute press freedom. There are conflicts over the correct balance between freedom of the press and individual rights to privacy and expression. The media themselves must struggle with their need to make a profit to survive and their ethical responsibility to cover unpopular persons and events.

Americans are very dependent upon the media for news. Exposure to the media influences peoples' political opinions and activism. The media either reinforce one's existing opinions or create opinions where there were none before.

Media Coverage of the Economy: Is It Impossible?

Media coverage of the economy is probably worse than its coverage of any other public policy, for several reasons. First, in both the press and the public, the level of economic understanding is low. Second, the press relies heavily upon government officials and financial documents for economic news. Third, there is a longstanding mutual distrust between the press and the business sector.

The election of Ronald Reagan, his attempts to implement supply-side economics, and the ensuing recession and recovery made the economy a major beat. It is now, as columnist Dom Bonafede notes, "the stuff of headlines. Rare is the front page that does not offer articles describing, explaining, analyzing, and correlating the twists and turns of employment, inflation, and production."[1]

The problem is that even with front-page coverage, the average person has had little economics education (although signs indicate that people want to understand the economy better). It's difficult for the media to educate the public on such a complex issue—one that not even the economists agree on. The print media have an advantage over the electronic media because they can provide more in-depth coverage. Said one TV representative, "Economics is a damn hard thing to put on television and is not easy to portray."[2] The networks say they don't have time for economics reporting because it's too complicated. Instead, they cite a few statistics, such as the level of unemployment, the Gross National Product, the inflation level, the rise in food prices, or the Dow Jones Industrial index. These statistics often seem contradictory, but the viewer is never "educated" about how they fit together. Sadly, then, the medium that reaches the most Americans is the least effective in informing them about one of the nation's most important policy issues.

This slack in TV coverage has been picked up by the country's leading newspapers and by magazines specializing in business. The *New York Times, Washington Post, Los Angeles Times,* and *Chicago Tribune* have expanded their business and financial sections and assigned their best reporters to the economic beat. Their stories have permeated the nation's newspapers, since many local newspapers, as we have seen, subscribe to their wire services and use their coverage as cues for deciding what ought to be published locally.

One common criticism of newspaper coverage of economic issues is that reporters rely too heavily upon economists. One professor at the Columbia University

[1] Dom Bonafede, "Reagan's Supply-Side Policies Push Economics Writers Into the Spotlight," *National Journal* (September 26, 1981), p. 1723.

[2] Quoted in Bonafede, *Ibid.*, p. 1727.

School of Journalism says that this causes more confusion than enlightenment:

There are always a lot of economists who are willing to talk. But this produces mutually contradictory statements which creep into the reporting. It's difficult to pin anything down. The reader can't be sure what's going on, let alone what is going to happen. If the interest rates drop, 10 different reasons are offered why. It all becomes tricky and mushy and a lot of journalists get lost in the mushiness. They report, "on the one hand this and on the other hand that."[3]

Coverage of the economy is said to be best in business-oriented newspapers, primarily the *Wall Street Journal*, and magazines such as *Fortune, Forbes,* and *Business Week.* Their advantage is that they have long had the talent, background, and experience to cover economic news. These publications have also benefited in the coverage of Reagan's supply-side economics because they were already familiar with its principles and did not regard them as new. Furthermore, business magazine writers are less likely to be biased against an economic approach that relies heavily on the business sector for implementation. (Recall that Lichter and Rothman found that the media elite regards the business community as far too powerful.) This is not to say that all business writers have endorsed supply-side economics; a number have not.

In general, the media elite—especially the Washington press corps—has been critical of supply-side economics because of its natural adversarial relationship with the president and its liberal philosophical bent. Not unexpectedly, when negative coverage led to a decline in public support for presidential economic goals, President Reagan criticized the press and tried to exert more control over the information his administration gave to the media. Reagan was particularly angry with budget director David Stockman for his "informal" conversations with a *Washington Post* writer. Stockman expressed doubts about certain aspects of supply-side economics even as he was publicly promoting them in Congress and before the public. These informal comments were published in the *Atlantic Monthly*, which sold very well when it hit the nation's newsstands. It was a classic example of the fine line between protection of a source and promotion of the public interest. Stockman thought the conversations were off the record; the *Post* writer understood them to be off the record for uses in the newspaper during the period in which the talks occurred.[4]

Economic issues can often influence international affairs, which is why presidents try to control leaks to the press. A leak about the possible imposition of a quota on foreign imports of Japanese or German cars at the very time the United States is pressuring those countries to spend more on defense would undoubtedly damage the negotiations. Press coverage of world economic issues is even more limited than coverage of domestic economic issues.[5] The world economy is more complex and difficult to understand, of course. The only hope for an informed public may be the public school systems, which have traditionally given little attention to teaching economics.

[3]*Ibid.*, p. 1724.

[4]Dom Bonafede, " 'Gross Misunderstanding,' " *National Journal* (November 21, 1981), p. 2084.
[5]Robert M. Batscha, *Foreign Affairs News and the Broadcast Journalists* (New York: Praeger 1975).

Americans rely most heavily on TV for their news; indeed, many rely on television exclusively. Yet TV is a visual medium, more a source of headlines than of in-depth coverage. People seeking in-depth coverage turn to the print media. There is concern today that too many Americans are relying on TV and getting only a superficial look at the important issues of the day, which may leave them open to manipulation by major TV networks and their broadcasting superstars. New technologies such as satellites and computers are changing the format of TV, radio, and newspapers, however, and the traditional roles of the different media may be changing.

Cross-ownership of the media and the formation of media conglomerates may be leading toward uniformity and standardization in the news. A contrary trend is the emergence of cable TV networks, specialized magazines, and public broadcasting networks for both radio and TV, which may indicate that the media are growing more specialized and diversified rather than more consolidated and standardized.

Decisions about what to call news and how to present it are left to reporters, editors and producers (gatekeepers), and media stars (anchorpersons). The power to decide what's news makes these individuals crucial actors in the policy agenda-setting process. This media elite is unrepresentative of the public at large, however, being more liberal, more educated, less religious, and more likely to come from the Northeast. Nevertheless, the majority of the population gives reporters relatively high marks for their coverage of the news.

The relationship between the media and government is both symbiotic and adversarial. The press is heavily dependent on the government for information about public affairs, and the government depends on the media to transmit information and maintain public confidence in our system. At the same time, government and the press remain suspicious of each other's motives. Much of this distrust stems from the Vietnam War and Watergate, during which both the press and the government misused each other.

In general, the media rely most heavily on middle-level bureaucrats for information. Coverage of the executive, legislative, and judicial branches varies with the medium. TV tends to focus on the president, newspapers on Congress, and neither very heavily on the courts, though this is changing.

Media coverage of economic and other issues differs because of variations in the predispositions of citizens and the press toward the issues, the technical nature of the issues, and the ease of presenting the issues to a mass public. The most difficult tasks are finding the right balance between freedom of the press and individual rights and between mutual dependency and suspicion on the part of government and the media.

KEY TERMS

background
beat system
cross-ownership
deep background
Federal Communications Commission (FCC)
fourth estate
freedom of the press
gatekeepers
general assignment (investigative reporting)
geographic zoning
leak
media conglomerate
media elite
narrowcasting
off-the-record
pack journalism
selective perception
umbrella hypothesis
video malaise
Washington information establishment

SUGGESTED READINGS

Altheide, David. *Creating Reality: How TV News Distorts Events*. Beverly Hills, Calif.: Sage Publications, 1976.

Friendly, Fred W. *The Good Guys, the Bad Guys, and the First Amendment*. New York: Random House, 1976.

Gans, Herbert J. *Deciding What's News: A Study of CBS Evening News, NBC Nightly News, Newsweek and Time*. New York: Pantheon, 1979.

Goldenberg, Edie N. *Making the Papers: The Access of Resource-Poor Groups to the Metropolitan Press*. Lexington, Mass.: D. C. Heath, Lexington Books, 1975.

Grossman, Michael B., and Kumar, Martha J. *Portraying the President: The White House and the News Media*. Baltimore, Md.: Johns Hopkins Press, 1981.

Heise, Juergen Arthur. *Minimum Disclosure: How the Pentagon Manipulates the News*. New York: W. W. Norton, 1979.

Phillips, Kevin P. *Mediacracy: American Parties and Politics in the Communication Age*. New York: Doubleday, 1975.

Rivers, William L. *The Other Government: Power and the Washington Media*. New York: Universe Books, 1982.

Robinson, Michael J. *Over the Wire and on TV: CBS and UPI in Campaign '80*. New York: Basic Books, Inc., 1982.

Roper, Burns W. *Public Perceptions of Television and Other Mass Media: A Twenty-Year Review 1959–1978*. New York: The Roper Organization, 1979.

Strouse, James C. *The Mass Media, Public Opinion, and Public Policy Analysis: Linkage Explorations*. Columbus, Ohio: Charles E. Merrill, 1975.

Williams, Frederick; LaRose, Robert; and Frost, Frederica. *Children, Television and Sex-Role Stereotyping*. New York: Praeger, 1981.

CHAPTER 11

CONGRESS

Ask the average citizen what Congress does and he or she would probably mention legislating or making laws. The image most people have is of the presiding officer sitting on the raised platform listening to the debate, gavel in hand, with the legislators arrayed in concentric semicircles around the podium. The perception of the Congress as a policymaking institution is certainly accurate, as far as it goes. Congress has a number of other functions, however, and some of them are quite important, although often overlooked.

In the course of a typical day, a legislator will perform a number of functions in several contexts. A Congress member's day may begin with a breakfast meeting with a small group of legislators who share a concern about an issue such as the maintenance of federal subsidies for tobacco farmers or how to help Frost Belt states secure a larger share of federal grant money. Following breakfast, the legislator goes to his/her suite of offices in one of the House or Senate office buildings. Here the legislator is briefed by staff members on what is scheduled on the legislative calendar for Congress and on the legislator's personal calendar for that day.

Much of the morning is spent in committee hearings or other legislative work such as discussing objectives and strategy with staff, lobbyists, constituents, colleagues, and perhaps legislative liaison personnel from the executive branch. Because the legislator may have to meet with a variety of people and more than one of the committees and subcommittees to which he/she is assigned may be meeting at the same time, the legislator may go to a hearing, ask a few questions, then rush to another committee room to help prepare a piece of legislation for the full chamber. At noon the houses of Congress convene. The legislator goes to the floor to answer the initial quorum call but is called from the floor to talk briefly with a group of students from his/her constituency who are visiting Washington. After posing with them for a group picture on the steps of the Capitol, the legislator returns to the floor, votes on an amendment, and then goes back to office via the subway that links the Capitol and the congressional office buildings.

A Congress member's day often begins with a breakfast meeting of a small group of legislators who share a concern about a specific issue and are interested in seeing their position adopted by the full Congress.

Having been told by a staffer who works in the party cloakroom that another **roll call vote** (*a recorded vote cast in a legislature*) is not likely for 45 minutes, the legislator goes to a recording studio operated for congressional use and cuts a tape to be sent to the radio stations back home. There is even time to meet with a reporter from the district, who asks questions about a press release put out by the legislator's staff earlier in the week.

During the remainder of the afternoon there are meetings with visiting constituents and staff, a swim in one of the pools that are open exclusively to members, and a meeting with several representatives of a group concerned about abortions. These activities are frequently interrupted by the ringing of bells calling members to the floor for roll calls.

That evening the legislator attends a banquet as the guest of some constituents who are in Washington attending the national convention of an organization they belong to. The legislator, after being recognized and saying a few words, slips away, goes back to the office, and changes into formal attire. The last event of the day is a reception at an embassy. It is important for the legislator to go to this function since he/she has been working with the governor's office to get a major manufacturing concern from this country to build a plant in the state that would hire several hundred of the legislator's constituents.

Four or five days a week for most of the year, members of Congress have days much like the hypothetical one outlined above. The other two or three days in most weeks, and much of the time when Congress is in recess, legislators have equally busy days back in their districts. These are spent traveling around the district, making speeches, listening to constituent complaints, and meeting with local leaders.

FUNCTIONS OF CONGRESS

Policymaking

Policymaking is the task the framers of the Constitution had in mind as the primary responsibility for the national legislature. For today's Congress, the workload of policymaking is massive. During the Ninety-Sixth Congress (1979–1980), 12,583 bills were introduced. Of the bills introduced, 929 were passed by the House and 977 were passed by the Senate. Of these, 613 public bills (legislation of general applicability) and 123 private bills (legislation aiding named individuals) were approved by both chambers and became law. In compiling this record, the House was in session for 1,876 hours. The Senate worked longer—if not harder—being in session for 2,324 hours.

The legislature can make its contribution to policy in several ways. One way is for a member or a committee to develop a new policy proposal. During the 1950s, for example, Senator Hubert Humphrey (D—Minn.) unveiled a proposal for sending young Americans abroad to share their skills with people in developing countries. This idea was subsequently embraced by the Kennedy administration and became known as the Peace Corps.

A second role for the legislature is to modify proposals developed in the executive branch. Although given a hearing, presidential proposals are only rarely rubber-stamped by Congress. Typically, presidents' requests are carefully scrutinized in one or more committees and often on the floor of one or both houses as well. During this process the bill may undergo extensive change. Consider, for example, what happened to the energy package that President Carter proposed in 1977. Several parts were deleted by Congress, and portions that remained in the final legislation bore the imprint of congressional involvement. Sometimes Congress intervenes to broaden a presidential proposal; at other times the legislation emerges from Congress minus some important elements—particularly those that are widely unpopular with the public.

In some notable instances, Congress has readily accepted the president's requests. This is most likely to happen when the nation faces a crisis. The other condition under which Congress is likely to pass legislation in the form sought by the president is when the parties interested in the bill have already compromised their differences and joined in support of the proposal.

Third, Congress can be a catalyst for social change. Between the time a new idea is seriously put forward and the time it is adopted, legislators can use committee hearings to keep the issue in the spotlight. Through these efforts, the public becomes increasingly aware both of what the legislator sees as an unmet need and of possible remedies. During this period of consciousness-raising, or policy incubation, the specifics of how the proposal would be transformed into a policy and implemented can be worked out.

The Eisenhower presidency provides an excellent illustration of how Congress can do much of the craftsmanship that precedes sweeping new programs. During the 1950s, when the president had a relatively brief agenda, Democrats in Congress were doing the groundwork for most of the items—particulary job training, health care, and civil rights—that were later enacted as part of the Great Society legislative package during the Johnson administration.[1]

During the Nixon years, Congress demon- strated its ability to play a fourth policy role. The conservative Nixon favored dismantling the War on Poverty, reining in school desegregation requirements, and reducing federal aid to education. Since these were ongoing programs authorized by Congress, the president could not unilaterally achieve his objectives. The concurrence of Congress was needed but the Democrat-controlled legislature refused to give it.[2] Thus, Congress can sustain existing programs in the face of presidential opposition either by ignoring the chief executive's proposals to reduce the programs' scope or by overriding vetoes of legislation that provides more financial support than the president wants.

Most people think of legislative policymaking as enacting legislation, but there are policy consequences even when Congress rejects proposals and refuses to act. For example, although a number of proposals have been introduced, Congress has never approved a constitutional amendment to allow prayer in public schools.

A final aspect of Congress's policymaking function is legitimation. The exploration of policy proposals, the debates focusing on the strengths, weaknesses, and potential implications of bills, the heightened public awareness that often results from the legislative process—all combine to promote acceptance of new policies. Americans' expectation that they will have an opportunity to participate in shaping the laws they live by are largely satisfied by the participation of our elected representatives.

Executive Oversight Executive *oversight* serves as a feedback loop for the policy process, *providing the legislature with information about executive branch implementation of programs it has approved.* When establishing a program, Congress sketches out the broad outlines of its intentions. The task of filling in the specifics is assigned to one or more offices in the bureaucracy. Consider, for example, the prohibition of discrimination based on sex. The relevant statute states simply that "No person in the United States shall, on the basis of sex, be excluded from participation in, be denied the benefits of, or be subjected to discrimination under any program or activity receiving federal financial assistance." The interpretation of this statute was assigned to the Department of Health, Education, and Welfare (now called the depart-

Congressional oversight of activities of the executive branch allows Congress to monitor how well the bureaucracy is carrying out legislative intent. In its investigation of the operations of the Environmental Protection Agency, Congress eventually filed charges against Rita M. Lavelle (left) for refusing to deliver certain information to Congress.

ment of Health and Human Services). HEW took three years to draft regulations, which fill up several triple-columned pages in the *Federal Register*.

Through oversight of the executive branch, Congress monitors how the bureaucracy is carrying out legislative intent. By reviewing program implementation, Congress can determine if the administration is more lax or more vigorous, more encompassing or too narrow, than had been intended. Likewise, Congress can discern whether the legislation fails to have the desired effect or produces unanticipated hardships. If problems are found, new legislation can be passed to correct the deficiencies. Evidence that the Civil Rights Act of 1957 was not facilitating the registration of black voters in the South led to the passage of three subsequent acts, which with increasing precision prohibited the techniques used to disenfranchise blacks. On the other hand, monitoring of the food stamp program has convinced Congress that, as originally enacted, the standards for participation were too broad. It was estimated that eligibility standards permitted as many as 41 million people to receive a grocery subsidy in 1975.[3] By redefining eligibility, Congress eliminated some potential beneficiaries.

Representation of Local Interests Members of Congress tend to have deep roots in the areas they represent, often having spent most of their lives in the district or state. Not surprisingly, this long association results in a special concern for the economic well-being of their constituency. Our national legislators learned long ago not to blatantly oppose the economic interests of their districts if they wish to be reelected.

Today, members of Congress try to secure federal projects for their districts. Indeed, a national survey conducted in conjunction with the 1978 congressional elections found that one voter in seven believed that a legislator's most important activity was to "make sure the district gets its fair share of government money and projects."[4] Rural districts are dotted with new post offices; cities are blessed with new federal office buildings, which in time may be named in honor of the legislator who secured the construction funds. These kinds of projects are tangible evidence of the legislator's effectiveness in bringing home the bacon. By participating in ground-breaking and ribbon-cutting ceremonies and releasing press announcements of federal grants coming to the district, legislators publicize their names and claim credit for the benefits conferred.

Constituent Liaison Activities A legislator also engages in activities designed to assist any constituent who has a problem. On Capitol Hill, the liaison function is more commonly referred to as *casework*. Each congressional office has one or more caseworkers, who *process requests and complaints from constituents*. Many of these communications from constituents concern a problem with the bureaucracy such as some holdup in getting veterans' or Social Security benefits.

When legislators receive letters seeking intervention with the bureaucracy, they are typically referred to the legislative liaison office of the appropriate agency with a "buck slip" (form letter) attached identifying the congressional office making the inquiry. Other letters request information—copies of bills, documents published by Congress or federal agencies, or materials relevant to a national debate topic.

Constituent liaison activities may aid legislators in their executive oversight efforts. Questions based on complaints from constituents can be asked of bureaucrats when they come before congressional committees seeking budget increases. The problems encountered by a constituent may prove to be a loose thread which, when pulled by a persistent legislator, exposes a widespread pattern of inefficiency or misfeasance.[5]

Most congressional offices take their casework very seriously. Many have a standing rule that every letter be acknowledged on the day it is received, even though it may take longer to fulfill the writer's request. It is easy to see why so much attention is given to casework. Unlike policymaking, in which a legislator's vote may please some constituents but alienate others, and oversight, which may displease segments of the bureaucracy and their powerful allies among interest groups, casework has very few costs to offset its sizable rewards.

Other Functions In addition to the activities described above, other functions are performed by Congress. Individual legislators and sometimes committees may function as representatives of economic interests. For example, many legislators from rural areas and the agriculture committees in the two chambers work to protect the interest of farmers just as interest groups such as the American Farm Bureau Federation and the National Farmers Union do. Similar patterns exist for oil, banking, the military, and some manufacturing interests. Economic interests that have a set of legislators or, even better, a committee to look out for them may enjoy better representation and more favorable policies than they could achieve even if they had unlimited resources to invest in lobbying.

Impeachment is another type of activity in which Congress members participate, though infrequently. The power to impeach presidents, vice-presidents, and federal judges for "high crimes and misdemeanors" is a powerful congressional sanction. In July, 1974, the House Judiciary Committee voted to recommend to the full House that Richard Nixon be impeached for 1) obstruction of justice in the Watergate investigation, 2) abuse of power in dealings with the FBI and the Internal Revenue Service, and 3) contempt of Congress for refusing to make available materials that Congress had subpoenaed.

Had the House concurred in the judgment of its Judiciary Committee and impeached the president, the trial on these charges would have been conducted before the Senate with the chief justice of the Supreme Court presiding. A two-thirds

Impeachment and conviction of high-ranking executive and judicial officials is a responsibility of Congress. The closest Congress has come to impeaching a president since the 1800s was when the House Judiciary Committee (above) voted to impeach Richard Nixon for his involvement in the Watergate affair. Nixon resigned before the full House could vote on the Committee's recommendation.

vote is needed to convict. In our history, only 1 president (Andrew Johnson) and 11 judges have been impeached; of these, 4 judges were convicted and removed from office.

The power to impeach a president or a judge, like other functions of legislators, places a tremendous responsibility in the hands of those we elect to Congress. This raises the important question of just who are these people that we entrust to make major policy decisions.

THE PERSONNEL OF CONGRESS

The 535 voting members of Congress (100 senators and 435 representatives)* are in some ways a diverse group, but their diversity is less than we would find if the membership of Congress were randomly drawn from the nation's population. The explanation for the types of people found in Congress does not lie in the Constitution—the preconditions specified there are minimal. A representative must be at least 25 and a senator at least 30 years of age. Both sets of legislators must be United States citizens—representatives for at least seven years and senators for nine years. Members of Congress must also reside in the state they represent, but there is no specification about how long they must have lived in the state before representing it in Congress. Robert Kennedy adopted New York as his home shortly before winning one of its Senate seats.

There is greater variety in other legislator characteristics, although certain trends are clearly apparent. The backgrounds of the men and women who serve in Congress are important to the extent that they influence how they vote on certain kinds of issues. In discussing the predominant characteristics in the backgrounds of members of Congress, we will be sensitive to the policy implications.

An important consideration in assessing the influence of background is whether Congress should be a place of passive or active representation.[6] In passive representation, the legislator shares the characteristics of the group that he or she represents. According to this perspective, only a woman could adequately represent the views of

women or a black, the views of blacks. Active representation occurs when a legislator articulates the interests of a group in society even though not a member of that group. Examples of active representation include the late Senator Hubert Humphrey's (D—Minn.) work on behalf of civil rights legislation designed to benefit blacks and Senator Edward Kennedy's interest in programs for the poor.

Occupations

Members of Congress are drawn disproportionately from a few job categories, and most occupations are substantially underrepresented. Lawyers are the group most overrepresented in Congress (see Table 11.1). While less than 1 percent of the workers in the United States are lawyers, approximately half of the national legislators in recent Congresses have been attorneys.

There are several reasons that so many lawyers are elected to Congress. Lawyers enjoy relatively high prestige, and they are experienced in working with statutes and in trying to resolve conflict. If defeated, they can usually return to their law practices, and even when they lose they may make new contacts that bring them new clients. The number of lawyers in Congress and state legislatures has become so great that many students who aspire to careers in politics go to law school believing that this will enhance their chances once they become candidates.

The second largest occupational group in Congress consists of people engaged in business or banking. There are also sizable numbers of educators and people who have spent their entire adult lives in some form of public employment. One former Congressmember believes there are too many career public servants now in Congress. He calls these members "Boy Scouts" and charges that they are "young kids who never earned a buck anywhere except at the public trough, and have no confidence in their ability to earn a living. They will always have no place to go [i.e., nothing to fall back on if defeated], and therefore they will always be frightened."[7]

The number of farmers serving in Congress continues to decline as America's population becomes increasingly urban. The number of farmers fell to 7 percent in 1983. That the number of farmers is decreasing may account for recent changes in agriculture policy. The subsidy

---

*In addition to the voting members, there are nonvoting delegates in the House from the District of Columbia, American Samoa, Guam, and the Virgin Islands, plus a resident commissioner from Puerto Rico.

TABLE 11.1

Occupations of Members of Congress

	92d Congress 1971–72	98th Congress 1983–84	Population
Attorneys	56%*	49%	0.3%
Banking and business	32	33	2.0
Public service	NA**	10	0.3
Educators	13	10	4.2
Farmers	9	7	1.8
Journalists	7	5	0.3
Medicine	1	1	0.7
Engineers	1	1	1.6
Ministers	0.4	1	0.3
Engineering/aeronautical scientists	0	2	0.3
Other	1	2	88.0

SOURCE: Computed from data reported in issues of *Congressional Quarterly Weekly Reports*.

*Columns for Congresses total more than 100 percent since some members list more than one occupation.

**NA = Not available.

farmers receive for not producing crops has been restricted, for example.

Clearly the groups most common in Table 11.1 are from higher status occupations. As a result, higher status citizen groups are more likely to find one of their own to bring their views before the Congress. Passive representation of this sort may be especially important on questions that directly affect an occupation's earning capacity. For example, lawyers have opposed proposals for national no-fault auto insurance, which would greatly reduce suits for damages caused by wrecks. Since such litigation is usually handled on a contingency basis with the lawyer receiving a third to a half of the settlement, no-fault legislation poses an economic threat, particularly to trial lawyers.

Affluence

As part of the reform movement to make Congress and its activities more open to public inspection, the financial assets of our national legislators have been made available for public inspection. These newly available data confirm suspicions that most members of Congress are well off. The reporting forms do not require legislators to reveal the exact size of their holdings and incomes; they indicate, rather, the nature and size of their holdings in broad categories. A conservative estimate is that there are at least 25 millionaires in the Senate. A mere handful had a net worth of less than $50,000.

Some wealthy legislators are the heirs of family fortunes, including the Senate's wealthiest member, John Heinz (R—Pa.), of the pickle and catsup family, followed by John Danforth (R—Mo.), whose family made its fortune with Ralston Purina. Others who amassed fortunes before entering politics include Senator Charles Percy (R—Ill.), who headed Bell and Howell before seeking public office; Senator Rudy Boschwitz (R—Minn.), who made his fortune in plywood; and Senator Bill Bradley (D—N.J.), who got his start playing basketball for the New York Knicks.

There are two perspectives on the policymaking consequences of having affluent decision-makers. Some argue that wealthy legislators will vote for the self-interest of their class so as to maintain if not enlarge income inequality.[8] Alternatively, there is evidence from popular voting on local bond referenda which suggests that the upper class is more willing than the middle class to support programs that primarily benefit the poor.[9] The active support by the Kennedy brothers of an array of social programs including national health insurance exemplifies this latter interpretation.

Religion

Twenty-six percent of the Congress is Roman Catholic, while approximately 7 percent is Jewish. Among Protestants, the largest denominations are Methodists (14 percent), Episcopalians (12 percent), Presbyterians (11 percent), and Baptists (9 percent). The religious groups that are overrepresented tend to be the higher status ones.

 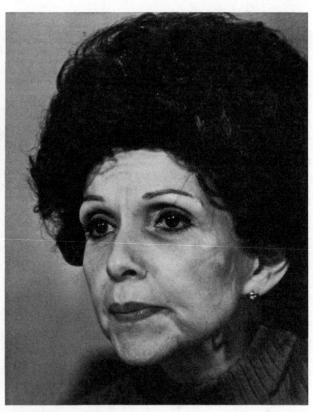

Relative to their proportional makeup in the population, women are underrepresented in Congress. Only two women senators, Nancy Kessebaum (R—Kansas) and Paula Hawkins (R—Florida) served in the 98th Congress.

A legislator's religion may influence his or her stands on several policy issues. Catholics have more often opposed programs that facilitate abortion and have sought legislation allowing parochial schools to receive federal education funds. Jewish legislators have been in the vanguard of those concerned about military aid to Israel and its neighbors. Fundamentalists have been more likely to introduce constitutional amendments intended to permit religious exercises in the public schools, while Catholic and Jewish members have tended to oppose such initiatives.

Gender

Like state legislatures, Congress is a predominantly male institution. In 1983 there were two women in the Senate and 21 in the House, the largest number of women to serve in Congress at one time.

In the past, many congresswomen succeeded their husbands when they died in office. Prior to 1940, half the women who had served in Congress arrived by this route, but between 1965 and 1976 only a fifth were widows of a previous incumbent.[10] Widows have tended to have less political experience than other congresswomen. They are also less likely to seek reelection and less likely to be lawyers.[11] Female legislators are more likely to support items designed to promote educational and occupational opportunities for women.

Race

In 1978 Edward Brooke (R—Mass.), the only black senator to serve in the last century, was defeated. However, the number of black representatives (20) has grown slowly. It is not likely in the foreseeable future that black representation in Congress will rise to 11 percent, the percentage of the general population that is black.

To maximize their influence, black representatives, along with the black nonvoting delegate from the District of Columbia, have created the

Black Caucus. This organization researches policy options of interest to blacks, encourages bloc voting by blacks, and helps focus public attention on black interests. Black representatives tend to be liberal and have actively supported a wide range of social programs as well as civil rights issues.

Age

The turnover in recent congresses—more than half the House members serving in the Ninety-Eighth Congress had been elected since 1974—has led to a decrease in the age of Congress members. In 1983 the mean age in the House was 45.5, 7.9 years below the Senate mean. Ages in the House ranged from 28 to 83. Don Nickles (R—Okla.) at 35 was the youngest senator, while 82-year-old John Stennis (D—Miss.) was the oldest. The average age of the House fell by seven years between 1971 and 1983.

As the number of retirees in the nation grows, we increasingly hear references to "grey power." Congress registered its responsiveness to older Americans in 1977 when it followed the leadership of 77-year-old Rep. Claude Pepper (D—Fla.) and repealed legislation that allowed employers to use 65 as the age for mandatory retirement.

Age may also lead legislators to respond differently to the funding crisis in Social Security. Older members, if representative of their age group, will want to keep Social Security mandatory and benefits high; younger members may be more likely to take the opposite side of these issues.

How much each of these factors—occupation, religion, gender, race, income, and age—affect each Congress member's vote on policy issues is often contingent on how closely they "match" the profile of the constituents back home who elect them.

CONGRESSIONAL ELECTIONS

They are the method of selecting policymakers and they enable the electorate to hold their leaders accountable. The use of elections to enforce accountability has certain preconditions. The first is that incumbents must find their jobs sufficiently attractive that they will attempt to hold on to them. Second, the electorate must evaluate incumbents and challengers on some dimension rel-

evant to policy. In this section we shall see to what extent elections are used to promote accountability and assess the factors that influence the outcomes of House and Senate races.

Security of House Incumbents

Members of the U.S. House of Representatives are among the most secure officeholders in any of the world's democracies. As can be seen in Table 11.2, at least 85 percent of the House incumbents who have sought reelection since 1950 have triumphed. In six of the last seven elections, the success rate has exceeded 90 percent, peaking at almost 97 percent in 1968.

This phenomenal success rate has been accompanied by a decline in the number of truly competitive districts.[12] Since 1966, the number of districts in which the representative wins less than 55 percent of the vote has decreased and the number of districts observers classify as "safe" has increased. This has occurred even while Republicans have been gaining strength in the South and Democrats have been making inroads in traditionally Republican strongholds in New England and the Midwest.

Susceptibility of Senate Incumbents

Since World War II, senators have been much less successful than representatives when running for reelection. Given that we assume that senators are more powerful compared to the more numerous and less prestigious representatives, the results for the Senate presented in Table 11.2 may come as a surprise. In only two elections since 1946 have senators fared better than representatives. How can we account for the interchamber differences in reelection rates?

Political scientists who have studied congressional elections have concluded that the major factor in these differences is the calibre of opposition.[13] Survey research carried out in 1978 found that candidates who ran against incumbent senators were almost as well known to the electorate as the incumbents. In contrast, representatives' challengers, even after the campaign, were recognized by less than half the voters. A similar disparity turns up if we consider how voters feel about candidates. The "feeling thermometer," which asks voters to place their attitudes about a candidate on a scale that runs from 0 (very negative) to 100 (very positive) is one method of getting voters' re-

TABLE 11.2

The Advantage of Incumbency in the House and Senate, 1946–1982

	House				Senate			
Year	Seeking Reelection	Defeated Primary	General	Percent Reelected*	Seeking Reelection	Defeated Primary	General	Percent Reelected*
1946	398	18	52	82.4	30	6	7	56.7
1948	400	15	68	79.2	25	2	8	60.0
1950	400	6	32	90.5	32	5	5	68.8
1952	389	9	26	91.0	31	2	9	64.5
1954	407	6	22	93.1	32	2	6	75.0
1956	411	6	16	94.6	29	0	4	86.2
1958	396	3	37	89.9	28	0	10	64.3
1960	405	5	25	92.6	29	0	1	96.6
1962	402	12	22	91.5	35	1	5	82.9
1964	397	8	45	86.6	33	1	4	84.8
1966	411	8	41	88.1	32	3	1	87.5
1968	409	4	9	96.8	28	4	4	71.4
1970	401	10	12	94.5	31	1	6	77.4
1972	390	12	13	93.6	27	2	5	74.1
1974	391	8	40	87.7	27	2	2	85.2
1976	384	3	13	95.8	25	0	9	64.0
1978	382	5	19	93.7	25	3	7	60.0
1980	398	6	31	90.7	29	4	9	55.2
1982	387	4	29	91.5	30	0	2	93.3
Mean				90.7				74.1

SOURCE: *Congressional Quarterly Weekly Report*, April 5, 1980, p. 908 and November 8, 1980, pp. 3302, 3320–3321, as published in Barbara Hinckley, *Congressional Elections* (Washington, D.C.: Congressional Quarterly Press, 1981), p. 39. Data for 1982 added by authors.

*Counting both primary and general election defeats.

actions to candidates. Voters are more than four times as likely to feel warmly toward House incumbents than they are to their challengers. Senators are more closely matched by their challengers. The same pattern exists if we look at whether voters have had contact with the candidates.

In essence, then, it appears that the differences in the reelection rates of House and Senate incumbents bear out an old adage of politics: "You can't beat somebody with nobody." House challengers are frequently "nobodies" who go through the campaign so underfunded that they have little contact with the voters and consequently evoke a positive response among only about 25 percent of the voters. Senate challengers run races that make them competitive with the incumbents by election day.

Factors in Voter Choice

A quarter of a century ago when political scientists began studying voter preferences in congressional elections, a very simple explanation of these preferences emerged. Congressional races were influenced by extraneous factors. In presidential election years, through the presidential "coattails" phenomenon, a popular candidate for the presidency would bring into office numerous House and Senate candidates who shared his party label. In off-year elections when the stimulus of a popular presidential candidate like Dwight Eisenhower was absent, voters responded in line with their partisan affiliations. From 1956 through 1962 at least 80 percent of the voters in House races chose their party's candidate. Since 1972, however, no more than 75 percent of the voters in House elections have stood behind their party's nominee. The growing number of defectors has created a more fluid situation in which party identification plays a lesser role in determining election outcomes.

Survey data on recent congressional elections reveals that party identification remains important, although the number of voters for whom it is determinative has declined. As discussed in chapter 6 party may be most important to voters who know little about either candidate.[14]

A second finding, one that is not terribly surprising, is that voters support the candidate they like best. Personal characteristics, experience, and—especially among incumbents—performance on the job are items that voters frequently cite when explaining what they like and dislike about candidates. Hinckley sums up the thrust of responses about likes and dislikes with the following: "People have a lot to say about liking incumbents, not too much to say about disliking them, and not much to say about challengers at all."[15]

The amount of contact voters have had with a candidate is a third factor likely to influence their predispositions. It seems logical that the factors that produce likes and dislikes derive from contacts with competing candidates. The kinds of contact that are related to voters' choices include having met the individual, having received something in the mail, and having seen the candidate on television. Incumbents realize how important

TABLE 11.3

Influence of Assessments of the Incumbent's Performance on Vote in 1978 House Elections*

Relevant Responses	Assessment of Performance		Distribution of Responses (%)	Voting for Incumbent (%)
General Job Performance				
89.7		Very good	22.1	98.0
		Good	48.5	88.0
		Fair	24.6	60.6
		Poor	3.9	19.2
		Very poor	0.9	33.3
District Services				
87.6	Expectations about incumbent's helpfulness in solving voter's problem	Very helpful	41.3	92.6
		Somewhat helpful	47.6	76.3
		Not very helpful	7.9	34.6
		It depends	3.2	81.0
21.5	Level of satisfaction with response to voter-initiated contact	Very satisfied	65.1	94.8
		Somewhat satisfied	27.5	80.5
		Not very satisfied	4.9	28.6
		Not at all satisfied	2.7	25.0
28.4	Level of friend's satisfaction with response	Very satisfied	84.2	89.7
		Somewhat satisfied	9.3	88.3
		Not very satisfied	1.0	0.0
		Not at all satisfied	5.4	60.0
	Could voter recall anything special incumbent did for the district?	Yes	31.1	86.3
		No	68.3	75.0
Voting and Policy				
56.9	General agreement or disagreement with incumbent's votes	Agree	25.1	97.2
		Agree somewhat	49.3	87.1
		Neither	15.6	62.9
		Disagree somewhat	7.2	51.6
		Disagree	3.8	25.0
16.1	Agreed or disagreed with vote on a particular bill	Agreed	69.4	94.0
		Disagreed	30.6	43.2
27.3	Which candidate would do better job on most important problem?	Incumbent	80.0	97.6
		Challenger	20.0	4.9
16.2	Ideological proximity	Closer to incumbent	56.2	92.6
		Closer to challenger	43.8	22.6

SOURCE: Gary C. Jacobson, "Incumbents' Advantages in the 1978 U.S. Congressional Elections," *Legislative Studies Quarterly*, 6 (May 1981), p. 188.
*n = 749

it is to maintain contact with their constituents. On average, House members spend parts of 23 weeks in their districts each year, and members of Congress send out more than 400 million pieces of mail in an election year.[16] Contact promotes familiarity with the candidates' names and familiarity is a factor in voter choice.

A fourth factor is the way an incumbent has performed the constituent liaison role or how a nonincumbent might be expected to perform in this sphere. Fifth, voters are somewhat more likely to vote for a candidate they believe to be closer to them ideologically.[17]

On a number of the items discussed thus far, the more favorable the voter's assessment of a representative's performance, the more likely the voter is to back the incumbent. This point is demonstrated by the figures in the last column of Table 11.3. This table also reveals that House incumbents are rated quite highly by voters in a broad range of areas. Gary Jacobson, who prepared this table, concludes that "Everything incumbents do appears to help them win support."[18] The only items in the table on which incumbents are not favored overwhelmingly by their constituents are ideological proximity and recall of special services performed by the incumbent for the district. These, however, do not appreciably weaken the incumbent. Only a sixth of the voters mentioned ideological proximity. On the other item, three-fourths of the voters who were unable to think of a special service nonetheless voted for the incumbent.

In explaining their votes in congressional races, voters infrequently discuss policy issues. In the 1978 survey, only 221 of 2,304 people questioned remembered how their representative had voted on a particular bill.[19] Of these, two-thirds supported the incumbent's action. The policymaking role, then, does not seem to be a determining factor in most voters' minds. Nonetheless, there are races in which a stand taken by the legislator becomes the key issue in the campaign. Incumbents in the South who were believed to be weak supporters of segregation were turned out of office by angry white voters a generation ago. In 1980, groups operating under the broad title of the Moral Majority claimed credit for defeating several liberal senators.

It is not always easy to make direct linkages between preferences of the voters and the policy stands taken by individual Congress members. As we shall see, another important factor—future ambition—may often intervene.

LEGISLATOR GOALS

Regardless of their background characteristics, the goals and interests of legislators influence their legislative performance. Richard Fenno has identified four basic goals that guide legislators in deciding how to allocate their time among the various demands confronting them.[20]

Reelection

One goal is to have a long career in the legislature. A person might correctly observe that since members of Congress rarely display a willingness to risk defeat, reelection is a goal for all but a few aged or jaded members. A useful distinction may be that while reelection is always a concern, some members have no other concern. The legislator for whom reelection is almost the exclusive concern is more likely to emphasize activities designed to promote favorable name recognition among constituents. This type of legislator may concentrate on being an effective constituent liaison, advertising his or her services as the constituents' intermediary in dealing with the bureaucracy.[21] The service-oriented legislator may bring services to constituents by establishing district offices where people can tell their problems to a sympathetic caseworker. These representatives may also spend more time in their districts.

The service orientation spills over into these members' legislative activities. Legislative efforts will be concentrated on the work of committees that provide jobs or other financial benefits for their districts. Examples are Agriculture, which is responsible for crop subsidies, Interior, which approves irrigation and reclamation projects and the use of federal land holdings for grazing, mining, and timbering (all of these are of concern to westerners), and Public Works, which authorizes all manner of federal construction projects. In return for promoting the economic interests of the district, the legislator hopes to receive praise from the media, campaign contributions, and votes.

Policymaking

A second goal of legislators is to participate in the shaping of public policy because of genuine interest in the subject matter rather than because of anticipated electoral payoffs. Policy-oriented legislators are likely to emphasize different functions than members who are concerned almost exclusively with reelection. Legislators can satisfy their policy interests by helping write and perfect legislation or by monitoring the implementation of programs previously passed by Congress. Legislators interested in establishing policies for financial institutions or in trying to devise answers to the problems faced by our deteriorating core cities have been attracted to committees such as Banking, Finance, and Urban Affairs (Banking, Housing, and Urban Affairs in the Senate). Since the most interesting policy questions are often marked by heated controversy, work on some policy-oriented committees may hurt a legislator's election chances. The House Education and Labor Committee has provided a fine arena in which outspoken Democrats and Republicans could square off on issues such as labor-management relations and federal aid to education. The Judiciary committees have dealt with the Equal Rights Amendment, abortion, and school busing to promote racial balance, all emotional issues. These kinds of issues are likely to divide one's constituents, so that regardless of which side the legislator endorses, some constituents will be alienated.

Many newer legislators have been elected following campaigns in which they emphasized their policy interests. When these members are in their districts, they prefer to debate or explain their positions. Their behavior is quite unlike that of service-oriented legislators, who use constituent contacts to seek out opportunities to be of service to their districts.[22] While many legislators begin their congressional careers concerned predominantly with policy, others only assign higher priority to this facet after a few years on the job when they have assured themselves that they can be reelected with less emphasis on constituent service.

Some legislators combine their policy interests with servicing their constituents. For example, a member interested in national defense policy who represents a district that has a number of military bases may find that pursuit of personal policy interests produces benefits for the district.

Influence in Congress

Third, some legislators' chief interest is to secure influence and prestige in their chamber. This goal can be realized in several ways—by being chosen to a position of party leadership (these jobs will be discussed shortly) or by working one's way up to a leadership position on a committee. Party leaders and those who chair committees and subcommittees have more influence than rank and file members on both the content of specific bills and on deciding which items will be placed on the policy agenda. They enjoy extra staff and receive more media attention. They also are in a position to advance or hinder the careers of their colleagues.

Party leaders tend to be selected from among their party's moderates. Some, notably, current Senate minority leader Robert Byrd (D—W.Va.) and one of his predecessors, Lyndon Johnson, were chosen largely because of their skill in helping other senators achieve their objectives.

Achieving a leadership position typically takes 10 to 20 years. A goal that can be attained earlier in the career of a legislator who aspires to become powerful in Congress is appointment to a prestigious committee. The most sought-after assignments are to committees dealing with spending, taxation, and, in the Senate, foreign policy. The committees that handle money in both chambers have extraordinary influence over a broad range of public policy. The near-universal breadth of these committees' responsibilities gives them a degree of control over the destinies of the pet projects of individual legislators and over the successes of the proposals of other committees. A member of the Appropriations Committee explained how other legislators behave toward members on Appropriations: "They are very polite to us. They've all got projects in over here and they know what we can do to them."[23]

Progressive Ambition

A fourth goal is to win higher office. Since World War II, the Senate has always boasted a number of serious aspirants to the presidency. Since 1970, an average of ten House members have given up their seats to run for the Senate or a governorship each election year.

A legislator who has progressive ambition will use his or her office to attract a larger following. Senators who believe that the mantle of the presidency fits them must become known nationally. For House members aspiring to become senators or governors, an essential step is to develop statewide name recognition.

The approach ambitious congress members take to further their political careers varies. Because of the president's role in foreign policy and the large stakes in this area, senators with presidential ambitions consider it valuable to serve on the Foreign Relations Committee, regardless of how active a part they take. Legislators who covet higher offices may work to develop an image of being responsive to broad economic interests or pledge loyalty to social principles broadly accepted within their party. One representative eager to move from the House to the Senate publicized his concern for his constituents—both those he represented and those he would like to represent as senator—by hiring a printer, buying a press, and churning out an endless stream of publications. He blanketed the state with these publications through the use of the *frank, the congressmember's authority to send mail at no charge by attaching a facsimile of his or her signature to the envelope.*

NORMS

Many aspects of legislative behavior are guided by *norms, unwritten, widely accepted standards of behavior.* Norms encourage legislators to perform unglamorous tasks that need to be done for the good of the chamber. A second function of norms is to promote good working relations among members. Since the decisions made in Congress at times involve the most controversial topics confronting society and can determine the political careers of protagonists, passions may run high. Some norms channel strong feelings so that opponents do not so poison the legislature's atmosphere that it ceases to function.

Since norms are unwritten, unofficial standards of behavior for legislators, they must also be enforced through informal means. Penalties assessed against flagrant norm violators include ostracism and loss of respect and influence. Norm violators may also find that their colleagues are unwilling to approve pet projects and legislation for them. Some of the more important norms are explained below.

Seniority

The *seniority norm allocates positions of committee leadership on the basis of members' length of continuous service in Congress.* It promotes stability by guaranteeing that members of Congress can, if they wish, remain on a committee year after year. A result of the seniority norm is that committees are generally chaired by the member of the majority party who has been on the committee the longest.

The seniority norm has reduced competition for committee chairs among a group of very ambitious people. It has also insured that those who lead committees and subcommittees have been exposed to the subject matter for which they are responsible.

Seniority is not, however, a guarantee that those who chair committees are well suited for the task. Some have been outstanding and could have won their posts through an election by committee members while others have been disinterested, dolts, or petty tyrants. A generation ago when committee leaders had few checks on their power, they could and occasionally did use their positions to obstruct the will of a majority of their fellow committee members, the Congress, and the American people. Today such unresponsiveness would not be tolerated; the members would choose a less senior but more democratic leader.

Specialization and Reciprocity

These two norms go hand in hand. *Specialization is the norm that encourages members of Congress to become experts in a few policy areas. Reciprocity is the norm that encourages legislators to help one another achieve their objectives.* Members are usually encouraged to specialize in some aspect of public policy dealt with by one of the committees on which they serve. As their chamber's specialist, they are responsible for reviewing legislative proposals in a particular sphere. They may also take the lead in developing legislation in their area of specialization. Senator Edmund Muskie (D—Maine), for example, dominated environmental politics for many years.

Specialization is also useful since it discourages widespread participation on most issues. If every member felt a need to speak out on every issue, the pace of Congress would be even slower that it is. Therefore, it is expected that members will not become actively involved in issues unless they have some expertise, their constituency is affected, or the issue is widely controversial. This aspect of specialization has been increasingly ignored by ambitious senators who feel they must speak out loudly and often to attract the media coverage necessary to make their dream of living in the White House a reality.

Specialization is not only useful to the chamber by providing it with experts who can challenge those from the bureaucracy and private interests; it also pays dividends to the specialists. Other members defer to specialists in their spheres of expertise, which gives them great influence in shaping congressional action on these items. This deference to the specialist is reflected in the norm of reciprocity.

Reciprocity also shows up in mutual log-rolling, in which members help one another pass legislation and obtain projects that will secure their positions with their voters. At its extreme, reciprocity results in public works bills that include a highway, federal building, or feasibility study for every state and most congressional districts.

Work Horse

When studying the Senate in the late 1950s, Donald Matthews observed that some of the senators who enjoyed greatest respect among their colleagues were largely unknown outside the institution.[24] The "work horses" who tended to the sometimes dull legislative work and saw to it that the Senate performed its responsibilities were held in high regard by other senators. In contrast, the "show horse" senators who courted the limelight, frequently made speeches, and traveled widely across the country were seen as dilettantes and were taken less seriously by other senators.

The approval given to the work horses is critical in getting members to perform the drudgery that often accompanies hearings, the perfection of legislative proposals, and oversight of the executive branch. If all members were show horses, the Senate would suffer in its dealings with the House and the executive branch.

Mutual Respect

Occasionally there are shouting matches on the floors of Congress, and in the past there have been rare outbursts of violence. Today the norms provide for behavioral patterns that allow legislators to disagree without being disagreeable. In an effort to keep disagreements from escalating, all statements made on the floor of either house are addressed to the presiding officer and not to one's opponent. A second feature is that speakers refer to one another by title and not by name. Going along with this is the custom of praising colleagues when referring to them. Thus, one refers to "the most distinguished senior senator from California" or "my esteemed colleague from Texas." This mode of address crosses party lines and helps keep partisanship from becoming too disruptive.

The norm of mutual respect also provides that legislators minimize personal criticisms of colleagues. Legislators have been very tolerant of some members' alcoholism, womanizing, and cheating the system. The houses of Congress reluctantly approve ethics requirements only when public pressures become irresistible.

Norms That Now Have Little Weight

Some norms that were once important are now largely ignored. Probably the best-known victim of changing times has been apprenticeship. This norm denied first-term legislators access to most of the desirable committees. It also prescribed that new legislators, like young children, should be seen and not heard. Legislators were expected to sit back and master the subject matter and proper behavior by observing what senior members did. They were not to become active participants in committee work or on the floor until they had been in Congress for several years.

These expectations were unacceptable to the more policy-oriented generation of legislators elected to Congress in the 1970s.[25] With the congressional workload increasing and the range of federal policies expanding, senior members acknowledge the need for full involvement of all members. This was particularly true in the Senate, where many established members are busy trying to fan the spark of presidential ambition into a brush fire of popular support.

Institutional patriotism is another norm which has become less important. Fenno has pointed out that many incumbents now seek reelection by running against Congress.[26] Representatives have discovered that they can capitalize on negative popular perceptions of Congress and its unpopular policy decisions while pointing out that they, as individuals, are among the few bright stars in what voters may see as a generally gloomy heaven. Once elected, however, they learn very quickly that one voice or vote is not sufficient to achieve their policy objectives. They must learn to work within the congressional organizational framework.

Prior to 1910, Speakers of the House had unlimited power to name committee members, designate committee chairpersons, and assign legislation to committees. Now Speakers (including the current Speaker, Tip O'Neill (D—Mass.) must strive to rule more by consensus than personal power.

CONGRESSIONAL ORGANIZATION

As mentioned in the previous section, there are two types of leaders in Congress: party leaders and committee leaders.

Party Leadership

In each chamber and for each party there is a separate leadership hierarchy (see Table 11.4). In the House, the presiding officer is the *Speaker of the House, who is selected from among the House membership and is the leader of the majority party*. Prior to the revolt against Speaker Joe Cannon (R—Ill.) in 1910, the Speaker had almost unlimited power to name committee members, designate committee chairpersons, and assign legislation to committees. Cannon's abuse of these powers (scholars call his term the era of czar rule) led to reforms which stripped the Speaker of most of his authority. Today the Speaker is much less powerful and must strive to rule by consensus rather than by strong-arming. They preside over House sessions and have limited authority in assigning legislation to committees. Speakers also participate in the scheduling of items for floor debate.

The legislators in each party also choose a *floor leader*. The *majority floor leader in the House is the heir apparent to the Speaker. The minority floor leader stands ready to become Speaker should the minority party win control of the legislature*. In the Senate, the floor leaders are the leaders of the minority and majority parties. Floor leaders try to encourage unity among their party's members on policy items on which there is a party position. Assisting the floor leaders are the whips. Each party has a chief whip who has several deputies. The *whip* organizations *are responsible for distributing information to party members on the legislation that will be voted on during the forthcoming week, along with relevant background information*. Whips also poll members before important roll calls to determine how the rank and file are likely to vote. They encourage members who plan to support the party's position to be present for roll calls.

The same organizational pattern is found in the Senate except that there is not a speaker. The Constitution provides that the vice-president is the Senate's presiding officer. In the absence of the vice-president, the chief officer is the president pro tempore, who by custom is the member of the majority party with the most years of service. Strom Thurmond (R—S.C.) held this position during the Ninety-Eighth Congress. In practice, neither of these people actually spends much time presiding over the Senate. The vice-president is likely to attend only when a close roll call vote is anticipated since he can vote only to break a tie.

Several committees play a role in the party hierarchy of Congress. The most important is the House Democratic Caucus, which is composed of all House Democrats. After lying dormant for almost half a century, the Caucus was revitalized by young, liberal Democrats who used it to impose greater partisan coherence. On the eve of the

TABLE 11.4

Party Leaders in the 98th Congress

Democrats	Republicans

House

Speaker—Thomas P. (Tip) O'Neill (Mass.)
Majority Leader—Jim Wright (Tex.)   Minority Leader—Robert Michel (Ill.)
Majority Whip—Thomas Foley (Wash.)   Minority Whip—Trent Lott (Miss.)
Caucus Chair—Gillis Long (La.)   Conference Chair—Jack Kemp (N.Y.)

Senate

Minority Leader—Robert Byrd (W.Va.)   Majority Leader—Howard Baker (Tenn.)
Minority Whip—Alan Cranston (Calif.)   Majority Whip—Ted Stevens (Alaska)
     President Pro Tempore—Strom
     Thurmond (S.C.)

Ninety-Fourth Congress, the Caucus removed three conservative southerners as committee chairs. The Caucus has also provided a forum for working out Democratic positions such as opposition to further military involvement in Southeast Asia. The chairperson of the Caucus is elected by the members; during the Ninety-Eighth Congress it was Gillis Long (D—La.).

The House Republican Conference, chaired in 1983 and 1984 by Jack Kemp (R—N.Y.), is similar to the Democratic Caucus. The Conference, however, has been less active as a force for reform or policymaking than the Caucus.

On the Senate side, James McClure (R—Idaho) chairs the Republican Conference and Robert Byrd (D—W.Va.) chairs the Democratic Conference. The Senate conferences do little except approve the roster of committee members.

Committee Leadership

In contrast with party leaders, who are chosen by the chamber membership of their party, leaders of committees and subcommittees are selected primarily on the basis of seniority. Seniority may be disregarded when a member is out of step with most party members on important policy questions or when a member already chairs another committee or subcommittee. The committees are always chaired by members of the majority party. The most senior minority party member is designated the ranking minority member and succeeds to the chair if there is a change in party control of the chamber. For example, when Republicans won control of the Senate in 1980, Strom Thurmond (R—S.C.), who had been the ranking mi-

nority member on the Judiciary Committee, became its chair.

Until quite recently, committee leaders were very powerful. Some behaved as autocrats and were able to block legislation they opposed and secure passage of most items they supported. For example, Howard Smith (D—Va.), conservative chair of the House Rules Committee during part of the 1950s and 1960s, blocked liberal legislation that he opposed by disappearing from Washington and refusing to hold hearings. Today, committee procedures and the authority of the chairperson are spelled out in written rules. The power of committee chairs has been further reduced by the distribution of much of their authority among members chairing subcommittees.

The revitalized House Democratic Caucus has also helped curb the undemocratic tendencies of some chairpersons. Junior legislators with strong policy interests often reject the leadership of their elders. As a result of these changes, proponents of new legislation must secure approval at many more points. It is no longer feasible for a few leaders to strike a bargain with the president and then secure congressional approval except on a few uncontroversial issues. All legislation has to work its way through the maze of congressional committees.

COMMITTEES

Many congressional functions can be carried out and all legislator goals can be met within the confines of the congressional committee system. Indeed, as Woodrow Wilson noted while he was still

TABLE 11.5

Matching Congressional Standing Committees and Their 1983 Partisan Makeup

House	Senate
Agriculture (26 D, 15 R)	Agriculture, Nutrition, and Forestry (10 R, 8 D)
Appropriations (36 D, 21 R)	Appropriations (15 R, 14 D)
Armed Services (28 D, 16 R)	Armed Services (10 R, 8 D)
Banking, Finance, and Urban Affairs (29 D, 17 R)	Banking, Finance, and Urban Affairs (10 R, 8 D)
Budget (20 D, 11 R)	Budget (12 R, 10 D)
District of Columbia (7 D, 4 R)	
Education and Labor (20 D, 11 R)	Labor and Human Relations (10 R, 8 D)
Energy and Commerce (27 D, 15 R)	Commerce, Science, and Transportation (9 R, 8 D)
Foreign Affairs (24 D, 13 R)	Foreign Relations (9 R, 8 D)
Government Operations (25 D, 14 R)	Governmental Affairs (10 R, 8 D)
House Administration (12 D, 7 R)	
Interior and Insular Affairs (25 D, 14 R)	Energy and Natural Resources (11 R, 9 D)
Judiciary (20 D, 11 R)	Judiciary (10 R, 8 D)
Merchant Marine and Fisheries (25 D, 14 R)	
Post Office and Civil Service (15 D, 9 R)	
Public Works and Transportation (30 D, 18 R)	Environment and Public Works (9 R, 7 D)
Rules (9 D, 4 R)	Rules and Administration (7 R, 5 D)
Science and Technology (26 D, 15 R)	
Small Business (26 D, 15 R)	Small Business (10 R, 9 D)
Standards of Official Conduct (6 D, 6 R)	
Veterans' Affairs (21 D, 12 R)	Veterans' Affairs (7 R, 5 D)
Ways and Means (23 D, 12 R)	Finance (11 R, 9 D)

a young scholar, most of the work of Congress is performed in committees. More recently, political scientists have documented Wilson's observation and have shown that Congress ratifies more than 90 percent of the recommendations of its committees.[27] Only issues that generate widespread interest (e.g., energy legislation) are likely to be fully aired on the House and Senate floors. Legislative proposals that are bottled up in committee are dead until the next Congress.

Standing committees *are the House and Senate committees that review and perfect legislative proposals.* The House currently has 22 standing committees, which are subdivided into approximately 150 subcommittees. In the Senate there are 16 standing committees with 101 subcommittees (see Table 11.5). All legislative proposals pass through one or more of these committees.

In addition to the standing committees, there are select committees, which are chartered to investigate a specific issue and function for a limited time. During recent Congresses, one select com-

mittee explored the assassinations of John Kennedy and Martin Luther King, Jr. in a search for evidence of conspiracies, and others investigated the activities of the CIA and FBI. Select committees gather evidence and ultimately file reports that may lead to the introduction of legislative proposals, but they do not prepare legislation themselves.

Another type of committee that lacks legislative authority is the joint committee, which is composed of members of both chambers. Joint committees, like standing committees, do not have limited lifetimes. They hold hearings to coordinate efforts between the two Houses in the policy area they are concerned with. Among the more important are the Joint Committee on Taxation and the Joint Economic Committee.

Committee Assignments
Since most legislation undergoes little modification once it leaves the committee and since committees help members attain their personal goals

and carry out the whole range of congressional functions, it is important to understand the process by which legislators are assigned to committees. In each chamber, the Democrats and Republicans have committees on committees. For Democrats in the House, this function is performed by the Steering and Policy Committee; for the Republicans by the Committee on Committees. Committees on committees handle this function for both Democrats and Republicans in the Senate.

After the November elections, newly elected members and incumbents who want to change their assignments make their preferences known to their party's committee on committees. Those who have just won a seat in Congress often journey to Washington to meet the leaders of their party in the chamber, the leaders of the committees they want to serve on, and the leader of their state party delegation, who is known as the ''delegation dean.'' Of the four committees on committees, the one for House Democrats is most subject to the control of the party leader since the Speaker chairs it and selects a third of the members. The Republicans in the House use a weighted voting system that results in states with large Republican delegations controlling the assignment process.

Every effort is made to appoint each new member to at least one of the committees he or she seeks. In the House, each representative is guaranteed one major committee assignment. In the Senate, no one is given a second important assignment until all other members of the party have at least one good assignment. Since these guidelines have gone into effect, new members have obtained much better committee assignments than previously. Among first-termers, those who want committee assignments to promote their reelection and those who are motivated by policy interests are about evenly divided.[28] Few freshmen voice other motivations. Attaining influence in the chamber is a goal of members who have some seniority.

For some committees, such as Appropriations and Commerce, there are far more requests than vacancies, while very few members seek assignment to the Veterans' Affairs, House Administration, or District of Columbia committees. When requests outnumber vacancies, senior members are usually chosen over newcomers.[29] Legislators from the same state as the person leaving the vacancy have an advantage since they can claim that their delegation is entitled to retain a seat on the committee. On the more desirable committees, all but the largest delegations are limited to a single seat, so newcomers may have to change their objectives if their delegation already has a person on a committee they desire. This limitation helps promote diversity and regional balance. Some committees do disproportionately attract members from certain kinds of districts, however; westerners are more likely to serve on Interior and coastal members on Merchant Marine and Fisheries, for example. An effort is made to distribute the few women and blacks across all types of committees so that these groups' input will be spread broadly.

Once appointed to a committee, a legislator can stay there for the remainder of his or her career. Since influence on a committee is determined by seniority, after a few years of service, legislators have little interest in exchanging assignments. Most committee transfers occur when legislators have a chance to secure appointments denied to them earlier or to move to one of their chamber's most sought-after committees, for which apprenticeships are usually necessary.[30]

Learning how to be an effective committee member is important to the personal career of each Congress member as well as to his or her constituents. Committee work is an integral part of each of the broad functions of Congress.

HOW CONGRESS CARRIES OUT ITS FUNCTIONS

Policymaking

Because the nation's founders distrusted the national government, they made policymaking very cumbersome. Several obstacles were created so that popular passions could not be quickly translated into public policy. One such obstacle is the **bicameral legislature** *composed of two chambers*. Policy shifts can be made only if there is widespread support that persists long enough for the proposed changes to make their way past the numerous points where approval is needed.

A Bill Becomes a Law The first step in the translation of an idea into a policy is the introduction of a bill (see Figure 11.1). With a few exceptions, this can be done in either the House or the

Senate. Any legislator can sponsor a bill by signing it and dropping it in the hopper at the front of the legislative chamber. A proposal may be drafted by presidential advisors, the legal staff of a federal department or agency, the legal counsel for an interest group, a legislator or his or her staff, Congress's own Office of Legislative Counsel, the staff of a committee or subcommittee, or a legislator's constituents. However, to be brought before Congress, regardless of who actually wrote it, the bill must be introduced by a member of Congress.

Upon being introduced, each proposal is assigned a number with an ''HR'' or ''S'' prefix, depending on whether the sponsor is a representative or a senator. It is then assigned to the appropriate committee. If it is a complex proposal that covers several topics, the bill may be assigned to more than one committee. Once assigned to a committee, it is then assigned by the chair to one of the committee's various subcommittees.

Most of the work is actually done at the subcommittee level. The first thing a subcommittee does with proposed legislation is seek input from the executive department or departments that would be involved in its implementation. At this stage there emerges what has come to be known as the *iron triangle*, a *closed system of information exchange among staff members of congressional committees, bureaucrats in the executive branch, and the clientele or interest groups affected by the agency*. These are the recognized experts in the policy area who play a large role in actually drafting the legislation.

Next the subcommittee schedules hearings. Groups and individuals interested in the legislation are invited to present their views. Care is taken to insure that all sides are allowed to testify, although the committee's chair may show some favoritism by scheduling testimony that supports his or her preference on the first day of hearings when media coverage is greatest. The hearings may provide new information, although often they do not. Other functions of hearings are to reassure interested parties of the openness of our decision-making process and to allow their representatives to articulate their perspectives. Transcripts of hearings are useful to courts and administrative offices in determining legislative intent when they are later called upon to interpret the legislation or devise rules for implementing it.

After the hearings, the subcommittee reviews the bill and may amend or even rewrite it. The process of putting legislation into the form in which it is reported to the full committee is called the ''mark-up.'' Of course, a second option after the hearings is to kill the legislation by taking no action on it. Although there is some variation among committees, the most common practice is for the full committee to accept the report of the subcommittee with little change. Exceptions to this practice occur when the legislation is controversial or deals with a topic that attracts a great deal of attention, such as energy bills or tax reform.

In the House of Representatives, once committee approval is given, most legislation goes to the Rules Committee. Oppenheimer has characterized these proceedings as a dress rehearsal since the leading proponents and opponents from the committee reporting the legislation present their arguments before Rules.[31] The questions asked by members of Rules may point up problems that should be cleared up before the legislation comes to the floor of the House.

The *Rules Committee* determines the procedural conditions under which the legislation will be debated when it comes before the full House. For each bill it reports on, it determines the time available for debate and whether amendments can be offered. Most legislation can be debated for two hours, with the time evenly divided between supporters and opponents. Typically an ''open rule'' is given to legislation, meaning that it can be amended. Occasionally legislation is given a ''modified open rule,'' which permits only certain specified amendments to be offered. A third option is a ''closed rule,'' which prohibits amendments. Traditionally, revenue bills from the Ways and Means Committee have been the main recipients of closed rules so as not to jeopardize the delicate compromises that are usually worked out at the committee level.

Now that Democrats on the Rules Committee are appointed by the Speaker, it is responsive to the preferences of party leaders. This is quite a change from the 1950s and 1960s, when Rules was chaired by conservative southern Democrats who used their positions to thwart liberal initiatives. When the committee delays in giving a rule today it is because the Democratic leadership has requested a delay to try to round up the votes necessary for passage.

Prior to floor debate, legislation is placed on

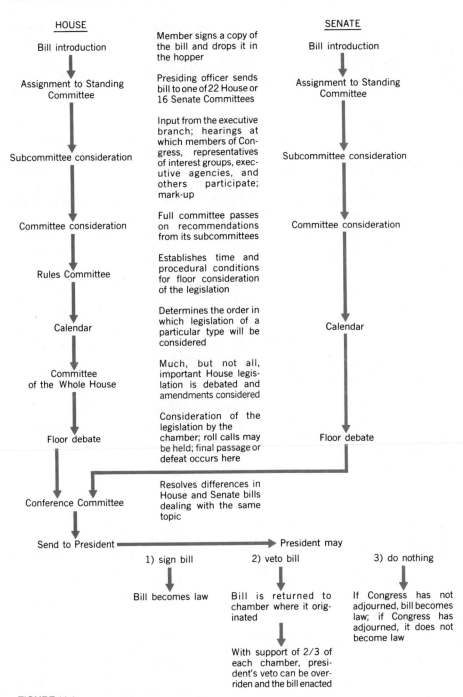

FIGURE 11.1
How a Bill Becomes a Law

one of six House Calendars. The Union Calendar is for Appropriations and tax measures. All other public bills (i.e., bills having general applicability) go on the House Calendar. Public bills that are not controversial, such as a bill to name a public building after a recently retired legislator, go on the Consent Calendar. Private bills that authorize the payment of claims to citizens who have suffered losses due to the actions of the federal government or that resolve an individual's immigration problems go on the Private Calendar. Each party has official objectors who monitor the items on the Consent and Private Calendars to insure that no controversial legislation slips by without the full review accorded bills on the House and Union Calendars. Legislation affecting the District of Columbia is also placed on a separate calendar.

If two-thirds of the representatives approve, a bill can come to the floor under suspension of the rules, thus bypassing the Rules Committee. Another method of circumventing the Rules Committee that may be attempted if Rules refuses to bring a measure to the floor is the discharge petition. If a majority of the House signs a petition asking that a bill stuck in the Rules Committee be brought to the floor for a vote, the petition is placed on the Discharge Calendar. This route is rarely used to produce legislation since any proposal that can command the support of a majority is unlikely to be held back by the Rules Committee.

Much House deliberation is carried out in the **Committee of the Whole House**, which is *a forum of all House members*. This is strictly a procedural technique in which formal rules for debate are relaxed to enable all members to participate. There are several reasons why activities are often conducted in the Committee of the Whole. First, 100 is a quorum in the Committee of the Whole while 218 constitutes a chamber quorum. It is of course easier to keep 100 representatives on the floor, which may be necessary to defeat opposition efforts to prevent action by questioning the presence of a quorum. Second, amendments rejected by the Committee of the Whole cannot be brought before the chamber. Third, since time-consuming roll calls are not permitted in the Committee of the Whole, suggested changes for which there is little support can be quickly dispensed with.

Following consideration by the Committee of the Whole, the chamber reconstitutes itself as the House. It is at this point that recorded votes can be taken on 1) amendments (including those approved in the Committee of the Whole), 2) a motion to recommit the bill to the committee that considered it, and 3) final passage. Roll calls are the indicators used most frequently in judging incumbents' policy preferences and job performance. Legislators are careful not to vote against their constituents' preferences too often or to miss too many roll calls. As John Kingdon discovered when talking to members of the House, they feel

they have some latitude in ignoring constituents' views but fear compiling a string of votes that would antagonize a large number of constituents.[32] Legislators also strive to be present for roll calls so that challengers cannot charge that they are only part-time legislators.

For most legislation either the House or the Senate can begin the process of consideration or a similar bill can be introduced simultaneously in both chambers. Exceptions to this general rule are tax bills, which the Constitution requires must originate in the House, and appropriations, which by tradition are approved by the House before being introduced in the Senate. The authors of the Constitution, believing that representation and taxation should be closely linked, restricted the introduction of new taxes to the House since its members could be more easily held accountable by the electorate, being directly elected by the people and having to seek reelection biennially. (Recall from chapter 3 that senators were initially elected by state legislatures.)

Once legislation is approved by one chamber it goes to the other, where the procedures of the first house are largely duplicated. The differences are that in the Senate, legislation does not pass through a Rules Committee before coming to the floor. Also, the Senate has no equivalent to the Committee of the Whole in the House. A third difference is that the Senate has only two calendars—General Orders, on which all legislation is listed, and the Executive Calendar, which is used for presidential nominations and treaties. All legislation coming to the Senate floor is open to amendment.

No time limits are imposed on debate in the Senate. The debate usually continues until participants agree that the arguments have been adequately aired. If a minority is deeply opposed to a piece of legislation, as the South was to civil rights bills in the 1960s, it may stage a **filibuster**, *an unlimited debate designed to forestall a vote on legislation that a majority approves of*. The minority hopes it can continue to discuss the legislation until the majority agrees to drop the issue and move on to other matters. The only way to break a filibuster is to invoke cloture by getting 60 members to vote to cut off debate. Until the late 1960s it was conservatives who resorted to filibusters. Recently liberals have staged talkathons to oppose proposals such as the deregulation of natural gas.

Before a bill can be sent to the president for his signature, it must be approved in identical form by both chambers. If, for example, the House approves a program for two years while the Senate specifies three years or the House funds a program with $2 billion while the Senate approves $2.2 billion, the bill is sent to a conference committee. A *conference committee is made up of senators and representatives from the committees that worked on the legislation who meet to resolve differences in the two chambers' versions of the bill.* A majority of the conferees from each chamber must agree to the compromises worked out in the conference committee. If compromises are achieved—and they usually are— then the agreement is taken back to both houses for ratification. No amendments are permitted at this stage.

Once a bill has been approved by the House and the Senate in identical form, it is sent to the president. If he signs it, the bill becomes a law. If the bill is unacceptable, the president can veto it by explaining his objections and returning it to the house that first approved the bill. The president, unlike most governors, does not have an item veto, which would allow him to accept part of a piece of legislation while rejecting other parts; it's all or nothing. If Congress is not in session, the president can kill a piece of legislation by exercising a pocket veto and not signing the bill within ten working days after it reaches him. When Congress is in session, bills become law if the president takes no action within ten working days.

When the president vetoes a bill, the proposal is typically dead until the next Congress unless the legislature is willing to remove the provisions the president objected to. It is possible, however, for Congress to override the president's veto. If two-thirds of both houses vote in favor of the legislation after the president returns it to them, it will be enacted despite the president's disapproval. Members of the president's party in Congress usually vote to support his position when he has vetoed a bill, so unless the president's position is widely unpopular, his veto will prevail. (Presidential vetos will be discussed in more detail in the next chapter.)

Considerations in Voting Several hundred times a year, members of Congress cast roll call votes, votes that are recorded. The diversity of topics on which legislators must vote—energy, civil rights, welfare, and foreign aid, to name but a few—is so

great that even the most conscientious members can arrive at decisions on the basis of their own study of the merits on only a few issues. It is not surprising, then, that legislators have devised techniques to help them carry out the highly visible job of voting on the floor.

The opinions of other legislators are one of the most important influences on voting. As John Kingdon suggests, when the issue is uncontroversial, the decision is simple: the legislator votes with the majority of his or her colleagues.[33] On other issues, legislators defer to the recommendations of their colleagues specializing in the relevant policy area. Thus, members of the committee that handled the legislation are a frequent source of information about the probable effects of the legislation. On issues with more regional thrusts, legislators are particularly likely to turn to colleagues from their state party delegation for voting cues.

Representatives report that a second very important influence on their voting is their constituents' preferences. This input may come through letters written by constituents to the legislator, petitions submitted to his or her office, responses to polls conducted by the legislator, signals picked up by the legislator or his or her staff members in the district, or the legislator's assumptions about how constituents would probably feel if they were aware of the issue. Whether a legislator endorses a trustee role (assigning higher priority to personal judgment than constituency preferences if they are in conflict) or a delegate role (voting as constituents desire regardless of personal feelings on the issue), they usually vote as they believe their constituents want them to.

The alignment of constituent preferences and the representative's roll call votes is especially close on issues considered important by the public. Only when legislators feel strongly about an issue will they knowingly vote against the preferences of the majority of the people they represent. It should be recognized, however, that on most roll calls legislators have a free hand since few of their constituents have opinions about most legislation.

Interest groups also influence the outcomes of some roll calls (see chapter 7). To be relevant to the legislator, an interest group should include some of the legislators' constituents, so group demands considered by a legislator often echo the

Congressmembers often gauge whether a majority of their constituents feel strongly about an issue on the basis of the amount of mail they receive, polls conducted in their district, or petitions delivered to them. Senator Dewey Bartlett (D-Okla.) received a 350-foot petition signed by more than 10,000 Oklahomans urging him to vote against the Panama Canal Treaty.

views of the constituents. Interest group influence may also be conveyed through other members of Congress. One strategy used by effective lobbyists is to gain the support of influential legislators, especially those who are recognized as experts on the subject of concern to the lobbyist.[34] Thus, the influence of an interest group may not be readily apparent because it is mediated through the activities of its legislative allies or members living in legislators' districts. When groups are active on opposing sides, they may cancel one another out so that observers attribute little influence to lobbying. When the issue does not produce group conflict, the legislators are likely to vote for the policy option favored by those who expect to derive a benefit, since they are the only active participants.[35]

Party affiliation is often a useful predictor of how a legislator will vote. Congress members profess a desire to vote with their party whenever they can without jeopardizing their electoral security.[36] However, in contrast to most European legislators, there is little pressure on American legislators to subordinate constituency demands to those of party. In fact, the primary obstacle to party voting is opposition to the party line from powerful forces in a legislator's constituency. Legislators who frequently experience this kind of cross-pressure do not always succumb to the voices they hear from back home, but they do have lower party loyalty scores than legislators for whom constituency expectations parallel the national party platform.[37]

Historically, party voting in Congress has been most prevalent in the years immediately after a realignment has produced a new majority party in Congress (see chapter 6). In part, this is because immediately after a realignment there tend to be fewer legislators who experience cross-pressures from constituency and party. Thus, members of Congress displayed high levels of party voting during the 1930s and in the decade after 1896.[38]

The type of policy also influences the level of party voting. Party-line voting has been more frequent on issues involving social welfare programs and government regulation of business or the economy.[39] The parties are less cohesive on civil liberties and foreign policy.

The conditions surrounding a vote are another factor influencing the extent to which members tow the party line. Party voting is more likely 1) on procedural than substantive matters, 2) when the party leaders have aggressively tried to line up votes, 3) when the issue is of low salience, or 4) when the vote is not recorded.[40]

Legislators may be influenced if the president takes a position on an issue, especially if they are of the president's party. Partisan pride coupled with an awareness that a president's failures may help bring down members of his party at the next election provide extra incentives to vote with the president. Legislative leaders in the president's party often serve as the conduit through which presidential preferences are conveyed to legislators. In the party that lost the last presidential election, chamber leaders attempt to rally support for their party's positions.

Finally, a legislator's staff may play a role in shaping his or her voting. Most members of Con-

Occasionally members of Congress switch party affiliation when their party's position on economic issues differs considerably from the position preferred by a significant majority of their constituents. Such was the case with Congressmember Phil Gramm (Texas) who switched from the Democratic to the Republican Party in 1983.

gress have one or more staffers responsible for analyzing each piece of legislation that comes to the floor. On most issues, a lobbyist's input is filtered through a staff member rather than going directly to the legislator. Members' legislative assistants also draw on the committee report accompanying the legislation, material provided by quasiparty organizations such as the Democratic Study Group, and the assistant's perception of what position would be preferred by the legislator's constituents and the legislator personally. In the absence of clear indicators on the last two factors, legislative assistants are free to inject their own preferences. If this cue does not come into conflict with some other cue, the staffer's recommendation will be followed.

Executive Oversight

Stein and Regens have established a useful schema to classify types of formal oversight.[41] The narrowest type of oversight is specific to an event and probes the causes of a particular problem such as the NASA test capsule fire that claimed the lives of three astronauts. A broader type, statutory oversight, reviews the way a piece of legis-

lation is being implemented or the impact of a program that Congress has established. Investigations with an even broader scope have as a target an entire agency such as the Central Intelligence Agency or an issue area such as labor racketeering. Oversight of the last two types, which is not event-specific, is likely to result in new legislation. Oversight may be conducted as a separate investigation or in the context of appropriations or reauthorization hearings.

When reviewing the implementation or consequences of previous policy decisions, committees draw on the research of their members and staff. At times this may even include the personal experiences of legislators or their constituents. Former Senator Frank Moss (D—Utah) posed as a bum seeking medical services in order to uncover abuses in federally funded health care programs. Private individuals and groups which monitor an agency's activities are also called on for evaluations and suggestions about needed remedial efforts. Likewise, committees may call on the General Accounting Office for evaluations. The GAO, under the leadership of the comptroller general, is an arm of the Congress that specializes in studies of bureaucratic efficiency and effectiveness (see chapter 13).

Only recently has Congress become extensively involved in executive oversight. This increased oversight activity may be a product of a number of

Congressmembers may at times conduct their own investigations of policy implementation. In order to determine the extent of abuse and fraud in federally-funded health care programs, Senator Frank Moss, chair of a Senate Special Committee on Aging, went into a medical clinic disguised as a bum. Although faking an ailment, he was given a number of prescriptions for it.

factors. Limitations on the number of committees and subcommittees an individual can chair have allowed a number of relatively junior members to become subcommittee leaders; some have used their positions and their growing autonomy to hire staff to probe bureaucratic activities.[42] Strains between the legislative and executive branches, particularly when there is a split situation in which the majority party in Congress does not control the presidency, encourage presidential opponents to use oversight hearings to embarrass the administration. Finally, controversial programs are receiving closer scrutiny.

The end product of oversight can range from extending a program without requiring modifications to terminating it—an option rarely exercised. When problems are uncovered, Congress is more likely to 1) modify the program (as it has done repeatedly in trying to contain the costs of Aid to Families with Dependent Children) or specify new standards to be applied by an agency (as in 1977 when the latitude of HEW in requiring busing as a corrective for school segregation was curtailed). Another option is for Congress to rewrite legislation to make more explicit what it expects the agency to do.

Legislative Veto Oversight, as discussed thus far, typically occurs a year or more after a program has been underway. This allows Congress to evaluate the implementation of legislation. From 1970–1983, Congress increasingly used the *legislative veto, legislative authority to keep regulations made by bureaucrats from going into effect.* This form of executive oversight had a much shorter fuse.

When legislation provided for a legislative veto, it in effect authorized Congress to throw a breaker switch. Such a veto authorized Congress or one of its committees to review the rules and regulations devised by the bureaucracy for carrying out a program before they took effect. If the Congress members responsible for the review disagreed with the proposed regulations, they vetoed them and the agency had to try again.

A 1983 Supreme Court decision raised questions about the constitutionality of the legislative veto. This ruling may have undone provisions of some 200 statutes. The full ramifications of this decision will not become clear until the court rules on some other cases involving a congressional veto. What is clear is that Congress will continue

to monitor the activities of the executive branch in order to make sure that regulations are in the best interest of their constituents back home.

Representation of Local Interests

Legislators can best represent local interests in their committees, for it is through the agencies that their committees deal with that legislators have the greatest influence. Bureaucrats realize that they are less likely to encounter hostility when seeking to expand their activities or justify their current operations if the legislators who authorize or appropriate funds for their operations are satisfied with the agency's responsiveness to the special needs of their constituents.

Members of Congress, especially those who are most concerned about reelection, are attracted to committees that interact with agencies already important to their constituents' well-being or to committees that would give them leverage over agencies they would like to see expand operations in their districts. Thus the legislator from a district containing several military installations may seek an Armed Services seat to guard against local base closings and seek additional military units. Legislators who do not have installations in their districts may be attracted to Armed Services in hopes that they can entice the Pentagon to locate a base in their district. Members of Congress might also seek improved crop supports or foreign markets for farmers in their districts, new dams and waterways, federal construction projects, and so forth.

Bringing millions of federal dollars and hundreds of construction jobs into a constituency is generally considered a major accomplishment. It is therefore not surprising that most legislators, regardless of party affiliation, ideology, or views on the virtues of a balanced budget, strive to protect their district's share of the federal pie. President Carter suffered one of his first congressional defeats when he proposed canceling some previously approved water projects.

The task of looking out for local interests is coming to involve more than simply trying to obtain authorization and funding for projects. During the 1970s, programs were created which distributed funds to local governments for job training, community development, law enforcement, as well as general revenue sharing on the basis of formulas written into the statutes. This has produced what Richard Nathan has called "politics by printout." Legislators can see how the communities they represent would fare under alternative formulas for dispensing the federal largess and then work to enact a favorable option. The ease with which computers can show the consequences of juggling funding formulas reduces prospects for significantly redistributing aid once a program is established. Therefore, to increase the funding for especially needy communities, it is usually necessary to enlarge the pie since representatives of districts that would lose funds will block reallocation. This, of course, has serious implications for efforts to balance the budget.

Members of Congress take pains to see that their efforts on behalf of their district's economy pay electoral dividends. When a new project is begun or dedicated, the representative is likely to participate in the festivities. They also put out press releases announcing the awarding of grants to district recipients. Even legislators who assign high priority to balancing the budget claim credit for federal projects in their districts. For example, conservative David Stockman, whom President Reagan appointed as director of the Office of Management and Budget and who became the administration's point man in the battle of the budget "worked hard to make certain that his Fourth District (of Michigan) constituents exploited the system. His office maintained a computerized alert system for grants and loans from the myriad agencies, to make certain that no opportunities were missed."[43]

Constituency Liaison Activities

The constituent service function differs from representation of local interests in that it involves provision of "particularized benefits for individuals or groups in (a legislator's) constituency"[44] as opposed to securing the benefits of federal programs for the district. The distinction is between casework and the pork barrel. A similarity is that both carry expected electoral payoffs.

Morris Fiorina reports that the constituent service function has grown apace with the expanded federal bureaucracy.[45] Indeed, he characterizes the symbiotic relationship he sees as "the Washington Establishment." According to Fiorina, an arrangement has been worked out under which bureaucrats resolve problems referred to them by members of Congress. In return, Congress supports an expanding bureaucracy. Members of Congress have created a "heads I win, tails you lose" situation. They can reap publicity by claiming credit for the creation of new programs. If the programs fail—perhaps because of careless legislative draftsmanship—Congress can pin the blame on the bureaucrats responsible for implementation.

Writing a member of Congress does not assure a favorable ruling from the bureaucracy, but it does guarantee that the bureaucracy will review the constituent's case. When constituents are denied benefits to which they are entitled because of bureaucratic bungling, a demonstration of interest by a congressional office usually corrects the situation. An inquiry from a congressional office may produce a favorable decision in a close case which could go either way. Interest from a congressional office may also cut red tape and expedite a decision.

Bureaucrats are more responsive to members of Congress than to the average citizen since it is Congress that controls their budgets and authorizes their programs. A failure to respond to an inquiry from a congressional office may come back to haunt the agency, particularly if the inquiry came from a legislator who serves on a committee that has authority over the agency's budget or programs. Inattention to an inquiry may provoke a grilling when agency officials make their annual pilgrimage up Capitol Hill to explain what they have done and make their requests for the next year. A dissatisfied legislator may go so far as to launch an investigation of the agency, in the course of which the skeletons in the closet will be put on public display.

After an agency looks into a legislative request, it responds to the legislator, who in turn notifies the constituent. If the constituent's request is fulfilled, the legislator wins a supporter for life. Indeed, the effect of successful handling of casework will probably be broader since the happy constituent will sing the praises of the legislator to friends and family. Voters who think they would get help from their representative, who have sought help, or whose friends have sought help are more likely to vote for an incumbent. The following passage illustrates what one service-oriented senator, Herman Talmadge (D—Ga.), did for his constituents:

Atlanta construction executive James Shepherd, 29,

credits Talmadge with saving his life after he broke his neck surfing off the coast of Brazil. Doctors said he would die unless carefully moved to the States. Commercial airlines wouldn't touch him. A call from Talmadge brought an Air Force C141 Medevac plane winging to Rio de Janeiro, a $40,000 flight for which the Shepherd family reimbursed the government.

'That's the kind of power seniority gives you,' reflects the once-paralyzed Shepherd, who now walks about with the help of a cane. 'If he hadn't done such a good job over the years for his people, he wouldn't have that power now. You have to respect him for that.'

Journalists also have sought his help in a pinch. James Townsend, an Atlanta magazine editor, once telephoned Talmadge's Senate office midair over Bermuda when military authorities refused to allow his Lear jet to land for lack of prior clearance. Within minutes of the call, Townsend laughs, the clouds parted and "they said, 'Let that boy land.'"

'By God, that's more than service. That's POWER!'[46]

CONGRESSIONAL REFORM

Congress in the 1980s is very different even from the Congress of 1970. Congress changed more during the 1970s than in any other decade in its history, with the possible exception of 1910 to 1920. The reforms occurred along a broad front. The objectives of the reformers were to 1) weaken the committee chairs, 2) make Congress more accountable to the public, 3) restore balance be-

tween Congress and the president, and 4) make the institution more efficient. After describing the major changes that have occurred in each of these areas (see Table 11.6), we will turn our attention to the agenda of additional changes that some reformers would like to see adopted.

Weakening Committee Chairs

Decentralization Following the 1910 revolt against Speaker Joe Cannon (R—Ill.), the presiding officer of the House was stripped of important powers such as control of the Rules Committee and authority to name committee members and their presiding officers. Into this vacuum came the committee chairs, who have been selected on the basis of seniority since 1910. Until the 1970s, the committee chairs were the oligarchs who ruled Congress. Those who combined resourcefulness with intelligence, political savvy, and a firm will were able to dominate their committees. They kept proposals they opposed from coming to the floor for a vote and bargained one-on-one with the president, extracting concessions from him before bringing his programs to the floor.

During much of the 1950s and 1960s, southern Democrats held a disproportionate share of the committee chairs. An an extreme example, in the Eighty-Sixth Congress (1959–1960), southerners comprised a third of all House and Senate Democrats, but due to their greater seniority they chaired 60 percent of the House committees and

TABLE 11.6

Congressional Reforms of the 1970s

1971–1972	Office of Technology Assessment created
	Computers authorized
1973–1974	Most House committee sessions made public
	War Powers Act passed
	Budget and Impoundment Control Act: passed; Budget Committees and Congressional Budget Office created
	Speaker authorized to name Democrats on Rules Committee
	Seniority norm weakened in House
	House subcommittees strengthened
	House Democrats give committee assignment function to Steering and Policy Committee
1975–1976	Filibuster cloture reduced to 60
	Most Senate committee sessions and conference committee sessions opened to public
1977–1978	New ethics rules adopted in both chambers
	Senate revised committee system
1979–1980	House floor roll calls reduced in number

63 percent of the Senate committees. Young northern liberals fretted under the constraints imposed by the conservative southerners. Particularly galling to the young liberals was the southerners' support for the Vietnam War and opposition to social and civil rights programs.

Challenges to the dominant position of House committee chairs culminated in a break with the seniority norm in 1974. When the Democrats organized the chamber, they overthrew the elderly southerners who chaired the Armed Services, Agriculture, and Banking and Currency Committees. In the vanguard of the reformers were many members who had capitalized on the Republican's Watergate embarrassment to capture seats. Although committee chairs or ranking minority members have not subsequently been pushed aside, the 1974 revolt has circumscribed the activities of committee leaders. They have become more democratic and deferential to the wishes and interests of even the most junior members. Today, committee leaders are confirmed by a vote of the full party membership in the caucus. Illustrative of the changes is a story that made the rounds in Washington a few years ago. A junior member is supposed to have observed that before 1974, young committee members laughed heartily at the chair's jokes; after the revolt, the committee chair laughed at the junior members' jokes.

A second blow at congressional oligarchs was to limit the number of committee and subcommittee chairs an individual could hold. A senator can chair no more than one full committee and two subcommittees. Prior to this 1977 reform, Howard Cannon (D—Nev.) had presided over a collection of ten committees and subcommittees. In the House, with its larger membership, an individual can chair only one committee or subcommittee. Thus, approximately 150 members of the majority party in the House preside over a unit. Virtually every majority party member with three terms or more of seniority leads a committee or subcommittee.

Evaluation Each of the three reforms discussed above has allowed more people to become involved in the work of Congress. This has reduced the ability of a few senior members to obstruct the work of Congress, but it should be recognized that the institution and the nation have paid a price for this. No longer can someone deliver legislation the way Wilbur Mills (D—Ark.) did. In his ca-

pacity as chair of the Ways and Means Committee, Mills could negotiate an agreement with the president and then see that the House carried out its end of the bargain. Those who want Congress to act must now touch many more bases than they had to in the past. This takes time, creates uncertainty, and reduces the likelihood of action. Bruce Oppenheimer, after a careful study of how the House has handled presidential energy packages, concludes that "without substantial leadership influence, the reformed House of the 1970s will find its main policy influence is limited to delaying and defeating policy initiatives, a role not very different from that played in the pre-reform period. The main difference will be in how this is done."[47]

Party Leadership Not all of the reforms of the 1970s decentralized power; some gave new authority to party leaders. A major move to strengthen the hand of the Democratic speaker has been to alter the way House Democrats get their committee assignments. Assigning Democrats to standing committees was previously the responsibility of the Democratic contingent of the Ways and Means Committee. In 1975 this authority was shifted to the Steering and Policy Committee, which the Speaker chairs. Other party leaders serving on this committee are the majority leader, the majority whip, the chair of the Democratic Caucus, and five other whips. The Speaker appoints the whips, representatives of the Black Caucus and the Women's Caucus, from among the recently elected Democratic representatives. By chairing the meetings and appointing nine of the members, the Speaker's influence over this critical process has been substantially increased.

The speaker also names the Democratic members of the Rules Committee, which schedules the work of the House. Unlike other committee members, the Rules Committee members' positions are not protected by seniority. This has converted the Rules Committee, with its two-to-one majority-party dominance, into a tool of the leadership, eliminating its ability to thwart the will of a substantial number of majority party members.[48]

Evaluation The steps taken to strengthen the hand of the party leadership have been insufficient to offset the decentralizing tendencies. Cover and Mayhew conclude that even rejuvenation of the

Caucus has weakened the party: "The revved-up House Democratic Caucus has been used less for making policy than for weakening committee chairpersons . . ."[49] Consequently, although Speaker Thomas "Tip" O'Neill has some powers that were denied to former Speaker Sam Rayburn (D—Tex.), he has been unable to exercise the degree of control over House Democrats during the Reagan administration that Rayburn enjoyed when he presided over the House during the last six years of the Eisenhower presidency. The House of the 1980s has far more members who have strong policy interests, and these representatives have a more secure power base to work from. Even the legendary Rayburn would have more difficulty leading today's disparate Democrats.

Strengthening Congress vis-à-vis the President

President Nixon's disdain for Congress finally provoked Congress to try to regain its position as an equal to the executive. Particularly galling to Congress had been its weakness in influencing the conduct of the war in Southeast Asia and presidential dominance of the budgetary process.

War Powers Often, rather than being allowed to play a consultative role, Congress was presented with an accomplished fact. In an effort to reassert its authority over American military activities, Congress passed the War Powers Act of 1973 (also see chapters 12 and 19).

In drafting this legislation, Congress tried to balance its desire to participate in the life-and-death decisions surrounding the use of military force with the need to respond quickly when America's national security is threatened. Accordingly, Congress did not seek a literal interpretation of the language of the Constitution, which authorizes Congress and Congress alone to declare war. In an age of missile warfare, such a response would come far too late. Therefore, the War Powers Act recognizes that the president may have to act before seeking approval from Congress.

If it is not feasible to obtain congressional approval before involving the United States in hostilities, the president is required to inform congressional leaders of the actions he has taken as soon as possible. Congress then has 60 days to approve

of what the president has done. If it concludes that the president acted improperly and fails to grant approval, the president must withdraw American troops as quickly as possible without unnecessarily endangering their lives. Allowing Congress to second guess the president may be unconstitutional as a result of a 1983 case involving the legislative veto. Congress could still, however, end U.S. participation in a war by cutting off funds.

Evaluation The United States has not become involved in extended hostilities since Congress approved the War Powers Act. One can argue that it is because Congress took this stand that American troops did not become involved in the civil wars in Angola.

The impact of the Act in a case in which troops are committed remains untested. Graham Allison argues that the Act would have had little effect on Vietnam if it had been on the books at the time.[50] He says that Congress would have approved President Johnson's requests in 1965. Indeed, greater congressional involvement in the early stages of the American build-up might have made it more difficult for legislators to become critics, since they would have had to publicly reverse their earlier decisions.

Budgetary Powers In an attempt to force Congress to eliminate categorical grant programs of which he disapproved, President Nixon impounded (refused to spend) large sums of money. This refusal to carry out the wishes of Congress—which, by the way, the president had agreed to by signing the legislation—brought to a head Congress's weakness in the budgetary process.

The Congressional Budget and Impoundment Control Act of 1974 makes several changes. If a president changes his mind and decides not to spend appropriated funds, he must now propose a rescission to Congress. If Congress does not approve the rescission within 45 days, the money must be spent. This provision may be an unconstitutional effort at a legislative veto but as yet this has not been determined by the Supreme Court.

More important than the restrictions placed on the president's ability to withhold appropriated funds were the new budgetary procedures Congress instituted. Prior to this legislation, neither house of Congress had a process for fully reviewing the government's income and outlays (revenues and expenditures). When the president sent his proposed budget to Congress, it was broken up into 13 pieces, each of which was scrutinized by an Appropriations subcommittee. The final budget was simply the sum of these parts; no effort was made to fit them into a package with a pre-set ceiling or to balance expenditures against revenues to keep the deficit below a certain level. The Budget Act changed all this. The new procedure called for specific targets to be established and timetables to be met. (These will be discussed in more detail in chapter 17.)

To carry out its new responsibilities, the Act mandated that Congress create a Budget Committee for each chamber. These committees in a sense oversee the work of the appropriations and revenue committees. (See chapter 17.)

To help the Budget Committees, a new service arm, the Congressional Budget Office, was created. The CBO's staff of economists provides the Budget Committees and Congress as a whole with an alternative source of economic forecasting. Prior to the creation of CBO, Congress had to rely on the executive branch's Office of Management and Budget for estimates of the costs, needs, and economic impacts of alternative courses of action.

Evaluation[51]   Reformers who hoped the new budgetary process would produce major changes have been disappointed. The new process has not led to a balanced budget as conservatives had expected, although linking expenditures to revenues may have kept deficits smaller than they would otherwise have been. Budget reform has not produced major reallocations from military to social spending as liberals had hoped, either. In retrospect, it was probably unrealistic to expect that procedural changes would alter substantive outcomes.

The new timetable has not been very effective either. In the first years after the new process was implemented, Congress was punctual in following the timetable. But since 1979 it has failed to make appropriations for some departments by the October 1 deadline (the start of the budget year).

The most completely realized goals of reformers have been improving the amount and quality of information available to Congress and restraining presidents' ability to impound funds.

Staffing   To better monitor the performance of the executive branch and to develop a competing base of expertise, Congress has greatly increased the size of its staff. Of course, not all staffers help strengthen Congress's position vis-a-vis the executive, but many do. From 1967 to 1981 the personal staff of members of Congress increased from 5,804 to 11,125.[52] This growth in staff also contributed to the decentralization of power discussed earlier.

Accountability

A basic premise of any government that claims to be responsive to the wishes of the public is that decision-makers be accountable to the masses. Accountability is supposed to be achieved, in part, with elections through which those who are out of step with public preferences or who have betrayed the public trust can be replaced. For members of the public to vote in a way that enforces accountability, they must have information available to base their judgments on.

Efforts to produce more abundant information for voters triggered a flood of openness reforms in the 1970s. These reforms brought into public view a variety of things that had previously been carried out behind closed doors or had simply not been reported on.

Openness   "Sunshine laws," which were initially adopted by states, have now been enacted by Congress. Today more than 90 percent of Congress's committee hearings are conducted in open session. Even conference committee deliberations and mark-ups, at which legislation is put in final form before being reported out by a committee, are usually open to the public. Prior to the mid-1970s, these proceedings were always conducted behind closed doors. Now sessions are closed only for specific reasons such as to allow legislators to be briefed on national security secrets. Opening up committee sessions allows reporters and incumbents' opponents to see what positions legislators take at two critical stages in the legislative process. Reporters and challengers are thus able to give to voters accounts of what they believe to be failures to represent the interests of the district or of the nation.

Television Coverage   After much soul-searching the House began television coverage of floor proceedings in 1979. In some media markets, congressional groupies can watch their laws being made. In allowing coverage, the House estab-

"Its a television first. Two committees are investigating each other."

The House of Representatives currently allows television coverage of its floor proceedings. However, the Senate has resisted televising its deliberations, fearing discussions may deteriorate into media events.

lished ground rules intended to minimize member embarrassment. Cameras must remain fixed on the person who is speaking and cannot roam the chamber to show inattentive members or the generally small chamber attendance.

A similar move is still under consideration by the Senate. Many Senators have resisted such a move, fearing some of their colleagues, with eyes on the presidency, would monopolize debate (see chapter 10).

Financial Reporting A basis for some ethics requirements has been the assumption that if legislators had to report their financial holdings, they would not place themselves in positions where it appeared they had a conflict of interest. Legislators are now required to report annually the value of their holdings in property, stocks, and outside earnings. The reporting is done by categories of value (less than $5,000, $5,000 to $15,000, and so forth) and by the nature of the holding (for example, real estate, securities, and commodity futures). Thus, while we do not know to the penny what a legislator's investment portfolio looks like, we can get a good idea.

Evaluation Openness reforms have met the objectives of their proponents and have brought into public view many activities that in the past were known only to members. It appears likely that making committees and conference committee activities visible to the media and the public has forced legislators to weigh the preferences of their constituents more heavily when making policy. Having to take stands in public, legislators more often behave like instructed delegates rather than trustees who rely chiefly on their own assessments when casting votes.

Has greater openness improved congressional operations? The answer to this question is essentially a value judgment. By increasing the number of decisions on which members must stand and be counted, the reforms have reduced the likelihood that legislators will respond to the call of their party.[53] On issues of interest to the constituency, the legislator will be reluctant to oppose the apparent preference of the voters back home. Even if few voters are aware at the time of how the legislator votes, legislators fear that in the future some challenger will trumpet the charge that the incumbent has betrayed the constituents' trust. Votes cast in committee, on the floor, or in conference can be used to back up the accusation.

If one believes that the public is usually correct in its preferences, then the greater attentiveness that legislators now pay to their constituents is reassuring. If on the other hand one suspects that the public generally pays little heed to political alternatives and is even less disposed to think through the long-term consequences of actions, one may find the greater number of legislators who behave as instructed delegates disconcerting. The problem with delegates is that they are often more concerned with their individual districts than with the nation as a whole.

Efficiency

Congress has rarely won praise for the speed with which it produces solutions. To the extent that it is a deliberative body, it will be slow. Most Americans, however, believe Congress should be a conduit through which presidential proposals flow with only minor impediments rather than an assembly in which presidential requests are closely scrutinized and, when found defective, rejected.[54] An image of Congress probably held by many Americans is that of a body unable to take any action because of delay tactics, such as the filibuster. During the 1970s, the Senate tried to curb the abuses of the filibuster and Congress took other steps to speed up the processing of legislative proposals.

Filibusters Prior to 1917 no process existed to cut off debate. Since then, it has been possible to invoke cloture and bring an issue to a final vote. Cloture has always required an extraordinary majority. In 1975 liberals succeeded in reducing the number of supporters needed to cut off debate from two-thirds of those actually in the chamber and voting to three-fifths of the Senate's members.

Electronic Voting With its 435 members, it takes about 45 minutes to conduct an oral roll call in the House. By adopting electronic voting, a procedure used for years in many state legislatures, the House cut the time required for each roll call by about two-thirds.

The time saved on each roll call has been offset by an increase in the number of roll calls. The number of recorded votes jumped by 64 percent in the first year the electronic apparatus was installed.[55] The frequency of roll calls continued to increase through 1978 when 834 were cast, two-and-a-half times the number cast six years earlier.

Roll call votes are conducted orally and recorded manually in the Senate. In the House, they are conducted electronically which has markedly increased the number of roll call votes taken there.

The number dropped after the use of roll calls as a delay tactic was restricted.

Having electronic voting capability may not fully account for the increase in House roll calls. Roll calls also became much more common in the Senate during the 1970s, even though they are still conducted orally there.

Computers[56] Congress lagged behind most banks, business houses, and the Dallas Cowboys in entering the computer age. But now computers are everywhere on Capitol Hill. Both Houses use computers to handle payroll and personnel. In the Senate they are also used to minimize the number of overlapping subcommittee meetings so that senators will do less rushing from one subcommittee to another.

Members can also use computers to set up files containing records of their casework and to store mailing lists. These records show which constituents have contacted them, the subject of the contact, and the legislator's response. Other data banks provide information on the current status of legislation and the availability of federal programs.

Representatives are allocated $12,000 annually for computer services. Approximately half the members, particularly junior ones from electorally marginal districts, have acquired their own personal computers.

Evaluation There is little evidence that Congress has become more efficient. Filibusters are still used by a wide range of ideological types to tie up the Senate. The time saved by electronic voting in the House has been more than offset by increases in the frequency with which issues are voted on.

Computers have certainly placed vast amounts of information at the fingertips of legislators and their staffs. Whether legislators are better informed or simply overwhelmed by information is uncertain. It is not clear that the use of computers results in qualitatively better decisions or in more efficient use of time and resources by legislators and their staffs.

Proposed Reforms

Despite the numerous changes of the 1970s, additional reforms have been proposed. Some of the suggested changes are designed to correct unanticipated consequences of some of the 1970s reforms.

Many representatives have their own personal computers in their offices with data files ranging from a list of which constituents have contacted them to a record of how much federal money has been allocated to projects in their district.

One perennial reform suggestion is that the congressional committee system be restructured. Predictably opposition to the resulting proposals has come from two sources: members, especially the chairs, of committees that would lose some of their responsibilities, and interest groups that have established a good working arrangement with a committee and do not want to see it disrupted.

Another suggested reform is more comprehensive registration of lobbyists. Proposals introduced in Congress in recent years would close loopholes in the legislation adopted in 1946 (see chapter 7). The theory behind this effort, which has been spearheaded by Common Cause, is that if groups that lobby are required to report their finances, the issues on which they have been active, and the identity of the legislators whom they have contacted, the glare of publicity will keep them in line.

The final reform effort to be discussed here is campaign finance. As we noted in chapter 9, people have long been suspicious that the big financiers of campaigns may enjoy a privileged position when legislation they are interested in comes before Congress. Some people, again led by Common Cause, have urged that public financing of campaigns, which has been used in presidential elections since 1976, be extended to congressional elections.

An alternative step toward reducing the significance of affluent groups would be to limit the total amount a candidate could take from political action committees (PACs). From 1972 to 1980, the share of the funding of House campaigns coming from PACs doubled, going from 14 to 28 percent, while the share from parties dropped from 17 to 6 percent.[57] The concern is that legislators will have a hard time serving the public interest when private groups play so large a role in financing their campaigns.

The impact of campaign contributions on the shaping of public policy is a topic that deserves more attention. The evidence that has been gathered suggests that contributions do induce legislators to view the giver's objectives more favorably. Research by Benjamin Ginsberg and John Green indicates that legislators who have not established a position of strong support or opposition to a group's objectives will become more supportive of the group after receiving campaign contributions from it. They estimate that "each $650 received from an interest by an uncommitted representative was associated with an additional roll call vote in support of the interests' position by that representative."[58] The apparent linkage between campaign contributions and the voting behavior of individual Congress members has lowered the public's opinion of Congress.

CONGRESS AND PUBLIC OPINION

Richard Fenno has pointed up an apparent anomaly in public evaluations of Congress.[59] Over the last decade, public opinion polls have found widespread disillusionment with Congress. For most of this period, fewer than one American in five who was surveyed reported a favorable evaluation of our national legislature. On the other hand, the same public that rates Congress so negatively reelects incumbent representatives more than 90 percent of the time. (The rate at which the public rejects sitting senators is more in line with the negative evaluations given the institution.) Why are we so fond of our representatives while being so critical of the institution in which they serve?

Several explanations have been offered. Parker and Davidson discovered that the public uses different criteria in evaluating Congress and its members.[60] The institution as a whole is judged in terms of its style and pace, the domestic policies it produces, and its relationship with the president. On all of these, the public generally gives Congress low scores. When people are asked to evaluate their individual legislator, they frequently comment on constituency service or personal attractiveness—items on which legislators score well. Only 3 percent of the people surveyed based their evaluation on policy issues, a dimension on which individual legislators as well as the institution are rated negatively.

A second explanation is based on an analysis that found that members of the House are evaluated along with state institutions such as the governor and the state legislature.[61] The president and the Supreme Court are evaluated along a different dimension. Thus, members of Congress seem to be evaluated for what they do locally. This evaluation is influenced by their attention to casework, by the projects they provide for the district, and by the image they promote when they are in the district. They effectively divorce themselves from things done by the federal government which are unpopular with the folks back home.

Finally, the variables that appear to be related to congressional popularity are largely beyond the control of the members of Congress. The national legislature is most popular when the economy is strong, when there has been a recent international crisis that evokes a rally-round-the-flag response from many Americans, and when the president proposes a limited agenda to Congress.[62] Presidents since Eisenhower have sent large numbers of programs to Congress. When Congress delays in enacting the president's requests, its popularity declines. The economic malaise that has characterized much of the period since the early 1970s also hurts congressional standing in the polls.

SUMMARY

Congress performs a number of important functions, including policymaking, executive oversight, the representation of local economic interests, and liaison services for constituents who are having problems with the bureaucracy. As members of Congress go about performing these functions, they attempt to attain their basic career goals. These goals, which may influence much of what a legislator does, are to secure reelection, to get power and prestige within the legislature, to shape policy, and to obtain higher office.

Much of the work of Congress is carried out in committees. The reforms of the 1970s decentralized power so that subcommittees and their leaders play a larger role at the expense of the party leaders and committee chairs who held greater power a generation ago. While party leaders have less influence over the outcome of deliberations, they still control the lawmaking schedule. They play critical roles in the complex procedure a bill must follow to become a law.

When voting on proposed legislation, the preferences of one's constituents and the recommendations from legislators who have expertise on the proposal carry great weight. On most bills, legislators have some discretion when voting. If their constituents do not give them a clear indication as to local preferences, legislators may be guided by cues from party leaders or interest groups. The openness reforms of the 1970s have reduced the arenas in which legislators can operate free from fears that they may be held accountable to their constituents at some future date.

While members of the House are greatly concerned about how their constituents evaluate them, incumbents are infrequently defeated. Indeed, since the mid-1960s, fewer House members have faced stiff competition. Senators are more likely to be defeated than are representatives. The primary cause of the differences in the reelection rates of the two chambers lies in the caliber of the opposition. Senators are more likely to face well-known, well-funded opponents than are House incumbents.

During the 1970s, Congress sought to reclaim some of the powers which it had allowed to gravitate to the president. In particular, it acted to limit the president's power over the budget and in the involvement of American troops in armed conflict abroad. The consequences of these reforms are not yet fully known.

Battling for Federal Bucks: What Happens When Pork, Norms, and Personalities Come Together[1]

As we have pointed out, a major activity of most members of Congress is trying to obtain a share of the federal budget for construction and pork barrel projects in their districts. Sometimes funds are for minor items such as the construction of a tiny rural post office or a few thousand dollars for a feasibility study for a larger project which is never undertaken. At other times, billions of federal dollars and the economic well-being of a large area are at stake.

Among the most lucrative projects and therefore the most aggressively sought are contracts to build major components of our national defense arsenal. Frequent players here include aircraft manufacturers and the legislators in whose districts or states these industrial giants are located. During 1982 one of the biggest defense items at stake was the contract for providing large cargo aircraft.

For years the military's need to rapidly move tanks, jeeps, and the other items needed when deploying a fighting force were met by Lockheed's C-5A, a monster of a plane the nose of which could be raised 90 degrees so that vehicles could be driven out and forklifts could be used to remove other materials. To meet new needs, Lockheed proposed to build a fleet of new planes for approximately $5 billion. The Boeing company proposed to modify unused 747s which had been built for commercial passenger use so that they could become giant cargo planes.

In hearings before Congress, Boeing pointed out that its modification proposal would be less expensive and quicker than the Lockheed package. But Pentagon experts, who also provided testimony, were unanimous in preferring the Lockheed product, which they said would better meet the needs of the military.

[1]This draws on Henry Eason, "McDonald Hurts in Lobbying for C-5," *Atlanta Journal-Constitution*, June 13, 1982.

The military, while not given everything it has on its shopping list, has been quite successful in at least being able to choose among items when it has been authorized to obtain new equipment. It was surprising, therefore, when a battle developed over which manufacturer would be given the contract for the cargo planes.

Despite expert testimony in favor of Lockheed, the Senate voted for Boeing by a three-to-two margin. Important to this decision was the aggressive lobbying campaign led by Democratic Senator Henry Jackson a 30-year veteran from Washington, the state in which Boeing is headquartered. Jackson was able to call in IOUs from many of his colleagues, and he also pointed out to many of the other senators that their states would also benefit if Boeing got the contract since among their constituents were subcontractors who would perform some of the work on the 747s. For example, Kansas senator Robert Dole (R) voted for the Boeing planes after being told that the work on the nose of the aircraft would be done in Wichita.

In the House, the point man in the Boeing effort was Norman Dicks (D—Wash). Since Dicks won reelection in 1980 with only 54 percent of the vote, he saw the outcome of the Boeing-Lockheed struggle as potentially critical for his political career. The leader of the Lockheed forces in the House should have been Armed Services Committee member Larry McDonald (D), a representative from Georgia, where the Lockheed assembly plant is located. It is at this point that personalities and norms entered in.

While Dicks is a fairly popular House member, McDonald has often failed to play by the unwritten reciprocity rules. McDonald, an active member of the John Birch Society, is more ideological than most members of Congress and far more conservative than most Democrats. In 1981, he had the poorest party loyalty record in Congress, voting with the majority of his party less than 10 percent of the time. This disloyalty to the party and unusual activities such as having his own organization for rooting out subversion have made McDonald something of an outcast within the Democratic party. Consequently, the ties of friendship and back-scratching which are so important in congressional decision-making were on the side of Boeing. The Georgia delegation sought to offset the Boeing advantage by having a legislator from a district adjacent to McDonald's assume leadership of the fight while McDonald concentrated on lining up votes among the Republicans with whom he frequently votes.

The Lockheed forces ultimately triumphed in the House. The key factor appeared to be the endorsement of Lockheed by President Reagan on the day before the critical vote was taken. Once the president's preferences became known, his supporters in the Senate also voted to grant Lockheed the contract, after a conference committee made the formal recommendation. As this story demonstrates, policymaking involves a lot of politicking, trading, and compromising among legislators who must be attuned to the interests of their respective constituents.

KEY TERMS

bicameral legislature
casework
Committee of the Whole
conference committee
filibuster
floor leaders
frank
House Rules Committee
iron triangles
legislative veto
norms
oversight
reciprocity
roll call vote
seniority
Speaker of the House
specialization
standing committees
whips

SUGGESTED READINGS

Dodd, Lawrence, and Oppenheimer, Bruce I., eds. *Congress Reconsidered* 2nd ed. Washington, D.C.: Congressional Quarterly Press, 1977.

Fenno, Richard F., Jr. *Congressmen in Committees.* Boston: Little, Brown, 1973.

Fenno, Richard F., Jr. *Home Style: House Members in Their Districts.* Boston: Little, Brown, 1978.

Jacobson, Gary C. *The Politics of Congressional Elections.* Boston: Little, Brown, 1983.

Jacobson, Gary C., and Kernell, Samuel. *Strategy and Choice in Congressional Elections.* New Haven, Conn.: Yale University Press, 1981.

Kingdon, John W. *Congressmen's Voting Decisions* 2nd ed. New York: Harper and Row, 1981.

Malbin, Michael J. *Unelected Representatives.* New York: Basic Books, 1980.

Matthews, Donald R. *U.S. Senators and Their World.* New York: W.W. Norton, 1973.

Sinclair, Barbara. *Congressional Realignment, 1925–1978.* Austin, Tex.: University of Texas Press, 1982.

THE PRESIDENCY: PROPOSING, POPULARIZING, AND IMPLEMENTING PUBLIC POLICY

The President as Policy Proposer ■ The President as Policy Popularizer ■ The President as Policy Implementor ■ The President's Supporting Cast ■ "Great" Presidential Performances: Why Would Anyone Want the Lead Role?

At certain times in American history, the presidency of the United States has been described as the most powerful office in the world. At other times, the presidency has been viewed as a weak institution and the president has been considered merely a pawn of Congress, the bureaucracy, or the courts. The strength or weakness of a president rests largely on his ability to propose, popularize, and implement public policies in reaction to the country's changing needs. This ability varies from one administration to the next. Rapid changes in the economy, world affairs, the makeup of Congress, and policymaking rules and procedures affect some presidential administrations more than others. Scandals, domestic crises, and the emergence of new groups and issues are also influential. The personality of the president is another factor.

Presidents today must confront issues that seem much more complex and interrelated than those that faced earlier presidents—energy, the environment, the economy, international relations, care of the nation's aged, sick, and poor, and protection of civil rights, to mention a few. Certainly George Washington did not face the burden of deciding whether to unleash a nuclear attack or of having to choose between clean air and energy dependence.

The nation's founders could never have predicted the changes that have taken place in our society, but in their design of the presidency they demonstrated a great deal of foresight and common sense. In Article II of the Constitution, they defined the powers of the president in broad terms, recognizing that the responsibilities of presidents would change as conditions in the nation changed.

Over the years, these powers have been defined more clearly through legislation, court interpretations, and everyday usage. When presidents overstep their powers, Congress or the courts act to return balance to the system—or the voters fail to return the president to office. If a president needs more authority in situations involving economic or foreign policy, Congress can draft legislation to grant it.

Sometimes the system is rebalanced too slowly or too quickly, but never in the history of the

United States have we been ruled by a dictator or a king, nor have we experienced a violent overthrow of government. President Ronald Reagan, in his inaugural address, remarked,

> *The orderly transfer of authority as called for in the Constitution routinely takes place as it has for almost two centuries and few of us stop to think how unique we really are. In the eyes of many in the world, this every-four-year ceremony we accept as normal is nothing less than a miracle.*[1]

Newly elected presidents, like the citizens who elected them, often have unrealistic expectations about what they can do and how fast they can do it. President John Kennedy's comments after being in office a short time reflect the rude awakening that new presidents get—and he had a Democratic Congress and a sympathetic public to work with:

> *In the first place, the problems are more difficult than I had imagined they were. Secondly, there is a limitation upon the ability of the United States to solve these problems. The responsibilities placed on the United States are greater than I imagined them to be, and there are greater limitations upon our ability to bring about a favorable result than I had imagined there to be . . . because there is such a difference between those who advise or speak or legislate and between the man who must select from the various alternatives proposed and say that this shall be the policy of the United States.*[2]

If we as citizens intend to influence public pol-

icy, we must understand the role of the presidency in proposing, advocating, and implementing policy. Just as importantly, we must understand the constraints and checks on those roles.

THE PRESIDENT AS POLICY PROPOSER

The founders believed that presidents should share with Congress a role in the policymaking process. Article II, Section 3, of the Constitution instructs the president to "give to Congress information of the State of the Union and to recommend to their Consideration such Measures as he shall judge necessary and expedient." Since then, Congress has further expanded the policy role of presidents, requiring them to give two other annual addresses, on the budget and the state of the economy. In each, the president identifies problems facing the nation, offers recommendations on how to deal with them, and challenges Congress to adopt those recommendations.

The State of the Union Message

Most recent presidents have preferred to give the State of the Union message in person before a joint session of Congress, but from 1797 to 1913 (Thomas Jefferson through Howard Taft) presidents sent their messages in writing to the Capitol. The president who began the modern tradition of personal appearances was Woodrow Wilson. Today, presidents are more than happy to

Presidents are instructed by the Constitution to give an annual State of the Union address. Recent presidents have chosen to deliver this message in person before a joint session of Congress and the nation's media.

go before Congress, if for no other reason than the press coverage they get both at home and abroad. In fact, some recent presidents have chosen to break their State of the Union message into several messages, thereby extending media coverage. In 1973, for example, President Nixon gave one general message and five "minimessages," each devoted to a specific, problem-ridden policy area.

The Budget Message

The president's annual budget message is often a more detailed policy statement than the State of the Union address. It states a president's policy priorities. By allocating different amounts of money to different agencies and functions, the president lets the people know which policies he considers most important.

The president's role in budgeting is a relatively new one. Before 1921, executive departments such as State, Agriculture, and Defense submitted their budget requests directly to Congress. As government grew and problems intensified, however, presidents realized that without the power to coordinate budget requests they could not develop consistent, cohesive policy proposals. The ***Budget and Accounting Act of 1921*** *created the Bureau of the Budget (now called the Office of Management and Budget) and gave it responsibility for consolidating the requests of each department into a single budget request to be submitted to Congress.* In 1939, Congress placed the Bureau under the direct control of the president in the ***Executive Office of the President,*** *the group of agencies that advise the president and help him carry out his duties.*

The president's budgetary power is important, but it is subject to constraints. The president cannot implement the budget. Only Congress can appropriate funds and thereby authorize expenditures from the federal treasury. Presidents are also restricted by budgetary commitments made by their predecessors. These "uncontrollables" sometimes make up more than half of the budget, leaving a president little room to set new priorities. (More will be said about this in chapter 17.)

The State of the Economy Message

Since 1946, when the Full Employment Act was passed by Congress, presidents have given annual addresses on the state of the economy. In these messages, they focus on the overall growth rate of the economy, the Gross National Product, the inflation rate, the unemployment rate, the produc-

tivity rate, the cost of living, and other economic indicators. A worsening economy can destroy a president, as it did Herbert Hoover and an improving economy can strengthen a president, as happened with Franklin Roosevelt.

Historically, presidents have been held accountable for the economy even though they do not have many formal powers to use in changing it. They do have the responsibility to identify problems and to suggest solutions such as tax increases, spending cuts, or job programs. And, of course, they can "jawbone"—try to persuade business and labor to voluntarily hold the line on wage and price increases. Presidents Truman and Nixon were granted the authority to impose wage and price controls, but these controls have been difficult to enforce and generally unpopular. Controls run counter to one of the nation's oldest, most cherished values—a free enterprise system without much government intervention.

Most control over the economy lies with the Congress and the Federal Reserve System, an independent agency composed of 12 individuals appointed for 14-year terms. Congress is responsible for taxing and spending decisions. The Federal Reserve Board determines the amount of money in circulation, which affects interest rates. (More about the role of the Federal Reserve Board will appear in chapter 17.)

Bill Drafting

Policies proposed in the president's three annual messages, like his other policy proposals, are generally drafted into bills by the president's staff. They are then sponsored by senior members of the president's political party in both the House and the Senate.

Over the years, presidents have tended to propose more policies to Congress, and get more passed, in the first year of their administrations than in the later years (see Figure 12.1). Many of these first-year policy proposals reflect major components of their campaign platforms.

A president's failure to propose legislation is regarded by members of Congress as a sign of weakness. They have come to expect presidents to play the primary role in policy initiation. One estimate is that between 50 and 80 percent of all bills introduced are initiated by the executive branch,[3] even though Article I of the Constitution states that "all legislative powers herein granted shall be vested in a Congress of the United States." Of

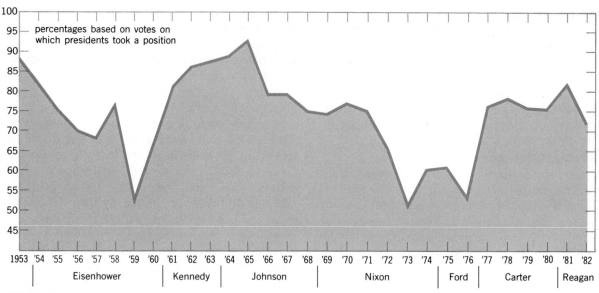

percentages based on votes on
which presidents took a position

| 1953 '54 '55 '56 '57 '58 '59 '60 '61 '62 '63 '64 '65 '66 '67 '68 '69 '70 '71 '72 '73 '74 '75 '76 '77 '78 '79 '80 '81 '82 |

Eisenhower　Kennedy　Johnson　Nixon　Ford　Carter　Reagan

FIGURE 12.1

Presidential Success on Congressional Votes 1953–1982*

SOURCE: Nadine Cohodas, "Presidential Support Study Shows Reagan Rating Fell 10 Percentage
Points in 1982," *Congressional Quarterly*, 41 (January 15, 1983), p. 95.

course, not all bills proposed by the president are passed by Congress and not all bills passed by Congress remain intact. However, if Congress changes or threatens to change the president's

While presidents play a major role as policy initiators, they must also work to get Congress members to go along with their proposals. Here President Johnson signs the Civil Rights Act of 1964 which his extensive lobbying efforts helped to pass.

policy proposals, he has a tool to send Congress back to the drawing board—the veto.

The Veto

The Constitution, in Article II, Section 7, gives the president the power to veto legislation passed by Congress. The *veto is the president's power to reject a bill and return it to Congress along with the reasons for his objections.* A president typically has two other options when he receives a bill—he can sign it and make it law or allow the bill to become law by neither vetoing nor signing it for ten working days. In the closing days of a congressional session the president has a fourth option. This is the *pocket veto—if a president receives a bill when ten days or less are left in the session, he can kill the bill by taking no action on it.* The Supreme Court has ruled that the pocket veto cannot be exercised when Congress is in a holiday recess.

Presidents have varied considerably in their willingness to use the veto (see Table 12.1) and their reasons for doing so. Nineteenth-century presidents often used the veto to control corruption and political patronage. Twentieth-century presidents have used the veto more as a tool of persuasion.

By vetoing legislation, the president is in effect proposing that a different policy be adopted by

Congress. To override a president's veto, the bill must receive a two-thirds vote in each house, which is often difficult to achieve. Since only about 4 percent of all presidential vetoes have been overridden by Congress (Table 12.1), the mere threat of a presidential veto often forces Congress to take the president's policy proposals to heart and modify its own policy preferences. But on occasion, especially when the Congress is not controlled by the president's own party, Con-

gress will attach riders that the president does not favor to a general bill that he has proposed. Congress does this knowing that he will probably not veto it because the general thrust of the bill is his. Unlike governors, presidents cannot veto one or more sections of a bill; they must accept or reject the entire package.

Calling Special Sessions of Congress

The Constitution also grants the president the power to call one or both houses of Congress into special session on "extraordinary occasions." If Congress is in recess, the president can reconvene it if a problem such as a declaration of war or confirmation of a treaty comes up that must be dealt with immediately. This power is not exercised as much today as it once was, primarily because Congress now meets year round. In the past, it was used by presidents to force a "do-nothing" Congress to deal with his policy proposals. Perhaps the best known such incident involved Democratic President Harry Truman, who called the Republican-controlled Eightieth Congress into special session to deal with legislative proposals they had ignored during the regular session.

Executive Orders

An *executive order* is "*a rule or regulation, issued by the President [personally, or by one of the executive departments under him] that has the effect of law . . . it is used to implement and give administrative effect to provisions of the Constitution, to treaties, and to statutes.*"[4] There is no constitutional or statutory delineation of this widely used presidential power, but it has been used since the presidency of Thomas Jefferson. Between 1907 and 1971, presidents issued 11,615 executive orders.[5]

The number of executive orders has greatly increased in recent years as Congress has given the president and other members of the executive branch greater discretionary powers. For example, in the 1960s and early 1970s Congress generally left to the president and the executive departments the power to govern the administration of federal grants-in-aid, determining who was eligible, how money would be distributed, and so on.

In the mid-1970s, a number of Congress members became worried that the president was exercising too much legislative power through executive orders. They began to tack on to new legislation a clause authorizing a legislative veto.

TABLE 12.1

Presidential Vetoes

President	Total Vetoes	Overridden
Washington	2	—
Adams	—	—
Jefferson	—	—
Madison	7	—
Monroe	1	—
Adams	—	—
Jackson	12	—
Van Buren	—	—
Harrison	—	—
Tyler	10	1
Polk	3	—
Taylor	—	—
Fillmore	—	—
Pierce	9	5
Buchanan	7	—
Lincoln	6	—
Johnson	29	15
Grant	93	4
Hayes	13	1
Garfield	—	—
Arthur	12	1
Cleveland	413	2
Harrison	44	1
Cleveland	170	5
McKinley	42	—
Roosevelt	82	1
Taft	39	1
Wilson	44	6
Harding	6	—
Coolidge	50	4
Hoover	37	3
Roosevelt	635	9
Truman	250	12
Eisenhower	181	2
Kennedy	21	—
Johnson	30	—
Nixon	43	6
Ford	66	12
Carter	29	2
Reagan (through 1/83)	15	2

SOURCE: From *The American Presidency* by Richard M. Pious. Copyright © 1979 by Basic Book, Inc., Publishers. Reprinted by permission of the publisher.

However, in 1983 the Supreme Court ruled the legislative veto unconstitutional.

Foreign and Defense Policy Initiation Powers

A number of presidential policy-initiation powers apply exclusively to foreign and defense policy. Some have been granted by the Constitution, including designation as commander-in-chief, the power to negotiate treaties, and the right to recognize foreign nations and receive their ambassadors. Others, such as executive agreements and executive privilege, have developed through custom and usage. All of these powers, however, may be checked by Congress and the courts.

Commander-in-Chief Article II, Section 2, of the Constitution designates the president as "Commander-in-Chief of the Army and Navy of the United States." The founders probably meant for the president to actually command the armed forces when in conflict—a natural expectation in light of the fact that General George Washington was the first president. In 1792, Washington, as president, personally led troops to quash the Whiskey Rebellion.

Modern presidents still "lead" the nation into combat, even though Congress is officially granted the power to declare war (Article I, Section 8). The interpretation of the president's constitutionally designated role as commander-in-chief has been expanded. For a long time, it has been assumed that a president has the right to initiate hostilities with foreign nations in order to "preserve and protect" the rights and property of American citizens. This view is summarized in a legal memorandum issued by the Department of State:

> *In the twentieth century the world has grown much smaller. An attack on a country far from its shores can impinge directly on the nation's security. . . . The Constitution leaves to the President the judgment to determine whether the circumstances of a particular armed attack are so urgent and the potential consequences so threatening to the security of the United States that he should act without formally consulting the Congress.*[6]

Many times in American history, presidents have ordered military forces into action against a foreign nation without any formal declaration of war by Congress. Korea and Vietnam stand out as two modern examples. However, such activities have been common throughout our history. In fact, in the more than 200 cases in which the president has committed armed forces abroad, Congress has officially declared war only five times: the War of 1812; the Mexican War (1846); the Spanish-American War (1898); World War I (1917); and World War II (1941). However, Congress has indirectly authorized many conflicts by either appropriating the funds to pay for them or retroactively giving the president authorization for what he had already done.

On occasion, presidents have also ordered the military into other nations when American lives

While George Washington literally served as commander-in-chief by leading U.S. troops in the Whiskey Rebellion, modern presidents command in a more figurative sense by ordering the military into action to preserve and protect the rights and property of American citizens.

or property were in danger. For example, in 1980, President Carter ordered a mission to recover 52 Americans held hostage by the Iranian government. Presidents have also ordered the military into other countries to administer their affairs when they failed to pay American creditors (for example, Cuba from 1906 to 1909, Nicaragua from 1912 to 1925, and Haiti from 1915 to 1934). At other times, American troops have been sent to aid regimes friendly to the United States, often to combat communism, which was the alleged purpose of Kennedy's Cuban Bay of Pigs invasion. Some refer to these uses of military power as "gunboat diplomacy."

Many members of Congress believed that our deep involvement in the unpopular Vietnam War began as far back as the late 1950s as a result of President Eisenhower's and his successors' overly-broad interpretation of the commander-in-chief role. That role was expanded during the term of Richard Nixon, and many members believed it was magnified too much. Nixon's tenure in office was called an *imperial presidency—the president was perceived as being too powerful as a result of his general misuse or abuse of presidential power.*

In 1973, Congress overrode Nixon's veto and enacted the *War Powers Act, which authorized congressional participation in decisions to use American armed forces abroad.* The Act states three conditions under which the president can commit armed forces: 1) a declaration of war by Congress; 2) specific statutory authorization; or 3) a national emergency created by an attack on the United States or its military forces. The Act also provides checks and balances by: 1) requiring the president to notify Congress within 48 hours after sending troops into another country; 2) establishing a device for an automatic cutoff of a "presidential," or undeclared, war within 60 days unless Congress authorizes the continuation of hostilities; 3) granting Congress the power to order withdrawal of American military personnel. The Act also requires the president to consult with Congress "in every possible instance" before committing troops abroad and to bring detailed reports to Congress of any such commitment.

The War Powers Act was first invoked in April 1975 when President Ford ordered American troops into Southeast Asia to help evacuate Americans from Cambodia and South Vietnam. It was also invoked in 1975 when Ford sent United States troops to recapture the United States merchant ship *Mayaguez* and its crew from Cambodia. In April 1980, some members of Congress accused President Carter of violating the Act by launching an unsuccessful mission to rescue American hostages in Iran without first notifying Congress. The Mayaguez and Iranian incidents led Congress to exclude rescue missions from coverage of the War Powers Act even though both presidents Ford and Carter presented detailed reports of the missions within two days of the occurrence, as required by law.

As part of his role as commander-in-chief, the president has also been granted a number of extraordinary emergency powers by Congress. Between 1930 and 1980, Congress passed some 500 federal statutes allowing a president during a crisis to temporarily seize property; organize and control the means of production; seize commodities; institute martial law; control all transportation and communications; restrict travel; regulate the operations of private enterprise; call up all the military reserves; and assign military forces abroad. The number of emergency powers on the books led one senator to remark,

> If the President were to make use of all the power available to him under the emergency statutes on the books, he could conduct a government without reference to usual constitutional processes. These powers taken together could form a basis for one-man rule.[7]

In another move to combat the "imperial presidency" and strengthen its own powers, Congress passed the *National Emergencies Act of 1976, which ended a number of "temporary" emergency powers of the president by declaring that the emergencies no longer existed as of September 1978.* The Act also laid out clear procedures to be followed in declaring future emergencies. These procedures still give the president the power to declare emergencies, but they provide for congressional review and establish that a majority vote in both the Senate and the House could end an emergency at any time.

Treaty-Making Powers A *treaty is a "formal agreement entered into between two or more [countries] for the purpose of creating or restricting mutual rights and mutual responsibilities."*[8] The Constitution, in Article II, Section 2, grants the president the "power, by and with the advice and consent of the Senate, to make treaties, provided two-thirds of the Senators present concur." In other words, the Consti-

In an unusual effort to add pomp and circumstance to the presidency, Richard Nixon authorized new gold-braided uniforms for the White House honor guard. Seen as too symbolic of Nixon's imperial presidency, these uniforms were eventually given to a high school band.

tution assigns the major role in initiating foreign policy to the president, although it gives the right to approve, disapprove, or revise treaties to the Senate.

Few times in history has the Senate failed to ratify treaties. They have rejected only about 1 percent of the treaties sent by the president, have amended or made specific reservations in about 15 percent, and have approved all the rest without change.[9] Some of the most memorable Senate rejections of treaties have been in modern times—Wilson's Treaty of Versailles ending World War I and the second Strategic Arms Limitation Treaty (SALT II) with Russia sponsored by Carter. The Senate nearly failed to ratify the Panama Canal Treaty drawn up by President Carter. It was debated for two years before the Senate finally approved it by a vote of 68 to 32, only one vote more than the required two-thirds majority. When presidents do not think they can get a two-thirds vote in the Senate, they often turn to another foreign policymaking device, the executive agreement.

The Executive Agreement An *executive agreement* is "*an international agreement between the President and a foreign head of state that, unlike a treaty, does not require Senate consent.*"[10] The authority to make such agreements has developed over time as presidents have broadly interpreted their constitutional power as commander-in-chief. Legally, an executive agreement is similar to a treaty and has

the force of law. Such agreements allow the president to 1) bypass a hostile or unreceptive Senate, especially one that is not controlled by the president's own political party; and 2) maintain secrecy, which is often important during wartime. Because of these advantages, presidents have used executive agreements far more than treaties.

Executive agreements were used by some of the nation's early presidents to buy land to accommodate the nation's westward expansion. Jefferson purchased Louisiana from France through an executive agreement, and Texas and Hawaii were annexed by the same means. More recent executive agreements have almost always involved trade and defense—negotiating for American military bases on foreign soil; selling arms and planes to other countries; or giving them economic aid in exchange for supporting the United States or fighting against communism.

During the Vietnam era, presidents misused their power to make executive agreements and their related power of executive privilege. *Executive privilege is the president's right to remain silent and refuse to give information to Congress on the grounds that keeping such information secret is vital to the national security.* As one presidential scholar noted,

> *What irked Congress in the 1960s and 1970s was that while the Senate was asked to ratify international accords on trivial matters, the White House arranged critically important mutual-aid and military-base agree-*

ments [with Ethiopia, Laos, Thailand, Korea, and South Vietnam] without even informing Congress.[11]

Because of presidential misuse, Congress passed the ***Case Act of 1972,*** *which requires that all executive agreements be submitted to Congress within 60 days of their execution for the sake of information.* The Case Act did not, however, grant Congress a veto power over such agreements. (The Supreme Court has repeatedly upheld a president's right to make executive agreements.)

Congress has another check on the president's executive agreement power—the authority to appropriate funds. For example, no economic aid can be given unless appropriated by Congress. Knowing this, presidents are careful not to enter into executive agreements that a large number of Congress members will fail to support.

Recognition of Foreign Governments   The president has the power to grant diplomatic recognition to foreign governments. This power is established in Article II, Section 3, which instructs the president to "receive ambassadors and other public ministers." Congress has no veto over this presidential power except an indirect one—refusal to fund programs to aid foreign countries.

A president's recognition of a country is an important policy statement. Recognition is usually routine, but it becomes troublesome when a government advocates an ideology such as communism that is contrary to that advocated by the United States. Jimmy Carter's official recognition of the People's Republic of China (Communist China) and his ordering the exchange of ambassadors was just such a situation. The action notified the world that the president considered the People's Republic and not the government of Taiwan the legitimate government of China, and that his foreign policies would be adjusted accordingly. Even though Carter's successor, Reagan, preferred a "two-China" policy, he did not "unrecognize" the People's Republic.

Presidents sometimes make foreign policy by withdrawing recognition of a foreign government whose actions they regard as contrary to the best interests of the United States or the world at large. Withdrawing recognition usually involves expelling the offending country's diplomats from the United States. President Eisenhower, for example, withdrew United States recognition of Cuba after Fidel Castro assumed power.

THE PRESIDENT AS POLICY POPULARIZER

The president is news: who he is, what he says, where he goes, what he does. . . . This man is the only nationally elected policy-maker in American government. . . . [He] is the ideological symbol of American democracy and nationhood.[12]

Americans tend to judge presidents by their ability to get things done—to get their policy proposals through Congress. To sell their proposals to Congress, the public, and other nations, presidents rely heavily on the prestige of the office itself, which gives them the ability to influence public opinion through personal appearances and the media.

Influencing Public Opinion

In his role as the nation's symbolic leader, the president can influence how the public feels about him in a number of ways. One is through his performance of ceremonial duties, which include acting as host to visiting royalty and heads of state; visiting foreign countries on goodwill trips; giving speeches on national holidays; receiving Boy and Girl Scouts, war veterans, or other groups; posing

Presidents have the power to grant diplomatic recognition to foreign governments. President Jimmy Carter's official recognition of the People's Republic of China marked a major shift in the nation's foreign policy.

TABLE 12.2

Ceremonial Activities: A Sampling of the Calendars of Presidents Ford and Carter

President Ford, March 10–March 16, 1975	Time Taken
Charitable Organizations: Easter Seal Girl	24 minutes
Youth Group: Voice of Democracy essay winners	5 minutes
Professional Delegations: Speech to 250 editors and publishers	45 minutes
Honorary Award Winners: Miss America	4 minutes
Maid of Cotton	11 minutes
White House Press Photographers Contest winners	5 minutes
Miscellaneous: Gridiron Club pictures (Washington News Corp)	5 minutes
Preparation of speech to be given to Gridiron Club	30 minutes
Total: 2 hours, 9 minutes	

President Carter, September 12–30, 1977		Time Taken
September 12	National Conference of Catholic Bishops	15 minutes
	National United Way Campaign	10 minutes
14	American Bible Society	5 minutes
15	Arrival ceremony for Raymond Barre, Prime Minister, France	30 minutes
	National Hispanic Heritage Week proclamation	15 minutes
	Recording Industry of America	5 minutes
20	Bill signing ceremony	15 minutes
22	Kiwanis International	5 minutes
23	Sickle-Cell Anemia Poster Child	5 minutes
28	Columbus Day proclamation	15 minutes
29	Chief Executives, Motion Picture Industries	10 minutes
30	Farm Family of the Year	5 minutes
	Supreme Court Justices ceremony	20 minutes
	Total: 2 hours, 35 minutes	

SOURCE: Merlin Gustafson, "Our Part-Time Chief of State," *Presidential Studies Quarterly*, 9 (Spring 1979), (Center for the Study of the Presidency) pp. 165–167.

for photographs; making proclamations; attending church or the Army-Navy football game; and traveling to scenes of national disasters (see Table 12.2). It is estimated that each month the president receives 1,000 to 1,500 requests for appearances and speaking engagements.[13] Because these events get national coverage by television, radio, and the press, it often appears that presidents spend more time on them than they really do.

Presidents use such occasions to build support for their policy proposals by personally interacting with groups and individuals. A study of the appointment calendars of presidents found that public relations and political considerations were decisive in determining who would be granted or denied presidential time.[14]

Personal interactions with the president are also important in influencing Congress members and foreign leaders. They, too, are flattered by the personal attention of a president. As one Congress member put it, "There is a great reverence for the Office of the Presidency, and the opportunity to invite people to the White House is very potent. . . . It's impossible to replicate."[15]

President Reagan successfully used this strategy to get his budget and tax cut proposals adopted by Congress in 1981. For example, he had a private chat at the White House with Representative Charles W. Stenhold, leader of a group of conservative Democrats, and also invited the entire Democratic conservative forum to breakfast at the White House. He attended a meeting of the House Republican caucus at the Capitol. Fifteen undecided members were flown to Camp David for hot dogs, hamburgers, and tax talk. Twelve of them later voted with Reagan.[16] Before the key votes were taken, he personally telephoned dozens of Congress members and met with many others.

Presidents use the media to stimulate support at the grassroots level. They hope voters, in turn, will urge their senators and representatives to go along with presidential policy proposals. The television press conference is one commonly used media technique. In *Media Power Politics*, Paletz and

Presidents are well aware that their personal interactions with members of Congress are often the key to congressional adoption of presidential policy preferences.

TABLE 12.3

Presidential-Press Honeymoon: Month of Termination and Reason

President	Month	Reason
Kennedy	4th	Press management charges over Bay of Pigs
Johnson	13th	Credibility questions about Vietnam
Nixon	11th	Agnew media assault
Ford	2nd	Nixon pardon
Carter	9th	Lance affair
Reagan	16th	Recession

SOURCE: Robert Locander, "Carter and the Press: The First Two Years," *Presidential Studies Quarterly,* 10 (Winter 1980), (Center for the Study of the Presidency) p. 107.

Entman stated,

> *The televised press conference is one of a president's more notable opportunities to enhance his power. . . . A president who dominates the press conference . . . gives the impression of a similar mastering of his office and of the political scene.*[17]

Presidents generally enter office enthusiastic about holding press conferences, but after their first really hostile questioning from the press, their enthusiasm wanes. Presidents' *honeymoons—periods of friendliness with the press early in their administration*—generally end after bad press about some policy decision or someone in their administration (see Table 12.3). Recent honeymoons have been as short as 2 months for Ford and as long as 16 for Reagan. Presidential press relations subsequently move into a *detachment phase* (generally the last two years of a term), in which *presidents leave most direct dealings with the press to members of their White House staff or their cabinet offi-*

cers.[18] But modern presidents cannot afford to stop holding press conferences. The press might speculate that the president has something to hide, which could cause his popularity to dip even further.

A safer but equally influential media technique to create grassroots support is the televised presidential address. (In the days before television, radio addresses such as the famous "fireside chats" given by Franklin Roosevelt served the same purpose.) Most appearances are during prime time and reach 60 to 80 million television viewers. Most addresses are also carried live by radio. In such appearances, the president talks directly to the people about a specific issue such as energy, Social Security, or taxes. There are no reporters to ask hostile questions to which the president might make an embarrassing reply. The networks almost always cover such addresses. For example, Johnson, Nixon, and Ford tried to obtain television time to address the nation on 45 occasions and received it 44 times from all three networks.[19] Beginning with the Ford administration, however, networks began to say no occasionally when the real purpose of the address appeared to be the president's personal campaign interests.

Whether it's a press conference or a television and radio address, the result is the same: the president gains several percentage points in public opinion polls. Consequently, many presidents stage such media events to precede congressional votes on their policy proposals. According to many media experts, the most successful presidential media lobbying effort was Reagan's appearance on television to explain his tax cut pro-

THE PRESIDENCY: PROPOSING, POPULARIZING, AND IMPLEMENTING PUBLIC POLICY

posal two days before the Congress voted. Reagan appealed to the public to "contact your senators and Congress [members]. Tell them of your support for this bipartisan proposal."[20] The public responded with an avalanche of pro-Reagan mail, telegrams, and telephone calls. The proposal passed, with 48 Democratic House members voting for it. The president's popularity in the polls shot up even higher than it already was.

Presidents find it increasingly difficult to maintain high popularity in the polls for more than a few months.* Every president since World War II has experienced widespread approval in the first few months following his inauguration, but sooner or later his standing in the polls begins to drop. Recent presidents have also had a more difficult time getting favorable press. One study found that every incumbent since Eisenhower had done slightly worse than his predecessor in attracting favorable press.[21] The exceptions were Ford, who could not possibly have gotten worse press than Nixon, and Reagan, whose honeymoon period was extended because of an assassination attempt. Reagan's personality and seeming ease with the press also gave him an advantage over his predecessors.

Some blame the press more than they blame the presidents for the phenomenon of worsening coverage, claiming that the press sets presidents up for falls. But presidents themselves help create this unrealistic expectation by their campaign promises. For example, an overwhelming majority of the population expected newly elected presidents Carter and Reagan to strengthen national defense and foreign policy, reorganize government agencies and make them run more efficiently, reduce the cost of government, and reduce unemployment. Are these realistic expectations of presidents? Hardly.

Building Support in Congress: Pork, Patronage, and Politicking

One of the president's most useful bargaining tools is his *preferment power—the power to award*

federal contracts to businesses and give federal grants to governments within a House member's district or a Senator's state. Ironically, Congress has bestowed this power on presidents over the years by granting them wide discretion to determine administrative details once Congress has authorized a program and appropriated the funds for it. This is also known as *pork barrel politics.*

Presidents often promise rewards to members of powerful committees and subcommittees in exchange for their support on certain policy proposals. President Johnson was particularly adept at using this strategy to get his Great Society programs passed. Presidents are also careful to see that the senator or representative whose district is getting a defense installation or urban development grant gets the credit and the publicity.

A president's failure to recognize the importance to Congress members of getting projects and jobs for their constituents can permanently damage his bargaining power with Congress. An example is President Carter's cancellation of 19 already-promised water projects. Carter intended to win points with the public for being cost-conscious and efficient. He did not anticipate the hostility his move created in Congress. Eventually he compromised and signed a bill that restored nine of the projects, having learned that he could not afford to ignore customs.

Another important bargaining tool is *patronage—the power to appoint top-level federal officials.* Article II, Section 2, of the Constitution grants the president the power to appoint "public Ministers and Consuls, Judges of the Supreme Court, and all other Officers of the United States," subject to Senate confirmation. Presidents build support in Congress by practicing **senatorial courtesy,** *conferring with the two senators from a state (especially those from his own party) before making a nomination to fill a federal position in that state.* These positions include judgeships, district attorney slots, customs officer positions, and regional directorships of key executive agencies such as the Department of Housing and Urban Development. Often, a president will ask senators to make several recommendations that would be acceptable to them as well as the president.

Presidents have a number of other jobs in Washington to hand out. Before each new administration, the House Post Office and Civil Service Committee publishes a document entitled *U.S. Government Policy and Supporting Positions.* More

---

*Researchers caution against strict comparisons of Gallup presidential popularity polls across time because of changes in the placement of the question: "Do you approve of the way _____ is handling his job as President?" Before 1956, the question was asked toward the end of a Gallup interview, which meant that a respondent's answer may have been biased by previous questions. Since 1956, the question has generally been the first question in a Gallup survey.

As leaders of their political party, presidents frequently hit the campaign trail on behalf of the party's congressional and gubernatorial candidates, particularly in states where the races are very close.

commonly known as the ***Plum Book***, this is *the official list of high-salaried government jobs the president will fill.* The 1980 Plum Book listed more than 3,000 positions ranging in pay from $50,112 to $69,630 annually. Shrewd presidents solicit senators' and representatives' recommendations for persons to fill these slots, recognizing the value of such appointments to Congress members who need to reward important campaign contributors and supporters.

Presidents can build credit with Congress members that can be used later by just plain "good politicking"—posing for photographs with Congress members; arranging VIP tours of the White House for important constituents; making a personal phone call or writing a personal letter to someone back home in the district; or soliciting a member's help in drafting an important policy proposal.

A president can be particularly helpful to members of Congress in their midterm election campaigns. As political party leader, a president can hit the campaign trail for a Congress member from the same party, formally endorse the member, and arrange for campaign funds from the national party treasury. A president can obtain party funds because he hand-picks the national party chairperson. Of course, if a president's popularity is low or he is too liberal or conservative for a particular Congress member's district, he does the member a favor by staying out of the campaign. A president may even promise not to campaign against a Congress member of the opposite party who has consistently supported the president's policy proposals, as Reagan did with the conservative southern Democrats ("boll weevils") who helped pass his 1982 budget and tax cuts.

The Power of Persuasion: Style, Personality, and Track Record

Richard Neustadt, in his book *Presidential Power*, says that what distinguishes one president from another is the ability to persuade, since all presidents have the same formal powers to exercise, the same tools of influence, and the same roles to perform. He defines a president's power of persuasion as the ability "to induce [members of Congress] to believe that what he wants of them is what their own appraisal of their own responsibilities requires them to do in their interest, not his."[22]

A president's social skills and knowledge of protocol help build confidence in his integrity and ability. Social ease and mutual respect can make bargaining easier. In Washington, ceremonial deference among powerful leaders is the norm, and press coverage of presidential entertaining is important in building the public's image of presidential style—his political persona, lifestyle, and personal congeniality.[23] President-watchers quickly contrast the style of a new president with that of his predecessor and predict how effective the new president will be in governing the nation. A recent example was the press's contrast of Carter and Reagan: "We went from Levi's to Gucci's, Willie Nelson to Bobby Short, cardigan sweaters to riding breeches, Coca-Cola to California wine, and barbecue to calamari."[24]

A president's social and political skills are inseparable; they are both part of his personality. In *The Presidential Character*, James David Barber notes that

> *Every story of Presidential [policymaking] is really two stories: an outer one in which a rational man circulates and an inner one in which an emotional man feels. The two are forever connected. Any real President is one whole man and his deeds reflect his wholeness.* [25]

According to Barber, the best predictor of a president's performance is his personality, which is largely shaped early in childhood. Barber's theory gained considerable credibility after Watergate: he had predicted that Nixon would be a bad president long before the burglary and cover-up that led to Nixon's resignation.

A president's track record can also enhance his power of persuasion. Nothing succeeds like success. A president's ability to sell a new policy proposal often depends on his previous sales successes. This is why a newly-elected president wants to move fast and win a few key votes—to get off on the right foot and become known as a mover and shaker. Another reason for this rush is the press's ritual of doing "first 100 days" stories. In one journalist's words, "Whatever the risks in reading events of the First 100 Days like scattered tea leaves, it does offer a convenient opportunity to take the measure of the new man in the White House and project what may be expected over the balance of his Administration." [26] No president wants to get bad press 100 days after taking office and be labeled a "do-nothing" president.

One way of looking at a president's track record is to separate domestic issues from foreign and defense issues. Presidential scholar Aaron Wildavsky has proposed a *"two presidencies" theory,* which suggests that the "United States has one president but two presidencies: one for domestic affairs and one for defense and foreign policy." [27] According to Wildavsky, presidents are better able to control the nation's defense and foreign policies than its domestic policies. Lee Sigelman confirmed this theory for presidents in general but noted that an individual president's success may vary. [28] Presidents Kennedy, Johnson, Ford, and Reagan were more successful in getting domestic policy proposals enacted by Congress; Eisenhower, Nixon (first term), and Carter, in defense and foreign policy proposals.

THE PRESIDENT AS POLICY IMPLEMENTOR

Article II of the Constitution states that "the executive power shall be vested in a President of the United States." Section 3 charges the president "to take care that the laws be faithfully executed." Presidents are expected to get the government machine going and to keep it going. If it doesn't operate well, they must find ways to repair it. But presidents often have little control over policy implementation, and yet it is in this stage of the policy process that a great deal can go wrong.

Managing and Motivating the Bureaucrats

Important in getting any job done are the people who do it and the management tools and administrative abilities that help them do it. Presidents have been given certain tools by the Constitution, Congress, and the courts, and they have developed others on their own. But each president's administrative style reflects his character, his previous experiences, and the precedents established by earlier presidents.

Appointment Powers   As we have seen, the Constitution grants the president the power to appoint. This important management tool allows a president to bring into power those who share his philosophies about how to best manage the government. Each president has his own ideas about what qualities appointees should have. For example, President Reagan's appointees were judged on five criteria: commitment to Reagan's objectives, integrity, competence, teamwork, and toughness. [29]

The president's appointment power does not extend deep into the bureaucracy. The federal government has some 2.1 million employees not appointed by the president. These civil service employees are hired, assigned, and promoted by departments and agencies under the supervision of the Office of Personnel Management (formerly the U. S. Civil Service Commission). They are hired through a merit system, not a patronage system. They are sometimes referred to collectively as the "permanent administration." They keep their jobs even when presidents change, and they often resist the efforts of new presidents to change administrative procedures. Nearly every president since Thomas Jefferson has campaigned on a platform of bureaucratic reform.

Presidents who have been overly critical of civil

servants either before or after taking office have often paid a price. Presidents can blame their failures on the permanent administration and try to attract public support by appearing to take on the bureaucracy. But they cannot get the cooperation of senior career officials if they antagonize them, and presidents need this cooperation to implement their policies. These permanent employees provide continuity in government activities. Some think an even greater number of federal employees should be permanent, criticizing a system that replaces its top officials every four years. No other democracy turns out such a large proportion of its officials when the administration changes. Most presidents would strongly disagree, however. They have experienced great frustration in tryng to control an enormous bureaucracy that seems to cause as many problems as it resolves.

A president's power to make appointments is restrained by a number of checks, both formal and informal. Approximately 800 of 3,000 appointees must be confirmed by the Senate. The Senate almost always honors a president's requests, particularly with regard to cabinet appointees. It generally considers the competence of the nominee and possible conflicts of interest rather than the nominee's politics. Confirmation, which requires a majority vote of the Senate, is often more difficult for judges and foreign ambassadors.

In selecting nominees, presidents must take into account the likelihood of Senate approval. Said one presidential aide: "If there are two candidates of equal qualifications but one of them is supported by a key Senator, then we will listen to that. We know better than to send a name to the Senate that is sure to be blocked."[30]

A president must also take into account a number of other considerations, including his promises to campaign contributors, supporters, and key interest groups; the maintenance of some geographical, racial, and gender balance; and the preferences of key party leaders. Besides, a president cannot always get the people he wants most to accept an appointment. Many first-choice people would have to take tremendous pay cuts and divest themselves of numerous business interests to work for the government. In the same way, presidents have difficulty keeping good people on board. Turnover among political appointees is high; they stay an average of only two years.

Removal Powers While the president's appointment power is constitutionally guaranteed, his power of removal is not. The removal power he does have has accrued over the years through common practice, congressional statutes, and judicial interpretations. For example, the president's power to remove cabinet secretaries was first exercised by Andrew Jackson through his own interpretation of the power to "faithfully execute the law." Congressional statutes permit presidential removal of civil servants "for cause only"—misconduct, delinquency, inefficiency, disability, or criminal conduct. The procedures for documenting "cause" are established in civil service regulations and monitored by the Merit System Protections Board. The procedures are regarded by many presidents as more trouble than they're worth. The exception is the power to remove government employees who go on strike. President Reagan dismissed some 15,000 air traffic controllers for going on strike in direct violation of federal statutes. Technically, he could have reinstated them by exercising his pardoning power (Article II, Section 2), but he chose not to. Since Ford's pardon of Nixon, presidents have been understandably cautious of exercising this power.

The removal of executive branch employees is influenced by the same political constituencies that affect a president's appointment powers. These constituencies include Congress members, interest groups, party leaders, and political supporters. Such groups can prevent the president from evicting a troublesome employee or force the president to remove someone he wanted to keep.

Management Limits Preventing tension between permanent civil servants and top-level political appointees such as cabinet secretaries, undersecretaries, and assistant secretaries is difficult for any new presidential administration. One reason is that presidents rarely reach into the ranks of the civil servants for their top-level appointees, choosing instead to bring in outsiders. This practice helps give credibility to an administration's promise to bring in new people with new ideas, but it can quickly alienate civil service employees if the new officials have poor management skills. And top-level officials are sometimes chosen more for their political skills or policy expertise than for managerial skills. In a study of presidential cabinet appointments from 1953 to 1976, James Best found that these types don't stay long because they soon learn that their main job as cabinet members is not to make policy decisions but to manage their departments.[31] And, as we have seen, the president as chief executive must manage the managers.

On the other hand, an outside cabinet appointee may be a superb manager, running the department with precision and bringing credit to the president. The longer cabinet members stay, however, the more likely it is that they will strengthen their identification with department employees and the department's constituents (i.e., interest groups) at the expense of identification with the president. As Clinton Rossiter observed,

> the President's hardest job is, not to persuade Congress to support a policy dear to his political heart, but to persuade the pertinent bureau or agency, even when headed by [persons] of his own choosing, to follow his direction faithfully and transform the shadows of the policy into the substance of a program.[32]

Staff Competition   Mixed signals from presidential appointees often occur when appointees compete for the attention of the president or the press. As the Executive Office of the President (described later in the chapter) has grown, competition between these staffers and the president's department and agency appointees has increased. Reputedly overbearing White House staffs of recent presidents have been blamed for much of the hostility that has developed between the president and his agencies and between the White House and Congress.

These limits on a president's power to manage the bureaucracy affect his ability to implement public policy. "The chief executive may be the captain of the ship; but he must function with a crew that is not entirely of his own choosing," says Joseph Kallenbach, author of *The American Chief Executive*.[33] The captain of the ship must sail it or sink with it, and if it is in need of repair, the captain must get it into port.

Repairing the System: Reorganization and Impoundment

Reorganization   Presidents and members of Congress have long recognized that any enterprise as large as the federal bureaucracy needs to be reorganized periodically to ensure greater effi-

ciency, economy, and responsiveness to citizens. Changing times may necessitate the creation of new departments and agencies to handle newly emerging problems, the abolition of old departments or agencies, or the adoption of new management techniques. At other times reorganization is used to respond to an active interest group.

Since 1932, Congress has passed a series of **legislative reorganization acts,** *which authorize presidents to propose executive reorganizations.* Under the acts (1932, 1939, 1949, and 1977), if neither house has vetoed a president's reorganization proposal in 60 days, it becomes effective. Between 1949 and 1980, presidents submitted 103 reorganization plans to Congress, 83 of which became effective.[34] Beginning with the 1977 act, presidents are prohibited from using reorganizations to create or eliminate a department; such proposals must go through the normal legislative process. A president is not prohibited from drafting such a proposal and then lining up congressional sponsors to introduce it in each house, however.

Congress has traditionally seen the purpose of reorganization to be cost-cutting. All reorganization acts since the 1939 act have required that each reorganization request include an itemized estimate of any reduction or increase in anticipated expenditures. Presidents, on the other hand, have seen the purpose of reorganization as improved management. President Franklin Roosevelt recognized that saving money "depends upon a change of policy, the abandonment of functions, and the demobilization of the staffs involved," all of which are outside the scope of most reorganization requests.[35] President Carter in 1977 requested that the itemized-savings requirements be deleted, proposing that efficiency measures such as improvements in management and the delivery of federal services be substituted. Congress, however, refused to buy this argument and kept the savings requirement in the 1977 act.

Presidents continue to use reorganization as a management tool for three primary reasons: 1) to demonstrate a commitment to efficient government, 2) to convince the bureaucracy that the White House is in charge; and 3) to avoid political obstacles that could occur in the regular legislative process.[36]

Impoundment   To get around budgetary obstacles, presidents beginning with Thomas Jefferson have occasionally used impoundment. *Impoundment is a president's refusal to spend funds that* *have been appropriated by Congress.* Impoundment has been used in the past to save money because of a change in events, as when a war ended and funds were no longer needed, or for managerial reasons, as when a project could be carried out in a more efficient way.[37]

Before Nixon's administration, impoundments were infrequent and usually did not involve large sums of money. But Nixon impounded about $18 billion that had been appropriated by Congress for water pollution control, urban aid, and other programs. Many members of Congress were irritated. They thought Nixon had usurped the power of Congress to legislate and he was, in effect, exercising an item veto. The result was the passage of the *1974 Congressional Budget and Impoundment Act.* This act *requires presidents to report delays in spending to Congress; gives either house the power to veto an expenditure deferral; and requires the approval of both the Senate and the House for a president to cancel any project for which Congress has already appropriated funds.* Some think the Impoundment Act was Congress's overreaction to a single individual—Nixon. The enormous amount of paperwork the Act has created for executive agency officials may lead to its revision.

THE PRESIDENT'S SUPPORTING CAST

The Cabinet

The *cabinet is the group that advises the president on matters of public policy. It is typically composed of the president, the vice president, and the heads of the executive departments—State, Treasury, Defense, Justice, Interior, Agriculture, Commerce, Labor, Health and Human Services, Housing and Urban Development, Treasury, Energy, and Education. In addition, a president may give cabinet status to any other official he chooses,* such as the U.S. ambassador to the United Nations, the U.S. trade representative, the director of the Office of Management and Budget, or the chair of the Council of Economic Advisers. Thus, the composition of the cabinet may change from one administration to the next.

George Washington started the custom of regularly calling together the vice president and department heads to ask for advice. Cabinet members today assist the president in two ways. First, they oversee the operations of the executive departments. Second, they help the president formulate policy and lobby Congress for its passage. Cabinet members are expected to function as

President Carter's cabinet was regarded as more representative of a cross section of Americans than the cabinets of his predecessors.

loyal advocates of the president's objectives. As supporting actors, they must take care not to upstage the president.

Presidents have varied greatly in how they have used their cabinets. Some have preferred to meet with members individually or in small groups. Carter, Reagan, and others have preferred to meet with cabinet members as a large group. Some have held cabinet meetings to boost their own morale when things are going badly; others have held meetings to thoroughly debate policy. But few have managed to avoid either favoring some cabinet members more than others or relying on their White House staff and personal advisers more than the cabinet. The longer presidents stay in office, the more likely they are to do both. The result is that they break their initial promise to heavily involve the cabinet in team policymaking.

Determined to avoid a similar fate, President Reagan organized his cabinet much differently than had his predecessors. He created five *cabinet councils, which are made up of cabinet members who deal with issues in the same policy area.* The councils cover commerce and trade, economic affairs, food and agriculture, human resources, and natural resources and the environment (see Table 12.4). Each council is chaired by the president, but sessions can be convened by the cabinet member serving as chair pro tem. The vice-president, counselor to the president, and the White House chief of staff serve as ex officio members of all five councils.

TABLE 12.4

**President Reagan's Cabinet Councils
(Policy Clusters)**

Council on Commerce and Trade*

Commerce Secretary, chair pro tem
Secretary of State
Treasury Secretary
Attorney General
Agriculture Secretary
Labor Secretary
Transportation Secretary
U.S. Trade Representative
Chairman, Council of Economic Advisers

Council on Economic Affairs*

Treasury Secretary chair pro tem
Secretary of State
Commerce Secretary
Labor Secretary
Transportation Secretary
Office of Management and Budget director
U.S. Trade Representative
Chairman Council of Economic Advisers

Council on Food and Agriculture*

Agriculture Secretary, chair pro tem
Secretary of State
Interior Secretary
Commerce Secretary
Transportation Secretary
U.S. Trade Representative

Council on Human Resources*

Health and Human Services Secretary, chair pro tem
Attorney General
Agriculture Secretary
Labor Secretary
Housing and Urban Development Secretary
Education Secretary

Council on Natural Resources and Environment*

Interior Secretary, chair pro tem
Attorney General
Agriculture Secretary
Transportation Secretary
Housing and Urban Development Secretary
Energy Secretary
Chairman, Council of Economic Advisers
Chairman, Council on Environmental Quality

SOURCE: "Reagan's Cabinet Councils May Have Less Influence Than Meets the Eye," *National Journal* (July 11, 1981), pp. 1244, 1245.

*Ex officio members include the vice-president, counselor to the president, and White House chief of staff.

Reagan's purpose in creating these councils was to make sure that cabinet officials did not develop a departmental stand as opposed to an adminis-

tration-wide stand. Said he, "We want our Cabinet Secretaries to have both the knowledge and the resolve to resist the protectionist attitudes of their departments."[43]

From a policy perspective, the purpose of the cabinet council system is to coordinate the formulation of policy decisions that affect more than one agency. According to one administration spokesperson, the councils are "the forum for the final arguing of or discussion of issues and policy decisions."[44] However, broad issues that affect the entire government and overall budgetary and fiscal matters are reviewed at meetings of the full cabinet.

Reagan presided over 19 full cabinet meetings and 6 cabinet council sessions in his first five months in office while he and his staff were formulating the budget and tax cut proposals. But Reagan's appearances became less frequent and cabinet infighting more frequent as it became more difficult to get Congress to adopt presidential policy preferences. Reagan, like his predecessors, has found cabinet governing difficult.

The Executive Office of the President

The Executive Office of the President is not really a single office. It is better visualized as an office composed of many "suites" which are periodically redesigned to better conform to the president's tastes and policy priorities (see Figure 12.2). For example, President Reagan virtually closed down the Council on Wage and Price Stability created by Ford because it conflicted with his preference for a free-enterprise economic system and his promise to reduce the amount of government intervention in the economy. Presidents have also periodically changed the job descriptions of managers, assistant managers, and other employees of various offices within the Executive Office to reflect their policy preferences, priorities, and management styles.

The White House Staff The *White House Office,* informally called the "White House staff," *has historically been responsible for facilitating and maintaining communication with Congress, the individual members of Congress, the heads of executive agencies, the press and other information media, and the general public.* By 1980, White House employees numbered 400 and running the office cost approximately $20 million a year.

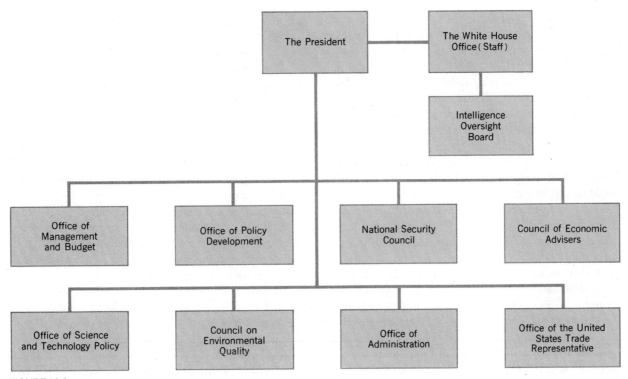

FIGURE 12.2

Executive Office of the President

SOURCE: General Services Administration, *The United States Government Manual 1981/82*, Washington, D.C.: U.S. Government Printing Office, 1981, p. 821.

More than the cabinet officials, the White House staff reflects a president's personality and style. Unlike cabinet members, staff members do not have to be confirmed by the Senate. Conse-quently, presidents are freer to bring in long-time friends, political supporters, or business acquaint-ances—people they trust and feel comfortable around. White House staff members are the pres-

A president's White House staff reflects his personality and style. President Reagan and his close aides project a formal image whereas President Carter and his aides reflected a more informal one.

ident's confidential advisers, whom he relies on in the daily workings of the executive branch. Among them are his "choreographers," "stagehands," "production crew," and "press agents." Together they help put the show on the road and keep it playing to a full audience.

To direct the staff, a president usually relies upon a handful of top aides and advisers with whom he is in daily contact. In recent years, a president's inner circle has typically included a chief of staff, deputy chief of staff, press secretary, counsel to the president, and assistant for national security affairs. There are also assistants heading the offices of public liaison, legislative affairs, political affairs, minority affairs, and intergovernmental affairs.

The dozen or so staff members closest to the president have a great deal of power because they control access to the president. They are often referred to as his "gatekeepers" or "palace guard." It can be damaging to a president if these bodyguards are too protective of him and keep out cabinet or agency officials or others who need to be let in. As we have seen, this has happened to a number of presidents. When it does happen, however, it results more from differing perspectives on the needs of the president than from a calculated power struggle. Presidential staff members emphasize personal loyalty and assess the president's best interests in terms of electoral politics, while cabinet members and Executive Office officials are more concerned with developing consistent and coherent policies.

Other Agencies of the Executive Office   The structures of executive agencies other than the White House Office are much more firmly established. This is because these agencies were originally created to manage and monitor specific programs and activities of the executive branch, many of which are technical in nature. The heads of these agencies are probably best described as the president's technical directors, and the personnel are policy experts rather than people experts like members of the White House staff. In fact, many positions in these agencies are civil service positions, such as budget analyst, budget examiner, and foreign policy analyst. Each agency is heavily involved in policy formation and execution. All agency personnel, whether they are appointed by the president or selected through the civil service system, are expected to be loyal to the president and committed to the implementation of his policy preferences and priorities.

The relative importance of these other agencies is often measured by whether or not the agency head is given cabinet status by the president. Almost all recent presidents have assigned cabinet status to the heads of the Office of Management and Budget, the Council of Economic Advisers, and the National Security Council.

The *Office of Management and Budget (OMB)* *helps prepare the federal budget, monitors spending, and conducts efficiency analyses.* It was called the Bureau of the Budget until 1970. In an executive order, Nixon renamed it and expanded its role to include numerous management responsibilities. Because of its almost daily contact with each executive department and agency, OMB is the president's best source of information about what is going on in the bureaucracy.

Through its role as preparer of the president's annual budget, OMB promotes and protects the president's policy preferences. Because of OMB's important policymaking role, the director appointed by the president must be confirmed by the Senate. Policymaking by OMB takes place both before and after the passage of the budget.

OMB helps ensure that the president maintains the power to submit his own budget to Congress by exercising its *legislative clearance* power: *every appropriations request submitted by a department or agency to Congress must receive the approval of OMB.* This rule helps prevent executive agencies from bypassing the president. OMB can also help the president get Congress to pass his budget. OMB staff members provide members of Congress with valuable budgetary information to help them explain their budget votes to constituents.

In its role as budget controller, OMB can ensure that agencies follow presidential priorities through its power to dispense funds. While agency funds are normally released on a quarterly basis, the president can order OMB to step up or slow down an agency's expenditure rate. (OMB's role in the budgetary process will be discussed further in chapter 17.)

OMB also has some management powers that can be used to make the government run more efficiently and economically. It can recommend that the president submit a reorganization proposal to Congress and help him draw up such a proposal.

It can also recommend that certain regulatory reforms be made, especially when it determines that the costs of certain regulations exceed their benefits or when it finds that agencies have not chosen to adopt the least burdensome regulations. When technological breakthroughs are made, OMB can recommend that new communication, information, and accounting systems be put into place to better monitor agency performance.

The **Council of Economic Advisers (CEA)** was created by the Employment Act of 1946. The purpose of the council is *to suggest policies that promote economic stability and full employment.*

The CEA is made up of three economists, who are appointed by the president with the advice and consent of the Senate. In addition, some 36 civil service employees, mostly economists, provide council members with the economic forecasts they need to make economic recommendations to the president.

The specific functions of the Council of Economic Advisers and its staff are to analyze the national economy, advise the president on economic developments, evaluate the economic programs and policies of the national government, recommend policies for economic growth and stability, and assist in the preparation of the president's annual economic report to Congress. In their taxing and spending recommendations, CEA members, like other members of the president's supporting cast, are expected to reflect the president's policy preferences and priorities.

The **National Security Council (NSC)**, created in 1947 and placed in the Executive Office in 1949, was established to *advise the president with respect to the integration of domestic, foreign, and military policies relating to national security.* Its members are the president, vice-president, secretary of state, and secretary of defense. Advisers required by law (statutory advisers) are the chair of the joint chiefs of staff and the director of the Central Intelligence Agency. The council is assisted by a staff of about 70 professionals. The executive director of the NSC is the assistant to the president for national security affairs. He is appointed by the president, but the appointment does not need Senate approval. The assistants for national security affairs prior to Reagan's Richard Allen have been quite visible (Henry Kissinger; Zbigniew Brzezinski). This reflected the growing importance of foreign policy and of the NSC itself.

The NSC resembles a cabinet council because it brings together all executive branch officials responsible for national security policy and attempts to coordinate their activities in line with presidential policy preferences and priorities. It is the president himself, as council chair, who determines the frequency and agenda of council meetings. Presidents have varied greatly in the role they have assigned to the National Security Council. Eisenhower, Nixon, and Ford relied more heavily on meetings of the full NSC than Truman, Kennedy, Johnson, Carter, or Reagan. But every president has occasionally used meetings of the full council to legitimize decisions arrived at informally or to offer symbolic reassurances to the public that security is one of the administration's highest priorities. Until recently, the council's activities were related almost exclusively to the military. However, the growing interrelationship between domestic and foreign policies, especially in economics, has broadened the council's focus.

The remaining "suites" in the Executive Office of the President are relatively new additions. The **Office of the United States Trade Representative** became part of the Executive Office in 1974, although it had existed since 1963. The trade representative, appointed by the president, is a cabinet-level official with the rank of ambassador. With the office staff, he or she is *responsible for directing all trade negotiations for the United States and for formulating all United States trade policy.* The office negotiates trade and commodity issues in the Organization for Economic Cooperation and Development, the United Nations Conference on Trade and Development, and other bilateral and multilateral institutions. It has become more important as the issue of free trade versus protection of American industry has intensified.

The **Office of Policy Development** became part of the Executive Office in 1978. This office *helps the president develop and coordinate domestic policy options and reviews the major policies of the administration.* Under Reagan, the office became more of a support mechanism to facilitate discussion and policymaking by the cabinet councils. The staff of each cabinet council includes personnel from the Office of Policy Development.

The **Council on Environmental Quality** was established in 1969 by the National Environmental Policy Act *to formulate and recommend national policies to improve the quality of the environment.* Traditionally, the council has prepared an annual report on environmental quality for Congress. The council consists of three members, who are appointed by the president with the advice and consent of the Senate. The chair, handpicked by the president, was assigned cabinet status by President Reagan, which reflects the council's important role in helping the president develop and sell his policy positions in the debate on renewal of the Clean Air Act.

The *Office of Science and Technology Policy* was created in 1976 by the National Science and Technology Policy, Organization, and Priorities Act. The office is *responsible for advising the president of scientific and technological considerations in areas of national concern, such as the economy, national security, health, foreign relations, and the environment.* This office has become involved in some lifestyle issues as well, particularly those involving scientific research that has ethical and moral implications, such as cloning, test tube babies, and experimentation with various drugs and surgical procedures.

The *Office of Administration* was created under President Carter's 1977 reorganization plan *to provide administrative support services to all the agencies in the Executive Office except the White House Office.* These services include information, personnel, and financial management; data processing; library services; records maintenance; and general office operations such as mail, messenger, procurement, and supply services.

Family and Friends: A President's "Kitchen Cabinet"

The president's *kitchen cabinet* is *"a group of informal advisers who hold only minor office, or no office at all, yet exert more influence on policy than the real Cabinet because of their closer personal relationships with the chief executive."*[40]

The term "kitchen cabinet" was first used to describe Andrew Jackson's close friends and advisers, who met him literally in the kitchen of the White House. All presidents turn to friends to avoid feeling isolated, to escape the bureaucracy, and to help them relax. Presidents also use their kitchen cabinets as sounding boards and places to let off steam without fear of public disclosure.

Each president's kitchen cabinet reflects his personality, working habits, and concept of governing, in the same way that his regular cabinet and the personnel of the Executive Office do.

Franklin D. Roosevelt, for example, assembled a "brain trust"—a fairly large group of academic and policy specialists to help him draw up the New Deal. Jimmy Carter's kitchen cabinet consisted of one man and one woman—Charles Kirbo, his personal lawyer and friend from Atlanta, and first lady Rosalynn Carter. President Carter occasionally invited Rosalynn to sit in on regular cabinet sessions and met with her once a week, privately, over lunch to discuss public policy.

Ronald Reagan's kitchen cabinet is composed of 12 to 15 wealthy, close-knit friends of long standing who socialize together, belong to many of the same clubs, transact business together, and share a conservative political ideology. However, they have no official connection with the administration.

The importance of these intimate networks of family and friends in the policymaking process should not be underestimated. As former Secretary of State Dean Rusk once observed,

> *The real organization of government at higher echelons is not what you find in textbooks or organization charts. It is how confidence flows down from the President. That is never put on paper. People don't like it. Besides, it fluctuates. People go up and people go down.*[41]

The Vice-President: The President's "Understudy"

According to the Constitution, the vice-president has only one executive role, which is to stand by in case the president dies or is disabled. He also presides over the Senate, but aside from these roles, he undertakes duties solely at the pleasure of the president. Thus, the vice-president has one primary role—successor to the president—and two secondary roles—presiding officer of the Senate, a legislative role, and stand-in for the president, an executive role. The vice-president's role in the policy process is very much dependent upon circumstances outside his control.

The Vice-President's Role as Presidential Successor As a possible successor, a vice-president must meet the same eligibility criteria as the president. A vice-president must be at least 35 years old, a natural born citizen, and a resident of the United States for 14 years (Article II, Section 1). Succession is permanent if the president dies, resigns, or is impeached, convicted, and removed from office. Succession is temporary if the president is ill or disabled. The importance of having qualified, prepared vice-presidents has been driven home in recent years. One president, John Kennedy, was assassinated in office, and two, Gerald Ford and Ronald Reagan, were victims of assassination attempts. Franklin Roosevelt died suddenly in office, and Richard Nixon resigned in midterm rather than be removed by Congress.

The Constitution (Article II, Section 1) clearly established the vice-president as the president's successor. It did not lay out the line of succession after the vice-president or spell out the procedures for declaring the president disabled. These uncertainties have since been cleared up by the Presidential Succession Act of 1947 and the Twenty-Fifth Amendment to the Constitution.

The *Presidental Succession Act of 1947* was passed by Congress immediately after Franklin Roosevelt's death. *The Act specifies that after the vice-president, the presidency passes to the Speaker of the House, then to the president pro tempore of the Senate, then to cabinet officials in the following order: secretaries of state, treasury, defense, the attorney general, the secretaries of interior, agriculture, commerce, labor, health and human services, housing and urban development, transportation, energy, and education.*

The *Twenty-Fifth Amendment* to the Constitution, ratified in 1967, *lays out two procedures for dealing with presidential disability. Under both procedures, the vice-president becomes acting president;* that is, he succeeds to the presidency only temporarily. Under the first procedure, the president notifies the Speaker of the House and the president pro tempore of the Senate, in writing, that he is unable "to discharge the powers and duties of his office." Under the second procedure, the vice-president and a majority of cabinet members or some other body designated by Congress by statute can declare the president unable to serve in that capacity. Either way, the vice-president serves as acting president until the president notifies Congress that he is no longer disabled. Under the second procedure, if the vice-president and a majority of the cabinet or other body do not agree that the president is ready to return, the decision goes to Congress. A two-thirds vote in both houses can keep the vice-president as acting president.

The Twenty-Fifth Amendment also clarifies how a new vice-president is to be chosen when that office becomes vacant. The president submits his choice for vice-president to Congress for approval, which takes a majority vote of both houses. This provision was first used when Nixon's vice-president, Spiro Agnew, resigned because of charges of corruption stemming from his term as governor of Maryland. Nixon nominated Gerald Ford, whose credentials were closely screened by Congress before his approval. The provision was used again when Ford nominated Nelson Rockefeller as his vice-president after Nixon resigned and Ford succeeded to the presidency.

Preparing the Vice-President for the Role of Successor: The President's Responsibility Until recently, presidents have neglected to prepare the vice-president for the presidency. One reason is that many presidents have seen vice-presidents as potential competitors for their job. This was especially the case before the passage in 1951 of the *Twenty-Second Amendment, which limits a president's tenure to two terms.* Before the Amendment, vice-presidents were given little to do to keep them from "upstaging" or perhaps even replacing the president. From presidents Van Buren to Eisenhower, not one vice-president was nominated by his political party for the presidency (except those who had already succeeded to the office because of the incumbent's death).

Another reason for neglect of the vice-president has to do with the method of selecting vice-presidential candidates. In some cases, the president has chosen his running mate strictly on the basis of regional, ideological, or ethnic characteristics in order to balance the ticket, so the working relationship between the two has been strained at best.

Since Eisenhower, presidents have taken a different attitude. One reason is that the vice-presidency is now a common route to the presidency (see Table 12.5). Johnson, Nixon, and Ford were vice-presidents before becoming president. The two-term limit has convinced presidents to play an important part in choosing a successor who shares their policy preferences and priorities. Assigning the vice-president meaningful responsibilities not only gets press coverage and builds up party support, it can also give the vice-president a head start in the race for the presidential nomination.

A second reason has been the expansion of the

TABLE 12.5

Vice-Presidential Successions to the Presidency: Permanent, Temporary, and "Almost"

Vice-President	Date	Situation
Permanent Successions		
John Tyler	1841	Death of President William Henry Harrison
Millard Fillmore	1850	Death of President Zachary Taylor
Andrew Johnson	1865	Assassination of President Abraham Lincoln
Chester A. Arthur	1881	Assassination of President James A. Garfield
Theodore Roosevelt	1901	Assassination of President William McKinley
Calvin Coolidge	1923	Death of President Warren G. Harding
Harry S. Truman	1945	Death of President Franklin D. Roosevelt
Lyndon B. Johnson	1963	Assassination of President John F. Kennedy
Gerald Ford	1974	Resignation of President Richard M. Nixon (in anticipation of removal by Congress)
Temporary Successions (Unofficial)		
Chester A. Arthur	2 months, 1881	President Garfield dying from gunshot wounds from an assassination attempt
Thomas R. Marshall*	17 months 1919–1921	President Woodrow Wilson suffering from a stroke that disabled him
Richard M. Nixon	1955	President Dwight Eisenhower had a heart attack
	1956	President Eisenhower had an ileitis operation
	1957	President Eisenhower had a brief cerebral blockage
George Bush	1 month, 1981	President Ronald Reagan recovering from a gunshot wound following an unsuccessful assassination attempt
"Almost" Successions (Missed Assassination Attempts)		
Martin Van Buren	1835	President Andrew Jackson shot at in rotunda of U.S. Capitol; assailant's pistols misfired
John N. Garner	1933	President Franklin D. Roosevelt shot at while riding in open car in Miami, Florida; assailant missed
Alben W. Barkley	1950	Two would-be assassins entered the Washington residence of President Harry Truman; were killed before reaching the president
Nelson Rockefeller	1975 (twice)	Would-be assassin aimed pistol at President Gerald Ford as he reached to shake her hand in Sacramento, California; gun grabbed before it fired by Secret Service agent
		President Ford shot at as he left a San Francisco hotel; bystander grabbed assailant's arm and shot was deflected

SOURCE: Abstracted from "Past Presidential Assassination Attempts," *Congressional Quarterly,* 39 (April 4, 1981), p. 582.
*First lady Edith Wilson was said to have really been president during this time.

presidency—the growth in both the number of problems presidents must deal with and the public's demands for solutions. Recent presidents have found vice-presidents useful in lightening their work load. Vice-presidents serve as members of the cabinet and the National Security Council, act as chairs of presidential task forces and study commissions, help sell the president's programs in Congress, and help formulate policy positions.

Finally, the growing incidence of assassination attempts has made presidents aware that they could be temporarily disabled at any time. They recognize that failure to prepare their vice-presidents to step in and carry on would reflect badly

on their presidency and damage their chances of reelection, if the attempt happened in their first term. (Many people were shocked, for example, to find out that Roosevelt never even informed Truman of the atomic bomb.)

The importance of the vice-president was finally recognized by President Carter. Carter gave his vice-president, Walter Mondale, an office within steps of the Oval Office, symbolizing the vice-president's importance. In addition, Carter gave Mondale full access to top-level memos and meetings and instructed his aides to work closely with Mondale's staff. Reagan has continued these practices.

Vice-presidents are often sent around the world as representatives of the president and the U.S. Vice-President George Bush made several trips to Europe for President Reagan.

Playing the Role of "Understudy": The Vice-President's Perspective One important rule for vice-presidents is "avoid stealing the show." It is never easy to be an understudy, especially when one wants so badly to be the star. Vice-presidents Hubert Humphrey and Nelson Rockefeller pushed hard to be "copresidents" but were boxed out of the action by the presidents under whom they served. On the other hand, Walter Mondale and George Bush played the traditional role of second-in-command and reaped personal political benefits. Bush, for example, served briefly as a stand-in for Ronald Reagan in the hours immediately after the assassination attempt:

Rushed back to Washington, [Vice-President Bush] declined to have his helicopter deliver him to the White House lawn for fear that it would be seen as an exercise of a presidential prerogative. Instead, he arrived by motorcade, in the conventional manner, and stepped into the President's ceremonial schedule with elaborate explanations that Reagan, in fact, remained in charge. . . . By minding his manners, Bush reaped rewards, such as being designated head of the White House crisis management team and chair of the Presidential Task Force on Regulatory Relief, and being sent to France to meet with newly elected President Francois Mitterand.[42]

Another important rule for vice-presidents to follow is to concentrate on selling the president's program to Congress and avoid presiding over the Senate. The Constitution designates the vice-president as the president of the Senate (Article I, Section 3). The vice-president can vote only in case of a tie and cannot participate in the floor debate. As presiding officer, his primary function is a parliamentary one, which requires impartiality.

Most vice-presidents have preferred to let the president pro tempore preside so that they can go about legislative liaison activities. The exception is when their vote may make the difference between passage or failure of a bill considered a high priority by the president.

The critics' evaluation of the overall presidential "production" is based upon the performance of both the president and his supporting cast—the cabinet, officials of his Executive Office, his "kitchen cabinet," and his vice-president. Few presidential productions have been judged "great."

"GREAT" PRESIDENTIAL PERFORMANCES: WHY WOULD ANYONE WANT THE LEAD ROLE?

Every few years, someone conducts a "presidential greatness" poll (see Table 12.6). Respondents to such surveys, usually historians and political scientists, each have their own criteria for judging greatness. Most agree, however, that the "great" presidents are those who have helped America through crises—periods of major economic, environmental, social, political, or ideological turmoil. Few presidents hold office under such con-

TABLE 12.6

Presidential "Greatness" Polls, 1962–1977

Schlesinger Poll 1962	U.S. Historical Society Poll 1977	
Great	**Ten Greatest Presidents**	**Votes**
(1) Lincoln	Lincoln	85
(2) Washington	Washington	84
(3) F. Roosevelt	F. Roosevelt	81
(4) Wilson	Jefferson	79
(5) Jefferson	T. Roosevelt	79
	Wilson	74
Near Great	Jackson	74
	Truman	64
(6) Jackson	Polk	38
(7) T. Roosevelt	J. Adams	35
(8) Polk	L. Johnson	24
(8) Truman	Cleveland	21
(9) J. Adams	Kennedy	19
(10) Cleveland	Madison	16
	J. Q. Adams	14
Average	Eisenhower	14
	Monroe	7
(11) Madison	Hoover	6
(12) J. Q. Adams	McKinley	4
(13) Hayes	Van Buren	2
(14) McKinley	Arthur	2
(15) Taft	Tyler	1
(16) Van Buren	Buchanan	1
(17) Monroe	Grant	1
(18) Hoover	Hayes	1
(19) Harrison	Taft	1
(20) Arthur	Coolidge	1
(20) Eisenhower	Nixon	1
(21) A. Johnson	W. Harrison	0
	Taylor	0
Below Average	Fillmore	0
	Pierce	0
(22) Taylor	A. Johnson	0
(23) Tyler	Garfield	0
(24) Fillmore	B. Harrison	0
(25) Coolidge	Harding	0
(26) Pierce	Ford	0
(27) Buchanan		

Failure

(28) Grant
(29) Harding

SOURCE: Thomas E. Cronin. *The State of the Presidency*, 2nd ed. (Boston: Little, Brown, 1980), pp. 387–388. Based on a table in Robert E. DiClerico, *The American President* (Englewood Cliffs, N.J.: Prentice-Hall, 1979), p. 332. Data from Arthur Schlesinger, Sr., "Our Presidents: A Rating by 75 Historians," *New York Times Magazine*, 29 July 1962, pp. 12ff.; U.S. Historical Society provided the results of its survey.

ditions—nor should we want them to—and therein lies a common criticism of these polls.

If the odds are so strongly against any president being regarded as great, especially in his lifetime, why do so many seek the job? Some say it is in the "perqs" (perquisites), the benefits that come along with the office: an annual salary of $200,000; a $50,000 expense account; elegant living quarters (the White House) complete with "help" (cooks, butlers, gardeners, florists, housekeepers), tennis courts, a heated pool, and a bowling alley; a private plane (Air Force One), two helicopters to help beat the traffic in busy Washington; a place in the country for weekend retreats (Camp David); 24-hour-a-day protection (Secret Service); and a great retirement plan.

Under the ***Former Presidents Act of 1958**, presidents receive an annual pension of $70,000 (tied to the pay rate of a cabinet member) and money for office space, phones, furnishings, supplies, equipment, a staff, and travel*. Former presidents also receive Secret Service protection for themselves, their wives, their widows (until their remarriage), and their children up to age 16. In 1981 alone, the cost of supporting ex-presidents Nixon, Ford, and Carter came to $11 million. It cost an additional $12.5 million to maintain the seven presidential libraries.[43]

Others say the real reason for wanting to be president is the ego, making it to the top in politics and securing lifetime recognition and a place in history. If nothing else, they are guaranteed that they will be first at something (see Table 12.7).

The challenge of occupying one of the world's most powerful offices and of meeting the country's changing needs and demands is probably the motivation for most of those who seek the nation's highest office.

SUMMARY

Since the administration of George Washington, presidents have been expected to propose solutions to problems, persuade Congress to adopt those proposals, and guide the government in carrying them out. The Constitution provides that the president share with Congress its role of making policy. The president proposes policy by:

1. giving State of the Union, budget, and state of the economy messages.

2. drafting bills, which are introduced in Congress by senior members of the president's party.

TABLE 12.7

Presidential "Firsts"

First to:	President
Wear false teeth	George Washington
Live in the White House	John Adams
Have illegitimate children	Thomas Jefferson
Be labeled the shortest president	James Madison
Be a college dropout	James Monroe
Be descended from a president (his father)	John Quincy Adams
Be the object of an assassination attempt (unsuccessful)	Andrew Jackson
Be born after the American Revolution	Martin Van Buren
Die in office	William Henry Harrison
Remarry while in office	John Tyler
Ban dancing and drinking at the presidential mansion	James Knox Polk
Not vote in any presidential election	Zachary Taylor
Have no interesting first in his life or career	Millard Fillmore
Be an alcoholic	Franklin Pierce
Be a lifelong bachelor; be gay	James Buchanan
Be assassinated	Abraham Lincoln
Never attend school	Andrew Johnson
Be a West Point graduate	Ulysses S. Grant
Win by one vote (185–184) in the electoral college	Rutherford B. Hayes
Be left handed	James Garfield
Be born outside the United States (Canada)	Chester A. Arthur
Be reelected after leaving office for a term	Grover Cleveland
Have electricity in the White House	Benjamin Harrison
Have an epileptic wife	William McKinley
Leave the continental United States during his term of office (to Panama)	Theodore Roosevelt
Become chief justice of the U.S. Supreme Court	William Howard Taft
Hold a Ph.D. in political science (from Johns Hopkins)	Woodrow Wilson
Speak over radio	Warren G. Harding
Be of Indian ancestry	Calvin Coolidge
Be born west of the Mississippi (Iowa)	Herbert Hoover
Appoint women to high administrative posts	Franklin Delano Roosevelt
Authorize the use of atomic weapons in warfare	Harry S. Truman
Have a press conference covered by movie and television cameras	Dwight D. Eisenhower
Be a Roman Catholic	John F. Kennedy
Be southern-born since Andrew Jackson	Lyndon Baines Johnson
Resign office	Richard Milhous Nixon
Be an Eagle Scout	Gerald R. Ford
Be born in a hospital	Jimmy Carter
Be a film actor	Ronald Reagan

SOURCE: Dennis Sanders, *The First of Everything.* Copyright © 1981 by Dennis Sanders. Reprinted by permission of DELACORTE PRESS.

Reagan's Changing Tax Policy: Cop-out or Compromise?

In 1981 Congress passed the largest tax cut in the history of the nation, $750 billion over five years. In 1982, it passed the largest tax increase in the country's history, $98.3 billion over three years. This was one of the most dramatic policy reversals ever to occur in such a short period. Both proposals were strongly supported by President Ronald Reagan.

Predictably, some observers saw the president's reversal as a cop-out. Conservative members of the president's own party saw it as an abandonment of supply-side economics, the philosophy on which the president was elected. Many Democrats saw the reversal as evidence that "Reaganomics" had failed and that it was bad policy to begin with. Still others saw it as pragmatic politics—a necessary step to reverse a badly sagging economy.

A mere eight months before the increase was passed, in his State of the Union address, Reagan had said "I will seek no tax increases this year and I have no intention of retreating from our basic program of tax relief." In making this promise, he rejected the advice of his top economic policy advisers and remained loyal to his position on supply-side economics. But projections of a federal deficit of more than $170 billion in fiscal year 1983, a nationwide unemployment rate of nearly 10 percent, and interest rates for consumers in the 16 to 19 percent range led Reagan to "temporarily" abandon pure supply-side approaches. Such a drastic shift in ideological position made it tough to promote the proposal. How did he do it?

His strategy was to "sell" the bill as a tax reform or tax compliance measure that affected businesses more than individuals. For example, he focused on sections of the bill that sought to stop tax cheating. (In 1981, some $87 billion of taxes owed were not paid.) He also focused on provisions that reduced or eliminated several corporate tax breaks, including the highly unpopular tax leasing provisions passed in 1981. Another selling point was that federal employees would be taxed for Medicare for the first time. (Nongovernment employees had been paying for two decades.) Finally, the president pushed the notion that some of the taxes that would most affect individuals would be on "luxury" items such as cigarettes and airline tickets.

These sales techniques were identical to the ones he had used a year earlier to cut taxes: appealing to the public on a nationwide televised address, inviting key members of Congress to the White House for personal conversations, and soliciting the help of business and housing groups such as the Chamber of Commerce and the National Association of Homebuilders in pressuring members of Congress to vote for the proposal. To each audience, Reagan posed a choice: "Would you rather reduce deficits and interest rates by raising revenue from those who are not now paying their fair share? Or would you rather accept larger budget deficits, higher interest rates, and higher unemployment?"[1]

The vote on the bill was close, and not at all along party lines. Voting for the tax increase were 103 Republicans and 123 Democrats; voting against it were 89 Republicans and 118 Democrats. The fact that the vote was taken only 75 days before the 1982 midterm congressional races made it especially tough for members of Congress to go along with the president since it is considered politically unwise to vote for a tax increase in an election year. But those who did considered it even more politically unwise not to. As the Democratic Speaker of the House put it, "It's [even] more unfortunate that there are more than 10 million Americans out of work, that millions of small business [owners] and small farmers are facing bankruptcy."[2]

The tax increase bill did not cure the nation's economic ills, but it demonstrates the president's important role in economic policymaking. It also shows how presidents react to the changing needs of the nation and often put the public's interests ahead of their own philosophical positions, knowing full well that the public may view a policy reversal as a cop-out instead of a compromise.

[1] Dale Tate, "President Hawks Tax Increase as Conferees Haggle Over Bill," *Congressional Quarterly*, 40 (August 14, 1982), p. 1947.
[2] Chronicle News Service, "Congress Passes $98 Billion Tax Bill," *Houston Chronicle*, August 20, 1982.

3. vetoing legislation passed by Congress.
4. calling special sessions of Congress.
5. issuing executive orders.
6. exercising his foreign and defense policy powers, which include serving as commander-in-chief of the army and navy, making treaties, using executive agreements, and recognizing foreign governments.

The president must popularize, or "sell," his proposals to Congress, the public, and sometimes to other nations. He influences public opinion through ceremonial duties, personal interactions, press conferences, and televised addresses. He builds support in Congress through pork barrel politics (awarding contracts in Congress members' districts in exchange for support), seeking recommendations from Congress in appointing federal officials, and campaigning on behalf of Congress members.

The president must also implement policy, as assigned by the Constitution. He does this by managing and motivating federal agencies, which may involve appointing or removing top-level offi-cials, reorganizing the federal bureaucracy, and impounding funds appropriated by Congress.

In his role as policy initiator, popularizer, and implementor, the president is supported by the cabinet, the Executive Office (which includes the White House staff), the vice-president, and a ''kitchen cabinet'' of family and close friends.

KEY TERMS

Budget and Accounting Act of 1921
cabinet
cabinet council
Case Act of 1972
Congressional Budget and Impoundment Control
*   Act of 1974*
Council of Economic Advisers (CEA)
Council on Environmental Quality
detachment period
executive agreement
Executive Office of the President
executive order
executive privilege
Former Presidents Act of 1958
honeymoon period
imperial presidency
impoundment
kitchen cabinet
legislative clearance
legislative reorganization acts
legislative veto
National Emergencies Act of 1976
National Security Council (NSC)
Office of Administration
Office of Management and Budget (OMB)
Office of Policy Development
Office of Science and Technology Policy
Office of the U.S. Trade Representative
patronage
Plum Book
pocket veto

preferment power
Presidential Succession Act of 1947
senatorial courtesy
treaty
Twenty-Fifth Amendment
Twenty-Second Amendment
two presidencies theory
veto
White House Office

SUGGESTED READINGS

Abshire, David M.; Moodie, Michael; and Nurn-berger, Ralph. *U.S. Global Leadership: The President and Congress.* New Brunswick, N.J.: Transaction Books, 1980.

Edwards, George. *Presidential Influence in Congress.* San Francisco: W. H. Freeman, 1980.

Fishel, Jeff. *Presidential Promises and Performance.* Washington, D.C.: Congressional Quarterly Press, 1981.

Genovese, Michael A. *The Supreme Court, The Constitution, and Presidential Power.* Washington, D.C.: University Press, 1980.

James, Dorthy Buckton. *The Contemporary Presidency.* New York: Pegasus, 1969.

Koenig, Louis W. *The Chief Executive,* 4th ed. New York: Harcourt, Brace, Jovanovich, 1981.

Nathan, Richard P. *The Administrative Presidency.* New York: John Wiley & Sons, 1983.

Porter, Roger B., ed. *The Economy and the President: 1980 and Beyond.* Englewood Cliffs, N.J.: Prentice-Hall, 1981.

Schlesinger, Arthur M., Jr. *The Imperial Presidency.* Boston: Houghton Mifflin, 1973.

Sindler, Allan P. *Unchosen Presidents: The Vice President and Other Frustrations of Presidential Succession.* Berkeley, Calif.: University of California Press, 1976.

Wayne, Stephen. *The Legislative Presidency.* New York: Harper and Row, 1978.

CHAPTER 13

THE BUREAUCRACY: BRINGING POLICY TO THE PEOPLE

The Public Perception ■ What Are Bureaucracies and Are They Inherently Bad? ■ The Organization of America's Government Bureaucracies ■ A Bureaucratic Web ■ How Well Do the Bureaucracies Perform? ■ The Complex Government Employment System ■ The Role of Bureaucrats in the Policy Process ■ Keeping the Bureaucrats Under Control

The word 'bureaucrat' has become a purely pejorative term connoting, in the public mind, inefficiency, ineptitude and even callous disregard for the rights and feelings of ordinary people.

President Jimmy Carter

It is not my intention to do away with government. It is rather to make it work—work with us—not over us; to stand by our side, not ride our back. Government can and must provide opportunity, not smother it.

President Ronald Reagan
Inaugural Address, 1981

Americans are tough on their public servants. The words of these two presidents reflect a hardening of public attitudes toward government employees (also called civil servants or bureaucrats). Americans today think less of bureaucrats but expect more—in responsiveness, efficiency, and productivity. Congress, presidents, and the courts have recognized these changing attitudes and responded by adopting policies to restructure the bureaucracy.

THE PUBLIC PERCEPTION

Many Americans view government employees as insensitive, inflexible, incompetent, agency oriented, impersonal, and lazy. They view government as inefficient, rigid, rule-dominated, wasteful, uncoordinated, unresponsive, and bogged down by paperwork and red tape.

How do such attitudes arise? The main source is the citizen's contact with government employees in daily life. When we mail a package at the post office, telephone an Internal Revenue Service branch with an income tax question, call the police to report a crime, ride a city bus or subway, have our garbage picked up, or attend a lecture at a public university, we come into direct contact with employees of our federal, state, and local governments. In addition, the food we eat, the medicine we take, the cars we drive, the gas we buy for our cars, the charges we pay for telephone calls, the toys we buy for our children, and the products we buy for our homes are all affected by

The negative attitude of most individuals toward government employees stems from an unpleasant encounter they have had with a bureaucrat in some government agency who appears to be inefficient, insensitive, or incompetent.

rules and regulations made and carried out by government employees. An unpleasant encounter with an unfriendly or seemingly inflexible bureaucrat makes an individual think all bureaucrats are that way and that government in general is not working well—especially if the scene is repeated frequently.

Citizens often fail to realize, however, that they, too, play an important role in the work of government employees. Many citizens are unfamiliar with the functioning of government agencies— what they do, how they do it, how many employees have been allocated by elected officials to do a job, what the legal limits on activities are, and so on. Citizens often expect bureaucrats to do things they have no authority to do. Citizens may also have conflicting expectations. They want more and better services, but they want to pay fewer taxes. They think government employees should not be able to strike to improve wage and job conditions, yet they may themselves belong to unions. They want government agencies to distribute services and enforce rules impartially, yet they are disgusted when a government employee refuses to bend the rules "just this once." While citizens may have an idea of how much the bureaucracy costs (often from politicians' campaign rhetoric), they have almost no idea whether they're getting their money's worth or whether programs, rules, and regulations work as they were intended to when they were passed. Most citizens are also unaware of the many checks and balances that have altered the bureaucracy as the needs and demands of the population have changed. Instead, they just assume the bureaucracy is untameable.

Actually, it is the bureaucracy that brings policy directly to the people—more so than the presidency, the Congress, or the courts. Since this is the level of government that most of us have direct contact with, it is important that we understand how it works—especially if we want to change it, as most of us will at some point in our lives.

WHAT IS A BUREAUCRACY AND ARE THEY INHERENTLY BAD?

A *bureaucracy* is a form of organization whose characteristics were first described by the German sociologist Max Weber in the *Theory of Social and Economic Organization.*[1] The characteristics are:

1. *a chain of command*   (hierarchy)
2. *division of labor among subunits*   (specialization)
3. *specification of authority for every position and unit by elaborate rules and regulations* (span of control)
4. *impersonality in executing tasks*   (neutrality)
5. *complete adaptation of the organization's structure, pattern of specialization and authority, and rules and regulations to the organizational goal*   (goal-orientation)
6. *flexibility in re-adapting organizational characteristics to changing organizational goals and circumstances*   (adaptability)

7. *predictability of behavior based on maintenance of records and observance of rules and regulations* (standardization)[2]

According to this definition, most agencies—public and private, government and business—are bureaucratic organizations. Whether it be the U.S. Department of Defense, the AFL-CIO, Delta Airlines, or McDonald's, the basic organization is similar. Each agency has a chain of command that defines goals and determines the best way to achieve them. The hierarchy's leaders decide which departments will do the tasks needed to accomplish the goals, coordinate the activities of specialized units, and make sure the goals remain clear to all. The leadership also identifies and reacts to changing conditions and the demands of those served by the organization while keeping the organization's basic framework the same to maintain consumers' trust. Isn't this a rational way to do business? Then why does the term "bureaucracy" bring to mind all forms of negative behavior? Why is it associated in the public's mind with government rather than private agencies when red tape pervades both?

What Makes Government Bureaucracy Different?

The government bureaucracy comes under attack precisely because it is not a single bureaucracy according to Weber's definition. In chapter 4 (Federalism) we saw that the American system of government is highly fragmented, consisting of a national government, 50 autonomous state governments, and thousands of local governments. Furthermore, because of the elaborate system of checks and balances, no single individual or group has total legal authority over all government sectors. As we saw in chapter 12 (The Presidency), the president does not have direct legal authority over all federal government employees, and he has *no* direct authority over the employees of state and local governments. In contrast, the board of directors of IBM has complete control over all employees of IBM no matter where they are or what they do. Thus, while the federal bureaucracy "has a highly developed division of labor, much specialization, a good deal of impersonality, and a huge accumulation of rules and regulations, no chain of command ties the whole 'system' together."[3]

Most Americans would not want such a tied-together system. They prefer the federal system of a national government and 50 state governments, choosing to give up the rationality of a single bureaucracy for the diversity built into federalism. Nonetheless, the American public has the right and the responsibility to demand responsiveness from government bureaucracies, even when they remain separate.

THE ORGANIZATION OF AMERICA'S GOVERNMENT BUREAUCRACIES

In 1980 the United States had 79,913 different governments. These governments employed 16,222,000 Americans. Of this total, state governments employed 23 percent; local governments, 59 percent; and the national government, 18 percent. The national government is the largest single employer, of course. There is only one federal government, but there are 50 state governments and 79,862 local governments. As we shall see, the federal government is itself composed of many different agencies, which are often considered separate bureaucracies (see Figure 13.1).

Executive Agencies

Even within the executive branch, there are many different administrative agencies. Not all of these agencies have the same status or prestige: a real "pecking order" exists (see Table 13.1). At the top are the cabinet-level departments.

Cabinet-Level Departments The 13 *cabinet departments comprise the largest and most visible of all the executive agencies. They are the first level of organization below the president.* They employ more than 60 percent of all federal employees. As we saw in chapter 12, the president appoints and the Senate confirms *secretaries, who head the cabinet departments* (the head of the Justice Department is called the attorney general). These department heads are in the official line of succession to the presidency. Directly under each secretary are undersecretaries, deputy undersecretaries, and assistant secretaries, most of whom are political appointees. The remainder of each department's employees are selected through competitive examinations.

Within each department are numerous subdivisions, which are referred to as bureaus, divisions, offices, or administrations. The logic of these sub-

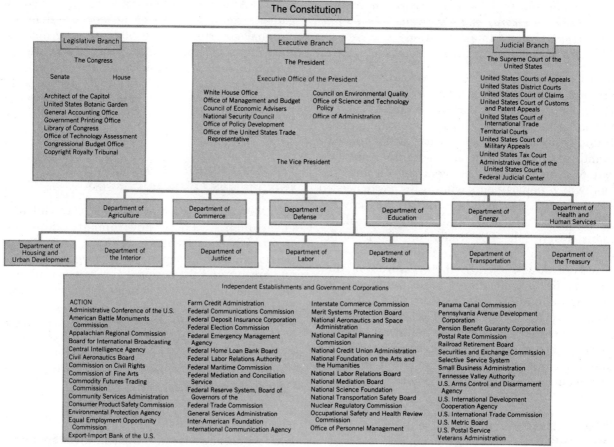

FIGURE 13.1

The Government of the United States

SOURCE: Office of the Federal Register, National Archives and Records Service, General Services Administration, *The United States Government Manual 1981/82*. Washington, D.C.: Government Printing Office, May 1, 1981, p. 815.

divisions depends upon the department and its functions. Some departments create subdivisions on the basis of their services, as with the Public Health Service division of the Department of Health and Human Services. Others are divided on the basis of the citizens they serve, as with the Bureau of Indian Affairs in the Department of Interior. Still others are organized on the basis of geography, as with the State Department's Bureaus of African Affairs, European Affairs, East Asian and Pacific Affairs, Inter-American Affairs, and Near Eastern and South Asian Affairs. Most department subdivisions are a mixture of all three. The organization of a typical cabinet-level department, Health and Human Services, is shown in Figure 13.2.

Cabinet-level departments, like executive agencies in general, have a pecking order that developed as they were created and determines their position in the line of succession to the presidency. As times change, new departments are created and older ones restructured. The departments and their years of origin are State, Treasury, and Defense (originally War, became Defense in 1949), 1789; Interior, 1849; Agriculture, 1862; Justice, 1870; Commerce, 1903; Labor, 1913; Health and Human Services (formerly Health, Education, and Welfare), 1953; Housing and Urban Development, 1965; Transportation, 1966; Energy, 1977; and Education, 1979. With the exception of the Department of Health and Human Services, the departments performing essential

TABLE 13.1

The "Pecking Order" in the Federal Bureaucracy

Most Prestigious

Executive departments.

Very Prestigious

Major agencies of the Executive Office of the President, such as the Office of Management and Budget; major independent agencies, such as the National Aeronautics and Space Administration, Central Intelligence Agency, Veterans Administration, International Communications Agency; Federal Reserve; military departments.

Moderately Prestigious

Independent agencies, such as the General Services Administration, Small Business Administration; major regulatory agencies, such as the Interstate Commerce Commission and Federal Communications Commission; government corporations, such as the Federal Deposit Insurance Corporation, Export-Import Bank, Tennessee Valley Authority; foundations; major administrations or bureaus within executive departments, such as the Federal Bureau of Investigation, Comptroller of the Currency, and Highway Administration.

Prestigious

Independent agencies, such as the Selective Service System, Equal Employment Opportunity Commission, National Transportation Safety Board, St. Lawrence Seaway Development Corporation; bureau heads within executive departments, such as director, Community Relations Service, and director of Public Roads.

Less Prestigious

Minor agencies, such as Renegotiation Board, Foreign Claims Settlement Commission; heads and deputy heads of principal constituent units within executive departments and agencies.

SOURCE: From *Politics, Position, and Power: The Dynamics of Federal Organization*, 3rd ed. by Harold Seidman. © 1980 by Oxford University Press, Inc. Reprinted by permission.

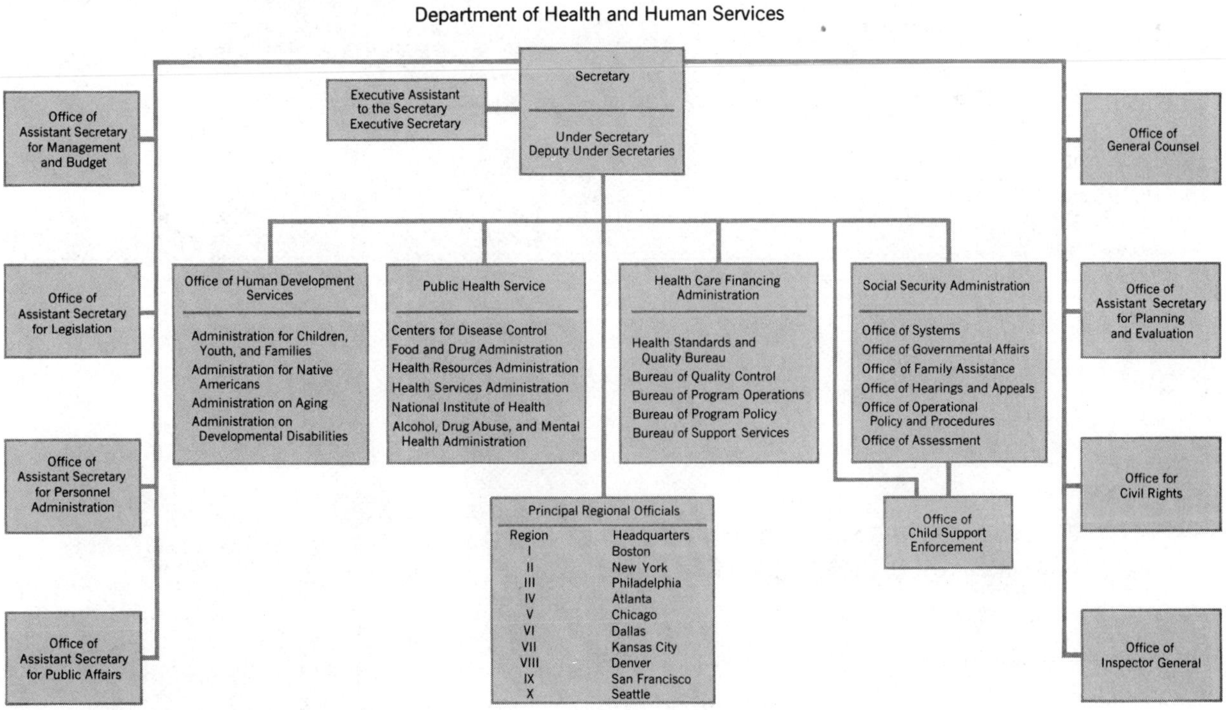

Department of Health and Human Services

FIGURE 13.2

Typical Organizational Structure of a Cabinet-Level Department of the Federal Government

SOURCE: Office of the Federal Register, National Archives and Records Service, General Services Administration, *The United States Government Manual 1981/82*. Washington, D.C.: Government Printing Office, 1981, p. 830.

TABLE 13.2

Estimated Size and Budgets of U.S. Government Executive Departments: 1982

Department	Personnel	Budget ($ millions)
Agriculture	87,000	$ 30,069
Commerce	32,700	3,064
Defense	892,600	199,027
Education	6,100	17,031
Energy	20,200	14,614
Health and Human Services	136,100	258,406
Housing and Urban Development	16,300	38,209
Interior	55,000	4,540
Justice	54,400	2,557
Labor	22,600	37,023
State	22,000	3,024
Transportation	69,100	23,984
Treasury	113,600	104,727

SOURCE: Executive Office of the President, Office of Management and Budget, *The United States Budget in Brief, Fiscal Year 1982* (Washington, D.C.: U.S. Government Printing Office, 1981), p. 86; *Special Analyses: Budget of the United States Government, Fiscal Year 1982,* p. 279.

government functions—the oldest departments—generally have the largest budgets and the most employees (see Table 13.2). A brief look at each department's functions may help explain why.[4]

State. Advises the president on the formation and execution of foreign policy; promotes the long-range security and well-being of the United States; determines and analyzes the facts relating to American overseas interests; negotiates treaties and agreements with foreign nations; speaks for the United States in the United Nations and in the more than 50 major international organizations to which the United States belongs.

Treasury. Performs four basic functions: formulates and recommends economic, financial, tax, and fiscal policies; serves as financial agent for the United States government; enforces the law; and manufactures coins and currency. Its subdivisions include, among others, the Bureau of Alcohol, Tobacco, and Firearms; United States Secret Service; Internal Revenue Service; Bureau of the Mint; Bureau of Engraving and Printing; and United States Customs Services.

Defense. Responsible for providing the military forces needed to deter war and protect the security of the country; its major elements are the Army, Navy, Marine Corps, Air Force, and the Joint Chiefs of Staff.

Justice. Enforces the federal law in the public interest; serves as public advocate in protecting citizens against criminals and subversion, ensuring the healthy competition of business in our free enterprise system, safeguarding the consumer, and enforcing drug, immigration, and naturaliza-

Activities of some cabinet-level departments:
(a) The State Department, the nation's oldest cabinet-level department, aids the president in negotiating treaties and agreements with foreign nations. (b) Scientists employed by the U.S. Geological Survey, a division of the Department of the Interior, monitor volcanic eruptions such as those of Mount St. Helen's. (c) The Bureau of the Census, a division of the Department of Commerce, collects extensive social and economic statistics on the nation's population every ten years. (d) The Center for Disease Control of the Department of Health and Human Services monitors outbreaks of diseases, ranging from strains of the common flu to new diseases like AIDS—acquired immune deficiency syndrome. (e) Federal aid to local communities for urban renewal projects is administered by the U.S. Department of Housing and Urban Development (HUD). (f) The U.S. Department of Energy sponsors research designed to make the nation less dependent on petroleum. Solar energy has been the focus of much of this research.

tion laws. Major subdivisions include the Antitrust Division, Civil Division, Civil Rights Division, Criminal Division, Tax Division, Federal Bureau of Investigation, Bureau of Prisons, Immigration and Naturalization Service, Drug Enforcement Administration, and United States Parole Commission.

Interior. Responsible for public lands and natural resources. Protects fish, wildlife, and land and water resources; preserves national parks and historical sites; and is responsible for American Indian reservations and for people who live in island territories under United States administration. The major subdivisions include the United States Fish and Wildlife Service, National Park Service, Bureau of Mines, Geological Survey, Office of Surface Mining Reclamation and Enforcement, Bureau of Indian Affairs, Bureau of Land Management, and Bureau of Reclamation.

Agriculture. Works to improve and maintain farm income and to develop and expand markets abroad for agricultural products. Safeguards and assures standards of quality in the daily food supply through inspection and grading services. Administers rural development, credit, and conservation programs to help carry out national growth policies. Helps landowners protect soil, water, forests, and other natural resources to maintain the country's production capacity. Helps curb poverty, hunger, and malnutrition. The major subdivisions are the Farmers Home Administration, Agricultural Cooperative Service, Animal and Plant Health Inspection Service, Food and Nutrition Service, Federal Crop and Insurance Corporation, Foreign Agricultural Service, Forest Service, and Soil Conservation Service.

Commerce. Encourages the nation's international trade, economic growth, and technological advancement. Administers programs to help increase exports, prevent unfair foreign trade competition, and assist the growth of minority businesses. Provides social and economic statistics and analyses for business and government. Maintains the merchant marines; grants patents and registers trademarks. Some of its major subdivisions are the International Trade Administration, Economic Development Administration, Maritime Administration, Minority Business Development Agency, National Oceanic and Atmospheric Administration, Patent and Trademark Office, Bureau of the Census, and Regional Action Planning Commissions.

Labor. Works to foster the welfare of wage earners, improve their working conditions, and advance their opportunities for profitable employment; administers more than 130 federal labor laws; protects worker's pension rights; sponsors job training programs; works to strengthen free collective bargaining; keeps track of changes in employment, price, and other national economic indicators; makes special efforts to help older workers, youth, minorities, and the handicapped. Major subdivisions include the Women's Bureau, Employment and Training Administration, Labor-Management Services Administration, Employment Standards Administration, Federal Contract Compliance Programs, Occupational Safety and Health Administration, and the Bureau of Labor Statistics.

Education. Establishes policy for, administers, and coordinates most federal assistance to education. The major subdivisions are federally aided corporations (such as Howard University and the National Technical Institute for the Deaf) and the divisions of Bilingual Education and Minority Language Affairs, Elementary and Secondary Education, Vocational and Adult Education, Special Education and Rehabilitation Services, Education for Overseas Dependents, and Post-Secondary Education.

Health and Human Services (originally Health, Education, and Welfare). Administers Title VI of the Civil Rights Act of 1964, which prohibits discrimination in federal grant programs and activities. Administers programs for the elderly, children and youth, Native Americans, persons with developmental disabilities, public assistance recipients, persons living in rural areas, and veterans. Protects the health of the nation against impure and unsafe foods, drugs, and cosmetics. Collects vital statistics; operates the Center for Disease Control; funds the Medicare and Medicaid programs; and operates the Social Security system. Major subdivisions are the Office of Human Development Services, Public Health Service, Health Care Financing Administration, and the Office of Child Support Enforcement.

Housing and Urban Development. Responsible for programs concerned with housing needs, fair housing opportunities, and the improvement and development of the nation's communities. Administers mortgage insurance programs, rental subsidy programs, and neighborhood rehabilitation and preservation programs. Some of its major subdivisions include the Community Development Block Grant Program, Urban Development Action Grant Program, Comprehensive Planning Assistance Program, Low Income Public Housing Program, and Government National Mortgage Association.

Transportation. Responsible for the nation's highway planning, development, and construction; also urban mass transit, railroads, aviation, and the safety of waterways, ports, highways, and oil and gas pipelines. Major subdivisions are the U.S. Coast Guard, Federal Aviation Administration, Federal Highway Administration, Federal Railroad Administration, National Highway Traffic Safety Administration, Urban Mass Transportation Administration, and the Saint Lawrence Seaway Development Corporation.

Energy. Responsible for the research, development, and demonstration of energy technology; marketing of federal power; energy conservation; the nuclear weapons program; regulation of energy production and use; and collection and analysis of energy data. Major subdivisions include fossil, nuclear, and other energy programs; Energy Information Administration; Federal Energy Regulation Commission; and the Southeastern, Alaska, Southwestern, Western, and other Power Administrations.

Independent Regulatory Commissions and Boards. In 1980, there were 13 *independent reg-*

ulatory agencies or commissions. These agencies *regulate important aspects of the economy to protect the public* (see Table 13.3).

Regulatory agencies differ from cabinet-level departments in several ways.[5] First, their function is quite different—they oversee and regulate the private economic sector. Second, they are headed by a commission or board (ranging in size from five to nine) instead of by a secretary. Third, they are more independent of both the president and Congress, because their terms of office are typically longer than the term of the president who appoints them or a single term of the senators who confirm them.

Criticism of these regulatory commissions has increased in recent years. Of all the federal agencies, they are perceived as the most guilty of reducing competition, removing funds from productive investment, and needlessly raising costs for both business and consumers. Critics contend that regulatory commissions make too many rules and regulations that in effect penalize industry.

However, consumer interest groups such as Common Cause and spokespersons such as Ralph Nader think regulatory agencies aren't tough enough. They claim that too many "independent" commissions are staffed by people who used to be in the industry they now regulate and that former commission employees often enter the industry they regulated and then reappear as industry lobbyists before the commission. After much pressure from consumer groups, Congress passed a law that prohibits former regulatory commission staffers from being involved with the agency for at least two years after they resign.

Independent Executive Agencies *Independent executive agencies are part of the executive branch, but are separate from any cabinet-level departments. These agencies vary greatly in form and function.* Some, such as the Central Intelligence Agency and the Veterans Administration, have a director. Others, such as the Postal Service and the Federal Election Commission, are governed by a small board or commission.

As with independent regulatory commissions, Congress has chosen to place independent executive agencies under the jurisdiction of something other than a cabinet-level department, for some very good reasons.[6] One is the desire to bring new approaches to certain policy problems. Another is to avoid the kind of pressure from clientele groups

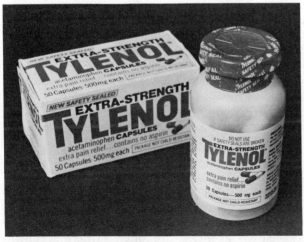

Independent regulatory commissions, like the Consumer Product Safety Commission, oversee and regulate the private sector to protect the public.

TABLE 13.3

Functions of Independent Regulatory Commissions

Commission	Date Created	Functions
Civil Aeronautics Board	1938*	Regulates the civil air transport industry within the U.S. and between the U.S. and foreign countries in the interest of the foreign and domestic commerce of the U.S., the postal service, and the national defense
Federal Communications Commission	1934	Regulates interstate and foreign communications by radio, television, wire, and cable; responsible for promoting the safety of life and property through the communications media
Federal Home Loan Bank Board	1932	Regulates savings and loan associations, which specialize in lending out money on homes and are the country's major private source of funds to pay for building and buying homes
Federal Maritime Commission	1961	Regulates the waterborne foreign and domestic offshore commerce of the U.S.; assures that U.S. international trade is open to all nations on fair and equitable terms
Federal Reserve System	1913	Regulates the nation's money supply by making monetary policy which influences the lending and investing activities of commercial banks and the cost and availability of money and credit
Federal Trade Commission	1914	Regulates business to prohibit unfair methods of competition and unfair or deceptive acts or practices, such as false advertising
Interstate Commerce Commission	1887	Regulates interstate surface transportation, including trains, trucks, buses, inland waterway and coastal shipping, and freight forwarders to provide the public with rates that are fair and reasonable
National Labor Relations Board	1935	Regulates business to protect employees' rights to organize and to prevent and remedy unfair labor practices
Securities and Exchange Commission	1934	Regulates the securities and financial markets (such as the stock market) to protect the interests of the public and investors against malpractice
Consumer Product Safety Commission	1972	Regulates products produced by business to protect the public against product-related deaths, illnesses, and injuries (standards of automobile safety, for example)
Commodity Futures Trading Commission	1974	Regulates trading on the futures exchanges as well as activities of commodity exchange members, public brokerage houses, commodity salespersons, trading advisers, and pool operators to ensure fair trade practices and to protect the rights of customers and the financial integrity of the marketplace
Nuclear Regulatory Commission	1974	Regulates and licenses the uses of nuclear energy to protect the public health and safety and the environment
Federal Energy Regulatory Commission (formerly Federal Power Commission)	1977	Regulates the transportation and sale of natural gas, the transmission and sale of electricity, the licensing of hydroelectric power projects, and the transportation of oil by pipeline

SOURCE: Office of the Federal Register, National Archives and Records Service, General Services Administration, *The United States Government Manual 1981/82* (Washington, D.C.: U.S. Government Printing Office, May 1, 1981), pp. 254, 459–616.

*Scheduled to be abolished by January 1, 1985.

that occurs in departments with strong clientele ties—Agriculture, Health and Human Services, and Education, for example. A third reason is to avoid presidential control—especially when the president is from a different political party than the majority of senators and representatives. Finally, some agencies, such as the National Aeronautics and Space Administration, don't fit in any existing department.

The rules and regulations made by independent executive agencies are often criticized. Critics contend that the public has no check on these agencies because voters don't elect the agency heads.

The National Aeronautic and Space Administration (NASA) is an example of an independent executive agency. Its functions do not fit into any existing cabinet-level department, although conceivably NASA could become part of the Department of Transportation if space flights via the shuttle become commonplace.

Government Corporations *Government corporations are, in effect, businesses operated by government.* Like private corporations, they can acquire, develop, and sell real estate and other kinds of property, acting in their own name rather than that of the national government. They can also bring suit in a court of law—or be sued—also in their own name.[7] Some, such as Amtrak, hope to make a profit; others, such as the Tennessee Valley Authority (an electric utility corporation) hope to at least break even. On the other hand, they are subject to federal budgetary and auditing controls and civil service statutes as a result of the Government Corporation Control Act of 1945.

Government corporations, like private corporations, are generally headed by a board of directors. They may be either independent agencies or subdivisions of a cabinet-level department. For example, the Government National Mortgage Association is under the Department of Housing and Urban Development. Like other agencies, government corporations evoke a mixture of criticism and support. As Harold Seidman notes, ''At one

and the same time the corporation represents the evils of government in business, and the virtues of business efficiency and organization in government.''[8]

Other Executive Agencies The executive branch has literally hundreds of other agencies. Seidman classifies these as foundations (e.g., National Science Foundation); institutions and institutes (e.g., National Institute of Health); claims commissions (e.g., Indian Claims Commission); conferences, interagency boards, councils, and committees (e.g., Consumer Advisory Council); statutory advisory boards (e.g., National Historical Publications Commission); joint executive-congressional commissions (e.g., Agricultural Trade Development Advisory Committee); and intergovernmental organizations (e.g., Advisory Commission on Intergovernmental Relations).

By now, the complexity and lack of unity of the federal bureaucracy should be apparent—and we haven't even discussed legislative and judicial bureaucracies. It is a common mistake to think of the bureaucracy exclusively in terms of the executive branch.

Legislative Agencies

Legislative agencies are information-gathering agencies in the legislative branch. During the 1960s and early 1970s, both houses of Congress greatly expanded their staffs. Some say this was to counter the growth of White House bureaucrats. Others say it was caused by the proliferation of standing sub-committees. The result was a 270 percent increase in the Congressional staff payroll.[9]

The intent of creating a professional congressional staff was to reduce Congress's reliance on lobbyists and executive branch bureaucrats for information—to create an independent research team and thereby improve the quality of data available to Congress members. However, as we saw in earlier chapters, what has emerged is the *iron triangle, a closed system of information exchange among staff members of congressional committees, bureaucrats in the executive branch, and the clientele or interest groups affected by the agency* (see Figure 13.3).

A number of other legislative information-gathering agencies are more independent, however. These agencies employ 21,000 persons.[10] Best known are the Congressional Budget Office (CBO) and the General Accounting Office (GAO). The CBO, established in 1974, provides Congress with basic budget data and analyses of alternative fiscal, budgetary, and programmatic issues. For example, the CBO may challenge figures on growth of the economy used by the executive branch's Office of Management and Budget in preparing the annual budget.

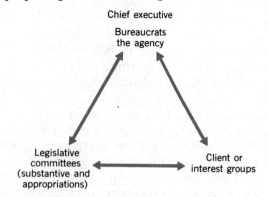

FIGURE 13.3

Iron Triangle Public Policy Subsystem

SOURCE: D.A. Cutchin, *Guide to Public Administration*, 1981, p. 54. Reproduced by permission of the publisher, F.E. Peacock Publishers, Inc., Itasca, Illinois.

The General Accounting Office, created in 1921, serves basically as the government's auditing and accounting agency. It is an independent, nonpolitical agency. The director, the comptroller general, and the deputy comptroller are appointed by the president with the advice and consent of the Senate for 15-year terms. The GAO has the authority to investigate matters relating to the receipt, disbursement, and application of public funds. It is also required to recommend more efficient and effective government operations after evaluating the impact of policy implementations.

The legislative branch has other important information-related agencies. The Library of Congress, established in 1800, was originally for the exclusive use of Congress, but it has been expanded so that it is now the nation's library. One department, the Congressional Research Service, is still reserved exclusively for Congress, however. The Office of Technology Assessment, created in 1972, gives Congress information about the probable influence of technological applications and identifies alternative technological methods of implementing specific programs. The Government Printing Office prints, binds, and distributes more than 25,000 agency publications.

Judicial Agencies

Judicial agencies are administrative agencies in the judicial branch. The number of government employees in the judicial branch has escalated rapidly in the past decade. By the end of 1980, the figure had reached 15,178. As Congress has expanded the number of courts to meet the increasing caseload (to be discussed in the next chapter), more clerical workers, stenographers, law clerks, court reporters, and probation officers have been hired. Many courts have had to hire court administrators just to manage the people and the paperwork.

The administration of the federal courts is the responsibility of the Administrative Office of the United States Courts, created by Congress in 1939. Its director and deputy director, who are appointed by the U.S. Supreme Court, are under the supervision of the U.S. Judicial Conference. This office is responsible for supervising the clerical and administrative personnel of the courts; keeping data on the dockets (cases scheduled); preparing quarterly statistical reports for delivery to the chief judges of the judicial circuits, the Judicial Conference, Congress, and the attorney general; determining pay for court employees; regulating the travel of judicial personnel; providing accommodations and supplies for court personnel; establishing and maintaining programs for the certification and utilization of court interpreters; and preparing the budget of the courts (except the Supreme Court).

Improvement of judicial administration is the responsibility of another judicial agency, the Federal Judicial Center. Created by Congress in 1967, the center is the judicial branch's agency for policy research, systems development, and continuing education.

A BUREAUCRATIC WEB

As this overview has shown, the federal government has no single bureaucratic hierarchy. It is, rather, a system of agencies, each of which is technically a bureaucracy with its own chain of command, divisions, rules and regulations, and tasks to perform. These agencies might be likened to the strands of a spider's web in that all are indirectly dependent on each other. It is no wonder that the average citizen is confused by it all.

State and Local Government Bureaucracies

State and local government bureaucracies have many of the same structural characteristics as the federal bureaucracies, primarily because they have used the federal government as their model. In general, the larger the state or local government, the more its bureaucratic structure is likely to resemble that of the federal government. However, the types of bureaucratic agencies adopted by state and local governments vary a great deal.

State Governments   State governments are organized as either strong executive systems or weak executive systems (see Figure 13.4). A *strong executive system* is one that clearly specifies authority for every position and unit through elaborate rules and regulations. The governor appoints the various department heads, and the state has few independent executive agencies or regulatory commissions. The trend among state governments, especially in the larger, wealthier states, is toward this type of organization. It seeks to promote administrative efficiency and bureaucratic accountability by eliminating duplication and clarifying lines of authority. The authority ultimately rests with an elected official. These same states have restruc-

tured their judicial systems by adopting unified court systems in which authority ultimately rests with elected state Supreme Court justices.

A *weak executive system is characterized by many separately elected executive officials* (secretary of state, attorney general, treasurer, agriculture commissioner), *a large number of independent boards and commissions* (public utility commissions, game and fresh water fish commissions, insurance and banking commissions), *and numerous legislative checks on the governor's power* (joint preparation of executive department budgets and approval of most appointments and removals). Most states with this form of bureaucratic organization gained their statehood in the Jacksonian era. The popular idea of the time was to guarantee citizen control of state government by separately electing as many state officials as possible.

Local Government Bureaucracies

Charles Press and Kenneth VerBurg identify four basic forms of local government structure: the strong-mayor council, weak-mayor council, council-manager, and commission plans[11] (see Figure 13.5). In the *strong-mayor council plan, the mayor, who serves full time, appoints all department heads and has the power to fire them as well. Thus, there is a clear chain of command.* This plan resembles the strong executive form of state organization. Council members serve only part time.

Under the *weak-mayor council plan,* which is generally found in small cities that have fewer employees and executive departments, *the council, rather than the mayor, hires and fires department heads and the city has numerous separately elected officials* (tax assessor, treasurer, auditor).

The *council-manager plan* is popular in cities with medium-sized populations (25,000 to 50,000). This structure is similar to that of a business corporation. Under this plan, *the voters (stockholders) elect the council (board of directors), which hires and fires the city manager (the chief executive).* Born out of the reform movement, this plan seeks to bring professional management to city hall to make government run more efficiently and economically.

The *commission plan* is a common organizational form for county and township governments. *Voters elect a number of commissioners, each of whom heads up a major commission, or department.* Individually, they serve as executive officials; collectively, they serve as the commission, or legislative officials. This form has few checks and balances

Strong Executive (Chief Executive Appoints Department Heads)

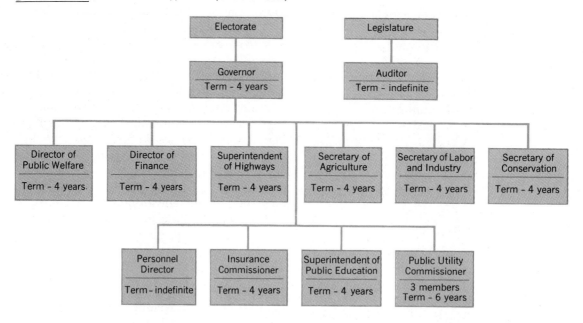

Weak Executive (Executive Power Split Between Governor and Other Elected Department Heads)

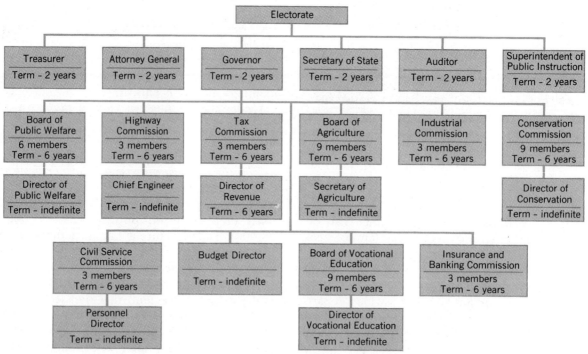

FIGURE 13.4

Different Types of State Government Administrative Organization

SOURCE: Thomas R. Dye, *Politics in States and Communities*, 4th ed. Englewood Cliffs, N.J.: Prentice-Hall, 1981, pp. 168–169; adopted from Frederic A. Ogg and P. Orman Ray, *Introduction to American Government*, 13th ed. by William H. Young (New York: Appleton-Century-Crofts, 1966), pp. 772–73.

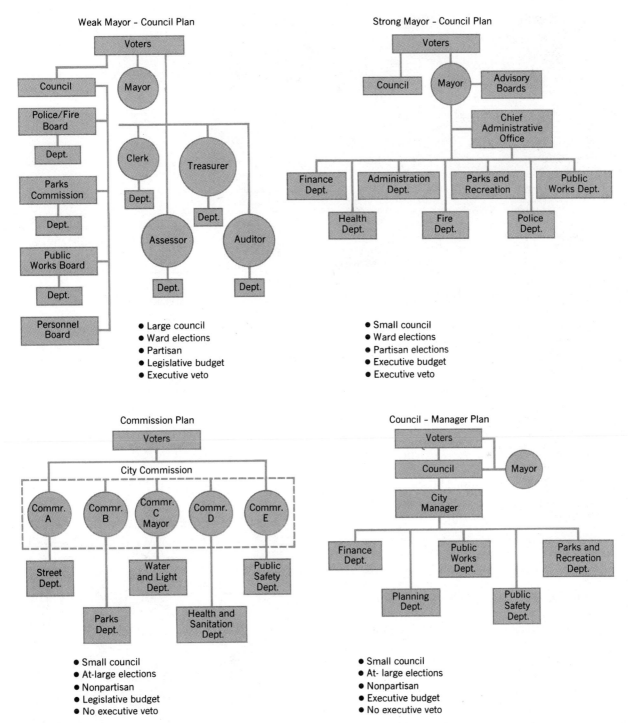

FIGURE 13.5

Basic Forms of Local Government Structure

SOURCE: Charles Press and Kenneth VerBurg, *State and Community Governments in the Federal System*. New York: John Wiley & Sons, 1979, p. 123.

Employees of local governments are perceived as more effective and efficient than federal employees primarily because they provide visible basic services such as police and fire protection, garbage collection, and pothole repair.

because the same officials comprise both the legislative and the executive branches.

State and local governments do not engage in activities related to national defense, mail, or space research and technology. State governments have much more responsibility for providing education, welfare, and highways than the national government does. Local governments are responsible for providing basic services such as police and fire protection, health care and hospitals, recreation, sewerage, and sanitation. As we shall see, local government bureaucracies are perceived by the public as doing the best job.

HOW WELL DO THE BUREAUCRACIES PERFORM?

In a major study of the public's evaluation of its bureaucracies, Katz *et al.* found that citizens rate the private sector's performance as equal to or better than the government's.[12]

Another study compared the public's rating of the responsiveness of institutions such as private voluntary organizations (the Salvation Army, for example), small businesses, local governments, the federal government, and large businesses. The institution that was rated ''least responsive'' by the most citizens (61 percent) was the federal government, followed closely by large businesses (58 percent). Rated ''most responsive'' were private voluntary organizations, followed by small businesses and local governments.[13] Two factors seem

to be at work here: size and geographical proximity. Citizens generally give higher ratings to smaller agencies closer to home. On the other hand, bureaucrats at each level view those at other levels as inferior.

"Something's cockeyed here... maybe I'll figure it out later."

Employees of the federal government and even federal elected officials generally view employees of state and local governments as not very professional. Federal employees were instrumental in getting Congress to pass the Intergovernmental Personnel Act of 1970, which created a grant program designed to improve state and local government personnel administration.

State and local employees and elected officials tend to view federal employees the same way most citizens do, as being out of touch with the real world and more concerned with rules and regulations than with people. As we saw in chapter 4 on federalism, most state and local government personnel view the rules and regulations made and carried out by federal employees as burdensome and in need of revision.

The truth is that bureaucrats from all levels of government interact frequently and depend on each other. Federal bureaucrats often rely upon state and local bureaucrats to implement federal grant-in-aid programs. Some scholars attribute the growth in the number of state and local government employees to federal grant policies.[14] In the same way, state and local bureaucrats rely heavily upon information and assistance from federal bureaucrats in carrying out programs. In a survey of 50 state agency administrators from 19 different agencies, for example, it was found that 70 percent relied upon federal agencies for information and that federal employees were the most common informational source.[15]

THE COMPLEX GOVERNMENT EMPLOYMENT SYSTEM

A former chairperson of the Consumer Product Safety Commission once wrote to Illinois Senator Charles Percy,

A manager in the executive branch of the federal government who finds it necessary to terminate an unproductive or non-contributing employee—or even an obstructing employee—must be prepared to spend 25 to 50 percent of his/her time for a period that literally may run from 6 to 18 months.[16]

The author of the article citing this letter concluded that if a small business employing ten people discharged workers for cause at the same rate as the federal government, it would fire only one person every 70 years.[17] To understand why this

problem exists, we need to review the historical development of the civil service system.

The Spoils System
Until the late nineteenth century, government employees were appointed by the president on the basis of political considerations. This was known as the **spoils system**—*selecting government employees on the basis of their political connections.* Who you knew was more important than what you knew in getting a government job.

The spoils system is often associated with President Andrew Jackson. While Jackson was one of its heaviest users, he was certainly not the first—or the last—president to select bureaucrats on the basis of politics. As we saw in the previous chapter, some government employees are still selected by patronage. President Reagan, for example, appointed 3,000 officials. We also saw that the president's power to appoint his own team (cabinet, White House staff) is seen as beneficial rather than harmful.

Civil Service Commission (1883–1978)
The shift from exclusive reliance upon patronage to a civil service system came with the passage of the Pendleton Act in 1883. Passage of the act was hastened by Charles J. Guiteau's assassination of President James Garfield after failing in his bid to be appointed general consul to Paris. Reformers, who had long opposed the spoils system, successfully pressured Congress to create a **merit system,** *a government employment system based on three principles: open competition for available jobs, occupational ability, and political neutrality.*

The Pendleton Act established the **Civil Service Commission,** making it *responsible for appointing civil servants on the basis of merit as determined by a competitive examination open to all.* The Act initially applied to some 14,000 positions, 12 percent of the total federal civil service. By 1978, more than 90 percent of all federal government employees were under some kind of merit system. Ironically, over the years it has been presidents who have increased the proportion of government jobs covered by civil service, thereby weakening later presidents' control over the bureaucracy. Until recently, almost every president engaged in **blanketing,** *bringing new groups of employees under civil service classification.*

Getting a government job—whether through competition or patronage—is not easy. Less than

TABLE 13.4
Categories of Governmental Employees

Category	Recruiting Process	Characteristics	Major Tasks	Educational Level
Political Appointments (Excepted Service) Top management	Appointed from political or civil service ranks; loyalty to administration in power often thought very important.	Relatively unrestricted by "red tape"; good education; much and varied experience.	Long-range planning; protection of values, methods, and personnel of agency from outside assault.	At least 4 years of college is common.
Competition-Based (General Service) Middle management	Administrative competence as tested by examination.	More devoted to rules of procedure than above; sometimes see both agency head and Congress as obstacles to good agency work.	Daily operations of agency.	At least 4 years of college, almost prerequisite.
Professional and technical staff	Formal examination or selection from list of licensed professionals.	Devoted to work; sometimes only dimly aware of political process and hostile to it; may be oriented more toward professional peers than to the agency.	Technical and professional tasks, such as those of the lawyer, engineer, geologist, accountant.	Usually at least 4 years of college; often graduate or professional degrees.
Clerical, manual, and routine worker staff.	Formal examination or straight hiring.	Some, but relatively low skills; often low aspirations; see government work as "a job."	Relatively routine, but essential to getting the agency's work done.	Most jobs, high school diploma or less.

SOURCE: Dale Vinyard, *The Presidency* (New York: Charles Scribner's Sons, 1971), p. 122; adapted from Charles Adrian and Charles Press, *The American Political Process* (New York: McGraw-Hill, 1965), p. 528.

4 percent of those who apply for *general service (GS) (competition-based)* jobs get them.[18] Even fewer of those hoping to get an *excepted service (political appointment)* job after a presidential election ever see their dreams fulfilled. A comparison of categories of federal employees who fall under each type of service (general and excepted) is shown in Table 13.4.

For entry into general service, an individual must first pass a competitive exam for the particular job he or she is seeking. General service, or general schedule, jobs are divided into 18 grades, with GS 1 the lowest and GS 18 the highest. Within each grade are pay steps based on seniority, time in grade, and skill.

The written exams used for general service jobs have increasingly come under attack as being 1) invalid—poor tests of the skills needed to perform the job; and 2) discriminatory toward minorities, who may be able to perform the task but not pass the written test because of poor linguistic skills.

After an applicant passes the exam, his or her name is placed on a register with the names of other passing applicants. They are ranked by test scores. In accordance with the practice of *veteran's preference, veterans are automatically given an extra five points, and disabled veterans are given an extra ten.* This practice is also attacked as highly discriminatory, especially to women and minorities—few of whom have served in the armed forces. (American veterans are still 98 percent male and 92 percent nonminority, even though this may eventually change since recent recruitment patterns have been less discriminatory.)

When a position in an agency opens up, according to the **rule of three,** *the top three names on the register are considered for that position.* The agency can hire any one of these individuals. The two candidates who aren't chosen remain at the top of the register until they get a job or the register expires and new exams are given.

How Meritorious is the Merit System?

In this century, the general service portion of the civil service system expanded rapidly. Civil service became weighted down with unproductive employees, often **street-level bureaucrats** *(those with whom citizens come in contact most often)* who no longer were offered real incentives to produce. No one feared job loss because of poor performance. For example, by 1977, 99.34 percent received "merit" pay raises;[19] the rate of meritorious performance was presumably somewhat lower. Government employees' average salaries were 20 percent higher than those in private industry because of "paper" reorganizations and alignments that created "new" jobs with higher grade classifications and, of course, higher wages.[20] Furthermore, fewer than one-seventh of 1 percent of tenured civil servants were fired for inefficiency or "cause."[21] Public employee unions were challenging the very principles upon which the merit system was built.

Civil Service Reform

The **Civil Service Reform Act of 1978** *was legislation designed to reform the civil service system*—again evidence of the American government's ability to react to changes and remedy shortcomings. President Jimmy Carter, during whose administration the Act was passed, said reform was necessary because "there is not enough merit in the merit system. There is inadequate motivation because we have too few rewards for excellence and too few penalties for unsatisfactory work."[22] The Act abolished the U.S. Civil Service Commission and replaced it with two agencies, the Office of Personnel Management and the Merit Systems Protection Board. The **Office of Personnel Management** *is responsible for recruiting, examining, training, and promoting federal employees on the basis of their knowledge, skills, and performance.* It also assures that affirmative action hiring policies are implemented. Unlike the Civil Service Commission,

the Office of Personnel Management is headed by a single director who is responsible to the president. The Office is intended to function as the president's arm for personnel management.

The **Merit Systems Protection Board** *is responsible for protecting the rights of federal employees.* It hears appeals by federal employees on adverse personnel actions such as removals, suspensions, and demotions. The Board also investigates and prosecutes merit system rule violations through its special counsel.

The most significant changes made by the Civil Service Reform Act of 1978 were those that 1) streamlined the procedures for firing or disciplining a federal employee, 2) established the Federal Labor Relations Authority to help improve relations between labor and management, 3) established a new performance-rating system based on nine merit principles, and 4) upgraded the pay scales for GS 13 to 15 (upper management) employees. Unlike the lower GS grades, high GS grades have typically lagged behind private sector management pay scales.

The most controversial component of the Civil Service Reform Act is the Senior Executive Service (SES), an idea dating from the late 1930s. The SES was originally intended to create an elite corps of 8,400 managers who could be moved from one agency to another. The possibility of salary bonuses of up to $10,000 and presidential awards of up to $20,000 for outstanding performance were the drawing cards. For top-level political appointees (cabinet-level department secretaries), SES was to provide more flexibility in managing their departments by letting them put SES members in the jobs where they were needed most and allowing them to demote those who were unsuitable to their positions.[23]

Initially, top-level general service employees (GS 16 to 18) were enthusiastic about the SES; 95 percent joined. But Congress soon placed a cap on federal salaries at $50,112, and bonuses were less than expected. The result has been a reluctance to join and a rush toward retirement by those who did join.

Critics of Congress's reductions in SES merit pay and bonuses say this signals a return to the civil service system as it was before: inflexible, lacking in incentives to increase productivity, and out of the control of top public policymaking officials. In the words of an administrator of the National Aeronautics and Space Administration,

''The bonus system must be there or some kind of tangible system must be there, if we are going to make the performance appraisal system work, which, in my mind, is the real key to the civil service reform being effected.''[24]

THE ROLE OF BUREAUCRATS IN THE POLICY PROCESS

In 1980 alone, bureaucrats churned out between 7,500 and 9,000 rules and regulations. They provided information on 4,423 bills considered by Congress and carried out 1,643 laws that Congress finally enacted.[25] Obviously, bureaucrats are heavily involved in all three stages of the policy process—formation, implementation, and evaluation. Some consider the bureaucracy a fourth branch of government.

Bureaucrats as Policy Formulators

The role of bureaucrats as policy formulators has greatly expanded in recent years, for several reasons. The increasing complexity of society and government and the accompanying technological revolution have created a larger, more specialized government work force. People with special expertise have become more influential because of their knowledge. More than any other factor, this control over information explains why bureaucrats' power is growing. Their use of a specialized language (jargon) makes it difficult for the average citizen or member of Congress to challenge their recommendations.

Congress has played a large role in expanding the policymaking role of bureaucrats by giving them a great deal of discretion in the details of how programs are administered once they are created by Congress.

By design, most laws are long on goals and short on ways and means. In other words, an act of Congress is only [the first step] in the process of creating or fine-tuning a federal program. Congress delegates the next step, the job of fleshing out the law through legally binding [rules and] regulations, to the executive departments and agencies (such as the Environmental Protection Agency or the Department of Health and Human Services).[26]

By having bureaucrats formulate rules and regulations, Congress saves itself the time and money that would be required to develop and debate de-

tailed guidelines for the thousands of bills considered each year. Congress also enjoys certain political advantages. ''Politically speaking, members would just as soon avoid addressing some of the controversial decisions involved in designing workable programs.''[27]

Presidents have also expanded the policymaking role of bureaucrats. President-sponsored reorganizations, authorizations for new positions, and continued expansions in permanent civil servant positions have made presidents as dependent as Congress upon bureaucratic technical expertise and information.

Bureaucrats as Policy Implementors

Policy implementation has been defined as *''the stage of [the policy process] between the establishment of a policy—such as the passage of a legislative act, the issuing of an executive order, the handing down of a judicial decision, or the [making] of a regulatory rule—and the consequences of the policy for people whom it affects.''*[28]

As George Edwards notes, policy implementation can involve a wide variety of actions on the part of bureaucrats: ''issuing and enforcing directives, disbursing funds, making loans, awarding grants, signing contracts, collecting data, disseminating information, analyzing problems, assigning and hiring personnel, creating organizational units, proposing alternatives, planning for the future, and negotiating with private citizens, businesses, interest groups, legislative committees, bureaucratic units, and even other countries.''[29]

A number of factors can affect bureaucratic implementation of policy. These include personal or professional biases of the bureaucrats; conflicts between top-level, middle-level, and street-level bureaucrats on how to do it; the level of funding; and the number of staff members assigned to the task. Other factors are the clarity of the policy decision itself; legal and social linkages between bureaucrats in the implementing agencies (hierarchical integration); and pressures (often conflicting) from important interest groups, the president's White House staff, Congress members, or other influential persons or groups.

Bureaucrats as Policy Evaluators

Policy evaluation involves *measuring the consequences of policy implementation efforts.* To make a coherent, rational evaluation of a program's or policy's effectiveness, a clear cause-and-effect relationship must be established between the actions of a government agency and their influence on a societal problem.[30] Policy evaluation allows citizens to hold public officials accountable for their policy decisions; just as importantly, it informs officials whether the old policy should be revised or replaced with a completely new one.

The evaluation of a program and its effectiveness are, once again, heavily dependent upon information that is developed by and under the control of bureaucrats. To evaluate any program, it is necessary to:

1. identify the program's goals;
2. construct a causal impact model (hypothesize as to what factors affect goal achievement, either positively or negatively);
3. develop an appropriate research design;
4. construct performance measures;
5. collect performance data; and
6. analyze and interpret the data.[31]

The importance of data in the evaluation process is clear. More than 70 federal agencies have the specific function of collecting or analyzing data. Bureaucrats in these agencies decide which data to collect and which performance indicators to use in demonstrating to Congress, the president, the public, and often the courts that a program is worth funding again at budget time.

Because the survival of an agency or program may depend on whether evaluations are positive or negative, evaluations conducted by the agency itself tend to recommend that a program be continued in essentially the same form. Evaluations conducted externally by the GAO or independent consultants are more likely to recommend changes. But even external evaluators must rely upon agency employees to furnish facts and figures. This conforms to the pattern we have stressed throughout the preceding discussion: control over information is the primary source of power for most bureaucrats. Bureaucratic power, however, is limited, as we shall see in the next section.

KEEPING THE BUREAUCRATS UNDER CONTROL

One check on the bureaucracy's power is the president. As we saw in chapter 12, he can manage the bureaucracy by appointing top-level bureaucrats, reorganizing departments and agencies, formulating the budget, issuing executive orders, impounding funds, and organizing special task forces and study commissions. He also has the ability to mold public opinion, of course.

Congress, too, has a constitutional mandate making it responsible for the bureaucracy. As we saw in chapter 11, Congress's powers and activities include holding committee and subcommittee hearings; passing legislation creating or abolishing agencies; approving reorganizations; passing authorization and appropriation acts; approving the budget; conducting special investigations; overseeing legislation; confirming personnel; and authorizing outside evaluations of bureaucratic performance.

The courts' control of bureaucratic activity lies in their power to interpret whether administrators are implementing policy in the public interest and consistent with legislative intent. By judicial rulings, courts can change administrative procedures. Court rulings have even changed the bureaucracy's composition by ordering agencies to comply with equal opportunity laws and affirmative action guidelines.

The public, too, can play a role in controlling the bureaucracy. Individually or as members of interest groups such as Common Cause, citizens can protest against bureaucratic activities before the media, Congress, the executive, and the courts. The public also has the right to comment on the need for any rule or regulation before it is adopted. Under the Administrative Procedures Act of 1946, an agency head is required to give advance notice in the *Federal Register* of an intent to make a rule or regulation, with enough information to enable the public to comment on the need for it or on its content. The **Federal Register** *is a government publication which reports all proposed, as well as approved, rules, regulations, and administrative orders of government agencies.* Of course, few individuals or groups take the time to comment on these rules and regulations, but the right still exists.

In the end, the public's best tool is the ballot box. Voting an official out of office lets elected officials in all branches of government know that the public is dissatisfied with the way government is being run. In the 1980 election, for example, a Republican candidate, Ronald Reagan, beat a Democratic incumbent, Jimmy Carter; a Republican majority emerged in the Senate for the first time since the 1950s; and a larger number of conservatives won seats in the House. These events were viewed by elected officials at all levels as an indication that the public wanted government to take a different direction. The early years of the Reagan administration show how the president and Congress responded to the voters' mandate to get the bureaucracy under control.

Cutting Back Government: The Early Reagan Years

In his inaugural address, President Reagan promised to "curb the size and influence of the federal establishment." He proposed reductions in the number of federal employees and the amount of paperwork, rules, and regulations. To accomplish these goals, he used his budgetary, appointment, and reorganization powers, his power to create special task forces and study commissions, and his power to issue executive orders.

Reducing the Number of Federal Employees Within minutes of taking office, Reagan signed an executive order imposing a freeze on federal hiring. A few days later he proposed to cut 32,900 federal employees by September 30, 1981, and another 63,100 by September 30, 1982. He instructed his Office of Management and Budget to use these figures in preparing the 1981 and 1982 budgets.[32] Congress approved many of Reagan's recommended 1981 budget revisions and personnel cuts.

Government employment at all levels had been expanding significantly for six decades. It was 2.6 million in 1920, 4.2 million in 1940, 8.6 million in 1960, and 16.3 million in October, 1980. Most of this growth has occurred at the state and local levels rather than the federal level, however. Federal employment has held relatively steady; it rose from 1.9 million in 1950 to 2.3 million in 1960, to 2.7 million in 1970, and to 2.8 million in 1980.[33] It dropped in 1981.

In the early 1980s, employment levels in state and local governments also dropped, which marked the first decline in total government employment since World War II. Labor experts attributed these declines to a recession and widespread citizen demands for reductions in the size of government.

Critics attacked Reagan's paring down of the federal bureaucracy for fear it would force out the newest employees, minorities, and women—the last to be hired are the first to be fired. *Reductions-in-force (RIFs), personnel cuts in the federal bureaucracy,* are generally made in the following sequence: 1) temporary workers, 2) employees on probation, 3) career employees in order of seniority, 4) nondisabled veterans, and 5) disabled veterans.[34]

Critics also questioned the net savings of the personnel cuts. The Reagan administration projected a $2 billion savings from job reductions alone. The Congressional Budget Office, however, estimated that the government would have to spend $34 million for severance pay, unemployment compensation, refunds of retirement contributions, unused leave, and pensions for unvoluntary retirees.[35] Even so, the estimated savings were huge.

Reducing Rules, Regulations, and Paperwork When President Reagan took office, he was well aware of two studies. One showed that the total cost of issuing and complying with federal regulations came to $121 billion in 1979—about $500 for each man, woman, and child in the United States.[36] The study also reported a sixfold increase in the budgets of 56 federal regulatory agencies between 1970 and 1979. Another study, by the Office of Management and Budget, showed that the public annually spent 786 million hours filling out federal forms.[37]

Immediately after taking office, Reagan attacked the regulatory maze by issuing directives to agencies and appointing sympathetic persons to various governmental posts and commissions. He created a Task Force on Regulatory Relief and named Vice-President George Bush as its chair. By August 1981, the task force had received more than 2,500 suggestions for regulatory relief. The 20 regulations rated by business as the most burdensome and costly (see Table 13.5) affect energy, the environment, the economy, and lifestyle. The agencies overseeing most of these unpopular regulations are the Environmental Protection Agency, the departments of Labor, Energy, and Health and Human Services, and the Nuclear Regulatory Commission.

Of course, not all 20 regulations are viewed as "terrible" by environmental protection groups, consumer groups, women, minorities, or labor groups. These groups contend that while some reforms are necessary, many regulations are needed

TABLE 13.5

The "Terrible 20": Regulations Rated as the Most Burdensome and Costly by the American Business Community (listed from highest to lowest)

1. Hazardous waste management rules that set up a nationwide system for classifying and handling hazardous products. Costs estimated by business at $3 billion initially and $2 billion annually.
2. Criteria standards for the national pollutant discharge elimination system, which governs permits for about 70,000 facilities. Annual costs estimated at $4 billion.
3. Licensing requirements for nuclear power plants. Costs range from several hundred million dollars per reactor to more than $1 billion.
4. The Clean Air Act's pre-treatment standards that tell what treatment industrial wastes must undergo before being discharged to publicly owned treatment plants. Business puts costs at $4 billion for the capital and $1 billion for maintenance and operation.
5. Notification and testing requirements for new chemical substances under the Toxic Substances Control Act. No cost estimate.
6. The cancer policy of the Occupational Safety and Health Act which set up a procedure for classifying and regulating possible carcinogens. Capital costs range from $9 billion to $85 billion; annual costs from $6 billion to $36 billion, according to industry.
7. Incremental pricing of natural gas to most interstate industrial gas users, which forces large industrial users of gas to pay more than residential users.
8. Regulations under the Davis-Bacon Act that require federally funded projects to pay prevailing wage rates in local areas. "Excessive" costs put at $770 million to $15 billion.
9. Residential conservation service program that requires utilities to tell customers of energy conservation techniques and offer "energy audits" of customers homes. Five-year costs projected at nearly $15 billion.
10. Coal conversion guidelines that tell large industries to switch from oil and natural gas to coal or an alternative fuel. Cost estimates: over $1 billion annually.
11. Energy consumption standards ordered by Congress for new residential, commercial and industrial buildings. Costs of $56 billion estimated over the next three decades.
12. Various standards and regulations applied to mining companies under the Mine Safety and Health Act. No cost estimate.
13. Regulations requiring employers in industry to take measures to conserve the hearing of workers exposed to certain noise levels. Annual cost: $250 million.
14. Rules governing the Medicaid and Medicare programs. No cost estimate.
15. Standards for worker exposure to hazardous substances, such as arsenic and lead. No cost estimate.
16. Proposed regulations requiring drug makers and pharmacists to provide consumer information on prescription drugs. Annual costs: $21 million to $80 million.
17. Proposed rules that would set up a historical record of chemicals that pose possible health or environmental risks. Record-keeping costs put at $500,000 to $20 million.
18. Rules requiring employers to develop affirmative action programs.
19. Food labeling policies of the Agriculture Department and the Food and Drug Administration.
20. Pension plan rules under the Employee Retirement Income Security Act.

SOURCE: Compiled by the U.S. Department of Commerce for the Presidential Task Force on Regulatory Relief at the beginning of the Reagan administration.

to protect people's health and safety: "Without stringent government regulation of the workplace and environment, business would pay little heed to environmental and health concerns."[38] These groups have successfully lobbied the president and Congress to delay action on the revision or elimination of affirmative action rules, nuclear licensing requirements, the Clean Air Act, hazardous waste management rules, and other environmental regulations.

During reform attempts, bureaucrats can come under cross-pressures from Congress and the president. For example, in response to intense lobbying by environmental groups against weakening regulations to clean up toxic wastes, four congressional committees (two in the Senate and two in the House) held hearings to "determine whether the Reagan administration was using deep budget cuts and regulatory 'reform' to retreat from its congressionally mandated pollution control duties."[39] Former EPA Director Anne Gorsuch Buford was "invited" to the Hill to respond to questions from committee members, many of whom had constituents who were against the revisions. The result was a delay in weakening the regulations, charges of cover-up and political

2 High Officials of E.P.A. Resign, Reportedly at White House Urging

Reagan Is Said to Want More Control of Agency Amid Rising Disputes

By DAVID BURNHAM
Special to The New York Times

WASHINGTON, Feb. 23 — The inspector general and chief administrator of the Environmental Protection Agency submitted their resignations today. The actions were taken at the request of the White House, according to a senior Reagan Administration official.

The inspector general, Matthew N. Novick, wrote a report critical of the agency's program for cleaning up toxic waste dumps that buttressed the position of its critics in Congress. But before that, the same critics accused him of not properly investigating charges of misconduct by a fellow agency official.

The other aide who resigned was John P. Horton, the agency's assistant administrator for administration, who was responsible for making the agency function. Many critics in Congress say the agency is ill managed. Mr. Horton is under investigation because of reports that he conducted his private business from his agency office. He has denied the charges.

Began With Contempt Move

The resignations were the latest development in a controversy about the agency's performance that erupted last December when the House held Anne McGill Burford in contempt of Congress

If high-level bureaucrats (appointed by the president) become unacceptable to a significant number of Congress members, presidents will ask them to resign, since they can no longer be effective as presidential liaisons with Congress.
(© The New York Times, February 24, 1983. Reprinted by permission.)

maneuvering on the part of the president and EPA officials, and the eventual dismissal of top level EPA administrators, including the director, as things got too hot for the president to handle. Other regulatory reforms were less controversial and more successful.

The regulations revised or eliminated during Reagan's first year saved taxpayers $6.8 billion, according to the Task Force on Regulatory Relief. The biggest savings came from eliminating strict bilingual education requirements, regulations on remodeling mass transit for the handicapped, and the requirement that air bags or automatic seat belts be installed in cars. Other major savings came from deferring EPA noise regulations and from easing Energy Department requirements that utilities convert to coal. Of course, not everyone agreed that these savings were good ones.

Reagan's real impact on regulatory reform came not so much from the rules and regulations he eliminated or revised but from those he prevented. Less than two months after his inauguration, Reagan issued Executive Order No. 12291, which centralized control over the regulatory process in the Office of Management and Budget.

The order mandated that executive agencies and departments (but not independent regulatory commissions) clear with OMB their intent to make a rule, and then the proposed rule itself, before releasing it for public comment.

The executive order also required that an agency conduct detailed *cost/benefit analyses* of alternative regulatory strategies. Such analyses *attempt to compare the costs of programs to the benefits they provide*. When proposing a major rule, unless forbidden by law, the agency was required to choose the least expensive strategy. (A major rule is one that is likely to have an effect of $100 million or more on the economy, lead to significant increases in costs or prices, or have adverse effects on competition.)

The effectiveness of the executive order is reflected in the following figures: 1) a drop by one-third in the number of pages in the *Federal Register*; 2) a 25 percent decrease in the number of rules published; and 3) a 50 percent drop in the number of major regulations published. But some are still skeptical of the order.

Groups such as the League of Women Voters greatly oppose OMB's clearance role. Spokespersons for the group argue that a regulation can be proposed by an agency and scrapped by OMB without the public ever having a chance to speak for or against the idea. OMB spokespersons say the clearance rule serves a different purpose—management and coordination.

Opponents of cost-benefit analysis argue that it is biased against regulatory activity. ''They complain that although costs can often be quantified with some precision, that is not true of benefits—particularly health and safety benefits such as injuries avoided or lives saved.''[40] Supporters say it's an objective method of weighing the pros and cons of regulation.

Another effective tool in reducing rules and regulations and subsequent paperwork is to decrease the number of rule-makers and regulators. Between 1981 and 1982, Reagan proposed and Congress approved a 4 percent drop in regulatory funding.

The Difficulty of Sustaining Bureaucratic Reform

Reagan's initial record in bureaucratic reform was impressive, but like other presidents he has had difficulty in moving beyond personnel and paper-work cuts to major regulatory reform. The problem with bureaucratic reform is always that once the most blatant personnel and regulatory excesses have been dealt with on a piecemeal basis, presidents must develop a coherent set of regulatory goals and a process for achieving them. The tough part, as the Reagan administration soon found out, is to find a balance between costs and benefits in social *and* economic policies—not just in the social programs. Without such a balance, regulatory reform seems unfair and the administration gets tagged as either ''pro-welfare'' or ''pro-business.'' This makes it difficult to achieve anything beyond superficial bureaucratic reform.

The System Works, But Why Can't We See It?

The bureaucracy does respond to the changing needs of the nation, formulating, implementing, and evaluating policies it regards as in the public interest. When a significant number of the nation's citizens and their elected representatives feel that bureaucratic actions are not in the public interest, the size and scope of the bureaucracy can be altered.

The problem is that most citizens cannot see any positive changes in government operations.

Regulating Used Car Sales: The Federal Trade Commission v. Congress

To most Americans, used car dealers are con artists who rip off the public. Used car sales are commonly perceived as riddled with deceptive acts and practices. Plenty of evidence suggests this image isn't far from the truth. A study by two state auto clubs has found that of 1,312 defects in a sample of used cars, only 87 (less than 7 percent) had been disclosed by dealers. Another study of used car dealers in Wisconsin has shown that only 17 percent gave buyers accurate information about the condition of cars offered for sale.[1] The National Association of Attorneys General reports that allegations of unfair and deceptive practices in used car sales are among the leading consumer complaints.

In response to the perceived need to protect consumers, the Federal Trade Commission (FTC) proposed a federal regulation requiring used auto dealers to inform customers of the condition of a car they were interested in buying. The rule required dealers to attach a sticker to each car's windshield detailing any known mechanical defects and stating the terms of any warranties offered. This rule represented nearly ten years of agency investigations, hearings, and deliberations. The FTC first started formulating the rule after the passage of the 1974 Magnusson-Moss Act, which required, in part, that the FTC decide whether to prescribe a consumer protection rule dealing with used car warranties. On September 30, 1981, the FTC finally submitted the regulation to Congress for approval; on May 26, 1982, Congress killed the regulation. Why did Congress reject a regulation that seemed to be so much in the public interest and that the FTC estimated would not cost much to implement (18 cents for printing the sticker plus the cost of filling it out)?

Opponents of the regulation claimed it was poorly written, unenforceable, and not in the public interest. They argued that the regulation, as written, excluded 50 percent of all used car sales—those occurring between

[1]Michael Wines, ''A Heavy Load,'' *National Journal*, January 2, 1982, p. 34.

Bureaucrats try to make policies in the public interest but not everyone agrees on what is the public interest. Such has been the case with attempts by the Federal Trade Commission to impose a regulation requiring used car dealers to inform customers of the condition of a car prior to its sale.

private individuals and not involving a dealer. Objecting specifically to the "known defects" portion of the regulation, the National Automobile Dealers Association complained that the rule would result in lawsuits from buyers whose cars had problems not listed on the sticker. To protect themselves against such lawsuits, elaborate inspections adding an average of $150 to the cost of each car would be necessary.[2] Dealers were also concerned about the regulation's seeming one-sidedness—the assumption that only car dealers engaged in deceptive practices. They pointed out that many a trade-in customer fixed up an old car just enough to get it to the lot, which left the dealers with some real clunkers. Finally, some opponents thought the federal government was overstepping its boundaries. They thought used car regulation should be a state responsibility.

Supporters of the proposed regulation interpreted it quite differently. One FTC commissioner said the regulation would not necessitate expensive inspections. Ironically, some thought this was reason enough to vote against the regulation. "If the dealer does not inspect the car, he/she will be conveying information about the car to the consumer, which is either incorrect or incomplete or both. That outcome is clearly of no benefit to consumers," said one senator.[3] A more convincing pro-regulation argument was that it would greatly benefit consumers and reputable used car dealers. As another senator explained, "The rule would benefit both consumers and the best and most principled dealers by offering customers more information, preventing potential complaints, and helping dealers compete against less principled [dealers]."[4] Still another proponent argued that vetoing the regulation would "send a message that we endorse shabby practices. We endorse cheating. We will take no action against those who would deliberately deceive."[5] Supporters also rejected arguments that the regulation would be too burdensome on the dealer. Said one Congress member in favor of the regulation, "There is no burden on the dealer that makes this rule particularly burdensome, except the burden of telling the truth to the used-car purchasers."[6]

In the end, Congress handily vetoed the FTC regulation in its first exercise of the legislative veto power over FTC regulations that it had granted itself a year earlier. Immediately, the Consumers Union of the United States announced plans to challenge the constitutionality of the legislative veto (congressional power to overturn a bureaucratic rule lacking a presidential signature if both houses adopt a resolution of disapproval). Other consumer groups, such as Public Citizen Congress Watch, saw the veto as "just an invitation to special interest groups to lobby Congress for changes in [FTC] regulations they don't like."[7] Some FTC bureaucrats vowed to write another regulation, this time requiring only the information about warranties since the dealers had not objected to that part of the original regulation. Ultimately the Supreme Court ruled the legislative veto unconstitutional which once again, put the ball in the FTC's court.

This example of the bureaucracy's role in formulating public policy shows that 1) bureaucracies do try to make policies in the public interest; and 2) not everyone agrees on the effect a policy will have once implemented or on its fairness; In this case, you must decide for yourself whether the bureaucrats (the FTC) or Congress initially made the best assessment about protecting the public interest at the used car lot.

[2]Judy Sarasohn, "Senate Overwhelmingly Acts to Block FTC Used-Car Rule," *Congressional Quarterly,* 40 (May 22, 1982), p. 1188.

[3]Judy Sarasohn, "FTC's Car Rule Falls Victim to First Congressional Veto," *Congressional Quarterly,* 40 (May 29, 1982), p. 1259.
[4]Sarasohn, "Senate Overwhelmingly Acts," *op. cit.,* p. 1188.
[5]*Ibid.*
[6]Sarasohn, "FTC's Car Rule Falls," *op. cit.*, p. 1259.
[7]Sarasohn, "Senate Overwhelmingly Acts," *op. cit.,* p. 1188.

They see only the defects in the administrative system. The problem is well stated by Gerald E. Caiden in "The Challenge to the Administrative State." Caiden observes:

> *The public does not know whether existing controls are adequate or not or whether they are breaking down and need to be strengthened. . . . They cannot really judge when things improve for as far as they are concerned, little changes. . . . They are inclined to exaggerate and generalize administrative defects that come to light and to believe the worst about what is supposed to happen behind the scenes. They cannot make the connection between big government and themselves.*[41]

As times have changed and government has become more complex, government employees have gotten more involved in the three stages of the policy process: establishing rules and regulations for programs created by Congress (formation); delivering government services (implementation); and collecting and analyzing data about program performance (evaluation).

The bureaucracy is kept under control by checks and balances, as is characteristic of our system of government. Ultimately, the impetus for change comes from the citizens who express their mandate at the ballot box.

SUMMARY

For the most part, the American public views government employees as impersonal and government as inefficient. This negative opinion is often a result of the ordinary citizen's direct contact with government employees in daily life. Although most public and private organizations have a bureaucratic structure, government comes under greatest attack because the federal system is fragmented and no single individual or group has legal authority over all government employees.

America's bureaucracy is a mix of national, state, and local governments. At the national level, the bureaucracy is most often identified as the agencies in the executive branch. These include cabinet departments, independent regulatory commissions, independent executive agencies, and government corporations. The bureaucracy extends to the legislative branch and the judiciary as well. State and local government bureaucracies are often patterned after those of the federal government.

Through the years the president, Congress, and the courts have adopted policies to make the bureaucracy more responsive to the needs of the American people. That policies can change is evident in the evolution of the government employment system, which was originally a system of political patronage. The Pendleton Act of 1883 created the Civil Service Commission and the foundation of a merit system. In response to changes in the system, the Civil Service Reform Act of 1978 was passed.

KEY TERMS

blanketing
bureaucracy
cabinet departments
Civil Service Commission
Civil Service Reform Act of 1978
commission plan
cost/benefit analysis
council-manager plan
excepted service jobs
Federal Register
general service jobs
government corporations
independent executive agencies
independent regulatory commissions
iron triangle
judicial agencies
legislative agencies
merit system
Merit Systems Protection Board
Office of Personnel Management
policy evaluation
policy implementation
reductions-in-force (RIFs)
rule of three
secretaries
spoils system
street-level bureaucrats
strong executive system
strong-mayor council plan
veteran's preference
weak executive system
weak-mayor council plan

Arnold, R. Douglas. *Congress and the Bureaucracy: A Theory of Influence.* New Haven, Conn.: Yale University Press, 1979.

Heclo, Hugh. *A Government of Strangers: Executive Politics in Washington.* Washington, D.C.: Brookings Institution, 1977.

Kaufman, Herbert. *Red Tape: Its Origins, Uses, and Abuses.* Washington, D.C.: Brookings Institution, 1977.

Kranz, Harry. *The Participatory Bureaucracy: Women and Minorities in a More Representative Public Service.* Lexington, Mass.: Lexington Books, 1979.

Larson, James W. *Why Government Programs Fail: Improving Policy Implementation.* New York: Praeger, 1980.

Lawson, Harry O.; Ackerman, H. R., Jr.; and Fuller,

Donald E. *Personnel Administration in the Courts.* Boulder, Colo.: Westview Press, 1979.

Lipsky, Michael. *Street-Level Bureaucracy: Dilemmas of the Individual in Public Services,* New York: Russel Sage Foundation, 1980.

Lynn, Laurence, C., Jr. *Managing the Public's Business: The Job of the Government Executive.* New York: Basic Books, 1981.

Meltsner, Arnold J. *Policy Analysis in the Bureaucracy.* Berkeley, Calif.: University of California Press, 1976.

Szanton, Peter, ed. *Federal Reorganization: What Have We Learned?* Chatham, N.J.: Chatham House Publishers, 1981.

Welborn, David M. *Governance of Federal Regulatory Agencies.* Knoxville, Tenn.: University of Tennessee Press, 1977.

CHAPTER 14

JUDICIARY

Court Functions ■ Supreme Court Personnel ■ Recruitment ■ Organization of the Court System ■ How a Suit Reaches the Supreme Court ■ Norms ■ Compliance with Court Decisions ■ Suggested Changes

People who feel that their rights are not being respected may angrily say that they will take their case all the way to the Supreme Court in order to obtain justice. This threat can rarely be carried out, but the fact that it is uttered provides some insight into the position occupied by the Supreme Court and the rest of the judiciary in many people's minds. Clearly, people look to the Supreme Court as a final authority on legal questions. The variety of issues that someone in society believes should be resolved through a judicial proceeding is virtually limitless.

Some questions brought before the courts are very specific, such as who was at fault in an automobile accident. Others have implications for millions of Americans, such as suits questioning the constitutionality of public and private employment practices as they affect women, the handicapped, and racial minorities. A third type of litigation concerns the proper balance of power within the political system. This category includes questions about the relationships between states and federal authority and whether the president can refuse to supply Congress with materials he has taped.

We begin this chapter with a discussion of the functions of the courts, paying particular attention to the unique responsibilities of the Supreme Court. The second section looks at the kind of individuals who have served on the Supreme Court and the process by which judges are selected for this and the lower federal courts. This will be followed by a section on the relationship of the Su-

The Supreme Court is regarded as the nation's final authority on legal questions. Through its rulings, it interprets the Constitution and adapts it to changing society.

preme Court to other courts and a description of the ways cases work their way up to the highest court in the land.

Attention will be paid to norms that seem to guide the behavior of judges. We will also review the variables related to judges' decision-making behavior. Finally, we will turn to a consideration of the way people react to Supreme Court decisions. Because of the controversial nature of a number of the issues brought to the Supreme Court for adjudication, segments of the public may be outraged by Court decisions. Examples over the last 30 years include decisions on the rights of defendants in criminal prosecutions, prayer in the schools, abortions, and school desegregation. The conditions under which court decisions are successfully implemented will be considered.

COURT FUNCTIONS

American courts fulfill two important functions for society: they help enforce the prevalent norms of behavior and they make policy. Many people who object to the outcome of Supreme Court cases argue that the Court should be restricted to enforcing the law and diligently avoid anything that smacks of judicial policymaking. The more prevalent view today is that Court decisions are unavoidably a part of the policy process. We will discuss norm enforcement first.

Norm Enforcement

Most of the cases filed in the nation's courts each year concern norm enforcement. The norm enforcement function is essential to avoid vigilante justice and other forms of self-help. Thus, we may go to court to get money owed to us or to prevent someone from harming us or our property. Environmentalists have sought *injunctions (court orders prohibiting certain actions)* to prevent the construction of dams, pipelines, and nuclear power plants. Governmental units go to court to condemn land to be used for public construction projects such as highways rather than forcibly turning people off their land. In the same way, most victims of crime leave it to the judiciary to determine who committed the crime and to assess the penalty. In some cultures, it is not uncommon for revenge to be carried out by a victim's next of kin, but in this country we turn to the government for help. It is because revenge is so rare that the feud that al-

most wiped out the Hatfields and McCoys remains part of American folklore a century later.

Norm enforcement also covers court proceedings that make official or legitimate actions that people of earlier generations either did without official sanction or that were handled by religious institutions. For example, one goes to court to adopt a child, to end a marriage, or to change a surname.

Societies have long realized that there must be an institution that has the authority to resolve disputes. Primitive societies often relied on a council of elders to carry out this function, while in parts of feudal Europe, the local noble had authority to settle disputes among his vassals. But in this country and most others today, if we cannot resolve differences with neighbors, merchants, or people who bump into us on the highway, we turn to the courts to decide who is at fault and what will be done to compensate the person who has been wronged. The dockets (lists of cases) of most trial courts are loaded with just these kinds of cases involving contracts and injuries.

Civil and Criminal Law For some kinds of wrongs, two types of punishment may be handed out. If the wrongdoer has violated the rights of another person and broken a law for which there are criminal penalties, then private as well as public litigation may follow. Having broken the law, the wrongdoer is subject to prosecution by the government in a criminal case. In these cases, which have titles such as *United States* v. *Smith* (if the defendant has violated federal law) or *California* v. *Smith* or *New York* v. *Smith* (if the defendant has violated state law), an arm of the government brings suit to enforce penalties against someone who has taken a life, hijacked an airplane, sold drugs, or plowed into another automobile.

For most offenses there can also be a private, civil action. These would be designated by a title such as *Jones* v. *Smith*, where Jones, the plaintiff, alleges some injury at the hands of Smith.

Suppose that Smith murders Jones. The state may prosecute Smith for murder under criminal law. In addition, Jones' heirs may sue Smith and seek damages under **tort law,** *which allows damages to those who have suffered because of wrongdoing by someone else.* Jones's widow and child could base their claim on the loss of the income that Jones would have generated had he not been killed. Similarly, if Brown runs a stop sign while drunk and hits

Green's car, the state can prosecute Brown for the laws that have been broken. While the penalty imposed by the state (a fine, imprisonment, or loss of a driver's license) may dissuade Brown from drinking and driving in the future, it does not pay for the repair of Green's car.* To obtain money to repair the damaged car (assuming that Brown cannot handle this with insurance and refuses to pay), Green can sue Brown under civil law.

The courts, then, are used by both the government and private citizens to enforce accepted standards of behavior. In the absence of the means for redress provided by the courts, violence would be more prevalent than it is and the adage that ''Might makes right'' would be the controlling principle of social relations.

Policymaking

The policymaking function derives from judges' responsibility to apply the law to the disputes that come before them. Many people believe this can be done without judges becoming policymakers. This perspective is symbolized by the presentation of Justice as blindfolded and holding a set of scales. People who favor this type of *mechanical jurisprudence believe a judge should have no discretion in applying the appropriate body of law to a particular case.* Indeed, the judge could be seen as simply a legal craftsperson. The judge takes the law as given and applies it dispassionately without regard for his or her personal preferences.

Not only is this mechanistic approach popular with a large share of the public, it is embraced by some judges. The classic statement of this perspective was made in a 1936 decision by Supreme Court Justice Owen Roberts:

> When an act of Congress is appropriately challenged in the courts as not conforming to the constitutional mandate the judicial branch of the Government has only one duty—to lay the Article of the Constitution which is invoked beside the statute which is challenged and to decide whether the latter squares with the former. All the court does, or can do, is to announce its considered judgment upon the question. The only power it has, if such it may be called, is the power of judgment.[1]

*Some judges when passing sentence will order that the defendant provide restitution to the injured party. This may be done through a lump sum payment or in weekly installments. This type of judgment combines restoration of the injured party with the state's interest in punishing lawbreakers.

Roberts's statement can easily be extended to cases that do not raise constitutional issues: the court lays the statute beside the activity in dispute and then judges whether the activity violates the statute.

While the mechanistic approach may accurately reflect much of what happens in most tribunals, it does not accurately describe the activity of the Supreme Court, a number of lower federal courts, and the highest courts in some states. In cases that reach the Supreme Court, there is often uncertainty about how to apply the law or the Constitution or about which of two conflicting sections of the Constitution takes precedence. The justices of the Supreme Court must frequently do more than judge whether a statute is constitutional or unconstitutional.

When hearing cases arising under relatively recent statutes, courts are often confronted with issues for which the legislature has not given clear guidance, and some litigation under older statutes raises issues that involve new technologies that the legislators who wrote the statutes could not have foreseen. In such cases, even if the court wishes to simply apply the terms of the statute to the particular situation, it must first decide what parts of the statute apply, if any. There may also be conflicts between a new statute and an earlier one which the legislature has not repealed.

Another problem for the advocates of mechanistic jurisprudence has been the vagueness of many statutes. Theodore Lowi has pointed out that Congress increasingly avoids standards and instead uses ambiguous guidelines when legislating.[2] Without clear standards to guide them, judges have become more willing to rely on their personal preferences since the statutes which they are applying allow them discretion. Furthermore, as we will see later in this chapter, presidents name to the federal bench men and women who share their policy preferences. Since having taken the ''correct'' stand on important issues is a factor in being appointed to a judgeship, it is hardly surprising that judges respond on the basis of their preferences when the law allows them this option.[3]

When confronted with ambiguities, the courts have little choice but to step in and complete the work left undone by the legislature and define the conditions under which the statute applies. Legislatures usually allow this kind of court activity to stand, but if there is widespread disagreement with the court's actions, the legislature occasionally amends the statute to reverse the court's decision.

Judicial Review   Probably the most important facet of the United States Supreme Court's policymaking function derives from its authority to exercise judicial review. This authority was not given to the Court by the Constitution but was assumed by Chief Justice John Marshall. *Judicial review* means that *the Court can declare an act of Congress to be in violation of the Constitution and therefore null and void.*

The Court first asserted the power to declare laws unconstitutional in *Marbury* v. *Madison.*[4] This suit grew out of the political conflict surrounding the election of 1800. When Thomas Jefferson narrowly defeated the incumbent, Federalist John Adams. The outgoing Federalists, who also lost control of both houses of Congress, tried to retain control of the judiciary. Stories are told that President Adams remained at his desk until midnight of the last day of his term signing the appointments for Federalists to serve in 16 newly created judgeships and 42 justice of the peace positions for the District of Columbia.

Some of the newly approved judicial appointments had not been delivered when the Jeffersonians assumed control of the government. Among these was the certificate naming William Marbury to the position of justice of the peace in the District of Columbia. The new secretary of state, James Madison, refused to deliver the appointment. Marbury sued Madison, asking that Madison be ordered to hand over the certificate. The Judiciary Act of 1789 had provided that a suit seeking a **writ of mandamus** (*an order for an official to carry out a nondiscretionary duty*) against federal officials would be heard by the Supreme Court under its original jurisdiction.

Chief Justice Marshall's handling of Marbury's petition was masterful. First, he pointed an accusatory finger at his political enemy Thomas Jefferson by ruling that Marbury was entitled to the appointment and Madison was wrong to withhold it. Second, however, he won for the Court the vast power of judicial review. For although Marshall's opinion said Marbury should get the appointment, the chief justice ruled that the Court could not grant the petitioner's request. The writ of mandamus could not be granted because Congress had breached the Constitution when it expanded the Court's original jurisdiction by giving

it the power to hear this type of case. Original jurisdiction is clearly stated in the Constitution and the only way to add to it would be through a constitutional amendment, not through the Judiciary Act.

The power of judicial review, like many extraordinary powers, has been used infrequently. After being unveiled in 1803, it was not used again in a federal case until the Dred Scott decision in 1857.[5] In that case, the Court held that Congress lacked the authority to ban slavery in the territories as it had tried to do in the Missouri Compromise.

Judicial Activism, Judicial Restraint   "Activism" and "restraint" are terms frequently used to characterize the role of the Court as policymaker. These terms refer to the willingness of the courts to strike down as unconstitutional actions of the legislative or executive branches. Those who practice *judicial activism are more willing to overturn the decision of another branch or level of government.* Thus, on today's Court, activist justices such as William Brennan or Thurgood Marshall are more inclined to hold acts of Congress or state legislatures to be unconstitutional. In contrast, justices such as William Rehnquist or Chief Justice Warren Burger practice *judicial restraint and more often defer to the policy decisions made by Congress or state legislatures.* Recent Republican presidents have sought to appoint strict constructionists who believe in restraint while Democratic presidents have named activists to the Supreme Court.

At issue here is the amount of deference the Supreme Court should give to other decisionmakers. When the Court strikes down an act of Congress for being unconstitutional, critics charge the judiciary with behaving as a super-legislature. Critics believe the courts should tamper with legislative enactments under only the most extreme conditions. While some disagree, the Supreme Court claims that it avoids deciding the constitutionality of an issue if there is some other basis for judgment (e.g., a statute) and holds a statute unconstitutional only when there is no way it can be interpreted as being in conformity with the Constitution.[6]

Should nonelected officials be able to block decisions that have been approved by a majority of the country's elected representatives and the president? Critics of judicial activism point out that federal judges are not directly accountable to the

A majority of the current Supreme Court justices, including Chief Justice Warren Burger (front center), is perceived as practicing judicial restraint and advocating strict construction (interpretation) of the Constitution.

public. Our system does not, however, give the courts an ultimate veto over legislative preferences. As we shall explain later, if enough legislators disagree with a court interpretation of a statute, they can reverse the judiciary. Congress can also propose a constitutional amendment to the states if two-thirds of the legislators disagree with a constitutional interpretation.

Conservatives as Activists   The nature of the issues before the Supreme Court has been an important factor in determining whether judicial activism or restraint have had liberal or conservative connotations. From the turn of the century until approximately 1940, the Court dealt primarily with cases of economic regulation. State and federal statutes seeking to regulate working conditions (maximum hours, minimum wages, and child labor) and New Deal efforts to revitalize the economy were among the highly controversial issues to come before the Court. On these types of cases, the conservative justices were the activists. In a long string of cases they disallowed federal and state regulations concerning working conditions. The Court ruled that states generally could not set wages or hours for workers because such legislation violated the freedom of an employer and an employee to agree to a contract setting the employee's wages, no matter how disadvantageous the contract might be to the employee.[7] Freedom of contract, the Court held, was a right protected by the due process clause of the Fourteenth Amendment.[8]

Conservative activists also applied a narrow definition of interstate commerce to strike down legislation. Congress tried to regulate various economic practices on the basis of its constitutional authority "to regulate commerce with foreign nations, and *among the several states,* and with the Indian tribes"[9] (italics added). The Supreme Court severely circumscribed these efforts by distinguishing the manufacturing process that occurred prior to interstate shipment from the shipment itself. Congress, the Court ruled, could only regulate shipment.[10]

During the 1930s, another basis was used to strike down some economic regulations—improper delegation of authority by the Congress. In the past, the courts declared legislation to be unconstitutional when Congress gave a vast grant of authority to the bureaucracy without providing sufficient guidance. Today the courts are no longer worried that Congress may allow the bureaucracy too much discretion. In the most famous case in which a grant of authority was ruled to be too broad, the Supreme Court invalidated a key component of President Roosevelt's program to stimulate the economy by holding the National Industrial Recovery Act to be unconstitutional.[11]

The conservative activists held the upper hand on the Court until the late 1930s. When Chief Justice Charles Hughes and Justice Owen Roberts made an ideological shift away from the four archconservatives and toward the Court's three liberals, the balance of power on the Court shifted, and so did the tone of its decisions. This realignment came in 1937 while Congress was considering President Roosevelt's proposal to add a justice to the Supreme Court for each sitting member who was over 70 years of age. Congress rejected the president's court-packing plan, but the ideological change in the Supreme Court's economic decisions was accelerated when the four staunch opponents of the New Deal were replaced over the next four years by liberals. In short order, the new liberal majority approved legislation on economic regulations that had been judged to be unconstitutional only a few years earlier.[12]

Liberals as Activists Once the pending agenda of economic regulations had been enacted and upheld as constitutional, the Court's docket came to contain increasing numbers of civil liberties cases. While the specific rights at issue varied from case to case, several common threads ran through many of them. Most suits challenged a state or local statute or practice and were filed by a member of a minority group who felt that the minority was being discriminated against. A second, less common type of case involved conservative challenges to efforts to expand the rights of minorities through the enactment of federal legislation.

In reviewing state legislation and practices that were alleged to be discriminatory, liberal justices like Hugo Black and William Douglas practiced judicial activism. These justices, who had believed it was improper for the Supreme Court to substitute its collective judgment for the economic policy preferences of state legislatures and Congress, perceived no need to exercise restraint when reviewing state legislation that touched on civil liberties and civil rights.

The suites in which liberals practiced judicial activism are described in detail in the next two chapters. At this point, we will simply indicate that the liberal majority used the equal protection clause of the Fourteenth Amendment to disallow state laws that denied blacks the vote and access to public accommodations and desegregated schools. Liberals used the First Amendment of the Bill of Rights as a battering ram to knock down community restrictions on religious proselytizing. Bill of Rights protections for people charged with crimes have gradually been applied to curtail various state practices and abuses.

The period of liberal dominance on the Supreme Court extended into the early days of the chief justiceship of Warren Burger, who was named to his post in 1969. During this period, it was conservatives who filed dissents urging greater restraint on the Court.

In summary, then, judicial activism and restraint are not ideals that most members of the court have adhered to consistently across issues. It appears that the approach a justice espouses is more a product of his or her policy preferences than of any deep-seated commitment to a particular notion of the proper relationship between the federal judiciary and the legislative branches of the state and national governments.

Activism was most pronounced between 1920–1939 and 1960–1977. In the first period of activism, the Court had a conservative majority while in the second period, liberals were dominant.

The Judiciary's Unique Role To some groups, the judiciary is a more accessible policy-making unit than are other branches of the government. Success before the legislature depends on the ability to persuade a majority of both houses of the desirability of one's position. As we pointed out in chapter 11, the fact that legislative proposals must gain approval at many stages stacks the deck in favor of those who prefer the status quo. In the same way, executive branch leaders are also generally more responsive to the politically influential than to the powerless. At lower levels of the bureaucracy there can be pockets of responsiveness to the disadvantaged, although in time this responsiveness may be eliminated if opposed by leaders in the administration.[13]

Since federal judges are appointed for life unless impeached for high crimes and misdemeanors, they are less subject to popular passions. Life tenure provides insulation from the preferences of the majority, so judges, if they wish, can make decisions based on the merits rather than on the basis of probable effects on potential voters and campaign contributors. Because of this freedom from reelection worries, the federal courts have led the way into a number of controversial areas.

SUPREME COURT PERSONNEL

When Sandra Day O'Connor took the oath as a justice of the Supreme Court, she became the hundred-and-second member but only the first woman to serve on the nation's highest tribunal. One of Justice O'Connor's colleagues is Thurgood Marshall, named to the Court in 1968 as its first black member.

Now that a woman serves on the Court, probably the only characteristic shared by all members

Justice Sandra Day O'Connor, appointed by President Ronald Reagan, is the first woman to serve on the Supreme Court.

is that they are lawyers, even though there is no requirement in the Constitution or the statutes restricting service on the Court to attorneys.

Education

Most justices have attended the nation's premier law schools. Of the last 27 justices (those appointed by President Franklin Roosevelt and his successors), a third attended Ivy League Schools (four went to Harvard, three to Yale, and two to Columbia).[14] Four were students at Big Ten law schools and three studied at leading West Coast law schools. Only one, James Byrnes, who was appointed in 1941, became a lawyer without graduating from law school. Generally, justices of the Supreme Court have been drawn from among the better educated members of the bar.

Occasionally presidential nominees to the Court have been opposed on the grounds that they were weak intellectually. In 1970, when this criticism was directed at G. Harrold Carswell, whom President Nixon had nominated, Senator Roman Hruska (R-Nebr.) argued, "Even if he were mediocre, there are a lot of mediocre judges and

people and lawyers. They are entitled to a little representation, aren't they, and a little chance?"[15]

Judicial Experience

Half of the justices who have begun service on the Supreme Court since 1937 had experience as judges on lower courts. Of these, eight had served on a United States Court of Appeals. Of today's justices, Chief Justice Burger and Associate Justices Blackmun and Stevens served as judges on the court of appeals before being elevated to the Supreme Court. Justices Brennan and O'Connor previously sat on state appellate courts. Prior experience on the bench is becoming increasingly common—five of the last seven justices were once judges.

Attorneys for the federal government are a second pool from which justices are frequently drawn. Presidents have often tapped high-ranking officials in the Department of Justice. Of the members of the Court in 1983, Rehnquist and Burger had worked as assistant attorney generals while White was a deputy attorney general in the Kennedy administration. Thurgood Marshall was serving as President Johnson's solicitor general at the time of his appointment. Of the current justices, only Lewis Powell was neither a judge nor a Justice Department official.

Political Experience

Current or recent holders of high public office constitute another set of potential Court nominees. As Table 14.1 shows, appointees of Democratic presidents are slightly more likely to have held elective office than appointees of Republican presidents. Elective office seems to be of decreasing importance as an incubator of future justices. Currently, the only justice who has held elective office is Sandra O'Connor, who once served in the Arizona legislature.

Success as a politician was a more important stepping-stone to the Court in the past. One for-

TABLE 14.1

Judicial and Political Experience of Justices Appointed to the Supreme Court Since 1945

	Experience as a Judge		Justice Department		Held Elective Office	
	Yes	No	Yes	No	Yes	No
Appointed by a						
Republican President	8	3	3	8	2	9
Democratic President	3	5	3	5	3	5

Source: Compiled from data in Lawrence Baum, *The Supreme Court* (Washington, D.C.: Congressional Quarterly, 1981), pp. 50–51.

mer president, William Howard Taft, served as chief justice from 1921 to 1930. Another nominee for the presidency, Charles Evans Hughes, served as an associate justice and later as chief justice.* Earl Warren was governor of California.

Other Characteristics

About half the justices appointed since the beginning of the New Deal were in their fifties when they took their places on the Court. The ages of justices of the last 46 years at the time of appointment ranged from 40 (William O. Douglas) to 64 (Lewis Powell). Because they have life tenure, a number of justices are likely to be over 70 years old at any given time. The Court that Franklin Roosevelt characterized as the "9 old men" had an average age of 71 in 1936, with 6 members aged between 70 and 80. Justice O'Connor's appointment reduces the average age of today's Court; prior to her appointment, the average age of the justices was 68.5. Although there is certainly not a direct relationship between age and opposition to change, the fact that justices tend to be elderly may retard the speed with which they embrace new ideas.

Most of the justices throughout the history of the Court have been from families of high social status. Less than 10 percent rose from modest beginnings.[16] Historically, most justices have come from politically active families, although this has been less true since the New Deal.

The membership on the Court has been comprised disproportionately of white, Anglo-Saxon, Protestant males. Through 1957, almost 90 percent of the justices' families had come from the British Isles. There have been relatively few Catholics, Jews, blacks, or women. No Hispanic has ever been appointed.

RECRUITMENT

Members of the Supreme Court as well as other federal judges are appointed by the president, subject to Senate confirmation. Few formal constraints are imposed on the president when he

*Justice Hughes was serving as governor of New York when appointed associate justice in 1910. Six years later he gave up his seat to accept the Republican presidential nomination, a race which he narrowly lost to Woodrow Wilson. President Hoover appointed Hughes to be chief justice in 1930.

makes these choices; nevertheless, a fairly regularized process has developed.

Supreme Court

When a justice dies or informs the president of an intention to retire, the attorney general, often a close friend of the president, develops a list of potential nominees (see Figure 14.1). The attorney general does some screening and a full background investigation is conducted by the FBI. The press speculates about the names on the list and tries to guess who will be the lucky nominee. With this kind of attention being given to the event, the president wants to avoid the embarrassment of having his nominee rejected by the Senate.

American Bar Association Recent presidents have allowed the American Bar Association to play a role in the screening process. The ABA's *Committee on the Federal Judiciary (CFJ)* *evaluates the judicial competence of those being considered for appointment.* Members of the CFJ contact lawyers who have observed the candidate in action and judges before whom the candidate has practiced. Under some presidents, such as Eisenhower, the CFJ has been able to veto potential nominees. Other presidents have simply treated the CFJ evaluation as one factor when making appointments.[17]

The CFJ reports the results of its research and its overall evaluation to the attorney general. In addition, the person chairing the CFJ is typically one of the witnesses called to testify by the Senate Judiciary Committee when it conducts its hearings on the nomination.

The judgment given by the Committee on the Federal Judiciary is an important element in the selection process. A president will think twice before sending to the Senate someone who has been labeled as unqualified. On the other hand, the CFJ has never obtained its objective of being allowed to make nominations to the president of lawyers whom it felt were qualified. It can only react to the names being considered.

Senate Approval The Senate Judiciary Committee conducts hearings to determine the fitness of nominees. When the hearings are over, the committee makes a recommendation to the full Senate, where approval is by a majority vote.

Despite prior explorations of the backgrounds

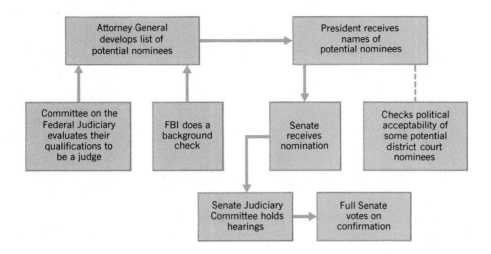

FIGURE 14.1

Selection Process for Federal Judges

of people being considered for appointment, three nominations were rejected between 1968 and 1970. This was the most concentrated series of rejections of presidential judicial nominations in more than a century. The first to be rejected was Abe Fortas, President Johnson's designee to replace Earl Warren as chief justice. Fortas was already a member of the Court, but his nomination encountered opposition when it was revealed that he might be guilty of behavior improper for a justice. A consideration that may have figured in the opposition of some Republicans to the Fortas nomination was the proximity of the presidential election. With the polls indicating that Richard

The Senate Judiciary Committee conducts hearings to determine the fitness of presidential nominees to the Supreme Court. The Committee, and later the full Senate, ultimately rejected Nixon's nominee, G. Harrold Carswell (center).

Nixon would be elected, Republicans had an incentive to delay confirmation of Fortas. Nixon's eventual victory meant that a conservative rather than the liberal Fortas would preside over the Court.

Liberals in the Senate counterattacked and rejected two of President Nixon's first three nominees. President Nixon had promised during the campaign that if elected he would name a conservative southerner to the Supreme Court. His first effort to deliver on this promise was thwarted when the Senate narrowly rejected Clement Haynsworth because he had failed to remove himself from consideration of a case involving a company in which he held stock. The case came before Haynsworth in his capacity as a member of the Fourth Circuit Court of Appeals. President Nixon then nominated G. Harrold Carswell, who was also a court of appeals judge. Carswell was rejected by the Senate when legal scholars and hundreds of lawyers raised serious questions about his competence.

Another consideration behind liberal senators' opposition to the two Nixon nominees was the conservative nature of the decisions handed down by these men in civil rights and labor cases. The AFL-CIO and the NAACP were active in rallying opponents to vote against confirmation. Particularly damaging to Carswell were some segregationist remarks he had uttered in a campaign decades earlier.

The experiences of Fortas, Haynsworth, and Carswell should provide two lessons for presidents as they consider whom to name to the Supreme Court. First, the president is poorly served if his attorney general fails to have the most searching examination of potential nominees' backgrounds conducted.

A second lesson is that the Senate will oppose nominees on the basis of policy disagreements. It appears, however, that policy disagreements alone are insufficient to defeat a nominee who is not otherwise tainted. Thus, a predominantly Democratic Senate approved the nomination of conservative William Rehnquist in 1971. A decade later, opposition to Sandra O'Connor among anti-abortion senators evaporated as she adroitly handled questions during the confirmation hearings.

Other Federal Courts

As with the Supreme Court, the president nominates judges to the federal district courts, the courts of appeals, and the specialized federal courts. Background checks are conducted by the FBI, and the ABA's Committee on the Federal Judiciary explores the qualifications of potential nominees. Nominees must be confirmed by the Senate; once confirmed, they serve for life unless impeached, or until they resigned.

Beginning with the Nixon administration, candidates for federal judgeships have had to complete an extensive questionnaire.[18] The questionnaire asks a number of personal questions and seeks information about candidates' professional activities. The FBI seeks to determine prospective nominees' political, economic, and social views, and since the rejection of the Carswell nomination, newspapers in cities where candidates have lived have been reviewed. In this way the FBI tries to avoid having damaging material of which it was unaware unearthed by diligent reporters.

While the general procedures for Supreme Court justices and the judges serving on lower federal courts are the same, there are a few differences in the considerations that influence the process. The CFJ applies somewhat lower standards when evaluating candidates for seats on lower courts. It is less concerned that these candidates—particularly those being considered for a district court judgeship—have bench experience, although it still prefers candidates who have good records as trial attorneys.

In addition to input from the CFJ and the FBI,

the president needs to get a reading on a candidate's political credentials, particularly for attorneys being considered for district court appointments. If one or both of the senators from the state in which the district court vacancy exists are of the same party as the president, then the norm of senatorial courtesy applies. *Senatorial courtesy requires that the president consult with senators in his party before making federal appointments in a state.* If the president fails to obtain the approval of a senator in his party before naming a judge in the senator's state, the senator can block the nomination by objecting to the Senate Judiciary Committee.

In states that do not have a senator of the president's party, the norm of senatorial courtesy does not apply, but there may be other political figures in the state whom the president should consult to promote the fortunes of his party and to build party unity. A federal judgeship is a most attractive political plum. If the president fails to consult his party's leaders in the state, they will be angry and may drag their feet when the president calls on them for help in getting his program through Congress. Because of such political considerations, the president usually selects someone whom his party's senators or other political influentials have recommended.

In light of the importance of political factors, it is hardly surprising that party affiliation is a factor in the nomination of federal judges. Recent presidents have awarded approximately 90 percent of their judicial nominations to lawyers who share their party allegiance.[19] A majority of the nominees have been active partisans.[20] Indeed, their efforts on behalf of their party probably figured in their being nominated to the bench.

Since presidents almost always choose candidates who are affiliated with their own party, there are differences in the characteristics of Democratic and Republican nominees. Each parties' chief executives are more likely to pick top lawyers who have characteristics similar to their party's followers. Accordingly, Democratic presidents are more likely to name blacks, Catholics, Jews, and people from relatively lower status backgrounds than are Republican presidents.[21] Democratic presidents have appointed a larger percentage of women to the federal bench than have Republican.

Satisfying the president's partisans in a state also plays a part in the choice of nominees to the circuit courts of appeals. Since each circuit covers several states, however, single senators cannot block appointments to which they object. There are unwritten rules which say that each state within a circuit should be represented by at least one member of the circuit court and that a departing judge should be replaced by someone from the same state, but these restrictions are less serious than those the president faces when filling district court vacancies.

The evaluations of the American Bar Association can be used by the attorney general, acting on behalf of the president, to eliminate potential appointees who are unqualified. An attorney who has been stamped as being unqualified by the ABA can be rejected without antagonizing the senator who advanced the person's name.

There has been debate over whether quality and representativeness are opposing values in staffing the federal bench. Leaders of organizations concerned with the legal interests of women and racial minorities have criticized President Reagan for infrequently venturing beyond the ranks of white males when naming judges. The counsel to President Reagan sought to deflect these criticisms, arguing that "[T]here are some people who think that courts should be staffed, if you will, on a basis of representativeness, and really, we think they should be staffed on the basis of qualifications."[22]

Since 1969, there has been relatively little difference in the quality of appointments as judged by the ABA, even though Republican and Democratic presidents' nominees differ on some characteristics. The great majority of the new federal jurists have been fairly evenly divided between the well qualified and qualified categories. Presidents Eisenhower, Kennedy, and Johnson tapped larger percentages of exceptionally well qualified candidates, but they also put forward the names of more unqualified nominees than their successors.

The reviews given by the Senate Judiciary Committee to nominations to the lower federal courts are fairly routine. However, the Republican majority on the Senate Judiciary Committee in the early 1980s inquired into nominees' stands on the issue of judicial activism or restraint. Opponents to the nomination bear the burden of proving the unsuitability of the candidate.

Appointments to judgeships below the Supreme Court have less potential for shaping policy. This fact plus the greater number of these appointments and the norm of senatorial courtesy combine to reduce the influence of the president over these appointments.

ORGANIZATION OF THE COURT SYSTEM

The Constitution provides for only one court: "The judicial power of the United States, shall be vested in one Supreme Court, and in such inferior Courts as the Congress may from time to time ordain and establish." The first Congress created a set of federal district courts, at least one for each state. As the country and its population have grown, additional district courts have been created until now there are 95 districts in the states and territories. Twenty-six states have only one district court while California, New York, and Texas have four each.

The ***federal district courts*** *are the trial courts in the federal system for most types of cases.* In these courts, one could see litigation as portrayed on television with lawyers and their clients sitting at tables before the judge and perhaps a jury empaneled in a jury box. It is in the trial court that the parties to the litigation (the plaintiff and the defendant) are present and witnesses are called to testify.

The ***courts of appeals*** *are federal courts where appeals are heard from people dissatisfied with outcomes in federal district courts and independent regulatory commissions.* The Circuit Courts of Appeals were created by Congress in 1891. For many years there was one Court of Appeals for the District of Columbia with the remainder of the country divided into ten other circuits, each with a minimum of three states. In October of 1981 the Fifth Circuit, which served Alabama, Florida, Georgia, Mississippi, Louisiana, and Texas, was divided. The division was necessitated by the heavy workload of the Fifth Circuit, due in part to the great number of civil rights cases that have arisen in the South. The three eastern states comprise the new Eleventh Circuit (see Figure 14.2).

In addition to the 95 district courts and the 12 courts of appeals, there are several federal courts that handle specialized types of cases. There is one separate court system to handle cases involving the misdeeds of military personnel and another for cases involving customs, international trade, and patent rights. The Court of International Trade is the trial court for these types of issues. As shown in Figure 14.3, there are appellate courts other than the circuit courts of appeals for military and trade cases. Finally, there are special courts that hear cases in which an individual has a claim against the United States government and in which citizens or corporations have disagreements with the Internal Revenue Service. While

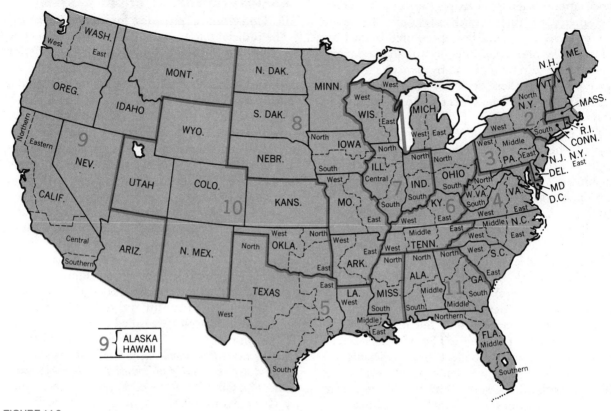

FIGURE 14.2

The States that Comprise the Circuit Courts of Appeals

SOURCE: Administrative Office of the United States Courts.

these specialized courts serve a function and permit the development of a set of judges who have expertise in complex subjects, the specialized courts handle a relatively small share of the federal judiciary's caseload.

Regardless of which court a federal case begins in, the last appeal is to the Supreme Court. The Supreme Court, although it devotes most of its attention to appellate matters, does have some items over which it exercises *original jurisdiction—it is*

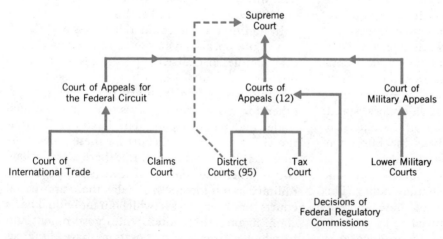

FIGURE 14.3

Federal Court System

the first court in which a case is heard. This dual responsibility distinguishes the Supreme Court from other courts. The district courts, for example, have only original jurisdiction, whereas the courts of appeals have only *appellate jurisdiction—authority to hear cases appealed from a lower court and to reverse lower court decisions.* The issues over which the Supreme Court has original jurisdiction are few and are identified in the Constitution. "In all cases affecting ambassadors, other public ministers and consuls, and those in which a state shall be a party, the Supreme Court shall have original jurisdiction. In all other cases before mentioned, the Supreme Court shall have appellate jurisdiction. . . ." Most of the cases in which the Supreme Court exercises its original jurisdiction involve disputes between two states, and even these are rare.

HOW A SUIT REACHES THE SUPREME COURT

Most of the lawsuits brought in this country begin and end in the state court system. Our nation has what is known as a *dual court system with parallel sets of federal and state trial and appellate courts.* Only under certain conditions are suits heard in federal court. One way is to bring suit in a federal district court, in which case the path outlined in Figure 14.3 may ultimately lead to a final resolution of the issues by the Supreme Court. The other path is to go through the state court system and then seek to obtain a hearing by the United States Supreme Court after the highest state court has handed down its decision.

Bringing Suit in Federal District Court

There are two bases for filing a suit in a federal district court. If a claim fails to meet one of these criteria, the litigation must take place in the state courts. The first grounds on which a litigant can turn to the federal court system is diversity of citizenship in a controversy that involves at least $10,000. *Diversity of citizenship means that the two parties to the case reside in different states.* Typically a suit is filed in the state in which the accident occurred or in which the defendant has his or her legal residence. One of the parties may prefer to have the case heard in federal district court rather than in the state trial court because of a fear that the judge or jury in the state trial court will be biased in favor of the litigant who lives in the state. This fear is probably out of date now that we all

watch the same television shows, read the same magazines, and travel among the states so freely. In the early days of the Republic, however, there may have been a sound basis for anticipating that litigants from other states or regions might not be treated fairly if they stood trial outside their home state.

In these diversity of citizenship cases, the federal judge who hears the case applies the same laws that would have been applied had the suit been brought in state court. Thus, there is no advantage of going into federal court to have different legal rights and requirements applied.

The limitation to suits of $10,000 or more is set so the federal courts will not be more overburdened than they already are. Without this limitation, every minor traffic accident involving a commuter who drives to work in another state might find its way into the federal courts.

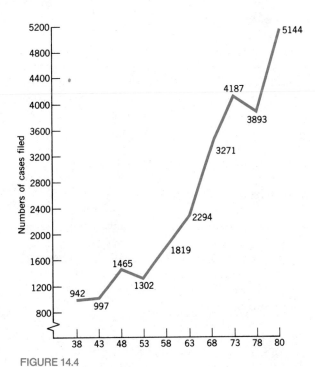

FIGURE 14.4

Cases Filed in Supreme Court at Five-Year Intervals, 1938–1980 Terms

SOURCE: Federal Judicial Center, *Report of the Study Group on the Caseload of the Supreme Court* (Washington, D.C.: Administrative Office of the U.S. Courts, 1972), p. A2 (1938–1968 terms); *United States Law Week*, 43 (August 13, 1974), p. 3085, and 48 (August 7, 1979), p. 3040. Data for 1968–1978 terms from Lawrence Baum, *The Supreme Court* (Washington, D.C.: Congressional Quarterly, 1981), p. 94.

The second basis for having a trial in federal district court is if a provision of a federal statute or the federal Constitution is at issue. Examples include cases in which one is charged with violating federal drug regulations, federal environmental protection legislation, the rights of minority students to attend desegregated schools, or the rights of women and minorities to have equal access to employment opportunities.

The workload of the federal district courts has grown rapidly in recent years (see Figure 14.4). There are now more than a quarter of a million suits a year filed in federal district courts. This is due in part to new legislation that has authorized federal involvement in an ever-widening circle of topics.[23] Civil rights, environmental protection, energy conservation, economic stimulation, and consumer protection are only some of the items now thought to be appropriate for federal regulation. In the not too distant past, there were few if any federal laws regulating these areas.

Court of Appeals

The party that loses before the district court can usually appeal to the court of appeals. An exception is that the government may not appeal a criminal case that it has lost. Only about one case in seven that is filed with a federal district court is appealed. The rate of appeals is much higher, however, in cases that actually go to trial.[24] This ratio has remained fairly constant in recent years, so the number of cases being appealed has risen at the same pace as the number of cases coming to the district courts.

Most cases decided by a court of appeals are heard by three-judge panels. Each panel is composed of three circuit court judges or of one member of a district court in that circuit and two court of appeals judges. In deciding cases, the judges may unanimously rule for one party or there may be a two-to-one split.

Suits that raise particularly important issues may be heard by the judges of a circuit sitting *en banc*. This means that all the court of appeals judges will participate in the decision.

Supreme Court

Unlike the courts of appeals, which must rule on all cases that are brought to them, the Supreme Court exercises tight control over the cases that reach it. The Supreme Court has been able to exercise discretion over which appeals to hear ever

since the creation of the courts of appeals in 1891. Some cases come from the lower federal courts, following the paths shown in Figure 14.3. Other cases come from the highest court in a state.

Cases decided by special three-judge district courts go immediately to the Supreme Court. Since 1970, the bulk of the hearings conducted by three-judge tribunals have involved civil rights issues.[25] The high court can choose to take appeals from district courts when an act of Congress has been held to be unconstitutional or when the United States is a party in a case.

Selecting Cases   Cases from the courts of appeals or the highest court in a state can come to the Supreme Court as an appeal as a matter of right or under writ of certiorari. Appeals to the Court are supposed to be a right and often involve cases in which a state or federal law has been struck down for being contrary to the federal constitution or federal statutes. In reality, however, even cases that involve questions of constitutionality can be rejected by the Supreme Court on the grounds that there is not a substantial federal question at issue.

The second procedure by which a case gets to the Supreme Court involves a writ of certiorari. Cases that do not qualify for an appeal as described above get to the Court, if at all, when a writ is granted. **Writs of certiorari** *are granted under the "rule of four": if at least four justices believe that the issues of a case raise important policy questions, they can request that a record of the lower court proceedings be forwarded so that they can decide the case.* Today, since the court can refuse appeals that raise no important federal question, the rule of four procedure also determines which appeals will be heard.

Many petitions for writs of certiorari come from prisoners who believe that in the course of being convicted they were denied due process. Such petitions are often hand-written by prisoners who have studied law books in prison libraries. Inmates' petitions are usually filed *in forma pauperis* which means that the usual expenses are waived because of the petitioner's poverty. Most of the landmark decisions in criminal law that are discussed in the chapter on civil liberties were handed down in cases that reached the Supreme Court through *in forma pauperis* proceedings. However, Howard Ball estimates that only one case in a hundred of this type is heard by the Supreme Court.[26]

The dockets of the nation's state and local courts are very crowded. Only a small percentage of these cases ever reaches the Supreme Court which usually selects only those with far-reaching policy ramifications.

The law clerks (outstanding recent law school graduates) review the thousands of petitions the Court receives each year and provide brief summaries for the justices. If a justice is interested in a case seeking a writ of certiorari, it goes on the "discuss list" along with the appeals as a matter of right. Meeting in private, the justices vote on which cases to schedule for oral arguments. When petitions from poor, unschooled prisoners are granted, the Court assures that the petitioner is served by competent counsel so that the issues of the case will be fully aired.

When appeals or writs of certiorari are granted, the attorneys for the two parties file written briefs. Briefs are legal documents in which attorneys present reasons for the Court to rule in favor of their client. The United States government, which is the most frequent litigant before the Supreme Court, is represented by the solicitor general, the third ranking member of the Justice Department.

The Supreme Court may also allow **amicus curiae** (friend of the court) briefs to be filed; these are *briefs submitted by interested parties who are not actually litigants in the case.* Because of its heavy workload, the Court generally rejects requests to file amicus briefs. An important exception is that the United States government is more likely to have its requests granted than are other interested parties. In the case that ruled that public schools that were segregated by law were unconstitutional, the attorney generals of southern states not parties to the suit were allowed to participate through amicus briefs.[27] Ideally, amicus briefs should introduce arguments or perspectives that the parties to the suit do not address.

In deciding which of the thousands of requests for hearings to accept, the members of the Court are guided by several considerations. Clearly, the case should be important. Beyond this, the Court may want to resolve differences between its circuits. Something seems basically unfair when the outcome of similar cases is different in, say, the Fifth and Eighth Circuits. This factor alone is insufficient, however, and the Court refuses to hear literally hundreds of cases in which one circuit's court of appeals defines legal requirements quite differently than the court of appeals for some other part of the country.[28]

Some justices may have strategic reasons for not wanting to clarify an ambiguous law. The decisions of a court of appeals are binding only on district courts within that circuit.

[J]ustices may vote to deny hearings in cases with decisions they dislike if they suspect that the Court would approve the undesired policy. As one member of the Court said, 'I'd much prefer bad law to remain the law of the Eighth Circuit or the State of Michigan than to have it become the law of the land.'[29]

This quotation introduces a factor that is often critical in determining whether a justice votes to hear a case. Justices who disagree with the decisions of lower courts are more likely to vote to grant a hearing than those who are satisfied with the outcome.

Oral Arguments In addition to the written briefs, justices hear oral arguments presented by opposing counsels. Typically only one attorney for each side participates in the oral argument. Since 1970, each side has been allowed one-half hour. An oral argument is intended to elaborate on the assertions and interpretations contained in

"TODAY'S AGENDA IS A TOUGH ONE, DEALING PRIMARILY WITH RELIGION IN THE PUBLIC SCHOOLS. BUT FIRST, LET US PRAY."

the brief. Attorneys may use notes but are not supposed to read their argument. At any time during a presentation, a justice may stop an attorney to ask for a clarification, an elaboration, a speculation on the impact of a decision, or an indication of how the attorney's position conforms with the decisions in other cases.

Decision On the Friday after an oral argument, the Court discusses the case in a conference to which only the nine justices are admitted. The chief justice begins the discussion and is followed by each of the associate justices in order of seniority. Voting on cases is in reverse order, with the most junior member of the Court announcing his or her position first and the chief justice going last.

Several factors may influence the justices as they go about the decision-making process. One consideration, which will be discussed in greater detail in the section on norms, is the Court's previous decisions on similar cases. Judges feel strongly that they should follow the precedent established in earlier cases and decide new litigation along the lines of earlier decisions.

When precedent is not controlling, perhaps because new legislation is being litigated, judges try

to determine what legislators hoped to accomplish through the law. To decipher legislative intent, jurists can turn to the committee hearings and floor debate in which the legislation was discussed and refined. If the intent of the legislature is clear and the objectives are not unconstitutional, the Court will try to apply the law as desired by the legislature.

Policy Preferences These kinds of efforts at objectivity are in keeping with proper judicial behavior as defined by those who favor judicial restraint and who perceive no legitimate policymaking role for the judiciary. Often, at least in cases before the Supreme Court, the justices have considerable latitude in deciding cases. Professor Lawrence Baum of Ohio State University notes that justices, like members of Congress, are often guided by individual notions of what constitutes good public policy.

Seldom is the law so clear on the issues faced by the Court that it dictates a particular decision. Choices among legally acceptable alternative policies must be based on other factors, and the justices' conceptions of good policy certainly are among these factors. Like other policymakers, members of the Supreme Court respond to policy choices largely in terms of their personal attitudes about policy. Indeed, policy preferences may play a larger role in the Court than in legislatures and administrative agencies.[30]

In a similar vein, Michigan State's Harold Spaeth uses as a heading "The Dominance of Personal Policy Preferences" in explaining justices' decisions. He points out that "it is significant that the Court's rules do not preclude any Justice from voting compatibly with his [or her] personal policy preferences."[31]

Generally, justices' decisions have reflected policy stands in line with those of the president who appointed them. Roosevelt's and Johnson's nominees sided with liberals while Eisenhower's and Nixon's appointees have generally been more conservative. If justices simply interpreted the laws and the Constitution free of policy preferences, we should not be able to so easily classify justices as liberal or conservative.

Presidential Disappointments Although presidents usually find jurists who will advance the chief executive's policy preferences, there are occasional exceptions. Probably the most notable

Chief Justice Earl Warren was a real disappointment to President Eisenhower who appointed Warren thinking he would be a conservative member of the Court. Instead, he was one of the most liberal justices to serve on the Court in recent times.

in recent years was Earl Warren. President Eisenhower appointed Warren as chief justice, expecting the former governor and state attorney general to be a conservative. Instead Warren led the Court into a wide range of policy areas it had previously avoided and greatly expanded federal standards at the expense of the states. The former attorney general helped usher in a series of new protections for those charged with violations of state law. Eisenhower was disappointed in his failure to anticipate Warren's votes as a justice.

Outspoken Harry Truman was even more critical of one of his nominees. Merle Miller reports the following conversation with the former president:

Miller: "What do you consider the biggest mistake you made as President?"
Truman: "Tom Clark was my biggest mistake. No doubt about it."
Miller: "I'm sorry, sir, I'm not sure I understand."
Truman: "That damn fool from Texas that I first made Attorney General and then put on the Supreme Court. I don't know what got into me. . . . He hasn't made one right decision that I can think of. And so when you ask me what was my biggest mistake, that's it. Putting Tom Clark on the Supreme Court of the United States."[32]

Even in the cases of Clark and Warren in which the justices did not vote on cases as their sponsor preferred, the justices did articulate policy preferences. Whether or not a justice decides cases as the president who made the nomination prefers, all justices allow their preferences to influence the stands they take.

Opinion Assignment When the chief justice is on the majority side, he decides who shall write the opinion of the Court. If the chief justice sides with the minority, the senior associate on the majority side traditionally assigns the opinion. Despite the secrecy that is supposed to shroud the conference discussions, stories have circulated charging Chief Justice Burger with infringing on the rights of associate justices to select authors. Woodward and Armstrong, in their best-seller *The Brethren*, report that when Justices Douglas and Brennan were the senior associates, they felt that Burger assigned authorship even when the conference discussion had seemed to show Burger's position to be in the minority.[33]

The power to decide who shall author the opinion of the Court is important since it is only the *majority opinion—the opinion of the majority of the justices*—that lower courts (to say nothing of the public or government agencies) are obligated to obey. For very important cases, the chief justice may write the decision himself to lend a bit of additional prestige to the ruling. Beginning with *Brown* v. *Board of Education* and extending through the 1971 busing case, the chief justice wrote the school desegregation decisions for the Court.[34]

Many people believe that another factor that can heighten the impact of a decision is for the Court to reach its decision unanimously. During the 17 years that the chief justice authored the major desegregation decisions, the Court spoke with one voice. Chief Justice Earl Warren was sensitive to the desirability of unanimity in *Brown* since it was obvious that millions of whites would object strongly to a demand that schools be integrated. He therefore worked long and hard to convince Kentuckian Stanley Reed, who preferred separation of the races, to vote with the majority.[35]

A second example of the importance of achieving unanimity in cases that are surrounded by the most intense controversy is *United States* v. *Nixon*.[36] This case was brought by Special Watergate Prosecutor Leon Jaworski in an effort to obtain tapes of conversations between President Nixon and his

Special Watergate Prosecutor Leon Jaworski successfully argued before the Supreme Court that President Nixon could not legally refuse to turn over tapes critical to the Watergate investigation. The Court's unanimity was regarded as a critical factor in forcing Nixon to obey the order.

account in making up the weekly assignment list. The chief justice may favor justices who usually agree with him by giving them the more important or more interesting decisions to pen while having his ideological opponents labor away on less significant cases.[39] Consider the retribution given to liberal Justice Brennan by conservative Chief Justice Burger, with whom Brennan frequently clashed.

Near the end of the term, the Court heard a case (Sakraidn v. Ag Pro, Inc.) involving a patent dispute over a waterflush system designed to remove cow manure from the floor of dairy barns. Referred to around the Court as the 'cow shit case,' it was of no significance, not even posing interesting questions in the arcane field of patent law. The conference was unanimous that there

aides in the Oval Office. Jaworski wanted to use the tapes in cases being prepared against Nixon staffers. While it can never be proved, there has been speculation that had the decision indicated divisiveness on the Court, Nixon might have refused to deliver the tapes since they contained statements that indicated the president's complicity in the cover-up and forced his resignation. With the Court, including the three members he had named, lined up unanimously against him, Nixon dared not ignore the direct order.

A final example of the importance of unanimity is provided by *Cooper v. Aaron.*[37] In this decision the Court refused to postpone desegregation in Little Rock, despite violent opposition. To emphasize the steadfastness of the Court's commitment to desegregation, the justices took the unusual step of all signing the opinion. Typically those who agree with the majority opinion of the Court are not even listed.

In less significant decisions, the chief justice or senior associate who is selecting the author is guided by other considerations. Work is distributed to ensure that the cases are disposed of expeditiously. A rapid writer like former Justice William O. Douglas might be given more cases than a slower worker like Harry Blackmun, whose pace has caused exasperation among his colleagues.[38]

Ideological alignments may also be taken into

The Supreme Court is more likely to issue a unanimous verdict when it anticipates that the ruling will be highly controversial and possibly even evoke violence. Such as the case with the Court's unanimous verdict in *Cooper* v. *Aaron* in which the Court refused to postpone desegregation of a Little Rock high school.

was no patent violation. The case would ordinarily go to the most junior Justice, Stevens. Instead, Burger assigned the 'cow shit case' to Brennan.

Brennan was insulted, but he refused to pass along the humiliation to his clerks. He did all the work on the five-page opinion himself.

*Later, when an insignificant Court of Claims case (*United States v. *Hopkins) was argued, Brennan decided to vote whichever way would leave him in the minority, 'so that bastard can't give me cases like this.'* [40]

Opinion assignments sometimes reflect justices' special interests. For example, Harry Blackmun, an avid baseball fan, wrote the majority opinion in St. Louis Cardinals outfielder Curt Flood's challenge to the reserve clause. [41] Blackmun relied on statistics from the Baseball Encyclopedia in writing a curious opinion that included the justice's list of all-time greats. Some justices develop expertise in particular areas and are given opinions to write whenever cases of this type reach the Court. There is much less specialization in the judiciary than in Congress and many state legislatures, however.

When assigning opinions, another consideration is to give the responsibility to a justice who can hold a fragile majority together. The decision might, for example, be written by a justice who has taken a moderate position on the case rather than one who has staked out a more extreme position. Positions taken by the members of the Court in the conference are subject to change; if the author of the majority opinion writes a decision that some members think goes too far, they may switch over. Justices change positions between the first conference vote and the final decision only about 10 percent of the time, however, and the conversion of a majority into a minority is rare. [42] A centrist justice is better able to keep the majority coalition intact and perhaps win over some who sided with the minority in conference.

Aside from the majority opinion of the court there are two other types of opinions. *Concurring opinions are prepared by justices who agree with the outcome reached by the Court but reject the reasons put forth by the majority. Dissenting opinions explain the reasoning behind the minority position.* While dissenting opinions have no authority, some have been accurate harbingers of things to come. Justice John Harlan's lone dissent in the case upholding the constitutionality of racially separate but equal fa-

cilities articulated what became the majority position 58 years later. [43]

When the justice assigned to write the majority opinion has completed a draft, it is circulated to the other justices. Authors of concurring and dissenting opinions can also send copies of their work to their colleagues. In the process of commenting on these tentative efforts, further negotiations may be conducted. To retain the support of a justice who sided with the author in conference or to win over a justice who was initially ambivalent or in the opposing camp, it may be necessary to modify some language in the opinion. Reading the authors' reasons for their stands may prompt further reflection by other justices; they may conclude that they no longer hold the preference they expressed in conference.

On some cases the justices in the majority are badly divided in the logic that leads them to a common result. When this occurs, no one opinion is endorsed by a majority of the justices. Uncertainty about the reasons behind the Court's decision makes it difficult for lower court judges confronted with similar cases to know how to conform with the high Court's intentions.

Announcing the Decision For many years Mondays were decision days. Today, there are so many decisions that the Court announces them several times a week during its October-through-June sessions. Because of the time required to fashion opinions, fewer decisions are made during the early weeks of a term.

Unlike legislators and top policymakers in the executive branch, the Supreme Court does not give copies of its decisions to media representatives beforehand. Copies of opinions are made available when the Court presents the decision. Historically, the full text of each decision was read by the author of the opinion in open court. Today, the number of decisions, the frequency of concurring and dissenting opinions, and the length of some decisions have prompted justices to usually present only a summary of the opinion orally.

The Court's method of announcing its decisions causes some problems. Reporters who cover the Court, particularly those who represent the print media, must rush to prepare their stories. Long, complex opinions cannot be fully digested before the story on the decision is filed for an afternoon newspaper or for the evening television news. Thus, coverage of Court decisions may focus exclusively on the outcome and ignore the reasoning behind the decision. Other reports may indicate that the Court has made a comprehensive ruling when the decision actually applies to a very narrow set of conditions. Fuller and more accurate treatment of the Court's decisions might head off some of the misperceptions and resulting antagonisms directed toward the Court.

Voting Blocs Since justices' policy preferences are important in determining how they will vote, it is not surprising that members who share ideological perspectives tend to vote together. Ideologically based blocs are rarely uniform; they tend to change from case to case. Nonetheless, the Court is usually divided into liberal and conservative blocs plus some swing justices who affiliate first with the conservatives and then with liberals, depending on the issues.

In the 1983 Court, the conservative bloc was dominated by Chief Justice Burger and associates Rehnquist, Blackmun, O'Connor, and Powell. The liberal bloc had been reduced to two justices, Brennan and Marshall. White and Stevens were less clearly aligned with either side.

During the first half-decade of the New Deal, the "nine old men" against whom President Roosevelt railed included a solid conservative bloc

"WHEN IT'S 6-TO-3, YOU'RE ONE OF THE THREE. WHEN IT'S 7-TO-2, YOU'RE ONE OF THE TWO. WHEN IT'S 8-TO-1, YOU'RE THE ONE. SIR, YOU ARE AN INCORRIGIBLE SPOILSPORT."

of only four members. The liberal bloc consisted of three justices, while Hughes and Roberts were the moderates who held the balance of power. When Hughes and Roberts began to vote with the three liberals—the so-called "switch in time that saved nine" since it undercut support for the court-packing plan—New Deal legislation ceased to be held unconstitutional.

Justices' voting behavior is sufficiently consistent that political scientists David Rohde and Harold Spaeth have succeeded in predicting how the Supreme Court will decide cases.[44] During the 1972 to 1973 term of the Court, they correctly predicted 90 percent of the individual justices' votes.

Issue Dimensions Like research that has sought to explain legislators' roll call voting behavior (see chapter 10), research into the voting behavior of Supreme Court justices has identified persistent issue dimensions. Rohde and Spaeth found that for the period 1958 to 1973, about 95 percent of the Supreme Court's decisions could be placed on one of three issue dimensions.

1. *Freedom* cases involving the rights of criminal defendants, national security, and the First Amendment freedoms of speech, press, and religion
2. *Equality* cases involving "discrimination on the basis of race, economic condition, or age, or for political reasons" in which equal protection under the law is frequently the central issue
3. *New Deal Economics* cases involving government regulation of activities that directly or indirectly affect the economy, e.g., "antitrust, mergers, bankruptcy, workers' compensation, state regulation of business, public utilities, federal regulation of securities, the reapportionment and districting of voting districts, natural resources," etc[45]

Some justices, such as Warren, Douglas, and Brennan, were liberal on all three dimensions while others, such as the Nixon appointees, were conservative on all three. Thirteen of the seventeen justices who served in the years studied by Rohde and Spaeth could be categorized as liberals (six) or conservatives (seven), with only four displaying ideological preferences that shifted with the nature of the issue. For example, Hugo Black, whom Rohde and Spaeth label a "populist," had a liberal voting record on cases raising issues of New Deal economics and freedom but voted conservatively when equality was the issue.

NORMS

Although less extensively explored in the judicial than the legislative setting, it is clear that the behavior of judges is guided in important ways by unwritten rules, or norms, that define what constitutes acceptable behavior.

Precedent

The most important norm governing judicial behavior is precedent, or *stare decisis* (Latin for "let the previous decision stand"), which *holds that judges should decide cases in conformity with earlier decisions*. The significance of precedent derives from the Anglo-American common law tradition. Hundreds of years ago the kings of England became concerned that different judges might be deciding similar cases differently. To minimize the likelihood that different judges would produce vastly different results, judges began to record the facts, outcomes, and reasoning behind their decisions—in other words, to write opinions. Thereafter, judges could consult the opinions of their colleagues and predecessors and make their own decisions in conformity with what had gone before. Today much of the judge-made law has been codified, i.e., collected and ratified in statutory form by the legislature.

Adherence to precedent may stem in part from the socialization process lawyers go through, which emphasizes the importance of this norm,[46] but there are also considerations of equity and its impact on the judiciary's authority. Current judges, like the judges of centuries ago, are concerned that failure to adhere to precedent would give an impression of arbitrariness or capriciousness. This would undermine respect for the judiciary, which might be more dangerous for the courts than for the other branches of the government in which the top policymakers are ultimately answerable to the electorate. To avoid the appearance of inconsistency—an effort often seen through by Court observers—a majority that disagrees with earlier policy stands typically does not overrule the previous cases. Instead, it justifies its arrival at a position seemingly at variance with what has gone before by distinguishing the case at issue from the precedent. The author of the opinion does this by showing how the facts or issues in the case being decided are slightly different from those of earlier cases.

Impact It should be clear that the weight of precedent is a conservative force. A court infrequently turns away from its past holdings. Consequently, new policy positions tend to be adopted slowly. (There have been some exceptions, such as the dramatic shifts registered by the Warren Court and the New Deal justices.)

The combination of precedent and life terms for federal jurists has caused some observers to conclude that Courts are frequently out of step with public preferences and the policy stands taken by other branches of government. One such example was pointed up by the difficulties New Deal reforms encountered with the Supreme Court during President Roosevelt's first term. More recently, the Supreme Court continued to broaden its definition of the obligations of school districts to correct past discrimination after a more conservative approach had come to pervade the White House. At other times, the Court may be ahead of the other branches, as it was in its initial decisions expanding the rights of criminal defendants, minority students confined to all-black schools, and women carrying unwanted fetuses.

Despite some clear examples of the Court being out of step with other branches, such instances tend to be short-lived. The gradual infusion of new blood through the replacement of retirees prevents the Court from being static—a new justice is named, on average, every other year. Jimmy Carter was the first president since Andrew Johnson not to appoint a justice.

Scholars who have compared the context of Supreme Court decisions with policies enunciated by Congress find that the judiciary is not often seriously at odds with Congress. Even after a critical election that produces a new congressional majority and the adoption of a long-frustrated policy agenda, the Court will be out of step with congressional policy positions for less than a decade.[47] Thus, a lag between the policy stands of the Court and those of other branches of government is not a continuing problem.

Courtesy Since the Court's nine members serve an average of 15 to 20 years (the ten who left the Court between 1962 and 1981 served an average of 17.8 years) and interact daily for nine months each year, it is imperative that they maintain a working relationship. The Court's subject matter makes this difficult, forcing justices to deal with the most controversial issues of the day. Moreover, the ideological constancy of most justices means that those who view the world from different perspectives will find themselves repeatedly at odds with one another.

While these conditions increase the possibility of ill-will, justices must resist the natural tendency to allow disagreements to degenerate into bitterness. They know the costs associated with permanently alienating other members of the Court, since at some future date one of these justices may hold the decisive vote in determining a case's outcome or whether the case will even be heard by the Court.

The members of the Court, therefore, have developed the practice of writing complimentary notes on the draft opinions of their colleagues even when they do not support the views expressed.[48] In addition, terms such as "the learned judge" are used by justices when referring to one another.

Reciprocity The practice of reciprocity also helps lubricate the wheels of justice. A justice may provide the fourth vote needed to grant certiorari even when they do not believe a case is of great import or involves a miscarriage of justice. For example, as the liberal bloc was reduced in size due to Nixon's appointment of conservatives, the leader of the liberals, William Brennan, sought to build ties to some of his less conservative brethren, such as Harry Blackmun:

> *The clerks in the Chief's [Chief Justice Burger] chambers joked that after Blackmun circulated certain opinions, Brennan would take him to lunch out of gratitude. . . . Even on the tax cases which Brennan hated, he gave extra consideration to them because they were Blackmun's area of expertise.*[49]

Apprenticeship The workload of the Court is too great and its personnel too few to permit a lengthy apprenticeship for new justices. They must quickly begin to write their share of opinions and fully participate in the Court. About the only accommodation made for apprenticeship is that a new justice's first majority opinion is written in a case that invokes a minor issue and on which the Court is unanimous.

COMPLIANCE WITH COURT DECISIONS

The Supreme Court often finds itself in an ironic position. It may be the only decision-maker accessible to those in society who lack political and economic power—the prisoners who believe they are unjustly incarcerated, the minority that feels it is denied rights enjoyed by the majority, the environmental activists facing a consortium of energy developers. The stakes are high when the Court hands down an unpopular decree. If the Court sides with the weak, particularly when the weak take an unpopular position, then it must be prepared to face down the opposition or see its mandate flouted. If the Court fails to see that its decrees are executed, the successful party has little to show for a substantial investment of time and money. Furthermore, if Court orders can be ignored with impunity, respect for the Court and for the government as a whole is reduced.

Despite the high stakes, the Supreme Court and other tribunals have few weapons, other than ordering imprisonment or fines, if forced to do battle with a party that has lost a suit and refuses to comply with the decision. This is particularly true when the Court's position is out of step with that of the Congress and the president and is vigorously opposed by a sizable share of the population. The Court's relatively weak position is pointed up in the classic challenge thrown down by President Andrew Jackson when he was angered by a ruling: "John Marshall [the chief justice] has made his decision, now let him enforce it."

Let us now review the important factors that handicap the Court's ability to secure compliance with its decisions.

Who Comes Before the Court?

One serious restraint on the Court is that it is more passive than the legislative or executive branches. It can keep cases off its agenda, but it cannot go out and bring before it cases on which it wants to rule. Many decisions of the Supreme Court and other appellate courts return the case to a lower court for further consideration in line with the appellate court's ruling. If the loser of a decision does not fully honor the terms of the decree, the court is not usually aware of the failure unless the successful party files a follow-up suit. Occasionally, as happened with some school desegregation and prison reform cases, lower courts have retained jurisdiction and required that school boards or prison authorities file periodic reports. These reports contain data that the judge can evaluate to determine whether the defendant is in compliance. This kind of extended monitoring is time-consuming and therefore undertaken rarely by trial courts and never by the Supreme Court. Requiring the successful party to return to court for further relief if the loser fails to comply places an unbearable burden on some parties, who may be unable to pay for additional litigation.

Who Is Bound?

A second difficulty for the judiciary is that its decrees are binding only on the parties to the litigation. Usually others who are in positions similar to the loser's will change their rules or practices to come into compliance. For example, many police departments started warning people they arrested of their right to remain silent and to have an attorney and that evidence they gave could be used against them at a trial after the Supreme Court held that confessions made in the absence of such warnings violated the Fifth and Sixth Amendments.[50] Although these other police departments were not defendants in the case and therefore technically had not been directed to provide those whom they arrested with these warnings, it was clear that prisoners who were not warned could file suit and their confessions would be disallowed and their convictions overturned.

When there is deep-seated feeling that the Supreme Court has erred on a highly emotional issue, those who are not parties to a suit may persist in their behavior until they are challenged and lose a court case. Over the last three decades numerous examples could be cited:

1. Even today there remain hundreds, if not thousands, of schools in which devotional exercises are conducted despite the Supreme Court prohibition.

2. Almost no school districts in the South desegregated in the immediate aftermath of the Supreme Court decision that segregation was unconstitutional.

3. Some police departments still abuse prisoners although such actions are clearly illegal.

Opposition to the prohibition of school prayers has been so great in a number of communities, particularly rural ones in which most people share the same religious beliefs, that local practices have gone unchallenged. Much the same situation prevailed with regard to southern school desegregation from 1954 until 1964. Even after it became clear that black plaintiffs would ultimately win if they sued school officials,* deep South districts asked to desegregate fought the request through the courts, availing themselves of all appeals, before allowing the first, token breaches in the walls of racial separation.

The refusal of many districts to desegregate until ordered to do so by a court continued beyond 1964 when Congress went on record in support of the position taken by the Supreme Court a decade earlier. Studies of districts (only four of which were in the South) ordered to desegregate during the 1970s show that all but one filed at least one appeal and eight went to the Supreme Court.[51] While some schools did negotiate desegregation plans with the Department of Health, Education, and Welfare (now Health and Human Services) during the latter half of the 1960s, those that had higher proportions of blacks and larger numbers of lower income citizens resisted until defeated in the courts.[52] Officials in a number of districts refused to negotiate, preferring to go through the expensive legal process. Stubborn resistance against long odds has continued to characterize the emotional issue of school desegregation.

There are at least two things to be learned from such recalcitrance. First, when opposition is deep and widespread, progress through the courts comes much like the advance of an army through inhospitable terrain defended by guerrillas. Broad strategies and objectives can be easily set forth on

---

*Although black plaintiffs often lost before southern-born federal district court judges, they would win on appeal. The refusal of some district court judges to rule in favor of blacks seeking to desegregate the schools despite clear precedent points up that the judicial commitment to *stare decisis* may, at times, give way to a judge's personal preferences.

a map but achieving objectives in the field is far more difficult. Advances come one by one as the opponents of the court-established policy are individually ordered to comply.* Consequently, even when school district A is ordered to desegregate or to eliminate Bible reading, adjoining districts B, C, and D may opt to continue similar practices until defeated in the courtroom.

Second, although people rail against the courts when they announce unpopular decisions, there is nonetheless an important symbolism attached to court decrees. School officials who were unwilling to negotiate a desegregation plan would comply with a court order directed specifically at them. They feared that a negotiated settlement might appear to their constituents to indicate less than total commitment to white supremacy, which had been the foremost value in the region's political culture for generations. The aura surrounding a direct court order was such, however, that school officials could and did comply. They told their constituents—and their constituents believed them—that the terms of a court order must be implemented.

What Must Be Done?
Unwillingness to implement a policy until specifically ordered to do so can throw a third roadblock in the path of court-made policy. Again, this occurs only when the local officials charged with compliance are steadfastly opposed to change. This occurred in some southern communities when they were ordered to allow prospective black voters to register or to desegregate their schools. Some officials restricted compliance to the individual plaintiffs, allowing those who had brought

*More than 15 years after the initial ruling that racially segregated schools went against the equal protection clause of the Fourteenth Amendment, the United States Department of Justice launched a comprehensive effort against the South's hold-out districts. Schools that refused to negotiate final desegregation plans in good faith were sued. The new twist was that all of the noncompliant districts in a state were named as defendants in a single suit. While it is possible to expedite enforcement by bringing a class action suit against the noncompliants, this approach is not one lightly undertaken. Except in Alabama, where a unique set of circumstances prevailed, a class action was not used earlier even though it was obvious that disobedience to the thrust of court holdings concerning desegregation was widespread. Moreover, the federal rules of procedure have made it more difficult to bring class action suits even should a plaintiff desire to do so.

suit to register or to attend a white school but continuing to reject the applications of other blacks. Had communities that gave this response remained adamant, it might have been necessary for there to be new litigation for each additional set of prospective voters or children wishing to attend desegregated schools. Instead, with varying degrees of gracelessness, communities that had taken the position of limiting implementation to the named plaintiffs backed off and undertook broader implementation.

Political Pressures
Some policies set forth by the Supreme Court have been so unpopular that forces have mobilized in Congress to reverse the outcome. If the decision that has angered members of Congress involves interpretation of a statute, then new legislation is all that is necessary to counter the Court decision. For example, Congress became impatient with Court-imposed delays in the construction of the Alaska pipeline stemming from a suit won by environmentalists.[53] An exasperated Congress barred courts from interpreting earlier laws to allow additional environmentalists' suits. The oil companies eager to tap the resources of Alaska's North Slope had won and immediately began construction.

If the provocative decision rests on an interpretation of the Constitution, it is more difficult, but not impossible, to countermand the Court. Reversing an unpopular constitutional interpretation requires that the Constitution be amended. This, you may recall, requires the approval of two-thirds of the members of both houses of Congress and ratification by three-fourths of the states. In the last quarter-century, amendments have been introduced in the Congress that would reverse Court decisions on prayer in the schools, redistricting legislative seats, abortion, and school desegregation. Some proposed amendments would alter the Court's jurisdiction and prohibit it from hearing particular kinds of cases. The effect of such proposals, if adopted, would be to leave the issue to the states. To embrace states rights in this fashion might allow states and communities to return to practices that had been barred by the Courts, such as school prayer.

None of the recent amendments designed to limit the Supreme Court's jurisdiction have been approved by Congress. That the Constitution has

Annoyed with court-imposed delays of construction of the Alaskan pipeline, Congress passed legislation prohibiting such delays. This is only one example of how the power of the courts can be checked and balanced by the other branches of government.

not been recently amended to undo Court decisions does not mean that it cannot happen, however. The Eleventh (removing the authority of the federal judiciary to hear suits brought against states) and Sixteenth Amendments (authorizing the levying of an income tax) were ratified to invalidate earlier Supreme Court decisions.

Factors Promoting Compliance

Despite the general problems facing those who seek to have policy made by the courts, certain conditions can enhance the likelihood that courts will be obeyed. Some factors that promote compliance are under the control of the courts while others are not. Considerations which are subject to influence by the courts will be considered first and then items beyond court control will be discussed.

We are, of course, interested here only in compliance with controversial policy decisions handed down by the courts. Popular decisions are likely to be carried out with a minimum of difficulty.

Factors Subject to Court Influence[54]

Policy Clarity   For the objectives of the Court to be achieved, it is essential that the decision be clearly articulated. If the statement of the parties' obligations is ambiguous, one should not be surprised that the court order evokes varying responses. For example, the Supreme Court's initial school desegregation decision did not define what was meant by "desegregation." Leaving this crucial term undefined resulted in a wide range of responses. Some districts completely merged black and white schools; others did nothing more than remove the requirement that the races be separated but actually permitted biracial enrollments only when blacks requested a transfer to the white

school. Only modest changes occurred until the Supreme Court ruled that by "desegregation" it meant that a school district must "convert promptly to a system without a 'white' school and a 'black' school, but just schools."[55] Thereafter, the proportion of the South's blacks attending schools with whites shot up. Outside the South, an unambiguous definition has not been imposed and, not surprisingly, racial balance in schools in the rest of the country is less common.

Specificity of Standards   Hand in hand with the need for a clear statement of policy is the need to have precise standards established by the Court. Imprecise standards allow those who oppose the policy to take steps so small that the policy goal is at best delayed. For example, the 1954 desegregation decision did not impose a timetable. Until this loophole was plugged 15 years later, it was quite acceptable for schools to desegregate at the rate of only one grade a year. Similarly, progress toward affirmative action goals in employment has been greater when decisions have specified goals and timetables.

Support from Other Branches of Government   The judiciary is most likely to encounter difficulties when its decisions are not supported by the other branches of the government. Criticism of Supreme Court decisions by the president may lead some people to think that noncompliance is not a serious matter and that they will not be punished. Certainly the outspoken opposition of Presidents Eisenhower and Nixon to Supreme Court desegregation decisions played a role in encouraging refusals to comply. Attacks on the Court by congressional leaders may also encourage noncompliance. The peacefulness with which unpopular decisions are implemented is also affected by whether local officials are supportive or vow unyielding opposition.[56]

The legislative and executive branches can undercut the impact of court decrees by limiting the ability of federal officials to act in conformity with court-established policy. Congress has not changed the Constitution or the law concerning abortions or school busing, but it has reduced the impact of court decisions in these areas by preventing federal officials from working to achieve the policy goals established by the courts. Federal funds cannot be used to pay for abortions or to require that school districts institute busing programs designed to promote racial balance. The rights established by the courts persist, but without the helping hand of the federal bureaucracy, they are beyond the grasp of many.

Monitoring The temptation to disobey the law increases as the probability of being caught decreases. If there is no traffic, we may be tempted to ease past a stop sign without stopping. A glimpse of a patrol car a block away is sufficient to make most of us model drivers, however. Similarly, even the most brazen thug will not knowingly rob a store in full view of the police. Along the same lines, court-made policy is more likely to be obeyed if there is a mechanism for monitoring compliance.

As pointed out earlier, judges occasionally monitor compliance by requiring periodic reports. For widespread monitoring of a policy decision that affects many in society, the responsibility must be given to a bureaucracy. But the courts cannot create a bureaucracy; this typically requires action by the legislature. Failure to assign monitoring responsibility reduces the likelihood that the noncompliant will be identified or punished. This reduces the anticipated costs, which, if high enough, would prompt compliance from some even though they object to the policy.

Let us look at an example. Although precise figures are unavailable, there is widespread noncompliance with decisions holding that classroom religious exercises violate the First Amendment. In the South, there is less compliance with this decision than with school desegregation or voting rights requirements, even though the civil rights decisions set off far more hostile reactions. The reason for greater noncompliance with school prayer decisions is largely a result of the absence of a federal monitoring agency.

Public Attitudes Very simply, if all other things are equal, there is less compliance with decisions that are unpopular. However, judges may feel obligated to hand down rulings even when they know there will be widespread resistance. Only occasionally do courts refuse to hear cases when there are bona fide litigants, although the discretionary nature of the Supreme Court's jurisdiction does allow it to avoid some issues.* The judicial system is more likely to have to deal with issues which other branches of government avoid. As was discussed, the way Supreme Court decisions are announced and reported by the media does not help promote support for its rulings.

SUGGESTED CHANGES

The Supreme Court has frequently been deeply involved in the most controversial issues. During the last generation the Court was often the first governmental institution to recognize a new right and order that unpopular changes be made. Many of the Court's most controversial decisions have required that local practices give way to national standards.

Those who prefer the frequently more conservative holdings of state courts have proposed the creation of a new court to which the Supreme Court would be subordinate. Called the Court of the States, this tribunal would be composed of the chief justices of the highest court in each state. Creation of this new tribunal would require a constitutional amendment.

It appears unlikely that such a super-court will be created since Congress can sometimes redirect the Supreme Court through the simpler legislative process. Also, although the Court majority may be a few years ahead of or behind public preferences, there is usually only a temporary disjunction between Court decisions and the policy

*Federal courts and most state courts will not give advisory opinions, so it is necessary that there be adversaries. The Supreme Court avoids what it considers to be political questions, although it has defined these differently at different points in our history. For example, the court refused to rule on the constitutionality of legislative apportioning plans in *Colegrove* v. *Green* (328 U.S. 549, 1946) because of its unwillingness to venture into this "political thicket." Sixteen years later, a bolder court plunged into the thicket even though some have suggested that it lacked an accurate map or compass.

Compliance with Supreme Court decisions is more certain if the ruling is popular. Where decisions are regarded as being out of touch with public sentiment, fears are expressed that the courts are too powerful, even tyrannical.

stands of the rest of the government and the public.

It is more likely that Congress will create a court between the courts of appeals and the Supreme Court. Chief Justice Burger has led a call for a new court which could reduce the workload of the Supreme Court. This new panel might screen appeals and decide which ones merit the attention of the high court or decide issues on which the courts of appeals in different circuits disagree.

SUMMARY

Many people believe the judiciary's function is not to make policy but simply to provide a forum for the enforcement of policies made by the other branches of government. This, however, is an untenable position. By interpreting and applying the standards set forth in the Constitution, legislation, and administrative decrees, courts are unavoidably caught up in the policymaking process. So long as legislators write broad, general laws,

the courts will have to fill in the gaps the legislators left in them.[57]

The way the judiciary responds to the policy questions confronting it depends on several factors. Jurists' attitudes about whether they should be activists or exercise restraint when reviewing legislative enactments are one consideration. Attitudes about the proper function of the judiciary are largely determined by the type of attorneys appointed to the bench by the president. The recruitment process almost always results in the selection of jurists who share the president's party affiliation. The justices' general ideological orientations, which roughly parallel party differences, are evident in the stands they take on many of the controversial issues the courts are called upon to resolve. The factors influencing Supreme Court justices' decisions are well enough understood that their votes can be predicted with remarkable accuracy.

The Supreme Court is the court of last resort. It has great latitude in deciding which of the thousands of cases on its docket to hear.

Most litigation is carried out in the courts of the

The Warren Court and Redistricting

When the late Earl Warren, chief justice of the United States Supreme Court from 1953 to 1969, was asked what he thought had been the most significant policy change launched during his tenure, he surprised many people. He did not cite the *Brown* v. *Board of Education* school desegregation case that launched the civil rights revolution or any of the suits expanding the rights of criminal defendants. Instead he pointed to the Court decisions that led to legislative redistricting.

In a series of decisions, the Warren Court established that legislative districts should have approximately equal populations. Throughout the 1960s and again following the 1970 and 1980 censuses, the legislative districts of members of the U.S. House, state legislatures, and various local bodies such as city councils, county commissions, and school boards have been redrawn to correct imbalances caused by population shifts.

By entering what an earlier court called the "political thicket" of redistricting, the Warren Court addressed a problem that no other unit of government had been willing to resolve. The Supreme Court forced states and communities that had not adjusted their legislative districts for decades to insure that all had equal representation.

The consequence of these decisions for Congress and state legislatures was to increase the number of legislators from cities and suburbs. In the South, the greater number of seats for urban areas facilitated the election of many new blacks and Republicans. Throughout the country urban legislators tended to be better educated, more likely to be professionals or blue-collar workers and less likely to be farmers.

The newly constituted legislatures took somewhat different approaches to certain policy questions than had their more heavily rural predecessors. Various studies have concluded that urban legislators are more likely to favor federal aid programs and to support efforts to redirect state expenditures from rural to urban needs. Frequently, urban legislators have also been more responsive to the needs of minorities.

---

50 states. For a case to be heard by a federal judge the litigants must be from different states or a question about the federal Constitution or federal law must be at issue.

When courts hand down unpopular decisions, there is often widespread noncompliance. Noncompliance is made easier by the court's largely passive role, by the fact that its decisions bind only the litigants, and by obstacles that can be raised by those who oppose the decision. Compliance is more likely when the requirements of a decision are clear, when there are specific standards against which to assess compliance, when compliance is monitored, and when there is support for the court's decision among other policymakers.

KEY TERMS

amicus curiae
appellate jurisdiction
Committee on the Federal Judiciary
concurring opinion
courts of appeals
dissenting opinion
diversity of citizenship
dual court system
federal district courts
injunctions
judicial activism
judicial restraint
judicial review
majority opinion
mechanical jurisprudence
original jurisdiction
senatorial courtesy
stare decisis
tort
writ of certiorari
writ of mandamus

SUGGESTED READINGS

Ball, Howard. *Courts and Politics: The Federal Judicial System.* Englewood Cliffs, N.J.: Prentice-Hall, 1980.

Glick, Henry R. *Courts, Politics, and Justice.* New York: McGraw-Hill, 1983.

Goldman, Sheldon, and Jahnige, Thomas P. *The Federal Courts as a Political System*. 2nd ed. New York: Harper and Row, 1976.

Grossman, Joel B. *Lawyers and Judges*. New York: John Wiley & Sons, 1966.

Jacob, Herbert. *Justice in America*. 3rd ed. Boston: Little, Brown, 1978.

Peltason, J. W. *Fifty-Eight Lonely Men*. Chicago: University of Illinois Press, 1971.

Rodgers, Harrell R., Jr. *Community Conflict, Public Opinion and the Law*. Columbus, Ohio: Charles E. Merrill, 1969.

Spaeth, Harold J. *Supreme Court Policy Making*. San Francisco: W. H. Freeman, 1979.

Ulmer, S. Sidney, ed. *Courts, Law, and Judicial Processes*. New York: Free Press, 1981.

CHAPTER 15

CIVIL RIGHTS

Voting ■ Education ■ Employment ■ Housing ■ Public Accommodations ■ Classificatory Schemes

The years since 1954 have seen remarkable changes in civil rights. Less than two generations ago, it was unthinkable to most Americans that they would ever witness what is commonplace today. A majority of adult women work outside of the home; black Americans are able to go to school, to work, and to play wherever their tastes and pocketbooks lead them; and bilingual education is offered in many areas. All of these situations would have been considered revolutionary just a few years ago.

During this period, the mainstream of American life has been broadened to include multitudes who had been excluded. The mainstream has not swept all of those who it has touched to a life of comfort, but it has eroded the dikes of prejudice and tradition that denied millions of Americans the opportunity to realize their potential. While all runners do not enter the race with equal talents and there are still more obstacles for some than for others, the possibilities for achievement and for participation in a variety of activities are greater now than ever before in our history.

Those who compare the present against the ideal may be disappointed. Many minorities still attend racially segregated schools, unemployment rates among blacks continue to be twice as high as those for whites, and blacks and women have much lower earnings than white males. Nonetheless, even the most pessimistic observer will acknowledge that many have come to enjoy new civil rights. It may help to illustrate the magnitude of the change if we read a factual account of one of the literally thousands of encounters that have marked the course of those who have fought the battle for equality.

In July, 1961, John Hardy, a Negro college student in Nashville, Tennessee, went down to Walthall County in southern Mississippi to help Negroes there register as voters. Walthall County had 4,400 white and 2,500 Negro residents of voting age. Virtually every white was on the voting rolls, but not a single Negro. Hardy set up a voters' school, instructing Negroes how to fill out the application form and how to interpret the long and complicated constitution of Mississippi to the satisfaction of the Walthall County registrar, John Q. Wood.

On September 7, 1961, Hardy accompanied two Negro residents of the county, Mrs. Edith S. Peters and Lucius Wilson, down to Wood's office in Tylertown.

424

In the relatively short period of two generations, blacks have been absorbed into the mainstream of American life and are no longer required to remain separate from whites. The Civil Rights movement of the 1960s played a key role in this process.

Hardy waited outside while the two applicants went in. Wood flatly refused to let them apply, saying only: "You all have got me in court." Hearing this, Hardy walked in and introduced himself politely. But he was not able to say much more than his name.

Registrar Wood pulled a gun out of a desk drawer and ordered Hardy to leave. As Hardy turned around and started to walk out, Wood hit him on the back of the head with the gun, swore at him and told him never to come back. Mrs. Peters and Wilson, who had watched the whole episode, helped Hardy out of the courthouse. His head was bleeding profusely, and he was staggering. After resting for a few minutes, Hardy found the county sheriff, Edd Craft, and told him what had happened. Craft arrested Hardy for breach of the peace. When Hardy tried to talk some more about it, Craft threatened to beat him within an inch of his life and locked him up in jail.[1]

That such a minor act—a request for an opportunity to register to vote—should stimulate so hostile a response is shocking. That this particular occurrence was neither unique nor as severe as some may be hard for those who did not live through the period to comprehend. Other episodes include:

1. the burning of a bus in Anniston, Alabama, that was carrying blacks calling themselves Freedom Riders who were challenging discrimination in interstate transportation;
2. punishment dealt out to Hispanic and Native American children in the Southwest and West who spoke their native language at school;
3. the first woman runner to enter the Boston Marathon being assaulted by a race official determined to keep the race an all-male event;
4. three civil rights activists being abducted by a crowd that included some law enforcement

The first woman to run in the Boston Marathon (1967) was assaulted by an official of the Boston Athletic Association who was determined to enforce a rule prohibiting women competitors from entering the race. Today, lots of women run in the annual event.

officials, murdered, and buried under an earthen dam near Philadelphia, Mississippi;

5. blacks who bought homes in numerous cities, North and South, being driven from them by mobs of angry white neighbors.

The main item of contention in civil rights policy has been whether to extend rights and protections enjoyed by some groups in society to those previously excluded from them. Thus the emphasis has been on broadening the coverage of existing rights rather than on recognizing new rights. While a number of aspects of this struggle will be discussed in the subsequent pages, the underlying theme that recurs again and again is that those who have been denied certain opportunities have petitioned the courts and Congress to recognize their right to equal treatment. Most of these claims have rested on the **equal protection clause** of the Fourteenth Amendment, *which states that "No state shall . . . deny to any person under its jurisdiction the equal protection of the laws."* Repeatedly at issue in equal protection cases has been whether the classification scheme being used is reasonable and acceptable, or arbitrary and unconstitutional.

Some distinctions that were once judged to be reasonable, such as separation of blacks and whites in schools and public facilities, have come to be viewed as indefensible. Others, such as treating men and women differently, have been discarded in some contexts but not others. Thus, women can now hold many jobs that were once denied to them, but in 1980 Congress rejected President Carter's proposal to make women as well as men subject to military draft registration. The story of the expansion of civil rights is one in which the discretion of states and private enterprise to treat some groups differently from others has been circumscribed.

In this chapter, the changing definitions of what rights are guaranteed by the equal protection clause will be explored. The groups to be considered are blacks, women, Hispanics, the handicapped, young adults, and the aged. The types of rights that will be reviewed are the ones that have ignited heated opposition both at the time that a group's rights were first officially recognized and then later when federal authorities began the implementation process. The topics dealt with here are suffrage, equal education opportunities, open housing, equal employment opportunities, and public accommodations.

VOTING

Along with freedom to express political views, the right to vote has been considered particularly important in a democracy. After all, a democratic regime derives its authority to govern from the public. If some part of the population is not allowed to participate in the selection of its leaders, one must question the legitimacy of the government. Aside from the issue of legitimacy, there is the practical consideration that groups which are not allowed to participate in the selection of the society's leaders will be disadvantaged when it comes to obtaining policies they favor. Those who cannot vote can neither reward elected officials who look out for their interests nor turn out of office those who prove unresponsive.

During the attempts to get Congress to protect blacks' right to vote, both civil rights leaders and public officials prophesied that once blacks were enfranchised, they could use the vote to eliminate racism from other aspects of American life. Martin Luther King, Jr. contended that

> *voting is the foundation stone for political action. With it the Negro can eventually vote out of office public officials who bar the doorway to decent housing, public safety, jobs, and decent integrated education. It is now obvious that the basic elements so vital to Negro advancement can only be achieved by seeking redress from government at local, state, and federal levels. To do this the vote is essential.* [2]

Individuals Not Owning Property

While blacks may have encountered more resistance on their way to the ballot box than have other groups, there were a number of predecessors in the history of broadening the suffrage. The first obstacle to political participation was the property-holding requirement that most states had when the new nation was established (see Table 15.1). Actions to remove this condition were carried out in individual state legislatures and were largely completed by 1830. Today property holding is a prerequisite to voting only on bond referenda in a few communities. The rationale for this requirement is that since higher property taxes will be needed to pay for the bonds, only those who directly bear the burden should determine whether it will be imposed.

TABLE 15.1

Removal of Obstacles to Political Participation

Obstacle	Method of Removal	Date
Property holding	State legislatures	1790–1830
Sex	Begun by state and territorial legislatures, completed by 19th Amendment	1890–1920
Race	Authorized by 15th Amendment, implemented pursuant to Civil Rights Acts of 1950s and 1960s	1870–1965
Young Adults	Approved of by three states, completed by 26th Amendment	1945–1971
Non-English Speaking	Voting Rights Act Amendments	1975

Women

The second major change came in response to the demands of the suffragettes. Some states and territories, beginning with Wyoming, relaxed prohibitions on women's voting during the late nineteenth century. With progress at the state level coming slowly, the decision was made to seek a national ban on the use of gender as a criterion for voting. Through the use of marches, pickets, and protests, pressures were mobilized that led to the adoption of the Nineteenth Amendment in 1920 guaranteeing women throughout the nation the right to vote.

Blacks

The extension of voting rights to women and the propertyless grew gradually until universally accepted, but there was a very different pattern in the extension of suffrage to blacks. Black suffrage was widespread for a generation or so following the Civil War, but then it plummeted and remained low until the mid-1960s. The Fifteenth Amendment, which was ratified in 1870, sought to enfranchise former slaves with its provision that "the right of citizens to vote shall not be denied or abridged by the United States or by any state on account of race, color, or previous condition of servitude." This amendment was widely implemented and thousands of blacks became voters. During the early 1870s the combination of newly registered blacks and the absence of whites (who were barred from political activities because of their efforts on behalf of the Confederacy) opened the way for blacks to win a number of public offices in the South. The Mississippi General Assembly chose two blacks to represent that state in the U.S. Senate while the House of Representatives had as many as seven popularly elected blacks in some years. Blacks were also elected to

dozens of seats in state legislatures and to a variety of local offices.

Disenfranchisement   Black political activity and office-holding declined during the 1890s as southern states, led by Mississippi, instituted impediments to black voter registration. Prospective

FROM THE PLANTATION TO THE SENATE.

Immediately following ratification of the Fifteenth Amendment (1870) granting blacks the right to vote, a significant number of southern blacks were elected to Congress, as well as to state and local offices. Such successes were short-lived as southern states quickly instituted impediments to black voter registration.

voters were required to demonstrate their literacy, an ability to interpret sections of the state constitution to the satisfaction of the local white registrar, or both. Since illiteracy was widespread among both blacks and whites, some states adopted a "grandfather clause" which exempted from literacy tests anyone whose ancestors had been registered prior to 1861. Requirements that an applicant demonstrate a comprehension of the state constitution or prove good character were often manipulated by county registrars to prevent most blacks but few whites from registering. Literate blacks might be turned away for inconsequential defects on their applications, while registrars completed the applications of illiterate whites. Thus in Macon County, Alabama, the home of the Tuskegee Institute, black applicants who held graduate degrees were judged to have flunked the literacy test. Elsewhere black applicants were rejected when they expressed their ages in years rather than months or when they underlined rather than circled "Mr.," "Mrs.," or "Miss" on their applications. Other potential registrants were dissuaded from attempting to register through threats or violence.

Even blacks who withstood harassment and discriminatory treatment by registrars and managed to get their names on the voting lists often discovered they had won a hollow victory. In the South the good government reform of using the direct primary to select party nominees was modified so that only whites could vote in the Democratic primary. Exclusion of blacks was rationalized on the grounds that the Democratic Party was a private organization and, as such, it could limit participation in the activities it sponsored just as a fraternal or religious group might. Since Democratic nominees rarely faced Republican opponents, blacks were excluded from the critical decision-making stage. They were allowed to participate only in the general election which, in the absence of partisan competition, was a meaningless referendum.

In reaction to the reformist Populist challenges of the mid-1890s, poll taxes were assessed as a prerequisite to voting. The collection of a few dollars a year for the right to vote eliminated the poor of both races from the electorate.

The combination of techniques designed to remove blacks as a political influence was very effective. In one dramatic example, the number of black voters registered in Louisiana was reduced from 130,334 in 1896 to 1,342 in 1904.[3] After

1898, no black was elected to Congress from the South until 1972. Thousands of state and local black officeholders were also replaced by whites and more than a half a century of virtually unchallenged white political leadership began.

Regaining the Vote The resurgence of black political participation began with a 1944 Supreme Court decision that sounded the death knell for the white primary.[4] The Twenty-Fourth Amendment brought an end to the collection of the poll tax as a prerequisite to voting in federal elections, and the Supreme Court declared it to be an unconstitutional impediment to state elections.[5] In 1957 the chief impetus for change shifted from the courts to Congress.

The 1965 Voting Rights Act marked the culmination of eight years in which Congress passed four statutes that sought to provide equal access to the ballot to southern blacks. Six southern states and selected counties in a seventh where black political participation was especially low were singled out.* These were areas in which less than half of the voting-age population was registered or had voted in the 1964 presidential election. In the areas covered, the legislation provided for the following:

1. Use of all types of tests and devices such as literacy tests and good character requirements was prohibited for five years.

2. Federal voting examiners could be dispatched to register qualified voters in counties that had a history of discrimination.

3. Federal poll watchers could be sent in to monitor elections in counties where there was a history of discrimination. The *preclearance provision stated that no changes affecting elections (e.g., location of polling places, redrawing of electoral districts, or laws relating to the conduct of elections or the manner in which public officials were to be selected) could be made until they were approved by either the United States Attorney General or the federal district court sitting in Washington, D.C.* (This provision was at the heart of the debate surrounding the 1982 extension of the Voting Rights Act.)

4. Discrimination was assumed to occur whenever less than half of the voting-age popula-

*The states were Alabama, Georgia, Louisiana, Mississippi, South Carolina, Virginia, and some counties in North Carolina.

TABLE 15.2

Areas Covered By Voting Rights Act of 1965 and Amendments

Entire States	Parts of States	
Alabama	California	(4 counties)
Alaska	Colorado	(1 county)
Arizona	Connecticut	(3 towns)
Georgia	Florida	(5 counties)
Louisiana	Hawaii	(1 county)
Mississippi	Idaho	(1 county)
South Carolina	Massachusetts	(9 towns)
Texas	Michigan	(2 townships)
Virginia	New Hampshire	(10 towns)
	New York	(3 counties)
	North Carolina	(40 counties)
	South Dakota	(2 counties)
	Wyoming	(1 county)

SOURCE: Based on information in Richard E. Cohen, "Will the Voting Rights Act Become a Victim of Its Own Success?" *National Journal,* August 1, 1981, p. 1365.

tion was unregistered or had failed to vote in the preceding presidential election.

The terms of the 1965 legislation were renewed in 1970 and 1975 and were approved for another 25 years in 1982. The 1970 extension banned the use of literacy tests nationwide; in 1975, this ban was made permanent. And while the terms of the racially oriented sections of the renewals of the Voting Rights Act still deal chiefly with the South, the "triggering mechanism" of less than 50 percent turnout or registration has made a number of counties outside of the South subject to the terms of this legislation (see Table 15.2).

In implementing the Voting Rights Act and its renewals, federal registrars have been sent into counties and states to enroll thousands of black voters. Thousands of federal agents have been sent to observe elections in scores of counties. Through 1980, almost 35,000 proposed changes affecting elections had been submitted to the attorney general for approval. While less than 3 percent of the proposed changes have been objected to, some of the rejections have been important in challenging legislative districting plans that would have minimized black representation in state legislatures and on local governing bodies.

By the time of the congressional debate on the 1982 extension, the concept of federal protection of blacks' voting rights was much less controversial. The House approved a ten-year extension by a vote of 389 to 24 with only 19 of the 108 southern representatives objecting. In contrast, when

this legislation was voted on in 1965, the margin of victory was 333 to 85 with 76 of 104 southerners registering their opposition. By the 1980s, the issue was not so much whether the lifetime of the legislation would be extended but to what degree it would concentrate on the South. Many southern legislators initially wanted to see the legislation—particularly the preclearance requirement, which they saw as a nuisance—made applicable nationwide. This effort subsided in the House when hearings on the legislation revealed that discrimination against blacks at the polls remained largely a southern phenomenon. That black voting rights, an issue which evoked so much hostility and violence only a generation ago, could command more than 90 percent support in Congress is a striking illustration of change in public attitudes.

Impact of Voting Rights Legislation   During the 1960s, numerous rallies staged by organizations such as Martin Luther King's Southern Christian Leadership Conference and the Student Non-Violent Coordinating Committee, hundreds of programs run by the Voter Education Project, and the concentrated efforts of hundreds of young adults who participated in the Mississippi Freedom Summer encouraged blacks to take an interest in politics and attempt to register. The proportion of southern voting-age blacks who were registered to vote rose from 25 percent in 1958 to more than 40 percent in the mid-1960s, climbing above 60 percent in the early 1970s[6] (see Figure 15.1). The most recent figures, which are for 1980, indicate that approximately 56 percent of the South's voting-age blacks are registered. Comparable figures for southern whites show a registration rate of 61 percent. The Voter Education Project estimated that two-thirds of the South's registered blacks actually voted in 1980, giving 90 percent of their votes to Jimmy Carter.[7] Clearly race is no longer a major factor in rates of political activity in the South.

Increased black political involvement has changed southern politics. While not wholly eliminated, racist campaign rhetoric has become much less common,[8] black communities have obtained a more equitable share of projects paid for with tax moneys,[9] and, perhaps most importantly, blacks have been selected for a variety of elective and appointive public offices. As of 1982 there were 2,601 black elected officials in the South;[10]

FIGURE 15.1

Voter Registration Rates Among Southern Blacks for Selected Years

SOURCES: Prepared from materials in Donald R. Matthews and James W. Prothro, *Negroes and the New Southern Politics* (New York: Harcourt, Brace & World, 1966), p. 18; *V.E.P. News*, 4 (January/February 1970), p. 3; U.S. Bureau of the Census, Current Population Reports, Series P-20, #359. "Voting and Registration in the Election of November 1980" (Washington, D.C.: Government Printing Office, 1981) p. 3.

before 1965 there were fewer than 100. Nationally, blacks now hold 20 seats in Congress (including 2 from the South), scores of seats in state legislatures (127 in the South), and hundreds of local offices (see Table 15.3). Significant local gains have been the election of blacks as mayors in Atlanta, Detroit, Los Angeles, New Orleans, Newark, Washington, D.C., and Chicago. The presence of black political officials, in addition to having great symbolic importance, insures that black policy preferences are at least brought to the attention of the decision-makers. Black preferences may still ultimately be rejected, but today they are at least given a hearing. As black votes have become important in southern politics, white legislators have become responsive to black interests.[11] At the local level the election of black officials and the importance of black votes in the electoral coalitions of white officials have often led to better services (such as more regular garbage pickup), new facilities in black communities, and improved public employment opportunities for black workers.

Today the primary obstacle to black political influence is no longer the overt denial of opportuni-

Detroit's Mayor Coleman Young is one of the nation's black mayors. A number of other large U.S. cities have elected blacks to their top political post.

TABLE 15.3
Black Elected Officials in Selected Offices in Eleven Southern States: December 1980

State	U.S. Representative			State Upper House			State Lower House			County Governing Boards			Municipal Mayors		
	1979	1980	Change	1979	1980	Change	1979	1980	Change	1979	1980	Change	1979	1980	Change
Ala.				3	3		13	13		16	22	+6	13	21	+8
Ark.				1	1		3	4	+1	30	35	+5	11	12	+1
Fla.							4	5	+1	2	2		7	9	+2
Ga.				2	2		21	21		17	21	+4	6	7	+1
La.				1	2	+1	9	10	+1	76	109	+33	11	12	+1
Miss.				2	2		15	15		26	26		18	18	
N.C.				1	1		3	3		18	24	+6	15	14	−1
S.C.							13	15	+2	28	38	+10	12	12	
Tenn.	1	1	1	3	3		9	9		44	44				
Tx.	1	1	1				14	13	−1	5	5		4	7	+3
Va.				1	1		4	4		23	35	+12	5	6	+1
Total	2	2		14	15	+1	108	112	+4	285	361	+76	102	118	+16

SOURCE: Richard A. Hudlin and K. Farouk Brimah, *What Happened in the South, 1980* (Atlanta: Voter Education Project, 1981), p. 17.

clude at-large elections in predominantly white communities that minimize the ability of black candidates to win office and municipal annexations that add white suburbanites to cities. Since black candidates often attract relatively few white votes, a black majority in the electorate may be required before blacks can win public office. The U.S. Attorney General refuses to approve annexations or changes in electoral districts that would reduce the likelihood that a black could win office. There is, however, no obligation for communities or states to maximize the number of seats on a legislative body which blacks can be reasonably expected to win.

Young Adults

The newest group in society to obtain the suffrage is young adults. In 1945 Georgia became the first state to extend the vote to citizens 18 years old. The rationale for this change was summed up in the slogan "If you're old enough to fight, you're old enough to vote." When Alaska and Hawaii joined the union, they also adopted lower voting ages—19 in Alaska and 20 in Hawaii. Uniformity was reestablished in 1971 with ratification of the Twenty-Sixth Amendment, which lowered the voting age to 18 throughout the country.

Some liberals deduced from the campus unrest of the 1960s and the demonstrations at the 1968 Democratic National Convention that newly enfranchised college-age voters would be an important source of support for liberal candidates. The voting age has not, however, had much impact. Youthful blue-collar voters have not shown the same preferences for change as activist students. Indeed, as campus concerns have become oriented less toward systemic reform and more toward vocations, the voting preferences of young adults have become much like those of their parents.[12]

The activism of young adults during the later years of the Vietnam War misled some observers to expect high levels of participation among the young. These expectations have not been met. Turnout for those under 21 has stayed lower than that for any other age group. Campbell observes that

in truth, young people are the least important age group among all voters. Young people have an abysmal turnout record, usually 15 points lower than the older electorate. Not even citizens over the age of 70 vote less than people between 18 and 30 (except in 1972).[13]

ties for black adults to register and cast a ballot. Instead the problem has become the dilution of potential black political power. The techniques that have been used to reduce black influence in-

Wolfinger and Rosenstone found that citizens aged 18 to 24 voted almost 30 percent less than people 37 to 69 years old.[14]

While there have been occasional instances of young candidates being elected—particularly in college towns—these instances remain rare. Greater political activity among the college-aged requires some policy that members of this group perceive as seriously disadvantaging them. The draft during the unpopular Vietnam War was such a policy. In the absence of a concern as salient as Vietnam, young adults have relatively little influence on election outcomes or policy decisions.

Language Minorities

Citizens whose native tongue is not English have been denied the right to vote in some areas. In the past, their inability to read English made it difficult to vote intelligently even if no other obstacles to voting existed. Congress first acted to remove obstacles for those with limited English as part of the 1964 Civil Rights Act. This legislation stated that anyone who had completed the sixth grade in an American school was presumed to be literate. The effect of this was to waive literacy requirements for Spanish-speaking adults who had been educated in Puerto Rico.

More sweeping changes were ushered in as part of the 1975 extension of the Voting Rights Act. Bilingual ballots and other election materials were required in areas where more than 5 percent of the adult population was of a single language minority and 1) less than half of the eligible population had registered or voted in the 1972 presidential election, or 2) the English literacy rate of the language minority was below the national rate. There are now areas where ballots and instructions are printed in Spanish, Japanese, Korean, and Chinese. Areas covered by the language provisions have to comply with the preclearance requirements. All of Texas and parts of 16 other states are affected by this portion of the 1975 Act.

EDUCATION

America has been called the land of opportunity. Realization of a person's full potential is widely considered to be influenced by education. Parents who want their children to have a better life have seen quality education as the key to a brighter future. As society becomes increasingly complex, it is imperative that young children receive a sound educational foundation. During the last quarter century or so there have been three groups that have challenged existing education policy as inequitable. These are blacks, women, and the handicapped.

Blacks

Just before the turn of the century the United States Supreme Court decided a public accommodations case which legitimized behavior affecting education practices. The results of this case remain influential today. In *Plessy* v. *Ferguson*, the Supreme Court ruled that the equal protection clause of the Fourteenth Amendment did *not* require that blacks have access to the same public facilities as whites.[15] Rather, in what came to be known as the **separate but equal doctrine**, *the Constitution was interpreted as tolerating racially segregated facilities so long as those for blacks were of the same quality as those used by whites.* This doctrine was used as the basis for segregation in many aspects of southern life.

The segregated schools that developed in southern and border states were anything but equal. White schools were better maintained, the texts used were newer, and they were more likely to be served by school buses and indoor plumbing than were black schools. White teachers and administrators were paid more than comparable blacks. In sum, much more was spent to educate the average white than the average black.

Beginning in the late 1930s, the courts began to chip away at the separate but equal edifice constructed on the foundation of *Plessy*. The first successful challenges by black plaintiffs came in suits directed at state higher education programs. At this level, it was not uncommon for states to make no pretense of providing equal facilities for blacks. There might be a medical school or law school at the state university for whites. When available, advanced training at the publicly supported black schools was far less comprehensive or of lower quality than that offered to whites. Seventeen states that operated segregated education facilities offered no graduate or professional training at their public black colleges.[16] Southern and border states paid to send black residents who wanted training not available at the state's public black schools to institutions in other states.

In 1938 the Supreme Court ruled that Missouri's offer to pay out-of-state tuition for a black who wanted to attend law school was insufficient to conform with the requirements of the equal protection clause.[17] In another case, the black plaintiff was ordered admitted to the University of Texas Law School despite the availability of a recently established, state-supported black law school.[18] In the Texas case, the Supreme Court noted that the black law school was inferior to the University of Texas facility on a number of quantitative dimensions such as size of library, range of courses, and number of faculty. The court went beyond these readily measurable items, however, and cited dimensions on which conditions at the black school could not be equalized, such as "the reputation of the faculty, experience of the administration, position and influence of the alumni, standing in the community, traditions and prestige."

Not until the early 1950s did black plaintiffs succeed in getting court orders directed at elementary and secondary school segregation. In the historic *Brown* v. *Board of Education* decision, the Supreme Court inaugurated the final struggle to desegregate schools that had previously been segregated by law. The unanimous *Brown* decision specifically overturned *Plessy*: "We conclude that in the field of public education the doctrine of 'separate but equal' has no place. Separate education facilities are inherently unequal."[19]

Implementation Communities in some border states moved quickly to implement *Brown* and desegregate their schools. The response in the South, however, took the form of massive resistance with almost no school boards voluntarily complied and with the state legislatures going on a rampage, passing laws designed to make desegregation more difficult to achieve. Legislation was enacted that 1) would close all public schools should even one be ordered to desegregate, 2) would make state-financed grants available to parents who wanted to send their children to private academies, and 3) sought to resurrect the myth that a state could interpose its authority between the federal government and local school systems to block desegregation. Ultimately these attempts failed but they illustrate the noncompliant attitudes that greeted the *Brown* decision.

From 1954 to 1964 schools in the South desegregated one at a time when ordered to do so by federal courts. Since the resources of private litigants (primarily the NAACP Legal Defense Fund) were limited and southern school systems numerous and adamant, very few black children were enrolled in white schools. A full decade after the Supreme Court struck down separate but equal schools, 97 percent of the South's black students continued to attend all-black schools.

This halting pace was accelerated after Congress approved the 1964 Civil Rights Act. This legislation authorized the attorney general to sue officials of segregated schools on behalf of black students and prohibited payment of federal aid to segregated facilities. The efforts of this dual attack on separate and unequal schooling were significantly advanced when the Supreme Court directed that a school board must "fashion steps which promise realistically to convert promptly to a system without a 'white' school and a 'Negro' school, but just schools."[20] Armed with this directive and with court decisions that grade-a-year plans and freedom of choice plans* were simply delay tactics, Justice Department lawyers and the Department of Health, Education, and Welfare negotiators fanned out across the South and won court orders or agreements from school districts to desegregate by the fall of 1970.

When the Nixon administration—which had come into office with the electoral votes of five southern states—sought to grant additional delays to some 30 Mississippi schools, the Supreme Court rejected the proposal in no uncertain terms.[21] The defendants and the South in general were instructed that further delays were intolerable and that full desegregation must be achieved immediately. The Court's impatience was visible as it ordered the Mississippi schools to desegregate in midyear.

When school opened in the fall of 1970 a set of conditions had been achieved that most white southerners—politicians and laypersons alike—had sworn would never come to pass. Almost every school system in the South had satisfied federal demands that it desegregate. Statistics gathered that fall showed that the South had changed

---

*These plans were adopted by many southern school systems once it was no longer possible to avoid desegregation altogether. Under grade-a-year plans, systems desegregated at the rate of one additional grade a year, usually beginning with the twelfth grade. Freedom of choice plans resulted in desegregation only when a black requested a transfer to a white school. Otherwise, students continued at the same schools as before desegregation.

TABLE 15.4

Proportion of Black Students in Schools with Fewer than 50 percent Blacks and 99 to 100 percent Blacks, 1968–1978

	1968	1970	1972	1974	1976	1978*
National						
0–49.9% Black	23.4	34.0 (33.1)	37.9 (36.3)	39.2	40.0	38.1
99–100% Black	39.7	24.2 (14.0)	20.5 (11.2)	19.5	17.9	22.2
South						
0–49.9% Black	18.4	40.1 (40.3)	46.3 (46.3)	47.1	47.1	44.2
99–100% Black	68.0	21.0 (14.4)	14.0 (8.7)	12.1	11.6	12.8
Border & D.C.						
0–49.9% Black	28.4	21.8 (28.7)	25.7 (31.8)	30.1	29.8	41.2
99–100% Black	25.2	49.6 (24.1)	46.6 (23.6)	42.5	38.1	29.1
North						
0–49.9% Black	27.6	37.2 (27.6)	41.5 (31.8)	42.4	42.5	30.7
99–100% Black	30.9	22.6 (11.7)	17.2 (10.9)	15.8	14.4	31.0

SOURCES: Data not in parentheses for 1970–1976 are from Office for Civil Rights, "Users' Guide and National and Regional Summaries," (Washington, D.C.: Department of Health, Education, and Welfare, 1978). This is a smaller sample of districts than was used in 1968. Data in parentheses for 1970–1972 are from a larger sample which is more equivalent to the 1968 figures. The larger sample includes many small districts in which there is little racial isolation. Therefore the numbers in parentheses indicate more extensive implementation of desegregation requirements. These data are from "Fall 1972 Racial and Ethnic Enrollment in Public Elementary and Secondary Schools" (Washington, D.C.: Office for Civil Rights, 1973). Data for 1968 from *HEW News,* U.S. Department of Health, Education, and Welfare, June 18, 1971; 1978 data are from *Distribution of Minority Pupils by Minority School Composition* (Alexandria, Va.: Killalea Associates, 1980).

*The 1978 data are not wholly comparable with those for earlier years, since 1978 figures are the proportion black in minority schools rather than proportion black in black schools.

from having the most segregated to having the most integrated schools in the nation. Only two years earlier, more than two-thirds of the region's black pupils attended all-black schools. By 1970, as shown in Table 15.4, this figure had dropped to 14 percent and by 1972 stood at less than 10 percent. Between 1968 and 1970 the proportion of the South's blacks in white majority schools more than doubled to 40.1 percent—more than 5 percentage points higher than the schools of the nation as a whole.

These dramatic changes did not come easily. In more than 200 districts, federal education funds were cut off in an attempt to force desegregation. Many other districts came into compliance only after federal judges threatened to enjoin payment of their state aid. Literally hundreds of districts desegregated only after losing suits, a number of which were contested all the way to the Supreme Court.

Northern Segregation As the schools of the South began educating black and white children in the same classrooms, attention gradually shifted to the widespread racial separation in nonsouthern schools. Challenging segregation in the North and West—which Table 15.4 clearly shows existed—proved difficult. The chief obstacle has been to prove that racial separation was the intent of public policy. In the absence of a history of statutory requirements that schools be segregated (as was found in the South), courts have been unwilling to assume that racial isolation is the product of discrimination. Consequently, outside of the South and border states plaintiffs have had to prove that segregation results from official action before they can secure relief. To win in court, the plaintiff must prove that the school board intended to keep blacks and whites apart.[22] If the plaintiff fails to prove *de jure segregation—that school authorities acted purposively to maintain segrega-*

tion—then the racial isolation will be considered *de facto segregation*, *the consequence of individuals' housing preferences*, for which there is no legal corrective. To develop the necessary evidence, painstaking research through decades of school board minutes and careful reconstruction of attendance maps are often necessary. That segregation is de jure may be demonstrated through evidence that racial separation was an objective of school board decisions concerning the location of new facilities or additions, the drawing of attendance zones, or the design of feeder patterns from elementary to junior high to high schools.

Despite the heavier burdens of proof, some desegregation suits have been won in northern and western cities. Denver, Detroit, Boston, Milwaukee, and Indianapolis are among the major nonsouthern communities that have been ordered to desegregate. Other northern districts are currently involved in litigation. Despite some successes, the figures in Table 15.4 show that schools outside the South continue to have higher levels of racial isolation.

To some extent the greater racial isolation in the North results from the fact that outside the South, blacks are served predominantly by central city school districts. Urban districts present greater logistical obstacles to desegregation. In designing big-city desegregation plans, one must consider traffic patterns and travel times, especially when, as in many cities, minorities are concentrated in ghettos near the heart of the city while whites are overrepresented on the periphery. Some cities that have relied on neighborhood schools have had to develop a transportation system to implement a desegregation plan. Rural southern districts have bused most of their students for years and could desegregate by simply modifying the busing patterns.

Another difficulty in desegregating urban areas that influences the North more than the South is that white public school enrollments in a number of cities are declining rapidly. Between 1970 and 1978, white enrollment in the Boston city schools declined from 62,014 (64 percent of the total) to 28,233 (40 percent). Two factors seem to account for these patterns. First, in recent years the black birthrate has exceeded that for whites, and second, the threat of desegregation induces many white parents to remove their children from city schools. Frightened whites may place their children in private schools or move to suburban dis-

Despite the difficulty of proving *de jure* (purposeful) segregation in northern and western cities, some desegregation suits have been won in these places. The desegration of Boston schools was one of the most widely publicized cases.

tricts that have small black enrollments. Escape by moving is feasible in the South as well as the North, but it may be more readily accomplished in the North because southern urban school districts tend to be larger and include portions of suburbia.[23]

Yet another factor in the more persistent racial isolation of the North has been the positions taken by Congress and recent presidents on this issue. Beginning with the Nixon administration, the Justice Department has not aggressively prosecuted school systems that seem to be segregated and has increasingly sided with school districts rather than with black plaintiffs suing for desegregation. This shift results in large part from policy directives from the White House.[24] For its part, Congress has passed legislation eliminating requirements for busing plans to correct racial isolation. In 1977 Congress prohibited the Department of Health, Education, and Welfare (since split into two departments—Education and Health and Human Services) from requiring school districts to bus children beyond the school nearest their home. Administrative enforcement is now restricted to voluntary approaches. These may include:

1. pairing, in which the student bodies of a predominantly white school and a nearby predominantly minority school are combined. Pairing of elementary schools might result in the first three grades attending what had been the white school while grades four through six attend the previously minority school.

2. the development of selected magnet schools with specialized curricula. One might emphasize math and science, another languages, and a third the performing arts. The idea behind magnet schools is that the uniqueness of their programs will attract a cross-section of the school districts' students.

3. majority to minority (M to M) transfers, which allow students to transfer from a school where their race is in the majority to one where they would be in the minority. Usually the school district provides transportation at no cost to the student.

Busing and the 1980s

Following the 1980 electoral gains by the Republican party, there has been a renewed push to circumscribe the use of busing. President Reagan has supported legislation which would prohibit the Justice Department from asking judges to require busing in suits filed by the attorney general on behalf of the United States. Similar legislation would have been enacted in 1980 had not President Carter threatened to veto it.

Also introduced in the Ninety-Seventh Congress (1981 to 1982) were proposals to prohibit federal courts from ordering busing as a remedy even in cases brought by private plaintiffs. Another proposal would allow existing busing court orders to be reconsidered and revoked. An even more sweeping bill would automatically terminate existing busing programs that had been imposed by judges. Also proposed was a constitutional amendment that would bar busing to promote racial balance. These bills, if enacted and not struck down as unconstitutional, would open the way to substantially reduce the amount of desegregation in many urban districts. They would write into law the widespread preference among whites for neighborhood schools.

The shift away from busing to achieve desegregation occurring in the White House and the halls of Congress is in step with public attitudes. Most Americans endorse the idea of school desegregation but not busing.[25] In mid-1981 only 12 percent of the nation's whites favored busing. Among blacks, only a slight majority (51 percent) supported it.

Recent Court Actions

During much of the last decade only the courts have continued to press for additional desegregation. But even the judiciary has circumscribed what it is willing to do. By making availability of a remedy contingent on proof that segregation was an objective of public officials, federal judges have largely precluded the possibility of demanding desegregation plans that would bring together the children of more than one district.[26] This creates a vicious circle of *white flight, in which whites move to the suburbs to avoid schools with heavy minority enrollments*; this results in higher percentages of blacks in the city schools, which causes more white flight. While white flight is but a part of the post-World War II exodus to the larger lots and newer facilities of suburbia, migration from central cities will be hastened by court-ordered desegregation as long as the suburbs are not included in efforts to devise a remedy. The upshot may be that desegregation plans that affect only central city schools may degenerate into futile efforts to apportion a shrinking number of white children across an increasingly black school system.

Two factors have the potential to check this drift. In some communities, such as Atlanta, blacks have come to question the utility of seeking racial balance among the schools in a system with few whites. Instead they have adopted as goals a share of the top administrative positions and better funding for ghetto schools.* Complementing declining support among blacks for desegregation in largely black districts is a Supreme Court ruling that once a school district desegregates, it is not obligated to continue redrawing its attendance zones to maintain racial balance among its schools.[27] The likely consequence of this decision is that urban systems may have racially balanced schools for a few years at most.

*In Atlanta, this change in emphasis came too late to maintain a biracial enrollment. By the 1978–1979 school year, Atlanta schools were only 10 percent white.

Post-Desegregation Discrimination

Most school systems have now brought their student assignment patterns into conformity with federal requirements, even though some racial tension often persists. Desegregation, however, has frequently been followed by more subtle efforts to reduce cross-racial student contact. Some schools instituted special education programs for slow learners when they implemented their final desegregation plan. The use of culture-bound evaluation instruments or simply having assignments made by teachers resulted in many of these programs being disproportionately black. In other schools, tracking and grouping policies had much the same effect: the college preparatory classes were disproportionately white while the lower track and special education classes were disproportionately black. Perhaps the saddest outcome of tracking has been that teachers may assume that students in "slow" classes *cannot* learn and therefore come to expect little of them.

Punishments have also been administered in a discriminatory manner in some schools. In some systems, blacks have been more harshly punished than whites for comparable offenses. In others, blacks have been suspended in disproportionate numbers.[28] A study by the Children's Defense Fund concluded that suspensions are one technique of inducing blacks to drop out of school.[29] For high schools, this method may be used to reduce black enrollments and contact between blacks and whites.

While blacks in a number of school districts perceive that they have been the victims of unequal applications of rules, whites often voice similar complaints. White students complain that white teachers seem to be afraid to discipline blacks. Thus, some whites contend that they are not only punished more severely than blacks for comparable acts but that the schools are not conducive to learning because teachers and administrators fail to maintain order.

A third component of *post-desegregation discrimination—acts designed to promote racial separation in an officially desegregated school system—*is the treatment accorded black educators. When forced to eliminate all-black schools, many districts demoted black principals or failed to renew their contracts. Hundreds of black teachers were also let go. Aside from the personal hardships experienced by black educators who were made subordinate to less experienced whites or who lost their jobs altogether, discriminatory personnel practices have negative consequences for a school system's educational program. Black children lose valuable role models and the presence of a sympathetic ear. White children also miss out on a valuable lesson if they do not see black administrators and teachers making decisions and interacting in a biracial environment.[30]

In summary, the desegregation of some school systems may have changed how racism is manifested, but discrimination has become much more difficult to prove.

Bilingual Education

A more recent issue than equity in the treatment of blacks concerns the kind of educational program that should be provided for students whose native tongue is not English. Millions of Spanish-speaking people have entered the United States through the porous Mexican-American border. In response to crises on the international scene, more than 100,000 Cubans came to Florida via the "freedom flotilla" in 1980, and thousands of refugees from Indochina and Haiti have also arrived recently. What are the obligations of schools to educate these children and others for whom English is a foreign tongue?

An answer to this question was provided by the Supreme Court in 1974 when it directed that schools provide *bilingual education to educate students in a language they can understand.*[31] To carry out this mandate, schools have had to determine the native language of their students and then establish programs to teach those not fluent in English. Educators and the parents of the students involved have disagreed on how this should be done. One issue has been whether schools should continue to help stir the melting pot or should instead promote cultural identity. A number of Hispanic leaders have preferred bilingual and bicultural programs designed to maintain students' Spanish fluency, teach them Hispanic culture, and also develop their competence in English. Oriental parents tend to be less interested in having the schools help maintain skills in the native tongue, preferring that their children master English as quickly as possible.

Some urban school systems have faced the task of trying to provide instruction to a dozen or more different language groups. This has entailed hiring additional staff and purchasing more materials, but these costs are only partially offset by ad-

ditional federal funds. Schools have therefore
tended to prefer programs that provide a rapid
transition to English so that these students can be
moved into regular classes. This has met with disapproval, especially by some Hispanic groups.

Another aspect of educating children who are
not fluent in English is the public schools' obligation to provide a free education to the children of
illegal aliens. A number of schools along the Mexican border objected to providing free schooling to
children who in the districts' view should not even
be in the country. The schools' objections that it
was expensive and unfair were rejected by the Supreme Court in 1982.

Equal Education Opportunities for Women

Title IX of the 1972 Education Amendments was
modeled on Title VI of the 1964 Civil Rights Act.
This legislation sought to do for women what the
earlier section had done for blacks and *eliminate sex
discrimination in schools and colleges.* The differences
in treatment accorded women and men bore some
similarities to distinctions based on race, but there
were also some differences. Title IX has focused
on inequities in employment practices, athletic
programs, course availability, and dress codes.

Probably the greatest similarity between
women and blacks concerns limited career opportunities. Both groups were and still are excluded
from most higher paying, prestigious policymaking positions. Very few of either group serve as
school superintendents or high school principals.
One explanation of the underrepresentation of
women in administration speculates that an "old
boy" network operates for the recruitment of administrators and that the selection process favors
coaches.

A second similarity in the treatment of blacks
and women by public school officials has been
that their concerns receive a disproportionately
small share of the school revenue. Women coaches
are often paid less than their male counterparts.
Less money is typically spent on women's athletic
teams than on comparable men's teams.

Course availability is another area in which discrimination has been a problem. In the past,
many school systems did not allow or encourage
girls to take vocational training in areas traditionally dominated by males, such as auto mechanics
or heating and air conditioning. These fields tend
to pay more than the secretarial jobs that girls
were encouraged to get training for. Today, train-

Title IX of the 1972 Education Amendments was designed to
eliminate sex discrimination in schools and colleges. Now,
female students cannot be excluded from auto mechanics
classes nor male students from home economics classes.

ing is usually available without regard to
gender.

A continuing problem, however, is the sexual
stereotypes that influence some school counselors.
Girls are unlikely to be encouraged to pursue nontraditional vocations and are still more likely than
boys to be dissuaded from studying math and sciences. To the extent that women are not encouraged to take advanced math courses, they are
handicapped when taking standardized exams
like the Scholastic Aptitude Test because of the
emphasis on quantitative skills. A weak performance on the math component limits one's choices
of colleges and universities and can prevent
dreams of a scholarship from being realized.

While it is difficult to obtain statistics to use in
evaluating the impact of Title IX, this legislation
has sparked some changes. Schools have greatly
expanded opportunities for female interscholastic
athletic competition. Between 1970 and 1977 the
number of girls involved in interscholastic high
school athletics rose from 268,500 to 1,965,000.
Steps are also being taken to place additional
women in administrative positions, but the proportion of women principals rose only 1 percentage point to 14 percent between 1974 and 1978.
There have been more marked changes in vocational enrollments, with the proportion of females
in traditionally male classes rising from 5 to 11
percent between 1972 and 1978.[32]

Title IX has also had an impact on the role of

women in colleges and universities. In the past, many of the best schools in the country were all male. Even at women's colleges, the top administrators were males. Coed schools usually placed little emphasis on women's athletics and male and female faculty members often earned different salaries. In the wake of Title IX have come greater opportunities in women's athletics, and comparability studies have led some women's salaries to be increased. Opportunities for women to be hired at good schools and to win promotions have expanded. Professional schools are seriously trying to attract female students, so now medical and law schools have sizable numbers of women enrolled.

Education Opportunities for the Handicapped

The newest group to demand greater sensitivity to educational needs has been the parents of handicapped children. The goals of these parents were brought closer to realization with the passage of the Education for Handicapped Children Act in 1974. This legislation obligates school systems to provide a free, appropriate education to the mentally and physically handicapped. Individualized educational programs are supposed to be developed for each handicapped child. To the extent possible, these children are *mainstreamed*, that is, *educated in classes along with nonhandicapped children.*

This legislation has increased costs for public schools. They now have to serve a clientele who previously were often ignored or educated in private or state-operated facilities (see Table 15.5). New, specially trained teachers have been employed. Some existing facilities have been modified and new ones have been built to provide access to students confined to wheelchairs.

Yet to be settled is whether public schools are obligated to provide a year-round curriculum for some or all special needs students rather than the 9- to 10-month programs provided for the non-

TABLE 15.5

Percentage of Handicapped Children Educated for Selected Years

Year	Percent
1965	25
1968	40
1972	39
1975	50
1979	50

SOURCE: Erwin L. Levine and Elizabeth M. Wexler, *PL 94-142 An Act of Congress* (New York: Macmillan, 1981), pp. 20–21, 25, 28, 80, 170, 180.

handicapped. Suits demanding 12-month services have been filed by parents of handicapped children. Such suits are based on the claim that without training during the summer, the gains made by handicapped children during the school year are lost. The response of school systems has typically been that the school year for the handicapped and the nonhandicapped should be equal.

Implications Legislation and court decisions requiring equitable education practices for additional groups have created strains in a number of school systems. Not only have schools been asked to change long-accepted practices, they have been called upon to spend additional funds that many districts do not have. Public unwillingness to pay higher taxes is apparent in the failure of numerous school bond referenda. Inability to raise additional revenues has meant that the implementation of bilingual education programs, equal opportunities for the handicapped, or additional women's athletic teams requires reallocation of scarce resources and evokes much controversy.

EMPLOYMENT

By the late 1960s, the top priority of many civil rights leaders had become the attainment of economic equality. The late Senator Hubert Humphrey (D-Minn.) pointed up the primacy of job opportunities during the Senate debate on the 1964 Civil Rights Act: "What good does it do [a black] to be accepted in a hotel that is too expensive for his modest income? How can a Negro child be motivated to take full advantage of integrated educational facilities if he has no hope of getting a job where he can use that education?"[33]

Equal employment opportunities have also been an important objective for many in the women's movement. Achievement of this goal requires equal pay for comparable work and the elimination of obstacles that have kept minorities and women out of higher paying jobs.

The primary policy impetus to these goals has been legislation. In 1963, Congress passed the Equal Pay Act, which stipulated that women should receive the same compensation as men when they had comparable seniority and did essentially similar jobs. In the same year, President Kennedy issued an executive order banning racial discrimination on federally funded construction projects. This was a first step toward dismantling the racial barrier that had kept most well-paid construction unions lily-white.

Title VII of the Civil Rights Act passed the next year provided more comprehensive protection for women and minority workers. This legislation has been the most important basis for efforts to increase the representation of women and minorities in job categories that in the past were almost exclusively the domain of white males. Title VII applied to a large number of private employers (about 75 percent of the labor force). Initially the provisions applied to all private employers and unions having more than 25 workers. In 1972 the minimum threshold for coverage was lowered to 15 workers and the law was also made applicable to state and local governments.

Enforcement

Two federal agencies were created to oversee the implementation of federal equal employment opportunity regulations. The Office of Federal Contract Compliance Programs (OFCCP) located in the Department of Labor monitors the employment practices of those who have contracts with the federal government. The Equal Employment Opportunity Commission (EEOC) enforces Title VII and its subsequent amendments.

The broad federal policy goals of equal employment opportunities have been pursued along several tracks. One heavily used approach has been for those who believe they have suffered discrimination to file complaints with the EEOC. A second approach has been for the EEOC or OFCCP to initiate a comprehensive compliance review. The OFCCP has investigated entire industries such as banking and insurance while the EEOC has limited itself to individual employers' practices and labor force. An advantage of compliance reviews is that they are more cost effective (that is, more people benefit from agency efforts) than investigations of individual complaints. Some of the large employers that have been subjected to compliance reviews include Western Electric, the United Steelworkers of America, and nine major steel producers. The Reagan administration has expressed less interest in the broader compliance reviews, so they are likely to become less frequent.

Litigation is a third approach. Suits charging employment discrimination can be filed by the federal government or by individuals. Inability to negotiate a settlement of either a complaint or problems unearthed in a compliance review may lead to litigation. If a pattern of discrimination is uncovered in a compliance review and the employer or union balks at taking corrective action, the EEOC can file a class action suit on behalf of all of those who have been mistreated. Private parties who despair of efforts to negotiate a settlement through either the EEOC or their state equal employment office (if there is one) can sue their employer or union.

Grievances

While there are a great many potential bases for alleging denial of equal employment opportunity, several problems are fairly common. These include maintaining separate seniority rosters for blacks or women and for white males. Separate rosters—which have been declared illegal—perpetuate past discrimination by denying minorities and women access to good jobs. Another issue involves recruitment and promotion practices that rely heavily on who you know. Under these conditions women and minorities, even should they apply for a position, may not receive serious consideration. Accordingly, remedies have frequently been directed at breaking the established pattern of recruitment and getting personnel officers to seek out and consider the merits of applicants from groups that in the past have been ignored.

A third issue has been the appropriateness of tests and prerequisites for employment. Some of these have required a certain amount of education or training while others have had strength or size requirements. Employers have been challenged to demonstrate that employment tests or requirements that exclude more black than white applicants or more female than male applicants are indeed necessary for the completion of the task.[34] Employment tests that do screen for characteristics related to job performance are permitted even if they disproportionately exclude minorities—unless there is evidence that the test was intended to be discriminatory.[35]

On-the-job harassment is a fourth type of equal employment problem. Minorities and women who have dared to break into jobs traditionally denied them have sometimes been subjected to verbal abuse from other workers and unfair treatment by supervisors. Sexual favors have been demanded of women—and occasionally men—as the price for career advancement. All such harassment has been declared illegal but that does not mean the problem has been eliminated.

Remedies

If discrimination in hiring or promotion practices is found, the employer may be directed to employ the plaintiff. Federal contractors who fail to take remedial action can be barred from future federal jobs, a financial penalty few would willingly accept.

A broader remedy would be to develop and institute an affirmative action plan. *Affirmative action plans specify what an employer will do to try to achieve a labor force more representative of the work force in the community.* Many federal contractors must file plans even though they have never been guilty of discrimination. Such plans may involve promises by the employer to advertise job openings in black or Hispanic publications or to send recruiters into minority neighborhoods, black schools, or women's colleges. Another component may be the establishment of goals and timetables for achieving a more diversified labor force. Goals and timetables specify dates by which the employer or union will try to have a certain proportion of minority or female workers on the job. The minority groups are blacks, Hispanics, Native Americans, and Asian Americans. The goals and timetables may be worked out through negotiations between employers and the EEOC or between unions and management.

A third source of hiring goals, one that has been frequently used in dealing with public agencies, has been the federal judiciary. Federal judges have established ratios for hiring minorities in police departments, city transit systems, fire departments, and prisons. For example, a police department may be told that a third or a half of all new officers hired must be black until the racial composition of the force approximates that of the community which it serves.

As part of the affirmative action plan, employers may have to make their criteria for employment and promotion more explicit so that reviewers can determine whether the procedures are free of bias and whether they have indeed followed the procedures they claim to abide by. More extensive record keeping is a frequent consequence of affirmative action: employers charged with discrimination must be able to document that they have fairly applied nondiscriminatory standards when making personnel decisions.

Another technique that benefits minorities involves earmarking a share of the governments'

contracts for minority contractors. In the Public Works Employment Act of 1977, Congress specified that a tenth of the funds provided by this legislation had to be spent for goods or services purchased from minority businesses. The Supreme Court approved this requirement as nondiscriminatory.[36] Earmarking a share of a government's expenditures for minority firms is intended to help them become established so that in the future they can compete with older, white-owned firms.

The wage policies of employers are another aspect of equality in employment that has been addressed by the federal government. As pointed out earlier, the Equal Pay Act required that men and women receive the same compensation when they carry out comparable tasks. A 1981 Supreme Court decision opened the door for more women to increase their earnings. The suit involved female guards at a county jail who were paid only 70 percent as much as male guards. The county justified the difference since the women guarded fewer prisoners and, unlike the male guards, did some clerical work. The Court ruled that the women could sue under Title VII of the 1964 Civil Rights Act—even though male and female guards did not perform exactly comparable jobs—since the pay rates were based on gender.[37]

The Reagan Approach

During the first half of the Reagan administration, federal efforts on behalf of women and minorities came under heavy fire. This resulted in part from a general effort to reduce federal regulations. Businesses have objected to the burden of equal employment opportunity requirements. An organization of representatives of 150 large concerns estimated that compliance with OFCCP requirements adds $1.2 billion annually to federal contracting expenses.[38] The OFCCP and EEOC have also been victims of budget cuts which reduce their ability to monitor compliance, resolve complaints, and launch investigations. Responsiveness to business objections in the Reagan administration and among Republicans in Congress may stem from the fact that businesses, and not minority groups, play major roles in the election of many Republicans.

Opposition to equal employment opportunity programs has taken a variety of forms during the early 1980s. First, President Reagan revoked new procedures adopted by the OFCCP in December of 1980. Second, representatives of the Reagan administration indicated a distaste for confrontation and a preference for pursuing equal employment opportunities through voluntary efforts. Third, the assistant attorney general for civil rights has disavowed the use of goals and timetables: "We no longer will insist upon or . . . support the use of quotas or any other numerical or statistical formulae designed to provide to nonvictims of discrimination preferential treatment based on race, sex, national origin or religion."[39] We see here a belief that the use of goals and timetables has overcompensated workers who belong to categories which in the past suffered discrimination.

Fourth, the OFCCP has proposed guidelines which would reduce contractors' obligations. Smaller contractors (those with fewer than 250 workers and contracts of less than $1 billion) would no longer have to file written affirmative action plans. This would eliminate the need to file plans for about three-fourths of the federal contractors, although the larger ones for whom coverage would continue hire the bulk of the workers now covered by plans.[40] In the past, contractors having contracts worth $50,000 and hiring 50 workers have had to submit affirmative action plans. Further impeding the OFCCP's ability to monitor how well employers comply with the law is a proposal to reduce the number of firms required to report on their hiring practices each year.

Evaluations Most civil rights groups have been critical of the changes the Reagan administration wants to make. They see the weakening or elimination of specific goals, timetables, and monitoring as seriously undercutting the government's ability to implement equal employment opportunity laws.[41] They flatly reject the Reagan preference for volunteerism. "Local governments and business have been reluctant to comply with affirmative action rules as it is. Without the government standing over them with a sledgehammer, they will do nothing," contends the head of the Atlanta office of the U.S. Commission on Civil Rights.[42] The head of the late Martin Luther King's Southern Christian Leadership Conference agrees: "Discrimination won't die accidentally. It has to be killed."[43]

Supporters of the changes proposed under Pres-

ident Reagan believe the programs can operate on a largely voluntary basis since the worst abuses have been eliminated. They also accept the contention that affirmative action can be counterproductive—the achievements of women or minorities who obtain good jobs may be discounted by some coworkers who attribute such advances to the favored status accorded these groups by Title VII of the Civil Rights Act. Others worry that if preference is given in hiring or promotions to minorities and women, it will undercut the concept that advancement should be based on merit. They fear that affirmative action accords special protection to mediocrity.

A heated dispute has arisen over the issue of how much responsibility the government, employers, and unions should have to correct discriminatory practices rooted in the past. Civil rights activists want aggressive action by federal authorities to help women and minorities catch up with white males and to break down old stereotypes that dissuade some employers from hiring and promoting minorities and women even in the absence of an intent to discriminate. Civil rights and feminist groups believe the goal of federal policy should be equality of results. This would be achieved if women and minorities were distributed evenly across job categories and income groups.

On the other side are those who feel the federal government is responsible only for assuring equality of opportunity. People who hold this attitude think that the federal government should do no more than sweep aside barriers designed to discriminate against minorities and women. This more conservative approach would tolerate a much slower attainment of wages and jobs comparable to those held by white males.

Reverse Discrimination

Pressures to have greater representation of minorities and women in job categories traditionally filled by white males have induced some employers to apply lower standards to minority or female applicants than to white male applicants. This has led to charges of *reverse discrimination—white males who have been passed over for promotions or selection to special training programs in favor of minorities or women who seem less qualified have charged that they are being discriminated against because they are white males.*

The best known reverse discrimination case so

The most famous reverse discrimination case involved a white male, Allan Bakke, who successfully challenged the University of California at Davis Medical School's admission policy requiring a number of slots be set aside for minority applicants. But the Court did rule that race could be considered as one factor in making a selection.

far involves not a job applicant but a man seeking admission to medical school. In a decision having some applicability to employment situations, the U.S. Supreme Court ruled that it was unconstitutional to set aside a certain number of slots in an entering medical school class for minority applicants.[44] Allan Bakke, a white male, challenged the procedure since some minorities accepted into the University of California at Davis Medical School had poorer records than he, yet he was rejected. The Court did not, however, prohibit all consideration of an applicant's race. Thus, in admitting educational or job applicants it may be permissible to consider a candidate's race or gender as a factor in making a selection and perhaps to add points (like the veteran's bonus) to the applications of minority candidates.[45]

The implications of *Bakke* were restricted in 1979 when the Supreme Court ruled on a suit filed by a white worker. In *United Steel Workers of America* v. *Weber*, the plaintiff challenged the agreement made between his union and Kaiser Aluminum, which reserved half of all slots in a training program for blacks.[46] Selection was based on seniority, but Weber was not selected even though he

had greater seniority than some of the blacks tapped for the better paying jobs. The high court decided that a program *voluntarily* entered into by a union and an employer that reserved at least half the slots in a training program for blacks was permissible. While the Civil Rights Act might not have required such a program, it certainly did not prohibit it as a short-term method of bringing the proportion of blacks in craft jobs up to the proportion of blacks in the area's labor force.

Impact Certainly at the level of tokenism many changes have been produced by equal employment opportunity programs. Just as almost every TV commercial that features a group scene will have at least one black, so almost every office has at least its token black and token woman. In some parts of the country there may also be a token Hispanic. These changes are of undeniable significance since they demonstrate that women and minorities can realistically aspire to some of the better jobs in the workplace.

Even tokenism has not come easily, and it certainly does not constitute full compliance for those who want to see equality of results. Statistics on the kinds of jobs held by minorities and women and the pay they receive shed light on the degree of equality achieved. Despite somewhat greater representation of women and minorities in good paying jobs in law, medicine, management, and engineering, most women and minorities continue to find jobs in the same fields as earlier generations did. Figure 15.2 shows the equity of nonwhite and female distribution across occupational categories. Scores below parity indicate that women or nonwhites constitute a smaller share of an occupational group (such as professional and technical) than of the total labor force. Scores above parity occur when nonwhites or women are overrepresented in an occupational category.

As Figure 15.2 shows, nonwhites are overrepresented among the ranks of such low paying occupations as laborers and service workers (many of whom are maids and cooks). They are substantially underrepresented among better paying jobs as managers, professionals, and craftsmen. A comparison with data for 1960 shows that, in the occupational categories in which nonwhites are underrepresented, the proportion of jobs held by nonwhites has nonetheless significantly increased.[47] Over the last two decades, the share of the jobs in which nonwhites are currently overrep-

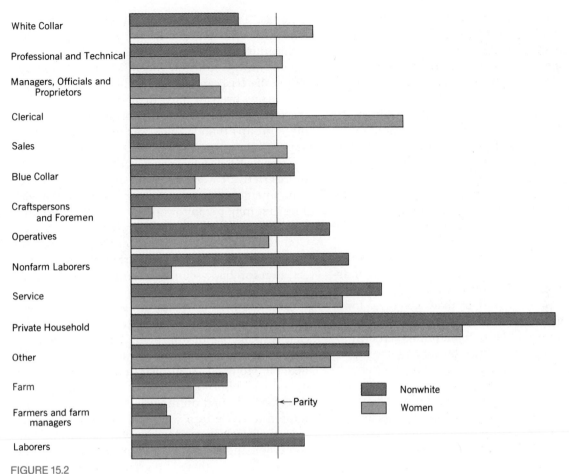

FIGURE 15.2

Underrepresentation or Overrepresentation of Nonwhite and Female Workers by Occupation, 1980

SOURCE: Computed from data in *Employment and Earnings*, 28 (January 1981), pp. 180–181.

resented has declined sizably. The one exception to these trends is the operatives category, in which nonwhites were somewhat more overrepresented in 1980 than in 1960.

Given the persistence in the job patterns among minorities and women, it would be surprising if past differences in pay did not persist. The disparities in pay that were evident in 1964 still exist. The gains registered by black families during the Johnson presidency have since eroded. Black family incomes hover at less than 60 percent of the amount earned by white families. Women also continue to earn an average of just under 60 percent as much as men.

Certain factors should be considered in evaluating statistics such as these. A larger portion of women than men work part-time. Also, some

working women are absent from the labor force for several years when they have children. A third factor, and this applies to minorities as well as women, is that even those in good paying jobs average less seniority than similarly placed males and therefore have lower earnings. The lower earnings of minorities are further attributable to the poor schools many of them attended, which failed to prepare them for highly skilled jobs. Also, members of minorities may have to enter the job market early to help support their families, which cuts short the education necessary for many better paying jobs. Thus, the inequities faced by one generation affect the life chances of the next.

Age Discrimination

In earlier times, the aged were revered as a source

of useful experience. In our society with its emphasis on new, improved products and its reliance on planned obsolescence as a mainstay of economic prosperity, the old are hurriedly pushed out of the labor force by eager, young, better trained workers. In recent years an octogenarian legislator, Rep. Claude Pepper (D-Fla.), has led efforts to protect the rights of older workers to hold jobs.

Efforts on behalf of job opportunities for older Americans have been of two types. One type parallels policy enactments on behalf of women and minorities. It has been made illegal to discriminate against job seekers because of their age. The other policy accomplishment was to ban mandatory retirement ages for most jobs.

While it is too soon to determine the consequences of these policies, elimination of mandatory retirement will result in some elderly people continuing to work rather than accept a lower standard of living on a fixed retirement income. Such a trend would become more marked if problems in the economy cause Social Security benefits to shrink or private pension plans to go bankrupt. High inflation is also likely to encourage older workers to stay in the labor force. The trade-off, in the absence of a full-employment economy, is that minorities, women, and young adults are most likely to be disappointed when seeking good jobs.

HOUSING

Residential patterns reveal the United States at its most segregated. In urban areas in the North as well as the South, the population of central cities is becoming increasingly black (and in some areas Hispanic), while the suburbs tend to be overwhelmingly white. This is not because minorities necessarily prefer the central city. In a number of urban areas the population of the core city is declining as minorities who can afford to do so follow whites out to suburbia. This movement of blacks to the suburbs does not seem to be a step toward racially heterogeneous neighborhoods, however. Instead, population changes in the suburbs follow the same pattern of racial succession that occurred in cities during the last couple of generations. The suburbs blacks have moved into have tended to be adjacent to central city ghettos. As the black population in a suburb rises, whites withdraw at an increasing rate.

Urban development thus continues to be homogeneous. The separation of blacks and whites follows the same pattern as the segregated ethnic communities that were common in earlier times. There have, however, been some differences. While the Irish and later the Italians and Eastern Europeans used to have their own communities, the force of law was less important in separating these groups than it once was for keeping blacks out of white communities.

Prior to 1948, whites in neighborhoods covered by restrictive covenants could go to court to prevent a neighbor from selling or leasing to a black. The first major step toward creating greater housing options for blacks came when the Supreme Court ruled that restrictive covenants (i.e., private contracts signed by a neighborhood's home owners) that forebade selling or renting to blacks were not legally enforceable.[48]

Over the next 20 years the federal government did little to promote open housing. Indeed, officials responsible for approving home loan guarantees made by the Veterans Administration and the Federal Housing Administration viewed racially mixed neighborhoods as risky investments and therefore frowned on making loans to blacks who wanted to move into white communities.[49] Other federal officials located federally subsidized low income housing so that it reinforced existing racial patterns rather than integrated neighborhoods. That is, projects were located where they attracted tenants of only one race.

Federal tolerance for residential segregation did not change until 1968. In that year the dormancy of Congress and the Supreme Court came to an abrupt end. The Court suddenly rediscovered the Civil Rights Act of 1866, which it interpreted in the case of *Jones* v. *Mayer* as guaranteeing blacks the same rights to purchase or rent housing as were enjoyed by whites.[50]

The *Jones* decision eclipsed the impact of the Open Housing Act of 1968. Members of Congress had acted in a more restrained manner, excluding from coverage rentals and sales handled by the owner. Thus, if a person sold his or her own home, it was still permissible under the legislation but not the *Jones* decision to refuse to sell to a black. Transactions handled by realtors, however, were to be carried out without consideration of the race of a prospective buyer or renter. In addition to admonishing realtors not to discriminate by steering (showing minorities homes in black but not white neighborhoods), the 1968 legislation sought to curb another practice that retards the evolution of biracial communities. The legislation prohibited block busting, in which realtors try to stimulate panic selling by whites at low prices by warning that blacks are moving into a neighborhood and prophesizing that property values will plummet. The block buster bought houses at less than their market value and then made a handsome profit by reselling to eager blacks.

The Open Housing Act took into account the prominent role played by financial institutions in the housing market. Regulating the behavior of realtors would have had less influence on the housing market if no steps had been taken to make mortgage money available to blacks and to whites willing to buy in changing or predominantly black neighborhoods. Banks, savings and loan institutions, and mortgage companies were forbidden to engage in redlining, a practice in which whole sections of a city would be ruled ineligible for loans, regardless of the financial characteristics of the loan applicant or the condition of the property in question. Mortgagees were warned not to use the race of an applicant or the racial composition of a neighborhood as criteria when considering loan applications.

Remaining Obstacles to More Heterogeneous Neighborhoods

Since 1968, when Congress and the Supreme Court embraced the goal of open housing, there have been only modest changes. Granted, token black families now live in more subdivisions and apartment complexes. The admonition not to discriminate against black loan applicants has enabled many blacks who opt to live in white communities to do so as home owners. Thus, open housing policy has had some effect. A number of other obstacles to racially integrated housing still exist, however.

Not to be ignored are lingering fear and prejudice. Many whites continue to fear that if large numbers of blacks move into their neighborhoods, property values will decline and the security of their possessions and the safety of their families will be endangered. Second, many members of both races simply prefer to live in racially homogeneous communities rather than confront greater cultural pluralism.

Third, economic limitations prevent some blacks who might like to move to a white neigh-

borhood from doing so. With the median income of black families less than 60 percent of the figure for whites, fewer blacks than whites can afford dwellings in the middle or upper price ranges. Until economic differences between the races are reduced, blacks will be disproportionately concentrated in less expensive housing while whites will cluster in more expensive housing.

There have been some attempts to use federal housing aid to offset the consequences of economic differences between blacks and whites. If federal authorities developed subsidized low income housing in the suburbs, the less affluent (who are disproportionately black) would be able to move into predominantly white areas. So far the federal Department of Housing and Urban Development (HUD) has generally avoided confrontation with suburban governments and therefore has infrequently tried to force suburbs to accept integrated subsidized housing projects.

In 1976 the Supreme Court stepped in where HUD feared to tread. In a suit brought by some Chicago blacks, the Court found HUD and the Chicago Housing Authority guilty of discrimination.[51] The defendants were ordered to develop a plan that would disperse future housing projects subsidized with federal funds throughout the urban area and not continue to locate them exclusively in the City of Chicago. This decision has yet to produce much change.

The Court's finding of discrimination in the location of Chicago public housing has not carried over to questions of zoning. The Supreme Court has approved local zoning ordinances requiring each residence to be situated on a large lot, even though the effect is to promote segregation.[52] If a suburban town zones all of its residential land for low density development, it becomes economically unfeasible for low income housing to be constructed within its borders. Low income housing is built only when relatively high density building is permitted, otherwise the price of land becomes prohibitive. In addition to large lot zoning, other zoning practices that disproportionately exclude minorities specify materials such as wooden shingles or ban multifamily units.

Builders have not been eager to develop communities offering housing across a range of prices. Their preference has been to build units within a relatively narrow price range and not to mix apartments and single-family residences. Developers perceive that mixing prices tends to pull

Thus far, the Supreme Court has not ruled unconstitutional local zoning ordinances requiring homes in certain sections of town to be built on very large lots in spite of the fact that such laws disproportionately exclude minorities from living there because of the high cost. Minorities tend to live in high density areas zoned for multi-family units (apartments).

down the price of the more expensive units. When efforts to develop new towns with a variety of housing prices and a mixture of styles (i.e., single family detached, townhouses, and multifamily units), and a leavening of commercial and light industrial uses near residences have encountered financial difficulties, the first component discarded has been lower income housing.

The success or failure of programs designed to promote racially heterogeneous neighborhoods is important for other aspects of American race relations. Integrated neighborhoods would lead automatically to integrated schools. Affordable homes in the suburbs that were accessible to blacks would make it possible for blacks to live closer to expanding job opportunities in suburban industrial parks, office buildings, and shopping malls.

Implementation There have been fewer changes in open housing than in the rights for minorities.[53] This is true in part because federal law is not actively enforced. For example, a survey conducted in 40 metropolitan areas concluded that a prospective black home buyer had a 75 percent chance of being discriminated against, while a black seeking a unit to rent had a 62 percent chance of encountering discrimination.[54]

HUD, which is responsible for carrying out the terms of the Open Housing Act, has had a poor record of resolving the discrimination complaints it receives. There has been little monitoring of the behavior of lending institutions to determine if they are complying with the law. Nor has HUD conducted many reviews to determine the degree of civil rights compliance in programs it funds.

HUD's unimpressive enforcement record may be a result of its limited authority. HUD can try to negotiate a settlement when it finds discrimination, but like the EEOC prior to 1972, HUD cannot file suit against a landlord or realtor who refuses to negotiate an acceptable plan. HUD can only refer the case to the Justice Department. Legislation that died in the Senate in 1980 after receiving House approval would have authorized HUD to go to court to protect the rights of minorities.

In addition to HUD's unaggressiveness in monitoring and enforcement, there are indications that some federal agencies may still not be treating minorities equally. Data for 1976 show that blacks and Hispanics on the average make larger down payments and have higher incomes and more assets than whites yet receive smaller loans from the Veterans Administration.

Women's Rights and the Housing Market

Lending institutions have traditionally discriminated against women when reviewing loan applications. Single women were treated as poorer credit risks than men with comparable financial profiles, making it more difficult for women to purchase homes. This obstacle has taken on added significance as the number of female-headed households has grown during the last 20 years.

A second aspect of discrimination against women affected the ability of two-breadwinner families to purchase housing. In assessing the size of a loan an applicant family could afford, only the husband's earnings were considered. Excluding the wife's salary from these computations reduced the size of the loan for which a family would be eligible and in some cases made it impossible for them to buy any home at all.

Both of these aspects of discrimination against women are now prohibited by the Equal Credit Opportunity Act. This Act requires lenders to treat the earnings of single women the same as those of male applicants and directs lenders to consider the combined earnings of families having two wage earners.

PUBLIC ACCOMMODATIONS

Two major efforts hve been made to eliminate barriers prohibiting access to public accommodations. The efforts were separated by a decade. The earlier legislative debate concerned whether private entrepreneurs had a right to deny service to blacks. More recently, legislation has made a number of facilities more accessible to the handicapped.

Racial Access

In the wake of *Plessy* v. *Ferguson*,[55] a whole range of segregated public services developed. Blacks were confined to the backs of buses and to separate railroad cars. They were restricted to specific seating areas in courthouses, theaters, and at sporting events. Access was denied to publicly supported golf courses, libraries, hospitals, parks, swimming pools, and other facilities reserved for whites. In some communities, separate facilities were provided for blacks, but in many there were none.

Private restauranteurs and motel operators in the South universally rejected black customers, although cafes sometimes served them on a carryout basis through the back door. Some filling stations provided segregated restroom facilities and water fountains, but many simply refused to provide these services to blacks. This made automobile travel in the South difficult for blacks. One needed to know the location of black hotels and restaurants and to hope that the filling stations at which one stopped would have a black restroom.

During the early 1960s, equal access to public accommodations stood along with school desegregation and suffrage as major objectives of the civil rights movement. Demands for public accommodations were dramatized by lunch counter sit-ins, which began in Greensboro, North Carolina, and spread across the South; by the Freedom Riders whose bus was burned in Anniston, Alabama; by kneel-ins at white churches; and by the picketing of many white-only facilities.

Economic pressures did succeed in winning negotiated settlements according blacks equal access to certain facilities. The first battle in the civil rights campaign, the boycott of the Montgomery bus system led by Martin Luther King, Jr., forced the local transit system to end its Jim Crow practices and allow blacks to sit anywhere on the buses. Some facilities in other communities, including restaurants, gradually agreed to serve blacks on an equal footing with whites.

After *Brown* v. *Board of Education*,[56] the weight of the Constitution tilted to the side of blacks demanding equal access to facilities supported by public taxes. A series of cases found the separate-but-equal doctrine to be inappropriate for the operation of public golf courses, parks, beaches, prisons, and other areas. Refusal to serve blacks in facilities owned or operated by the state or its agents was thus subject to successful attack under

Private restauranteurs in the South used to universally reject black customers. Passage of Title II of the 1964 Civil Rights Act ended such practices by treating them as violations of the interstate commerce clause of the Constitution.

the equal protection clause of the Fourteenth Amendment.

In the sphere of privately owned businesses that catered to the public, however, the major blow to discrimination occurred in Title II of the 1964 Civil Rights Act. The legal theory on which this legislation rests is the commerce clause of Article I, Section 8 of the Constitution.[57] Congress treated denial of services to blacks as an impediment to the free flow of commerce among the states. It therefore forebade discrimination against blacks 1) by private businesses which catered to interstate travelers, and 2) by businesses that moved a substantial proportion of their goods in interstate commerce. The first provision covered operators of hotels, motels, restaurants, and theaters in the convention areas of central cities and along major highways. The latter provision, thanks to America's extensive transportation network, seemingly encompasses almost all businesses in the country.[58]

During the first year or so after this legislation was passed, there was some reluctance to comply. This gave way as the courts upheld the constitutionality of the statute. Some die-hard entrepreneurs reincorporated their businesses as private clubs which any white could join by paying a nominal fee but from which all blacks were excluded; but in light of the controversy that had surrounded enactment of the public accommodations section, compliance came surprisingly readily. Within a short time blacks were sitting wherever they liked at sporting events, movies, and concerts and being served in hotels, motels, and restaurants. Soon black access to services and entertainment was limited only by the same factors which limit white patronage—personal taste and money.

The remaining vestiges of the segregation that once characterized virtually every aspect of southern life are now confined to private clubs. There continue to be private country clubs and social clubs, including fraternities and sororities, that limit their membership to whites. While social pressures are occasionally brought to bear on these clubs and their members—particularly members nominated for high public office—the restrictions on membership practiced by such organizations are legal.[59] The Supreme Court has accepted private organizations as being protected by one's right to associate with whomever one chooses.

Private schools are an exception to the right of private organizations to practice racial selectivity. The Court has held that private schools are covered by the terms of the Civil Rights Act of 1866, which guarantees the rights of blacks to enter into contracts.[60] (This is the same statute relied on in *Jones* v. *Mayer*, the open housing case.) The school's policy of rejecting black applicants was judged to be an illegal barrier to black parents who wanted to accept the offer of a contract to provide an education. The offer was considered to be more public than private since it was made in the yellow pages of the telephone directory and in mass mailings.

The Reagan administration reopened one aspect of the relationship between public policy and private schools that had seemed to be settled. President Reagan proposed restoring the eligibility of private schools and colleges that practice racial discrimination for tax deductions. This would allow donors to count as deductions on their federal income tax returns contributions to schools found to practice discrimination. In 1983, the Supreme Court disallowed such deductions.

Access for the Handicapped

The issue of access for blacks stimulated controversy before being adopted as public policy. Thereafter, it was implemented with less resistance than most programs designed to attain equal treatment for blacks. In contrast, relatively little controversy accompanied imposition of requirements that public buildings and conveyances be made accessible to the handicapped. The implementation of provisions designed to expand the mobility of the handicapped has, however, been marked by delays and opposition.

A particularly important distinction between these two sets of rights may be that by complying with the public accommodations statute, private businesses acquired a new market and public officials could save a little money by eliminating duplication of services. Compliance with legislation for the handicapped, on the other hand, typically entails added expense. Ramps may have to be added to curbs and public buildings, and city buses may have to be adapted to accommodate wheelchairs.

The basis for requiring that public facilities be made accessible to those in wheelchairs is the Rehabilitation Act of 1973. It provides that "no otherwise qualified handicapped individual . . . shall

The Rehabilitation Act of 1973 required that public facilities be made accessible to those in wheelchairs. This law was not enforced until handicapped citizens mounted extensive protests.

. . . be excluded from participation in . . . any program or activity receiving federal financial assistance." Thus, the federal government has used its funding as leverage to force local implementation of handicapped rights, just as it used Title VI to promote school desegregation and Title IX to secure equal rights for women in public education.

For four years, the Department of Health, Education, and Welfare delayed issuing the regulations specifying how the Rehabilitation Act would be implemented for four years. Indeed, regulations were not published until there was a sit-in at the offices of the secretary of HEW by handicapped citizens.

Publication of the guidelines has set off a public debate over the cost efficiency of the requirements (previously discussed in Chapter 4). The handicapped counter these arguments by contending that it is inappropriate to attach a price tag to rights. Moreover, wheelchair users are not the only beneficiaries of easier access to public transit and buildings. The elderly, pregnant women, and others who have impaired mobility can use the

ramps and elevators. One way to resolve this argument would be for the federal government to pay any additional costs attributable to this policy. The taxpayers revolt and disenchantment with many federal programs make this an unlikely alternative.

CLASSIFICATORY SCHEMES

As has been demonstrated, the Supreme Court has frequently struck down laws and practices that treat minorities or women differently than whites or males. In evaluating such cases, the Court has ruled that classification schemes based on race are inherently suspect, and presumably unconstitutional; they are therefore given the closest scrutiny by the courts. Indeed, except for affirmative action plans, which are intended to promote more equitable treatment of blacks and other minorities by offsetting the consequences of past discrimination, racial classifications are almost invariably struck down.

The Reagan administration's attack on affirmative action is premised in part on the notion that even benign uses of racial classifications violate the Fourteenth Amendment's equal protection clause. Opponents of affirmative action contend that they want the Constitution to be totally colorblind. Proponents assert that without affirmative action, change will come much slower.

Leaders of women's rights groups would like to see comparable stringency applied to schemes that make distinctions on the basis of gender. So far, the Supreme Court has been unwilling to equate gender equality with racial equality. Instead, cases raising the issue of gender equality have turned on the issue of whether the sex-based classification advanced an important government objective: "To withstand constitutional challenge, previous cases establish that classifications by gender must serve important government objectives and must be substantially related to achievement of these objectives."[61]

Applying this obviously imprecise yardstick, the Court has invalidated statutes providing benefits to widows but not widowers and alimony to divorced women but not men. The Court has not, however, found a constitutional violation in the congressional decision to register men but not women for the draft.

Congress determined that any future draft, which would be facilitated by the registration scheme, would be char-

acterized by a need for combat troops. . . . The fact that Congress and the Executive have decided that women should not serve in combat fully justifies Congress in not authorizing their [women's] registration, since the purpose of registration is to develop a pool of potential combat troops. . . . "the gender classification is not invidious, but rather realistically reflects the fact that the sexes are not similarly situated" in this case. . . . The Constitution requires that Congress treat similarly situated persons similarly, not that it engage in gestures of superficial equality.[62]

Differential Impact in the Absence of Classifications

When evaluating statutes that have a different impact on minorities and whites or females and males but do not classify by race or sex, the Court's response has been the same as it was when classifications were based on race or gender. Thus, it is insufficient for plaintiffs to show that a preference is given to veterans in filling public jobs or that an employment test eliminates disproportionate numbers of women or minorities. For the procedure or test to be struck down by the courts, the plaintiff must prove that the overexclusion of minorities or women was intentional. The requirement that plaintiffs prove an intent to discriminate has spread beyond employment cases and has been used to evaluate practices affecting education which, on their face, are not discriminatory. The difference in the rates at which minorities and whites or women and men participate in an activity can indicate that a law or procedure is not affecting all people equally. This alone, however, is insufficient to have the procedure or statute invalidated.

By using an *intent test that invalidates laws or practices only if they were designed to discriminate,* the courts have shown that they are satisfied with the creation of equality of opportunity. Equality of results—the goal of activist groups—need not be achieved. Minority and women's groups have preferred that courts apply an *effects test, in which all a plaintiff would have to prove is that a law or practice was discriminatory, regardless of the intent of those who designed it.* A differential effect is usually easier to prove than an intent to discriminate.

Congress has already shown its willingness to move in the direction of the effects test. In its 1982 extension of the Voting Rights Act of 1965, it adopted the effects test as the standard for determining whether governmental structures and policies dilute minority voting strength. Undoubtedly, in the 1980s the success of various groups fighting for what they regard as their civil rights will hinge on whether legislative bodies—and ultimately the courts—apply the effects test.

SUMMARY

The Supreme Court has led the way in expanding the rights of Americans to vote, to an equal education, to fair housing practices, to public accommodations, and to equal employment opportunities. Blacks, other racial minorities, and women have received guarantees from the federal government which have enabled them to do many things denied them in the past. In addition, the handicapped have achieved new rights of access and rights to education.

While the courts have typically been the institution to inaugurate changes in this policy area, the bureaucracy often plays an important role in determining the impact of changes. This has been particularly true of education, employment, and voting rights.

There have been indisputable and significant changes during the last generation. Millions of blacks have achieved the right to vote and have played critical roles in determining the outcomes of thousands of elections. Thousands of schools have been desegregated, hundreds of bilingual education programs have been instituted, and opportunities for female students in academics and athletics have been substantially broadened.

The range of jobs available to minorities and women has been expanded to cover virtually everything done by white males. Only a few gender-related differences remain with women still excluded from combat positions in the armed forces and the linebacker corps of the National Football League. Women do, however, serve in many capacities in the military, including duty at sea, and female sports writers must be given equal access to post-game interviews.

The right of access of minorities to tax-supported facilities and to businesses that cater to the public is universal. Women now have access to businesses such as posh clubs that once had male-only rules. The number of places accessible to people confined to wheelchairs has been increased markedly.

In summary, then, although not all obstacles have been removed, the changes that have occurred are little short of revolutionary. Changes that millions of opponents swore would never come to pass have been widely implemented. Perhaps even more notable has been the adoption and implementation of changes that most Americans did not even contemplate a generation ago. As different groups of Americans have risen up to demand their civil rights, the equal protection of the laws clause of the Constitution has been applied to grant them equality, at least of opportunity.

The Drawn-Out Struggle Against the White Primary*

Of the many techniques adopted to keep southern blacks from playing an important role in politics, one of the most effective was the white primary. In Texas, the white primary was adopted after Ku Klux Klan candidates ran poorly in the Democratic primary in San Antonio. In 1923, in response to Klan lobbying, the Texas legislature excluded blacks from voting in Democratic primaries. Since there were rarely any serious Republican candidates in the South, the important decisions about who would hold office were made in the Democratic primary. The Democratic nominee was then routinely swept to victory in the general election.

When L. A. Nixon, a black El Paso doctor, was denied a ballot in the 1924 primary, he filed suit charging that the state law which limited primary participation to whites violated the equal protection clause of the Fourteenth Amendment. Three years later, the U.S. Supreme Court agreed and struck down the Texas statute.[1]

Immediately the Texas legislature convened and passed a law which authorized "every political party . . . through its state executive committee . . . to prescribe the qualifications of its own members." The Democratic State Executive Committee promptly limited membership and thereby the right to participate in primaries to whites. Consequently when Dr. Nixon sought to vote in 1928, he was again turned away.

In a second suit brought by the El Paso doctor, the Supreme Court concluded that the Democratic party leadership was acting as an agent of the state and therefore this version of the white primary violated the equal protection clause prohibition on racial discrimination carried out by states.[2]

Following this second decision, the State Democratic Convention, meeting in 1932, voted to exclude blacks from party primaries. A suit challenging this action was decided by the Supreme Court in 1935.[3] In this case, the Court noted that the party and not the state paid for the primary, provided the ballots and counted the ballots. Moreover, the exclusion of blacks was done pursuant to a decision by the party and not in any way as a result of state law. The Supreme Court therefore did not find this version of the white primary to be unconstitutional.

In 1941 in a Louisiana case dealing with fraud in the election of members of Congress, the Supreme Court for the first time ruled that the federal government could regulate state primary elections under Section 2 of Article 1 of the Constitution. This provides that federal representatives shall be "chosen . . . by the people in the several states."

With the federal government now willing to regulate some aspects of primary elections, a black Houston dentist, Lonnie Smith, attempted to vote in the Democratic primary. After being refused, he brought suit. In *Smith* v. *Allwright* (1944), the Supreme Court overturned the decision it had handed down nine years earlier because of the integral role in the election process played by primaries in Texas.[4] Thus, 20 years after Dr. Nixon was kept from voting in a Texas primary, the Supreme Court finally fully acknowledged the unconstitutionality of the white primary.

In a flurry of activity, several southern states tried to find a way around the *Smith* decision. South Carolina repealed some 150 laws dealing with primaries in hopes that doing so would sufficiently sever any ties which

*This draws on materials in V. O. Key, Jr. *Southern Politics* (New York: Vintage Books, 1949), chapter 29, and Steven F. Lawson, *Black Ballots* (New York: Columbia University Press, 1976), chapter 2.

[1] *Nixon* v. *Herndon*, 273 U.S. 536 (1927).
[2] *Nixon* v. *Condon*, 286 U. S. 73 (1932).

[3] *Grovey* v. *Townsend*, 295 U.S. 45 (1935).
[4] *Smith* v. *Allwright*, 321 U.S. 649 (1944).

could be used to demonstrate that the discrimination constituted state action. Arkansas used a complicated procedure in 1946 in which four primaries were held in consecutive weeks. There were separate primaries for federal and nonfederal contests. Each of these primaries was preceded by a preferential primary. In some localities blacks who sought to vote in primaries were simply refused by local election officials.

When the South Carolina law was challenged in court, the judge, a South Carolinian, urged the leaders of his state to "rejoin the Union. It is time to fall in step with the other states and to adopt the American way of conducting elections."

Minorities, whether racial, gender, age, language, or other have always had to fight for their civil rights. Ultimately, this struggle which generally begins at the local or state level, ends up in the national arena. There actions by Congress or the Courts make it clear that all individuals are entitled to certain basic civil rights.

KEY TERMS

affirmative action plans
bilingual education
de facto *segregation*
de jure *segregation*
effects test
equal protection clause
intent test
mainstream
post-desegregation discrimination
preclearance
reverse discrimination
separate-but-equal doctrine
Title IX
white flight

SUGGESTED READINGS

Garcia, C. R., and R. D. de la Garza. *The Chicago Political Experience: Three Perspectives.* North Scituate, Mass.: Duxbury Press, 1977.

Garrow, David J. *Protest at Selma.* New Haven, Conn.: Yale University Press, 1978.

Githens, Marianne, and Prestage, Jewel L., eds. *A Portrait of Marginality.* New York: David McKay Company, 1977.

Keech, William. *The Impact of Negro Voting.* Chicago: Rand McNally, 1968.

Key, V. O., Jr. *Southern Politics.* New York: Random House, Vintage, 1949.

Kluger, Richard. *Simple Justice.* New York: Alfred A. Knopf, 1976.

Lawson, Steven F. *Black Ballots: Voting Rights in the South, 1944–1969.* New York: Columbia University Press, 1976.

Levine, Erwin L., and Wexler, Elizabeth M. *PL 94–142: An Act of Congress.* New York: Macmillan, 1981.

Orfield, Gary. *Must We Bus?* Washington, D.C.: Brookings Institution, 1978.

Rodgers, Harrell R., Jr., and Bullock, Charles S., III. *Law and Social Change.* New York: McGraw-Hill, 1972.

Yarmolinsky, Adam; Liebman, Lance; and Schelling, Corinne S., eds. *Race and Schooling in the City.* Cambridge, Mass.: Harvard University Press, 1981.

CHAPTER 16

CIVIL LIBERTIES

Constitutional Bases for Civil Liberties ■ First Amendment Freedoms ■ Abortion
■ Rights of Criminal Defendants

A major feature that distinguishes democracies from totalitarian regimes is the concern for civil liberties. In our nation's 200-year history, an extensive list of rights has developed. Many of the rights we currently enjoy are quite new, having been recognized by the courts or written into law by Congress only within the last generation or two. Typically these new rights have expanded on original guarantees included in the Constitution and its *Bill of Rights, the first ten amendments*. Another important basis for some recently acknowledged rights has been the due process clause of the Fourteenth Amendment. The Supreme Court has held that this provision extends many of the protections of the Bill of Rights to the state level.

As with most other significant policy changes, the broadening of our civil liberties has become enveloped in clouds of controversy. Each time the canopy of guaranteed rights has been expanded to cover new groups or activities, there have been those who have opposed it. Consequently, a newly protected right that was boldly declared has often been implemented only grudgingly. When the passage of time has not eroded the intensity of op-

position, the Supreme Court has sometimes ultimately adopted more restrictive interpretations of what the Constitution required than it appeared to do initially.

Another result of the opposition to new definitions of civil liberties is that the rights described remain ideals to some extent. They sketch out what protections American citizens should have. Constant vigilance may be required to actually secure the enjoyment of these rights. People may have to be willing to go to court to obtain reaffirmation and to have those who would unjustly curb their freedoms rebuked. People have risked their lives and fortunes first to define and subsequently to enforce these basic guarantees of freedom, participation, and fairness of treatment. The lengths to which Americans have gone to win and protect these rights point up their importance.

Civil liberties encompass such essential facets of our democratic political system as our rights to free expression and to worship as we please. Other civil liberties include protections designed to insure that those accused of crimes receive fair trials. Enforcement of these guarantees can play a critical role in determining whether a person can enjoy the life, liberty, and pursuit of happiness promised in the Declaration of Independence.

Civil liberties, then, are protections of our rights as individuals. Sometimes people get the false impression that civil liberties are nothing more than a collection of loopholes that the devious in society exploit to do things that ''good Americans'' should not be doing. For example, we have probably all heard impassioned criticism of court decisions that have allowed seemingly guilty people to go free. Many of us have probably wished at least momentarily that a person who was saying, showing, or selling something we found offensive could be forced to stop.

While we may be troubled when those we disagree with exercise their rights, we should keep in mind that civil liberties do not just protect those we consider to be deviants. If law enforcement officers are allowed to ignore the rights of those accused of crimes, then what is there to protect innocent people arrested through some kind of mix-up? Similarly, if the government is allowed to silence those with whom we disagree, it is not inconceivable that it might sanction those who express views similar to our own. It is civil liberties protections that restrict the government's authority to unreasonably restrict our behavior.

CONSTITUTIONAL BASES FOR CIVIL LIBERTIES

The rights to be discussed in this chapter are derived from six amendments to the Constitution. Freedom of expression (i.e., freedom of speech, the press, religion, and assembly) is guaranteed in the First Amendment. Protections for those who are accused of criminal activities are set forth in the Fourth, Fifth, Sixth, and Eighth Amendments. The Supreme Court has gradually extended these protections, using the guarantees of the federal Constitution to invalidate state laws that infringe on these rights. The due process clause of the Fourteenth Amendment has provided the basis for applying these protections below the national level.

The Supreme Court has repeatedly used the due process prohibition (''nor shall any state deprive any person of life, liberty, or property without due process of law'') as a vehicle to extend the rights of Americans. The reference to states in the Fourteenth Amendment has been picked up on by the courts and interpreted to mean that a number of federal rights also exist at the state level. For example, the First Amendment protects freedom of expression and religion only from infringement by Congress. The due process clause extends these protections to the level of the states.

In the remainder of this chapter we will demonstrate what these sections of the Constitution have come to mean. As previously indicated, their meaning today is the product of an evolutionary process. All the sections of the Constitution that will be dealt with in this chapter are more than 100 years old, yet most of the interpretations discussed here have been set forth only since World War II. The basic structure of the Constitution changes slowly through the amendment process, while its meaning changes through interpretations made by each generation of jurists. In reading this chapter be sensitive to the shifts in the ways the Supreme Court has interpreted the unchanging language of the Bill of Rights.

FIRST AMENDMENT FREEDOMS

The First Amendment is stated as an absolute: ''Congress shall make *no law* respecting an establishment of religion or prohibiting the free exercise thereof; or abridging the freedom of speech, or of the press; or of the right of the people peaceably to assemble, and to petition the government for a redress of grievances'' (emphasis added).

If indeed the prohibitions contained in this amendment were absolute, there would be very little to say at this point in the text. It would be sufficient to quote the amendment and then indicate that the courts have, with unceasing vigilance, struck down as unconstitutional all attempts to restrict expression, assemblage, and religious practices. The absolutist terms of the prohibition have not, however, been applied absolutely. The courts have tolerated a number of actions by Congress and state legislatures that punish certain types of expression, prohibit some forms of assembly, and prevent some religious practices. Other attempted infringements have run afoul of the constitutional protections. We will now discuss what is forbidden and what infringements are permitted.

Freedom of Speech

Our legal system owes a great deal to the **common law**, *the system of judge-made law that developed in England before the United States was colonized.* Common law recognized that there are some types of speech for which one can be punished.

Sedition is one type of speech that democratic governments have frequently tried to curb. The government has historically been allowed to punish those who say or publish things that are believed to threaten its stability.

Obscenity is a second type of speech that is not protected by the First Amendment. Again, there is a long history of governments prohibiting the dissemination of certain kinds of sexually oriented materials in order to protect public morals. John Cleland's bawdy classic *Fanny Hill: Memoirs of a Woman of Pleasure* was banned for almost two centuries. Works by James Joyce, D. H. Lawrence, and others were once considered to be pornographic and were only distributed through underground channels.

Another exception to free speech that has a long history has been "fighting words." Neither courts nor legislatures have identified a list of words or phrases so provocative that their use will threaten the peace. Nonetheless, there are numerous statutes prohibiting the use of words that are likely to set off a fight or catalyze an audience into a rampaging mob.

Defamation of character is the fourth type of speech that can be regulated. The courts have historically found that no useful purpose is served by the dissemination of falsehoods. This type of misinformation is a far cry from the free and open political discussions that the Founding Fathers wanted to protect from government interference.

In dealing with cases involving these possible exceptions to the First Amendment guarantees, the Courts have had to adjust to changes in public attitudes concerning what constitutes acceptable behavior. They have also had to contend with new communication techniques. When the Bill of Rights was ratified, literacy was limited and therefore many Americans, particularly those in rural areas or along the frontier, relied heavily on the spoken word to communicate. Increased literacy rates, the availability of printed materials, and now radio, television, pictures, movies, satellite communications, and so forth have reduced public reliance on face-to-face speech as the primary mode of communication. To what extent do the guarantees of the First Amendment apply to these alternative methods of communication? In the sections of this chapter dealing with free speech and free press, the distinctions between the two types of communication will at times be blurred since the courts have extended similar protections to the spoken and the printed word.

A few justices have taken an **absolutist approach**—*they have taken the words of the First Amendment literally and voted to strike down as unconstitutional all attempts to restrict expression or punish people for what they have said, published, or distributed.* In the view of some other justices, freedom of expression occupies a **preferred position**—*laws that infringe on free-*

Freedom of speech controversies frequently involve the censoring, or banning, of materials that some find offensive but others find perfectly acceptable.

dom of expression are presumed to be unconstitutional and subjected to the most exacting scrutiny. Usually courts presume that laws are constitutional and the burden is on critics to prove that they are unconstitutional. In cases restricting expression, attorneys for the state must demonstrate that it is essential to curb certain kinds of speech or writing.

More commonly, judges confronted with cases involving claims of violation of freedom of speech or press have taken a less one-sided perspective when balancing competing values. The balancing tests most frequently used by the Supreme Court, the clear and present danger test, and the gravity of evil test will be explained shortly.

Sedition   Cases involving criticism of the government or its policies are of great importance. A mainstay of a democratic regime is that citizens be allowed to debate the wisdom of its policies and the merits of its officials, but many people believe that there is some point at which criticism may go too far. Public officials whose policies are under fire may claim that the criticisms are unfair or inaccurate and that they make it difficult for them to govern. In wartime or when criticism is directed at the design and implementation of national security policy, government leaders may see criticism as treasonous. Often supporters and opponents of government policy divide along partisan lines, which brings in another dimension. Government leaders may lump together their foreign rivals and domestic political opponents and conclude that they are all working against the national good, which government leaders see as represented by the policies of their party.

Since the stakes are so much higher during wartime, it is not surprising that the government has been most concerned about sedition during such periods. Congress first attempted to curb political criticism in 1798 when the Federalist majority enacted the Alien and Sedition Acts. The sedition statute was used against publishers who supported Jeffersonian criticisms of the way the Adams administration was dealing with France and England. The Supreme Court was never asked to rule on this statute since the law was repealed when President Jefferson and his partisans won control of the government in 1800.

The Supreme Court's earliest attempt to specify the point at which political speech goes too far and becomes punishable grew out of World War I. In *Schenck* v. *United States*, the defendant was charged

under the Espionage Act of 1917 with trying to incite unrest among draftees.[1] Based on a review of the conditions surrounding Schenck's activities (the distribution of a leaflet intended to cause insubordination by questioning the legality of the draft and urging noncompliance), the Supreme Court upheld the constitutionality of the statute and Schenck's conviction. Pointing up the situational nature of free speech, Justice Holmes made the frequently quoted statement that "The most stringent protection of free speech would not protect a man in falsely shouting fire in a crowded theater and causing a panic." The test Holmes suggested is "whether the words used are used in such circumstances and are of such a nature as to create a clear and present danger that they will bring about the substantive evils that Congress has a right to prevent. It is a question of proximity and degree." The *clear and present danger* test has since been used by some justices in determining whether the freedom of expression guarantee can be abridged; conditions surrounding the expression are taken into account.

In the *Schenck* case the Supreme Court upheld the government's right to punish those who are critical of it. The entry of the United States into World War I followed a congressional declaration of war so that there was no question of the legality of American involvement as there was in the 1960s in Vietnam. In providing for the common defense, a nation can, within poorly defined limits, prevent activities by fifth columnists. On the other hand, Schenck and others who believed that American participation was a mistake had a right to criticize government policy. They certainly had a right to lobby against the declaration of war and might have been able to continue voicing their opposition. Where Schenck apparently ran afoul of the law and went beyond actions protected by the First Amendment was in urging draftees to disrupt the war effort.

Since fears about national security increase when international tensions rise, it is not surprising that on the eve of World War II Congress again sought to limit the expression of attitudes at variance with American foreign policy. The Smith Act of 1940 prohibited advocacy or teaching that there was a "duty, necessity, desirability, or propriety of overthrowing any government in the United States by force of violence. . . ." Although passed in response to Nazi aggression in Europe, the statute was used chiefly after the war against members of the Communist party. The Smith Act was upheld in *Dennis* v. *United States*, in which leaders of the Communist party were charged with conspiring to overthrow the government "as speedily as circumstances would permit."[2] In approving punishment for advocating the overthrow of the government, the Court elaborated on the balancing that should occur when applying the clear and present danger test. "In each case [courts] must ask whether the gravity of the evil discounted by its improbability, justifies such invasion of free speech as is necessary to avoid the danger." The "gravity of the evil" (i.e., overthrow of the government) was judged to be sufficiently great to sustain the conviction of the Communist party leaders, even though their likelihood of success was small.

The scope of *Dennis* was clarified in 1957 when the Supreme Court ruled in *Yates* v. *United States* that it was Congress's intent to prohibit an *action*, overthrow of the government, and not to limit advocacy of an abstract doctrine.[3] To teach the desirability of overthrowing the government without calling for action is thus an acceptable exercise of free speech. To rule otherwise would preclude a broad sweep of political discussion from constitutional protection. Indeed, discussions in dormitory rooms and over faculty lunches could make participants liable for prosecution should they speculate that perhaps problems with the political system could not be readily redressed through the ballot box. Had the Supreme Court upheld the *Yates* conviction, then reiteration of Thomas Jefferson's statement that "the tree of liberty must be refreshed from time to time, with the blood of patriots and tyrants" might make one liable to punishment.

As postwar paranoia receded and as it became increasingly clear that the microscopic Communist party in the United States had little likelihood of winning political power through violent or peaceful means, the courts came to assign greater weight to the freedom of speech guarantee and less significance to the need to punish seditious speech.

Obscenity Obscenity is not subject to constitutional protection. For those who argue that the concern of the drafters of the Bill of Rights was to protect political expression, obscenity is clearly beyond the pale. For example, Chief Justice Warren Burger has written "in our view, to equate the free and robust exchange of ideas and political debate with commercial exploitation of obscene material demeans the grand conception of the First Amendment and its high purposes in the historic struggle for freedom."[4] Justice Paul Stevens has made an argument similar to Burger's: "Every school child can understand why our duty to defend the right to speak remains the same. But few of us would march our sons and daughters off to war to preserve the citizen's right to see 'Specified Sexual Activities' exhibited in the theaters of our choice."[5]

In contrast, for Justices Black and Douglas, who read the First Amendment as an absolute ban on limiting speech, obscenity deserved the same protection as a political address. Justice William Douglas, in a 1973 dissent, reminded his colleagues that

there was no recognized exception to the free press at the time the Bill of Rights was adopted which treated 'obscene' publications differently from other types of papers, magazines, and books. So there are no constitutional guidelines for deciding what is and what is not 'obscene.' The Court is at large because we deal with tastes and standards of literature. What shocks me may be sustenance for my neighbor.[6]

Over the years the Supreme Court has pursued a frequently confusing course between these two extremes. As with other constitutional issues, conflicts between values are the issue. Proponents of obscenity laws justify them in terms of the protec-

THE WALL STREET JOURNAL

tion of public morals, the fear that consumers of pornography may be incited to commit rape and murder, and the right not to be exposed to sexually explicit materials that one finds offensive. Opponents argue that unrestrained censorship might prohibit the circulation of classics, films, artwork, and writings widely perceived to have merit. They would agree with Justice Douglas that whether something is obscene is frequently a matter of taste and that they prefer to grant too much rather than too little artistic license. Except for those who embrace the absolutist approach, the issue is one of where to draw the line. Where does art, creativity, or genius end and smut begin? Neither the clear and present danger nor the gravity of the evil test is of use to the courts in resolving this question.

The confusion over what is obscene and therefore subject to regulation and what is not and thus protected by the freedom of speech guarantee has made the Supreme Court the *de facto* censor for the country. Over the years, dozens of convictions of booksellers, theater operators, and publishers have been appealed to the Supreme Court. In the words of Justice William Brennan, "one cannot say with certainty that material is obscene until at least five members of this Court, applying inevitably obscure standards, have pronounced it so."[7]

The Supreme Court's continuing role in passing upon the constitutionality of convictions under state and federal laws is attributable to its inability to establish a clear standard that will narrow the range of disputes between prosecutors and those who make and sell sexually oriented materials. Obscenity cases typically generate a number of opinions, and often no one justice can muster the support of a majority of the members. In one of the most candid admissions of the difficulties surrounding obscenity cases, Justice Potter Stewart wrote that "I shall not today attempt further to define the kinds of material I understand to be obscene; and perhaps I never could succeed in intelligibly doing so. But I know it when I see it. . . ."[8]

The Supreme Court's first attempt to define the boundary between obscenity and free speech came in *Roth* v. *United States*.[9] The Court applied the **balancing test**, *considering competing interests when reaching its decision*. In this case, the Court protected communication that had some social importance. Excluded was material that the average person applying contemporary community stan-

dards believed appealed to the prurient (sexual) interest. In reaching a decision, the jury was asked to consider the work as a whole and not just selected passages of a book or scenes from a movie. This was intended to guard against Victorian standards of prudery that would ban a work in its entirety for containing a single racy passage or nude.

Nine years later the Court elaborated on the *Roth* standards and set forth three elements that must be proven before something can be declared obscene. In reviewing a Massachusetts decision banning *Fanny Hill*, a book written two centuries ago, the Supreme Court held that to be obscene something must 1) appeal to the prurient interest, 2) be patently offensive, that is, in conflict with community standards on sex, and 3) have no redeeming social value.[10] To be banned in Boston, or any place else, a work must be found guilty on all three counts. If it has some social value, it could still be published and distributed even if patently offensive. Like many other phrases that the Supreme Court has used when trying to define obscenity, "social value" is broad and imprecise. At a minimum it includes anything that can be argued to have artistic or literary merit or that has political significance.

Modification of the *Fanny Hill* decision began almost immediately. State obscenity laws were upheld when their objective was to prevent sexually explicit materials from falling into the hands of young people or when there was "an assault upon individual privacy by publication in a manner so obtrusive as to make it impossible for an unwilling individual to avoid exposure to it."[11] Moreover, the Court held that people have a right not to receive offensive materials through the mails.[12]

With the modification of the *Fanny Hill* standards, the Supreme Court ceased trying to set standards for determining what is obscene. Instead each case is reviewed separately, with each justice applying his or her personal definition of what is unacceptable.

Another issue has been what community's standards are to be applied—the small town in which the prosecution is brought, the state in which the suit is filed, or the nation as a whole? In 1964 the Warren Court* indicated that a single national

*Commentators on the Supreme Court break up its history into segments by referring to periods using the name of the chief justice. Thus, the tenure of Chief Justice Earl Warren, 1953–1969, is called the Warren Court.

standard should be applied in evaluating potentially obscene materials.[13] The more conservative Burger Court took a different view in *Miller* v. *California*.

Our nation is simply too big and too diverse for the court to reasonably expect that such standards could be articulated for all 50 states in a single formulation. . . . It is neither realistic nor constitutionally sound to read the First Amendment as requiring that the people of Maine or Mississippi accept public depiction of conduct found tolerable in Las Vegas or New York.[14]

The application of local standards results in broader definitions of obscenity than would be tolerated if a universal standard were used. A difficulty with allowing local tastes to determine obscenity is that publishers and movie makers may have their works evaluated on the basis of literally thousands of different standards. The potential variation in local standards has now been partially checked. When a south Georgia prosecutor won a conviction against a theater owner for showing *Carnal Knowledge*, the Supreme Court overturned the jury decision that this violated local contemporary community standards.[15] Thus movies with some nudity or magazines like *Playboy* seem not to be obscene, regardless of local standards. Apparently only hard-core pornography—which Justice Stewart claimed to recognize when he saw it—can be banned.

Another aspect of the free speech and obscenity issues involves the conflict between personal privacy and the authority of the government to ban obscene materials. Again the Court has shifted its stand. In *Stanley* v. *Georgia*, it approved a greater latitude for what a person could have in his or her home than for what might be displayed or sold to the public. "If the First Amendment means anything; it means that a State has no business telling a man, sitting alone in his home, what books he may read or what films he may watch. Our whole constitutional heritage rebels at the thought of giving government the power to control men's minds."[16]

While a person may have a right to read or view whatever titillates his or her fancy so long as it is done at home, this right does not extend to suppliers who would use the mail to distribute materials. This inconsistency led Justice Hugo Black to chide the majority that the right to possess obscene materials apparently applies only "when a man writes salacious books in his attic, prints them in his basement, and reads them in his living room."[17]

The Court's vacillation on standards brings us back to the issue of vagueness. In our legal system, people expect to be able to know beforehand whether a contemplated action would be illegal. The imprecision and frequent changes in defining obscenity have produced a wide grey area in which it is difficult, if not impossible, to predict whether a magazine, book, or movie would be considered obscene according to local, contemporary standards. This makes conditions particularly difficult for those who produce materials that are distributed nationwide.

The cracks and crevices of this imprecise and changing policy are well suited to zealous local prosecutors who want to curry public favor by bringing suit against local booksellers and theater operators. An arrest for selling or showing obscene material often prompts the owner of the business to remove the offending material rather than get involved in a lengthy court battle to determine whether it is obscene. The result is a victory for those who have a relatively broad definition of obscenity.

Fighting Words A third basis for curbing speech is when a speaker seeks to incite an audience to riot and it appears that the effort may succeed.[18] In essence, the clear and present danger standard developed to evaluate communications advocating the overthrow of the government has been applied to situations of civil unrest.

For authorities to cut short an expression of opinion, the speaker must be the instigator of the potential violence. Speakers or protest marchers who are themselves peaceful and who do not seek to provoke violence cannot be prevented from acting simply because authorities fear their opponents may become unruly.[19] So long as the speaker or protestors are peaceful, the primary responsibility of the police is to protect their right of expression. One suspects that police are more likely to agree with those opposing an unpopular idea and act to end the speech or protest rather than protect it, Supreme Court holdings notwithstanding.

Libel and Slander At the time the First Amendment was drafted, it was well established that a person whose reputation was damaged by libelous (printed) or slanderous (spoken) state-

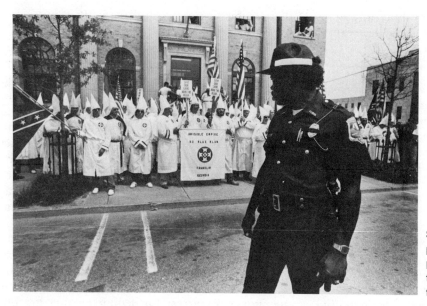

So long as protestors are peaceful, the primary responsibility of the police is to protect their right of expression, no matter how offensive their message may be to the general public.

ments could collect damages. The person whose reputation was hurt could sue not only the person who made the initial statement but also everyone who repeated it. There is no indication that the First Amendment was intended to abrogate the right recognized by common law to protect one's reputation.

Only in the last 20 years have courts restricted the rights of plaintiffs to recover damages resulting from the publication of false information. A major modification has been the denial of recovery to plaintiffs whom the courts concluded had voluntarily entered the limelight, even when it is acknowledged that the material published about them is false. The Supreme Court has ruled as follows:

> The constitutional guarantees require, we think, a federal rule that prohibits a public official from recovering damages for a defamatory falsehood relating to his official conduct unless he proves that the statement was made with "actual malice"—that is, with knowledge that it was false or with reckless disregard of whether it was false or not. [20]

Behind the more stringent standard that is applied to suits by public officials is the presumption that by seeking or holding public office one foregoes some of the protections enjoyed by private citizens. Free and full debate concerning public officials is sufficiently important that the publication of falsehoods is tolerated as long as the publisher is unaware of the error or, as a reasonable individual, does not suspect the statement is false. This degree of latitude insures that the press will not feel constrained to practice self-censorship. Another consideration is that public officials have better access to the media than most people, which they can use to try to correct misinformation.

The need to prove malice has been extended beyond those who hold public office to include people who are public figures. [21] This extension has given rise to a number of suits in which one of the issues is who falls into the category of "public figure." This is much less well-defined than "public official," which means one who holds public office. A key factor in determining whether a person is a public figure is the extent to which the plaintiff has courted public attention. Thus, the Supreme Court ruled that the ex-wife of the heir to the Firestone tire fortune could sue *Time* magazine for an article that incorrectly labeled her an adulteress. [22] That the plaintiff was a party in a well-publicized trial did not make her a public figure.

Corporate Speech   Publications of corporate entities and professionals have recently joined communications by individuals under the protection of the First Amendment. This new guarantee applies to corporate attempts to influence election outcomes or the advertising of goods or services.

Campaign finance laws allow corporations to establish political action committees (PACs), so-

In a 1981 landmark case, Carol Burnett won a libel suit against the *National Enquirer*. Prior to the decision, the courts had made it very difficult for public figures to win libel suits.

licit contributions from their officers and administrators, and use these funds on behalf of candidates. The use of funds collected by PACs has been ruled to be appropriate in federal elections.

The Supreme Court has also ruled that freedom of speech permits corporations to participate in local referenda. The majority decision noted that "the inherent worth of the speech . . . does not depend upon the identity of the source, whether corporation, association, union, or individual."[23]

Freedom of expression for businesses and those engaged in business or professional pursuits has been expanded beyond the sphere of political activity. In the 1970s, the Supreme Court backed away from earlier decisions holding that advertising, or commercial speech, was not protected by the First Amendment. Efforts to prohibit advertisment relating to birth control were ruled to be unconstitutional. The Court then built on this decision and struck down regulations by state licensing boards that banned advertising of prices by professionals for goods or services. Licensing boards have argued that advertising fees for services (such as lawyers' fees for divorces) or for goods (prices for prescription drugs or eye glasses) can be misleading or result in cost-cutting through reductions in quality. The Supreme

Court has not found such arguments to be compelling.[24] Consumers have benefited from this "right to advertise."

Freedom of the Press

Totalitarian governments and a free press cannot coexist. A basic function of a free press is to monitor the activities of the government and to criticize what it believes to be foolish, misguided, inefficient, or illegal. In the absence of an aggressive press that can publish what it believes to be the truth, citizens will be poorly informed and less able to evaluate the quality of the government and its policies. If information critical of government leaders and policies was spread only through word of mouth, those in power would be able to cover up their failures and break the laws almost without fear of punishment.

A critical issue for freedom of the press is ***prior restraint***, *prohibitions that prevent the publication of some kinds of information.* Under what conditions, if any, can the government keep information from being disseminated? Attempts to forbid publication have been premised on several important considerations. Some judges have tried to prevent publication of information about particularly vicious crimes on the grounds that it may make it difficult to select the unbiased jury guaranteed to defendants by the Sixth Amendment.

Concern about insuring a defendant a fair trial has been cited as sufficient reason to exclude the press from a pretrial hearing at which the defendant challenged the admissibility of evidence that the prosecution wanted to use at the trial. The Court emphasized that the right to a public trial is designed to protect the defendant from secret proceedings; since the defendant waived the right to have the public in attendance, the press could be excluded.[25]

The Supreme Court is less willing to uphold judges' efforts to restrict publication of materials that come out in the course of a trial. Applying the clear and present danger test, the Supreme Court refused to prohibit publication of information about a trial of a person charged with the murder and sexual assault of six people. According to the Court, the defendant's lawyers failed to prove that prior restraint was necessary to insure the defendant a fair trial. The Court concluded that "the barriers to prior restraint remain high and the presumption against its use continues intact.''[26] Nor is it permissible to exclude the press from a trial (as distinguished from a pretrial hearing) even if both defendant and prosecutor prefer that the press not be present.[27] And while television stations do not have rights to coverage equal to those enjoyed by the print media, the Supreme Court has ruled that televising a trial does not infringe on a defendant's rights.[28]

National security has been proposed as a second reason for prior censorship. One of the most celebrated cases in which this rationale was rejected involved the federal government's attempt to keep the *New York Times* and other newspapers from publishing excerpts from the Pentagon Papers, an extensive Defense Department analysis of American involvement in Vietnam. The government's claims were swept aside in a six to three decision stating that ''any system of prior restraints of expression comes to this Court bearing a heavy presumption against its constitutional validity. The government thus carries a heavy burden of showing justification for the imposition of such restraint.''[29] In this case some justices pointed to the absence of any statute that specifically prohibited publication; others ruled against the government since it was not clear that publication would ''result in direct, immediate, and irreparable damage to our nation or its people.''

Vietnam and Watergate made reporters more suspicious of the information they received from officials in the higher reaches of the executive branch and destroyed the old convention that reporters would not publish stories that the chief executive believed might damage national security. This changed relationship was evident in efforts in 1979 to publish an article explaining how to make a hydrogen bomb. The attorney general asked the courts to prohibit publication. A generation earlier, people had been executed for treason for giving the Russians information about how nuclear weapons were designed. It should be noted that the material in the article did not draw upon secret documents, although there was some question about whether the documents should have been declassified. The Supreme Court did not rule on the issues in this case since it became moot when similar materials were published in several newspapers.

Protection of Sources A yet-to-be-resolved issue that threatens to restrict what papers publish and television broadcasts is whether courts can force a reporter to reveal confidential sources. On one side is the claim that information bearing on the possible commission of a crime should be made available to a grand jury or trial jury. This conflicts with reporters' claims that they should enjoy a privileged position like the lawyer-client or doctor-patient relationship so that they can keep the identity of their sources and the content of communication with their sources secret. Reporters argue that if communications with sources are not entitled to confidentiality, informants will not talk as openly. This would limit the information that could be gathered and published. A judge's order that reporters identify their source of information about criminal activities forces reporters to choose between professional ethics and punishment for contempt of court. Some reporters have served time in jail for refusing to obey judges' directives.

The Supreme Court has generally come down on the side of the needs of the criminal justice system: ''It is clear that the First Amendment does not invalidate every incidental burdening of the press that may result from the enforcement of civil or criminal statutes of general applicability.''[30] An elaboration of the rationale for this decision noted that the burden would be relatively small and that reporters had the same duty as other citizens to come forth with relevant information.

> *Nothing before us indicates that a large number or percentage of* all *confidential news sources . . . would in any way be deterred by our holding that the Constitution does not, as it never has, exempt the newsman from performing the citizen's normal duty of appearing and furnishing information relevant to the grand jury's task. The preference for anonymity of those confidential informants involved in actual criminal conduct is presumably a product of their desire to escape criminal prosecution, and this preference, while understandable, is hardly deserving of constitutional protection.*[31]

To the extent that the confidentiality of reporters' sources is protected, it depends on state ''*shield laws*.'' Approximately half the states have adopted such legislation, *which places some restrictions on the ability of a grand jury or a prosecutor to compel the revelation of sources or information.* Many reporters would like to see a federal statute enacted that would provide universal protection.

Availability of Information Despite the

chilling effect of holding a few reporters in contempt, the press today appears to be reasonably healthy. The Freedom of Information Act (FOIA) has opened up innumerable federal documents to reporters. While not all materials of federal agencies have been made public, the exceptions are limited and subject to court challenges.

The likelihood that journalists can obtain reports, analyses, and communications relating to most federal activities probably discourages some questionable government activities that would be embarrassing if made public. Since the FOIA can force the release of so much information, it also encourages federal officials to voluntarily explain their actions and the reasons for them. Contributing to these two tendencies was the exceptional role of the *Washington Post* in exploring the events surrounding the break-in at the Democratic National Committee headquarters at the Watergate hotel. Since President Nixon's downfall, his successors have been more candid with the press. One need only compare the speed with which the Carter administration acknowledged the aborted April 1980 attempt to rescue 53 Americans held hostage by student revolutionaries in Iran with the Nixon administration's denials of American invasions into Cambodia.

Access to the Media People who have been denied access to the media have argued that such denials restrict the free flow of ideas which they believe is protected by the First Amendment.

The Supreme Court has affirmed the right of those who have been attacked personally on the radio to respond.[32] This right is guaranteed by the Federal Communications Commission's fairness doctrine. The Supreme Court has, however, struck down a state law requiring newspapers to extend a similar right to candidates for public office who were attacked editorially.[33] The basis for distinguishing these cases seems to be the limited number of broadcast frequencies and the role of the federal government in allocating broadcast licenses (see chapter 10).

An individual's right to reply to critical statements broadcast about him or her does not extend to a right to buy time for political advertising.[34] Once a political campaign is under way, however, the fairness doctrine of the Federal Communications Commission requires that broadcasters sell time to all candidates, even those who espouse unpopular or hate-filled doctrines.

It appears from these and other decisions that there is no general right of access to the media by those who feel they have been wronged by earlier published or broadcasted statements. Many broadcasters do offer an opportunity for the expression of contrary viewpoints and many newspapers publish opposing views in letters columns. Whether to disseminate views at variance with those of the publisher or broadcaster seems to be determined largely by the media.

Freedom of Assembly

The First Amendment has been applied to political expression that takes a form other than the spoken or written word. This is sometimes called "symbolic speech" and may be accorded protection under the freedom of assembly guarantee of the First Amendment.

Relatively powerless groups have frequently gone into the streets to try to influence decision-makers. Marches and pickets have been used to show how a group feels about an issue, to solidify the commitment of group members, and to produce change.

On one side in this clash of values are those who see union picketing, politically oriented rallies, marches, and so forth as forms of expression deserving the same broad protections given the written and spoken word in political debates. Opponents of this view are concerned that those not involved in the protest be able to go about their activities without undue inconvenience. Toward this end, many communities require that a group planning activities that will block streets and sidewalks obtain a parade permit, thereby alerting the city so that it can provide police to protect marchers from hecklers and redirect traffic away from the line of march.

While there is a legitimate interest in knowing about rallies beforehand, parade permit requirements have sometimes been used to prevent activities by those representing locally unpopular views. The Supreme Court has required that parade licensing ordinances be narrowly drawn so that protests cannot be denied simply because a group's goals are unpopular.[35] The right to peacefully march and protest has been generally upheld even for protestors who have no march permit.[36]

Guilt by Association In many regimes, people are punished for belonging to organizations seen as subversive by those in power. Communist regimes have not tolerated organizations critical of the state. Governments whose power is derived from the tanks and bayonets of the military rather than from the votes of citizens often allow little dissent.

In dictatorships, people are often punished because of the friends they keep. During much of the Cold War era, citizens of Soviet Bloc countries were discouraged from fraternizing with visiting westerners. Being seen talking to Americans might lead to a nocturnal visit by the secret police and a term in the Gulag Archipelago.

Americans have sometimes been ostracized for having unconventional friends who hold unpopular beliefs. Indeed, local officials have at times punished people who associated with groups that threatened accepted patterns of behavior and belief. Organizers who came into the South during the 1960s to challenge segregation were harassed by police, who gave them tickets or arrested them, ostensibly for speeding, reckless driving, loitering, and other charges. The federal government has sometimes been guilty of similar practices, as in its clandestine surveillance of civil rights leader Martin Luther King, Jr.

More serious offenses by federal authorities have denied people freedom because of their membership in certain unpopular groups. The largest operation of this sort was the internment of thousands of Americans of Japanese descent during World War II. The basis for this action was the fear that Japanese-Americans living on the

West Coast might include spies and saboteurs. These fears proved to be unfounded; the Nisei 442nd Infantry made up of soldiers of Japanese descent was "the most decorated and casualty-ridden American military unit in World War II."[37] Nonetheless, the Supreme Court upheld the forced removal and imprisonment of citizens guilty of nothing other than Japanese ancestry. It accepted President Roosevelt's rationale that "the successful prosecution of the war requires every possible protection against espionage and against sabotage to national-defense material, national-defense premises, and national-defense utilities. . . ."[38]

Punishment because of membership in a political rather than an ethnic group has been meted out to some members of the Communist party. In the early 1960s, the Supreme Court upheld the conviction of a person whose crime was to be a knowing active member of the Communist party.[39] The Court was careful to indicate that mere membership alone would be insufficient for conviction under the Smith Act. Knowledgeable membership (awareness of the objectives of a subversive organization) plus active participation were necessary to sustain a conviction. This decision appears to have been a unique aberration.

Freedom of Religion

Careful reading of the First Amendment reveals two separate components affecting religion. Both the establishment of a state religion and interfer-

The imprisonment of thousands of Americans of Japanese descent during World War II was one of the most dramatic examples of government denial of individual freedom in out nation's history. At the time, the Supreme Court upheld this action as essential for national security.

ence with citizens' religious practices are prohibited. It is not surprising that the Bill of Rights reflects such concern for religious freedom when we remember that a number of the colonists braved the seas and came to an unknown land to escape religious persecution in Europe. Massachusetts was settled by the Puritans, Pennsylvania by Quakers, and Maryland by Catholics—all of whom suffered in England at the hands of adherents of the state religion. Even on this continent Roger Williams established Rhode Island after the leaders of the Massachusetts colony charged him with heresy.

Establishment Clause In this country we have no official state religion. The significance of the "establishment" clause has been in determining whether state revenue can be used 1) by organizations that have a religious affiliation or 2) by public institutions to promote religious beliefs. Most of the court decisions in this area have involved education policies.

Aid to Parochial Schools In areas where many parents send their children to parochial schools, politicians may seek support by using public revenues to finance some services for parochial students, thereby reducing the financial burden on these families. The rationale underlying state aid to parochial schools has been that this assistance promotes a legitimate state interest in having an educated citizenry who can function intelligently in political affairs. In cases in which public revenues provide goods or services, the issue is whether such assistance breaches the "wall between Church and state" established by the First Amendment.[40]

An early case of this sort challenged a Louisiana statute that provided free textbooks to students attending parochial as well as public schools. Governor Huey Long, a Baptist from the northern part of the state, hit upon free textbooks as a policy that would attract both poor Protestants in his part of the state and poor Catholics from southern Louisiana to his political machine. The Supreme Court reasoned that a state's interest in the education of the young was sufficient to sustain Long's free textbook policy.[41]

That the state or federal government may contribute some kinds of goods and services to schools having religious affiliations has now become well established. One key feature of the "child benefit theory" that is used to justify public aid is that the assistance be intended to help *students*, not the religious group that operates the facility. That the tax dollars used to provide textbooks, bus transportation, or other services relieve a burden the religious body or parochial students' parents would otherwise have to bear is disregarded.

A consideration in applying the child benefit theory is the notion of state neutrality toward religion. In approving a New Jersey statute allowing public financing of school buses for students at parochial schools, Justice Hugo Black explained the

Freedom of religion is one of our most basic civil liberties. Even so, many Americans find nontraditional religious groups such as the Hare Krishnas objectionable and would like to see their freedoms limited.

proper state attitude toward religion: "[The First] Amendment requires the state to be a neutral in its relations with groups of religious believers and non-believers; it does not require the state to be their adversary. State power is no more to be used so as to handicap religions than it is to favor them."[42]

Finally, it would be inappropriate for the state to help one denomination but not others. Therefore, the neutrality doctrine requires that benefits for children be available to all types of church-related schools if they are offered to any nonpublic schools.

When the federal government began playing a larger role in public education with passage of the 1965 Elementary and Secondary Education Act, provision was made for parochial schools to receive some of the benefits. By making funds available to whoever educated needy children regardless of whether they attended public or private schools, the Johnson administration won the crucial support of the United States Catholic Conference.

In 1971 the Supreme Court sought to establish limits on the assistance that can be given parochial schools. In striking down state aid to defer the costs of salaries of teachers of secular subjects in parochial schools, the Court established a three-part test for determining constitutionality: "First, the statute [granting aid] must have a secular legislative purpose; second, its principal or primary effect must be one that neither advances nor inhibits religion, . . . finally, the statute must not foster 'an excessive government entanglement with religion.' "[43] Salary supplements were held to be an excessive entanglement between government and religion. One problem with the statutes was that they provided for government review to insure that religious values did not become intertwined with secular subjects. Thus, there would have been a relatively high degree of government involvement in the running of parochial schools. A second defect was that parents of parochial school children might become politically active in trying to increase the supplement given the parochial teachers. Finally, the Pennsylvania statute gave aid directly to the schools and so did not conform with the tenet that the benefit should be conferred directly on the child rather than passing through the hands of parochial school administrators.

Excessive entanglement has also been used to prohibit state funding for counselors, special education teachers, maps, and laboratory equipment for church-related schools.[44] States can, however, pay for the testing, diagnosis, and therapy of private school students if these do not occur on the campus of private schools.[45]

Several types of public funding for church-related colleges and universities have been approved, including loans and grants to teachers, research grants, and funds for building construction. Some states provide all students who want to go to college in the state with a grant to pay tuition at private or public schools. While all of these programs would seem to benefit church-related schools, they have not been found to constitute "excessive government entanglement with religion." An important distinction between institutions of higher education with religious ties and parochial schools is that religious training is more central to the purpose of the latter than the former.

Propagation of Religious Beliefs   A series of cases have challenged the use of tax-supported facilities for various kinds of religious exercises. A number of these have dealt with religious training during school hours and classroom devotionals. The Supreme Court has held that voluntary religious instruction by privately hired teachers cannot be provided in school facilities during school hours.[46] Also held to violate the establishment clause have been a requirement that a nondenominational prayer written by the state board of regents be read aloud daily[47] and a state requirement that at least ten verses from the Bible be read at the beginning of each school day.[48]

In contrast with these prohibitions, the Supreme Court has approved programs for off-campus religious instruction. The decision in *Zorach* v. *Clawson*, which provided for voluntary religious training during school hours but not in tax-supported facilities, was rationalized on the basis that "We are a religious people whose institutions presuppose a Supreme Being."[49]

The important feature here seems to be whether the religious activity takes place on school property. Whether participation is compulsory or optional has no bearing on the court's decision. Since the constitutional terminology has been interpreted as prohibiting the promotion of all religion, not just the promotion of a specific doctrine or faith, it is not acceptable to grant equal time to various beliefs or to try to use bland language

The Supreme Court's rulings against school prayer have been among its most controversial. Polls show a significant number of Americans favor setting aside a few minutes of each school day for voluntary private prayer.

when praying in hopes that no one will be offended.

Many Americans find the prohibition of school prayer unacceptable. Numerous school districts, especially in the South, have continued classroom devotionals despite their unconstitutionality.[50] Proposals to amend the Constitution to ''put God back in the classroom'' (as proponents like to say) are frequently introduced in Congress.

Perhaps in response to the public's negative reception of its school prayer ruling, in 1983 the Court ruled that prayer sessions in Congress and in state legislatures, even when led by government-paid chaplains, do not violate the constitutionally-required separation of church and state. It is possible that the reasoning behind this ruling may eventually be extended to prayer in public schools.

Free Exercise Clause As with the freedom of speech clause, the Supreme Court has not interpreted the free exercise of religion clause literally. It has accepted certain requirements derived from states' police powers although these contradict some sects' religious practices. State police powers can be used to protect the health, safety, welfare, and morals of the population. This has provided the basis for prohibiting polygamy and snake handling despite claims by the affected groups that such practices are important to their beliefs. State law may also require that children be vaccinated against certain contagious diseases, even if this is consistent with their parents' religious beliefs.

The Court has also upheld Sunday closing laws even though this forces Orthodox Jews to forego two days of business while their Gentile competitors need close down only one day.[51]

Despite these limitations on the free exercise of religion, many statutes have been struck down because they force some people to choose between obedience to the law and their religious principles. For example, the Amish cannot be forced to comply with state school attendance laws,[52] nor can children of Jehovah's Witnesses be required to salute the flag and recite the pledge of allegiance.[53] It is also improper to deny unemployment compensation to a Seventh Day Adventist who loses a job for refusing to work on Saturday.[54]

Conscientious Objectors An issue having great salience during the Vietnam conflict was the basis for claiming conscientious objector status. In earlier wars, members of sects that held pacifism as one of their tenets were exempted from combat roles, either serving as noncombatants such as stretcher bearers or providing alternative service in hospitals or mental health institutions. During

The newest type of conscientious objector is the individual who opposes the draft and military service not for any religious reason but because of a personal objection to war.

the 1960s, a new type of conscientious objector appeared. Some were members of nonpacifist denominations although they personally objected to war. Others opposed war even though they belonged to no recognized religious body and indicated uncertainty when asked if they believed in God or a Supreme Being. Another set of young men sought conscientious objector status since they were unwilling to bear arms in Vietnam although they said that they would fight to defend the United States in the case of an enemy attack.

The Supreme Court interpreted the statute dealing with conscientious objectors broadly and held that those who objected to war were covered if their "belief in a relation to a Supreme Being [was] . . . sincere and meaningful [and] occupie[d] a place in the life of its possessor parallel to that filled by the orthodox belief in God of one who clearly qualifies for exemption."[55] Potential draftees who objected to Vietnam but not to war in general were not eligible under the law for conscientious objector status.[56]

ABORTION

Since the 1970s, there has been a raging debate over what, if any, right a pregnant woman has to obtain an abortion. On one side, pro-choice groups argue that a woman's right to control the use of her body entitles her to rid herself of an unwanted fetus. Opposing this view are right-to-life groups that believe human life begins at the moment of conception so that abortion is murder.

This controversy was triggered by the 1973 Supreme Court decision in *Roe* v. *Wade*.[57] This decision invalidated the Texas statute that banned abortions except to save the mother's life, a provision common among states at that time. The Supreme Court fashioned a decision that explicitly weighed competing values. The right to obtain an abortion was premised on the notion of a right to privacy. In *Roe*, the Court interpreted the Fourteenth Amendment's guarantee of personal liberty to include a right to privacy that "is broad enough to encompass a woman's decision whether or not to terminate her pregnancy."

This right to privacy is not absolute, but must be tempered by opposing state concerns. One of these is to protect the health of the woman and the other is a concern for the unborn. The *Roe* decision sidesteps the difficult question of when life begins, but it does recognize that the controlling

concern can change during the course of a pregnancy. Since mortality rates for women who have abortions soon after conception are lower than for women who give birth, the woman's right to an abortion is supreme during the first trimester. During the second trimester, the state may establish some standards, such as allowing abortions only in hospitals. During the last trimester, abortions can be prohibited except to protect the mother's life or health.

Subsequent decisions have invalidated state laws that require married women to obtain the approval of their husbands and minors to get their parent's permission before having an abortion.[58] A state may, however, require that a minor tell her parents that she is pregnant before getting an abortion since the parents may be able to provide valuable background information to the physician.[59] The Utah law that required that the parents of a minor be notified did not allow the parents to prevent the abortion.

Right-to-life advocates have sought to reverse *Roe* by getting changes through Congress. One proposal has been to amend the Constitution to prohibit abortions except to protect the life of the mother. Amending the Constitution is neither easy nor quick since extraordinary majorities are required in both houses of Congress and among the states. A speedier technique for reducing the number of abortions has been to deny public funds for this use. Administrators of the Medicaid program were willing to use federal funds to pay for abortions for women on welfare. Since 1976, however, Congress has amended appropriations acts to prohibit the use of federal money for most abortions.[60] These are known as the Hyde Amendments, after Rep. Henry Hyde (R-Ill.), the sponsor. The impact of limiting federal money for abortions is quite significant, since before these restrictions were imposed, several hundred thousand poor women had availed themselves of this program. The poor can still obtain abortions, but except in a handful of states where state aid is available, they must pay for the procedure using their own limited resources.

Pro-choice supporters have pointed out that denying federal assistance will not keep all poor women who want an abortion from obtaining one. A woman who cannot afford to have the procedure performed in a hospital or clinic may seek out an illegal abortionist where she will run a much higher risk of infection and complications.

Alternatively, if unable to procure an abortion, an unwanted child may be brought into the world by a mother who cannot afford it. Such children may become a burden on the state, drawing Aid to Families with Dependent Children, Food Stamps, and Medicaid while living in public housing and eating free breakfasts and lunches in school.

Since the annual Hyde Amendments do nothing to keep those who can afford abortions from getting them, right-to-life groups have adopted a new approach. They are supporting legislation that would pinpoint the moment of conception as the time when life begins. Should this legislation be adopted and then found to be constitutional by the Supreme Court, all abortions would be illegal and the persons who performed them would be considered murderers.

RIGHTS OF CRIMINAL DEFENDANTS

The level of concern at the end of the eighteenth century for the rights of those charged with crimes is indicated by the fact that four of the ten amendments in the Bill of Rights address this topic. The scope of the protections incorporated into the Bill of Rights was limited, however, to infringements by the federal government. Defendants charged with violations of state laws or local ordinances were entitled only to such protections as the laws of their state and its constitution provided.

Since the 1930s, a steady stream of cases filed by convicts has come to the Supreme Court. Basically these suits have been of two types. One type of case has asked the Supreme Court to extend the rights enjoyed by defendants charged with violating federal law to those charged with breaking state or local laws. The potential impact of extending federal constitutional protections to state trials is great—for every federal criminal prosecution there are approximately 100 state prosecutions.

In the other type of case, defendants have asked the court to more broadly interpret the protections included in the Bill of Rights. The Warren Court (1953–1969) frequently expanded the rights of criminal defendants in both directions. The Burger Court (since 1969) has on a number of occasions narrowed the application of decisions rendered by its predecessor, although it has not yet explicitly overturned any of the more expansive Warren Court doctrines.

In the area of the rights of criminal defendants, as with the First Amendment freedoms, the courts try to balance competing values. The notion that confession is good for the soul and therefore the police should be allowed to pressure suspects into confessing has few adherents in modern America. We look negatively at the kangaroo courts, unrestrained secret police, and torture chambers of authoritarian regimes. We accept the idea that a person is entitled to a fair trial. It is generally agreed that defendants have a right to confront their accusers, to subpoena witnesses on their own behalf, to have an impartial judge or jury, and to have a trial held in open court.

Despite general support for these protections in our criminal justice system, there has been disagreement over some other features. Some judges (including Chief Justice Warren Burger) and many people in the general public believe that some current interpretations of the Bill of Rights harm law-abiding citizens by making it too difficult to obtain convictions. Many critics believe the Supreme Court has gone too far in overturning convictions because of what they consider to be legal technicalities. There is a widespread perception that the Supreme Court has so redefined the rights of suspects that it interferes with the work of the police. Moreover, the protections of suspects' rights that have been required by the Supreme Court have contributed to a more general impression that the courts are too lax when dealing with criminals (See Table 16.1). This has given credibility to the stories we have all heard about suspects who were out of jail before their victims were out of the hospital.

The perception that the rights of suspects have been given precedence over the rights of citizens to be secure against attack and burglary impairs respect for the courts and the political system. Ultimately, if enough people come to doubt that the legal system is effective, mob rule can result. If the courts are seen as releasing the guilty rather than punishing them, victims and their friends may resort to self-help. In the context of the justice system, self-help means personal vengeance, vigilante justice, and lynch law.

The extension of federal protections to defendants charged with violating state statutes has been accomplished under the due process clause of the Fourteenth Amendment. Before this Amendment was ratified, the Supreme Court had ruled that the Bill of Rights applied only to the federal gov-

TABLE 16.1

Attitudes about the Treatment of Criminals by the Courts (in percentages)

Question: "Do courts deal too harshly or not harshly enough with criminals?"

	Not Enough	Right	Too Harsh	No Opinion
1965	48	34	2	16
1968	63	19	2	16
1969	75	13	2	10
1973	74	13	5	8

SOURCE: George H. Gallup, *The Gallup Poll* (Wilmington: Scholarly Resources, Inc., 1972, 1978).

ernment. The Supreme Court has interpreted the Amendment's prohibition ''nor shall any State deprive any person of life, liberty, or property, without due process of law'' to mean that certain minimum standards of fairness must be met in all trials. When these minimum protections are not extended to defendants, the conviction will be overturned. The state can prosecute the defendant again, but it must first institute whatever changes are necessary to bring its procedures into line with constitutionally guaranteed rights.

The conclusion that the due process clause requires adherence to certain procedures in state trials has come incrementally. Indeed, it was more than half a century after the ratification of the Fourteenth Amendment before the Supreme Court first determined that the due process clause applied to defendants in state criminal trials. Gradually the requirements stemming from this constitutional provision have been expanded. The protections that have come to be required are those that the Bill of Rights made applicable to federal prosecutions almost two centuries ago. The number of items spelled out in the Bill of Rights that must now be followed in state prosecutions has been expanded to include all the major protections enjoyed by the defendants in federal cases.

Right to Counsel

The right to be represented at a trial by an attorney used to be a much narrower guarantee than it is today. As conceived at the time of the Bill of Rights, this provision insured that a defendant could hire an attorney for a trial. Those who could not afford professional counsel were left on their own to do the best they could. The meaning of this guarantee has been substantially enlarged

for federal prosecutions and subsequently applied to state trials.

The first of the state right-to-counsel cases was a highly publicized trial in Scottsboro, Alabama. A group of illiterate, indigent, black youths were charged with raping two white women who were riding with them on a freight train. The defendants could not afford to hire a lawyer and the trial court judge failed to appoint one, ignoring the provision of Alabama law that called for indigent defendants in rape cases to be furnished with counsel. Recognizing the unfairness of having common citizens confronted by trained prosecutors, the Supreme Court ruled that states must pay for lawyers to represent impoverished defendants in capital cases.[61]

In 1938, the right of an indigent to have an attorney provided was expanded to include all federal criminal prosecutions.[62] A quarter of a century later, this interpretation of the Sixth Amendment guarantee was extended to require that an attorney be provided for any person charged with a felony in a state court, not just those facing possible execution.[63] More recently, right to counsel at public expense has been applied to misdemeanor cases that could result in the defendant receiving a jail sentence.[64] The state need not provide an attorney in misdemeanor cases where no imprisonment is possible, even though there may be a penalty.[65] Thus, a consideration in whether the state must provide an attorney is the severity of the possible punishment.

The right to have a lawyer present is not restricted to the trial. Those who are suspected of crimes are entitled to have an attorney present when they are being questioned by the police. In one case, the conviction of a child murderer on the basis of incriminating statements made to police when they were transporting the defendant by car was overturned.[66] The defendant revealed where the victim's body lay after police officers played upon his conscience by pointing out the need to give the child a decent burial. This confession could not be used in court because it was given in the absence of the defendant's attorney.

The right-to-counsel provision currently means, then, that a defendant is entitled to legal representation during the essential parts of the adversary process from the initial questioning on through an appeal. Anyone who cannot afford a lawyer will be provided with one free of charge.

Failure by state or federal officials to honor these rights provides grounds for overturning the conviction. If the overturned conviction rested in part on a confession made when counsel was not present, it cannot be used in the second trial.

Self-Incrimination

The prohibition against *self-incrimination—testimony given by a person against himself or herself*—in the Fifth Amendment was designed to protect those charged with crimes from being tortured into admitting guilt. Self-incriminating testimony is excluded from trials.

Initially, this protection was applicable only to federal prosecutions. It was first used in state trials to throw out confessions when it was clear they were not given voluntarily. For example, a conviction was overturned because the confession was obtained by beating the suspect.[67] Other state cases reversed by the Supreme Court during the 1940s involved threats of violence, continuous questioning by teams of police, and psychological pressures. Another line of cases excluded the testimony of defendants under such ''special circumstances'' as mental deficiency or illiteracy.

In *Miranda* v. *Arizona*, the Supreme Court used the protection against self-incrimination to establish warning procedures for suspects.[68] On the rationale that being arrested and interrogated mobilizes coercive pressures against a person, the Court sought to insure that whatever a suspect told police was conveyed with full knowledge of the possible consequences. The *Miranda* decision was based on an extension of the earlier notion that involuntary admissions of guilt should not be used to convict a defendant. Chief Justice Warren, writing for the Court, explained that

> it is obvious that such an interrogation environment is created for no purpose other than to subjugate the individual to the will of the examiner. This atmosphere carries its own badge of intimidation. . . . The circumstances surrounding in-custody interrogation can operate very quickly to overbear the will of one merely made aware of his privilege [to have an attorney present] by his interrogators. Therefore, the right to have counsel present at the interrogation is indispensable to the protection of the Fifth Amendment privilege under the system we delineate today.

For interrogations to be free of the taint of involuntary self-incrimination, a number of safeguards were imposed. Prior to any interrogation, suspects must be warned as follows:

> You have the right to remain silent. Anything you say can and will be used against you in a court of law. You have the right to talk to a lawyer and have him present with you while you are being questioned. If you cannot afford to hire a lawyer, one will be appointed to represent you before any questioning, if you wish. You can decide at any time to stop the questioning and not answer any questions or make any statements.

Anyone who has watched a cops and robbers show on television has heard the *Miranda* warning given suspects when they are arrested.

Under *Miranda*, the prosecution has the burden

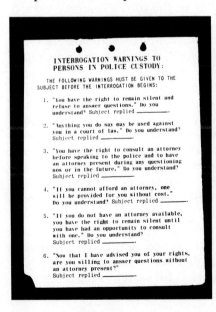

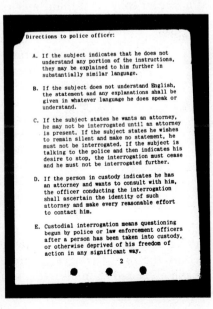

In *Miranda* v. *Arizona*, the Supreme Court ruled that prior to any interrogation, a suspect must be informed of certain rights to protect him or her from involuntary self-incrimination.

of proving that any confession made by a suspect without an attorney present was given after the defendant knowingly waived the rights provided for in this decision. Therefore, a person who has been arrested can agree to talk to police and even confess without having an attorney present—and many people charged with crimes still do this.

If a defendant's *Miranda* rights are violated, then a conviction based on the confession will be reversed on appeal. The prosecution can retry the case, but it must use something other than the defendant's confession.

Police have been highly critical of *Miranda*. Many of them would like to see the self-incrimination protection restricted to instances in which physical or psychological coercion were used to extract confessions. They contend that because of procedural errors, which they would categorize as trivial, the convictions of guilty parties have been set aside. These claims have coincided with popular perceptions that Supreme Court decisions have tied the hands of the police.

In response to this kind of criticism, the Burger Court has limited *Miranda*. If a defendant who has voluntarily confessed in the absence of *Miranda* warnings retracts that statement and offers a different version of what happened at the trial, the prosecutor can introduce the earlier confession to impeach the later statements.[69] This use of the confession is permitted even though the confession could not otherwise be introduced as evidence.

In evaluating the acceptability of confessions, the Supreme Court has now added a second consideration to the earlier concern about voluntariness. The majority of the Court has held that

> *when involuntary statements or the right against compulsory self-incrimination are involved, a second justification for the exclusionary rule has also been asserted—protection of the courts from reliance on untrustworthy evidence. . . . We find the arguments in favor of admitting the testimony quite strong. For, when balancing the interests involved, we must weight the strong interest under any system of justice of making available to the hearer of fact all concededly relevant and trustworthy evidence which either party seeks to adduce.[70]*

Despite the controversy surrounding *Miranda*, the decision has not been overturned by the conservative Burger Court. Officers are still obligated to inform defendants of their rights at the time of an arrest. However, the scope of the *Miranda* protection has been narrowed as the Court has identified conditions under which an improperly obtained confession can nonetheless be used. *Miranda* is not an absolute prohibition of the use of incriminating evidence.

The protection against self-incrimination applies to both oral testimony and to personal records that a person has in his or her possession. It does not apply to tax or bank records held by someone else, such as an accountant. Nor can the protection be claimed if the government waives its right to prosecute. That testimony might be embarassing is an insufficient excuse if the prosecutor grants immunity from prosecution. Failure to testify once immunity has been granted is punishable by fines and imprisonment for contempt of court.

Search and Seizure   The Fourth Amendment prohibits unreasonable searches by law enforcement officers. If the police have a search warrant, they can carry out the search the warrant provides for even if the owner or occupant of the property objects. Warrants are issued by magistrates or judges if they conclude that "probable cause" exists. That means that the police must explain not only what they plan to look for but also why they think it is on the premises they want to search.

Grossman and Wells identify five conditions in which searches can be legally carried out in the absence of a warrant.[71] First, a person who agrees to allow the police to search a home or business cannot later object to the use of evidence turned up in the search. A second exception allows police to search an individual who is being arrested and the area immediately surrounding the individual. In the absence of a warrant, however, it is improper to search the entire building in which an arrest is made. Third, no warrant is needed if the evidence is clearly visible so that no searching needs to be done. A fourth exception allows warrantless searches under what the courts call "exigent (urgent) circumstances." Police need not break off chasing a suspect in order to obtain a warrant. Nor do they need to stand by and merely observe a suspicious character and wait for a crime to be committed. Instead, police are authorized to carry out limited stop and frisk procedures to protect themselves and the public. Finally, the authority to search an automobile without a warrant is broader than the authority to search a building. The Fourth Amendment, then, is not an absolute prohibition—it guards citizens from *unreasonable* searches by authorities.

The penalty for conducting unreasonable searches is similar to that imposed when a confession has been improperly obtained. Under the *exclusionary rule, improperly seized evidence is excluded from a trial and a conviction based on the use of this evidence is thrown out.* This rule has applied to federal proceedings since 1914.[72]

The Fourth Amendment protection was extended to cover state prosecutions in *Mapp* v. *Ohio.*[73] Using the same standards in state and federal court when determining the admissibility of evidence eliminated one type of problem. Federal authorities could no longer take evidence improperly seized and therefore inadmissible in a federal trial and turn it over to local prosecutors, nor could federal attorneys use evidence illegally seized by state or local authorities.

Police have argued that when they turn up contraband, drugs, or weapons used to commit crimes, this clear evidence of a defendant's wrongdoing should not be kept from the jury because of what they perceive to be a technicality. The Burger Court has, over the years, narrowed the impact of the *Mapp* decision by upholding the legality of various searches. For example, searches without warrants or probable cause at permanent checkpoints several miles from the Mexican border have been upheld. Materials seized using

vague warrants for items "at this [time] unknown" have been admitted as evidence.[74] Likewise, the Court has ruled that random boarding of boats by law enforcement officials along waterways with easy access to the open seas does not violate the privacy rights of boat owners. This 1983 ruling was aimed at curtailing drug smuggling.

Operating from this perspective, the Court has concluded that little additional deterrence results from having federal courts review state court decisions on Fourth Amendment questions. Therefore, if a state court rejects a defendant's request that evidence be excluded, the federal courts will no longer second-guess the state court decision on the constitutionality of the search. A number of liberals worry that state courts may apply less rigorous standards when confronted with questions about the propriety of searches.

The application of the exclusionary rule to unreasonable searches has frequently prompted critics to raise the question asked by Justice Cardozo more than a half-century ago: "Is the criminal to go free because the constable has blundered?"[75] Those who oppose exclusion think that the right of suspects to be secure from searches not supported by a warrant should be subordinant to the responsibility of police to apprehend and punish lawbreakers. Critics go on to point out that excluding improperly obtained evidence neither helps the victim of the crime nor punishes the police officers who violated the Fourth Amendment.

Searches without warrants or probable cause around border areas have been upheld by the Supreme Court.

The sole effect may be to release someone because of the illegally seized evidence that the police know is guilty.

One's home is still protected from a search unless it is authorized by a warrant or conditions exist that make obtaining a warrant impractical. In striking down the laws of 23 states that permitted police to enter a person's home without a warrant to make a felony arrest, Justice John Paul Stevens wrote that, "It is a 'basic principle of Fourth Amendment law' that searches and seizures inside a home without a warrant are presumptively unreasonable."[76] Such protections apply with much less force to public places.

Wiretaps The courts and Congress have dealt with the legality of wiretaps of telephone conversations as an aspect of the Fourth Amendment prohibition on illegal searches. Initially, the Supreme Court did not exclude evidence gained through a wiretap since the conversations could be recorded without trespassing on the defendant's property.[77] Congress prohibited wiretapping in 1934, but on the eve of World War II, President Franklin Roosevelt authorized wiretaps in the interest of national security. Congress has subsequently provided that wiretapping and electronic surveillance can be used in investigations of organized crime. Wiretaps on conversations of American citizens can be conducted legally only if authorized by a warrant. As with searches, warrants are issued if the police can show that probable cause exists. Evidence obtained through an illegal wiretap cannot be used in a trial. These standards apply at the state as well as the federal level.

The states conduct far more wiretaps than do federal authorities. The most common type of offense for which wiretaps are used is gambling. Drug cases are a distant second.

Death Penalty An eye for an eye, a tooth for a tooth, a life for a life. This notion of justice has a long Judeo-Christian heritage. Approximately two-thirds of the states have had statutes prescribing execution as the penalty for certain crimes. In 1972 the Supreme Court ruled in *Furman* v. *Georgia* that such legislation was unconstitutional, not necessarily because it was a violation of the Eighth Amendment prohibition against cruel and unusual punishment, but because of the arbitrary way the penalty was exacted.[78] The death penalty was disproportionately imposed on the poor and the black—those least able to obtain expensive legal representation.

Since 1975 the Supreme Court has reviewed a number of states' post-*Furman* death penalty statutes. Beginning with *Gregg* v. *Georgia,*[79] the Court has been willing to condone the death penalty under some circumstances. The Georgia statute provided for a separate sentencing decision following a conviction. After reaching a decision on sentencing, a jury could impose the death penalty only for one of ten specified aggravating circumstances. In addition, Georgia law stipulates that the death penalty can be imposed only if the jury further concludes that none of five mitigating circumstances accompanied the act (see Table 16.2). The Court believed it was important that the death penalty statute provide guidance to juries when they contemplated imposing the death sentence to prevent the randomness and arbitrariness characteristic of the application of pre-*Furman* statutes.

In *Gregg* the Supreme Court noted that the death penalty was appropriate for a murder "outrageously or wantonly vile, horrible, or inhuman in that it involved torture, depravity of mind, or an aggravated battery to the victim." The Court further held that "in part, capital punishment is an expression of society's moral outrage at particularly offensive conduct. This function may be unappealing to many, but it is essential in an ordered society that asks its citizens to rely on legal processes rather than self-help to vindicate their wrongs."

In acknowledging a societal benefit produced by exacting the ultimate penalty, the Court rejected opponents' argument that the death penalty has no value as a deterrent. The Court's response to this contention was that studies of deterrence "simply have been inconclusive."

In reviewing post-*Furman* death penalty statutes, the Supreme Court has rejected the argument that executions violate the Eighth Amendment's prohibition of cruel and unusual punishment, pointing out that more than two-thirds of the states enacted new death penalty statutes after *Furman* declared existing statutes unconstitutional. Congress also imposed the death penalty for acts of air piracy in which someone is killed. In California the death penalty was approved in a referendum. The decision of the California voters coincides with the preferences of at

TABLE 16.2

Aggravating and Mitigating Factors to be Considered by Georgia Juries When Imposing the Death Penalty

Aggravating Factors	Mitigating Factors—Applicable to All Covered Offenses: Murder, Treason, and Espionage
A. Treason and Espionage 1. Defendant has been convicted of another such offense, for which a sentence of death or life imprisonment was authorized. 2. Defendant created grave risk of substantial danger to the national security. 3. Defendant created grave risk of death to another person. **B. Murder** 1. The death, or injury resulting in death, occurs during the commission, or flight from eight specified offenses: escape, espionage, three explosive offenses involving personal injury or property damage, kidnapping, treason, and aircraft hijacking. 2. Conviction of another offense, either state or federal, for which the sentence of death or life imprisonment was authorized by statute. 3. Previous conviction of two or more separate offenses involving serious bodily harm. 4. Defendant created grave risk of death to another person in addition to the victim. 5. Crime was committed in an especially heinous, cruel, or depraved manner. 6. Defendant paid for the crime to be committed. 7. Defendant was paid to commit the crime. 8. The victim was the president, vice-president, or another listed government official.	1. Defendant was under the age of eighteen at the time of the commission of the offense. 2. Defendant's mental capacity was significantly impaired. 3. Defendant acted under unusual and substantial duress. 4. Defendant had a relatively minor part in the crime in which the killing was committed by another participant. 5. The defendant could not reasonably have foreseen that his conduct would cause or create a great risk of causing death.

SOURCE: Joel B. Grossman and Richard S. Wells, *Constitutional Law and Judicial Policy Making*, 2nd ed. (New York: Wiley, 1980), p. 945.

least a plurality of Americans as indicated by public opinion surveys (see Table 16.3).

The Court has struck down statutes that make the death penalty mandatory for specified types of murder.[80] Juries must be given some discretion in imposing the death penalty when there are mitigating circumstances, but they should also be given some guidance such as the Georgia law provides. Another limitation on the death penalty is that it must not be disproportionate to the crime for which it is imposed. Therefore the state can take the life of a murderer but not a rapist.[81]

There are now, as there were before *Furman,* hundreds of inmates on death rows across the country. The execution of Gary Gilmore by a Utah firing squad in 1977 has not signaled the start of the blood bath some observers anticipated. Instead, both state and federal judges have been

TABLE 16.3

Attitudes on Capital Punishment (in percentages)

	Favor	Undecided	Don't Favor
1957	47	3	50
1960	51	13	36
1965	45	12	43
1966	42	11	47
1972	50	9	41
1974	64	—	36
1976	65	7	28

SOURCE: George H. Gallup, *The Gallup Poll* (Wilmington: Scholarly Resources, Inc., 1972, 1978).

careful to allow appeals so that arguments that might save a defendant's life can be considered. In fact, some conservatives have criticized the seemingly unending set of procedural hurdles that must be cleared before a death sentence can be carried out. In 1983 the Supreme Court addressed the delay issue and ruled that federal appeals courts may speed up the process of handling last-minute requests for delays in the executions of death row inmates as long as the merits of the legal arguments raised by those inmates have been considered.

Juvenile Justice At the turn of the century, reformers removed juveniles charged with crimes from the process used for adults. The role of the judge in a juvenile proceeding was to be more like that of parent. The judge was to gather as much information as possible before making a decision that would be in the best interest of the child. The justice system was to function as a forgiving parent and the youngster who ran afoul of the law was to be given a fresh chance upon coming of age. Young offenders' names were kept out of the press and the records concerning their misdeeds were kept secret.

However, as is often the case when society's values change, the bold ideas of yesterday's reformers are now regarded by some as outmoded and undesirable. This has been the fate of the juvenile court reforms. The Supreme Court has decided that the informality of the juvenile justice process does not provide defendants with necessary due process protections. Under the old reform system youthful offenders did not have to be indicted by a grand jury, were not entitled to representation by an attorney, had no right to confront witnesses against them, and had no appeal from the decision.

The key case in this area, *In re Gault,*[82] made it clear that the outcome of the juvenile process could be harsher than that of the adult criminal justice sytem. The defendant was sent to a reform school for as long as six years for making an obscene telephone call. The maximum penalty for an adult was a two-month sentence and a 50-dollar fine.

The Supreme Court has since concluded that constitutional protections must be extended to juveniles, observing that "under our Constitution, the condition of being a boy does not justify a kangaroo court." Therefore, in

proceedings to determine delinquency which may result in commitment to an institution in which the juvenile's freedom is curtailed, the child and his parent must be notified of the child's right to be represented by counsel retained by them, or if they are unable to afford counsel, that counsel will be appointed to represent the child.

The execution of Utah death row inmate Gary Gilmore in 1977 following the Supreme Court's ruling that executions do not violate the Eighth Amendment's prohibition of cruel and unusual punishment, did not bring about a vast number of executions because of the lengthy appeals process. In 1983, the Court ruled that such appeals could be speeded up as long as the merits of the legal arguments raised by the inmate are considered.

The *Gault* decision also required that *Miranda*-like warnings be given youthful suspects to protect them from self-incrimination.

Other Issues in Criminal Rights The application to the states of protections incorporated in the Bill of Rights has not been made complete. Some procedures can be followed in state criminal trials that would be unacceptable at the federal level. The concept of "fair trial" determines whether a protection applies to state procedures. If the Supreme Court decides that defendants can receive a fair trial despite state procedure being at variance with federal procedure, then the differences can remain. For example, state juries need have no more than 6 members—compared to 12 for federal juries—but unanimity is required of smaller juries. Nor is it necessary that defendants in state trials be indicted by a grand jury. Such practices do not deny a defendant due process.

As the discussion of search and seizure, self-incrimination, and right to counsel cases indicates, the Court has substantially expanded its definition of what is encompassed by the due process clause of the Fourteenth Amendment. This gradual expansion process was predicted by Justice Felix Frankfurter more than three decades ago.

> [D]ue process, unlike some legal rules, is not a technical conception with a fixed content unrelated to time, place, and circumstances. Expressing as it does . . . respect enforced by law for that feeling of just treatment which has been evolved through centuries of Anglo-American constitutional history and civilization, 'due process' cannot be imprisoned within the treacherous limits of any formula.[83]

It is certainly possible that a newly constituted majority may, at some time, ban capital punishment or require that state trial courts have 12 members.

An alternative future, one that seems more likely given the current makeup of the Supreme Court, would be a narrower interpretation of the requirements of due process. The flexibility to which Frankfurter refers need not provide a one-way street to ever greater protection for defendants in criminal cases. As has been shown in this section, the Burger Court has set limits to the requirements of *Miranda* and *Mapp* that some people see as reducing the due process guarantees established by the Warren Court.

SUMMARY

A major concern of the state legislators asked to approve the Constitution drafted in 1787 was the lack of limitations on governmental power. To secure ratification, supporters of the new Constitution agreed to add a set of amendments that have come to be known as the Bill of Rights. The main thrust of these first ten amendments has been to secure civil liberties for the American public.

Among these civil liberties, the most important in the early 1980s are:

1. freedom of expression.
2. freedom of assembly.
3. freedom of religion.
4. the right to a fair trial.
5. a woman's right to control her body.

The scope of the protections provided by the Bill of Rights has changed substantially over time. The changes have been of two types. First, these protections, which were initially designed to limit the federal government, have gradually been applied to the states. One by one, most of the terms of the Bill of Rights have been held to be applicable to state activities under the due process clause of the Fourteenth Amendment.

Second, the scope of the guarantees have been broadened. The Supreme Court—especially during the years when Earl Warren was chief justice—has interpreted the unchanging words as establishing new rights. In the last couple of decades, for example, the Court has determined that women have a right to an abortion under certain circumstances, that some capital punishment statutes are unconstitutional, and that school prayers are inappropriate.

As the Supreme Court has gone about defining the civil liberties protected by the Constitution, it has usually been confronted with conflicting values. Indeed, both parties to a case often base their positions on a claimed constitutional right. In sorting through these claims, the Court has rarely recognized a right as being absolute. Instead, a variety of balancing procedures have been developed. The standards used by the Courts have usually been imprecise; when a series of decisions are reviewed across time, it may appear that the Supreme Court has behaved inconsistently. In reality, it has adapted to the changing needs of society.

KEY TERMS

absolutist approach
balancing test
Bill of Rights
clear and present danger
common law
exclusionary rule
preferred position
prior restraint
self-incrimination
shield laws

SUGGESTED READINGS

Cushman, Robert F. *Leading Constitutional Decisions.* 16th ed. Englewood Cliffs, N.J.: Prentice-Hall, 1982.

Dolbeare, Kenneth M., and Hammond, Phillip E. *The School Prayer Decisions.* Chicago: University of Chicago Press, 1971.

Goldman, Sheldon. *Constitutional Law and Supreme Court Decision-Making Cases and Essays.* New York: Harper and Row, 1982.

Grossman, Joel B., and Wells, Richard S. *Constitutional Law & Judicial Policy Making.* 2nd ed. New York: John Wiley & Sons, 1972.

Lewis, Anthony. *Gideon's Trumpet.* New York: Vintage Books, 1964.

Milner, Neal A. *The Court and Local Law Enforcement.* Calif.: Sage Publications, 1971.

Muir, William K., Jr. *Prayer in the Public Schools.* Chicago: University of Chicago Press, 1967.

Woodward, Bob, and Armstrong, Scott. *The Brethren.* New York: Simon & Schuster, 1979.

CHAPTER 17

THE BUDGET: THE GOVERNMENT'S MOST IMPORTANT POLICY DECISION

The Budget's Importance ■ What's Different About Government Budget? ■ The Shape of the United States Budget ■ Revenue: The Government's Income ■ The Expenditure Side of the Budget ■ When Expenditures Exceed Revenues: Deficits and Debt ■ The Budgetary Process: Playing a High-stakes Game ■ Politics, the Economy, and Lifestyle

A *budget* is a plan for meeting program goals that explains how much money is needed and how it will be spent over a given time period. A government needs a budget just as an individual or business does. A budget is also a management tool. Setting taxing, spending, and borrowing limits is a way to make government and its agencies accountable to the citizenry. It helps ensure that the government spends the taxpayers' money in the public interest.

Because it shows how government spends money, a budget is a statement of the nation's policy priorities—what the government considers most important. Indeed, formulating the budget is the most important policy decision government can make. This chapter will show you, the taxpayer, how this policy decision is made.

THE BUDGET'S IMPORTANCE

Budgeting serves different purposes for different people.

For an accountant, it is a means of tracking government finances; for an economist, it is a means of manipulating revenue and expenditures to influence the production of goods and services. A political scientist's budget is one in which some people pay so that others may benefit; a public administrator's budget is a source of funding for government agencies and programs.[1]

For most interest groups, the budget identifies who are the winners and losers in the mad scramble for funding for programs, services, and facilities. To some citizens, the budget (and the policy priorities set by it) is evidence that elected officials are doing what's right. For others, the budget may be proof that government is wasteful, inefficient, or unresponsive to the people's needs.

Regardless of how one views the budget, few would disagree that governmental decisions on the budget are the heart of the policymaking process. This holds true whether one is talking about the national budget or the budgets of state and local governments. The mayor of Minneapolis once described budgeting as "the World Series of government."[2]

Taxing and spending decisions are often highly political and extremely controversial. Because choices must be made among multitudes of different programs, competition is keen. ''The budgetary process is a political process conducted in the political arena for political advantage,'' says Thomas Lynch in *Public Budgeting in America.*[3] Deciding which activities to allocate money to is difficult. Such decisions are influenced as much or more by political variables as by economic variables.

Of course, to spend money, one must have the money to spend. Thus, the budget has two sides—a revenue side and an expenditure side. Public budgeting involves selecting expenditure priorities and the means of reaching them (ways to raise revenues). A *deficit* *occurs when expenditures exceed revenues,* as is often the case with the national government and some state and local governments. As we shall see, governments, like individuals, often have to borrow money to make ends meet. Government borrowing, deficits, and the national debt have historically been controversial topics splitting along political and ideological lines.

Changes in the nation's budget closely mirror changes in the country's demographic, social, economic, ideological, and political characteristics. Lance LeLoup has described the phenomenon:

> *A budget tells much about a nation: its health, wealth, problems, and priorities. It reveals the size of the public sector compared with the private sector and degree of government control of the economy. It reveals the proportion of national resources devoted to defense and to human resources. It reveals a set of social choices developed over a period of many years. It reveals national policies on food stamps, nuclear power plants, space probes, and tax loopholes.*[4]

The importance of budgets to a nation cannot be overstated. More than 200 years ago, Alexander Hamilton, in *The Federalist* papers, referred to money as the vital principle of politics.[5] This assessment holds true today. As one contemporary scholar notes, ''The money trail [the budget] provides the most reliable, most direct, path to the nerve centers in government and politics.''[6]

WHAT'S DIFFERENT ABOUT GOVERNMENT BUDGETS?

Individuals, businesses, and governments all budget time, dollars, energy, and other resources, each for the same reason. Drawing up a budget

and sticking to it can help one control one's affairs or put one's household, business, or government in order. But government budgeting differs from private budgeting in a number of ways:

1. the amount of resources available
2. motives
3. measurement of success
4. consumption of goods produced
5. expected returns on investments
6. control of the economy
7. decision-making structure.[7]

Amount of Resources Available

Governments have much greater resources (income) than individuals and corporations. Government technically can tap all resources in a society, even though the United States government does not. For example, the government could tax one's total earnings instead of allowing deductions for certain expenditures. Compared to individuals and businesses, government certainly has a wide range of revenue sources to use if it chooses. Of course, government has to serve more people and a wider range of needs.

Motives

The primary motive of individuals and industry is to make a profit. If a product does not yield a profit, the company that manufactures it will stop producing it. The primary role of government, however, is to promote and protect the general

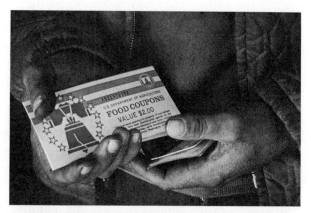

One of the roles of our government is to promote and protect the general welfare of all people. Consequently, government provides some programs, such as food stamps, to those who need them but cannot help pay for them.

State-owned liquor stores are one type of government activity that can produce a profit. These profits help pay for services the state provides that are unprofitable, such as social welfare programs.

welfare of all people, regardless of whether all can pay for its services. Consequently, government must provide a number of services and programs that never produce a profit. Some government programs exist to serve those who simply do not have enough money for food, clothing, housing, and health care.

Of course, other programs or activities can produce a profit, such as sale of alcoholic beverages by state-owned liquor stores or sale of electricity by government-owned utility companies. These profits help pay for the unprofitable services the government must provide. When governments end up with huge surpluses, however, taxpayers are quick to criticize them for collecting more than they need. As a result, governments often spend surpluses, rather than reduce taxes because it is too politically difficult to raise them again. And taxpayers often forget that governments, too, need to save "for a rainy day."

Measurement of Success

Private companies are judged largely in terms of dollars and cents—their net financial gain at the end of a fiscal year. A *fiscal year is a yearly accounting period; it does not necessarily coincide with the calendar year.* Governments provide many programs whose value cannot be measured in dollar costs and dollar returns. As we saw in chapter 13 (The Bureaucracy), it is almost impossible to conduct meaningful cost-benefit analyses on many government activities. "There is no ready means of comparing the net value of a life saved through cancer research and one enemy death on the battlefield; these units simply cannot be equated," note Robert Lee and Ronald Johnson.[8]

Consumption of Goods Produced

Goods produced by the private sector are generally for a narrow segment of the population, while government-produced goods are largely for society as a whole. The Ford Motor Company's cars are used only by the persons buying the cars. The Defense Department intercontinental ballistic missile system, on the other hand, is "consumed" by everyone. These sorts of goods or services are called *public*, or *collective*, *goods*—*their benefits are shared by everyone.* Public goods cannot be denied to anyone merely because he or she refuses to pay for them. The city fire department cannot decide to let some houses burn because their occupants have not paid their property tax. The problem created by public goods is one of pricing. If Ford's cars don't sell, the company can lower the price, give out rebates, or try other measures. But if taxpayers revolt because they think taxes are too high for the services they are getting, how can a government determine which services taxpayers think are too costly in relation to the benefits received? "Without the pricing mechanism, consumer preferences, as expressed by the public's willingness to purchase goods and services, are not identifiable."[9]

Expected Returns on Investments

Individuals and businesses generally expect their investments to be efficient. In other words, they expect to get back at least a dollar's worth of goods or services for every dollar spent. Governments, in contrast, often spend money on goods and services such as work incentive payments that will directly aid the recipients but only indirectly aid the government. The government may recover some money in taxes paid by the individual recipient and benefit from the build-up of human capital, but it does not expect to recover a dollar for every dollar paid out. Thus, governments do not always expect efficient returns on their expenditures. They are often more concerned with **equity**—*getting services to those who are least able to pay for them but most in need of assistance.*

Ability to Control the Economy

An important distinction between government and the private sector is the government's responsibility for controlling the economy. As we saw in chapter 2, government is officially charged with ensuring full employment and continued economic growth. Governmental decisions affect economic conditions that influence corporations.

As we shall see later, the government's economic policymaking falls into two categories: monetary policy and fiscal policy. **Monetary policy** *is designed to promote national economic goals by controlling the amount of money in circulation.* Monetary policy is largely the domain of the Federal Reserve Board. **Fiscal policy** *involves decisions regarding the taxing, spending, and borrowing of the government.* It is the responsibility of the president and the Congress.

Together, monetary and fiscal policymaking affect the nation's employment levels, **gross national product**, or **GNP** *(the monetary value of all goods and services produced)*, the stability of price levels, and the **balance of payments** *(the balance between income and expenditures resulting from trade with foreign nations)*. As far as the economy is concerned, the private sector is at the mercy of the government—although the private sector can and does lobby the government to influence policies.

Decision-making Structures

Budgetary decision-making in the private sector is much more centralized than it is in the government sector. As we saw in chapters 4 (Federalism) and 13 (The Bureaucracy), the fact that our maze of agencies and bureaucracies is highly decentralized along with the intergovernmental nature of government finances make it more difficult for governments to budget. Corporations can stop producing economically unprofitable goods such as Edsels and DeSotos. Governments, however,

have more trouble deciding what programs to begin or end.[10]

It is important to keep these differences between governments and the private sector in mind as you evaluate the taxing, spending, and borrowing activities of the governments that serve you (national, state, city, county, school district, or other special districts). Budgeting in the public sector is clearly somewhat different than budgeting in the private sector, even though the processes are the same in many respects. Because the motives of the two sectors differ, evaluations of the budgeting process are carried out differently as well.

THE SHAPE OF THE UNITED STATES BUDGET

A comparison of the 1980 and 1984 budgets (see Figure 17.1) shows how both sides of the budget have changed in recent years. On the revenue side, reliance upon individual and corporation income taxes declined while reliance upon borrowing and excise taxes increased. (An **income tax** *is a tax on income from all sources*; an **excise tax** *is a tax on the manufacture, transportation, sale, or consumption of goods*.) This change was attributable largely to presidential and congressional reaction to the tax revolt that spread across the nation after passage of California's Proposition 13, which cut state and local taxes for Californians. The cut in income taxes also reflected Reagan's commitment to his economic recovery program. Reagan wished to restore strength and growth to the economy "by reducing the existing tax barriers that discourage work, savings, and investment."[11] Under the Economic Recovery Tax Act of 1981, individual income taxes were cut by 23 percent over a three-year period beginning in October 1981. This tax cut quickly became very controversial when the nation slumped into a recession and the federal deficit grew larger.

On the expenditure side, the biggest proportional cut came in grants to states and localities, which dropped from 16 to 11 percent of all expenditures. This downward trend in grants began in 1978 under Carter, but the rate of cutback was speeded up under Reagan as part of his New Federalism program. As we saw in chapter 4, the New Federalism program was designed to take the federal government out of policy areas such as education, highways, and welfare that had been the re-

California's Proposition 13 tax revolt and similar movements in states across the nation sparked taxing and spending cuts at the national level as well.

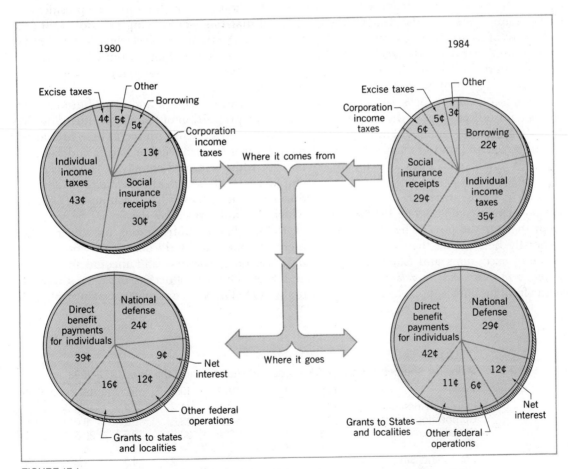

FIGURE 17.1

The Budget Dollar—Where It Comes From and Where It Goes (Fiscal Years 1980 and 1984, Estimated)

sponsibility of state governments in the early days of the nation.

REVENUE: THE GOVERNMENT'S INCOME

Benjamin Franklin once said, "The only two sure things in life are death and taxes." Americans are living longer today, but they are also paying more taxes. The average family in 1980 contributed almost a fourth of its income (22.7 percent) to taxes. This figure almost doubled in the relatively short span of 27 years, and it doesn't include indirect taxes such as those on alcohol, gas, and tobacco.

Taxes as a Revenue Source

The federal tax system relies predominantly on income and payroll taxes. The individual income tax is a tax on income received from salaries, wages, profits, rents, interest, dividends, and other sources. Most of us are acutely aware of this tax, especially around April 15, the deadline for filing an income statement with the Internal Revenue Service (IRS). The income tax has not always been the number-one source of income, however. It was not until passage of the Sixteenth Amendment (1913) that the national government was clearly authorized to impose an income tax. Before the Civil War, customs duties were the primary source of revenue.

The income tax is a *progressive tax*—*it is based on one's ability to pay*. The income tax rate for the rich is higher than that for the poor. The rich, however, are generally better able than the poor to take advantage of exceptions and *loopholes*, *legal deductions permitted in determining taxable income*. Everyone benefits from loopholes, however; the most common one is the standard deduction built into the tax tables.

The corporate income tax is another important federal revenue source. It was enacted in 1909. This is a tax levied on corporations on the basis of their annual net income. The corporate income tax is levied at a flat rate. A lower rate is applied to the first $50,000 as a concession to smaller businesses. This tax is probably the most complicated and controversial federal tax because of the difficulty in determining how to measure net income. Deciding what constitutes legitimate expenses for a corporation is also controversial. For example, should businesses be able to deduct three-martini lunches? The recognition that some of the nation's largest corporations were paying virtually no corporate income taxes led President Reagan to propose that Congress close corporate taxation loopholes, some of which it did. The president estimated that this would bring an additional $7.2 billion into the treasury. Nevertheless, the share of federal revenues that comes from corporate taxes has been shrinking steadily for several decades (see Table 17.1).

Social insurance taxes and contributions make up a large proportion of federal revenue, and they are the fastest growing source. These are largely payroll taxes (taxes levied on wages and salaries), most of which are paid equally by employers and employees. The largest of these taxes is Old-Age, Survivors, and Disability Insurance (OASDI), which was authorized by the Social Security Act of 1935. These contributions provide a retirement income for elderly persons, income for totally disabled workers, and income for spouses and minor children of deceased wage earners. Actually, OASDI is a compulsory savings plan de-

TABLE 17.1

Major Tax Sources of Federal Revenues and Their Share of the Total: 1952–1983

Taxes	1952	1960	1970	1980	1981	1982	1983
Individual Income	42.2%	44.0%	46.9%	47.2%	47.7%	48.3%	47.2%
Corporation Income	32.1	23.2	17.0	12.5	10.2	8.0	6.6
Social Insurance**	9.8	15.9	23.0	30.5	30.5	32.6	35.5
Excise	13.4	12.6	8.1	4.7	6.8	5.9	6.4
Estate and Gift	1.2	1.7	1.9	1.2	1.1	1.3	0.9
Other	1.4	2.5	3.0	3.9	3.7	4.0	3.5

SOURCE: *New York Times*, March 20, 1983; based on data from the Office of Management and Budget.
*Totals may not equal 100 percent due to rounding.
**Includes Social Security, Me

signed to provide for an increasingly aging population. One problem with this tax, as we have seen in earlier chapters, is that fewer young workers are paying in while a larger number of retirees are drawing out. Also, funds have not been invested wisely, so Social Security taxes must constantly be increased.

Another type of social insurance tax is unemployment insurance, which was also authorized by the Social Security Act of 1935. This is a tax on the payroll of employers of four or more workers; if the employees lose their jobs, they receive some form of payment from the government. The Department of the Treasury holds the funds, but it is up to each state to determine the amount to be paid to unemployed persons in their states, for how long, and under what conditions.

In general, payroll taxes are earmarked to pay for the nation's income security programs and are placed in separate trust funds. Unlike income tax revenue, which can be spent for virtually any function, payroll taxes support direct payments to individuals for retirement and unemployment.

Excise taxes on the manufacture, transportation, sale, or consumption of goods are one of the oldest sources of federal revenue guaranteed under the Constitution. Immediately after the Constitution was ratified, Congress placed excise taxes on carriages, liquor, snuff, sugar, and auction sales. The most common excise taxes levied today are those on tobacco, liquor, cars, gasoline, telephone calls, telegrams, airports, airline tickets, and oil earnings.

Customs duties, which are levied on imports, are another of the oldest revenue sources. But as of 1980, they provided only about 1 percent of all federal revenue. Other common tax sources are estate and gift taxes. These are, in effect, taxes on the transfer of wealth such as land, stocks, bonds, and mortgages.

The only new tax of any significance is the windfall profits tax, a type of excise tax created by Congress in 1980 after deregulation of crude oil. But most of the federal tax system originated earlier in this century. Our current big revenue-producing taxes and the dates they were first imposed are:

1. corporation income tax—1909
2. individual income tax—1913
3. estate tax—1916

4. gift tax—1924
5. payroll taxes (Social Security, unemployment insurance)—1935
6. windfall profits tax—1980

These taxes were stimulated by changes in society and the economy. The country shifted from an agricultural to a manufacturing and service economy. Wealth came to be measured more in terms of income than of property. Welfare or social service functions became the primary responsibility of the federal government rather than the family or state and local governments. As a consequence, taxes on income, payroll, and wealth replaced excise taxes and customs duties as the biggest producers of federal revenues.

Nontax Revenue Sources

Commonly lumped together into a category called "Miscellaneous Receipts," *nontax revenue sources* contribute between 1 and 2 percent of all budget receipts. Examples of such revenue sources are *government-owned enterprises such as the Postal Service and Government Printing Office; sales of government products and land such as abandoned armed forces installations; rental of land and equipment; fines and penalties such as those imposed for violating environmental standards; gifts to the government such as art or land for parks; and interest on government loans such as those made to students.*

Borrowing as a Revenue Source

At first, one may think of borrowing as an expenditure rather than a revenue. But when the government borrows, it gets money (revenue) immediately. Eventually the government has to pay it back, of course, and it pays back more than it borrows because of interest costs. In the short run, however, borrowing is clearly a way to raise revenue.

Governments borrow money for the same reasons individuals do: to make ends meet during a crisis, to undertake expensive capital projects that cannot be financed out of current revenues, to refinance maturing debts, and to invest in hopes of making more money in the long run. The Constitution gives Congress the power to borrow in Article I, Section 8.

In recent years, the amount of federal borrowing has increased dramatically. Between 1965 and 1969, the average amount borrowed annually was

$19.9 billion. The estimated amount borrowed in 1982 was $164.1 billion. One must be careful about making such comparisons across time because inflation effectively reduces the dollar's value, but the increase in government borrowing is still impressive. Government borrowing as a percentage of all borrowing in the public and private sectors increased from 25 percent in 1965 to 42 percent in 1980.

Government borrowing falls into three categories: 1) direct federal borrowing to cover the deficit and off-budget spending programs (the transactions of certain federally owned entities such as the Postal Service and the Synthetic Fuels Corporation, which are kept separate from the regular budget); 2) loans whose repayment is guaranteed by the federal government such as student educational loans and housing mortgages; and 3) loans by such government-created enterprises as the Government National Mortgage Association.[12] Loan guarantees promise that the federal government will pay off a loan if the borrower does not. Many loan programs are designed to give those with no credit or bad credit (students, veterans, the poor) a chance to improve their credit rating. Loans are, in effect, the government's investment in society. They help build up the nation's human capital.

The government borrows from individuals, commercial banks, foreign central banks, other financial institutions and businesses, and the *Federal Reserve System*, *the banking regulatory system that establishes banking policies and controls the amount of currency in circulation.* It does so by selling treasury bills, notes, certificates, and bonds; U.S. Savings Bonds; and treasury foreign currency notes, bonds, and certificates. Almost all federal borrowing is conducted by the Treasury Department. In 1976, 24 percent of all federal debts were held by government agencies and trust funds; 15 percent by the Federal Reserve banks; 12 percent by other American investors such as corporations, insurance companies, and pension funds; and 6 percent by state and local governments. Only 11 percent of the federal government's borrowing is from foreign and international investors.[13]

THE EXPENDITURE SIDE OF THE BUDGET

The expenditure side of the budget has grown faster than the revenue side, which explains the increase in borrowing. Government spending has skyrocketed, regardless of which growth measure one uses. In current dollars (unadjusted for inflation), spending rose from $140 billion in 1966 to $655.2 billion in 1981. In constant dollars (adjusted for inflation), spending climbed from just over $100 billion to almost $200 billion. Spending as a percentage of the gross national product increased during this time from 17 to 23 percent. (This is probably the most accurate measure of the growth of government spending.) Americans are concerned about increases in federal government spending and the rising debt level, as we shall discuss later in the chapter.

Defense versus Social Programs

Expenditures say a great deal about the nation's policy priorities. Changes in expenditure patterns closely parallel changes in the demographic, so-

The debate over budget priorities historically has centered on the relative amounts that should be spent on national defense and social programs. This is often referred to as the "guns versus butter" debate.

cial, and political characteristics of the population. The percentage of total spending for non-defense-related federal operations increased sharply in the mid-1960s. This was a result of the passage of the Great Society programs after a period of racial unrest and Vietnam War protests. At the same time, spending for national defense declined. The priority clearly shifted from military spending to human resource spending. In the 1970s, federal spending for benefits to individuals (Social Security, Supplemental Security Income, food stamps, public assistance) surpassed defense spending and became the most expensive item in the federal budget. This change reflected our aging population and a shift in societal roles and values as women entered the work force, the number of female-headed households increased, and divorce rates rose. Defense spending jumped sharply in the 1980s with the election of Reagan. Reagan ran on a platform of improving the defense system and reducing spending for social welfare programs.

The debate over budget priorities historically has centered on the relative amounts that should go to national defense and social programs. This is often referred to as the "guns versus butter" dispute. John Gist has found that since fiscal year 1969 there has been a tradeoff between national defense and individual income security.[14] As one goes up, the other goes down. Gist predicts that by 1985 defense will once again become the largest single component in the budget.

Interest Payments

The third most costly item in the budget next to income security ($282 billion in FY 1984) and defense ($245 billion in FY 1984) is interest payments, which cost over $100 billion in FY 1984. Interest payments are one of the fastest growing categories of federal spending, as you could probably have guessed, knowing how fast federal borrowing has increased in recent years.

Health Expenditures

Another increasingly expensive function is health. Health spending jumped 64 percent between 1980 and 1984 and now makes up about 11 percent of all expenditures ($90.6 billion in FY 1984). Included in this category are two costly programs—Medicare (aid for the elderly and disabled) and Medicaid (health care for the poor). It is estimated that Medicaid expenses alone will increase at an *annual* rate of 33 percent in the 1980s.

Many of these items, particularly income security, health, and interest payments, are in a sense uncontrollable. Lance LeLoup defines **uncontrollable spending** as *spending that cannot be increased or decreased without changes in existing law*.[15] Such changes are generally difficult and painful for elected officials to make because they must deal with those whose benefits are reduced. LeLoup notes that the growth in federal spending is almost completely attributable to growth in uncontrollable items. These items include fixed costs such as multiyear contracts and obligations; entitlement

The two most expensive government health care programs are Medicare (aid for the elderly and disabled) and Medicaid (health care for the poor).

programs such as Social Security that permit any eligible person to draw benefits; and formula grants to state and local governments.

The greater the proportion of all expenditures that is uncontrollable, the less flexibility there is for changes in the budget. The percentage of uncontrollable expenditures increased from 54 to 77 percent between 1970 and 1980. It was partially in an attempt to reverse the pattern of increasing uncontrollable expenditures that President Reagan introduced his New Federalism program (discussed in chapter 4). While this program reduced uncontrollables somewhat, the problem remains.

WHEN EXPENDITURES EXCEED REVENUES: DEFICITS AND DEBT

The United States has not had a balanced budget (revenues equaling expenditures) since 1969. Every year the federal government runs a deficit, spending more than it takes in (Figure 17.2), and every year the national debt gets larger. The *national debt is the total amount of all debt issues outstanding (all borrowed monies that have not yet been repaid).* On October 22, 1981, the national debt broke the trillion dollar mark ($1,000,000,000,000) for the first time. One newspaper account of the event explained the defi-

cit this way: "It's about $4,700 for every American man, woman, and child and it's such a big number that someone counting it out, one dollar every second, would be 31,688 years older when the task was completed."[16]

Deficits: Good or Bad?

Some view deficit spending as desirable, others as harmful. Advocates contend that deficit spending is a way to stimulate a sluggish economy by increasing purchasing power. This is sometimes called the "pump-priming" theory. Proponents argue that the deficits can be repaid with surpluses during periods of prosperity, which will help control inflation. This argument was first popularized in the 1930s by British economist John Maynard Keynes. Other supporters of deficit spending argue that a growing national debt is not so bad because most of it is held internally. This is the "we owe it to ourselves" rationalization.

Critics of deficit spending argue that a growing national debt crowds out private investors. Arthur Burns, former chairman of the board of governors of the Federal Reserve System, once testified that continued deficit spending places enormous strains on money and capital markets. According to Burns, "interest rates shoot up, many private

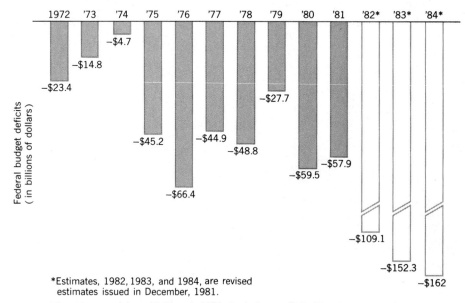

*Estimates, 1982, 1983, and 1984, are revised estimates issued in December, 1981.

Note: Years end June 30 through 1976, thereafter on Sept. 30.

FIGURE 17.2

Federal Budget Deficits

SOURCE: *Chicago Tribune*, December 29, 1981; based on data from OMB. Copyrighted 1981, Chicago Tribune. Used with permission.

borrowers are crowded out of the market, savings funds are diverted from mortgage lenders and the stock market turns weak."[17]

Other critics of excessive deficit spending argue that a large national debt unfairly burdens future generations. As one United States senator put it,

This is the crime: the generation that controls the economy of this nation today and those who have important government responsibility are callously and mercilessly burdening the livelihood and earnings of the generations that will follow us with a tremendously oppressive national debt.[18]

What to Do When Deficits Get Out of Hand

During the depths of the recession of 1981 and 1982, the director of the Congressional Budget Office (CBO), Alice Rivlin, appeared before the Senate Budget Committee and painted a grim picture of the economy. She characterized it as "floundering . . . snared in a vicious cycle of high interest rates, low growth, high unemployment, sagging government revenues, rising spending demands and upward spiraling deficits."[19] It was the "upward spiraling deficits" that most concerned policymakers of both parties.

CBO predicted that in FY 1982 (an election year for many members of Congress), the deficit would range between $110 billion and $112 billion, $3 to $8 billion more than was first expected. Furthermore, deficits were predicted to range between $141 billion and $151 billion in FY 1983 and between $145 billion and $160 billion in FY 1984 and FY 1985. (Even these predictions greatly underestimated the actual deficits, which exceeded $200 billion in FY 1983). These projections were mind-boggling to nearly everyone. Many agreed with the senator who said, "It is now clearly apparent that the current economic policies of this administration aren't working."[20]

But not everyone could agree on what to do to get the deficit under control. The CBO director recommended cutting defense spending, cutting "sacred cow" entitlement programs such as Social Security, and raising taxes. A senator from Michigan recommended an "economic summit" meeting, to be attended by the president, congressional leaders from both parties, and the chairman of the Federal Reserve Board. A number of state legislatures, the National Taxpayers Union, and the National Tax Limitation Committee recommended a constitutional amendment to balance the federal budget. These preferences represent three possible responses: 1) reform the tax structure; 2) cut back expenditures; or 3) mandate a balanced budget.

Reform the Tax Structure Recommendations on reforming the tax structure typically range from toughening the tax compliance laws, closing loopholes, and raising taxes on certain items, to revamping the whole tax structure with a flat-rate income tax (to be discussed in more detail at the end of the chapter). Some are more far-reaching than others, but all are politically sensitive.

Cut Back Expenditures Another way to get deficits under control is to cut back expenditures. Again, this is easier said than done. Proponents of spending cutbacks point out that it's unfair to ask taxpayers to pay more taxes if, at the same time, no effort is made to tighten the belt on spending. The difficulty is in deciding what to cut. Entitlement programs are the toughest to reduce because they largely benefit middle-class Americans such as retired persons, students, veterans, and

Entitlement programs, such as farm subsidies, are often the toughest for Congress to cut because they primarily benefit middle-class Americans—a very large group of voters.

farmers. Another difficulty is Congress's institutional tendency toward higher spending.

Mandate a Balanced Budget An intriguing approach to getting deficits under control is to amend the Constitution to make a balanced budget mandatory, thereby outlawing deficit spending. In 1975, the National Taxpayers Union (NTU) began a drive to force Congress to consider such an amendment. Part of the NTU's strategy was to threaten calling a constitutional convention on the issue. Recall from chapter 3 that under Article V of the Constitution, a convention must be called if two-thirds of the states (34) request one. Then Congress must decide whether or not to accept the amendment proposed by the constitutional convention.

By January, 1982, 31 states had called for such a convention and nine others were threatening to do so. (Most state and local governments are required by their constitutions or charters to have balanced budgets.) This move by the states, in combination with huge deficits, led Congress to take the issue up on its own. The Senate passed such a proposal in August, 1982, but the House did not, so the issue is still being discussed. It is very controversial.

Supporters of such an amendment argue that "the lack of a balanced budget means that the federal government is without a guiding policy, and is merely a collection of emphases built on the theory of 'something for everybody.' " They argue that "without a fixed inherent policy, the government flounders, inefficiency flourishes, and mistrust in the government's ability to govern efficiently and rationally, justifiably grows."[21] Supporters of the amendment also see it as giving members of Congress a way to fend off constituents' requests for money. Senator Strom Thurmond of South Carolina, a supporter, said "Because of the amendment, members can tell constituents, 'We can't spend more.' "[22]

Opponents of a constitutional amendment refer to it as "the game of constitutional cop-out."[23] They see it as more of a bookkeeping or statutory matter than a constitutional matter. Economists, in particular, are opposed to using the Constitution as a vehicle for ensuring economic stability: "It's blasphemy to clutter [that] elegant charter with bookkeeping strictures," said Nobel laureat James Tobin.[24] Critics are particularly concerned about the inflexibility of a balanced budget mandate—the inability to adjust for changes or na-

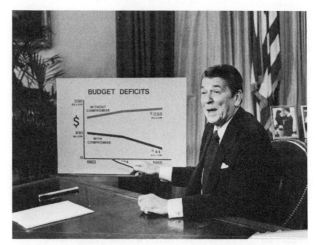

Much of the debate among policymakers as to how to solve the nation's economic problems centers on the rapid growth of federal budget deficits.

tional crises. Opponents see it as unenforceable anyway, since "there's no provision to keep Congress from doctoring its books to obtain a balanced budget by shifting certain spending areas 'off-budget.' "[25] Since 1973, Congress has increasingly moved agencies off-budget, so that off-budget spending now makes up one-third of all government spending.[26]

In spite of the opposition, the idea remains alive because deficits are still a fact of life. And there's an "almost universally held conviction that most of our serious economic ills—inflation, high interest rates, recession—can be traced to deficit spending."[27]

The taxpayers are somewhat responsible for the difficulties presidents and Congress have in balancing the budget. A 1981 survey by Louis Harris helps explain why. Citizens were asked, "If the only way to have a chance to balance the federal budget by 1984 were to make sharp cuts in certain programs, would you favor such cuts, or would you favor not balancing the federal budget?"[28] The majority of the population regarded certain programs as more important than balancing the budget: federal aid to the elderly, poor, and handicapped—83 percent; Social Security—78 percent; federal health programs—62 percent; federal aid to education—56 percent; and defense spending—51 percent. As we have shown, most of these programs are expensive and uncontrollable. The results indicate that the budgetary process reflects the wishes of the population. Maybe we should reexamine our policy preferences from a larger economic perspective—or, alternatively, reevaluate our criticism of budget deficits. Otherwise, presidents and Congresses will continue to face the impossible task of reconciling uncontrollable spending with balancing the budget.

THE BUDGETARY PROCESS: PLAYING A HIGH-STAKES GAME

John Wanat compares budgeting to a chess game:

> *[In chess], no one can predict ahead of time which player will win. But in the course of the match, a judgement can be made of the techniques used, the strategies employed, and the styles characterizing each player. This information can help in estimating how the match will develop. . . .*[29]

If we want to have an impact on the ''game's'' final outcome, we must familiarize ourselves with the times various phases of the game are played, the players involved in each phase, the roles each plays, and their game-winning strategies.

The Budget Timetable

Budgeting is a multiyear activity (see Figure 17.3). For example, budgeting for fiscal year 1984 actually began in March 1982, some 19 months before the start of the fiscal year. (Fiscal year 1984 runs from October 1, 1983 to September 30, 1984.) If you wish to participate in the budgetary process, you've got to be ready much earlier than you probably imagined.

The budget cycle has four phases: 1) executive preparation and submission; 2) congressional authorization and appropriation (formal adoption); 3) implementation and control of the enacted budget; and 4) review and audit.

This may seem simple enough, but the process

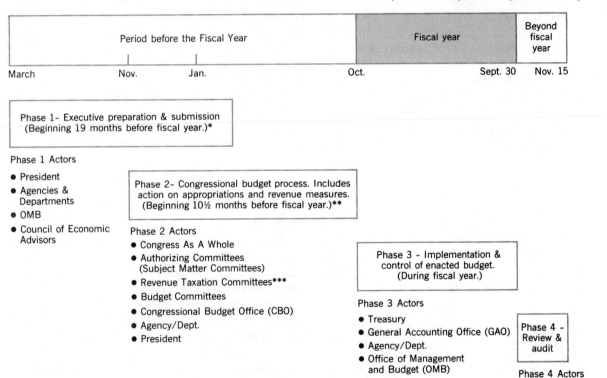

FIGURE 17.3

Summary of Major Steps in the Budget Process and the Government Actors Involved

SOURCE: United States General Accounting Office, *A Glossary of Terms Used in the Federal Budget Process*. Washington, D.C.: GAO, March 1981, p. 7.

is complicated by the fact that each phase of a fiscal year budget overlaps different phases of other fiscal years. For example, while the budget execution phase is going on for FY 1984, Congress is considering appropriations for FY 1985, the executive branch is preparing the preliminary estimates for spending in FY 1986, and the General Accounting Office is reviewing and auditing spending that took place in FY 1983. Fortunately, the process is more manageable than it seems because the key players differ in each phase.

Phase 1: Executive Preparation and Submission   The key players in this phase are the president, the various executive departments and agencies, the Office of Management and Budget, and the president's Council of Economic Advisers. This phase runs from March of one year to January of the next, when the president formally submits his proposed budget to Congress.

The President's Role   The president's role in budgeting is a relatively new one, formalized by passage of the Budget and Accounting Act of 1921. Before 1921, executive departments such as State, Agriculture, and Defense submitted their budget requests directly to Congress. Presidents had neither the power nor the responsibility to coordinate all the requests into a single budget document. As government grew and problems intensified, however, it became apparent that presidents needed the power to coordinate budget requests in order to develop consistent, cohesive policy proposals.

During budget preparation, the president sets down the guidelines that will be used by the agencies and the Office of Management and Budget in estimating their spending needs. As Robert Lorsch describes the process,

> He may say, 'submit a balanced budget to Congress,' or he may say, 'a balanced budget isn't necessary, but don't let it go in the red over 20 billion.' Whatever his instructions, they are generally quite broad, though occasionally he might take an interest in one or two particular agencies (e.g., Carter's interest in creating a Department of Education; Reagan's interest in abolishing it).[30]

The president's role in the preparation phase, then, is to let agencies know his basic policy priorities and philosophies about appropriate taxing, spending, and borrowing (deficit) levels. Presidents tend to leave most details of the actual drawing up of the executive budget to the Office of Management and Budget.

The president is most visible when he actually submits the budget to Congress. By law, the budget must be submitted no later than 15 days after Congress convenes in January. This is a big media event that usually lasts for a couple of weeks as television, radio, and newspapers report the reactions of various members of Congress. These reactions help the president to identify who he will have to lobby during Phase 2, the congressional approval stage.

The Role of the Departments and Agencies   The actual formation of budget estimates begins at the agency level after the president has announced his spending preferences. Individual organizational units such as the Census Bureau in the Department of Commerce review current operations, program objectives, and future plans. By October 15, all executive, legislative, and judicial agencies have submitted their initial budget requests to the Office of Management and Budget (see Table 17.2). Throughout this preparation, there is a continuous exchange of information among various federal agencies, OMB, and the president. The Treasury Department and other agencies keep posted about revenue estimates and economic projections. It's still difficult to predict how much to request, however, because the fiscal year for which they are drawing up spending plans does not begin for more than a year. As we know, the economy and the political scene can change a great deal in a year's time.

The goal of most agencies is to get more money. At the absolute minimum, they want to protect their base, the amount of money they received the previous year. Their measure of success is the size of their increment, the percentage increase from the previous year's base. Sometimes, however, a department head may prefer not to increase appropriations for a particular program. If public opinion on a program has soured, as happened with the Comprehensive Education and Training Act (CETA) program, a request for more appropriations may risk greater alienation of the public and hamper the administration of the program as it already exists.

The strategies agencies use to protect and expand their base vary according to the agency's size, the importance of the function performed, the clientele served, and the personal aggressive-

TABLE 17.2

Executive Branch Budget Timetable

Timing	Action to Be Completed
April–June (March)*	Conduct spring planning review to establish presidential policy for the upcoming budget.
June	OMB sends policy letters to the agencies.
September 1	Smaller agencies submit initial budget request materials.
September 15	Cabinet departments and major agencies submit initial budget request materials.
October 15	Legislative branch, judiciary, and certain other agencies submit initial budget request materials.
September–January (September)*	OMB and the president review agency budget requests and prepare the budget documents.
January	The president transmits the budget during the first 15 days of each regular session of Congress.
January–February	OMB sends allowances letters to the agencies.
April 10 (February)*	The president transmits an update of the budget estimates. (Note: transmittal is often requested to be made earlier than the required date.)
July 15 (June)*	The president transmits an update of the budget estimates. (Note: transmittal is often requested to be made earlier than the required date.)

SOURCE: United States General Accounting Office, *A Glossary of Terms Used in the Federal Budget Process*. Washington, D.C.: GAO, March, 1981, p. 4. Based on information from OMB Circular No. A-11, Rev. (June 3, 1980).

*Months in parentheses indicate when agencies are expected to submit review materials to OMB.

ness of department heads. Small departments often have a tough time when competing with such giants as the Department of Defense or Department of Health and Human Services. Agencies and programs that always seem to fare well are known as "sacred cows."

One soon learns certain tricks of playing the game. The classic explanation of agency strategies is Wildavsky's *The Politics of the Budgetary Process*.[31] He says that for an agency to be successful it must 1) cultivate an active clientele of powerful interest groups who will pressure the president and Congress to keep a program alive and well; 2) develop confidence among other government officials by giving reliable information, playing it straight, making friends with elected officials and their staffs, and compromising when necessary; and 3) know when and how to use different strategies. For example, if an agency wants merely to defend its base (guard against cuts in old programs), then it should choose among strategies such as the following:

1. Cut a popular program you perform, but make the cuts in such a way that they have to be put back.

2. Cut less visible items such as office or general administrative expenses or promotional activities.

3. Claim it's all or nothing. Assert that if a cut is made, the entire program will have to be scrapped (but be careful lest the program be cut!).

4. Claim the request is down to the penny. You are squeezed against the wall and any cuts will simply reduce effectiveness.

On the other hand, if an agency wishes to expand its base and perhaps add a new program or service, Wildavsky recommends strategies such as these:

1. Use the "wedge" tactic. Begin a program with an insignificant amount of money and later claim that it would be terrible to lose the money already spent by not finishing the job. Or, request a small sum for research and use the research to justify the feasibility of the big new project (also known as the "foot in the door" tactic).

2. Claim that the request is temporary. Temporary expenditures or programs usually turn out to be permanent.

3. Demonstrate a backlog that with current staff and funding cannot be cleared up, which will mean there is a need for new appropriations.

4. Use computer-type information to show the need for more funds. Who can doubt the "objective," "pure" data spewed out of a computer?

5. If possible, claim that the project pays for itself or makes a profit.

6. If necessary, claim that a crisis exists which can be met only through a new program, expenditure, etc. This is often a necessary strategy when you need sizeable new appropriations rather than minimal increases.

Wildavsky's strategies apply not only to an agency's relations with Congress, but with the Office of Management and Budget as well. In the budget preparation phase, agencies use a number of these techniques to convince OMB of the merit and necessity of their budget requests.

OMB's Role   The Office of Management and Budget was originally created as the Bureau of the Budget under the Budget and Accounting Act of 1921. OMB is responsible for consolidating the individual agency requests into "the president's budget." OMB is the liaison between the president and the executive departments. It relays the president's budget guidelines to individual agencies in August or September of the year preceding the fiscal year, holds hearings with agency heads in November, and listens to their appeals in December. OMB makes the final recommendations to the president in late December.

Putting agency requests together is not an easy task. Invariably, when the initial requests are added, the amount exceeds the ceiling established by the president. OMB has to pare down these requests. The reasons OMB typically gives for cutting back requests range from removing unintended benefits to consolidating programs and reducing overhead. In spite of the difficult task of cutting back agency requests, OMB always manages to produce the several-hundred-page budget document in time for the president to submit it to Congress.

Phase 2: Congressional Adoption of the Budget   Before the ink is dry, members of Congress react to the president's budget—and strongly. By responding to a president's newly proposed budget, Congress is merely flexing its muscle and defending its constitutionally delegated "power of the purse." But then it spends

the next nine months (January through September) compromising with the president. Congress generally ends up revising the president's overall requests downward by only 2 or 3 percent.[32]

Before the Congressional Budget and Impoundment Control Act of 1974, the congressional approval phase was highly fragmented. One scholar likened it to a Humpty Dumpty whose pieces were never put back together again.[33] John Ellwood and James Thurber described the old congressional budget process this way:

> *Each year Congress would take the president's total budget, chop it up into small pieces, and parcel them out among committees and subcommittees that would work on them with little regard for the impact their particular changes might have on the whole. Indeed, few within Congress were even aware of the emerging totals.*[34]

The lack of control over the budget along with sharp increases in spending, deficits, and uncontrollables, the need to control fiscal policy (which couldn't be done with a fragmented budgetary process), the lack of budgetary information other than that provided by OMB, and frustration with President Nixon's frequent impounding of funds enabled the **Congressional Budget and Impoundment Control Act** to sail through Congress. The act

1. *established a timetable for congressional budget action* (see Table 17.3);

2. *established the House and Senate Budget Committees;*

3. *created the Congressional Budget Office (CBO), the congressional counterpart to OMB; and*

4. *established procedures to control presidential impoundment of funds.*

Impoundment *is the refusal by a president to spend funds that have already been appropriated for a program by Congress.*

While the reforms imposed a new time clock and introduced some new players, the game remains basically the same. Congress's primary responsibilities are still authorizing programs by passing authorization legislation (see Table 17.4) and funding programs by passing an appropriations bills. The difference the reforms made was to improve the information Congress had to work with and to establish some agreed-upon totals for

TABLE 17.3
Congressional Budget Timetable

Action to Be Completed	On or Before
President submits current services budget to Congress	January
President submits annual budget message to Congress	15 days after Congress meets
Congressional committees make recommendations to Budget committees	March 15
Congressional Budget Office reports to Budget committees	April 1
Budget committees report first budget resolution	April 15
Congress passes first budget resolution	May 15
Legislative committees complete reporting of authorizing legislation	May 15
Congress passes all pending bills	7 days after Labor Day
Congress passes second budget resolution	September 15
Congress passes budget reconciliation bill	September 25
Fiscal year begins	October 1

SOURCE: Lance T. LeLoup, *The Fiscal Congress: Legislative Control of the Budget* (Westport, Conn.: Greenwood Press, 1980), p. 27; based on information from the House Budget Committee.

revenue, expenditures, and debt through passage of concurrent budget resolutions.

Information-gathering generally takes place between January 15 and April 15. The key congressional players are the standing committees (subject matter committees such as Agriculture, Defense, and Foreign Relations) in each house. Other key players are the Congressional Budget Office and the House and Senate Budget Committees. The key executive players are the secretary of the Treasury, director of OMB, chairpersons of the president's Council of Economic Advisers, and department heads who may be called to testify before a standing committee to justify their agency budget requests.

By March 15, the standing committees must submit to the Budget Committees their estimates for spending in the upcoming fiscal year. By April 1, the CBO must submit its annual report to the Budget Committees. This report outlines alternative spending patterns and revenue levels associated with different budget options and their budgetary implications.

The House and Senate Budget Committees review data from economic forecasts, standing committees, the president's budget, and the CBO. By April 15, the Budget Committees present both houses with the ***First Concurrent Resolution***, *which proposes targets for taxation, spending, and borrowing levels.* For the next month, the various standing committees and finance committees debate the proposed resolution. The president and his main

lobbying agency (OMB) try to get the resolution revised if it varies markedly from the president's proposed budget.

Once the First Concurrent Resolution is adopted (no later than May 15), Congress can turn to authorizing and appropriating. The deadline for passage of all authorizing legislation and appropriations bills is September 14. The House and Senate Appropriations Committees take the authorizations from the various subject matter committees and decide how much to appropriate to each. This is similar to OMB's consolidation of individual agency budget requests into one comprehensive budget document. At the same time, the Finance Committees (the House Ways and Means and the Senate Finance Committees) are busy preparing tax legislation and spending bills for entitlement programs such as Social Security, Medicare, and Medicaid.

During the appropriations stage, agency heads are brought in to testify. Also, committee members are lobbied by the president, his top White House staff officials, and high-level OMB personnel. Even Congress members who are not themselves on the Appropriations Committee actively lobby their colleagues to be sure programs benefitting their constituents do not fall by the wayside.

Traditionally, the Appropriations Committees have been powerful, but recently a great deal of their power has shifted to the Budget Committees. (In contrast, the Finance Committees have lost lit-

TABLE 17.4

Principal Duties and Functions of Participants in the Congressional Budget Process

President	Authorizing Committees (Standing; Subject Matter)	Appropriations Committees	Revenue Committees	Budget Committees	Congressional Budget Office
—Submits executive budget and current services estimates. —Updates budget estimates in April and July. —Signs or vetoes revenue, appropriations, and other budget-related legislation. —May propose the deferral or rescission of appropriated funds.	—Prepare views and estimates on programs within jurisdiction. —Report authorizing legislation for the next fiscal year. —Include CBO cost estimates in reports accompanying their legislation. **Limitations:** 1. Legislation providing contract or borrowing authority is effective only as provided in appropriations. 2. Entitlements cannot become effective before next fiscal year.	—Report regular and supplemental bills. —After adoption of a budget resolution, allocate budget authority and outlays among their subcommittees. —Provide five-year projections of outlays in reports accompanying appropriations, and compare budget authority with amounts provided in latest budget resolution. —Can be directed by second budget resolution to report reconciliation bill repealing new or existing budget authority. —Review rescission and deferral proposals of the president. **Limitation:** After second resolution is adopted, spending cannot exceed amount set by Congress.	—Submit views and estimates on budget matters in their jurisdiction. —Can be directed by second resolution to report legislation changing tax laws. **Limitation:** Legislation cannot cause revenues to fall below level set in the second resolution.	—Report two or more concurrent resolutions on the budget each year. —Allocate new budget authority and outlays among House and Senate committees. —Monitor congressional actions affecting the budget. —Advise Congress on the status of the budget.	—Issues reports on annual budget. —Estimates cost of bills reported by House and Senate committees. —Issues periodic scorekeeping reports on status of the congressional budget. —Assists the budget, revenue, appropriations, and other committees. Issues five-year budget projections.

SOURCE: Allen Schick, *Congress and Money: Budgeting, Spending and Taxing.* Washington, D.C.: The Urban Institute, 1980, Table 2, p. 8.

tle of their power to these newer committees.) The Budget Committees are responsible for the final budget activities—passage of the Second Concurrent Resolution (which is binding) and reconciliation. The **Second Concurrent Resolution** *sets a ceiling on expenditures and a floor on receipts (tax and nontax*

revenue). If the second resolution is different from the first, the Budget Committees must prepare **reconciliation legislation** *to reconcile amounts in tax and spending legislation for a fiscal year with the ceilings required by the Second Concurrent Resolution.* Congress must adopt it by September 25, giving the president only five days to review the bill and sign it. When Congress cannot complete the reconciliation process by the start of the fiscal year (about 85 percent of the time), it must pass a *continuing resolution*. *This is a stopgap measure that usually authorizes agencies to spend at the same level as in the previous fiscal year.*

Reconciliation was the device Reagan used to cut the FY 1981 and 1982 budgets. Fearing that going through the Appropriations Committees would take too long, Reagan's congressional leaders used reconciliation to bypass these committees and speed up the cuts. The Budget Committees prepared amendments to previously passed concurrent resolutions (permissible under the Congressional Budget and Impoundment Control Act) and submitted them to Congress as a whole for approval. These amendments instructed the House and Senate standing committees to prepare the cuts, rather than the Appropriations Committees. Because of Reagan's successful lobbying and the increased Republican membership in Congress, the amendments passed. This established spending ceilings in the authorizing legislation. That left the Appropriations Committees only the option of voting further cuts in these programs. Angry, these bypassed committee members attacked the reconciliation process and the power of the Budget Committees, arguing that reconciliation made the standing committees into little appropriations committees and the Appropriations Committees into subcommittees of the Budget Committees.[35]

Criticisms of the reconciliation process reflect a new era of the congressional budget process. The Budget Committees are playing a significant role in the congressional appropriations process, which has historically been the exclusive domain of the Appropriations Committees. As is true after any change, there is already talk of reforming the 1974 act.

Phase 3: Budget Implementation and Control   During the third phase, the funds appropriated by Congress are spent by the agencies. This phase coincides with the fiscal year, October 1 to September 30, and is sometimes called the "budget execution" phase (see Figure 17.4). Most of the key players in this phase—in the Treasury Department, OMB, the individual departments and agencies, and the president—are from the executive branch. The key player from the congressional team is the General Accounting Office (GAO), whose primary role is to countersign and monitor checks written by the Treasury Department. Congress itself in recent years has occasionally entered the game when presidents or agencies have used their discretionary spending tools—impoundment, reprogramming, and transfers—to alter the outcome of the game outlined by Congress in its appropriations legislation.

Once the appropriations bill is passed, the Treasury, with the approval of GAO, in effect creates an account for each agency from which the agency can withdraw funds. The agency cannot go wild and spend most of its money in the first quarter of the fiscal year, however. OMB has the power of *apportionment*—*it decides the pace at which agencies can spend funds.* It usually apportions them on a quarterly basis. This power is intended to control agency requests for additional or supplemental funds near the end of the fiscal year. It is also intended to give OMB the power to make agencies set aside funds for contingencies and to make sure that agencies spend money efficiently. OMB advises the president when an agency does not need to spend all the money Congress gave it due to changes in the economy, technological innovations, policy changes, or other developments. It is then up to the president to decide whether to use his power of impoundment and refuse to spend funds that have already been appropriated for a program.

Under the impoundment control provisions of the 1974 act, a president, with the approval of Congress, can withhold appropriated funds for fiscal or other policy reasons or because he has determined that all or part of an appropriation is not needed to carry out a program. Presidents can make two types of impoundments: rescissions and deferrals. *Rescissions* *cancel existing budget authority for a certain program and thus eliminate the expenditure of those funds. Deferrals delay expenditures for certain functions.* Congress generally regards presidential deferral requests more favorably than rescission requests, but impoundment often creates great tension between the presidential and congressional teams.

Agencies often reinterpret congressional budgetary decisions by reprogramming or transferring funds. *Reprogramming* *is a procedure that gives executive officials some latitude in shifting funds within an appropriation account, moving them from one program to another.*[36] Congressional control over reprogram-

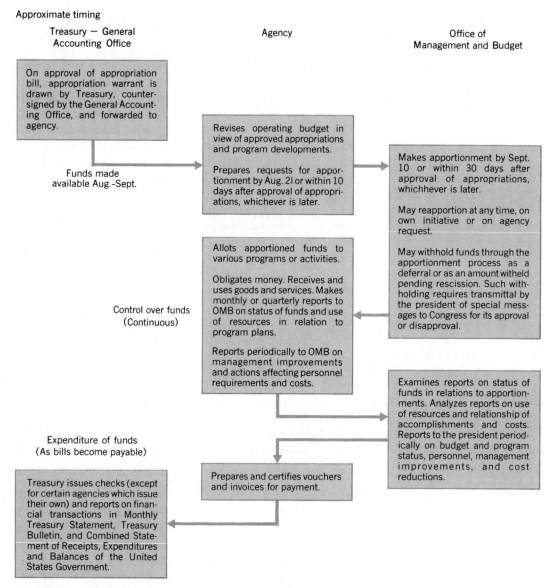

FIGURE 17.4

Phase 3—Implementation and Control of Enacted Budget

SOURCE: United States General Accounting Office, *A Glossary of Terms Used in the Federal Budget Process*. Washington, D.C.: GAO, March 1981, p. 12–13.

ming lies in the ***oversight committees***, *appropriations and authorizing committees that have the power to monitor the operation of an agency or program*—and in the CBO with its "scorekeeping reports" that track agency spending. ***Transfers*** *involve shifting funds between appropriations accounts*.[37] Transfer power must be statutorily conferred on agency officials by Congress. In practice, much reprogramming and transferring goes unnoticed by Congress, but these fund-

ing shifts are sometimes detected by the GAO during the audit and review phase.

Phase 4: Audit Review and Evaluation
Phase 4, the final step in the budget process, occurs after the fiscal year is over. It may last up to 12 months. The key player during this phase has traditionally been the General Accounting Office, a member of the congressional team.

The GAO's role is to audit and evaluate government programs. To do this, it has 5,200 staff members posted throughout the federal establishment. The Comptroller General, as head of the GAO, reports the staff's findings and recommendations for corrective action to Congress, OMB, and the agencies involved. He also monitors the president's proposed rescissions and deferrals and reports to Congress any illegal agency reprogramming or transferring of funds uncovered by GAO audits.

Evaluation has become just as important a function as auditing. In 1980, the GAO spent $197.3 million and issued 935 reports on issues ranging from the herbicide Agent Orange used in Vietnam to changes in calculating Social Security benefits.[38] The GAO claimed to have saved the taxpayers $3.7 billion. Of course, the GAO is only as successful as Congress makes it by adopting its recommendations for saving.

Executive agencies and OMB have also become more involved in the evaluation phase of the budgetary process. Studies of the impact of expenditures provide extremely useful information that aids them in future budget preparations. The need to demonstrate effectiveness and efficiency of past expenditures and agency operations has led to the development of a number of new budgeting techniques. Each is designed to make the budgetary process more scientific, objective, and rational—to take the politics out of the process. Some of the more popular new techniques have been:

1. *Planning-Programming-Budgeting Systems (PPBS).* *This technique requires an agency to identify program objectives, develop methods of measuring program outputs, calculate total program costs over the long run, prepare detailed multiyear program and financial plans, and analyze the costs and benefits of alternative program designs.*[39]

2. *Management By Objective (MBO).* *This technique requires an agency to determine its average work output (products, services), list the areas of performance in which improvement is necessary or desirable, estimate how much measurable improvement can be achieved during the next fiscal year, and consider whether organizational changes would contribute to a greater effectiveness.*[40] It was used by federal agencies during the Nixon administration in the 1970s.

3. *Zero-Base Budgeting (ZBB).* *This technique requires an agency to start from ground zero—to identify every program or function it controls; evaluate the cost and intrinsic merits of each and the alternatives to each; rank each function in terms of funding priority; and assess each function on a dollar-value basis. This technique assumes no money base in the budget and requires every function to be justified.*[41] It was proposed during President Carter's administration but was never fully implemented.

In spite of efforts to make budgeting more scientific, as Thomas Murphy concludes, "budgeting will never be a science."[42] It will always be based somewhat on the last year's assessment because those doing the budgeting can never completely erase from their memories the priorities and funding levels of the previous year—nor would it be in the best interest of the citizens for them to do so, because the start-up cost would be exorbitant. The real benefits of these new budgetary evaluation techniques have been better definitions of policy options and clearer statements of performance goals.

In the end, however, none of these budget approaches can make value choices. These choices must be made by elected officials. Politics is an inherent and important part of the budgetary process, one that makes the whole system accountable to the citizenry. Politics is also involved in decisions affecting the overall economy of the nation, both the public and the private sectors.

POLITICS, THE ECONOMY, AND LIFESTYLE

To tell how healthy or sick the economy is, the government uses indicators such as inflation, recession, gross national product, Consumer Price Index, unemployment rate, Index of Industrial Production, and housing starts. From these widely publicized figures, we get a sense of the economy's condition. For example, we know things are going well if we hear that inflation and the consumer and production price indices are down and housing starts and industrial production are up.

The state of the economy and how we are faring in it affect our votes for presidents, senators, representatives, and even local officials who may be closely associated with national officials. This explains why elected officials, particularly at the national level, become more concerned about the economy close to election time.

Edward Tufte, in *Political Control of the Economy*, found strong statistical evidence that the outcomes of national elections since 1946 have been affected by the condition of the economy in the period immediately preceding election time.[43] A healthy economy generally keeps incumbents in office; a bad economy turns them out. Obviously, there is a great political incentive to reduce inflation and unemployment levels and increase disposable personal income (income minus tax and nontax payments to the government).

The Employment Act of 1946 mandated federal government involvement in the making of economic policies. It charged government to

> *create and maintain, in a manner calculated to foster and promote free competitive enterprise and the general welfare, conditions under which there will be afforded useful employment opportunities, including self-employment for those able, willing and seeking to work, and to promote maximum employment, production, and purchasing power.*

To alter inflation, employment, and personal income levels, the government may make policies of two types: fiscal and monetary.

Fiscal policy is in the hands of the president and the Congress. Their fiscal tools are governmental taxing, spending, and borrowing. How they use these tools is determined through the budget process, as described earlier in this chapter.

Monetary policymaking tools are in the hands of the Federal Reserve Board. The "Fed" is made up of seven individuals appointed by the president and confirmed by the Senate for 14-year terms. The Fed uses a number of policy tools to control the amount of money in circulation and the availability of credit, as will be discussed later.

While fiscal and monetary policymaking activites differ, they are not independent of each other. The president and Congress often make fiscal policy in reaction to the Federal Reserve's monetary policy, and vice versa. The policies made directly affect the lifestyle and standard of living of a large number of Americans. Some benefit; others lose. Some are happy; others are bitter and angry. Such was the case in the early years of the Reagan administration when the president and Congress adopted taxing and spending cuts and the Federal Reserve tightened credit and forced up interest rates.

Fiscal Policy Changes and the Individual

Changes in tax policy which affected millions of Americans were part of the Economic Recovery Tax Act of 1981. A review of some of the major provisions demonstrates how shifts in fiscal policy can affect our lifestyles.[44] Included were provisions for:

1. Individual income-tax rate cuts. Reduced all individual income tax rates by 5 percent as of October 1, 1981, 10 percent as of July 1, 1982, and an additional 10 percent as of July 1, 1983.

2. Indexing. Automatically adjusted income taxes to offset inflation every year, beginning in 1985.

3. Marriage deductions. Allowed two-earner married couples filing joint returns to deduct 5 percent of up to $30,000 of the lesser of their two incomes; made rates for married individuals more similar to those for single individuals.

4. Child care. Increased from 20 to 30 percent the maximum tax credit for child and dependent day-care expenses in connection with the taxpayer's employment for those earning $10,000 or less.

5. Sale of home. Extended from 18 to 24 months the period an individual is allowed to defer taxes on proceeds from the sale of a home before buying another.

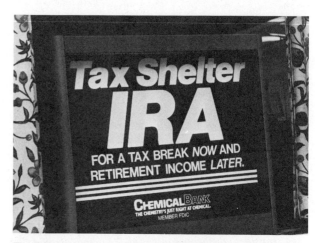

The Economic Recoverty Tax Act of 1981 allows individuals to open Individual Retirement Accounts (IRAs) and deduct their payments into these accounts from their taxable income regardless of whether they are already covered by an employer-sponsored retirement plan.

6. Individual Retirement Accounts (IRA). Increased the amount an individual can deduct for annual contributions to his or her personal retirement fund and extended eligibility to include individuals who are already covered by an employer-sponsored retirement plan.

Most of these individual tax breaks (along with many business tax breaks) are tax loopholes, technically referred to as "tax expenditures." The 1974 Budget Reform Act defines tax expenditures as revenue losses from any special exclusion, exemption, or deduction from income taxes, or from tax law provisions that provide a special credit, a preferential rate of tax, or a deferral of tax liability.

The Economic Recovery Tax Act handed out some $82 billion in new tax breaks to go along with the $266 billion that already existed. The ten largest tax expenditures for fiscal 1982 are shown in Table 17.5. A 1980 study by the Congressional Research Service concluded that if all tax expenditures were eliminated, average tax rates could be cut by approximately one-third.[45] But many loopholes are popular (e.g., deductions for Social Security payments, home-mortgage interest, credits for child care, and certain business depreciation tax breaks), which makes it difficult for elected officials to eliminate them. Senator Nancy Landon Kessebaum remarked, "Tax loopholes, once enacted, tend to outlive Methuselah, regardless of their effect on the public good."[46]

Another feature of the 1981 tax laws is likely to become equally popular—and equally difficult to eliminate. That feature is **tax indexing**, *the automatic adjusting of income taxes to inflation.* Indexing is designed to eliminate bracket creep. Bracket creep occurs when inflation pushes taxpayers into higher tax brackets and takes away more of their income. Under the new tax law, beginning in 1985, individual tax brackets, the personal exemption, and the zero tax bracket rate will be adjusted annually by the average increases in the Consumer Price Index over the preceding 12 months.

Spending cuts were another important part of the fiscal policy adopted by the president and Congress in 1981. The budget reconciliation bill cut FY 1982 government spending by $35 billion. Some 70 percent of these cuts were in programs

TABLE 17.5

Top 10 Tax Expenditures* ("Loopholes")

The 10 largest tax expenditures for fiscal 1982, according to the Congressional Budget Office, are:**

1. Exclusion from taxable income of pension plan contributions and earnings—$30.2 billion. The entire benefit goes to individuals.
2. Deductibility of home mortgage interest payments—$25.3 billion, all for individuals.
3. Deductions for state and local non-business taxes other than on owner-occupied homes—$23.1 billion. All goes to individuals.
4. Ten percent investment tax credit for investment in new plant and equipment—$20.8 billion ($17.3 billion for corporations, $3.4 billion for individuals).
5. Preferential tax rate on capital gains other than for agriculture, timber, iron ore and coal—$20 billion. Individuals will receive $19 billion; corporations, $1 billion.
6. Exclusion of employer contributions for medical insurance premiums and employee health care—$16.6 billion, all for individuals.
7. Exclusion of Social Security benefits from taxable income—$13.7 billion, all for individuals.
8. Deductibility of property tax on owner-occupied homes—$10.7 billion, all for individuals.
9. Deductibility of charitable contributions, other than for education and health—$9 billion ($8.6 billion for individuals, the rest for corporations).
10. Reduced tax rates on the first $100,000 of corporate income—$7.6 billion, all for corporations.

SOURCE: Pamela Fessler, "Congress Urged to Scrutinize Tax Breaks That Cost U.S. Billions in Lost Revenues," *Congressional Quarterly*, January 30, 1982, p. 156.

*Revenue losses attributable to provisions of the federal income tax laws that allow a special exclusion, or deduction from gross income, or that provide a special credit, preferential tax rate, or deferral of tax liability.

**These estimates were made in March 1981, prior to enactment of the Economic Recovery Tax Act of 1981. Since that law reduced individual income tax rates—therefore lowering the value of many deductions—certain tax expenditures for fiscal 1982 could cost less than these estimates.

affecting the poor. But this figure is misleading and must be placed in a broader, comparative perspective. According to the 1980 census, 30 million Americans, or 13 percent of the population, live on incomes at or below the poverty line. In the FY 1982 budget proposed by Carter before leaving office, programs directed at the poor made up $120.13 billion of a total budget of $739.3 billion, or 16 percent of all expenditures. The reconciliation bill of 1981 cut only $24.5 billion (20 percent) out of the poverty budget and left poverty programs with 13 percent of the total budget outlays.[47] Excluded from these cuts were social "safety net" programs such as Social Security, Medicare, railroad retirement, Supplemental Security income, veterans benefits, and basic unemployment benefits.

The major poverty programs that were reduced or eliminated (amounting to well over half of all the budget cuts) were:

1. Housing assistance (cut $11.6 billion). Reduced the number of new subsidized housing units; reduced rent subsidies for low-income families by requiring a higher contribution from renters.

2. CETA public service jobs (cut $3.8 billion). The temporary jobs program was eliminated.

3. Food stamps (cut $1.7 billion). Toughened eligibility requirements; reduced the benefits to the working poor.

4. School lunches (cut $1.4 billion). Raised eligibility requirements; eliminated special milk programs; cut federal subsidies for school meals; restricted summer funding programs.

Many of these programs were unpopular with a large number of middle-class Americans, who viewed them as wasteful, fraud-ridden, and unfairly burdensome to the average taxpayer. In reaction, Congress and the president adopted a social spending policy aimed at aiding only those who cannot work—the genuinely disabled, mothers with small children, and the elderly without income.

This fiscal policy package of taxing and spending cuts was controversial and has already been revised. But at the time it was adopted, it represented what a majority of elected officials thought was the best way to reduce inflation and stimulate economic growth.

The problem confronting fiscal policymakers today is stagflation, high levels of inflation *and* unemployment. Economists and elected officials disagree about how to solve it. Those who believe in Keynesian solutions accept the fact that these two conditions will always exist and attempt to keep them as stable as possible. The Keynesian approach is to alter the demand side of the economic equation. Advocates argue, for example, that if unemployment is rising too fast, government should make up for the decline in private-sector investment by increasing government spending to maintain high levels of investment, employment, and income.

Another group of economists favor supply-side solutions. They reject the Keynesian notion of a natural trade-off between inflation and unemployment, contending instead that there is a natural rate of unemployment. Furthermore, trying to use fiscal and monetary policies to reduce unemployment beyond this point breeds inflation without changing unemployment. Supply-side economists say the solution is stimulating production.

One of the most controversial budget cuts during the early years of the Reagan administration was in the school lunch program.

They advocate cutting taxes, increasing individual incentives to produce, and stimulating investment and savings. Higher investment, they say, will mean greater production, more jobs, and more tax revenue for the government.

Supply-side economic approaches of recent years have fared little better than Keynesian approaches of the past. The proponents of both theories argue that the shortcomings are not of the theories, but of their implementation. In other words, they argue that the politics involved in the implementation and unforeseen external events compromise and change the theories. For example, supply-siders under Reagan claimed that the delay in cutting taxes (after spending cuts had already been imposed) slowed instead of hastened economic recovery because consumers were not spending and investing tax savings to offset "lost" federal dollars. They also complained that the Federal Reserve Board kept interest rates too high too long, which discouraged investment by the private sector. Some supply-side purists extended their attack to President Reagan, whom they regarded as abandoning the theory when he proposed tax hikes to shrink the deficit. (Private sector investment is a key part of supply-side theory.) The same kind of implementation explanations for failures of Keynesian theories could be cited. The truth is that taxing and spending decisions fall into the broader domestic policy arena. Economist Robert J. Samuelson describes this situation well:

> Ever since the Great Depression, domestic policy has increasingly revolved around two central purposes. The first is to monitor and manage the national economy to achieve low unemployment, low inflation, and maximum growth. The second is to marshal the nation's resources to achieve a higher degree of social justice; in practice, that has meant abolishing poverty, ending discrimination, and assuring fairer economic treatment among groups.[48]

What this means is simply that what makes economic sense often does not make sense in practical human terms. The difficulty is in finding the right balance.

Monetary Policy Changes and the Individual

For individuals, the direct effects of monetary policy are reflected in interest rates and the ease or difficulty of getting credit. When interest rates are high, many of us cannot afford to buy homes or new cars or start small businesses, and buying on credit becomes too expensive. If money is tight, those who have a low income may have a tough time getting a major credit card such as Master Card, VISA, or American Express.

The Federal Reserve Board makes the monetary policy decisions that affect our ability to borrow. The Fed controls the **money supply**—*the total amount of currency, bank deposits, and other forms of what economists regard as money.* The Fed exercises this control because of its authority over the credit-rating and lending activities of the nation's banks, primarily its commercial banks. To reduce the amount of money in circulation, which is usually done to combat inflation, the Fed

1. raises the **reserve requirement** (*the portion of a bank's assets that must be deposited in one of the 12 Federal Reserve banks across the nation*);

2. raises the **discount rate** (*the rate of interest Federal Reserve banks charge to commercial banks that borrow from them*);

3. sells government securities to increase the size of reserves of the Federal Reserve banks. (*The process of buying or selling government bonds and bills is called an* **open market operation**.)

The Fed would do the reverse if it wanted to put more money in circulation to combat a recession.

In recent years, the Federal Reserve Board has regarded inflation as more dangerous to the economy than unemployment. In October, 1979, the Board announced that in the future, its major effort would be to control inflation. It set lower annual targets for monetary growth. Those who support the Fed's inflation-fighting priority argue that during the 1970s,

> unprecedented spurts upward in the cost of living undermined our system, halted the traditional rise of our standard of living, reduced our ability to compete in the world, warped American values by mocking the thrifty and rewarding the [wasteful], and wiped out the value of life savings.[49]

Inflation-fighting monetary policy satisfies private investors, the public, and elected officials until inflation comes under control, interest rates skyrocket, and unemployment lines get longer. This is exactly what happened by the end of 1981. Inflation had fallen to an annual rate of 6 percent, but unemployment had risen to 8 percent and interest rates were at record levels. Members of Congress whose constituents made their living in the housing and automobile industries, small business, or farming began to publicly criticize the Fed for not bringing interest rates down. One House member from Texas even introduced a resolution calling for the impeachment of the entire seven-member board of governors.

The conflicts between the president, Congress, and the Fed intensified in 1982 as unemployment rates approached World War II levels and deficit projections grew bigger and bigger. The chairperson of the Federal Reserve Board publicly criticized the president and Congress for adopting budgetary policies that perpetuated huge deficits.

The president and Congress retaliated by instructing the Fed to reconsider its tight-money policy which, in their estimation, kept interest rates too high to promote economic recovery. Such battles between public policymakers are not new and will always exist. They simply represent the difficulties of finding the right balance between monetary and fiscal policies.

The problem of coordinating the Fed's monetary policies with the fiscal policies of the president and Congress is that they don't see through the same glasses. The Fed's prescription is heavily economic in character. The president and Congress see through bifocals, the top half of which is an economic prescription, and the bottom half of which is purely political.

What's Best for Raising Revenue—Progressive or Flat-Rate Income Taxes?

In the annual surveys conducted by the Advisory Commission on Intergovernmental Relations, the public consistently rates the federal income tax as being one of the most unfair taxes. Because of its perceived unfairness, an underground economy (in which people receive income that they don't report to the Internal Revenue Service) has flourished (see Table). Estimates are that the United States Treasury loses between $90 billion to $150 billion yearly because of unreported income. The extensiveness of this underground economy makes people even more critical of the income tax. It also contributes significantly to the nation's deficit, the ever-widening gap between expenditures and revenues. Yet the income tax remains the federal government's most lucrative source of revenue. Obviously, the challenge is how to improve the income tax system to make it fairer and more lucrative.

Our current progressive income tax system permits numerous deductions and exemptions. It also taxes individuals on a graduated scale at rates ranging from 12 percent in the lowest income bracket to 50 percent in the highest income bracket. The basic principle is that those who have higher incomes should pay a greater percentage in taxes than those with lower incomes.

The problem with the progressive income tax system as it has evolved is that many taxpayers believe the wealthy do not pay considerably more because they benefit from loophole deductions. As one representative has said,

People see those who make a lot more money than they do not paying any taxes at all, and they say 'Hey, is that fair?' . . . *This growing sense that some taxpayers are carrying the burden for those with the most creative accountants has brought with it widespread tax evasion [which contributes to the deficit].* [1]

The progressive tax system, with its brackets, exemptions, and deductions, is also terribly confusing. The legislative director of the National Taxpayers Union says that "Wading through the tax code is getting to be pretty near impossible."[2] He is probably right. The current tax code is composed of 7,000 pages of regulations, deductions, and exemptions. Four out of ten taxpayers hire professionals ranging from H. R. Block to expensive tax accountants to fill out their returns. It is estimated that over $60 billion a year is spent by people complying with or taking advantage of IRS regulations.[3] What can or should be done to improve the public's confidence and support for the income tax?

A popular alternative is a flat-rate income tax system, which would allow no deductions and no exemptions and require every taxpayer to pay at the same rate. A number of flat-rate tax proposals have already been introduced in Congress. Proponents argue that it would be

[1] Pamela Fessler, ''Flat-Rate Tax Plan Advanced as Radical Cure for Problems of Existing Revenue System,'' *Congressional Quarterly*, 40 (June 5, 1982), p. 1331.
[2] *Ibid.*, p. 1332.
[3] William Safire, ''Flat Tax Fair, Efficient, Adaptable,'' *Houston Chronicle*, May 4, 1982.

America's Underground Economy* (Unreported Income)

Source	Individuals Not Reporting	Annual Tax Loss**
Business Activity	Doctors, lawyers, building contractors, salespersons, retail store operators, independent contractors	$26 billion
Capital Gains	Sellers of real estate, commodities, and securities	$9.1 billion
Dividends & Interest	Holders of stocks, bonds, savings, CD's, money market certificates	$8.2 billion
Partnerships & Small Business Corporations	Owners, stockholders	$7.2 billion
Pensions	Eligible beneficiaries	$2.8 billion
Wages & Salaries	Moonlighters, household workers, farm workers, service personnel (recipients of cash payments)	$4.8 billion
Non-filers	People failing to file an income tax return	$4.9 billion
Illegal Sector	Persons involved in drugs, gambling, and prostitution	$ 8 billion

SOURCE: Pamela Fessler, "Stricter Tax Compliance Seen as Easy Way to Lift Revenues," *Congressional Quarterly*, June 26, 1981, p. 1521–22.

*The underground economy is all income not reported to the IRS. It results in lost tax revenues—monies that would have been paid into the U.S. Treasury.

**FY 1981.

fairer, much simpler to understand, an impetus to productivity, and a more lucrative revenue source. It would be fairer because it would eliminate many deductions perceived by the public as benefiting the rich. It would be simpler because it would substitute a single across-the-board rate (suggestions range from 10 to 19 percent) for the current maze of multiple tax brackets. It would also simplify filing procedures; some have speculated that the entire tax form could be printed on a single postcard. The flat-rate tax would improve productivity by making it unprofitable for individuals to invest their money in nonproductive tax shelters. Finally, it would bring more money into the Treasury by eliminating one of the incentives to participate in the underground economy.

Not everyone is sold on the idea. Opponents see it as a scheme to aid the rich. Senator Russell Long, member of the Senate Finance Committee, says: "If you're rich, you'll love it; if you're not rich, look out!"[4] In an attempt to deal with this complaint, a number of the flat-rate tax proposals have provided for sizeable personal exemptions for lower income individuals to ensure that they pay little, if any, tax. Opponents of this "hybrid" flat-rate tax system cite studies by the Joint Committee on Taxation and the Tax Analysis Division of the Congressional Budget Office which show that such strategies reduce the taxes paid by the poor and the rich but leave middle-class taxpayers "holding the bag."[5] The middle class would suffer because they would lose the deductions for home mortgage interest, consumer installment interest, union dues, medical bills, moving expenses, alimony, and educational expenses. Ironically, middle-class tax-

In spite of the Internal Revenue Service's annual attempt to simplify the income tax reporting form, most Americans still find it terribly confusing. This makes proposals for a flat-rate income tax appealing to many despite the fact that popular deductions might be eliminated.

[4] Russell B. Long, "Flat-Rate Tax: 'If You're Rich, You'll Love It,'" *Houston Chronicle*, July 19, 1982.

[5] *Ibid.*

payers seem to think that only "fat cats" benefit from loopholes!

In spite of the objections to the flat-rate tax plan, a number of policymakers support its basic principles. As usual, however, no one agrees on how to draw up a plan. No matter how strong the economic arguments, revamping the tax system is difficult because of the politics involved.

Few members of Congress really believe that a pure flat-rate tax system will ever be enacted. In the short term, there are three stumbling blocks: 1) whether a certain amount of earnings should be exempted; and, if so, how much; 2) how to protect home mortgage holders; and 3) whether to allow continued deductions for charitable contributions. These are highly volatile issues. At the heart of each is the question of what is fair and equitable. How do you measure these concepts? Unfortunately, the individual who defined fairness as "You pay more than I do" may be all too correct.

The flat-rate tax proposal has already aroused opposition from powerful special interest groups: recipients of charitable contributions, homeowners, the housing industry, institutions financing housing construction, the buyers and sellers of tax shelters, tax lawyers and accountants, and, last but not least, politicians who raise campaign funds from special interests by seeking to retain existing tax loopholes or to create new ones.[6]

While few expect a pure flat-rate tax system to be adopted by Congress (one scholar went so far as to say "it does not have the chance of the proverbial snowball"[7]), many expect that the income tax system will be reformed somewhat because of the attention the debate has aroused. Still, making tax policy is one of the most difficult and most important tasks confronting policymakers. Each voter has his or her own ideas about what a fair and equitable tax system should be.

Having to balance economic considerations with political considerations will continue to be one of the most difficult obstacles to making public policy in the 1980s.

[6]Milton Friedman, ''How Flat is Flat?'' *Newsweek*, 100 (August 2, 1982), p. 52.
[7]*Ibid.*

SUMMARY

Government budgeting differs from private budgeting in many ways, including the amount of resources available, the government's ability to control the economy, and the decision-making structure. A government's budget reveals the nation's problems and priorities. Because money is power, the budget is a government's most important policy decision.

The United States budget has changed greatly over the years. Before the Civil War, customs duties were the primary source of revenue. Today, however, income and payroll taxes bring in most of the revenue. Government borrowing has also increased dramatically. The expenditure side of the budget has grown faster than the revenue side. In the 1960s, government spending shifted from defense to human resources, reflecting a change in the nation's priorities. Since 1969, expenditures have exceeded revenues. Recent presidents have tried to balance the budget or at least reduce the national debt, but with little or no success.

Budgeting is a multiyear activity occurring in four phases: 1) executive preparation and submission, 2) congressional authorization and appropriation, 3) implementation and control (this phase coincides with the fiscal year, October 1 to September 30), and 4) review and audit. The players and strategies differ in each phase, and a phase of one fiscal year overlaps other phases of other fiscal years.

Politics plays an important role in the budgetary process and makes the whole system accountable to the citizenry. To closer it is to election time, the more concerned politicians become about the economy. To change inflation, employment, and personal income levels, the government may change monetary or fiscal policy. These changes affect the amount of income taxes people pay, the kinds of benefits available under government programs such as Social Security, food stamps, and unemployment insurance, and people's ability to get credit for buying a home or car or investing in a business.

KEY TERMS

apportionment
balance of payments
budget
Congressional Budget and Impoundment Control Act of 1974
continuing resolution

deferrals
deficit
discount rate
equity
excise tax
Federal Reserve System
First Concurrent Resolution
fiscal policy
fiscal year
gross national product (GNP)
impoundment
income tax
loophole (tax expenditure)
management by objective (MBO)
monetary policy
money supply
national debt
nontax revenue sources
open market operations
oversight committee
planning-programming-budgeting systems (PPBS)
progressive tax
public (collective) goods
reconciliation legislation
reprogramming
rescissions
reserve requirement
Second Concurrent Resolution
tax indexing
transfers
uncontrollable spending
zero-base budgeting (ZBB)

SUGGESTED READINGS

Berman, Larry. *The Office of Management and Budget and the Presidency, 1921–1979*. Princeton, N.J.: Princeton University Press, 1979.

Borcherding, Thomas E., ed. *Budgets and Bureaucrats: The Sources of Government Growth*. Durham, N.C.: Duke University Press, 1977.

Boskin, Michael J., and Wildavsky, Aaron, eds. *The Federal Budget: Economics and Politics*. San Francisco, Calif.: Institute for Contemporary Studies Press, 1982.

Break, George R. *Financing Government in a Federal System*. Washington, D.C.: Brookings Institution, 1980.

Derthick, Martha. *Uncontrollable Spending for Social Services Grants*. Washington, D.C.: Brookings Institution, 1975.

Hall, Robert E., and Rabushka, Alvin. *Low Tax, Simple Tax, Flat Tax*. New York: McGraw-Hill, 1983.

Havemann, Joel. *Congress and the Budget*. Bloomington, Ind.: Indiana University Press, 1978.

Pfiffner, James. *The President, the Budget and Congress: Impoundment and the 1974 Budget Act*. Boulder, Colo.: Westview Press, 1979.

Schick, Allen. *Congress and Money: Budgeting, Spending, and Taxing*. Washington, D.C.: Urban Institute, 1980.

Wholey, Joseph. *Zero-Base Budgeting and Program Evaluation*. Lexington, Mass.: Lexington Books, 1978.

CHAPTER 18

DOMESTIC SOCIAL POLICY

Categories of Policy ■ Self-Regulation ■ Regulation ■ Distribution ■ Redistribution

In a very real sense, much of the material in this book has been leading up to this chapter. While the reader may not have perceived a gradual yet continuous crescendo, many of the topics discussed in earlier chapters play a part in the policy process. A brief review will help you see how earlier materials fit together to affect policy-making and implementation.

Congress, the presidency, and the courts are clearly all important in shaping the laws, decisions, and executive orders that form the skeleton of public policy. The bureaucracy through the process of implementing policy decisions, the courts when interpreting and applying the law, and even Congress when tinkering with its earlier output all have a hand in fleshing out the skeletal form in which most policy decisions are initially enunciated. Figure 18.1 shows how these components fit together.

At both the adoption and implementation stages, decision-makers are responsive not only to each other but to the array of forces discussed in earlier chapters. Political parties, through their platforms and the pressures exerted by their lead-ers in the White House and Congress, are important in determining which issues will be placed on the policy agenda and what alternatives will be considered in seeking solutions. In making these choices, party leaders are, to varying degrees, responding to public opinion, interest groups, and, ultimately, the electorate. Not all of the constraints that policymakers work within are imposed by people. In selecting among alternatives—indeed, when deciding what the alternatives are—policymakers are limited by the Constitution and, to a lesser extent, by our federal form of government.

With so many factors impinging on the making of public policy, it is not surprising that the process can be exceedingly complex. The steps by which Congress passes a law (see Figure 11.1, for example) outline the process for only one of the four institutions that is likely to become involved in making and implementing any controversial policy.

Although the nation's founders did not foresee the development of our contemporary bureaucracy, much of the complexity of the process is not

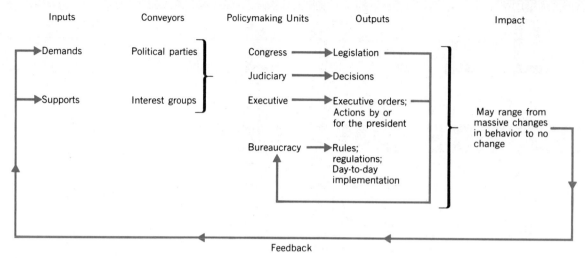

FIGURE 18.1
Policy Input-Output Model

without design. They intentionally weighted the odds toward inaction. This was done through the separation of powers, which gave the executive, legislative, and judicial institutions each a role in making and carrying out policy. Because of this design, policy objectives are most likely to be realized when all three institutions support a goal.

Policymaking in our system is further complicated by the division of authority between the states and the national government. Under federalism, the national government holds sway in some areas, such as the regulation of the interstate flow of goods, passengers, television signals, and so forth. In other policy areas, such as education, both state and federal law play a part. In these realms, the objectives of the two levels of government will sometimes be indentical, as when both appropriate money to improve education or build sewage treatment plants. At other times the two may conflict, as in Buckeye, Louisiana, where a federal judge ordered some students to attend a racially mixed school in a nearby city while a state judge forbade them to attend that school and ordered them to continue going to school in Buckeye. Policy of a third type, such as traffic regulations, is left exclusively to state and local governments.

Since public policy is the product of a variety of forces, some introductory American government texts reserve the discussion of public policy exclusively for the last chapter or two. As you are well aware by this time, we have woven a discussion of three policy areas into the fabric of this book. Ad-

ditionally, in chapters 15 and 16 we analyzed civil rights and civil liberties policy. In this chapter we briefly review the major components of some of the important federal programs that we have not dealt with elsewhere.

CATEGORIES OF POLICY

Demands for public policy can be divided into two categories, or patterns—consensual or conflictual.[1] A **consensual demand pattern** *exists when there is a high level of agreement among those in society who are interested in the policy area.* This need not mean that the public unanimously favors the policy put forth

The policy objectives of different levels of government may conflict, as in Buckeye, Louisiana. There a federal judge ordered some students to attend a racially mixed school in a nearby city while a state judge ordered them to continue going to school in Buckeye.

by the government. More than likely a sizable share of the public is supremely happy as it goes through life totally ignorant of even the existence of the issue, to say nothing of the ramifications of alternative decisions which the government might take. When there is a consensual demand pattern, there are no organized groups actively opposing the action being urged on the government. An example of this situation would be pensions or hospitals for ex-military personnel, two programs not opposed by any important segment of society.

In a *conflictual demand pattern*, *opposing groups are trying to influence Congress, the courts, or the bureaucracy to adopt their position.* For example, natural gas producers have sought the authority to charge consumers prices equal to the prices on the world market. Consumer groups have fought vigorously to limit prices. Another illustration of conflictual demand involves pollution standards for automobile exhaust. Environmentalists have urged the implementation of standards significantly limiting the amount of emissions in automobile exhaust. Car manufacturers, citing costs and technological problems, have displayed equal commitment in seeking to postpone bringing their products into compliance with these standards.

In response to demands, public officials make policy decisions. Officials can either choose among the demands which they receive, or they can delegate the authority to decide to some other group. Thus policymakers themselves may make

an *allocation, passing out benefits to a set of interested participants.* These goodies may include funds for highways, education grants, sewage treatment plants, or new federal facilities. In instances of policy *delegation, the policymakers specify the objectives of a program and establish broad guidelines for achieving these goals, but leave it up to some other group—typically a bureaucratic unit or a private organization—to make the actual decisions.* For example, in the clean air legislation, Congress established the standards to be achieved but left it up to the states to determine how they would go about meeting the standards.

Table 18.1 shows how the two types of demands and the two types of responses can be combined to create four types of policies. When the demand pattern is consensual (that is, when those who are interested in the policy agree about what it should be) and the government delegates authority to make decisions, the product will be self-regulation. In this situation, a private group is allowed to make policy in the sphere it is interested in. If governmental authority is delegated on a topic on which there is disagreement among those interested in the outcome, the product is regulation. Here a governmental agency is directed to specify the rules and procedures that must be followed by those involved. For example, the Environmental Protection Agency establishes standards for handling hazardous wastes and the clean-up of abandoned sites at which wastes have been dumped.

When the legislature is allocating benefits and

Support for mass transit construction, like this subway in Boston, is an example of an allocation policy response since federal legislators determined which among the many applicants for mass transit funds would actually be funded.

TABLE 18.1
Policy Classification Scheme

Policy Supply Pattern	Demand Pattern	
	Consensual	Conflictual
Delegation	Self-regulation	Regulation
Allocation	Distribution	Redistribution

SOURCE: Based on Michael T. Hayes, *Lobbyists and Legislators* (New Brunswick, N.J.: Rutgers University Press, 1981), p. 30.

costs itself rather than having the bureaucracy do it, and if the demand pattern is consensual, distributive policies will be produced. An example is the federal program to pay a share of the costs of constructing sewage treatment plants—the goal of having cleaner water being one to which few in society object. When there is disagreement as to which values should be incorporated into public policy, but the legislature makes the allocation, the resulting policies are redistributive. The use of federal revenues to provide Aid to Families with Dependent Children or to pay for housing, food stamps, or health care for the poor are examples of redistributive programs.

The ways in which supply and demand patterns intersect should become clearer as we discuss specific program areas in the four categories.

SELF-REGULATION

Some groups want the government to leave them alone to take care of their own business. The best known examples are occupational groups such as doctors and lawyers, but there are others, including realtors, morticians, and cosmetologists. What these groups want most from government is the power to set standards for working as a member of their occupation. To practice law or medicine or to prepare bodies for burial, for example, one must meet certain standards of competency. Often these include a minimum amount of education, experience, or both. Typically, potential members must also pass a licensing examination. These standards are imposed by law, but the actual implementation of the requirements is delegated by the legislature to a board of examiners made up of practitioners. To illustrate, a portion of the bar exams that law school graduates must pass in order to practice law is designed, administered, and graded by lawyers serving on state bar examination committees.

An obvious advantage for members of licensed

occupations is that the number of practitioners can be limited. By increasing the education or experience requirements or making the examination more difficult, the number of new entrants into the occupation can be restricted so that competition does not become so great that practitioners are forced to reduce their fees.

One may ask why legislatures have turned the authority to regulate occupational entry over to various professions. The answer is that representatives of these professions have convinced legislators that delegation of state authority to the groups will serve the public interest. Leaders of the profession argue that licensing and the establishment of standards exclude the unqualified and the dishonest from mistreating or bilking the public. They also contend that professionals themselves are the best qualified to determine the skills or knowledge needed to practice a profession.

Occupational groups can persuade the government to delegate its authority to them because the request is noncontroversial; i.e. the demand pattern is consensual. The people currently engaged in the occupation perceive an economic advantage and perhaps a certain amount of prestige in state licensing. When licensing is instituted there is typically a "grandfather provision" that automatically licenses all current practitioners. As a result, support for regulation is nearly unanimous. One might argue that licensing restricts entry and will probably lead to higher prices for consumers, but such consequences seem so remote and insignificant to most people that they do not actively oppose the delegation of authority.

REGULATION

Regulatory policy is policy for which the legislature or judiciary has established broad guidelines and left the specific implementation to a bureaucracy. It is likely to be produced when the legislature is unwilling to decide between powerful competing groups. Rather than deciding for labor and against business or for grain producers and against livestock raisers, the legislature may enact legislation that establishes some broad, vague parameters. The fleshing out of the program enacted by the legislature is left up to an agency or department such as the National Labor Relations Board or the Department of Agriculture.

After legislation has been enacted and responsibility for preparing regulations and guidelines has been assigned to an agency, group conflict may be played out in another arena. As discussed in chapter 13 (Bureaucracy), group representatives try to influence regulatory agency officials to draft regulations favorable to their group's positions. The group that loses in the regulation-writing stage may go back to the legislature and request that it overrule the agency with new legislation. This was done when Congress forbade the Federal Trade Commission to ban saccharin even though the FTC had concluded that the artificial sweetner could be hazardous.

DISTRIBUTION

Distributive policies spread government benefits such as funds or projects to a certain share of the public without making it apparent to other groups that they are sharing in the costs. In other words, all active participants appear to win and none to lose. Of course only in *Alice in Wonderland* and road races in which all finishers get T-shirts do all players win. Ultimately, someone has to pick up the tab—but more about that in a moment.

Legislators prefer distributive policies because they are a source of federal funding for their constituents. *Pork barrel legislation, which provides funding for projects in legislators' districts*, is a form of distributive policy. Building a stretch of interstate highway, a new federal building, or a dam creates job opportunities for construction firms and troops of local construction workers. As the payrolls cycle and recycle through the business community, they can be a major factor in the economic health of a congressional district.

The economic fallout from pork barrel projects may go beyond the construction work. Reclamation dams in the West store up water that can be used to transform arid land into fertile fields. Dams built by the Tennessee Valley Authority provide electricity and form lakes that can be used

by boating enthusiasts. Elsewhere, interstate highways may become arteries sustaining narrow strips of commercial and industrial development reaching far out into suburbia and beyond.

Pork barrel legislation is carefully designed so that most, if not all, members of Congress have an incentive to support it. This is achieved by including a great many projects in the legislation to ensure that most states and congressional districts will have a stake in passing it. In congressional jargon, these pieces of legislation are known as "Christmas tree" bills because there is something there for virtually everyone. If a legislator objects to some part of the bill, then he or she jeopardizes the programs that benefit his or her district.

The high priority which members of Congress assign to the development of distributive legislation is clear in the rules of the House. The Public Works Committee, which each year produces the most lavishly decorated Christmas tree bill, is one of the few committees that can meet while the full House is in session without obtaining special permission.

The reason for insuring that the project-laden Public Works bill passes without undue delay should be clear. Morris Fiorina and Roger Noll have argued that securing projects for the district is the type of activity most likely to help legislators get reelected.[2] Taking a stand on a controversial policy issue will probably antagonize some of a legislator's voters, but bringing federal dollars and jobs into the district will be roundly applauded. Even strong advocates of budget balancing typically make an exception when proposals to cut funding would hurt *their* districts. Some members of Congress even joke that foreign aid is anything that is not given to their districts.

As you might expect, challengers running against incumbents sometimes criticize the current officeholder for failing to get a fair share of the federal boodle for the district. Eulau and Karps assert that a legislator's success in obtaining federal funds is an important measure of his or her responsiveness to the needs of constituents.[3] Responsiveness is, of course, a basic tenet of a representative form of government.

The myth that distributive policies have no losers rests on an erroneous assumption. Ultimately, someone has to pay for the dams, highways, sewage treatment plants, and so forth. The perception that there are no losers is fostered by the insignificance (and at times, total absence) of organized opposition to pork barrel legislation. Generally no one bears enough of the cost to make opposition worthwhile. The funds are collected through the federal revenue system and then doled out in such a way that no one can trace what becomes of his or her tax payment, and few people feel that they are paying for someone else's project. Moreover, program benefits are usually distributed so that most congressional districts have one or more projects which would be jeopardized by a cut in funding.[4] Thus, there are the beneficiaries who actively pursue their goals and there are those who will bear the cost, but the cost is so negligible to the individual that few complain.

This pattern has changed slightly in recent years. Regional disagreements over how federal dollars should be distributed lie at the heart of the North-South, or Frost Belt-Sun Belt, conflict in Congress.

Having laid out some of the basic features of distributive programs, we turn now to a discussion of the primary provisions of some of the more important federal undertakings in this area. The programs to be discussed here are education, housing, Social Security, and home loan guarantees.

Education

Postsecondary Higher Education Federal aid to education takes several forms. At the postsecondary level, federal grants and loans have been instrumental in the building programs of many colleges and universities. From the time the Soviets launched Sputnik until the 1970s, funding under the National Defense Education Act (NDEA) and other legislation was an important source of fellowships for graduate students. The National Science Foundation, although sharply reduced in size by the Reagan administration, has funded university-run programs for training and upgrading the skills of public school teachers.

Federal programs have also opened college gates to thousands of undergraduates. Basic Education Opportunity Grants have provided money for economically deprived young people to pay tuition and other fees. Middle-class students have, over the years, been eligible for federal loan programs that require no payments while the student is in

school. Once out of school, interest is assessed, but at a lower rate than would generally be charged by a private lender. Under some loan programs, such as one created by the NDEA, students who became teachers had a portion of their loans forgiven. An older program was the "GI Bill" of World War II (which has reappeared in various forms). This gave living allowances to veterans to enable them to go to school.

Another set of federal programs was created to prevent an anticipated shortage of health care professionals. Responding to projections that the United States was facing a potential shortage of doctors, Congress enacted legislation reducing the costs that medical schools or aspiring doctors would otherwise have to bear. It has been estimated that federal aid pays as much as 60 percent of the cost of medical education.[5]

The federal government has provided two other types of aid that are important to colleges and universities. One of these is the oldest form of aid, having begun in 1862. In that year, the Morrill Act gave federal lands to state colleges to support the teaching of agricultural and mechanical subjects. This is the basis for the land grant institutions.

The last type of federal support for higher education is research grants. Until the cutbacks by the Reagan administration, the National Institute of Education, National Institute of Mental Health, and other funding agencies were major sources of research money. Indeed, federal funds supported more than half of the research carried out in institutions of higher learning.[6]

Public Education At the elementary and secondary level, federal aid has taken a form quite different from the scholarships, loans, and building programs provided at the postsecondary level. During the 1950s and 1960s, there was widespread support among educators for federal aid to pay teachers' salaries and build classrooms to accommodate the baby boom youngsters. Such legislation has never been passed.

Instead of meeting the requests of state and local school officials, who would like to have money to use as they see fit, the federal government has developed a series of *categorical grant programs, which provide money that can only be used for purposes specified by Congress or executive agencies*. Thus, beginning with the Smith-Hughes Act of 1917, there

Federally-funded educational programs targeted to Indian children living on reservations are examples of categorical grant programs whose designs have been determined by federal officials, rather than state and local officials.

have been federal aid programs for vocational education. The federal government has also provided free lunches and breakfasts for poor children and subsidized lunches for all children. In addition, there have been programs to pay for bilingual education, education on Indian reservations, education for the handicapped, and aid to schools that are desegregating. The federal dollars are insufficient, however, to pay the total costs of these programs.

Besides programs designed for a specific purpose, there is the "impact aid program," which has been broadened to provide assistance to most of the nation's school districts. The "impact" the federal government seeks to alleviate is the supposed extra burden that the federal government's presence creates for a school system. This burden may be created by federal land holdings in the school district, since these lands are not subject to local property taxation. Since property taxes are an important revenue source for most school districts, the federal government compensates districts for lost tax money by paying a certain amount for each student whose parents live on federal land (e.g., military bases), work for the federal government, or live in public housing. Recent presidents have proposed cutting or eliminating the impact aid program. It is almost universally popular among school officials and members of Congress, however, so these proposals have never gotten very far.

Federal aid to education underwent a major transformation in 1965 with the passage of the Elementary and Secondary Education Act (ESEA). This legislation was the culmination of a 20-year effort to develop a larger role in education for the federal government. At the urging of President Lyndon Johnson, a one-time school teacher, Congress approved a massive aid program. The rationale for ESEA was to improve the calibre of education offered to the children of low-income families. The bulk of the funds went for compensatory education; they were distributed on the basis of the number of low-income children in a school district and the state's per-pupil expenditures. By directing aid to poor children, ESEA finessed one of the main sticking points that had derailed earlier efforts to pass federal aid bills. Congress authorized private schools that enrolled low-income students to participate in the program. This overcame the opposition of the Catholic church, which had objected to earlier proposals that made no provision for helping parochial education.[7]

Table 18.2 shows the pattern of education funding for every state. Clearly there are interstate differences. Since federal funds are heavily oriented toward the disadvantaged, they play a larger role in the budgets of poor states. Mississippi, the poorest state in the nation, relies most heavily on federal aid. We also see from this table that state aid generally plays a more important role in the South, although in our newest state (Hawaii), state aid accounts for the largest share of the budget. States in a crescent running from New England (led by New Hampshire) through the Midwest rely most heavily on local property taxes. You may recall that most of the midyear school closings and teacher strikes of recent years have

TABLE 18.2

Revenue and Nonrevenue Receipts of Public Elementary and Secondary Schools, by Source and by State: 1977–1978
(Amounts in thousands of dollars)

State	Total Revenue and Nonrevenue Receipts	Revenue Receipts		
		Federal Percent of Total	State Percent of Total	Local and Other* Percent of Total
1	2	3	4	5
United States	**$84,969,058**	9.5	43.0	47.6**
Alabama	1,083,386	16.6	61.5	21.9
Alaska	321,337	14.1	67.3	18.6
Arizona	1,028,884	8.8	44.3	46.9
Arkansas	580,025	16.5	48.4	35.1
California	9,458,394	9.8	38.8	51.4
Colorado	1,287,275	6.5	38.7	54.9
Connecticut	1,086,375	5.3	24.0	70.7
Delaware	260,845	11.1	66.4	22.5
District of Columbia	293,590	31.6	—	68.4
Florida	2,711,364	11.4	50.6	37.9
Georgia	1,556,415	14.6	48.2	37.2
Hawaii	348,015	16.2	82.8	1.0
Idaho	297,547	15.0	45.1	39.9
Illinois	4,523,773	8.6	37.7	53.7
Indiana	1,882,486	6.1	51.5	42.4
Iowa	1,180,751	6.0	39.7	54.3
Kansas	757,789	9.3	35.3	55.4
Kentucky	882,472	17.2	62.5	20.2
Louisiana	1,291,854	14.9	53.9	31.2
Maine	381,082	9.1	46.1	44.8
Maryland	1,801,226	8.1	38.8	53.2
Massachusetts	2,742,978	5.0	30.3	64.7
Michigan	4,093,284	7.6	41.3	51.0
Minnesota	2,020,427	5.9	56.8	37.3
Mississippi	607,123	24.4	55.8	19.8
Missouri	1,524,717	10.3	35.0	54.7
Montana	361,770	9.6	51.7	38.7
Nebraska	579,161	7.2	16.1	76.7
Nevada	266,445	9.8	34.0	56.2
New Hampshire	292,853	7.1	6.3	86.6
New Jersey	3,167,372	6.6	41.6	51.7
New Mexico	484,765	18.3	65.0	16.7
New York	8,767,421	7.1	37.0	55.9
North Carolina	1,609,173	14.0	63.2	22.8
North Dakota	233,278	11.2	44.0	44.9
Ohio	3,723,942	6.2	41.0	52.8
Oklahoma	1,007,369	12.4	55.0	32.6
Oregon	1,137,821	10.1	29.1	60.8
Pennsylvania	4,843,168	8.7	44.5	46.8
Rhode Island	305,721	9.2	31.6	59.2
South Carolina	708,336	21.1	46.8	32.1
South Dakota	236,947	14.2	18.1	67.7
Tennessee	1,294,373	12.5	49.4	38.1
Texas	4,735,430	10.6	51.2	38.1
Utah	576,596	9.6	54.8	35.5
Vermont	189,333	7.4	27.5	65.0
Virginia	1,830,542	12.1	37.2	50.8
Washington	1,794,769	9.9	58.0	32.1
West Virginia	568,645	12.4	61.1	26.5
Wisconsin	2,038,519	5.8	34.4	59.8
Wyoming	211,895	7.0	30.8	62.2

SOURCE: Reprinted in W. Vance Grant and Leo J. Eiden, *Digest of Education Statistics, 1980* (Washington, D.C.: U.S. Government Printing Office, 1980), p. 70; based on data from U.S. Department of Health, Education, and Welfare, National Center for Education Statistics, *Revenues and Expenditures for Public Elementary and Secondary Education, 1977–78.*
*Local and other revenue receipts include revenue receipts from local and intermediate sources, gifts, and tuition and fees from patrons. **Because of rounding, percents may not add to 100.0.

occurred in these states. Inability to secure approval of bond proposals has left some schools unable to meet payrolls and teacher demands because of their heavy reliance on local efforts.

Education is frequently cited as one of the policy areas that should be the responsibility of the states under the Tenth Amendment since the Constitution does not assign it to the national government. As Table 18.2 makes evident, federal dollars play a role in the financing of education in every state—and probably every school district. School officials have had few qualms about accepting federal dollars. Tenth Amendment arguments, then, are raised only by people who object to federal demands such as the requirement that there be no discrimination because of race, sex, national origin, or handicap. These requirements are the ''strings'' attached to federal funds.

Housing

Beginning with the New Deal, the federal government has funded programs that have housed millions of American families. Many of these programs distribute benefits not just to the families who get housing but to those in the housing industry such as builders, construction workers, and realtors. Both low- and middle-income families have benefited.

Programs for the Low Income As part of President Franklin Roosevelt's effort to create work and stimulate the economy, funds were first appropriated in 1937 to allow communities to acquire land and build housing for the poor. Such units have since been built in communities large and small across the country. In major cities, public housing has taken the form of high-rise apartments, while in small towns it may consist of duplexes or quadriplexes dispersed throughout the community. These spartan units provide structurally sound dwellings that, because of a federal subsidy, rent for substantially less than one would pay for a less habitable privately owned tenement or shack. Rent for these units is based on a family's size and income. If a family's income rises or its size shrinks so that it ceases to be eligible for public housing, it must move out.

Since the rent for public housing is below the market level, there are waiting lists for the units in most communities. This is an important distinction between low-income housing and many other federal programs for the poor. Public housing is not an entitlement program. Not all people who qualify can participate because the low-income housing program has never had enough funds to handle everyone who is eligible. This shortage is not being alleviated, since in recent years relatively few family units have been built. Most new construction is of small apartments for the elderly.

The popularity of public housing among the poor should not obscure the difficulties it has encountered in some large cities. Some high-rise apartments have not been adequately policed; tenants have been terrorized by gangs and the buildings have been vandalized by vagrants and drug addicts. The most extreme case was St. Louis's Pruitt-Igoe Project. Hailed as the prototype for high density urban developments, conditions at Pruitt-Igoe became so bad that the tenants moved out and other families refused to move in. After unsuccessful efforts to rehabilitate the buildings and their image in the community, they were dynamited by local authorities.

Builders, developers, and realtors were never strong supporters of public housing since they did not profit from it. Since the 1960s they have prevailed on Congress to shift away from publicly owned and operated housing for the poor and to institute programs that provide for greater private sector involvement. Builders have liked ''turnkey projects'' in which units are privately constructed

Public policies do not always produce the intended results. High-density public housing projects, once thought to be ideal, are now regarded as undesirable. The Pruitt-Igoe Project in St. Louis was finally dynamited by local officials after numerous attempts to rehabilitate it failed.

Loans guaranteed by the Federal
Housing Administration (FHA) and the
Veteran's Administration (VA) are
examples of distributive federal
programs largely benefitting
middle-class Americans.

and then turned over to public authorities to operate.

Some landlords have been quite supportive of programs in which the federal government subsidizes the rent payments of low-income families living in privately owned dwellings. Realtors, developers, and builders have liked mortgage subsidy programs in which federal funds paid a share of the interest charges, thereby bringing the monthly payment down to a level at which a new stratum of society was able to buy a home.

As the role of the private sector in meeting the housing needs of the poor has expanded, the housing industry has changed from opposing to supporting federal aid. These groups have become the leading advocates of low-income housing programs.

Their support was insufficient, however, to keep the Reagan administration from substantially reducing the number of new subsidized units. Moreover, the Reagan administration wants to raise the eligibility standards for those who get financial assistance for their housing. President Reagan is also considering gradually phasing out the program under which private landlords are paid subsidies for housing 1.5 million low-income families.[8]

Programs for the Middle Income   At about the time the federal government began paying for public housing projects, legislation was passed that completely changed the way middle-income

families financed their homes. The Federal Housing Administration, created in 1934, guarantees the repayment of certain loans made by banks and savings and loan institutions. Loans guaranteed by FHA have required relatively small down payments (as low as five percent), have been for extended periods (up to 40 years), and are repaid in equal monthly installments. These features were quite different from the typical pre-FHA loan which required a substantial down payment (often as much as 50 percent), and were for relatively short periods (ten years or less). In addition, the full principal of these loans was due at one time. In case of default on FHA loans, the agency pays off the loan and repossesses the house, thereby relieving the lender of any financial risk.

The FHA approach (later adopted by the Veterans' Administration loan program for former military personnel) was so popular that it became the model for the entire home finance industry. Not until the raging inflation of the late 1970s and the accompanying spiraling interest rates did lenders turn away from FHA-type long-term fixed-rate mortgages.

Most people think of distributive policies as payments made to individuals or groups by the government. This perspective is too limited for a proper understanding of the federal role in middle-class housing. An important aspect of federal assistance to the middle class is the tax advantages enjoyed by home owners. By allowing home buyers to deduct the amount they pay for interest and property taxes, the federal government foregoes $39 billion in revenue, which serves as a subsidy for the buyer.[9] For most people buying a home, this is the largest deduction claimed and may be the only factor that makes it worthwhile for them to file the long form of the 1040 income tax return. Moreover, it is the tax break that makes it reasonable for many families to buy rather than to rent.

Social Security

Social Security has grown until it has become the largest program in the federal government. Benefits totaling approximately $120 billion are annually paid out to some 36 million beneficiaries.

As it was designed, Social Security is part social insurance and part a game of passing on deficits to the next generation. Almost all workers pay a share of their earnings into Social Security. The employees' contributions are matched by their employers. In 1983 employees and employers each paid 7 percent of the employees' first $38,100 in earnings into the system. Both the tax rate and the amount of earnings on which it is levied have risen, with increases being particularly large in recent years.

Although we speak of Social Security as if it were a single fund with a single purpose, it actually has three components. One pays benefits to qualified retired workers who paid into the sys-

tem, to their spouses, and to their dependents who are still children. A second component pays disability benefits to former contributors who are no longer able to work. The third and newest portion is the Medicare program, which was added in 1965 to help pay some of the medical expenses of the elderly.

The retirement part of Social Security has periodically been in financial trouble since the 1970s. Prior to that time, there were so many workers paying into the system that there was always plenty of money to give to beneficiaries. During the 1970s, the ratio of workers to retirees began to drop as the number of retirees increased, a process accelerated by the early retirements that many employers encouraged. Contributions to the system were further reduced by the high rate of unemployment. By 1981 the ratio of workers to beneficiaries was down to 3.3 contributors for each beneficiary, and projections suggested it would continue dropping. The solvency of the retirement fund was further weakened by increases in the benefits paid. In 1972 there was a 20 percent jump in payments, which continued to rise thereafter since a cost of living adjustment (COLA) was instituted in that year.

The troubles encountered by the Social Security system point up a frequent misconception. Although often referred to as a social insurance program, it is also partially a program to pass the

The Social Security program is part social insurance and part a game of passing on deficits to the next generation. But a declining birth rate poses real problems for the future since there will be fewer workers paying into the system to support larger numbers drawing out retirement pay.

buck to the next generation. From its earliest days, the system has paid out more to many beneficiaries than they contributed. For example, a worker who made the maximum contribution every year from the time Social Security was begun would have paid in $12,791 by the end of 1980. Many retirees draw out that amount in three years, and a person receiving the maximum benefit would have gotten back more than he or she ever contributed in a little over a year and a half. Public misperception is so widespread that only 15 percent of a national sample thinks it will receive more in benefits than it contributed.[10] The difference between what a person contributes while working and what he or she receives back during retirement is founded by the money collected from current workers.

A longer range problem for Social Security is that the declining birthrate will result in relatively few workers paying into the system when the post-World War II baby boom generation retires early in the next century. It has been estimated that a deficit as large as $1.5 trillion may be amassed over the next 75 years.[11]

Early in the Carter administration (1977) when Social Security was first threatened with bankruptcy, the tax rate and the amount of earnings on which the tax was levied were increased (see Table 18.3). Despite projections made at that time that estimated these changes would provide enough money to keep the system operating into the next century, by late 1982 the retirement fund was having to borrow from the other funds to keep afloat.

In trying to promote the solvency of Social Security, President Reagan quickly got Congress to eliminate benefits for college-age dependents of recipients. His initial attempts to institute changes which would produce greater savings, such as raising the retirement age, immediately encountered fierce congressional opposition. Resolution of the Social Security funding crisis was delayed until 1983 while a bipartisan commission worked up recommendations. Once the commission had submitted its report, Congress moved with uncharacteristic speed and adopted several major modifications. The major changes which were designed to save $165 billion by the end of the decade are listed below.

1. For the first time taxes would be levied on the Social Security benefits received by more affluent retirees, defined as individuals with earnings above $25,000 annually or couples earning more than $32,000. This is a step toward redefining Social Security as a need-based program, thereby introducing something of a redistributive element.

2. Federal employees hired after January 1, 1984, must contribute to Social Security rather than to the separate retirement system

TABLE 18.3

Social Security Taxes

Calendar Year	Tax Rate (percent)	Wage Base*	$10,000 Wage Earner		$20,000 Wage Earner		Maximum Wage Earner	
			Annual Contributions	Increase Over Prior Year	Annual Contributions	Increase Over Prior Year	Annual Contributions	Increase Over Prior Year
1977	5.85	$16,500	$585	—	$ 965.25	—	$ 965.25	—
1978	6.05	17,700	605	$20.00	1,070.85	$105.60	1,070.85	$105.60
1979	6.13	22,900	613	8.00	1,226.00	155.15	1,403.77	332.92
1980	6.13	25,900	613	—	1,226.00	—	1,587.67	183.90
1981	6.65	29,700	665	52.00	1,330.00	104.00	1,975.05	387.38
1982	6.70	32,400	670	5.00	1,340.00	10.00	2,170.80	195.75
1983	6.70	35,100	670	—	1,340.00	—	2,351.70	180.90
1984	7.00	38,100	700	30.00	1,400.00	60.00	2,667.00	315.30
1985	7.05	41,100	705	35.00	1,410.00	70.00	2,897.55	344.85
1986	7.15	44,100	715	10.00	1,430.00	20.00	3,153.15	255.60
1987	7.15	47,100	715	—	1,430.00	—	3,367.65	214.50
1988	7.51	50,100	751	36.00	1,502.00	72.00	3,762.51	394.86
1989	7.51	53,400	751	—	1,502.00	—	4,010.34	247.83
1990	7.65	57,000	765	14.00	1,530.00	28.00	4,360.50	350.16

SOURCE: Portions from *Congressional Quarterly Weekly Report* (Washington, D.C.: Congressional Quarterly, Inc., 1980), Vol. 38, Dec. 20, 1980, p. 3627; updated and expanded by authors to reflect 1983 legislative changes.

*Amounts for 1982–1990 are based on economic predictions.

for federal workers. The latter has paid more generous benefits than Social Security.

3. In changes which will affect today's college students, the age at which full benefits become available will be raised to 66 in 2009 and 67 in 2027. In these same years, workers who retire at age 62 will receive 75 percent and then 70 percent of the full benefits, compared with the current 80 percent. These changes were explained as being appropriate because of increasing life expectancy since the adoption of Social Security.

4. Some of the increases in Social Security taxes which were approved in 1977 will take affect one or two years earlier.

5. The cost of living adjustments will be delayed from July to January and the rate of wage increases will be used if it is lower than the consumer price index increases. In the past the latter has been used, which has meant that during recessions, benefits have risen rapidly even as active workers have seen their wage increases decline.

Among the consequences of these reforms is that Social Security in the future will replace a smaller share of the retirees' wages than in the past. Proponents of cutting benefits justify their position by noting that Social Security was never intended to cover all of a retiree's needs. Instead it was intended to supplement money from private pensions, annuities, and savings. However, less than half of the public and barely a third of those nearing retirement (ages 55 to 64) have resources other than Social Security.[12] As Social Security becomes less generous, workers will need to carefully consider whether they want to set aside more of their earnings for retirement or plan to experience substantial reductions in their lifestyles when they retire.

The reforms adopted in 1983 rejected organized labor's proposal to use general revenues to maintain high benefit levels. Conservatives have opposed this idea since they fear that Congress would give in to public pressures and raise benefits without increasing Social Security taxes and thereby contribute to still higher program deficits.

Projections are that Social Security will now be fiscally sound until early in the next century when the generation born during the post-World War II baby boom retires. This growth in beneficiaries, which will be accompanied by a decline in the number of contributors, will again cause money to be paid out faster than it is taken in. Today's student will be deeply affected by whatever action Congress ultimately takes to resolve the problems which wait just over the horizon.

Medicare Medicare was part of President Lyndon Johnson's Great Society program. It was designed to pay a share of the medical expenses of retirees. Benefits are paid out of a fund operated by Social Security that workers and their employ-

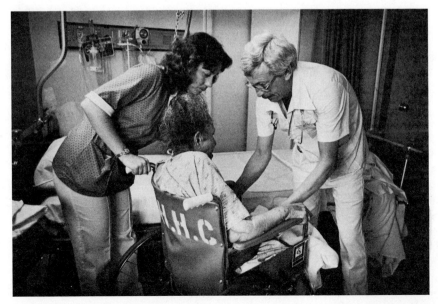

The Medicare program is designed to pay a share of the medical expenses of retirees. The program is one of the fastest growing, most controversial of all federal distributive programs.

ers make small contributions to in each pay period.

For participants (people over 65), Medicare pays most of the costs for as many as 90 days a year in the hospital, 100 days in a nursing home, and 100 home visits by a nurse or therapist. If they wish, Medicare participants can pay a nominal monthly charge and in return the federal government will pay up to 80 percent of their doctor's fees after the patient pays the first $75 each year. Shifting much of the costs of medical care for the elderly to the federal government has resulted in the elderly receiving much more health care than they formerly did.

In 1981 Medicare helped some 28.5 million people at a cost of $42.5 billion.[13] Experts predict that it will cost more than $100 billion by the end of this decade with costs rising 13 percent a year as the population ages. The financial health of Medicare has been endangered by the syphoning off of some of its funds to pay for Social Security retirement benefits. The Congressional Budget Office has predicted that Medicare will go broke before the end of the decade and will have a deficit of $400 billion by 1995. These staggering deficits are projected despite steps being taken by the Reagan administration to curb Medicare expenses.

Changes made under President Reagan require that Medicare patients pay a larger amount before their hospital expenses are picked up by the government. In other changes, the reimbursement given to nursing homes has been pared back and the premium raised for those who choose optional coverage to pay for their doctor's bills. Even greater changes were recommended by the president in 1983. If adopted by Congress, Medicare expenses would rise for most participants, although patients who had prolonged hospital stays would find a larger share of their expenses covered than is now the case.

The Reagan proposal would move Medicare in the direction of catastrophic insurance where the patient is expected to bear a larger share of the burden for relatively minor hospital costs. In the case of long-term treatment, the maximum one would pay under the Reagan plan is $1,529.50. Under present law, patients must pay $13,475 for 150 days of hospitalization and thereafter Medicare pays nothing.

Proposals before Congress could replace Medicare payments to health care providers with a voucher system. Under this system, the elderly would be able to choose vouchers with which to purchase health insurance. If they purchased a cut-rate plan, they could pocket the difference, and those who bought deluxe plans would have to pay extra expenses out of their own money. Supporters claim that allowing beneficiaries to shop for their health insurance rather than simply having the federal government pick up the tab would create competition among sellers, which would reduce costs. Moreover, since health care providers could not simply bill the government as they do now, they would prescribe fewer x-rays and lab tests. They might also emphasize keeping patients well through preventive medicine rather than simply treating the sick.

Opponents question whether the voucher system would result in savings.[14] The healthy might select cheaper plans but the infirm would want full coverage, so the total costs would be unchanged. Insurers might refuse to cover the unhealthy. There is also a question of whether most Americans can behave as informed consumers when it comes to health care. Finally, what about people who select less comprehensive plans but then get sick and exhaust their benefits and their savings?

REDISTRIBUTION

With *redistributive policies*, as with distributive policies, the government provides a set of benefits. The difference is that with redistributive policies, *the government takes from one group in society in order to give to another group.* Perhaps the most important distinction is that with redistributive policies, many people know they are being taxed so that the government can help others in society. As we mentioned earlier, even in distributive programs some people get back less than they contribute while others get back more. But distribution programs spread the benefits so widely that few people know that they, their state, or their community is being shortchanged. The availability of computerized data now allows members of Congress to determine with greater precision whether their constituents are receiving as much as they are paying. This knowledge, coupled with the funding cutbacks of the Reagan era, may result in a perception that more programs are redistributive and fewer are distributive. Should this happen, it would in effect raise the stakes associated with congressional decisions, and more of the issues before Congress would be considered controversial.

Another feature that distinguishes distributive from redistributive programs is that the latter are usually perceived as taking from the rich (or at least the middle class) in order to give to the poor. Some of the affluent in society counter such proposals with the criticism that it is demeaning and counterproductive to give people something rather than make them work for it. This approach, coupled with the attitude that "I got mine through hard work and so should everybody else," has meant that programs considered to be redistributive have met strong political opposition from conservatives. Policies that benefit the wealthy—such as the 1981 tax reform package that virtually eliminated the corporate income tax—are generally not thought to be redistributive, even though one can argue that they take from the middle class and give to the upper class.

The programs to be discussed in this section are those that target money, goods, or services to those of lower income. Over the last 50 years, redistributive programs, which are sometimes called social welfare programs, have been among the most divisive to come before Congress.[15] The mainstream of the Democratic party has believed that the government is responsible for maintaining a threshold below which no one will be allowed to sink. The components of this minimally acceptable lifestyle are secured through programs designed to provide the poor with money, food, shelter, and health care. The Republican party has initially opposed these programs. However, once enacted, Republicans have not typically sought to repeal them, but have voted against expanding them and at times have favored imposing a ceiling to contain costs.

In predicting how legislators will respond to social welfare programs, ideology may be an even better distinguishing feature than party. Conservatives are more likely than liberals to believe that the beneficiaries of redistributive policies are undeserving. They are more prone to attribute the plight of the poor to personal deficiencies such as laziness, drunkenness, or irresponsibility. Liberals, on the other hand, see poverty as more a product of forces beyond the control of the poor, such as an economy that fails to provide a suffi-

cient number of decent paying jobs and an educational system that fails to impart literacy skills to some of the nation's students. Liberals are drawn to programs that give benefits directly to low-income families. Conservatives believe in a *trickle-down approach*, *which holds that if public programs help the affluent, the result will be a strengthened economy that will, in time, improve conditions for the poor.* For example, the trickle-down approach would predict that giving tax breaks to industry, as was done in 1981, would encourage industrial expansion, stimulate the economy, and create new jobs, which would reduce unemployment among the poor.

Let us now turn to some of the more important redistributive programs. We will discuss those that have grown rapidly over the last decade in cost and number of people served. As cost and clientele size have shot upward, opposition has become more outspoken, and the programs have become more controversial.

Aid to Families with Dependent Children

The AFDC program was launched during the New Deal. It was intended to provide relatively short-term benefits to mothers and their young children in female-headed households. The rationale for the program was that a widow and her children would need assistance until the last child matured. At that point, the children could work and care for their mother. At the time that AFDC was approved, it was taken as a matter of course that the mother would stay at home with her youngsters rather than take a job outside the home.

AFDC has changed substantially since it was created. Only 2 percent of today's beneficiaries are widows and their children. Most live in households in which the father either never has resided or has deserted. For many AFDC families, the expectation that participation in the program would last only until the children matured has gone unfulfilled. Not infrequently, before one generation has reached maturity, a daughter has become pregnant and she and her child continue living with the infant's grandmother. For thousands of people, AFDC has become a way of life. Desertions, teenage promiscuity, the weakening of traditional sexual mores, and high divorce rates have all had a hand in the growth in AFDC rolls and program costs (see Figure 18.2). Another aspect

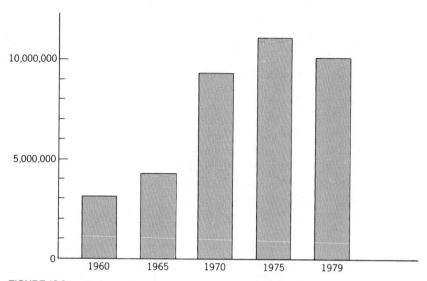

FIGURE 18.2

Numbers of Recipients of Aid to Families with Dependent Children (AFDC)

SOURCE: U.S. Bureau of the Census, *Statistical Abstract of the United States* (Washington, D.C.: U.S. Government Printing Office, for years shown).

of the program that has changed over the years is the racial composition of the recipients; more than 40 percent of those receiving AFDC money are black.

As AFDC costs have risen, political opposition has grown. Critics have charged that since AFDC payments are made on a per-capita basis, the program encourages poor women to have babies. Moreover, since in many states eligibility is limited to households in which there is no adult male present, critics claim that AFDC encourages illegitimacy and desertion. The "no male in the household" rule may prompt a father who is unable to find work to leave his family so that they will be eligible for AFDC.

Unlike most other redistributive programs, AFDC benefits vary from state to state. The federal government pays part of the cost, but states also contribute a share. The federal government pays for at least half of each state's AFDC costs, and in a number of states the federal share approaches two-thirds. The monthly maximum for a mother and three children ranges from $140 per month in Texas to $569 in Oregon.

The U.S. Department of Agriculture pegged the poverty level for a family of four at $8,410 in the year for which AFDC payments are reported in Table 18.4. As can be calculated from this table, in no state do welfare payments for a family of four exceed the poverty level. It therefore does

not seem likely that there are many women getting rich off of welfare by having babies.

State variations in payments have led to demands from some sectors that AFDC be taken over by the federal government. Providing a standard benefit nationwide would remove the inducement for a poor family to move to a state with higher benefits. Under the Reagan administration, federalization of AFDC seems unlikely. Recall from chapter 4, Reagan's New Federalism plan called for returning total responsibility for AFDC back to the states, though Congress has opposed this plan.

Even though the federal government does not bear the full burden of AFDC, rapidly rising costs have prompted members of Congress to search for techniques to reduce spending on the program. Adult AFDC recipients are required to sign up for work-training programs once their youngest child reaches six years of age. After completing job training, it is hoped that they can get a job and become self-supporting. Although the backers of the Work Incentive Program that provides the training anticipated that it would dramatically reduce AFDC rolls, this has not occurred. The training has not prepared enrollees for good paying jobs, and welfare mothers who take jobs often lose benefits worth more than they earn.[16] The sluggish economy of recent years has made job hunting very difficult for those who complete the Work In-

TABLE 18.4

AFDC Benefit Levels: The States Decide

The states set their own benefit levels for the Aid to Families with Dependent Children program, and the federal government makes supporting grants that vary according to per-capita income and the level of state benefits. The table shows the maximum monthly benefit by state for families of four with no other income, total benefits, and the federal percentage as of July 1980.

	Maximum Benefit	Total Benefits	Federal Share		Maximum Benefit	Total Benefits	Federal Share
Alabama	$148	$ 6,952,314	65.00%	Montana	$331	$ 1,624,678	60.31%
Alaska	514	2,327,104	50.00	Nebraska	370	3,426,326	52.91
Arizona	244	3,415,226	57.19	Nevada	314	964,307	50.00
Arkansas	188	4,226,623	65.00	New Hampshire	392	2,229,174	56.78
California	563	177,154,478	50.00	New Jersey	414	47,318,473	50.00
Colorado	361	6,850,206	50.00	New Mexico	267	3,596,990	65.00
Connecticut	553	18,176,226	50.00	New York	476	134,821,243	50.00
Delaware	312	2,663,315	50.00	North Carolina	210	12,940,770	64.04
District of Columbia	349	7,503,873	50.00	North Dakota	408	1,333,886	57.16
Florida	230	16,910,306	54.38	Ohio	327	46,572,725	50.11
Georgia	193	12,135,545	63.06	Oklahoma	349	7,593,049	59.60
Hawaii	546	7,597,846	50.00	Oregon	569	13,449,646	50.73
Idaho	367	2,117,034	61.89	Pennsylvania	395	64,686,201	50.16
Illinois	350	61,505,901	50.00	Rhode Island	432	5,453,191	53.12
Indiana	327	11,551,280	52.53	South Carolina	229	6,323,408	65.00
Iowa	419	12,182,798	51.74	South Dakota	361	1,576,162	65.00
Kansas	390	7,574,948	50.00	Tennessee	148	7,029,650	65.00
Kentucky	235	11,800,251	64.52	Texas	140	10,905,333	53.72
Louisiana	187	9,772,020	65.00	Utah	429	4,318,355	64.52
Maine	352	4,958,189	65.00	Vermont	553	2,759,491	64.88
Maryland	326	19,055,492	50.00	Virginia	360	13,815,987	51.71
Massachusetts	444	40,229,841	50.00	Washington	536	22,375,919	50.00
Michigan	501	88,893,439	50.00	West Virginia	249	4,700,651	63.73
Minnesota	486	17,897,089	50.71	Wisconsin	529	30,555,129	53.27
Mississippi	252	5,084,707	65.00	Wyoming	340	724,541	50.00
Missouri	290	15,753,306	55.96				

SOURCE: *National Journal* (Washington, D.C.: Government Research Corporation, 1981), Vol. 13, Sept. 19, 1981, p. 1673; based on data from the Social Security Administration.

centive Program, even though they would like to find jobs.

A second effort to control costs involves trying to force AFDC childrens' fathers to support their offspring. By using Social Security numbers to track down fathers who have deserted their families, some $2.2 billion in support payments have been extracted.[17]

Recent efforts to substantially reduce AFDC rolls have not had notable success. The Reagan administration's tightening of the eligibility criteria caused an estimated 700,000 people to lose benefits in 1981, but since these people tended to be relatively better off, they received smaller benefits and the savings were relatively modest.

Another 1981 change allowed states to implement the "workfare" program which President Reagan had embraced while serving as California's governor. Workfare requires that able-bodied recipients register for public jobs, for which they are paid the minimum wage. There is evidence that this approach does reduce AFDC rolls.

Food Stamps

Unlike AFDC, which provides cash that a family can spend as it likes, the food stamps program provides coupons that can only be redeemed for approved items. Food stamps also differ from AFDC in that they are paid for entirely by federal funds.

From its beginning in 1961 as a pilot program involving fewer than 100,000 people, food stamps was expanded to replace the surplus commodities program. The earlier program had given the needy allotments of food from the store of goods that American farmers overproduced. Relying on overproduction to feed the poor meant that recipients had no choice about what they got and also that they did not usually have a balanced diet. Deficiencies in the surplus commodity approach contributed to the decision to make food stamps available nationwide in 1974 while the commodities program was phased out. By 1981, more than 23 million Americans were using food stamps for a share of their food budget at a cost of almost $11 billion.

Growth in food stamps usage was accelerated by the elimination of the purchase requirement in 1977. Initially, food stamps had to be purchased, the subsidy being the difference between the purchasing power of the stamps and what a person paid for them. In 1976, for example, the average user received stamps worth 24 dollars more each month than he or she paid for them.[18] Now users are given stamps equal to the subsidy they are entitled to. In 1981, the monthly subsidy averaged $40 per person. The amount of the subsidy is determined by a family's size and resources.

One controversial area has been determining how to calculate family resources. To qualify for food stamps one need not be totally destitute. Recipients can own a car, a home, and have a few other valuables. Food stamps are also available to people who hold jobs, the amount that can be earned while retaining eligibility depending on the number of dependents (see Table 18.5).

Skyrocketing costs and Reagan administration efforts to balance the budget have spurred attempts to reduce eligibility. Efforts to curb the costs of the program are in keeping with public preferences. In 1981, 61 percent of a national survey thought that too much was being spent on the program.[19] Program standards have been modified to eliminate most college students and workers on strike, groups that Congress concluded suffered from self-imposed deprivations. Other reforms have stemmed from complaints of middle-class taxpayers who claim to have witnessed food stamp recipients buying choice cuts of meat and then loading their groceries into expensive automobiles. These misuses of stamps have prompted Congress to make eligibility standards more restrictive by reducing the income and amount of property one can have and still participate in the program. It has also been proposed that able-bodied recipients be required to work on public projects in return for their stamps.

During 1981, attempts to cut back eligibility were more than offset by high unemployment rates (see Figure 18.3). As people lost their jobs, they became eligible for food stamps. It is estimated that a 1 percentage point rise in the unemployment rate produced a million more food stamp users.

A not particularly imaginative effort to control costs has been for Congress to put a spending cap (or ceiling) on the amount of federal money available for food stamps. This approach has been ineffective since when it becomes obvious that the amount set aside for the program is insufficient, Congress has relented and appropriated additional funds. In fiscal 1980, Congress ultimately approved $10.7 billion for food stamps, $4.5 billion more than the ceiling previously imposed for that year. The problem with ceilings is that they have been set on the basis of economic assumptions that have proven to be woefully off target. Unemployment rates and inflation have both run well ahead of the projections used in fashioning the spending cap.

TABLE 18.5

Who Receives Food Stamps?

Almost 22 million people—1 of every 10 Americans—received food stamps last year. What kind of people are they? Data from the Agriculture Department and from a report by the Senate Agriculture, Nutrition and Forestry Committee shed some light.

Participants

Average household size: 3.17 people
Households with at least one child: 57 percent
Households with one or more members age 60 or older: 25 percent
Households with a member on strike: 0.3 percent of all cases
Student recipients: 0.2 percent
Recipients under 18: 54 percent
Households headed by women: 69 percent
Households headed by women age 60 or over: 14 percent
Households headed by women 16 to 65 who work: 11 percent
Female-headed households that also receive AFDC: 30 percent

Income and Assets

Average gross annual income of food stamp households: $3,900
Households with gross annual income of less than $3,600: more than 50 percent
Households with gross annual income of less than $4,800: almost 75 percent
Households with gross annual income of more than $9,000: less than 3 percent
Households with gross annual income of more than $12,000: 0.6 percent
Households with no liquid assets: 60 percent*
Households with liquid assets of less than $1,500: 95 percent*
Households that do not own a car: 64 percent
Households that own or are buying their own homes: 29 percent (compared with 67 percent of all households)

Race and Ethnic Origin	*Regional Distribution*
White: 48.8 percent	Mid-Atlantic: 32 percent
Black: 29.4 percent	Southeast: 20 percent
Hispanic: 9.4 percent	Midwest: 15 percent
American Indian: 0.9 percent	West: 12 percent
Pacific Islander: 0.1 percent	Southwest: 11 percent
All other: 0.4 percent	New England: 5 percent
Unknown: 11 percent	Mountain and Plains: 4 percent

SOURCE: *National Journal* (Washington, D.C.: Government Research Corporation, 1981), Feb. 21, 1981, p. 309.

*Liquid assets are possessions or paper holdings (e.g., stocks, savings bonds) which can be converted into cash.

Since attempts to control costs have had little success, a crackdown on program abuses has been urged. Some conservatives estimate that as much as a billion dollars a year, or almost a tenth of the program's budget, is being used improperly.[20] Catching unqualified users and putting an end to the underground markets in which food stamps are traded for goods other than food is difficult.

Despite congressional and presidential concern about the cost of food stamps, the program appears to be in a somewhat more secure position than some other redistributive programs. The favored position of food stamps is a result of its linkage to agricultural interests. The increased purchasing power that food stamps produce creates additional demand for food products. In Congress, a coalition of liberals concerned about the poor and rural legislators representing farming districts has formed to seek approval of food stamps and crop supports in tandem. This broadening of the base of support for food stamps could conceivably bring about a situation like the one that now exists for low-income housing, in which important economic interests derive so much benefit from the program that they play an important role in maintaining it. However, if crop subsidies are eliminated as part of the Reagan policy of cutting back on federal involvement, the glue that has held the urban liberal-rural farmer coalition together might dissolve.

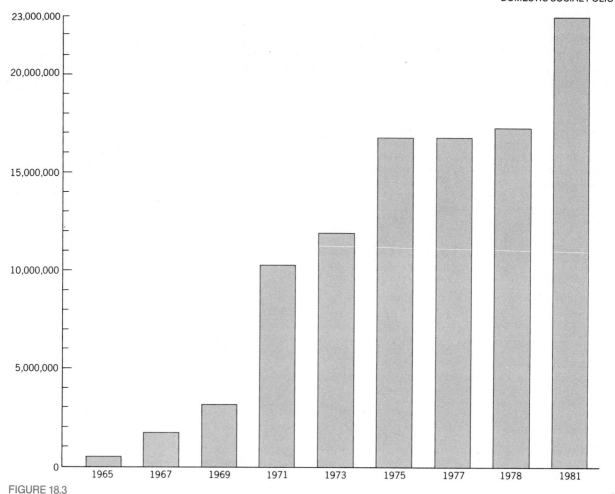

FIGURE 18.3

Numbers of Food Stamp Recipients

Source: U.S. Bureau of the Census, *Statistical Abstract of the United States* (Washington, D.C.: U.S. Government Printing Office, for years shown).

Medicaid

The third major redistributive program with seemingly uncontrollable costs is Medicaid. Created in 1965, Medicaid has paid for many of the medical bills of welfare recipients. Like AFDC, Medicaid is paid for jointly by the states and the federal government. The federal contribution is about 55 percent of the total cost, but the exact state-federal mix varies from state to state. In fiscal 1981, the total cost of Medicaid exceeded $25 billion, about twice as much as it cost six years earlier. The share of the cost assessed against the states has risen from an initial 22 percent in the mid-1960s to 45 percent today.

A number of federal and state officials have been appalled by the cost increases. As far back as

1976, the chair of the National Governors' Conference Medicaid Task Force warned that Medicaid "will surely bankrupt the states and the federal Treasury unless substantial reforms are undertaken, both at the state and federal levels."[21] The experience of one state illuminating. The cost of the state Medicaid contribution in Georgia shot up from $7 million in 1967 to about $650 million in 1982.[22]

Augmenting concern about Medicaid's price tag has been a suspicion that Medicaid patients get better treatment than many middle-class families can afford. Since their medical bills are paid by the government, Medicaid patients do not have to consider cost when getting treatment. The middle class, who must rely on health insurance and personal resources, may have to postpone treatment until they can afford it.

The rising costs are partially due to increases in program usage by the poor once they become informed of its benefits. High costs, then, are an indicator that the program is achieving its objective. Poor people are now obtaining health services that they previously could not afford. Critics, however, complain that a major component of costs is needless overuse.

Program design has also contributed to rising costs. Although outpatient treatment may be less expensive, Medicaid coverage has often been contingent on hospitalization. An example popular with President Reagan involved a child who remained in the hospital rather than at home at a cost of $6,000 versus $1,000 because Medicaid would pay the full hospital bill but nothing to defray the cost of home care.[23] Once in the hospital, a Medicaid patient may be given more expensive treatment than his or her condition merits (such as placement in an intensive care unit) since the costs can be passed on to the government. Medicaid thus helps fill the tens of thousands of beds that would otherwise be empty in American hospitals every day—which explains hospital association lobbying efforts for the program.

Reagan Administration Changes The least painful way to control costs is to insure that funds are not lost through fraud. Among the perpetrators of fraud have been laboratories that bill the government for tests not run or overcharge for analyses that are carried out. Some doctors have also charge the government for services not performed and for services performed but not needed. The elimination of fraud would save hundreds of millions of dollars annually.

Another cost-cutting approach has been to limit the amount a provider of health care can collect from Medicaid for specific services. *Prospective reimbursement*, which some states have adopted, *establishes a set of maximum rates that Medicaid will pay*. In communities with competing health care providers, Medicaid patients either patronize the doctors and hospitals whose charges conform to the Medicaid scale or they have to pay a share of the cost themselves. In California, the state has contracted with selected hospitals to set the costs for treatments. Hospitals and doctors have generally opposed prospective reimbursement.

Federal budget cuts have caused some state governments to impose their own reforms. To cut costs, some states are reducing the amounts they pay nursing home operators, doctors, and pharmacists. They are also reducing the number of days of hospital coverage, the number of prescriptions, and the number of doctor visits for which Medicaid will pay. Another step has been to charge patients small amounts per doctor visit or prescription. The response taken to the trimming of federal aid varies from state to state.

War on Poverty

The three programs of redistribution discussed thus far are all what some would call ''alleviative'' approaches to poverty. The aim of these programs is for the government to relieve poor people of some expenses. Although early alleviative programs like AFDC were expected to provide relatively short-term assistance to individual families, it is now recognized that many of the current beneficiaries of these programs will never be self-supporting.

President Lyndon Johnson's War on Poverty, the center piece of his Great Society package, was intended to be a new approach to poverty. It was supposed to help large numbers of poor people escape from the cycle of poverty. The arsenal of the War on Poverty contained two major types of weapons: education for young people and job training for adults.

Education for the Young Education was supposed to provide a ladder on which the children of the lower class could climb into the middle class. That the creators of the War on Poverty should emphasize education is hardly surprising since this route has been taken by the offspring of millions of immigrants who came to this country with nothing but the clothes on their backs.

The education component of the smorgasbord of War on Poverty programs provided services to a wide range of age groups. Probably the most popular program has been Head Start, which is for poor preschoolers. This program is designed to expose children to things common in middle-class homes but often missing in ghetto tenements or sharecroppers' shotgun shacks. Head Start pupils are taught the alphabet, how to count, names for colors, months, days of the week, and so forth, which permits them to enter the public schools on a more equal footing with middle-income class-

The Head Start program was designed to expose children from poverty environments to things common in middle-class homes so that they might enter public school on a more equal footing. It has been one of the most successful of the federal government's redistributive policies.

mates. Recent research indicates that the effects of Head Start are long lasting, with the alumni of this program performing better in math classes, dropping out less often, failing less often, and being arrested less often than comparable youths who did not attend a Head Start program.[24]

Other programs have been aimed at other age groups. Work-study has provided funding to pay college students who need to work part-time. The War on Poverty also initiated a program to teach illiterate adults to read.

Job Training for Adults The second major thrust of the War on Poverty was to prepare the unemployed for productive jobs. Some of the programs had as another objective the teaching of attitudes and behaviors desired by employers. Participants in such programs were instructed in the importance of personal grooming, punctuality, and dependability.

Two job programs were created to prepare teenagers for work. One, the Neighborhood Youth Corps (NYC), was aimed primarily at students who needed summer jobs or part-time jobs during the school year. Designers of the NYC hoped that income from these jobs would be enough to keep cash-starved youngsters from dropping out of school to get full-time employment. Some recent dropouts also got NYC jobs. These participants were counseled to return to school and graduate.

The other program was aimed at dropouts in their teens and early twenties. In the Job Corps,

full-time work was combined with counseling. The initial Job Corps concept was based on the Civilian Conservation Corps of the New Deal era and, like the CCC, put corpsmembers to work in rural areas, often on conservation projects in national parks and forests. Most Job Corps recruits came from big city slums, however, and found adaptation to wilderness areas difficult. Likewise, people living near Job Corps camps found the recruits different and frightening. The Job Corps has since been reoriented with training now occurring in urban areas. The rural conservation work was turned over to the Youth Conservation Corps, which was created after the War on Poverty. Since their establishment in the 1960s, millions of young people have participated in the Job Corps and NYC.

As we mentioned in the context of the AFDC program, welfare mothers were another component of the unemployed that was singled out for job training. Welfare mothers were required to register for training as a condition for the continuation of benefits. (Mothers of preschoolers are exempted from having to register.)

Training of large numbers of low-income individuals was the objective of programs authorized by the Manpower Development and Training Act (MDTA). About 60 percent of those who participated in MDTA programs were given classroom instruction in skills for specific jobs and in behaviors that would make prospective employers more willing to hire them. The remaining 40 percent of the MDTA enrollees acquired skills through on-the-job training. That is, they were given jobs in which they were expected to learn by doing.

Finally, the War on Poverty ushered in a number of programs that provided money to state and local governments to enable them to hire paraprofessionals. The unemployed were hired as aides to work in schools, hospitals, and playgrounds.

In 1974 most of these programs were lumped together by the Comprehensive Employment and Training Act. This block grant legislation made funds available to states and "prime sponsors," subunits of states having populations of at least 100,000 such as cities, counties, or sets of counties. Operating within broad guidelines, prime sponsors can decide how the money is to be used. They can decide whether to stress on-the-job training or classroom instruction, programs for teenagers or for adults, and so forth.

Evaluation Billions of dollars have been spent on job training programs since the mid-1960s, but the effectiveness of these efforts is difficult to determine. When unemployment is high, there may be no jobs for those who have completed training programs. If the economy is healthy, employers are eager to hire and are willing to pay for a larger share of the training themselves rather than relying on government programs.

Acknowledging that the health of the economy has a lot to do with the ability of those who have completed job training to find work, some things can still be said about these programs.[25] First, they often failed to teach marketable skills. This shortcoming may have resulted from a failure to anticipate the needs of employers and may be partially due to program design. The job training programs have placed greater emphasis on the number of people participating than on the level of training given. The trade-off has been to run a greater number of people through programs quickly rather than deal with fewer trainees for extended periods. For program enrollees who have very few marketable skills and are functionally illiterate, a few months of training is not adequate preparation for jobs in our complex, automated society. People who complete short training programs are frequently prepared only for low-skill, entry-level jobs, and the pool of people eligible for such employment exceeds the demand. Moreover, the pay for such jobs is so low that a person may be able to make as much or even more by not working. Taking a job for example, may cause a welfare mother to lose AFDC benefits, Medicaid, and unearned income tax credits. Because she has a job, she may have to employ a babysitter, pay for transportation to and from work, and buy additional clothing. If taking a job does not provide much more than could be received by not working, there is little incentive to work.

The unconclusive evidence on the effectiveness of job training programs made them prime targets for budget cuts during the early years of the Reagan administration. But when unemployment rates rose rapidly, he too, endorsed a new job training program but one heavily reliant upon the private sector.

The health of the economy has a lot to do with the ability of those who have completed federally-funded job training programs to find work.

Community Action Programs An important feature of the War on Poverty was the effort to involve poor people in implementing the program. The War on Poverty specified that there should be "maximum feasible participation" of the poor since it was assumed that they would know what needed to be done to help others like themselves.

Operationalizing the maximum feasible participation concept involved providing federal funds to Community Action Programs. In the CAPs, representatives of a community's poor made decisions on how to allocate funds, and established agencies such as legal services offices, family planning clinics, programs for the elderly, day care centers, and so forth.

Allowing program beneficiaries to decide how funds should be spent was a novel idea. Previous redistribution programs had been categorical in nature—acceptable uses of funds had been carefully specified either by Congress in the enabling legislation or by bureaucratic personnel in the executive agency responsible for the program's implementation.

Turning money over to poor people with few strings attached soon became a controversial issue. Local officials were angered when they discovered that the CAP funds went directly to low-income community groups, bypassing city hall. With their funding not under the control of city or county political leaders, the CAPs could criticize public officials without fear of retaliation. Particularly disconcerting to elected officials were the legal services corporations created by CAPs which could block or challenge public policy by going to court. Political leaders, not surprisingly, sought to redirect federal aid so they could distribute funds to bolster their positions and at the same time cut the ground out from under their strident critics in the ghettos.

The money going to the CAPs and other War on Poverty programs was also eyed jealously by officials in older federal agencies. To demonstrate his support of the War on Poverty and to free this crusade from a thwarting "business as usual" implementation, President Johnson assigned overall responsibility for the program to a newly created White House unit, the Office of Economic Opportunity (OEO). Existing departments such as Labor and Health, Education, and Welfare, which would have administered the programs in the absence of OEO, continued to snipe at OEO

mistakes. In time, they succeeded in demolishing the agency. They then picked up the pieces, integrating them into their operations.[26]

Evaluation of the War on Poverty Like other programs designed to bring about some redistribution of income, the War on Poverty has been heavily criticized. With the heating up of the war in Vietnam, President Johnson's attention turned away from the poverty struggle. When Richard Nixon succeeded Lyndon Johnson as president, the War on Poverty was almost defenseless against attack.

To what extent are the charges that the War on Poverty failed accurate? Have federal efforts to alleviate poverty produced some successes? As often happens in debates over policy issues, the answer depends on who you ask and which data they select to evaluate.

Government data show a decline in the proportion of the population that lives below the low-income level over the last two decades (see Figure 18.4). In the early 1960s almost 40 million Americans or 22 percent of the population lived in poverty. Within two years after passage of the 1964 Economic Opportunity Act, 7.5 million people rose out of poverty and the proportion of the population that was poor dropped by 4 percent. The share of the population which was poor continued to decline, bottoming out at 11.2 percent in 1974. Then there was little change until 1980, when there was a jump to 13 percent, the highest poverty rate in more than a decade.

One possible contributor to the sharp drop in the low-income population from 1964 to 1969 was the influence of the Vietnam War on the economy. As is always the case during wartime, a larger share of the population is in the armed services, which brought down the unemployment rate. Demands for equipment and supplies for the military kept factories busy, which further cuts into unemployment.

The ending of American involvement in the Vietnam War and a worsening of the economy did not result in a marked increase in the poor people, however. For this reason, many have concluded that not only were the War on Poverty and other welfare programs of the 1960s important in improving the economic condition of many people, but that they continued to work even when the economy faltered.

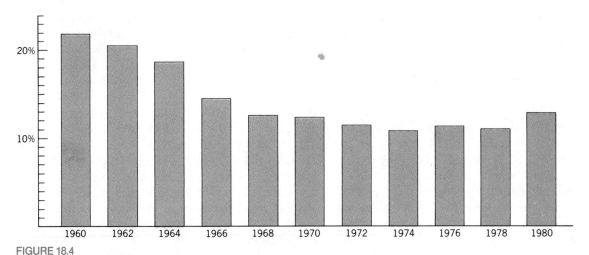

FIGURE 18.4

Proportion of the Population Below the Poverty Level

SOURCE: 1960–1978 data from U.S. Bureau of the Census, Current Population Reports, Series P-60, No. 124, *Characteristics of the Population Below the Poverty Level, 1978* (Washington, D.C.: U.S. Government Printing Office, 1979), p. 16; 1980 data from Series P-60, No. 127, *Money, Income, and Poverty Status of Families and Persons in the United States, 1980* (Washington, D.C.: U.S. Government Printing Office, 1981), p. 27.

Some economists believe that data such as those reported in Figure 18.4 actually understate the government's success in reducing poverty. In calculating the share of the population that falls below the poverty level, government analysts consider only cash income. They exclude *in-kind benefits* such as food stamps, Medicaid, and subsidized housing. If in-kind benefits are included with income, it is estimated that there may be as few as 8 million poor people.[27]

Whether one accepts this estimate, the figure of 29.3 million based on the U.S. Department of Agriculture definition, or some higher figure, there are some points on which there is widespread agreement. There is little question that Medicaid has given the poor far better access to health care and that because of food stamps poor Americans are now better fed than they were a generation or more earlier. Therefore, while the distribution of income may not have changed substantially, access to some of the basic needs of life has been broadened.

As President Reagan began implementing his platform, which called for reducing federal spending for social programs, Democrats charged that he was threatening to undo the achievements of the two previous decades. Cuts in social programs, they warned, would deny needy families the food, health care, and money on which they depended heavily.

The rejoinder from the president's camp was that benefits for the "truly needy" were not being cut off. The program participants who lost benefits—some one million AFDC recipients, one million food stamp recipients, and a million Medicaid recipients—tended to be those whose income levels put them at the upper range of people eligible for these programs. Futhermore, the president's supporters claimed that most of the cuts simply eliminated money that in the past had been used for fraudulent purposes. Finally, President Reagan contended that the poor would be helped more by a sound economy (the trickledown approach) than by welfare programs. According to this logic, the poor may suffer some short-term dislocations, but in time they, along with the rest of society, will be better off because of stable economic conditions.

Critics of the president's reductions in social program spending point out that since many poor people are not in the labor force, economic stabilization and a stronger demand for labor will not help them. The poor child born out of wedlock to a high school dropout will be hungry in the absence of a food program. The impoverished elderly widow will not get a job no matter how busy the nation's factories are. The 9.8 million poor who are under 15 years of age and the 3.9 million who are 65 or older will not receive more income even if the health of the economy is restored. They may, however, be benefited by bringing inflation under control, which has been done.

The budget-cutting of the early 1980s further threatens the marginal existence of some who hover just above the poverty line. Cutbacks in Social Security or other programs will make it impossible for some families to survive financially. High unemployment or renewed higher rates of inflation compound the problem. If the economic situation degenerates, the programs that in the past have provided money, food, shelter, and medical care will be less able to cope. Increased need may coincide with decreased resources for alleviating need.

The impact of poverty programs can also be assessed on a very different dimension. Particularly as a result of the Community Action Programs, a group of ambitious and talented poor people were able to achieve secure positions in the middle class. Although they are not a large proportion of the millions of poor people, a number of individuals obtained jobs in local poverty programs and then had the drive and skills needed to become administrators. Some picked up bachelors and graduate degrees along the way. Many who began with poverty agencies have moved on to other agencies of state, local, and national government. In other words, poverty programs have often served as paths of upward mobility for some of their participants.

SUMMARY

In this chapter we established a framework for classifying policy. This is useful, at least for many domestic programs, in helping us understand why Congress responds dissimilarly to different policy demands. Proposals that are perceived as redistributing goods or money are difficult to enact and are never wholly secure from attack. In contrast, proposals that distribute benefits or are perceived as spreading benefits widely across society stir up less opposition and tend to be approved easily by Congress. Conflict over distributive programs tends to occur when the idea is first proposed. If enacted, they quickly come to be broadly accepted and are generally extended and expanded with only minor opposition. Only a major effort to redefine governmental responsibilities is likely to produce a serious reevaluation of program desirability. When this occurs, as with the Reagan administration's New Federalism proposal, the consensual demand pattern will be interrupted at least briefly.

When there are opposing forces, Congress often makes policy without resolving the conflict, creating a regulatory body that is authorized to mediate between opponents. Thus, regulatory policy simply transfers the site of the conflict from the halls of Congress to the paneled hearing rooms of a regulatory agency or perhaps to marble court chambers.

A number of major distributive and redistributive social welfare programs have been undertaken during the last half-century. Among the important federal distributive programs were aid to education at both the college and public school levels, public housing, loan guarantee programs to help middle-income people purchase houses, Social Security, and Medicare.

Redistributive programs provide assistance to the needy in society. Among the more important have been Aid to Families with Dependent Children, food stamps, Medicaid, and the War on Poverty. These programs have proven to be more expensive than initially expected, and a number of proposals for reducing expenses have been offered. Conservatives generally want to cut the budgets of these programs, whereas liberals fear the possible consequences of budget reductions. Evaluations of the success of federal anti-poverty programs vary, depending on the perspective one adopts in assessing them.

The Evolution of Social Security

Social Security has become the most expensive program operated by the U.S. government. Because of the rate at which the cost for Social Security has grown, the question of how to keep the system from going bankrupt has been a heated political controversy in recent years.

When it was created during the New Deal, no one anticipated the mammoth size to which it would grow. Contributions and benefits were small at the outset. From its creation until 1949, employers and employees contributed only 1 percent of the employees' wages to the system.

Social Security is a distributive program which passes out benefits to a wide range of people. Until recently no one worried about the funding of these benefits. For many years it was the kind of program members of Congress loved because they could win favor among their constituents by increasing the benefits. This practice began in 1939 before Social Security had even begun to pay retirees, when Congress expanded coverage to include dependents of beneficiaries. Later, benefits were increased, often just before an election, so that the elderly, whose rate of voting is among the highest of any age group, would not have time to forget who their friends were. To cite an extreme example of how increasing benefits burdened the system, the first person to receive a Social Security check was ultimately paid almost $21,000 before she died. She had paid only $22 into the fund.[1]

In 1972 Congress soared to new heights of generosity. Led by Wilbur Mills (D—Ark.), who chaired the Ways and Means Committee which was responsible for Social Security legislation, Congress increased the benefits substantially and tied future increases in benefits to the consumer price index. This meant that the purchasing power of Social Security benefits would no longer be reduced by inflation. Mills had a reputation of being fiscally conservative. Why did he guide legislation through Congress which has done more than anything else to create the crisis in Social Security? There is a simple answer. Mills hoped to win the Democratic nomination for the presidency in 1972 and he saw the elderly as an important source of support. Moreover, at that time it did not look like Mills' ambitions would cause financial problems. The retirement fund was so sound that economists were predicting that it might have a surplus of as much as $1 trillion by the turn of the century.

No one foresaw the Arab oil embargo. As prices for petroleum products reached unheard-of levels, they pulled up the inflation rate, which forced Social Security to pay higher benefits. High fuel costs also reduced demand for various products, which resulted in economic dislocations causing widespread unemployment. The thousands of workers who lost their jobs ceased paying into the retirement fund just at the time inflation was depleting the reserves at an alarming rate.

Less than five years after Mills made Social Security inflation-proof, the fund was nearing bankruptcy. Under the prodding of President Carter, one of the largest tax increases in American history was approved in 1977. The president proudly announced that the new schedule for increasing Social Security taxes would make the fund financially healthy into the twenty-first century. Again our leaders failed to anticipate the ravages of inflation and unemployment.

In 1982, Social Security ran out of money. It was able to pay benefits to retirees only by borrowing money from the funds for Medicare and the disabled. Borrowing coupled with the rising health care costs have now jeopardized the soundness of the Medicare fund.

Soon after taking office, President Reagan recognized the dangerous condition of Social Security financing. However, his efforts to reduce costs by raising the retirement age and eliminating some payments were rejected by a bipartisan coalition in Congress. The president named a special commission which included some

Recognizing that the Social Security system was in danger of going bankrupt, President Reagan appointed a bipartisan commission whose recommendations were quickly adopted by Congress.

[1]Harry Anderson, et al., "The Social-Security Crisis," *Newsweek*, January 2, 1983, pp. 20, 22.

members of Congress from both parties to come up with a solution.

Shortly after the 1982 midterm Congressional election, the bipartisan commission made its report. Although its recommendations were wholly pleasing to virtually no one, they were quickly adopted with only minor changes by Congress and signed into law. (The major terms of the legislation to save Social Security are outlined in this chapter.) It was unthinkable that the system not be saved and so Congress moved rapidly to resolve the crisis well in advance of the 1984 elections. When Congress must be the bearer of bad tidings, as it was

here when it tapped new sources of revenue, it wants to give the voters ample time to forget who is responsible.

As a result of the changes, Social Security has taken a step toward becoming a redistributive program since its more affluent beneficiaries must pay taxes on a share of what they receive. Congress also stepped back from its pattern of increasing generosity. The cost of living element has been made more conservative and during the first part of the next century, the age for receiving benefits will be raised. Consequently, when today's students retire, it will take longer before they receive back as much as they contributed.

KEY TERMS

allocation
categorical grant programs
conflictual demand pattern
consensual demand pattern
delegation
distributive policies
in-kind benefits
pork barrel legislation
prospective reimbursement
redistributive policies
regulatory policies
trickle-down approach

SUGGESTED READINGS

Anderson, James E.; Brady, David W.; and Bullock, Charles S., III. *Public Policy and Politics in America.* 2nd ed. Monterey, Calif.: Brooks/Cole Publishing Company, 1984.

Bailey, Stephen K., and Mosher, Edith K. *ESEA: The Office of Education Administers a Law.* Syracuse, N.Y.: Syracuse University Press, 1968.

Donovan, John C. *The Politics of Poverty.* 3rd ed. Washington, D.C.: University Press of America, 1980.

Eidenberg, Eugene, and Morey, Roy D. *An Act of Congress.* New York: W. W. Norton, 1969.

Hayes, Michael T. *Lobbyists and Legislators.* New Brunswick, N.J.: Rutgers University Press, 1981.

Olson, Mancur. *A New Approach to the Economics of Health Care.* Washington, D.C.: American Enterprise Institute, 1982.

Palmer, John L., and Sawhill, Isabel V. *The Reagan Experiment.* Washington, D.C.: Urban Institute Press, 1982.

PRESIDENT ASSAILS LIBYA OVER CHAD

He Says He Does Not Foresee 'Participating Militarily' in Defending Government

CHAPTER 19

THE CHANGING FACE OF AMERICAN FOREIGN POLICY

A Fragmented World ■ The Omnipotent Presidency ■ The Omnipotent Ideology ■ An Eroding Consensus ■ A Foreign Policy Partnership ■ A Foreign Policy Agenda

A FRAGMENTED WORLD

Like domestic policymaking, foreign policymaking can be exceedingly complex. The political forces within our nation at the local, state, and federal levels are an elaborate and sometimes bewildering combination of individuals, groups, institutions, and policy objectives. With foreign policymaking, yet another level is added: the international arena, with its more than 150 sovereign nations, the majority of them proud, fiercely independent political units recently freed from colonial bondage.

If the making of domestic policy can produce headaches, foreign policy can lead to migraines. Within the nation, the citizens at least have a common set of laws, regulations, institutions, and customs that help buffer the sharp edges of political conflict. In the international realm, however, the norms of common understanding that transcend national borders are few in number and dependent upon the voluntary cooperation of each

nation. The monopoly over the use of the military and police enjoyed by leaders within the nation to enforce decisions, if necessary, has no equivalent at the international level. Without this global monopoly, it is impossible to enforce legal conformity among nations. The United Nations (UN) has occasionally fielded limited multinational peacekeeping forces, most dramatically in the Korean War (1950 to 1953, fought largely on the UN side by the U.S. Army); however, the global police force envisaged in Article 43 of the UN Charter has continued to be an idealistic hope of world federalists. What nations possess but the world lacks is, in the words of one scholar, a "central guidance capability."[1]

Within the United States, political disputes are normally arbitrated by jurists, legislators, executive officers, and bureaucrats at the three levels of domestic government. Their decisions depend upon interpretations of the law, norms of compromise and conciliation, and, ultimately, the authority vested in them by virtue of their offices. In contrast, international political disputes are usually dealt with, but not always resolved, through the art of *diplomacy (peaceful negotiations between na-*

The United States, as a member of the United Nations, occasionally provides troops for multinational peacekeeping forces when the UN authorizes their formation. U.S. Marines, along with French and Italian troops, were part of a peacekeeping force sent to Lebanon in August, 1982 following an Israeli invasion of Lebanon.

tions); through ***covert action*** *(secret intervention in the affairs of other countries to advance a nation's interests)*; or through the outright use of military force (e.g., sending in the Marines). The earth today remains a world of independent nations, with few signs of evolution toward common global rules and means of enforcement. (Over the past decade, though, several observers have emphasized the presence of increasingly powerful centripetal forces at work—particularly "the onrush of economic transnationalism," with its worldwide network of multinational corporations.[2])

The international setting thus presents a natural source of frustration for political leaders, especially for the president, whose role has become crucial in world affairs in large part because of the danger of a nuclear attack. This unique danger from abroad has caused presidents to focus inordinate attention on foreign policy, even though they may have been elected as a result of domestic policy promises. "Domestic policy . . . can only defeat us," commented President John F. Kennedy on this paradox, "foreign policy can kill us."[3]

THE OMNIPOTENT PRESIDENCY

Foreign affairs, then, complicate life for the nation and its leaders. Until recently, however, policymaking in this area was considered chiefly a presidential prerogative. In terms of the policy process, this ironically made foreign policy decisions easier for the president than most domestic policy decisions—although the former were often more far-reaching in import and risk for the na-

tion and the world. The chief executive enjoyed the luxury of broad discretion on international decisions, a freedom from the hurly-burly of public and interest group scrutiny and even close examination by Congress, the institution envisaged by the founding fathers as a vital constitutional check on executive power. In short, the decision-making process was simpler even if the substance of decisions was often more difficult.

This deference to the presidency in foreign policy may be cast in terms of the policy classification scheme presented earlier in Table 18.2 (p.520). In a nutshell, the demand pattern in foreign policy has been overwhelmingly consensual. This agreement has been evident, first, in the widespread belief throughout most of this century that "the president knows best" when it comes to foreign policy, and, second, in the ***containment doctrine***, the almost universally accepted view that *the main tenet of American foreign policy must be isolation of communism behind its "iron curtain" boundaries of 1945.* Only in the past decade have these premises undergone a fundamental reevaluation.

Deference to the presidency in foreign affairs was reflected in one of the most beguiling slogans in American politics: "politics stops at the water's edge." Clothed more formally in the concept of ***bipartisanship***, this approach to foreign policy rested on the notion that *the United States must present a united front in its relations with other nations, supported by Democrats and Republicans alike without extensive debate.* Partisan or institutional wrangling over foreign policy would be unseemly, detrimental to our interests, confusing to foreigners, and unpatriotic. Foreign nations that perceived dis-agreements among our leaders might seek to exploit them. In a word, the judgment of the president would have to be trusted.

Beyond this rationale of speaking with one clear voice to other nations, congressional and public abdication to the president in foreign affairs stemmed from his greater capacity to gather and analyze information relevant to decisions of international consequence. How could the Congress, let alone the public, possibly match the resources of the executive bureaucracy, with its Central Intelligence Agency (CIA), surveillance satellites and reconnaisance airplanes, embassies in almost every country, global military presence, and the like? The president knew best because presumably he knew the most.

On top of this, the world had become a more dangerous place to live. Two hundred years ago, Thomas Paine could write: "Not a place upon earth might be so happy as America. Her situation is remote from all the wrangling world. . . ." Since 1954, however, the Soviet Union has had the capability to strike the United States with nuclear Intercontinental Ballistic Missiles (ICBMs). Every year, new Soviet submarines are constructed, each of which is armed with enough warheads to annihilate our major population centers. Near our coasts, these enemy missiles can reach their targets in a matter of minutes. The ability to respond to an international crisis with dispatch has thus become more important than it was when the Atlantic and Pacific Oceans provided some protection. In the popular phrase, the world has shrunk—and so has our time for making foreign policy decision. In this setting, the organizational attributes of hierarchy associated with the executive branch gain favor over the more decentralized legislative branch.

The sense of urgency in foreign policy has been heightened by the series of prolonged crises endured by the United States in the modern era, from World War II through the continual Cold War. The showdown with the Soviets in 1962 over their attempted placement of missiles in Cuba, 90 miles from our shore, took us to the brink of nuclear war. The red telephone on the president's desk that connects him to his military commanders has become a key symbol of presidential power in our nuclear age.

Other forces have combined to further enhance the preeminance of the presidency in foreign affairs. The Constitution, of course, provides the president with certain prerogative powers in designating him the commander-in-chief in Article II, Section 2, but less explicit sources of power have fed this wellspring. The tendency of the press (especially the electronic media) to focus on the president has magnified his importance enormously. So probably has the exaltation of this office in many civics textbooks. Nor should psychological explanations of deference to the president be ignored; as human beings living in stressful times, we may subconsciously desire reassurance that the chief executive can indeed protect us from the dangers we face. Time and again citizens have put their faith in a "strong leader" in periods of grave national distress.

The leeway allowed presidents in foreign affairs may be seen in their exercise of five important powers: to make agreements abroad; to conduct warfare; to engage in covert action; to spend money; and to control information. Their preeminence in these areas has often led to foreign policy by executive fiat—an "imperial presidency," to coin historian Arthur M. Schlesinger, Jr.'s famous phrase.

United States Commitments Abroad

In Article II, Section 2, the Constitution states that the president "shall have power, by and with the advice and consent of the Senate to make treaties, provided two-thirds of the Senators present concur. . . ." The language is clear. As one legal scholar put it, "The Founders made unmistakably plain their intention to withhold from the President the power to enter into treaties all by himself. . . ."[4] The Senate was meant to be a strong partner in the making of commitments overseas, but in the modern era (as discussed in chapter 12), presidents and lesser members of the executive branch have often involved this nation in significant foreign obligations without the advice and consent of the Senate or the counsel of the House.

An examination of American diplomacy from 1946 to 1973 reveals the existence of over 6,000 agreements signed between the United States and other sovereign nations.[5] In 1972, for example, the United States signed agreements on the following topics (among many others):

Presidents play a key role in the foreign policymaking process, often attending summits, or conferences, of world leaders. The annual summit of the seven most industrialized western nations was held at Williamsburg, Virginia in 1983.

1. Television and radio facilities (Saudi Arabia)
2. Trade—strawberries (Mexico)
3. Satellite tracking station (Canada)
4. Whaling—international observer scheme (Japan)
5. Education program for agrarian reform (Philippines)
6. Protection of migratory birds (Mexico)
7. Atomic energy—cooperation for civil use (Japan)
8. Military assistance (Malaysia)
9. Air transport services (Czechoslovakia)
10. Seabed arms control (Multilateral)
11. Cultural exchanges (USSR)
12. Scientific and technical cooperation (USSR)
13. Weather station (Honduras)
14. Prevention of foot-and-mouth disease (Costa Rica)

Seven percent of these 6,000 commitments took the form of executive agreements entered into by the executive branch drawing in whole or in part upon a claim of constitutional authority vested in the president. Only 6 percent of the commitments took the form of treaties. The vast majority (87 percent) were **statutory agreements,** *international agreements made pursuant to existing congressional legislation.*

Designed to be the primary means of reaching agreements with other nations, treaties have been ratified only infrequently. That they have been replaced by another legislative procedure—the statutory agreement—may calm the fears of some regarding presidential abuse of the agreement-making power. After all, a legislative—indeed a two-chamber—check remains in place. Recent findings suggest, however, that congressional involvement in the agreement-making process is superficial. Congress does participate procedurally insofar as it legislates broad guidelines requested by the executive branch, but its substantive knowledge of the intended foreign commitments is often deficient. As shown in chapter 11, members of Congress are often too busy to examine the details of public policy proposals, including international agreements.

Still more troubling to some observers of foreign policy is the use of the executive agreement. Under a claim of constitutional prerogatives that are often ill-defined, the executive branch has entered into many important international pacts with the stroke of a pen in the seclusion of executive offices, far from the halls of the Congress with its bothersome habit of public debate.

The classic example comes from the administration of Franklin D. Roosevelt. In 1940, Roosevelt signed an agreement with Great Britain (imperiled by an anticipated German invasion) to provide 50 antiquated United States destroyers in exchange for selected British naval bases in the Caribbean. This was a sweeping commitment, providing legal grounds for a German declaration of war against the United States. The treaty process, however, was bypassed: Roosevelt's signature sealed the pact. In this instance, the end result was unquestionably worthwhile but the procedure adopted had the effect of eroding the agreement-making procedure established by the Constitution. This single invasion of the Senate's treaty powers provided a precedent for future interventions in areas ranging from military and economic commitments abroad to those dealing with transportation, communications, and a host of other policy areas.

Military commitments overseas have proven to be the most sensitive policy decisions. In the five administrations following the Roosevelt years (Truman through Nixon), presidents increasingly used executive agreements instead of treaties for significant military pacts (see Table 19.1). Solely by executive decision, the United States has sent military missions to or established bases in Latin America, Africa, the Far East, the Near East, and the islands of Diego Garcia and the Azores. By one estimate, of the 151 military commitments made by Presidents Truman, Eisenhower, Kennedy, Johnson, and Nixon, nearly half (48 per-

cent) seemed to warrant closer inspection by Congress.[6]

Through the years, members of Congress have expressed frustration over the demise of the treaty procedure. Former chairperson of the Senate Committee on Foreign Relations, J. William Fulbright (D—Ark.) complained, ''The Senate is asked to convene solemnly to approve by a two-thirds vote a treaty to preserve cultural artifacts in a friendly neighboring country. At the same time, the chief executive is moving military men and material around the globe like so many pawns in a chess game.''[7] The full Committee concluded in a 1969 report that ''We have come close to reversing the traditional distinction between the treaty as the instrument of a major commitment and the executive agreement as the instrument of a minor one.''[8]

The problem is further broadened by less obvious forms of the executive agreement, including pacts whose existence is a secret tightly held by the executive branch; verbal ''promises'' and ''understandings'' between nations; and agreements made by various bureaucratic officials without the knowledge of the president or the Department of State. Instances of such agreements are, respectively, President Nixon's 1973 secret message to North Vietnamese Premier Pham Van Dong promising postwar reconstruction aid in exchange for a peace agreement in the Vietnam

TABLE 19.1

The Dominance of Executive Agreements over Treaties in the Making of Significant Military Commitments Abroad

Administration	Significant Military Treaties (T)	Significant Military Executive Agreements (EA)	Executive Agreement Index EA/T + EA**
Truman	17	18	.51
Eisenhower	7	20	.74
Kennedy	1	3	.75
Johnson	4	13	.76
Nixon	3	19	.86
Total	32	73	

SOURCE: Loch Johnson and James M. McCormick, "Foreign Policy by Executive Fiat," *Foreign Policy*, 28, (Fall 1977), p. 120.

*This table summarizes the use of military treaties and executive agreements for the period 1946–1974; statutory agreements, which are more numerous but less controversial, are not analyzed here.

**The numbers in this column represent for each administration the proportion of significant military executive agreements, compared to the total number of significant military treaties and executive agreements. This Executive Agreement Index ranges from 0 to 1; the higher the index, the greater the reliance on executive agreements for major military commitments.

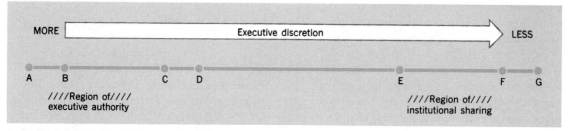

A—Secret, verbal executive agreements ("understandings," "promises")

B—Secret, written executive agreements (kept from Congress)

C—Secret verbal or written agreements (shared with select Congressional committees)

D—Unclassified executive agreements

E—Statutory agreements

F—Agreements pursuant to treaties

G—Treaties

FIGURE 19.1

International Agreement-Making: a Continuum of Executive Discretion

War; Secretary of State Henry Kissinger's 1975 "understanding" with Israel and Egypt on the placement of United States "monitoring" personnel in the Sinai Peninsula; and some 30 military agreements between the Department of Defense and the Republic of South Korea from 1972 to 1976. In each case, Congress and the American people learned of the hidden compacts only long after their completion.

In 1776, Thomas Jefferson urged, "On the subject of treaties, our system is to have none with any nation, as far as can be avoided."[9] With an ironic twist, his wish has been practically granted; the treaty is an all but discarded procedure. (Significant exceptions recently include the Panama Canal Treaties of 1977 and Strategic Arms Limitation Talks treaties, *SALT* I, passed in 1972, and Salt II, proposed in 1979 but subsequently tabled in the Senate.) Jefferson might be dismayed, however, by what has taken its place: international commitments often based on loosely worded statutes and hidden transactions (see Figure 19.1).

War-Making Powers

While the treaty power was designed to be shared, the nation's founders vested the war powers almost exclusively in the Congress. Article I, Section 8 of the Constitution states that Congress shall have the power to declare war; to raise and support armies; to provide and maintain a navy; to make rules for the government and regulation of the armed forces; to provide for calling forth,

organizing, arming, and disciplining the militia; and to make all laws necessary and proper for executing the foregoing powers.

The founders did designate the president as commander-in-chief of the army and navy, but their intention was to provide him with a mantle of authority to repel sudden attacks against the United States. James Madison was adamant in his resolve that the power to make war be lodged in the legislature. In a letter to Jefferson in 1789, he wrote: "We have already given in example one effectual check to the Dog of War by transferring the power of letting him loose from the Executive to the Legislative body, from those who are to spend to those who are to pay."[10]

In spite of these original intentions, presidents of the twentieth century have repeatedly used military force—usually in Latin America—without congressional approval. American soldiers have landed on foreign territory well over 100 times without a declaration of war. This has been called **gunboat diplomacy**, *political intervention using overt military force*. Flexing his commander-in-chief muscles in 1941, President Franklin Roosevelt ordered the United States Navy to defend Iceland and Greenland, to escort convoys bound for Britain, and to shoot on sight any German or Italian warships on the Western Atlantic. In essence, this amounted to an undeclared naval war in the Atlantic well before the Congress had declared war on the Axis powers. In 1950, President Truman took the country to war in Korea, again with no authorization from Congress. The president had

The Gulf of Tonkin Resolution passed in 1964 by Congress at the urging of President Johnson allowed the president to take all necessary steps, including use of armed force, to protect American interests in Indochina. This resolution allowed Johnson and his successor, Nixon, to escalate the Vietnam War without direct congressional declaration of war.

"simply usurped authority," influential Senator Robert Taft (R—Ohio) declared at the time.[11]

Most controversial of all was President Lyndon Johnson's escalation of the war in Vietnam. When North Vietnamese patrol boats allegedly fired torpedoes against American destroyers in the Gulf of Tonkin in 1964, Johnson immediately requested from Congress authority to respond. With only two days of hearings and debate, the Congress voted 533 to 2 to grant the president broad discretionary powers. In the **Gulf of Tonkin Resolution**, *the president was allowed to "take all necessary steps, including the use of armed force" in Indochina.* His undersecretary of state later called this the "functional equivalent" of a congressional declaration of war—despite disclaimers from Capitol Hill that the vote was meant only to allow Johnson authority to relieve the immediate threat to our forces in that region.[12] Certainly the legislative debate at the time showed no comprehension that the president would soon commit half a million troops in a full-scale war in Indochina.

The Quiet Option

Impatient with diplomacy and sometimes wary of sending in the Marines, presidents have frequently turned to a third option: covert action (CA). Hidden and quiet (if successful), CA offers a powerful temptation to presidents seeking quick solutions—without debate—to hard problems. Not least among its supposed virtues is the **doctrine of plausible denial**—*presidents attempt (often unsuccessfully) to implement covert actions in a way that conceals official involvement, which permits them to deny culpability in case the operation is exposed.*

Like executive agreements and presidential expansion of the war powers, covert action has grown by custom, with minimal statutory and no constitutional foundation. The 1947 National Security Act, which created the Central Intelligence Agency, the nation's chief covert-action arm, establishes a mandate for intelligence collection and analysis. Nothing in the law, however, provides authority for CA—beyond the mischievous phrase requiring the CIA to "perform such other functions and duties related to intelligence . . . as the National Security Council (NSC) may from time to time direct."

Drawing upon this ambiguous wording, presidents, their advisers, and CIA officials have exercised the CA option to its full limits through a variety of covert operations—none of which (until December, 1974) they were even required to report to Congress. This "dark side" of government may as well have been the dark side of the moon, as far as Congress was concerned.

Political covert actions *encompass various secret relationships with influential foreign personalities (called "agents of influence"), operations to manipulate foreign economies, and, most commonly, deception and propaganda programs in support of American foreign policy.*

In the past, political covert action has been used (among other examples) to assist pro-Western political factions in Italy, Greece, West Germany, and the Philippines (consistently during the Cold War), as well as pro-Western groups in Iran (1951–1953), Ecuador (1959–1963), and—most thoroughly documented—Chile (1958–1973). Each of the last three cases led to a military coup. (Whether or not the coup in Chile would have occurred anyway, without CIA encouragement, is a matter of dispute.) Occasionally, the agency has resorted to "spoiling operations" or "dirty tricks" during election campaigns to foil candidates suspected to be unfriendly toward the United States.

Propaganda is the most frequently employed covert activity and includes clandestine and unat-

Political Covert Action: American Involvement in Chile.

In Chile, CIA political covert action involved the extensive use of propaganda, as well as other means designed to influence public opinion and sway the outcome of national elections. (see Table 19.2). The objective of the various spoiling operations (some of them financed by the American corporation International Telephone and Telegraph [ITT] through CIA conduits) was to discredit leftist political groups in Chile, led by Salvador Allende, and to strengthen non-Marxist groups. In the 1964 presidential elections in Chile, the CIA spent more than $3 million, financing over half of the campaign expenses incurred by the Christian Democratic Party.[1] (On a per capita basis, if a foreign government had spent a similar amount of money in our 1964 presidential election, its investment would have totaled some $60 million, or $35 million more than candidates Lyndon Johnson and Barry Goldwater actually spent combined.)

Covert Action Expenditures in Chile, 1963–1973 (to nearest $100,000)

Propaganda for elections and other support for political parties	$8,000,000
Producing and disseminating propaganda and supporting mass media	$4,300,000
Influencing Chilean institutions: (labor, students, peasants, women) and supporting private sector organizations	$ 900,000
Promoting military coup d'etat Less than	$ 200,000

SOURCE: "Intelligence Activities: Covert Action," *Hearings*, Senate Select Committee on Intelligence, 94th Cong., 1st Sess., 7 (December 4 and 5, 1975), Exhibit 1, p. 95.

In the 1964 election in Chile, the CIA (under presidential orders) covertly subsidized news and television services with an anti-Allende slant; disseminated anti-Marxist leaflets and wall posters (3,000 a day); and, among other things, flooded radio news programs and provincial newspapers with anti-communist propaganda. The CIA-backed Christian Democrats won the election by 56 percent of the vote.

In 1970, Allende ran for president again and, once more, the CIA instigated a series of political CAs against his candidacy (though with less intensity than in 1964). Agents were hired to paint slogans on walls evoking images of communist firing squads; posters warned of the end of religion and family life if the Allende forces came to power. This time, however, the operations failed and Allende won a plurality in the presidential election. Since no candidate had won a majority, according to Chilean law the national Congress had to choose between the first- and second-place finishers.

This gave the Nixon administration and the CIA a final opportunity to thwart an Allende victory. Two plans were proposed, known as Track I and Track II. The first included more political covert actions, particularly propaganda and economic pressure. The second involved the plotting of a coup to prevent the accession to power of Allende. Neither track succeeded, and in October, 1970, Allende was elected by a vote of 153 to 35 in the Chilean Congress.

This clear internal support for Allende failed to deter the Nixon administration. On the eve of Allende's win, the U.S. Ambassador in Chile warned the incumbent Christian Democratic president, Eduardo Frei, that "once Allende comes to power we shall do all within our power to condemn Chile and the Chileans to utmost deprivation and poverty."[2] Now that Allende was president, the White House and the CIA turned to an array of covert action policies designed to "make the economy scream."[3]

The *40 Committee, a subcommittee of the National Security Council in charge of approving covert action proposals*, immediately endorsed the expenditure of $7 million to continue the anti-Allende operations. Most of this money went into the coffers of the Christian Democratic party and other non-Marxist groups and toward the stimulation of antigovernment strikes. Additional increments of money were approved by the 40 Committee over the next three years. Then on September 11, 1973, Allende was murdered in a military coup whose perpetrators apparently had no connection with the CIA. With the establishment of a military junta, United States covert actions in Chile were scaled down drastically.

As the Chile case illustrates, propaganda programs have often operated arm-in-arm with various political maneuvers to discredit perceived enemies of the United States.

---

[1]This figure and the following discussion is based on "Covert Action in Chile, 1963–1973," Staff Report, Senate Select Committee on Intelligence, 94th Cong., 1st Sess. (December 18, 1975); and "Intelligence Activities: Covert Action," *Hearings*, Senate Select Committee on Intelligence, 94th Cong., 1st Sess., 7 (December 4 and 5, 1975) p. 11.

[2]"Alleged Assassination Plots Involving Foreign Leaders," *Interim Report*, (November 20, 1975), p. 231, note 2.
[3]*Ibid.*, p. 227.

tributable support for radio programs, pro-Western newspapers, periodicals, and books, media placements, leaflet distribution, publishing operations, and the like—a great tide of information flowing secretly from Washington through hundreds of hidden channels and into media outlets around the world from which, as one observer has noted, "not even the most powerful government in the world can dictate where it will go."[13] The elusive character of propaganda can lead to *blow back* or *replay, in which false information directed at our enemies abroad finds its way back to our shores to deceive our own citizens.*

Paramilitary (PM) covert action consists of secret warlike operations and has always been the riskiest form of the so-called "quiet option" (as if fighting wars was ever secret or quiet). These operations may consist of *support to groups engaged in insurgency fighting; the funding of paramilitary training activities, including counter-terrorist training; the dispatch of CIA military advisers (often "sheep-dipped," that is, dressed in civilian attire); and the direct or indirect shipment of arms, ammunition, or other military equipment abroad.*

In the past, CIA PM operations have supported Ukrainian guerrillas (1949–1953); Polish resistance organizations (1950–1952); Albanian insurgents (1949–1952); Tibetan rebels (1953–1959); and *inter alios*, splinter groups on mainland China and North Korea (1950–1954). Paramilitary operations were also mounted to subvert leftist regimes in Guatemala (successfully, in 1954) and Cuba (unsuccessfully, first in 1961 with the Bay of Pigs invasion and later with various sabotage and assassination operations). The most recent PM operations of large-scale were conducted in Indochina (1955–1974) and Central America (1982–present).

Assassination is one of the most controversial forms of PM covert action. A recent Senate investigation of the CIA revealed that the Agency had plotted the deaths of foreign leaders, including Patrice Lumumba of the Congo (now Zaire) and Fidel Castro of Cuba.[14] The missions failed, sometimes because other plotters struck first (as with Lumumba, who was killed by a rival faction within his own country), or because the target was too elusive or well protected (Castro). The assassination schemes involved approaches to foreign policymaking that went far beyond those usually discussed in textbooks on American government.

The instruments of murder given to secret agents to dispose of Lumumba were sent by diplomatic pouch from the United States to our embassy in the Congo. The deadly package contained rubber gloves, gauze masks, a hypodermic syringe, and lethal biological material requisitioned by the CIA from an Army Chemical Corps installation in Maryland. As one CIA officer admitted to Senate investigators, "I knew it wasn't for somebody to get his polio shot up to date."[15] The toxic material was to be injected into some substance that would reach the mouth of the African leader, "whether it was food or a toothbrush." The result would be quick death.

As fear mounted in the United States government over the consequences of communism spreading from Cuba throughout the Western Hemisphere, the covert actions against Castro grew more frequent—and more lethal. The several plots planned at CIA headquarters included treating a box of Castro's favorite cigars with a toxin so potent it would cause death immediately upon being placed to the lips; concocting highly poisonous tablets that would work quickly when immersed in just about anything but boiling soups; contaminating a diving suit with a fungus guaranteed to produce a chronic skin disease called Madura foot and offering the suit as a gift to Castro; constructing an exotic seashell which could be placed in reefs where Castro often skin dived and then exploded at the right moment from a small submarine nearby; and providing an agent with a ballpoint pen which contained a hypodermic needle filled with the deadly poison Blackleaf-40 and had so fine a point that it could pierce the skin of the victim without his knowledge.

The CIA used contacts with underworld figures whose criminal talents and Cuban connections (from earlier Havana gambling days) were deemed valuable. Mobster John Rosselli went to Florida on behalf of the agency in 1961 and 1962 to assemble assassination teams of Cuban exiles who would infiltrate their homeland and try to kill Castro. Rosselli in turn called upon two other crime figures, Chicago gangster Sam Giancana and the Cosa Nostra chieftain for Cuba, Santos Trafficante. Giancana's specific role was to locate someone in Castro's entourage who could drop poison pills into the Cuban leader's food; Trafficante would serve as courier to Cuba and on the island would help make arrangements for the murder. Rosselli was to be the primary link among the recruited assassins, the syndicate figures, and the CIA.

In the Dominican Republic, various dissident groups requested weapons from the CIA. In March 1961, for instance, a request was passed for 50 fragmentation grenades, 5 rapid-fire weapons, and 10 64-mm. antitank rockets. Through State Department channels travelled information about the dissidents and their requests, disguised with references to a picnic:

> . . . the members of our club [i.e., dissidents] are now prepared in their minds to have a picnic [coup]. Lately they have developed a plan for the picnic, which just might work if they could find the proper food [weapons]. They have asked us for a few sandwiches [guns]. . . . Last week we were asked to furnish three or four pineapples [fragmentation grenades] for a picnic in the near future. . . .[16]

Eventually, three .38 caliber pistols were sent to the CIA station chief in the Dominican Republic, using a diplomatic pouch, and these "sandwiches" were then passed on to dissidents. Later, three .30 caliber M1 carbines stored in the U.S. Consulate were also given to the dissidents.

In no case was an American finger actually on the trigger of any weapon aimed at a foreign leader (though officials of the United States clearly initiated assassination plots against Castro and Lumumba). Technically, neither the CIA nor any other agency of the American government murdered a foreign leader; but, through others, the government had tried.

Whether the CIA acted on its own as a "rogue elephant" in these missions or followed presidential orders is disputed. The answer may never be known, for memories fade, conveniently or otherwise, and concrete evidence remains concealed behind layers of plausible denial or lost in missing documents. One thing, though, is clear: the plots were never approved by or even made known to the Congress or the American people at the time. Only with the congressional investigations of the CIA in 1975 did these past policies come to light.

The Power of the Purse

Conventionally, Congress is considered the guardian of the purse strings, and properly so, since the Constitution declares in Article I, Section 9, "No money shall be drawn from the Treasury, but in Consequence of Appropriations made by Law. . . ." But just as congressional war-making powers have eroded, so have its spending powers. This side of presidential aggrandizement has been most visible in the practice of impoundment (see chapter 12), which is in essence an item veto, nowhere granted to the president by the Constitution (although the Confederate Constitution contained such a provision).

Most controversial impoundments have been of domestic funds. Indeed one of the articles of impeachment against President Nixon grew from his practice of impounding funds for school aid, medical research, and hospital construction—all politically sensitive programs. Presidents, however, also have frozen moneys appropriated for national security purposes, chiefly various weapons systems. In 1949, President Truman impounded $615 million appropriated by Congress for an Air Force group larger than he preferred; the next year, his administration cancelled the carrier Forrestal after funds had been appropriated.[17] In 1956, the Department of Defense impounded appropriations by Congress earmarked for 20 bombers.[18] In 1959, the failure to spend funds appropriated for Polaris submarine construction, Marine Corps operations, and other military projects was examined by the Senate Armed Services Committee. "Last year the Congress appropriated $1,300,000,000 extra . . ." the hearings disclosed, "and 58 percent was not spent at all. . . ."[19]

Information as Power

One of the most popular clichés of this age is also one of the most accurate: information is power. Since our nation was founded, much of the tension between the branches has arisen from the executive branch's reluctance to keep Congress informed of its decisions. For a system of checks and balances to work, an informed Congress has been and always will be essential. Normally, the legislative quest for information proceeds informally as representatives and their staffs question officials in the executive branch over the telephone, over luncheon and conference tables, by letter, and by other means. Often the probing takes a stricter turn, through hearings or field inquiries, or, most formally, through full-fledged investigations with sworn depositions from witnesses, the use of subpoenas, and swarms of young attorneys serving as legislative consultants. Among the better known foreign policy inquiries conducted by Congress in the modern era have been the investigations into the intelligence failure at Pearl Harbor (1945), the firing of General Douglas MacArthur (1951), and abuses by United States intelligence agencies (1975).

The chief obstacles confronted by Congress in its efforts to obtain information about executive decisions have been the doctrine of executive privilege, the executive classification system, and bureaucratic footdragging. Executive privilege, as shown in chapter 12, is proclaimed most commonly on grounds that the sanctity of private discussions between the president and his advisors must be preserved. This practice of denying legislators information on executive policymaking was exercised vigorously by the Eisenhower administration, less so by the Kennedy and Johnson administrations, then, in the words of historian Schlesinger, "with a vengeance" by the Nixon administration.[20] In 1973, Nixon's attorney general, Richard G. Kleindienst, proclaimed in a congressional hearing that the blanket of executive privilege covered every member of the executive branch; none of some 2.5 million employees could be compelled to testify before Congress if the president objected!

The Ford administration two years later informed a House subcommittee that the doctrine of executive privilege extended to the private sector, too. Through his attorney general, President Ford ordered three corporate executives to resist a congressional subpoena to testify on *Operation SHAMROCK, a secret United States intelligence operation conducted from 1947 to 1975 involving the interception of international cable communications sent and received by American citizens.* Just as Kleindienst had retreated from his stance in the face of congressional outrage, so did the corporate executives, who decided to appear before Congress as directed by the House of Representatives.

Against the few executive retreats, however, stands a long history of stony silence from the White House and the bureaucracy. In 1975, for example, neither the House Intelligence Committee nor the Senate Intelligence Committee was ever successful in forcing Secretary Kissinger to testify in public on past United States covert actions abroad. Even when the House committee

subpoenaed a memorandum written by a Kissinger subordinate on a less sensitive subject (our policy toward Cyprus), the secretary of state blocked any response to the subpoena, stating through an aide that "we must preserve the confidentiality of the decision-making process."[21]

The classification system has been equally frustrating to Congress. In the name of "national security" and the need for secrecy, officials in the executive branch daily stamp documents "Confidential," "Secret," and "Top Secret," and apply scores of other little known "compartmentations" that effectively remove them from the public domain. Even the most aggressive legislators are frequently unable to gain access to documents sealed by special classifications. The authority for such classifications comes from executive orders issued by presidents since 1951 (and earlier for military agencies). As one expert on bureaucracies has observed, "Inevitably, bureaucratic caution and self-interest lead executive agencies to classify many more documents as secret than security interests actually require since the penalties attached to unauthorized disclosure may be severe,

In the name of "national security," officials in the executive branch stamp documents "Secret" which effectively removes them from public or congressional scrutiny.

while overclassification is not likely to be punished.''[22]

If all other efforts to monopolize information fail, the executive branch usually resorts to the stall. The 1975 intelligence investigation is a case in point. In the early weeks of their inquiry, the House and Senate investigative committees generated long lists of documents they required to complete the probe. For months thereafter, the executive branch dragged its feet in a hundred different ways to avoid relinquishing evidence. Paper warfare was underway.

The intelligence agencies in the Department of Defense used a popular bureaucratic technique to keep the legislators at bay: they sent several truck loads of documents (mostly irrelevant) to the committees, in hopes of bogging down the staff in minutiae. The technique was remarkably successful. For its part, the Federal Bureau of Investigation (FBI) simply misled Congress about the existence of some key documents, sending its investigators back to Capitol Hill empty-handed.

In sum, an important contributor to the rise in presidential power has been the vast network of information sources available to the White House (including more than a dozen major intelligence agencies), and the executive branch's success in monopolizing this information through proclamations of executive privilege, the establishment of classification barriers, and the use of well-honed tactics of delay.

Together these five powers intertwined to form a branch of government so massive that it overshadowed the legislature and produced a weakened form of representative government on Capitol Hill. In the ''invitation to struggle''[23] between Congress and the presidency that the Constitution represents, the executive branch—for the moment—had proven the stronger. The ax blows of Vietnam and Watergate, however, dramatically altered power relations in the federal government.

THE OMNIPOTENT IDEOLOGY

If an institutional deference to the presidency represented one key component of the consensus behind American foreign policymaking prior to the Vietnam War, a second component was the anticommunist philosophy shared by most Americans and virtually all their leaders. World War II, which accelerated the growth of presidential

power so dramatically, also produced for the United States an ideological opponent in the Soviet Union of even greater military might (and inscrutability) than the German Third Reich.

Joining with the Soviet Union (or U.S.S.R.) temporarily in an alliance against Hitler, we found ourselves in 1945 at odds with the Soviets in practically every significant dimension of human activity. Whereas the United States extolled the virtues of a free-market economy, the Soviets preferred a centrally controlled, planned economy; whereas we professed strong religious beliefs, the ''godless communists'' denounced religious tenets; whereas we claimed to respect and honor the sovereignty of other nations (despite various transgressions to the contrary, as in Chile in 1964), the Soviets immediately seized the political and police apparatus in Eastern Europe and established a Moscow-directed hegemony over these ''satellite'' nations. Still weary from defeating the Axis, the United States now braced itself against this new perceived threat. In 1947, diplomat George F. Kennan recommended publicly (though anonymously in a now famous article signed ''X'') what he had been advising the nation's leaders privately for some years, namely, a ''long-term, patient but firm and vigilant containment of Russian expansive tendencies.''[24] America was introduced to the containment doctrine.

On March 12, 1947, President Truman proclaimed what came to be known as the **Truman Doctrine:** ''*it must be the policy of the United States to support free peoples who are resisting attempted subjugation by armed minorities or outside pressures.''* Through this application of the containment doctrine, the decision was made to aid nations threatened by the Soviets, beginning in 1947 with Greece (where Soviet-sponsored Marxist guerillas were thwarted) and Turkey.

Closer study of Lenin's writings, with its anti-Western rhetoric, coupled with the aggressive speeches and behavior of Stalin (and later Khrushchev) added to the uneasiness in the West. The explosion in 1949 of a Soviet atomic bomb raised fears that we stood in mortal danger from this new world power. As a top-secret report prepared for President Eisenhower concluded in 1954:

It is now clear that we are facing an implacable enemy whose avowed objective is world domination by what-

ever means at whatever cost. There are no rules in such a game. Hitherto acceptable norms of human conduct do not apply. If the U.S. is to survive, long-standing American concepts of 'fair play' must be reconsidered. We must develop effective espionage and counterespionage services. We must learn to subvert, sabotage and destroy our enemies by more clever, more sophisticated and more effective methods than those used against us. It may become necessary that the American people will be made acquainted with, understand and support this fundamentally repugnant philosophy.[25]

The huge missiles constructed by the Soviets and their dazzling achievements in space exploration (Sputnik, the first earth satellite, was launched in 1957) further fueled Western anxieties.

To some, we seemed to be in a struggle for our very existence; either we or the Soviets would be destroyed. In the mathematical game-theory language popular at the time, it was a *"zero-sum game" with no compromises and only one winner.* Politicians and others often reduced the complicated relationship between the two superpowers to simplistic slogans, depicting a kind of global superbowl of ideological conflict which pitted the Christian free world against the godless, totalitarians headquartered in the Kremlin. It was a battle between "Jesus Christ and the hammer-and-

sickle," summed up Representative Mendel Rivers (D-S.C.), chairperson of the House Armed Services Committee from 1965 to 1971.[26] Comparable exaggerations on the Soviet side contributed to the siege mentality in both countries during this "Cold War."

The Soviets were not the only communists who caused concern. Just as threatening to some proponents of containment was the People's Republic of China (or "Red China" as it was colloquially called by most Americans during the 1950s and 1960s), with its population of 600 million and Marxist revolutionary leaders, who in 1949 drove pro-American Chinese factions off the Asian mainland to exile on the island of Taiwan. During the Cold War, Republicans and Democrats alike worried (in the words of Townsend Hoopes) that from China an "evil ideology would flow like a contagious lava" across the Far East.[27] This force, too, had to be contained.

The conventional wisdom of this era is summed up in the **domino theory,** *which suggested that the communists, if they were not contained, would conquer one nation after another until the last one—the United States—fell.* To protect ourselves, the United States continued to provide economic, military, and covert assistance to countries resisting communist expansion.

One of the most catastrophic events in American history, the Vietnam War, was justified on the basis of the domino theory. This theory holds that if communists are not contained, they will conquer one nation after another until they rule the world.

The battleground has often been (and continues to be) the **Third World,** *the diverse group of nations outside both the Western and the Sino-Soviet blocs.* Driven by this intense anticommunism, the United States directed or supported coups and assassination plots in many small, weak, and remote nations. Like the communists, we had few successes and many failures, most conspicuously in the Bay of Pigs. The United States fought to stalemate a major though undeclared war in Korea against Chinese and North Korean communists during which, in one view, "we lost 30,000 dead . . . to save face . . . and it was undoubtedly worth it."[28] And, in what became the most catastrophic event in American history since the Civil War, we engaged indigenous communists in Indochina from 1964 to 1975 in a losing military effort that cost over 57,000 American lives, 300,000 wounded and maimed, and $175 billion.

The domino theory lives on today in the Reagan administration. A few years before his election as president in 1980, Ronald Reagan resurrected the world view that had been so pervasive in the 1950s and 1960s:

> *The Communist master plan, as we know it from published reports, from intelligence sources and from our own painful experience, is to isolate free nations, one by one, stimulating and supplying revolution without endangering their own troops. What they did in Vietnam was simply to follow the plan they have pursued in many countries around the world. . . . There is a Communist plan for world conquest, and its final step is to conquer the United States.*[29]

Once in office, his administration expressed fears that guerrilla rebellions in El Salvador would lead to communism in that country. In the 1980s, though Americans were more skeptical; Vietnam had eroded the foreign policy consensus that had dominated our view of world affairs since 1945.

AN ERODING CONSENSUS

The war in Vietnam, with its grievous toll in blood and treasure, its revelations of government deception, its uncertain management and ambiguous objectives, caused a wave of revulsion across the United States. The young, called upon to fight the war, rebelled; public officials began to question the judgment and the truthfulness of the president and his advisers. By 1970, a leading member of the Senate Foreign Relations Committee declared, "The myth that the Chief Executive is the fount of all wisdom in foreign affairs today lies shattered on the shoals of Vietnam."[30]

On the heels of the failure in Vietnam came the near-impeachment and resignation of President Nixon in 1974 during the Watergate crisis. Institutional deference to the president as a given in the conduct of foreign affairs quickly became a subject of reappraisal.

The Cold War took on a new appearance, too.

The historical deference of Congress and the public to the president in the conduct of foreign affairs was eroded significantly by the Vietnam War and the Watergate crisis.

The Sino-Soviet split in 1962 suggested that the communist world was polycentric rather than ruled by the Soviet politburo. A major U.S.-Soviet arms accord ratified in 1963, the Nuclear Test-Ban Treaty, began an era of warmer relations between the two superpowers. The Cold War continued to thaw, with interruptions, over the next decade, reaching warm points in 1972 with the successful negotiation of SALT I and again in 1974 when President Nixon (whose early political fortunes, ironically, were built upon an unalloyed hostility toward the USSR) visited the Soviet Union and paved the way for further accords on nuclear weapons, which were signed at Vladivostok later in the year. *Détente, the relaxation of tensions between the superpowers,* became the order of the day.

The views of many Washington decision-makers on the Cold War, however, were shaped more by the experiences of the Vietnam War than by apparent divisions within the communist camp. They began to reason that a zero-sum view of communism led only to needless entanglements in regions far removed from American shores and American interests. As one United States senator (himself once a Cold War warrior) recalled, "[It was] only with our deep embroilment in that misbegotten war in Asia that I began to see where the excesses of this old notion had led us and what a catastrophic cause it had been."[31]

Over the past decade, then, the once-strong consensus in foreign affairs has changed significantly. The presidency has been revived since the Watergate scandal, and containment remains the dominant philosophy among the foreign policy elite. Indeed, sharp-tongued anticommunist rhetoric is once more in vogue with the advent of the Reagan administration and the neoconservative movement. But the once solid consensus on foreign policy, supported by the doctrines of bipartisanship and containment, no longer exists.

Institutionally, in place of a presidency all-knowing and omnipotent in foreign affairs stand a Congress searching for a partnership role in policymaking and a public more skeptical of White House appeals and declarations. Ideologically, in place of a reflex willingness to intervene with Cold War fervor against Marxist regimes anywhere on the globe, there is a more reflective attitude (short of a clear and present danger to the United States) on the part of Congress and the public about the costs of intervention.

A FOREIGN POLICY PARTNERSHIP

The congressional pursuit of a full partnership in foreign policy is readily apparent in the recent proliferation of various legislative "reporting" requirements and other statutes fashioned by Congress to trim presidential powers. Through law as well as less formal pressure, Congress has attempted to force the executive branch to keep legislators more fully informed of foreign policy decisions—often down to the details. ("Micromanagement," complains one bureaucrat, echoing the views of many.[32]) As Senator Arthur Vandenberg (R—Mich.) once put it, the Congress now demands to be in on the "take-offs," not just the "crash landings," in foreign policy.[33]

In several important instances, Congress went beyond a basic demand for information and invoked various "legislative veto" provisions (declared unconstitutional by the Supreme Court in June 1983); (see chapters 11 and 12). This response from Capitol Hill—a noisy, if bloodless, "revolution" in foreign policymaking—may be summarized in terms of the five key powers presented earlier.

Agreement-Making

In 1968, four long years after the Gulf of Tonkin Resolution, President Johnson hastily requested the Senate to approve a broadly worded resolution on foreign aid. On the eve of a summit meeting of Western Hemisphere leaders in Punta del Esta, Johnson sought congressional support for costly new agreements with the nations of Latin America. The Senate Foreign Relations Committee refused to act quickly and instead passed by a vote of nine to zero a substitute resolution stating that new foreign aid initiatives in Latin America would be given due consideration in accordance with the Committee's normal legislative timetable. In so doing, the Foreign Relations Committee went beyond words (some of its members had already spoken up against Johnson and the Vietnam War during hearings held in 1966) to deeds in an effort to restore a constitutional balance between the branches in the conduct of foreign policy. Distrust of Lyndon Johnson had created a mood of skepticism—even defiance—on Capitol Hill.

The next year the Senate passed, 70 to 16, a *National Commitments Resolution*, which stated,

"Be it resolved, that it is the sense of the Senate that a national commitment by the United States to a foreign power necessarily and exclusively results from affirmative action taken by the executive and legislative branches of the United States government through means of a treaty, convention, or other legislative instrumentality specifically intended to give effect to such a commitment."

One of the leading lights in the legislative resurgence was Senator Clifford Case (R—N.J.), a member of the Senate Foreign Relations Committee. During the Vietnam War, he was mortified by the inability of Congress to keep track of the commitments President Johnson and his advisers were making in Indochina. His frustration eventually led to the Case-Zablocki Act, in which he and Representative Clement Zablocki (D—Wisc), chairman of the House International Relations Committee, joined to pass a reporting requirement forcing the Department of State (and, since 1976, all agencies) to inform Congress of agreements negotiated with other nations (see chapter 12). The Congress had taken steps, however tentative and cautious, to monitor more closely the agreement-making process.

Subsequent efforts failed, however. Congress was unwilling to pass the **Case Amendment** *requiring congressional approval for military agreements* or the **Treaty Powers Resolution** of 1976, which *mandated the use of the treaty procedure for all "significant" international agreements.* Congress was prepared, though, to tighten supervision over the export of military weapons by the executive branch. Senator Gaylord Nelson (D—Wisc.) and Representative Jonathan B. Bingham (D—N.Y.) joined in 1974 to pass the **Nelson-Bingham Amendment** *that required the president to forward to Congress a complete description of any defense item or service costing $25 million or more (reduced to $7 million or more in 1976) intended for overseas sale. The report had to arrive on Capitol Hill before the executive branch was allowed to issue the letter of offer abroad, and the sale had to be stopped promptly if, within 30 days, both chambers of Congress voted down the proposal by simple majorities.* As Thomas Franck and Edward Weisband have commented, the Nelson-Bingham Amendment "worked a profound transformation in arms exports policy."[34]

Congress had similar successes in its efforts to gain the right of prior consultation in the fields of human rights and nuclear sales. With the passage of the **Harkin Amendment** in 1975 (sponsored by Thomas Harkin, D—Iowa), *either chamber of Congress could end foreign aid to a country over the president's objection if by majority vote it decided that the prospective recipient was engaged in "a consistent pattern of gross violations of internationally recognized human rights" and that the aid was unlikely to reach needy people.* The **Nuclear Non-proliferation Act** of 1978 *gave Congress veto power over nuclear exports, should both chambers vote to negate a sale within a 60-day waiting period.* When all of these legislative veto provisions were struck down by the Supreme Court in 1983, Congress began to seek new—and old—ways to supervise the executive branch. Enacting statutes with greater detail, leaving less room for executive discretion, was one remedy proposed. This, however, is more easily said than done.

War-Making

Determined in the midst of the Vietnam War to regain control of the war powers, the Senate passed in 1968 an amendment to the Military Appropriations bill introduced by Senator Frank Church (D—Idaho). Adopted 73 to 17 the **Church Amendment** *prohibited the use of any funds in the bill for the introduction of United States combat troops into Laos or Thailand.* In 1970, Senator John Sherman Cooper (R—Ky.) joined with Senator Church in the **Cooper-Church Amendment** *to add Cambodia to the list.* With these amendments, the Senate sought to block further escalation of the Vietnam War and to demonstrate that war powers could be regained through a tighter legislative grip on the purse strings.

The major attack on presidential war-making, however, came four years later in 1973 with the passage of the War Powers Act (see chapter 12). Congress, henceforth, would know about United States involvement in war within 48 hours after the first shots and would have to formally approve any prolongation of the hostilities. There would be no more "silent" troop build-ups like the one that occurred in Indochina during 1965.

Whether Congress actually regained its lost war powers through this initiative is disputed. Certainly President Nixon saw the Act as a threat to presidential power, and he vetoed it. His veto was overridden by a cliff-hanging 4 votes in the House and 13 in the Senate. Still, the 48 hours allowed the president arguably gives him more explicit war-making power than ever before. The Constitution states that Congress shall declare war; now, for two days at any rate, the president may engage in combat without congressional debate—or even awareness.

The War Powers Act, then, does seem to provide the president with considerable leeway for two days, as well as some room for maneuvering in support of counterinsurgency opportunities. Of course, as weapons technology increases in sophistication and as payloads grow larger, 48 hours could mean the lifetime of the planet. And in longer military engagements, the legislature—once informed—is apt to "rally 'round the flag" and support our troops in the field, guided by information about the battle conditions provided by the executive branch itself. (As usually happens in a military engagement, President Ford's popularity in the polls surged upward 11 percentage points after the *Mayaguez* incident.) In short, the War Powers Act has obvious flaws, but it does set in place a mandatory vote by the Congress on the merits of any United States armed conflict extending beyond a brief period. However, the legislative veto ruling of the Supreme Court may render this provision unconstitutional as well.

Covert Action

Before December, 1974, the executive branch was under no legal obligation to report covert actions to Congress. Sometimes the CIA would brief selected members, sometimes not. Allen W. Dulles, director of the agency from 1953 to 1961, told the Warren Commission that when he was at the agency's helm he felt obliged to tell the truth only to one person: the president.[35] Nor did Congress seek information. Members apparently assumed it was better to avoid political risks by remaining ignorant of controversial operations.

In December, 1974, however, Congress passed an amendment to the Foreign Assistance Act co-sponsored by Senator Harold E. Hughes (D—Iowa) and Representative Leo J. Ryan (D—Ca.). The *Hughes-Ryan Act required the president to approve in writing all important covert actions and then to inform Congress of these decisions.* The act read:

No funds appropriated under the authority of this or any other Act may be expended by or on behalf of the [CIA] for operations in foreign countries, other than activities intended solely for obtaining necessary intelligence, unless and until the President finds that each such operation is important to the national security of the United

States and reports, in a timely fashion, a description and scope of such operation to the appropriate committees of the Congress. . . .

Exactly one year later, at the height of the congressional investigations into the CIA, Congress, in the **Clark Amendment** (named for sponsor Richard Clark, D—Iowa), took aim at a specific covert action operation and *prohibited, over strong presidential objections, the use of any funds for covert actions in Angola.* An attempt by President Reagan to repeal this amendment failed.

In the aftermath of the CIA investigations, Senate (1976) and House (1977) intelligence committees were created to more attentively monitor CA and other intelligence operations. Interest in intelligence oversight reached its peak in 1980, with the adoption of the **Intelligence Accountability Act**. This law advanced the legislative role in the intelligence field further than ever before. It *demanded for Congress prior notification of significant intelligence operations, not just notification "in a timely fashion," as prescribed by Hughes-Ryan, as well as access to all intelligence information deemed necessary for its conduct of legislative oversight, not just on important covert actions.* In short, irrevocable decisions (*faits accomplis*) from the executive branch and executive privilege were forbidden at least when it came to intelligence policy. An ambiguous preamble in the statute raised questions about an executive escape hatch—the president could apparently determine if the law was consistent with constitutional "authorities and duties"[36]—but Congress had nevertheless put some heavy artillery in place for better control over intelligence policy (and without recourse to a legislative veto.)

In 1982, Congress passed the **Boland Amendment** (named after its chief sponsor, chairperson of the House Committee on Intelligence, Edward P. Boland, D—Mass.). This statute stated that *none of the funds provided to the intelligence agencies could be used "to furnish military equipment, military training or advice, or other support for military activities, to any group or individual, not part of a country's armed forces, for the purpose of overthrowing the Government of Nicaragua or provoking a military exchange between Nicaragua and Honduras."* In a word, the Congress sought to head off rumored plans by the Reagan administration to use paramilitary operations launched from Honduras against the Marxist regime in Nicaragua. Apparent efforts by the administration to circumvent this law in 1983 led the vice chairman of the Senate Intelligence Committee, Daniel Patrick Moynihan (D—N.Y.), to warn of a "crisis of confidence . . . between the Committee and the intelligence community."[37] Congress tightened the language of the Boland Amendment in 1983 to make plainer still its wish to prohibit covert actions in Nicaragua.

Drawing the Purse Strings

Few executive branch policies are cost-free; each decision normally requires the expenditure of funds from the federal treasury. To control the flow of funds is to control policymaking. The Cooper-Church Amendment was a dramatic move by Capitol Hill designed to limit the president's war-making abilities. In 1974, the Congressional Budget and Impoundment Control Act represented a far more sweeping effort to regain control over government spending practices (see

chapter 11). With this statute in place, presidents could no longer quietly bury funds appropriated for specific weapons systems and other expenditures related to foreign affairs.

Secrecy

During the period of legislative resurgence from 1968 to the present, a major target of congressional wrath was executive secrecy. The several new reporting requirements passed by Congress were crafted to keep the legislature informed of executive decisions. The Case-Zablocki Act, The Nelson-Bingham Amendment, the Congressional Budget Act, and the rest (see Table 19.2) all forced the executive branch to disclose policy to Congress within specific time limits. The laws and resolutions described here are only a few of the many that were instituted. These included the important *Electronic Surveillance Act of 1978, which requires a judicial review of presidential requests for wire-*

TABLE 19.2

Landmarks in the Legislative Resurgence, 1964–1982: A Selective Summary

	International Agreements	War	Covert Action	Money	Secrecy
1964		Vietnam			
1966		Vietnam Hearings			
1968	Punta del Esta rejection	Church Amendment			
1969		National Commitments Resolution			
1970		Cooper-Church Amendment			
1971					N.Y. Times v. U.S.
1972	Case-Zablocki Amendment				
1973		War Powers Act			Watergate
1974	Nelson-Bingham Amendment		Hughes-Ryan Amendment	Congressional Budget Act	
1975	Harkin Amendment		Clark Amendment		intelligence investigations
1976			Senate Intelligence Committee		
1977			House Intelligence Committee		
1978	Nuclear Non-proliferation Act				Electronic Surveillance Act
1980			Intelligence Accountability Act		
1982			Boland Amendment		

taps on American citizens. Prior to this law, presidents could order wiretaps simply by claiming that an individual threatened internal security through an alleged association with foreign intelligence agents or operations. The list of related resolutions is extensive and the point is clear: Congress wants to know about decisions in the White House and the bureaucracy. While it may no longer veto executive actions, Congress will no doubt continue to insist on executive branch fidelity to reporting requirements.

Congress made it clear in other less formal ways that it would steadfastly oppose efforts to conceal information. The House Subcommittee investigation in 1975 into Operation SHAMROCK cast aside President Ford's expansive use of executive privilege and subpoenaed the corporate executives implicated in illegal surveillance of cable communications. In 1975, the Senate and House Intelligence investigation committees, through hard negotiations, achieved access to executive documents never before shared with the Congress— most notably, National Security Council decision memoranda. As one of the Senate Committee staff aides recalled, "there were no classes of documents that the Committee did not obtain, although it agreed that in general the names of agents and their methods of conducting certain intelligence activities should remain in executive custody."[38] The 1980 Intelligence Accountability Act seemed to reject placing even these two categories of information in exclusive executive custody, but again, ambiguous language in the preamble regarding the sanctity of intelligence sources and methods left the issue cloudy.

The Supreme Court, too, whittled away at executive secrecy in foreign affairs. It declared in New York Times *v.* U.S. (the Pentagon Papers case) *that the Times had the right to print leaked and highly classified documents on the Vietnam War over the president's objection, since—in this instance at least— publication was unlikely to result (in the words of Justice Potter Stewart) "in direct, immediate, and irreparable damage to our nation or its people."*[39]

Beyond Containment

An ideological revolution took place along with this institutional one. An increasing number of legislators (although probably less than a majority) seemed unwilling to view the world through a Cold War prism. Drawing away from an emphasis on confrontation between the Soviet Union and the United States, prominent political figures declared nationalism—not communism—to be the engine of change around the globe. "What about the force of nationalism?" questioned then-Senator Walter F. Mondale (D—Minn.) in a hearing with Secretary Kissinger in 1975. The Senator was unwilling to accept Kissinger's warning about Soviet dominance over African nations such as Angola. More likely, he thought, the proud nations of this continent would reject outside interference from Moscow or anywhere else.[40]

Moreover, some members of Congress were far more concerned with internal problems than with external "threats" from small, developing nations. "When they [the Reagan administration] get ready to send helicopters to El Salvador, they talk about saving the country from Communism," testified Representative Barbara Mikulski (D—Md.) before a Senate subcommittee. "I want them to start talking about saving the country from birth defects. I'm talking about children in my district who are more likely to die of birth defects than from some communist who's going to come up the Chesapeake Bay."[41] Though the Reagan administration continued to cling to a Cold War philosophy, one change had occurred: politics no longer stopped at the water's edge.

An Executive-Legislative Compact

In terms of the supply pattern presented in Table 18.2 (p. 520), legislative decision-makers (as the preceeding summary suggests) were inclined until recently to grant the executive branch broad leeway on matters of foreign policy. Congress, though, has rarely been fully passive.

Even before the Vietnam War, some legislators monitored selected foreign affairs decisions with an eagle's eye, forcing changes in policy by the executive branch. Former Congressmember Otto Passman (D—La.), for example, had no love for foreign aid, which he viewed as a redistributive "give away" program that had no advantages for the United States. From his powerful post as chairperson of the Appropriations Subcommittee on Foreign Operations, he regularly cut the State Department aid bill.

Instances of legislative involvement, however, have been uncommon exceptions to the usual mood of quiescent bipartisanship characteristic of this century. The successful stand of Henry Cabot

Lodge (R—N.H.) against President Woodrow Wilson's desire to join the League of Nations represented a last hurrah for legislative assertiveness in foreign affairs until the late 1960s. For the most part, on key decisions regarding the use of military force, the establishment of military bases abroad, covert intervention, and other important issues, foreign policy by executive fiat has been the rule. Most of the key allocation decisions were made by the executive branch.

At the beginning of the new era of a foreign policy partnership between the two branches, remnants of the traditional deference to the presidency remained. Despite his skepticism about foreign aid, Representative Passman could still ask on the House floor in 1974, "Mr. Speaker, if we cannot trust the President of the United States, who can we trust?"[42] During the debate on the War Powers Act, Senator Jacob Javits (R—N.Y.) said to Senator Barry Goldwater (R—Ariz.), "So really you are opposed to my bill because you have less faith in Congress than you have in the President. Isn't that true?" Responded Goldwater, "To be perfectly honest with you, you are right."[43] Even by 1980, when the experiment in foreign policy partnership was in full swing, Goldwater, as the new chairpersons of the Senate Committee on Intelligence, said, "I don't even like to have an intelligence oversight committee. I don't think it's any of our business."[44]

The role of foreign policy lapdog, though, has been discarded by most members of Congress. This has produced strains in the American political system as the "supply pattern" shifts from delegation to presidential authority toward an allocation partnership. Having two disparate institutions decide allocation policies has inevitably proven more complicated than having one, especially since foreign policy decisions tend frequently to be redistributive; that is, American citizens usually have to give up something without necessarily seeing tangible benefits in return, as when we give foreign aid to a poor nation that then votes against us in the United Nations. Policies like the Nuclear Test Ban Treaty and the General Agreement on Tariff and Trade, both signed in 1963, are distributive; they benefit everyone by banning radioactive explosions in the atmosphere and by enhancing world trade. Some forms of foreign aid can also be distributive, as when recipients pay back loans with interest. Often, however,

National security decisions are especially controversial because the appropriations process is not a zero sum game. Money spent on defense is money not spent on domestic programs.

our aid programs appear more like a one-way street, even though it could be argued that by enhancing the economic and defense security of other nations, we make the world a safer place—a definite benefit to ourselves.

Especially controversial are national security decisions. Money spent on guns is money taken away from butter—and housing, and mass transit systems, and the like. The $175 billion "redistributed" in the jungles of Vietnam might have gone a long way toward restoring antiquated industrial plants and deteriorating cities within our own country.

So a more assertive Congress now demands a larger say in both distributive and—particularly—redistributive decisions. The president, once relatively free of foreign policy kibitzers on Capitol Hill, must now contend with a multitude of voices and votes in the decision process. The dispersal of power in Congress during the past decade, discussed in chapter 11, further complicates decision-making for presidents. As former Secretary of State Dean Rusk has ruefully observed, during his service with Presidents Kennedy and Johnson, the chief executive could count on five legislators to tell him how Congress would react to an administration proposal. Now, in place of these five "whales," Congress is more like "535 minnows swimming around in a bucket."[45]

Another source of institutional conflict is the different constituencies represented by the president and legislators—that is, national versus local. These two perspectives were illustrated recently during a dispute over the settlement of claims by Czechoslovakia.

Czech immigrants to the United States filed claims against the Communist regime in Czechoslovakia for confiscation of their property in the postwar period. To encourage the Czech government to pay these claims, the United States government froze in a New York bank $200 million worth of Czech gold found by American troops in 1945 in Germany, which had been stolen by the Nazis from Prague. The State Department initially refused to return this gold until the Czech government settled the claims filed by the newly naturalized United States citizens from Czechoslovakia. As we moved into the era of détente, however, the State Department was more willing to settle the matter with limited payment to the claimants. Representatives in Congress intervened, seeking full payment for the claimants, who were now voters in congressional districts. These different perspectives, détente for the State Department and the satisfaction of citizen grievances for Congress made the conduct of foreign policy far more complicated for the professional diplomats, but, one could argue, far more just to our citizens. In this case, a fortuitous rise in the price of gold made the Czech gold sufficiently valuable that the Czech government agreed to pay the claimants in full in return for the gold. Unpredictable changes in the gold market had allowed a distributive outcome.[46]

What has arisen in the last decade, then, is a new openness in the approach to foreign policymaking in the United States. Institutionally, this openness brings Congress, and with it the public, more directly into deliberations on international matters; ideologically, it questions the zero-sum assumptions of the Cold War. The British statesman, James Bryce, once observed,

In a democracy the people are entitled to determine the ends or general aims of foreign policy. History shows that they do this at least as wisely as monarchs or oligarchies, or the small groups to whom, in democratic countries, the conduct of foreign relations has been left, and that they have evinced more respect for moral principles.[47]

For those who share this view, the new openness is a blessing. But those who believe that foreign policy is too intricate for Congress or the people to fathom, that the job should be left to the president and his corps of professional diplomats, must regard this evolution as a misfortune.

What is most obvious about foreign policymaking in the United States is the need for a ceasefire between branches, as called for recently by President Carter's Undersecretary of State, Warren Christopher. We need, he argues, an **executive-legislative compact** in foreign affairs. "As a fundamental precept," he writes, "the compact would call for *restraint on the part of the Congress—for Congress to recognize and accept the responsibility of the Executive to conduct and manage foreign policy on a daily basis.*" He properly stresses that the executive branch *must be prepared to provide Congress "full information and consultation"* and that *"broad policy should be jointly designed."* For its part, *Congress should only rarely, in extreme circumstances, attempt "to dictate or overturn Executive decisions and action. . . ."*[48] The challenge is to strike this proper balance.

A FOREIGN POLICY AGENDA

Imagine that you have just been elected president. What follows is only a brief sample of the pressing foreign policy problems that you would inherit on Inauguration Day.

Defense Policy

Perhaps nothing a president faces creates a greater dilemma for him than defense policy. On the one hand, the protection of the American people from external threats is a vital duty of the commander-in-chief. On the other hand, the production of weapons represents a tremendous drain on the national treasury (see Figure 19.2), and these weapons hold the potential for annihilating the

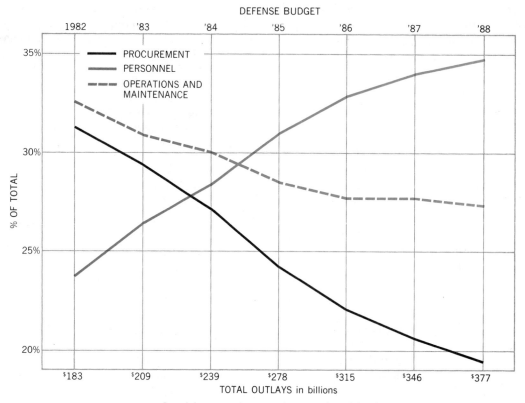

DEFENSE BUDGET

FIGURE 19.2

The Rising Cost of U.S. Weapon Procurement

SOURCE: *Time*, March 7, 1983, p. 13. Copyright 1983 Time Inc. All rights reserved. Reprinted by permission from *Time*.

human race, should a full-blown nuclear war ever erupt.

The central defense question has always been: How much is enough? The answer depend upon a host of variables. Among them is how extensive one thinks our military commitments abroad ought to be, which in turn is tied closely to how fully one embraces the containment doctrine.

For those who believe the United States must oppose Marxist regimes and rebellions whenever and wherever they appear, the costs will be enormous, for the world is large and warfare is expensive. Similarly, for those who wish to surpass the Soviets in nuclear weaponry rather than settle for a rough parity (''essential equivalence''), the costs may be exorbitant, for the Soviets are unlikely to let us achieve superiority over them any more than we would allow them superiority over us. The end result of a quest for superiority, critics contend, is only all-out, unwinnable arms races.

Defense policy, then, like all other policies discussed in this book, can be reduced to assump-

The arms race between the Soviets and the U.S. is an expensive contest. The goal of each is superiority rather than parity (equality).

tions about the world we live in (zero-sum versus détente, for example). These assumptions lead to policy priorities (covert action over international trade, say) and specific programs. Decision-makers in Washington and attentive citizens across the land often have differing views on these assumptions, priorities, and programs—especially on how much money ought to be diverted away from their favorite programs. The result is considerable "pulling-and-tugging"—in short politics, which columnist William F. Buckley, Jr., once aptly described as a "debate about the future."

What makes the debate over the future of defense policy all the more heated are the great costs involved. The money used for defense is money taken from other societal needs. The essence of politics lies in this competition for limited resources—the struggle over "who gets what how," in political scientist Harold Lasswell's famous definition of politics.

The Reagan administration, with its leery outlook on American-Soviet relations, proposed to raise the defense budget by 10 percent in 1983, including a 40 percent increase in spending on nuclear weaponry. Even the Republican-led Senate Budget Committee (with several members up for reelection in 1984) balked at this increase and slashed the request in half.

The House of Representatives and the American people seemed to agree more with the Senate Budget Committee than with the president. A *New York Times*/CBS News Poll in early 1983 revealed that 48 percent of those surveyed thought the United States was spending too much on new weapons, compared with 25 percent who said spending levels were about right. Only 11 percent wanted more money spent on new weapons systems.[49]

Opposition to further spending for nuclear weapons is most conspicuous in the *nuclear freeze movement, a bipartisan coalition of officials and citizens formed in 1982 to support a mutual, verifiable halt in the production of nuclear weapons by both superpowers.* A *Newsweek* poll in 1983 indicated that 64 percent of those surveyed favored a freeze.[50]

President Reagan, however, saw the movement as a "very dangerous fraud," smacking of "appeasement."[51] Freeze advocates, though, denied an interest in appeasement, claiming that they sought a money-saving, risk-reducing agreement

with the Soviets to stop the nuclear arms race. The heart of their argument was that both super-powers already had more than enough nuclear warheads to maintain *deterrence, the strategic theory that a sufficient threat of devastating military retaliation against an enemy will prohibit attacks.* Indeed, as Chairperson of the Senate Appropriations Committee and freeze leader Mark O. Hatfield (R—Oreg.) noted in 1982, the United States has 9,000 nuclear warheads arming its weapons triad of submarines, bombers, and ICBMs, compared to 7,000 for the Soviets. Moreover, just two United States submarines, said Hatfield, carried enough warheads to "knock out every major Russian city."[52]

Regardless of this capacity for "overkill," nuclear-weapons assembly lines in the Soviet Union and the United States (see Figure 19.3) continue to turn out additional warheads at an estimated rate of one a day.

As president, what would your answer be in the defense field to the question: How much is enough?

International Economic Policy

At the end of World War II, the United States stood in an enviable—and unusual—position. Our country was preeminent in military and economic power among the war-wracked nations of the world. We enjoyed this preeminence for over two decades, but inevitably the countries of Western Europe and Japan emerged as fierce competitors in the international marketplace. Indeed, the United States contributed to its competitors' welfare by providing financial and technical assistance to shore up these nations against communist influence (especially with the Marshall Plan for European economic recovery initiated in 1947).

Scores of newly independent nations have sought their fair share of the marketplace, too. Though mostly still poor, several of these nations have developed a capacity to compete with the richer countries in the sale of selected products. They also supply such critical materials as tin, bauxite, rubber, and oil.

The emergence of healthy economies around the world has not been strictly bad news for the United States. New markets mean jobs for Americans. Forty percent of our agricultural product is now sold in overseas markets. The nonaligned countries are our fastest growing markets; only

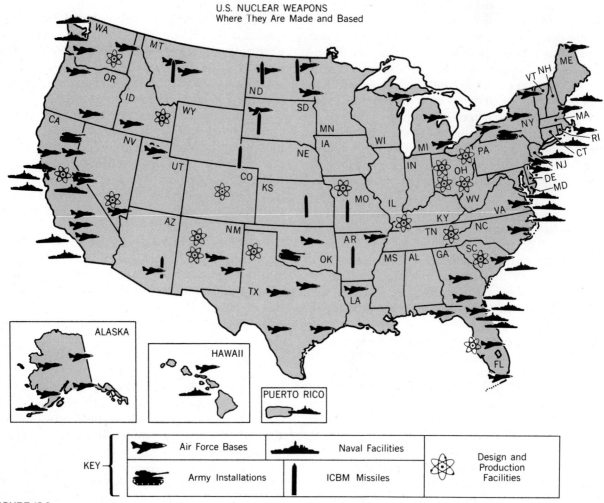

FIGURE 19.3

U.S. Nuclear Weapons: Where They Are Made and Based

SOURCE: Center for Defense Information; Reprinted in *Pacific Daily News*, May 10, 1983, p. 10.

Japan exports more to them than we do. Still, the United States now has to struggle for international economic gains that we once took for granted. This has led to acute anxieties about some industries in our country, particularly during periods of domestic recession.

Western Europe

Practically since the establishment of the North Atlantic Treaty Organization (NATO) in 1949, commentators have debated the strength of the Western Alliance. Despite occasionally gloomy prognostications, NATO has remained a strong military, political, and economic association of states. Its most serious challenges today, as always, concern defense and trade matters.

On defense, NATO leaders have attempted to achieve an appropriate balance of forces in Western Europe to counter a Soviet military build-up, especially in intermediate-range nuclear forces (INFs). Despite mass protests in England and West Germany, the United States, with the compliance of NATO leaders, considered placing nuclear Pershing II and cruise missiles on Western European soil to balance Soviet SS-20 nuclear missiles in Eastern Europe. The fast-flying Pershing IIs in Europe would reduce Soviet reaction time to only six minutes in case of attack.

The United States now has to struggle for international economic gains that we once took for granted as the competition from other nations, like Japan, has intensified.

Negotiations in Geneva over the appropriate number of missiles to place, if any, were prolonged and heated with NATO allies often in disagreement. To protect slowly achieved ties of economic cooperation and relaxed emigration policies with the Soviets, many Western European leaders were reluctant to engage in Cold War rhetoric and practices to the degree espoused by the Reagan administration. Détente held greater appeal in Bonn than in Washington, and European leaders were more inclined to seek negotiated settlements through compromise on defense agreements. With respect to INFs, the Reagan administration showed signs in 1983 of moderating its initial demand for the removal of all SS-20s in exchange for an American pledge to keep Pershing IIs and cruise missiles out of Europe (the ''zero option''). In consultation with NATO allies, the United States began to search for a reasonable compromise with the Soviets on INF balances.

Similarly, on trade issues, the Reagan administration struck a note of stronger discord with the Soviets than some of our NATO allies were pre-

pared to accept. The president preferred to broaden restrictions on trade with the Soviet bloc, especially on items that might have national security implications such as heavy-axle trucks that could carry weapons. In contrast, West Germany warned the United States in 1983 against creating strains in NATO through conflict over East-West commercial transactions. West Germany did not want to jeopardize opportunities to improve its economy through trade with the Soviets or plans to construct an oil pipeline from Russia that promised to bring added fuel supplies.

Critics of the Reagan administration's approach to defense and trade policy in Europe contended that the tougher our stances were toward the Soviets, the further they drove us from our NATO allies. As president, what would be your position on INF deployment in Europe? What restrictions would you place on trade with the Soviets by American and West European business?

The Developing World

Three-quarters of the world's population lives in the developing regions of Latin America, Asia,

Africa, and the Middle East. Our foreign policy leaders must decide what part of America's resources should be used to improve our relationships with these countries. Economic realities alone suggest that it would be foolish to ignore them. More of our exports go to developing nations than to Japan and the European market combined. Our destiny is bound to the future of

U.S. attempts to control the commercial transactions of our allies create strain in these otherwise-friendly relationships. For example, the Reagan administration antagonized its NATO allies by imposing a ban on European resale of American-made equipment to the Soviets for its pipeline being built to carry natural gas from Siberia to Western Europe. The Reagan administration ultimately backed off on this issue.

these poor countries and, most critics agree, strengthening the world economy augments our own well-being. Moreover, American ideals would seem to favor efforts by the United States to address the evils of world hunger and poverty.

Still, the question remains of precisely what our role should be in the developing world. Should we adopt a policy of "benign neglect," as some recommend, or should we offer technical and financial assistance? How much? What about overt, or covert, intervention to curb Marxist rebellions?

Our recent levels of foreign assistance are "modest," according to Secretary of State George P. Schulz of the Reagan administration.

"The total cost in tax dollars for all our security and economic assistance programs in the developing countries," said Secretary Schulz in 1983, "is $43.91 per person." In contrast, he noted, "we Americans spend $104 per person a year for TV and radio sets, $35 per person per year for barbershops and beauty parlors, $97 per person per year for soap and cleaning supplies, and $21 per person per year for flowers and potted plants."[53] The richest nation in the world, the United States ranks twelfth of the 17 Western nations dispensing foreign aid as measured in terms of the percentage of GNP spent on aid programs.[54]

In 1982, debate over the wisdom of direct intervention in the developing world heated up as new revolutions and counter-revolutions took place in Central America. The Reagan administration reportedly came down on the side of covert intervention against Nicaraguan leftists (the Sandinistas), and covert as well as overt intervention (supplying weapons and training) against El Salvadoran leftists.[55] Failure to respond to Marxist challenges in Central America would be tantamount to a policy of appeasement, argued officials in the Reagan administration. Critics disagreed. "It's as though nobody has read about the Bay of Pigs," said one senator.[56]

Guerilla warfare in Central America is only one of several thorny issues in the developing world. The following problems would also be on your presidential agenda:

1. How far should the United States proceed toward the establishment of cordial relations toward China? In December, 1978, President Carter entered into formal diplomatic relations with the People's Republic. Since then, progress toward closer ties has been slow and uneven, and trade between the two nations actually began to decline in 1982. To what extent would you attempt to improve relations with China to gain a tactical advantage against the Soviet Union? Would you sell weapons to the People's Republic? If so, how would that affect American-Taiwanese relations?

2. The quality of American relations in Africa has varied over the years. During the Ford administration, Secretary of State Henry Kissinger was refused permission to visit Nigeria. A few years later, President Carter

was warmly received on an African tour, perhaps in part because he appointed a black to be United States Ambassador to the United Nations. This signaled a sympathy for the principle of majority rule in a continent ruled by white European minorities. How far would you go toward embracing that principle in Africa? Would you risk alienating the white leaders of South Africa, who practice *apartheid (a system of racial segregation)*, when that country holds rich mineral resources that might be important to us strategically?

3. For 30 years, the Middle East has been embroiled in a series of wars. In 1978, the Carter administration was able to achieve peace between Israel and Egypt for the first time in their modern history through the Camp David accords. This peace framework must now be used to achieve a broader peace, drawing in all the parties of this troubled region. How would you approach what has probably been the most difficult and enduring problem of modern diplomacy, resolving the twin issues of Palestinian rights and Israeli security?

None of these policy problems has an easy solution, and the partial agenda presented here is merely a sampling of a wide range of decisions foreign policymakers must face. Little wonder presidents seem to age so rapidly in office.

Though some of the problems you would face as president would be comparable to those faced by your predecessors, others would be novel. Institutional conflict between the Congress and the presidency would continue, for it is inherent in the system of shared powers devised by the nation's founders. A grave concern for Soviet intentions will continue, too, as long as the U.S.S.R. is capable of destroying our society. These enduring aspects of American foreign policy have become all the more complicated, however, for the world has become more complex, interdependent, and dangerous since the days of the early Cold War.

The birth of a hundred new nations in the postwar period has, in the words of historian Harvey A. DeWeerd, balkanized the globe into "small, poor, but overmilitarized states struggling for power." The result is a world that is "unmanageable."[57] Some of these nations appear determined to manufacture their own nuclear weapons, and that the possibility exists that within this century a half-dozen new nuclear powers—some harboring ancient feuds with regional neighbors—will come into existence. Weapons technology is also reaching the point at which miniaturization of nuclear weapons will soon be possible, which raises the prospect of delivering H-bombs in hat boxes.

In terms of the three major policies addressed in this book alone—changing lifestyles, energy shortages, and a fluctuating economy—our government is confronted with a difficult foreign policy agenda. The disparity in lifestyles between the poor and the wealthy nations has created resentment throughout the developing world. Economist Robert L. Heilbroner has compared the world to "an immense train, in which a few passengers, mainly in the advanced capitalist world, ride in first-class coaches, in conditions of comfort unimaginable to the enormously greater numbers jammed into the cattle cars that make up the bulk of the train's carriages."[58] The use of violence by desperately poor nations can be anticipated in the future until the wealthier countries more effectively help the economic development of these regions.

The United States continues to be plagued by energy dependence, too. We now import even more OPEC oil than we did in 1973, when the nation first realized the extent of its vulnerability to shut-offs in the flow of foreign oil. Six percent of the earth's population, we use over one-third of the annual energy production in the world—a profligate consumption in the eyes of other nations.

Economically, our system continues to respond sluggishly, alternating between high inflation and high unemployment. Only lately have we begun to realize the importance of competing more vigorously in the world marketplace against skillful traders like the Japanese. As with everything else in our society, we can no longer carry out commerce within the splendid isolation of our own borders, wide though they are.

These and other recent developments make our efforts to balance relations with the Soviet Union during the height of the Cold War seem like child's play. Our government will require all the knowledge, wisdom, patience, and citizen advice it can muster to meet these challenges. The old formulas have failed to make the world a peaceful place. The new formulas—an executive-legislative compact in foreign affairs, a global perspective that goes beyond the slogans of the Cold War, and a greater concern for the destiny of the poor nations—remain untested.

SUMMARY

For most of this century, there was an institutional consensus that American foreign policy was a presidential prerogative. Members of Congress, Republicans and Democrats alike, were expected to follow the president's lead in relations with other countries, freeing him from the constraints of extensive partisan wrangling. The leeway allowed presidents in foreign affairs was evident in their expansive exercise of five important powers, including power to make agreements abroad; to conduct warfare; to engage in covert action; to spend money; and to control information.

Since World War II, the making of American foreign policy has been guided by an ideology based on the containment doctrine, a commitment to resist Soviet expansionism wherever it appeared.

The war in Vietnam and the Watergate scandal, however, brought about a profound reappraisal of this institutional and ideological consensus. Institutionally, in place of a presidency omniscient and omnipotent in foreign affairs, we now have a Congress searching for a partnership role in policymaking and a public more skeptical of White House appeals and declarations. Ideologically, in place of a reflex willingness to intervene with Cold War fervor against Marxist regimes anywhere on the globe, there is a more reflective attitude on the part of Congress and the public about the costs of intervention.

KEY TERMS

apartheid
bipartisanship
blow back or replay
Boland Amendment
Case Amendment
Church Amendment
SALT
Clark Amendment
containment doctrine
Cooper-Church Amendment
covert action (CA)
détente
deterrence
diplomacy
doctrine of plausible denial
domino theory
Electronic Surveillance Act of 1978
executive-legislative compact
40 Committee
Gulf of Tonkin Resolution
gunboat diplomacy
Harkin Amendment
Hughes-Ryan Act
Intelligence Accountability Act
National Commitments Resolution
Nelson-Bingham Amendment
New York Times v. U.S.
nuclear freeze movement
Nuclear Non-proliferation Act
Operation SHAMROCK
paramilitary (PM) covert action
political covert action
statutory agreements
Third World
Treaty Powers Resolution
Truman Doctrine
zero-sum game

SUGGESTED READINGS

Bertsch, Gary K., and McIntyre, John, eds. *National Security and Technology Transfer: The Strategic Dimensions of East-West Trade*. Boulder, Co.: Westview Press, 1983.

Crabb, Cevil V., and Holt, Pat M. *Invitation to Struggle: Congress, the President, and Foreign Policy*. Washington, D.C.: Congressional Quarterly Press, 1980.

Gaddis, John Lewis. *Strategies of Containment: A Critical Appraisal of Postwar America's National Security Policy*. New York: Oxford University Press, 1982.

Gelb, Leslie H., and Betts, Richard K. *The Irony of Vietnam: The System Worked*. Washington, D.C.: Brookings Institution, 1979.

Johnson, Loch. *The Making of International Agreements: Congress Confronts the Presidency*. New York: New York University Press, 1984.

Lifton, Robert Jay, and Falk, Richard. *Indefensible Weapons*. New York: Basic Books, Inc., 1982.

Marchetti, Victor, and Marks, John D. *The CIA and the Cult of Intelligence*. New York: Alfred A. Knopf, 1974.

Waltz, Kenneth N. *Foreign Policy and Democratic Politics: The American and British Experience*. Boston: Little, Brown, 1967.

Wyden, Peter. *Bay of Pigs: The Untold Story*. New York: Simon & Schuster, 1979.

Yergen, Daniel, and Hillenbrand, Martin, eds. *Global Security: A Strategy for Energy and Economic Renewal*. Boston: Houghton Mifflin, 1982.

APPENDIX

THE DECLARATION OF INDEPENDENCE

When in the Course of human events, it becomes necessary for one people to dissolve the political bands which have connected them with another, and to assume among the Powers of the earth, the separate and equal station to which the Laws of Nature and of Nature's God entitle them, a decent respect to the opinions of mankind requires that they should declare the causes which impel them to the separation.

We hold these truths to be self-evident, that all men are created equal, that they are endowed by their Creator with certain unalienable Rights, that among these are Life, Liberty and the pursuit of Happiness. That to secure these rights, Governments are instituted among Men, deriving their just powers from the consent of the governed, That whenever any Form of Government becomes destructive of these ends, it is the Right of the People to alter or to abolish it, and to institute new Government, laying its foundation on such principles and organizing its powers in such form, as to them shall seem most likely to effect their Safety and Happiness. Prudence, indeed, will dictate that Governments long established should not be changed for light and transient causes; and accordingly all experience hath shown, that mankind are more disposed to suffer, while evils are sufferable, than to right themselves by abolishing the forms to which they are accustomed. But when a long train of abuses and usurpations, pursuing invariably the same Object evinces a design to reduce them under absolute Despotism, it is their right, it is their duty, to throw off such Government, and to provide new Guards for their future security.—Such has been the patient sufferance of these Colonies; and such is now the necessity which constrains them to alter their former Systems of Government. The history of the present Great Britain is a history of repeated injuries and usurpations, all having in direct object the establishment of an absolute Tyranny over these States. To prove this, let Facts be submitted to a candid world.

He has refused his Assent to Laws, the most wholesome and necessary for the public good.

He has forbidden his Governors to pass Laws of immediate and pressing importance, unless suspended in their operation till his Assent should be obtained; and when so suspended, he has utterly neglected to attend to them.

He has refused to pass other Laws for the accomodation of large districts of people, unless those people would relinquish the right of Representation in the Legislature, a right inestimable to them and formidable to tyrants only.

He has called together legislative bodies at places unusual, uncomfortable, and distant from the depository of their Public Records, for the sole purpose of fatiguing them into compliance with his measures.

He has dissolved Representative Houses repeatedly, for opposing with manly firmness his invasions on the rights of the people.

He has refused for a long time, after such dissolutions, to cause others to be elected; whereby the Legislative Powers, incapable of Annihilation, have returned to the People at large for their exercise; the State remaining in the mean time exposed to all the dangers of invasion from without, and convulsions within.

He has endeavoured to prevent the population of these States; for that purpose obstructing the Laws of Naturalization of Foreigners; refusing to pass others to encourage their migration hither, and raising the conditions of new Appropriations of Lands.

He has obstructed the Administration of Justice, by refusing his Assent to Laws for establishing Judiciary Powers.

He has made Judges dependent on his Will alone, for the tenure of their offices, and the amount and payment of their salaries.

He has erected a multitude of New Offices, and sent hither swarms of Officers to harass our People, and to eat out their substance.

He has kept among us, in times of peace, Standing Armies without the Consent of our legislature.

He has affected to render the Military independent of and superior to the Civil Power.

He has combined with others to subject us to a jurisdiction foreign to our constitution, and unacknowledged by our laws; giving his Assent to their acts of pretended legislation:

For quartering large bodies of armed troops among us:

For protecting them, by a mock Trial, from Punishment for any Murders which they should commit on the Inhabitants of these States:

For cutting off our Trade with all parts of the world:

For imposing taxes on us without our Consent:

For depriving us in many cases, of the benefits of Trial by Jury:

For transporting us beyond Seas to be tried for pretended offences:

For abolishing the free System of English Laws in a neighbouring Province, establishing therein an Arbitrary government, and enlarging its Boundaries so as to render it at once an example and fit instrument for introducing the same absolute rule into these Colonies:

For taking away our Charters, abolishing our most valuable Laws, and altering fundamentally the Forms of our Governments:

For suspending our own Legislature, and declaring themselves invested with Power to legislate for us in all cases whatsoever.

He has abdicated Government here, by declaring us out of his Protection and waging War against us.

He has plundered our seas, ravaged our Coasts, burnt our towns, and destroyed the lives of our people.

He is at this time transporting large armies of foreign mercenaries to compleat the works of death, desolation and tyranny, already begun with circumstances of Cruelty & perfidy scarcely paralled in the most barbarous ages, and totally unworthy the Head of a civilized nation.

He has constrained our fellow Citizens taken Captive on the high Seas to bear Arms against their Country, to become the executioners of their friends and Brethren, or to fall themselves by their Hands.

He has excited domestic insurrections amongst us, and has endeavoured to bring on the inhabitants of our frontiers, the merciless Indian Savages, whose known rule of warfare, is an undistinguished destruction of all ages, sexes and conditions.

In every stage of these Oppressions We have Petitioned for Redress in the most humble terms: Our repeated Petitions have been answered only by repeated injury. A Prince, whose character is thus marked by every act which may define a Tyrant, is unfit to be the ruler of a free People.

Nor have We been wanting in attention to our British brethren. We have warned them from time to time of attempts by their legislature to extend an unwarrantable jurisdiction over us. We have reminded them of the circumstances of our emigration and settlement here. We have appealed to their native justice and magnanimity, and we have conjured them by the ties of our common kindred to disavow these usurpations, which, would inevitably interrupt our connections and correspondence. They too have been deaf to the voice of justice and of consanguinity. We must, therefore, acquiesce in the necessity, which denounces our Separation, and hold them, as we hold the rest of mankind, Enemies in War, in Peace Friends.

We, therefore, the Representatives of the United States of America, in General Congress, Assembled, appealing to the Supreme Judge of the world for the rectitude of our intentions, do, in the Name, and by the Authority of the good People of these Colonies, solemnly publish and declare, That these United Colonies are, and of Right ought to be Free and Independent States; that they are Absolved from all Allegiance to the British Crown, and that all political connection between them and the State of Great Britain, is and ought to be totally dissolved; and that as Free and Independent States, they have full Power to levy War, conclude Peace, contract Alliances, establish Commerce, and to do all other Acts and Things which Independent States may of right do. And for the support of this Declaration, with a firm reliance on the Protection of Divine Providence, we mutually pledge to each other our Lives, our Fortunes and our sacred Honor.

THE CONSTITUTION OF THE UNITED STATES

We the people of the United States, in Order to form a more perfect Union, establish Justice, insure domestic Tranquility, provide for the common defense, promote the general Welfare, and secure the Blessings of Liberty to ourselves and our Posterity, do ordain and establish this CONSTITUTION for the United States of America.

ARTICLE I

Section 1. All legislative Powers herein granted shall be vested in a Congress of the United States which shall consist of a Senate and House of Representatives.

Section 2. The House of Representatives shall be composed of Members chosen every second Year by the People of the several States, and the Electors in each State shall have the Qualifications requisite for Electors of the most numerous Branch of the State Legislature.

No Person shall be a Representative who shall not have attained to the Age of twenty-five Years, and been seven Years a Citizen of the United States, and who shall not, when elected, be an inhabitant of that State in which he shall be chosen.

Representatives and direct Taxes shall be apportioned among the several States which may be included within this Union, according to their respective Numbers, which shall be determined by adding to the whole Number of free Persons, including those bound to Service for a Term of Years and excluding Indians not taxed, three fifths of all other Persons. The actual Enumeration shall be made within three Years after the first Meeting of the Congress of the United States, and within every subsequent Term of ten Years, in such Manner as they shall by Law direct. The Number of Representatives shall not exceed one for every thirty Thousand, but each State shall have at Least one Representative; and until such enumeration shall be made, the State of New Hampshire shall be entitled to chuse three, Massachusetts eight, Rhode-Island and Providence Plantations one, Connecticut five, New-York six, New Jersey four, Pennsylvania eight, Delaware one, Maryland six, Virginia ten, North Carolina five, South Carolina five, and Georgia three.

When vacancies happen in the Representation from any State, the Executive Authority thereof shall issue Writs of Election to fill such Vacancies.

The House of Representatives shall chuse their Speaker and other Officers; and shall have the sole Power of Impeachment.

Section 3. The Senate of the United States shall be composed of two Senators from each State, chosen by the Legislature thereof, for six Years; and each Senator shall have one Vote.

Immediately after they shall be assembled in Consequence of the first Election, they shall be divided as equally as may be into three Classes. The Seats of the Senators of the first Class shall be vacated at the Expiration of the second Year, of the second Class at the Expiration of the fourth Year, and of the third Class at the Expiration of the sixth Year, so that one-third may be chosen every second Year; and if Vacancies happen by Resignation, or otherwise, during the Recess of the Legislature of any State, the Executive thereof may make temporary Appointments until the next Meeting of the Legislature, which shall then fill such Vacancies.

No Person shall be a Senator who shall not have attained to the Age of thirty Years, and been nine Years a Citizen of the United States, and who shall not, when elected, be an Inhabitant of that State in which he shall be chosen.

The Vice President of the United States shall be President of the Senate, but shall have no vote, unless they be equally divided.

The Senate shall chuse their other Officers, and also a President pro tempore, in the absence of the Vice President, or when he shall exercise the Office of the President of the United States.

The Senate shall have the sole Power to try all Impeachments. When sitting for that purpose, they shall be on Oath or Affirmation. When the President of the United States is tried, the Chief Justice shall preside; And no person shall be convicted without the Concurrence of two thirds of the Members present.

Judgment in Cases of Impeachment shall not extend further than to removal from Office, and disqualification to hold and enjoy any Office of honor, Trust, or Profit under the United States: but the Party convicted shall nevertheless be liable and subject to Indictment, Trial, Judgment, and Punishment, according to Law.

Section 4. The Times, Places and Manner of holding Elections for Senators and Representatives, shall be prescribed in each state by the Legislature thereof; but the Congress may at any time by Law make or alter such Regulations, except as to the Places of Chusing Senators.

The Congress shall assemble at least once in every Year, and such Meeting shall be on the first Monday in December, unless they shall by Law appoint a different Day.

Section 5. Each House shall be the Judge of the Elections, Returns and Qualifications of its own Members, and a Majority of each shall constitute a Quorum to do Business; but a smaller number may adjourn from day to day, and may be authorized to compel the Attendance of absent Members, in such Manner, and under such Penalties, as each House may provide.

Each House may determine the Rule of its Proceedings, punish its Members for disorderly Behavior, and with the Concurrence of two thirds, expel a Member.

Each House shall keep a Journal of its Proceedings, and from time to time publish the same, excepting such Parts as may in their Judgment require Secrecy; and the Yeas and Nays of the Members of either House on any question shall, at the Desire of one fifth of those Present, be entered on the Journal.

Neither House, during the Session of Congress, shall, without the Consent of the other, adjourn for more than three days, nor to any other Place than that in which the two Houses shall be sitting.

Section 6. The Senators and Representatives shall receive a Compensation for their Services, to be ascertained by Law, and paid out of the Treasury of the United States. They shall in all Cases, except Treason, Felony, and Breach of the Peace, be privileged from Arrest during their Attendance at the Session of their respective Houses, and in going to and returning from the same; and for any Speech or Debate in either House, they shall not be questioned in any other Place.

No Senator or Representative shall, during the Time for which he was elected, be appointed to any civil Office under the Authority of the United

States, which shall been created, or the Emoluments whereof shall have been increased, during such time; and no Person holding any Office under the United States shall be a Member of either House during his continuance in Office.

Section 7. All Bills for raising Revenue shall originate in the House of Representatives; but the Senate may propose or concur with Amendments as on other bills.

Every Bill which shall have passed the House of Representatives and the Senate, shall, before it become a Law, be presented to the President of the United States; if he approve he shall sign it, but if not he shall return it, with his Objections, to that House in which it shall have originated, who shall enter the Objections at large on their Journal, and proceed to reconsider it. If after such Reconsideration two thirds of that House shall agree to pass the bill, it shall be sent, together with the objections, to the other House, by which it shall likewise be reconsidered, and if approved by two thirds of that House, it shall become a Law. But in all such Cases the Votes of both Houses shall be determined by Yeas and Nays, and the Names of the Persons voting for and against the Bill shall be entered on the Journal of each House respectively. If any Bill shall not be returned by the President within ten Days (Sunday excepted) after it shall have been presented to him, the Same shall be a Law, in like Manner as if he had signed it, unless the Congress by their Adjournment prevent its Return, in which Case it shall not be a Law.

Every Order, Resolution, or Vote to which the Concurrence of the Senate and House of Representatives may be necessary (except on a question of Adjournment) shall be presented to the President of the United States; and before the Same shall take Effect, shall be approved by him, or being disapproved by him, shall be repassed by two thirds of the Senate and House of Representatives, according to the Rules and Limitations prescribed in the Case of a Bill.

Section 8. The Congress shall have Power To lay and collect Taxes, Duties, Imposts and Excises, to pay the Debts and provide for the common Defence and general Welfare of the United States; but all Duties, Imposts and Excises shall be uniform throughout the United States;

To borrow money on the credit of the United States;

To regulate Commerce with foreign Nations, and among the several States, and with the Indian Tribes;

To establish an uniform Rule of Naturalization, and uniform Laws on the subject of Bankruptcies throughout the United States;

To coin Money, regulate the Value thereof, and of foreign Coin, and fix the Standard of Weights and Measures;

To provide for the Punishment of counterfeiting the Securities and current Coin of the United States;

To establish Post Offices and post Roads;

To promote the Progress of Science and useful Arts, by securing for limited Times to Authors and Inventors the exclusive Right to their respective Writings and Discoveries;

To constitute Tribunals inferior to the Supreme Court;

To define and punish Piracies and Felonies committed on the high Seas, and Offences against the Law of Nations;

To declare War, grant Letters of Marque and Reprisal, and make Rules concerning Captures on Land and Water.

To raise and support Armies, but no Appropriation of Money to that Use shall be for a longer Term than two Years;

To provide and maintain a Navy;

To make Rules for the Government and Regulation of the land and naval forces;

To provide for calling forth the Militia to execute the Laws of the Union, suppress Insurrections and repel Invasions;

To provide for organizing, arming, and disciplining the Militia, and for governing such Part of them as may be employed in the Service of the United States, reserving to the States respectively, the Appointment of the Officers, and the Authority of training the Militia according to the discipline prescribed by Congress;

To exercise exclusive Legislation in all Cases whatsoever, over such District (not exceeding ten Miles square) as may, be Cession of particular States, and the acceptance of Congress, become the Seat of Government of the United States, and to exercise like Authority over all Places purchased by the Consent of the Legislature of the States in which the Same shall be, for the Erection of Forts, Magazines, Arsenals, dock-Yards, and other needful Buildings;—And

To make all Laws which shall be necessary and proper for carrying into Execution the foregoing Powers, and all other Powers vested by this Constitution in the Government of the United States, or in any Department or Officer thereof.

Section 9. The Migration or Importation of such Persons as any of the States now existing shall think proper to admit, shall not be prohibited by the Congress prior to the Year one thousand eight hundred and eight, but a tax or duty may be imposed on such Importation, not exceeding ten dollars for each Person.

The privilege of the Writ of Habeas Corpus shall not be suspended, unless when in Cases of Rebellion or Invasion the public Safety may require it.

No Bill of Attainder or ex post facto Law shall be passed.

No capitation, or other direct, Tax shall be laid unless in Proportion to the Census or Enumeration herein before directed to be taken.

No Tax or Duty shall be laid on Articles exported from any State.

No Preference shall be given by any Regulation or Revenue to the Ports of one State over those of another: nor shall Vessels bound to, or from, one State, be obliged to enter, clear, or pay Duties in another.

No Money shall be drawn from the Treasury, but in Consequence of Appropriations made by Law; and a regular Statement and Account of the Receipts and Expenditures of all public Money shall be published from time to time.

No Title of Nobility shall be granted by the United States: And no Person holding any Office of Profit or Trust under them, shall, without the Consent of the Congress, accept of any present, Emolument, Office, or Title, of any kind whatever, from any King, Prince, or foreign State.

Section 10.   No State shall enter any Treaty, Alliance, or Confederation; grant Letters of Marque and Reprisal; coin Money; emit Bills of Credit; make any Thing but gold and silver Coin a Tender in Payment of Debts; pass any Bill of Attainder, ex post facto Law, or Law impairing the Obligation of Contracts, or grant any Title of Nobility.

No State shall, without the Consent of the Congress, lay any Imposts or Duties on Imports or Exports, except what may be absolutely necessary for executing its inspection Laws: and the net Produce of all Duties and Imposts, laid by any State on Imports or Exports, shall be for the Use of the Treasury of the United States; and all such Laws shall be subject to the Revision and Control of the Congress.

No State shall, without the Consent of Congress, lay any duty of Tonnage, keep Troops, or Ships of War in time of Peace, enter into any Agreement or Compact with another State, or with a foreign Power, or engage in War, unless actually invaded, or in such imminent Danger as will not admit of delay.

ARTICLE II

Section 1. The executive Power shall be vested in a President of the United States of America. He shall hold his Office during the Term of four years, and, together with the Vice-President, chosen for the same Term, be elected, as follows:

Each State shall appoint, in such Manner as the Legislature thereof may direct, a Number of Electors, equal to the whole Number of Senators and Representatives to which the State may be entitled in the Congress; but no Senator or Representative, or Person holding an Office of Trust or Profit under the United States, shall be appointed an Elector.

The Electors shall meet in their respective States, and vote by Ballot for two persons, of whom one at least shall not be an Inhabitant of the same State with themselves. And they shall make a List of all the Persons voted for, and of the Number of Votes for each; which List they shall sign and certify, and transmit sealed to the Seat of the Government of the United States, directed to the President of the Senate. The President of the Senate shall, in the Presence of the Senate and House of Representatives, open all the Certificates, and the Votes shall then be counted. The Person having the greatest Number of Votes shall be the President, if such Number be a Majority of the whole Number of Electors appointed; and if there be more than one who have such Majority, and have an equal Number of Votes, then the House of Representatives shall immediately chuse by Ballot one of them for President; and if no Person have a Majority, then from the five highest on the List the said House shall in like Manner chuse the President. But in chusing the President, the Votes shall be taken by States, the Representation from each State having one Vote; a quorum for this Purpose shall consist of a Member or Members from two-thirds of the States, and a Majority of all the States shall be necessary to a Choice. In every Case, after the Choice of the President, the Person having the greatest Number of Votes of the Electors shall be the Vice President. But if there should remain two or more who have equal votes, the Senate shall chuse from them by Ballot the Vice-President.

The Congress may determine the Time of chusing the Electors, and the Day on which they shall give their Votes; which Day shall be the same throughout the United States.

No person except a natual-born Citizen, or a Citizen of the United States, at the time of the Adoption of this Constitution, shall be eligible to the Office of President; neither shall any Person be eligible to that Office who shall not have attained to the Age of thirty-five years, and been fourteen Years a Resident within the United States.

In Case of the Removal of the President from Office, or of his Death, Resignation, or Inability to discharge the Powers and Duties of the said Office, the same shall devolve on the Vice President, and the Congress may by Law provide for the Case of Removal, Death, Resignation, or Inability, both of the President and Vice President, declaring what Officer shall then act as President, and such Officer shall act accordingly, until the disability be removed, or a President shall be elected.

The President shall, at stated Times, receive for his Services a Compensation, which shall neither be increased nor diminished during the Period for which he shall have been elected, and he shall not receive within that Period any other Emolument from the United States, or any of them.

Before he enter on the execution of his Office, he shall take the following Oath or Affirmation:— "I do solemnly swear (or affirm) that I will faithfully execute the Office of President of the United States, and will, to the best of my Ability, preserve, protect, and defend the Constitution of the United States."

Section 2. The President shall be Commander in Chief of the Army and Navy of the United States,

and of the Militia of the several States, when called into the actual Service of the United States; he may require the Opinion, in writing, of the principal Officer in each of the executive Departments, upon any subject relating to the Duties of their respective Offices, and he shall have Power to Grant Reprieves and Pardons for Offences against the United States, except in Cases of Impeachment.

He shall have Power, by and with the Advice and Consent of the Senate, to make Treaties, provided two thirds of the Senators present concur; and he shall nominate, and by and with the Advice and Consent of the Senate, shall appoint Ambassadors, other public Ministers and Consuls, Judges of the supreme Court, and all other Offices of the United States, whose Appointments are not herein otherwise provided for, and which shall be established by Law: but the Congress may by Law vest the Appointments of such inferior Officers, as they think proper, in the President alone, in the Courts of Law, or in the Heads of Departments.

The President shall have Power to fill up all Vacancies that may happen during the Recess of the Senate, by granting Commissions which shall expire at the End of their next Session.

Section 3. He shall from time to time give to the Congress Information of the State of the Union, and recommend to their Consideration such Measures as he shall judge necessary and expedient; he may, on extraordinary occasions, convene both Houses, or either of them, and in Case of Disagreement between them, with respect to the Time of Adjournment, he may adjourn them to such Time as he shall think proper; he shall receive Ambassadors and other public Ministers; he shall take Care that the Laws be faithfully executed, and shall Commission all the Officers of the United States.

Section 4. The President, Vice President and all civil Officers of the United States, shall be removed from Office on Impeachment for, and Conviction of, Treason, Bribery, or other high Crimes and Misdemeanors.

ARTICLE III

Section 1. The judicial Power of the United States, shall be vested in one Supreme Court, and in such inferior Courts as the Congress may from time to time ordain and establish. The Judges, both of the supreme and inferior Courts, shall hold their Offices during good Behaviour, and shall, at stated Times, receive for their Services, a Compensation, which shall not be diminished during their Continuance in Office.

Section 2. The judicial Power shall extend to all Cases, in Law and Equity, arising under this Constitution, the Laws of the United States, and treaties made, or which shall be made, under their Authority;—to all Cases affecting ambassadors, other public ministers and consuls;—to all cases of admiralty and maritime Jurisdiction;—to Controversies to which the United States shall be a Party;—to Controversies between two or more States;—between a State and Citizens of another State;—between Citizens of different States,—between Citizens of the same State claiming Lands under Grants of different States, and between a State, or the Citizens thereof, and foreign States, Citizens or Subjects.

In all Cases affecting Ambassadors, other public Ministers and Consuls, and those in which a State shall be Party, the supreme Court shall have original Jurisdiction. In all the other Cases before mentioned, the supreme Court shall have appellate Jurisdiction, both as to Law and Fact, with such Exceptions, and under such Regulations as the Congress shall make.

The trial of all Crimes, except in Cases of Impeachment, shall be by Jury; and such Trial shall be held in the State where the said Crimes shall have been committed; but when not committed within any State, the Trial shall be at such Place or Places as the Congress may by Law have directed.

Section 3. Treason against the United States, shall consist only in levying War against them, or in adhering to their Enemies, giving them Aid and Comfort. No Person shall be convicted of Treason unless on the Testimony of two Witnesses to the same overt Act, or on Confession in open Court.

The Congress shall have power to declare the Punishment of Treason, but no Attainder of Treason shall work Corruption of Blood, or Forfeiture except during the Life of the Person attainted.

ARTICLE IV

Section 1. Full Faith and Credit shall be given in each State to the public Acts, Records, and judicial Proceedings of every other State. And the Congress may be general Laws prescribe the Manner in which such Acts, Records and Proceedings shall be proved, and the Effect thereof.

Section 2. The Citizens of each State shall be entitled to all Privileges and Immunities of Citizens in the several States.

A Person charged in any State with Treason, Felony, or other Crime, who shall flee from Justice, and be found in another State, shall on demand of the executive Authority of the State from which he fled, be delivered up, to be removed to the State having Jurisdiction of the crime.

No Person held to Service or Labour in one State, under the Laws thereof, escaping into another, shall, in Consequence of any Law or Regulation therein, be discharged from such Service or Labour, but shall be delivered up on Claim of the Party to whom such Service or Labour may be due.

Section 3. New States may be admitted by the Congress into this Union; but no new State shall be formed or erected within the Jurisdiction of any other State; nor and State be formed by the Junction of two or more States, or parts of States, without the Consent of the Legislatures of the States concerned as well as of the Congress.

The Congress shall have Power to dispose of and make all needful Rules and Regulations respecting the Territory or other Property belonging to the United States; and nothing in this Constitution shall be construed as to Prejudice any Claims of the United States, or of any particular State.

Section 4. The United States shall guarantee to every State in this Union a Republican Form of Government, and shall protect each of them against Invasion; and on Application of the Legislature, or the Executive (when the Legislature cannot be convened) against domestic Violence.

ARTICLE V

The Congress, whenever two-thirds of both Houses shall deem it necessary, shall propose

Amendments to this Constitution, or, on the Application of the Legislatures of two-thirds of the several States, shall call a Convention for proposing Amendments, which, in either Case, shall be valid to all Intents and Purposes, as part of this Constitution, when ratified by the Legislatures of three-fourths of the several States, or by Conventions in three-fourths thereof, as the one or the other Mode of Ratification may be proposed by the Congress; Provided that no Amendment which may be made prior to the Year One thousand eight hundred and eight shall in any Manner affect the first and fourth Clauses in the Ninth Section of the first Article; and that no State, without its Consent, shall be deprived of its equal Suffrage in the Senate.

ARTICLE VI

All Debts contracted and Engagements entered into, before the Adoption of this Constitution, shall be as valid against the United States under this Constitution, as under the Confederation.

This Constitution, and the Laws of the United States which shall be made in Pursuance thereof; and all Treaties made, or which shall be made, under the Authority of the United States, shall be the supreme Law of the Land; and the Judges in every State shall be bound thereby, any Thing in the Constitution or Laws of any State to the Contrary notwithstanding.

The Senators and Representatives before mentioned, and the Members of the several State Legislatures, and all executive and judicial Officers, both of the United States and of the several States, shall be bound by Oath or Affirmation to support this Constitution; but no religious Test shall ever be required as a qualification to any Office or public Trust under the United States.

ARTICLE VII

The Ratification of the Conventions of nine States shall be sufficient for the Establishment of this Constitution between the States so ratifying the same.

Done in Convention by the Unanimous Consent of the States present the Seventeenth Day of September in the Year of our Lord one Thousand seven hundred and Eighty seven, and of the Independence of the United States of America the Twelfth. In Witness whereof We have hereunto subscribed our names.

Articles in Addition to, and Amendment of, the Constitution of the United States of America. Proposed by Congress, and Ratified by the Legislatures of the Several States, Pursuant to the Fifth Article of the Original Constitution.

AMENDMENT I [1791]

Congress shall make no law respecting an establishment of religion, or prohibiting the free exercise thereof; or abridging the freedom of speech, or of the press; or the right of the people peacably to assemble, and to petition the Government for a redress of grievances.

AMENDMENT II [1791]

A well regulated Militia, being necessary to the security of a free State, the right of the people to keep and bear Arms shall not be infringed.

AMENDMENT III [1791]

No Soldier shall, in time of peace, be quartered in any house, without the consent of the Owner, nor in time of war, but in a manner to be prescribed by law.

AMENDMENT IV [1791]

The right of the people to secure in their persons, houses, papers, and effects, against unreasonable searches and seizures, shall not be violated, and no Warrant shall issue, but upon probable cause, supported by Oath or affirmation, and particularly describing the place to be searched, and the persons or things to be seized.

AMENDMENT V [1791]

No person shall be held to answer for a capital or otherwise infamous crime, unless on a presentment or indictment of a Grand Jury, except in cases arising in the land or naval forces, or in the Militia, when in actual service in time of War or public danger; nor shall any person be subject for the same offence to be twice put in jeopardy of life or limb; nor shall be compelled in any criminal case to be a witness against himself, nor be deprived of life, liberty, or property, without due process of law; nor shall private property be taken for public use, without just compensation.

AMENDMENT VI [1791]

In all criminal prosecutions, the accused shall enjoy the right to a speedy and public trial, by an impartial jury of the State and district wherein the crime shall have been committed, which district shall have been previously ascertained by law, and to be informed of the nature and cause of the accusation; to be confronted with the witnesses against him; to have compulsory process for obtaining witnesses in his favor, and to have the Assistance of Counsel for his defence.

AMENDMENT VII [1791]

In suits at common law, where the value in controversy shall exceed twenty dollars, the right of trial by jury shall be preserved, and no fact tried by a jury, shall be otherwise reexamined in any Court of the United States, than according to the rules of the common law.

AMENDMENT VIII [1791]

Excessive bail shall not be required, nor excessive fines imposed, nor cruel and unusual punishments inflicted.

AMENDMENT IX [1791]

The enumeration in the Constitution, of certain rights, shall not be construed to deny or disparage others retained by the people.

AMENDMENT X [1791]

The powers not delegated to the United States by the Constitution, nor prohibited by it to the States, are reserved to the States respectively, or to the people.

AMENDMENT XI [1798]

The Judicial power of the United States shall not be construed to extend to any suit in law or equity, commenced or prosecuted against one of the United States by Citizens of another State, or by Citizens or Subjects of any Foreign State.

AMENDMENT XII [1804]

The Electors shall meet in their respective States and vote by ballot for President and Vice-President, one of whom, at least, shall not be an inhabitant of the same State with themselves; they shall name in their ballots the person voted for as President, and in distinct ballots the person voted for as Vice-President, and they shall make distinct lists of all persons voted for as President, and of all persons voted for as Vice-President, and of the number of votes for each, which lists they shall sign and certify, and transmit sealed to the seat of the government of the United States, directed to the President of the Senate;—The President of the Senate shall, in the presence of the Senate and House of Representatives, open all the certificates and the votes shall then be counted;—The person having the greatest number of votes for President, shall be the President, if such number be a majority of the whole number of Electors appointed; and if no person have such majority, then from the persons having the highest numbers not exceeding three on the list of those voted for as President, the House of Representatives shall choose immediately, by ballot, the President. But in choosing the President, the votes shall be taken by states, the representation from each state having one vote; a quorum for this purpose shall consist of a member or members from two-thirds of the states, and a majority of all the states shall be necessary to a choice. And if the House of Representatives shall not choose a President whenever the right of choice shall devolve upon them, before the fourth day of March next following, then the Vice-President shall act as President, as in the case of the death or other constitutional disability of the President.—The person having the greatest number of votes as Vice-President, shall be the Vice President, if such number be a majority of the whole number of Electors appointed, and if no person have a majority, then from the two highest numbers on the list, the Senate shall choose the Vice-President; a quorum for the purpose shall consist of two-thirds of the whole number of Senators, and a majority of the whole number shall be necessary to a choice. But no person constitutionally ineligible to the office of President shall be eligible to that of Vice-President of the United States.

AMENDMENT XIII [1865]

Section 1. Neither slavery nor involuntary servitude, except as a punishment for crime whereof the party shall have been duly convicted, shall exist within the United States, or any place subject to their jurisdiction.

Section 2. Congress shall have power to enforce this article by appropriate legislation.

AMENDMENT XIV [1868]

Section 1. All persons born or naturalized in the United States, and subject to the jurisdiction thereof, are citizens of the United States and of the State wherein they reside. No State shall make or enforce any law which shall abridge the privileges or immunities of citizens of the United States; nor shall any State deprive any person of life, liberty, or property, without due process of law; nor deny to any person within its jurisdiction the equal protection of the laws.

Section 2. Representatives shall be apportioned among the several States according to their respective numbers, counting the whole number of persons in each State, excluding Indians not taxed. But when the right to vote at any election for the choice of electors for President and Vice-President of the United States, Representatives in Congress, the Executive and Judicial officers of a State, or the members of the Legislature thereof, is denied to any of the male inhabitants of such State, being twenty-one years of age, and citizens of the United States, or in any way abridged, except for participation in rebellion, or other crime, the basis of representation therein shall be reduced in the proportion which the number of such male citizens shall bear to the whole number of male citizens twenty-one years of age in such State.

Section 3. No person shall be a Senator or Representative in Congress, or elector of President and Vice-President, or hold any office, civil or military, under the United States, or under any State, who, having previously taken an oath, as a member of Congress, or as an officer of the United States, or as a member of any State legislature, or as an executive or judicial officer of any State, to support the Constitution of the United States, shall have engaged in insurrection or rebellion against the same, or given aid or comfort to the enemies thereof. But Congress may by a vote of two-thirds of each House, remove such disability.

Section 4. The validity of the public debt of the United States, authorized by law, including debts incurred for payment of pensions and bounties for services in suppressing insurrection or rebellion, shall not be questioned. But neither the United States nor any State shall assume or pay any debt or obligation incurred in aid of insurrection or rebellion against the United States or any claim for the loss or emancipation of any slave; but all such debts, obligations, and claims shall be held illegal and void.

Section 5. The Congress shall have the power to enforce, by appropriate legislation, the provisions of this article.

AMENDMENT XV [1870]

Section 1. The right of citizens of the United States to vote shall not be denied or abridged by the United States or by any State on account of race, color, or previous condition of servitude—

Section 2. The Congress shall have power to enforce this article by appropriate legislation.

AMENDMENT XVI [1913]

The Congress shall have power to lay and collect taxes on incomes, from whatever source derived, without apportionment among the several States, and without regard to any census or enumeration.

AMENDMENT XVII [1913]

The Senate of the United States shall be composed of two Senators from each State, elected by the people thereof, for six years; and each Senator shall have one vote. The electors in each State shall have the qualifications requisite for electors of the most numerous branch of the State legislatures.

When vacancies happen in the representation of any State in the Senate, the executive authority of such State shall issue writs of election to fill such vacancies: *Provided*, That the legislature of any State may empower the executive thereof to make temporary appointments until the people fill the vacancies by election as the legislature may direct.

This amendment shall not be so construed as to affect the election or term of any Senator chosen before it becomes valid as part of the Constitution.

AMENDMENT XVIII [1919]

Section 1. After one year from the ratification of this article the manufacture, sale, or transportation of intoxicating liquors within, the importation thereof into, or the exportation thereof from the United States and all territory subject to the jurisdiction thereof for beverage purposes is hereby prohibited.

Section 2. The Congress and the several States shall have concurrent power to enforce this article by appropriate legislation.

Section 3. This article shall be inoperative unless it shall have been ratified as an amendment to the Constitution by the legislatures of the several States, as provided in the Constitution, within seven years from the date of the submission hereof to the States by the Congress.

AMENDMENT XIX [1920]

The right of citizens of the United States to vote shall not be denied or abridged by the United States or by any State on account of sex.

Congress shall have power to enforce this article by appropriate legislation.

AMENDMENT XX [1933]

Section 1. The terms of the President and Vice-President shall end at noon on the 20th day of January, and the terms of Senators and Representatives at noon on the 3d day of January, of the years in which such terms would have ended if this article had not been ratified; and the terms of their successors shall then begin.

Section 2. The Congress shall assemble at least once in every year, and such meeting shall begin at noon on the 3d day of January, unless they shall by law appoint a different day.

Section 3. If, at the time fixed for the beginning of the term of the President, the President elect shall have died, the Vice-President elect shall become President. If a President shall not have been chosen before the time fixed for the beginning of his term, or if the President elect shall have failed to qualify, then the Vice-President elect shall act as President until a President shall have qualified; and the Congress may by law provide for the case wherein neither a President elect nor a Vice-President elect shall have qualified, declaring who shall then act as President, or the manner in which one who is to act shall be selected, and such person shall act accordingly until a President or Vice-President shall have qualified.

Section 4. The Congress may by law provide for the case of the death of any of the persons from whom the House of Representatives may choose a President whenever the right of choice shall have devolved upon them, and for the case of the death of any of the persons from whom the Senate may choose a Vice-President whenever the right of choice shall have devolved upon them.

Section 5. Sections 1 and 2 shall take effect on the 15th day of October following the ratification of this article.

Section 6. This article shall be inoperative unless it shall have been ratified as an amendment to the Constitution by the legislatures of three-fourths of the several States within seven years from the date of its submission.

AMENDMENT XXI [1933]

Section 1. The eighteenth article of amendment to the Constitution of the United States is hereby repealed.

Section 2. The transportation or importation into any State, Territory, or possession of the United States for delivery or use therein of intoxicating liquors, in violation of the laws thereof, is hereby prohibited.

Section 3. This article shall be inoperative unless it shall have been ratified as an amendment to the Constitution by conventions in the several States, as provided in the Constitution, within seven years from the date of the Submission hereof to the States by the Congress.

AMENDMENT XXII [1951]

No person shall be elected to the office the President more than twice, and no person who has held the office of President, or acted as President, for more than two years of a term to which some other person was elected President shall be elected to the office of the President more than once.

But this Article shall not apply to any person holding the office of President when this Article was proposed by the Congress, and shall not prevent any person who may be holding the office of President, or acting as President, during the term within which this Article becomes operative from holding the office of President or acting as President during the remainder of such term.

AMENDMENT XXIII [1961]

Section 1. The District constituting the seat of Government of the United States shall appoint in such manner as the Congress may direct:

A number of electors of President and Vice President equal to the whole number of Senators and Representatives in Congress to which the District would be entitled if it were a State, but in no event more than the least populous State; they shall be in addition to those appointed by the States, but they shall be considered, for the purposes of the election of President and Vice President, to be electors appointed by a State; and they shall meet in the District and perform such duties as provided by the twelfth article of amendment.

Section 2. The Congress shall have power to enforce this article by appropriate legislation.

AMENDMENT XXIV [1964]

Section 1. The right of citizens of the United States to vote in any primary or other election for President or Vice President, for electors for President or Vice-President, or for Senator or Representative in Congress, shall not be denied or abridged by the United States or any State by reason of failure to pay any poll tax or other tax.

Section 2. The Congress shall have the power to enforce this article by appropriate legislation.

AMENDMENT XXV [1967]

Section 1. In case of the removal of the President from office or his death or resignation, the Vice President shall become President.

Section 2. Whenever there is a vacancy in the office of the Vice President, the President shall nominate a Vice President who shall take the office upon confirmation by a majority vote of both houses of Congress.

Section 3. Whenever the President transmits to the President pro tempore of the Senate and the Speaker of the House of Representatives his written declaration that he is unable to discharge the powers and duties of his office, and until he transmits to them a written declaration to the contrary, such powers and duties shall be discharged by the Vice President as Acting President.

Section 4. Whenever the Vice President and a majority of either the principal officers of the executive departments, or of such other body as Congress may by law provide, transmit to the President pro tempore of the Senate and the Speaker of the House of Representatives their written declaration that the President is unable to discharge the powers and duties of his office, the Vice President shall immediately assume the powers and duties of the office as Acting President.

Thereafter, when the President transmits to the President pro tempore of the Senate and the Speaker of the House of Representatives his written declaration that no inability exists, he shall resume the powers and duties of his office unless the Vice President and a majority of either the principal officers of the executive departments, or of such other body as Congress may by law provide, transmit within four days to the President pro tempore of the Senate and the Speaker of the

House of Representatives their written declaration that the President is unable to discharge the powers and duties of his office. Thereupon Congress shall decide the issue, assembling within 48 hours for that purpose if not in session. If the Congress, within 21 days after receipt of the latter written declaration, or, if Congress is not in session, within 21 days after Congress is required to assemble, determines by two-thirds vote of both houses that the President is unable to discharge the powers and duties of his office, the Vice President shall continue to discharge the same as Act-

ing Presidnt; otherwise, the President shall resume the powers and duties of his office.

AMENDMENT XXVI [1971]

Section 1. The right of citizens of the United States who are eighteen years of age or older, to vote shall not be denied or abridged by the United States or by any State on account of age.

Section 2. The Congress shall have power to enforce this article by appropriate legislation.

The Seneca Falls Declaration of Sentiments and Resolutions

July 19, 1848
(*The History of Woman Suffrage*, ed. by E. C. Stanton, S. B. Anthony and M. J. Gage, Vol. I, p. 70 ff.)

Though Frances Wright, Ernestine Rose, and others had championed the cause of woman's rights early in the century, the immediate origin of the woman's rights movement of the mid-century was in the anti-slavery crusade. When at the World Anti-Slavery Convention in London, in 1840, a group of American women delegates found themselves excluded, they determined that the cause of emancipation affected them as well as slaves. The Seneca Falls Convention was the first of its kind ever held. On the early woman's rights movement, see *The History of Woman Suffrage*, Vol. I; E. A. Hecker, *Short History of Women's Rights;* B. A. Rembaugh, *The Political Status of Women in the United States;* T. Stanton and H. S. Baltch, *Elizabeth Cady Stanton;* A. D. Hallowell, *Life and Letters of James and Lucretia Mott;* K. Anthony, *Margaret Fuller.* Some interesting comments on the philosophical implications of the movement are in T. V. Smith, *The American Philosophy of Equality.*

1. DECLARATION OF SENTIMENTS

When, in the course of human events, it becomes necessary for one portion of the family of man to assume among the people of the earth a position different from that which they have hitherto occupied, but one to which the laws of nature and of nature's God entitle them, a decent respect to the opinions of mankind requires that they should declare the causes that impel them to such a course.

We hold these truths to be self-evident: that all men and women are created equal; that they are endowed by their Creator with certain inalienable rights; that among these are life, liberty, and the pursuit of happiness; that to secure these rights governments are instituted, deriving their just powers from the consent of the governed. Whenever any form of government becomes destructive of these ends, it is the right of those who suffer from it to refuse allegiance to it, and to insist upon the institution of a new government, laying its foundation on such principles, and organizing its powers in such form, as to them shall seem most likely to effect their safety and happiness. Prudence, indeed, will dictate that governments long established should not be changed for light and transient causes; and accordingly all experience hath shown that mankind are more disposed to suffer while evils are sufferable, than to right themselves by abolishing the forms to which they are accustomed. But when a long train of abuses and usurpations, pursuing invariably the same object, evinces a design to reduce them under absolute despotism, it is their duty to throw off such government, and to provide new guards for their future security. Such has been the patient sufferance of the women under this government, and such is now the necessity which constrains them to demand the equal station to which they are entitled.

The history of mankind is a history of repeated injuries and usurpations, on the part of man toward woman, having in direct object the establishment of an absolute tyranny over her. To prove this, let facts be submitted to a candid world.

He has never permitted her to exercise her inalienable right to the elective franchise.

He has compelled her to submit to laws, in the formation of which she had no voice.

He has withheld from her rights which are given to the most ignorant and degraded men—both natives and foreigners.

Having deprived her of this first right of a citizen, the elective franchise, thereby leaving her without representation in the halls of legislation, he has oppressed her on all sides.

He has made her, if married, in the eye of the law, civilly dead.

He has taken from her all right in property, even to the wages she earns.

He has made her, morally, an irresponsible being, as she can commit many crimes with impunity, provided they be done in the presence of her husband. In the covenant of marriage, she is compelled to promise obedience to her husband, he becoming, to all intents and purposes, her master—the law giving him power to deprive her of her liberty, and to administer chastisement.

He has so framed the laws of divorce, as to what shall be the proper causes, and in case of separation, to whom the guardianship of the children shall be given, as to be wholly regardless of the happiness of women—the law, in all cases, going upon a false supposition of the supremacy of man, and giving all power into his hands.

After depriving her of all rights as a married woman, if single, and the owner of property, he has taxed her to support a government which recognizes her only when her property can be made profitable to it.

He has monopolized nearly all the profitable employments, and from those she is permitted to follow, she receives but a scanty remuneration. He closes against her all the avenues to wealth and distinction which he considers most honorable to himself. As a teacher of theology, medicine, or law, she is not known.

He has denied her the facilities for obtaining a thorough education, all colleges being closed against her.

He allows her in Church, as well as State, but a subordinate position, claiming Apostolic authority for her exclusion from the ministry, and, with some exceptions, from any public participation in the affairs of the Church.

He has created a false public sentiment by giving to a world a different code of morals for men and women, by which moral delinquencies which exclude women from society, are not only tolerated, but deemed of little account in man.

He has usurped the prerogative of Jehovah himself, claiming it as his right to assign for her a sphere of action, when that belongs to her conscience and to her God.

He has endeavored, in every way that he could, to destroy her confidence in her own powers, to lessen her self-respect and to make her willing to lead a dependent and abject life.

Now, in view of this entire disfranchisement of one-half the people of this country, their social and religious degradation—in view of the unjust laws above mentioned, and because women do feel themselves aggrieved, oppressed, and fraudulently deprived of their most sacred rights, we insist that they have immediate admission to all the rights and privileges which belong to them as citizens of the United States.

In entering upon the great work before us, we anticipate no small amount of misconception, misrepresentation, and ridicule: but we shall use every instrumentality within our power to effect our object. We shall employ agents, circulate tracts, petition the State and National legislatures, and endeavor to enlist the pulpit and the press in our behalf. We hope this Convention will be followed by a series of Conventions embracing every part of the country.

2. RESOLUTIONS

WHEREAS. The great precept of nature is conceded to be, that "man shall pursue his own true and substantial happiness." Blackstone in his Commentaries remarks, that this law of Nature being coeval with mankind, and dictated by God himself, is of course superior in obligation to any other. It is binding over all the globe, in all countries and at all times; no human laws are of any validity if contrary to this, and such of them as are valid, derive all their force, and all their validity, and all their authority, mediately and immediately, from this original; therefore,

Resolved, That all laws which prevent woman from occupying such a station in society as her conscience shall dictate, or which place her in a position inferior to that of man, are contrary to the great precept of nature, and therefore of no force or authority.

Resolved, That woman is man's equal—was intended to be so by the Creator, and the highest good of the race demands that she should be recognized as such.

Resolved, That the women of this country ought to be enlightened in regard to the laws under which they live, that they may no longer publish their degradation by declaring themselves satisfied with their present position, nor their ignorance, by asserting that they have all the rights they want.

Resolved, That inasmuch as man, while claiming for himself intellectual superiority, does accord to woman moral superiority, it is pre-eminently his duty to encourage her to speak and teach, as she has an opportunity, in all religious assemblies.

Resolved, That the same amount of virtue, delicacy, and refinement of behavior that is required of woman in the social state, should also be required of man, and the same transgressions should be visited with equal severity on both man and woman.

Resolved, That the objection of indelicacy and impropriety, which is so often brought against woman when she addresses a public audience, comes with a very ill-grace from those who encourage, by their attendance, her appearance on the stage, in the concert, or in feats of the circus.

Resolved, That woman has too long rested satisfied in the circumscribed limits which corrupt customs and a perverted application of the Scriptures have marked out for her, and that it is time she should move in the enlarged sphere which her great Creator has assigned her.

Resolved, That it is the duty of the women of this country to secure to themselves their sacred right to the elective franchise.

Resolved, That the equality of human rights results necessarily from the fact of the identity of the race in capabilities and responsibilities.

Resolved, That the speedy success of our cause depends upon the zealous and untiring efforts of both men and women, for the overthrow of the monopoly of the pulpit, and for the securing to women an equal participation with men in the various trades, professions, and commerce.

Resolved, therefore, That, being invested by the creator with the same capabilities, and the same consciousness of responsibility for their exercise, it is demonstrably the right and duty of woman, equally with man, to promote every righteous cause by every righteous means; and especially in regard to the great subjects of morals and religion, it is self-evidently her right to participate with her brother in teaching them, both in private and in public, by writing and by speaking, by any instrumentalities proper to be used, and in any assemblies proper to be held; and this being a self-evident truth growing out of the divinely implanted principles of human nature, any custom or authority adverse to it, whether modern or wearing the hoary sanction of antiquity, is to be regarded as a self-evident falsehood, and at war with mankind.

The Presidents of the United States of America

	Term of Office	Political Party	State of Residence	Inauguration Age	Sessions of Congress	VP	Cabinet	Prior Service Congress	Prior Service Gov.	Prior Service General
George Washington	1789–1797	Fed.	Va.	57	1– 4					X
John Adams	1797–1801	Fed.	Mass.	61	5– 6	X				
Thomas Jefferson	1801–1809	Dem.–Rep.	Va.	57	7–10	X	X		X	
James Madison	1809–1817	Dem.–Rep.	Va.	57	11–14		X	X		
James Monroe	1817–1825	Dem.–Rep.	Va.	58	15–18		X	X	X	
John Q. Adams	1825–1829	Dem.–Rep.	Mass.	57	19–20		X	X		
Andrew Jackson	1829–1837	Dem.	Tenn.	61	21–24			X	Xa	X
Martin Van Buren	1837–1841	Dem.	N.Y.	54	25–26	X	X	X	X	
William Harrison	1841	Whig	Ind.	68	27		X	X	Xa	
John Tyler	1841–1845	Dem.*	Va.	51	27–28	X		X	X	
James K. Polk	1845–1849	Dem.	Tenn.	49	29–30			X	X	
Zachary Taylor	1849–1850	Whig	La.	64	31					X
Millard Fillmore	1850–1853	Whig	N.Y.	48	31–32	X		X		
Franklin Pierce	1853–1857	Dem.	N.H.	50	33–34			X		X
James Buchanan	1857–1861	Dem.	Pa.	65	35–36		X	X		
Abraham Lincoln	1861–1865	Rep.	Ill.	52	37–38			X		
Andrew Johnson	1865–1869	Union†	Tenn.	56	39–40	X		X	X	
Ulysses Grant	1869–1877	Rep.	Ohio	46	41–44		X			X
Rutherford Hayes	1877–1881	Rep.	Ohio	54	45–46			X	X	X
James A. Garfield	1881	Rep.	Ohio	49	47			X		X
Chester Arthur	1881–1885	Rep.	N.Y.	50	47–48	X				X
Grover Cleveland	1885–1889	Dem.	N.Y.	47	49–50				X	
Benjamin Harrison	1889–1893	Rep.	Ind.	55	51–52			X		X
Grover Cleveland	1893–1897	Dem.	N.Y.	55	53–54				X	
William McKinley	1897–1901	Rep.	Ohio	54	55–56			X	X	
Theodore Roosevelt	1901–1909	Rep.	N.Y.	42	57–60	X			X	
William Taft	1909–1913	Rep.	Ohio	51	61–62		X		Xa	
Woodrow Wilson	1913–1921	Dem.	N.J.	56	63–66				X	
Warren Harding	1921–1923	Rep.	Ohio	55	67			X		
Calvin Coolidge	1923–1929	Rep.	Mass.	51	68–70	X			X	
Herbert Hoover	1929–1933	Rep.	Calif.	54	71–72		X			
Franklin Roosevelt	1933–1945	Dem.	N.Y.	51	73–78				X	
Harry Truman	1945–1953	Dem.	Mo.	60	79–82	X		X		
Dwight Eisenhower	1953–1961	Rep.	N.Y.	62	83–86					X
John Kennedy	1961–1963	Dem.	Mass.	43	87–88			X		
Lyndon Johnson	1963–1969	Dem.	Texas	55	88–90	X		X		
Richard Nixon	1969–1974	Rep.	Calif.	56	91–93	X		X		
Gerald Ford, Jr.	1974–1977	Rep.	Mich.	61	93–94	X		X		
James E. Carter	1977–1981	Dem.	Ga.	52	95–96				X	
Ronald Reagan	1981–	Rep.	Calif.	69	97–				X	

*Elected on Whig ticket, affiliated with congressional Democrats.
†Elected on Unionist and Republican slates
aDenotes territorial governorship.
SOURCE: From Thomas E. Cronin, *The State of the Presidency*, 2nd ed., p. 382. Copyright © 1980 by Thomas E. Cronin. Reprinted by permission of Little, Brown and Company.

THE EMANCIPATION PROCLAMATION

January 1, 1863

Whereas, on the twentysecond day of September, in the year of our LORD one thousand eight hundred and sixty two, a proclamation was issued by the President of the United States, containing, among other things, the following towit:

"That on the first day of January, in the year of our Lord one thousand eight hundred and sixty-three, all persons held as slaves within any State or designated part of a State, the people whereof shall then be in rebellion against the United States, shall be then, thenceforward, and forever free; and the Executive Government of the United States, including the military and naval authority thereof, will recognize and maintain the freedom of such persons, and will do no act or acts to repress such persons, or any of them, in any efforts they may make for their actual freedom.

"That the Executive will, on the first day of January aforesaid, by proclamation, designate the States and parts of States, if any, in which the people thereof, shall on that day be, in good faith, represented in the Congress of the United States by members chosen thereto at elections wherein a majority of the qualified voters of such State shall have participated, shall in the absence of strong countervailing testimony, be deemed conclusive evidence that such State, and the people thereof, are not then in rebellion against the United States."

Now, therefore, I, Abraham Lincoln, President of the United States, by virtue of the power in me invested as Commander-in-Chief, of the Army and Navy of the United States in time of actual armed rebellion against authority and government of the United States, and as a fit and necessary war measure for suppressing said rebellion, do, on this first day of January, in the year of our Lord one thousand eight hundred and sixty three, and in accordance with my purpose so to do publicly proclaimed for the full period of one hundred days, from the day first above mentioned, order and designate as the States and parts of States wherein the people thereof respectively, are this day in rebellion against the United States, the following, towit:

Arkansas, Texas, Louisiana, (except the Parishes of St. Bernard, Plaquemines, Jefferson, St. Johns, St. Charles, St. James Ascension, Assumption, Terrebonne, Lafourche, St. Mary, St. Martin, and Orleans, including the City of New-Orleans) Mississippi, Alabama, Florida, Georgia, South-Carolina, North-Carolina, and Virginia, (except the fortyeight counties designated as West Virginia, and also the counties of Berkley, Accomac, Northampton, Elizabeth-City, York, Princess Ann, and Norfolk, including the cities of Norfolk and Portsmouth; and which excepted parts are, for the present, left precisely as if this proclamation were not issued.

And by virtue of the power, and for the purpose aforesaid, I do order and declare that all persons held as slaves within said designated States, and parts of States, are, and henceforward shall be free; and that the Executive government of the United States, including the military and naval authorities thereof, will recognize and maintain the freedom of said persons.

And I hereby enjoin upon the people so declared to be free to abstain from all violence, unless in necessary self-defence; and I recommend to them that, in all cases when allowed, they labor faithfully for reasonable wages.

And I further declare and make known that such persons of suitable condition, will be received into the armed service of the United States to garrison forts, positions, stations, and other places, and to man vessels of all sorts in said service.

And upon this act, sincerely believed to be an act of justice, warranted by the Constitution, upon military necessity, I invoke the considerate judgment of mankind, and the gracious favor of Almighty God.

In witness whereof, I have hereunto set my hand, and caused the seal of the United States to be affixed.

Done at the City of Washington, this first day of January, in the year of our Lord one thousand eight hundred and sixty three, and of the Independence of the United States of America the eighty-seventh.

By the President: ABRAHAM LINCOLN
WILLIAM H. SEWARD, Secretary of State.

GLOSSARY

ABSCAM (*Arab Scam*) a nationwide undercover effort by the FBI to identify corrupt public officials.

absolutist approach the view that interprets the First Amendment's guarantee of freedom of expression literally and would therefore allow no abridgements.

affirmative action actions taken to increase employment opportunities for minority groups that were disadvantaged in the past because of discrimination and poor educational opportunities.

allocation policy decisions that provide benefits such as federal funds to a set of interested participants.

amateur activist activists drawn into party work, not by material incentives, but by their concern about public policy and their sense of civic duty.

American System a plan designed to stimulate a sagging American economy by imposing a protective tariff, maintaining a national bank, and providing transportation between cities and farms at federal expense. Identified with Henry Clay and the Whig party.

American Voter model an interpretation of American voting behavior developed by a group of scholars at the University of Michigan; the model relies on the normal vote analysis and minimizes the role of issues.

amicus curiae litigation strategy major litigation strategy in which an interest group is not a sponsor of the litigation but merely a "friend of the court," an interested party which wishes to present its viewpoints about a case.

Annapolis Convention the second meeting of delegates to address problems arising in the states because of deficiencies in the Articles of Confederation. This meeting called for the Philadelphia Convention which wrote the Constitution of 1789.

Anti-Federalists those who opposed the ratification of the Constitution of 1789.

apartheid a system of racial segregation practiced in white-ruled South Africa.

appellate jurisdiction authority to hear cases appealed from a lower court and to reverse lower court decisions.

apportionment allocation of funds for each agency by the Office of Management and Budget by specific time periods or projects, usually on a quarterly basis.

attitudes long-term, fairly stable products of political socialization; they directly influence public opinion and political participation.

Australian ballot a secret ballot prepared, distributed, and tabulated by government officials at public expense.

background information given to a reporter by a public official or private individual that can be attributed to a general source (e.g., "an administration official") but not to the specific individual supplying the information.

balance of payments the net balance between the country's income and expenditures resulting from its business and trade relations with foreign countries.

balancing test the attempt by the Supreme Court to consider competing interests when reaching a decision.

beat system   the system of assigning reporters to regularly and exclusively cover the institutions, issues, or individuals most likely to be the sources of news of interest to the public.

bicameralism   the principle of a two-house legislature as contrasted with the unicameralism of the Articles of Confederation Congress.

bilingual education   programs for educating children whose native tongue is not English.

Bill of Rights   the first ten amendments to the Constitution.

bipartisanship   an approach to foreign policy based on the notion that the United States must present a united front in its relations with other nations, supported by Democrats and Republicans alike without extensive debate.

blanketing   the presidential practice of bringing new groups of employees under civil service classification.

block grant   a payment to a state or local government by the national government for a general function such as health, education, or community development.

blow back or replay   a dangerous side-effect of propaganda, in which fake information directed at our enemies abroad finds its way back to our shores to deceive our own citizens.

Boland Amendment   passed in 1982, this law prohibits covert action designed to overthrow the leftist government of Nicaragua.

bonus plan   a reform of the electoral college proposed by a task force in 1978 that would create a national bonus of 102 electoral votes to be awarded to the candidate polling the most votes nationwide.

budget   a plan for meeting program goals, including an estimate of receipts needed and expenditures anticipated within a definite future time period, usually one year.

Budget and Accounting Act of 1921   created the Bureau of the Budget and gave it responsibility for consolidating the requests of each department into a single budget request to be submitted to Congress.

bureaucracy   an administrative system characterized by a hierarchical chain of command, a high degree of specialization, standardized rules of procedure, impersonality, goal orientation and adaptability to changing goals, and highly predictable behavior.

cabinet   composed of the president, vice president, the heads of the executive departments (State, Treasury, Defense, Justice, Interior, Agriculture, Commerce, Labor, Health and Human Services, Housing and Urban Development, Transportation, Energy, Education) and any other official the president chooses to give cabinet status. The cabinet advises the president on matters of public policy.

cabinet council   a group created during the Reagan administration which is made up of cabinet members who deal with issues in the same policy area. There are five: commerce and trade, economic affairs, food and agriculture, human resources, and natural resources and the environment.

campaign strategy   the over-all approach to a campaign; it involves resource management—how candidates, media, trends, events, money, bases of support, issues, and modern campaign technology are blended together.

Case Act of 1972   requires that all executive agreements be submitted to Congress within 60 days of their execution for the sake of information.

Case Amendment   an unsuccessful legislative proposal introduced in 1973 which would have required congressional approval for military agreements with other nations.

casework   legislators' processing of complaints and requests for assistance from constituents.

categorical grant   federal funds made available to state and local governments for a specific, narrowly defined program.

caucus   a closed meeting of party leaders to nominate party candidates or develop strategies for implementing public policies.

Changing American Voter model   a revisionist interpretation of American voting behavior which dwelled on changes noted in the voters from 1964 on and relied somewhat more than the *American Voter* model on issues in explaining the voting decision.

check-off trust fund   the source of public funding for presidential contests, established by the Revenue Act of 1971, which gave taxpayers the option of contributing one dollar of their income taxes to finance presidential elections.

checks and balances   a modification of the doctrine of separation of powers whereby each branch of the government exercises a check upon the other.

Church Amendment   a legislative effort in 1968 to control the war powers through a tighter grip on the purse strings, specifically by prohibiting the use of funds for the introduction of United States combat troops into Laos or Thailand during the Vietnam War.

Civil Service Reform Act of 1978   legislation designed to reform the civil service system. This act abolished the U.S. Civil Service Commission created under the Pendleton Act and replaced it with two agencies: the Office of Personnel Management and the Merit Systems Protection Board.

Clark Amendment   passed in 1975, this law prohibits covert action in Angola.

clear and present danger   the test used by some justices that considers the conditions surrounding expression of opinions in determining whether the freedom of expression guarantee can be abridged.

client states   foreign governments that depend heavily on the United States for military, political, and economic aid.

closed primary   a primary in which "a party test" is made to gain access to the ballot—a voter may vote only in the primary of the party in which he or she is registered.

coalition   an alliance of different groups or factions.

commission plan   one of the four basic forms of local government structure, commonly used for county and township governments. Voters elect a number of commissioners, each of whom heads a major commission or department. Individually, they serve as executive officials; collectively, they serve as the commission, or legislative officials.

Committee of the Whole   forum of all House members in which much of the legislation is considered and amendments are offered.

Committee on the Federal Judiciary   an arm of the American Bar Association that evaluates the suitability of nominees for federal judgeships.

Committees of Correspondence   the communications network established in the 1770s to organize a Colonial response to English authority.

common law   the system of judge-made law that developed in England prior to the colonization of the United States. English common law was the basis for the initial legal system in the sections of the country settled by the British.

concurring opinion   an opinion written by a judge who agrees with the majority opinion but disagrees with the rationale set forth in the majority opinion.

confederation   a system of government in which inde-

pendent state governments create and assign policy-making powers to a central (national) government.

conference committee   committee composed of members of the House and Senate that meets to resolve differences in the versions of legislation passed by the two chambers.

conflictual demand pattern   situation in which competing interests disagree about what policy the government should pursue.

Congressional Budget and Impoundment Act of 1974   established a new congressional budget process designed to strengthen the hand of Congress in controlling budget outlays and in setting national policies and priorites.

conjugal socialization   the peer influence of husband and wife on each other.

consensual demand pattern   situation in which all interested parties agree with a government policy.

constitution   a nation's policy about policymaking. It defines how policy will be made and who will make it. It contains fundamental law, allocates power and responsibility, and provides ways for conflicts within the political system to be resolved.

containment doctrine   the commitment to resist Soviet expansionism wherever it appears around the world.

Continental Congresses   meetings of delegates from the colonies beginning in 1774. The first and second Continental Congresses provided an organized resistance to English authority and provided a national government of the former colonies until 1781.

continuing resolution   resolution passed by Congress when it cannot complete the reconciliation process by the start of the fiscal year. It is a stopgap measure that usually authorizes agencies to spend at the same level as in the previous fiscal year.

controlled media   the paid media, the content and scheduling of which the purchaser can control.

convention   a meeting of party delegates to nominate party candidates, make party policy, and prescribe rules for the conduct of the party's business.

Cooper-Church Amendment   in 1970, an extension to Cambodia of the principle in the earlier Church Amendment.

cost/benefit analysis   a decision-making technique that attempts to assign a dollar figure to a program in relationship to the services it provides.

Council of Economic Advisors (CEA)   a council of economists whose purpose is to analyze the national economy, advise the president on economic development, evaluate the economic programs and policies of the national government, recommend to the president policies for economic growth and stability, and assist in the preparation of the president's annual economic report to Congress.

Council on Environmental Quality a council established in 1969 by the National Environment Policy Act to develop and recommend national policies to improve the quality of the environment.

council-manager plan one of the four basic forms of local government structure, most popular in medium-sized cities. The voters elect the council, which hires and fires the city manager.

courts of appeals federal courts that hear appeals from federal district courts and independent regulatory commissions.

covert action (CA) secret intervention in the affairs of other nations to advance United States interests.

creative federalism President Johnson's program to combat domestic problems by expanding the role of the national government and soliciting the help of the private sector.

critical election a rare type of political event that elicits great depth and intensity of electoral involvement and produces a dramatic and durable realignment between the parties.

cross-cutting requirements requirements attached to each federal grant. There are some 59 of these requirements.

cross-ownership the situation that exists when a company owns media in several different sectors of the communications industry.

culture all of the parts of the environment created by humans—language, institutions, myths, and so forth.

de facto segregation school segregation which is the result of individual choices and is in no way the product of racially based policies of the school system.

de jure segregation segregation required by law, as distinguished from segregation resulting from public choices about where to live.

Declaration of Independence a document adopted by the Second Continental Congress on July 4, 1776 formally declaring the independence of the colonies from England and explaining the justification for the separation.

deep background information given to a reporter by a public official or private individual for use by the reporter only on the reporter's own authority.

deferral a type of impoundment in which expenditures for certain functions are withheld or delayed.

deficit the amount by which expenditures exceed revenues in a fiscal year.

delegated powers powers specifically granted to the national government in the Constitution.

delegation policy decisions in which one unit of government authorizes another governmental or quasi-governmental unit to act.

detachment period phase in White House press relations when a president leaves most of his dealings with the press to members of his staff or cabinet.

détente the relaxation of tensions between the superpowers.

deterrence the strategic theory that a sufficient threat of devastating military retaliation against an enemy discourage a foe from attacking.

diffuse support the sort of bedrock support the government requires to persist through time, as distinct from the more specific support an individual might give to a leader, institution, or policy.

diplomacy peaceful negotiations between nations.

direct popular vote plan a reform proposed for the electoral college by Senator Birch Bayh—presidents would be elected by direct popular vote and a run-off election between the top two vote-getters would be held if no candidate received 40 percent of all votes cast.

direct primary an intraparty election in which the voters select the candidates who will run under the party's label in the subsequent general election.

discount rate the rate of interest Federal Reserve Banks charge to commercial banks that borrow from them.

dissenting opinion an opinion that disagrees with the decision reached by the majority.

distributive policies government policies that spread benefits such as funds or projects to a share of the public without making it apparent to other groups that they are sharing in the costs.

diversity of citizenship one criterion for bringing a suit in a federal district court. It requires that the parties not be citizens of the same state.

doctrine of plausible denial the implementation of

covert operations such that official involvement is concealed and can be denied in case the operation is exposed.

domino theory   the view that the communists, if not contained, would conquer one nation after another until the United States fell.

dual court system   the system of separate state and federal courts found in the United States.

dual federalism rulings   court interpretations of the relative powers of the national and state governments in the federal system which held that the governments were coequal sovereigns, each having responsibility for different policy areas.

effects test   standard that minorities and women's groups think courts should use so that proof of discrimination would require nothing more than showing that minorities or women are disadvantaged.

election   the final stage of the leadership selection process when public officials are formally chosen.

Electronic Surveillance Act of 1978   legislation providing for a confidential judicial review of executive branch requests for wiretaps based on the alleged association of domestic citizens with foreign intelligence agents or operations.

elitism   the theory that only a handful of citizens have the real power to influence the public policymaking process. These citizens are from the higher socioeconomic levels of society and hold important positions in the country's industrial, financial, military, or governmental institutions. These elites must be aware of and respond to the needs of the masses to maintain the system of government that keeps them in power.

entitlement grant   a grant available automatically to eligible recipients who meet requirements and conditions established by congressional statute.

equal protection clause   portion of the Fourteenth Amendment which provides that ''No state shall . . . deny to any person within its jurisdiction the equal protection of the laws.'' This has been relied on heavily by those who have sought civil rights that they had previously been denied.

equity   an economic principle that usually refers to fairness in the distribution of services—getting services to those who are least able to pay for them but most in need of assistance.

excepted service (ES) jobs   government jobs available through political appointment. These are usually top-level jobs filled by the president.

excise taxes   taxes on the manufacture, transportation, sale, or consumption of goods. Excise taxes are levied on goods such as liquor, tobacco, and gasoline without regard to the individual's ability to pay.

exclusionary rule   the rule that improperly obtained evidence or confessions are not to be used to obtain convictions.

executive agreement   an agreement between the president and a foreign country or head of state that does not require Senate approval.

Executive Office of the President   a group of top agencies that advise the president and assist him in carrying out his duties.

executive order   a rule or regulation issued by the president or one of the executive departments that has the effect of law.

executive privilege   the president's right to remain silent and refuse to give information to Congress or a court on the grounds that keeping such information secret is vital to national security.

executive-legislative compact   a tacit agreement between the branches that they will try to work in harmony through joint planning of policy and equal access to information, but with day-to-day management by the executive branch and minimal interference by the Congress at this stage.

external evaluation   a policy evaluation conducted by public or private research institutions, either under contract to the government or by independent individuals or citizen groups. It is intended to determine whether a government policy achieved its stated objective once it was implemented.

extradition   a legal process by which a person accused of a crime in one state who has fled to another is returned to officials in the state where the crime was allegedly committed.

faithless elector   an elector pledged to a presidential candidate who votes for someone else.

fat cats   contributors who make large contributions to political campaigns.

Federal Communications Commission (FCC)   an independent regulatory agency created in 1934 and charged with the regulation of interstate and foreign communications by radio, TV, telephone, telegraph, and cable.

federal district courts courts in which most suits brought in the federal judicial system are originally heard.

Federal Register a United States government publication in which all presidential proclamations, reorganization plans, and executive orders must be published. In addition, every agency must publish a statement of its organization and general policy and give advance notice of an intent to make a rule or regulation, with enough information to enable the public to comment on the need for it or its content.

Federal Reserve System the banking regulatory system that establishes banking policies and controls the amount of credit available and currency in circulation in the United States.

federal system of government a system of government in which power is divided between a central government (national government) and regional governments (the fifty state governments).

federalism A geographical distribution of power. It was one of the most important compromises reached at the Constitutional Convention—governmental powers were divided between a national government and the state governments. It represents a particularly appropriate compromise between concentration of power and decentralization of power.

Federalist papers a series of articles written by Hamilton, Madison, and Jay as a part of the campaign to secure the ratification of the Constitution in New York. They constitute one of our most important sources on the intent of the Constitution framers and one of the most important American contributions to original political theory.

Federalists at first this name was given to supporters of the Articles of Confederation who favored a reliance on state legislatures, and preferred state power to power concentrated at the national level. After the Constitutional Convention, supporters of the Constitution of 1789 became known as Federalists. A political party adopted the name in 1793.

filibuster in the Senate, an attempt to kill legislation through unlimited debate by preventing a vote from being taken on the legislation's merits; also known as talking a bill to death.

First Concurrent Resolution resolution presented by the Budget Committees of each house of Congress on April 15 proposing targets for taxation, spending, and borrowing levels.

fiscal policy government economic policy based on decisions about the taxing, spending, and borrowing of government.

fiscal year (FY) a yearly accounting period; it does not necessarily coincide with a calendar year.

floor leaders the leaders of the Senate majority and minority parties, the House minority party, and the heir apparent to the Speaker in the majority House party.

formal measures of public opinion expressions of public opinion which must be taken into account by government—examples are primaries, elections, referenda, public hearings, citizen's advisory boards, and petitions.

Former Presidents Act of 1958 provides that former presidents receive an annual pension of $70,000 (tied to the pay rate of a cabinet member) and money for office space, phones, furnishings, supplies, equipment, a staff, and travel. Former presidents also receive Secret Service protection for themselves, their wives and widows, and their children up to age 16.

formula-based grant a grant distributing moneys to all eligible jurisdictions on the basis of a formula set by Congress.

40 Committee a subcommittee of the National Security Council in charge of reviewing important covert action proposals.

fourth estate the media, often referred to as the fourth branch of government because they have so much power.

frank the authority that members of Congress have to send official mail at no cost by attaching a facsimile of their signature to the envelope.

freedom of the press a right guaranteed in the First Amendment to the United States Constitution: "Congress shall make no law . . . abridging the freedom . . . of the press." Freedom of the press is also protected by the Fourteenth Amendment to the Constitution and by the 50 state constitutions.

free-enterprise system economic system in which private individuals and businesses, not government, decide what to produce, how to produce it, and who will get the product.

front porch campaign a campaign in which the candidates stayed at home as delegations of influential persons from around the country came to call on them. Is no longer a wise campaign strategy.

"full faith and credit" clause　Article IV, Section 1, of the U.S. Constitution, which obliges states to give "full faith and credit . . . to the public acts, records, and judicial proceedings of every other state."

gatekeepers　editors and publishers who decide what is news.

general assignment reporters　reporters who are either assigned stories by their editor or suggest their own stories and have them okayed by their editor. They are most likely to be investigative or interpretive reporters.

general revenue-sharing grant　a lump sum of money returned to state and local governments from the national government with no strings attached.

general service (GS) jobs　also known as General Schedule jobs; government jobs available on a competitive basis.

geographic zoning　the newspaper technique of printing different news stories and distinctive advertisements for different sections and neighborhoods of large metropolitan areas.

government corporations　businesses operated by government.

grant-in-aid　cash payment from one level of government to another, usually from the national government to state and local governments, for a specific purpose.

Great Compromise or *Connecticut Compromise*　resolved the most important conflict at the Constitutional Convention by providing for a bicameral Congress with one house representing population and the other representing states.

gross national product (GNP)　the monetary (market) value of all goods and services produced in a country in a given year.

Gulf of Tonkin Resolution　a resolution passed by Congress in 1964 allowing President Johnson to "take all necessary steps, including the use of armed force" in Indochina.

gunboat diplomacy　political intervention abroad using overt military force.

Harkin Amendment　passed in 1975, this statute allows either chamber of Congress to end foreign aid to a country over the president's objection, if by majority vote it decides that the prospective recipient is engaged in the violation of human rights and that the aid is unlikely to reach needy people.

honeymoon period　the period of friendly relations between the president and the press during the initial phase of an administration.

House Rules Committee　schedules legislation for debate in the House and specifies the amount of time for the debate and whether the legislation can be amended.

Hughes-Ryan Act　passed in 1974, this statute requires the president to approve in writing all important covert actions and then to inform Congress of these decisions.

imperial presidency　any presidential administration that is perceived as being too powerful because of its general misuse or abuse of presidential power, especially war powers and secrecy.

implied powers　powers of the national government that are not specifically spelled out in the Constitution but are inferred from powers that are spelled out.

impoundment　the power of a president to refuse to spend funds that have already been appropriated for a program.

income tax　a tax on income received from salaries, wages, profits, rents, interest, dividends, and other sources. The national government taxes both individual and corporate income, although at different rates.

independent executive agencies　agencies that are not placed under the jurisdiction of a cabinet-level department.

independent regulatory commissions　the agencies outside the major executive departments responsible for overseeing and regulating certain activities in the private sector.

independent spending　campaign spending uncoordinated with the campaign organization of the candidate benefiting from the effort, which is thus not subject to the spending ceilings and rules of presidential campaigns.

inflation　an economic condition in which prices and wages rise sharply and employment levels are high.

informal measures of public opinion　expressions of public opinion which have no official status—public opinion polls are a good example.

injunctions　court orders prohibiting certain actions or behaviors.

in-kind benefits　noncash benefits such as food stamps.

inside lobbying strategies activities that rely on the internal legislative and political needs of Congress members and the cultivation of relationships in order to exert influence; these activities include contacting policymakers, providing information, drafting legislation, testifying at congressional hearings, and forming coalitions.

integrated political culture the type of political culture that exists when people within the nation have similar or compatible orientations that are in basic harmony with existing political institutions.

Intelligence Accountability Act passed in 1980, this law demanded for Congress prior notification of significant intelligence operations (not after the fact as prescribed by its precursor, the Hughes-Ryan Act), as well as access to all intelligence information deemed necessary for its conduct of legislative oversight (not just on important covert actions).

intent test standard used by the courts in some discrimination cases which invalidates laws or practices only if it is shown that they were designed to discriminate.

interest group an organized group of citizens who share the same views about what type of policy the government should adopt on a specific issue.

intergroup lobbying an interest-group strategy of forming coalitions with other groups who share public policy preferences; it is an instance of lobbyists lobbying each other.

internal evaluation a policy evaluation conducted by government through case studies, committee hearings and investigations, or internal audits. The purpose is to determine whether the policy achieved its stated objectives once it was implemented.

interpreted Constitution or unwritten Constitution the meaning of the Constitution which goes beyond its literal words. Government officials and the people have expanded the Constitution by using it and by interpreting it to solve the problems of the day.

interstate compact an agreement between two or more states which must be approved by Congress if it involves a federal policy domain.

investigative reporting in-depth gathering of the news to protect the public interest; is usually directed at government or business and engaged in by general assignment reporters.

invisible primary an informal process of assessing candidacies that takes place long before the first caucus or primary is held.

iron triangles three-way alliances between middle-level bureaucrats, congressional staff members, and lobbyists based on the mutual benefits they receive from sharing information and common interests.

judicial activism a relatively greater willingness by some judges to substitute their policy preferences for those expressed by the legislative or executive branches. This usually involves a court holding the policies adopted by another branch of government to be unconstitutional.

judicial agencies administrative agencies within the judicial branch, such as the Administrative Office of the U.S. Courts and the Federal Judicial Center. The agencies are responsible for supervising the day-to-day operations of the federal court system and recommending ways to improve it.

judicial restraint relatively greater willingness by a judge to defer to the wishes expressed by a legislature or executive and, therefore, to reject challenges to the constitutionality of these actions.

judicial review the power of the United States Supreme Court to void acts of Congress or state legislatures by ruling that they are not in keeping with the national Constitution.

Kemp-Roth supply-side economics proposal a proposal in the 1980 Republican platform calling for a 10 percent across-the-board cut in individual taxes each year for three consecutive years and a limit on government spending to a fixed share of the GNP, with that percentage being reduced by 1 percent a year for three consecutive years.

Keynesian economic theory (also known as demand-side economics) an economic theory that focuses on influencing individual and government buying (consumption) patterns to stabilize the economy.

kitchen cabinet an informal group of friends and advisors to the president who may actually exert more influence on policy than the real cabinet by virtue of their close personal relationship with the president.

layer-cake federalism an analogy of dual federalism that views government as a three-layer cake. Each layer (national, state, and local) is assigned responsibility for different policy areas; there is no overlap of authority between the different layers.

leak information given to the press that was not intended for official publication at that particular time.

legislative agencies information-gathering agencies in the legislative branch such as the Congressional Budget Office, the General Accounting Office, the Library of Congress, and the Government Printing Office.

legislative clearance the power of the Office of Management and Budget to approve any appropriations request of a department or agency before it can be submitted to Congress.

legislative reorganization acts a series of acts passed by Congress since 1932 authorizing presidents to propose executive reorganizations.

legislative veto the right of Congress to veto orders, rules, or program regulations devised by the president or executive agencies within a certain time period (generally 60 to 90 days). It has been declared unconstitutional by the Supreme Court.

lobbying the pressuring of legislative, executive, or judicial policymakers by a person or group acting as the representative of an organized group for the purpose of influencing public policy.

Lodge-Gossett plan a reform of the electoral college, also known as the proportional plan, that would abolish the office of elector and allocate each state's electoral vote on the basis of the popular vote.

loophole (tax expenditure) legal deduction or exemption permitted in determining taxable income.

mainstream to place mentally or physically handicapped children in regular classrooms for a portion of the day.

majority opinion an opinion endorsed by a majority of a court's judges. The majority opinion sets precedent.

management by objective (MBO) budgetary technique that requires an agency to determine its average work output, list the areas of performance where improvement is necessary or desirable, estimate how much measurable improvement can be achieved during the next fiscal year, and consider whether organizational changes would contribute to greater effectiveness.

marble-cake federalism an analogy that describes the American system of government as a marble cake because the functions of each level of government (national, state, local) are interrelated.

mechanical jurisprudence the notion that judges' personal preferences play no role in determining the outcomes of cases.

media conglomerate a large corporation with diversified nonmedia holdings that buys into the media industry as well.

media elite journalists and broadcasters at the nation's most influential national media outlets, such as the *New York Times, Washington Post, Wall Street Journal, Time Magazine, Newsweek, U.S. News & World Report,* the news departments at CBS, NBC, ABC, PBS, and the wire services, AP and UPI.

medialities events, developments, or situations to which the media have given importance by emphasizing, expanding, or featuring them in such a way that their real significance has been modified, distorted, or obscured.

merit system the selection and promotion of government employees based on the principles of open competition for available jobs, occupational ability, and political neutrality.

Merit Systems Protection Board created by the Civil Service Reform Act of 1978, the Board is responsible for protecting the rights of federal employees.

mixed economic system a system in which the private sector (consumers and producers) and the public sector (government) both take an active part in the economy. Government's role is to ensure full employment and continued economic growth.

Monday-morning-quarterback model analyses of presidential election outcomes which appear on television and in newspapers, magazines, and books in the days and weeks immediately following the election.

monetarism an economic theory that focuses on controlling the nation's money supply (availability of credit) as a means of stabilizing the economy.

monetary policy policy designed to promote national economic goals such as full employment, growth in the gross national product, price stability, and equilibrium in the balance of payments by controlling the amount of money that is in circulation at any time.

money supply the total amount of currency, bank and savings deposits, and other forms of what economists regard as money.

moral change change in cultural, religious, or ethical values.

Mount Vernon Conference the first meeting of delegates from the states to address policy questions that were not being adequately handled by the Articles of Confederation Congress.

Mundt-Coudert plan a reform of the electoral college, also known as the district plan, that would divide each state's electoral vote so that the candidates would receive two votes for carrying a state and one vote for carrying a district.

narrowcasting   directing media programming and advertising toward homogeneous audiences.

National Commitments Resolution   a resolution passed in 1969 as a warning to the president that all significant commitments abroad should be made only with executive and legislative participation in the decision.

national debt   the total outstanding debt owed by the government.

National Emergencies Act of 1976   legislation that ended a number of "temporary" emergency powers of the president by declaring that the emergencies no longer existed as of September, 1978.

National Security Council (NSC)   the president's primary advisory group in the area of defense and foreign policy.

Nationalists   the name given to those who favored a stronger national government for the United States during the 1780s. The Articles of Confederation represented a defeat for them, but the Constitution of 1789 was their victory.

negative advertising   the public relations campaign strategy of attacking the opposition and attempting to damage its credibility.

Nelson-Bingham Amendment   passed in 1974, this law required the president to forward to Congress a complete description of any defense item or service costing $25 million or more (reduced to $7 million or more in 1976) intended for overseas sales. Congress then had 30 days to stop the sale by simple majority votes in both chambers.

new federalism   theory of federalism that advocates strengthening the power of state and local governments by reducing the power of the national government and thereby restoring balance to the federal system.

New Jersey Plan   the Small-State or Paterson plan submitted as a rival to the Virginia plan. It provided for a unicameral Congress with representation by states, a plural executive, and a national judiciary. It was a Nationalist revision of the Articles of Confederation and very influential in Convention deliberations on the Constitution of 1789.

new politics   politics based on a candidate-centered campaign. The old politics was based on a party-centered campaign.

New York Times v. *U.S.*   the celebrated "Pentagon Papers" case of 1971 in which the Supreme Court concluded that the *Times* had the right to print classified government documents on the Vietnam War since, in this instance, publication was unlikely to result "in direct, immediate, and irreparable damage to our nation or its people."

1974 Congressional Budget and Impoundment Act   requires presidents to report delays in spending to Congress; gives either house the power to veto an expenditure deferral; and requires the approval of both the Senate and the House for a president to cancel any project for which Congress has already appropriated funds.

nomination   the authoritative designation of an individual as a candidate for public office.

nonpartisan primary   a primary in which candidates do not run under a party symbol. It is an elimination contest in which the candidates who file are reduced to a number twice as large as the seats to be filled— these are thus "qualified" to run in the general election.

nontax revenue sources   revenues from government-owned enterprises, sales of government products and land, rentals of land and equipment, fines and penalties, gifts to the government, and interest on government loans.

normal vote   an estimate of the vote in a presidential contest based entirely on what social scientists know about the impact of party identification on the electorate's voting behavior.

norms   unwritten rules that guide behavior.

nuclear freeze movement   a bipartisan coalition of officials and citizens formed in 1982 to support a mutual, verifiable halt in the arms race and reduction in the production of nuclear weapons by both superpowers.

Nuclear Non-proliferation Act   passed in 1978, this law gives Congress veto power over nuclear exports, should both chambers vote to negate a sale within a 60-day waiting period.

office block ballot   a ballot which groups candidates according to the office they seek.

Office of Administration   provides administrative support services to all within the Executive Office of the President except the White House Office.

Office of Management and Budget   the executive agency that helps prepare the federal budget, monitors spending, and conducts efficiency analyses.

Office of Personnel Management created by the Civil Service Reform Act of 1978, this office is responsible for recruiting, examining, training, and promoting federal employees on the basis of their knowledge, skills, and performance. It is also responsible for making sure that affirmative action policies are implemented.

Office of Policy Development the office that helps the president formulate domestic policy options and reviews the major policies of the administration.

Office of Science and Technology Policy the office responsible for advising the president on scientific and technological aspects of policy areas of national concern, such as national security and the environment.

Office of the U.S. Trade Representative the office responsible for negotiating and formulating U.S. trade policy.

off-the-record information given to a reporter by a public official or private individual with the understanding that it will not be reported, but merely used to help the reporter develop a broader understanding of an issue or event.

open market operations the purchase or sale of governmental bonds by the Federal Reserve; it is a monetary policy tool.

open primary a primary system in which the voter may vote in either party's primary.

Operation SHAMROCK a secret United States intelligence operation conducted from 1947 to 1975 involving the interception of international cable communications sent and received by American citizens.

opinions short-term, relatively current evaluations of the political world.

Organization of Petroleum Exporting Countries (OPEC) an organization of the countries in the Middle East and elsewhere that produce most of the world's oil. It meets regularly to decide how much oil to produce and what price to charge its customers.

original jurisdiction refers to the court in which a case is first heard.

outcome-oriented litigation strategy major litigation strategy adopted by interest groups wanting to modify specific decisions made by the executive branch or to redefine statutes in a more favorable light.

outside lobbying strategies strategies designed to mobilize group members in the home districts of Congress members in order to demonstrate that an issue is important to many people back home and to sug-

gest that at election time the interest group will not forget how the senator or representative voted on the issue.

oversight the process, usually involving committee hearings, through which the legislature monitors the way the executive branch is implementing programs.

oversight committee a congressional committee which monitors the general operation of an agency or program; generally it also serves as the authorizing committee for that agency's programs.

pack journalism the tendency of different media representatives to cover the same stories from a similar perspective.

paramilitary (PM) covert action secret warlike operations which may consist of support to groups engaged in insurgency fighting; the funding of paramilitary training activities; the dispatch of CIA military advisers; and the direct or indirect shipment of arms, ammunition, or other military equipment abroad.

partisan primary a primary in which candidates must run under a party symbol.

party column ballot a ballot which lists all of the candidates, for whatever office they are seeking, in a column under the party label. This ballot usually provides an opportunity to check one box and vote a straight ticket.

party image the mental picture a voter has of a party.

party in office party members who hold elective or appointive public office at any level of government; also referred to as the party in government.

party in the electorate organized group and mass public followers of the political parties.

party organization formally-chosen party officials, including everyone from the chairman of the national committee to the members of the local party precinct committee who make and carry out decisions in the name of the party.

party platform statement of a political party's positions on selected policy issues.

party professionals (old pros) the old style of party activists who value winning and see their role as peacekeepers, coalition builders, and policy compromisers.

patronage appointment appointments made strictly on the basis of party loyalty and party service.

Philadelphia Convention or ***Constitutional Convention of 1787*** a meeting called by the Articles of Confederation Congress at the request of the Annapolis Convention to propose amendments to the Articles; instead it abandoned the Articles and prepared the Constitution of 1789.

planning-programming-budgeting systems (PPBS) budgetary technique that requires an agency to identify program objectives, develop methods of measuring program outputs, calculate total program costs over the long run, prepare detailed multiyear program and financial plans, and analyze the costs and benefits of alternative program designs.

Plum Book the official list of high-salaried government jobs that an incoming president has the authority to fill. Its official title is *U.S. Government Policy and Supporting Positions.*

pluralism the theory that any citizen has the power to influence policy, particularly if he or she is a member of an interest group. Since the same citizens are not interested in every policy issue, the same people do not influence every policy issue. No one group of people holds all the power.

plurality requirement dictates that the candidate who receives the largest number of votes, not necessarily a majority, be declared the winner.

pocket veto a type of presidential veto. If the president receives a bill when ten days or less are left in the session he can simply let the bill die by refusing to take action on it.

policy evaluation the measuring of the impact or consequences of policy implementation. Policy evaluation allows citizens to hold public officials accountable for their policy decisions, and it informs officials whether the old policy should be revised or replaced with a completely different one.

policy formation the identification of a particular need and the adoption of a policy to meet that need. While policy formation depends on individuals or groups telling government officials what they want or don't want, the power to adopt the policy lies exclusively with government officials.

policy implementation the actual carrying out of a policy decision by government officials.

policy triangles sets of interested parties from congressional sub-committees, the executive branch, and pressure groups that establish policy in a subject area also known as iron triangles.

policy-making process the ongoing process of policy formation, policy implementation, and policy evaluation.

political action committee (PAC) the political arm of a business, labor, professional or other interest group which raises funds on a voluntary basis from members or employees in order to contribute funds to candidates or political parties.

political boss the leader of a political machine.

political consultants the new professionals who sell their skills in modern campaign technology.

political covert action secret relationships with influential foreign personalities, operations to manipulate foreign economies, and, most commonly, deception and propaganda programs in support of American foreign policy.

political culture the core of basic values acquired through political socialization.

political ideology an abstract view of the world, an elaborate, inter-related, and far-reaching set of attitudes about politics.

political interest group an organization whose members share the same views about what type of policy the government should adopt on a specific issue.

political machines well-organized, tightly-knit, hierarchical party organizations whose power stems from their ability to provide personal benefits in exchange for party loyalty and support. They were prevalent in the nation's largest cities in the nineteenth and early twentieth centuries.

political participation actions taken to indirectly or directly influence policy.

political party a group of individuals, often having some measure of ideological agreement, who organize to win elections, operate government, and determine public policy.

political power the ability to influence the public policymaking process.

political socialization the process through which the individual acquires his or her particular political orientations—knowledge, feelings, and evaluations regarding his or her political world.

politics the struggle to make policies that meet the needs and demands of citizens. Politics involves conflict and compromise over who gets what, when, where, and how.

popular sovereignty the idea that ultimate political authority rests with the people, who retain the power to create, alter, or abolish government.

pork barrel legislation legislation providing funding for projects in a legislator's district.

post-desegregation discrimination any discriminatory actions taken by a school system intended to promote racial separation within an officially desegregated system.

power the ability to determine who gets what, when, where, and how.

precinct a manageable region or geographical area for counting election ballots and for administering the election process.

preclearance provision of the Voting Rights Act of 1965 and subsequent years that requires communities covered by this legislation to obtain approval from the Justice Department before making changes in their election laws or procedures.

preferment power the power to award federal contracts to businesses and give federal grants to governments within a House member's district or a senator's state. Also known as *pork barrel politics.*

preferred position the view held by some justices that freedom of expression is so important to a democracy that attempts to restrict it will be presumed to be unconstitutional.

Presidential Succession Act of 1947 specifies that after the vice president, the presidency passes to the Speaker of the House, then to the president pro tempore of the Senate, then to cabinet officials in the following order: secretary of state, treasury, defense, the attorney general, the secretaries of interior, agriculture, commerce, labor, health and human services, housing and urban development, transportation, energy, and education.

primary relationships relationships that are close, personal, and involve a high level of interaction—peer relationships are a good example.

printout politics a system of federal aid distribution in which funds are allocated on the basis of formulas set in Congress rather than by federal agencies. Congress members get computer printouts showing how much money will go to their districts under each proposed formula which often determines which one they will vote for.

prior restraint prohibitions that prevent the publication of some kinds of information; they are rarely tolerated by the courts.

"privileges and immunities" clauses two clauses in the Constitution (Article IV and the Fourteenth Amendment) that establish that citizens of all states shall be treated equally.

productivity decline the situation that exists when fewer and fewer things are produced for the same amount of labor and money.

progressive tax also known as a graduated tax; a tax based on one's ability to pay. The tax rate increases as income increases.

project-based grant a grant that state and local governments must compete for to get the limited funds set aside for a specific program.

prospective reimbursement method of paying for health care through Medicaid that establishes maximum rates for procedures and services.

prospective voting voting in an election on the basis of the performance anticipated from a challenger.

public-interest group an interest group that seeks programs and policies which benefit everyone in society, not just those who formally belong to the group.

public opinion the complex of preferences expressed by a significant number of persons on an issue of general importance.

public or collective goods goods or services the benefits of which are shared by everyone.

public policy any decision, backed by the authority of a government, that determines who in the population gets what, where, when, and how.

purist activists a political party workers who are so committed to their ideology or principles that they find it difficult to compromise and would rather be right than to win.

recession an economic condition in which the economy slows down, wages and prices do not rise as rapidly, but the unemployment rate increases sharply.

reciprocity norm that encourages legislators to help one another achieve their objectives.

reconciliation legislation legislation prepared by Congress to reconcile amounts in tax and spending legislation for a fiscal year with the ceilings required by the Second Concurrent Resolution.

recruitment identifying leaders either by going to potential candidates and urging them to run or by making the party available to politicians who have already decided to run.

redistributive policies policies that provide benefits for one group in society by charging the cost against another group.

reductions-in-force (RIFs) personnel cuts in the federal bureaucracy.

regulatory policies policies for which the legislature or the judiciary establishes its objectives in broad terms and then leaves it up to a bureaucracy to establish the specifics of implementation.

reprogramming the use of funds by agency officials for purposes other than those for which they were appropriated.

rescission type of impoundment that cancels all or part of an existing appropriation for a certain program and thus prohibits the expenditure of those funds.

reserve requirement the portion of a bank's assets that must be deposited in one of the 12 Federal Reserve Banks across the nation. The Feds can raise and lower this amount to affect the money supply.

resocialization the process of revising, replacing, or supplementing the individual's set of acquired political orientations.

"responsible" party system one in which parties offer a clear-cut choice on policy and officials follow their party's line once elected.

retrospective voting voting in an election on the basis of the record of the incumbent in the previous years of his administration.

reverse discrimination the practice of discriminating against whites, particularly males, in order to increase opportunities for minorities and previously disadvantaged groups.

role change a basic alteration in the distribution of roles in society; a recent example is the entry of a large number of women into what were formerly considered men's jobs in carpentry, law, medicine, and other fields.

role equity equal political and economic opportunities for men and women.

roll call votes recorded votes cast in a legislature.

rose garden campaign a style of presidential campaign in which the president declines debates and campaign travel while keeping himself before the public in media appearances from the rose garden of the White House.

rule of three practice followed by the Office of Personnel Management when notified that a position has opened up. The hiring agency is sent the names of the top three applicants from a register for that position arranged by civil service exam scores. Any of the three individuals can be hired by the agency. The other two remain at the top of the register until they get a job or the register expires and new exams are given.

run-off primary a nominating system used by ten southern states which requires a second run-off primary between the top two candidates if no candidate secures a majority in the first primary.

SALT Strategic Arms Limitation Talks.

Second Concurrent Resolution binding budget resolution setting a spending ceiling and revenue floor for the fiscal year.

secondary relationships relationships that involve formal interactions between members of the same clubs, professional groups, unions, and business or trade associations.

secretaries cabinet-level department heads (except for the head of the Justice Department, who is the attorney general).

selective perception the tendency of individuals to see and hear only what they want and to screen out or ignore other messages and information presented to them by the media.

self-incrimination testimony given by a person against himself or herself.

senatorial courtesy the presidential practice of conferring with the senators from a state (especially those from his own political party) before making a nomination to fill a federal position in that state.

seniority norm that allocates positions of committee leadership and offices in the congressional office buildings on the basis of members' length of continuous service in Congress.

separate-but-equal doctrine interpretation of the equal protection clause of the U.S. Constitution in effect from 1896 to 1954 that allowed for segregated public facilities so long as equal quality was available to the two races.

separation of powers the principle that the three great functions of government (legislative, executive, and judicial) be assigned to separate and independent agencies to avoid a dangerous concentration of power.

Shay's Rebellion a debtors' revolt in the state of Massachusetts in 1786 and 1787 that frightened many of the nation's leaders and is believed to be the most important catalyst for writing a new Constitution providing a stronger national government.

shield laws legislation that allows reporters to refuse to reveal the identity of their confidential sources.

social contract   an agreement between the ruler and the ruled, with both having mutual obligations. The contract theory appeared prominently in the work of John Locke, which influenced the Declaration of Independence.

Social Security system   an insurance program administered by the federal government to provide a retirement income for the elderly, income for totally disabled workers, and income for widows and minor children of deceased workers. It also provides health insurance for the elderly through Medicare.

social service state or *welfare state*   the situation that exists when government plays a large role, through economic and social programs, in protecting individual security and general welfare. All of the world's industrialized nations have adopted this concept to at least some degree; in the United States the concept gained acceptance during the Great Depression.

socialization   the process by which individual citizens acquire societal values.

sovereignty   the long standing notion that a nation or state is defined by its absolute power to make and enforce policy within its boundaries.

Speaker of the House   the leader of the majority party who presides over the House of Representatives.

specialization   norm that encourages members of Congress to participate in relatively few subject areas but to become experts in those they do serve in.

spoils system   the system of selecting government employees on the basis of political connections.

stagflation   an economic condition characterized by the simultaneous existence of high unemployment and high inflation. During such a period, the growth of the economy is sluggish and the dollar decreases in value.

standing committees   the 22 House and 16 Senate committees that review and perfect legislative proposals.

stare decisis   a judicial norm that holds that judges should decide cases in conformity with earlier decisions. Also known as precedent.

statutory agreements   international commitments entered into by the United States pursuant to existing congressional legislation.

straw poll   an informal assessment of public opinion, usually taken by newspapers. They were a forerunner of modern public opinion polls, but they lacked their scientific reliability.

street-level bureaucrats   the civil service employees with whom most citizens come in direct contact, either by phone, letter, or in person.

strict constructionist   the idea that government is forbidden to adopt a policy for which a specific and explicit constitutional authorization cannot be found.

strong executive system   state government organizational framework characterized by a clear span of control with ultimate authority resting with the governor; such a system is designed to promote administrative efficiency and bureaucratic accountability.

strong-mayor council plan   one of the four basic forms of local government structure. The mayor serves full time and has strong appointment and budgetary powers.

subculture   a group within society with the same status, background, interests, and goals.

supply-side economics   an economic theory popularized during the Reagan administration that focuses on stimulating supply (production) rather than demand (consumption).

synthetic fuels (synfuels)   fuels produced from coal, tar sands, oil shale, garbage, and other sources. Synfuels are regarded as the alternative to oil and other nonrenewable fossil fuels.

tax indexing   automatic adjustment of income taxes to offset inflation every year.

Third World   the diverse nations that lie outside the Western and the Sino-Soviet blocs.

Three-Fifths Compromise   resolved sectional differences on how slaves should be considered in computing representation and taxes in the Constitution of 1789 by counting slaves as three-fifths of one person for both representation and taxes.

Title IX   1972 legislation designed to eliminate sex discrimination in schools and colleges.

tort   an injury or wrong.

trade association   an organization composed of businesses operating in the same field.

trade states   foreign governments whose primary interaction with the United States is commercial.

transfers   the shifting of funds from one appropriated account to another.

treaty   a formal agreement between two or more countries that establishes or limits mutual rights and responsibilities, usually within some definite time frame.

Treaty Powers Resolution a failed attempt by some senators in 1976 to require use of the treaty procedure for all "significant" international agreements.

trickle-down approach economic theory, more likely to be embraced by conservatives than liberals, that holds that benefits conferred on the affluent will in time improve conditions for the poor.

Truman Doctrine an application of the containment doctrine through the provision of aid to nations threatened by the Soviet Union, beginning with Greece and Turkey in 1947.

Twenty-Fifth Amendment ratified in 1967, it lays out two procedures for dealing with presidential disability. Under both procedures, the vice president temporarily succeeds to the presidency.

Twenty-Second Amendment ratified in 1951, this Amendment limits a president's tenure in office to two terms, thereby ending his need to compete for the office a third time.

two presidencies theory theory proposed by Aaron Wildavsky that the United States has one president but two presidencies: one for domestic affairs and one for defense and foreign policies.

umbrella hypothesis the hypothesis that there is still competition in the newspaper industry, even though the number of cities with competing dailies is declining, because of the existence of suburban newspapers, weekly newspapers, "shoppers," and other specialized media.

umbrella organization a broad-based group to which a number of other organizations belong.

uncontrollable spending government spending, particularly in the areas of income security (entitlement programs), health, and interest payments, that cannot be increased or decreased without changing an existing law.

uncontrolled media the free media, the content of which are largely under the control of the working professionals but which may be influenced or even manipulated by an effective campaign strategy.

unconventional participation types of political participation that have not gained wide acceptance in the United States—violence, civil disobedience, and protest behavior.

unitary system of government a system of government in which all policymaking powers are assigned to the central government.

veteran's preference the practice of giving veterans an extra five points and disabled veterans an extra ten points on the civil service exam.

veto the president's power to reject and return a bill unsigned to Congress along with the reasons for his objections.

video malaise a feeling of cynicism and mistrust toward the media caused by constant exposure to the press's negativism and crisis orientation.

Vietnamization the gradual turning of the conduct of hostilities against the North Vietnamese over to the South Vietnamese.

Virginia Plan the Large-State or Randolph Plan submitted to the Constitutional Convention at the beginning of deliberations. It was the most important single influence on the Convention. It provided for a bicameral Congress with representation based on population, an expansion of national powers, and both an independent executive and a national judiciary.

War Powers Act of 1973 legislation authorizing Congress to participate with the president in making the decision to use American armed forces abroad. The Act provides that the president can commit forces only under three conditions: 1) a declaration of war by Congress; 2) specific statutory authorization; or 3) a national emergency created by an attack on the United States or its military forces.

Washington information establishment the government publicists who are the primary source of information for the Washington press corps.

Watergate takes its name from a White-House-approved burglary of the national Democratic party headquarters in the Watergate complex by seven men during the 1972 election, but it stands for a variety of illegal acts committed by officers and agencies of the Nixon administration.

weak executive system state government organization characterized by many separately elected executive officials, a large number of independent boards and commissions, and numerous legislative checks on the governor's power.

weak-mayor council plan one of the four basic forms of local government structure, usually found in small cities that have relatively few employees and executive departments. The council rather than the mayor has strong appointment and budgetary powers; the mayor serves mainly as the figurative head, presiding at council meetings and performing ceremonial acts.

whips assistant to the floor leaders responsible for maintaining party discipline on roll calls and distributing information about the legislature's agenda.

white flight movement of whites to the suburbs to avoid the higher concentrations of minorities found in some central cities.

White House Office informally called the White House staff, the White House Office is part of the Executive Office of the President. The staff is responsible for maintaining communication with Congress, the heads of executive agencies, the press, and the general public.

winner-take-all rule a tradition by which the candidate with a plurality of votes in a state gets all of that state's electoral votes.

winnowing process the process by which the number of presidential candidates is narrowed down so that only a few remain by convention time.

writ of certiorari request to have the records sent to the Supreme Court from a lower court so that the decision of the latter can be reviewed.

writ of mandamus a court order commanding an official to perform an act that he or she is legally required to perform.

zero-base budgeting (ZBB) budgeting technique that requires an agency to start from ground zero—to identify every program or function it controls, evaluate the cost and intrinsic merits of each and alternatives to each; rank each function in terms of funding priority; and assess each function on a dollar-value basis.

zero-sum game a term from mathematical game-theory, popular in the 1950s among scholars, indicating a policy of pure confrontation between nations with no compromises and only one winner.

NOTES

Chapter 1

1. Excellent overviews of the policy-making process can be found in James E. Anderson, *Public Policy-Making*, 2d ed. (New York: Holt, Rinehart & Winston, 1979), and Thomas R. Dye, *Understanding Public Policy*, 4th ed. (Englewood Cliffs, N.J.: Prentice-Hall, 1981).
2. This definition is based on one developed by Harold D. Lasswell in his famous book *Politics: Who Gets What, When, How* (New York: McGraw-Hill, 1936).
3. John Herbers, "Experts See More Flight to Suburbs," *Houston Chronicle*, June 9, 1980.
4. "Planner Sees a Return to Urban Centers," *Houston Chronicle*, December 13, 1979.
5. William Greidner and Barry Sussman, "The American Spirit: National Opinion Survey Finds a View of Hope, Not Malaise," *Houston Chronicle*, December 23, 1979.
6. James W. Singer, "Undervalued Jobs—What's a Woman (and the Government) to Do?" *National Journal*, May 24, 1980, p. 858.
7. *Ibid.*
8. U.S. Department of Commerce, Bureau of the Census, *Statistical Portrait of Women in the United States—1978* (Washington, D.C.: Government Printing Office, 1980), p. 1.
9. "Demographics of the Eighties," *American Demographics*, January 1980; Leon F. Bouvier and Cary B. Davis, cited in Judy Wiessler, "A Changing Society," *Houston Chronicle*, October 2, 1982.
10. Richard Polenberg, "Sameness, and Same Old Differences," *Houston Chronicle*, March 20, 1980.
11. Greidner and Sussman, *op. cit.*
12. "The American Women's Opinion Poll, 1980." Conducted by the Roper Organization for Virginia Slims.
13. Robert J. Samuelson, "Fragmentation and Uncertainty Litter the Political Landscape," *National Journal*, October 20, 1979, p. 1726.
14. Richard E. Cohen, "The Political System Attempts to Cope with Public Loss of Faith in Government," *National Journal*, January 19, 1980, p. 110.
15. *Ibid.*, p. 116.
16. Jack W. Germond and Jules Witcover, *Blue Smoke and Mirrors: How Reagan Won and Why Carter Lost the Election of 1980* (New York: The Viking Press, 1981), pp. 316–317.
17. Samuelson, *op. cit.*, pp. 1726–1736.
18. James Reston, "Statistics on Voters Troubling," *Houston Chronicle*, January 5, 1980.
19. *Ibid.*
20. Cited by Reston in *Ibid.*
21. Samuelson, *op cit.*, p. 1726.
22. *Ibid.*
23. Nelson W. Polsby, Introduction to "Politics, Parties, and 1980," special issue of *National Journal*, 1979.
24. Curtis Gans, quoted in Samuelson, *op. cit.*, p. 1728.
25. Richard Scammon, quoted in *Ibid.*
26. Samuelson, *op. cit.*, p. 1736.
27. Thomas R. Dye and L. Harmon Zeigler, *The Irony of Democracy* (Belmont, Calif.: Wadsworth Publishing Co., 1970), p. 1.
28. Robert A. Dahl, *Pluralist Democracy in the United States* (Chicago: Rand McNally, 1967), p. 24.

Chapter 2

1. Jenkin Lloyd Jones, "How Large Can the Welfare Mass Grow?" *Houston Chronicle*, May 26, 1980.
2. Robert S. McNamara, "Will We Face Up to the New Balance of Wealth?" *Newsweek*, November 19, 1979, p. 144.
3. John Maynard Keynes, *General Theory of Employment, Interest, and Money* (New York: Harcourt, Brace & World, 1936).
4. Arthur M. Schlesinger, Jr., "Can We Control Our World?" *Newsweek*, November 19, 1979, p. 136.
5. Survey by the Roper Organization, June 2–9, 1979.
6. Robert J. Samuelson, "Monetarism Maligned," *National Journal*, February 27, 1982, p. 385.
7. *Ibid.*
8. Robert J. Samuelson, "Friends and Enemies," *National Journal*, July 17, 1982, p. 1265.

9. Robert S. Ozaki, *Inflation, Recession . . . And All That* (New York: Holt, Rinehart & Winston, 1972), p. 23.

10. The Advertising Council, U.S. Department of Commerce, and U.S. Department of Labor, "The American Economic System, and Your Part in It," *Houston Chronicle,* July 3, 1977.

11. Vernon E. Jordan, Jr., "Is Equality Possible?" *Newsweek,* November 19, 1979, p. 140.

12. Schlesinger, *op. cit.,* p. 136.

13. William Greider, "The Education of David Stockman," *The Atlantic,* 248 (December 1981), p. 46.

14. Daniel Yergin, "Energy: Crisis and Adjustment," excerpt from *Global Insecurity: A Strategy for Energy and Economic Renewal* (Boston: Houghton Mifflin, 1982), *Houston Chronicle,* August 1, 1982.

15. Robert Burns, "Crisis Is Gone but the Changes Remain," *Houston Chronicle,* February 24, 1982.

16. *Ibid.*

17. *Ibid.*

18. Everett Carll Ladd, "Clearing the Air: Public Opinion and Public Policy on the Environment," *Public Opinion,* 5 (February/March 1982), p. 20.

19. Robert Burns, "Americans Take Conservation to Heart," *Houston Chronicle,* February 26, 1982.

20. Richard Corrigan, "Economic War Over Oil Also Looms at the State Level," *National Journal,* March 22, 1979, p. 2137.

21. Samuel O. Hancock, "Plans for Energy Independence," *Houston Chronicle,* August 1, 1982.

22. "Breaking Up the Energy Department May Not Be All That Easy," *National Journal,* January 2, 1982, p. 39.

23. "Expert Predicts Third Energy Crisis," *Houston Chronicle,* July 12, 1982.

24. Daniel Yankelovich and Bernard Leftwitz, "National Growth: The Question of the 80's," *Public Opinion,* 3 (December/January 1980), p. 55.

25. *Ibid.,* p. 47.

26. *Ibid.,* p. 52.

27. *Ibid.,* p. 56.

28. Geoffrey Godbey, "Things of the Leisure Mass," *Public Opinion,* 2 (August/September 1979), p. 47.

29. "Opinion Roundup: The 70's: For Every Yes, a No," *Public Opinion,* 3 (December/January 1980), p. 25.

30. *Ibid.,* p. 37.

31. *Gallup Report,* No. 198, March 1982.

32. U.S. Congress, Joint Economic Committee, *Economic Review of the U.S.* (Washington, D.C.: Government Printing Office, 1979).

33. American Productivity Center, *Productivity: Challenge of the 80's* (Houston: American Productivity Center, November 1979), p. 4.

34. "Opinion Roundup: Women in the 70's," *Public Opinion,* 3 (December/January 1980), pp. 33, 34.

35. Poll is cited in David E. Rosenbaum, "Racial Quotas in America," *Houston Chronicle,* September 25, 1977.

36. Steven V. Roberts, "More and More White Males Claiming They Are Victims of Reverse Discrimination," *Houston Chronicle,* November 27, 1977.

37. William Raspberry, "Bakke Ruling Ambiguity Welcome," *Houston Chronicle,* July 4, 1978.

38. Robert J. Samuelson, "Pension Tension," *National Journal,* May 17, 1980, p. 822.

39. Dale Tate, "Tackling Social Security: Is 1980 the Year of Decision?" *Congressional Quarterly Weekly Report,* January 12, 1980, p. 67; Robert J. Samuelson, "Retirement Politics—Will Mandatory Pensions Meet the Elderly's Needs?" *National Journal,* May 31, 1980, p. 894.

40. Linda E. Demkovich, "In Treating the Problems of the Elderly, There May Be No Place Like Home," *National Journal,* December 22, 1979, p. 2155.

41. Alexis de Tocqueville, *Democracy in America,* 2 vols. (1835; New York: Vintage Books, 1954).

42. Patricia McCormick, "High School Students Change Some Views in Recent Years," *Houston Chronicle,* December 8, 1979.

43. Laurence E. Lynn, Jr., *Designing Public Policy* (Santa Monica, Calif.: Goodyear, 1980), p. 21.

44. James E. Anderson, *Public Policy-Making,* 2d ed. (New York: Holt, Rinehart & Winston, 1979), p. 27.

45. Robert Eyestone, *From Social Issues to Public Policy* (New York: John Wiley & Sons, 1978), p. 3.

46. Advisory Commission on Intergovernmental Relations, *Citizen Participation in the American Federal System* (Washington, D.C.: Government Printing Office, 1979).

47. Anderson, *op. cit.,* p. 42.

Chapter 3

1. J. Franklin Jameson, *The American Revolution Considered as a Social Movement* (Princeton, N.J.: Princeton University Press, 1967).

2. Clinton Rossiter, *1787: The Grand Convention* (New York: The Macmillan Company, 1966), p. 148.

3. Max Farrand, *The Framing of the Constitution of the United States* (New Haven, Conn.: Yale University Press, 1967), p. 68.

4. Max Farrand, ed., *The Records of the Federal Convention of 1787,* rev. ed.: 4 vols. (New Haven, Conn.: Yale University Press, 1966).

5. *Ibid.,* vol. I, p. 17.

6. *Ibid.,* vol. I, pp. 20–23.

7. *Ibid.,* vol. I, pp. 242–245.

8. For other plans, see *Ibid.,* vol. III, pp. 591–630.

9. *Ibid.,* vol. II, p. 137.

10. Charles A. Beard, *An Economic Interpretation of the Constitution of the United States* (New York: The Macmillan Company, 1913), p. 324.

11. See, for example, Robert E. Brown, *Charles A. Beard and the Constitution* (Princeton, N.J.: Princeton University Press, 1956); and Forrest McDonald, *We the People: The Economic Origins of the Constitution* (Chicago: University of Chicago Press, 1958). Beard himself said that he did not write *the,* but *an,* economic interpretation.

12. Max Farrand, ed., *Records, op. cit.,* vol. 1, p. 48. See Richard Hofstadter, *The American Political Tradition* (New York: Alfred A. Knopf, 1948) for an excellent essay on the backgrounds and values of the nation's founders, pp. 3–17.

13. David G. Smith, *The Convention and the Constitution* (New York: St. Martin's Press, 1965), p. 31.

14. Forrest McDonald and Ellen Shapiro McDonald, eds., *Confederation and Constitution, 1781–1789* (Co-

lumbia S.C.: University of South Carolina Press, 1968), p. 220.

15. Alfred A. Kelly and Winfred A. Harbison, *The American Constitution: Its Origins and Development* (New York: W.W. Norton, 1955), pp. 219–223.

16. *Congressional Quarterly Weekly Report*, February 3, 1979, pp. 189–194; Robert A. Diamond, ed., *Powers of Congress* (Washington, D.C.: Congressional Quarterly, Inc., 1976), pp. 211, 214, 218; Malcolm E. Jewell and Samuel C. Patterson, *The Legislative Process in the United States*, 3d ed. (New York: Random House, 1977), pp. 330–331; John R. Schmidhauser, ed., *Constitutional Law in the Political Process* (Chicago: Rand McNally, 1963), pp. 184–187.

17. Robert H. Jackson, *The Struggle for Judicial Supremacy* (New York: Random House, 1941), pp. 96–104.

18. Richard C. Cortner, *The Supreme Court and Civil Liberties Policy* (Palo Alto, Calif.: Mayfield Publishing Company, 1975), pp. 33–79.

19. Robert L. Lineberry, *American Public Policy* (New York: Harper and Row, 1977), p. 209.

20. *Congressional Quarterly Weekly Report*, February 17, 1979, pp. 273–279; *Congressional Quarterly Almanac*, XXVII (1971), pp. 758–759; *Congressional Quarterly Almanac*, XXIII (1967), pp. 461–464.

Chapter 4

1. Rochelle L. Stanfield, "What Has 500 Parts, Costs $83 Billion and is Condemned by Almost Everybody?" *National Journal*, January 3, 1981, p. 4.

2. Advisory Commission on Intergovernmental Relations, *In Brief: The Federal Role in the Federal System: The Dynamics of Growth*, Report No. B-4 (Washington, D.C.: Government Printing Office, December, 1980), p. 4.

3. Carol S. Weissert, "The Big Squeeze: Government by Trade-off," *Intergovernmental Perspective*, 6 (Spring 1980), p. 1.

4. Daniel J. Elazar, "First Principles," in *The Federal Polity*, Daniel J. Elazar ed. (New Brunswick, N.J.: Travachin Books, 1974), p. 3.

5. *Texas v. White*, 7 Wall. 700 (1869).

6. Cited in Deil S. Wright, *Understanding Intergovernmental Relations* (North Scituate, Mass.: Duxbury Press, 1978), p. 22.

7. Morton Grodzins, "The Federal System," in *American Government: Readings and Cases*, Peter Woll ed. (Boston: Little, Brown, 1972), p. 125.

8. Stanfield, *op. cit.*, p. 4.

9. *Federal-State-Local Relations: Federal Grants-in-Aid*, House Report No. 2533, House Committee on Government Operations, 85th Congress, 2nd Session, p. 7.

10. George E. Hale and Marian L. Palley, *The Politics of Federal Grants* (Washington, D.C.: Congressional Quarterly Press, 1981), pp. 18–21.

11. *Ibid.*, p. 8.

12. *Ibid.*

13. *Ibid.*, p. 7.

14. Thomas R. Dye, *Politics in States and Communities*, 4th ed. (Englewood Cliffs, N.J.: Prentice-Hall, 1981), p. 48.

15. Hale and Palley, *op. cit.*, p. 11.

16. Carl W. Stenberg, "Federalism in Transition: 1959–79," *Intergovernmental Perspective*, 6 (Winter 1980), p. 18.

17. *Ibid.*, p. 7.

18. Michael C. Mitchell, "National Events in 1979: The New Austerity Takes Hold," *Intergovernmental Perspective*, 6 (Spring 1980), p. 9.

19. *Ibid.*

20. Stenberg, *op. cit.*, p. 12.

21. Advisory Commission on Intergovernmental Relations, *op. cit.*, p. 12.

22. Stenberg, *op. cit.*, p. 12.

23. Monroe W. Karmin, "Growth Policy Stresses Better Handling of Federal Programs," syndicated column, *Chicago Daily News*, February 5, 1978.

24. Stephanie J. Becker, "1980 Spotlights Rebalancing Federalism," *Intergovernmental Perspective*, 7 (Winter 1981), p. 4.

25. Advisory Commission on Intergovernmental Relations, *op. cit.*, p. 4.

26. "Block Grants: An Old Republican Idea," *Congressional Quarterly*, May 14, 1982, p. 449.

27. Rochelle L. Stanfield, "Ready for 'New Federalism,' Phase II? Turning Tax Sources Back to the States," *National Journal*, August 22, 1981, p. 1492.

28. Rochelle L. Stanfield, "Block Grants Look Fine to States; It's the Money That's the Problem," *National Journal*, May 9, 1981, p. 831.

29. Rochelle L. Stanfield, "Reagan's Policies Bring Cities, States Together in Marriage of Convenience," *National Journal*, December 19, 1981, p. 2224.

30. Harrison Donnelly, "Reagan Changes Focus With Federalism Plan," *Congressional Quarterly Weekly Report*, January 30, 1982, p. 152.

31. Dan Pilcher, "Sorting Out the Federal System: The Choices," *State Legislatures* (February 1982), p. 17.

32. Jack A. Meyer, "Private Sector Initiatives and Public Policy: A New Agenda," in *Meeting Human Needs: Toward a New Public Philosophy*, Jack A. Meyer ed. (Washington, D.C.: American Enterprise Institute, 1982), p. 6.

Chapter 5

1. William S. Gilbert, "Iolanthe II," quoted in "Liberal and Conservative," in Bergen Evans, *Dictionary of Quotations* (New York: Delacorte Press, 1968), p. 385.

2. *The Rodgers and Hammerstein Song Book* (New York: Simon and Schuster, Williamson Music, Inc., 1968), pp. 169–171.

3. James C. Davies, *Human Nature in Politics: The Dynamics of Political Socialization* (New York: John Wiley & Sons, 1963), p. 175.

4. Richard M. Merelman, "Democratic Politics and the Culture of American Education," with a comment by M. Kent Jennings and reply by Merelman, *American Political Science Review*, 74 (June 1980), pp. 319–431.

5. M. Kent Jennings and Richard G. Niemi, *The Political Character of Adolescence: The Influence of Families and Schools* (Princeton, N.J.: Princeton University Press, 1974), pp. 246, 328.

6. Bruce A. Campbell, "A Theoretical Approach to Peer Influence in Adolescent Socialization," *American Journal of Political Science*, 24 (May 1980), pp. 324–344.

7. Sidney Kraus and Dennis Davis, *The Effects of Mass Communications on Political Behavior* (University Park, Pa.: Pennsylvania State University Press, 1976), pp. 8–47.
8. Doris A. Graber, *Mass Media and American Politics* (Washington, D.C.: Congressional Quarterly Press, 1980), p. 122.
9. National Institute of Mental Health, *Television and Behavior*, 2 vols. (Rockville, Md.: National Institute of Mental Health, 1982).
10. V.O. Key, Jr., *Public Opinion and American Democracy* (New York: Alfred A. Knopf, 1961), pp. 8, 14.
11. Bernard Hennessy, *Public Opinion*, 4th ed. (Monterey, Calif.: Brooks/Cole Publishing Company, 1981), p. 4.
12. Robert S. Erikson, Norman R. Luttbeg, and Kent L. Tedin, *American Public Opinion: Its Origins, Content, and Impact* (New York: John Wiley & Sons, 1980), p. 4.
13. Robert E. Lane and David O. Sears, *Public Opinion* (Englewood Cliffs, N.J.: Prentice-Hall, 1964), pp. 6–16.
14. Lester W. Milbrath, *Political Participation* (Chicago: Rand McNally, 1965), p. 18.
15. Sidney Verba and Norman H. Nie, *Participation in America* (New York: Harper and Row, 1972), p. 31.
16. Richard G. Smolka, *Election Day Registration: The Minnesota and Wisconsin Experience in 1976* (Washington, D.C.: American Enterprise Institute, 1977).
17. Norman H. Nie and Sidney Verba, "Political Participation," in Fred I. Greenstein and Nelson W. Polsby, eds., *Nongovernmental Politics*, vol. 4 of the *Handbook of Political Science* (Reading, Mass.: Addison-Wesley, 1975), p. 69.

Chapter 6

1. Everett Carll Ladd, ed. "Opinion Roundup: Election '82," *Public Opinion* 5 (December/January) 1983, p. 21.
2. Frank J. Sorauf, Party Politics in America, 4th ed. (Boston: Little, Brown, 1980), p. 6.
3. V.O. Key, Jr., *Politics, Parties, and Pressure Groups*, 5th ed. (New York:

Thomas Y. Crowell Co., 1964), pp. 163–165.
4. Jack C. Plano and Milton Greenberg, *The American Political Dictionary*, 3d ed. (Hinsdale, Illinois: The Dryden Press, 1972), p. 132.
5. Sorauf, *op. cit.*, p. 7.
6. *Ibid*, p. 8.
7. Clinton Rossiter, *Parties and Politics in America* (Ithaca, N.Y.: Cornell University Press, 1960), p. 3.
8. For an excellent summary of these theories, see Sorauf, *op. cit.*, pp. 38–40.
9. Gerald Pomper, "Party Loyalty and Party Choice," in David W. Abbott and Edward T. Rogowsky, eds., *Political Parties*, 2d ed. (Chicago: Rand McNally, 1978). p. 264.
10. Richard Hofstadter, *The Idea of a Party System* (Berkeley, Calif.: University of California Press, 1969), pp. 70–71.
11. James McGregor Burns, *The Deadlock of Democracy: Four-Party Politics in America* (Englewood Cliffs, N.J.: Prentice-Hall, 1963).
12. Walter Dean Burnham, *Critical Elections and the Mainsprings of American Politics* (New York: W.W. Norton & Co., 1970).
13. Steven J. Rosenstone, Roy L. Behr, and Edward H. Lazarus, *Third Party Voting in America,* to be published and copyright ©1984 by Princeton University Press. Fig. 1.1 reprinted by permission of Princeton University Press.
14. Cornelius P. Cotter and Bernard C. Hennessy, *Politics Without Power: The National Party Committees* (New York: Atherton, 1964).
15. Sarah McCally Morehouse, *State Politics, Parties and Policy* (New York: Holt, Rinehart & Winston, 1980).
16. Peter B. Clark and James Q. Wilson, "Incentive Systems: A Theory of Organizations," *Administrative Science Quarterly*, 6 (September 1961), pp. 129–166.
17. Gordon Henderson, *An Introduction to Political Parties* (New York: Harper and Row, 1976), p. 133 ff.
18. Raymond E. Wolfinger, "Why Political Machines Have Not Withered Away and Other Revisionist Thoughts," in David W. Abbott and Edward T. Rogowsku, eds., *Political Parties*, 2d ed. (Chi-

cago: Rand McNally, 1978), pp. 51–76.
19. Norman H. Nie, Sidney Verba, and John R. Petrocik, *The Changing American Voter* (Cambridge, Mass.: Harvard University Press, 1979), p. 270 ff.
20. David S. Broder, *The Party's Over: The Failure of Politics in America* (New York: Harper and Row, 1971).

Chapter 7

1. V.O. Key, Jr., *Politics, Parties, and Pressure Groups*, 5th ed. (New York: Thomas Y. Crowell Co., 1964), p. 18.
2. Carol S. Greenwald, *Group Power: Lobbying and Public Policy* (New York: Praeger, 1977), p. 20.
3. *Ibid.*, p. 50.
4. Alexander Hamilton, James Madison, and John Jay, *The Federalist Papers: A Collection of Essays Written in Support of the Constitution of the United States*, ed. Roy P. Fairfield, 2d. ed. (New York: Doubleday, Anchor Books, 1966), p. 17.
5. E.E. Schattschneider, *The Semisovereign People* (New York: Holt, Rinehart & Winston, 1960).
6. Timothy B. Clark, "The Public and the Private Sectors—The Old Distinctions Grow Fuzzy," *National Journal*, January 19, 1980, p. 104.
7. Jim Craig, "Too Many Voices: Hispanic Lobby Not Able to Present United Front," *Houston Post*, May 14, 1981.
8. William J. Lanouette, "The Many Faces of the Jewish Lobby in America," *National Journal*, May 13, 1978, pp. 748–756.
9. Jeffrey M. Berry, *Lobbying for the People: The Political Behavior of Public Interest Groups* (Princeton, N.J.: Princeton University Press, 1977), p. 7.
10. *Ibid.*, p. 29.
11. "Public Interest Groups: Balancing the Scales," *The Washington Lobby*, 3d ed. (Washington, D.C.: Congressional Quarterly Press, October 1979), p. 172.
12. David Vogel, "The Public-Interest Movement and the American Reform Tradition," *Political Science Quarterly*, 95 (Winter 1980–81), p. 623.

13. Berry, *op. cit.*, p. 288.
14. Key, *op. cit.*, p. 105.
15. Joyce Gelb and Marian Lief Palley, "Women and Interest Group Politics: A Comparative Analysis of Federal Decisionmaking," *The Journal of Politics*, 41 (May 1979), pp. 362–392.
16. Sue Bessmer, "Anti-Obscenity: A Comparison of the Legal and the Feminist Perspectives," *The Western Political Quarterly*, 34 (March 1981), pp. 143–155.
17. Lisa B. Belkin, "For State and Local Governments, Washington Is the Place to Be," *National Journal*, September 6, 1980, p. 1486.
18. Dennis S. Ippolito and Thomas G. Walker, *Political Parties, Interest Groups, and Public Policy: Group Influence in American Politics* (Englewood Cliffs, N.J.: Prentice-Hall, 1980), p. 308.
19. Barry M. Hager, "Biographical Sketches of Men and Women Who Lobby Congress for Departments," *Congressional Quarterly Weekly Report*, March 4, 1978, p. 583.
20. Elizabeth Wehr, "Reagan's Team on the Hill Getting Members' Praise for Hard Work, Experience," *Congressional Quarterly Weekly Report*, May 2, 1981, p. 750.
21. Bill Keller, "In a Bull Market for Arms, Weapons Industry Lobbyists Push Products, Not Policy," *Congressional Quarterly Weekly Report*, October 25, 1980, p. 3203.
22. Michael R. Gordon, "The Image Makers in Washington—PR Firms Have Found a Natural Home," *National Journal*, May 31, 1980, p. 885.
23. Key, *op. cit.*, p. 141.
24. Norman J. Ornstein and Shirley Elder, *Interest Groups: Lobbying and Policymaking* (Washington, D.C.: Congressional Quarterly Press, 1978), p. 3.
25. Greenwald, *op. cit.*, p. 64.
26. *Ibid.*
27. Bill Keller, "Castoff Congressmen Find More Money and Less Misery Lobbying Former Colleagues," *Congressional Quarterly Weekly Report*, December 20, 1980, p. 3648.
28. "1946 Lobby Act Is Narrowly Interpreted," *Current American Government*: *Spring 1981 Guide* (Washington, D.C.: Congressional Quarterly, Inc., 1981), p. 113.
29. James MacGregor Burns, J.W. Peltason, and Thomas E. Cronin, *Government by the People*, 11th ed. (Englewood Cliffs, N.J.: Prentice-Hall, 1981), pp. 193–194.
30. Bill Keller, "Congressional Rating Game Is Hard to Win," *Congressional Quarterly Weekly Report*, March 21, 1981, p. 507.
31. Ippolito and Walker, *op. cit.*, p. 323.
32. Maxwell Glen, "Liberal Political Action Committees Borrow a Page from the Conservatives," *National Journal*, July 4, 1981, p. 1198.
33. Karen O'Connor, *Women's Organizations' Use of the Courts* (Lexington, Mass.: Lexington Books, 1980), p. 4.
34. *Ibid.*

Chapter 8

1. James W. Davis, *Presidential Primaries: Road to the White House* (Westport, Conn.: Greenwood Press, 1980).
2. Arthur T. Hadley, *The Invisible Primary* (Englewood Cliffs, N.J.: Prentice-Hall, 1976), p. 2.
3. The list is based on quotes from *Ibid.*, pp. 14–19.
4. Richard A. Watson, *The Presidential Contest* (New York: John Wiley & Sons, 1980), p. 14.
5. Donald R. Matthews, "Winnowing," in *Race for the Presidency: The Media and the Nominating Process*, James David Barber ed. (Englewood Cliffs, N.J.: Prentice-Hall, 1978), pp. 66–71.
6. "Face Off: A Conversation with the Presidents' Pollsters Patrick Caddell and Richard Wirthlin," *Public Opinion*, 3 (December/January 1981), pp. 2–13, 63, 64.
7. Gerald M. Pomper, with Susan S. Lederman, *Elections in America: Control and Influence in Democratic Politics*, 2d ed. (New York: Longman, 1980), pp. 173, 174.
8. Congressional Quarterly, Inc., *National Party Conventions: 1831–1972* (Washington, D.C.: Congressional Quarterly, Inc., 1976), p. 7.
9. Quoted in Larry J. Sabato, *The Rise of Political Consultants: New Ways of Winning Elections* (New York: Basic Books, Inc., 1981). The next five paragraphs borrow heavily from Sabato's work.
10. *Ibid.*, p. 128.
11. Michael J. Robinson, "The Media in 1980: Was the Message the Message?" in *The American Elections of 1980*, Austin Ranney ed. (Washington, D.C.: American Enterprise Institute, 1981), p. 191. The Robinson essay has heavily influenced this section on media.
12. The text of the Reagan-Carter debate is printed in the appendices of David Broder, Lou Cannon, Haynes Johnson, Martin Schram, Richard Harwood, and the staff of the *Washington Post*, *The Pursuit of the Presidency 1980* (New York: Berkley Books, 1980); the quote is on p. 399.
13. Richard E. Cohen, "Costly Campaigns: Candidates Learn That Reaching Voters is Expensive," *National Journal*, April 16, 1983, p. 782.

Chapter 9

1. In chapter 8 we relied on a number of journalistic accounts of the 1980 election. Examples of authors of illustrative sources include David Broder, Jack W. Germond, Jules Witcover, Elizabeth Drew, and Theodore White.
2. Angus Campbell, Philip E. Converse, Warren E. Miller, and Donald E. Stokes, *The American Voter* (New York: John Wiley & Sons, 1960).
3. Norman H. Nie, Sidney Verba, and John R. Petrocik, *The Changing American Voter* (Cambridge, Mass.: Harvard University Press, 1979).
4. V.O. Key, Jr., "A Theory of Critical Elections," *Journal of Politics*, 17 (February 1955), pp. 3–18; Ruth C. Silva, *Rum, Religion and Votes* (University Park, Pa.: Pennsylvania State University Press, 1962).
5. Nie, Verba, and Petrocik, *op. cit.*, pp. 45, 318.
6. Angus Campbell, Philip E. Converse, Warren E. Miller, and Donald Stokes, *Elections and the Po-*

litical Order (New York: John Wiley & Sons, 1966), p. 123.

7. Arthur H. Miller and Martin P. Wattenberg, "Policy and Performance Voting in the 1980 Election"; Warren E. Miller, "Policy Directions and Presidential Leadership: Alternative Interpretations of the 1980 Presidential Election"; Gregory B. Markus, "Political Attitudes During an Election Year: A Report on the 1980 NES Panel Study"; and John R. Petrocik, Sidney Verba, with Christine Schultz, "Choosing the Choice and Not the Echo: A Funny Thing Happened to The Changing American Voter on the Way to the 1980 Election." All four papers were prepared for delivery at the Annual meeting of the American Political Science Association, New York, September 3–6, 1981.

8. "1980 Results: What the Election Showed," Public Opinion, 3 (December/January 1981), pp. 21–44.

9. The statistics on the issues in the 1980 election come from W. Miller, op. cit., pp. 10–41, and Markus, op. cit., pp. 7–13.

10. Winner Take All: Report of the Twentieth Century Fund Task Force on Reform of the Presidential Election Process, with a background paper by William R. Keech (New York: Holmes & Meier Publishers, 1978), pp. 3–13.

11. Wallace S. Sayre and Judith R. Parris, Voting for President (Washington, D.C.: Brookings Institution, 1970); Alexander M. Bickel, Reform and Continuity (New York: Harper and Row, 1971); Congressional Quarterly, Inc., Elections '80 (Washington, D.C.: Congressional Quarterly, Inc., 1980), pp. 29–41.

12. Thad L. Beyle, "Gubernatorial Campaign Costs Entering the 1980's," unpublished paper prepared for delivery at the annual meeting of the Midwest Political Science Association, Milwaukee, Wisconsin, April 30, 1981.

13. James MacGregor Burns, J.W. Peltason, and Thomas E. Cronin, Government by the People, 11th ed. (Englewood Cliffs, N.J.: Prentice-Hall, 1981), pp. 193–194.

14. Dom Bonafede, "Costly Campaigns: Consultants Cash In As Candidates Spend What They Must," National Journal, April 16, 1983, p. 789.

Chapter 10

1. "Nation's Press is 'Full of Itself,' Former Editor Tells Publishers," Houston Chronicle, April 17, 1982.

2. "Former NBC News Chief Says Press Serving Better Than Ever," Houston Chronicle, May 1, 1982.

3. Thomas Carlyle, as quoted by Dom Bonafede, "A New Elite," National Journal, December 19, 1981, p. 2250.

4. Theodore White in The Making of the President, 1972, quoted in Donald L. Shaw and Maxwell E. McCombs, The Emergence of American Political Issues: The Agenda Setting Function of the Press (St. Paul, Minn.: West Publishing Co., 1977), p. 6.

5. John Immerwahr and John Doble, "Public Attitudes Toward Freedom of the Press," Public Opinion Quarterly, 46 (Summer 1982), p. 177.

6. Edwin M. Yoder, Jr., " 'Voluntary Censorship' Has Its Hazards, Too," Houston Chronicle, March 24, 1982.

7. Gallup Report, No. 196 (January 1982), pp. 34–36.

8. Thomas Patterson and Robert McClure, The Unseeing Eye: The Myth of Television Power in National Elections (New York: G.P. Putnam's Sons, 1976), p. 138.

9. Dom Bonafede, "The Press Does Some Soul Searching in Reviewing its Campaign Coverage," National Journal, November 29, 1980, pp. 2034–2035.

10. Dom Bonafede, "The Washington Press—An Interpreter or a Participant in Policy Making?" National Journal, April 24, 1982, p. 721.

11. "Networks' Heyday in TV Coming to a Close?" U.S. News & World Report, April 5, 1982, p. 62.

12. Ron Powers, "Eyewitless News," Columbia Journalism Review, 16 (May/June 1977), pp. 17–23.

13. "TV News Programs," Journalism Quarterly, 59 (Spring 1982), pp. 74–79.

14. M.T. Malloy, quoted in David L.

Altheide, Creating Reality: How TV News Distorts Events (Beverly Hills, Calif.: Sage Publications, 1976), p. 20.

15. Anne Rawley Saldich, Electronic Democracy: Television's Impact on the American Political Process (New York: Praeger, 1979), p. 36.

16. Jenkin Lloyd Jones, "Media Brought to the Woodshed," Houston Chronicle, May 22, 1982.

17. Judith Lemon, "Dominant or Dominated? Women on Prime-Time Television," in Hearth and Home: Images of Women in the Mass Media, Gaye Tuchman, Arlene Kaplan Daniels, and James Benét (eds.). (New York: Oxford University Press, 1978), p. 52.

18. Study by Neil Vidmar and Milton Rokeach, "Archie Bunker's Bigotry: A Study in Selective Perception and Exposure," Journal of Communication, 24 (Winter 1974), pp. 36–47; cited by Thomas R. Dye in Who's Running America? 2d ed. (Englewood Cliffs, N.J.: Prentice-Hall, 1979), pp. 108–109.

19. Julian Hale, Radio Power: Propaganda and International Broadcasting (Philadelphia: Temple University Press, 1975), p. ix.

20. David Shaw, Journalism Today: A Changing Press for a Changing America (New York: Harper and Row, 1977), pp. 4–5.

21. Anthony Smith, Goodbye Gutenberg: The Newspaper Revolution of the 1980s (New York: Oxford University Press, 1980), p. 55.

22. Shaw, op. cit., p. 55.

23. Ibid., p. 73.

24. Ibid., p. 88.

25. Stephen Hess and Milton Kaplan, The Ungentlemanly Art: A History of American Political Cartoons (New York: The Macmillan Company, 1975), p. 13.

26. Charles Manatt, quoted in Shaw, op. cit., p. 78.

27. Patterson and McClure, op. cit., pp. 51–53.

28. See Maxwell E. McCombs and Donald L. Shaw, "Stimulating the Unseen Environment," Journal of Communications, 26 (Spring 1976), pp. 18–22; D. Charles Whitney and Lee B. Becker, " 'Keeping the Gates' for Gatekeepers: The Effects of Wire

News,'' *Journalism Quarterly*, 59 (Spring 1982), pp. 60-65.

29. Benjamin M. Compaine, *Who Owns the Media? Concentration of Ownership in the Mass Communications Industry* (New York: Harmony Books, 1979), p. 34.

30. James H. Rosse, *Economic Limits of Press Responsibility*, Studies in Industry Economics, No. 56 (Stanford, Calif.: Department of Economics, Stanford University, 1975).

31. Doris A. Graber, *Mass Media and American Politics* (Washington, D.C.: Congressional Quarterly Press, 1980), p. 35.

32. Bernard Roshco, *Newsmaking* (Chicago: University of Chicago Press, 1975), p. 9.

33. Lou Cannon, *Reporting: An Inside View* (Sacramento, Calif.: California Journal Press, 1977), p. 15.

34. *Ibid.*, p. 16.

35. Edith Efron, ''Why Speech on Television is *Not* Really Free,'' *TV Guide*, 12, April 11, 1964.

36. Graber, *op. cit.*, pp. 63-64.

37. Leo C. Rosten, *The Washington Correspondents* (New York: Harcourt, Brace, 1937), pp. 149-150.

38. Quoted in Cannon, *op. cit.*, p. 34.

39. John L. Hulteng, *The News Media: What Makes Them Tick?* (Englewood Cliffs, N.J.: Prentice-Hall, 1979), p. 40.

40. Leon V. Sigal, *Reporters and Officials: The Organization and Politics of Newsmaking* (Lexington, Mass.: D.C. Heath, 1973).

41. David L. Paletz and Robert M. Entman, *Media Power Politics* (New York: The Free Press, 1981), p. 20.

42. Rosten, *op. cit.*, p. 352.

43. Mark Fishman, *Manufacturing the News* (Austin, Tex: University of Texas Press, 1980), p. 8.

44. Saldich, *op. cit.*, p. 37.

45. Stephen Hess, *The Washington Reporters* (Washington, D.C.: The Brookings Institution, 1981); S. Robert Lichter and Stanley Rothman, ''Media and Business Elites,'' *Public Opinion*, 4 (October/November 1981), pp. 42-46, 59-60.

46. S. Robert Lichter and Stanley Rothman, ''Media and Business Elites,'' *Public Opinion*, 4 (October/November 1981), pp. 59-60.

47. Everett Carll Ladd, ed., ''Opinion Roundup: Hyping the Media,'' *Public Opinion*, 4 (October/November 1981), p. 36.

48. Dom Bonafede, ''The Washington Press—Competing for Power with the Federal Government,'' *National Journal*, April 17, 1982, p. 666.

49. Ron Powers, *The Newscasters* (New York: St. Martin's Press, 1977), pp. 3-4.

50. Paletz and Entman, *op. cit.*, p. 24.

51. Sigal, *op. cit.*, p. 293.

52. Charles S. Steinberg, *The Information Establishment: Our Government and the Media* (New York: Hastings House, 1980), p. 38.

53. *Ibid.*, p. 59.

54. *Ibid.*, p. 76.

55. Hess, *op. cit.*, p. 17.

56. Steinberg, *op. cit.*, p. 77.

57. Charles Peters, *How Washington Really Works* (Reading, Mass.: Addison-Wesley, 1980), pp. 25-26.

58. Hess, *op. cit.*, p. 100.

59. *Ibid.*

60. ''CBS Stands By Its Story—Sort Of,'' *Newsweek*, July 26, 1982, p. 77.

61. Cannon, *op. cit.*, p. 217.

62. John Herbers, ''The Media vs. Reagan's Message,'' *Houston Chronicle*, May 9, 1982.

63. Paletz and Entman, *op. cit.*, p. 88.

64. Bob Woodward and Scott Armstrong, *The Brethren* (New York: Simon & Schuster, 1979).

65. Paletz and Entman, *op. cit.*, p. 101.

Chapter 11

1. James L. Sundquist, *Politics and Policy* (Washington, D.C.: Brookings Institution, 1968).

2. Gary Orfield, *Congressional Power* (New York: Harcourt, Brace, 1975).

3. James E. Anderson, David W. Brady, and Charles S. Bullock, III, *Public Policy and Politics in America* (North Scituate, Mass.: Duxbury Press, 1978), p. 144.

4. Barbara Hinckley, *Congressional Elections* (Washington, D.C.: Congressional Quarterly, 1981), p. 49.

5. Cf. John R. Johannes, ''Casework as a Technique of U.S. Congressional Oversight of the Execu-

tive,'' *Legislative Studies Quarterly*, 4 (August 1979), pp. 325-351.

6. Frederick C. Mosher, *Democracy and the Public Sector* (New York: Oxford University Press, 1968), pp. 11-13.

7. Former Representative Otis Pike (D-N.Y.), quoted in Kathy Sawyer, ''Former Rep. Otis Pike: The New Boy on the Bus,'' *Washington Post*, October 5, 1979.

8. Harrell R. Rodgers, Jr., *Crisis in Democracy* (Reading, Mass.: Addison-Wesley, 1978), pp. 73 ff.

9. James Q. Wilson and Edward Banfield, ''Public-Regardingness as a Value Premise in Voting Behavior,'' *American Political Science Review*, 58 (December 1964), pp. 876-887.

10. Irwin H. Gertzog, ''Changing Patterns of Female Recruitment to the U.S. House of Representatives,'' *Legislative Studies Quarterly*, 4 (August 1979), p. 432.

11. Charles S. Bullock, III and Patricia L.F. Heys, ''Recruitment of Women for Congress: A Research Note,'' *Western Political Quarterly*, 25 (September 1972), pp. 416-423.

12. David R. Mayhew, ''Congressional Elections: The Case of the Vanishing Marginals,'' *Polity*, 6 (1974), pp. 295-317.

13. Barbara Hinckley, ''House Reelections and Senate Defeats: The Role of the Challenger,'' *British Journal of Political Science*, 10 (October 1980), pp. 441-460; Alan I. Abramowitz, ''A Comparison of Voting for U.S. Senator and Representative in 1978,'' *American Political Science Review*, 74 (September 1980), pp. 633-640.

14. M. Margaret Conway and Mikel L. Wyckoff, ''The Kelley-Meier Rule and Prediction of Voter Choice in the 1974 Senate Election,'' *Journal of Politics*, 42 (November 1980), pp. 1146-1152.

15. Hinckley, *Congressional Elections*, *op. cit.*, p. 44.

16. Figures on trips home are for the Ninety-Fourth Congress, Glenn R. Parker, ''Sources of Change in Congressional District Attentiveness,'' *American Journal of Political Science*, 24 (February 1980), p. 115.

17. John Sullivan and Eric Uslaner,

"Congressional Behavior and Election Marginality," *American Journal of Political Science*, 22 (August 1978), pp. 536–553.

18. Gary C. Jacobson, "Incumbents Advantage in the 1978 U.S. Congressional Elections," *Legislative Studies Quarterly*, 6 (May 1981), pp. 183–200.

19. Hinckley, *Congressional Elections*, op. cit., p. 44.

20. Richard F. Fenno, Jr., *Congressmen in Committees* (Boston: Little, Brown, 1973), chapter 1.

21. Morris P. Fiorina, *Congress: Keystone of the Washington Establishment* (New Haven, Conn.: Yale University Press, 1977).

22. Richard F. Fenno, Jr., *Home Style: House Members in Their Districts* (Boston: Little, Brown, 1978).

23. Fenno, *Congressmen*, op. cit., p. 3.

24. Donald Matthews, *U.S. Senators and Their World* (New York: Norton, 1973), p. 95.

25. Herbert B. Asher, "The Learning of Legislative Norms," *American Political Science Review*, 67 (June 1973), pp. 499–513.

26. Fenno, Jr., *Home Style*, op. cit., pp. 163–168.

27. James W. Dyson and John W. Soule, "Congressional Committee Behavior on Roll Call Votes: The U.S. House of Representatives," *Midwest Journal of Political Science*, 14 (November 1970), pp. 626–647; Anne L. Lewis, "Floor Success as a Measure of Committee Performance in the House," *Journal of Politics*, 40 (May 1978), pp. 460–467.

28. Charles S. Bullock, III, "Motivations for U.S. Congressional Committee Preferences," *Legislative Studies Quarterly*, 1 (May 1977), pp. 201–212.

29. Kenneth A. Shepsle, *The Giant Jigsaw Puzzle* (Chicago: University of Chicago Press, 1978), p. 213; Charles S. Bullock, III, "House Committee Assignments," in *The Congressional System: Notes and Readings* 2d ed., Leroy N. Rieselbach ed. (North Scituate, Mass.: Duxbury Press, 1979), p. 73.

30. Irwin N. Gertzog, "The Routinization of Committee Assignments in the U.S. House of Representatives," *American Journal of Political Science*, 20 (November 1976), p. 698; Nicholas A. Masters, "Committee Assignments in the House of Representatives," *American Political Science Review*, 55 (June 1961), pp. 345–357.

31. The discussion of the Rules Committee relies heavily on Bruce I. Oppenheimer, "The Rules Committee: New Arm of Leadership in a Decentralized House," in *Congress Reconsidered*, Lawrence C. Dodd and Bruce I. Oppenheimer eds. (New York: Praeger, 1977), pp. 96–116.

32. John W. Kingdon, *Congressmen's Voting Decisions* (New York: Harper and Row, 1973), pp. 41–42.

33. Ibid., pp. 230–232.

34. H. Owen Porter, "Legislative Experts and Outsiders: The Two-Step Flow of Communication," *Journal of Politics*, 36 (August 1974), pp. 703–730.

35. Michael T. Hayes, "The Semi-Sovereign Pressure Groups: A Critique of Current Theory and an Alternative Typology," *Journal of Politics*, 40 (February 1978), pp. 138–161.

36. Matthews, op. cit., p. 123; Randall Ripley, *Party Leaders in the House of Representatives* (Washington, D.C.: Brookings Institution, 1967), p. 143.

37. David R. Mayhew, *Party Loyalty Among Congressmen* (Cambridge, Mass.: Harvard University Press, 1966); Julius Turner, *Party and Constituency Pressures on Congress* (Baltimore, Md.: John Hopkins University Press, 1951), rev. ed. by Edward V. Schneier, Jr. (1970).

38. David W. Brady, "Critical Elections, Congressional Parties, and Clusters of Policy Change," *British Journal of Political Science*, 8 (1978), pp. 79–99.

39. Barbara Sinclair, *Congressional Alignment, 1925–1978* (Austin, Tex.: University of Texas Press, 1982); Aage R. Clausen, *How Congressmen Decide* (New York: St. Martin's Press, 1973).

40. Lewis A. Froman, Jr. and Randall B. Ripley, "Conditions for Party Leadership: The Case of the House Democrats," *American Political Science Review*, 59 (March 1965), pp. 52–63.

41. Robert M. Stein and James L. Regens, "Empirical Typology of Congressional Oversight" paper presented at the Annual Meeting of the Southwest Political Science Association, Houston, Tex., April 12–15, 1978.

42. Fred Kaiser, "Oversight of Foreign Policy: The U.S. House Committee on International Relations," *Legislative Studies Quarterly*, 2 (August 1977), pp. 255–280.

43. William Greider, "The Education of David Stockman," *Atlantic*, 248 (December 1981), p. 30.

44. Heinz Eulau and Paul D. Karps, "The Puzzle of Representation: Specifying Components of Responsiveness," *Legislative Studies Quarterly*, 2 (August 1977), p. 241.

45. Fiorina, op. cit., pp. 39–49.

46. Art Harris, "Drawlin' and Brawlin'," *Washington Post*, August 23, 1980.

47. Bruce I. Oppenheimer, "Policy Effects of U.S. House Reform: Decentralization and the Capacity to Resolve Energy Issues," *Legislative Studies Quarterly*, 5 (February 1980), p. 28.

48. Bruce I. Oppenheimer, "The Rules Committee," op. cit., pp. 96–116.

49. Albert D. Cover and David R. Mayhew, "Congressional Dynamics and the Decline of Competitive Congressional Elections," in *Congress Reconsidered*, 2d ed., Lawrence C. Dodd and Bruce I. Oppenheimer eds. (Washington, D.C.: Congressional Quarterly, 1981), p. 80.

50. Graham T. Allison, "Making War: The President and Congress," in *The Presidency Reappraised*, 2d ed., Thomas E. Cronin and Rexford G. Tugwell eds. (New York: Praeger, 1979), pp. 228–247.

51. This section draws on Lance T. Le Loup, *The Fiscal Congress* (Westport, Conn.: Greenwood Press, 1980) and Allen Schick, *Congress and Money* (Washington, D.C.: Urban Institute, 1980).

52. Norman I. Ornstein, Thomas E. Mann, Michael J. Malbin, and John F. Bibby, *Vital Statistics on*

Congress, 1982 (Washington, D.C.: American Enterprise Institute, 1982), p. 110.

53. Cf. Froman and Ripley, *op. cit.*, pp. 52–63.

54. John S. Saloma, III, *Congress and the New Politics* (Boston: Little, Brown, 1969), pp. 8–14; Roger H. Davidson, David M. Kovenock, and Michael K. O'Leary, *Congress in Crisis* (Belmont, Calif.: Wadsworth Publishing Co., 1966), pp. 52–53.

55. John F. Bibby, Thomas E. Mann, and Norman J. Ornstein, *Vital Statistics on Congress, 1980* (Washington, D.C.: American Enterprise Institute, 1980), p. 90.

56. This section draws on Stephen E. Frantzich, "Computerized Information Technology in the U.S. House of Representatives," *Legislative Studies Quarterly*, 4 (May 1979), pp. 255–280.

57. Ornstein, Mann, Malbin, and Bibby, *op. cit.*, p. 69; Bibby, Mann, and Ornstein, *op. cit.*, p. 24.

58. Benjamin Ginsberg and John Green, "The Best Congress Money Can Buy: Campaign Contributions and Congressional Behavior," paper presented at the Annual Meeting of the American Political Science Association, Washington, D.C., August 31–September 3, 1979, p. 13.

59. Richard F. Fenno, Jr., "If, as Ralph Nader says, Congress Is 'The Broken Branch,' How Come We Love Our Congressman So Much?" In *Congress in Change*, Norman J. Ornstein ed. (New York: Praeger, 1975), pp. 277–287.

60. Glenn R. Parker and Roger H. Davidson, "Why Do Americans Love Their Congressmen So Much More Than Their Congress?" *Legislative Studies Quarterly*, 4 (February 1979) pp. 53–61.

61. Timothy E. Cook, "Legislative vs. Legislator: A Note on the Paradox of Congressional Support," *Legislative Studies Quarterly*, 4 (February 1979), pp. 43–52.

62. Glenn R. Parker, "Some Themes in Congressional Popularity," *American Journal of Political Science*, 21 (February 1977), pp. 93–109.

Chapter 12

1. "President Reagan's Inaugural Address," *Congressional Quarterly Weekly Report*, January 24, 1981, p. 186.

2. From a radio and television interview, December 16, 1982. Cited in Marian D. Irish, James W. Prothro, and Richard J. Richardson, *Politics of American Democracy*, 7th ed. (Englewood Cliffs, N.J.: Prentice-Hall, 1981), p. 309.

3. Louis Fisher, *Presidents and Congress: Power and Policy* (New York: Free Press, 1972), p. 54.

4. Jack C. Plano and Milton Greenberg, *The American Political Dictionary*, 3d ed. (Hinsdale, Ill.: Dryden Press, 1972), p. 197.

5. Fisher, *op. cit.*, pp. 50–52.

6. Leonard C. Meeker, "The Legality of U.S. Participation in the Defense of Vietnam," *Department of State Bulletin*, 28 (March 1966), pp. 484–485.

7. Comments of Senator Frank Church (D-Idaho), quoted in Thomas E. Cronin, "A Resurgent Congress and the Imperial Presidency," *Political Science Quarterly*, 95 (Summer 1980), p. 213.

8. Plano and Greenberg, *op. cit.*, p. 390.

9. Irish, Prothro, and Richardson, *op. cit.*, p. 314.

10. Plano and Greenberg, *op. cit.*, p. 372.

11. Cronin, *op. cit.*, p. 213.

12. David L. Paletz and Robert M. Entman, *Media Power Politics* (New York: Free Press, 1981), p. 55.

13. Dom Bonafede, "That's Mike Deaver at the Hub of Ronald Reagan's Presidential World," *National Journal*, August 15, 1981, p. 1464.

14. Merlin Gustafson, "Our Part-Time Chief of State," *Presidential Studies Quarterly*, 9 (Spring 1979), p. 168.

15. Elizabeth Wehr, "Public Liaison Chief Dole Reaches to Outside Groups to Sell Reagan's Programs," *Congressional Quarterly Weekly Report*, June 6, 1981, p. 978.

16. Elizabeth Wehr, "White House Lobbying Apparatus Produces Impressive Tax Vote Victory,"

Congressional Quarterly Weekly Report, August 1, 1981, p. 1372.

17. Paletz and Entman, *op. cit.*, p. 59.

18. Michael Grossman and Martha Kumar, *Portraying the President: The White House and the News Media* (Baltimore: Johns Hopkins University Press, 1981).

19. Paletz and Entman, *op. cit.*, p. 65.

20. "President Reagan's TV Address on Tax Bill," *Congressional Quarterly Weekly Report*, August 1, 1981, p. 1405.

21. Grossman and Kumar, *op. cit.*, cited by Michael Jay Robinson and Margaret Sheehan, "Brief Encounters with the Fourth Kind: Reagan's Press Honeymoon," *Public Opinion*, 3 (December/January, 1981), p. 59.

22. Richard E. Neustadt, *Presidential Power: The Politics of Leadership from FDR to Carter* (New York: John Wiley & Sons, Inc., 1980), p. 35.

23. Dom Bonafede, "The Reagan's Bring a New Ambience to the Washington Social Scene," *National Journal*, June 6, 1981, p. 1021.

24. *Ibid.*, pp. 1021–1024.

25. James David Barber, *The Presidential Character: Predicting Performance in the White House* (Englewood Cliffs, N.J.: Prentice-Hall, 1977), p. 7.

26. Dom Bonafede, "From a 'Revolution' to a 'Stumble'—The Press Assesses the First 100 Days," *National Journal*, May 16, 1981, p. 879.

27. Aaron Wildavsky, "The Two Presidencies," in Aaron Wildavsky, ed., *Perspectives on the Presidency* (Boston: Little, Brown, 1975), p. 448.

28. Lee Sigelman, "A Reassessment of the Two Presidencies Thesis," *Journal of Politics*, 41 (November 1979), pp. 1195–1205.

29. Dick Kirschten, "Wanted: 275 Reagan Team Players: Empire Builders Need Not Apply," *National Journal*, December 6, 1980, p. 2078.

30. *Ibid.*, p. 2079.

31. James J. Best, "Presidential Cabinet Appointments: 1953–1976," *Presidential Studies Quarterly*, 11 (Winter 1981), p. 64.

32. Clinton Rossiter, *The American*

Presidency, rev. ed. (New York: Mentor Books, 1980), pp. 55–56.

33. Joseph Kallenbach, *The American Chief Executive: The Presidency and the Governorship* (New York: Harper and Row, 1966), p. 387.

34. Louis Fisher and Ronald C. Moe, "Presidential Reorganization Authority: Is It Worth the Cost?" *Political Science Quarterly*, 96 (Summer 1981), p. 306.

35. *Ibid.*, p. 305.

36. *Ibid.*, p. 317.

37. Cronin, *op. cit.*, p. 215; Louis Fisher, *Presidential Spending Power* (Princeton, N.J.: Princeton University Press, 1975); and James P. Pfiffner, *The President, the Budget, and Congress: Impoundment and the 1974 Budget Act* (Boulder, Colo.: Westview Press, 1979).

38. Dick Kirschten, "White House Strategy," *National Journal*, February 21, 1981, p. 302.

39. Dick Kirschten, "Reagan's Cabinet Councils May Have Less Influence Than Meets the Eye," *National Journal*, July 11, 1981, pp. 1242, 1244.

40. Bill Stall, "Reagan's 'Kitchen Cabinet': A Tough-Minded Group Bound Together by Loyalty and a Belief in Business Enterprise," syndicated column, *Houston Chronicle*, September 6, 1981.

41. Richard M. Pious, *The American Presidency* (New York: Basic Books, Inc., 1979), p.363.

42. Dick Kirschten, "George Bush— Keeping His Profile Low So He Can Keep His Influence High," *National Journal*, June 20, 1981, p. 1096.

43. Malvina Stephenson, "Senators Trying to Cut Back 'Imperial' Former Presidency," *Houston Chronicle*, July 15, 1981.

Chapter 13

1. Max Weber, *The Theory of Social and Economic Organization*, Talcott Parsons, ed. A.M. Henderson and Talcott Parsons, trans. (New York: Oxford University Press, 1974).

2. Summary of Weber's theory in Robert C. Fried, *Performance in American Bureaucracy* (Boston: Little, Brown, 1976).

3. *Ibid.*, p. 34.

4. Office of the Federal Register, National Archives and Records Service, General Services Administration, *The United States Government Manual 1981/82* (Washington, D.C.: Government Printing Office, May 1, 1981).

5. George J. Gordon, *Public Administration in America* (New York: St. Martin's Press, 1978), p. 11.

6. Kenneth J. Meier, *Politics and the Bureaucracy: Policymaking in the Fourth Branch of Government* (North Scituate, Mass.: Duxbury Press, 1979), pp. 19–23.

7. Gordon, *op. cit.*, p. 13.

8. Harold Seidman, *Politics, Position, and Power: The Dynamics of Federal Organization*, 3d ed. (New York: Oxford University Press, 1980), p. 265.

9. Connie Wright, "Members Say Congress Works Harder, Does Less," *Nation's Cities Weekly*, 3 (March 24, 1980), p. 10.

10. Meier, *op. cit.*, p. 30.

11. Charles Press and Kenneth Verburg, *State and Community Governments in the Federal System* (New York: John Wiley & Sons, 1979), pp. 121–131.

12. Daniel Katz, Barbara A. Gutek, Robert L. Kahn, and Eugenia Barton, *Bureaucratic Encounters: A Pilot Study in the Evaluation of Government Services* (Ann Arbor, Mich.: Institute for Social Research, 1975).

13. Survey commissioned by the American Enterprise Institute for Public Policy Research, conducted by the Roper Center for Public Policy Research. Cited in Dick Kirschten, "Reaganomics Puts Business on the Spot; Now It Must Either Put Up or Shut Up," *National Journal*, December 19, 1981, p. 2232.

14. Daniel Elazar, *American Federalism: A View From the States* (New York: Thomas Y. Crowell Co., 1972), pp. 53–77.

15. Robert P. McGowan and Stephen Loveless, "Strategies for Information Management: The Administrator's Perspective," *Public Administration Review*, 41 (May/June 1981), pp. 331–339.

16. Letter to Senator Charles Percy, appearing in Leonard Reed, "Firing a Federal Employee: The Impossible Dream," in *The Culture of Bureaucracy*, Charles Peters and Michael Nelson eds. (New York: Holt, Rinehart & Winston, 1979), p. 201.

17. Reed, *Ibid.*, p. 200.

18. Charles Peters and Michael Nelson, "Government Service, Civil and Otherwise," in Peters and Nelson, *op. cit.*, p. 185.

19. *Ibid.*

20. Marjorie Boyd, "What's Wrong with the Civil Service?" in Peters and Nelson, *op. cit.*, p. 195.

21. Reed, in Peters and Nelson, *op. cit.*, p. 200.

22. Quoted in David H. Rosenbloom, "Public Personnel Reforms," *Policy Studies Journal*, 9 (Special Issue No. 4, 1981), p. 1232.

23. William J. Lanouette, "SES— From Civil Service Showpiece to Incipient Failure in Two Years," *National Journal*, July 18, 1981, p. 1299.

24. *Ibid.*, p. 1298.

25. Michael Wines, "A Heavy Load," *National Journal*, January 2, 1982, p. 34.

26. "Regulation and the Public Trust," *The National Voter*, 31 (Winter 1982), pp. 1–2.

27. *Ibid.*, p. 2.

28. George C. Edwards, III, *Implementing Public Policy* (Washington, D.C.: Congressional Quarterly Press, 1980), p. 1.

29. *Ibid.*, p. 2.

30. Gordon, *op. cit.*, p. 375.

31. Adapted from David Nachmias, *Public Policy Evaluation* (New York: St. Martin's Press, 1979), p. 12.

32. William J. Lanouette, "Reagan Has Some Help in His Two-Front War to Reduce the Federal Payroll," *National Journal*, April 11, 1981, p. 610.

33. William Serrin, "Government Employment Declining for the First Time Since World War II," *Houston Chronicle*, December 27, 1981.

34. "How the Rules Work for Federal Job RIFs," *Congressional Quarterly Weekly Report*, November 14, 1981, p. 2222.

35. Laura B. Weiss, "Confusion on Federal Layoff Angers Employees'

36. Hill Allies as Reagan Cuts Begin to Bite," *Congressional Quarterly Weekly Report*, November 14, 1981, p. 2222.

36. Study by Murray L. Weidenbaum reported in Donald Lambro, "Government Regulation Cost Put at $141 Billion," *Houston Chronicle*, November 29, 1979.

37. Susan M. Kuziak, "Bothered by Too Much Paperwork? OMB Thinks It Has the Answer," *National Journal*, November 27, 1980, p. 1988.

38. Laura B. Weiss, "Administration Takes Sweeping Action: Reagan, Congress Planning Regulatory Machinery Repair," *Congressional Quarterly Weekly Report*, March 7, 1981, p. 409.

39. Kathy Koch, "EPA Budget, Staff Cut Plans Stir Concern on Capitol Hill," *Congressional Quarterly Weekly Report*, October 10, 1981, p. 1957.

40. Timothy B. Clark, "Do the Benefits Justify the Costs? Prove It, Says the Administration," *National Journal*, August 1, 1981, p. 1382.

41. Gerald E. Caiden, "The Challenge to the Administrative State," *Policy Studies Journal*, 9 (Special Issue No. 4, 1981), p. 1151.

Chapter 14

1. *United States* v. *Butler*, 299 U.S. 1, 62–63 (1936).

2. Theodore J. Lowi, *End of Liberalism*, 2d ed. (New York: W.W. Norton, 1979).

3. Jethro Lieberman, *The Litigious Society* (New York: Basic Books, Inc., 1981); Robert Carp and C.K. Rowland, *Politics and Policy Making in the Federal District Courts* (Knoxville: University of Tennessee Press, 1983).

4. *Marbury* v. *Madison*, 1 Cr. 137 (1803).

5. *Scott* v. *Sandford*, 19 How. 393 (1857).

6. *Ashwander* v. *Tennessee Valley Authority*, 297 U.S. 288 (1936).

7. In the best known exception, the Court upheld a state law establishing maximum hours for women on the grounds that this was an appropriate means of protecting public health. *Muller* v. *Oregon*, 208 U.S. 412 (1908).

8. *Lochner* v. *New York*, 198 U.S. 45 (1905).

9. Article I, Section 8 of the Constitution.

10. *United States* v. *E.C. Knight Co.*, 156 U.S. 1 (1895).

11. *Schechter Poultry Corp.* v. *United States*, 295 U.S. 495 (1935).

12. Minimum wages for women were approved in *West Coast Hotel Co.* v. *Parrish* (300 U.S. 379, 1937); minimum wages and maximum hours for men and a ban on child labor were upheld in *United States* v. *Darby Lumber Co.* (312 U.S. 100, 1941); a broader definition of the commerce clause allowed some reformulations of the New Deal recovery legislation to stand (*National Labor Relations Board* v. *Jones and Laughlin Steel Corp.* (301 U.S. 1, 1937).

13. For an example of bureaucratic resistance to the wishes of the president and his top advisers, see the discussion of the implementation of school desegregation in the early days of the Nixon administration in Harrell R. Rodgers, Jr. and Charles S. Bullock, III, *Coercion to Compliance* (Lexington, Mass.: Lexington Books, 1976). For a more general discussion of the problems a president may have in exerting his will over a bureaucracy which opposes him, see Joel D. Aberbach and Bert A. Rockman, "Clashing Beliefs within the Executive Branch: The Nixon Administration Bureaucracy," *American Political Science Review*, 70 (June 1976), pp. 456–468.

14. These figures and others dealing with justices appointed since 1937 are based on data from Lawrence Baum, *The Supreme Court* (Washington, D.C.: Congressional Quarterly Press, 1981), pp. 50–51.

15. "Senate Begins Debate on Carswell Nomination," *Congressional Quarterly Weekly Report*, 28 (March 20, 1970), p. 776.

16. Much of this draws on the analysis of the backgrounds of Supreme Court justices appointed between 1789 and 1957 in John Schmidhauser, "The Justices of the Supreme Court: A Collective Portrait," *Midwest Journal of Political Science*, 3 (February 1959), pp. 1–57.

17. For this and other information on the role of the CFJ, see Joel B. Grossman, *Lawyers and Judges* (New York: John Wiley & Sons, 1966), chapters 4 through 6.

18. Sheldon Goldman and Thomas P. Jahnige, *The Federal Courts as a Political System*, 2d ed. (New York: Harper and Row, 1976), p. 51.

19. Sheldon Goldman, "Characteristics of Eisenhower and Kennedy Appointees to the Lower Federal Courts," *Western Political Quarterly*, 18 (December 1965), pp. 755–762; Goldman and Jahnige, *op. cit.*, pp. 57–61; Nadine Cohodas, "Reagan Slow in Appointing Women, Blacks, Hispanics to Federal Judiciary Seats," *Congressional Quarterly Weekly Report*, December 26, 1981, p. 2561.

20. Goldman and Jahnige, *op. cit.*, p. 72.

21. *Ibid.*, pp. 70–73.

22. Quoted in Cohodas, *op. cit.*, p. 2560.

23. Figures showing the growth in litigation in the federal courts are graphically presented in Howard Ball, *Courts and Politics: The Federal Judicial System* (Englewood Cliffs, N.J.: Prentice-Hall, 1980), pp. 82–98.

24. Jerry Goldman, "Federal District Courts and the Appellate Crisis," *Judicature*, 57 (1973), pp. 211–213.

25. *Ibid.*, p. 104.

26. *Ibid.*, p. 106; also see Baum, *op. cit.*, pp. 83–84.

27. *Brown* v. *Board of Education* (347 U.S. 483, 1954) brought together four sets of litigants who had filed separate suits in federal district courts in Delaware, Kansas, South Carolina, and Virginia. Since the issues were essentially the same in all four cases, the Supreme Court treated them as one case. The Supreme Court decision bears the name of Linda Brown, a black Topeka student, and her parents because they came first alphabetically among the plaintiffs.

28. *Commission on Revision of the Federal Court Appellate System, Structure and*

Internal Procedures: Recommendations for Change (Washington, D.C.: Government Printing Office, 1975), p. 101.

29. Baum, *op. cit.*, p. 90.
30. *Ibid.*, p. 124.
31. Harold J. Spaeth, *Supreme Court Policy Making* (San Francisco: W.H. Freeman, 1979), p. 113.
32. Merle Miller, *Plain Speaking* (New York: Berkley, 1973), p. 225.
33. Bob Woodward and Scott Armstrong, *The Brethren* (New York: Simon & Schuster, 1979), pp. 170–172, 415–420.
34. The busing case was *Swann* v. *Charlotte-Mecklenburg County Board of Education*, 402 U.S. 1 (1971).
35. Richard Kluger, *Simple Justice* (New York: Alfred A. Knopf 1976), pp. 680–699.
36. *United States* v. *Nixon*, 481 U.S. 683 (1974).
37. *Cooper* v. *Aaron*, 358 U.S. 1 (1958).
38. Woodward and Armstrong, *op. cit.*, p. 224.
39. Elliot E. Slotnick, "Who Speaks for the Court? Majority Opinion Assignments from Taft to Burger," *American Journal of Political Science*, 23 (February 1979), pp. 60–77.
40. *Ibid.*, p. 419.
41. See *ibid.*, pp. 189–192, for an extended discussion of the writing of the opinion in *Flood* v. *Kuhn*, 407 U.S. 258 (1972).
42. Saul Brenner, "Fluidity on the United States Supreme Court: A Reexamination," *American Journal of Political Science*, 24 (August 1980), pp. 526–535.
43. The case in which Justice Harlan dissented was *Plessy* v. *Ferguson*, 163 U.S. 537 (1896).
44. David W. Rohde and Harold J. Spaeth, *Supreme Court Decision Making* (San Francisco: W.H. Freeman, 1976), pp. 145–155.
45. *Ibid.*, pp. 129–131, quotes from p. 130.
46. Theodore L. Becker, *Political Behavioralism and Modern Jurisprudence* (Chicago: Rand McNally, 1964).
47. Robert A. Dahl, "Decision-Making in a Democracy: The Supreme Court as a National Policy-Maker," *Journal of Public Law*, 6 (Fall 1957), pp. 279–295; Richard Funston, "The Supreme Court

and Critical Elections," *American Political Science Review*, 69 (September 1975), pp. 795–811.
48. Cf. Woodward and Armstrong, *op. cit.*, p. 215.
49. *Ibid.*, p. 362.
50. *Miranda* v. *Arizona*, 384 U.S. 436 (1966).
51. Charles V. Willie and Susan L. Greenblatt, eds., *Community Politics and Educational Change: Ten School Systems under Court Order* (New York: Longman, 1981).
52. Rodgers and Bullock, *op. cit.*, chapter 4.
53. The primary suit, *Morton* v. *Wilderness Society*, 479 F.2d 842 (1973), barred construction because it would require more than the 50-foot-wide right-of-way authorized by Congress in the Mineral Leasing Act of 1920.
54. Relevant to this section are materials in Charles S. Bullock, III and Charles Lamb, eds., *Implementing Civil Rights* (Monterey, Calif.: Brooks/Cole, 1983); Daniel A. Mazmanian and Paul A. Sabatier, eds., *Effective Policy Implementation* (Lexington, Mass.: Lexington Books, 1981).
55. *Green* v. *County School Board of New Kent County*, 391 U.S. 430 (1968).
56. Willie and Greenblatt, *Community Politics and Educational Change*, especially chapter 13.
57. Theodore Lowi has urged that the courts take up the sword against poorly defined delegations of authority made by Congress. He wants the Supreme Court to invalidate legislation which makes broad, vague grants of power to the bureaucracy. Theodore J. Lowi, *op. cit.*, pp. 300–302. The Supreme Court last struck down a delegation of authority for being too vague in *Schechter Poultry Corp.* v. *United States*, 295 U.S. 495 (1935).

Chapter 15

1 Anthony Lewis, *Decade of Decision* (New York: New York Times, 1964), pp. 126–127.
2. Quoted in David J. Garrow, *Protest at Selma* (New Haven, Conn.: Yale University Press, 1978), p. 238.

3. Charles Silberman, *Crisis in Black and White* (New York: Random House, Vintage, 1964), p. 23.
4. *Smith* v. *Allright*, 321 U.S. 649 (1944).
5. *Harper* v. *Virginia Board of Elections*, 383 U.S. 663 (1966).
6. Harrell R. Rodgers, Jr. and Charles S. Bullock, III, *Law and Social Change* (New York: McGraw-Hill, 1972), p. 25.
7. Richard A. Hudlin and K. Farouk Brimah, *What Happened in the South, 1980* (Atlanta: Voter Education Project, 1981), p. 30.
8. Earl Black, *Southern Governors and Civil Rights* (Cambridge, Mass.: Harvard University Press, 1976).
9. William Keech, *The Impact of Negro Voting* (Chicago: Rand McNally, 1968).
10. *National Roster of Black Elected Officials*, 12 (Washington, D.C.: Joint Center for Political Studies, 1982), pp. xvi–xvii.
11. Charles S. Bullock, III, and Susan A. MacManus, "Policy Responsiveness to the Black Electorate," *American Politics Quarterly*, 9 (July 1981) pp. 357–364; Charles S. Bullock, III, "Congressional Voting and the Mobilization of a Black Electorate in the South," *Journal of Politics*, 43 (August 1981), pp. 662–682.
12. Bruce A. Campbell, *The American Electorate* (New York: Holt, Rinehart & Winston, 1979), p. 229.
13. *Ibid.*, p. 228.
14. Raymond Wolfinger and Steven Rosenstone, *Who Votes?* (New Haven, Conn.: Yale University Press, 1980), p. 38.
15. *Plessy* v. *Ferguson*, 163 U.S. 537 (1896).
16. Richard Kluger, *Simple Justice* (New York: Alfred A. Knopf, 1976), p. 169.
17. *Missouri ex rel. Gaines* v. *Canada*, 305 U.S. 337 (1938).
18. *Sweatt* v. *Painter*, 339 U.S. 629 (1950).
19. *Brown* v. *Board of Education*, 347 U.S. 483 (1954).
20. *Green* v. *County School Board*, 391 U.S. 430 (1968).
21. *Alexander* v. *Holmes*, 396 U.S. 19 (1969).
22. *Dayton Board of Education* v. *Brinkman*, 433 U.S. 406 (1977).

23. Gary Orfield, *Must We Bus?* (Washington, D.C.: Brookings Institution, 1978), pp. 62–63.

24. Leon E. Panetta and Peter Gall, *Bring Us Together* (Philadelphia: Lippincott, 1971).

25. CBS News—*New York Times* Poll, June 30, 1981, p. 15.

26. *Milliken* v. *Bradley*, 418 U.S. 717 (1974).

27. *Pasadena* v. *Spangler*, 427 U.S. 424 (1976).

28. Charles S. Bullock, III and Joseph Stewart, Jr., "Implementing Equal Education Opportunity Policy: A Comparison of the Outcomes of HEW and Justice Department Efforts," *Administration and Society*, 12 (February 1981), pp. 427–446.

29. Children's Defense Fund, *Children Out of School* (Washington, D.C.: Children's Defense Fund, 1974).

30. *Columbus Board of Education* v. *Penick*, 439 U.S. 1348 (1979).

31. *Lau* v. *Nichols*, 414 U.S. 563 (1974).

32. "Report Finds Gains from Title IX," *Atlanta Journal-Constitution*, October 18, 1981.

33. *Congressional Record*, 88th Congress, 2d Session, 110 (1964), p. 6547.

34. *Griggs* v. *Duke Power Co.*, 401 U.S. 424 (1971).

35. *Washington* v. *Davis*, 426 U.S. 229 (1976).

36. *Fullilove* v. *Klutznick*, 488 U.S. 488 (1980).

37. *County of Washington* v. *Gunther*, U.S. 49 L.W. 4623 (1981).

38. Timothy B. Clark, "Affirmative Action May Fall Victim to Reagan's Regulatory Reform Drive," *National Journal*, July 1, 1981, p. 1250.

39. "Black Congressmen Blast New Approach to Fair Employment," *Atlanta Journal*, September 24, 1981.

40. Nadine Cohodas, "Affirmative Action Assailed in Congress, Administration," *Congressional Quarterly Weekly Report*, September 12, 1981, p. 1752.

41. On policy implementation, see Paul Sabatier and Daniel Mazmanian, "The Implementation of Public Policy: A Framework of Analysis," *Policy Studies Journal*, 8:4 (1980), pp. 538–560; Charles S. Bullock, III, "The Office for Civil Rights and Implementation of Desegregation Programs in the Public Schools," *Policy Studies Journal*, 8:4 (1980), pp. 597–616.

42. Quoted in Susan Wells and Ann Woolner, "Under Reagan, Affirmative Action Fight Won't Die Down," *Atlanta Journal-Constitution*, October 18, 1981.

43. *Ibid.*

44. *University of California Regents* v. *Bakke*, 438 U.S. 265 (1978).

45. *Personnel Administrator* v. *Feeney*, 442 U.S. 256 (1979).

46. *United Steel Workers of America* v. *Weber*, 443 U.S. 193 (1979).

47. James E. Anderson, David W. Brady, and Charles S. Bullock, III, *Public Policy and Politics in America*, 2d ed. (Monterey, Calif.: Brooks/Cole, 1984), "Civil Rights," chapter 6, Table 4.

48. *Shelley* v. *Kramer*, 334 U.S. 1 (1948).

49. Rodgers and Bullock, *op. cit.*, chapter 6.

50. *Jones* v. *Mayer*, 392 U.S. 409 (1968).

51. *Hills* v. *Gautreaux*, 425 U.S. 284 (1976).

52. *Belle Terre* v. *Boraas*, 416 U.S. 1 (1974).

53. Much of this section draws on Charles M. Lamb, "Federal Implementation of Equal Housing Opportunity," in Charles S. Bullock, III and Charles M. Lamb, eds., *Implementing Civil Rights* (Monterey, Calif.: Brooks/Cole, 1983), chapter 6.

54. William Raspberry, "Far from Fair Housing," *Washington Post*, June 12, 1980.

55. *Plessy* v. *Ferguson*, 163 U.S. 537 (1896).

56. *Brown* v. *Board of Education*, 347 U.S. 483 (1954).

57. Congress chose the commerce clause rather than the equal protection clause as the constitutional basis for the public accommodations legislation since many years earlier the Supreme Court had ruled that the equal protection clause did not apply to private business (*Civil Rights Cases*, 109 U.S. 3, 1883).

58. *Katzenbach* v. *McClung*, 379 U.S. 294 (1964).

59. *Sullivan* v. *Little Hunting Park*, 396 U.S. 229 (1969).

60. *Runyon* v. *McCrary*, 427 U.S. 160 (1976).

61. *Craig* v. *Boren*, 429 U.S. 190 (1976).

62. *Rostker* v. *Goldberg*, U.S. 49 L.W. 4798 (1981).

Chapter 16

1. *Schenck* v. *United States*, 249 U.S. 47 (1919).

2. *Dennis* v. *United States*, 341 U.S. 494 (1951).

3. *Yates* v. *United States*, 354 U.S. 298 (1957).

4. *Miller* v. *California*, 413 U.S. 15 (1973).

5. *Young* v. *American Mini Theaters, Inc.*, 427 U.S. 50 (1976).

6. *Miller* v. *California*, 413 U.S. 15 (1973).

7. *Paris Adult Theater* v. *Slaton*, 413 U.S. 49 (1979).

8. *Jacobellis* v. *Ohio*, 378 U.S. 184 (1964).

9. *Roth* v. *United States*, 354 U.S. 476 (1957).

10. *Memoirs* v. *Massachusetts*, 383 U.S. 413 (1966).

11. *Redrup* v. *New York*, 386 U.S. 767 (1967).

12. *Rowan* v. *United States Post Office*, 397 U.S. 728 (1970).

13. *Jacobellis* v. *Ohio*, 378 U.S. 184 (1964).

14. *Miller* v. *California*, 413 U.S. 15 (1973).

15. *Jenkins* v. *Georgia*, 418 U.S. 153 (1974).

16. *Stanley* v. *Georgia*, 394 U.S. 557 (1969).

17. *United States* v. *Reidel*, 402 U.S. 351 (1971).

18. *Feiner* v. *New York*, 340 U.S. 315 (1951).

19. *Terminiello* v. *Chicago*, 337 U.S. 1 (1949); *Gregory* v. *Chicago*, 394 U.S. 111 (1969).

20. *New York Times* v. *Sullivan*, 376 U.S. 254 (1964).

21. *Associated Press* v. *Walker*, 388 U.S. 130 (1967).

22. *Time, Inc.* v. *Firestone*, 424 U.S. 448 (1976).

23. *First National Bank of Boston* v. *Bellotti*, 435 U.S. 765 (1978).

24. *Bates* v. *State Bar of Arizona*, 433 U.S. 350 (1977).
25. *Gannett Co., Inc.* v. *De Pasquale*, 443 U.S. 368 (1979).
26. *Nebraska Press Association* v. *Stuart*, 427 U.S. 539 (1976).
27. *Richmond Newspapers, Inc.* v. *Virginia*, 448 U.S. 555 (1980).
28. *Chandler* v. *Flordia*, 449 U.S. 560 (1981).
29. *New York Times* v. *United States*, 403 U.S. 713 (1971).
30. *Branzberg* v. *Hayes*, 408 U.S. 665 (1972).
31. *Ibid.*
32. *Red Lion Broadcasting Co.* v. *FCC*, 395 U.S. 367 (1969).
33. *Miami Herald Publishing Co.* v. *Tornillo*, 418 U.S. 241 (1974).
34. *Columbia Broadcasting System* v. *Democratic National Committee*, 412 U.S. 94 (1973).
35. *Shuttlesworth* v. *Birmingham*, 394 U.S. 147 (1969).
36. *Edwards* v. *South Carolina*, 372 U.S. 229 (1963).
37. Michael Barone, Grant Ujifusa, and Douglas Matthews, *The Almanac of American Politics, 1980* (New York: Dutton, 1979), p. 219.
38. Executive Order No. 9066.
39. *Scales* v. *United States*, 367 U.S. 203 (1961).
40. *Everson* v. *Board of Education*, 330 U.S. 1 (1947).
41. *Cochran* v. *Louisiana*, 281 U.S. 370 (1930).
42. *Everson* v. *Board of Education*, 330 U.S. 1 (1947).
43. *Lemon* v. *Kartzman*, 402 U.S. 602 (1971).
44. *Meek* v. *Pittenger*, 421 U.S. 349 (1975).
45. *Wolman* v. *Walter*, 433 U.S. 229 (1977).
46. *McCollum* v. *Board of Education*, 333 U.S. 203 (1948).
47. *Engle* v. *Vitale*, 370 U.S. 421 (1962).
48. *Abington School District* v. *Schempp*, 374 U.S. 203 (1963).
49. *Zorach* v. *Clawson*, 343 U.S. 306 (1952).
50. Kenneth M. Dolbeare and Phillip E. Hammond, *The School Prayer Decisions* (Chicago: University of Chicago Press, 1971), chapter 3.
51. *Braunfeld* v. *Brown*, 366 U.S. 599 (1961).
52. *Wisconsin* v. *Yoder*, 406 U.S. 205 (1972).

53. *West Virginia State Board of Education* v. *Barnette*, 319 U.S. 624 (1943).
54. *Sherbert* v. *Verner*, 374 U.S. 398 (1963).
55. *United States* v. *Seeger*, 380 U.S. 163 (1965).
56. *Gillette* v. *United States*, 401 U.S. 437 (1971).
57. *Roe* v. *Wade*, 410 U.S. 113 (1973).
58. *Planned Parenthood of Central Missouri* v. *Danforth*, 428 U.S. 52 (1976).
59. *H.L.* v. *Matheson*, U.S. 67 L.Ed 2d 388 (1981).
60. *Harris* v. *McRae*, 448 U.S. 297 (1980). The limitations imposed by the Hyde Amendments have been approved by the courts since, while a woman has a constitutional right to obtain an abortion, it is optional whether public funds will be made available for this purpose.
61. *Powell* v. *Alabama*, 287 U.S. 45 (1932).
62. *Johnson* v. *Zerbst*, 304 U.S. 458 (1938).
63. *Gideon* v. *Wainwright*, 372 U.S. 335 (1963).
64. *Argersinger* v. *Hamlin*, 407 U.S. 25 (1972).
65. *Scott* v. *Illinois*, 440 U.S. 367 (1979).
66. *Brewer* v. *Williams*, 430 U.S. 387 (1977).
67. *Brown* v. *Mississippi*, 297 U.S. 278 (1936).
68. *Miranda* v. *Arizona*, 384 U.S. 436 (1966).
69. *Harris* v. *New York*, 401 U.S. 222 (1971).
70. *Michigan* v. *Tucker*, 417 U.S. 433 (1974).
71. Joel B. Grossman and Richard S. Wells, *Constitutional Law and Judicial Policy Making*, 2d ed. (New York: John Wiley & Sons, 1980), pp. 789–791.
72. *Weeks* v. *United States*, 245 U.S. 618 (1914).
73. *Mapp* v. *Ohio*, 367 U.S. 643 (1961).
74. *Anderson* v. *Maryland*, 427 U.S. 463 (1976).
75. *People* v. *Defore*, 242 N.Y. 13 (1926).
76. *Payton* v. *New York*, 445 U.S. 573 (1980).
77. *Olmstead* v. *United States*, 277 U.S. 438 (1928).

78. *Furman* v. *Georgia*, 408 U.S. 238 (1972).
79. *Gregg* v. *Georgia*, 428 U.S. 153 (1976).
80. *Woodson* v. *North Carolina*, 428 U.S. 280 (1976).
81. *Coker* v. *Georgia*, 433 U.S. 584 (1977).
82. *In re Gault*, 387 U.S. 1 (1967).
83. *Joint Anti-Fascist Refugee Committee* v. *McGrath*, 341 U.S. 123 (1951).

Chapter 17

1. Allen Schick, ed., *Perspectives on Budgeting* (Washington, D.C.: American Society for Public Administration, 1980), p. 15.
2. Thomas D. Lynch, *Public Budgeting in America* (Englewood Cliffs, N.J.: Prentice-Hall, 1979), p. 2.
3. *Ibid.*
4. Lance LeLoup, *Budgetary Politics*, 2d ed. (Brunswick, Ohio: Kings Court Communications, 1980), p. 4.
5. *Ibid.*, p. 1.
6. Henry Bretton, *The Power of Money* (Albany, N.Y.: State University of New York Press, 1980), p. XVIII.
7. Robert D. Lee and Ronald W. Johnson, *Public Budgeting Systems*, 3d ed. (Baltimore, Md.: University Park Press, 1983), pp. 2–4.
8. *Ibid.*, p. 3.
9. *Ibid.*
10. *Ibid.*, p. 4.
11. Office of Management and Budget, Executive Office of the President, *Fiscal Year 1982 Budget Revisions* (Washington, D.C.: Government Printing Office, March 10, 1981), p. M-2.
12. Timothy B. Clark, "Reagan's Assault on Federal Borrowing—Making Room for the Private Sector," *National Journal*, October 17, 1981, p. 1860.
13. David J. Ott and Attiat F. Ott, *Federal Budget Policy*, 3d ed. (Washington, D.C.: Brookings Institution, 1977), p. 110.
14. John R. Gist, "The Reagan Budget: A Significant Departure from the Past," *Policy Studies*, 14 (Fall 1981), p. 742.
15. LeLoup, *op. cit.*, p. 70.
16. "National Debt Tops $1 Trillion—That's $1,000,000,000,000," *Houston Post*, October 23, 1981.

17. Quoted in Ott and Ott, *op. cit.*, p. 107.
18. Senator John L. McClellan, quoted in Ott and Ott, *op. cit.*, p. 108.
19. "Budget Office Foresees 3 Year Flood of Red Ink," *Houston Chronicle*, July 28, 1982.
20. *Ibid.*
21. William B. Cannon, "Reform of Federal Financing Policy: A Suggested Guide to Governmental Action," in *Federal Budget and Social Reconstruction*, Marcus G. Raskin ed. (Washington, D.C.: Institute for Public Policy Studies, 1978), p. 55.
22. Nadine Cohodas, "Senate Narrowly Approves Balanced Budget Amendment, But House Adoption Doubtful," *Congressional Quarterly Weekly Report*, August 7, 1982, p. 1887.
23. Quote from the *Wall Street Journal*, cited by Henry Hyde in "What Price a Balanced Budget?" *Houston Chronicle*, July 23, 1982.
24. Michael A. Lerned, "A Juggernaut Slows Down," *Newsweek*, August 9, 1982, p. 17.
25. Arthur Wiese, "Balanced Budget Amendment Gaining Congressional Support," *The Houston Post*, April 18, 1982.
26. James T. Bennett and Thomas D. Lorenzo, *Underground Government: The Off-Budget Public Sector* (Washington, D.C.: Cato Institute, 1983).
27. Hyde, *op. cit.*
28. Everett Carll Ladd, "Opinion Roundup: The Public Reacts to the Reagan Legislative Agenda," *Public Opinion*, 4 (December/January 1982), p. 28.
29. John Wanat, *Introduction to Budgeting* (North Scituate, Mass.: Duxbury Press, 1978), p. 54.
30. Robert S. Lorsch, *Public Administration* (San Francisco: West Publishing Co., 1979), p. 248.
31. Aaron Wildavsky, *The Politics of the Budgetary Process*, 3d. ed. (Boston: Little, Brown, 1979), chapter 3.
32. Mark W. Huddleston, "Assessing Congressional Budget Reform: The Impact on Appropriations," *Policy Studies Journal*, 9 (Autumn 1980), pp. 81–86.
33. Carl P. Chelf, *Public Policymaking in America: Difficult Choices, Limited Solutions* (Santa Monica, Calif.: Goodyear, 1981), p. 59.
34. John W. Ellwood and James A. Thurber, "The Politics of the Congressional Budget Process Re-Examined," in *Congress Reconsidered* 2d ed., Lawrence C. Dodd and Bruce I. Oppenheimer eds. (Washington, D.C.: Congressional Quarterly Press, 1981), p. 248.
35. Richard E. Cohen, "Budget Express Leaving the Station Without the Appropriations Committee," *National Journal*, July 4, 1981, p. 1211.
36. Louis Fisher, *Presidential Spending Power* (Princeton, N.J.: Princeton University Press, 1975), pp. 75–76.
37. Dennis S. Ippolito, *The Budget and National Politics* (San Francisco: W.H. Freeman, 1978), p. 151.
38. Jay Perkins, "Who Watches the Watchers? Congressional Agency Cuts Costs, But Some Say It Oversimplifies," *Houston Post*, July 14, 1981.
39. D.A. Cutchin, *Guide to Public Administration* (Itasca, Ill.: F.E. Peacock Publishers, 1981), p. 74.
40. Thomas P. Murphy, *Contemporary Public Administration* (Itasca, Ill.: F.E. Peacock Publishers, 1981), p. 438.
41. *Ibid.*, pp. 443–444.
42. *Ibid.*, p. 443.
43. Edward R. Tufte, *Political Control of the Economy* (Princeton, N.J.: Princeton University Press, 1978), p. 136.
44. Pamela Tessler, "Reagan Tax Plan Ready for Economic Test," *Congressional Quarterly Weekly Report*, August 8, 1981, pp. 1433–1436.
45. Pamela Tessler, "Congress Urged to Scrutinize Tax Breaks That Cost U.S. Billions in Lost Revenues," *Congressional Quarterly Weekly Report*, January 30, 1982, p. 157.
46. *Ibid.*, p. 156.
47. Poverty programs figures are from Harrison Donnelly, "Millions of Poor Face Losses Oct. 1 as Reconciliation Bill Spending Cuts Go into Effect," *Congressional Quarterly Weekly Report*, September 26, 1981, pp. 1834–1835. Carter's and Reagan's proposed budget outlay figures are from Joseph A. Pechman, ed., *Setting National Priorities: The 1982 Budget* (Washington, D.C.: Brookings Institution, 1981), p. 3. The revised FY 1982 total budget outlay figure is from Dale Tate, "New Reagan Budget Cuts Face Stiff Fight," *Congressional Quarterly Weekly Report*, September 26, 1981, p. 1820.
48. Robert J. Samuelson, "Beyond Our Reach," *National Journal*, January 9, 1982, p. 74.
49. William Safire, "In Praise of the Current Recession," *Houston Chronicle*, February 9, 1982.

Chapter 18

1. The discussion of the conceptual scheme draws on Michael T. Hayes, *Lobbyists and Legislators* (New Brunswick, N.J.: Rutgers University Press, 1981), pp. 29–39; Theodore J. Lowi, "American Business, Public Policy, Case Studies, and Theory," *World Politics*, 16 (June 1964), pp. 677–715; Robert H. Salisbury and John P. Heinz, "A Theory of Policy Analysis and Some Preliminary Applications," in *Policy Analysis in Political Science*, Ira Sharkansky ed. (Chicago: Markham, 1970), pp. 39–60.
2. Morris P. Fiorina and Roger G. Noll, "Majority Rule Models and Legislative Elections," *Journal of Politics*, 41 (November 1979), pp. 1081–1104; Morris P. Fiorina, *Congress: Keystone of the Washington Establishment* (New Haven, Conn.: Yale University Press, 1978), chapter 3.
3. Heinz Eulau and Paul D. Karps, "The Puzzle of Representation: Specifying Components of Responsiveness," *Legislative Studies Quarterly*, 2 (August 1977), p. 245.
4. R. Douglas Arnold, *Congress and the Bureaucracy* (New Haven, Conn.: Yale University Press, 1979).
5. Elizabeth Wehr, "Carter, Congress Seek Ways to Improve U.S. Health Care," *Congressional Quarterly Weekly Report*, May 12, 1979, p. 889.
6. James E. Anderson, David W. Brady, and Charles S. Bullock,

III, *Public Policy and Politics in America* (North Scituate, Mass.: Duxbury Press, 1978), p. 275.

7. Eugene Eidenberg and Roy D. Morey, *An Act of Congress* (New York: W.W. Norton, 1969), pp. 66–69.

8. "Reagan Studies Ways to Eliminate Rental Subsidy Program for Poor," *Atlanta Journal Constitution*, November 5, 1981.

9. "Home Tax Breaks Up Prices, Study Says," *Atlanta Journal-Constitution*, October 10, 1981.

10. CBS-*New York Times* Poll, July 16, 1981.

11. Pamela Fessler, "Threat of Bankruptcy Spurs Action on Social Security Bill; Long Term Changes Studied," *Congressional Quarterly Weekly Report*, September 19, 1981, p. 1776.

12. CBS-*New York Times* Poll, July 16, 1981.

13. Pamela Fessler, "Soaring Health Care Costs for the Elderly: A Problem Growing Worse Every Year," *Congressional Quarterly Weekly Report*, November 28, 1981, p. 2338.

14. Linda E. Demkovich, "Health Insurers Favor Budget Cutting—But Not If It Means They Must Pay More," *National Journal*, November 21, 1981, p. 2070.

15. Aage Clausen, *How Congressmen Decide* (New York: St. Martin's Press, 1973); Barbara Sinclair, *Congressional Realignment, 1925–1978* (Austin, Tex.: University of Texas Press, 1982).

16. See, for example, Gilbert Y. Steiner, *The State of Welfare* (Washington, D.C.: Brookings Institution, 1971), pp. 68–71.

17. Newsletter from Senator Sam Nunn (January, 1981), p. 8.

18. Anderson, Brady, and Bullock, *op. cit.*, p. 144.

19. Peter Goldman, "Bracing for Reagan's Cuts," *Newsweek*, February 23, 1981, p. 19.

20. "U.S. to Bolster War on Food Stamp Fraud," *Atlanta Journal*, October 29, 1981.

21. Quoted in John K. Iglehart, "The Rising Cost of Health Care—Something Must Be Done, But What?" *National Journal*, October 16, 1976, p. 1462.

22. Linda Parham, "State May End Families' Free Medicaid Rides," *Atlanta Journal-Constitution*, December 19, 1981.

23. Fessler, "Soaring Health Care," *op. cit.*, p. 2340.

24. Spencer Rich, "Lasting Gains Are Found from Pre-School Start," *Washington Post*, November 30, 1979.

25. For a fuller discussion of the shortcomings of manpower training programs, see Charles S. Bullock, III, "Expanding Black Economic Rights," in *Racism and Inequality*, Harrell R. Rodgers, Jr. ed. (San Francisco: W.H. Freeman, 1975), pp. 100–109, and the sources cited there.

26. Anderson, Brady, and Bullock, *op. cit.*, p. 142.

27. "Experts Differ on How Many Are Poor," *Congressional Quarterly Weekly Report*, April 18, 1981, p. 669.

Chapter 19

1. Richard A. Falk, *A Study of Future Worlds* (New York: Free Press, 1975), pp. 156–157.

2. The phrase is from Richard Rosecrance and Arthur Stein, "Interdependence: Myth or Reality?" *World Politics*, 76 (October 1973), p. 22.

3. Cited by Aaron Wildavsky, "The Two Presidencies," *Trans-Action*, 4 (December 1966), p. 2.

4. Raoul Berger, "The Presidential Monopoly of Foreign Relations," *Michigan Law Review*, 71 (1972), p. 39.

5. These figures and the following discussion are based on a series of articles by Loch Johnson and James M. McCormick: "Foreign Policy by Executive Fiat," *Foreign Policy*, 28 (Fall 1977), pp. 117–138; "The Making of International Agreements: a Reappraisal of Congressional Involvement," *Journal of Politics*, 40 (May 1978), pp. 468–478; and "The Democratic Control of International Commitments," *Presidential Studies Quarterly*, 8 (Summer 1978), pp. 275–283.

6. Johnson and McCormick, "Foreign Policy by Executive Fiat," *ibid.*, p. 121.

7. Subcommittee on Separation of Powers, Senate Judiciary Committee, "Congressional Oversight of Executive Agreements," *Hearings*, 92nd Cong., 2nd Sess. (1972), p. 249.

8. "National Commitments," Senate Report 91–129, 91st Cong., 1st Sess., April 16, 1969, p. 28.

9. Cited by Louis Henkin, *Foreign Affairs and the Constitution* (Mineola, N.Y.: Foundation Press, 1972), p. 372.

10. Julian P. Boyd, ed., *The Papers of Thomas Jefferson*, 17 vols. (Princeton, N.J.: Princeton University Press, 1955), vol. 15, p. 397.

11. *Congressional Record*, 82nd Cong., 1st Sess., 97 (January 5, 1951), p. 57.

12. Testimony of Nicholas Katzenbach, "U.S. Commitments to Foreign Powers," *Hearings*, Senate Foreign Relations Committee, 90th Cong., 1st Sess. (1967), p. 82.

13. "Notes and Comments," *The New Yorker*, 54 (February 27, 1978), p. 26.

14. "Alleged Assassination Plots," *op. cit.*

15. *Ibid.*, p. 41.

16. *Ibid.*, p. 199.

17. Mary Louise Ramsey, "Impoundment," Legislative Reference Service, Library of Congress, May 10, 1968, p. 4; and Report No. 1406, 87th Congress, 2nd Sess. (1962), p. 5.

18. Edwin S. Corwin, *The President: Office and Powers, 1787–1957,* rev. ed. (New York: New York University Press, 1957), p. 137.

19. Norman J. Small, "Constitutional Power of the President to Order the Impounding of Appropriated Funds," Legislative Reference Service, Library of Congress, August 25, 1959, p. 6.

20. Arthur M. Schlesinger, Jr., *The Imperial Presidency* (Boston: Houghton Mifflin, 1973), p. 247.

21. David Binder, "Kissinger Backed in House Dispute," *New York Times*, October 14, 1975.

22. Francis E. Rourke, "The United States," in *Government Secrecy in Democracies*, Itzhak Galnoor ed. (New York: New York University Press, 1977), p. 118.

23. Corwin, *op. cit.*, p. 171.

24. "The Sources of Soviet Conduct," *Foreign Affairs*, 25 (July 1947), p. 575.

25. "Foreign and Military Intelligence," *Final Report*, Senate Select Committee on Intelligence, 94th Cong., 2nd Sess., I (April 26, 1976), p. 9.

26. Charles McCarry, "Ol' Man Rivers," *Esquire*, 74 (October 1970), p. 171.

27. Townsend Hoopes, *The New Republic*, 181 (September 1, 1979), p. 34.

28. Thomas C. Schelling, *Arms and Influence* (New Haven, Conn.: Yale University Press, 1966), p. 124.

29. From a book entitled *Ronald Reagan's Call to Action*, cited by David Broder, "The One Worry About Reagan," *Washington Post*, February 11, 1981.

30. Frank Church (D—Idaho), *Congressional Record*, December 8, 1970, p. S40455.

31. Senator Frank Church, quoted by Loch Johnson, "Operational Codes and the Prediction of Leadership Behavior: Senator Frank Church at Midcareer," in *A Psychological Examination of Political Leaders*, Margaret G. Herman ed. (New York: Free Press, 1977), p. 110.

32. Author's interview with a high-ranking CIA official, Washington, D.C., December 16, 1978.

33. James Reston, "Bewildered Congress Faces World Leadership Decision," *New York Times*, March 14, 1947.

34. Thomas M. Franck and Edward Weisband, *Foreign Policy by Congress* (New York: Oxford University Press, 1979), p. 99.

35. Quoted by Tom Braden, "What's Wrong with the CIA?" *Saturday Review*, 2 (April 5, 1975), p. 14.

36. Loch Johnson, "The CIA: Controlling the Quiet Option," *Foreign Policy*, 39 (Summer 1980), p. 150.

37. Kim Rogal, "Congress vs. the C.I.A.," *Newsweek*, April 11, 1983, p. 50.

38. John Elliff, "Congress and the Intelligence Community," in *Congress Reconsidered*, Lawrence C. Dodd and Bruce J. Oppenheimer eds. (New York: Praeger, 1977), p. 203.

39. 403 U.S. 713, argued June 26, 1971, and decided June 30, 1971.

40. "Angola," *Hearings*, Senate Select Committee on Intelligence, 94th Cong., 2nd Sess. (November 21, 1975).

41. Judy Mann, "Hunger," *Washington Post*, March 5, 1982.

42. *Congressional Record*, October 7, 1974, p. H.9996.

43. "War Powers Legislation," *Hearings*, Senate Committee on Foreign Relations, 92nd Cong., 1st Sess. (1972), p. 393.

44. George Lardner, Jr., "CIA Attacks Freedom of Information Law at Senate Hearings, Asks to be Exempted," *Washington Post*, July 22, 1981.

45. Author's interview, University of Georgia, Athens, Georgia, March 31, 1982. The "whales" included Senators Everett Dirksen (D—Ill.), Hubert H. Humphrey (D—Minn.), Robert Kerr (D—Okla.), Richard B. Russell (D—Ga.), and Speaker of the House Sam Rayburn (D—Tex.).

46. Loch Johnson, "Legislators as Diplomats: The Czechoslovak Gold Dispute," *Journal of Legislation*, 9 (Winter 1982), pp. 36-51.

47. James Bryce, "Democracy and Foreign Policy," in *Readings in Foreign Policy*, Robert A. Goldwin ed. (New York: Oxford University Press, 1959), p. 17.

48. Warren Christopher, "Ceasefire Between the Branches: A Compact in Foreign Affairs," *Foreign Affairs*, 60 (Summer 1982), p. 999.

49. William E. Schmidt, "Poll Shows Lessening of the Fear That U.S. Military is Lacking," *New York Times*, February 6, 1983.

50. "A Newsweek Poll: Arms Wrestling," *Newsweek*, January 31, 1983, p. 17.

51. "Excerpts from President's Speech to National association of Evangelicals," *New York Times*, March 9, 1983.

52. "Pro and Con," *U.S. News & World Report*, April 5, 1982, p. 55.

53. Bernard Gwertzman, "A Citizen Pays $43 for Aid, Schultz Says, And $35 for Hairdos," *New York Times*, February 25, 1983.

54. Charles W. Kegley, Jr. and Eugene R. Witkopf, *American Foreign Policy: Pattern and Process* (New York: St. Martin's Press, 1979), p. 93.

55. Martin Tolchin, "Key House Member Fears U.S. Breaks Law on Nicaragua," *New York Times*, April 14, 1983.

56. An anonymous member of the Senate Intelligence Committee, cited in Patrick E. Tyler, "Congressional Concern on U.S. Objectives in Nicaragua Persist," *Washington Post*, January 1, 1983.

57. Cited by Richard J. Barnet, *Real Security: Restoring American Power in a Dangerous Decade* (New York: Simon & Schuster, 1981), p. 137.

58. Robert L. Heilbroner, *An Inquiry into the Human Prospect* (New York: Norton, 1975), p. 39.

Credits

berg/Sygma. 211, 216 and 217: UPI. 218: Michael Evans/Sygma. 220: Courtesy of Mount Vernon Associates, Inc. 223: Woodfin Camp & Associates.

Chapter 9
Opener: Courtesy of Smithsonian Institution Archives; Karl Schumacher/The White House; Michael Evans/The White House. 231: Michael Evans/Sygma. 233: Left, Bettye Lane/Photo Researchers; right, Owen Franken/Stock, Boston. 236, 238, and 239: UPI. 243: Right, UPI; left, Dirk Halstead/Contact Press Images. 248: Library of Congress. 249: Wide World. 259: Arthur Grace/Sygma.

Chapter 10
Opener: Courtesy of The New York Times; NBC News; Time Magazine; S. Kupferberg; The Washington Post; ABC News; Bill Fitz-Patrick/The White House. 267: Mark Godfrey/Archive Pictures. 269: Arthur Grace/Sygma. 270: UPI. 272: Courtesy ABC-TV. 279: Sam Lafata/Black Star. 280: Left, Courtesy ABC News; right, Mark Godfrey/Archive Pictures. 281: James A. Karales/Peter Arnold. 282: Paul Conklin. 285: Top left, Chid Hires/Liaison Agency; top center, Stephen J. Sherman/Picture Group; top right, Jim Pozarik/Liaison Agency; bottom left, Courtesy ABC News; bottom center, Courtesy WNET/THIRTEEN and WETH/26; bottom right, Courtesy CBS News. 288: Sidney Harris. 290: Michael Evans/The White House.

Chapter 11
Opener: Courtesy of S. Kupferberg. 296 and 298: Wide World. 299: J.P. Laffont/Sygma. 302: Left, Paul Conklin; right, Owen Franken/Sygma. 310: George Tames/New York Times Pictures. 318: UPI. 319: Left, Wide World; right, UPI. 326: Sidney Harris. 327: UPI. 328: Paul Conklin.

Chapter 12
Opener: Courtesy of The White House; Eastman Kodak Company, News Service; Architect of The Capitol. 334: Paul Conklin. 336: UPI. 338: *Washington and His Staff at Fort Cumberland, Maryland*, attributed to Kemmelmeyer. The Metropolitan Museum of Art. 340: UPI. 341: Contact Press Images. 343: Karl Schumacher/The White House. 345 and 349: UPI. 351: Left, Paul Conklin; right, Contact Press Images. 357: R. Bossu/Sygma.

Chapter 13
Opener: Courtesy of The Department of Energy; The Pentagon; California Department of Water. Resources. 364: Benyas Kaufman/Black Star. 368: a, UPI; b, Roger Jensen/USGS; c, Ellis Herwig/Stock, Boston; d, Courtesy The Centers for Disease Control; e, Patricia H. Gross/Stock, Boston; f, Mark Antman/The Image Works. 371: Mark Antman/The Image Works. 373: NASA. 378: Top, Martin A. Levick/Black Star; bottom, by permission of Bill Mauldin and Wil-Jo Associates, Inc. 388: Read D. Brugger/The Picture Cube.

Chapter 14
Opener: Courtesy of Library of Congress; Agency of Development and Community Affairs, Montpelier, Vermont; The Supreme Court Historical Society. 393: J.P. Laffont/Sygma. 397: Courtesy the Supreme Court Historical Society. 399: UPI. 401: Wide World. 407: Michael D. Sullivan. 408: Sidney Harris. 409: Fred Ward/Black Star. 410: Left, UPI; right, Burt Glinn/Magnum. 412: Sidney Harris. 417: Ellis Herwig/Stock, Boston. 419: Peter Southwick/Stock, Boston.

Chapter 15
Opener: Courtesy of Alyeska Pipeline Service Company; Rose Skytta/Jeroboam; Ira Wyman/Sygma; Library of Congress; UPI. 424: Top left, Library of Congress; top right, Arthur Grace/Stock, Boston; bottom, UPI. 426: Library of Congress. 429: Jim West. 434: Ira Wyman/Sygma. 437: Mimi Forsyth/Monkmeyer. 442: Wide World. 446: Left, Betsy Cole/The Picture Cube; right, Taurus Photos. 447: Library of Congress. 449: Rose Skytta/Jeroboam.

Chapter 16
Opener: Courtesy of S. Kupferberg; National Archives; The Port of New York Authority; Thomas England/Photo Researchers; Susan Kuklin/Photo Researchers. 457: Jim Anderson/Woodfin Camp & Associates. 459: From *The Wall Street Journal*, by permission of Cartoon Features Syndicate. 462: Thomas England/Photo Researchers. 463: Wide World. 466: Library of Congress. 467: UPI. 469: Left, Susan Kuklin/Photo Researchers; right, Martin Levick/Black Star. 473: Michael Stratford. 475: David E. Kennedy. 478: Akhtar Hussein/Woodfin Camp & Associates.

Chapter 17
Opener: Courtesy of J. L. Atlan/Sygma; Sygma; The Federal Reserve. 484: Michael Hayman/Black Star. 485: Arthur Grace/Stock, Boston. 487: Tony Korody/Sygma. 490: Paul Conklin. 491: Joel Gordon. 493: Mark Godfrey/Archive Pictures. 494: J.L. Atlan/Sygma. 504: Martin Levick/Black Star. 506: George Cohen/Gamma-Liaison. 509: Arthur Glauberman/Photo Researchers.

Chapter 18
Opener: Courtesy of California Department of Water Resources; Travenol Laboratories, Inc; United States Department of Agriculture; Atlanta Chamber of Commerce. 514: Wide World. 515: J. Holland/Stock, Boston. 519: Michal Heron/Woodfin Camp & Associates. 521: Wide World. 522: Peter Vandermark/Stock, Boston. 523: Erika Stone/Photo Researchers. 525: Frank D. Smith/Jeroboam. 534: Alan Carey/The Image Works. 535: Michael Dressler/TIME Magazine. 539: UPI.

Chapter 19
Opener: Courtesy of The White House; The New York Times. 544: Milner/Sygma. 546: L.J. Atlan/Sygma. 549: Wide World. 553 and 555: UPI. 556: Mark Godfrey/Archive Pictures. 562: Ellen Skat/The Picture Cube. 564: UPI. 567: Left, Jim West; right, Tass from Sovfoto.

INDEX